COMPETITION LAW

A Practitioner's Guide

i.m. Bríd

COMPETITION LAW

A Practitioner's Guide

NATHY DUNLEAVY

LL.B. (Dub), LL.M. (Maastricht)
of King's Inns and Gray's Inn, Barrister
Attorney at Law (New York)

Consultant Editor

PAUL SREENAN SC

Bloomsbury Professional

Published by
Bloomsbury Professional
Maxwelton House
41–43 Boltro Road
Haywards Heath
West Sussex
RH16 1BJ

Bloomsbury Professional
The Fitzwilliam Business Centre
26 Upper Pembroke Street
Dublin 2

ISBN 978 1 84766 687 1

© Bloomsbury Professional 2010

This work is intended to be a general guide and cannot be a substitute for professional advice. Neither the authors nor the publisher accept any responsibility for loss occasioned to any person acting or refraining from acting as a result of material contained in this publication.

British Library Cataloguing-in-Publication Data
A catalogue record for this book is available from the British Library

Typeset by Marie Armah-Kwantreng, Dublin, Ireland
Printed and bound in the United Kingdom by CPI William Clowes, Beccles, NR34 7TL

FOREWORD

I write this foreword in the week when the government has published the outline of the 'Joint EU-IMF Programme for Ireland'. Significantly, among its provisions are requirements concerning the removal of restrictions on competition in 'sheltered sectors' of the economy, first among them the legal profession.

This detail provides further confirmation, if confirmation were needed, of the central role of freely competitive markets in a developing economy. Enforcement of competition requires the backing of the law.

For my own part, I continue to marvel at the pre-eminence achieved, over an astonishingly short number of years, of competition law as a major independent field of study and practice. For example, the Irish Society for European Law, of which I am President, organises a regular and well-attended Competition Law Forum.

To give point to the novelty of this field of study, I can recall that, as a barrister in the early 1990's, it was exceedingly difficult to persuade even our very best judges that competition rules could prevail over normal legal rights and individual property rights in particular. Opposing counsel was able to portray reliance on the competition rules as something disreputable to be derided as a 'Euro-defence'. Sir Robert Megarry had, of course, urged the English courts to *'scrutinise a Euro-defence with care'* (*ICI v Berk Pharmaceuticals* [1981] 2 CMLR 91).

That sort of scepticism is a thing of the past. We have brought competition law home, with the passing in 1991 of our first Competition Act and the establishment of our own Competition Authority. Competition Law has come of age.

Hence the need for accessible textbooks. Nathy Dunleavy has provided our practitioners with a striking and most valuable *vade mecum*. His approach is original. Each subject is treated as a question, a sort of catechism of competition law. The presentation is reminiscent of Halsbury. Each proposition is stated clearly, in simple terms and without unnecessary academic qualifications and sub-clauses. Crucially for the practitioner, he backs each statement with an authority. He cites both European and Irish cases.

A central and distinguishing feature of competition law is that it is really, in certain respects at any rate, economics disguised as law. At certain points law, and economics tend to merge. At least, the practitioner—and the judge—must be able to grasp basic principles of economics. Our system of enforcement is essentially by means of a private action, even when the Competition Authority is the mover. This is radically different from the system of enforcement at European level, where the courts are called on to review Commission decisions and principles of judicial review require a degree of deference to the decision-maker. Our system, therefore, places a premium on judicial understanding of the underlying economics. Nathy Dunleavy has been able to treat difficult and subtle concepts such as dominant position, product markets, substitutability, tying abuses and predatory pricing with assurance and to bring clarity to them.

I appreciate being asked to write this foreword. I wish Nathy the success with this work that his industry and application deserves.

Nial Fennelly
Supreme Court

PREFACE

My aim in this book has been to provide a resource for practitioners and others interested in EU competition law. To this end, the book employs the device of a *Questions & Answers* format, to which competition law seems particularly conducive. The primary purpose has been to address the main areas of EU competition law, including the antitrust rules, merger control, State aid law and other areas such as the intersection between competition law and the public procurement rules, as well as enforcement.

It was apparent to me at the outset that the book should also provide a national perspective. National courts and competition authorities play a central role in the enforcement of Articles 101 and 102 of the Treaty on the Functioning of the European Union, while the national judge has recently been described by Commissioner Almunia as 'increasingly one of the key actors' in the field of State aid. My own limitations meant that there was a choice between two EU Member States and I have chosen to include both. Given the similarities in the legal systems of Ireland and the UK, there are, it is hoped, interesting parallels to be drawn in areas such as private enforcement, with both systems containing similar procedural rules and adopting a like approach to remedies. Other crossovers can be seen in Irish and UK domestic competition law, for example, in what are the early cases on criminal enforcement in each jurisdiction, *DPP v Duffy* [2009] 3 IR 613 and *R v Whittle* [2008] EWCA Crim 2560. The national perspective, while weaved through at various points, is most pronounced in Chapters 5 and 6 on public enforcement and private enforcement respectively. Where I thought it helpful, I have also incorporated reference to US antitrust law, the influence of which is difficult to ignore in this field.

It goes without saying that the book is not intended to be relied on for legal advice. This is particularly so with respect to the *Summaries* appearing at the start of each question, which are intended merely as an aid to the reader in identifying key issues rather than an attempt to condense the law to a few bullet points.

I have endeavoured to update the law to 1 September 2010 but it was possible to take into account a number of subsequent developments, including coverage of the first margin squeeze case before the Court of Justice in Case C-280/08P *Deutsche Telekom v Commission* and a number of other significant judgments, such as those in Case C-550/07P *Akzo Nobel v Commission* and Case T-155/06 *Tomra Systems v Commission*.

I have incurred a number of debts in writing this book. I am grateful to several colleagues who provided comments and insights from their extensive experience including, from the Irish Bar, Eileen Barrington, Catherine Donnelly, Niamh Hyland, John McCarroll, Paul Anthony McDermott and Jonathan Newman; Philip Andrews of McCann FitzGerald; and Elizabeth Harwick in London. Niamh Cleary of Trinity College Dublin and Zeldine Niamh O'Brien, barrister, provided invaluable research assistance as the book neared completion.

I would also like to thank former colleagues in New York, Brussels and London, in particular Juan Rodriguez of Sullivan & Cromwell, who provided a number of helpful comments on the book and Bob Osgood, also of S&C, and Christopher Bright of Shearman & Sterling.

I was honoured that Mr. Justice Nial Fennelly agreed to write the foreword. His immense contribution to competition law, in particular as an Advocate General at the Court of Justice and a judge of the Supreme Court of Ireland, requires no introduction.

My greatest debt in these respects is owed to Paul Sreenan SC, who acted as consultant editor. Paul was a great source of encouragement and guidance throughout and generously made himself available to discuss difficult questions. As well as making numerous suggestions for ways to improve the work, he read and commented on the entirety of the text. The book would have been significantly poorer without the contribution of someone with his range of experience and intellectual rigour. Of course, he is not responsible for errors in the book, which are mine alone.

The process of working with Bloomsbury Professional was a pleasure from start to finish. I am grateful to all at Bloomsbury who worked on the book and especially to Amy Hayes, who ran the project with great skill and dedication. Marie Armah-Kwantreng did a superb and speedy job in typesetting the manuscript.

Finally, on a personal note, I would like to mark my sincere thanks to friends and family, especially Joe Dunleavy, Kieron Dunleavy and my wife, Catherine.

Nathy Dunleavy

Dublin, November 2010

CONTENTS – SUMMARY

Contents

TABLE OF CASES

Numerical List of General Court Cases

Numerical List of Court of Justice Cases

European Commission Merger Regulation Decisions

European Free Trade Association Court

European Court of Human Rights

Irish Cases and Decisions

UK Cases and Decisions

TABLE OF EU TREATIES AND LEGISLATION

Table of Equivalence (select provisions)

Treaty on the Functioning of the European Union ('TFEU')

Old numbering of the EC Treaty	TFEU Numbering
Article 16	Article 14
Article 28	Article 34
Article 31	Article 37
Article 49	Article 56
Article 73	Article 93
Article 80	Article 100
Article 81	Article 101
Article 82	Article 102
Article 86	Article 106
Article 87	Article 107
Article 88	Article 108
Article 89	Article 109
Article 95	Article 114
---	Article 194
Article 300	Article 218
Article 195	Article 228
Article 225	Article 256
Article 226	Article 258
Article 227	Article 259
Article 230	Article 263
Article 232	Article 265
Article 234	Article 267
Article 235	Article 268
Article 242	Article 278
Article 243	Article 279
Article 249	Article 288
Article 254	Article 297
Article 287	Article 339
Article 288	Article 340
Article 299(2), second, third and fourth sub-paragraphs	Article 349
Article 308	Article 352

Treaty on European Union ('TEU')

Old numbering TEU/EC Treaty	New TEU Numbering
Article 2 TEU	Article 3
Article 10 EC is substantially replaced by the new Article 4(3) TEU	Article 4
Article 5 EC	Article 5
Article 6 TEU	Article 6

EU Directives

TABLE OF NATIONAL LEGISLATION

United Kingdom – Secondary Legislation

TABLE OF GUIDELINES, NOTICES AND OTHER INFORMAL TEXTS

UNITED STATES

INTERNATIONAL AGREEMENTS

Chapter 1

SCOPE OF EU COMPETITION LAW

Chapter 1

SCOPE OF EU COMPETITION LAW

1. WHAT IS AN 'UNDERTAKING' FOR PURPOSES OF EU COMPETITION LAW?

Summary

- Articles 101 and 102 and other competition law provisions only apply to 'undertakings'. This term is not defined in the Treaties but has been interpreted by the courts.

- Doubts as to whether an entity is an undertaking usually arise only in respect of public entities or entities linked to the State.

- The context in which the entity is operating must be considered. An entity may be an undertaking for some activities but not others.

- The key issue is whether an entity is engaged in 'economic activity'.

- The defining characteristic of 'economic activity' is the *offering* of goods or services on a market.

- Tasks in the public interest which form part of 'the essential functions of the State' fall outside the scope of economic activity – e.g. administration of sickness benefit based on the principle of national solidarity.

- Any entity, regardless of its legal status or funding arrangements, can qualify as an undertaking.

- Other factors, such as whether the entity is profit-making, may be relevant but are not usually decisive to the analysis.

1. That an entity is an 'undertaking' is a crucial threshold question for application of the competition rules of the Treaty. Article 101(1) of the Treaty on the Functioning of the European Union ('TFEU') prohibits anti-competitive agreements 'between undertakings', decisions by 'associations of undertakings'[1] and concerted practices (between undertakings).[2] Article 102 covers 'any abuse by one or more undertakings of a dominant position'.

---

1. The concept of an association of undertakings is discussed further in Question 15.
2. Article 101(1) does not explicitly state that 'concerted practices' have to be between undertakings but this is clear from the way in which Article 101 has been interpreted by the Court of Justice, which has defined a concerted practice as 'a form of co-ordination between undertakings' (see, e.g., Case 48/69 *ICI v Commission ('Dyestuffs')* [1972] ECR 619, [1972] CMLR 557, para 64). The Irish Supreme Court has similarly made clear that section 4 of the Competition Act 1991 (now section 4 of the Competition Act 2002) only applies to 'multilateral' actions or activity (see *Chanelle Veterinary Limited v Pfizer (Ireland) Limited* [1999] 1 IR 365, 419).

2. The term 'undertaking' also arises in Article 106. Article 106(2) provides a potential derogation from the application of the EU competition rules for undertakings entrusted by the State with the performance of a service of general economic interest. State aid under Article 107 can arise when 'certain undertakings' are favoured. The term 'undertaking' is also used in the Merger Regulation.[3]

3. The term 'undertaking' is not defined in the Treaty and so it has been left to the courts to interpret its meaning. They have given the term a wide and functional meaning. The meaning of an undertaking is contextual rather than absolute, *i.e.* whether an entity is an undertaking is judged by the activity in which it is engaged, not by any permanent characteristic in its make-up. Consequently, an entity may be an undertaking when it engages in one activity and not be an undertaking when it carries out a different function.

What is meant by 'economic activity'?

4. The Court of Justice has defined the concept of an 'undertaking' in the following terms:

> [The] concept of an undertaking encompasses *every entity* engaged in an *economic activity*, regardless of the legal status of the entity and the way in which it is financed.[4]

5. The key question in assessing if an entity is an undertaking is whether it engages in 'economic activity'. In many cases, there is little doubt that a particular entity carries out an economic activity. Businesses and companies, of whatever size, engaged in commercial activity will generally satisfy this criterion. However, as the case law shows, the 'economic activity' criterion cannot always be applied so easily and 'it seems to be very difficult to lay down a precise formula by which an entity may be classified' as an undertaking.[5] This is particularly so with respect to entities linked to the State or which carry out functions of a public nature.

6. To constitute an economic activity, the entity must be involved in offering goods or services. It is not sufficient that it acts only as a purchaser. An economic activity is one 'which consists in *offering* goods or services on a given market and which could, at least in principle, be carried on by a private actor in order to make profits'.[6]

---

3. Regulation (EC) No 139/2004 on the control of concentrations between undertakings [2004] OJ L24/1 (the 'Merger Regulation').

4. Case C–41/90 *Höfner & Elser v Macrotron GmbH* [1991] ECR I–1979, [1993] 4 CMLR 306, para 21 (emphasis added).

5. *Hemat v The Medical Council* [2006] IEHC 187, para 41 (McKechnie J) (appeal dismissed, *Hemat v The Medical Council* [2010] IESC 24).

6. Case C–475/99 *Ambulanz Glöckner v Landkreis Südwestpfalz* [2001] ECR I–8089, [2002] 4 CMLR 726, opinion of Advocate General Jacobs, para 67 (emphasis added). See also, e.g., Case C–113/07P *SELEX Sistemi Integrati SpA v Commission* [2009] ECR I–2207, [2009] 4 CMLR 1083, para 69; Case C–35/96 *Commission v Italy ('CNSD')* [1998] ECR I–3851, [1998] 5 CMLR 889, para 36.

7.   The Union courts have employed different methods of determining whether an entity is an undertaking engaged in economic activity. They have asked whether the activity at issue could be performed by private entities. For example, in *Ambulanz Glöckner*, health organisations providing emergency and ambulance services were held to be undertakings, the Court of Justice finding that '[s]uch activities have not always been, and are not necessarily, carried on by such organisations or by public authorities'.[7] However, given that '[a]lmost all activities are capable of being carried on by private operators'[8] whether on a stand-alone basis, through contract or delegation of governmental power, including what would traditionally have been viewed as public functions, it has become more difficult to identify which activities are part of the State's 'essential functions'. At most, it would appear that the fact that an activity may be carried out by a private entity can be evidence that the activity in question may be described as an economic activity.[9]

8.   Another tool used by the Union courts has been to focus on the actual participation of an entity in a market or the carrying on by the entity of an activity in a market context. For example, in *Pavlov*, the Court of Justice stated that 'any activity consisting in offering goods and services *on a given market* is an economic activity'.[10] As Advocate General Maduro further explained in *FENIN*:

> It is not the mere fact that the activity may, in theory, be carried on by private operators which is decisive, but the fact that the activity is carried on under market conditions. Those conditions are distinguished by conduct which is undertaken with the objective of capitalisation, which is incompatible with the principle of solidarity. That allows it to be determined whether a market exists or not, even if the legislation in force prevents genuine competition emerging on that market. By contrast, where the State allows partial competition to arise, the activity in question necessarily implies participation in a market.[11]

9.   In other cases the EU courts have been able to classify certain activities as non-economic. The Court of Justice has held that 'activities which fall within the exercise of public powers are not of an economic nature'.[12] So entities are not

---

7.   Case C–475/99 *Ambulanz Glöckner v Landkreis Südwestpfalz* [2001] ECR I–8089, [2002] 4 CMLR 726, para 20.

8.   Case C–205/03P *FENIN v Commission* [2006] ECR I–6295, [2006] 5 CMLR 559, opinion of Advocate General Maduro, para 12. See also Case E–5/07 *Private Barnehagers Landsforbund v EFTA Surveillance Authority* [2008] 2 CMLR 818, para 80 (adding that the specific circumstances under which the activity was being performed had to be taken into account).

9.   See, e.g., Case C–82/01 *Aéroports de Paris v Commission* [2002] ECR I–9297, [2003] 4 CMLR 609, para 82.

10. Cases C–180/98 etc., *Pavlov* [2000] ECR I–6451, [2001] 4 CMLR 30, para 75 (emphasis added).

11. Case C–205/03P *FENIN v Commission* [2006] ECR I–6295, [2006] 5 CMLR 559, opinion of Advocate General Maduro, para 13.

12. Case C–113/07P *SELEX Sistemi Integrati SpA v Commission* [2009] ECR I–2207, [2009] 4 CMLR 1083, para 70.

undertakings when they exercise sovereign or administrative functions 'that are typically those of a public authority'[13] or can be classed as 'a task in the public interest which forms part of the essential functions of the State'.[14]

10. In finding that entities were not undertakings, the EU courts have focused in some cases on the fact that the function fulfilled by the activity is a 'social' one or is based on the principle of 'solidarity' (defined by one Advocate General as 'the inherently uncommercial act of involuntary subsidisation of one social group by another'[15]). This focus has allowed entities operating sickness funds,[16] compulsory work insurance schemes[17] and public kindergartens[18] to fall outside the Treaty's competition rules. The courts have also considered the overall nature, aim and rules to which the activities in question are subject, finding, for instance, that an entity carrying out air traffic control with the collection of charges was not an undertaking.[19]

Is each activity of the entity considered separately?

11. The approach to interpreting the concept of an undertaking has been 'functional'. The focus should be on the activities in which the entity is engaged. The notion of an undertaking is 'a relative concept in the sense that a given entity might be regarded as an undertaking for one part of its activities while the rest fall outside the competition rules'.[20]

12. This functional approach can raise difficult questions. What if an entity exercises public powers that have an impact on a market on which it participates? Is the entity an undertaking when exercising its regulatory functions?

13. In *MOTOE*, the Court of Justice held that while some of the activities of the Automobile and Touring Club of Greece (ELPA) fell within the exercise of public authority (it had a power of authorisation for motorcycling events), this did not prevent it from being considered an undertaking in respect of the remainder of its

---

13. Case C–364/92 *SAT Fluggesellschaft v Eurocontrol* [1994] ECR I–43, [1994] 5 CMLR 208, para 30.
14. Case C–343/95 *Cali & Figli v SEPG* [1997] ECR I–1547, [1997] 5 CMLR 484, para 22.
15. Case C–70/95 *Sodemare SA v Regione Lombardia* [1997] ECR I–3395, [1997] 3 CMLR 591, opinion of Advocate General Fennelly, para 29.
16. Cases C–264/01 etc *AOK Bundesverband* [2004] ECR I–2493, [2004] 4 CMLR 1261.
17. Case C–218/00 *Cisal* [2002] ECR I–691, [2002] 4 CMLR 833.
18. Case E–5/07 *Private Barnehagers Landsforbund v EFTA Surveillance Authority* [2008] 2 CMLR 818, para 83 (by establishing a system where every child increased the costs incurred, the State was not seeking to engage in gainful activity but was 'fulfilling its duties towards its own population in the social, cultural and educational fields').
19. Case C–364/92 *SAT Fluggesellschaft v Eurocontrol* [1994] ECR I–43, [1994] 5 CMLR 208, para 30. See also Case C–343/95 *Cali & Figli v SEPG* [1997] ECR I–1547, [1997] 5 CMLR 484, para 23 (referring to the nature, aim and rules of the activity).
20. Case C–475/99 *Ambulanz Glöckner v Landkreis Südwestpfalz* [2001] ECR I–8089, [2002] 4 CMLR 726, opinion of Advocate General Jacobs, para 72.

activities. ELPA was an undertaking when it engaged in the organisation and commercial exploitation of motorcycling events. The fact that ELPA also had the function of giving consent to authorisations for those events did not prevent it from being an undertaking when it carried out its commercial activities.[21] The Court went on to hold that the power to give those consents could not itself be classified as an economic activity.[22] While ELPA could not then be found to be in breach of competition law when it exercised its public powers, the Court held that the Greek rule that enabled ELPA to authorise motorcycling events when it participated in organising such events itself, fell foul of Article 102 in conjunction with Article 106.[23]

14. In some cases it may not be possible to separate one activity from the core exercise of public powers carried out by the entity. In *SELEX*, the Court of Justice considered whether Eurocontrol, an agency with tasks including airspace management and the development of air safety, was an undertaking with respect to some of its activities. The General Court had held that the provision by Eurocontrol of assistance to national administrations (for example, by drafting contract documents) was separable from its core public functions as such assistance had only an indirect relationship with air safety. As this assistance constituted an offer of services on the market for advice, it was held by the General Court to be an economic activity.[24] This separation of Eurocontrol's activities was rejected by the Court of Justice which found that the provision of assistance was 'closely linked' to Eurocontrol's public task of technical standardisation with a view to achieving air safety and so it was 'connected' with the exercise of its public powers.[25] It was not necessary to show that the provision of assistance was 'essential or indispensable' to ensure air navigation safety; what mattered was that the activity was 'connected' with Eurocontrol's exercise of public powers.[26]

15. In *Panda*, the Irish High Court found that in exercising public powers to vary a waste management plan, four local authorities were acting as undertakings. The local authorities were also active in the market for the collection of household

---

21. Case C–49/07 *MOTOE v Elliniko Dimosio* [2008] ECR I–4863, [2008] 5 CMLR 790, para 26.
22. Case C–49/07 *MOTOE v Elliniko Dimosio* [2008] ECR I–4863, [2008] 5 CMLR 790, para 46. This finding was made in the context of applying Article 106(2), with the Court holding that ELPA was not an undertaking entrusted with a service of general economic interest. Earlier at para 43, however, the Court had held that ELPA was, by virtue of the same public power to consent to authorisations for organising motorcycling events, an undertaking which was granted special rights by the Member State within the meaning of Article 106(1).
23. Case C–49/07 *MOTOE v Elliniko Dimosio* [2008] ECR I–4863, [2008] 5 CMLR 790, paras 48–53. See also Question 125.
24. Case T–155/04 *SELEX Sistemi Integrati SpA v Commission* [2006] ECR II–4797, [2007] 4 CMLR 372.
25. Case C–113/07P *SELEX Sistemi Integrati SpA v Commission* [2009] ECR I–2207, [2009] 4 CMLR 1083, para 76.
26. Case C–113/07P *SELEX Sistemi Integrati SpA v Commission* [2009] ECR I–2207, [2009] 4 CMLR 1083, para 79.

waste, in which context they were clearly acting as undertakings. The decision to vary the plan was aimed at affecting that market directly. McKechnie J held:

> In those circumstances it is clear that the Variation is of an economic, rather than of an administrative, nature. It seeks to substantially reorder the market as it currently exists. Were the respondents exclusively involved in the regulation of the waste market, e.g. merely imposing charges or conditions on licences and/or overseeing the market for compliance, they would not be undertakings.[27]

16.   In other words, where a public body makes a regulatory decision that directly affects the commercial dynamics of the market in which it operates as an undertaking, the exercise of the regulatory power itself will constitute an economic activity. At the time of writing, an appeal in *Panda* was pending before the Supreme Court.[28]

May an entity be an undertaking when it purchases goods or services?

17.   Although each activity must be considered separately, it is the offering of goods or services that is the characteristic feature of an economic activity. Purchasing activities must therefore be considered in light of downstream activities. In *FENIN*, the Court of Justice held that public management bodies which ran the Spanish health system, including three ministries of the Spanish government, were not undertakings when they carried out purchasing activities. The management bodies were large purchasers of medical goods and equipment. It was argued that the act of purchasing was itself an economic activity but the Court did not consider purchasing in isolation. The Court found that 'the nature of the purchasing activity must be determined according to whether or not the subsequent use of the purchased goods amounts to an economic activity'.[29]

---

27.   *Nurendale Ltd t/a Panda Waste Services v Dublin City Council* [2009] IEHC 588, para 63.

28.   The judgment in Case C–113/07P *SELEX Sistemi Integrati SpA v Commission* [2009] ECR I–2207, [2009] 4 CMLR 1083 was delivered after argument closed in *Panda* and so is not referred to in the *Panda* judgment. For comment on *Panda*, see Andrews and Gorecki, 'Market Regulation and Competition; Law in Conflict: A View from Ireland, Implications of the Panda Judgment' ESRI Working Paper No. 353 (September 2010) arguing that the local authorities in *Panda* were not undertakings when they varied the waste management plan. One difficulty for the High Court (which it may not have faced had EU competition law applied) was that it could not invoke a national law equivalent of Article 106(1) to find that the Variation, or the law that gave the power to the local authorities to make the Variation, was itself in breach of the competition rules in conjunction with such an equivalent rule (the Competition Act 2002 does not contain an equivalent to Article 106). The only way to enforce competition law against the local authorities was to find that they were undertakings when they adopted the Variation. McKechnie J also held (para 157) that by adopting the Variation the local authorities had acted *ultra vires*. See also the related case, *Greenstar Ltd v Dublin City Council* [2009] IEHC 589. Cf *Global Knafaim Leasing Limited v The Civil Aviation Authority* [2010] EWHC 1348 (Admin) (Collins J found that the exercise of a fleet lien power granted by statute to BAA was not a breach of competition law; the question whether BAA was an undertaking when exercising the statutory power was not addressed).

29.   Case C–205/03P *FENIN v Commission* [2006] ECR I–6295, [2006] 5 CMLR 559, para 26.

18. As had been explained by the General Court in *FENIN*:

>   Whilst an entity may wield very considerable economic power, even giving rise to a
>   monopsony, it nevertheless remains the case that, if the activity for which that entity
>   purchases goods is not an economic activity, it is not acting as an undertaking for the
>   purposes of Community competition law and is therefore not subject to the
>   prohibitions laid down in Articles [101(1) and 102].[30]

19. The Court of Justice held that FENIN's alternative plea, that the provision of
     medical treatment was itself an economic activity, which meant that the purchasing
     activity was economic in nature, was inadmissible as the argument was raised by
     FENIN for the first time at the appeal stage.[31]

20. It may be difficult to identify precisely how goods or services procured by a public
     body are ultimately used if the body is engaged in offering some goods or services
     downstream, whereas other of its downstream activities are non-economic.
     Potentially, such an entity could use the procured goods or services for both
     economic and non-economic activities. It seems at least arguable that in this
     situation the entity is acting as an undertaking when it makes purchases.

21. Various other specific factors may be relevant, although one factor or another is
     not generally determinative of whether an entity is acting as an undertaking.

Is the legal form or public law status of the entity relevant?

22. The legal form of the entity is irrelevant to its classification as an undertaking. The
     concept is not confined to companies or other corporate bodies. It extends to
     entities including partnerships, trade associations (which may be undertakings
     themselves or associations of undertakings), professional bodies and agricultural
     cooperatives, among others. An individual may qualify as an undertaking if
     engaged in an economic activity. Individual lawyers[32] and individual doctors[33]
     have been held to be undertakings.

23. The legal status of an entity linked to the State is irrelevant in determining whether
     it is an undertaking:

>   It is of no importance that the State carries out the said economic activities by way of
>   a distinct body over which it may exercise, directly or indirectly, a dominant influence

---

30. Case T–319/99 *FENIN v Commission* [2003] ECR II–357, [2003] 5 CMLR 34, para 37.
31. Case C–205/03P *FENIN v Commission* [2006] ECR I–6295, [2006] 5 CMLR 559, para 21.
     Advocate General Maduro (paras 38 and 57 of his opinion) had considered that this plea was
     admissible and that the case should have been remitted to the General Court to determine on
     the facts whether or not the activities of the Spanish healthcare bodies were economic in
     nature.
32. Case C–309/99 *Wouters* [2002] ECR I–1577, [2002] 4 CMLR 913.
33. Cases C–180/98 etc *Pavlov* [2000] ECR I–6451, [2001] 4 CMLR 30.

... or that it carries out the activities directly through a body forming part of the State administration. [34]

24. The fact that the entity in question has public law status does not prevent it being an undertaking. The legal framework within which the entity enters agreements and takes decisions and the classification given to that framework by the national legal system are irrelevant as far as the application of the EU competition rules is concerned.[35]

25. On this basis, any of, for example, a State-owned company, a government agency, a local authority, a government department or a minister[36] could potentially qualify as an undertaking.

Is profit a factor?

26. A non-profit entity involved in offering goods or services on the market may be in competition with other operators who do seek to make a profit. In such a case, the non-profit entity may be an undertaking. A non-profit entity offering goods or services on a market might even be in competition with another non-profit entity.[37] While the fact that an activity is not-for-profit is therefore not decisive of an entity's classification as an undertaking, it can be a relevant factor in determining whether or not the activity engaged in is of an economic nature.[38] Similarly, the fact that the entity receives no remuneration for the services it provides may indicate that the activity is non-economic but again, this is unlikely to be decisive.[39]

Is a public service objective a factor?

27. That the goods or services in question are offered in pursuit of a public service objective may indicate a non-economic activity but, again, this is not usually decisive. In *Albany*, a compulsory pension fund, although non-profit making and pursuing a social objective, qualified as an undertaking. It was relevant that the

---

34. Case 118/85 *Commission v Italy* [1987] ECR 2599, [1988] 3 CMLR 255, para 8. See also, e.g., Case T–196/04 *Ryanair Ltd v Commission* [2008] ECR II–3643, [2009] 2 CMLR 137, paras 91–92 (the fact that a public authority was the owner of an airport in public ownership did not mean that it was not engaged in economic activity when it provided airport facilities to airlines in return for a fee).

35. See, e.g., Case C–35/96 *Commission v Italy ('CNSD')* [1998] ECR I–3851, [1998] 5 CMLR 889, para 40.

36. See *Greally v Minister for Education* [1995] 3 IR 481, 484 (Costello P in the Irish High Court noting that a government Minister could be an undertaking depending on the activity engaged in).

37. See Case C–49/07 *MOTOE v Elliniko Dimosio* [2008] ECR I–4863, [2008] 5 CMLR 790, paras 27–28.

38. See Case C–113/07P *SELEX Sistemi Integrati SpA v Commission* [2009] ECR I–2207, [2009] 4 CMLR 1083, para 116.

39. See Case T–155/04 *SELEX Sistemi Integrati SpA v Commission* [2006] ECR II–4797, [2007] 4 CMLR 372, para 90.

amount of the benefits provided by the fund depended on the financial results of the investments made by it, the fund operated in accordance with the principle of capitalisation, the fund could grant exemption from affiliation where an employer gave its workers benefits of at least an equivalent level and the fund was in competition with insurance companies.[40]

Can entities subject to the public procurement rules be undertakings?

28.   There is no exemption from the competition rules for contracting authorities that are subject to the public procurement rules. Such entities may be undertakings if they are engaged in economic activity. Whether a contracting authority is considered to be an undertaking when it procures goods or services will depend on the use to which it puts those goods or services and whether that latter activity is economic.[41]

Can an employee be an undertaking?

29.   An individual employee is not considered to be an undertaking as the employee is acting on behalf of its employer and so is not himself an independent undertaking. Rather, the employee forms a single economic unit with its employer.[42] However, if an employee, in parallel with his duties to the employer, pursues his own economic interests, he may be considered an undertaking in that context. An ex-employee carrying on a business through firms he controls may be an undertaking.[43]

Are trade unions undertakings?[44]

30.   There is no blanket exemption for trade unions from competition law. Whether a trade union will be subject to competition law will depend on the context in which it is acting. The Court of Justice recognised in *Albany* that certain restrictions of competition were inherent in collective agreements between organisations representing employers and workers. The Court recognised that 'the social policy objectives pursued by such agreements would be seriously undermined if

---

40.   Case C–67/96 *Albany* [1999] ECR I–5751, [2000] 4 CMLR 446, paras 81–84. See also Case C–244/94 *FFSA v Ministère de l'Agriculture et de la Pêche* [1995] ECR I–4013, [1996] 4 CMLR 536, para 20; Cases C–115/97 etc *Brentjens* [1999] ECR I–6025, [2000] 4 CMLR 566, paras 73–87.

41.   See Case C–205/03P *FENIN v Commission* [2006] ECR I–6295, [2006] 5 CMLR 559, para 26. The application of the competition rules to contracting authorities is considered in more detail in Question 134.

42.   See, e.g., Case C–22/98 *Becu* [1999] ECR I–5665, [2001] 4 CMLR 968, para 26.

43.   See *Reuter/BASF* [1976] OJ L 254/40, [1976] 2 CMLR D44 (the individual engaged in economic activity through the firms which remained under his control, by exploiting the results of his own research and as commercial adviser to third parties). See also *Lennon v Doran* (Irish High Court, unreported, 20 February 2001) (pointing out that merely being a shareholder would not qualify an individual to be an undertaking).

44.   See separately Question 15 on when bodies such as professional representative organisations are associations of undertakings.

management and labour were subject to Article [101(1)] of the Treaty when seeking jointly to adopt measures to improve conditions of work and employment'.[45] The agreements therefore fell outside the scope of Article 101.[46]

31.   Rather than providing a general exclusion from the scope of the competition rules for collective agreements, the exclusion provided for in *Albany* would seem to apply only to collective agreements with a given purpose, in particular that of improving conditions of work and employment. In *Van der Woude*, Advocate General Fennelly stated that the exception for collective agreements had to be narrowly construed and that collective agreements that appreciably restricted competition would not be immune from antitrust scrutiny.[47] Outside the context of collective agreements of a type considered in *Albany*, the standard analysis would seem to apply to trade unions in deciding whether they are acting as undertakings.

Are contracts with consumers subject to Article 101?

32.   Contracts between a company and a final consumer are not caught by Article 101 because a final consumer, who does not engage in offering goods or services on a market, is not an undertaking within the meaning of the case law of the Court of Justice. However, a contract between a supplier and distributor would be subject to Article 101. Although the distributor is acting only as a purchaser pursuant to the contract with the supplier, its subsequent economic activity of offering the goods for resale makes it an undertaking.

Ireland

Is the meaning of 'undertaking' in Irish law different to that in EU law?

33.   The term 'undertaking' is also used in Irish competition law. It is defined in section 3(1) of the Competition Act 2002 as 'a person being an individual, a body corporate or an unincorporated body of persons engaged for gain in the production, supply or distribution of goods or the provision of a service'.

34.   The reference to 'for gain' in the Irish definition of an undertaking does not require that the entity be profit making. In *Deane v VHI*, finding that the State health insurer, the VHI, was an undertaking, the Supreme Court held that the term

---

45.   Case C–67/96 *Albany* [1999] ECR I–5751, [2000] 4 CMLR 446, para 59.

46.   See also Cases C–115/97 etc *Brentjens* [1999] ECR I–6025, [2000] 4 CMLR 566, paras 45–62; Case C–219/97 *Drijvende Bokken* [1999] ECR I–6121, [2000] 4 CMLR 599, paras 35–52. See also *Greally v Minister for Education* [1995] 3 IR 481, 484 (a teaching union was not an undertaking where it was not engaged in any commercial activity but was rather providing a service for its members for a common purpose).

47.   See Case C–222/98 *Van der Woude* [2000] ECR I–7111, [2001] 4 CMLR 93, opinion of Advocate General Fennelly, para 32. See also Case C–271/08 *Commission v Germany*, opinion of Advocate General Trstenjak of 14 April 2010, paras 54–62; judgment of 15 July 2010 (the award of pension contracts for local authority employees to undertakings designated in an agreement between a trade union and local authority employer association, without a call for tender, was in breach of the public procurement rules).

connotes 'merely an activity carried on or a service supplied ... which is done in return for a charge or payment'.[48] It is arguable that this constitutes a potential difference with the EU law meaning of an undertaking, as in the EU law context an entity can be considered an undertaking even if it does not issue a charge or receive payment.[49]

35.   While the imposition of a charge or payment seems to be a prerequisite for an entity to be engaged 'for gain', the fact that it issues a charge does not necessarily mean that it is an undertaking. In *Carrigaline*,[50] it was held that the Minister for Transport, Energy and Communications, in granting licences for television transmission, was engaged in no more than a regulatory or administrative function and the fact that he imposed a charge for the granting of the licence did not of itself mean that he was 'engaged for gain'. Keane J, as he then was, held it would be a 'misuse of language' to describe the imposition of charges for a broadcasting license as the provision of a service for payment or to consider the licensing authority to be in any meaningful sense 'engaged for gain'. The fact that the Minister charged a fee of 5 per cent of turnover in addition to an initial levy in respect of certain types of license did 'not convert him from a regulator into a person providing a service for payment'. These charges enabled the Minister, on behalf of the public, to recoup some of the expenses of administering the licensing regime and whether this left him with a surplus or loss could not 'affect the legal capacity in which he receives the annual levy which is solely that of a regulator and administrator'. The learned judge cited the Court of Justice decision in *Eurocontrol* in support of his findings.[51]

36.   The Competition Authority has found that in negotiating with pharmacy bodies about the prices of drugs and purchasing pharmacy services from private undertakings, the Health Service Executive was not an undertaking as it did not receive any payment from patients for drugs dispensed under the scheme and so was not acting 'for gain'.[52]

37.   Despite the definition of an undertaking in the Competition Act 2002 and the absence of a definition in the EU Treaties, the recent practice of the Supreme

---

48.   *Deane v VHI* [1992] 2 IR 319, 332 (Finlay CJ) (interpreting section 3(1) of the Competition Act 1991, which contains identical language to section 3(1) of the 2002 Act). See also *Greally v Minister for Education* [1995] 3 IR 481, 484 (tying the provision of services for gain to 'doing so in the course of trade').

49.   See Case T–155/04 *SELEX Sistemi Integrati SpA v Commission* [2006] ECR II–4797, [2007] 4 CMLR 372, para 90 (upheld, Case C–113/07P *SELEX Sistemi Integrati SpA v Commission* [2009] ECR I–2207, [2009] 4 CMLR 1083, para 117).

50.   *Carrigaline Community Television Broadcasting Co. Ltd v Minister for Transport, Energy and Communications* [1997] 1 ILRM 241.

51.   *Carrigaline Community Television Broadcasting Co. Ltd v Minister for Transport, Energy and Communications* [1997] 1 ILRM 241, 291; Case C–364/92 *SAT Fluggesellschaft v Eurocontrol* [1994] ECR I–43, [1994] 5 CMLR 208.

52.   Competition Authority Enforcement Decision (ED/01/08), *Alleged anticompetitive conduct by the Health Service Executive relating to the administration of the Community Drugs Schemes* (10 October 2008) para 2.31.

Court has been simply to follow the EU courts' approach to the meaning of an undertaking when applying Irish law. In the *Credit Unions* case, Fennelly J assessed whether the Irish League of Credit Unions was an undertaking for purposes of the Competition Act 2002 with reference to the Court of Justice's jurisprudence on the meaning of an undertaking, without any suggestion that the term had a different meaning in Irish competition law.[53] In *Hemat*, Fennelly J said that it was 'patent' that the Oireachtas had used the language of Articles 101 and 102 in sections 4 and 5 of the Competition Act 2002 and that accordingly, 'the judgments of the Court of Justice must be taken as authoritative in the interpretation of notions such as "undertaking" and "association of undertakings"'.[54]

38.   As in EU law, an entity can be an undertaking under the Competition Act even if it is not-for-profit. In the *Credit Unions* case, it was accepted that credit unions were undertakings for purposes of the Competition Act 2002, even though they advocated a not-for-profit philosophy.[55]

UK

39.   The term 'undertaking' is also used in the Competition Act 1998 but it is not defined in that Act. Section 60 of the 1998 Act provides that questions of UK competition law under the Act should be dealt with in a manner consistent with corresponding EU law questions and that the courts must ensure there is no inconsistency with EU law, as laid down by the Treaties and the European courts, when interpreting the relevant parts of the Act. The Chapter I and II prohibitions in the 1998 Act are framed in similar terms to Articles 101 and 102 and so the meaning of 'undertaking' in the 1998 Act should be interpreted in accordance with the EU jurisprudence on the meaning of that term.

40.   The meaning of an 'undertaking' was considered by the Competition Appeal Tribunal ('CAT') in *BetterCare*.[56] The CAT had to consider whether two Northern Irish health trusts were undertakings for purposes of the Competition Act 1998 when they ran residential care homes and contracted out the provision of social care to private companies (they were accused of abusing a dominant position). The CAT concluded that the trusts were undertakings both in the purchasing of

---

53.   See *Competition Authority v O'Regan* [2007] IESC 22, [2007] 4 IR 737, paras 84–87.
54.   *Hemat v The Medical Council* [2010] IESC 24, para 37. The preamble to the Competition Act 2002 speaks of a new Act to make provision for competition rules 'by analogy with' Articles 101 and 102 and the criminal law offences set out in sections 6 and 7 of the Act apply where there is a breach either of section 4 or 5 of the Act or Article 101 or 102.
55.   *Competition Authority v O'Regan* [2007] IESC 22, [2007] 4 IR 737. For comment on the recent approach of the Irish courts to the meaning of an undertaking and more generally on the application of economic theory in Irish competition cases, see Andrews, 'Post Modern Judgments of Ireland's Competition Court: From Appalachian Coal to Socony Vacuum (and Back Again)' [2011] *European Competition Law Review* (forthcoming).
56.   *BetterCare Group Limited v Director General of Fair Trading* [2002] CAT 7, [2002] CompAR 299.

services from BetterCare and in the provision of their own statutory homes. The CAT took the view that the definition of 'economic activity' as established by the case law of the Court of Justice was not exhaustive and, referring to the opinion of Advocate General Jacobs in *Cisal*,[57] it suggested a key consideration was whether the entity was 'in a position to generate the effects which the competition rules seek to prevent'.[58] It went on to discuss how the competition rules apply not only to suppliers but also to purchasers of goods and services and that where a buyer has significant market power – e.g. where it has a monopsony – it is capable of abusing a dominant position through its purchasing practices alone. However, the applicability of this broader approach to the application of competition law in the State health care sector must now be doubted in light of the narrower approach of the Court of Justice in the subsequent judgment in *FENIN*.[59]

41. Examples of entities that have been held *not* to be undertakings

Entity	Basis of finding
Eurocontrol, an international organisation founded by a number of Member States, which provides air traffic control services in return for which it levies charges.	'[T]asks in the public interest aimed at contributing to the maintenance and improvement of air navigation safety'.[60]
Entities managing social security systems subjecting self-employed persons in non-agricultural occupations to compulsory social protection.	Exclusively social function based on the principle of solidarity.[61]
A company set up by the public port authority to carry out anti-pollution surveillance services in the port of Genoa.	'Task in the public interest which forms part of the essential functions of the State as regards protection of the environment in maritime areas'.[62]
Associations of sickness funds, which provided benefits to employees who, according to German law, were obliged to be insured.	Exclusively social function founded on the principle of solidarity; conclusion not altered by the fact the funds engaged in some competition to attract members.[63]
Entities providing compulsory insurance for work accidents.	Principle of solidarity; amount of benefits and contributions supervised by the State; compulsory affiliation; exclusively social function.[64]
A municipal authority granting exclusive concessions to undertakers.	Article 101 did 'not apply to contracts for concessions concluded between communes acting in their capacity as public authorities and undertakings entrusted with the operation of a public service'.[65]
Bodies responsible for the operation of the Spanish national health system.	Nature of purchasing activity dependent on the use to which goods were put.[66]

---

57.   Case C–218/00 *Cisal* [2002] ECR I–691, [2002] 4 CMLR 833.
58.   *BetterCare Group Limited v Director General of Fair Trading* [2002] CAT 7, [2002] CompAR 299, para 190.
59.   Case C–205/03P *FENIN v Commission* [2006] ECR I–6295, [2006] 5 CMLR 559.

Entity	Basis of finding
Non-profit, ELPA, which represented the International Motorcycling Federation in Greece and was vested with certain public powers.	Not an undertaking entrusted with a service of general economic interest when exercising statutory powers to give authorisation for motorcycling events.[67]

42. Examples of entities that have been held to be undertakings

Entity	Basis of finding
Members of the Dutch Bar.	The fact that the profession was regulated did not alter the economic nature of the activities.[68]
Medical specialists.	They were paid by patients for their services and assumed the financial risks of pursuing their activity.[69]
A public employment agency.	Employment procurement was an activity not necessarily carried out by public entities.[70]
Customs agents.	They offered, for payment, services including carrying out of customs formalities and assumed the financial risks of the activity.[71]

---

60. Case C–364/92 *SAT Fluggesellschaft v Eurocontrol* [1994] ECR I–43, [1994] 5 CMLR 208, para 27.
61. Case C–159, 160/91 *Poucet and Pistre v Assurances Générales de France and Cancava* [1993] ECR I–637, paras 18–19.
62. Case C–343/95 *Cali & Figli v SEPG* [1997] ECR I–1547, [1997] 5 CMLR 484, paras 22–23.
63. Cases C–264/01 etc *AOK Bundesverband* [2004] ECR I–2493, [2004] 4 CMLR 1261, paras 51–57.
64. Case C–218/00 *Cisal* [2002] ECR I–691, [2002] 4 CMLR 833, paras 38–46.
65. Case 30/87 *Bodson v Pompes Funèbres des Regions Libèrè SA* [1988] ECR 2479, [1989] 4 CMLR 984.
66. Case C–205/03P *FENIN v Commission* [2006] ECR I–6295, [2006] 5 CMLR 559, para 26.
67. Case C–49/07 *MOTOE v Elliniko Dimosio* [2008] ECR I–4863, [2008] 5 CMLR 790, paras 46–47.
68. Case C–309/99 *Wouters* [2002] ECR I–1577, [2002] 4 CMLR 913, para 49. The case arose out of regulations of the Dutch Bar which prohibited lawyers from practising in full membership with accountants.
69. Cases C–180/98 etc *Pavlov* [2000] ECR I–6451, [2001] 4 CMLR 30, paras 75–77.
70. Case C–41/90 *Höfner & Elser v Macrotron GmbH* [1991] ECR I–1979, [1993] 4 CMLR 306, paras 22–23.
71. Case C–35/96 *Italy v Commission ('CNSD')* [1998] ECR I–3851, [1998] 5 CMLR 889, para 37.

Entity	Basis of finding
A compulsory pension fund.	It was set up by a collective agreement between organisations representing management and labour in particular sectors and made compulsory by the public authorities. Although non-profit making and pursuing a social objective, it qualified as an undertaking: the amount of the benefits provided by the fund depended on the financial results of the investments made by it; the fund could grant exemption from affiliation where an employer gave its workers benefits of at least an equivalent level; and the fund was in competition with insurance companies.[72]

Key Sources

Case C–41/90 *Höfner & Elser v Macrotron GmbH* [1991] ECR I–1979, [1993] 4 CMLR 306.

Case C–159, 160/91 *Poucet and Pistre* [1993] ECR I–637.

Case C–364/92 SAT *Fluggesellschaft v Eurocontrol* [1994] ECR I–43, [1994] 5 CMLR 208.

Case C–343/95 *Cali & Figli v SPEG* [1997] ECR I–1547, [1997] 5 CMLR 484.

Case C–67/96 *Albany* [1999] ECR I–5751, [2000] 4 CMLR 446.

Cases C–180/98 etc *Pavlov* [2000] ECR I–6451, [2001] 4 CMLR 30.

Case C–309/99 *Wouters* [2002] ECR I–1577, [2002] 4 CMLR 913.

Case C–218/00 *Cisal* [2002] ECR I–691, [2002] 4 CMLR 833.

Cases C–264/01 etc *AOK Bundesverband* [2004] ECR I–2493, [2004] 4 CMLR 1261.

Case C–205/03P *FENIN v Commission* [2006] ECR I–6295, [2006] 5 CMLR 559.

Case C–49/07 *MOTOE v Elliniko Dimosio* [2008] ECR I–4863, [2008] 5 CMLR 790.

Case C–113/07P *SELEX Sistemi Integrati SpA v Commission* [2009] ECR I–2207, [2009] 4 CMLR 1083.

---

72.   Case C–67/96 *Albany* [1999] ECR I–5751, [2000] 4 CMLR 446, paras 80–87.

2. WHEN IS A PARENT COMPANY LIABLE FOR COMPETITION LAW INFRINGEMENTS OF A SUBSIDIARY?

Summary

- The key issue is whether the parent company exercises decisive influence over the subsidiary so that they are considered to form one undertaking.

- Where the parent owns 100 per cent of the subsidiary (or almost 100 per cent), the parent is presumed to be responsible for competition law infringements of the subsidiary.

- This presumption can be rebutted if there is sufficient evidence to show that the subsidiary determined its conduct on the market autonomously.

- For shareholdings of less than 100 per cent, the higher the parent's shareholding, the more likely that it has decisive influence.

- However, decisive influence can also be found at lower levels, depending on the circumstances; this has included the imposition of liability on a parent company holding only 50 per cent of the capital of an infringing subsidiary.

- A 'passive' shareholding, where the parent is not involved in the management of the subsidiary, may escape liability but the parameters of this 'defence' are unclear.

1. This question frequently arises in practice, in particular in cartel cases.[73] The parent company of a corporate group often seeks to argue, on appeal from a Commission decision, that it has no responsibility for cartel activity engaged in by one of its subsidiaries and so should not be an addressee of the decision. For the purpose of applying and enforcing an infringement decision, it can only be addressed to legal persons on whom fines can be imposed, a narrower category than undertakings in the broad sense.[74] This requirement can make the identification of the appropriate addressee a complex exercise in some cases and involve the extension of liability to a parent entity.

2. The extension of liability to the parent can have significant financial consequences as its higher turnover (being the turnover of its corporate group) can then be used as the basis for the calculation of the fine. The Commission can impose a fine of up to 10 per cent of turnover of the participating undertaking for breach of the competition rules.[75]

---

73. The question whether a subsidiary is responsible for antitrust infringements of a parent company has also arisen in private actions, where claimants have sought to establish the court's jurisdiction on the basis of the subsidiary's liability. See Question 107.
74. See Cases T–305/94 etc *Limburgse Vinyl Maatschappij NV v Commission* [1999] ECR II–931, [1999] 5 CMLR 303, para 978.
75. Council Regulation (EC) No 1/2003 on the implementation of the rules on competition laid down in Articles 81 and 82 of the Treaty [2003] OJ L1/1, Article 23(2). (contd .../)

3.   The starting point for imposing liability for infringement of competition law is the principle of personal responsibility, according to which the entity that infringes the competition rules must answer for the infringement.[76] However, it is well established that a parent company, which itself did not participate in the infringement, will be responsible for the acts of its subsidiary where the two entities are considered to form one undertaking. Technically, this is not a question of the imputation of *liability* to the parent, rather, the analysis holds that the parent and the subsidiary are one and the same undertaking. It is, therefore, the subsidiary's *conduct* that is imputed to the parent, resulting in it being primarily liable.

4.   The parent and subsidiary will be considered to form one undertaking where it is shown that the parent exercises decisive influence over the subsidiary. Decisive influence will be found in particular 'where the subsidiary, although having separate legal personality, does not decide independently upon its own conduct on the market, but carries out, in all material respects, the instructions given to it by the parent company'.[77] It is for the Commission to demonstrate that there is decisive influence on the basis of factual evidence, including, in particular, any management power held by the parent in the subsidiary.[78] A finding of decisive influence may be based on a number of different factors. The ownership level of the parent is of crucial importance.

Is a parent company automatically liable for the actions of a 100 per cent owned subsidiary?

5.   When the parent holds 100 per cent of the capital in the subsidiary, a rebuttable presumption will apply that the parent does in fact exercise decisive influence over the subsidiary. This was reiterated by the Court of Justice in *Akzo*.[79] That case involved an appeal against the Commission's decision in the *Choline Chloride Cartel*. Several 100 per cent-owned subsidiaries of the parent of the Akzo group, Akzo Nobel NV, participated in the cartel. Even though Akzo Nobel NV was not itself a participant, the Commission decided to address its decision jointly and severally to Akzo Nobel NV and the relevant subsidiaries. One consequence of this was that for purposes of setting a fine, the Commission took account of the market share of the Akzo group as a whole.

---

75.   (contd) In setting the fine, the Commission might also take into account the corporate group's higher market share; see Commission Guidelines on the method of setting fines imposed pursuant to Article 23(2)(a) of Regulation No 1/2003 [2006] OJ C210/2 ('Commission Guidelines on Fines') para 22.

76.   See Case C–49/92P *Commission v Anic Partecipazioni SpA* [1999] ECR I–4125, [2001] 4 CMLR 602, para 145.

77.   Case 48/69 *ICI v Commission ('Dyestuffs')* [1972] ECR 619, [1972] CMLR 557, para 133.

78.   Case T–314/01 *Avebe BA v Commission* [2006] ECR II–3085, [2007] 4 CMLR 9, para 136.

79.   Case C–97/08P *Akzo Nobel NV v Commission* [2009] ECR I–8237, [2009] 5 CMLR 2633. For an earlier statement of the presumption, see Case C–286/98P *Stora Kopparbergs Bergslags AB v Commission* [2000] ECR I–9925, [2001] 4 CMLR 370, para 29.

6.   The Court of Justice, upholding an earlier decision of the General Court dismissing Akzo's appeal,[80] pointed out that the fact a parent company and its subsidiary formed a single undertaking enabled the Commission to address a decision imposing fines for breach of Article 101 to the parent, without having to establish that the parent company itself was involved in the infringement. The Court held that in the case of a 100 per cent subsidiary, 'there is a rebuttable presumption that the parent company does in fact exercise a decisive influence over the conduct of its subsidiary'.[81] The parent had the burden of rebutting that presumption by adducing 'sufficient evidence to show that its subsidiary acts independently on the market'.[82] That evidence should relate to 'the organisational, economic and legal links between the subsidiary and itself which are apt to demonstrate that they do not constitute a single economic entity'.[83]

How can the presumption of parental liability be rebutted?

7.   It is open to the parent to rebut the presumption in a given case 'based on conclusions derived from common experience, by demonstrating that it exercised restraint and did not influence the market conduct of its subsidiary'.[84] Relevant factors in rebutting the presumption could include, among others, whether the subsidiary has independent access to finance, an individual credit rating, independence in deciding investments and whether it is free to source raw materials itself. In *Akzo*, Advocate General Kokott agreed that the presumption might be rebutted where, for example, the parent company was an investment company and behaved like a pure financial investor, where the parent company held 100 per cent of the shares for only a short period or where the parent company was prevented for legal reasons from fully exercising 100 per cent control.[85]

8.   The parent's conduct during the Commission's investigation, for example, the fact that it contested the Commission's decision to send documents to it, cannot be used to rebut the presumption.[86]

9.   It has been argued in one case that the General Court has been contradictory in applying the presumption by holding on the one hand that the presumption may be

---

80.   Case T–112/05 *Akzo Nobel NV v Commission* [2007] ECR II–5049, [2008] 4 CMLR 321.
81.   Case C–97/08P *Akzo Nobel NV v Commission* [2009] ECR I–8237, [2009] 5 CMLR 2633, para 60. For application of the presumption in the Article 102 context, see, e.g., Case T–301/04 *Clearstream Banking AG v Commission* [2009] 5 CMLR 2677.
82.   Case C–97/08P *Akzo Nobel NV v Commission* [2009] ECR I–8237, [2009] 5 CMLR 2633, para 61.
83.   Case C–97/08P *Akzo Nobel NV v Commission* [2009] ECR I–8237, [2009] 5 CMLR 2633, para 65.
84.   Case C–97/08P *Akzo Nobel NV v Commission* [2009] ECR I–8237, [2009] 5 CMLR 2633, opinion of Advocate General Kokott, para 75.
85.   Case C–97/08P *Akzo Nobel NV v Commission* [2009] ECR I–8237, [2009] 5 CMLR 2633, opinion of Advocate General Kokott, fn 66.
86.   Case T–12/03 *Itochu Corp v Commission* [2009] ECR II–883, [2009] 5 CMLR 1375, para 56.

rebutted with evidence that the subsidiary acted independently and on the other, holding that the role of a parent company is to ensure that the subsidiaries within a group of companies are run as one, in particular through budgetary control. That, it is argued, effectively gives rise to a non-rebuttable presumption.[87] It can be expected that this argument and other aspects of the workings of the presumption will be the subject of future cases. As things stand however, the presumption seems to be a difficult one to rebut.[88]

How are majority-owned companies treated?

10.   The EU courts have applied the presumption of decisive influence where the parent owns slightly less than 100 per cent of the subsidiary. In *Elf Aquitaine*, the General Court held that the presumption applies in the case of a 98 per cent subsidiary.[89]

11.   In *Avebe*, the General Court held that the presumption could apply in the context of an unincorporated entity that was jointly owned by two companies, each of which had a 50 per cent stake and joint management power. The General Court found that this situation was analogous to one in which a single parent company held 100 per cent of its subsidiary and that the economic and legal links between the subsidiary and the parents formed a sufficient basis for the presumption of decisive influence to apply. The two 50:50 shareholders together with the subsidiary were held to form one undertaking in the context of which the unlawful conduct of the subsidiary could be imputed to the two parent companies.[90]

12.   What then are the boundaries of the presumption? What if, say, one company held 51 per cent of the capital in a subsidiary with the remainder widely dispersed and with the majority shareholder having the right to appoint half of the management of the subsidiary. Could the presumption apply in this case? In the UK *Construction Bid Rigging* decision, the OFT interpreted *Avebe* as authority for the view that the presumption was not confined to situations of 100 per cent (or almost 100 per cent) ownership by a parent.[91] However, it can be argued that *Avebe* did not extend the scope of the presumption to shareholders below 100 per cent (or almost 100 per cent). Invoking the presumption was rooted in the fact that there was total joint control by two entities, which amounted to 100 per cent ownership (even if that was on a joint basis). Although the General Court considered the management control of the parents to be relevant to the establishment of the presumption, there

---

87.   This argument is made in Case C–520/09P *Arkema France SA v Commission* (pending), appealing Case T–168/05 *Arkema SA v Commission,* judgment of 30 September 2009.

88.   See Bourke, 'Parental Liability for Cartel Infringements' *The Antitrust Chronicle* (November 2009) 1, 5 (noting that the Commission systematically considers any evidence advanced to rebut the presumption but that in reality the evidence presented tends to be weak).

89.   See Case T–174/05 *Elf Aquitaine SA v Commission,* judgment of 30 September 2009.

90.   Case T–314/01 *Avebe BA v Commission* [2006] ECR II–3085, [2007] 4 CMLR 9, paras 135–141.

91.   CA98/02/2005 *Bid rigging in the construction industry in England,* OFT decision of 21 September 2009, para III.24; appeals pending before the Competition Appeal Tribunal.

is no suggestion in *Avebe* that the presumption would apply where the parental holding was materially below 100 per cent, whether singly or jointly.

13.   It would be a significant extension of the presumption to apply it to a single shareholder that held 51 per cent of the subsidiary's capital or, even, 65 per cent or 75 per cent or higher. It should be remembered that the presumption is an exception to the primary rule that it is for the Commission to demonstrate that the shareholder exercises decisive influence on the basis of factual evidence, in particular any management power it has in the subsidiary. Under that primary rule, it is not sufficient for the Commission to show that the shareholder merely has the ability to exercise decisive influence.[92]

14.   Even if the presumption does not apply, the shareholder and subsidiary can be found to constitute one undertaking where the Commission adduces sufficient evidence to show that the shareholder exercises decisive influence over the subsidiary. The Commission must demonstrate such decisive influence on the basis of factual evidence.[93] The Commission will be seeking to adduce evidence of the same kinds of factors that a parent company seeking to rebut the presumption of decisive influence would argue did not exist. Relevant evidence would include the level of the shareholding and the nature of the links between the parent and the subsidiary, for example, the composition of the board of directors[94] and the extent to which the parent company is involved in commercial dealings of the subsidiary with third parties and, more generally, how it influences the commercial policy of the subsidiary.[95]

How are shareholdings of 50 per cent and below treated?

15.   Could a 50 per cent shareholder or even a minority shareholder be considered to form a single undertaking with the company in which it holds shares for purposes of imposing liability under Article 101 or 102? Under the Merger Regulation, the acquisition of less than majority shareholdings can trigger a filing requirement as the test of control in that context includes 'negative control'. Under this concept, one company can 'control' another if it has the ability to veto important business

---

92.   See Case T–314/01 *Avebe BA v Commission* [2006] ECR II–3085, [2007] 4 CMLR 9, para 136. Note, however, a different view taken by the OFT in the *Construction Bid Rigging* case, where it held that a shareholder's 'clear ability' to exercise control over a majority-owned subsidiary would be sufficient to give rise to the presumption. The OFT extrapolated this holding from the conclusion in *Avebe* that two 50 per cent shareholders could be presumed to have determined their subsidiary's marketing policy jointly (CA98/02/2005 *Bid rigging in the construction industry in England*, OFT decision of 21 September 2009, para III.19–24; appeals pending before the Competition Appeal Tribunal).

93.   See Case T–314/01 *Avebe BA v Commission* [2006] ECR II–3085, [2007] 4 CMLR 9, para 136.

94.   See, e.g., Cases C–189/02P etc *Dansk Rørindustri v Commission* [2005] ECR I–5425, [2005] 5 CMLR 796, para 120.

95.   See, e.g., Case 107/82 *AEG-Telefunken v Commission* [1983] ECR 3151, [1984] 3 CMLR 325, paras 51–52.

decisions, such as the adoption of the budget, even if it holds only a small percentage of shares. It is deemed to exercise decisive influence by virtue of such a veto power.[96]

16. It does not yet seem to be established whether this concept of negative control applies in the Article 101/102 context.[97] The courts may have less difficulty in finding that a subsidiary and a parent with significantly less than a 100 per cent shareholding form one undertaking when the Commission seeks to impose liability for infringements of competition law by the subsidiary. In contrast, where the 'single undertaking' argument is employed in an attempt to avoid the application of the competition rules (for example, a minority shareholder arguing that it forms one undertaking with a subsidiary with the result that Article 101 does not apply to agreements between them), it seems less likely to succeed. In *Gosme/Martell-DMP*, the Commission considered a similar structure to that in *Avebe*. In deciding whether Article 101 could be disapplied in the case of an agreement between one of two 50 per cent owners of a subsidiary and the subsidiary, it found that the parent and subsidiary were independent undertakings. In reaching this conclusion, the Commission pointed to some of the same features which the General Court had emphasized in reaching an opposite conclusion in *Avebe*, including that the parent companies each held 50 per cent of the capital and could each nominate half of the supervisory board members. These factors suggested that one of the parents was not itself in a position to control the commercial activity of the subsidiary.[98] These differences in approach highlight the contextual nature of the concept of an undertaking which, in the Article 101 context, 'must be understood as designating an economic unit *for the purpose of the subject-matter of the agreement in question*'.[99]

Can a trade association and its members constitute a single economic unit?

17. The imputation of unlawful conduct from one entity to the other has been extended beyond the parent-subsidiary context to include a trade association and its members as one economic unit. Applying the parent-subsidiary analysis to the trade association context in *Metsä-Serla*, the Court of Justice held that the trade association was obliged to follow the instructions of its members and unable to act on the market independent of them. It effectively formed an economic unit with each member and in such a case the members were jointly and severally liable for fines imposed on the trade association.[100]

---

96. See Question 66.
97. See Whish, *Competition Law* (6th edn, 2009) 93.
98. *Gosme/Martell-DMP* [1991] OJ L185/23, [1992] 5 CMLR 586, para 30. See also, *Ijsselcentrale* [1991] OJ L28/32, [1992] 5 CMLR 154, in which the Commission found that a subsidiary did not form an economic unit with one or more of four parent companies.
99. Case C–217/05 *Confederación Española de Empresarios de Estaciones de Servicio v CEPSA* [2006] ECR I–11987, [2007] 4 CMLR 181, para 40 (emphasis added).
100. Case C–294/98 *Metsä-Serla Oyj v Commission* [2000] ECR I–10065, paras 27, 28, 36.

Can passive investments give rise to antitrust liability?

18. If a parent company holds shares merely for investment purposes and is not involved in the day-to-day running of the subsidiary's business, will it still be liable for the antitrust infringements of the subsidiary? The starting point is again the level of the parent's shareholding. If the parent holds 100 per cent or close to this amount of the capital in the subsidiary, the presumption that it forms one undertaking with the subsidiary will apply. It is up to the parent to adduce sufficient evidence to rebut this presumption. In the *Dutch Bitumen Cartel*, one parent company, Kuwait Petroleum Corporation ('KPC'), argued that it should not be an addressee of the Commission's infringement decision as it took a passive role with respect to its subsidiaries outside Kuwait, including the Dutch subsidiary that had been involved in the cartel. As KPC indirectly held 100 per cent of the shares in the subsidiary, the presumption that it exercised decisive influence over the subsidiary applied. The Commission considered that insufficient evidence was submitted to rebut the presumption. The Commission rejected the argument that KPC was merely an investment vehicle, pointing out that it received financial reports about its subsidiaries based outside Kuwait and, as well as having played an essential role in structuring the group's business outside Kuwait, KPC retained the power to change that structure if it wished to do so.[101]

19. KPC appeared to be too 'hands-on' to avoid the presumption of liability for its subsidiary's actions. However, an investment vehicle may be able to avoid liability where it does not have any meaningful input in its portfolio companies. In *Spanish Raw Tobacco*, the Commission held that a parent company did not exercise decisive influence over a 100 per cent subsidiary where its interest in the subsidiary was of a 'purely financial nature'.[102] In stating in an appeal against the decision in the *Monochloroacetic Acid Cartel* that the parent company there was 'not simply an investment vehicle that merely serves to invest capital in companies whose commercial operation it then leaves to those companies,'[103] the General Court also seems to imply that a sufficiently 'passive' investor might not be subject to the presumption that it is part of the same undertaking as its subsidiary. In *Akzo* Advocate General Kokott also suggested that a 100 per cent shareholder might be able to rebut the presumption of decisive influence on the basis that it behaved purely as a financial investor.[104] This 'passive investor defence' may be of interest to private equity companies and others with significant investments in companies which they do not themselves manage on a day-to-day basis.[105]

---

101. Case COMP/F/38.456 *Dutch Bitumen Cartel* [2007] 5 CMLR 617, paras 223–226.
102. Case COMP/C.38.328/B.2 *Raw Tobacco Spain*, Commission Decision of 20 October 2004, paras 376, 383.
103. Case T–175/05 *Akzo Nobel NV v Commission* [2009] 5 CMLR 2774, para 18.
104. Case C–97/08P *Akzo Nobel NV v Commission* [2009] ECR I–8237, [2009] 5 CMLR 2633, opinion of Advocate General Kokott, fn 66.
105. See, e.g., Case T–45/07 *Unipetrol v Commission* (pending) (applicant arguing that its holding of all the shares of a company that participated in the *Butadiene Rubber* cartel was of a purely financial nature).

What are the implications of imputation of a subsidiary's conduct to a parent company?

20.   Where the Commission makes a finding that the competition rules have been breached by a company that forms a single economic entity with a parent company, it can choose whether to address its infringement decision and impose a fine only on the subsidiary or the parent or both. The Commission has a discretion whether to address itself to the parent company and it does not have to justify its choice.[106]

21.   The inclusion of a parent company as an addressee of the Commission's decision can have significant consequences. It may result in a much higher fine being imposed as the maximum fine is based on the turnover of each undertaking deemed to have participated in the infringement.[107] If the turnover of the parent group is used as the basis, as opposed to the subsidiary that was primarily involved in the infringement, the potential maximum fine can be calculated relative to 10 per cent of the total turnover of the consolidated corporate group. There is also a risk of higher fines for any future infringements as the Commission can impose additional penalties for repeat infringements. If a different subsidiary is involved in a future breach of the competition rules, that could be considered a repeat infringement with a potential 100 per cent uplift in the fine for the new infringement.[108]

Key Sources

Case C–97/08P *Akzo Nobel NV v Commission* [2009] ECR I–8237, [2009] 5 CMLR 2633.

Case T–314/01 *Avebe BA v Commission* [2006] ECR II–3085, [2007] 4 CMLR 9.

Case 107/82 *AEG-Telefunken v Commission* [1983] ECR 3151, [1984] 3 CMLR 325.

Commission Guidelines on the method of setting fines imposed pursuant to Article 23(2)(a) of Regulation No 1/2003 [2006] OJ C210/02.

---

106.   See, e.g., Cases T–236/01 etc *Tokai Carbon Co. Ltd. v Commission* [2004] ECR II–1181, [2004] 5 CMLR 1465, para 285.
107.   Regulation 1/2003, Article 23(2).
108.   See Commission Guidelines on Fines [2006] OJ C210/2, para 28.

3.   **WHEN A SUBSIDIARY IS SOLD, WHO HAS RESPONSIBILITY FOR BREACHES OF COMPETITION LAW COMMITTED BY THE SUBSIDIARY BEFORE THE SALE?**

Summary

- If the seller had decisive influence over the subsidiary, it is liable for anti-competitive conduct that took place prior to the sale. However the Commission has a discretion to address a fine to the subsidiary or the seller.

- If proceedings would normally have been addressed to the subsidiary in its own right, then liability will pass with it.

1.   By the time an infringement decision has been adopted, the entity or undertaking that participated in the anti-competitive conduct or agreement may no longer exist or it may have been sold. Which entity then has responsibility for the breach of competition law and payment of any fines?

2.   In the context of the enforcement of the EU competition rules by the Commission, this question is one of EU law and domestic law rules on the liability of companies for actions of their organs is not relevant.[109]

3.   The starting point for imposing liability for infringement of competition law is the principle of personal responsibility, according to which the entity that infringes the competition rules must answer for the infringement.[110] As discussed in Question 2, when a parent company and its subsidiary form one undertaking, the actions of the subsidiary are imputed to the parent so that the parent, as well as the subsidiary, has personal responsibility. In this case, the Commission can choose whether to address an infringement decision to one or both entities and its practice in many cases has been to address it to both.[111]

4.   The basic rule in the case of an infringing entity that has been sold was stated by the Court of Justice in *Cascades*:

> It falls, in principle, to the legal or natural person managing the undertaking in question when the infringement was committed to answer for that infringement, even if, when the Decision finding the infringement was adopted, another person had assumed responsibility for operating the undertaking.[112]

---

109. Case T–134/94 *NMH Stahlwerke GmbH v Commission* [1999] ECR II–239, para 44.
110. See Case C–49/92P *Commission v Anic Partecipazioni SpA* [1999] ECR I–4125, [2001] 4 CMLR 602, para 145.
111. The Commission typically lists the addressees at the end of its decisions. See, e.g., COMP/ 39.125 *Car Glass*, Commission Decision of 12 November 2008, 187–189.
112. Case C–279/98P *Cascades SA v Commission* [2000] ECR I–9693, para 78. See also Case C–286/98P *Stora Kopparbergs Bergslags AB v Commission* [2000] ECR I–9925, [2001] 4 CMLR 370, para 37.

5.   Assume that an undertaking (T), which participated in a cartel, has been sold by its
      former parent company (S), to a new company (P). Which entities are now
      responsible for breaches of competition law committed by T before the sale?

What if the Seller was not responsible?

6.   If S was not liable before the sale because it did not exercise decisive influence
      over T, and the infringement decision could only have been addressed to T in its
      own right but for the sale, then responsibility for T's anti-competitive conduct
      taking place before the sale will attach to T and pass with T when it is sold. If T as
      an entity no longer exists, for example if it has been dissolved or subsumed into
      another of P's subsidiaries, the infringement decision would be addressed to P.[113]

What if the Seller was responsible?

7.   Assume that S was responsible for the cartel conduct of T before its sale, for
      example because S owned 100 per cent of the shares in T and there were no
      arguments that could credibly be made that S did not exert decisive influence over
      T. In this case, S will remain liable for the period before the sale. It falls on the
      Seller, as the legal person managing T when the infringement was committed, to
      answer for that infringement, even if, when the decision finding the infringement
      was adopted, P had assumed responsibility for operating T.[114]

8.   However, the Commission has a discretion in deciding to which entity it will
      address its infringement decision. It may choose to address the decision to S or T,
      regardless of the fact that T has now been sold to P.[115] If the Commission decision
      is addressed to T, as a practical matter, this will likely mean that its new owner, P,
      shoulders the financial burden of a fine.

**What if the Purchaser had itself been involved in the cartel before it acquired the
Target?**

9.   In *Stora*, the Court of Justice held that P could not be liable for conduct of T before
      the acquisition even though P could not have been unaware that T participated in

---

113. See, e.g., Cases T–259/02 etc *Raiffeisen Zentralbank Österreich AG v Commission* [2006]
     ECR II 5169, [2007] 5 CMLR 1142, paras 334–335 (the word 'prior' in para 334 in the
     English language report should read 'after') (appeals dismissed Cases C–125/07 etc
     Raiffeisen Zentralbank Österreich AG v Commission [2009] ECR I–8681).
114. See, e.g., Case T–161/05 *Hoechst GmbH v Commission* [2009] 5 CMLR 2728, para 61
     (noting that in such cases, the principle of personal responsibility cannot be called into
     question by the principle of economic continuity).
115. Cases T–259/02 etc *Raiffeisen Zentralbank Österreich AG v Commission* [2006] ECR II
     5169, [2007] 5 CMLR 1142, para 331 (appeals dismissed Cases C–125/07 etc *Raiffeisen
     Zentralbank Österreich AG v Commission* [2009] ECR I–8681; see para 82).

the cartel because P itself was active in the cartel through another subsidiary.[116] However, if T no longer exists, then P can be made liable in this situation.[117]

If the infringing entity ceases to exist, who is responsible?

10.   Other than in the context of the sale of a company, where the infringing entity has ceased to exist, either in law or in economic terms, another entity can be made responsible. If this were not possible, 'undertakings could escape penalties by simply changing their identity through restructurings, sales or other legal or organisational changes'.[118] It is also essential to be able to identify an entity to whom the infringement decision can be addressed where the infringing entity has become insolvent or is otherwise unable to pay a fine. A decision by the Commission imposing a fine can only be addressed to a legal person.[119]

11.   In *ETI*, the Court of Justice applied the principle of 'economic continuity' to find that the imposition of penalties for the entirety of an infringement on the economic successor of the entity that had commenced the infringement would not be precluded. The latter part of an infringement of the competition rules had been carried out by the economic successor of the entity that had commenced the infringement even though that original infringing entity, while no longer operating in the economic sector concerned, was still in existence. The fact that both entities were owned by the same public entity, the Italian Ministry of the Economy and Finance, was a key factor in finding that it would be permissible for the penalty in respect of the entire infringement to be imposed on the entity which was the economic successor.[120]

How should an acquiror minimise the risk of inheriting competition law infringements?

12.   The allocation of liability for breaches of competition law is an important question in the sale and purchase of companies and businesses. Exposure for cartel conduct, in particular, in the form of fines and private damages actions can be significant. Given the secret nature of cartels, it can be difficult for a potential purchaser to identify possible antitrust liability through the due diligence process. It is important then for a potential purchaser to identify the likelihood of antitrust liability, whether it or the seller will be responsible for any fines or damages and

---

116. Case C–286/98P *Stora Kopparbergs Bergslags AB v Commission* [2000] ECR I–9925, [2001] 4 CMLR 370, para 39.
117. Cases T–259/02 etc *Raiffeisen Zentralbank Österreich AG v Commission* [2006] ECR II 5169, [2007] 5 CMLR 1142, para 334 (appeals dismissed Cases C–125/07 etc *Raiffeisen Zentralbank Österreich AG v Commission* [2009] ECR I–8681).
118. Case C–280/06 *Autorità Garante della Concorrenza e del Mercato v ETI SpA* [2007] ECR I–10893, [2008] 4 CMLR 277, para 41.
119. See Cases T–305/94 etc *Limburgse Vinyl Maatschappij NV v Commission* [1999] ECR II–931, [1999] 5 CMLR 303, para 978.
120. See Case C–280/06 *Autorità Garante della Concorrenza e del Mercato v ETI SpA* [2007] ECR I–10893, [2008] 4 CMLR 277, para 51.

how it can protect itself in the transaction documents through warranties and indemnities.[121]

Key Sources

Case C–286/98P *Stora Kopparbergs Bergslags AB v Commission* [2000] ECR I–9925, [2000] 4 CMLR 370.

Case C–279/98P *Cascades SA v Commission* [2000] ECR I–9693.

Cases T–259/02 etc. *Raiffeisen Zentralbank Österreich AG v Commission* [2006] ECR II 5169, [2007] 5 CMLR 1142.

Case C–280/06 *Autorita Garante della Concorrenza e del Mercato v ETI SpA* [2007] ECR I–10893, [2008] 4 CMLR 277.

---

121. See Question 81.

4.   IS IT A DEFENCE TO SHOW THAT A BREACH OF COMPETITION LAW WAS REQUIRED BY A GOVERNMENTAL AUTHORITY?

Summary

- State compulsion is recognised as a defence to the application of Articles 101 and 102.

- However, the exemption is applied narrowly – the undertaking must be compelled to act anti-competitively.

- It is insufficient that the national legislation or governmental authority permits, approves or even encourages the anti-competitive behaviour. It must compel it.

- State compulsion can be evidenced by (i) a binding national rule or (ii) where the national legal framework eliminates the possibility of competition.

1.   The competition rules only apply to anti-competitive conduct engaged in by undertakings 'on their own initiative'.[122] If undertakings are compelled to act in an anti-competitive manner by the State, then Articles 101 and 102 will not apply to the undertakings. State compulsion could be exercised through a requirement in national legislation or where national legislation creates a legal framework which itself eliminates any possibility of competitive activity on the part of undertakings.[123]

2.   The competition rules may apply if a State measure does not preclude an undertaking from engaging in autonomous conduct.[124] If national legislation provides that anti-competitive conduct is allowed, this is not sufficient to disapply the competition rules. Similarly, national legislation that encourages or approves of anti-competitive conduct is not sufficient. The State measure must nullify the undertaking's autonomy.[125]

3.   The State compulsion doctrine is interpreted strictly so that an undertaking seeking to rely on it must truly be compelled to act in an anti-competitive manner. This will be difficult for an undertaking to show where its State compulsion argument is based on anything less than a binding provision of national law. In a case involving an appeal against a Commission decision that Greek ferry operators had fixed prices, it was argued by the ferry operator that the legislative and

---

122. Case C–18/99 *Régie des télégraphes et des téléphones v GB-Inno-BM SA* [1991] ECR I–5941, para 20.
123. See Cases C–359 & 379/95P *Commission v Ladbroke Racing Ltd.* [1997] ECR I–6265, [1998] 4 CMLR 27, para 33.
124. See Cases C–359 & 379/95P *Commission v Ladbroke Racing Ltd.* [1997] ECR I–6265, [1998] 4 CMLR 27, para 34.
125. Cf the position in US federal antitrust law, under which private action can be exempted from the reach of the federal antitrust laws where it is authorized by a State law, without a requirement of compulsion (see, e.g., *Southern Motor Carriers Rate Conference, Inc. v United States* 471 US 48, 105 S Ct 1721 (1985)).

regulatory framework in Greece restricted the autonomy of shipping companies to set prices. Rejecting those arguments, the General Court noted that:

> [In] the absence of any binding regulatory provision imposing anti-competitive conduct, the Commission is entitled to conclude that the operators in question enjoyed no autonomy only if it appears on the basis of objective, relevant and consistent evidence that that conduct was unilaterally imposed upon them by the national authorities through the exercise of irresistible pressure, such as, for example, the threat to adopt State measures likely to cause them to sustain substantial losses.[126]

4.   In *BIDS*, it was noted by Advocate General Trstenjak that meat processors who agreed that certain plants would be closed were not acting under State compulsion. The fact that a market study recommending a reduction in the number of beef processors was financed by the Irish government and that a task force formed by the Minister for Agriculture called on the beef industry to implement the market study was not in itself sufficient to amount to State compulsion.[127]

5.   Even if undertakings are compelled to act in a certain way that is anti-competitive, to the extent the State measure leaves room for residual competition, the competition rules will apply to that residual area.[128] In the *Dutch Tobacco* case, the Court of Justice rejected the argument that Dutch legislation on tobacco made all forms of competition impossible. While this legislation left limited scope for competition, the tobacco manufacturers could still have competed on prices to retailers. Instead, they collectively agreed to margins and rebates given to retailers, so doing collectively what they said they could not do individually.[129]

6.   The State compulsion argument has been unsuccessfully raised in several cases before the Commission.[130]

What types of State measure are covered?

7.   The parameters of the types of measure that can be relied upon to establish State compulsion have not been fully elaborated in the cases. The central requirement is that the measure is binding, as per, for example, the reference to a 'binding regulatory provision'[131] or 'national law or if the [national law] creates a legal

---

126. Case T–65/99 *Strintzis Lines Shipping SA v Commission* [2003] ECR II–5433, [2005] 5 CMLR 1901, para 122 (appeal dismissed, Case C–110/04P *Strintzis Lines Shipping SA v Commission* [2006] ECR I–44).

127. Case C–209/07 *Competition Authority v BIDS* [2008] ECR I–8637, [2009] 4 CMLR 310, opinion of Advocate General Trstenjak at para 95. The Court of Justice agreed with the Advocate General's conclusions but it did not address the state compulsion argument.

128. See Cases 40/73 etc *Suiker Unie UA v Commission* [1975] ECR 1663, [1976] 1 CMLR 295, para 24.

129. See Cases 240/82 etc *Stichting Sigarettenindustrie v Commission* [1985] ECR 3831, [1987] 3 CMLR 661, para 36.

130. For a brief overview of these cases, see Whish, *Competition Law* (6th edn, 2009) 134–135.

131. Case T–65/99 *Strintzis Lines Shipping SA v Commission* [2003] ECR II–5433, [2005] 5 CMLR 1901, para 122.

framework eliminating any possibility of competitive conduct'.[132] National legislation, whether primary or secondary, would clearly be covered, as would binding orders issued by a government but a measure lacking compulsion, such as guidelines or recommendations or even non-binding State measures encouraging anti-competitive conduct[133] could not be relied on in making the State compulsion argument. It is doubtful that a condition imposed in a public contract under the public procurement rules, requiring the contractor to engage in conduct or agreements that were found to infringe the competition rules, would satisfy the required element of compulsion.

8.   It has not been conclusively established if a binding measure of a State outside the EU can be relied on to make out the State compulsion argument but this possibility has at least been countenanced by the courts.[134]

May the State measure itself breach EU law?[135]

9.   EU Member States have a duty under Article 4(3) TEU (which is substantially similar to the former Article 10 TEC) not to adopt measures that could jeopardise the attainment of the Union's objectives. This includes measures that undermine the effectiveness of the Union's competition rules. If, for example, a national measure gives rise to agreements that infringe Article 101, then Article 4(3) TEU can be applied in combination with Article 101 to make the national measure unenforceable. National courts and designated competition authorities that have the power to apply Articles 101 and 102 can make this determination.[136]

10.   If a finding is made that a national law breaches EU law in this way, how does this affect an undertaking which seeks to invoke the national law in its State compulsion defence to a charge that it has breached EU competition law? Once the decision to set aside the national law is made definitive, the national measure cannot be relied on in arguing State compulsion. However, up until such time, the defence based on that national law is potentially available.[137]

Ireland

11.   The Competition Act 2002 makes specific provision for a State compulsion defence in respect of criminal proceedings. In proceedings for the offence of a

---

132. Cases T–191/98 etc *Atlantic Container Line AB v Commission* [2003] ECR II–3275, [2005] 4 CMLR 1283, para 1130.
133. See, e.g., Case 43&63/82 *VBVB v Commission* [1984] ECR 19, [1985] 1 CMLR 27, para 40.
134. See, e.g., Cases T–191/98 etc *Atlantic Container Line AB v Commission* [2003] ECR II–3275, [2005] 4 CMLR 1283, paras 1131–1150 (the General Court considered whether certain agreements and practices were required by US law, concluding that there was no such requirement). Foreign state compulsion is recognised as a defence in US federal antitrust law (see, e.g., *Interamerican Refining Corp. v Texaco Maracaibo, Inc.* 307 F Supp 1291 (D Del 1970)).
135. See also Question 135.
136. See Regulation 1/2003, Article 5; Case C–198/01 *CIF* [2003] ECR I–8055, [2003] 5 CMLR 829, paras 48–50.
137. See Case C–198/01 *CIF* [2003] ECR I–8055, [2003] 5 CMLR 829, paras 54–55.

breach of section 4/Article 101, it is a good defence to prove that the alleged agreements or conduct were entered into 'pursuant to a determination made or a direction given by a statutory body'.[138] This is also a good defence in proceedings for the offence of a breach of section 5/Article 102.[139] It is not clear whether the measure relied on must be legally binding in order for the defence to be successful. Certainly, the terms 'determination' and 'direction' seem to fall short of legally binding action. The defence can also be invoked in a private action for damages based on a breach of section 4 or 5 but the Act is silent as to whether the defence can be invoked in a damages claim based on a breach of Article 101 or 102.[140] Whereas the EU law principle of equivalence dictates that a claimant basing a damages action on a breach of Article 101/102 would have equivalent rights as provided for in the Act in respect of claims based on breaches of sections 4 and 5, it is doubtful that the defendant could rely on the principle of equivalence to invoke the defences specifically provided for in section 4/5 actions.

12. Bodies that fall under the definition of 'statutory body' are specifically listed in the Act. They are the Commission for Taxi Regulation, the Broadcasting Commission of Ireland, the Commission for Energy Regulation, the Commission for Aviation Regulation, ComReg, the National Consumer Agency and the Health Insurance Authority.[141]

UK

13. In contrast to the Irish Act, the Competition Act 1998 does not specifically recognise a State compulsion defence. Given that section 60 of the Competition Act 1998 provides for the application of UK competition law to be dealt with in a manner consistent with corresponding questions of EU competition law, it is likely that a State compulsion defence along the lines of that in EU law would be recognised.

Key Sources

Cases C–359, 379/95 *Commission v Ladbroke Racing Ltd.* [1997] ECR I–6265, [1998] 4 CMLR 27.

Case T–65/99 *Strintzis Lines Shipping SA v Commission* [2003] ECR II–5433, [2005] 5 CMLR 1901.

Case C–198/01 *Consorzio Industrie Fiammiferi (CIF) v Autorità Garante della Concorrenza e del Mercato* [2003] ECR I–8055, [2003] 5 CMLR 829.

Ireland

Competition Act 2002, ss 6(5), 7(2), 14(9)

---

138. Competition Act 2002, s 6(5).
139. Competition Act 2002, s 7(2).
140. See Competition Act 2002, s 14(9).
141. See Competition Act 2002, Schedule 1, column 1.

5.   ARE THERE LIMITATION PERIODS FOR THE APPLICATION OF EU
     COMPETITION LAW?

Summary

• There is a five-year limitation period for imposing fines for breach of Articles
  101 and 102.

• For continuing infringements, time does not start to run until the day on which
  the infringement ends.

• Enforcement actions by the Commission or national authority interrupt the
  limitation period and start time running afresh.

• Following an infringement decision, the Commission has five years to enforce
  it. This period may be interrupted subject to a total limitation period of ten
  years.

1.   Limitation periods for imposing fines or penalties for breaches of EU competition
     law are contained in Regulation 1/2003.[142] Article 25(1) of Regulation 1/2003
     establishes a five-year limitation period for imposing fines for breaches of Articles
     101 and 102. A three-year limitation period applies to infringements of provisions
     concerning requests for information or the conduct of inspections.[143]

2.   Article 25(2) of Regulation 1/2003 states:

     > Time shall begin to run on the day on which the infringement is committed. However,
     > in the case of continuing or repeated infringements, time shall begin to run on the day
     > on which the infringement ceases.

3.   Infringements of competition law are often of a type that could potentially be
     viewed as constituting separate agreements and concerted practices over time. A
     cartel, for example, may last over a number of years and be the subject of
     developing agreements and understandings. The EU courts recognised that the
     concept of a single continuous infringement could be applied in such cases. The
     General Court noted in 1989 in respect of appeals in the *Polypropylene* cartel case:

     > Those schemes were part of a series of efforts made by the undertakings in question in
     > pursuit of a single economic aim, namely to distort the normal movement of prices on
     > the market in polypropylene. It would thus be artificial to split up such continuous
     > conduct, characterized by a single purpose, by treating it as consisting of a number of

---

142. Previously, similar limitation periods were found in Regulation (EEC) 2988/74 concerning
     limitation periods in proceedings and the enforcement of sanctions under the rules of the
     European Economic Community relating to transport and competition [1974] OJ L319/1.

143. Regulation 1/2003, Article 25(1)(a).

separate infringements. The fact is that the applicant took part – over a period of years – in an integrated set of schemes constituting a single infringement, which progressively manifested itself in both unlawful agreements and unlawful concerted practices.[144]

4. Applying the concept of a single continuous infringement allows the Commission to avoid questions about the limitation period. However, the Commission cannot employ the concept to circumvent the limitation period for imposing fines. In an appeal against the Commission decision in the *Choline Chloride* cartel, the General Court held that the Commission had failed to show that the European and global cartels constituted a single and continuous infringement. There was an absence of any temporal overlap in the implementation of the two cartels, they pursued different objectives and were implemented by dissimilar methods, and there was no evidence that the European producers intended to adhere to the global arrangements in order to divide the EEA market.[145] Fines imposed in respect of the global cartel were held to be time barred.[146] The General Court made the more general point that anti-competitive agreements do not form a single continuous infringement just because they are concluded in the same industry sector.[147]

5. An undertaking may be held responsible for an overall antitrust infringement, such as a cartel, even though it is shown to have participated directly only in one or some of the constituent elements of that cartel if it knew, or must have known, that the collusion in which it participated was part of an overall plan and that the overall plan included all the constituent elements of the cartel.[148]

6. As a general rule, the characterisation of certain unlawful actions as constituting one and the same infringement also affects the penalty that may be imposed. A finding that multiple infringements exist may entail the imposition of a number of separate fines. This may be advantageous to the undertakings involved if some of the infringements are time-barred.[149]

---

144. Case T–1/89 *Rhône-Poulenc SA v Commission* [1991] ECR II–867, [1992] 4 CMLR 84, para 126 (upheld on appeal, Case C–49/92P *Commission v Anic Partecipazioni SpA* [1999] ECR I–4125, [2001] 4 CMLR 602, noting at para 81 that infringement of Article 101 'may result not only from an isolated act but also from a series of acts or from continuous conduct').

145. Cases T–101 & 111/05 etc *BASF AG v Commission* [2007] ECR II–4949, [2008] 4 CMLR 347, para 209.

146. Cases T–101 & 111/05 etc *BASF AG v Commission* [2007] ECR II–4949, [2008] 4 CMLR 347, para 210.

147. Cases T–101 & 111/05 etc *BASF AG v Commission* [2007] ECR II–4949, [2008] 4 CMLR 347, paras 179–180. See also Case T–446/05 *Amann & Söhne GmbH & Co. KG v Commission*, judgment of 28 April 2010, para 92.

148. Case T–19/05 *Boliden AB v Commission*, judgment of 19 May 2010, para 61; Cases T–305/94 etc *Limburgse Vinyl Maatschappij NV v Commission* [1999] ECR II–931, [1999] 5 CMLR 303, para 773.

149. See Cases T–101 & 111/05 etc *BASF AG v Commission* [2007] ECR II–4949, [2008] 4 CMLR 347, para 158.

When is the limitation period interrupted?

7.   Article 25(3) provides that any action taken by the Commission or a national competition authority for purposes of the investigation or proceedings in respect of an infringement interrupts the limitation period. An investigation by the Commission or a national competition authority will often commence at a time when the alleged infringement is still continuing so that the limitation period will not yet have begun to run and the initiation of the investigation will, in any event, suspend the running of the limitation period.

8.   Each interruption starts time running afresh. However, the limitation period expires at the latest after 10 years if the Commission has not imposed a fine or periodic penalty payment.[150] This provision is subject to the rule that the limitation period is suspended for the duration of any appeals against the Commission's decision.[151]

9.   The limitation periods contained in Article 25 of Regulation 1/2003 cover only the imposition of fines and periodic penalty payments. The Commission may still take infringement decisions (without the imposition of a fine or payment) outside of these periods. Article 7(1) provides that '[if] the Commission has a legitimate interest in doing so, it may also find that an infringement has been committed in the past'. In the *GVL* case, the Court of Justice found that the Commission had a sufficiently 'legitimate interest' in taking an infringement decision where there was a real danger of a resumption of the anti-competitive practice and it was necessary to clarify the legal position.[152]

10.   A more difficult question is whether the Commission can impose structural or behavioural remedies in respect of an infringement decision taken outside the Article 25 limitation periods. Those limitation periods apply only to powers in Articles 23 and 24 of Regulation 1/2003, which cover, respectively, only 'fines' and 'periodic penalty payments'. A remedy such as, for example, an order to make available an essential facility arising out of a finding of abuse of dominance, would not fall within either category.[153]

Is there a limitation period for taking previous infringements into account for purposes of increasing the fine?

11.   The Commission is entitled to take into account repeat infringements of competition law as an aggravating factor in increasing the fine.[154] The General

---

150. Regulation 1/2003, Article 25(5).
151. Regulation 1/2003, Article 25(6).
152. See Case 7/82 *Gesellschaft zur Verwertung von Leistungsschutzrechten mbH (GVL) v Commission* [1983] ECR 483, [1983] 3 CMLR 645, paras 27–28.
153. In the past, there might have been a stronger argument that structural and behavioural remedies constituted a 'penalty' under Article 1 of Regulation 2988/74 and so were covered by the limitation periods in that Regulation, however, it was held that only pecuniary penalties were covered in respect of Regulation 2988/74 (see Cases T–22 & 23/02 *Sumitomo Chemical Co. Ltd v Commission* [2005] ECR II–4065, [2006] 4 CMLR 42, para 60).
154. Commission Guidelines on Fines [2006] OJ C210/2, para 28; e.g., Cases C–204/00P etc *Aalborg Portland A/S v Commission* [2004] ECR I–123, [2005] 4 CMLR 251, para 91.

Court examined in *BASF (Choline Chloride)* whether there was a limitation period on what previous infringements could be considered. It was argued that some of the activity taken into account was in the 'distant past' (as far back as 1964). The General Court found that the fact that no time limit was laid down for considering previous infringements did not breach the principle of legal certainty and that the Commission could not be bound by any limitation period in considering whether to increase the fine for recidivism. However it also held that the Commission 'may … take into consideration the indicia which tend to confirm such a propensity, including, for example, the time which has elapsed between the infringements at issue'.[155]

12. The Commission has a wide discretion in appraising repeated infringements[156] and, in calculating a fine, there would not appear to be any obstacle to it taking account, as an aggravating factor, of previous infringement decisions taken under Article 7 of Regulation 1/2003 that did not involve the imposition of a fine.[157]

What are the limitation periods for the enforcement of penalties?

13. Once an infringement decision is taken, the Commission has five years to enforce it.[158] Time runs from the date the decision is made final. The limitation period can be interrupted, starting time to run afresh, if there is a decision varying the original amount of the fine or penalty or refusing an application for variation or 'by any action of the Commission or of a Member State, acting at the request of the Commission, designed to enforce payment of the fine or periodic penalty payment'.[159] The limitation period is suspended for the period during which time to pay is allowed or where ordered by the Court of Justice.[160]

14. It is a general principle of EU law related to the principle of sound administration that the Commission must act within a reasonable time when it adopts decisions following administrative proceedings relating to competition policy.[161] However, in light, in particular, of the total limitation period of ten years, 'there is no room for consideration of the Commission's duty to exercise its power to impose fines within a reasonable period'.[162] The limitation period alone will determine whether the Commission acted in time in imposing a fine.

---

155. Cases T–101 & 111/05 etc *BASF AG v Commission* [2007] ECR II–4949, [2008] 4 CMLR 347, para 67.
156. See, e.g., Case T–161/05 *Hoechst GmbH v Commission* [2009] 5 CMLR 2728, paras 141–142.
157. See Case T–122/04 *Outokumpu Oyj v Commission* [2009] ECR II–1135, paras 55–59 (previous infringement decision under the ECSC Treaty, which did not involve the imposition of a fine, taken into account).
158. Regulation 1/2003, Article 26(1).
159. Regulation 1/2003, Article 26(3).
160. Regulation 1/2003, Article 26(5).
161. See, e.g., Case T–213/00 *CMA CGM v Commission* [2003] ECR II–913, [2003] 5 CMLR 268, para 317.
162. Case T–213/00 *CMA CGM v Commission* [2003] ECR II–913, [2003] 5 CMLR 268, para 324.

What limitation periods apply in private actions?

15.   The limitation periods applicable to private actions claiming damages or other remedies based on a breach of EU competition law are a matter for the relevant national law, subject to the principles of equivalence and effectiveness.[163]

Key Sources

Regulation 1/2003, Articles 7, 25, 26.

Cases T–101 & 111/05 etc. *BASF AG v Commission* [2007] ECR II–4949, [2008] 4 CMLR 347.

---

163.   See Question 117.

6.   WHEN DOES AN AGREEMENT OR PRACTICE HAVE A SUFFICIENT CROSS-BORDER IMPACT THAT IT 'MAY AFFECT TRADE BETWEEN MEMBER STATES'?

Summary

- A cross-border effect is required for the EU competition rules to apply.

- A *potential* effect on inter-State trade is sufficient.

- This cross-border effect is usually found without much difficulty.

- Agreements among parties in only one Member State may still have sufficient cross-border effect to invoke Article 101.

- The effect on trade must be appreciable (*De minimis* exception: combined EU market share of not more than 5 per cent and combined turnover of not more than €40 million).

1.   This is a jurisdictional requirement which outlines the boundary between areas covered by EU law and the laws of the Member States. Articles 101 and 102 each have a requirement that there be an effect on trade between member States before those provisions are applicable. The Court of Justice summarised the rationale for the requirement in *Hugin:*

> Community law covers any agreement or any practice which is capable of constituting a threat to freedom of trade between Member States in a manner which might harm the attainment of the objectives of a single market between the Member States, in particular by partitioning the national markets or by affecting the structure of competition within the Common Market. On the other hand, conduct the effects of which are confined to the territory of a single Member State, is governed by the national legal order.[164]

2.   The effect on trade between Member States therefore serves as a criterion to define the scope of EU competition law as against that of national competition law.[165] If the effect on trade requirement in Article 101 or 102 is not met, then the EU competition rules do not apply.

3.   The effect on trade requirement took on new significance under Council Regulation 1/2003. Where a Member State court or competition authority applies national competition law to agreements or conduct which may affect trade between Member States, they must also apply Article 101, or Article 102 in the case of abuse of a dominant position.[166] In this case, the court or competition authority cannot prohibit under national competition law an agreement that would not breach Article 101.[167] This carries with it an obligation to notify the Commission

---

164. Case 22/78 *Hugin Kassaregister AB v Commission* [1978] ECR 1869, [1979] 3 CMLR 345, para 17.
165. Case C–425/07P *AEPI v Commission* [2009] ECR I–3205, [2009] 5 CMLR 1337, para 50.
166. Regulation 1/2003, Article 3(1).
167. Regulation 1/2003, Article 3(2).

at least thirty days before an infringement decision is taken.[168] The Commission has the power to take over such a case from the national authority.[169]

4.   The Commission has published guidelines, which aim to set out the principles developed by the Union courts in relation to the concept of an effect on trade between Member States.[170]

5.   Agreements that restrict imports or exports between Member States are an obvious example of an effect on trade between Member States. However, many agreements and practices that may not at first appear to have a cross-border element have been found to satisfy the effect on trade requirement. Historically, the Commission and the courts have not had much difficulty in finding this element of Article 101 or 102 to be met.

6.   Article 101(1) does not require that each individual clause in an agreement should be capable of affecting intra-Union trade. It is only where the agreement as a whole is capable of affecting trade that it is necessary to examine which are the clauses of the agreement which have as their object or effect the restriction or distortion of competition.[171]

What is included in the concept of 'trade'?

7.   The concept of 'trade' is a wide one. It includes all types of economic activity. It covers trade in goods and services. The concept even extends to the transfer of profits from a subsidiary to a parent company located in another Member State.[172]

8.   It is not necessary that the trade that is the object of the anti-competitive agreement or conduct itself be affected; it is sufficient if there is an indirect effect on trade in related goods or services. For example, an agreement restricting the sale of a raw material, which was not itself exported, was capable of affecting trade in the finished product, which was exported.[173] Where restrictions concerning intermediate products are concerned, it is necessary to consider whether trade in the final product is affected.

9.   The fact that an agreement encourages an increase, even a large one, in the volume of trade between Member States will not save it from the application of Article 101 if it otherwise affects the normal pattern of trade.[174]

---

168. Regulation 1/2003, Article 11(4).
169. Regulation 1/2003, Article 11(6).
170. Commission Guidelines on the effect on trade concept contained in Articles 81 and 82 of the Treaty, [2004] OJ C101/81 ('Commission Guidelines on Effect on Trade').
171. Case 193/83 *Windsurfing International Inc. v Commission* [1986] ECR 611, [1986] 3 CMLR 489, para 96.
172. *ABI* [1987] OJ L43/51, [1989] 4 CMLR 238, para 46.
173. Case 123/83 *Bureau national interprofessionnel du cognac v Clair* [1985] ECR 391, [1985] 2 CMLR 430.
174. See Cases 56 & 58/64 *Consten SaRL and Grundig Verkaufs GmbH v Commission* [1966] ECR 299, 341.

Is a potential effect sufficient?

10. Articles 101 and 102 are couched in terms of agreements or conduct that *may* affect trade between Member States. An actual effect on trade is not necessary. It is sufficient to show a potential effect, although this must be more than merely hypothetical or speculative:[175]

> If an agreement, decision or practice is to be capable of affecting trade between Member States, it must be possible to foresee with a sufficient degree of probability, on the basis of a set of objective factors of law or of fact, that they may have an influence, direct or indirect, actual or potential, on the pattern of trade between Member States in such a way as to cause concern that they might hinder the attainment of a single market between Member States. Moreover, that effect must not be insignificant.[176]

Can agreements or conduct concerning only one Member State have an effect on inter-State trade?

11. Agreements or conduct involving parties in only one Member State are capable of affecting trade between Member States. A particular concern of the Treaty rules on competition is to prevent the partitioning of national markets, which can be achieved by a restrictive agreement covering only one Member State. When an agreement extends over the whole of the Member State's territory, it may, by its nature, reinforce the partitioning of national markets and therefore have an effect on trade between Member States. For example, 'by its nature, a clause designed to prevent a buyer from reselling or exporting goods he has bought is liable to partition the markets and consequently to affect trade between Member States'.[177]

12. The Court of Justice has often applied a generous interpretation of the effect on trade requirement where the agreement covered only one State. In *Pronuptia*, bridal wear franchisees were restricted from setting up a shop outside a particular area. Although the undertakings were all based in the same Member State and it must have been doubtful that a franchisee would want to open a shop in another Member State, the Court of Justice was satisfied that the effect on trade criterion was met.[178] In a case involving a banking cartel in Austria, the General Court held that there was an effect on trade between Member States. The cartel was made up of committees in different regions of the country but there was an overall effect in Austria as a whole. The General Court noted that there was 'a strong presumption that a practice restrictive of competition applied throughout the territory of a

---

175. Commission Guidelines on Effect on Trade [2004] OJ C101/81, para 43. See also Case T–29/05 *Deltafina SpA v Commission*, judgment of 8 September 2010, paras 166–177 (rejecting an argument that the Commission breached paragraph 43 of the Commission Guidelines on Effect on Trade [2004] OJ C101/81).
176. Case C–475/99 *Ambulanz Glöckner v Landkreis Südwestpfalz* [2001] ECR I–8089, [2002] 4 CMLR 726, para 48.
177. Cases C–89/85 etc *Ahlström Osakeyhtiö v Commission ('Wood Pulp II')* [1993] ECR I–1307, [1993] 4 CMLR 407, para 176.
178. Case 161/84 *Pronuptia de Paris GmbH* [1986] ECR 353, [1986] 1 CMLR 414, para 26.

Member State is liable to contribute to compartmentalisation of the markets and to affect intra-Community trade'.[179]

13. It has also been held by the Court of Justice that even where there is no partitioning of markets, an agreement between undertakings established in only one Member State and covering only the market of that State affects trade between Member States if it concerns, even partly, a product imported from another Member State, even where the parties to the agreement obtain the product from a company belonging to their own group.[180] The same principle is applicable in the context of Article 102, so the fact that the conduct of a dominant undertaking relates only to the marketing of products in a single Member State is not sufficient to preclude the possibility that trade between Member States might be affected.[181]

14. There have also been cases where agreements covering the whole of a Member State did not result in an inter-State effect on trade. In *Bagnasco*, the Court of Justice considered whether restrictive standard bank conditions imposed in Italy met the effect on trade requirement. The economic activities involved had a very minor impact on trade between Member States, with only limited participation in Italy by subsidiaries or branches of non-Italian financial establishments. There was nothing to justify the conclusion, with a sufficient degree of probability, that the restrictions would have an appreciable effect on inter-State trade.[182]

Can agreements concluded outside the EU have an effect on trade between EU Member States?

15. An effect on trade may also be found where all the relevant parties are located outside the EU. This was the situation in *Wood Pulp II*, which involved an agreement to fix prices of wood pulp among undertakings, all of which were located and had registered offices outside the EU. The undertakings did not trade the goods at issue between Member States, merely exporting them to the EU but the Court of Justice had little difficulty in finding that Article 101 applied.[183]

---

179. Cases T–259/02 etc *Raiffeisen Zentralbank Österreich AG v Commission* [2006] ECR II 5169, [2007] 5 CMLR 1142, para 181 (appeals dismissed, Cases C–125/07 etc *Raiffeisen Zentralbank Österreich AG v Commission* [2009] ECR I–8681, para 39).

180. See Cases 240/82 etc *Stichting Sigarettenindustrie v Commission* [1985] ECR 3831, [1987] 3 CMLR 661, para 49.

181. Case C–49/07 *MOTOE v Elliniko Dimosio* [2008] ECR I–4863, [2008] 5 CMLR 790, para 42.

182. Cases C–215 & 216/96 *Bagnsaco v BPN* [1999] ECR I–135, [1999] 4 CMLR 624, para 52. See also, e.g., Case C–393/08 *Sbarigia v Azienda USL RM/A*, judgment of 1 July 2010, para 32 (Italian legislation in relation to opening periods of pharmacies in a specific municipal area of Rome could not affect trade between Member States within the meaning of Articles 101 and 102).

183. See Cases C–89/85 etc *Ahlström Osakeyhtiö v Commission ('Wood Pulp II')* [1993] ECR I–1307, [1993] 4 CMLR 407, para 142.

Is there an appreciability requirement?

16. The Court of Justice has established that for Article 101 or 102 to be invoked, the effect on inter-State trade must not be insignificant.[184] So the agreement or practice must be capable of appreciably affecting trade between Member States.[185] In applying Article 102, the assessment of whether the effect on trade between Member States is appreciable must take account of the conduct of the dominant undertaking.[186]

17. There is a separate requirement that the effect on competition be appreciable. This will depend on a number of factors, including the market position of the parties. A rough rule of thumb is that an undertaking with a market share of 5 per cent or more is usually capable of having an appreciable effect on competition. However, this analysis is not scientific.[187]

18. The Commission has noted that 'the stronger the market position of the undertakings concerned the more likely it is that an agreement or practice capable of affecting trade between Member States can be held to do so appreciably'.[188] The Commission holds the view that agreements – even those containing hardcore restrictions[189] – are not capable of appreciably affecting trade between Member States when the following conditions are met:[190]

•   The aggregate market share of the parties on a relevant market in the EU does not exceed 5 per cent;

     AND

•   *For horizontal agreements* – aggregate EU-wide turnover of the parties in the products covered by the agreement does not exceed €40 million.

•   *For vertical agreements* – the supplier's turnover in the covered products does not exceed €40 million.

---

184. A similar rule has not been established in relation to the State aid rules (see, e.g., Case T–227/01 *Territorio Histórico de Álava v Commission*, judgment of 9 September 2009, para 148).

185. See, e.g., Cases C–125/07 etc *Raiffeisen Zentralbank Österreich AG v Commission* [2009] ECR I–8681, paras 36, 37, 46.

186. Case C–49/07 *MOTOE v Elliniko Dimosio* [2008] ECR I–4863, [2008] 5 CMLR 790, para 41.

187. See further Question 19.

188. Commission Guidelines on Effect on Trade [2004] OJ C101/81, para 45.

189. Commission Guidelines on Effect on Trade [2004] OJ C101/81, para 50.

190. Commission Guidelines on Effect on Trade [2004] OJ C101/81, para 52. See also Case 5/69 *Völk v Vervaecke* [1969] ECR 295 and Case 1/71 *Cadillon v Höss* [1971] ECR 351, [1971] CMLR 420, para 9 (exclusive dealing agreements providing for absolute territorial protection may escape the prohibition in Article 101(1) in view of the 'weak position' of the parties on the market).

The same presumption applies where during two successive years, the turnover threshold was not exceeded by more than 10 per cent and the market share threshold not by more than 2 per cent.

Where the agreement by its nature is capable of affecting trade between Member States (e.g., an import agreement) and the above thresholds are exceeded, the Commission assumes that the effect is appreciable.[191]

Key Sources

Commission Notice, Guidelines on the effect on trade concept contained in Articles 81 and 82 of the Treaty [2004] OJ C101/81.

Case 161/84 *Pronuptia de Paris GmbH* [1986] ECR 353, [1986] 1 CMLR 414.

---

191. Commission Guidelines on Effect on Trade [2004] OJ C101/81, para 53.

7. **DOES UK OR IRISH COMPETITION LAW HAVE A REQUIREMENT THAT THERE BE AN APPRECIABLE EFFECT ON TRADE?**

Summary

UK

- The antitrust provisions of the Competition Act 1998 apply when there is an effect on trade within the United Kingdom.

- Decisions of the CAT and High Court have taken different approaches as to whether there must be an appreciable effect on trade within the UK.

Ireland

- The antitrust provisions of the Competition Act 2002 refer to trade 'in the State or in any part of the State'. There does not appear to be appreciability requirement.

---

1. It may be necessary to examine, particularly if there is no effect on trade between Member States, whether a potentially anti-competitive agreement or practice might violate the competition law of the country with which it is connected. Each national law will have its own jurisdictional requirements.

UK

2. The Chapter I prohibition in the Competition Act 1998 prohibits anti-competitive agreements and practices which 'may affect trade within the United Kingdom' and have an anti-competitive object or effect 'within the United Kingdom'.[192] Similarly, the Chapter II prohibition provides that an abuse of dominance is prohibited 'if it may affect trade within the United Kingdom'.[193] On the face of the legislation, there is no requirement to show that the effect on UK trade is 'appreciable'. However it has been accepted that an appreciable effect on competition is required.[194]

3. In *Aberdeen Journals*,[195] the CAT considered whether a test of appreciability should be read into the Act. This case involved an appeal from a decision of the OFT that Aberdeen Journals had abused a dominant position in the market for newspaper advertising in the Aberdeen area by engaging in below cost selling with a view to eliminating a competitor. Aberdeen Journals argued that the OFT was

---

192. Competition Act 1998, s 2(1).
193. Competition Act 1998, s 18(1).
194. See, e.g., *P&S Amusements Ltd v Valley House Leisure Ltd* [2006] EWHC 1510 (Ch), [2006] UKCLR 876, para 23; Whish, *Competition Law* (6th edn, 2009) 336–337.
195. *Aberdeen Journals Limited v The Office of Fair Trading* [2003] CAT 11, [2003] Comp AR 67.

required to show a causal connection between the abuse and a material effect on trade within the UK. The CAT rejected the general assertion that a test of appreciability should be read into the Competition Act. The CAT pointed out that the test of appreciability incorporated into Articles 101 and 102 had the purpose of demarcating the jurisdictional line between Union law and national law:

> [Since] we are already dealing, under domestic law, with conduct which takes place within the United Kingdom, there is no need to import into section 18(1) of the 1998 Act the rule of 'appreciability' under Community law, the essential purpose of which is to demarcate the fields of Community law and domestic law respectively. In terms of section 60(1) of the 1998 Act, that seems to us to be a 'relevant difference'[196] between the 1998 Act and the provisions of Community law.[197]

4. The CAT felt supported in its view that there was no additional appreciability test in national law by the fact that section 40 of the Act provided for 'conduct of minor significance' to be made immune from fines. Regulations making the Chapter II prohibition inapplicable to undertakings with turnover of less than £50 million had been adopted and an undertaking (such as Aberdeen Journals) that did not come within this exception could not 'claim to benefit from a further *de minimis* rule to be read into section 18(1)'.[198]

5. The conclusion of the CAT that there is no appreciability requirement has been doubted in the subsequent High Court decision in *P&S Amusements*.[199] This involved a summary judgment application in which the defendant tenant had argued that a beer tie to which he was subject constituted an abuse of a dominant position. The defendant relied on *Aberdeen Journals* in arguing that it was not necessary to show that the effect on trade was appreciable. Although the case was decided on other grounds (and so comments on the requirement that the effect on trade be appreciable are *obiter*), Chancellor Morritt stated that he had 'considerable misgivings' about the CAT's conclusion in *Aberdeen Journals* and also doubted that it should be transposed to the context of the Chapter I prohibition. The Chancellor asked, 'What is the purpose of imposing such a requirement to the application of the section at all if it does not have to be satisfied to an extent greater than the minimal?'[200]

---

196. Section 60(1) provides that as far as possible, having regard to 'relevant differences' between the provisions concerned, questions arising under Part 2 of the 1998 Act in relation to competition within the UK are dealt with in a manner consistent with the treatment of corresponding questions arising in EU law.

197. *Aberdeen Journals Limited v The Office of Fair Trading* [2003] CAT 11, [2003] Comp AR 67, para 460.

198. *Aberdeen Journals Limited v The Office of Fair Trading* [2003] CAT 11, [2003] Comp AR 67, para 461.

199. *P&S Amusements Ltd v Valley House Leisure Ltd* [2006] EWHC 1510 (Ch), [2006] UKCLR 876.

200. *P&S Amusements Ltd v Valley House Leisure Ltd* [2006] EWHC 1510 (Ch), [2006] UKCLR 876, para 22.

6.   In support of the CAT's approach in *Aberdeen Journals*, it can be argued that the requirement of an appreciable effect on trade for EU law to apply is for the purpose of making the jurisdictional choice *between* EU law and national law. Once the choice is made in favour of national law, in deciding whether it applies, it can be argued that it does not make sense to adopt a similar requirement of appreciability because that is what is done with Articles 101 and 102. At this stage, there is no choice *between* the national law and another law to be made. It can also be argued that if an agreement has an appreciable effect on competition in the UK, then it may be expected that trade will also be appreciably affected.[201]

Ireland

7.   The Competition Act 2002 does not contain a requirement of an appreciable effect on trade. Section 4 of the Competition Act 2002 applies to anti-competitive agreements and practices 'which have as their object or effect the prevention, restriction or distortion of competition in trade in any goods or services in the State or in any part of the State'. Section 5 applies to the abuse of a dominant position 'in trade for any goods or services in the State or in any part of the State'.

8.   The question whether an additional requirement of appreciability (whether in respect of an effect on trade or competition) should be read into section 4 or 5 of the 2002 Act does not appear to have been recently examined by the courts. However earlier Competition Authority decisions on the application of section 4 of the Competition Act 1991 did not find any need for an additional test of appreciability. One decision concerned an agreement between a milk producer and a distributor (essentially a milkman). The producer argued that by analogy with EU competition law, section 4 should not apply to agreements with individual milkmen because the arrangement did not have an appreciable impact on the market, with each milkman covering an area of only 300–400 households. Reliance was also placed on the producer's low market share, amounting to less than 5 per cent of domestic milk supply in the State. The Authority did not address the appreciability argument in detail but simply concluded that section 4 was applicable as '[t]he agreement has effect within the State'.[202] A similar approach has been taken to appreciability arguments in other decisions of the Competition Authority.[203]

9.   Given the relatively small size of the Irish economy and the proximity of Northern Ireland in particular, it can be expected that many Irish-based agreements and

---

201. See also Bailey, 'Appreciable Effect on Trade within the United Kingdom' [2009] *European Competition Law Review* 353.

202. Dec No 480 *Snowcream Ltd/John Greene*, Competition Authority Decision of 15 April 1997, para 13.

203. See, e.g., Dec No 590 *Cadbury Ireland Sales Limited/Retailers/Standard Loan Agreement*, Competition Authority Decision of 25 June 2001, paras 15 and 18. See also McCarthy and Power, *Irish Competition Law: The Competition Act 2002* (2003) paras 3.36–3.38.

practices of an anti-competitive nature will have an appreciable effect on inter-State trade, thereby invoking the EU competition rules.[204]

Key Sources

UK

Aberdeen Journals Limited v The Office of Fair Trading [2003] CAT 11.

P&S Amusements Ltd v Valley House Leisure Ltd [2006] EWHC 1510 (Ch), [2006] UKCLR 876.

---

204. See, e.g., *Competition Authority v O'Regan* [2004] IEHC 330 (Kearns J, as he then was, concluding that there was an appreciable effect on trade between Member States and so EU rather than Irish law applied, in particular given the potential for entry into the Irish market by credit unions in Northern Ireland) (reversed on other grounds, *Competition Authority v O'Regan* [2007] IESC 22, [2007] 4 IR 737).

8.   DOES EU COMPETITION LAW APPLY TO AGREEMENTS AND ACTIVITIES OUTSIDE THE EU?

Summary

- The EU competition rules will apply where an agreement or practice is implemented in the EU or where it produces effects inside the EU.

- The fact that all parties to the agreement or practice are located outside the EU does not matter.

- Similarly, the EU competition rules can apply to agreements relating to imports and exports with third countries.

- When applying Article 101, it should first be considered whether the agreement or practice has the object of restricting competition in the EU.

- If the object is not anti-competitive, effects in the EU should be examined. Such effects may be direct or indirect but should be appreciable.

1.   This question concerns the extra-territorial application of EU competition law. It arises not only with respect to agreements and practices to which Article 101 may apply but also in the context of Article 102 and the Merger Regulation. The Union courts have taken a broad approach to the issue so that once effects are potentially generated within the EU, an agreement or practice will be subject to EU competition law.

2.   If an agreement is concluded and the parties to it are located outside the EU, it can still be caught by EU competition law if it is implemented in the EU. In *Wood Pulp I*, it was held that although the activities in question took place outside the Union, as they were implemented inside the Union, Article 101 applied. The Commission had found that wood pulp producers, all of whom were located outside the Union, had engaged in concerted practices contrary to Article 101 relating to prices charged to customers within the Union. The Court of Justice pointed out that an agreement or concerted practice had two elements, its formation and its implementation:

> If the applicability of prohibitions laid down under competition law were made to depend on the place where the agreement, decision or concerted practice was formed, the result would obviously be to give undertakings an easy means of evading those prohibitions. The decisive factor is therefore the place where it is implemented.[205]

3.   This approach focuses on the implementation of the agreement or practice. There is also the broader 'effects' doctrine, which would apply EU competition law as long as the agreement or activity generated effects in the EU, regardless of whether it was actually implemented in the EU. This is a broader test than implementation, which itself would be caught by an effects test. In *Gencor*, the General Court

---

205. Cases 89/85 etc *Ahlström Osakeyhtiö v Commission ('Wood Pulp I')* [1988] ECR 5193, [1988] 4 CMLR 901, para 16.

examined the jurisdiction of the Merger Regulation over the merger of South African mining interests of a South African and English company. The General Court held that the Merger Regulation applied to all concentrations with a Community dimension and it was not necessary that 'the undertakings in question must be established in the Community or that the production activities covered by the concentration must be carried out within Community territory'.[206] The General Court compared the Union's jurisdiction over concentrations with that of Article 101, finding from *Wood Pulp I* that the criterion as to the implementation of an agreement was satisfied by mere sale of products within the Union, irrespective of the location of the sources of supply or production.[207] As the parties to the concentration made sales in the EU and the turnover thresholds were met, the Merger Regulation applied. The General Court went on to hold that this conclusion was compatible with public international law and that the application of the Merger Regulation was justified 'when it is foreseeable that a proposed concentration will have an immediate and substantial effect in the Community'.[208] While it did not endorse the effects doctrine explicitly, the General Court did rely on it.[209]

4.   The likelihood is that whether the implementation doctrine or the effects doctrine applies, the scope of application of EU competition law will usually be the same. The position is described in Bellamy & Child as follows:

> [The] Court in *Gencor* did not enunciate the qualified effects doctrine in substitution for the implementation doctrine as the basis of Community jurisdiction, but as placing a boundary on the jurisdiction that might otherwise result from application of the implementation doctrine. Formally, therefore, jurisdiction over undertakings outside the Community must satisfy both doctrines; but in practice, at the Community level, this seems unlikely to produce a different result from application of the effects doctrine alone.[210]

Does EU competition law apply to import and export agreements?

5.   If an agreement or practice outside the EU relates to imports into the EU, it may well have the requisite effect on trade between Member States. For example, a provision which restricted the freedom of wholesalers to import citrus fruit directly from third countries by requiring them to go through an import auction

---

206. Case T–102/96 *Gencor Ltd v Commission* [1999] ECR II–753, [1999] 4 CMLR 971, para 79.
207. On the application of EU competition law to agreements and abuses of dominance involving undertakings outside the EU, see also Commission Guidelines on Effect on Trade [2004] OJ C101/81, paras 100–109.
208. Case T–102/96 *Gencor Ltd v Commission* [1999] ECR II–753, [1999] 4 CMLR 971, para 90. The General Court did not provide any authority for this proposition of international law.
209. The effects doctrine has its origins in US antitrust law. See, e.g., *Timberlane Lumber Co. v Bank of America*, 549 F 2d 597, 608–609 (9th Cir 1976).
210. Roth and Rose (eds) *Bellamy & Child European Community Law of Competition* (6th edn, 2008) (hereafter, 'Bellamy & Child') para 1.113.

was in breach of Article 101 as it was 'liable to interfere with the natural movement of trade and thus to affect trade' between Member States.[211]

6.   Agreements concerning exports from the EU to third countries are less likely to invoke EU competition rules. However, such agreements may be caught if they contain restrictive provisions such as a ban on the re-importation of goods into the Union where there is a real possibility that a sufficiently large quantity of goods, such as to have an appreciable effect on competition, would be re-imported. While such an agreement would not generally be considered to have, of its nature, an anti-competitive object under Article 101, the economic and legal context should be examined to determine whether its effect violates Article 101. This may be the case where the market has an oligopolistic structure or where there is a significant difference in the price of the product inside and outside the EU.[212]

7.   An agreement by undertakings that compete within the EU to export surplus quantities to countries outside the EU could be considered as having as its object the restriction of competition within the EU, where the exported quantities might otherwise have been sold inside the EU.[213]

Key Sources

Commission Guidelines on the effect on trade concept contained in Articles 81 and 82 of the Treaty [2004] OJ C 101/81, paras 100–109.

Cases 89/85 etc *Ahlström Osakeyhtiö v Commission ('Wood Pulp I')* [1988] ECR 5193, [1988] 4 CMLR 901.

Case T–102/96 *Gencor Ltd v Commission* [1999] ECR II–753, [1999] 4 CMLR 971.

---

211. Case 71/74 *Frubo v Commission* [1975] ECR 563, [1975] 2 CMLR 123, para 38.
212. See Case C–306/96 *Javico International v Yves Saint Laurent Parfums SA* [1998] ECR I–1983, [1998] 5 CMLR 172, paras 21–24.
213. See Commission Guidelines on Effect on Trade [2004] OJ C101/81, para 105.

9. DOES EU COMPETITION LAW APPLY IN THE EEA?

Summary

- Competition rules that mirror the EU rules are contained in the EEA Agreement.

- This applies between the EU and Iceland, Liechtenstein and Norway.

- Switzerland is not included.

1. The European Free Trade Association ('EFTA') is made up of Iceland, Liechtenstein, Norway and Switzerland. In 1992, the EFTA States, the European Communities and the Member States signed the European Economic Area ('EEA') Agreement, which entered into force on 1 January 1994.[214] It is this agreement that contains competition provisions substantially similar to those in the TFEU. The EEA Agreement was not ratified by Switzerland, so the EFTA countries that are party to it are now Iceland, Liechtenstein and Norway.

2. Articles 53, 54 and 59 of the EEA Agreement mirror Articles 101, 102 and 106 of the TFEU. Article 53 of the EEA Agreement applies to anti-competitive agreements and practices 'which may affect trade between Contracting Parties' and which have an anti-competitive object or effect 'within the territory covered' by the Agreement. Article 54 covers abuses of a dominant position insofar as they 'may affect trade between Contracting Parties'.

3. The EEA Agreement provided for an EFTA Surveillance Authority and an EFTA Court of Justice. Both bodies were established by the EFTA Surveillance and Court Agreement entered into by Iceland, Liechtenstein and Norway. The role of the EFTA Surveillance Authority is similar to that of the Commission. The EFTA Court has similar judicial review powers vis-à-vis the EFTA Surveillance Authority as the General Court has over decisions of the Commission.

4. The uniform interpretation of provisions in the EEA Agreement that correspond to those in the TFEU is provided for in two ways. Article 6 of the EEA Agreement provides that such provisions shall be interpreted in conformity with rulings of the Court of Justice given before the date of the EEA Agreement. Article 3(2) of the EFTA Surveillance and Court Agreement provides that the EFTA Surveillance Authority and the EFTA Court 'shall pay due account to the principles laid down by the relevant rulings by the Court of Justice' given after the date of the EEA Agreement. As the EFTA Court has noted in a case interpreting Article 53 of the EEA Agreement:

    > It is a fundamental objective of the EEA Agreement to achieve and maintain uniform interpretation and application of those provisions of the EEA Agreement that correspond to provisions of the EC Treaty.[215]

---

214. Agreement on the European Economic Area [1994] OJ L1/3.

215. Case E–8/00 *Landsorganisasjonen i Norge v Kommunenes Sentralforbund* [2002] Rep EFTA Ct 114 [2002] 5 CMLR 160, para 39.

5.   The EFTA Surveillance Authority has jurisdiction over conduct or agreements affecting only trade between EFTA States. However, where conduct or agreements affect trade between both EFTA and EU States, the Commission has jurisdiction and it may apply both the EU Treaties and the EEA Agreement.[216] The domestic courts of each of Iceland, Liechtenstein and Norway have power to apply the EEA competition rules.[217] The European Commission's jurisdiction in merger control includes the EFTA States so once the relevant thresholds in the Merger Regulation[218] are triggered, the Commission has exclusive jurisdiction.[219]

Key Sources

Agreement on the European Economic Area [1994] OJ L1/3.

---

216. Agreement on the European Economic Area, Article 56.
217. See Bellamy & Child (6th edn, 2008) para 1.090.
218. Council Regulation (EC) No 139/2004 on the control of concentrations between undertakings [2004] OJ L24/1.
219. Agreement on the European Economic Area, Article 57(2)(a).

10. HOW IS THE 'RELEVANT MARKET' DEFINED FOR COMPETITION LAW PURPOSES?

Summary

• Market definition is a crucial element in the application of competition law.

• Markets must be defined before market share, an important indicator of market power, can be quantified.

• Both a relevant product market and a geographic market must be defined.

• Working out the degree of substitutability between products is the basis for market definition. Demand-side substitutability is usually more important but supply-side factors are also relevant.

• The so-called SSNIP test is a tool to measure substitutability. It asks whether a hypothetical monopolist could profitably raise prices by 5–10 per cent or whether this would cause a significant amount of sales to be lost to a competitor, in which case the competitor is in the same market.

1. Market definition is of crucial importance in competition law. It is 'a tool to identify and define the boundaries of competition between firms'[220] and courts have emphasised the importance of a robust market definition in cases brought by antitrust regulators and private plaintiffs.[221] Market definition has traditionally provided the framework for identifying which firms compete against each other and what competitive constraints they face. The level of market share held by a firm, together with the concentration levels in the market, is often used as a first indication of its market power.[222] As well as the general importance of market shares in making a competitive assessment, the application of the various block exemption Regulations depends on the market shares of the parties falling below

---

220. Commission Notice on the definition of relevant market for the purposes of Community competition law [1997] OJ C 372/5 ('Commission Notice on Market Definition') para 2.

221. See, e.g., *Rye Investments Ltd v Competition Authority* [2009] IEHC 140, paras 7.19–7.21 (Cooke J rejecting the Irish Competition Authority's market definition in processed cheese as 'inadequate and unsound'); *Chester City Council v Arriva plc* [2007] EWHC 1373 (Ch), [2007] UKCLR 1582, para 188 (Rimer J, rejecting the plaintiff's market definition of a local bus market in an abuse of dominance case, required that the market definition be made out 'in a cogent and principled way' and that the court be provided with 'compelling justification' for the market definition proposed by the plaintiff); *United States v Oracle Corporation* 331 F Supp 2d 1098 (ND Cal, 2004) (Walker CJ emphasising that market definition was 'critical' in a case challenging a merger).

222. For a discussion of indicators of market power, see Bishop and Walker, *The Economics of EC Competition Law* (3rd edn, 2010) para 3.12 *et seq* (noting indicators of market power other than market shares and concentration levels to include barriers to entry and potential competition, barriers to expansion, countervailing buyer power, product differentiation and the nature of the oligopolistic interaction between firms).

certain thresholds.[223] Market shares can also be relevant to the amount of any fine imposed.[224]

2.   In order to establish market shares, the relevant market must first be defined.[225] There are two relevant markets that should be defined – the product market and the geographic market.

3.   The requirement for a market definition to be set out by the Commission or national competition authority is less stringent with regard to hardcore restrictions of Article 101, such as price fixing or market sharing. Such arrangements will typically be found to have an anti-competitive object in breach of Article 101, regardless of the exact market definition or market shares of the parties.[226]

4.   In applying Article 102, 'the proper definition of the relevant market is a necessary precondition ... since, before an abuse of a dominant position is ascertained, it is necessary to establish the existence of a dominant position in a given market, which presupposes that such a market has already been defined'.[227] Market share provides a useful first indication of whether an undertaking is dominant and a very high market share – say 50 per cent[228] – may, in itself, be evidence of a dominant position.

5.   In applying the Merger Regulation, 'a proper definition of the relevant market is a necessary precondition for any assessment of the effect of a concentration on competition'.[229] The Commission's starting point is to define the markets in which the transaction has an impact and market share is once again an important part of the analysis.

6.   Whereas the parties under investigation often argue for a wide market definition, the Commission and other antitrust regulators have a tendency to define markets narrowly, hence producing higher market shares.

7.   Despite their importance, market definition and market shares are not the whole of the story. Other measurements of competition and other econometric tests may be as or more important in carrying out an analysis of competition. To take just one example, in a bidding market, market shares may underestimate or overestimate

---

223. See Question 22 on block exemption Regulations.

224. Commission Guidelines on Fines [2006] OJ C210/2, paras 18, 22.

225. See, e.g., Case C–234/89 *Delimitis v Henninger Bräu AG* [1991] ECR I–935, [1992] 5 CMLR 210, para 16.

226. Although subject to the agreement or practice having an appreciable effect on competition and inter-state trade. On the relaxation of the requirement for a precise market definition where the agreement has an anti-competitive object, see, e.g., Case T–213/00 *CMA CGM v Commission* [2003] ECR II–913, [2003] 5 CMLR 268, paras 213, 215.

227. Case T–29/92 *Vereniging van Samenwerkende Prijsregelende Organisaties in de Bouwnijverheid v Commission* [1995] ECR II–289, para 74.

228. Case C–62/86 *AKZO Chemie BV v Commission* [1991] ECR I–3359, [1993] 5 CMLR 215, para 60. See further, on when an undertaking is dominant, Question 53.

229. Case C–68/94 and C–30/95 *France v Commission ('Kali & Salz')* [1998] ECR I–1375, [1998] 4 CMLR 829, para 143.

the extent to which two firms act as competitive constraints on each other. Competitive dynamics might be more accurately assessed by carrying out an analysis of bidding data, establishing, for example, if one firm's price is lower when the other also participates in a bid.

How is the product market defined?[230]

8. A central factor in defining the product market (and the geographic market) is the concept of substitutability:

> The concept of the relevant market in fact implies that there can be effective competition between the products which form part of it and this presupposes that there is a sufficient degree of interchangeability between all the products forming part of the same market in so far as a specific use of such products is concerned.[231]

9. Demand-side substitution involves consumers switching from one product to another in response to a change in the relative price of those products:

> A relevant product market comprises all those products and/or services which are regarded as interchangeable or substitutable by the consumer, by reason of the products' characteristics, their prices and their intended use.[232]

10. If consumers are able to switch to an available substitute then it is unlikely that price increases will be profitable and in this way demand-side substitution works as a disciplining force on suppliers of a given set of products. If a sufficient degree of substitutability arises between two products, this would indicate that they are part of the same market.

11. According to the Commission, 'demand substitution constitutes the most immediate and effective disciplinary force on the suppliers of a given product'[233] and the importance of demand-side substitution has been confirmed by the Union courts:

> As the Commission stated in the notice on market definition, companies are subject to three main sources of competitive constraints: demand substitutability, supply substitutability and potential competition. From an economic point of view and for the definition of the relevant market, demand substitution constitutes the most immediate and effective disciplinary force on the suppliers of a given product, in particular in relation to their pricing decisions. Substitutability must therefore be looked at not only from the supply side but also from the demand side, which remains, in principle, the most effective assessment criterion.[234]

---

230. See generally, Bishop and Walker, *The Economics of EC Competition Law* (3rd edn, 2010) Ch 4.
231. Case 85/76 *Hoffmann-La Roche & Co. AG v Commission* [1979] ECR 461, [1979] 3 CMLR 211, para 28.
232. Commission Notice on Market Definition [1997] OJ C 372/5, para 7.
233. Commission Notice on Market Definition [1997] OJ C 372/5, para 13.
234. Case T–177/04 *easyJet Airline Co. Ltd. v Commission* [2006] ECR II–1931, [2006] 5 CMLR 663, para 99.

12.   The EU Notice on market definition adopts the SSNIP ('small but significant non-transitory increase in price') test as a tool for determining which products are substitutable for each other.[235] This test asks whether consumers of product A would switch to other products in the face of a permanent relative price increase of between 5 per cent and 10 per cent by a hypothetical monopolist of product A. If consumers switch to, say, Product B, then this tends to indicate that B is in the same market as A.

13.   The Commission sets out in the Notice on Market Definition the types of evidence that it considers relevant in assessing whether different products are demand substitutes. These include:[236]

- Evidence of substitution in the recent past.

- Quantitative tests designed for market definition – e.g. a test based on similarity of price movements over time.

- The views of customers and competitors.

- Consumer preferences.

- Switching costs and barriers to switching.

- Different categories of customers and price discrimination.

14.   Supply-side substitution also plays a role in the analysis. Even if consumers could not react to a price increase by switching products, producers may be able to react to such a move by a competitor by switching the products they produce. The resulting increase in supply may render any attempted price increase unprofitable, even if there is limited demand-side substitution.[237]

What is the 'Cellophane Fallacy'?

15.   The SSNIP test assumes that the prevailing prices on the market are competitive. However, the use of the SSNIP test can create difficulties in the context of Article 102. To apply Article 102 it must be established that a firm is dominant. In this case, the test should not ask whether a hypothetical monopolist could profitably raise price with reference to current prices. Economic theory suggests that a profit-maximising firm will already have set prices at the highest level its customers can bear so that a further price increase will result in lost sales. Using the standard SSNIP test, a monopolist could show that relative to current prices, a 5 per cent to 10 per cent increase would result in lost sales to other products and hence, that those other products must form part of the same market. However, this analysis exaggerates the size of the market as the products to which consumers switch are false substitutes. This is known as the 'cellophane fallacy' after the US *du Pont* case.[238] Du Pont argued that cellophane competed in a wider market including other flexible packaging materials such as waxed paper, showing high

---

235. See Commission Notice on Market Definition [1997] OJ C 372/5, paras 15–19.
236. See Commission Notice on Market Definition [1997] OJ C 372/5, paras 37–43.
237. See Commission Notice on Market Definition [1997] OJ C 372/5, paras 20–23.
238. *United States v E.I. du Pont de Nemours & Co.* 351 US 377, 76 S.Ct. 994 (1956).

cross-elasticities of demand between cellophane and those other products. The Court failed to recognise that a high own-price elasticity (the extent of switching from a product after a price rise) might mean that the firm was already exercising monopoly power.

16.   The application of the SSNIP test to Article 102 should focus on whether a price rise would be profitable relative to *competitive* prices rather than current prevailing prices. The existence of the cellophane fallacy means that market definition in Article 102 cases needs to be carefully considered and it may be necessary to rely on a number of methods for checking the robustness of possible alternative market definitions.[239]

How is the geographic market defined?

17.   The relevant geographic market may be worldwide, EEA-wide, national, regional, local etc. depending on the nature of the products and the ease with which consumers can source them and competitors can supply them from other areas. The Commission summarises the geographic market as follows:

> The relevant geographic market comprises the area in which the undertakings concerned are involved in the supply and demand of products or services, in which the conditions of competition are sufficiently homogeneous and which can be distinguished from neighbouring areas because the conditions of competition are appreciably different in those area.[240]

18.   The geographic market can range from a local one[241] to a worldwide market.[242]

19.   For the purposes of defining the geographic market in the context of the Merger Regulation, the General Court has said that:

> ... account must be taken of a number of factors, such as the nature and characteristics of the products or services concerned, the existence of entry barriers, consumer preferences, the existence, in the area concerned as compared with neighbouring areas, of appreciable differences in the market share of undertakings, or price differences.[243]

20.   The SSNIP test can also be used in defining the geographic market by asking if consumers of a particular product in one area would switch their purchase to a supplier of the product in another area in the face of a permanent 5 per cent to 10 per cent price increase. If consumers would switch then the alternative area is in the same market as the area under consideration.

---

239. DG Competition Discussion Paper on the application of Article 82 of the Treaty to exclusionary abuses (December 2005) paras 13, 18–19.
240. Commission Notice on Market Definition [1997] OJ C 372/5, para 8.
241. See, e.g., *Blemings v David Patton Ltd.* [2001] 1 IR 385, 418 (the Irish High Court finding that the relevant geographic market for the provision of broiler growing services was within a fifteen mile radius of a monopolist purchaser).
242. See, e.g., Case T–26/02 *Daiichi Pharmaceutical Co Ltd v European Commission* [2006] ECR II–713, [2006] 5 CMLR 169, para 78 (worldwide vitamins market accepted).
243. Case T–151/05 *Nederlandse Vakbond Varkenshouders (NVV) v Commission* [2009] ECR II–1219, [2009] 5 CMLR 1613, para 52.

21. In its Notice on Market Definition, the Commission identifies the following factors to be considered in defining the relevant geographic market:[244]

   • Past evidence of diversion of orders to other areas.

   • Basic demand characteristics.

   • Views of customers and competitors.

   • Current geographic pattern of purchases.

   • Trade flows/pattern of shipments.

   • Barriers and switching costs associated with diverting orders to companies located in other areas.

What first steps can be taken to define the relevant market in practice?

22. In practice, it is often necessary to come to a working market definition quickly, for example, when a company needs to make its own assessment as to whether an agreement or practice might be anti-competitive; establishing whether a company in fact holds a dominant position; or carrying out an analysis of whether a potential merger would raise competition concerns.

23. Before carrying out a substitutability analysis focusing on the factors discussed above, it is worth conducting a search to establish whether market definitions in the sector have already been made by the Commission, other antitrust regulators or the courts. It should be kept in mind that markets can change over time, so previous findings do not necessarily continue to apply. It is also worth examining how business people define the markets or by what yardstick market share is assessed in the industry. This information is often available in internal documents such as business plans, strategy presentations etc. In addition, external reports on the industry by market research firms such as Frost & Sullivan will often include market definitions and share data. These internal company documents and external consultant reports are often used by the Commission when carrying out an investigation.

24. Market shares will typically be attributed according to the value or volume of sales made but there is no one correct measure of share. The most appropriate measure will depend on the circumstances. The Commission often considers both value and volume information[245] and in merger control, the Commission requests that the parties supply both kinds of data.[246] Data based on value of sales is often the most

---

244. Commission Notice on Market Definition [1997] OJ C 372/5, para 45–50.
245. See, e.g., Case COMP/C–3/37.990 *Intel*, Commission Decision of 13 May 2009, paras 837–852 (appeal pending, Case T–286/09 *Intel v Commission*); COMP 38.784 *Wanadoo España v Telefónica*, Commission Decision of 4 July 2007, paras 245–246 (share of broadband provision in terms of both revenue and number of subscribers) (appeals pending, Case T–336/07 *Telefónica v Commission* and Case T–398/07 *Spain v Commission*).
246. Form CO relating to the Notification of a Concentration pursuant to Regulation (EC) No 139/2004 (Annex I to Commission Regulation (EC) No 802/2004 implementing Council Regulation (EC) No 139/2004 on the control of concentrations between undertakings [2004] OJ L133/1) s 7.2, 7.3.

appropriate indicator of market strength, particularly in respect of differentiated products but in other areas, data based on volume may be used. For example, market shares have been calculated by volume in respect of sales of video game consoles.[247] In some industries, a measure of market share other than one based on sales by value or volume may be appropriate. For example, in the market for fund administration, market shares have been calculated based on the amount of assets under custody[248] and in mining industries, market shares based on capacity have been considered.[249]

When may a standard market definition approach not be applicable?

25. Defining markets based on direct substitutability provides a relatively straightforward formula for approaching a competition analysis. However, it does not always produce results that accurately identify the competition issues. For example, when considering competition in input markets, it may be necessary to consider indirect substitution, *i.e.* whereas the inputs themselves may not be directly substitutable, the final products they end up in may be directly substitutable. Consumers may switch their choice of final product in reaction to a price increase in one of the inputs.[250]

26. Another situation where market definition may be less straightforward involves products with spare parts and aftermarkets. Take, for example, printers. In deciding which printer to purchase, consumers may factor in not only the price of the printer but also the cost of purchasing ink cartridges in the future. In this case, it may be appropriate to include the primary product (the printer) and the secondary product (the cartridge) in the market definition.

Key Sources

Commission Notice on the definition of relevant market for the purposes of Community competition law [1997] OJ C 372.

Case T–151/05 *Nederlandse Vakbond Varkenshouders (NVV) v Commission* [2009] ECR II–1219, [2009] 5 CMLR 1613.

Case T–213/00 *CMA CGM v Commission* [2003] ECR II–913, [2003] 5 CMLR 268.

---

247. *Nintendo* [2003] OJ L255/33, [2004] CMLR 421, paras 73–74 (partly upheld on appeal, Case T–13/03 *Nintendo Co., Ltd v Commission* [2009] ECR II–947, [2009] 5 CMLR 1421).
248. M.3207 *State Street Corporation/Deutsche Bank Global Securities*, Commission Decision of 16 January 2003, para 20.
249. M.2420 *Mitsui/CVRD/Caemi*, Commission Decision of 30 October 2001 (market shares in iron ore markets were calculated based on capacity as well as sales; see, e.g., paras 171, 174).
250. See the example discussed in Veljanovski, 'Markets without substitutes: substitution versus constraints as the key to market definition' [2010] *European Competition Law Review* 122, 123.

11. WHAT CHANGES TO EU COMPETITION LAW AND POLICY WERE BROUGHT ABOUT BY THE LISBON TREATY?

Summary

- The substantive competition and State aid rules have not changed (there are two minor amendments to the State aid rules on specific points).

- There is a question mark about whether the status of a system of undistorted competition as a fundamental objective of the EU has been downgraded, with repeal of Article 3(1)(g) TEC and the adoption of a new Protocol on competition. It remains to be seen how the EU courts interpret these changes and whether there will be any consequences for the interpretation and application of the EU competition rules.

1. The Treaty of Lisbon entered into force on 1 December 2009. The most immediately noticeable change that this new treaty brought about was to abolish the Treaty establishing the European Community ('TEC') and replace it with the Treaty on the Functioning of the European Union ('TFEU'). The rules relevant to competition are now to be found in the TFEU, as well as in an amended Treaty on European Union ('TEU').

2. The substantive antitrust rules are renumbered but they remain the same in substance. Articles 81, 82 and 86 of the TEC are now, respectively, Articles 101, 102 and 106 TFEU.

3. The State aid rules which were contained in Article 87, 88 and 89 TEC are now to be found in Article 107, 108 and 109 TFEU. Those rules remain largely the same, apart from two minor changes. Article 107(2)(c) TFEU provides that the Council may, five years after entry into force of the Lisbon Treaty, repeal the automatic exemption for aid for regions that were affected by the division of Germany. Article 107(3)(a) adds to the categories of aid that may be declared compatible with the internal market, aid granted to overseas territories of EU Member States.

4. Another change that potentially affects competition law is the repeal of Article 3 TEC. Article 3(1)(g) TEC had provided that the activities of the Community would include 'a system ensuring that competition in the internal market is not distorted'. The substance of this provision has been moved to a Protocol on the internal market and competition, annexed to the TEU and TFEU. The Protocol provides as follows:

    THE HIGH CONTRACTING PARTIES,

    CONSIDERING that the internal market as set out in Article 3 of the Treaty on European Union includes a system ensuring that competition is not distorted,

    HAVE AGREED that:

    To this end, the Union shall, if necessary, take action under the provisions of the Treaties, including under Article 352 of the Treaty on the Functioning of the European Union.

    This protocol shall be annexed to the Treaty on European Union and to the Treaty on the Functioning of the European Union.[251]

5.   The substance of Article 3(1)(g) TEC is essentially preserved. Article 51 TEU provides that 'the Protocols and Annexes to the Treaties shall form an integral part thereof'.

6.   Article 3(3) TEU now states that one of the aims of the Union is to achieve a 'highly competitive social market economy, aiming at full employment and social progress, and a high level of protection and improvement of the quality of the environment'.

7.   Article 3(1)(g) TEC had been described as embodying the 'fundamental objective of undistorted competition'.[252] The Union courts often referenced Article 3(1)(g) when applying EU competition law. While Article 3(1)(g) did not produce legal obligations in itself, the courts applied it in conjunction with other Treaty provisions. For example, in *CIF*, the Court of Justice pointed to Article 3(1)(g) as one of the bases (together with Article 10 TEC (the substance of which is now in Article 4(3) TEU) and Article 101) for its conclusion that a national competition authority had to disapply national legislation that required undertakings to engage in anti-competitive conduct.[253]

8.   There has been some debate about whether the removal of the substance of Article 3(1)(g) TEC to a Protocol could adversely affect the promotion of competition in the Union and 'water down' the meaning and application of EU competition law.[254] Similar questions could be raised about the effect of Article 3(3) TEU and how it might be read together with the Protocol. One can imagine, for example, an argument being made for a broader interpretation of the Article 106(2) derogation on the basis of the Union objective in Article 3(3) TEU of a 'highly competitive *social market* economy'.[255] It might also be argued that undistorted competition is no longer a fundamental objective of the Union, given the removal of this activity from a prominent position at the front of the EC Treaty to a Protocol. Against this, it can be argued that any change in emphasis is meaningless and that the move to a

---

251. Protocol (No 27) on the internal market and competition, annexed to the TEU and TFEU.
252. Cases T–259/02 etc *Raiffeisen Zentralbank Österreich AG v Commission* [2006] ECR II 5169, [2007] 5 CMLR 1142, para 255.
253. Case C–198/01 *CIF* [2003] ECR I–8055, [2003] 5 CMLR 829, para 51. See also, e.g., Case C–484/08 *Caja de Ahorros y Monte de Piedad de Madrid v Asociación de Usuarios de Servicios Bancarios (Ausbanc)*, judgment of 3 June 2010, para 47 (the Court of Justice explaining that Article 3(1)(g) was limited to indicating an objective which had to be specified in other provisions of the Treaty, in particular those concerning competition rules).
254. See, e.g., Riley, 'The EU Reform Treaty and the Competition Protocol: Undermining EC Competition Law' *CEPS Policy Brief* (September 2007); Petit and Neyrinck, 'A Review of the Competition Law Implications of the Treaty on the Functioning of the European Union' *CPI Antitrust Journal* (January 2010).
255. Emphasis added.

Protocol is without significance, given Article 51 TEU, which provides that Protocols form an integral part of the Treaties.

Key Sources

Treaty on the Functioning of the European Union, Articles 101–109.

Treaty on European Union, Article 3(3).

Protocol (No 27) on the internal market and competition, annexed to the TEU and TFEU.

Chapter 2

ARTICLE 101

Information Exchange and Interlocking Directors

Compliance

Horizontal Cooperation and Joint Trading

Vertical Agreements

Chapter 2

ARTICLE 101

12. MUST AGREEMENTS BE IN WRITING TO BE CAUGHT BY ARTICLE 101?

Summary

- No.

- There are no formal requirements.

- An agreement can be express or implied.

- A 'nod and a wink' is sufficient.

1. For there to be an agreement within the meaning of Article 101, it is sufficient that at least two undertakings have expressed their joint intention to conduct themselves on the market in a specific way.[1] The concept of an agreement in Article 101 'centres around the existence of a concurrence of wills between at least two parties, the form in which it is manifested being unimportant so long as it constitutes the faithful expression of the parties' intention'.[2]

2. The decisive component is the 'concurrence of wills'. The form of an agreement does not matter; what matters is that two or more undertakings cooperate to distort competition, not *how* they cooperate. Not surprisingly, the most egregious violations of Article 101, such as price fixing, are not usually the subject of written agreements. The prohibition in Article 101 extends to all kinds of agreements or understandings, formal or informal, written or oral, legally enforceable or unenforceable. It covers both horizontal agreements (between competitors) and vertical agreements (between undertakings at different levels of the supply chain). The fact that a clause intended to restrict competition has not been implemented by the contracting parties is not sufficient to remove it from the prohibition in Article 101(1).[3]

3. The following types of agreements have all been held to fall within Article 101:

- 'Gentlemen's agreements'.[4]

- Informal understandings.[5]

---

1. See, e.g., Case 41/69 *ACF Chemiefarma NV v Commission* [1970] ECR 661, para 112.
2. Case T–41/96 *Bayer AG v Commission* [2000] ECR II–3383, [2001] 4 CMLR 126, para 69.
3. Cases C–89/85 etc *Ahlström Osakeyhtiö v Commission ('Wood Pulp II')* [1993] ECR I–1307, [1993] 4 CMLR 407, para 175.
4. See, e.g., Case 41/69 *ACF Chemiefarma NV v Commission* [1970] ECR 661, para 112; Case 44/69 *Buchler & Co. v Commission* [1970] ECR 733, para 25; Case C–113/04P *Technische Unie BV v Commission* [2006] ECR I–8831, [2006] 5 CMLR 1223, paras 116–119.
5. *National Panasonic* [1982] OJ L354/28, [1983] 1 CMLR 497, paras 43, 47.

- Settlement of litigation.[6]

- Oral agreements.[7]

- Guidelines adhered to by another party.[8]

- The constitution of a trade association.[9]

4.   The fact of agreement does not have to be expressed. An agreement can be implicit in the parties' behaviour.[10] An agreement may consist not only of an isolated act, but also of 'a series of acts or from continuous conduct'.[11]

5.   The concepts of an agreement and a concerted practice are distinct from each other but they may overlap such that it is not necessary, nor may it practically be possible, to define the point at which an agreement ends and a concerted practice begins.[12] This allows the Commission to categorise a single infringement as a decision and a concerted practice. As the Court of Justice noted in *Anic*:

> ... [a] comparison between that definition of agreement and the definition of a concerted practice ... shows that, from the subjective point of view, they are intended to catch forms of collusion having the same nature and are only distinguishable from each other by their intensity and the forms in which they manifest themselves.[13]

---

6.   *Penneys* [1978] OJ L60/19, [1978] 2 CMLR 100.
7.   Case 28/77 *Tepea BV v Commission* [1978] ECR 1391, [1978] 3 CMLR 392, para 41; Cases C–101 & 110/07 *Coop de France bétail et viande v Commission* [2008] ECR I–10193, [2009] 4 CMLR 743.
8.   *Anhesuer-Busch – Scottish & Newcastle* [2000] OJ L 49/37, [2000] 5 CMLR 75.
9.   *Nuovo CEGAM* [1984] OJ L99/29, [1984] 2 CMLR 484.
10. *Viho/Toshiba* OJ 1991 L287/39, [1992] 4 CMLR 180, para 22.
11. Case C–49/92P *Commission v Anic Partecipazioni SpA* [1999] ECR I–4125, [2001] 4 CMLR 602, para 81.
12. Case T–7/89 *Hercules v Commission* [1991] ECR II- 1711, para 264.
13. Case C–49/92P *Commission v Anic Partecipazioni SpA* [1999] ECR I–4125, [2001] 4 CMLR 602, para 131.

13. CAN MERE ACQUIESCENCE BY ONE UNDERTAKING TO UNILATERAL CONDUCT OF ANOTHER UNDERTAKING RESULT IN AN 'AGREEMENT' UNDER ARTICLE 101?

Summary

- Unilateral conduct by one undertaking may give rise to an agreement under Article 101 where acquiesced to, explicitly or tacitly, by the other undertaking.

- Relevant factors in assessing whether there is a sufficient degree of acquiescence include whether the parties' interests are aligned.

- Where one party can implement a policy unilaterally, it is doubtful that an agreement will be inferred from acquiescence by the other party.

1. Genuinely unilateral conduct does not raise issues under Article 101 and if such conduct is to be challenged under the antitrust rules, this must be done by showing an abuse of a dominant position under Article 102. However, conduct entered into or terms dictated by one party, which may appear unilateral in nature, could give rise to an agreement for purposes of Article 101 if the other party acquiesces, resulting in a concurrence of wills. This can arise, in particular, in vertical relationships between a manufacturer and distributor, when the distributor at least tacitly accepts what appear to be anti-competitive measures adopted unilaterally by the manufacturer.

2. In *Sandoz*, a manufacturer sent invoices to its suppliers with the words 'exports prohibited' systematically inserted on them. The Court of Justice found that this term became part of the agreement between the manufacturer and suppliers, given the suppliers' tacit acquiescence with the export ban. The suppliers continued to place new orders without protest against the clause and *de facto* complied with the export ban.[14] In other cases, what appears to be acquiescence may even be interpreted as full co-operation as, for example, in the OFT's decision on a double-glazing cartel. A manufacturer sent faxes to distributors setting out a price increase and suggesting that it be co-ordinated. The distributors did not object to this and in fact implemented the increase. The OFT viewed this response to go beyond tacit acquiescence and to constitute 'full co-operation'.[15]

3. There are limits to the extent to which acquiescence will result in an agreement, as illustrated by *Bayer-Adalat*, in which it was held that there was no agreement as a concurrence of wills had not been proved.[16] Wholesalers in Spain and France bought supplies of Bayer's Adalat drug and exported them to the UK. The drug was more expensive in the UK so the wholesalers were able to undercut Bayer's UK distributors. Bayer unilaterally reduced the volumes of sales it made to the

---

14. Case C–277/87 *Sandoz v Commission* [1990] ECR I–45, [1989] 4 CMLR 628.
15. OFT Decision No. CA98/08/2004 *Double Glazing Cartel* (8 November 2004) para 243.
16. Case T–41/96 *Bayer AG v Commission* [2000] ECR II–3383, [2001] 4 CMLR 126 and Case C–2 & 3/01P *BAI v Bayer AG* [2004] ECR I–23, [2004] 4 CMLR 653.

French and Spanish wholesalers. The aim of this action was to partition national markets and the practical effect of the reduction in supplies was that the Spanish and French wholesalers had less Adalat to export to the UK.

4.   The Commission adopted a decision finding that an export ban was tacitly incorporated into the agreements between Bayer and the French and Spanish wholesalers. According to the Commission, the wholesalers' acquiescence in the export ban was evidenced by their awareness of Bayer's motives and the fact that they did not react against the export ban but instead aligned their conduct to Bayer's policy of preventing parallel imports to the UK.[17]

5.   The General Court overturned the Commission decision[18] and a further appeal to the Court of Justice upheld the findings of the General Court.[19] The General Court noted that 'a distinction should be drawn between cases in which an undertaking has adopted a genuinely unilateral measure, and thus without the express or implied participation of another undertaking, and those in which the unilateral character of the measure is merely apparent'.[20] Here, the Commission had not shown that Bayer actually imposed an export ban on the wholesalers or that it systematically monitored the export of Adalat. The Commission was wrong to view a reduction in orders by the wholesalers as proof that they adhered to the export ban; in fact, the wholesalers had continued to try to obtain supplies of Adalat for export. There was no agreement about an export ban and the goals of Bayer and its wholesalers were different, with the export ban not in the latter's interest. The wholesalers 'adopted a line of conduct demonstrating a firm and persistent intention to react against a policy that was fundamentally contrary to their interests'.[21]

6.   The Court of Justice reiterated that unilateral action of itself was not sufficient to give rise to an agreement for purposes of Article 101. It drew a distinction between 'what is only the expression of a unilateral policy of one of the contracting parties',[22] which could not form the basis of an agreement for purposes of Article 101 and the situation of tacit acceptance, which could give rise to an agreement:

> For an agreement within the meaning of [Article 101(1)] of the Treaty to be capable of being regarded as having been concluded by tacit acceptance, it is necessary that the manifestation of the wish of one of the contracting parties to achieve an anti-competitive goal constitute an invitation to the other party, whether express or implied, to fulfil that goal jointly, and that applies all the more where … such an agreement is not at first sight in the interests of the other party.[23]

---

17. IV/34.279/F3 *Adalat* [1996] OJ L 201/1, paras 176–185.
18. Case T–41/96 *Bayer AG v Commission* [2000] ECR II–3383, [2001] 4 CMLR 126.
19. Case C–2 & 3/01P *BAI v Bayer AG* [2004] ECR I–23, [2004] 4 CMLR 653.
20. Case T–41/96 *Bayer AG v Commission* [2000] ECR II–3383, [2001] 4 CMLR 126, para 71.
21. Case T–41/96 *Bayer AG v Commission* [2000] ECR II–3383, [2001] 4 CMLR 126, para 129.
22. Case C–2 & 3/01P *BAI v Bayer AG* [2004] ECR I–23, [2004] 4 CMLR 653, para 101.
23. Case C–2 & 3/01P *BAI v Bayer AG* [2004] ECR I–23, [2004] 4 CMLR 653, para 102.

7.   The Court went on to state that:

> ... the mere fact that a measure adopted by a manufacturer, which has the object or effect of restricting competition, falls within the context of continuous business relations between the manufacturer and its wholesalers is not sufficient for a finding that such an agreement exists.[24]

8.   The English courts have applied the *Bayer-Adalat* judgments in different contexts. In *Unipart*, the Court of Appeal considered whether an alleged margin squeeze was part of an agreement between a mobile network operator, Cellnet, and Unipart, an independent service provider which purchased airtime from Cellnet. Applying the *Bayer-Adalat* judgments and in light of the facts, it was clear that Unipart had not agreed to a margin squeeze as part of its contract nor could it be found to have tacitly acquiesced in such a policy on the part of Cellnet. The alleged margin squeeze was therefore truly unilateral.[25]

9.   In *Sel-Imperial*, it was alleged that there was an agreement in breach of Article 101 and/or the Chapter I prohibition between a body, BSI, that developed an industry standard entailing a specification for automotive vehicle body repair and various undertakings that were involved in developing the standard and which allegedly entrusted the interpretation of the standard to BSI and agreed to adopt that interpretation. The defendant sought to strike out the claim and alternatively sought summary judgment, arguing on this point that there was no meeting of minds and that BSI's interpretation of the standard was a unilateral action. Roth J distinguished the approach taken in *Bayer-Adalat* and *Unipart*. Whereas the Article 101 issues in those cases arose in the context of vertical relationships where the parties were not actual or potential competitors, the allegation here related to an agreement that involved BSI and a number of undertakings, including several motor insurers (which presumably were horizontal competitors), to give up their independent right to determine whether a part complied with the relevant standard. Whether such an agreement existed was a matter of fact to be determined at the trial.[26]

Key Sources

Case C–277/87 *Sandoz v Commission* [1990] ECR I–45, [1989] 4 CMLR 628.

Case T–41/96 *Bayer AG v Commission* [2000] ECR II–3383, [2001] 4 CMLR 126.

Cases C–2 & 3/01P *BAI v Bayer AG* [2004] ECR I–23, [2004] 4 CMLR 653.

---

24.   Case C–2 & 3/01P *BAI v Bayer AG* [2004] ECR I–23, [2004] 4 CMLR 653, para 141.

25.   *Unipart Group Ltd v 02 (UK) Ltd (formerly BT Cellnet Ltd)* [2004] EWCA Civ 1034, [2004] UKCLR 1453, paras 97–108 (a breach of Article 102 was not pleaded).

26.   *Sel-Imperial Ltd v British Standards Institution* [2010] EWHC 854 (Ch), [2010] UKCLR 493, paras 23–35 (Roth J).

14. WHAT IS A 'CONCERTED PRACTICE'?

Summary

- A concerted practice falls short of an agreement (but may also overlap).

- It involves knowing substitution of practical cooperation for the risks of competition.

- Concerted practices are often based on exchanges of information or meetings between competitors. A single meeting or document may be sufficient.

- To prove a concerted practice, as well as concertation, a causal connection between subsequent market conduct and the concertation must be shown.

- However, the causal connection will be presumed if there is evidence of concertation and the parties remain active on the market. The parties can rebut the presumption by adducing contrary proof but this may be difficult.

- Parallel conduct may be strong evidence of a concerted practice.

1. A concerted practice falls short of an agreement or a decision but may exist if there is contact between undertakings, which has the object or effect of influencing their conduct on the market. A simple example is where one competitor indicates a future price increase to another but the two companies do not enter into any agreement as such. Were concerted practices not part of Article 101, it could prove difficult to establish coordination among undertakings in certain cases, particularly in the cartel context where participants will often be careful enough to leave no evidence of an actual agreement.

2. The Court of Justice has defined a concerted practice as:

    A form of coordination between undertakings which, without having reached the stage where an agreement properly so-called has been concluded, knowingly substitutes practical cooperation between them for the risks of competition.[27]

3. In *Suiker Unie,* the Court of Justice clarified that the terms 'coordination' and 'cooperation' do not require 'the working out of an actual plan'.[28] The Commission, describing a concerted practice in *Soda Ash*, noted that '[an] infringement of [Article 101] may well exist where the parties have not even spelled out an agreement in terms but each infers commitment from the other on the basis of conduct'.[29]

4. Where competitors inform each other in advance of conduct they are going to adopt, this may result in a concerted practice. An example is one company informing a competitor of a future price increase. Another example would be

---

27. Case 48/69 *ICI v Commission ('Dyestuffs')* [1972] ECR 619, [1972] CMLR 557, para 64.
28. Cases 40/73 etc *Suiker Unie UA v Commission* [1975] ECR 1663, [1976] 1 CMLR 295, para 173.
29. *ICI/Solvay (Soda Ash)* [1991] OJ L152/1, [1994] 4 CMLR 454, para 59.

where one competitor indicates to another the value of a tender it intends to submit for a public contract. The elements of an actual agreement may not exist but it may be possible to infer a concerted practice if the subsequent behaviour of the parties could only have resulted from them acting together. The position was described by the Court of Justice in *Suiker Unie*:

> The criteria of coordination and cooperation laid down by the case-law of the court, which in no way require the working out of an actual plan, must be understood in the light of the concept inherent in the provisions of the Treaty relating to competition that each economic operator must determine independently the policy which he intends to adopt on the common market including the choice of the persons and undertakings to which he makes offers or sells.
>
> Although it is correct to say that this requirement of independence does not deprive economic operators of the right to adapt themselves intelligently to the existing and anticipated conduct of their competitors, it does however strictly preclude any direct or indirect contact between such operators, the object or effect whereof is either to influence the conduct on the market of an actual or potential competitor or to disclose to such a competitor the course of conduct which they themselves have decided to adopt or contemplate adopting on the market.[30]

5.   The principle that each undertaking must independently decide how it acts on the market is 'a concept inherent in the [Treaty] provisions relating to competition'[31] and has been used by the EU courts on numerous occasions in providing a rationale for their decisions.

6.   Proving a concerted practice does not require a showing that an undertaking has formally undertaken, in respect of other competitors, to adopt a particular course of conduct or that the competitors have colluded over their future conduct on the market. It is sufficient that, by its statement of intention, the competitor has eliminated or substantially reduced uncertainty as to the conduct to expect of the other on the market with the result that competition between them is restricted.[32]

What is the burden of proof to establish a concerted practice?

7.   As the fifth recital of Regulation 1/2003 states, it should be for the party or the authority alleging an infringement of the competition rules to prove the infringement. It is then for the undertaking or association of undertakings invoking the benefit of a defence against a finding of an infringement to demonstrate that the conditions for applying the defence are satisfied. If the defendant succeeds in this, the party or authority seeking to prove the infringement will have to resort to other evidence.

8.   The Court of Justice acknowledged in *Hüls* that the concept of a concerted practice 'implies, besides undertakings' concerting with each other, subsequent

30.   Cases 40/73 etc *Suiker Unie UA v Commission* [1975] ECR 1663, [1976] 1 CMLR 295, paras 173–174.

31.   Case C–209/07 *Competition Authority v BIDS* [2008] ECR I–8637, [2009] 4 CMLR 310, para 34.

32.   See, e.g., Case C–194/99P *Thyssen Stahl AG v Commission* [2003] ECR I–10821, para 81.

conduct on the market, and a relationship of cause and effect between the two'.[33] So, the party seeking to show a breach of Article 101 must prove (i) concertation and (ii) subsequent conduct on the market caused by the concertation.

9. The Court of Justice has developed a presumption, according to which, if there is evidence of concertation, the parties then have the burden of proving that their subsequent conduct was not caused by the concertation:

> The presumption must be that the undertakings taking part in the concerted action and remaining active on the market take account of the information exchanged with their competitors for the purposes of determining their conduct on that market. That is all the more true where the undertakings concert together on a regular basis over a long period.[34]

10. This presumption has the consequence that once concertation and a continuing presence on the market are shown, the Commission does not have to show a causal connection between the concertation and subsequent conduct or that the concertation had any effects restrictive of competition.[35]

11. The limits of this presumption were examined in the *T-Mobile* case, in which the question was raised whether the presumption must be applied by national courts or whether national rules of evidence could be used when applying Article 101, subject to the principles of equivalence and effectiveness. The Court of Justice ruled that the presumption of a causal connection stemmed from Article 101 itself as interpreted by the Court and that in applying Article 101, any interpretation provided by the Court was binding on national courts.[36] The Court also found that the presumption of a causal connection between the concerted practice and subsequent conduct on the market applied even if the concerted action was the result of only one meeting between the undertakings.[37]

12. It should be remembered that as with agreements that have an anti-competitive object, there is no need to examine the effects of a concerted practice once its anti-competitive object is established.[38] To establish that a concerted practice has an anti-competitive object, 'it is sufficient that it has the potential to have a negative impact on competition'.[39]

33. Case C–199/92P *Hüls v Commission* [1999] ECR I–4287, [1999] 5 CMLR 1016, para 161.
34. Case C–199/92P *Hüls v Commission* [1999] ECR I–4287, [1999] 5 CMLR 1016, para 162; see also Case C–49/92P *Commission v Anic Partecipazioni SpA* [1999] ECR I–4125, [2001] 4 CMLR 602, para 121.
35. See Case C–199/92P *Hüls v Commission* [1999] ECR I–4287, [1999] 5 CMLR 1016, para 167.
36. See Case C–8/08 *T-Mobile Netherlands BV* [2009] ECR I–4529, [2009] 5 CMLR 1701, paras 50–52.
37. See Case C–8/08 *T-Mobile Netherlands BV* [2009] ECR I–4529, [2009] 5 CMLR 1701, paras 54–62.
38. See Case C–49/92P *Commission v Anic Partecipazioni SpA* [1999] ECR I–4125, [2001] 4 CMLR 602, para 123.
39. Case C–8/08 *T-Mobile Netherlands BV* [2009] ECR I–4529, [2009] 5 CMLR 1701, para 31.

13. The standard of proof is the balance of probabilities, the General Court having rejected the argument that proof must be beyond reasonable doubt when the Commission imposes heavy fines.[40]

May parallel conduct give rise to a concerted practice?

14. Parallel conduct may be 'strong evidence'[41] of a concerted practice, for example where competitors raise their prices at around the same time and by a similar amount. However, similar price movements do not of themselves give rise to a concerted practice. In many markets, competitors will quite legitimately take a unilateral decision to respond to changes in competitors' prices.

15. In oligopolistic markets, tacit collusion (or 'conscious parallelism') may be a rational choice dictated by factors including the market structure. If a price cut in such a market is met by similar cuts by competitors, then prices fall and the respective market shares of the competitors remain the same. Each firm in the market individually comes to the conclusion that it is useless to cut prices. This in turn results in price stability as members of the oligopoly mimic each other's price movements. This economic theory can explain how undertakings price the same and are aware of this, without violating Article 101.[42]

16. In the past, the Commission has sought to apply Article 101 in such cases involving oligopolistic markets, arguing that parallel conduct of this type is evidence of a concerted practice. In *Wood Pulp*, the Commission found that wood pulp producers had engaged in an illicit concerted practice.[43] It relied on evidence that the major wood pulp producers had announced price increases almost simultaneously and subsequently raised prices in parallel.

17. On appeal, the Court of Justice considered that where a finding of an infringement was based solely on parallel conduct, without any supporting documentary evidence of concertation, a strict approach would have to be taken in concluding that there was in fact a concerted practice. It held that parallel conduct was not itself proof of a concerted practice unless that conclusion was the 'only plausible explanation for such conduct'.[44] In this case, concertation was not the only plausible explanation for the parties' conduct. The Court considered that the system of price announcements could be viewed as a 'rational response' to market dynamics and was also explained by the high degree of market transparency and the 'oligopolistic tendencies' of the market.[45]

---

40. See Case T–53/03 *BPB v Commission* [2008] ECR II–1333, [2008] 5 CMLR 1201, para 64.
41. Case 48/69 *ICI v Commission ('Dyestuffs')* [1972] ECR 619, [1972] CMLR 557, para 66.
42. For a more detailed discussion of oligopolistic economic models, see Bishop and Walker, *The Economics of EC Competition Law* (3rd edn, 2010) para 2.020 *et seq.*
43. *Wood Pulp* [1985] OJ L85/1, [1985] 3 CMLR 474.
44. Cases 89/85 etc., *Åhlström Osakeyhtiö v Commission ('Wood Pulp II')* [1993] ECR I–1307, [1993] 4 CMLR 407, para 71. See also Case T–53/03 *BPB plc v Commission* [2008] ECR II–1333, [2008] 5 CMLR 1201, para 143.
45. Cases 89/85 etc., *Åhlström Osakeyhtiö v Commission ('Wood Pulp II')* [1993] ECR I–1307, [1993] 4 CMLR 407, para 126.

18. The general distinction between unilateral conduct and agreements or concerted practices that fall within Article 101(1) has been described by the General Court in the following terms:

> [A] distinction should be drawn between cases in which an undertaking has adopted a genuinely unilateral measure, and thus without the express or implied participation of another undertaking, and those in which the unilateral character of the measure is merely apparent.[46]

19. One commentator has suggested that in practice it seems to be 'almost impossible for concerted practice to be deduced from evidence focusing solely on parallel conduct'.[47]

How likely are stand-alone concerted practice cases?

20. The Commission's recent practice has tended not to identify stand-alone concerted practices. Rather, where the Commission makes a finding of a concerted practice, it is typically found as part of a single continuous infringement where an agreement is also established.[48] The concepts of 'agreement' and 'concerted practice' are fluid and may overlap. A typical explanation is as follows:

> [It] may not even be possible realistically to make any such distinction [between an agreement and a concerted practice], as an infringement may present simultaneously the characteristics of each form of prohibited conduct, while considered in isolation some of its manifestations could accurately be described as one rather than the other. It would, however, be artificial analytically to sub-divide what is clearly a continuing common enterprise having one and the same overall objective into several different forms of infringement.[49]

21. This approach potentially allows the Commission to establish a longer duration for the infringement than it otherwise could if it had to establish precisely what conduct amounted to a concerted practice and when exactly an agreement was formed. The Commission does not appear to have taken any recent Article 101 cases solely on the basis of a concerted practice[50] and so unless there is evidence of

---

46. Case T–41/96 *Bayer AG v Commission* [2000] ECR II–3383, [2001] 4 CMLR 126 (upheld on appeal, Case C–2 & 3/01P *BAI v Bayer AG* [2004] ECR I–23, [2004] 4 CMLR 653). See also *Polypropylene* [1986] OJ L230/1, [1988] 4 CMLR 347, para 87 ('The importance of the concept of a concerted practice does not thus result so much from the distinction between it and an 'agreement' as from the distinction between forms of collusion falling under [Article 101(1)] and mere parallel behaviour with no element of concertation').

47. Alese, 'The Economic Theory of Non-Collusive Oligopoly and the Concept of Concerted Practice Under Article 81' [1999] *European Competition Law Review* 379, 383.

48. For a recent example, see Case COMP/39406 *Marine Hoses*, Commission decision of 28 January 2009, para 272 (on appeal, Case T–146/09 *Parker ITR Srl v Commission* and Case 148/09 *Trelleborg AB v Commission*, pending).

49. Case COMP/39406 *Marine Hoses*, Commission decision of 28 January 2009, para 259 (on appeal, Case T–146/09 *Parker ITR Srl v Commission* and Case 148/09 *Trelleborg AB v Commission*, pending).

50. See Petit, 'Agreements, Decisions of Associations of Undertakings and Concerted Practices', presentation available at http://professorgeradin.blogs.com.

collusion, it is unlikely that the Commission will pursue an Article 101 case on the basis of a concerted practice alone.

Key Sources

Case 48/69 *ICI v Commission ('Dyestuffs')* [1972] ECR 619, [1972] CMLR 557.

Cases 40/73 etc *Suiker Unie UA v Commission* [1975] ECR 1663, [1976] 1 CMLR 295.

Case C–199/92P *Hüls v Commission* [1999] ECR I–4287, [1999] 5 CMLR 1016.

Case C–49/92P *Commission v Anic Partecipazioni SpA* [1999] ECR I–4125, [2001] 4 CMLR 602.

Case C–8/08 *T-Mobile Netherlands BV* [2009] ECR I–4529, [2009] 5 CMLR 1701.

---

15. WHAT IS AN 'ASSOCIATION OF UNDERTAKINGS'?

Summary

- The Treaty does not define an 'association of undertakings'.

- It is usually an entity that consists of undertakings of the same type and may represent their interests in economic matters. Often, members of the association follow its rules or recommendations.

- Several of the cases on associations of undertakings have dealt with professional bodies. If it is not fulfilling social functions based on the principle of solidarity or exercising typically public powers, a professional body may be considered an undertaking or association of undertakings. This is particularly likely where it is involved in representing the commercial interests of its members.

- Rules adopted by a professional body can escape the Article 101 prohibition where they are necessary for the proper functioning of the profession in the particular Member State.

1. Like the term 'undertaking', the concept of an 'association of undertakings' is not defined in the Treaty. The concept was explained as follows by Advocate General Léger in *Wouters*:

> The concept of association of undertakings is not defined by the Treaty. As a general rule, an association consists of undertakings of the same general type and makes itself responsible for representing and defending their common interests vis-à-vis other economic operators, government bodies and the public in general.

> The concept of an association of undertakings does, however, play a particular role in Article [101(1)] of the Treaty. It seeks to prevent undertakings from being able to evade the rules on competition on account simply of the form in which they coordinate their conduct on the market. To ensure that this principle is effective, Article [101(1)] covers not only direct methods of coordinating conduct between undertakings (agreements and concerted practices) but also institutionalised forms of cooperation, that is to say, situations in which economic operators act through a collective structure or a common body.[51]

2. In *Sel-Imperial*, Roth J provided the following general explanation of an association of undertakings:

> In addition to agreements and concerted practices, art 101 applies to decisions by 'associations of undertakings'. This is a term of art under art 101(1). It is not to be confused with association in the sense of several independent undertakings associating together, for example in meetings or on a particular project or venture. An 'association of undertakings' here refers to a representative or cooperative body or entity, usually with members, whose rules or decisions or recommendations are

---

51. Case C–309/99 *Wouters* [2002] ECR I–1577, [2002] 4 CMLR 913, opinion of Advocate General Léger, paras 61–62.

followed, whether as a matter of obligation or practice, by its members or those whom it represents.[52]

3.   To qualify as an association of undertakings, it is not necessary that the association is itself engaged in economic activity. If the entities that make up the association are themselves engaged in economic activity so as to be undertakings, then the association can constitute an 'association of undertakings'. In *Hemat*, Fennelly J explained that in its jurisprudence on the meaning of an undertaking and an association of undertakings, the Court of Justice:

> has refrained from laying down a set of rules from which it could be deduced a *priori* whether a particular body was an association of undertakings. Rather the underlying principle is that the competition rules apply to any body whether an individual undertaking or an association of undertakings provided that it is engaged in economic activity. The association of undertakings is in a slightly different situation, insofar as it is not normally engaged in the activity itself. But the principle remains.[53]

4.   The concept of an association of undertakings is not limited to any particular type of organisation. However it has been noted that an association of undertakings 'cannot be incorporeal or notional' or 'hypothetical'.[54] As well as trade associations, the term can cover entities such as agricultural cooperatives[55] and professional regulatory bodies representing the interests of a profession.

5.   In the leading case of *Wouters*, the Court of Justice considered whether the General Council of the Bar of The Netherlands was an association of undertakings. There was little difficulty in finding that individual lawyers were themselves undertakings as they provided legal services for a fee and bore the financial risks attached to performing those activities and so were clearly engaged in economic activity. The question then was whether the General Council of the Bar was an association of undertakings when it adopted a regulation providing that lawyers could not enter into partnerships with non-lawyers. The other possibility was that it was a public authority not subject to competition law.[56]

6.   The Court of Justice found that the Dutch Bar was not fulfilling a social function based on the principle of solidarity, nor was it exercising powers which are typically those of a public authority. Rather, it acted as the regulatory body of a profession, the practice of which constituted an economic activity. The fact that it regulated the practice of the profession could not in itself exclude the Bar from the scope of Article 101. Other factors supported the conclusion that the Bar did not fall outside the scope of Article 101. There was no public interest criteria considered in adopting the regulation at issue. The Bar was to act in the interests of

52. *Sel-Imperial Ltd v British Standards Institution* [2010] EWHC 854 (Ch), [2010] UKCLR 493, para 36 (Roth J).

53. *Hemat v The Medical Council* [2010] IESC 24, para 52.

54. *Nurendale Ltd t/a Panda Waste Services v Dublin City Council* [2009] IEHC 588, para 66 (McKechnie J).

55. Case 61/80 *Coöperatieve Stremsel-en Kleurselfabriek v Commission* [1981] ECR 851, [1982] 1 CMLR 240.

56. Case C–309/99 *Wouters* [2002] ECR I–1577, [2002] 4 CMLR 913, paras 56–57.

the profession and given its impact on the conduct of lawyers on the market, the regulation did not fall outside the sphere of economic activity. Therefore, in adopting the regulation, the Bar was an association of undertakings within the meaning of Article 101, regardless of the fact that its constitution was regulated by public law.[57] The regulation was a decision of an association of undertakings.[58]

7.   In 2004, the Commission found that the Belgian Architects' Association had infringed Article 101 by adopting a minimum fee scale for architects, entitled 'Ethical Standard No 2'. The Commission found that the association was an association of undertakings within the meaning of Article 101 when it adopted the fee scale. It was not fulfilling a social function based on the principle of solidarity or carrying out a typically public function. It was clear from *Wouters* that 'a professional association must be considered to be an association of undertakings within the meaning of Article [101] when it adopts rules constituting the expression of the intention of the delegates of members of a profession that they should act in a particular manner in carrying on their economic activity'.[59]

8.   In *Hemat*, the Irish High Court held that in issuing a guide on ethical conduct, which placed restrictions on advertising, the Irish Medical Council was not an association of undertakings.[60] This finding was upheld on appeal. In contrast to *Wouters*, in issuing a guide on ethical conduct which restricted advertising, the Medical Council was not acting in the interests of its members but rather acted solely in the public interest. In the Supreme Court, Fennelly J emphasised that the Medical Council was required by statute to act in the public interest and that had it been motivated by the economic interests of the medical profession, it would be abusing its power and acting *ultra vires*.[61] Fennelly J acknowledged that the restriction on advertising fell within the economic field and was capable of restricting competition. However, the special context of medical advertising had to be considered. There was an 'indisputable public interest in discouraging the promotion of unproven or fraudulent medical practices' and ultimately the learned judge was satisfied that in adopting the restriction on advertising the Medical Council was predominantly motivated by considerations of the interests of patients and so the restrictions 'were only incidentally concerned with economic matters'.

---

57.   Case C–309/99 *Wouters* [2002] ECR I–1577, [2002] 4 CMLR 913, paras 58–65.
58.   Case C–309/99 *Wouters* [2002] ECR I–1577, [2002] 4 CMLR 913, para 71. The Court went on to hold that the regulation did not infringe Article 101 (see para 12 below).
59.   *Belgian Architects' Association* [2005] OJ L4/10, [2005] 4 CMLR 677, para 44.
60.   *Hemat v The Medical Council* [2006] IEHC 187. Although not addressing competition law, cf. Cases 266 & 267/87 *The Queen v Royal Pharmaceutical Society of Great Britain, ex parte Association of Pharmaceutical Importers* [1989] ECR 1295, [1989] 2 CMLR 751 (the Court of Justice held that measures adopted by a professional body for pharmacy, which laid down ethical rules applicable to all members of the profession and which had a committee upon which national legislation had conferred disciplinary powers, may have constituted 'measures' within the meaning of Article 34 TFEU (ex 28 EC)).
61.   *Hemat v The Medical Council* [2010] IESC 24, para 57.

The Medical Council could not therefore be considered an association of undertakings.[62]

Is the fact that a body is composed of members of the profession/industry relevant?

9. In a number of cases, the fact that a professional body was made up entirely of members of the profession or appointed exclusively by the profession, has been a factor supporting the conclusion that the body was an association of undertakings.[63] In *Wouters*, the governing bodies of the Dutch Bar were composed exclusively of members of the Bar elected by members of the profession;[64] in *CNSD*, an association of customs agents was composed entirely of customs agents and the Italian Minister for Finance could not intervene in appointments;[65] and in *Pavlov*, an association of medical specialists was composed exclusively of self-employed medical specialists, whose economic interests it defended.[66]

10. Outside appointments will not necessarily prevent a body being considered an association of undertakings. In the *Belgian Architects* case, the Commission found that the Belgian Architects' Association could not escape the application of Article 101 because half of the members of its national council were appointed by the government. It was highly likely that these appointees would also be registered architects bearing in mind that they were selected from groups linked to the architecture profession. In any event, the other half of the national council, including the chairman, was directly elected by the profession.[67]

11. When will external influence in the composition of a professional body be sufficient to bring it outside the scope of Article 101? In a case involving the setting of road-haulage tariffs in Italy, the Court of Justice concluded that proposals of tariffs by a central committee could not be regarded as falling within the scope of Article 101. A majority of the members of the committee were representatives of public authorities, with a minority representing industry

---

62. *Hemat v The Medical Council* [2010] IESC 24, paras 61–68. See also *Kenny v Dental Council* [2004] IEHC 105, [2009] 4 IR 321 (Gilligan J holding that the Dental Council was not an undertaking when making a scheme for auxiliary dental workers; for discussion of this decision, arguing that the rule at issue could have been viewed as falling within the economic sphere, as had the Council provided a scheme for the recognition of denturists and permitted them to legitimately engage in a limited form of dental practice, this would have had obvious competitive implications, see Hogan, 'Regulatory Bodies as Associations of Undertakings' (2005) 27 *Dublin University Law Journal* 329); *Easy Readers Ltd v Bord na Radharcmhastori* [2003] IEHC 93 (Smyth J finding that the regulatory body for opticians was not an undertaking; the question as to whether it might have been an association of undertakings was not addressed in the judgment).
63. On competition in the professions, see the Commission Report on Competition in Professional Services COM(2004) 83 final.
64. See Case C–309/99 *Wouters* [2002] ECR I–1577, [2002] 4 CMLR 913, para 61.
65. See Case C–35/96 *Commission v Italy ('CNSD')* [1998] ECR I–3851, [1998] 5 CMLR 889, para 42.
66. Cases C–180/98 etc., *Pavlov* [2000] ECR I–6451, [2001] 4 CMLR 30, para 88.
67. *Belgian Architects' Association* [2005] OJ L4/10, [2005] 4 CMLR 677, para 42.

associations, and the obligation on the committee to observe various criteria was set out in law.[68] In *Hemat*, it was held that the Medical Council was not an association of undertakings, even though a majority of its members appeared to be undertakings themselves. McKechnie J declined to countenance the 'numbers game', concluding that the 'decisive and ultimate question must always centre on the nature of the activity carried on'.[69] This approach was approved in the Supreme Court. Fennelly J noted the Court of Justice holding in *Pavlov* that 'a decision taken by a body having regulatory powers within a given sector *might* fall outside the scope of [Article 101] of the Treaty where that body is composed of a majority of representatives of the public authorities and where, on taking a decision, it must observe various public-interest criteria'.[70] Fennelly J took the view that the Court of Justice had not laid down any rule of general application regarding composition of bodies and distinguished the Medical Council from the bodies at issue in *Wouters* and *Pavlov*.[71]

Are rules which are necessary for the functioning of a profession exempt from competition law?

12. In *Wouters*, although the Dutch Bar Council was an association of undertakings, the Court of Justice held that the regulation adopted by the Bar Council, which prohibited partnerships between lawyers and non-lawyers, did not infringe Article 101. It held that a decision by an association of undertakings would not infringe Article 101, despite its restrictive effects, where it was necessary for the 'proper practice' of the profession in the Member State concerned. That was so in light of factors such as the importance placed in The Netherlands on the duty on lawyers to act for clients in complete independence and in their sole interest and to avoid all risk of conflict of interest and the duty to observe strict professional secrecy. The Court's finding in this respect was not that the rule was capable of justification under Article 101(3) but rather that it did not infringe Article 101(1) in the first place.[72]

May associations of undertakings make recommendations about fees?

13. Whereas the *Wouters* exception allowing rules necessary for the proper practice of a profession might apply to some restrictive rules of professional organisations, it

---

68. Case C–96/94 *Centro Servizi Spediporto Srl v Spedizioni Marittima del Golfo Srl.* [1995] ECR I–2883, [1996] 4 CMLR 613, paras 23–25.
69. *Hemat v The Medical Council* [2006] IEHC 187, paras 58–59.
70. Cases C–180/98 etc *Pavlov* [2000] ECR I–6451, [2001] 4 CMLR 30, para 87 (emphasis added).
71. *Hemat v The Medical Council* [2010] IESC 24, paras 59–60.
72. Case C–309/99 *Wouters* [2002] ECR I–1577, [2002] 4 CMLR 913, paras 100–110. Cf Case T–144/99 *Institute of Professional Representatives v Commission* [2001] ECR II–1087, [2001] 5 CMLR 77, para 78 (where it was not shown that an absolute prohibition of comparative advertising was objectively necessary in order to preserve the dignity and rules of conduct of the profession concerned, the rule fell within the scope of Article 101(1)).

is doubtful that it would apply to the fixing of fees. Rules and recommendations on fees have been condemned by the Commission and the national competition authorities.

14. In the *Belgian Architects* case, the Commission examined whether a recommended scale of fees adopted by the Belgian Architects Association breached Article 101. The scale set out a table in which the key to fixing architects' fees was a set percentage of the value of the building work, by category of work and by expenditure bracket. Although described as a 'guideline', the Commission found that the scale had an intentional rule-making tone with statements including 'that all architects are obliged to set their fees at a level determined at the very least by...'[73] On the question of whether the scale was necessary for the proper functioning of the profession, one of the arguments made by the association was that the scale was useful as a guideline in fielding inquiries from parties to the contract or from a court. The Commission rejected this argument, noting that information on prices could be provided in other ways, for example through independent parties such as consumer associations or through surveys.

15. The French Competition Authority has prohibited the French Architects' Association from elaborating and distributing fee scales.[74] In the UK, the OFT concluded in 2001 that the Royal Institute of British Architects' indicative fee guidance could facilitate collusion. The OFT subsequently accepted new fee guidance based on historical information gathered by an independent body and the collation of price trends that did not provide a lead on current year's prices.[75]

16. In Ireland, the Competition Authority carried out an investigation into the way in which fees for hospital consultants' services are negotiated between consultants and private health insurers.[76] It concluded that the actions of the consultants' representative body, the Irish Hospital Consultants Association ('IHCA'), in the context of those negotiations breached section 4(1) of the Competition Act 2002. No litigation ensued as a settlement was reached between the Authority and the IHCA. The Competition Authority subsequently published a note setting out its view of the application of competition law in respect of collective negotiations relating to the setting of medical fees.[77] The Authority was of the view that

---

73. *Belgian Architects' Association* [2005] OJ L4/10, [2005] 4 CMLR 677, para 57. See also, Case 45/85 *Verband der Sachversicherer eV v Commission* [1987] ECR 405, [1988] 4 CMLR 264, para 32 (the Court of Justice rejected the argument that a recommendation by an association of German insurers to its members to raise premiums was not binding and therefore fell outside Article 101, finding that it was a decision within the meaning of Article 101 as it reflected the association's aim to coordinate the pricing of its members).

74. French Conseil de la Concurrence Decision no. 97D45 of 10 June 1997.

75. OFT Case Closures, *Royal Institute of British Architects* (14 March 2003).

76. Cf the treatment of collective negotiations between unions and employers, which fall outside the scope of Article 101 when aimed at improving conditions of work and employment. See Case C–67/96 *Albany* [1999] ECR I–5751, [2000] 4 CMLR 446, para 59 and Question 1.

77. The Competition Authority, Guidance in respect of Collective Negotiations relating to the Setting of Medical Fees (10 January 2007).

decisions or recommendations by any representative body to coordinate or facilitate the coordination of fees or other commercial terms amongst doctors was a breach of the Competition Act, potentially open to criminal prosecution.[78] The Authority views such arrangements in the same was as price fixing, with no real prospect of exemption under section 4(5) (the equivalent of Article 101(3)).

Are partnerships subject to Article 101?

17. An agreement between members of a genuine partnership will not be subject to Article 101 or equivalent national provisions as it is not an agreement between independent undertakings. The partnership will itself be considered as a single undertaking. However the partnership must be *genuine*, with the partners sharing the financial risk. Several factors may be relevant to this assessment. For example, in respect of a group of anaesthetists, the Office of Fair Trading found that the group would be treated as a single undertaking:

> if it operates and presents itself as a single entity on the market, for example, where the members generate profits for the common benefit of the group, operate under a common name, share administrative functions such as joint billing, have a bank account (or accounts) in the name of the group and/or a single set of accounts is produced in respect of the group's commercial activities.[79]

Key Sources

Case C–309/99 *Wouters* [2002] ECR I–1577, [2002] 4 CMLR 913.

Cases C–180/98 etc *Pavlov* [2000] ECR I–6451, [2001] 4 CMLR 30.

Hemat v The Medical Council [2010] IESC 24.

---

78. See The Competition Authority, Guidance in respect of Collective Negotiations relating to the Setting of Medical Fees (10 January 2007) paras 3.5–3.6. Cf *Hickey v Health Service Executive* [2008] IEHC 290, [2009] 3 IR 156, paras 91–92 (Finlay Geoghegan J holding *obiter* that a clause in an agreement between the Minister for Health and pharmacists providing that the Minister would set prices after consultation with a committee of the Irish Pharmaceutical Union, did not give rise to a concerted practice or decision by an association of undertakings in relation to price under section 4 of the Competition Act 2002 as the final decision on payment was to be made unilaterally by the Minister).
79. OFT Non-infringement decision, *Anaesthetists' groups* (15 April 2003).

16. What constitutes a 'decision' for purposes of the Article 101 'decision by an association of undertakings'?

Summary

- There are no formal requirements for a 'decision' to be taken.

- A 'decision' does not have to be binding on members of the association.

- Rules, activities and even recommendations of an association may be sufficient to give rise to a 'decision' within the meaning of Article 101.

1. There are no formal requirements for a 'decision' to be taken by an association of undertakings. If the activities or rules of an association breach Article 101, the exact form those measures take is not decisive. Any act of the association which has the objective or effect of influencing the commercial behaviour of the members of the association may constitute a 'decision'. The application of Article 101 will not be affected whether the activities of an association are categorised as a decision or an agreement where they 'are calculated to produce the results which [Article 101] aims to suppress'.[80]

2. A decision of an association of undertakings does not have to be binding on its members, where it is actually complied with:

    > [A] measure may be categorised as a decision of an association of undertakings for the purposes of Article [101(1)] even if it is not binding on the members concerned, at least to the extent that the members to whom the decision applies comply with its terms.[81]

3. Recommendations issued by the association that purport to be non-binding, may give rise to an Article 101 violation if they are actually complied with.[82] For example, in *Verband der Sachversicherer*, it was argued that a 'recommendation' by an association of insurance companies to raise premiums for fire insurance was not a 'decision' as it was non-binding. However, the Court of Justice looked beyond the non-binding label. In light of its mandatory terminology, the fact that it was quickly implemented and the fact that the statutes of the association

---

80. Cases 96/82 etc *IAZ International Belgium v Commission* [1983] ECR 3369, [1984] 3 CMLR 276, para 20.

81. Case T–325/01 *DaimlerChrysler AG v Commission* [2005] ECR II–3319, [2007] 4 CMLR 559, para 210; See also Cases 209/78 etc. *Heintz van Landewyck SARL v Commission ('FEDETAB')* [1980] ECR 3125, [1981] 3 CMLR 134, paras 88–89.

82. See, e.g., *Fenex* [1996] OJ L181/28, [1996] 5 CMLR 332 (Dutch association of freight forwarders had a practice of circulating recommended tariff increases); *SCK* [1995] OJ L312/79 (association of firms which hired out mobile cranes published cost calculations and recommended rates based on them, with an obligation to give preference to other members when hiring or hiring out cranes and to charge 'reasonable' rates).

empowered it to coordinate the activities of its members, the Court concluded that the recommendation was a 'decision' within the meaning of Article 101.[83]

4.   A recommendation, even if it has no binding effect, cannot escape Article 101(1) 'where compliance with the recommendation by the undertakings to which it is addressed has an appreciable influence on competition in the market in question'.[84]

5.   A typical example of a decision by an association of undertakings is that of a trade association.[85] Such a decision is often treated more as if it were an agreement between the members of the association. Trade associations often feature in cartel cases.[86] They may provide a 'cover' for the cartel's activities and facilitate coordination between competitors through organised meetings and the exchange of commercially sensitive information.[87] The rules promulgated by a trade association or its membership rules may violate Article 101.[88] The trade association might itself enter into an anti-competitive agreement on behalf of its members.[89] The trade association, as well as its members, can be found to infringe Article 101(1).

Key Sources

Case 45/85 *Verband der Sachversicherer e.V. v Commission* [1987] ECR 405, [1988] 4 CMLR 264.

Case T–325/01 *DaimlerChrysler AG v Commission* [2005] ECR II–3319, [2007] 4 CMLR 559.

---

83.   See Case 45/85 *Verband der Sachversicherer eV v Commission* [1987] ECR 405, [1988] 4 CMLR 264, paras 29–32. See also, *Competition Authority v Licensed Vintners Association* [2009] IEHC 439, [2010] 1 ILRM 374 (the announcement of a one-year price freeze by two trade associations of publicans was found to breach an earlier settlement with the Competition Authority pursuant to which the associations undertook not to recommend prices to their members or otherwise breach section 4 of the Competition Act 2002).

84.   Cases 96/82 etc *IAZ International Belgium v Commission* [1983] ECR 3369, [1984] 3 CMLR 276, para 20. See also Question 15, paras 14–16 (price recommendations by professional associations).

85.   For a general discussion, see Reid, 'EU Competition Law and Trade Associations' in Greenwood (ed), *The Challenge of Change in EU Business Associations* (2003) Ch 6.

86.   See, e.g., Case 246/86 *Belasco v Commission* [1989] ECR 2117, [1991] 4 CMLR 96 (roofing felt cartel coordinated through the Cooperative of Belgian Asphalt Producers).

87.   See, e.g., *Bundesverband Deutscher Verstahlhandel eV* [1980] OJ L62/34, [1980] 3 CMLR 193.

88.   See, e.g., *National Sulphuric Acid Association* [1980] OJ L260/24, [1980] 3 CMLR 429; *BPICA* [1977] OJ L299/18, [1977] 2 CMLR 43.

89.   See Case 272/85 *ANTIB v Commission* [1987] ECR 2201, [1988] 4 CMLR 677 (Association of Independent Waterways Workers entering into an anti-competitive agreement).

17. ARE THERE CERTAIN TYPES OF AGREEMENTS THAT WILL, BY THEIR
NATURE, HAVE AN ANTI-COMPETITIVE OBJECT?

Summary

- Certain types of agreements such as horizontal price fixing, market sharing and output restrictions are generally considered, of their nature, to have an anti-competitive object.

- If the object is anti-competitive, it is unnecessary to consider the effect to find a breach of Article 101(1).

- It is unnecessary to show a direct link between the anti-competitive object and consumer prices.

- A subjective intention of the parties to restrict competition may be a relevant factor in finding an anti-competitive object but their intention not to restrict competition is irrelevant.

- An agreement will not breach Article 101 if it is not capable of having an appreciable effect on competition or an appreciable effect on trade between Member States.

- An agreement with an anti-competitive object may be capable of exemption under Article 101(3).

1.   Article 101(1) prohibits agreements or conduct that have as their object or effect the prevention, restriction or distortion of competition. An anti-competitive object *or* effect suffices. As the Court of Justice stated in *Anic*:

> It is settled case-law that, for the purposes of applying Article [101(1)] of the Treaty, there is no need to take account of the concrete effects of an agreement once it appears that it has as its object the prevention, restriction or distortion of competition.[90]

2.   An agreement with an anti-competitive object can fall within Article 101(1) even if it has not yet been put into effect.[91] Similarly, a provision with an anti-competitive object that is not in fact enforced or implemented may still violate Article 101:

> The fact that a clause prohibiting exports, which by its very nature constitutes a restriction of competition, has not been implemented by the distributor with which it has been agreed does not prove that it has had no effect, because … its existence may create a 'visual and psychological' effect which contributes to a partitioning of the market, and accordingly the fact that a clause which is intended to restrict competition

---

90. Case C–49/92P *Commission v Anic Partecipazioni SpA* [1999] ECR I–4125, [2001] 4 CMLR 602, para 99.
91. See, e.g., Case C–209/07 *Competition Authority v BIDS*, [2008] ECR I–8637, [2009] 4 CMLR 310 (the case arose from an action by the Irish Competition Authority seeking prevent anti-competitive agreements being implemented).

has not been implemented by the contracting parties is not sufficient to remove it from the prohibition in Article [101(1)] of the Treaty.[92]

3.   It has been suggested that if an agreement does not have an object which *of its nature* restricts competition, then the analysis should turn to effect,[93] although in practice, the Commission has often found it unnecessary to distinguish between object and effect.

How is the object of an agreement or practice determined?

4.   The object of an agreement is determined by examining 'the precise purpose of the agreement, in the economic context in which it is to be applied'.[94] This requires an objective assessment of the aims of the agreement and 'regard must be had inter alia to the content of its provisions, the objectives it seeks to attain and the economic and legal context of which it forms a part'.[95] The subjective intent of the parties to restrict competition may be a relevant factor in concluding that the object is anti-competitive but this is not a necessary condition or a determinative factor.[96] That the parties acted *without* any subjective intention of restricting competition is irrelevant.[97]

5.   The Commission has explained that where the anti-competitive object is not clear-cut on the face of the agreement, it may be necessary to consider a range of factors in determining the object:

> These factors include, in particular, the content of the agreement and the objective aims pursued by it. It may also be necessary to consider the context in which it is (to be) applied and the actual conduct and behaviour of the parties on the market. In other words, an examination of the facts underlying the agreement and the specific circumstances in which it operates may be required before it can be concluded whether a particular restriction constitutes a restriction of competition by object. The way in which an agreement is actually implemented may reveal a restriction by object

---

92.   Case T–77/92 *Parker Pen Ltd v Commission* [1994] ECR II–549, [1995] 5 CMLR 435, para 55. See also, Case T–43/92 *Dunlop Slazenger v Commission* [1994] ECR II–441, [1994] 5 CMLR 201, para 61 (irrelevant to the application of Article 101(1) whether an export ban was implemented by the parties).

93.   See Bellamy & Child (6th edn, 2008) para 2.098.

94.   Case 56/65 *Société Technique Minière v Maschinenbau Ulm GmbH* [1966] ECR 235, 249 [1966] CMLR 357, 375.

95.   Cases C–501/06P etc, *GlaxoSmithKline Services Unlimited v Commission* [2009] ECR I–9291, [2010] 4 CMLR 50, para 58.

96.   Commission's Guidelines on the application of Article 81(3) of the Treaty [2004] OJ C101/97 ('Commission Guidelines on Article 101(3)') para 22; Cases C–501/06P etc, *GlaxoSmithKline Services Unlimited v Commission* [2009] ECR I–9291, [2010] 4 CMLR 50, para 58; Case C–551/03P *General Motors BV v Commission* [2006] ECR I–3173, [2006] 5 CMLR 4491, paras 77–78.

97.   Case C–209/07 *Competition Authority v BIDS* [2008] ECR I–8637, [2009] 4 CMLR 310, para 21.

even where the formal agreement does not contain an express provision to that effect.[98]

6.   An agreement may be regarded as having a restrictive object even if it does not have the restriction of competition as its sole aim but also pursues other legitimate objectives.[99]

Is it necessary to show detriment to consumers?

7.   It is unnecessary for a finding of restriction by object to show that final consumers will be deprived of some advantage of effective competition in terms of supply or price. As the Court of Justice held in the *GlaxoSmithKline* dual pricing case, there is nothing in Article 101 itself to indicate that only those agreements which deprive consumers of certain advantages may have an anti-competitive object. Furthermore, 'Article [101] aims to protect not only the interests of competitors or of consumers, but also the structure of the market and, in so doing, competition as such',[100] so no showing of detriment to consumers was necessary. The agreements in question, which were intended to limit parallel imports by charging a higher price for GSK products sold to Spanish distributors for re-export than those for sale in Spain, had an anti-competitive object.[101]

What types of agreements can generally be said to have an anti-competitive object?

8.   Certain types of agreements will usually have an anti-competitive object and a fairly cursory analysis can conclude that they violate Article 101(1). In *Consten & Grundig*, the Court of Justice held that an agreement that prohibited exports within

---

98. Commission Guidelines on Article 101(3) [2004] OJ C101/97, para 22. For an example of a case in which some of these factors were applied to conclude that an agreement did not have an anti-competitive object, see *Bookmakers' Afternoon Greyhound Services Ltd v Amalgamated Racing Ltd* [2009] EWCA Civ 750, [2009] UKCLR 863 (Thirty-one racecourses organised to grant exclusive rights to a distributor to show footage in betting shops; the aim of the arrangement was to sponsor a new entrant and viewed in the economic and legal context, the object was not restrictive of competition).

99. See Cases 56 & 58/64 *Consten SaRL and Grundig Verkaufs GmbH v Commission* [1966] ECR 299, 342; Case C–551/03P *General Motors BV v Commission* [2006] ECR I–3173, [2006] 5 CMLR 9, para 64; Case C–209/07 *Competition Authority v BIDS* [2008] ECR I–8637, [2009] 4 CMLR 310, para 21.

100. Cases C–501/06P etc, *GlaxoSmithKline Services Unlimited v Commission* [2009] ECR I–9291, [2010] 4 CMLR 50, para 63. The Court of Justice overruled an earlier finding of the General Court that a showing of consumer detriment was required (Case T–168/01 *GlaxoSmithKline Services Unlimited v Commission* [2006] ECR II–2969, [2006] 5 CMLR 1589, para 119 *et seq*).

101. Cases C–501/06P etc, *GlaxoSmithKline Services Unlimited v Commission* [2009] ECR I–9291, [2010] 4 CMLR 50, paras 54–64. However, the agreements benefited from exemption under Article 101(3). See also Case C–8/08 *T-Mobile Netherlands BV* [2009] ECR I–4529, [2009] 5 CMLR 11, para 39 (the Court of Justice clarifying that for an agreement or concerted practice to have an anti-competitive object, there does not need to be a direct link between the agreement/practice and consumer prices).

the Union of its nature restricted competition, whatever its actual effects.[102] Agreements involving horizontal price fixing, market sharing and output limitations can generally be considered by their nature to have as their object the restriction of competition.[103] The Commission considers that agreements that are black-listed in its block exemption regulations or identified as hardcore restrictions in its guidelines and notices generally constitute restrictions of competition by object.[104]

9.   Despite the fact that certain types of agreements will usually be considered by the courts to have an anti-competitive object, there is no *presumption* that such agreements have an anti-competitive object. The 'burden of proving an infringement of Article [101(1)] or Article [102] of the Treaty shall rest on the party or the authority alleging the infringement'.[105] So, while as a practical matter, certain types of agreements will generally be considered to have an anti-competitive object, it is for the party seeking to prove the infringement to show that the agreement does indeed have an anti-competitive object and that the other conditions for the application of Article 101 are met.[106]

10.   With that caveat in mind, the following types of agreements are generally considered to have an anti-competitive object:[107]

Horizontal agreements

- Price fixing.

- Market sharing (allocating customers, territories or markets).

- Agreed output restrictions among horizontal competitors.

- Bid rigging agreements.

---

102. Cases 56 & 58/64 *Consten SaRL and Grundig Verkaufs GmbH v Commission* [1966] ECR 299.

103. There may be exceptions. See, e.g., *Visa International – Multilateral Interchange Fee* [2002] OJ L318/17, [2003] 4 CMLR 283 (an agreement that fixed the interchange fee for cross-border payment transactions using VISA cards was found by the Commission not to constitute a restriction of competition by object but rather had a restrictive effect; the Commission granted an exemption under Article 101(3) noting at para 79 that that it was 'not the case that an agreement concerning prices is always to be classified as a cartel and thus as inherently non-exemptible').

104. Commission Guidelines on Article 101(3) [2004] OJ C101/97 para 23.

105. Regulation 1/2003, Article 2.

106. See, e.g., Case C–260/07 *Pedro IV Servicios SL v Total España SA* [2009] ECR I–2437, [2009] 5 CMLR 1291, para 82.

107. As Whish states, classifying agreements of a particular type as generally giving rise to a restrictive object 'may require refinement from time to time to exclude from the 'object' category some types of agreements that are not so obviously restrictive of competition as others' (Whish, *Competition Law* (6th edn, 2009) 122). A similar caveat could be added in respect of the list produced here.

- Exchanges of information on current or future prices designed to facilitate the implementation of a price fixing agreement.[108]

- Collective boycotts.[109]

Vertical agreements

- Fixed and minimum resale price maintenance.[110]

- Restrictions providing absolute territorial protection, in particular by placing a ban on passive sales.[111]

- Agreements aimed at preventing or restricting parallel exports.[112]

11. The above types of agreements will *generally* be considered to have an anti-competitive object. However, this approach is 'subject to the proviso that the legal and economic context of the agreement to be examined does not preclude application of this standardised assessment'.[113]

---

108. See Cases T–25/95 etc *Cimenteries CBR SA v Commission* [2000] ECR II–491, [2000] 5 CMLR 204, para 1531 (the Commission had shown that agreements on the exchange of price information were designed to facilitate the implementation of a price fixing agreement, so it did not have to show in addition that the exchanges of price information themselves resulted in a restriction of competition). See also Draft Commission Guidelines on the applicability of Article 101 of the Treaty on the Functioning of the European Union to horizontal co-operation agreements SEC(2010) 528/2 ('Commission 2010 Draft Horizontal Cooperation Guidelines') paras 67–68 (suggesting that the sharing of future prices and current prices that reveals future conduct should be considered a restriction of competition by object).

109. See, e.g., the *Pre-insulated Pipe* cartel, which featured a collective boycott, discussed in Cases C–189/02P etc *Dansk Rørindustri v Commission* [2005] ECR I–5425, [2005] 5 CMLR 796. But see *R (Cityhook Ltd) v Office of Fair Trading* [2009] EWHC 57 (Admin), [2009] UKCLR 255, paras 126–142 (Foskett J noting the uncertainty as to whether collective boycotts by purchasers are object-based restrictions of competition). There is also a distinction to be made between a collective boycott that is a part of, or comparable to, a cartel-type agreement and joint purchasing and joint selling arrangements that pursue a legitimate aim. See Questions 36 and 37 on joint purchasing and joint selling respectively.

110. See, e.g., Case 243/83 *Binion & CIE v AMP* [1985] ECR 2015, [1985] 3 CMLR 800, para 44 (resale price maintenance was in itself a restriction of competition within the meaning of Article 101). Fixed and minimum resale price maintenance is considered to be a hardcore restriction in Article 4 of Commission Regulation (EU) No 330/2010 on the application of Article 101(3) of the Treaty on the Functioning of the European Union to categories of vertical agreements and concerted practices [2010] OJ L102/1.

111. See, e.g., Cases 56 & 58/64 *Consten SaRL and Grundig Verkaufs GmbH v Commission* [1966] ECR 299; Case C–279/87 *Tipp-Ex v Commission* [1990] ECR I–261; Case C–306/96 *Javico International v Yves Saint Laurent Parfums SA* [1998] ECR I–1983, [1998] 5 CMLR 172.

112. See Cases C–501/06P etc, *GlaxoSmithKline Services Unlimited v Commission* [2009] ECR I–9291, [2010] 4 CMLR 50.

113. Cases C–501/06P etc. *GlaxoSmithKline Services Unlimited v Commission* [2009] ECR I–9291, [2010] 4 CMLR 50, opinion of Advocate General Trstenjak, para 91.

12. The list above is by no means exhaustive of agreements that can have an anti-competitive object. Other types of agreements may on their facts be found to have an anti-competitive object. For example, in *Jones v Ricoh*, the English High Court found that a clause in a confidentiality agreement had an anti-competitive object and effect and breached Article 101. The agreement prevented one company and its affiliates from approaching clients or prospective clients of another company, with which it had a business relationship, while it held confidential information of the latter. Roth J held that the clause went far beyond any possible view of what was necessary to protect confidential information. Although the context of a confidentiality agreement was not one normally held to give rise to an agreement regarded as anti-competitive by object, it was held that this agreement exceptionally came within that category.[114]

How can an agreement with an anti-competitive object be defended under Article 101?

13. Once it is established that an agreement by its object restricts competition, it is caught by Article 101(1) and it is unnecessary to consider its effects in the market. Such an agreement could still escape the reach of Article 101(1) if (i) it does not have an appreciable effect on competition or (ii) it does not have an appreciable effect on trade between Member States. Agreements that contain hardcore restrictions cannot benefit from the *de minimis* exception for agreements of minor importance (which assumes that certain agreements do not have an appreciable effect on competition), no matter how small the market shares or turnover of the parties.[115] Nevertheless, it would still be open to an undertaking to argue that the agreement did not have an appreciable effect on competition.[116] The more likely escape route would be that the agreement does not appreciably affect trade between Member States. Such a finding will usually bring the agreement outside Article 101(1) even if it contains hardcore restrictions.[117] Of course, national equivalents of Article 101 might still apply. In the case of cartels covering several Member States, the Commission considers that, by their nature, they have an appreciable effect on trade between Member States.[118]

14. If an agreement with an anti-competitive object cannot be brought outside Article 101(1), the only way it can be saved is by the exemption in Article 101(3).[119] It is

---

114. *Jones v Ricoh UK Limited* [2010] EWHC 1743 (Ch) paras 41–42.
115. See the Commission Notice on agreements of minor importance which do not appreciably restrict competition under Article 81(1) of the Treaty establishing the European Community *(de minimis)* [2001] OJ C368/13 ('*De Minimis* Notice') para 11.
116. See Case 5/69 *Völk v Vervaecke* [1969] ECR 295, [1969] CMLR 273; European Commission Guidelines on Vertical Restraints [2010] OJ C130/1 ('Commission Guidelines on Vertical Restraints') para 10 (acknowledging that an appreciable effect on competition must be shown even in the case of hardcore restrictions).
117. See Commission Guidelines on Effect on Trade [2004] OJ C101/81, para 50.
118. Commission Guidelines on Effect on Trade [2004] OJ C101/81, paras 64–65.
119. See Cases T–374/94 etc *European Night Services Ltd v Commission* [1998] ECR II–3141, [1998] 5 CMLR 718, para 136.

doubtful that agreements constituting hardcore object-based restrictions of competition, such as price fixing agreements, would benefit from the Article 101(3) exemption in practice. However, exemption is a theoretical possibility for any kind of agreement as 'in principle, no anti-competitive practice can exist which, whatever the extent of its effects on a given market, cannot be exempted, provided that all the conditions laid down in Article 101(3) of the Treaty are satisfied'.[120]

What kind of an agreement was involved in the *BIDS* case?

15. The decision of the Court of Justice in the *BIDS* case provides a useful illustration of some of the above points in practice.

16. The ten principal meat processors in Ireland formed the BIDS company with the aim of reducing capacity in the meat processing industry. A number of reports had identified significant overcapacity in the sector. BIDS drew up a standard contract for achieving the exit of processors, the 'goers', who would be paid compensation by the processors who remained in the market, the 'stayers'.

17. The standard terms and one specific agreement were notified to the Irish Competition Authority, which took the view that they were anti-competitive and applied to the High Court for an order restraining the implementation of the agreements. The High Court dismissed the application but on appeal, the Supreme Court made a reference to the Court of Justice, seeking clarification on the compatibility of the arrangements with Article 101.

18. The Court of Justice reiterated that in assessing an agreement under Article 101, there is 'no need to take account of its actual effects once it appears that its object is to prevent, restrict or distort competition within the common market'.[121]

19. BIDS argued that the aim of the arrangements was not in fact anti-competitive but rather its purpose was to rationalise the beef industry to make it *more* competitive by reducing, but not eliminating, production overcapacity. This argument was rejected, the Court holding that even if it could be established that the parties acted without any subjective intention of restricting competition, this was irrelevant to the question whether the agreement had an anti-competitive object.[122]

20. BIDS also argued that the concept of infringement by object, rather than effect, should be interpreted narrowly and limited to horizontal price fixing agreements or agreements to limit output or share markets. BIDS argued that the arrangements here could not be equated to agreements to 'limit production' within the meaning of Article 101(1)(b), which referred to limitation of total market output, rather than a limitation of output of certain operators who voluntarily withdrew from the

---

120. Case T–17/93 *Matra Hachette SA v Commission* [1996] II-ECR 595, para 85.

121. Case C–209/07 *Competition Authority v BIDS* [2008] ECR I–8637, [2009] 4 CMLR 310, para 16.

122. See Case C–209/07 *Competition Authority v BIDS* [2008] ECR I–8637, [2009] 4 CMLR 310, para 21.

market. The Court rejected these points, noting that the list of agreements in Article 101(1) was not exhaustive. The aim of the BIDS arrangements was to enable a number of undertakings to adopt a common policy with the object of encouraging some of them to leave the market, thereby reducing overcapacity, which affected the profitability of the processors by preventing them from achieving economies of scale. The Court held:

> That type of arrangement *conflicts patently* with the concept inherent in the EC Treaty provisions relating to competition, according to which each economic operator *must determine independently* the policy which it intends to adopt on the common market. Article [101(1)] is intended to prohibit *any* form of coordination which deliberately substitutes practical cooperation between undertakings for the risks of competition.[123]

21.   The Court pointed out that the matters relied on by BIDS could only be taken into account, if at all, in connection with an assessment under Article 101(3). That matter has subsequently been left to the Irish High Court to decide.[124]

22.   The decision in the BIDS case reiterates that once it is shown that an agreement has an anti-competitive object, it will fall foul of the Article 101(1) prohibition, whatever the surrounding circumstances or claimed pro-competitive motivations for the agreement. Such pro-competitive elements can only be taken into account when applying Article 101(3). However, it should be remembered that the relevant legal and economic context of the arrangement should be considered in the initial assessment of whether there is an anti-competitive object.

How does the EU approach of designating some agreements as having an anti-competitive object compare with that in the US?

23.   In applying section 1 of the Sherman Act, the US courts draw a distinction between agreements that are *per se* illegal and those that must be examined more closely under the so-called rule of reason. Examples of *per se* illegality include price fixing, bid rigging and market sharing. Resale price maintenance used to be *per se* illegal until the Supreme Court ruled in 2007 that it should be assessed under the rule of reason.[125] Where an agreement is unlawful *per se*, it is unnecessary to consider its effects in the market as it is automatically illegal.

24.   In US federal antitrust law, the rule of reason is applied to arrangements that are not clearly illegal. The rule involves the application of a balancing act, weighing up pro and anti-competitive effects. If the anti-competitive effects outweigh the pro-competitive effects, the arrangement violates the antitrust laws and *vice versa*.

---

123. Case C–209/07 *Competition Authority v BIDS* [2008] ECR I–8637, [2009] 4 CMLR 310, para 34 (emphasis added).
124. The Court of Justice judgment was considered by the Supreme Court, which referred the case back to the High Court to consider the application of Article 101(3). See *Competition Authority v Beef Industry Developments Society Limited* [2009] IESC 72. At the time of writing, the case was pending in the High Court.
125. *Leegin Creative Leather Products, Inc. v PSKS, Inc.* 551 US 877 (2007), overruling *Dr. Miles Medical Co. v John D. Park & Sons Co.* 220 US 373 (1911).

25.   Although the European courts have eschewed the adoption of the US terminology, the way that Article 101 is applied in practice is similar to the US *per se*/rule of reason dichotomy. However, an important difference is that agreements found to have an anti-competitive object under Article 101(1) can be exempted under Article 101(3) (even if this is not a realistic possibility for some agreements such as price fixing and market sharing) whereas, in the US, agreements that are *per se* illegal cannot be exempted.[126]

Key Sources

Case C–209/07 *Competition Authority v Beef Industry Development Society Ltd.* ('BIDS') [2009] 4 CMLR 310.

Cases C–501/06P etc, *GlaxoSmithKline Services Unlimited v Commission* [2009] ECR I–9291, [2010] 4 CMLR 50.

---

126.   See further, Lasok, 'Recent Developments in the Rule of Reason in EC Antitrust Law' [2008] *Competition Law Journal* 226.

18. WHAT FACTORS ARE IMPORTANT IN ASSESSING WHETHER AN AGREEMENT HAS AN ANTI-COMPETITIVE EFFECT?

Summary

- There is no presumption that a particular agreement has an anti-competitive effect. It is up to the Commission or other party seeking to enforce Article 101 to show that there is such an effect.

- The competitive effects of an agreement should be considered in the market context in which it applies.

- A range of factors may be relevant in determining whether the agreement has an anti-competitive effect. Some of the most important include:

  - Whether the agreement is horizontal or vertical;

  - The market shares of the parties and competitors;

  - Buyer power;

  - Barriers to entry and expansion.

- But the particular circumstances and market dynamics need to be examined closely.

1. If an agreement or concerted practice does not have as its object the restriction of competition, then its effect must be examined to determine if it gives rise to an appreciable 'prevention, restriction or distortion' of effective competition.[127]

2. There is no presumption that a particular agreement has an anti-competitive effect. It is up to the Commission or other regulator or party seeking to show an infringement of Article 101 to establish that the agreement or practice has an anti-competitive effect.[128] Both the actual and potential effect of the agreement must be

---

127. See, e.g., Case C–8/08 *T-Mobile Netherlands BV* [2009] ECR I–4529, [2009] 5 CMLR 1701, para 28. The concept of 'effective competition' (or 'workable competition') is used in applying Articles 101 and 102. For examples of the use of the term 'effective competition', see Cases C–501/06P etc, *GlaxoSmithKline Services Unlimited v Commission* [2009] ECR I–9291, [2010] 4 CMLR 50, para 63; Case T–321/05 *AstraZeneca AB v Commission,* judgment of 1 July 2010, para 239; Case C–26/76 *Metro SB-Großmärkte GmbH & Co. KG v Commission ('Metro I')* [1977] ECR 1875, [1978] 2 CMLR 1, paras 20–21 (describing workable competition as 'the degree of competition necessary to ensure the observance of the basic requirements and the attainment of the objectives of the Treaty, in particular the creation of a single market achieving conditions similar to those of a domestic market. In accordance with this requirement the nature and intensiveness of competition may vary to an extent dictated by the products or services in question and the economic structure of the relevant market sectors'.); Commission Guidelines on Article 101(3) [2004] OJ C 101/97, para 47. For a detailed discussion of the concept of effective competition, see Bishop and Walker, *The Economics of EC Competition Law* (3rd edn, 2010) Ch 2.

128. Regulation 1/2003, fifth recital and Article 2.

considered.[129] It is not necessary that competition be restricted between the parties to the anti-competitive agreement or conduct. An agreement can restrict competition within the meaning of Article 101(1) even if the restriction of competition is between a party to the agreement and a third party.[130]

3.   In assessing the competitive effect, the agreement should be considered in its wider context by examining 'in particular the economic context in which the undertakings operate, the product or services covered by the agreement and the actual structure of the market concerned'.[131]

4.   A distinction should be made between horizontal agreements (between undertakings at the same level in the supply chain, *i.e.* competitors) and vertical agreements (between undertakings at different levels in the supply chain, e.g. a manufacturer and a distributor). Generally speaking, horizontal agreements are much more likely to produce anti-competitive effects than vertical agreements, which are often pro-competitive even when both firms have market power and the agreement imposes restrictions on one or both.

5.   In horizontal relationships where the firms are producing competing substitute products, each firm would prefer the other to price higher and thereby soften price competition. In vertical relationships, in which the parties produce complementary products or play complementary roles (e.g. a supplier and distributor), each firm prefers the other to lower its price as demand rises as the price of complementary products falls. This has the effect of lowering prices overall and so the incentives of the parties to a vertical agreement can generally be viewed as pro-competitive.[132] Restrictions in vertical agreements may play an important role in achieving positive competitive effects. To take one example, if a manufacturer wishes to enter a new territory, it may have to grant a local distributor territorial protection if it is to be incentivised to make the initial investment required to establish a sales platform for the product in that territory.[133] Without the restriction, the product may not enter the market at all.

6.   In examining the competitive effects of an agreement or practice, it is necessary to consider the degree of competition that would have existed in the absence of the agreement or practice.[134] This is the 'counterfactual' analysis. So, one can ask whether the agreement restricts actual or potential competition that would have

129. See, e.g., Case C–238/05 *Asnef-Equifax v Ausbanc* [2006] ECR I–11125, [2007] 4 CMLR 224, para 50.

130. See Cases 56 & 58/64 *Consten SaRL and Grundig Verkaufs GmbH v Commission* [1966] ECR 299, 339.

131. Cases T–374/94 etc *European Night Services Ltd v Commission* [1998] ECR II–3141, [1998] 5 CMLR 718, para 136. See also Case 56/65 *Société Technique Minière v Maschinenbau Ulm GmbH* [1966] ECR 235, 249–250, [1966] CMLR 357, 375–376.

132. See Bishop and Walker, *The Economics of EC Competition Law* (3rd edn, 2010) para 5.037; European Commission Guidelines on Vertical Restraints [2010] OJ C130/1, para 98.

133. See Commission Guidelines on Vertical Restraints [2010] OJ C130/1, para 106 *et seq.*

134. Case 56/65 *Société Technique Minière v Maschinenbau Ulm GmbH* [1966] ECR 235, 250, [1966] CMLR 357, 375.

existed without the agreement or, in the case of effects on intra-brand competition (*i.e.* competition between distributors of the same brand), in the absence of the particular contractual restraint.[135]

7. Various factors might be relevant to the assessment of competitive effects of a particular agreement or practice, including:

- The market shares of the parties and those of competitors.

- Countervailing buyer power.

- Whether the agreement is part of a network of similar agreements.

- Barriers to entry.

- Barriers to expansion.

- Existence of potential competitors.

- Customer loyalty to incumbent operators.

- The pro-competitive effects of the agreement.

- Realistic commercial alternatives for the parties in the absence of the agreement.

- The nature of the product.

- Maturity of the market.

8. What factors are relevant and what weight should be attributed to them will depend on the particular circumstances. Emphasis should be placed on the economic effects of the agreement. This effects-based approach to Article 101(1) is evident in the Commission's block exemption regulations and various guidelines on the application of Article 101.[136]

9. It may be helpful to consider an illustration of the assessment of an agreement's effect on competition in an economic context. A good example is the decision of the Court of Justice in *Delimitis*, which concerned a vertical agreement.[137]

10. The agreement at issue constituted a beer tie, pursuant to which Mr. Delimitis, a publican, agreed to purchase his beer exclusively from the Henninger brewery. The compatibility of the agreement with Article 101 was raised in German proceedings between Delimitis and the brewery over amounts claimed as being owed by the publican following termination of the parties' contract. The German court made an Article 267 reference to the Court of Justice raising a number of questions about the compatibility of the beer supply agreement with Article 101.

11. The Court of Justice first pointed out that the exclusive purchasing obligation had advantages both for the supplier (a guaranteed outlet, the ability to plan sales over

---

135. See Commission Article 101(3) Guidelines, paras 17–18.
136. See also Bellamy & Child (6th edn, 2008) para 2.062 *et seq.*
137. Case C–234/89 *Delimitis v Henninger Bräu AG* [1991] ECR I–935, [1992] 5 CMLR 210. See also the similar earlier case, Case 23/67 *Brasserie de Haecht v Consorts Wilkin-Janssen* [1967] ECR 407, [1968] CMLR 26.

a period and organise production and distribution effectively) and the tied publican (access to supplies under favourable conditions, guaranteed supply, the supplier's assistance in guaranteeing product quality and customer service) and concluded that the agreement did not have the object of restricting competition. Therefore, its effect had to be assessed in the context in which it occurred.

12. The court was particularly concerned with the issue of barriers to entry and expansion. It considered whether the market for the sale of beer in licensed premises in Germany was one that was difficult for new suppliers to enter or for existing suppliers to increase their market share. The existence of a network of beer tie agreements was relevant to this issue but it was only one factor. Consideration also had to be given to other matters, such as the legal rules and agreements on the acquisition of companies and establishment of outlets and the minimum number of outlets necessary for the economic operation of a distribution system; the presence of independent wholesalers not tied to beer producers who are active on the market (as a new entrant could use such a wholesaler's sales networks to distribute beer); and the competitive conditions on the relevant market, considering the number and size of competitors, the level of market concentration and the extent of customer loyalty to existing brands 'for it is generally more difficult to penetrate a saturated market in which customers are loyal to a small number of large producers than a market in full expansion in which a large number of small producers are operating without any strong brand names'.[138]

13. If that analysis concluded that there were entry barriers, then it was necessary to consider the extent to which the agreement entered into by the brewery in question contributed to that effect. If the effect were insignificant, then the brewery's agreements did not fall within Article 101(1). That would depend on several factors, including the market position of the contracting parties, the number of outlets tied to the brewery in relation to the total number of public houses in the market and the duration of the agreement as compared to the average duration of other beer supply contracts.

14. The two-stage analysis in *Delimitis*, (i) whether there are significant barriers to entry/expansion and (ii) whether the agreement contributes to those barriers, is applicable to exclusive purchasing agreements in general[139] although it is not necessarily applicable to other types of agreements. The wider relevance of the case is that it illustrates how a full analysis of the effects of an agreement in its economic and legal context must be made to determine if Article 101(1) applies. That analysis may involve an examination of the commercial options realistically open to the parties in the absence of the agreement, which may bring the pro-competitive effects of the agreement into the analysis.[140]

---

138. Case C–234/89 *Delimitis v Henninger Bräu AG* [1991] ECR I–935, [1992] 5 CMLR 210, para 22.
139. See Bellamy & Child (6th edn, 2008) para 2.083.
140. See, in particular, *Cases* T–374/94 etc *European Night Services Ltd v Commission* [1998] ECR II–3141, [1998] 5 CMLR 718.

What are the implications if the effects of an agreement change over time?

15. As competitive conditions may change over time, so too may the effect of an agreement for purposes of Article 101. For example, a R&D agreement between two competitors might not raise issues under Article 101 (and indeed benefit from a block exemption)[141] when entered into at a time when their combined market share was low but may be problematic two years later when they occupy over 50 per cent of the market. Conversely, it has been held by the English Court of Appeal that an agreement which breaches Article 101 and is therefore unenforceable would become enforceable once it ceased to have the effects prohibited by Article 101.[142]

16. Given that the application of Article 101 is down to an undertaking's self-assessment in the first instance, this places the burden on an undertaking to monitor agreements the effects of which change over time.

Key Sources

European Commission Guidelines on Vertical Restraints [2010] OJ C130/1.

Commission's Guidelines on the application of Article 81(3) of the Treaty [2004] OJ C 101/97.

Case C–234/89 *Delimitis v Henninger Bräu AG* [1991] ECR I–935, [1992] 5 CMLR 210.

Cases T–374/94 etc *European Night Services Ltd v Commission* [1998] ECR II–3141, [1998] 5 CMLR 718.

---

141. Commission Regulation No 2659/00 on the application of Article 81(3) to categories of research and development agreements [2000] OJ L304/7.
142. *Passmore v Morland plc* [1999] ICR 913, [1999] 1 CMLR 1129, para 27 ('… an agreement which is within the prohibition in Article [101(1)] at the time when it is entered into—because, in the circumstances prevailing in the relevant market at that time, it does have the effect of preventing, restricting or distorting competition—may, subsequently and as the result of a change in those circumstances, fall outside the prohibition contained in that Article—because, in the changed circumstances, it no longer has that effect') (Chadwick LJ).

19. **WHEN CAN IT BE ASSUMED THAT THE EFFECT ON COMPETITION IS NOT 'APPRECIABLE'?**

Summary

- An agreement falls outside Article 101 if it is not capable of having an appreciable effect on competition.

- A *de minimis* effect can be presumed where the parties' combined share of the relevant market does not exceed 10 per cent in the case of actual or potential competitors.

- Where the parties are not actual or potential competitors, a *de minimis* effect can be presumed where each party has a market share that does not exceed 15 per cent.

- This *de minimis* exception does not apply to agreements containing hardcore restrictions but such agreements may fall outside Article 101(1) if they do not have an appreciable effect on competition.

- The *de minimis* exception should be applied with caution as, depending on the particular market features, shares below the *de minimis* thresholds could still result in an appreciable effect.

1. In addition to requiring an appreciable effect on trade between Member States,[143] the effect on competition must be 'appreciable' for the Article 101(1) prohibition to apply. This principle was established in the *Völk* case. The rationale for this *de minimis* rule is that an agreement is not capable of hindering the attainment of a single market and so falls outside Article 101(1) 'when it has only an insignificant effect on the markets, taking into account the weak position which the persons concerned have on the market of the product in question'.[144] Even agreements containing hardcore restrictions, for example, an exclusive dealing agreement with absolute territorial protection, may fall outside Article 101(1) where the parties have a weak market position. This was the case in *Völk*, where a restrictive agreement between a German washing machine manufacturer and its exclusive distributor in Belgium and Luxembourg did not have an appreciable effect on competition where the manufacturer produced less than 0.5 per cent of washing machines in Germany.

2. The Commission has issued guidelines in a *De Minimis* Notice[145] setting out its view that agreements, which *do* affect trade between Member States, do not appreciably restrict competition if certain conditions are met. The Notice applies

---

143. See Question 6.
144. Case 5/69 *Völk v Vervaecke* [1969] ECR 295, [1969] CMLR 273, para 5/7.
145. Commission Notice on agreements of minor importance which do not appreciably restrict competition under Article 81(1) of the Treaty establishing the European Community (*de minimis*) ('Commission *De Minimis* Notice') [2001] OJ C368/13.

different market share thresholds, depending on whether the parties are competitors (actual or potential) or non-competitors:

- Agreements between actual or potential competitors are presumed *de minimis* if the combined market share of the parties on a relevant market does not exceed 10 per cent.

- Agreements between parties that are not actual or potential competitors are presumed *de minimis* if the market share held by each of the parties on a relevant market does not exceed 15 per cent.[146]

3. If there is doubt as to whether the parties are competitors or non-competitors, the 10 per cent threshold applies.[147]

4. A type of marginal relief is provided in respect of agreements where the market share thresholds are not exceeded by more than 2 percentage points during two successive calendar years.[148]

5. Where competition is restricted by the cumulative effect of agreements for the sale of goods or services entered into by different suppliers or distributors, the above thresholds are reduced to 5 per cent for both competitors and non-competitors (but a cumulative foreclosure effect is considered unlikely if less than 30 per cent of the relevant market is covered by the parallel network of agreements).[149]

6. The Commission will not fine undertakings which assume in good faith that the *De Minimis* Notice applies to an agreement. Although not binding, the Notice is intended to give guidance to the courts and competition authorities of the Member States on the application of Article 101.[150]

7. The benefit of the *De Minimis* Notice does not apply to agreements containing hardcore restrictions.[151] However, as noted in para 19.1 above, such agreements could still fall outside the scope of Article 101(1) if they do not have an appreciable effect on competition.[152] In comparison, the Commission considers that even agreements containing hardcore restrictions can benefit from its negative rebuttable presumption that there is no appreciable effect on trade between Member States where the parties' combined market share does not exceed 5 per cent and combined turnover is not more than €40 million in the products

---

146. Commission *De Minimis* Notice, para 7(b).
147. Commission *De Minimis* Notice, para 7(a).
148. Commission *De Minimis* Notice, para 9.
149. Commission *De Minimis* Notice, para 8. See also Case C–234/89 *Delimitis v Henninger Bräu AG* [1991] ECR I–935, [1992] 5 CMLR 210.
150. Commission *De Minimis* Notice, para 4.
151. Commission *De Minimis* Notice, para 11.
152. In addition to Case 5/69 *Völk v Vervaecke* [1969] ECR 295, [1969] CMLR 273, see Commission Guidelines on Vertical Restraints [2010] OJ C130/1, para 10; Case 1/71 *Cadillon v Höss* [1971] ECR 351, [1971] CMLR 420, para 9; Bellamy & Child (6th edn, 2008) para 2.129.

concerned (or, in vertical agreements, the supplier's turnover is not more than €40 million).[153]

8.   The *de minimis* principle must be applied with some degree of caution. There may be situations where undertakings with market shares below those in the *De Minimis* Notice can be found to have an appreciable effect on competition. For example, in a fragmented market, a party's share of less than 5 per cent may be sufficiently significant relative to competitors to enable it to have an appreciable effect on competition.[154]

Key Sources

Commission Notice on agreements of minor importance which do not appreciably restrict competition under Article 81(1) of the Treaty establishing the European Community (*de minimis*) [2001] OJ C368/13.

Case 5/69 *Völk v Vervaecke* [1969] ECR 295, [1969] CMLR 273.

Cases 100–103/80 *SA Musique Diffusion française v Commission* [1983] ECR 1825, [1983] 3 CMLR 221.

---

153. Commission Guidelines on Effect on Trade [2004] OJ C101/81, paras 50–52.
154. See, e.g., Cases 100–103/80 *SA Musique Diffusion française v Commission* [1983] ECR 1825, [1983] 3 CMLR 221 (competitors with shares of less than 4 per cent each were held to have an appreciable effect on interstate trade). The analysis would also be applicable to the issue of appreciable effect on competition. For a discussion about situations where there may be doubt as to the application of the *de minimis* rule, see Vaughan, Lee, Kennelly and Riches, *EU Competition Law: General Principles* (2006) para 186.

20. CAN A CLAUSE THAT BREACHES ARTICLE 101 BE SEVERED FROM THE REMAINDER OF THE AGREEMENT?

Summary

- The provisions of an agreement that violate Article 101 are void.

- The remainder of the agreement may survive, depending on the applicable severance rules. These will depend on the law governing the agreement.

1. Article 101(2) provides that any agreements or decisions prohibited by Article 101 'shall be automatically void'. The Court of Justice has interpreted this to mean that only the individual provisions of an agreement that violate Article 101 are void.[155] The remainder of the agreement may be enforceable. This depends on the law governing the agreement and how it approaches the question of severability.

2. In Ireland, the Competition Act 2002 specifically provides for severance in section 4. However the courts will only sever the offending provision of a contract if the remainder can survive and it will not rewrite the contract.[156] Section 4(6) of the 2002 Act provides as follows:

   > The prohibition in subsection (1) shall not prevent the court, in exercising any jurisdiction conferred on it by this Act concerning an agreement, decision or concerted practice which contravenes that prohibition and which creates or, but for this Act, would have created legal relations between the parties thereto, from applying, where appropriate, any relevant rules of law as to the severance of those terms of that agreement, decision or concerted practice which contravene that prohibition from those which do not.[157]

3. English law permits the illegal provision of the contract to be severed with the remainder continuing in force. Whether the agreement survives will depend on the effect of severing the particular provisions:

   > [In] applying Article [101] to an English contract, one may well have to consider whether, after the excisions required by the Article of the Treaty have been made from the contract, the contract could be said to fail for lack of consideration or on any other

---

155. See Case 56/65 *Société Technique Minière v Maschinenbau Ulm GmbH* [1966] ECR 235, 250 [1966] CMLR 357, 376; confirmed by the Court of Justice in Case 319/82 *Société de Vente de Ciments et Bétons de l'Est SA v Kerpen & Kerpen GmbH* [1983] ECR 4173, [1985] 1 CMLR 511, para 11.

156. See McDermott, *Contract Law* (2001) paras 16.96–16.108. See also, generally, Clark, *Contract Law in Ireland* (6th edn, 2008) 476–480.

157. Competition Act 2002, s 4(6).

ground, or whether the contract would be so changed in its character as not to be the sort of contract the parties intended to enter into at all.[158]

4.   In *Byrne*, one of the cases in the *Crehan* litigation involving a beer tie with a minimum purchase obligation, the Court of Appeal considered the doctrine of severance in the competition law context in more detail. It reviewed the approach to severance in *Chemidus* and other cases, which formulated the question in ways including (i) is that which is unenforceable part of the main purpose and substance?; (ii) does the deletion alter entirely the scope and intention of the agreement?; or (iii) does the deletion leave the rest of the deed a reasonable arrangement between the parties?[159]

5.   The issue in *Byrne* was whether the invalidity of the minimum purchase requirement, which breached Article 101, made the remainder of the agreement, including an option to extend the lease on the pub, invalid. In deciding that the offending clause could not be severed, the Court of Appeal stated:

> Each agreement must be viewed according to its own nature and terms ... In our view, the nature and terms of the present option leads to a wider view of the substance of the conditions imposed, and a condition of due performance of the tie and minimum purchasing requirement must be viewed as at least one integral aspect of the substance of the consideration, without which it would amount as a whole to something quite different...

> ... The issue is not how significant the conditions are on the facts of any particular case, but whether as a matter of interpretation and law the conditions go to the substance of the consideration or to substantially the whole or main consideration ....

> ... if ... the tie and minimum purchasing requirement are invalid under Article [101](1) and (2), it follows that the option ceases also to have any validity.[160]

6.   More recently, in the context of employment law, the Court of Appeal approved the following three-part severance test, which partly draws on *Chemidus* and which may well be applicable in the competition law context and more generally going forward:

> [A] contract which contains an unenforceable provision nevertheless remains effective after the removal or severance of that provision if the following conditions are satisfied:

> 1 The unenforceable provision is capable of being removed without the necessity of adding to or modifying the wording of what remains.

---

158. *Chemidus Wavin Limited v Societe pour la Transformation et l'Exploitation des Resines Industrielles SA* [1978] 3 CMLR 514, 520, [1977] FSR 181, 187 (Buckley LJ).

159. *Byrne v Inntrepreneur Beer Supply Co Ltd* [1999] ECC 455, [1999] UKCLR 110, para 158 (discussing *Amoco Australia Pty Ltd v Rocca Bros Motor Engineering Co. Pty Ltd* [1975] AC 561).

160. *Byrne v Inntrepreneur Beer Supply Co Ltd* [1999] ECC 455, [1999] UKCLR 110, paras 166–168.

2 The remaining terms continue to be supported by adequate consideration.

3 The removal of the unenforceable provision does not so change the character of the contract that it becomes 'not the sort of contract that the parties entered into at all'.[161]

Key Sources

Chemidus Wavin Limited v Societe pour la Transformation et l'Exploitation des Resines Industrielles SA [1978] 3 CMLR 514, [1977] FSR 181.

---

161. *Sadler v Imperial Life Assurance Co of Canada Ltd* [1988] IRLR 388, 391–392 (Crawford QC), approved by the Court of Appeal in *Beckett Investment Management Group Ltd v Hall* [2007] EWCA Civ 613, [2007] ICR 1539, para 40. A severance clause in the agreement will not necessarily operate to save the remainder of the agreement where deletion of the void clause entirely alters the scope and intetion of the agreement (*Richard Cound Ltd v BMW (GB) Ltd* [1997] EuLR 277). For further discussion of severance in English law, see Brealey and Green eds, *Competition Litigation: UK Practice and Procedure* (2010) paras 18.02–18.32. On the application of the doctrine of severability in the Article 102 context, see *English Welsh & Scottish Railway Ltd v E. ON UK plc* [2007] EWHC 599 (Comm), [2007] UKCLR 1653, para 29 (exclusionary terms in a coal carriage agreement could not be severed as the agreement would have a fundamentally different nature without those terms).

21. **WHAT CONDITIONS MUST BE SATISFIED FOR THE ARTICLE 101(3) EXEMPTION TO APPLY?**

Summary

- Four conditions must be fulfilled to invoke Article 101(3):

  (i)   Efficiency gains;

  (ii)   Fair share of benefits to consumers;

  (iii) Indispensability of restrictions;

  (iv)   No elimination of competition.

- Alternatively, it is enough to show that an agreement comes within the terms of a block exemption to avail of the Article 101(3) exemption.

1. Any agreement, decision or concerted practice caught by Article 101(1) can be exempted from the Article 101 prohibition if it fulfils the four conditions in Article 101(3). The General Court has emphasised that, in principle, there are no anti-competitive restrictions that are not capable of exemption provided that the conditions in Article 101(3) are satisfied.[162] So even an agreement containing hardcore restrictions such as price fixing and market sharing could benefit from the Article 101(3) exemption, even if it is highly doubtful that such an agreement would be exempted in practice. This position is in contrast to US federal antitrust law, where certain types of agreements are deemed to be *per se* illegal without the possibility of exemption.

2. Article 101(3) provides that the provisions of Article 101(1):

    may, however, be declared inapplicable in the case of:

    — any agreement or category of agreements between undertakings,

    — any decision or category of decisions by associations of undertakings,

    — any concerted practice or category of concerted practices,

    which contributes to improving the production or distribution of goods or to promoting technical or economic progress, while allowing consumers a fair share of the resulting benefit, and which does not:

    (a)   impose on the undertakings concerned restrictions which are not indispensable to the attainment of these objectives;

    (b)   afford such undertakings the possibility of eliminating competition in respect of a substantial part of the products in question.

3. So, the four cumulative conditions that must be met to satisfy Article 101(3) are:

    - **Efficiency gains.** The agreement must contribute to improving the production or distribution of goods or contribute to promoting technical or economic progress.

---

162. See Case T–17/93 *Matra Hachette SA v Commission* [1994] ECR-II 595, para 85.

- **Fair share for consumers.** Consumers must receive a fair share of the resulting benefits.

- **Indispensability of restrictions.** The restrictions must be indispensable to the achievement of these objectives.

- **No elimination of competition.** The agreement must not afford the parties the possibility of eliminating competition in respect of a substantial part of the products in question.

4.   Article 101(3) recognises that an agreement with anti-competitive effects may also have pro-competitive effects. For example, such an agreement may result in efficiency gains, creating additional value by lowering the cost of producing a product, improving the quality of the product or creating a new product. Competition law performs a balancing act, asking whether the anti-competitive effects of such an agreement are outweighed by its pro-competitive effect.

5.   Since the coming into effect of Regulation 1/2003 on 1 May 2004, it is no longer possible to apply to the Commission for an exemption under Article 101(3).[163] Undertakings must themselves consider whether agreements and conduct to which they are party violate Article 101(1) and whether the exemption in Article 101(3) is applicable. The courts and designated competition authorities of the Member States can apply Article 101(3).[164] Previously, only the Commission had this jurisdiction.

6.   The Commission will still consider whether Article 101(3) applies when it takes decisions under Article 101. The Commission published guidelines in 2004, which set out its interpretation of the conditions for exemption in Article 101(3).[165]

7.   Article 101(3) applies to certain categories of agreement and concerted practice by way of block exemption Regulations. Where a block exemption Regulation applies, it is not necessary to show that the four Article 101(3) conditions are satisfied; it is sufficient to show that the agreement in question comes within the terms of the block exemption. However, the Commission and the designated competition authorities of the Member States have the power to withdraw the benefit of a block exemption where the Article 101(3) conditions are not

---

163. Article 53(3) of the EEA Agreement is identical to Article 101(3) and is also now directly applicable in national courts, with the possibility of individual exemption by the Commission or the EFTA Surveillance Authority removed (see Decision of the EEA Joint Committee No 130/2004, [2005] OJ L64/57, which amended parts of the EEA Agreement).
164. In Ireland, only the courts have power to apply Article 101, including Article 101(3) (see SI No. 525 of 2007 European Communities (Implementation of the Rules on Competition Laid Down in Articles 81 and 82 of the Treaty) (Amendment) Regulations 2007, in which no authority is designated as having power to apply Article 5 of Regulation 1/2003, meaning that only the courts have this power). In the UK, the OFT and the various sectoral regulators have the power to enforce Article 101(3) (see SI 2004 No. 1261 Competition Act 1998 and Other Enactments (Amendment) Regulations 2004).
165. Commission Guidelines on Article 101(3) [2004] OJ C101/97.

fulfilled.[166] National courts do not have this power unless specifically designated as competition authorities for the purpose.[167] Where a block exemption applies to an agreement, the bock exemption itself will provide the Commission's view of when Article 101(3) applies.

How are the four conditions of Article 101(3) applied in practice?

8.   The first step is to apply Article 101(1) as Article 101(3) is only relevant if the agreement would otherwise breach Article 101(1). The four conditions in Article 101(3) are cumulative, *i.e.*, each must be satisfied for Article 101(3) to apply.[168] If it is obvious that one of the conditions is not fulfilled, then no further analysis is required – the agreement or conduct will not benefit from the Article 101(3) defence. Where the four conditions are met, the exception applies and cannot be made dependent on any other conditions.

9.   The burden of proving that Article 101(3) applies is on the undertaking seeking to avail itself of the exemption.[169]

10. In making a self-assessment of the application of Article 101(3), market structure should be examined and a calculation and assessment of efficiencies made. This may require sophisticated economic analysis, involving, for example, an examination of cost structures in the market. This may be required, in particular, to work out whether consumers will receive a fair share of the efficiencies generated (condition 2).

How does Condition 1 – Efficiency Gains – apply?

11. To be capable of exemption under Article 101(3), an agreement must contribute to improving the production or distribution of goods or to promoting technical or economic progress. The evidence and factual arguments must show that the agreement contributes 'appreciable objective advantages of such a kind as to compensate for the resulting disadvantages for competition'.[170] Efficiencies are not viewed from the perspective of the parties to the agreement and cost savings that benefit only those parties do not count. There must be a benefit to the Union

---

166. Regulation 1/2003, Article 29(2). In Ireland, the Competition Authority and, in respect of functions assigned to it, ComReg, have this power (SI No 195 of 2004 European Communities (Implementation of the Rules on Competition laid down in Articles 81 and 82 of the Treaty) Regulations 2004, as amended by SI 525 of 2007, r 4). In the UK, the OFT and sectoral regulators have these powers (see SI 2004 No. 1261 Competition Act 1998 and Other Enactments (Amendment) Regulations 2004).

167. Neither the Irish nor the UK courts have been designated as competition authorities for purposes of withdrawing the benefit of a block exemption.

168. See, e.g., Cases 43 &63/82 *VBVB v Commission* [1984] ECR 19, [1985] 1 CMLR 27, para 61; Cases T–528/93 etc *Metropole télévision SA v Commission* [1996] ECR II–649, [1996] 5 CMLR 386, para 93.

169. Regulation 1/2003, Article 2.

170. Cases C–501/06P etc, *GlaxoSmithKline Services Unlimited v Commission* [2009] ECR I–9291, [2010] 4 CMLR 50, para 92.

interest. Nevertheless, parties to the agreement are not precluded from making some profit from the provision in respect of which efficiencies are claimed.[171] The benefit to the Union interest need not necessarily be in the relevant market the subject of the agreement but may also arise in related markets.[172] Benefits must be sufficient to outweigh the restriction of competition.[173]

12. Efficiency claims must be sufficiently substantiated, with the parties required to provide details of the efficiencies' scope and show when they will occur and how they derive from the agreement.[174] It is necessary to show that the claimed efficiencies arise from the agreement.[175] According to the Commission, this causal connection must be direct.[176] It is not necessary that the efficiencies arise in the same Member State where the parties are established but it is uncertain whether the Article 101(3) exemption can be availed of when the only efficiencies from the agreement arise outside the EU.

13. In its Guidelines on Article 101(3), the Commission draws a distinction between (i) cost efficiencies and (ii) qualitative efficiencies, whereby value is created in the form of new or improved products, increased product variety etc. The same agreement may give rise to various types of efficiencies.

14. Examples of cost efficiencies include:

 •   Development of new production technologies and methods.

 •   Synergies (through combining existing assets, leading to reduced production costs).

 •   Economies of scale.

 •   Economies of scope.

 •   Better planning of production, stock optimisation.

15. Examples of qualitative efficiencies include:

 •   Higher quality products.

 •   Products with novel features.

 •   More rapid dissemination of technology.

---

171. See Cases C–501/06P etc, *GlaxoSmithKline Services Unlimited v Commission* [2009] ECR I–9291, [2010] 4 CMLR 50, paras 111–120. It was argued that profits resulting from the provision that restricted parallel imports were required for R&D investment in the pharmaceutical industry and it was held unnecessary for an appreciable objective advantage to arise that all profit generated by the restriction be invested in R&D.
172. See Case T–86/95 *Compagnie générale maritime v Commission* [2002] ECR II–1011, [2002] 4 CMLR 1115, para 130.
173. See Case 45/85 *Verband der Sachversicherer eV v Commission* [1987] ECR 405, [1988] 4 CMLR 264, para 61.
174. See Commission Guidelines on Article 101(3) [2004] OJ C101/97, para 51.
175. See, e.g., Case T–29/92 *Vereniging van Samenwerkende Prijsregelende Organisaties in de Bouwnijverheid v Commission* [1995] ECR II–289, para 291.
176. See Commission Guidelines on Article 101(3) [2004] OJ C101/97, para 54.

- The introduction of new or improved products more quickly.

16. Qualitative efficiencies can be achieved through different types of agreements, including:

   - R&D agreements.

   - Licensing agreements.

   - Joint production agreements.

   - Distribution agreements.

How does Condition 2 – Fair share of benefit to consumers – apply?

17. This 'pass on' provision requires a showing that a fair share of the benefit that results from an agreement will go to consumers.

18. The term 'consumers' includes all consumers, direct or indirect, whether final end users or intermediate buyers of a product such as wholesalers. It will not be necessary to show that an end user will receive a fair share of the efficiencies generated by the agreement if an intermediate consumer receives the benefit. It is the effect on consumers as a whole in a given market that is relevant, not the effect on individual consumers. So, even if some consumers are disadvantaged by the agreement, if the overall effect on consumers is positive, the second condition may be fulfilled.[177]

19. According to the Commission, the net effect of the agreement must at least be neutral from the perspective of consumers affected by it in each relevant market. If consumers are worse off following the agreement, the second condition will not be satisfied.[178] It has been noted that the Commission appears to go beyond the requirements of Article 101(3) here, under which it is sufficient if the objective benefits of an agreement outweigh the restriction of competition and consumers receive a fair share of those benefits.[179] Also, the Commission's view that there should be at least a neutral effect in each relevant market does not appear to equate with the position of the Union courts that effects in different markets, including those not concerned by the agreement, can be taken into account.[180]

20. It is possible that an agreement that results in higher prices could still be viewed as passing on a sufficient benefit to consumers where, for example, it allows a new improved product to come to the market more quickly.[181]

---

177. See Case C–238/05 *Asnef-Equifax v Ausbanc* [2006] ECR I–11125, [2007] 1 CMLR 224, paras 68–72.

178. Commission Guidelines on Article 101(3) [2004] OJ C101/97, para 85.

179. See Bellamy & Child (6th edn, 2008) para 3.054.

180. See Case T–86/95 *Compagnie générale maritime v Commission* [2002] ECR II–1011, [2002] 4 CMLR 1115, para 130 ('… Article 85(3) of the Treaty envisage[s] exemption in favour of, amongst others, agreements which contribute to promoting technical or economic progress, without requiring a specific link with the relevant market'); Case T–213/00 *CMA CGM v Commission* [2003] ECR II–913, [2003] 5 CMLR 268, para 227.

181. Commission Guidelines on Article 101(3) [2004] OJ C101/97, para 89.

21.   As the Commission notes, the second condition involves a sliding scale: the greater the restriction of competition, the greater the efficiency pass-on to consumers must be. Where it is not obvious what the outcome is, *i.e.*, where there are significant anti-competitive effects and pro-competitive effects, a careful analysis of the second condition is required.[182]

22.   Cost efficiencies may in some circumstances lead to increased output and lower prices for affected consumers. Cost efficiencies may allow the undertakings to increase profits by expanding output and this may result in a benefit being passed on to consumers. In assessing whether consumers receive a fair share of cost efficiencies, the following factors should be taken into account:[183]

*   The characteristics and structure of the market.

*   The nature and magnitude of the efficiency gains.

*   The elasticity of demand.

*   The magnitude of the restriction of competition.

23.   Consumers are more likely to benefit from a reduction in variable costs as opposed to fixed costs because they are more likely to result in lower consumer prices and be achieved in the short term. This is because a firm will base pricing decisions according to variable cost, *i.e.* cost that varies depending on the amount of production, rather than its fixed costs, which remain stable regardless of production.

24.   Consumers can also receive a fair share of the benefit through new and improved products, which might compensate for price increases. However it may be difficult to work out whether a benefit is passed on as this involves a value judgment. It is necessary to consider whether the claimed efficiencies will create 'real value' for consumers that will compensate for anti-competitive effects.[184]

How does Condition 3 – Indispensability of restrictions – apply?

25.   The agreement must not impose restrictions that are not indispensable to the attainment of the efficiencies created by the agreement. According to the Commission's Article 101(3) Guidelines, this implies a two-fold test. First, the restrictive agreement must be reasonably necessary to achieve the efficiencies. There must be no other economically practicable and less restrictive means to achieve the claimed efficiencies. For example, in *Matra Hachette*, restrictions in a manufacturing joint venture agreement were found to be indispensible where

---

182. Commission Guidelines on Article 101(3) [2004] OJ C101/97, paras 90–92.
183. Commission Guidelines on Article 101(3) [2004] OJ C101/97, para 96.
184. Commission Guidelines on Article 101(3) [2004] OJ C101/97, paras 102–104.

penetration of the market by the parties on an individual basis could only be achieved at a loss.[185]

26. Second, the individual restrictions that flow from the agreement must be reasonably necessary for the attainment of the efficiencies. The nature and intensity of any restriction must be reasonably necessary to produce the claimed efficiencies. A restriction is indispensable if its absence would eliminate or significantly reduce the efficiencies or make it significantly less likely that they would materialize. For example, a non-compete agreement in an industry restructuring plan that prevents the re-entry of parties that exit the industry might be indispensable.[186] Hard core restrictions, such as price fixing and absolute territorial protection,[187] are unlikely to be considered indispensable.[188]

How does Condition 4 – No elimination of competition in a substantial part of the market – apply?

27. The agreement must not afford the undertakings in question the possibility of eliminating competition in respect of a substantial part of the products concerned. It is necessary to examine the degree to which competition will be reduced by the agreement, which requires an assessment of the degree of competition existing prior to the agreement. The more that competition is already reduced, the less of a restriction required for the restrictive agreement to be unable to avail of the Article 101(3) exemption. The analysis requires consideration of the various sources of competition in the relevant market (the geographic as well as the product market has to be considered), the market shares of the participants,[189] the level of competitive constraint imposed on the parties to the agreement and the impact of

---

185. Case T–17/93 *Matra Hachette SA v Commission* [1994] ECR II–595, para 138.

186. See *Competition Authority v Beef Industry Developments Society Limited* [2009] IESC 72, Kearns P stating: 'I am satisfied that the incorporation of restrictive covenants in an agreement designed to rationalise an industry by means of a reduction in capacity may be justified as indispensable if the reduction in capacity is a valid objective of the arrangements and if the means of reducing capacity are proportionate to the aims being sought. A non-compete clause is entirely appropriate to secure such arrangements and to prevent players who are paid to leave the industry from re-entering and acquiring capacity from non-licensed producers. The necessity of restrictive covenants to underpin a reduction in capacity has been acknowledged by the Commission itself in the *Dutch Bricks* case'. The case was remitted to the High Court to apply Article 101(3).

187. See Case 258/78 *Nungesser KG v Commission* [1982] ECR 2015, [1983] 1 CMLR 278, paras 76–78 (absolute territorial protection for seeds for maize production went beyond what was indispensable for improving production or distribution or promoting technical progress).

188. See Commission Guidelines on Article 101(3) [2004] OJ C101/97, paras 73–82.

189. See Cases 209/78 etc *Heintz van Landewyck SARL v Commission* [1980] ECR 3125, [1981] 3 CMLR 134, paras 187–189.

the agreement on that competitive constraint. Both actual and potential competition is relevant, which requires an analysis of entry barriers.[190]

Key Sources

Commission's Guidelines on the application of Article 81(3) of the Treaty [2004] OJ C 101/97.

Case C–238/05 *Asnef-Equifax v Ausbanc* [2006] ECR I–11125, [2007] 1 CMLR 224.

---

190. See Commission Guidelines on Article 101(3) [2004] OJ C101/97, paras 105–116.

22. To which agreements does Article 101(3) apply by way of block exemption?

Summary

- The Commission has power to adopt block exemptions that exempt from Article 101 certain types of agreements.

- Commission block exemptions cover the following areas and are summarised below:

  - Vertical agreements;

  - Specialisation (or joint production) agreements;

  - Research & Development agreements;

  - Technology transfer agreements;

  - Motor vehicle distribution agreements;

  - Rail, Road and Inland Waterway agreements;

  - Liner shipping companies (consortia);

  - Insurance.

- Rules in Ireland provide for the adoption of block exemptions in respect of Section 4 of the Competition Act 2002.

- Block exemptions can be adopted in the UK in respect of the Chapter I prohibition in the Competition Act 1998.

1. An alternative route for an agreement to be exempted from the application of Article 101(1) is to come under one of the block exemptions adopted by the Council and the Commission. The Commission is empowered to adopt block exemption Regulations pursuant to a number of EU Regulations.[191]

2. If an agreement satisfies all the conditions in a particular block exemption, then Article 101 does not apply to it. If an agreement does not fulfil all the conditions in the block exemption, this does not mean that it automatically violates Article 101. The Article 101 analysis would have to be carried out in the usual way and the agreement could also still benefit from Article 101(3).

3. Some block exemptions apply to particular industry sectors, while others are of more general application, applying to particular types of agreements in different industries. The Commission has published guidelines on the application of a number of the block exemptions.

---

191. These include Regulation No 19/65/EEC, Regulation (EEC) No 2821/71, Regulation (EEC) No 3976/87, Regulation (EEC) No 1534/91 and Regulation (EEC) No 479/92.

4.   The below table provides an overview of block exemptions currently in force.

Block exemption	Details
Vertical agreements Reg 330/10; expires 31/5/22[192]	Applies to agreements between two or more undertakings operating at different levels of the production and distribution chain and relates to conditions under which the parties may purchase, sell or resell certain goods.
	To avail of the exemption, the supplier's share must not exceed 30 per cent of the relevant market on which it sells the contract goods or services and the market share held by the buyer must not exceed 30 per cent of the relevant market on which it purchases the contract goods or services (Article 3(1)).
	The exemption does not apply if the vertical agreement contains certain hardcore restrictions (Article 4).
	The Commission has also adopted Guidelines on Vertical Restraints.[193]
Specialisation agreements Reg 2658/00; expires on 31/12/10[194]	At the time of writing, a new block exemption regulation for specialisation agreements had not yet been adopted. As Regulation 2658/2000 was due to expire on 31 December 2010, a new regulation was expected to be published before that date. Revised horizontal cooperation Guidelines were also expected to be published.[195] A draft block exemption for specialisation agreements was published for consultation in May 2010.[196] That draft maintained the position in Regulation 2658/2000 that the block exemption would apply if the combined market share of the parties to the specialisation agreement was not more than 20 per cent on any relevant market. The exemption is also subject to the agreement not containing certain hardcore restrictions.
	The 2010 draft also provided that the exemption covered three types of agreement relating to conditions under which production of products is specialised:
	Unilateral specialisation agreements – one party agrees to cease (or refrain from) producing a product and purchase it from a competitor, who agrees to supply the product.
	Reciprocal specialisation agreements – two or more parties agree, on a reciprocal basis, to cease (or refrain from) producing certain but different products and to purchase these products from the other parties, who agree to supply them.
	Join production agreements – two or more parties agree to produce certain products jointly.
R&D agreements Reg 2659/00; expires on 31/12/10[197]	At the time of writing, a new block exemption regulation for R&D agreements had not yet been adopted. As Regulation 2659/2000 was due to expire on 31 December 2010, a new Regulation was expected to be published before that date. A draft block exemption for R&D agreements was published for consultation in May 2010.[198]
	That draft maintains the position in Regulation 2659/2000 that when the parties are not competitors, the exemption applies for the duration of the R&D and continues for seven years from marketing of the products, where the results are jointly exploited.

R&D agreements Reg 2659/00; expires on 31/12/10[197] (contd)	Where the parties are competitors, the exemption lasts for the same periods only if at the time of entering the R&D, the parties' combined market share does not exceed 25 per cent. The exemption continues as long as the combined market share of the parties does not exceed 25 per cent of the relevant market for the contract products or contract processes.

The exemption is also subject to the agreement not containing certain hardcore restrictions.

Technology transfer agreements Reg 772/04; expires 30/4/14[199]	Exempts patent, know-how and software copyright licensing agreements where the licensor permits the licensee to exploit the licensed technology for the production of goods or services.

When the undertakings are competitors, their combined share must not exceed 20 per cent on the affected relevant technology and product market. When the parties are not competitors, the market share of each must not exceed 30 per cent on the affected relevant technology and product market (Article 3).

The market share of a party on the relevant technology market(s) is defined in terms of the presence of the licensed technology on the relevant product market(s). A licensor's market share on the relevant technology market shall be the combined market share on the relevant product market of the contract products produced by the licensor and its licensees.

The exemption is also subject to the agreement not containing certain hardcore restrictions. There is a different list depending on whether the undertakings are competitors or not (Article 4).

The Commission has published Guidelines on the application of the block exemption.[200]

Motor vehicle distribution Reg 461/10; expires 31/5/23[201]	Regulation 461/2010 provides an exemption for vertical agreements relating to the conditions under which the parties may purchase, sell or resell spare parts for motor vehicles or provide repair and maintenance services for motor vehicles, which fulfil the requirements for an exemption under the Vertical Agreements Block Exemption Regulation (Regulation 330/2010) and which do not contain certain hardcore restrictions relating to restrictions on the method of selling and the placing of trade marks or logos on components or spare parts (Article 5).

The Commission may by regulation declare that, where parallel networks of similar vertical restraints cover more than 50 per cent of a relevant market, Regulation 461/2010 shall not apply to vertical agreements containing specific restraints relating to that market.

Regulation 1400/2002[202] continues to apply to vertical agreements and concerted practices relating to the conditions under which the parties may purchase, sell or resell new motor vehicles until 31 May 2013. Regulation 461/2010 applies to such agreements with effect from 1 June 2013.

There are different market share thresholds in Regulation 1400/2002 (Article 3):

• 30 per cent (buyer's share) where there is an exclusive supply obligation.

Motor vehicle distribution Reg 461/10; expires 31/5/23[201] (contd)	• 40 per cent (supplier's share) for quantitative selective distribution systems for the sale of new motor vehicles. • Otherwise, 30 per cent (supplier's share). The Commission has adopted Supplementary Guidelines to be read together with Regulation 461/2010.[203]
Rail, Road & Inland Waterway Reg 169/09; indefinite duration[204]	Regulation 169/2009 sets out certain exceptions to the application of the competition rules. There is an exemption from Article 101(1) for certain types of technical agreements and for small and medium-sized undertakings in road and inland waterway (Article 3). There are size limits based on tonnage: the total carrying capacity of groupings cannot exceed 10,000 tonnes for road transport and 500,000 tonnes for inland waterway (with individual capacities not exceeding 1,000 tonnes for road and 50,000 for inland waterway).
Liner consortia Reg 906/09; expires 25/4/15[205]	Commission Regulation 906/2009 allows shipping lines to enter into extensive cooperation for the purpose of providing joint maritime cargo transport services ('consortia'), exempting such arrangements from the application of Article 101.[206] To qualify for exemption, the combined market share of the consortium members in the relevant market upon which the consortium operates shall not exceed 30 per cent calculated by reference to the total volume of goods carried in freight tonnes or 20-foot equivalent units (Article 5). Regulation 906/2009 was adopted pursuant to Council Regulation 246/2009.[207] The Commission has also adopted Guidelines setting out the application of the competition rules to the maritime transport sector.[208]
Insurance Reg 267/10; expires 31/3/17[209]	Regulation 267/2010 exempts from the application of Article 101 certain types of insurance agreements on: • Joint calculations and distribution of information necessary for (i) the calculation of the average cost of covering a specified risk in the past or (ii) construction of mortality tables, and tables showing the frequency of illness, accident and invalidity in connection with insurance involving an element of capitalization. • The joint carrying-out of studies on the probable impact of general circumstances external to the interested undertakings, either on the frequency or scale of future claims for a given risk or risk category or on the profitability of different types of investment, and the distribution of the results of such studies. There are various conditions for application of the exemption, e.g., that tables and studies do not identify the insurance undertakings concerned or any insured party. For co-insurance or co-reinsurance pools created exclusively to cover new risks, the exemption applies for three years from the date of the first establishment of the pool, regardless of the market share of the pool. For others, the exemption remains in place as the combined market share of the undertakings does not exceed (i) for co-insurance pools, 20 per cent of any relevant market, (ii) for co-reinsurance pools, 25 per cent of any relevant market (Article 6).

192. Commission Regulation (EU) No 330/2010 on the application of Article 101(3) of the Treaty on the Functioning of the European Union to categories of vertical agreements and concerted practices [2010] OJ L102/1. See further Question 43.
193. Commission Guidelines on Vertical Restraints [2010] OJ C130/1.
194. Commission Regulation (EC) No 2658/2000 on the application of Article 81(3) of the Treaty to categories of specialisation agreements [2000] OJ L304/3.
195. These would replace the Commission Guidelines on the applicability of Article 81 of the EC Treaty to horizontal cooperation agreements [2001] OJ C3/2 ('Commission 2001 Horizontal Cooperation Guidelines'). In May 2010, the Commission published the Commission 2010 Draft Horizontal Cooperation Guidelines SEC(2010) 528/2.
196. Available on the Commission's website.
197. Commission Regulation (EC) No 2659/2000 on the application of Article 81(3) of the Treaty to categories of research and development agreements [2000] OJ L304/7.
198. Available on the Commission's website.
199. Commission Regulation (EC) No 772/2004 on the application of Article 81(3) of the Treaty to categories of technology transfer agreements [2004] OJ L123/11.
200. Commission Guidelines on the application of Article 81 of the EC Treaty to technology transfer agreements [2004] OJ C101/2.
201. Commission Regulation (EU) No 461/2010 on the application of Article 101(3) of the Treaty on the Functioning of the European Union to categories of vertical agreements and concerted practices in the motor vehicle sector [2010] OJ L129/52.
202. Commission Regulation (EC) No 1400/2002 on the application of Article 81(3) of the Treaty to categories of vertical agreements and concerted practices in the motor vehicle sector [2002] OJ L203/30.
203. Commission Supplementary guidelines on vertical restraints in agreements for the sale and repair of motor vehicles and for the distribution of spare parts for motor vehicles [2010] OJ C138/16.
204. Council Regulation (EC) No 169/2009 of 26 February 2009 applying rules of competition to transport by rail, road and inland waterway [2009] OJ L61/1.
205. Commission Regulation (EC) 906/2009 on the application of Article 81(3) of the Treaty to certain categories of agreements, decisions and concerted practices between liner shipping companies (consortia) [2009] OJ L256/31.
206. For an overview of Regulation 906/2009, see Prisker, 'Commission adopts new block exemption regulation for liner shipping consorita' (2010) 1 *Competition Policy Newsletter* 8.
207. Council Regulation (EC) No 246/2009 of 26 February 2009 on the application of Article 81(3) of the Treaty to certain categories of agreements, decisions and concerted practices between liner shipping companies [2009] OJ L79/1.
208. Commission Guidelines on the application of Article 81 of the EC Treaty to maritime transport services [2008] OJ C245/2 ('Commission Maritime Transport Guidelines'). The exemption from EU competition rules for liner conferences, which had been set out in Regulation 4056/86, was abolished with effect from 18 October 2008. See Council Regulation (EC) No 1419/2006 repealing Regulation (EEC) No 4056/86 laying down detailed rules for the application of Articles 85 and 86 of the Treaty to maritime transport, and amending Regulation (EC) No 1/2003 as regards the extension of its scope to include cabotage and international tramp services [2006] OJ L269/1.
209. Commission Regulation (EU) No 267/2010 on the application of Article 101(3) of the Treaty on the Functioning of the European Union to certain categories of agreements, decisions and concerted practices in the insurance sector [2010] OJ L83/1. See also Communication from the Commission on the application of Article 101(3) of the Treaty on the Functioning of the European Union to certain categories of agreements, decisions and concerted practices in the insurance sector [2010] OJ C82/20.

Ireland

5.   Under section 4(3) of the Competition Act 2002, the Competition Authority has
     the power to declare that a certain category of agreements, decisions or concerted
     practices are compatible with the conditions in section 4(5), which mirrors Article
     101(3).[210] Agreements or conduct falling within such a declaration shall not then
     be prohibited under section 4(1).[211] Any person aggrieved by the making of a
     section 4(3) declaration may appeal to the High Court within 28 days of
     publication and the High Court may confirm, annul or amend the declaration.[212]

6.   The Authority has made a number of section 4(3) declarations. At the time of
     writing, the following declarations were in effect:

     •   Vertical Agreements (expires 30 November 2010).[213]

     •   Motor fuels (expires 30 November 2010).[214]

     •   Exclusive purchasing of LPG (expires 31 March 2015).[215]

7.   The Authority carried out a consultation in summer 2010 in respect of the vertical
     agreements and motor fuels exemptions, with a view to determining whether these
     exemptions should be replaced when they expired on 30 November 2010.

UK

8.   The OFT may recommend to the Secretary of State the adoption of a block
     exemption from the Chapter I prohibition for particular categories of agreements.
     It is then for the Secretary of State to adopt the block exemption.[216] A block
     exemption for public transport ticketing schemes, which allows bus operators to
     agree public transport ticketing schemes, has been adopted under the Competition
     Act 1998.[217]

---

210. Section 4(3), as amended by section 23 of the Communications Regulation (Amendment)
     Act 2007 also makes provision for ComReg to issue declarations.
211. Competition Act 2002, s 4(2).
212. Competition Act 2002, s 15.
213. Competition Authority Declaration No. D/03/001 in Respect of Vertical Agreements and
     Concerted Practices (5 December 2003, last amended 17 May 2010); Competition Authority
     Notice N/03/002 in respect of Vertical Agreements and Concerted Practices (5 December
     2003; amended 17 May 2010).
214. Competition Authority Decision No. D/08/001 issuing a Declaration pursuant to section 4(3)
     of the Competition Act 2002 to a category of exclusive purchasing agreements in respect of
     motor fuels (1 July 2008; amended 17 May 2010).
215. Competition Authority Declaration No. D/05/001 in respect of Exclusive Purchasing
     Agreements for Cylinder Liquefied Petroleum Gas (8 March 2005; amended 31 March
     2005).
216. Competition Act 1998, s 6(1), s 6(2).
217. The block exemption was adopted in 2001 and amended with effect from 2006. See SI 2005
     No 3347 Competition Act 1998 (Public Transport Ticketing Schemes Block Exemption)
     (Amendment) Order 2005. The OFT consulted on extending this block exemption in 2010 as
     it was due to expire in February 2011.

9.   Provision is also made in the Competition Act 1998 for declarations to be made by the Treasury (in respect of agreements related to investment business)[218] and the Secretary of State (in respect of certain broadcasting agreements)[219] that certain agreements are not caught by the Chapter I prohibition.

---

218. See Financial Services Act 1986, s 127(2), s 127(3), as inserted by Schedule II of the Competition Act 1998.
219. See Broadcasting Act 1990, s 194(a)(3), s 194(a)(4), as inserted by the Schedule II of the Competition Act 1998.

23. WHAT ARE COMMON FEATURES OF A CARTEL?

Summary

- A ringleader.

- A monitoring mechanism.

- A punishment mechanism.

- The cartel may be coordinated through a trade association.

- A 'consultant' is sometimes used to facilitate the cartel.

- Depending on the industry, cartels may be organised on a global basis.

1. Among antitrust enforcers, cartels are seen as the most egregious of violations of competition law, 'the supreme evil of antitrust'.[220] This is borne out by the growing number of jurisdictions adopting criminal sanctions for cartel conduct. As the Irish High Court recently put it, it is:

    > ... clear beyond argument and must be so declared that cartels operate one of the most serious forms of anti-competitive behaviour which exists, inflicting the most harm on customers, consumers and the public alike.[221]

2. The most common forms of cartel conduct include horizontal price fixing, market allocations, bid rigging and agreed output restrictions. Often a cartel will combine two or more of these practices.

3. Cartels are presumed to have detrimental effects on the economy, raising prices, restricting supply and making products far more expensive than they would otherwise be. Meanwhile, the cartel members generate excessive profits. The Commission has described the effect of cartels as follows:

    > Cartels shield their participants from competition. This allows the participants to charge higher prices and to remove the pressure on them to improve the products they sell or find more efficient ways in which to produce them. Their customers (companies and consumers) end up paying higher prices for lower quality and narrower choice. This also adversely affects the competitiveness of the economy as a whole.[222]

4. Working out the economic impact that cartels produce, in particular establishing the exact extent to which prices are inflated because of the cartel's activity, is a complex task. Although it usually publishes lengthy decisions when it finds that a cartel has infringed competition law, the Commission rarely draws any conclusions about the cartel's precise economic impact. This issue poses a

---

220. *Verizon Communications v Law Offices of Curtis v Trinko*, 540 US 398, 408 (2004).
221. *Director of Public Prosecutions v Duffy* [2009] IEHC 208, [2009] 3 IR 613, para 27 (McKechnie J).
222. http://ec.europa.eu/comm/competition/cartels/overview/index_en.cfm.

particular problem for claimants in private damages actions when attempting to quantify the damage that the cartel has caused them.[223]

5.   The Commission has expended considerable effort in recent years in tackling cartels, evidenced by the number of infringement decisions it has taken and the ever higher fines it imposes. The Commission contains a specific Directorate to deal with cartels, Directorate G. The detection of cartels also owes much to the success of the Commission's leniency programme. There seems to be a growing awareness of cartel enforcement among business in Europe and it has been noted that cartel participants have increasingly recognised the illegal nature of their behaviour with the focus in appeals against Commission decisions being the nature of the evidence, the administrative procedure and the level of fines imposed.[224]

6.   Cartels come in all shapes and sizes. Some may be fairly loosely arranged, an agreement made over a few drinks to fix prices, with nothing written down. Others may be more elaborate, with regular meetings, implementation of the cartel agreement by a dedicated 'coordinator' and documents in sophisticated code created.

7.   Cartels sometimes have a ringleader or instigator who is responsible for its organisation and who may have coerced others into joining the cartel or remaining in it. Being a ringleader typically attracts an additional fine from the European Commission[225] and removes the possibility of that company receiving immunity from fines.[226]

8.   Cartels often involve executives at different levels of seniority, who carry out different tasks. Senior managers of the cartel members may meet to establish general principles of the cartel, while more junior executives may monitor the implementation of the cartel.[227]

9.   Economic theory suggests that cartels are inherently unstable. The cartel seeks to maintain an artificially high cartel price. If one participant lowers its price and increases output, it will gain additional market share. There is therefore an incentive to cheat on the cartel.[228]

---

223. See 111.13, 111.29.
224. Bellamy & Child (6th edn, 2008) para 5.006.
225. See, e.g., COMP/C.39181 *Candle Waxes* [2009] OJ C295/17, Press Release IP/08/1434 of 1 October 2008 (ringleader's fine increased by 50 per cent); Commission Guidelines on the method of setting fines imposed pursuant to Article 23(2)(a) of Regulation No 1/2003 [2006] OJ C210/02, para 23.
226. Commission Notice on Immunity from fines and reduction of fines in cartel cases [2006] OJ C298/17, para 13.
227. See, e.g., *Citric Acid* [2002] OJ L239/18, [2002] 5 CMLR 24, para 71 (high level strategic 'Masters' meetings and more technically oriented 'Sherpa' meetings).
228. See, e.g., Bishop and Walker, *The Economics of EC Competition Law* (3rd edn, 2010) para 5.017.

10. The structural features of the market may affect the likelihood of cartels forming. Certain market characteristics may facilitate collusion among competitors. These may include:

    - A concentrated market structure, e.g. there are a small number of suppliers in the market, each of which has a high market share.

    - A high degree of market transparency. A transparent market where, for example, competitors can easily determine what price each is selling at, may facilitate cartel behaviour as it allows deviations from the cartel agreement to be easily detected and punished, thereby providing a disincentive for cartel members to cheat and thereby making the cartel more stable.

    - High barriers to entry.

    - A limited number of alternative suppliers.

    - Homogenous products.

    - Limited buyer power.

    - Stable supply and demand conditions.

    - Opportunities for repeated interaction and similar firm characteristics.

11. If a market is transparent and particularly if there is price transparency, deviations from the cartel agreement can be monitored more easily. Cartels may also include specific built-in monitoring mechanisms which involve exchanges of data on the prices charged by each participant, volumes of sales, market share reports, customer lists etc. A monitoring or reporting system allows the effectiveness of the cartel and each participant's adherence to the agreement to be monitored.[229]

12. An ability to punish those members of the cartel who deviate is also important to preserving the cartel's stability. An effective punishment mechanism is a deterrent against deviation in the first place. Punishment could take different forms, for example:

    - The other members of the cartel may engage in a temporary price war or increase output temporarily.

    - A 'compensation' system, whereby a cartel member who cheats and exceeds its allowed market share is forced to pay financial compensation or purchase products from a cartel member that has underperformed.

    - If the cartel members are also involved in other markets that are not subject to the cartel agreement, retaliation could take place in those markets, for example, refusing to supply the deviator with an essential input.

13. Trade associations are often used as a cover for illicit cartel meetings.[230] Given this, a company's participation in any trade association should be handled with

---

229. See, e.g., Case COMP/E–1/37.370 *Sorbates* (1 October 2003) para 113 (fine reduced on appeal, Case T–410/03 *Hoechst GmbH v Commission* [2008] ECR 881, [2008] 5 CMLR 839).

230. See, e.g., Case COMP/E–1/36.212 – *Carbonless paper*, [2004] OJ L115/1, para 83 ('The EEA-wide planning and coordination of the cartel took place at the general cartel meetings convened under the cover of the official meetings of the trade association') (contd\...)

care and executives attending trade association meetings should adhere to the company's antitrust compliance guidelines. The association itself may be found to breach competition law where it is an association of undertakings (or an undertaking) under Article 101.[231]

14. Cartels sometimes utilise the services of a 'consultant' to coordinate the activities of the cartel. This might be a third party, often someone with connections to the industry, such as a former employee of one of the cartel members or an outside consultancy firm. In *AC-Treuhand*, the General Court confirmed that an undertaking that played an accessory role in a cartel is jointly liable for the infringement of Article 101.[232] The Swiss consulting company, AC-Treuhand, had provided logistical assistance to a cartel in organic peroxides, audited a quota system agreed among the cartelists and provided advice on how to avoid cartel detection. The same firm was found to have played a similar role in a cartel in the plastic additives sector, organizing cartel meetings and making its offices available for such meetings. It was fined €348,000 by the Commission.[233]

15. In the *Marine hose* cartel, an independent consultant was employed full time to coordinate the activities of the cartel around the world. He was subsequently jailed in the UK.[234] In Ireland, an individual who was alleged to have performed the role of 'referee' or 'facilitator' in the *Home Heating Oil* cartel case, though himself not a trader, was charged with aiding and abetting another undertaking in engaging in price fixing. The individual pleaded guilty and received a six month suspended prison sentence.[235]

16. As commerce has become more globalised, so too have cartels. This trend can be seen in the growing number of international cartels detected by competition authorities worldwide and the increased cooperation between the authorities in conducting cartel investigations. For example, in the *Marine hose* cartel, in May 2007, the US Antitrust Division and the FBI arrested eight executives in Houston from the United Kingdom, France, Italy and Japan and conducted multiple searches in the United States. On the same day, the EU and UK authorities conducted searches in several European locations. This was followed by the

---

230. (contd) (partly overturned on appeal, Cases T–109/02 etc. *Bolloré SA v Commission* [2007] ECR II–947, [2007] 5 CMLR 66).
231. See, e.g., Case 246/86 *Belasco v Commission* [1989] ECR 2117, [1991] 4 CMLR 96.
232. Case T–99/04, *AC-Treuhand AG v Commission* [2008] ECR II–1501, [2008] 5 CMLR 13. See also Case T–29/05 *Deltafina SpA v Commission*, judgment of 10 September 2010, paras 45–64, 425–436 (confirming the liability of a firm that was not active in the relevant market in which the cartel operated; here, the company operated in a downstream market).
233. COMP 38.589 *Heat Stabilisers*, Commission decision of 11 November 2009.
234. See *R v Whittle* [2008] EWCA Crim 2560 and OFT press release 72/08, *Three imprisoned in first OFT criminal prosecution for bid rigging*, 11 June 2008. See, also, Case COMP/37.857 *Organic peroxide* [2005] 5 CMLR 579, paras 95–105 (appeal dismissed Case T–120/04 *Peróxides Orgánicos SA v Commission* [2006] ECR II–4441, [2007] 4 CMLR 4).
235. See the note of the case on the Competition Authority's website at http://www.tca.ie/EN/ Enforcing-Competition-Law/Criminal-Court-Cases/Home-Heating-Oil.aspx.

Japanese Fair Trade Commission carrying out searches in Japan. Such cooperation also requires coordination with respect to whistleblowers:

> The Commission also holds the view that international cooperation with other competition authorities, which is of major importance for the detection and investigation of international cartels, requires that obligations of immunity applicants under different jurisdictions have to be coordinated.[236]

Key Sources

Case T–99/04, *AC-Treuhand AG v Commission* [2008] ECR II–1501, [2008] 5 CMLR 13.

Case COMP/E–1/37.370 *Sorbates*, Commission Decision of 1 October 2003.

Case COMP/39406 *Marine Hoses*, Commission Decision of 28 January 2009.

---

236. Case COMP/39406 – *Marine Hoses*, Commission Decision of 28 January 2009, para 69 (on appeal, Case T–146/09 *Parker ITR Srl v Commission* and Case 148/09 *Trelleborg AB v Commission*, pending).

24. How should a businessperson react at a meeting of competitors that turns into a cartel meeting?[237]

Summary

- Mere attendance at a cartel meeting creates a presumption that the undertaking subscribes to the cartel.

- Such an undertaking should publicly distance itself from the cartel (proving that the other participants understood its position) or act as a whistleblower and report the cartel to the authorities.

1. Any company or executive seeking to avoid potential antitrust liability should distance itself as quickly and effectively as possible from any conversations or meetings with competitors that involve price fixing or other cartel subject matter. The most effective way to do this would be never to have contact with one's competitors but this may not be realistic in many industries. It is of course legitimate to meet with competitors in the normal course, for example at a trade association meeting or social event. However anything that could be interpreted as a cartel should be avoided at all costs.

2. The very fact of attendance at a meeting that involved cartel discussions can result in a finding of a breach. The Court of Justice has held that once attendance is established, the undertaking is presumed to have subscribed to the meeting's anti-competitive initiatives.[238] The Commission has the burden of proving that the undertaking attended the meeting but it is then for the undertaking to put forward evidence to establish that its participation in the meeting was without any anti-competitive intention. The reason for the presumption is that 'having participated in the meeting without publicly distancing itself from what was discussed, the undertaking has given the other participants to believe that it subscribed to what was decided there and would comply with it'.[239]

3. The burden of rebutting the presumption that it participated in the cartel can be met in one of two ways, by the undertaking 'publicly' distancing itself from the anti-competitive scheme or blowing the whistle:

    > [A] party which tacitly approves of an unlawful initiative, without publicly distancing itself from its content or reporting it to the administrative authorities, effectively encourages the continuation of the infringement and compromises its discovery. That

---

237. See the following sound advice from a US lawyer in answer to a similar question: 'Not gleefully. Instead, the law-abiding competitor should behave conspicuously, encouraging the noisy departure of its key personnel in attendance. Spilling a Mai Tai upon departing is an example of such conspicuous behaviour' (Disner, *Antitrust: Questions, Answers, Law and Commentary* (3rd edn, 2007) 163).
238. See Case C–49/92P *Commission v Anic Partecipazioni SpA* [1999] ECR I–4125, [2001] 4 CMLR 602, para 96.
239. Case C–204/00P etc *Aalborg Portland A/S v Commission*, [2004] ECR I–123, [2005] 4 CMLR 251, para 82.

complicity constitutes a passive mode of participation in the infringement which is therefore capable of rendering the undertaking liable in the context of a single agreement.[240]

4. Faced with a situation where an executive is at a meeting with competitors, which though starting out innocuously changes to a discussion about prices, how should the executive react? The executive should leave such a meeting immediately and make clear to the other participants that the company has no intention of taking part in discussions or agreements that could breach competition law. Whether these actions will be sufficient to satisfy the first of the two alternate conditions for rebutting the presumption of participation in the cartel – to show that the undertaking has 'publicly' distanced itself from the cartel – will come down to the evidence.

5. The Court of Justice has stated that the undertaking should demonstrate that it had indicated to its competitors that it was participating in the meeting 'in a spirit that was different from theirs'.[241] So, would documentary evidence of a quick exit from a cartel meeting and communication of a firm rejection to the other participants be sufficient? This will depend on what exactly the evidence proves. The crucial point is whether the other participants in the cartel understood that the undertaking had the intention to distance itself from the unlawful agreement.[242] This test suggests that the company's own notes about its actions in leaving a meeting and turning its back on a cartel will be of limited use. Documentary evidence showing that this is what the other meeting participants understood would be more important.

6. Ultimately, each case will depend on the circumstances. It will be easier for an undertaking to show that it did not participate in a cartel where it only attended the first meeting of what was a long-running cartel and the notes of one of the cartelists show that it left in protest. Proving that it publicly distanced itself may be more difficult if the cartel was of short duration and the meeting in which it participated was the main focus point of the cartel agreement.

7. Given the likely difficulty of producing such evidence, the safer route would be to satisfy the second test and blow the whistle by informing the competition authorities. This leaves little doubt about the undertaking's intention to distance itself from the cartel. Even if the company is found to have participated in the cartel, at least it can apply for leniency and put itself in a position to obtain an exemption or reduction in any fines that are imposed.

---

240. Case C–204/00P etc *Aalborg Portland A/S v Commission*, [2004] ECR I–123, [2005] 4 CMLR 251, para 84.
241. Case C–199/92 *Hüls AG v Commission* [1999] ECR I–4287, [1999] 5 CMLR 1016, para 155.
242. Case C–510/06P *Archer Daniels Midland Co v Commission (Sodium Gluconate)* [2009] ECR I–1843, [2009] 4 CMLR 889, para 120.

8.   It is no defence for the company to argue that although it attended the cartel meeting, it did not act on the outcome of the meeting. It must publicly distance itself or blow the whistle.[243]

Key Sources

Case C–199/92 *Hüls AG v Commission* [1999] ECR I–4287, [1999] 5 CMLR 1016.

Case C–204/00P etc *Aalborg Portland A/S v Commission* [2004] ECR I–123, [2005] 4 CMLR 251.

Case C–510/06P *Archer Daniels Midland Co v Commission (Sodium Gluconate)* [2009] ECR I–1843, [2009] 4 CMLR 889.

---

243. See Case C–204/00P etc *Aalborg Portland A/S v Commission,* [2004] ECR I–123, [2005] 4 CMLR 251, para 85.

25. WHAT ARE TYPICAL FORMS OF PRICE FIXING?

Summary

- Article 101 prohibits the fixing of any element of price, not just the ultimate price charged.

- The fixing of discounts, surcharges etc. amounts to as serious an infringement as the fixing of headline prices.

1. Article 101 specifically lists as incompatible with the common market agreements, decisions and concerted practices that 'directly or indirectly fix purchase or selling prices or any other trading conditions'. Price fixing agreements between competitors are one of the most common types of competition violations investigated by the European Commission and national competition authorities. Although in theory any kind of agreement, including one to fix prices, can be defended under Article 101(3), in practice, it is extremely difficult for a horizontal price fixing agreement to benefit from the exemption.

2. Price fixing agreements may take many forms. It is not necessary that the agreement or understanding pertain to the ultimate price charged for a product. A conspiracy to agree on pricing policies or to fix a range of prices or an element of the price, such as a discount or surcharge, is still price fixing. The word 'price' has a broad meaning, encompassing any matter relating to the cost of goods or services offered or the quality or value of those goods or services such as credit terms or practices, discounts and warranties. Article 101(1) catches any agreement that directly or indirectly suppresses price competition.

3. The following is a non-exhaustive list of elements of pricing, the fixing of which will result in a breach Article 101:

    - Sales prices.[244]

    - Price floors.[245]

    - Price ranges.[246]

    - Price targets.[247]

    - Reference prices and prices of standard products.[248]

---

244. See, e.g., Case 41/69 *ACF Chemiefarma v Commission* [1970] ECR 661, paras 132–134.
245. See, e.g., *Polypropylene* OJ 1986 L230/1, [1988] 4 CMLR 347; *IFTRA Aluminium* [1975] OJ L228/3, [1975] 2 CMLR D20 (an agreement not to offer prices below published prices).
246. See, e.g., Cases IV/33.126 and 33.322 – *Cement* OJ 1994 L343/1, para 16; COMP/F/38.645 – *Methacrylates* [2006] OJ L322/20, para 101.
247. See, e.g., *Welded Steel Mesh* [1989] OJ L260/1, [1991] 4 CMLR 13, para 166.
248. See, e.g., Case COMP/39.165 – *Flat glass* OJ 2008 C 127/9, paras 88–96.

- List prices.[249]
- Price increases.[250]
- Discounts.[251]
- Rebates.[252]
- Surcharges.[253]
- Interest rates.[254]
- Other credit terms.[255]
- Profit margins.[256]

4. An example of a 'plain vanilla' price fixing cartel is *Professional Videotapes*, in which the Commission found that the three main producers of certain types of professional videotapes formed a cartel to increase or stabilise prices. They achieved this by holding a number of meetings where the prices of professional videotapes were discussed and agreed and three rounds of price increases were organised. Commercially sensitive information was exchanged to facilitate and monitor the implementation of the price fixing agreement.[257]

5. Price fixing is often combined with a range of other restrictions, each of which would singly give rise to a breach of Article 101. In *Pre-Insulated pipes*, the cartel not only fixed prices but also engaged in bid rigging, the allocation of market shares, allocations of customers, using standards to prevent the introduction of new technology which would have led to lower prices and the payment to smaller competitors to leave the market.[258]

---

249. Even if the parties are still free to offer discounts and industry practice is to negotiate price irrespective of list prices. See, e.g., *Franco-Japanese Ballbearings Agreement* [1974] OJ L343/19, [1975] 1 CMLR D8.

250. See, e.g., COMP/F/38.645 – *Methacrylates* [2006] OJ L322/20, paras 100–107.

251. See, e.g., Case 246/86 *Belasco v Commission* [1989] ECR 2117, [1991] 4 CMLR 96, paras 21–23; COMP/39165 *Flat Glass*, Commission Decision of 28 November 2007.

252. See, e.g., Cases 209/78 etc. *Heintz van Landewyck SARL v Commission ('FEDETAB')* [1980] ECR 3125, [1981] 3 CMLR 134, paras 142–146.

253. See, e.g., IV.34.503 *Ferry Operators – Currency surcharges* [1997] OJ L26/23, [1997] 4 CMLR 798; *Air passenger fuel surcharge cartel*, see OFT press release 113/07 of 1 August 2007, available on the OFT website.

254. See, e.g., Case COMP/36.571/D–1 *Austrian Banks – 'Lombard Club'* [2004] OJ L56/1, [2004] 5 CMLR 399 (fines reduced on appeal, Cases T–259/02 etc *Raiffeisen Zentralbank Österreich AG v Commission* [2006] ECR II 5169, [2007] 5 CMLR 1142; further appeals dismissed, Cases C–125/07 etc *Raiffeisen Zentralbank Österreich AG v Commission* [2009] ECR I–8681).

255. See, e.g., *Vimpoltu* [1983] OJ L200/44, [1983] 3 CMLR 619; Case COMP/36.571/D–1 *Austrian Banks – 'Lombard Club'* [2004] OJ L56/1, [2004] 5 CMLR 399.

256. See, e.g., Cases 209/78 etc. *Heintz van Landewyck SARL v Commission ('FEDETAB')* [1980] ECR 3125, [1981] 3 CMLR 134.

257. Case COMP 38.432 *Professional videotapes*, Commission Decision of 20 November 2007.

258. *Pre-Insulated Pipe Cartel* [1999] OJ L24/1, [1999] 4 CMLR 402.

6.   Indirect price fixing may also violate competition law. For example, a retailer who provides its supplier with pricing information in circumstances where it is foreseeable that the information will be used to influence market conditions and is then passed on to another retailer can form the basis for a finding of price fixing between the three parties. This was the position in the English case, *Toys and Games/Replica Football Kits*.[259]

---

259. *Argos v Office of Fair Trading* [2006] EWCA Civ 1318, [2006] UKCLR 1135.

26. MAY COMPETITORS AGREE ON TERMS OF SALE OTHER THAN PRICE?

Summary

- The Article 101 prohibition applies to the fixing of any trading conditions.

- The voluntary adoption of standard terms may be justified in particular circumstances where it facilitates the comparison by customers of different products.

1.   As well as price fixing, Article 101 prohibits competitors agreeing on other terms. Article 101(1)(a) specifically prohibits agreements or concerted practices which 'directly or indirectly fix purchase or selling prices *or any other trading conditions*'.

2.   An example of an infringement involving restrictions on both price and other trading conditions can be seen in *Vimpoltu*.[260] Through a decision of a trade association, importers of Dutch tractors agreed to observe maximum discounts and standard delivery and payment terms. Where credit was given, a minimum interest rate would be charged. There was an agreement that the net price of delivery to dealers was to be for delivery to the showroom or warehouse including the costs of preparation or delivery normally borne by the importer. Restrictions were also imposed on sales promotions.

3.   Additional examples of 'other trading conditions', the fixing of which has infringed Article 101, include entry by the auction houses, Sotheby's and Christie's, into a common plan that included an agreement not to give vendors at auction guarantees as to the minimum price,[261] an agreement to prohibit bulk deliveries of certain types of Armagnac[262] and as part of the *Marine Hose* cartel, the harmonization of sales conditions such as payment terms, guarantees and the discouragement of long-term and global contracts and agreements on dealing with exchange rates, internet bidding and penalties.[263] As indicated by these examples, the fixing of non-price trading terms is often used as an ancillary restriction to a cartel agreement.

4.   Although the prohibition with respect to trading conditions in Article 101(1)(a) seems clear, it belies the reality that the adoption of standard terms can be pro-competitive and beneficial to customers in certain circumstances. For example, standard contract terms can minimise transaction costs by allowing customers to make a like-for-like comparison of different offerings on the basis of price without having to distinguish between other more detailed terms, which could make comparisons less useful. However, if such standard terms are to be provided, their

---

260. *Vimpoltu* [1983] OJ L200/44, [1983] 3 CMLR 619.

261. COMP/37.784 *Fine Art Auction Houses* [2006] 4 CMLR 90, para 76.

262. *Pabst & Richarz/BNIA* [1976] OJ L231/24, [1976] 2 CMLR D63.

263. COMP/39406 *Marine Hoses*, Commission decision of 28 January 2009 (appeals pending, Case T–146/09 *Parker ITR Srl v Commission* and Case 148/09 *Trelleborg AB v Commission*).

adoption should be voluntary rather than compulsory so as to minimise the possibility of being found in breach of the competition rules. These types of agreements should be distinguished from standardisation or standard-setting agreements, which involve the adoption of particular industry standards in respect of technical or quality requirements. Such arrangements may also raise issues under Article 101.[264]

5. Agreements fixing trading conditions may also be ancillary to and necessary for the effective functioning of agreements that are compatible with Article 101, for example with respect to collective purchasing or collective selling pools. Such agreements may require a more sophisticated Article 101 analysis to determine whether they are caught by Article 101(1) and if so, whether they can avail of the Article 101(3) exemption.[265]

6. It should be remembered that agreements that are considered as price fixing agreements do not always focus on the headline price to be charged. Other elements of the amount that the customer will be charged, which may less obviously appear to constitute part of the price, may be fixed and in this case, the agreement is treated as a price fixing agreement.[266]

Key Sources

Vimpoltu [1983] OJ L200/44, [1983] 3 CMLR 619.

COMP/39406 *Marine Hoses*, Commission Decision of 28 January 2009.

---

264. See Commission 2001 Horizontal Cooperation Guidelines [2001] OJ C3/2, paras 159–178; Commission 2010 Draft Horizontal Cooperation Guidelines SEC(2010) 528/2, para 252 *et seq.*
265. See on joint purchasing and joint selling, Questions 36 and 37 respectively.
266. See Question 25 for examples.

27. CAN AGREEMENTS TO RESTRICT OUTPUT OR IMPOSE QUOTAS ON PRODUCTION BE DEFENDED UNDER ARTICLE 101?

Summary

- An agreement among competitors to restrict output falls squarely within Article 101(1).

- Such an agreement may be a standalone restriction or ancillary to a cartel agreement, in which case it will be condemned under Article 101(1) without any realistic possibility of exemption under Article 101(3).

- Where an agreement to restrict output is made due to industry-wide overcapacity (so-called 'crisis cartels'), the agreement will still be treated as one with an anti-competitive object caught by Article 101(1) but may stand a better chance of exemption under Article 101(3).

1. Article 101(1)(b) specifically refers to agreements that 'limit or control production, markets, technical development, or investment'. It is generally unlawful for competitors to agree upon limitations involving either production or supply with respect to goods and services. An agreement to restrict output may constitute a standalone horizontal conspiracy. It is also often used as a mechanism to reinforce a market allocation or price fixing cartel – if the volume of output is artificially reduced, there is less chance of price competition breaking out.

2. The Commission has consistently found quota agreements, whereby parties agree to limit the volume of the goods they produce or sell, to violate Article 101. Quotas often aim to keep the market shares of cartel members at a set level,[267] which may be based on the market shares obtained in previous years and other market conditions such as capacity constraints. In some industries, a market share quota may be a more straightforward means of achieving a stable cartel than naked price fixing, where participants may still have an incentive to compete in ways other than by price. Market share based on volumes may also be easier to monitor than prices, where cheating cartelists can more easily hide discounts that they provide to customers.

3. Quota agreements often provide for an enforcement mechanism, whereby, for example, a company that exceeds its quota must make a penalty payment[268] or the

---

267. See, e.g., *Car Glass,* Commission Decision of 12 November 2008; *Vitamins* [2003] OJ L6/1, [2003] CMLR 1030 (incorporating volume control mechanisms known as 'budgets') (fines reduced on appeal, Case T–15/02 *BASF v Commission* [2006] ECR II–497); *Benelux Flat Glass* [1984] OJ L212/13, [1985] CMLR 350 (market share quotas used to maintain the 'status quo' in sharing the Benelux market).

268. See, e.g., COMP 37.370 *Sorbates* [2005] 5 CMLR 2054, para 116 (fine reduced on appeal, Case T–410/03 *Hoechst v Commission* [2008] ECR II–881, [2008] 5 CMLR 839); *Citric Acid* [2002] OJ L239/18, [2002] 5 CMLR 24, para 110 ('the principle that overselling participants would have to compensate those who undersold played a central role in the cartel arrangement') (contd \...)

compensation mechanism may be more elaborate, for example, requiring the party who has exceeded its quota to buy products from other members of the cartel.[269]

What are 'crisis cartels'?

4.   An agreement among competitors to limit production is generally considered to be a hardcore restriction of Article 101. However, certain industries, in particular heavy industry where demand may be 'lumpy' and levels of investment high, may from time to time be affected by long-term overcapacity resulting from changes in demand. One possible response for industries in this situation is to have competing undertakings enter into 'restructuring agreements' or 'crisis cartels' to address the overcapacity problem and return the industry to competitiveness. Such arrangements will invariably fall squarely within Article 101(1) but they may be defensible under Article 101(3).

5.   Crisis cartels have been considered in a number of Commission decisions and court judgments. In the *Stichting Baksteen* case, the Commission examined a restructuring agreement involving the Dutch brick industry.[270] The major producers agreed to a collective reduction in production, with compensation provided for parties who suffered losses due to closures. This naked restriction of competition was found to fall within Article 101(1) but the Commission granted an exemption for five years under Article 101(3) after the agreement was amended to remove production quotas. It was a condition of the exemption that the parties did not disclose to each other data regarding individual outputs or deliveries.

6.   In *Synthetic Fibres*, the Commission considered an agreement between manufacturers of synthetic fibre to reduce production capacity.[271] The industry was unprofitable due to overcapacity and the agreement was aimed at bringing production back in line with demand. The Commission found that the agreement was contrary to Article 101(1) but it granted an exemption. Market forces had failed by themselves to achieve capacity reductions necessary to re-establish and maintain in the longer term an effective competitive structure. Following implementation of the agreement, consumers would benefit from a healthier and more competitive industry in the long term, while in the short term, sufficient competition would remain.

7.   The Court of Justice confirmed in the *BIDS* case that crisis cartels fall squarely within the Article 101(1) prohibition.[272] The Irish meat processing industry was

---

268. (cont) (appeal mainly dismissed, Case T–59/02 *Archer Daniels Midland v Commission* [2006] ECR II–3627, [2006] 5 CMLR 1528; further appeal partly upheld and fine reduced, Case C–511/06P *Archer Daniels Midland Co v Commission (Citric Acid)* [2009] ECR I–5843, [2009] 5 CMLR 1963).

269. See, e.g., *Vitamins* [2003] OJ L6/1, [2003] CMLR 1030, paras 196, 225 (requirement to 'slow down' if selling above quota and, if above quota at the end of the year, requirement to purchase vitamins from others to compensate them for the corresponding shortfall in their allocation).

270. *Stichting Baksteen* [1994] OJ L131/15, [1995] 4 CMLR 646.

271. *Re Synthetic Fibres* [1984] OJ L207/17, [1985] 1 CMLR 787.

272. Case C–209/07 *Competition Authority v BIDS* [2008] ECR I–8637, [2009] 4 CMLR 310.

affected by overcapacity and the ten principal meat processors in Ireland formed a company, BIDS, with the aim of reducing that overcapacity. A number of producers would exit the industry and be compensated in return by those who remained. On a preliminary reference from the Irish Supreme Court, the Court of Justice held that arrangements of this type had an anti-competitive object and so fell squarely within the Article 101(1) prohibition. However, there was a possibility that the arrangements could benefit from the Article 101(3) exemption. The application of Article 101(3) to BIDS is currently pending before the Irish High Court.[273]

8.   The case law of the Union courts and Commission decisions show that restructuring agreements will typically be found to infringe Article 101(1) on the basis that such agreements have an anti-competitive object. However, the Article 101(3) exemption may apply, as it has done in several Commission decisions.

Key Sources

Car Glass, Commission Decision of 12 November 2008.

COMP 37.370 *Sorbates* [2005] 5 CMLR 2054.

Re Synthetic Fibres [1984] OJ L207/17, [1985] 1 CMLR 787.

Stichting Baksteen [1994] OJ L131/15, [1995] 4 CMLR 646.

Case C–209/07 *Competition Authority v Beef Industry Development Society Ltd.* *('BIDS')* [2008] ECR I–8637, [2009] 4 CMLR 310.

---

273. See *Competition Authority v Beef Industry Developments Society Limited* [2009] IESC 72, remitting the case to the High Court for it to consider the application of Article 101(3).

28. MAY COMPETITORS ALLOCATE DIFFERENT TERRITORIES OR CUSTOMERS BETWEEN THEMSELVES WITHOUT INFRINGING THE COMPETITION RULES?

Summary

- No.

- An agreement among horizontal competitors to share markets or customers is a hard core violation of Article 101.

- An agreement dividing markets on a global basis will still be caught by Article 101 if the conditions for its application are satisfied.

- A limited exception allows non-compete agreements of a limited duration that are ancillary to the sale of a business.

1. Article 101(1)(c) specifically prohibits agreements, decisions and concerted practices that 'share markets or sources of supply' while Article 101(1)(b) refers to agreements that 'limit ... markets'.

2. A market allocation agreement may take different forms. Markets may be allocated on a geographic basis, by product or service type or by customer. In procurement markets, allocation may involve the division of different lots among the competitors.

3. The allocation of markets or customers between horizontal competitors is a hard-core violation of Article 101 and is in the same category of egregious conduct as price fixing. Allocating markets by territory is a serious distortion of competition, as, if competitors agree to stay out of each others designated geographic markets, the result is that there will be no competition at all in those areas.

4. An obvious form of market sharing in the EU is to segment markets by country. From the cartel's perspective, this may be more effective than simple price fixing, as the presence of a competitor in a territory in which he is not supposed to operate is more easily monitored than adherence to a fixed price. The *Cement* cartel followed the principle of the 'home market' according to which the companies only sold product in their own countries and the export of cement within Europe was prohibited. As a note written by a cartel member put it: 'It is a club: object: protection of home markets – rule: everyone respects his home markets and exports excess production under general consensus'.[274]

5. A similar 'home market rule' was adopted in the *Peroxygen Products* cartel, with each producer limiting sales to end-users in those Member States where it possessed production facilities, a restriction which was 'all the more remarkable given the very considerable price differences' between each country.[275]

---

274. *Cement* [1994] OJ L343/1, [1995] 4 CMLR 327, para 34.
275. *Peroxygen products* [1985] OJ L35/1, [1985] 1 CMLR 481, para 10.

6.   In *E.ON/GDF*, the two main gas companies in Germany and France entered into an agreement in 1975 that they would not enter each other's home markets and they continued to apply this agreement even after gas markets had been liberalised up to 2005.[276]

7.   Market sharing of this type on the basis of Member State is of particular concern in the EU context as it directly challenges a fundamental Treaty goal of promoting an internal market and leads to the insulation of markets along national lines.

8.   The division of global markets by competitors may also violate Article 101, at least where it results in effects in the EU. For example, if three competitors divide the world into three markets – Europe, Asia and the rest of the world – and each takes a region for itself, this is a blatant market allocation agreement that violates Article 101 because it restricts competition within the EU. An example of such a market-sharing agreement is seen in the *Gas Insulated Switchgear* cartel, where markets in Japan and Europe were allocated to a Japanese and European block of companies respectively.[277]

9.   Another form of prohibited market sharing is the allocation of customers.[278] Market sharing agreements sometimes take the form of 'non-aggression agreements' or 'status quo' agreements where competitors agree not to compete aggressively for each other's main customers or give assurances to each other that they will not target specific clients.[279] The parties to the cartel might also agree who is to supply each customer and provide that quotes given by the other parties to the customer will be higher than that of the chosen supplier. In *Polypropelene* this involved 'the quoting by producers other than the regular suppliers of a particular customer, if approached, of prices somewhat higher than the target, so as to avoid the danger of 'customer tourism' (the customer going to a new supplier in the hope of obtaining a more favourable price than the one quoted by the traditional supplier)'.[280]

10.   Other forms of prohibited market sharing include agreements between competitors to allocate markets on the basis of product type,[281] the allocation by a group of purchasers of suppliers, *i.e.* an agreement that certain purchasers would purchase

276. *E.ON/GDF* [2009] OJ C248/5.
277. COMP/F/38.899 *Gas Insulated Switchgear*, Commission Decision of 24 January 2007 (appeal pending, Case T–117/07 *Areva v Commission*).
278. See, e.g., COMP/37.533 *Choline Chloride*, Commission Decision of 9 December 2004; COMP F/38.368 *Synthetic Rubber*, Commission Decision of 29 November 2006, para 130.
279. See Case COMP 38.638 *Butadiene Rubber and Emulsion Styrene Butadiene Rubber*, Commission Decision of 29 November 2006, para 130.
280. *Polypropelene* [1986] OJ L230/1, [1988] CMLR 347.
281. See, e.g., Case COMP 38.338 *Needles* [2005] 4 CMLR 792 (fines reduced on appeal, Case T–36/05 *Coats Holdings v Commission* [2007] ECR II–110, [2008] 4 CMLR 45; Case T–30/05 *Prym v Commission*, judgment of 12 September 2007; further appeals dismissed, Case C–468/07P *Coats Holdings Ltd v Commission* [2008] ECR I–127, [2009] 4 CMLR 301; Case C–534/07P *William Prym GmbH & Co. KG v Commission* [2009] ECR I–7415, [2009] 5 CMLR 2377).

from only certain suppliers (a 'buyer's cartel')[282] and the allocation of sales volumes or market shares.[283]

11. As with other hardcore cartel agreements and conduct, it is very unlikely that a market allocation agreement would benefit from the Article 101(3) exemption.

Are non-compete agreements in the context of a business sale permissible?

12. A limited exception to the general prohibition on non-compete and market allocation agreements does apply in the context of the sale of a business. An ancillary non-compete restriction on the vendor will not be incompatible with Article 101 if it can be regarded as necessary for the agreement to be workable. Non-competes in the context of the sale of a business are justified as without them, the vendor would be free to attempt to win customers of the sold business immediately after the sale. This would completely undermine the rationale for the purchaser agreeing to buy the business in the first place. However, the scope and duration of the non-compete must not go beyond what is necessary to ensure the efficacy of the agreement.[284]

13. Where a non-compete obligation is considered to be ancillary to the sale of the business, then Article 101 will not apply to it. To be considered 'ancillary', the duration of the non-compete must be reasonable. The Commission considers that non-competes of three years are justified where goodwill and know-how are transferred and two years where the sale only includes goodwill.[285] However, the Commission does not consider that non-competes are necessary where the sale is limited to physical assets or exclusive industrial and commercial property rights.[286] The geographic scope should be limited to the area in which the business was

---

282. See Case COMP/38.238 *Raw Tobacco Spain*, Commission Decision of 20 October 2004 (appeals pending, Cases T–24/05 etc *Standard Commercial Corporation v Commission*) and Case COMP/38.321 *Raw Tobacco Italy*, Commission Decision of 20 October 2005 (appeals pending Cases T–11/06 etc *Romana Tabacchi v Commission*). This should be distinguished from a legitimate joint purchasing agreement, which may still fall foul of Article 101 but which is more likely to benefit from the Article 101(3) exemption. See Question 36.

283. See, e.g., COMP/E–1/37.027 *Zinc Phosphate* [2003] OJ L153/1, [2003] 5 CMLR 731, para 66 (appeals dismissed, Case T–33/02 *Britannia Alloys & Chemicals Ltd v Commission* [2005] ECR II–4973, [2006] 4 CMLR 1046, Case T–52/02 *SNCZ v Commission* [2005] ECR II–5005, [2006] 4 CMLR 1069, Case T–62/02 *Union Pigments AS v Commission* [2005] ECR II–5057, [2006] 4 CMLR 1105, Case T–64/02 *Dr. Hans Heubach GmbH & Co. KG v Commission* [2005] ECR II–5137, [2006] 4 CMLR 1157; further appeal dismissed, Case C–76/06P *Britannia Alloys & Chemicals Ltd v Commission* [2007] ECR I–4405, [2007] 5 CMLR 251); COMP/38.695 *Sodium Chlorate*, Commission Decision of 11 June 2008, para 73 (appeal pending, Case T–343/08 *Arkema France v Commission*; Case T–299/08 *Elf Aquitaine v Commission*).

284. For an example of a national court addressing a non-compete in the context of a business sale, see *RGDATA v Tara Publishing Co. Ltd.* [1995] 1 ILRM 453.

285. Commission Notice on restrictions directly related and necessary to concentrations [2005] OJ C56/24 ('Commission Ancillary Restraints Notice') para 20.

286. Commission Ancillary Restraints Notice [2005] OJ C56/24, para 21.

active, to include territories into which expansion was planned at the time of the sale.[287] Restrictions on the purchase of stakes in competing companies, solicitation of customers or using confidential information of the business are similarly justified on the same basis and for the same periods.[288]

---

287. Commission Ancillary Restraints Notice [2005] OJ C56/24, para 22.
288. Commission Ancillary Restraints Notice [2005] OJ C56/24, paras 25, 26.

29. WHAT CONSTITUTES BID RIGGING AMOUNTING TO A HARDCORE VIOLATION OF THE COMPETITION RULES?

Summary

- Bid rigging is a hardcore violation of the competition rules and is treated as being as egregious as price fixing.

- The most common form of bid rigging is probably 'cover bidding' or 'cover pricing', where conspirators work out in advance who the 'winner' will be and the others submit a false or 'cover' bid.

- Cover bidding will breach Article 101 even if the undertaking that submitted the cover bid would not have made a genuine bid anyway.

- Other forms of bid rigging include bid rotation and bid suppression.

- The award of sub-contracts may be used as compensation for partaking in the conspiracy.

1. Bidding markets exist in various sectors of the economy and public authorities regularly put bids out to tender under the public procurement rules.

2. Agreements among tenderers to rig bids, whether for private or public tenders, are hardcore restrictions of Article 101(1). As the Commission noted in 1973:

> In a system of tendering, competition is of the essence. If the tenders submitted by those taking part are not the result of individual economic calculation, but of knowledge of the tenders by other participants or of concertation with them, competition is prevented, or at least distorted and restricted.[289]

3. Bid rigging can take different forms. It might involve outright agreements not to compete in particular bids; the use of 'cover' bidding, where the 'winner' is chosen in advance and other members of the cartel submit false bids with a higher price; or different tenders may be rotated among the cartel.

4. Depending on the features of the cartel, the bid rigging may result in price fixing, market allocations or agreed output restrictions or include elements of all of these practices. The main forms of bid rigging are now summarised.[290]

---

289. IV/26 918 *European sugar industry* [1973] OJ L 140/17, [1973] CMLR D65.

290. In general, see, e.g., Irish Competition Authority, The Detection and Prevention of Collusive Tendering (November 2009); US Department of Justice, Price Fixing, Bid Rigging and Market Allocation Schemes: What They Are and What To Look For, available on the DOJ website http://www.justice.gov/atr; OECD Guidelines for Fighting Bid Rigging in Public Procurement (March 2009); Anderson and Kovacic, 'Competition Policy and International Trade Liberalisation: Essential Complements to Ensure Good Performance in Public Procurement Markets' (2009) 18 *Public Procurement Law Review* 67; Szilagyi, 'Bidding Markets and Competition Law in the European Union and the United Kingdom: Part 1' [2008] *European Competition Law Review* 16.

What is 'cover pricing' (or 'cover bidding')?

5. Where cover pricing is utilised, the competitors have worked out in advance which one of them will 'win' the bid. The 'winning' bidder submits its bid at an agreed price or at a price or on terms which it knows will be lower or better than the cover bids. The other parties to the agreement in turn submit token bids at a higher price or include terms which it is known will be unacceptable to the purchaser running the tender. Cover bidding aims to give the impression of genuine competitive bidding, when in fact the bidding process is rigged.

6. This method of bid rigging has the advantage for the losing bidders of making it seem that they are in fact trying to obtain the business, which may be important for obtaining future bids from the same purchaser. This type of bid rigging was used in *Elevators and Escalators*, where the agreed 'winner' would inform the other members of the cartel of its price and they would then submit complementary bids that were too high to be accepted.[291]

7. Cover pricing was a particularly prevalent feature in the UK *Construction* case, the OFT noting that cover pricing was a 'widespread and endemic practice ... carried out in a relatively standard way'.[292] In an earlier case, *Apex Asphalt*, the CAT upheld the OFT's finding of a bid rigging cartel in the flat roofing sector. The collusive tendering here also featured cover bids. The CAT noted that in a selective tendering process, where the contracting authority invited a restricted number of bidders to submit quotes, 'any interference with the selected bidders' independence can result in significant distortions of competition'.[293]

How does a bid rotation scheme operate?

8. In a bid rotation conspiracy, all parties to the cartel agreement submit bids but take turns being the 'winning' bidder with the lowest price. Bids are rotated on a systematic or rotating basis. The terms of the rotation may vary. For example, competitors may take turns winning contracts according to the size of the contract, allocating equal amounts to each conspirator or allocating volumes that correspond to the size or market share of each of the tenderers.

---

291. Case COMP 38/823 *Elevators and Escalators*, Commission Decision of 21 February 2007, paras 161, 191, 315, 316, 349, 443, 447 (appeals pending, Cases T–145–147/07 *Otis SA v Commission*; Case T–151/07 *KONE Corporation v Commission*). Other examples include *Building and construction industry in the Netherlands* [1992] OJ L92/1, [1993] 5 CMLR 135 and COMP/F/38.899 *Gas Insulated Switchgear*, Commission Decision of 24 January 2007 (appeal pending, Case T–117/07 *Areva v Commission*).
292. CA98/02/2005 *Bid rigging in the construction industry in England*, OFT decision of 21 September 2009, 395 (appeals pending before the CAT).
293. *Apex Asphalt and Paving Co Ltd v Office of Fair Trading* [2005] CAT 4, para 211. See also *Makers UK Ltd v Office of Fair Trading* [2007] CAT 11, concerning the same bid rigging practices.

How does a bid suppression scheme operate?

9. Bid suppression takes place when suppliers agree among themselves to abstain from bidding or to withdraw bids. This ensures that the allocated company 'wins' the bid.

How may sub-contracting be used as part of bid rigging?

10. In addition to the above forms of collusive tendering, a bid rigging scheme might also feature a sub-contracting element whereby competitors who agree not to bid or to submit a cover bid are awarded subcontracts as 'compensation' from the 'winning' bidder.

Is open joint bidding permissible?

11. Bid rigging should be distinguished from situations where two or more competitors are open about the fact that they are submitting a joint bid. Such joint bidding would usually be acceptable under the competition rules. However, the line between what is permissible and what is prohibited is not always clear-cut. Five individuals and three companies were prosecuted under the Irish Competition Act 2002 for entering into agreements to share waste collection markets and customers. It appears that the defendants came together and openly submitted joint bids in respect of tenders. The defendants were all acquitted by a jury.[294]

Is 'cover pricing' a hardcore violation when the company providing the cover price would not have bid competitively in any event?

12. What if the company submitting the cover price would not have submitted a competitive bid in any event? It may not have been capable of carrying out the work that was called for in the tender, say, because of resources issues.

13. It may wish to submit a bid anyway, partly to be seen to be participating so that the contracting authority believes that the undertaking wishes to participate in future bids. The undertaking providing the cover price in this situation may ask where is the harm in its actions, especially given that it would not otherwise have submitted a bid.

14. Defendants in the OFT's *Construction* case claimed that cover pricing was a historic and industry-wide practice that was generally understood not to be illegal. For the most part, its purpose was seen as enabling a company to provide a bid that appeared plausible and to be close enough to the winning bid that the company would be considered for any future tenders. As one of the defendants described:

> The practice of cover pricing appears historically to have been prevalent within the industry and … helping out a competitor by providing a cover price where that competitor did not have a desire (or the capacity) to undertake a project seems to have been accepted commercial custom and practice … Putting in tenders based on a cover

---

294. Details of the case are discussed in *Director of Public Prosecutions v Bourke Waste Removal Limited* [2010] IEHC 122.

price, on projects which a contractor did not wish to win, enabled a rapport to be maintained with the client, whereas 'returning' tenders (*i.e.* sending them back to the clients without pricing them) ran the risk that the company would be dropped from the list of contractors invited to bid in future.[295]

15.   It was argued that there would always be a number of competing bids in each tender so that the winning price would be a competitive price anyway. On this view the practice of cover bidding was not fraudulent or anti-competitive. These arguments did not convince the OFT, which referred to the CAT decision in *Apex Asphalt*, in which the CAT pointed out that the submission of false bids gave to the procuring entity:

> the mistaken impression that all of the tenderers had submitted competitive bids independently and were genuinely interested in carrying out the work.

> The fact that the parties to the concerted practices may not have considered the anti-competitive nature of their conduct, and therefore may not have appreciated that the object or effect of that conduct was anti-competitive, is not a relevant consideration when considering the existence of an infringement.[296]

16.   While ignorance of illegality was no defence, in coming to its starting point for the imposition of fines in the *Construction* case, the OFT did take account of the defendants' arguments to the effect that there was general widespread ignorance in the industry about the illegal nature of cover pricing.[297]

Key Sources

Case COMP 38/823 *Elevators and Escalators*, Commission decision of 21 February 2007.

UK

Apex Asphalt and Paving Co Ltd v Office of Fair Trading [2005] CAT 4.

No. CA98/02/2005 Bid rigging in the construction industry in England, OFT Decision of 21 September 2009.

---

295.   CA98/02/2005 *Bid rigging in the construction industry in England,* OFT Decision of 21 September 2009, para IV.570–571 (appeals pending before the CAT).

296.   *Apex Asphalt and Paving Co Ltd v Office of Fair Trading* [2005] CAT 4, [2005] CompAR 507, para 253.

297.   CA98/02/2005 *Bid rigging in the construction industry in England,* OFT Decision of 21 September 2009, para VI.173 (appeals pending before the CAT).

30. WHAT TOOLS CAN A PROCURER UTILISE TO DETECT BID RIGGING?

1.   Bid rigging in public procurement tenders or private tenders, like other cartel behaviour, can be extremely difficult to detect. The best method of detection is undoubtedly the whistleblower. Absent that, procuring entities themselves and competitors participating in auctions who are not part of the cartel, may be best placed to detect signs of bid rigging. The following features may be indicative of bid rigging:[298]

- The same company always wins a particular procurement (this is more suspicious if one or more companies continually submit unsuccessful bids).

- The same suppliers submit bids and each seems to take a turn being the winner.

- There is a pattern of geographic allocation, e.g. some bidders never seem to win in a particular area.

- Some bids are much higher than published price lists, previous bids by the same firms or engineering cost estimates.

- Fewer than the normal number of competitors submit bids.

- A company appears to be bidding substantially higher on some bids than on other bids, with no apparent cost differences to account for the disparity.

- There is a significant price difference between the winning bid and all other bids, without any apparent explanation for this difference.

- There are sudden price increases or changes in prices or discounts offered.

- Bid prices drop whenever a new or infrequent bidder submits a bid.

- A successful bidder subcontracts work to competitors that submitted unsuccessful bids on the same project.

- A company withdraws its successful bid and subsequently is subcontracted work by the new winning contractor.

- Suppliers meet before tenders are submitted and the contracting authority is not present.

- Suppliers that are expected to tender do not.

- Tenders are similar – e.g. identical spelling errors, miscalculations.[299]

---

298. See also, e.g., Irish Competition Authority, The Detection and Prevention of Collusive Tendering (November 2009); OECD, Detecting Bid Rigging in Public Procurement, available on the OECD website. For a discussion of economic tools that can be used to detect bid rigging in procurement markets, focusing in particular on cover bidding in road construction procurement, see Porter and Zona 'Detection of Bid Rigging in Procurement Auctions' (1993) 101 *Journal of Political Economy* 518.

299. In one US case, a bid rigging conspiracy was uncovered and successfully prosecuted after a procurement official noticed the same typographical error (an unnecessary word) in the bid letters of two competing companies: 'Please give us a call **us** if you have any question' (see OECD Report, *Public Procurement:* The Role of Competition Authorities in Promoting Competition (DAF/COMP(2007)34) (8 January 2008) 158).

2.   The detection of bid rigging is not a scientific process. If a contracting authority or other bidder detects what they believe to be bid rigging, they should contact the relevant antitrust authority, in Ireland, The Competition Authority, in the UK, the OFT.[300] It would be prudent to make a note of any relevant conversations or events and details of the suspicious bids.

Key Sources

Irish Competition Authority, The Detection and Prevention of Collusive Tendering (November 2009).

OECD, Detecting Bid Rigging in Public Procurement.

---

300. In Sweden, the Swedish Competition Authority has, since 1 September 2007, also taken over responsibility for the supervision of public procurement, which may make cartel enforcement in the procurement context more efficient.

31. WHAT STEPS CAN A PROCURING ENTITY TAKE TO TRY TO PREVENT BID RIGGING?

1. There are steps that public authorities and private procurers can take in the design and operation of tenders which may help to minimise the opportunity for tenderers to engage in bid rigging. These include the following:

    - Where possible, procurers could try to lower barriers to entry by avoiding unnecessarily restrictive pre-qualification criteria, ensuring that such criteria are proportionate and taking other measures to lower the cost of participation in tenders, for example, through the use of electronic systems. Such measures may encourage the participation of small and medium sized enterprises ('SMEs'), in particular.

    - Procurers should not release confidential information that could impact on competition. The Court of Justice has stated that to achieve the objective of opening up public procurement to undistorted competition, 'it is important that the contracting authorities do not release information relating to contract award procedures which could be used to distort competition, whether in an ongoing procurement procedure or in subsequent procedures'.[301]

    - Procurers should not release the identities of bidders to each other.

    - A procurer should not disclose its own internal estimate for the contract before the award is made.

    - Line item bids, rather than lump sum bids, should be sought, where this is feasible.

    - Where feasible, larger projects could be divided into a few smaller projects and this may also encourage the participation of SMEs. However, it is possible that more frequent bids might actually encourage collusion. In contrast if there is a long gap between tenders, it may make it more difficult for a cartel to operate in stability. While encouraging the participation of SMEs is pro-competitive, the decision to split contracts must comply with the principle of equal treatment and not be indirectly discriminatory.

    - Contracting authorities could require that bidders identify joint venturers, partners and subcontractors upfront. Under Regulation 25 of the Irish Public Sector Regulations, a contracting authority is entitled to ask each tenderer whether it intends to subcontract any share of the contract that might be awarded to it but there is no mention of whether a contracting authority may ask for the identity of intended sub-contractors.[302] The UK Public Sector Regulations enable a contracting authority to require a bidder to identify any person to whom it proposes sub-contracting any part of the contract.[303] The

---

301. Case C–450/06 *Varec SA v Belgium* [2008] ECR I–581, [2008] 2 CMLR 687, para 35.
302. SI No 329 of 2006 European Communities (Award of Public Authorities' Contracts) Regulations 2006, r 25.
303. SI 2006 No. 5 The Public Contracts Regulations 2006, r 45.

underlying directive provides that the contracting authority *may* ask for this information.[304]

- Requiring a 'certificate of non-collusion'.[305]

May subcontracting be prohibited?

2. Some guidance on tender design suggests that bids should be free of subcontracting and that winning bidders should not be allowed to subcontract part of the contract.[306] While this would negate the possibility of compliant cartel members being 'compensated' through the award of a subcontract, it does not seem compatible with the EU public procurement regime. First, recital 32 to Directive 2004/18/EC provides that 'it is advisable to include provisions on subcontracting' in order to encourage the participation of SMEs.[307] This provision recognises the important pro-competitive effect that sub-contracting can play.

3. Second, an outright ban on subcontracting does not appear permissible in EU law, following the Court of Justice decision in the *Siemens* case. This involved a tender stipulating that a maximum of 30 per cent of the contract could be subcontracted, with a ban on subcontracting in respect of certain work. Whereas subcontracting might be prohibited where the capacity of subcontractors to carry out the work had not been verified at the time of the contract award, the Court held that contracting authorities could not exclude a firm solely because the firm proposed to rely on the resources of others for performing the contract.[308]

---

304. Directive 2004/18/EC on the coordination of procedures for the award of public works contracts, public supply contracts and public service contracts, Article 25.
305. See Prasifka, 'Making Competition Work in Public Procurement,' presentation of 3 July 2008, available at http://www.tca.ie/controls/getimage.ashx?image_id=2117, at 7.
306. See, e.g., OECD Report, *Public Procurement: The Role of Competition Authorities in Promoting Competition* (DAF/COMP(2007)34) (8 January 2008).
307. Directive 2004/18/EC on the coordination of procedures for the award of public works contracts, public supply contracts and public service contracts, recital 32.
308. Case C–314/01 *Siemens AG Österreich* [2004] ECR I–2549, [2004] 2 CMLR 601, para 43.

32. WHAT INFORMATION MAY BE LEGITIMATELY SHARED AMONG COMPETITORS?

Summary

- The exchange of competitively sensitive information among competitors can breach Article 101.

- A one-way flow of information may be sufficient to breach competition law.

- Information exchanges to support a cartel are treated the same way as a cartel and will generally give rise to a restriction of competition by object.

- For most other data exchanges, an assessment of their competitive effects should be made. A useful rule of thumb is to ask whether the information is normally of a type one would be happy for a competitor to have access to.

- Relevant factors include:

  - Market structure (oligopoly; transparent market; homogeneous products; stable demand);

  - The type of information exchanged (is it commercially sensitive? aggregated/disaggregated; historic/recent/present, future);

  - Mechanics of the exchange (frequency; whether shared with customers).

- The exchange of information on prices and other strategically important data is usually the most problematic.

- If the exchange of information between competitors is of such a type that it would normally raise issues under Article 101, the fact that the information could have been obtained from another source may not make a difference.

- Information exchanges caught by Article 101(1) may be defensible under Article 101(3).

1. Not all information exchanges raise competition concerns and the dissemination of much commercial information is pro-competitive. The more information that is made available to consumers, the better informed their choices will be. The publication of information is also important to enable businesses, investors, governments and others to make important decisions on matters such as investments. The practice of benchmarking, whereby undertakings measure their own performance against a standard of best practice in the industry, relies on the exchange of information. Such exchanges may have a pro-competitive effect by enabling undertakings to act more efficiently on the market. Similarly, the compilation of statistics on market sales over time may be beneficial by allowing undertakings to plan better for the future. Such information exchanges should usually be carried out through a third party, rather than directly.

2. Nevertheless, information exchanges can result in liability under Article 101. There must be an agreement, concerted practice or a decision of an association of

undertakings for an information exchange to come within the ambit of Article 101. For this to occur, it is not always necessary that information flows in two directions. A concerted practice within the meaning of Article 101 may arise where information is imparted from one competitor to another, the party that merely received the information being equally liable for a breach of Article 101.[309] As the General Court noted in *Cement*:

> ... the concept of concerted practice does in fact imply the existence of reciprocal contacts. That condition is met where one competitor discloses its future intentions or conduct on the market to another when the latter requests it or, at the very least, accepts it.[310]

3.   Whether a violation of Article 101(1) arises depends on the specific economic and factual context.[311] The attendance of an undertaking at a single meeting at which information is exchanged may be sufficient to give rise to a concerted practice in breach of Article 101.[312]

4.   Information exchanges that fall within Article 101(1) may be defensible under Article 101(3) if the conditions for application of the exemption are satisfied.

5.   Special consideration should be given to the exchange of information in the context of the proposed sale of a company or business. A potential purchaser, which may be a competitor, must carry out due diligence and gain access to certain information about the target to enable it to decide whether to make an offer. However, restrictions may have to be put in place in respect of particularly sensitive material.[313]

---

309. See, e.g., Cases T–202/98 etc *Tate & Lyle plc v Commission* [2001] ECR II–2035, [2001] 5 CMLR 859, para 58 (appeal dismissed, Case C–359/01P *British Sugar plc v Commission* [2004] ECR I–4933, [2004] 5 CMLR 329); OFT Press Release 34/10, RBS agrees to pay £28.5 million penalty for disclosing pricing information to competitor (30 March 2010), detailing the agreement by Royal Bank of Scotland to pay a fine for breach of competition law by the unilateral disclosure of pricing information relating to loans to Barclays Bank, which took account of the information in determining its own pricing of loans.

310. Cases T–25/95 etc *Cimenteries CBR SA v Commission* [2000] ECR II–491, [2000] 5 CMLR 204, para 1849 (however, the Court noted in the same paragraph that the recipient of the information, Lafarge, had requested the meeting at which the information was exchanged and that its attitude could not be reduced to 'the purely passive role of a recipient of the information').

311. See, e.g., *Bouygues Télécom SA v Union Fédérale des Consommateurs – Que Choisir* [2008] ECC 32 (the French Supreme Court found that the Paris Court of Appeal had failed to investigate in an empirical manner whether, from 1997 to 2003, the regular exchange of retrospective information between the three enterprises operating in the market, in relation to certain information not published by the Telecommunications Regulation Authority, had the purpose or real or potential effect of enabling each operator to adapt to the anticipated behaviour of its competitors and thereby distort or restrict in a significant manner the competition in the market in question).

312. See Case C–8/08 *T-Mobile Netherlands BV* [2009] ECR I–4529, [2009] 5 CMLR 1701, para 59.

313. See further Question 80.

What information exchanges are clearly anti-competitive?

6.   If information is exchanged among competitors for the purpose of facilitating an anti-competitive practice, such as monitoring the adherence of members of a cartel to a price fixing agreement, then the information exchange is assessed together with the practice that it supports. The exchange of information for the purpose of implementing a price fixing agreement would, in the same way as the price fixing agreement, generally be treated as a restriction of competition by object.[314] This will be so even if the information exchanged is in the public domain or historical, the Court of Justice noting in *Cement* that this interpretation of Article 101(1) was

> based on the consideration that the circulation of price information limited to the members of an anti-competitive cartel has the effect of increasing transparency on a market where competition is already much reduced and of facilitating control of compliance with the cartel by its members.[315]

7.   In its 2010 Draft Horizontal Guidelines, the Commission has suggested that information exchanges between competitors of individualised data regarding intended future prices or quantities, as well as exchanges on current conduct that reveals intentions on future behaviour, would in themselves constitute restrictions of competition by object, even when the exchange did not take place to support a cartel.[316] It is questionable whether this view is supported by the case law of the EU courts on Article 101.[317]

How should the effect of information exchanges be analysed?

8.   Assuming that the information exchange is not a restriction by object, it should be considered whether it might have an anti-competitive effect. An important principle of EU competition law is that each economic operator should independently decide on its course of action on the market. That requirement strictly precludes:

> any direct or indirect contact between such operators, the object or effect whereof is either to influence the conduct on the market of an actual or potential competitor or to disclose to such a competitor the course of conduct which they themselves have decided to adopt or contemplate adopting on the market, where the object or effect of

---

314. See, e.g., Cases T–25/95 etc *Cimenteries CBR SA v Commission* [2000] ECR II–491, [2000] 5 CMLR 204, para 1531. See also Commission Maritime Transport Guidelines [2008] OJ C245/02, para 42.

315. Cases C–204/00P etc *Aalborg Portland A/S v Commission* [2004] ECR I–123, [2005] 4 CMLR 251, para 281.

316. Commission 2010 Draft Horizontal Cooperation Guidelines SEC(2010) 528/2, para 68.

317. Although see Case T–16/98 *Wirtschaftsvereinigung Stahl v Commission* [2001] ECR II–1217, [2001] 5 CMLR 310, para 44 ('information exchange agreements are not generally prohibited automatically but only if they have certain characteristics relating, in particular, to the sensitive and accurate nature of recent data exchanged at short intervals'). See also, Camesasca, Schmidt and Clancy, 'The EC Commission's Draft Horizontal Guidelines: Presumed Guilty when Having a Chat' (2010) 1 *Journal of European Competition Law and Practice* 405.

such contact is to create conditions of competition which do not correspond to the normal conditions of the market in question, regard being had to the nature of the products or services offered, the size and number of the undertakings and the volume of the said market.[318]

9. Data exchanges between competitors may make it easier for them to predict each other's behaviour and adjust their own. So, an information exchange may be contrary to Article 101 where it results in anti-competitive effects.

10. To establish whether anti-competitive effects result from information exchange, a full market analysis should be made. A number of factors will be relevant to the assessment. The Court of Justice stated in *Asnef-Equifax* that:

> ... the compatibility of an information exchange system ... with the Community competition rules cannot be assessed in the abstract. It depends on the economic conditions on the relevant markets and on the specific characteristics of the system concerned, such as, in particular, its purpose and the conditions of access to it and participation in it, as well as the type of information exchanged – be that, for example, public or confidential, aggregated or detailed, historical or current – the periodicity of such information and its importance for the fixing of prices, volumes or conditions of service.[319]

11. This can be distilled into three main items of inquiry: (i) market structure; (ii) the type of information exchanged; and (iii) the mechanics of the exchange.[320]

How is the market structure relevant?

12. Market structure is an important element in considering the effect of an exchange of information:

> The level of concentration is particularly relevant since, on highly concentrated oligopolistic markets, restrictive effects are more likely to occur and are more likely to be sustainable than in less concentrated markets. Greater transparency in a concentrated market may strengthen the interdependence of firms and reduce the intensity of competition.[321]

13. Information exchange among three competitors who together hold the vast majority of the market is much more likely to be problematic than an exchange among three competitors who together have only a minority share in a highly competitive market.[322] In its decision in the *UK Tractor* case, the Commission

---

318. Case C–49/92P *Commission v Anic Partecipazioni SpA* [1999] ECR I–4125, [2001] 4 CMLR 602, para 117.

319. Case C–238/05 *Asnef-Equifax v Ausbanc* [2006] ECR I –11125, [2007] 4 CMLR 224, para 54.

320. See also Commission 2010 Draft Horizontal Cooperation Guidelines SEC(2010) 528/2, paras 69–87.

321. Commission Maritime Transport Guidelines [2008] OJ C245/02, para 48.

322. See also Commission 2010 Draft Horizontal Cooperation Guidelines SEC(2010) 528/2, para 71 ('For an information exchange to be likely to have appreciable restrictive effects on competition, the companies involved in the exchange have to cover a sufficiently large part of the relevant market').

emphasised the oligopolistic nature of the market in finding that the exchange of detailed information about sales and market shares broken down by product, territory and time period was a breach of Article 101.[323] The greater the transparency in the market, the more likely there will be a collusive outcome from an information exchange.[324]

14. The Commission also points out that the structure of supply and demand on the market is an important consideration. Relevant factors are the number of competitors, the stability of their market shares and the existence of any structural links between competitors.[325] Competition concerns are more likely to arise in homogeneous product markets than differentiated product markets.

Which types of information are most problematic to exchange?

15. The exchange of commercially sensitive information is more likely to breach Article 101 than other types of information. A good barometer in practice is sometimes to ask whether one would normally be happy for a competitor to have access to the information or whether it would be regarded as a business secret. Information on items such as price, costs, capacity, production volumes, customers and future strategy is often highly commercially sensitive.

16. A number of factors are relevant in assessing the commercial sensitivity of information. Aggregate data that combines data from several sources and produces information that is not identifiable on an individual basis is much less likely to be problematic than individual data identifying the particular undertaking to which it relates. For example, if a trade association collects capacity utilisation rates for a particular industry and then publishes the information to its members, it is less likely to be commercially sensitive if produced on the basis of average capacity utilisation rates for a particular part of the industry than, say, specific percentages for each undertaking that is a member of the association.

17. Even if data is provided on an aggregated basis, it should not be in such a form that it can be disaggregated 'so as to allow undertakings directly or indirectly to identify the competitive strategies of their competitors'.[326] The Commission gives the example of aggregated capacity data in liner shipping, pointing out that it could be disaggregated when combined with individual announcements by line carriers, allowing undertakings to identify the market positions and strategies of its competitors.[327]

18. Historical data is less likely to be competitively sensitive and so its exchange is less problematic. The speed with which data loses its competitive sensitivity will

323. *UK Agricultural Tractor Registration Exchange* [1992] OJ L68/19, [1993] 4 CMLR 358 (appeal dismissed Case T–35/92 *John Deere Ltd v Commission* [1994] ECR II–957; further appeal dismissed, Case C–7/95P *John Deere Ltd v Commission* [1998] ECR I–3111, [1998] 5 CMLR 311).
324. Commission 2010 Draft Horizontal Cooperation Guidelines SEC(2010) 528/2, para 74.
325. Commission Maritime Transport Guidelines [2008] OJ C245/02, para 49.
326. Commission Maritime Transport Guidelines [2008] OJ C245/02, para 52.
327. Commission Maritime Transport Guidelines [2008] OJ C245/02, para 53.

depend on the particular industry, the types of data and the extent to which the data is aggregated. For example, price information that is a year old is unlikely to be sensitive but a strategy statement dated a year ago may continue to be competitively sensitive where its contents have not been made public and are still relevant to the company's future behaviour.

19. In general, the most sensitive information relates to prices and quantities, followed by information about costs and demand. In certain industries, technical R&D information may be the most sensitive.[328] By indicating the strategy an undertaking intends to adopt, the exchange of this type of information may reduce rivalry among competitors and restrict competition.

Does the advance publication of a price list raise competition law issues?

20. The advance publication of a price list, released in the normal course for legitimate purposes and shared with customers, will not usually raise concerns under Article 101. The fact that advance publication is standard practice in the industry, is requested by customers and that the price list is published widely to include customers, are all factors tending to show that the publication serves a legitimate business purpose. Prices simply have to be communicated. If competitors adjust their behaviour based on a rival's price list that was made public, they can say that they are simply exercising their 'right to adapt themselves intelligently to the existing and anticipated conduct of their competitors'.[329]

21. However the exchange of price lists among competitors, where the information is not also shared with customers, is liable to breach Article 101. As the Commission stated in *Glass Containers*:

> It is contrary to the provisions of Article [101(1)] for a producer to communicate to his competitors the essential elements of his price policy such as price lists, the discounts and terms of trade he applies, the rates and date of any change to them and the special exceptions he grants to specific customers.[330]

22. That the exchange of information could, of itself, result in a breach of Article 101(1) was confirmed by the Court of Justice in *John Deere*. The information exchanged among UK tractor suppliers, organised through a trade association, did not even extend to exact prices but allowed the competitors to work out each other's sales of tractors. In a highly concentrated market, this was held to prevent competition through the increased transparency and increased barriers to entry.[331]

23. In *Wood Pulp II*, the Court of Justice considered whether the system of quarterly price announcements by wood pulp producers in itself constituted a breach of

---

328. Commission 2010 Draft Horizontal Cooperation Guidelines SEC(2010) 528/2, para 81.
329. Cases 40/73 etc *Suiker Unie UA v Commission* [1975] ECR 1663, [1976] 1 CMLR 295, para 174.
330. *Glass Containers* [1974] OJ L160/1, [1974] 2 CMLR D50, para 43.
331. *UK Agricultural Tractor Registration Exchange* [1992] OJ L68/19, [1993] 4 CMLR 358 (upheld on appeal Case T–35/92 *John Deere Ltd v Commission* [1994] ECR II–957; upheld on further appeal, Case C–7/95P *John Deere Ltd v Commission* [1998] ECR I–3111, [1998] 5 CMLR 311).

Article 101. The Commission had considered that the price announcements had been introduced deliberately to enable the producers to ascertain what their competitors would charge in the coming quarters and also that this made the market artificially transparent. The Court of Justice rejected the proposition that the price announcements themselves constituted breaches of Article 101:

> [The] communications arise from the price announcements made to users. They constitute in themselves market behaviour which does not lessen each undertaking's uncertainty as to the future attitude of its competitors. At the time when each undertaking engages in such behaviour, it cannot be sure of the future conduct of the others.[332]

24. In reviewing the *Linpac/DS Smith* merger the UK Competition Commission was concerned that headline price announcements, which were a common feature of the corrugated sheet market, might lead to coordination among suppliers.[333] Ultimately, the Competition Commission found that this was not the case for reasons including that the headline price announcement, which was an announcement of intended price increases, provided only limited information about the actual price that would be charged. Although this analysis was carried out in the context of merger control, the concerns expressed about price announcements are equally applicable to an Article 101 analysis.

Is it legitimate to obtain information from a competitor if it could have been obtained from another source anyway?

25. If an exchange of information would otherwise breach Article 101, then the fact that the information could have been obtained from some other source does not necessarily justify the exchange.

26. In *COBELPA/VNP*, the Commission found that the exchange of prices, discounts and other terms of supply among competitors in the printing paper and stationary industry breached Article 101. It was irrelevant to this finding that the undertakings could have obtained the price information of their competitors through other sources. The Commission pointed out that 'this would have been a more complicated and time-consuming method'. Rather, it found that it could 'be assumed that the spontaneous notification of all significant information on prices artificially alters the conditions of competition and establishes between competitors a system of solidarity and mutual influence'.[334] Similar statements have been made in other cases.[335]

---

332. Cases 89/85 etc., *Åhlström Osakeyhtiö v Commission ('Wood Pulp II')* [1993] ECR I–1307, [1993] 4 CMLR 407, para 64.
333. Competition Commission, *A report on the completed acquisition of Linpac Containers Ltd by DS Smith Plc* (21 October 2004).
334. Commission Decision 77/592/EEC *COBELPA/VNP* [1977] OJ L242/10, [1977] 2 CMLR D28, para 30.
335. See Commission Decision 78/252/EEC *Vegetable Parchment* [1978] OJ L70/54, [1978] 1 CMLR 534, para 68; Commission Decision 82/367/EEC *Hasselblad* [1982] OJ L161/18, [1982] 2 CMLR 233, para 49, appeal Case 86/82 *Hasselblad (GB) Limited v Commission* [1984] ECR 883, [1984] 1 CMLR 559.

27. The alternative source of the information at issue in *COBELPA/VNP* would likely have been customers and obtaining information from this source would have been 'more complicated and more time consuming' than a direct exchange between competitors. However if the information that is exchanged is genuinely available in the public domain and is equally easy (and costless) for everyone to access, its direct exchange is unlikely to constitute an infringement of Article 101.[336]

Key Sources

Commission's Guidelines on the application of Article 81 of the EC Treaty to maritime transport services [2008] OJ C245/02.

UK Agricultural Tractor Registration Exchange [1992] OJ L68/19, [1993] 4 CMLR 358.

Case C–238/05 *Asnef-Equifax v Ausbanc* [2006] ECR I –11125, [2007] 4 CMLR 224.

Case C–8/08 *T-Mobile Netherlands BV v Raad van Bestuur van de Nederlandse Mededingingsautoriteit* [2009] ECR I–4529, [2009] 5 CMLR 1701.

---

336. See Commission 2010 Draft Horizontal Cooperation Guidelines SEC(2010) 528/2, para 82.

33. IS IT PERMISSIBLE TO OBTAIN DETAILS OF A COMPETITOR'S PRICES FROM ONE'S OWN CUSTOMERS?

Summary

- In general, it is legitimate for an undertaking to learn about a competitor's price from contacts in the normal course with its own customers.

- However, if a customer is used as a conduit to transfer price information from one competitor to another or if the information exchange is used to augment an anti-competitive agreement, it will come within the Article 101(1) prohibition and may constitute hardcore cartel conduct.

1. In general, it is legitimate for an undertaking to learn about the prices charged by a competitor from conversations or contacts in the normal course with its own customer. Often, such an exchange is pro-competitive, where, for example, the customer provides information about lower prices of the supplier's competitor in the hope of obtaining a better offer from that supplier. In this situation, there is no agreement with an anti-competitive object or effect that would breach Article 101.

2. Competition issues could arise if the provision by the customer of pricing information was a means for the suppliers to coordinate their pricing. If that were the aim of the exchange, then this could amount to price fixing.

3. If the two competing suppliers were already engaged in a price fixing cartel, by providing the prices of one supplier to the other, the customer may enable the receiving party to monitor compliance with the cartel.

4. The provision of its own pricing information by a distributor to a manufacturer can breach Article 101 where the manufacturer uses the information to inform its distributors of prices charged by other distributors. This device was used in *Hasselblad*, with the exchange of price lists and business secrets used to augment market partitioning.[337] As the Commission noted, no objections will normally be raised under competition law merely because a manufacturer asks its sole distributors for their price lists and for information regarding their terms of business (price rebates, bonuses, etc.). However, Hasselblad used the information it received to inform its sole distributors of the prices charged by the other sole distributors. This exchange of information was designed to prevent exports or to remove the incentive for them.

5. In *Toys and Games*, the English Court of Appeal upheld a decision of the CAT which had upheld a finding by the OFT of a breach of the Chapter I prohibition.

---

337. Commission Decision 82/367/EEC *Hasselblad* [1982] OJ L161/18, [1982] 2 CMLR 233, para 49 (appeal partly dismissed, Case 86/82 *Hasselblad (GB) Limited v Commission* [1984] ECR 883, [1984] 1 CMLR 559).

The Court of Appeal confirmed that the exchange of information at issue was a breach of the Chapter I prohibition, approving the following proposition:

> [If] (i) retailer A discloses to supplier B its future pricing intentions in circumstances where A may be taken to intend that B will make use of that information to influence market conditions by passing that information to other retailers (of whom C is or may be one), (ii) B does, in fact, pass that information to C in circumstances where C may be taken to know the circumstances in which the information was disclosed by A to B and (iii) C does, in fact, use the information in determining its own future pricing intentions, then A, B and C are all to be regarded as parties to a concerted practice having as its object the restriction or distortion of competition. The case is all the stronger where there is reciprocity: in the sense that C discloses to supplier B its future pricing intentions in circumstances where C may be taken to intend that B will make use of that information to influence market conditions by passing that information to (amongst others) A, and B does so.[338]

6. The Court of Appeal did consider, *obiter*, that the CAT may have gone too far in suggesting that if a retailer (A) privately discloses to a supplier (B) its future pricing intentions 'in circumstances where it is reasonably foreseeable that B might make use of that information to influence market conditions' and B then passes that pricing information on to a competing retailer (C), that is a sufficient basis for concluding that A, B and C all breached the Chapter I prohibition, even if A did not in fact foresee what was reasonably foreseeable or C did not appreciate the basis on which A had provided the information.[339] The Court had in mind here the statement of the Court of Justice in *Bayer-Adalat* that 'it is necessary that the manifestation of the wish of one of the contracting parties to achieve an anti-competitive goal constitute an invitation to the other party, whether express or implied, to fulfil that goal jointly'.[340]

Key Sources

Commission Decision 82/367/EEC *Hasselblad* [1982] OJ L161/18, [1982] 2 CMLR 233.

Argos Ltd v Office of Fair Trading [2006] EWCA Civ 1318, [2006] UKCLR 113.

---

338. *Argos Ltd v Office of Fair Trading* [2006] EWCA Civ 1318, [2006] UKCLR 113, para 141.
339. *Argos Ltd v Office of Fair Trading* [2006] EWCA Civ 1318, [2006] UKCLR 113, para 140.
340. Case C–2 & 3/01P *BAI v Bayer AG* [2004] ECR I–23, [2004] 4 CMLR 653, para 102.

34. **IF A DIRECTOR OR OFFICER OF A COMPANY SITS ON THE BOARD OF DIRECTORS OF A COMPETITOR COMPANY, DOES THIS RAISE COMPETITION LAW ISSUES?**

Summary

- There is no rule of EU law prohibiting interlocking directorships.

- However, interlocking directorships may give rise to competition law issues.

- In particular, an interlocking directorship could facilitate collusion.

- Interlocking directors and the relevant companies should have procedures in place to ensure that the risk of competition problems arising is minimised.

1.   A director or officer who sits on the boards of two different companies is often referred to as an interlocking director or officer. The question arises whether this creates an antitrust problem when the two companies are competitors or potential competitors.

2.   There is no rule of EU competition law preventing a board member of one company sitting on the board of a competitor company. However, such an arrangement may create competition law risks and it is important that the necessary precautions are taken to limit exposure to antitrust liability. Consideration should also be given to whether competition laws in individual Member States or outside the EU[341] specifically address the question of interlocking directorships (there are no specific competition rules prohibiting interlocking directorships in Ireland or the UK). Similarly, there may be corporate law rules and fiduciary duties issues at the national law level that need to be addressed.

What circumstances give rise to interlocking directorships?

3.   Interlocking directorships are not generally prevalent in industry but they are not unknown and interlocks have been fairly common in some sectors, such as banking and insurance. Where a company acquires a minority investment in a competitor, it may gain the right to nominate a member of the board. The minority shareholding may, in itself, lessen the incentives of both firms to compete vigorously against each other, thereby raising issues under the antitrust rules.[342] This effect may be exacerbated if each holds a minority share in the other (cross-

---

341. For example, in the United States, section 8 of the Clayton Act prohibits interlocking directors and officers in certain circumstances.

342. See, e.g., Cases 142 & 156/84 *British American Tobacco v Commission* [1987] ECR 4487, [1988] 4 CMLR 424, paras 37–39 (a minority investment in a competitor may 'serve as an instrument for influencing the commercial conduct of the companies'; this would be true in particular where the shareholding agreement provided for commercial cooperation between the two companies or created a structure likely to be used for such cooperation; this could result in a breach of Article 101); (contd \...)

shareholdings). Interlocking directorships in this situation may further add to the adverse impact on competition.

4.   Non-executive directors often sit on the boards of several companies and it may be that such a person ends up on the boards of two companies that compete against each other. Given the fast pace at which industry develops and markets evolve, a company that is not a competitor today may become one tomorrow.

5.   There are different types of arrangements that can be considered as interlocking directorships other than the simple scenario where one director sits on the board of two competing companies. For example, there may be a 'secondary interlock' where two directors of two different companies come together when they sit on the board of a third company.[343] Another example might be where two competitors enter into a production joint venture and a director from each firm sits on the board of the joint venture.

6.   Non-executive interlocking directorships should be less problematic than interlocks involving directors who are involved in the day to day running of a business. In general, interlocks involving directors or officers in such hands-on positions create significant risk and should be avoided.

What competition law issues might arise with interlocking directors?

7.   The principal concern is that the interlocking directorship could facilitate collusion. Inside knowledge can change the way a company behaves. The concern is that a person who serves on the boards of two competitors may act as a conduit for collusion or the exchange of competitively sensitive information. This could raise serious issues under Article 101. If one of the firms is dominant, Article 102 issues could also arise.

8.   Where the interlocking directorship leads to collusion, there will be little doubt that there is a competition law infringement. Even absent collusion, Article 101 could still be breached if certain types of information are exchanged. Information exchanges may allow the competitors to respond to each other's behaviour and in this way form the basis of a concerted practice or agreement that is contrary to Article 101. Whether competition issues arise will depend on the facts and one of the crucial elements is what exact information the interlocking director is exposed to and how that information is used. Any information that is competitively sensitive could raise issues.

9.   An interlocking directorship could also be pointed to by an antitrust authority as an ancillary method of supporting an anti-competitive agreement, where, for

---

342. (contd) IV/33.440 *Warner Lambert/Gillette* [1993] OJ L116/21 (the acquisition by a dominant company of a 22 per cent stake in a competitor gave rise to an abuse of dominance in breach of Article 102). Minority investments in competitors may give rise to 'control' within the meaning of the Merger Regulation if the minority shareholder has the possibility to exercise decisive influence over the target. See further Question 66.

343. See Wood, 'Interlocking Directorships – Measuring the Antitrust Risks' *Competition Law Insight* (September 2004).

example, it allows the interlocking director to monitor compliance with a price-fixing agreement between the two companies.

10. Interlocking directorships may be considered as a factor in attributing the market share of one undertaking to another for purposes of establishing a dominant position under Article 102.[344] Interlocks might also be a factor leading to a finding that two or more undertakings occupy a position of collective dominance in the context of Article 102.

What guidelines should interlocking directors follow to minimise antitrust risk?

11. Where interlocking directorships occur, appropriate measures should be taken to ensure that the relevant people are aware of the antitrust risks posed and proper guidelines should be put in place. This may involve a special briefing by a lawyer. The content of detailed guidelines should be tailored for the particular circumstances.

12. One of the biggest risks is that a regulator would argue that the interlock facilitated the exchange of competitively sensitive information which gave rise to a breach of Article 101. Any guidelines that are drawn up for the director should highlight the types of information the exchange of which is problematic, which could include:

- Prices.
- List prices.
- Price floors.
- Discounts.
- Methods by which discounts are determined.
- Surcharges.
- Other terms and conditions offered to customers.
- Price trends.
- Bids.
- Customer names or details.
- Names or details of distributors or suppliers.
- Markets into which the company sells or intends to sell.
- Margins.
- Costs.
- Plans about strategy, marketing etc.
- Any similar types of information.

---

344. See Cases 40/73 etc *Suiker Unie UA v Commission* [1975] ECR 1663, [1976] 1 CMLR 295, para 378.

How have interlocking directorships been treated in merger cases?

13.   Interlocking directorships (along with minority shareholdings) have been examined as part of the competitive assessment by the Commission of concentrations under the Merger Regulation. Typically, they have been assessed together with other factors rather than being the focus of the competitive assessment themselves.

14.   In a number of cases, the elimination or reduction of interlocking directorships has been one of the conditions for clearance of a merger. For example, in *Nordbanken/ Postgirot*, the Commission placed conditions on the clearance of the acquisition of Swedish bank Nordbanken of Postgirot, which owned and operated one of Sweden's two giro payment systems, the other of which, Bankgirot, was owned by a number of Swedish banks. Nordbanken was a shareholder in Bankgirot and was represented on its board. This would have given Nordbanken access to information and influence over the strategy of the only rival of a company that it was acquiring. As well as having to reduce its shareholding in Bankgirot to 10 per cent, Nordbanken agreed that all of its representatives on the boards, working groups and any other Bankgirot bodies would resign and that no commercial information available to those bodies would be made available to Nordbanken.[345]

15.   In *Generali/INA* the Commission was concerned that the transaction would lead to a dominant position in the life insurance sector in Italy. Clearance was made conditional on the parties eliminating some interlocking directorships with competing insurers and reducing others.[346]

16.   Other merger cases in which remedies have included the severing or reduction of interlocking directorships include *Thyssen/Krupp*[347], *Allianz/AFG*[348] and the determination of the Irish Competition Authority in *SRH/FM104*.[349]

What is the US approach to interlocking directors?

17.   It is worth briefly commenting on the US position as section 8 of the Clayton Act contains a specific interlocking director provision. It prohibits the same 'person' from serving as a director or officer of two competing corporations where each corporation meets certain financial thresholds.[350] The 'person' requirement can be met by either an individual director serving on both boards or a corporation that employs different individuals who sit on both boards. Historically, section 8 has

---

345.   COMP/M.2567 *Nordbanken/Postgirot*, Commission decision of 8 November 2001, para 60.

346.   COMP/M.1712 *Generali/INA*, Commission decision of 12 January 2000.

347.   COMP/M.1080 *Thyssen/Krupp*, Commission decision of 8 May 1998.

348.   COMP/M.1082 *Allianz/AFG*, Commission decision of 2 June 1998.

349.   M03/033 *Scottish Radio Holdings/Capital Radio Productions*, Determination of the Irish Competition Authority of 23 February 2004.

350.   See 15 USC § 19(a)(2). There is a *de minimis* threshold, updated annually, for the competitive sales of either corporation, which was $2,584,100 in 2010. Section 8 does not apply to banks, banking associations or trust companies but such entities are subject to the Depository Institution Management Interlocks Act, 12 USC §§ 3201–08.

not produced a great deal of litigation, one possible reason being that where concerns arise, the resignation of the interlocking director from one of the boards is a sufficient remedy.

18.   There have been recent high profile investigations with this result. For example, in 2009, two directors of Apple, who also sat on the board of Google, stepped down from Google's board following an investigation by the Federal Trade Commission.[351] While Apple and Google would not have been competitors historically, this changed with Google's development of an operating system that may compete with Apple's Mac OS X operating system and both companies have also been developing applications for mobile phones.

19.   It is doubtful as a practical matter that the US regulators would seek to enforce section 8 of the Clayton Act where the interlocks were in two non-US companies.

20.   As with Article 101 in the EU, interlocking directorships in the US may also raise issues under section 1 of the Sherman Act.

---

351. See 'Levinson Leaves Google Board Amid FTC Inquiry' *The New York Times*, 12 October 2009.

35. **WHAT SHOULD BE CONTAINED IN A COMPETITION LAW COMPLIANCE MANUAL?**

Why have a competition law compliance policy?

1. The adoption of a competition law compliance policy and compliance training should help to prevent breaches of competition law occurring in the first place.

2. Failure to comply with EU and national competition law can have serious consequences:

    *   Very high financial penalties – the Commission has imposed enormous fines on companies involved in cartel activity in recent years, for example:

Case	Total fines[352]	Largest individual fine
Car Glass (2008)	€1.4 billion on 4 companies	€896 million
Gas (2009)	€1.1 billion	€553 million
Elevators & Escalators (2007)	€992 million	€480 million
Vitamins (2001)	€790 million	€462 million
Gas Insulated Switchgear (2007)	€750 million	€396 million

    *   Criminal sanctions for individuals in certain countries, including in Ireland and the UK (up to 5 years imprisonment in each jurisdiction).

    *   Private damages actions brought by persons who suffered loss as a result of the anti-competitive conduct.

    *   Invalidity of agreements, as any agreement that breaches Article 101 or equivalent national rules may be declared void, in whole or in part.

    *   More indirect consequences such as loss of management time in dealing with an investigation, adverse press publicity etc.

3. The adoption of a competition law compliance manual or policy will not exempt a business from application of the competition rules. However, the fact that an undertaking has sought to prevent antitrust breaches through a compliance programme might be considered by the Commission as a mitigating factor in setting a fine (although it is not obliged to consider such factors in mitigation).[353]

4. The circulation of a competition law compliance manual within the company is not particularly effective on its own. The document may end up in a drawer and

---

352. Figures have been adjusted following court appeals, where relevant.
353. See, e.g., Case T–352/94 *Mo Och Domsjö AB v Commission* [1998] ECR II–1989, para 417.

never be read or taken seriously. There is no substitute for live training seminars, where issues can be discussed. The most effective programmes will not simply announce that price-fixing and cartels are illegal and will not be tolerated; rather, effective training should tackle the 'grey areas' that may not strike everyone as blatant breaches of the antitrust rules, e.g. the exchange of certain types of information with a competitor that is not as commercially sensitive as prices. The more open the discussion, the more effective the training will be.

5.   In an ongoing case before the English courts, a company that was fined for breach of competition law is seeking to recover the amount of the fine from the directors and employees who engaged in anti-competitive behaviour.[354] Whether the employees received competition law compliance training might be a relevant consideration in such cases.

What format should the company's competition law compliance policy take?

6.   Different companies adopt different kinds of competition law compliance policies and guidelines. The appropriate format of such a document will depend on the nature of the company's business, the markets in which it operates, the size of the organisation etc. It may be sensible to place emphasis on particular areas that are important for the company. For example, if the entirety of the company's business is carried out in bidding markets, then a detailed outline of competition issues that frequently arise in tenders may be useful. There is no 'one-size fits all' competition policy.

7.   A common goal of every company statement of competition law compliance is that it be read and understood by all those to whom it is addressed. Practical guidelines that avoid unnecessary legalese are likely to be more effective than a mini-treatise on Articles 101 and 102. The following is a sample draft competition law policy/guidelines. It is written in a fairly generic style. A more detailed document, tailored to specific circumstances, may be required in practice.

Antitrust Policy and Guidelines

Message from the Chief Executive

The Company is committed to the principles of free and fair competition and it is the Company's policy to comply with the competition and antitrust laws in all countries where we do business.

It is crucially important that all our employees are aware of the way in which competition laws impact on our business. A breach of these laws can have significant consequences, including potential imprisonment for individuals. Any person who breaches the relevant competition laws may be subject to disciplinary measures, including dismissal. It is the responsibility of each employee, director and officer to ensure that they comply with competition law.

---

354. See *Safeway Stores Limited v Twigger* [2010] EWHC 11 (Comm), [2010] Bus LR 974; Question 124.

I would ask you to familiarise yourself with our competition law policy contained in this document and by attending the training sessions that will be arranged by the legal department. It is very important that you fully understand your responsibilities. The success of our compliance policy is essential to the best interests of the Company and I therefore ask for your full support and cooperation in this sensitive area.

Madam X

CEO

About this document

(i) You should at all times be guided by this policy with respect to compliance with competition laws. If you have any doubts, it is your duty to seek advice from the Company's legal department. In complying with the policy, please consider the following:

DO	DO NOT
Study this document.	Put this document in a drawer and ignore it.
Report anything unusual.	Presume you know how to deal with every situation.
Follow procedures at all times.	Delay in reacting to a situation.

(ii) This document contains guidelines. They are obviously couched in general terms, as it would be impossible to develop guidelines that cover every situation that can arise. If you have any doubt or questions about a particular situation, please contact a member of the legal department at [*telephone number*].

The Company makes business decisions independently

(iii) In carrying out our business and in our dealings with customers, suppliers and other partners, the Company takes decisions independently and must be seen to do so. This is an important principle that you should keep in mind in reading this document.

(iv) In setting prices or other terms of sale, it is legitimate to take account of a competitor's price or term only if that information was obtained from a published price list or other legitimate source **but it can never be obtained from the competitor**. You must keep a record of the source of all price information about competitors that you obtain.

Sensitive Information

(v) There should not be any discussions or coordination of any type with competitors about commercially sensitive information, including:

- Prices

- Discounts

- Methods by which discounts are determined

- Other terms and conditions offered to customers

- Price trends

- Bids

- Customer names or details

- Names or details of distributors or suppliers

- Markets into which the company sells or intends to sell

- Margins

- Costs

- Plans about strategy, marketing etc.

- Any similar types of information

(vi) The above is not an exhaustive list of problematic information but gives you an indication of the most serious kinds of competition law violations, which include price fixing, bid rigging and market allocation.

(vii) Not only must you not discuss, provide or solicit commercially sensitive information, you must also not accept it if offered to you by a competitor.

Meetings with Competitors

(viii) If any sensitive information is discussed in the presence of a competitor, you should immediately interrupt to point out that it is the Company's policy never to discuss such matters with competitors and thereby bring the conversation to an end. If the matter persists, you should leave immediately, ensuring that any minute records your objection and departure (for example, if this arises in a trade association meeting). In all cases, you should also report the matter by calling a lawyer in the legal department.

(ix) Contacts with competitors should be kept to a minimum. Any proposed meetings with a competitor must have a legitimate purpose that is not commercially sensitive and must be discussed in advance with the legal department. If such a meeting is sanctioned, an agenda should be prepared in advance, discussions at the meeting should be confined to subjects on the agenda and a minute of the meeting kept. Meeting minutes produced by others should be read carefully and corrected if they are inaccurate.

(x) Where meetings take place in the context of a trade association, the above guidelines continue to apply. Be aware that the competition authorities place particular focus on trade association meetings and are sometimes suspicious that such meetings are used as a 'cover' to exchange sensitive information or engage in anti-competitive discussions. An agenda for trade association meetings should be agreed in advance, followed at the meeting and a minute of the meeting should be kept. Again, meeting minutes produced by others should be read carefully by you and corrected if they are inaccurate.

(xi) Where you encounter a competitor in another context, for example, at a social function, remember that these guidelines continue to apply fully. The regulators can point to a meeting in a bar or airport as the source of an anti-competitive exchange of information as equally as a formal meeting.

Legitimate business transactions with competitors

(xii) Occasionally, our business involves selling or purchasing quantities of stock to or from a competitor. If this need arises, any discussions and exchange of information must be limited to what is necessary for purposes of that particular transaction. You must not go beyond this and the above guidelines continue to apply.

Competition Law Training

(xiii) An integral part of the Company's competition law compliance involves the provision of training for staff.[355] Each relevant employee must be provided with a copy of this document as soon as possible and must be provided with appropriate training within 90 days of taking up their position. It is the responsibility of the director of each business unit to ensure this.

(xiv) Competition law training courses are arranged by the in-house legal department and take place four times a year. Employees should attend a training session at least every two years. Attendance records are maintained for these sessions.

(xv) Each employee must sign a certification every year which states that (i) they have read and understand the Company's competition law policy and guidelines; (ii) they have attended a competition law training session within the previous two years; and (iii) they are unaware of any instance of a possible breach of competition law or have reported any such matters to the legal department.

(xvi) Competition law audits of the various business units will be arranged by the legal department and carried out periodically.

Consulting the legal department

(xvii) As noted, these guidelines cannot hope to cover all situations that arise in practice. It is perfectly natural that you may have questions about the application of the competition rules to specific circumstances that arise from time to time. In these situations, please contact a lawyer in the legal department as quickly as possible and before proceeding with the matter before you. In some countries where we operate, written communications with in-house lawyers are not privileged so it is recommended that you make contact by telephone when you wish to discuss a competition law question. The legal department can be reached at [*telephone number*].

Specific guidelines for a dawn raid

The following procedures should be followed if the Company receives an unannounced inspection by a competition authority – a *dawn raid*.

---

355. In many businesses, competition law issues may not be relevant to certain technical staff, who could be exempted from training.

Dealing with the arrival of investigators – Reception and Security staff should take particular note

The team carrying out the dawn raid, whether from the European Commission or another authority, will likely arrive unannounced and will usually ask for a particular individual. They will not necessarily ask to see a Company lawyer. So, in addition to contacting the person they request, **you should contact the legal department immediately** to inform them of the situation.

You should check the identity of the investigators by asking them to produce formal identification.

You should ask the investigators to wait in the reception area until the person they have asked to see has arrived. However, if the investigators have a warrant, they cannot be prevented from entering and remaining in offices of their choice. If they insist on entering offices, you should not obstruct them but ensure that they are accompanied at all times by a member of our staff.

Guidelines aimed at in-house lawyers

You should call our external competition lawyers immediately and arrange for them to arrive promptly at the Company.

You should check the investigators' authority to conduct the raid. This will be a notice setting out the subject matter and purpose of the investigation. If they do not have such a document or if it is irregular in any way, they should be asked to leave.

You should ask the investigators to wait until external lawyers arrive before beginning the raid. The investigators may or may not agree to this but are unlikely to wait more than half an hour before requiring access to offices and files. The in-house team should use this time to deal with uncontroversial matters such as describing the Company's internal organisation or identifying the executives who are to deal with the investigators' inquiries.

Assuming that it is not open to challenge, study the authorisation document produced by the investigators. Discuss it with them to ensure that you understand its scope and what documents and files are relevant to it and which ones are outside its scope.

You should produce all relevant documents and files that are relevant to the subject matter of the investigation as set out in the authorisation. The investigators can access computers, emails and other electronically stored data and may ask for passwords. You should be cooperative in providing them with this information.

Keep a note of all documents and files that the investigators copy and get them to sign this note. The investigators may ask to remove original documents in certain cases. You should never allow them to do this unless you first have the opportunity to copy the documents.

Investigators may ask for oral explanations but they are not entitled to ask questions about behaviour not revealed on the face of documents. Any answers you give should be brief. If you do not know the answer or cannot give a brief answer, decline to answer and offer to supply the information later in writing. If possible, you should not answer questions without an outside lawyer being present.

You may ask for your answers to be minuted and you are entitled to a copy of the investigator's minute. Ensure such minutes are consistent with your own notes. Be aware that anything you say might be used in evidence.

As a general rule, you are entitled to withhold communications to or from the Company's external legal advisors. If the investigation is being carried out by the OFT in the UK or the Competition Authority in Ireland and is not an investigation directed by the Commission, you may also withhold communications with in-house legal advisors.

After the raid, review the notes of the proceedings and documents given to the investigators. Follow up any incomplete or unanswered questions and correct any inaccuracies in the information given.

Officials also have the power to enter domestic premises and so can enter an employee's home if business documents (including on computers or other electronic devices) are kept there. A warrant has to be produced. If officials have reasonable grounds to believe that an employee's personal vehicle contains relevant information, a warrant could be obtained to search the vehicle. If faced with a raid on personal property, the above guidelines should be followed where possible.

36. MAY A NUMBER OF COMPETITORS AGREE TOGETHER TO PURCHASE PRODUCTS FROM ONLY ONE SUPPLIER?

Summary

Joint purchasing is often pro-competitive, allowing undertakings to obtain better terms than would be available to individual purchasers.

If the joint purchasers are not competitors downstream, Article 101 will usually not apply.

If the arrangement is really a disguised cartel, it will be condemned under Article 101.

In many cases, a more detailed analysis under Article 101 has to be carried out. The following factors may be relevant:

- Competitive effects should be considered in both the purchasing market and the downstream selling market.

- Where the combined share is less than 15 per cent in each of these markets, anti-competitive effects are unlikely.

- Restrictions (e.g. minimum purchasing requirements) should not go beyond what is necessary to ensure the joint purchasing arrangement functions properly.

- If the joint purchasers have buyer power, concerns may include:

  - Savings are not passed on to customers downstream;

  - Competitors on the selling markets face cost increases as suppliers seek to recoup the discounts given to the joint purchasers;

  - The joint purchasers have an incentive to coordinate behaviour downstream, a particular concern if they achieve a high level of commonality of costs through joint purchasing;

  - Foreclosure of competitors, raising of rivals' costs.

- If the agreement is caught by Article 101(1), the Article 101(3) exemption may be applicable.

Vertical agreements that arise out of the joint purchasing agreement should be considered separately.

1. Joint purchasing involves two or more undertakings coming together to make purchases, whether through a joint purchasing company, an association or more informal cooperation. It may involve the joint purchasing of goods for resale or joint purchasing of raw materials. It can take the form of an agreement on what prices the purchasers are prepared to pay or an agreement to purchase wholly or mainly through the joint arrangements.[356]

---

356. See Bellamy & Child (6th edn, 2008) para 5.124.

2. If the purchasers are not in competition with each other downstream, Article 101 does not usually apply, unless they have a particularly strong position on the purchasing market so that adverse effects on competition are created on that market.[357]

3. At the other end of the scale, if the joint purchasing arrangement does not truly concern joint purchasing but, rather, is used as a front for a cartel, it will be treated as such and will by its object breach Article 101(1) with no realistic possibility of exemption under Article 101(3).[358] In *Raw Tobacco Italy*, the Commission imposed fines totalling €56 million on four Italian tobacco processors in respect of their operation of a buyer's cartel through which they colluded on their overall purchasing strategy, agreeing purchase prices and allocating suppliers, as well as rigging bids in public auctions.[359] It may not always be clear whether a particular agreement really involves legitimate joint purchasing or a buyer's cartel.[360]

4. Apart from these two extremes, joint purchasing is often pro-competitive. It is usually aimed at the creation of buying power which can lead to lower prices for consumers. The fact that joint purchasing agreements are often pro-competitive may partly explain the dearth of competition cases dealing with the question.[361] While suppliers to joint purchasers sometimes ask if there is a competition argument to attack what they may see as an arrangement by purchasers which 'squeezes' them, such cases are often difficult to make out in practice.

5. However, if the firms engaging in joint purchasing have market power, joint purchasing may produce anti-competitive effects and be caught by Article 101. The agreement should be analysed in its legal and economic context and the availability of the Article 101(3) exemption should be considered. As well as the horizontal element of the joint purchasing agreement, the vertical element with suppliers should also be assessed under Article 101.

---

357. See Commission 2001 Horizontal Cooperation Guidelines [2001] OJ C3/2, para 24; *P&I Clubs, IGA* [1999] OJ L125/12, [1999] 5 CMLR 646, para 66.

358. See Commission 2001 Horizontal Cooperation Guidelines [2001] OJ C3/2, para 124.

359. COMP/38.281 *Raw Tobacco Italy* [2006] OJ L353/45 (on appeal with respect to fines, Case T–11/06 *Romana Tabacchi v Commission*, Case T–12/06 *Deltafina v Commission*).

360. See *R (Cityhook Ltd) v Office of Fair Trading* [2009] EWHC 57 (Admin), [2009] UKCLR 255, para 58 (an OFT case review panel thought that an arrangement concerned joint purchasing but a case team strongly disagreed and thought the arrangement was a buyer's cartel; see also the discussion of collective boycotts by Foskett J at paras 126–142).

361. A number of earlier decisions of the Irish Competition Authority dealt with joint purchasing. See, e.g., Dec No 354 *Musgraves Ltd./Licensee and Franchise Agreements*, Competition Authority Decision of 19 September 1994 (exclusive purchasing arrangement with elements of joint buying met the conditions for a license under section 4(2) of the Competition Act 1991); Dec No 578 *Dublin Institute of Technology Joint Purchasing Agreement*, Competition Authority Decision of 28 January 2000 (joint purchasing agreement did not breach section 4(1) of the Competition Act 1991 given the very small market share of the joint purchasers and the fact that suppliers were not prevented from negotiating individually with the purchasers).

6.   Effects on competition in two different markets should be considered: (i) the purchasing market in which the cooperation takes place; and (ii) the downstream market, where the joint buyers are active as sellers.

7.   If the combined share of the parties in each of these markets is less than 15 per cent, it is unlikely that the joint purchasing arrangement would fall within the Article 101(1) prohibition and even if did, at this level of market power, the Article 101(3) exemption would usually apply.[362] If the joint purchasers are not active on the same relevant market downstream, Article 101(1) will rarely apply unless they have significant market power in the purchasing market, which could be used to harm the position of other players in their respective selling markets.[363]

What are the main competition concerns with joint purchasing?

8.   Concerns about joint purchasing arise where the purchasers have a sufficient degree of market power. One concern is that lower prices obtained through joint purchasing will not be passed on to customers downstream. The more market power that joint purchasers enjoy on the downstream selling market, the greater their incentive to coordinate their behaviour as sellers. This may be facilitated where the products that are jointly purchased represent a significant proportion of the costs of the product to be sold downstream. The joint purchasing will then result in a high degree of commonality of costs among the competitors (also a potential problem with joint production).[364]

9.   This was the situation in the *Sulphuric Acid* case. Producers of sulphuric acid formed a buying pool to purchase sulphur, which accounted for up to 80 per cent of the production cost of sulphuric acid. The 'equalising effect' of the joint purchasing arrangement on the price of sulphur was felt in the price of sulphuric acid and other products of which sulphuric acid was a constituent chemical. Price competition was largely eliminated between the members of the purchasing pool selling sulphuric acid. Although Article 101(1) was invoked, the arrangement was exempted under Article 101(3).[365]

10. If the joint purchasing agreement does not have a particularly close or direct connection with the product or service supplied downstream, there is unlikely to be a commonality of costs issue and this may support the argument that the agreement should not be caught by Article 101(1). An example might be where a number of private hospitals form a joint purchasing group to buy computers.[366]

---

362. Commission 2001 Horizontal Cooperation Guidelines [2001] OJ C3/2, para 130; Commission 2010 Draft Horizontal Cooperation Guidelines SEC(2010) 528/2, para 203.

363. See Commission 2001 Horizontal Cooperation Guidelines [2001] OJ C3/2, para 123.

364. See the example given by the Commission at para 217 of the Commission 2010 Draft Horizontal Cooperation Guidelines SEC(2010) 528/2, noting that an agreement between two retailers, with a combined share of 25–40 per cent on the purchasing market and 60 per cent on the selling market, to jointly purchase products amounting to 80 per cent of their costs would likely provide the retailers with the ability to coordinate their behaviour on the selling market, where entry by new competitors into that market is not likely. This purchasing agreement would be unlikely to fulfil the conditions for the application of Article 101(3).

365. *National Sulphuric Acid Association* [1980] OJ L260/24, [1980] 3 CMLR 429.

366. Cf US Department of Justice and Federal Trade Commission Statements of Antitrust Enforcement Policy in Health Care (August 1996) s 7.

11. Another concern with joint purchasing may arise when competitors of the joint purchasers face cost increases, for example because a supplier tries to recover price reductions to the joint purchasing group by increasing prices to other purchasers. There is also a risk that joint purchasers with market power on the purchasing market will force suppliers to reduce the range or quality of products they produce, which may lead to anti-competitive effects such as quality reductions, lessening of innovation efforts or ultimately sub-optimal supply.[367] In assessing the level of market power enjoyed by the joint purchasers, the number and intensity of links between them will be relevant.[368]

12. Significant buying power among the joint purchasers may also lead to foreclosure of competing buyers by limiting their access to efficient suppliers. This further weakens competition in the downstream selling market. The Commission considers that such foreclosure is only possible if there are a limited number of suppliers and there are barriers to entry on the supply side of the upstream market.[369]

13. A further concern is that the exchange of information between the parties to a joint purchasing agreement may facilitate coordination with regard to sales prices and output and thereby lead to a collusive outcome on the selling market.[370]

14. These examples illustrate the interdependencies between the purchasing and selling markets and explain why competitive effects in both markets must be considered.[371] A challenge to a joint purchasing agreement under Article 101 may be more credible where significant interdependencies between the purchasing market and the selling market can be shown.

How are restrictions placed on the parties to the agreement considered?

15. Other important factors in considering the application of Article 101 include whether the participants are free to obtain supplies other than through the joint purchasing agreement and any ancillary restrictive practices. Restrictions included as part of a joint purchasing agreement should not go beyond what is necessary to ensure that the agreement functions properly. In *Gøttrup-Klim*, the Court of Justice found that a purchasing cooperative was not caught by Article 101(1) even though its members could not participate in competing forms of cooperation and were therefore discouraged from obtaining supplies elsewhere. The members of the cooperative had limited purchasing power and so the restriction was justifiable in order to make the agreement effective; it did not 'go beyond what is necessary to ensure that the cooperative functions properly and maintains its contractual power in relation to producers'.[372]

---

367. Commission 2010 Draft Horizontal Cooperation Guidelines SEC(2010) 528/2, para 197.
368. Commission 2010 Draft Horizontal Cooperation Guidelines SEC(2010) 528/2, para 206.
369. Commission 2010 Draft Horizontal Cooperation Guidelines SEC(2010) 528/2, para 198.
370. Commission 2010 Draft Horizontal Cooperation Guidelines SEC(2010) 528/2, para 210.
371. See Commission 2001 Horizontal Cooperation Guidelines [2001] OJ C3/2, paras 128–129.
372. Case C–250/92 *Gøttrup-Klim v Dansk Landbrugs Grovvareselskab AmbA* [1994] ECR I– 5641, [1996] 4 CMLR 191, para 40.

16. The Commission adopted a similar approach in *P&I Clubs*, in holding that there was no restriction of competition where the members of a pooling agreement for insurance were not actual or potential competitors because they were unable to insure alone the risks covered by the pool. The Commission found that the restrictions imposed on the parties, including the requirement that they jointly purchase reinsurance, were indispensable to the proper functioning of the claim sharing agreement (without the joint purchase of reinsurance, most of the clubs would not have been able to obtain reinsurance up to the level that was obtained jointly) and were not covered by Article 101(1).[373]

17. If a joint purchasing agreement is contrary to Article 101(1), the indispensability of the restrictions contained in the agreement will be one of the four conditions to be satisfied for the Article 101(3) exemption to apply.

Is countervailing supplier power relevant?

18. If the joint purchasers face suppliers who have significant market power, this may be a factor in the Article 101 assessment. Supplier power was considered by the Commission in the *Eurovision* case, which examined the compatibility with Article 101 of the European Broadcasting Union, composed of public service broadcasters who jointly acquired television rights. The Commission noted the holders of broadcasting rights to sporting events were often 'rather powerful' and 'in an extremely strong situation with regard to television rights' and that this had resulted in a transfer of profits away from the broadcasters and towards upstream rights owners.[374] The Commission granted an exemption under Article 101(3) but this decision was overturned on appeal.

How is the vertical element assessed?

19. Even if the horizontal aspect of the joint purchasing agreement does not breach Article 101, it should also be examined whether the vertical aspects of the agreement create competition difficulties. This could arise, for example, where the joint purchasers agree to buy exclusively from a particular supplier and competing suppliers are foreclosed from a significant part of the market. In this case, the vertical agreement between the joint purchaser and supplier that might breach Article 101.[375]

How is Article 101(3) applied to joint purchasing agreements?

20. A joint purchasing agreement that is caught by Article 101(1) may well be exempted under Article 101(3), in particular in light of efficiencies it may

---

373. See *P&I Clubs, IGA* [1999] OJ L125/12, [1999] 5 CMLR 646, paras 67, 82–84.
374. Case IV/32.150 – *Eurovision* [2000] OJ L151/18, paras 52–53 (annulled on appeal on other grounds, Case T–185/00 *Métropole Télévision SA (M6) v Commission* [2002] ECR II–3805, [2003] 4 CMLR 707; subsequent appeal dismissed, Case C–470/02P *Union européenne de radio-télévision (UER) v Commission* [2004] OJ C314/2).
375. See Question 44 on the assessment of vertical agreements.

generate. Purchasing agreements can lead to cost savings, facilitate economies of scale and ultimately result in lower prices for consumers.

21. The availability of the Article 101(3) exemption will depend on factors such as the structure of the market and the restrictive nature of the agreement. The four cumulative conditions for application of Article 101(3) must be satisfied.[376]

22. The combined market shares of the parties are an important factor. A fair share of the economic benefits of the agreement must be passed on to customers for the exemption to apply. This is less likely to occur where the parties have significant market power on the selling markets.[377]

23. If the parties are obliged to source all or most of their supplies through the joint purchasing agreement, this may negate the exemption, unless this element of exclusivity is required to make the agreement worthwhile. In *Sulphuric Acid*, the Commission considered that the requirement of members of a purchasing pool to source at least 25 per cent of their requirements of sulphur through the pool was 'a restriction without which the Pool's strong negotiating position with the suppliers would be eroded to too great an extent'.[378] It was therefore compatible with Article 101(3).

24. Other restrictions that are not truly necessary, such as a restriction on how the purchased products can be used or restrictions on resale, will negate the application of the Article 101(3) exemption.

25. Finally, a joint purchasing agreement that distorts the structure of demand in the market, for example by imposing a maximum purchase price on members, may negate the application of the Article 101(3) exemption.[379]

Key Sources

Commission's Guidelines on the applicability of Article 81 of the EC Treaty to horizontal cooperation agreements [2001] OJ C 3/2, paras 115–138.

Draft Commission Guidelines on the on the applicability of Article 101 of the Treaty on the Functioning of the European Union to horizontal co-operation agreements SEC(2010) 528/2, paras 189–219.

Decision 80/917 *National Sulphuric Acid Association* [1980] OJ L260/24, [1980] 3 CMLR 429.

Case C–250/92 *Gøttrup-Klim v Dansk Landbrugs Grovvareselskab AmbA* [1994] ECR I–5641, [1996] 4 CMLR 191.

P&I Clubs, IGA [1999] OJ L125/12, [1999] 5 CMLR 646.

---

376. See Question 21.
377. Commission 2001 Horizontal Cooperation Guidelines [2001] OJ C3/2, para 132; Commission 2010 Draft Horizontal Cooperation Guidelines SEC(2010) 528/2, para 214.
378. Decision 80/917 *National Sulphuric Acid Association* [1980] OJ L260/24, [1980] 3 CMLR 429, para 49.
379. See, e.g., *Belgian Industrial Timber,* Commission Fifth Report on Competition Policy (1975) paras 36–37.

37. How are joint selling agreements treated under Article 101?

Summary

- Joint selling that results in the fixing of prices or the allocation of markets will generally be considered to give rise to a restriction of competition by object within the meaning of Article 101(1).

- If the agreement does not have an anti-competitive object, its effect on competition must be examined. If the combined market share of the participants is below 15 per cent, it is unlikely that Article 101(1) applies. If the parties have market power, the economic impact of the agreement needs to be considered.

- Particular areas of concern in joint selling agreements include information exchanges that produce a collusive outcome and commonality of costs affecting the scope for price competition.

- If the agreement falls within Article 101(1), it may still benefit from Article 101(3).

1. Companies may engage in joint selling to generate efficiencies in the distribution of their goods. This might be done by setting up a joint sales company, agency or sales office, by competitors agreeing to distribute each other's products or through some other similar form of cooperation. Such agreements are sometimes used to facilitate the entry into a new geographic market.[380] Joint selling may extend to joint determination of all aspects of selling goods, including setting prices, or it may be more limited in nature, encompassing only aspects such as distribution, after-sales service or advertising. The Commission considers all of these arrangements under the rubric of 'commercialisation agreements'.[381]

2. Joint selling by undertakings that are not actual or potential competitors in the products covered by the agreement will not breach Article 101 (although if the agreement contains vertical restraints, these would need to be assessed separately).[382] This might arise, for example, if two companies arrange joint sales of complementary products that do not compete.

3. In its 2010 Draft Horizontal Cooperation Guidelines, the Commission identifies four main competition concerns with joint selling agreements:

    - Price fixing.

    - Market allocation.

---

380. See Question 38.
381. Commission 2001 Horizontal Cooperation Guidelines [2001] OJ C3/2, para 139; Commission 2010 Draft Horizontal Cooperation Guidelines SEC(2010) 528/2, para 220. Two particular aspects of commercialisation agreements, the legitimacy of using joint selling to break into a new geographic area and the joint selling of media rights to sporting events, are considered in Questions 38 and 40 respectively.
382. Commission 2001 Horizontal Cooperation Guidelines [2001] OJ C3/2, paras 24, 143.

- Output limitation.

- Information exchanges resulting in a collusive outcome.[383]

4.   The Commission suggests that where the agreement involves price fixing or market allocation, it is likely to restrict competition by object and fall squarely within Article 101(1), regardless of the market power of the parties. The Commission takes a sceptical view of such joint selling agreements that extend to fixing sales prices:

> A major competition concern about a commercialisation agreement between competitors is price fixing. Agreements limited to joint selling generally have the object of coordinating the pricing policy of competing manufacturers or service providers. In this case they not only eliminate price competition between the parties on substitute products but also restrict the total volume of products to be delivered by the parties within the framework of a system for allocating orders. Such agreements are therefore likely to have as their object a restriction of competition within the meaning of Article 101(1).[384]

5.   Joint distribution agreements may result in market partitioning, in particular in reciprocal arrangements (the parties distribute each other's products) where the parties are active in different geographic markets and deliberately allocate markets or customers between them. Such agreements are also generally considered to have an anti-competitive object. If the agreement is not reciprocal, it is less likely to have the object of restricting competition but it should still be considered whether the agreement is a basis for a mutual understanding between the parties that they will avoid entering each other's markets.[385] If the market or customer allocation is objectively necessary for the parties to enter each other's markets, it can be argued that the agreement does not have an anti-competitive object and may even fall outside Article 101(1) altogether.[386]

6.   Despite the Commission's suggestion that joint selling agreements involving price fixing or market allocation will give rise to a restriction of competition by object, it may not always be clear whether a joint sales agency or sales joint venture will be considered as falling squarely within Article 101(1). On one view, an agreement which results in a joint price being set clearly involves 'price fixing' and this is indicated by the Commission in the examples it provides in its guidelines.[387] However, in rejecting a complaint that the *Opodo* online travel portal

---

383. Commission 2010 Draft Horizontal Cooperation Guidelines SEC(2010) 528/2, paras 225–228.

384. Commission 2010 Draft Horizontal Cooperation Guidelines SEC(2010) 528/2, para 229. A similar statement was made in the Commission 2001 Horizontal Cooperation Guidelines [2001] OJ C3/2, para 144.

385. Commission 2010 Draft Horizontal Cooperation Guidelines SEC(2010) 528/2, para 231.

386. Commission 2001 Horizontal Cooperation Guidelines [2001] OJ C3/2, para 147; Commission 2010 Draft Horizontal Cooperation Guidelines SEC(2010) 528/2, para 232–233.

387. Commission 2001 Horizontal Cooperation Guidelines [2001] OJ C3/2, para 157; Commission 2010 Draft Horizontal Cooperation Guidelines SEC(2010) 528/2, paras 247–250.

joint venture among nine European airlines breached Article 101(1), the Commission distinguished the arrangement from a 'joint selling joint venture', the mere creation of which would lead to the coordination of the competitive behaviour of its shareholders.[388] This was not the case with Opodo, as marketing and other agreements with the participating airlines were negotiated separately and kept confidential. Opodo was not by any means the sole source of distribution for the airlines and there was no evidence that the airlines would seek to channel their sales through Opodo given the options of travel agents and direct selling which continued to apply.[389] In another example, in *UEFA Champions League*, the Commission treated 'price fixing' by a joint selling entity not as a restriction with an anti-competitive object but rather one with an anti-competitive effect.[390]

7.   If the agreement does not restrict competition by object, it should be examined whether its effect is anti-competitive. The agreement is unlikely to fall within Article 101(1) where the parties' combined market share is not more than 15 per cent.[391] Above that level, the agreement should be assessed in its legal and economic context in considering if it is caught by Article 101(1) and can benefit from Article 101(3). The nature of the agreement together with other structural factors in the relevant market are relevant.

8.   Concerns may arise because the arrangement leads to the exchange of commercially sensitive information. The likely restrictive effects on competition of information exchange will depend on the characteristics of the market and the data shared.[392] Another concern is that by making common a significant input to the parties' cost base, the scope for price competition in the market is limited.[393] This could be the case if marketing and distribution account for a significant part of the cost of a particular product.

9.   Restrictions may be placed on the parties to the joint selling arrangement, for example, clauses requiring exclusive supply or the payment of exit fees. To avoid falling within Article 101(1), such restrictions must be limited to what is necessary to ensure that the arrangement functions properly and in particular to ensure that it has a sufficiently wide commercial base and a certain stability in its

---

388. Case COMP/A.38321/D2 – *TQ3 Travel Solutions GmbH/Opodo Limited*. The Commission decision of 9 December 2002 rejecting the complaint is available on the Commission's website.

389. The Commission therefore distinguished the Opodo case from *SCPA – Kali und Salz* [1973] OJ L 217/3 and *Floral* [1980] OJ L39/51, [1980] 2 CMLR 285. See also the discussion in Van Bael & Bellis, *Competition Law of the European Community* (5th edn, 2010) 485–486.

390. COMP/C.2–37.398 *Joint selling of the commercial rights of the UEFA Champions League* [2003] OJ L291/25, [2004] 4 CMLR 9, para 114 (the Commission did not explain why the arrangement was considered a restriction of competition by effect rather than by object).

391. Commission 2010 Draft Horizontal Cooperation Guidelines SEC(2010) 528/2, para 235; Commission 2001 Horizontal Cooperation Guidelines [2001] OJ C3/2, para 149.

392. Commission 2010 Draft Horizontal Cooperation Guidelines SEC(2010) 528/2, para 240.

393. Commission 2010 Draft Horizontal Cooperation Guidelines SEC(2010) 528/2, paras 237–240. Commission 2001 Horizontal Cooperation Guidelines [2001] OJ C3/2, para 146.

membership.[394] The indispensability of restrictions is also relevant when considering the application of Article 101(3).

10. If the agreement falls within the Article 101(1) prohibition, it should be examined whether the Article 101(3) exemption can be claimed. Joint selling agreements may generate significant efficiencies so the Article 101(3) exemption may be available in many cases. The four cumulative conditions for application of Article 101(3) must be satisfied.[395] These include that restrictions must not go beyond what is necessary to achieve efficiency gains. The efficiency gains that can be taken into account in assessing a joint selling agreement under Article 101(3) will depend on the nature of the activity. The Commission has noted that joint distribution is more likely to generate significant efficiencies for producers of widely distributed consumer products than for producers of industrial products that are bought by a limited number of customers.[396] The Commission has stated that price fixing or market allocation will be considered indispensible only under exceptional circumstances.[397]

Key Sources

Commission's Guidelines on the applicability of Article 81 of the EC Treaty to horizontal cooperation agreements [2001] OJ C 3/2, paras 139–158.

Draft Commission Guidelines on the on the applicability of Article 101 of the Treaty on the Functioning of the European Union to horizontal co-operation agreements SEC(2010) 528/2, paras 220–251.

Case COMP/A.38321/D2 – *TQ3 Travel Solutions GmbH/Opodo Limited.*

---

394. See Case C–399/93 *Oude Luttikhuis v Verenigde Coöperatieve Melkindustrie Coberco BA* [1995] ECR I–4515, [1996] 5 CMLR 178, paras 14–16 (joint selling by a milk cooperative).
395. See Question 21.
396. See Commission 2001 Horizontal Cooperation Guidelines [2001] OJ C3/2, para 151.
397. Commission 2010 Draft Horizontal Cooperation Guidelines SEC(2010) 528/2, para 244.

38. IS IT LEGITIMATE FOR COMPETITORS TO COOPERATE THROUGH A JOINT SELLING AGREEMENT IN ORDER TO BREAK INTO A MARKET IN A DIFFERENT GEOGRAPHIC REGION?

Summary

- If the agreement results in the joint setting of prices, it will almost always come within Article 101(1).

- If the evidence shows that the parties would not have entered the new market without joint selling, this may bring the agreement outside Article 101(1). This will depend on the circumstances and the nature of any restrictions.

- The beneficial effects of joint selling, such as savings on distribution costs, may be relevant to the application of Article 101(3).

- The use of joint selling to enter the EU market will be assessed under Article 101. Joint selling used for exporting outside the EU will not usually be subject to Article 101 but may be caught by the antitrust laws of other jurisdictions.

1. The first issue that should be checked in assessing the joint selling agreement is whether the parties are in fact competitors. If they are not actual or potential competitors, Article 101 is unlikely to apply.

2. Assuming the parties are competitors, then the agreement should be analysed under Article 101. The argument that without the joint selling agreement, the parties would not be able to enter the new geographic market, may be relevant but does not provide a categorical defence of the agreement in itself. According to the Commission, where the agreement involves 'price fixing' or market allocation, it will generally be considered to restrict competition by object within the meaning of Article 101(1).[398] If the agreement falls short of jointly setting prices or allocating markets, it will only be subject to Article 101(1) where the parties have market power. If so, the overall impact of the agreement on the market must be analysed.

3. With respect to what market should market power be assessed? Say that joint sales will only be made in a particular geographic market (Region Y) where, at present, none of the parties to the agreement have any sales. It could be argued that they have no market power in Region Y and so the agreement should not be caught by Article 101(1). However, the likely approach of the Commission would be that the parties are at least potential competitors in Region Y and therefore Article 101 does apply.[399] An argument that might be available in defence of the agreement is that the parties would never enter Region Y unless they were able to cooperate

---

398. Commission 2010 Draft Horizontal Cooperation Guidelines SEC(2010) 528/2, paras 229–231.
399. Cf the example given at para 158 of the Commission 2001 Horizontal Cooperation Guidelines [2001] OJ C3/2.

through a joint selling agreement, as entry would be too costly to pursue on an individual basis.

4. In *Floral*, the three largest compound fertilizer producers in France set up a company to sell their products in Germany. The parties argued that before the joint distribution agreement, their exports to Germany had been negligible, the cost of carriage was a natural barrier to exporting alone and that use of the joint network would save on distribution costs.

5. The Commission, rejecting these arguments, found that in the absence of the joint selling agreement, the three companies could offer compound fertilizers for sale in Germany in competition with each other. Undertakings of the size involved were not forced to cooperate with each other to establish sales in Germany. They had adequate output available for sale and plants that were capable of supplying for export to Germany and they had already shown that they had the requisite know-how and resources to market their fertilizers in other EU countries independently of each other. While there was no explicit agreement to sell all their products bound for the German market through the company, this is what occurred. Whereas the producers sold their products to the joint selling company at different prices, the end price established in Germany for each party's products was the same. Competition was therefore eliminated and Article 101(1) infringed. There were no countervailing benefits to warrant an exemption under Article 101(3) for an agreement such as this in an oligopolistic market. In particular, there was no evidence of beneficial effects in distribution that might offset the restriction of competition.[400]

6. Where the joint selling agreement is truly necessary to enable one or more parties to enter a new market, then the agreement is unlikely to raise issues. As the Commission notes in its 2010 draft guidelines:

    > A commercialisation agreement is normally not likely to create competition concerns if it is objectively necessary to allow one party to enter a market it could not have entered individually or with a more limited number of parties than the ones effectively taking part in the co-operation, e.g., because of the costs involved.[401]

Can joint selling agreements outside the EU be caught by Article 101?

7. Agreements by companies outside the EU to establish a joint selling arrangement in the EU can also be caught by Article 101(1). In *Asnac* the Commission found that an agreement by six US producers of soda ash to jointly export natural soda ash through the Ansac company, at uniform prices and conditions, breached Article 101. An exemption was not available, the Commission taking the view that the companies were capable of marketing their products individually in the EU.[402]

---

400. *Floral* [1980] OJ L39/51, [1980] 2 CMLR 285.
401. Commission 2010 Draft Horizontal Cooperation Guidelines SEC(2010) 528/2, para 232.
402. *Ansac* [1991] OJ L152/54.

8.   Joint selling in respect of export markets outside the EU will not usually infringe Article 101 provided there is no ban on re-importation.[403] The Commission has approved agreements for the joint marketing of goods outside the EU.[404] In some circumstances, EU law may not have jurisdiction over such agreements. However, the agreement might be subject to antitrust rules in jurisdictions outside the EU.

Key Sources

Floral [1980] OJ L39/51, [1980] 2 CMLR 285.

Ansac [1991] OJ L152/54.

Cobelaz/Fébelaz [1986] OJ L276/13.

---

403. But see *Centraal Stikstof Verkoopkantoor* [1978] OJ L242/15 which involved a joint selling arrangement in respect of both the Dutch market and export markets. In finding that the arrangement breached Article 101, the Commission did not appear to draw a distinction between its effects on the Dutch market and the export markets. Bellamy & Child (6th edn, 2008) at para 5.108 suggest that the Commission left open the possibility of the application of Article 101 to joint sales arrangements for resale to third countries.
404. See *Cobelaz/Fébelaz* [1986] OJ L276/13.

39. IS IT LEGITIMATE FOR COMPETITORS TO ENGAGE IN A JOINT ADVERTISING CAMPAIGN?

Summary

- The competitive assessment of joint advertising agreements is similar to joint selling agreements.

- The main concern is that the agreement will lead to the coordination of pricing or otherwise limit competition.

- Joint advertising that disparages competing goods and encourages consumers to purchase a product from one particular Member State may breach Article 101.

1. The Commission views joint advertising agreements as part of the broader category of 'commercialisation agreements' along with joint selling. The main antitrust concern with joint advertising is the same as with joint selling – that such agreements lead to the coordination of prices or, by making common a significant cost, limit the scope for price competition.[405] In certain industries, joint advertising may lead to users' impression of a homogenous product where individual advertising would have allowed product differentiation and fostered competition.[406]

2. If the parties do not have market power, which is likely to be the case where their combined market share is less than 15 per cent, joint advertising that does not include price fixing will not usually be caught by Article 101.[407] Otherwise, the competitive effects of the agreement in its legal and economic context should be analysed.

3. One of the leading cases on joint advertising is *Milchförderungsfonds*.[408] The German dairy industry set up a fund, which promoted the export of milk and other dairy products and used subsidised sales and brand advertising campaigns for this purpose. Both of these methods were found to infringe Article 101(1) by artificially strengthening the position of the German dairies in markets in the EU vis-à-vis their competitors. The Commission drew a distinction between generic and brand advertising – the former was acceptable as it benefited all dairy producers but in this case, the promotion of the German products had the effect of discouraging consumers from buying non-German products. Had the advertising promoted special characteristics of the products, even if those features were typically German, there would not have been an anti-competitive effect. It seems

---

405. Commission 2001 Horizontal Cooperation Guidelines [2001] OJ C3/2, para 146; Commission 2010 Draft Horizontal Cooperation Guidelines SEC(2010) 528/2, para 238.

406. See *Roofing Felt* [1986] OJ L232/15, [1991] 4 CMLR 130, paras 72, 74 (upheld on appeal, Case 246/86 *Belasco v Commission* [1989] ECR 2117, [1991] 4 CMLR 96).

407. See Commission 2001 Horizontal Cooperation Guidelines [2001] OJ C3/2, para 149; Commission 2010 Draft Horizontal Cooperation Guidelines SEC(2010) 528/2, para 235.

408. *Milchförderungsfonds* [1985] OJ L35/35, [1985] 3 CMLR 101.

then that joint advertising that disparages competing goods and adversely affects the internal market may be particularly problematic under Article 101.

4.   The Commission has noted that restrictions placed on advertising may limit an important aspect of competition. In *Vimpoltu,* the Commission found that a decision of a trade association, by which importers of Dutch tractors agreed to observe maximum discounts and standard delivery and payment terms, was in breach of Article 101(1). The decision included restrictions on sales promotions, which prevented importers from introducing such schemes without informing the trade association's secretariat and fellow importers in advance.[409]

Key Sources

Milchförderungsfonds [1985] OJ L35/35, [1985] 3 CMLR 101.

Vimpoltu [1983] OJ L200/44, [1983] 3 CMLR 619.

---

409. *Vimpoltu* [1983] OJ L200/44, [1983] 3 CMLR 619.

40. HOW IS THE JOINT SELLING OF MEDIA RIGHTS TO SPORTING EVENTS TREATED UNDER ARTICLE 101?

Summary

- The joint selling of media rights to sporting events can raise Article 101 concerns, including that such arrangements:

    - Reduce or eliminate price competition among providers;

    - Foreclose broadcasters where only one media package is put up for sale;

    - Reduce output.

- However, joint selling of media rights may be necessary to create a new product.

- It may be possible to structure joint selling of sports rights in such a way that the arrangement is brought outside Article 101(1), for example, by creating different packages of rights and ensuring that different technology providers (such as Internet and mobile) have access to content.

- Even if caught by Article 101(1), such arrangements may benefit from the Article 101(3) exemption because they provide consumers with better products and reduce the transaction costs and financial risks for broadcasters.

1.   The rationale for jointly selling media rights to sporting events is obvious. Take, for example, a national football league such as the English Premier League. The commercial feasibility of selling separately the rights to each game or the rights owned by a particular club is doubtful and the attractiveness of creating packages of games is clear from a seller, buyer and end-user perspective. However, by selling the rights jointly in packages, price competition among the owners of the rights is reduced or eliminated. Joint selling can also result in the foreclosure of broadcasters from access to content. The competition difficulties created by the joint selling of sports broadcasting rights have been addressed in a number of cases.[410]

What approach was taken in *UEFA Champions League*?

2.   The Commission's decision in *UEFA Champions League* involved the joint selling of broadcasting rights to the latter stages of the UEFA Champions League.[411] The Commission objected to the original joint selling arrangements, notified in 1999, because UEFA sold all Champions League TV rights in one package to a single

---

410. For a detailed discussion of the application of completion law to sport, see Lewis and Kennelly, 'EC and UK Competition Rules and Sport' in Lewis and Taylor, *Sport: Law and Practice* (2nd edn, 2008) Ch B2. See also Case C–519/04P *Meca Medina v Commission* [2006] ECR I–6991, confirming the application of Articles 101 and 102 to sport.

411. COMP/C.2–37.398 *Joint selling of the commercial rights of the UEFA Champions League* [2003] OJ L291/25, [2004] 4 CMLR 9.

broadcaster on an exclusive basis for up to four years at a time. The sale of the entire rights on an exclusive basis for a long period had the effect of reinforcing the position of the incumbent TV broadcasters, which were the only providers with the financial strength to purchase entire packages. This lead to unsatisfied demand from other broadcasters and a lack of attractive offers made to customers, while Internet and phone providers were denied access to key sports content altogether.

3.   UEFA proposed a new arrangement, pursuant to which UEFA would still sell the rights centrally. The rights would be split into different packages, Internet and phone providers would be offered access to content and the sale of broadcasting rights, which would proceed through a public tender procedure, would not be for longer than three years at a time. This arrangement was still caught by the Article 101(1) prohibition, in particular because its effect was to reduce price competition:

> UEFA's joint selling arrangement has the effect that through the agreement jointly to exploit the commercial rights of the UEFA Champions League on an exclusive basis through a joint selling body, UEFA prevents the individual football clubs from individually marketing such rights. This prevents competition between the football clubs and also between UEFA and the football clubs in supplying in parallel media rights to the UEFA Champions League to interested buyers in the upstream markets. This means the third parties only have one single source of supply. Third-party commercial operators are therefore forced to purchase the relevant rights under the conditions jointly determined in the context of the invitation to bid, which is issued by the joint selling body. This means that the joint selling body restricts competition in the sense that it determines prices and all other trading conditions on behalf of all individual football clubs producing the UEFA Champions League content. In the absence of the joint selling agreement the football clubs would set such prices and conditions independently of one another and in competition with one another. The reduction in competition caused by the joint selling agreement therefore leads to uniform prices compared to a situation with individual selling.[412]

4.   There was also an anti-competitive effect by virtue of restrictions placed on the clubs in utilizing media rights that had not been transferred to UEFA and there was still a negative effect on broadcasters downstream.[413]

5.   The Commission exempted the arrangement under Article 101(3), noting that it had numerous benefits. The ability to purchase rights through one source would benefit media companies by making it easier to put media packages together and reducing transaction costs and financial risks; football clubs would find it much easier to deal with a joint selling agency; and viewers would benefit from better-packaged products.[414]

---

412. COMP/C.2–37.398 *Joint selling of the commercial rights of the UEFA Champions League* [2003] OJ L291/25, [2004] 4 CMLR 9, para 114.
413. See COMP/C.2–37.398 *Joint selling of the commercial rights of the UEFA Champions League* [2003] OJ L291/25, [2004] 4 CMLR 9, paras 115–116.
414. COMP/C.2–37.398 *Joint selling of the commercial rights of the UEFA Champions League* [2003] OJ L291/25, [2004] 4 CMLR 9, paras 136–197. Cf *UIP* [1989] OJ L226/25 (the Commission granted an exemption under Article 101(3) for a joint distribution and licensing joint venture by film producing companies who together had a 20 per cent market share. (contd \...)

What approach was taken in *FA Premier League*?

6.   In *FA Premier League* the Commission assessed arrangements for the sale of media rights to English Premier League matches.[415] A single entity, owned by the clubs in the Premier League, had the exclusive right to negotiate media rights to matches played by the clubs, and offered them every three years by way of competitive tender.

7.   The Commission expressed a preliminary view that these arrangements infringed Article 101(1), in particular because the joint sales organisation could restrict output and create foreclosure problems on downstream markets, for example, by the sale of large packages of rights. In response, the Premier League made successive proposals for changes to the arrangements, designed to reduce output restrictions and enhance the scope for *ex ante* competition for rights, including a prohibition on any one purchaser (alone or in association with others) buying all the packages and a limit on the duration of rights agreements up to three years. The commitments included providing the rights in six packages; providing for increased mobile and radio rights; the ability of clubs to exploit certain TV, Internet and mobile rights on a deferred basis; and a requirement that bids for each package would have to be made separately, with no direct or indirect link to other packages allowed as part of a bid.[416] Ultimately the Commission was satisfied that the varied arrangements did not infringe Article 101(1). An important consideration for the Commission was to ensure that existing operators in the market were not foreclosed from the possibility of acquiring relevant rights and using them as part of their broadcasting service.

What approach was taken in *German Bundesliga*?

8.   The *German Bundesliga* case involved the central marketing of the media rights in respect of matches in the first and second national football divisions in Germany.[417]

9.   The Commission had preliminary concerns that the league association, under the marketing agreements with the clubs, determined the price and the nature and scope of exploitation of the media rights. The clubs were prevented from dealing independently with television and radio operators and sport-rights agents. In particular, the clubs were prevented from taking independent commercial decisions about the price for their rights.

---

414. (contd) Certain modifications, such as making the venture available to other film producers, were required. The Commission noted that the venture would increase the efficiency of film distribution and these benefits would be passed on to consumers. The market power among a small number of purchasing exhibitors was a countervailing factor).
415. COMP/C.2–38.173 *Re FA Premier League* [2007] CEC 2138.
416. COMP/C.2–38.173 *Re FA Premier League* [2007] CEC 2138, para 36.
417. COMP/C.2/37.214 *Joint Selling of the Media Rights to the German Bundesliga ('DFB')* [2005] OJ L134/46.

10.   The Commission took the view that the joint marketing arrangements could have an adverse effect on the relevant downstream television market. The commitments offered by the league led to the relevant rights being offered in several packages in a transparent and non-discriminatory manner. The duration of the agreement entered into would not exceed three seasons. The Commission concluded that these commitments introduced competition into the marketing of the relevant rights between the league and the clubs and allowed for new club branded products. These commitments reduced the scope and duration of future marketing deals and provided a transparent non-discriminatory marketing procedure. Ultimately, the arrangements were not found to breach Article 101(1).

What approach was taken in Racecourse Association and Bookmakers' Afternoon?

11.   Two English cases highlight how the joint selling of media rights may be necessary to enable a new product to be launched or a new entrant to enter the market.

12.   *Racecourse Association v OFT* involved the collective sale of certain media rights by 49 racecourses to bookmakers other than licensed betting offices, for distribution in combination with betting services.

13.   The OFT had found the agreement to breach the Chapter I prohibition and that decision was appealed. The CAT considered whether this collective selling or collective negotiation was 'necessary' for the creation of the new product in respect of which the racecourses were selling media rights. It considered whether the necessary critical mass of rights could have been assembled by individual negotiation with racecourse owners rather than by a process of collective negotiation, dismissing the idea of individual negotiation as 'a triumph of theory over commercial reality'.[418] The CAT concluded that the collective negotiation was necessary for the achievement of the legitimate commercial objective of creating a new product and that there was no infringement of the Chapter I prohibition.

14.   In *Bookmakers' Afternoon* a similar conclusion about the requirement of collective selling to create a new product was made. Thirty-one racecourses had set up a joint venture to establish a distributor to sell media rights to licensed betting offices ('LBOs'). Previously, media rights from all sixty racecourses in the UK had been sold through only one distributor. With the introduction of the new entrant, LBOs now had to purchase rights from two distributors in order to carry coverage of all racecourses. Consequently, the LBOs' costs rose. They argued that the new joint venture was contrary to Article 101. The High Court rejected the application[419]

---

418.   *Racecourse Association v Office of Fair Trading* [2005] CAT 29, [2006] CompAR 99, para 170.

419.   *Bookmakers' Afternoon Greyhound Services Ltd v Amalgamated Racing Ltd* [2008] EWHC 1978 (Ch), [2009] UKCLR 547.

and the Court of Appeal upheld that decision, finding that there was no breach of Article 101(1).[420]

15. The arrangement did not have the object or effect of restricting competition. It introduced new competition into a situation where previously there had only been one competitor in the upstream market. To achieve the viable new entrant:

> ... the broadcaster would have to acquire LBO media rights for a minimum number of racecourses on an exclusive basis. It is not something that any racecourse could have achieved by itself. Given that the incumbent operator was dominated by the interests of the purchasers in the downstream market, given the high cost of entry, and given the very long period in which no other operator had shown any interest in entry to these markets ... it was obviously necessary that the new entrant would have to be promoted by or in association with a number of racecourses, and that it would need to be protected, at the stage of its establishment, from competition from the incumbent, since otherwise it would never get off the ground.[421]

16. This approach is not dissimilar to the Commission's guidelines on production agreements, in which it acknowledges that there may be a need for cooperation to achieve market entry:

> [Cooperation] between firms which compete on markets closely related to the market directly concerned by the cooperation, cannot be defined as restricting competition, if the cooperation is the only commercially justifiable possible way to enter a new market, to launch a new product or service or to carry out a specific project.[422]

Key Sources

Joint selling of the commercial rights of the UEFA Champions League [2003] OJ L291/25, [2004] 4 CMLR 9.

Re FA Premier League [2006] 5 CMLR 25.

Joint Selling of the Media Rights to the German Bundesliga ('DFB') [2005] 5 CMLR 26.

Racecourse Association v Office of Fair Trading [2005] CAT 29, [2006] CompAR 99.

Bookmakers' Afternoon Greyhound Services Ltd v Amalgamated Racing Ltd [2009] EWCA Civ 750, [2009] UKCLR 863.

---

420. *Bookmakers' Afternoon Greyhound Services Ltd v Amalgamated Racing Ltd* [2009] EWCA Civ 750, [2009] UKCLR 863.
421. *Bookmakers' Afternoon Greyhound Services Ltd v Amalgamated Racing Ltd* [2009] EWCA Civ 750, [2009] UKCLR 863, para 85 (Lloyd LJ).
422. Commission 2001 Horizontal Cooperation Guidelines [2001] OJ C3/2, para 87. See also Commission 2010 Draft Horizontal Cooperation Guidelines SEC(2010) 528/2, para 157.

41. Do B2B ELECTRONIC MARKETPLACES RAISE COMPETITION LAW ISSUES?

Summary

B2B electronic marketplaces are usually seen as pro-competitive but they may also raise antitrust concerns in areas including:

- Information exchange.

- Joint purchasing or joint selling concerns.

- Exclusivity resulting in foreclosure.

- Article 102.

1. Business-to-business (B2B) marketplaces (or 'e-marketplaces' or 'electronic platforms') are electronic trading exchanges for selling and buying goods and services over the Internet. They usually have pro-competitive aspects, increasing choice for buyers and reducing transaction costs. However, B2B marketplaces can also raise antitrust concerns.[423]

2. These concerns may include that (i) B2B markets, with their significant flow of online information, might facilitate collusion; (ii) they could result in the foreclosure of third parties who were excluded from the exchange; and (iii) buyers or sellers will club together to 'bundle' their purchases or sales in a way liable to fall within the scope of Article 101(1) of the Treaty.

3. The Commission has provided guidance on the competitive impact of B2B markets in statements following informal settlements of a number of cases.

4. In the *Volbroker* case, the Commission made a number of comments about information exchanges.[424] The case involved the creation of a joint venture called Volbroker.com between subsidiaries of six major banks that would develop and market an electronic brokerage service for trading among banks in foreign currency options. The Commission noted that the parents of the joint venture had given a number of assurances that negated antitrust concerns. These assurances could be read as informal guidelines about information exchange in B2B platforms:

   - None of the exchange's staff or management would have any contractual or other obligation towards any of the parents and vice versa.

---

423. Depending on the structure, the establishment of the B2B marketplace may give rise to a full-function joint venture subject to the Merger Regulation [2004] OJ L24/1. See, e.g., COMP/M.2374 *Telenor/ErgoGroup/DnB/Accenture/JV*, Commission Decision of 2 May 2001. See further Kirch, 'The Internet and EU Competition Law' [2006] *Journal of International Trade Law and Policy* 18.

424. Commission Press Release IP/00/896, Commission approves the Volbroker.com electronic brokerage joint venture between six major banks (31 July 2000).

- The exchange's staff and management would be in a geographically distinct location from that of the parents.

- The representatives of the parents on the board of the exchange would not have access to commercially sensitive information relating to each other or to third parties.

- The parents would not have access to the information technology and communication systems of the exchange.

- The parents would also ensure that the staff and management of all the parties understood and appreciated the importance of maintaining the confidentiality of sensitive commercial information and that sanctions for breach would be spelled out.

5. The risk that inappropriate information exchanges would be facilitated by B2B exchanges is an obvious concern. In addition to the types of safeguards mentioned by the Commission in the *Volbrocker* case, limitations on the exchange of information could be achieved through 'technical solutions like firewalls or encryption technology, or through contractual provisions, such as rules limiting the frequency of information exchanges and/or controlling the level of data aggregation and age of the information exchanged'.[425] In its informal clearance of the *GF-X* exchange (facilitating the sale of air freight capacity between air freight forwarders and air freight carriers), the Commission noted that the exchange was set up in such a way as to prevent the exchange of commercially sensitive information between participants. In particular, sales negotiations would be conducted on a bilateral basis and as such would not reveal more information than was made available to buyers under the existing sales channels.[426]

6. Further antitrust concerns could be raised if there are exclusionary rules that limit competitors from using the B2B or that unduly impede the development of competing B2B exchanges by preventing shareholders or participants from using competing exchanges.[427] Such restrictions could be contained in the constituent agreements setting up the B2B.

7. In its statements on the antitrust issues surrounding B2B marketplaces, the Commission has noted other potential concerns. For example, in its press release clearing the *Covisint* B2B automotive marketplace, it noted that negative competitive effects could outweigh efficiencies and that this may be the case in particular where there is discrimination against certain classes of users leading to

---

425. Capobianco, 'Information Exchange under EC Competition Law' [2004] *Common Market Law Review* 1247, 1256.

426. Commission Press Release IP/02/1560, Commission clears GF-X air freight trading platform between several European airlines (28 October 2002).

427. See, e.g., Commission Press Release IP/02/943, Commission clears electronic multi-bank trading platform for foreign exchange products (27 June 2002) (in finding that the B2B did not breach Article 101(1), the Commission noted that the 'banks participating in the platform remain free to sell their financial products via other trading platforms or other distribution channels'.)

foreclosure or where buyers or sellers club together to 'bundle' their purchases or sales in a way liable to fall within the scope of Article 101(1).[428]

8.   The Commission has also noted that B2B marketplaces could raise concerns under Article 102. A particular concern is that e-markets may create so-called network effects. As their value for individual users rises with the number of users, this may result in a dominant position of a network operator if the network effects are strong enough to induce all market participants to use the same network. In addition, risks of market dominance may arise from efforts to impose the exclusive use of a given e-market or to prevent access of all interested buyers and sellers to it.[429]

Key Sources

Volbroker.com – Commission Press Release IP/00/896 of 31 July 2000.

GF-X air freight trading platform – Commission Press Release IP/02/1560 of 28 October 2002.

Commission Communication, Enhancing Trust and Confidence in Business-to-Business Electronic Markets, SEC(2004) 930.

---

428. Commission Press Release IP/01/1155, Commission clears the creation of the Covisint Automotive Internet Marketplace (31 July 2001). See also, Commission Press Release IP/02/761, Commission approves the creation of the inreon online reinsurance exchange (24 May 2002).
429. Commission Communication, Enhancing Trust and Confidence in Business-to-Business Electronic Markets, SEC(2004) 930, 6.

42. MAY COMPETITORS COLLABORATE FOR THE PURPOSES OF RESEARCH AND DEVELOPMENT?

Summary

•   R&D agreements between competitors can benefit from a block exemption if their combined share in the products capable of being improved or replaced by the contract products does not exceed 25 per cent at the time the R&D agreement is entered into. The exemption continues as long as the combined share does not exceed 25 per cent.

•   R&D agreements falling outside the block exemption should be analysed under Article 101(1). Many R&D agreements will not raise competition issues. The main concerns that could be raised include that there will be a reduction or slowdown in innovation, the parties will coordinate their behaviour or compete less aggressively outside the R&D collaboration or the agreement will give rise to foreclosure concerns.

1.   Research and development agreements between competitors may benefit from the R&D block exemption. If the agreement falls outside the block exemption, an analysis should be made to determine if it breaches Article 101.

2.   At the time of writing, the Commission's new R&D block exemption Regulation, which will replace Regulation 2659/2000[430] which expires on 31 December 2010, had not yet been adopted. The Commission produced a draft block exemption Regulation in 2010, which contains many of the same features as Regulation 2659/2000.[431]

What are the conditions for application of the R&D block exemption?

3.   The block exemption applies to

(a) joint research and development of products or processes and joint exploitation of the results of that research and development;

(b) joint exploitation of the results of research and development of products or processes jointly carried out pursuant to a prior agreement between the same parties; or

(c) joint research and development of products or processes excluding joint exploitation of the results.[432]

---

430. Commission Regulation (EC) No 2659/2000 on the application of Article 81(3) of the Treaty to categories of research and development agreements [2000] OJ L304/7.

431. Commission's Draft Regulation on the application of Article 101(3) of the Treaty on the Functioning of the European Union to categories of research and development agreements (May 2010) ('2010 Draft R&D Block Exemption Regulation').

432. Regulation 2659/2000, Article 1(1); 2010 Draft R&D Block Exemption Regulation, Article 2(1).

4. The application of the exemption depends on whether the parties are competitors. Where the parties are not competitors, the exemption applies for the duration of the research and development and where the results are jointly exploited, the exemption continues for seven years from the time the goods are first marketed.[433]

5. Where the parties are competitors, the exemption shall apply for the same periods only if the parties' combined share of the relevant market for the products capable of being improved or replaced by the contract products does not exceed 25 per cent at the time the R&D agreement is entered into.[434]

6. The exemption continues as long as the combined share of the parties does not exceed 25 per cent of the relevant market for the contract products.[435] If the combined share rises to between 25–30 per cent during the period of exemption, the exemption continues for two years following the year in which the 25 per cent threshold was first exceeded. If the combined share rises above 30 per cent, there is only a one-year grace period.[436]

7. The exemption does not apply if the R&D agreement contains hardcore restrictions, which include restrictions on the parties carrying out R&D independently, limitations of output, fixing of sales prices and restrictions on territories into which a party can make passive sales.[437]

8. The following are further requirements for the application of the R&D block exemption:[438]

    •   All the parties must have access to the results of the R&D (there is an exception for research institutes, academic bodies) ('equal access' is required in the 2010 draft).

    •   If the agreement does not provide for joint exploitation, each party must be free to exploit the results but such right may be limited to certain technical fields of application where the parties were not competitors on entering the R&D (the 2010 draft amends this slightly, providing that the R&D agreements must stipulate that each party be granted access to any pre-existing know-how of the other parties, if this know-how is indispensible for exploiting the results).

---

433. Regulation 2659/2000, Article 4(1); 2010 Draft R&D Block Exemption Regulation, Article 4(1).

434. Regulation 2659/2000, Article 4(2); 2010 Draft R&D Block Exemption Regulation, Article 4(2).

435. Regulation 2659/2000, Article 4(3); 2010 Draft R&D Block Exemption Regulation, Article 4(3).

436. Regulation 2659/2000, Articles 6(2), 6(3); 2010 Draft R&D Block Exemption Regulation, Articles 7(2), 7(3).

437. Regulation 2659/2000, Article 5; 2010 Draft R&D Block Exemption Regulation, Article 5.

438. Regulation 2659/2000, Articles 3(2)–3(5); 2010 Draft R&D Block Exemption Regulation, Articles 3(3)–3(6).

- Any joint exploitation must relate to results which are protected by IP rights or constitute know-how and which are indispensible for the manufacture of the contract products or the application of the contract processes.

- Undertakings with responsibility for manufacture must be required to fulfil orders for supplies from all the parties, except where the R&D agreement also provides for joint distribution.

9. The Commission's 2010 draft added a further requirement, that the parties must agree that prior to starting the R&D, they will disclose all existing and pending intellectual property rights insofar as they are relevant for the exploitation of the results of the R&D by other parties.[439]

How is the relevant market defined?[440]

10. If the product of the R&D agreement is intended to compete with existing products, then the relevant market for calculating the market share for purposes of the block exemption (and considering the effects of the agreement where the block exemption is not applicable) will be the relevant market for the existing products. If a new product will be developed, the relevant market is the market in which the new product will compete.

11. The R&D might also aim at a significant change of existing products so that it is difficult to analyse how the newly developed product will compete with existing products. The Commission has noted the difficulty of market definition in this case:

> If the R&D efforts aim at a significant change of existing products or even at a new product replacing existing ones, substitution with the existing products may be imperfect or long-term. It may be concluded that the old and the potentially emerging new products do not belong to the same relevant market. The market for existing products may nevertheless be concerned, if the pooling of R&D efforts is likely to result in the coordination of the parties' behaviour as suppliers of existing products, for instance because of the exchange of competitively sensitive information relating to the market for existing products.[441]

12. When the R&D concerns technology as well as a new product, the relevant technology market, consisting of the intellectual property that is licensed and its close substitutes, also has to be defined. Market shares in technology markets can be derived by dividing the licensing income generated by the parties by the total licensing income from all licensors in that technology market.[442] Where such a calculation is not practical, shares could be calculated on the basis of sales of products or services incorporating the licensed technology on the downstream

---

439. 2010 Draft R&D Block Exemption Regulation, Article 3(2).
440. See also Question 10.
441. Commission 2010 Draft Horizontal Cooperation Guidelines SEC(2010) 528/2, para 108.
442. Commission 2010 Draft Horizontal Cooperation Guidelines SEC(2010) 528/2, paras 110–112. See also Commission Guidelines on the application of Article 81 of the EC Treaty to technology transfer agreements [2004] OJ C101/2, paras 19–25.

product markets. All sales on the relevant market would be taken into account, irrespective of whether the product incorporated a licensed technology.[443]

13. What if the R&D agreement is intended to produce a new product that results in an entirely new market? In this situation, it may be necessary to consider a future market. This might arise, for example, with the development of a new drug that is expected to produce a treatment for a disease that currently is untreatable. In analysing the competitive effects of drugs in R&D in the merger context, the Commission has noted that in a situation such as this, the definition of the market is less clear-cut than in the case of existing markets. In this context, market definition could be based 'either on the existing ATC[444] classes or it can be guided primarily by the characteristics of future products as well as by the indications to which they are to be applied'.[445] The Commission has also suggested that different R&D poles can be analysed to establish whether after the collaboration, there will be a sufficient number of remaining R&D poles.[446] Where the R&D will create entirely new demand, the agreement is treated as one between non-competitors and so can benefit from the block exemption irrespective of market share for a period of seven years after the product is first put on the market.[447]

What competition concerns might be raised by R&D agreements that do not benefit from the block exemption?

14. If the R&D agreement does not meet the conditions for application of the block exemption, it must be analysed under Article 101. Horizontal research and development agreements are often considered to be pro-competitive and the Commission has previously acknowledged that 'most R&D agreements do not fall under Article [101(1)]'.[448] Such collaborations can advance technical progress and bring benefits to consumers in the form of new and better products and processes and lower prices. R&D collaboration may be especially important in developing new products in areas such as pharmaceuticals and biotechnology.

15. The following types of R&D will not generally be caught by Article 101:

   •   R&D 'at a rather early stage, far removed from the exploitation of possible results'.[449]

---

443. Commission 2010 Draft Horizontal Cooperation Guidelines SEC(2010) 528/2, para 119.
444. This is the Anatomical Therapeutic Classification, which groups medicines according to therapeutic qualities/intended use.
445. COMP/M.1878 *Pfizer/Warner Lambert*, Commission Decision of 22 May 2000.
446. Commission 2010 Draft Horizontal Cooperation Guidelines SEC(2010) 528/2, para 114. The Commission states at para 116 that where R&D poles cannot be indentified, the competitive assessment should be limited to existing products and/or technology markets which are related to the R&D cooperation in question.
447. Commission 2010 Draft Horizontal Cooperation Guidelines SEC(2010) 528/2, para 120.
448. Commission 2001 Horizontal Cooperation Guidelines [2001] OJ C3/2, para 55.
449. Commission 2010 Draft Horizontal Cooperation Guidelines SEC(2010) 528/2, para 123. See also Commission 2001 Horizontal Cooperation Guidelines [2001] OJ C3/2, para 55.

- R&D between non-competitors.[450]

- Outsourced R&D involving research institutes, academic bodies, specialised R&D companies.[451]

- Where the R&D products will not be jointly exploited.[452]

16.   R&D agreements may restrict competition in certain circumstances, particularly if the cooperation goes beyond pure research and development and extends to joint production and marketing. The main concerns identified by the Commission are:[453]

- A reduction or slowdown in innovation, leading to fewer or worse products coming to the market as well as delay in new products.

- A reduction of competition between the parties outside of the R&D collaboration or more likelihood of anti-competitive coordination on these markets.

- Foreclosure problems if the R&D features a key technology, one of the parties has significant market power and there is exclusive exploitation of the R&D results.[454]

- An R&D agreement that is merely a disguised cartel will be treated as a restriction of competition by object.

17.   As noted above, Article 101 will not usually apply if the parties are not actual or potential competitors. The 2010 draft R&D block exemption Regulation defines a potential competitor in the context of a R&D collaboration as an undertaking that would, on realistic grounds, 'in case of a small but permanent increase in relative prices be likely to undertake, within not more than three years, the necessary additional investments or other necessary switching costs to supply a product, technology or process capable of being improved or replaced by the contract product or contract process on the relevant geographic market'.[455] The Commission further explains:

> If the parties are not able to carry out the necessary R&D independently, the R&D agreement will normally not have any restrictive effects on competition. This can apply, for example, to companies bringing together complementary skills,

450. However, if the R&D relates to an exclusive exploitation of results and one of the parties has significant market power with respect to key technology, foreclosure effects could be produced. See Commission 2001 Horizontal Cooperation Guidelines [2001] OJ C3/2, para 56.

451. Commission 2001 Horizontal Cooperation Guidelines [2001] OJ C3/2, para 57; Commission 2010 Draft Horizontal Cooperation Guidelines SEC(2010) 528/2, para 125.

452. Commission 2001 Horizontal Cooperation Guidelines [2001] OJ C3/2, para 58; Commission 2010 Draft Horizontal Cooperation Guidelines SEC(2010) 528/2, para 126.

453. Commission 2010 Draft Horizontal Cooperation Guidelines SEC(2010) 528/2, para 121.

454. See the example at para 142 of the Commission 2010 Draft Horizontal Cooperation Guidelines SEC(2010) 528/2.

455. 2010 Draft R&D Block Exemption Regulation, Article 1(16). See also Regulation 2659/2000, Article 2(12).

technologies and other resources. The issue of potential competition has to be assessed on a realistic basis. For instance, parties cannot be defined as potential competitors simply because the co-operation enables them to carry out the R&D activities. The decisive question is whether each party independently has the necessary means as to assets, know how and other resources. [456]

18.   An R&D agreement that is caught by Article 101(1) may benefit from the Article 101(3) exemption if the conditions for exemption are satisfied. Many R&D agreements will generate significant efficiency gains and so may well benefit from the exemption if gains are passed on to consumers.[457]

Key Sources

Commission Regulation (EC) No 2659/2000 on the application of Article 81(3) of the Treaty to categories of research and development agreements [2000] OJ L304/7.

Commission's Draft Regulation on the application of Article 101(3) of the Treaty on the Functioning of the European Union to categories of research and development agreements (May 2010).

Commission's Guidelines on the applicability of Article 81 of the EC Treaty to horizontal cooperation agreements [2001] OJ C 3/2.

Draft Commission Guidelines on the on the applicability of Article 101 of the Treaty on the Functioning of the European Union to horizontal co-operation agreements SEC(2010) 528/2, paras 105–143.

---

456. Commission 2010 Draft Horizontal Cooperation Guidelines SEC(2010) 528/2, para 124. See also Commission 2001 Horizontal Cooperation Guidelines [2001] OJ C3/2, para 56.
457. See Question 21.

43. WHAT ARE THE CONDITIONS FOR APPLICATION OF THE VERTICAL AGREEMENTS BLOCK EXEMPTION?

Summary

- The block exemption applies if:

  (i)   the supplier's market share is not more than 30 per cent of the market on which it sells the contract goods or services; and

  (ii) the buyer's share of the market on which it purchases goods or services is not more than 30 per cent.

What are vertical agreements?

1. For purposes of applying the competition rules, agreements between undertakings may be either horizontal or vertical in nature. An agreement between two undertakings at the same level of the supply chain, for example an agreement between two wholesalers, is horizontal. An agreement between undertakings at different levels of the supply chain is vertical in nature. An example is an agreement between a supplier and a distributor. The main types of vertical agreements include:

    - Distribution agreements.

    - Supply agreements.

    - Franchise agreements.

    - Licensing agreements.

    - Agency agreements.[458]

2. Vertical agreements containing restrictive elements are much less likely to raise competition concerns than restrictive horizontal agreements. The Commission has explained the difference as follows:

    > Vertical restraints are generally less harmful than horizontal restraints. The main reason for the greater focus on horizontal restraints is that such restraints may concern an agreement between competitors producing identical or substitutable goods or services. In such horizontal relationships, the exercise of market power by one company (higher price of its product) may benefit its competitors. This may provide an incentive to competitors to induce each other to behave anti-competitively. In vertical relationships, the product of the one is the input for the other, in other words, the activities of the parties to the agreement are complementary to each other. The exercise of market power by either the upstream or downstream company would therefore normally hurt the demand for the product of the other. The companies involved in the agreement therefore usually have an incentive to prevent the exercise of market power by the other.[459]

---

458. 'True' agency agreements, pursuant to which the agent simply negotiates on behalf of the principal, fall outside the scope of Article 101. See Question 45.

459. Commission Guidelines on Vertical Restraints [2010] OJ C130/1, para 98.

3.   Nevertheless, vertical agreements may in some cases adversely affect competition when the undertaking imposing a vertical restraint has market power. A firm with market power could use vertical restraints to raise the costs of its rivals. This could occur, for instance, if it can use its market power to enforce an exclusivity clause on buyers, thereby foreclosing its rivals from access to those buyers.[460] When the undertaking imposing the vertical restraint does not have sufficient market power, the vertical agreement may benefit from the block exemption.

What are the conditions for application of the block exemption on vertical agreements?

4.   A new vertical agreements block exemption, Regulation 330/2010, entered into force on 1 June 2010 and will expire on 31 May 2022.[461] It takes a similar approach to the previous block exemption that applied to vertical agreements, Regulation 2790/1999.[462] Where an agreement which entered into before 31 May 2010 would benefit from exemption under the Regulation 2790/1999 but would not meet the criteria for exemption under the Regulation 330/2010 (as discussed below, the market share requirements are more rigorous in Regulation 330/2010), Regulation 2790/1999 can continue to be availed of until 31 May 2011.[463]

5.   The block exemption applies to certain types of vertical agreements that are assumed to benefit from the Article 101(3) exemption. The assumption is based on the likelihood that efficiency-enhancing effects of the agreement, such as a reduction in transaction and distribution costs of the parties and an optimisation of their sales and investment levels, will outweigh any anti-competitive effects. The block exemption should be read together with the Commission Guidelines on Vertical Restraints.

6.   Availability of the exemption depends on the market power of the parties. Specifically, the exemption applies only if the market share of the supplier does not exceed 30 per cent of the relevant market on which it sells the contract goods or services and the market share of the buyer on the purchasing market does not

---

460. The potential negative effects of vertical restraints are discussed in Question 44.

461. Commission Regulation (EU) No 330/2010 on the application of Article 101(3) of the Treaty on the Functioning of the European Union to categories of vertical agreements and concerted practices [2010] OJ L102/1. In respect of Irish competition law, see Competition Authority Notice in Respect of Vertical Agreements and Concerted Practices, as amended on 17 May 2010, which was due to expire on 30 November 2010. In the UK, an exemption from the Chapter I prohibition in the Competition Act 1998 for vertical agreements generally was removed by SI 2004 No 1260 Competition Act 1998 (Land Agreements Exclusion and Revocation) Order 2004. That still left in place an exemption for Land Agreements, which was removed by the SI 2010 No 1709 Competition Act 1998 (Land Agreements Exclusion Revocation) Order 2010, which applies from 6 April 2011.

462. Commission Regulation (EC) No 2790/1999 on the application of Article 81(3) of the Treaty to categories of vertical agreements and concerted practices [2000] OJ L304/7.

463. Regulation 330/2010, Article 9.

exceed 30 per cent.[464] This is a change from Regulation 2790/1999, which applied as long as the supplier's market share was not above 30 per cent.[465]

7.   Certain financial thresholds also apply. The exemption applies to vertical agreements entered into by an association of undertakings and its members or between the association and its suppliers only if the members are retailers and none of them, together with its connected undertakings, has a turnover of more than €50 million.[466]

8.   When the parties to the agreement are competitors, the exemption only applies if the arrangements are non-reciprocal and (i) the supplier is a manufacturer and a distributor of goods, while the buyer is a distributor and not a competing undertaking at the manufacturing level or (ii) the supplier is a provider of services at several levels of trade, while the buyer provides its goods or services at the retail level and is not a competing undertaking at the level of trade at which it purchases the contract services.[467]

What restrictions are impermissible?

9.   The entire agreement will lose the benefit of the block exemption if it contains hardcore restrictions. Article 4 provides that the exemption shall not apply to vertical agreements which, directly or indirectly, in isolation or in combination with other factors under the control of the parties, have as their object:

(a)   the restriction of the buyer's ability to determine its sale price, without prejudice to the possibility of the supplier to impose a maximum sale price or recommend a sale price, provided that they do not amount to a fixed or minimum sale price as a result of pressure from, or incentives offered by, any of the parties;

(b)   the restriction of the territory into which, or of the customers to whom, a buyer party to the agreement, without prejudice to a restriction on its place of establishment, may sell the contract goods or services, except:

(i)   the restriction of active sales into the exclusive territory or to an exclusive customer group reserved to the supplier or allocated by the supplier to another buyer, where such a restriction does not limit sales by the customers of the buyer,

(ii)   the restriction of sales to end users by a buyer operating at the wholesale level of trade,

(iii)   the restriction of sales by the members of a selective distribution system to unauthorised distributors within the territory reserved by the supplier to operate that system, and

(iv)   the restriction of the buyer's ability to sell components, supplied for the purposes of incorporation, to customers who would use them to manufacture the same type of goods as those produced by the supplier;

---

464.   Regulation 330/2010, Article 3(1). See Article 7 for rules on calculating market shares.
465.   Regulation 2790/1999, Article 3(1). Article 3(2) had provided that the buyer's share applied instead where the agreement contained exclusive supply obligations.
466.   Regulation 330/2010, Article 2(2).
467.   Regulation 330/2010, Article 2(4).

    (c) the restriction of active or passive sales to end users by members of a selective distribution system operating at the retail level of trade, without prejudice to the possibility of prohibiting a member of the system from operating out of an unauthorised place of establishment;

    (d) the restriction of cross-supplies between distributors within a selective distribution system, including between distributors operating at different level of trade;

    (e) the restriction, agreed between a supplier of components and a buyer who incorporates those components, of the supplier's ability to sell the components as spare parts to end-users or to repairers or other service providers not entrusted by the buyer with the repair or servicing of its goods.[468]

10.   Subject to certain specified exceptions,[469] the exemption does not apply to non-compete obligations exceeding five years or those with an indefinite duration or, with limited exceptions, restrictions on the buyer's ability to manufacture or trade in goods or services after termination of the agreement or restrictions on members of a selective distribution system selling brands of particular competing suppliers.[470] If the agreement contains any of these kinds of clauses, the rule of severability applies so that only the offending clause loses the benefit of the block exemption.[471]

Does the block exemption apply to vertical agreements providing for the assignment of intellectual property rights?

11.   Article 2(3) of Regulation 330/2010 provides that the block exemption applies to vertical agreements containing provisions which relate to the assignment or use of intellectual property rights ('IPRs'), provided that those provisions do not constitute the primary object of such agreements and are directly related to the use, sale or resale of goods or services by the buyer or its customers. The Guidelines on Vertical Restraints go on to explain that the block exemption applies to vertical agreements containing provisions on IPRs where five conditions are fulfilled:

    (a) The IPR provisions must be part of a vertical agreement, that is, an agreement with conditions under which the parties may purchase, sell or resell certain goods or services;

    (b) The IPRs must be assigned to, or licensed for use by, the buyer;

    (c) The IPR provisions must not constitute the primary object of the agreement;

    (d) The IPR provisions must be directly related to the use, sale or resale of goods or services by the buyer or its customers. In the case of franchising where marketing forms the object of the exploitation of the IPRs, the goods or services are distributed by the master franchisee or the franchisees;

---

468. Regulation 330/2010, Article 4.
469. Regulation 330/2010, Articles 5(2), 5(3).
470. Regulation 330/2010, Article 5(1).
471. Commission Guidelines on Vertical Restraints [2010] OJ C130/1, para 71.

(e) The IPR provisions, in relation to the contract goods or services, must not contain restrictions of competition having the same object as vertical restraints which are not exempted under the Block Exemption Regulation.[472]

Key Sources

Commission Regulation (EU) No 330/2010 on the application of Article 101(3) of the Treaty on the Functioning of the European Union to categories of vertical agreements and concerted practices [2010] OJ L102/1.

European Commission Guidelines on Vertical Restraints [2010] OJ C130/1.

---

472. Commission Guidelines on Vertical Restraints [2010] OJ C130/1, para 31.

44. IF A VERTICAL AGREEMENT DOES NOT COME WITHIN THE BLOCK EXEMPTION, HOW WILL IT BE ANALYSED UNDER ARTICLE 101?

1.   The Guidelines on Vertical Restraints set out the Commission's view of the methodology for applying Article 101 and the approach to be taken to particular kinds of vertical restraints. Even if a vertical agreement falls within Article 101(1), it may still benefit from the Article 101(3) exemption. The assessment of whether a vertical agreement has the effect of restricting competition is to be made by comparing the actual or likely future situation on the relevant market with the vertical restraints in place and the situation that would have transpired without the restraints. A reduction of intra-brand competition (between distributors of the same brand), is unlikely to have negative competitive effects on consumers if there is significant inter-brand competition (competition between competing brands).[473] The Commission summarises its approach as follows:

> In the assessment of individual cases, the Commission will take, as appropriate, both actual and likely effects into account. For vertical agreements to be restrictive of competition by effect they must affect actual or potential competition to such an extent that on the relevant market negative effects on prices, output, innovation, or the variety or quality of goods and services can be expected with a reasonable degree of probability. The likely negative effects on competition must be appreciable. Appreciable anticompetitive effects are likely to occur when at least one of the parties has or obtains some degree of market power and the agreement contributes to the creation, maintenance or strengthening of that market power or allows the parties to exploit such market power.[474]

2.   The following is a brief summary of the approach taken in the Guidelines on Vertical Restraints.

Potential negative effects of vertical agreements[475]	Foreclosure of suppliers or buyers by raising barriers to entry or expansion.
	Reduction of inter-brand competition by softening competition between the supplier and its competitors and/or facilitation of collusion.
	Reduction of intra-brand competition between distributors of the same brand by softening competition between the buyer and its competitors and/or facilitation of collusion.
	Creating obstacles to market integration, in particular limitations on the possibilities for consumers to purchase goods or services in any Member State they choose.
Factors in considering negative effects[476]	A reduction of inter-brand competition is more problematic than a reduction in intra-brand competition.
	Exclusive arrangements are generally more anti-competitive than non-exclusive arrangements.
	Restraints for non-branded goods and services are generally less harmful than restraints affecting branded goods and services.

---

473. Commission Guidelines on Vertical Restraints [2010] OJ C130/1, para 102 (referring to inter-brand competition remaining 'fierce').
474. Commission Guidelines on Vertical Restraints [2010] OJ C130/1, para 97.

Factors in considering negative effects[476] (contd)	A combination of vertical restraints generally aggravates their negative effects.
Possible justifications for vertical restraints[477]	To solve a 'free-rider' problem – e.g., one distributor may free-ride on another's promotional efforts.
	To open up or enter new markets.
	The 'certification free-rider issue' – the supplier needs to have its product launched only at premium resellers.
	The 'hold-up problem' – the investor may not commit to needed investment without particular distribution arrangements being in place.
	Transfer of significant know-how to the distributor may justify a non-compete (the 'specific hold-up problem that may arise in the case of transfer of substantial know-how').
	The 'vertical externality issue'. If a retailer is pricing too high, this may create a 'double marginalisation problem' which could be avoided by imposing a maximum resale price on the retailer. To increase the retailer's sales efforts, selective distribution, exclusive distribution or similar restrictions may be helpful.
	'Economies of scale in distribution' can be achieved by limiting the number of distributors.
	'Capital market imperfections'. Where loans are provided by the supplier to the distributor and vice versa, this may require quantity forcing or non-competes.
	To achieve 'uniformity and quality standardisation', e.g. creating a brand image through selective distribution or franchising.
	'The case is in general strongest for vertical restraints of a limited duration which help the introduction of new complex products or protect relationship-specific investments'.[478]
Relevant factors in assessing vertical restraints[479]	Nature of the agreement – nature and duration of restraints and the percentage of total sales on the market affected by those restraints.
	Market position of the parties – market share, competitive advantages over competitors etc. are relevant to assessing market power.
	Market position of competitors – market share etc. is relevant; the stronger the position of competitors and the greater their number, the less likely that the parties will be able to individually exercise market power and foreclose the market or soften competition.
	Market position of buyers of the contract products – do customers have buyer power that can prevent the parties from exercising market power and thereby solve a competition problem that would otherwise have existed?
	Entry barriers.
	Maturity of the market – negative effects are more likely in a mature market.
	Level of trade – if restrictions are more in intermediate goods, this is less likely to be problematic than where restrictions are placed on distributors of final products.

Relevant factors in assessing vertical restraints[479] (contd)	Nature of the product – negative effects are more likely with heterogeneous, less expensive products that resemble more a one-off purchase.
	Other factors, e.g., if there is a network of similar agreements; is the agreement imposed rather than agreed; regulatory environment; behaviour such as price leadership, price discrimination, previous cartel behaviour in the industry.
Article 101(3)[480]	Restrictive vertical agreements may well produce efficiencies that outweigh negative competitive effects. The four cumulative conditions for application of the Article 101(3) exemption must be fulfilled.
Types of vertical restraints[481]	Single branding.
	Exclusive distribution.
	Exclusive customer allocation.
	Selective distribution.
	Franchising.
	Exclusive supply.
	Upfront access payments.
	Category management agreements.
	Tying.
	Resale price restrictions.

Key Sources

European Commission Guidelines on Vertical Restraints [2010] OJ C130/1.

---

475. Commission Guidelines on Vertical Restraints [2010] OJ C130/1, para 100.
476. Commission Guidelines on Vertical Guidelines [2010] OJ C130/1, paras 102–105.
477. Commission Guidelines on Vertical Guidelines [2010] OJ C130/1, para 107.
478. Commission Guidelines on Vertical Guidelines [2010] OJ C130/1, para 108.
479. Commission Guidelines on Vertical Guidelines [2010] OJ C130/1, paras 111–121.
480. Commission Guidelines on Vertical Guidelines [2010] OJ C130/1, paras 122–127.
481. These particular restraints are analysed at paras 128–229 of the Commission Guidelines on Vertical Restraints [2010] OJ C130/1.

45. DOES ARTICLE 101 APPLY TO AGENCY AGREEMENTS?

Summary

- If the agency relationship is genuine, with the economic risk remaining with the principal, Article 101 will not apply to obligations imposed on the agent as to contracts he negotiates and concludes on behalf of the principal.

- The terms of the agency contract and the surrounding circumstances should be examined to determine if the agent assumes sufficient economic risk to bring the agency within Article 101.

- Provisions concerning the relationship between the agent and principal remain subject to Article 101. Certain of these, such as post-contract non-competes, could be problematic.

1. The Commission's Guidelines on Vertical Restraints define an agent as follows:

> An agent is a legal or physical person vested with the power to negotiate and/or conclude contracts on behalf of another person (the principal), either in the agent's own name or in the name of the principal, for the:
>
> — purchase of goods or services by the principal, or
>
> — sale of goods or services supplied by the principal.[482]

2. In a genuine agency, since the principal bears the commercial and financial risks related to the selling and purchasing of the contract goods and services all obligations imposed on the agent in relation to the contracts concluded and/or negotiated on behalf of the principal fall outside Article 101(1).[483]

3. A genuine agency is one in which the agent 'may in principle be treated as an auxiliary organ forming an integral part' of the principal's undertaking.[484] The agent is then treated as forming part of the same economic unit as the principal.[485] The key factor is that the agent does not himself bear (more than a negligible amount of)[486] economic risk.

---

482. Commission Guidelines on Vertical Restraints [2010] OJ C130/1, para 12.
483. Commission Guidelines on Vertical Restraints [2010] OJ C130/1, para 18.
484. Cases 40/73 etc *Suiker Unie UA v Commission* [1975] ECR 1663, [1976] 1 CMLR 295, para 480.
485. Strictly speaking, an independent agent may remain a separate undertaking (see Commission Guidelines on Vertical Restraints [2010] OJ C130/1, para 19; Bellamy & Child (6th edn, 2008) para 2.020). Cf Case C–217/05 *Confederacion Espanola de Empresarios de Estaciones de Servicio v CEPSA* [2006] ECR I–11987, [2007] 4 CMLR 181, opinion of Advocate General Kokott, para 46 ('even if he is in law a separate entity, an agent is not necessarily to be regarded as an undertaking for the purposes of Article [101] as regards the transactions he negotiates on behalf of his principal ... It is only to the extent that the agent acts as an independent economic entity on the market for the principal's goods and services without constituting an economic unit with the latter that Article [101] and the block exemptions are at all applicable').
486. Case C–217/05 *Confederacion Espanola de Empresarios de Estaciones de Servicio v CEPSA* [2006] ECR I–11987, [2007] 4 CMLR 181, para 61.

4.   To determine whether an agent can be considered to form an economic unit with his principal, one should first look at the terms of the agency contract, 'in particular, in the clauses ... implied or express, relating to the assumption of the financial and commercial risks linked to sales of goods to third parties'.[487] The question of risk should be assessed 'with regard to the economic reality of the situation rather than the legal form'[488] and will depend on the circumstances of each case.

5.   In its Guidelines on Vertical Restraints, the Commission states that the agreement will generally be considered to be an agency agreement if property in the contract goods bought or sold does not vest in the agent, or the agent does not himself supply the contract services and where the agent:

• Does not contribute to supply and purchase costs.

• Does not maintain stock at its own cost or risk.

• Does not take responsibility for product liability (unless the agent is himself at fault).

• Does not take responsibility for the customer's non-performance of the contract, with the exception of the loss of the agent's commission, unless the agent is liable for fault.

• Is not directly or indirectly obliged to invest in sales promotion.

• Does not make market-specific investments in equipment, premises or training of personnel.

• Does not undertake other activities within the same product market required by the principal, unless these activities are fully reimbursed by the principal.[489]

6.   This list is not exhaustive and other factors may be relevant in assessing whether the agent has assumed a sufficient degree of risk in the particular circumstances. In *Volkswagen*, for example, agreements between Volkswagen and its dealers were caught by Article 101 because the dealers assumed some financial risk linked to transactions they concluded on behalf of Volkswagen. The dealers repurchased vehicles upon the expiry of leasing contracts and their principal business of sales and after-sales services was carried on, largely independently, in their own name and for their own account.[490] In contrast, in *DaimlerChrysler*, agents of Mercedes-Benz did not constitute separate undertakings, where they were prevented by the terms of the agency agreements from holding stocks of vehicles for sale. Unlike the Volkswagen dealers, these agents did not bear the risk of cars held in stock and

---

487. Case C–217/05 *Confederacion Espanola de Empresarios de Estaciones de Servicio v CEPSA* [2006] ECR I–11987, [2007] 4 CMLR 181, para 46.

488. Commission Guidelines on Vertical Restraints [2010] OJ C130/1, para 17.

489. Commission Guidelines on Vertical Restraints [2010] OJ C130/1, para 16.

490. Case C–266/93 *Bundeskartellamt v Volkswagen AG and VAG Leasing GmbH* [1995] ECR I–3477, [1996] 4 CMLR 505.

remaining unsold.[491] It was Mercedes-Benz which determined the conditions applying to car sales, in particular the sales price, and which bore the risks attached to selling cars.

7. It is only the provisions governing the sale or purchase of the contract goods or services that fall outside Article 101(1), which continues to apply to provisions concerning the relationship between the agent and principal. The Commission discusses how Article 101(1) might apply to such provisions, noting that the agreement

> ... may contain a provision preventing the principal from appointing other agents in respect of a given type of transaction, customer or territory (exclusive agency provisions) and/or a provision preventing the agent from acting as an agent or distributor of undertakings which compete with the principal (single branding provisions). Since the agent is a separate undertaking from the principal, the provisions which concern the relationship between the agent and the principal may infringe Article 101(1). Exclusive agency provisions will in general not lead to anti-competitive effects. However, single branding provisions and post-term non-compete provisions, which concern inter-brand competition, may infringe Article 101(1) if they lead to or contribute to a (cumulative) foreclosure effect on the relevant market where the contract goods or services are sold or purchased. Such provisions may benefit from the Block Exemption Regulation,[492] in particular when the conditions provided in Article 5 of that Regulation are fulfilled. They can also be individually justified by efficiencies under Article 101(3).[493]

8. The Commission Guidelines on Vertical Restraints also point out the danger of a genuine agency being used as a means to facilitate collusion. This could occur if a number of principals use the same agents and collectively prevent other principals from using those agents or when the agents are used to coordinate strategy or exchange sensitive information among the principals.[494]

Key Sources

European Commission Guidelines on Vertical Restraints [2010] OJ C130/1.

Case C–266/93 *Bundeskartellamt v Volkswagen AG and VAG Leasing GmbH* [1995] ECR I–3477, [1996] 4 CMLR 505.

Case T–325/01 *DaimlerChrysler AG v Commission* [2005] ECR II–3319, [2007] 4 CMLR 559.

Case C–217/05 *Confederacion Espanola de Empresarios de Estaciones de Servicio v CEPSA* [2006] ECR I–11987, [2007] 4 CMLR 181.

---

491. Case T–325/01 *DaimlerChrysler AG v Commission* [2005] ECR II–3319, [2007] 4 CMLR 559, paras 97, 102.
492. Commission Regulation (EU) No 330/2010 on the application of Article 101(3) of the Treaty on the Functioning of the European Union to categories of vertical agreements and concerted practices [2010] OJ L102/1 ('Vertical Agreements Block Exemption').
493. Commission Guidelines on Vertical Restraints [2010] OJ C130/1, para 19 (references omitted).
494. Commission Guidelines on Vertical Restraints [2010] OJ C130/1, para 20.

46. MAY A SUPPLIER IMPOSE RESALE PRICES ON ITS DISTRIBUTORS?

Summary

- The imposition of fixed and minimum resale prices is generally considered a hardcore restriction of Article 101.

- Agreements containing such restrictions will not benefit from the block exemption for vertical agreements.

- However, the imposition of fixed or minimum resale prices may generate efficiencies in certain cases and the Article 101(3) exemption might apply.

- Imposing maximum prices or recommending fixed resale prices is less problematic.

- If the supplier's share is not more than 30 per cent, an agreement recommending the resale price or fixing a maximum resale price can benefit from the block exemption for vertical agreements.

- Above that level, a competitive assessment should be carried out.

- Recommended/maximum resale prices are potentially problematic where the supplier has significant market power.

1. Agreements or concerted practices having as their direct or indirect object the establishment of fixed or minimum resale prices or price levels ('RPM') fall squarely within the specific prohibition in Article 101(1)(a) to 'directly or indirectly fix purchase or selling prices' and are considered to be a hardcore restriction of Article 101. RPM is generally considered to be a restriction of competition by object.[495] The imposition of minimum or fixed resale prices is considered to be a hardcore restriction and agreements containing such clauses will not benefit from the block exemption for vertical agreements.[496]

2. RPM may restrict competition in a number of ways, including: (i) facilitating collusion between suppliers by enhancing price transparency and making it easier to detect deviations by a supplier from an agreed price; (ii) it may undermine a supplier's incentive to cut prices as a fixed resale price will prevent it from benefiting from expanding sales; (iii) RPM may facilitate collusion among distributors as they may be able to force or convince suppliers to fix prices above the competitive level; (iv) RPM may soften competition more generally between suppliers and/or distributors; and (v) RPM may be introduced by a supplier to

---

495. See, e.g., Case 243/83 *Binion & CIE v AMP* [1985] ECR 2015, [1985] 3 CMLR 800, para 44 (resale price maintenance was in itself a restriction of competition within the meaning of Article 101); COMP/37.975 *Yamaha*, Commission Decision of 16 July 2003, para 127 (RPM was a restriction by object) and paras 141, 146; Commission Guidelines on Vertical Restraints [2010] OJ C130/1, para 48 ('In the case of contractual provisions or concerted practices that directly establish the resale price, the restriction is clear cut').

496. Regulation 330/2010, Article 4(a).

foreclose smaller rivals as the increased margin offered to distributors through RPM may entice them to favour the brand of that supplier when advising customers.[497]

3. According to the Commission, RPM gives rise to the presumption that the agreement is unlikely to fulfil the conditions of Article 101(3).[498] However, the Commission has recognised that RPM may be justifiable in certain cases where it generates efficiencies and that undertakings have the possibility to plead an efficiency defence under Article 101(3) in an individual case.[499] For example, where a manufacturer introduces a new product, RPM may be helpful to establish the product during an introductory period of expanding demand. In a franchise network, the imposition of fixed resale prices may be necessary to coordinate a short-term low price campaign. In the case of experience or complex products, RPM may enable retailers to provide a certain level of pre-sale services, which could not be achieved otherwise as other retailers might 'free-ride' on the pre-sales efforts. [500]

4. Resale price maintenance that is achieved through indirect means is also a hardcore restriction. If a distributor is 'in reality' bound to adopt minimum or fixed prices, then the fact that there is no direct clause or statement to that effect will not make the RPM any less objectionable.[501]

5. Can RPM fall outside Article 101 if it does not have an appreciable effect on competition? Even where each party's market share is not more than 15 per cent, the *De Minimis* Notice, which would then usually apply, is not applicable if the agreement contains RPM.[502] However, it has been suggested that 'where the supplier's market share is very small any potential effect on competition may not be appreciable and thus the agreement could fall outside Article 101(1)'.[503]

6. In Ireland, specific rules apply to the unilateral conduct of non-dominant firms in the grocery sector. Regardless of whether they have market power, 'grocery goods undertakings' are prohibited from engaging in certain behaviour, including fixed or minimum resale price maintenance.[504]

7. In the United States, RPM had been considered to be *per se* illegal under the federal antitrust laws until a decision of the Supreme Court in 2007 overruled that

---

497. For discussion of these and other potential negative effects of RPM, see the Commission Guidelines on Vertical Restraints [2010] OJ C130/1, para 224.

498. Commission Guidelines on Vertical Restraints [2010] OJ C130/1, para 223.

499. Commission Guidelines on Vertical Restraints [2010] OJ C130/1, para 223.

500. Commission Guidelines on Vertical Restraints [2010] OJ C130/1, para 225

501. See Case C–260/07 *Pedro IV Servicios SL v Total España SA* [2009] ECR I–2437, [2009] 5 CMLR 1291, para 81.

502. Commission *De Minimis* Notice [2001] OJ C368/13, para 11(2)(a).

503. Bellamy & Child (6th edn, 2008) para 6.050.

504. Competition Act 2002, s 15B, as inserted by the Competition (Amendment) Act 2006.

position and held that minimum RPM should in future be assessed under the 'rule of reason'.[505]

Is it permissible to recommend resale prices or impose maximum resale prices?

8. Recommended resale prices and the imposition of maximum resale prices are not considered to be hardcore restrictions of Article 101 or give rise to a restriction of competition by object. In *Pronuptia*, the Court of Justice held that the fact a franchisor makes price recommendations to its franchisees does not constitute a restriction of competition, as long as there is no concerted practice between the franchisor and the franchisees or between the franchisees themselves for the actual application of such prices.[506]

9. Agreements in respect of recommended or maximum resale prices can benefit from the block exemption for vertical agreements if the market shares of each of the supplier and purchaser are not more than 30 per cent.[507] Above that level, the competitive effects of the arrangement have to be considered.

10. Two potential anti-competitive effects are suggested by the Commission: (i) a maximum or recommended resale price could be used as a focal point and be followed by most or all resellers, resulting in a reduction of price competition; or (ii) maximum or recommended prices may soften competition or facilitate collusion among suppliers.[508]

11. An important factor in the assessment is the degree of market power of the supplier. The stronger the supplier's position, the more reluctant resellers may be to deviate from a price recommended by the supplier. The recommended or maximum price can therefore become a focal point for resellers.[509]

12. If the arrangement comes within Article 101(1), the Article 101(3) exemption could be applicable. Potential positive effects include that the imposition of maximum prices helps to ensure that the particular brand competes more forcefully with other brands.[510]

Key Sources

European Commission Guidelines on Vertical Restraints [2010] OJ C130/1.

---

505. *Leegin Creative Leather Products, Inc. v PSKS, Inc.* 551 US 877 (2007), overruling *Dr. Miles Medical Co. v John D. Park & Sons Co.* 220 US 373 (1911).
506. Case 161/84 *Pronuptia de Paris GmbH* [1986] ECR 353, [1986] 1 CMLR 414, para 27. See also Case T–67/01 *JCB Service v Commission* [2004] ECR II–49, [2004] 4 CMLR 1346, paras 121–133 (resale prices were recommended by the manufacturer but it was not established that resale prices were fixed).
507. Regulation 330/2010, Article 3(1); Commission Guidelines on Vertical Restraints [2010] OJ C130/1, para 226.
508. Commission Guidelines on Vertical Restraints [2010] OJ C130/1, para 227.
509. Commission Guidelines on Vertical Restraints [2010] OJ C130/1, para 228.
510. Commission Guidelines on Vertical Restraints [2010] OJ C130/1, para 229.

47. **DO 'MOST FAVOURED NATION' CLAUSES OR 'ENGLISH CLAUSES' IN CONTRACTS BETWEEN A SUPPLIER AND DISTRIBUTOR BREACH COMPETITION LAW?**

Summary

- A MFN clause usually provides that the supplier will provide the purchaser with price/terms as good as it provides to other purchasers. An English clause usually gives the supplier a right of first refusal to meet better offers obtained by the purchaser.

- MFN and English clauses should be analysed in their economic and legal context to determine if they raise issues under Article 101.

- MFN clauses may have pro-competitive effects, for example, enabling purchasers to benefit from lower prices and increased competition among suppliers.

- MFN clauses may also have anti-competitive effects, for example, resulting in the alignment of prices among suppliers.

- English clauses, by allowing a purchaser to 'shop around' may ameliorate some of the negative effects of an exclusive purchasing obligation.

- However, such clauses may have negative effects, for example, they could facilitate collusion among suppliers where the purchaser is made to reveal the source of a competing offer.

What are 'MFN' and 'English' clauses?

1. A 'Most Favoured Nation' ('MFN') clause in a contract between a supplier and distributor would typically provide that the supplier will offer as good a price or terms to that distributor as it offers to any of its other distributors. The distributor therefore ensures that it will receive terms that are at least as favourable as any other distributor. A MFN clause could also work the other way, with a distributor promising a supplier that it will give it terms that are at least as favourable or prices that are at least as high, as it gives to similar suppliers.

2. Under an 'English' clause, a buyer is typically required to inform a supplier of any better offers it receives (and possibly the source of those offers) for the supply of similar goods. The buyer can accept the better offer only if the supplier refuses to match it. Such a clause might feature in an exclusive purchasing contract. Another form of English clause operates beyond the duration of an agreement by applying to subsequent agreements, effectively giving the supplier a right of first refusal for those subsequent agreements.

How are MFN clauses assessed under Article 101?

3.   MFN clauses are not generally considered to have an anti-competitive object. The effects of the particular clause in its legal and economic context would need to be analysed to establish whether the clause raises issues under Article 101.

4.   In some circumstances MFN clauses might be viewed as a device to facilitate collusion. Take a MFN clause that benefits buyers, where the supplier guarantees that the buyer will receive at least as good a price as offered to other customers. If all suppliers in an oligopolistic market include such MFN clauses, this may result in price stabilisation at uncompetitive levels because no supplier has an incentive to offer a discount.[511] MFN clauses could also be used to facilitate collusion if used by a price leader. The MFN clause could operate as a 'cooperative' gesture with the price leader effectively indicating that competitors can raise their price to the same level. The price leader will retaliate through a price war if they do not follow but at the same time, if they do follow, the price leader will not lower its prices.[512]

5.   The EU case law and guidance on MFN clauses is sparse. Among the few cases involving MFN clauses, the compatibility of MFN clauses with Article 101 was considered by the Commission in its examination of a network of agreements between the major Hollywood studios and a number of European pay-TV stations. The clauses were contained in 'output deals' between the studios and the stations, pursuant to which a studio would agree to sell all of its output for a particular period. The MFN clause would give a studio the right to enjoy the most favourable terms agreed between a pay-TV company and any one of the studios. Although the studios withdrew the clauses, the Commission had taken the preliminary view that the cumulative effect of the clauses was to align the prices paid to the studios. This was particularly so because any increase agreed with a studio triggered a right to parallel increases in the prices of the other studios. The Commission considered that the cumulative effect of these arrangements was an anomalous way of setting prices that was at odds with the basic principle of price competition.[513] As this case did not result in a formal decision, there is little in the way of legal analysis that can be taken from it. However, it appears that the Commission was particularly concerned about the cumulative effect of a network of MFN clauses, resulting in the risk of the alignment of prices in a range of commercial agreements.[514]

6.   MFN clauses can also be viewed as pro-competitive. Where a MFN clause is given by a supplier to a purchaser, the purchaser benefits from lower prices where other purchasers drive the supplier's price downwards, which they may be able to do by playing that supplier off against others. Even if the MFN clause or a network of such clauses could result in the alignment of prices or facilitate tacit collusion,

---

511. See Monti, *EC Competition Law* (2007) 341.
512. See Monti, *EC Competition Law* (2007) 341.
513. Commission Press Release IP/04/1314, Commission closes investigation into contracts of six Hollywood studios with European pay-TVs (26 October 2004).
514. MFN clauses imposed by a dominant purchaser/supplier might raise issues under Article 102 if it could be shown that they represented unfair trading conditions in the circumstances.

such collusion may well be too unstable to survive. Against this, there may well be a loss in competition if the MFN clause is required to be removed.[515]

7.   In *Pedro IV*, the Court of Justice acknowledged that a MFN clause in a fuel supply contract did not distort competition. The exclusive supply agreement was between Total and a company that ran a service station in Barcelona, Pedro IV. A clause in the agreement provided that Total was to determine the price of the fuel which it supplied to Pedro IV on the most advantageous terms agreed by it with other service stations in Barcelona and guarantee that the price would never be higher than the average of the prices fixed by other suppliers with a significant presence on the market. The Court of Justice simply acknowledged that this clause concerned the price that Pedro IV was to pay for the fuel, 'the determination of which comes within the competence of the parties and does not distort competition'.[516] While there was no detailed analysis of the effects of the MFN clause, the Court's terse conclusion indicates that it did not see any reason for concern over the clause.

How are English clauses treated under Article 101?

8.   When it is part of an exclusive purchasing agreement, an English clause could be viewed as ameliorating any restrictive effect of such an agreement. It gives the purchaser an opportunity to benefit from competition despite the exclusivity agreement. The Court of Justice has acknowledged this, noting of the English clause at issue in *Hoffmann-La Roche* that 'there is no doubt whatever that this clause makes it possible to remedy some of the unfair consequences' of an exclusive purchasing agreement.[517]

9.   English clauses can also give rise to concerns under Article 101. If the clause requires the buyer to reveal the identity of the supplier making the better offer, it may increase transparency on the market and facilitate collusion among suppliers. In *BP/Kemi*, the Commission considered that an English clause restricted competition because it provided a supplier with information about prices of its competitors that it would not otherwise be able to obtain.[518] In this case, DDSF was required to obtain all of its requirements of ethanol from BP Kemi. This exclusive purchasing obligation was tempered by an English clause which both parties argued protected the interest of DDSF, as it could obtain cheaper supplies of ethanol when the conditions for application of the clause were met. However, the Commission found that the clause was of limited practical value as the conditions for it coming into play were onerous. For example, it only applied if the quantity offered by the competitor corresponded to DDSF's total annual requirements. Smaller purchases could not be made under the clause. Even if the

---

515. See Monti, *EC Competition Law* (2007) 342.
516. Case C–260/07 *Pedro IV Servicios SL v Total España SA* [2009] ECR I–2437, [2009] 5 CMLR 1291, para 77.
517. Case 85/76 *Hoffmann-La Roche & Co. AG v Commission* [1979] ECR 461, [1979] 3 CMLR 211, para 104.
518. *BP Kemi/DDSF* [1979] OJ L286/32, [1979] 3 CMLR 684, para 64.

English clause was triggered, DDSF was still required to make certain minimum purchases from BP Kemi so the purchasing obligation was relaxed only to a limited extent.

10. An English clause may also operate in a similar way to an exclusivity agreement. Depending on the market power of the parties, it may result in foreclosure of other suppliers as the supplier who is party to the agreement with the English clause is effectively able to maintain total exclusivity with the distributor buyer (at least where it is prepared to meet any price offered to the purchaser as covered by the clause). Therefore, an English clause may have the same effect as a single branding agreement, with the buyer induced to concentrate its order for a particular type of product with one supplier.[519]

11. If an English clause applies to subsequent agreements that a buyer will enter into, essentially giving the incumbent supplier a right of first refusal over the new agreement, it means that other suppliers are at a disadvantage and so the period for which competition is affected is extended.[520] Such a clause is likely to be caught by Article 101(1).

12. An English clause involving a dominant company may be found to be a breach of Article 102. It is essentially a qualified form of exclusive dealing. Such a clause was condemned in *Hoffmann-La Roche*, the Court of Justice noting that it enabled Roche to obtain sensitive information about the market and its competitors.[521]

Key Sources

BP Kemi/DDSF [1979] OJ L286/32, [1979] 3 CMLR 684.

Case 85/76 *Hoffmann-La Roche & Co. AG v Commission* [1979] ECR 461, [1979] 3 CMLR 211.

Case C–260/07 *Pedro IV Servicios SL v Total España SA* [2009] ECR I–2437, [2009] 5 CMLR 1291.

---

519. Commission Guidelines on Vertical Restraints [2010] OJ C130/1, para 129.
520. See Bellamy & Child (6th edn, 2008) para 6.159.
521. Case 85/76 *Hoffmann-La Roche & Co. AG v Commission* [1979] ECR 461, [1979] 3 CMLR 211, paras 102–108.

48. MAY A SUPPLIER APPOINT AN EXCLUSIVE DISTRIBUTOR TO A PARTICULAR AREA?

Summary

- An exclusive distribution agreement may benefit from the block exemption for vertical agreements if the market share thresholds are not exceeded and the other conditions in the block exemption are met.

- If the agreement is not covered by the block exemption, an analysis must be carried out to determine if the agreement breaches Article 101.

- Important factors include the market share of the supplier and its competitors and whether the distributor is distributing the products of more than one supplier.

- A restriction on 'passive sales' is a hardcore restriction of Article 101 and will bring the agreement outside the block exemption and likely be caught by Article 101(1).

- Exclusive distribution may also generate efficiencies and even if caught by Article 101(1), may benefit from the Article 101(3) exemption.

1.   In an exclusive distribution agreement, the supplier usually agrees to appoint only one distributor to sell its products in a particular territory or to a particular class of customers (the latter is termed an 'exclusive customer allocation agreement' by the Commission).[522] The distributor is usually restricted from making active sales into other exclusively allocated territories. This can be contrasted with selective distribution, where the restriction on the appointment of distributors is linked to the nature of the product and distributors are restricted from selling to non-authorised distributors, leaving only appointed dealers and final customers as possible buyers.[523] The distributors are not allocated exclusive territories or customer groups in selective distribution.

2.   The Commission has described the main potential competition concerns of exclusive distribution arrangements as follows:

> The possible competition risks are mainly reduced intra-brand competition and market partitioning, which may facilitate price discrimination in particular. When most or all of the suppliers apply exclusive distribution, it may soften competition and facilitate collusion, both at the suppliers' and distributors' level. Lastly, exclusive distribution may lead to foreclosure of other distributors and therewith reduce competition at that level.[524]

3.   Exclusive distribution agreements can benefit from the block exemption for vertical agreements. The market share thresholds, which are 30 per cent for each

---

522. Commission Guidelines on Vertical Restraints [2010] OJ C130/1, para 168.
523. Commission Guidelines on Vertical Restraints [2010] OJ C130/1, para 174.
524. Commission Guidelines on Vertical Restraints [2010] OJ C130/1, para 151.

of the supplier and the distributor, cannot be exceeded.[525] Even if the market shares of the parties are below these thresholds, the agreement will not benefit from the block exemption if it contains any of the hardcore restrictions prohibited by Article 4 of Regulation 330/2010. When exclusive distribution is combined with selective distribution, the block exemption will apply only if active selling in other territories is not restricted.[526]

4. If the exclusive distribution agreement does not benefit from the block exemption, a competition analysis should be carried out to determine whether the agreement falls within Article 101(1) and if so, whether it can avail of the Article 101(3) exemption. As the Court of Justice stated in *L'Oréal* (in the context of selective distribution but also applicable to exclusive distribution):

    > In order to decide whether an agreement is to be considered as prohibited by reason of the distortion of competition which is its object or its effect, it is necessary to consider the competition within the actual context in which it would occur in the absence of the agreement in dispute. To that end, it is appropriate to take into account in particular the nature and quantity, limited or otherwise, of the products covered by the agreement, the position and the importance of the parties on the market for the products concerned, and the isolated nature of the disputed agreement or, alternatively, its position in a series of agreements.[527]

5. The Commission identifies in the Guidelines on Vertical Restraints a number of factors that may be important in the analysis. One such factor is the market position of the supplier and its competitors. A loss of intra-brand competition (competition between distributors of the same brand) as a result of the exclusive distribution arrangement is only problematic if there is limited competition between different brands (inter-brand competition). The higher the market share of the supplier and the more significant its market power, the weaker the degree of inter-brand competition and the more likely that the protection conferred by exclusive distribution will distort competition.[528]

6. The Commission is also attuned to the risk of collusion where there are a small number of strong competitors, each of whom operates an exclusive distribution network. If one distributor is granted exclusive distribution rights in respect of two or more important competing products, this may substantially reduce inter-brand competition between those products. The Commission notes that such a distributor will have an incentive not to pass any price reduction in one brand to consumers as this will affect sales and margins on other brands. This in turn may disincentivise producers from engaging in price competition in the first place. The Commission states that such 'cumulative effect' situations may be reason to withdraw the benefit of the block exemption where the market shares of the individual supplier and retailer are below the 30 per cent thresholds.[529]

---

525. Regulation 330/2010, Article 3(1).
526. Commission Guidelines on Vertical Restraints [2010] OJ C130/1, para 152.
527. Case 31/80 *L'Oréal v PVBA De Nieuwe AMCK* [1980] ECR 3775, [1981] 2 CMLR 235, para 19.
528. Commission Guidelines on Vertical Restraints [2010] OJ C130/1, para 153.
529. Commission Guidelines on Vertical Restraints [2010] OJ C130/1, para 154.

7.   The level at which the exclusive distribution takes place is also important. If the exclusive distributor is a wholesaler, which can sell to downstream retailers without restriction, it is unlikely there will be appreciable anti-competitive effects. However, restrictions at the retail level may be more problematic, especially when applied to large territories 'since final consumers may be confronted with little possibility of choosing between a high price/high service and a low price/low service distributor for an important brand'.[530]

8.   The Commission recognises the potential for exclusive distribution to generate efficiencies, for example, where investments by distributors are required to build up a new brand or through savings generated by economies of scale in transport costs.[531] The extent to which efficiencies are generated will be an important factor in considering the availability of the Article 101(3) exemption.

9.   If an exclusive distribution agreement contains hardcore restrictions, it will fall outside the block exemption (even if the parties are below the market share thresholds) and may well breach Article 101. Certain restrictions on resale are not considered to be hardcore restrictions. These are outlined in Article 4 of Regulation 330/2010 and include a restriction of active sales into the territory of another exclusive distributor and the restriction of sales by the members of a selective distribution system to unauthorised distributors within the territory reserved by the supplier to operate that system.[532] Two hardcore restrictions that frequently arise in the context of exclusive distribution are resale price maintenance (the imposition of fixed or minimum resale prices)[533] and territorial restrictions on resale.[534]

Key Sources

European Commission Guidelines on Vertical Restraints [2010] OJ C130/1.

---

530. Commission Guidelines on Vertical Restraints [2010] OJ C130/1, para 159.
531. Commission Guidelines on Vertical Restraints [2010] OJ C130/1, para 164.
532. Regulation 330/2010, Articles 4(b)(i), 4(b)(iii).
533. See Question 46.
534. See Question 49.

49. MAY A SUPPLIER BAN AN EXCLUSIVE DISTRIBUTOR IN ONE MEMBER STATE FROM MAKING SALES INTO ANOTHER MEMBER STATE?

Summary

- A ban on 'passive sales' is a hardcore restriction of Article 101.

- An agreement that prohibits the distributor from making 'active sales' outside its designated territory can still benefit from the block exemption. If the agreement falls outside the exemption, the ban on active sales would have to be analysed under Article 101 along with the other effects of the agreement.

1. The application of Article 101 to resale restrictions on a distributor will depend on whether they relate to 'active' or 'passive' sales. Active sales are those where the distributor seeks out customers. Passive sales involve unsolicited requests originating from the customer. The Commission considers that sales made through the Internet are generally passive sales so that, for example, if a customer contacts a distributor having viewed its website, any resulting sales are passive. However, online advertising may give rise to active selling, for example where the distributor pays a search engine to display advertisements specifically to users in a particular territory.[535]

2. A ban on passive sales is generally considered to be a hardcore restriction of Article 101. Such restrictions, which limit parallel trade in the EU, are typically considered to have an anti-competitive object and so will usually fall squarely within the Article 101(1) prohibition with little chance of an exemption under Article 101(3). Although it is unlikely in practice that an agreement restricting passive sales would not be found to have an anti-competitive object, it should not simply be assumed that the agreement has an anti-competitive object, as 'in order to assess the anti-competitive nature of an agreement, regard must be had *inter alia* to the content of its provisions, the objectives it seeks to attain and the economic and legal context of which it forms a part'.[536]

3. The Commission has imposed considerable fines in respect of agreements containing restrictions on passive sales.[537] It has emphasised that a distributor must be free to respond to unsolicited orders from outside its allocated territory:

    > The restriction of competition which results from the obligation to resell in a specific country may itself affect trade between Member States to an appreciable degree owing

---

535. For the Commission's definition of active sales and passive sales and its treatment of Internet sales restrictions, see Commission Guidelines on Vertical Restraints [2010] OJ C130/1, paras 51–54.

536. Case C–501/06P *GlaxoSmithKline Services Unlimited v Commission* [2009] ECR I–9291, [2010] 4 CMLR 50, para 58.

537. See, e.g., involving a €30 million fine, Case T–67/01 *JCB Service v Commission* [2004] ECR II–49, [2004] 4 CMLR 1346 (appeal dismissed, Case C–167/04P *JCB Service v Commission* [2006] ECR I–8935, [2006] 5 CMLR 1303); a fine of €102 million imposed by the Commission, reduced to €90 million on appeal, Case T–62/98 *Volkswagen AG v Commission* [2000] ECR II–2707, [2000] 5 CMLR 853 (upheld on appeal, Case C–338/00 *Volkswagen AG v Commission* [2003] ECR I–9189, [2004] 4 CMLR 351).

to the fact that the subsequent seller is established in the common market, within which he must remain free to sell the goods where he wishes depending on the circumstances and, *inter alia*, on the prices quoted to him.[538]

4.   An agreement may breach Article 101 even if the territory allocated to the distributor is one outside the EU. A prohibition on such a distributor from making sales within the EU may breach Article 101 if that prohibition has the effect of preventing, restricting or distorting competition within the Union and is liable to affect the pattern of trade between Member States.[539]

5.   The export ban does not have to be explicit. A requirement that the distributor refer orders from customers outside its territory back to the supplier or to other distributors or to obtain approval from the supplier would be sufficient to give rise to a breach.[540] Mere acquiescence on the part of the distributor to the export ban may also suffice.[541]

6.   The treatment under Article 101 of territorial restrictions on active sales is different to restrictions on passive sales. Regulation 330/2010 itself recognises that restrictions on a distributor engaging in active selling outside its territory may be legitimate. Article 4(b)(i) of the Regulation provides that 'the restriction of active sales into the exclusive territory or to an exclusive customer group reserved to the supplier or allocated by the supplier to another buyer, where such a restriction does not limit sales by the customers of the buyer' is not a hardcore restriction and that the block exemption can apply to agreements containing such clauses.

Key Sources

European Commission Guidelines on Vertical Restraints [2010] OJ C130/1.

---

538. 82/866/EEC *Rolled Zinc Products and Zinc Alloys* [1983] 2 CMLR 285, 292.
539. Case C–306/96 *Javico International v Yves Saint Laurent Parfums SA* [1998] ECR I–1983, [1998] 5 CMLR 172, para 28.
540. See, e.g., IV/29.395 *Windsurfing International* [1983] OJ L229/1, [1984] 1 CMLR 1, paras 111–112 (sole importers prevented from active and passive selling; supplier approval required for sales outside the allocated territory).
541. See further Question 13.

50. HOW ARE SELECTIVE DISTRIBUTION AGREEMENTS TREATED UNDER ARTICLE 101?

Summary

- A selective distribution system may benefit from the block exemption for vertical agreements if the conditions for the exemption are met. However, if there are restrictions on sales to end users or cross-supplies to other authorised distributors, the block exemption cannot be availed of.

- Selective distribution based on qualitative criteria will be assumed to fall outside Article 101(1) if the nature of the product necessitates selective distribution, distributors are chosen on the basis of objective qualitative criteria and the criteria are necessary.

- Assuming that a competition analysis must be carried out, a particular concern is the potential cumulative effect of selective distribution networks operated by different suppliers. This could reduce competition between brands and result in the foreclosure of distributors.

1. Selective distribution systems are common. The supplier restricts the number of distributors based on criteria related to the product and imposes restrictions on resale, with distributors entitled to sell only to other authorised distributors or end-users. The goods that are the subject of a selective distribution system are typically branded, final products. This form of distribution is used, for example, for selling luxury products, where the method of sale is an important part of the brand's image.

2. There is a specific exemption for selective distribution agreements under the block exemption for vertical agreements, Regulation 330/2010. If the conditions for application of the exemption are met, the benefit of the block exemption will not be lost if the agreement restricts the sales by the members of a selective distribution system to unauthorised distributors within the territory reserved by the supplier to operate that system.[542] However a restriction on active or passive sales to end users or a restriction on making cross-supplies to other authorised dealers will be considered a hardcore restriction. The entire agreement with lose the benefit of the block exemption if such a restriction is included.[543] The block exemption will not apply to a clause in a vertical agreement that imposes any direct or indirect obligation causing the members of a selective distribution system not to sell the brands of particular competing suppliers.[544]

3. If a particular selective distribution agreement does not benefit from the block exemption (e.g. where the market share thresholds are exceeded), it should be

---

542. Regulation 330/2010, Article 4(b)(iii).
543. Regulation 330/2010, Article 4(c), 4(d).
544. Regulation 330/2010, Article 5(1)(c).

analysed whether the agreement is caught by the Article 101 prohibition and if so whether it can avail of the Article 101(3) exemption.

4. The main competition concern with selective distribution is that it will reduce intra-brand competition, in particular by foreclosing certain kinds of distributors who may have lowered prices. Where there are parallel networks of selective distribution systems, this may facilitate collusion among suppliers or buyers. On the other hand, selective distribution may have pro-competitive elements. It rewards investment by distributors and prevents free-riding by discounting distributors. It may also be an important element in establishing a product's brand recognition.

5. If the criteria for appointing distributors is purely qualitative, e.g. the distributor must provide a certain level of after-sales service, selective distribution will generally be considered to fall outside Article 101(1), provided that three conditions are met. These three conditions, which follow from the case law of the Union courts and are repeated in the Guidelines on Vertical Restraints are:

• The nature of the product necessitates selective distribution;

• Distributors are chosen on objective qualitative criteria which are laid down uniformly for all potential resellers and are not applied in a discriminatory fashion; and

• The criteria must not go beyond what is necessary.[545]

6. The Court of Justice has rejected the argument that the exclusion of certain distributors from a selective distribution system is a unilateral act by the supplier that does not fall within Article 101. In *AEG-Telefunken*, the Court held that the supplier's refusals to admit certain distributors was caught by Article 101 as:

> ... even refusals of approval are acts performed in the context of the contractual relations with authorized distributors inasmuch as their purpose is to guarantee observance of the agreements in restraint of competition which form the basis of contracts between manufacturers and approved distributors. Refusals to approve distributors who satisfy the qualitative criteria ... therefore supply proof of an unlawful application of the system if their number is sufficient to preclude the possibility that they are isolated cases not forming part of systematic conduct.[546]

7. Assuming that the arrangement does not fall outside the scope of Article 101(1), a competition analysis would have to be undertaken to assess the effects of the selective distribution and to ascertain whether the Article 101(3) exemption was available. The market position of the supplier and its competitors is of central importance as a reduction in intra-brand competition will be problematic only if there is limited inter-brand competition.[547] If competitors operate similar selective

---

545. Commission Guidelines on Vertical Restraints [2010] OJ C130/1, para 175; and, e.g., Case C–26/76 *Metro SB-Großmärkte GmbH & Co. KG v Commission ('Metro I')* [1977] ECR 1875, [1978] 2 CMLR 1, para 20; Case 31/80 *L'Oréal v PVBA De Nieuwe AMCK* [1980] ECR 3775, [1981] 2 CMLR 235, paras 15–16.

546. Case C–107/82 *AEG-Telefunken v Commission* [1983] ECR 3151, [1984] 3 CMLR 325, para 39.

547. Commission Guidelines on Vertical Restraints [2010] OJ C130/1, para 177.

distribution networks, there may be a cumulative foreclosure effect of distributors, for example, online resellers that may be very price competitive.[548] The Commission may consider withdrawing the benefit of the block exemption where different selective distribution systems produce such cumulative anti-competitive effects but it acknowledges that such cumulative effects problems are unlikely to arise unless more than 50 per cent of the market operates on the basis of selective distribution.[549] Concerns will increase if each of the top five suppliers operate selective distribution and their combined share is more than 50 per cent. The Commission suggests that the Article 101(3) exemption may not apply in this situation:

> If all five largest suppliers apply selective distribution, competition concerns may arise with respect to those agreements in particular that apply quantitative selection criteria by directly limiting the number of authorised dealers or that apply qualitative criteria, such as a requirement to have one or more brick and mortar shops or to provide specific services, which forecloses certain distribution formats. The conditions of Article 101(3) are in general unlikely to be fulfilled if the selective distribution systems at issue prevent access to the market by new distributors capable of adequately selling the products in question, especially price discounters or online-only distributors offering lower prices to consumers, thereby limiting distribution to the advantage of certain existing channels and to the detriment of final consumers.[550]

8. Other potentially relevant considerations in assessing selective distribution networks include the extent to which there is buyer power among dealers, which may increase the risk of collusion and the imposition of selection criteria on the supplier, with the effect of foreclosing other distributors;[551] and the imposition of non-compete obligations on distributors (*i.e.* a requirement that they not sell the products of other suppliers), which could result in the foreclosure of suppliers.[552]

Key Sources

European Commission Guidelines on Vertical Restraints [2010] OJ C130/1.

Case C–26/76 *Metro SB-Großmärkte GmbH & Co. KG v Commission ('Metro I')* [1977] ECR 1875, [1978] 2 CMLR 1.

---

548. Commission Guidelines on Vertical Restraints [2010] OJ C130/1, para 178.
549. Commission Guidelines on Vertical Restraints [2010] OJ C130/1, para 179.
550. Commission Guidelines on Vertical Restraints [2010] OJ C130/1, para 179.
551. Commission Guidelines on Vertical Restraints [2010] OJ C130/1, para 181.
552. Commission Guidelines on Vertical Restraints [2010] OJ C130/1, para 183.

51. HOW ARE FRANCHISE AGREEMENTS TREATED UNDER ARTICLE 101?

Summary

- Franchise agreements can benefit from the block exemption for vertical agreements.

- Restrictions that are required for the protection of know-how and expertise, such as non-compete obligations, and restrictions necessary to protect the reputation of the franchise network, usually fall outside Article 101(1).

- Restrictions that confer territorial protection or result in market sharing or restrictions that prevent price competition between franchisees will typically fall within Article 101(1).

- If a clause in a franchise agreement falls within Article 101(1), it may still benefit from the Article 101(3) exemption. The more important the transfer of know-how involved, the more likely that restrictions will be exempted Article 101(3).

1. Franchise agreements usually involve the licensing of intellectual property rights relating to trademarks, know-how etc. by a franchisor to a franchisee for the distribution of goods or services. The franchisor usually also provides the franchisee with commercial or technical assistance. The franchisee will assume the financial risk of his own business and pay a royalty or fee to the franchisor. Franchise agreements may take different forms and apply to the manufacture of goods, the provision of a service or the distribution of goods.

2. The Court of Justice examined franchise agreements under Article 101 in the *Pronuptia* case. The franchisee sought to avoid paying royalties by arguing that the distribution franchise agreement was in breach of Article 101 and the German court hearing the case made a preliminary reference on the issue. The Court held that the compatibility of franchise agreements with Article 101 depended on the clauses in the agreement. The Court recognised that obligations that were necessary to underpin the franchise relationship would not be caught by Article 101(1). There were two essential elements of the franchise relationship:

> First, the franchisor must be able to communicate his know-how to the franchisees and provide them with the necessary assistance in order to enable them to apply his methods, without running the risk that that know-how and assistance might benefit competitors, even indirectly. It follows that provisions which are essential in order to avoid that risk do not constitute restrictions on competition for the purposes of [Article 101(1)]. That is also true of a clause prohibiting the franchisee, during the period of validity of the contract and for a reasonable period after its expiry, from opening a shop of the same or a similar nature in an area where he may compete with a member of the network. The same may be said of the franchisee's obligation not to transfer his shop to another party without the prior approval of the franchisor; that provision is intended to prevent competitors from indirectly benefiting from the know-how and assistance provided.

Secondly, the franchisor must be able to take the measures necessary for maintaining the identity and reputation of the network bearing his business name or symbol. It follows that provisions which establish the means of control necessary for that purpose do not constitute restrictions on competition for the purposes of [Article 101(1)].

The same is true of the franchisee's obligation to apply the business methods developed by the franchisor and to use the know-how provided.

That is also the case with regard to the franchisee's obligation to sell the goods covered by the contract only in premises laid out and decorated according to the franchisor's instructions, which is intended to ensure uniform presentation in conformity with certain requirements. The same requirements apply to the location of the shop, the choice of which is also likely to affect the network's reputation. It is thus understandable that the franchisee cannot transfer his shop to another location without the franchisor's approval.[553]

3.   The first type of restriction covers non-compete clauses and restrictive covenants and the Court accepted that such restrictions could operate not only during the term of the franchise agreement but also 'for a reasonable period after its expiry'. In general, a period of twelve months from the termination of the agreement is considered reasonable.[554] In some cases, a non-compete clause that applies after the expiry of the agreement may not be justified, in particular where the know-how provided by the franchisor includes a large element of general commercial techniques and where the franchisee already had experience in the area.[555] It seems that a 'cautious, case-specific analysis' should be undertaken to establish whether the non-compete obligation falls outside Article 101(1).[556]

4.   As to the second type of restriction, the Commission has upheld restrictions on the sale of the franchise goods to resellers outside the franchise network. If such restrictions were not allowed, many of the obligations in the franchise agreement would be rendered meaningless as the goods could be passed on to resellers who had no access to the franchisor's know-how and were not bound by the same obligations which were necessary in order to establish and maintain the originality and reputation of the network and its identifying marks.[557] In the Guidelines on Vertical Restraints, the Commission recognises that 'the more important the transfer of know-how, the more likely it is that the restraints create efficiencies and/or are indispensable to protect the know-how and that the vertical restraints fulfil the conditions of Article 101(3)'.[558]

---

553. Case 161/84 *Pronuptia de Paris GmbH* [1986] ECR 353, [1986] 1 CMLR 414, paras 16–19.
554. Cf, e.g., *Vendo plc v Adams* [2002] NI 95 (eighteen month non-compete was reasonable). This case discusses a number of English authorities on similar issues.
555. See *Charles Jourdan* [1989] OJ L35/31, [1989] 4 CMLR 581, para 27.
556. *Pirtek (UK) Ltd v Joinplace Ltd* [2010] EWHC 1641 (Ch) para 53 (Briggs J). Note also, para 59 ('Once it is established that, taken as a whole, the know-how and assistance provided by a franchisor to a franchisee ... is of an extent and type likely to turn that franchisee or principal into an effective competitor of the franchisor', the post-termination non-compete clause would not breach competition law).
557. *Yves Rocher* [1987] OJ L8/49, [1988] 4 CMLR 592, para 46.
558. Commission Guidelines on Vertical Restraints [2010] OJ C130/1, para 190(a).

5.   The Guidelines on Vertical Restraints also recognise that certain restrictions related to intellectual property rights ('IPRs') will usually be covered by the block exemption.[559] The block exemption will only apply where the other conditions for its application, including the 30 per cent market share thresholds, are met.[560] In that context, the following IPR-related obligations are generally considered necessary to protect the franchisor's IPRs and where such obligations fall under Article 101(1), are also covered by the block exemption:

(a)   An obligation on the franchisee not to engage, directly or indirectly, in any similar business;

(b)   An obligation on the franchisee not to acquire financial interests in the capital of a competing undertaking such as would give the franchisee the power to influence the economic conduct of such undertaking;

(c)   An obligation on the franchisee not to disclose to third parties the know-how provided by the franchisor as long as this know-how is not in the public domain;

(d)   An obligation on the franchisee to communicate to the franchisor any experience gained in exploiting the franchise and to grant the franchisor, and other franchisees, a non-exclusive licence for the know-how resulting from that experience;

(e)   An obligation on the franchisee to inform the franchisor of infringements of licensed intellectual property rights, to take legal action against infringers or to assist the franchisor in any legal actions against infringers;

(f)   An obligation on the franchisee not to use know-how licensed by the franchisor for purposes other than the exploitation of the franchise;

(g)   An obligation on the franchisee not to assign the rights and obligations under the franchise agreement without the franchisor's consent.[561]

6.   Certain other restrictions in a franchise agreement, which are not related to the essential character of franchising, may fall within Article 101(1). These include restrictions on the locations in which a franchisee can operate, which can result in territorial protection and market sharing, and provisions that prevent franchisees from engaging in price competition with each other.[562] The Court of Justice recognised in *Pronuptia* that a potential franchisee might only engage in the business in the first place if guaranteed a certain degree of protection from competition on the part of the franchisor or franchisee. However, this could only be considered when applying Article 101(3).[563]

Key Sources

European Commission Guidelines on Vertical Restraints [2010] OJ C130/1.

Case 161/84 *Pronuptia de Paris GmbH* [1986] ECR 353, [1986] 1 CMLR 414.

---

559. Commission Guidelines on Vertical Restraints [2010] OJ C130/1, para 44; Regulation 330/ 2010, Article 4(3).
560. See Question 43.
561. Commission Guidelines on Vertical Restraints [2010] OJ C130/1, para 45.
562. Case 161/84 *Pronuptia de Paris GmbH* [1986] ECR 353, [1986] 1 CMLR 414, para 23.
563. Case 161/84 *Pronuptia de Paris GmbH* [1986] ECR 353, [1986] 1 CMLR 414, para 24.

Chapter 3

ARTICLE 102

Chapter 3

ARTICLE 102

52. WHAT ARE THE ELEMENTS OF ARTICLE 102?

Summary

- A dominant position.

- Held in the common market or a substantial part of it.

- Abuse of the dominant position.

- An effect on trade between Member States.

- Article 102 applies only to undertakings.

1. Article 102 first sets out the general prohibition on an abuse of dominance and then includes four particular ways in which abuse may occur. This is a non-exhaustive list of abusive conduct.[1]

2. Article 102 states as follows:

    > Any abuse by one or more undertakings of a dominant position within the internal market or in a substantial part of it shall be prohibited as incompatible with the internal market in so far as it may affect trade between Member States.

    > Such abuse may, in particular, consist in:

    > (a) directly or indirectly imposing unfair purchase or selling prices or other unfair trading conditions;

    > (b) limiting production, markets or technical development to the prejudice of consumers;

    > (c) applying dissimilar conditions to equivalent transactions with other trading parties, thereby placing them at a competitive disadvantage;

    > (d) making the conclusion of contracts subject to acceptance by the other parties of supplementary obligations which, by their nature or according to commercial usage, have no connection with the subject of such contracts.

3. A central idea within the case law on Article 102 is that a dominant undertaking has 'a special responsibility not to allow its conduct to impair genuine undistorted competition'.[2] A dominant undertaking therefore may be prevented from engaging in certain types of activity which can legitimately be carried out by non-dominant

---

1. See, e.g., Case C–333/94P *Tetra Pak International SA v Commission* [1996] ECR I–5951, [1997] 4 CMLR 662, para 37.
2. Case 322/81 *Michelin NV v Commission* [1983] ECR 3461, [1985] 1 CMLR 282, para 57.

firms. The actual scope of the dominant firm's special responsibility will depend on the circumstances.[3] It seems that firms in a position of 'superdominance', described by Advocate General Fennelly as a position of 'overwhelming dominance verging on monopoly', may face a 'particularly onerous special obligation'.[4]

4. In contrast to the position under Article 101, where an undertaking otherwise caught by the Article 101 prohibition can benefit from an exemption under Article 101(3), Article 102 does not provide for any formal exemption mechanism. However, it may be possible to show that otherwise abusive conduct is objectively justified.[5]

5. The Irish equivalent of Article 102 is section 5 of the Competition Act 2002, which applies to any abuse 'in trade for any goods or services in the State or in any part of the State'.[6] The same four categories of abuse listed in Article 102 are also included in section 5.[7]

6. The equivalent UK provision is section 18 of the Competition Act 1998. It provides that 'any conduct on the part of one or more undertakings which amounts to the abuse of a dominant position in a market is prohibited if it may affect trade within the United Kingdom'.[8] Again, the same four categories of abuse from Article 102 are repeated.[9]

What elements must be established to make out an infringement of Article 102?

7. The following elements must be established to make out an abuse of a dominant position under Article 102:

    i. The entity is an undertaking;

    ii. Holding a dominant position;

    iii. Held within the internal market or a substantial part of it;

    iv. The dominant position is abused; and

    v. There is an effect on trade between Member States.

8. First, Article 102 applies only to undertakings so an entity must come within the meaning of that term in respect of the activity about which allegations of an abuse

---

3. Case C–333/94P *Tetra Pak International SA v Commission* [1996] ECR I–5951, [1997] 4 CMLR 662, para 24.
4. Cases C–395 & 396/96P *Compagnie Maritime Belge Transports SA v Commission* [2000] ECR I–1365, [2000] 4 CMLR 1076, opinion of Advocate General Fennelly, para 137. The CAT followed this opinion in *Napp Pharmaceutical Holdings Ltd v Director General of Fair Trading* [2002] CAT 1, [2002] CompAR 13, para 219.
5. See Question 55, paras 14–18.
6. Competition Act 2002, s 5(1).
7. Competition Act 2002, s 5(2).
8. Competition Act 1998, s 18(1).
9. Competition Act 1998, s 18(2).

of dominance are made. The meaning of an undertaking is discussed in Question 1.

9. Second, it must be established that the undertaking holds a dominant position on a relevant market or, in the case of collective dominance, that two or more undertakings together occupy a dominant position. Article 102 does not provide a definition of dominance but the concept has been the subject of extensive case law. A number of factors are relevant in assessing dominance and these are discussed in Question 53.

10. Third, the dominant position must be held 'within the internal market or in a substantial part of it'. This does not appear to be an alternative test in any meaningful sense. If the phrase 'within the internal market' is meant to suggest that the dominant position is held in the common market as a whole,[10] then nothing is really added to the second part of the test, as once it is shown that the dominant position is held in a 'substantial part,' this is sufficient. In practice, cases in which this has become an issue have focused on whether the dominant position is held in a substantial part of the common market.

11. Whether a dominant position is held in a substantial part of the common market will depend on the circumstances. The dominant position within a relevant market will first have been defined. The question then is whether that relevant market constitutes a substantial part of the common market. The key question is the economic importance of the particular territory, as emphasised by the general test laid down by the Court of Justice in *Suiker Unie*:

> For the purpose of determining whether a specific territory is large enough to amount to 'a substantial part of the common market' within the meaning of Article [102] the pattern and volume of the production and consumption of the said product as well as the habits and economic opportunities of vendors and purchasers must be considered.[11]

12. The share of the common market taken up by the area may be an important factor. In *Suiker Unie* itself, the area covered by Belgium and Luxembourg was considered to be a substantial part of the common market in respect of sugar. It accounted for around 5 per cent of the total common market and this, together with other criteria such as high freight rates and consumer habits, was sufficient for the Court of Justice to conclude that the Belgo-Luxembourg market was sufficiently substantial.[12]

13. The courts generally tend to find that the territory of a Member State will be sufficiently large to constitute a substantial part of the common market[13] but much

---

10. See *Cutsforth v Mansfield Inns Ltd.* [1986] 1 WLR 558, 567.
11. Cases 40/73 etc. *Suiker Unie UA v Commission* [1975] ECR 1663, [1976] 1 CMLR 295, para 371.
12. Cases 40/73 etc. *Suiker Unie UA v Commission* [1975] ECR 1663, [1976] 1 CMLR 295, paras 370–375.
13. See, e.g., Case C–203/96 *Dusseldorp BV* [1998] ECR I–4075, [1998] 3 CMLR 873, para 60; Case C–52/07 *Kanal 5 Ltd v STIM* [2008] ECR I–9275, [2009] 5 CMLR 2175, para 22.

smaller areas have also been found to satisfy the test. In some cases the particular economic importance of the area has been decisively important. In finding that the port of Genoa was a substantial part of the common market in *Port of Genoa*, the Court of Justice relied on the volume of traffic in the port and its importance in relation to maritime trade as a whole in Italy.[14]

14. If a particular area is not economically significant within a Member State, its geographic size may nevertheless indicate that it is a substantial part of the common market. This was the view of Advocate General Jacobs in arguing in *Ambulanz Glöckner* that the German Land of Rheinland-Pfalz was a substantial part of the common market in respect of ambulance services, even though, in contrast to *Port of Genoa*, it could not be said that such services were either important or unimportant for the German economy. The Court was entitled to find that an area of 20,000 km^2, with a population of 4 million and therefore larger than some Member States, was a substantial part of the common market.[15]

15. Fourth, there must be an abuse of the dominance to give rise to a violation of Article 102.

16. The most common forms of abuse, which are discussed in separate questions in this chapter, include:

- Tying and bundling (Question 56)

- Price discrimination (Question 57)

- Predatory pricing (Question 58)

- Fidelity rebates (Question 59)

- Excessive pricing (Question 60)

- Refusals to deal (Questions 61–63)

- Margin squeeze (Question 64)

---

14. Case C–179/90 *Merci convenzionali porto di Genova SpA* [1991] ECR I–5889, [1994] 4 CMLR 422, para 15. Cf *Re Anley Maritime Agencies Ltd* [1999] Eu LR 97 (Northern Irish High Court stating, *obiter*, that it would have great difficulty in accepting that the Warrenpoint Harbour Authority enjoyed an alleged dominant position in a substantial part of the common market in respect of activities at Warrenpoint harbour).

15. Case C–475/99 *Ambulanz Glöckner v Landkreis Südwestpfalz* [2001] ECR I–8089, [2002] 4 CMLR 726, opinion of Advocate General Jacobs, paras 127–129, approved by the Court of Justice at para 38. See also, Case 30/87 *Bodson v Pompes funèbres des régions libérées* [1988] ECR 2479, [1989] 4 CMLR 984 (a group of undertakings with exclusive concessions for funeral services in 10 per cent of French communes which represented more than a third of the population could occupy a dominant position in a substantial part of the common market). But Cf *Cadbury Ireland Ltd v Kerry Co-operative Creamery Ltd* [1982] ILRM 77 (the Irish High Court (Barrington J) doubting that the area of a local authority, north County Kerry, was a substantial part of the common market) and *Cutsforth v Mansfield Inns Ltd.* [1986] 1 WLR 558 (in respect of the management of public houses, the North of England held not to be a substantial part).

17.   There are many other ways in which a dominant undertaking might abuse a dominant position, including:[16]

- Using regulatory powers to limit competition.[17]

- Instituting oppressive litigation, the aim of which was to limit competition.[18]

- Making misrepresentations in relation to patent filings in order to obtain additional patent protection to which the dominant undertaking was not entitled and keep manufacturers of generic drugs out of the market.[19]

- Selective deregistering of the marketing authorisations for a drug so as to exclude parallel imports.[20]

- Entering into an exclusive supply contract (especially if for a long duration and even if the dominant undertaking's counterparty willingly accepts the contract).[21]

- English clauses (requiring that the purchaser gives the dominant supplier the opportunity to match any lower offer received by the purchaser).[22]

- Entering into an agreement that breaches Article 101.[23]

---

16.   For other forms of abuse, see, e.g., Bellamy & Child (6th edn, 2008) para 10.145 *et seq.*

17.   *Nurendale Ltd t/a Panda Waste Services v Dublin City Council* [2009] IEHC 588, para 140 (McKechnie J holding that local authorities abused a dominant position by varying a waste management plan, which had the potential to foreclose the market to all competition) (appeal to the Supreme Court pending). Cf *Global Knafaim Leasing Limited v The Civil Aviation Authority* [2010] EWHC 1348 (Admin) (in considering if aircraft charges levied by BAA were abusive, Collins J commenting that as BAA's power had been granted by statute, 'it would be extraordinary if it fell foul of competition law' (para 80) and that 'the proportionate use of the power means it does not amount to an abuse and there is no evidence from which I could properly find a weakening of competition' (para 84)).

18.   Case T–111/96 *ITT Promedia NV v Commission* [1998] ECR II–2937, [1998] 5 CMLR 491, paras 55–61, 72–73 (the General Court accepting the appropriateness of the Commission view that before litigation would constitute an abuse under Article 102, it was 'necessary that the action (i) cannot reasonably be considered as an attempt to establish the rights of the undertaking concerned and can therefore only serve to harass the opposite party and (ii) it is conceived in the framework of a plan whose goal is to eliminate competition'). See also *Sandisk Corporation v Koninklijke Philips Electronics* [2007] EWHC 332 (Ch), [2007] Bus LR 705, para 46 (Pumfrey J finding that litigation to enforce patents would be potentially abusive only 'if the patent is obviously not infringed or if the patent is invalid and in either case the patentee either knows or believes that to be the case').

19.   Case T–321/05 *AstraZeneca AB v Commission,* judgment of 1 July 2010, paras 352–367.

20.   Case T–321/05 *AstraZeneca AB v Commission*, judgment of 1 July 2010, para 864.

21.   See, e.g., Case 85/76 *Hoffmann-La Roche & Co. AG v Commission* [1979] ECR 461, [1979] 3 CMLR 211, paras 86, 90.

22.   See Case 85/76 *Hoffmann-La Roche & Co. AG v Commission* [1979] ECR 461, [1979] 3 CMLR 211, paras 102–108.

23.   See Question 54, para 4.

- A breach by the owner of a patent essential to a technical standard to license on fair, reasonable and non-discriminatory ('FRAND') terms.[24]

18. It is not unusual for an abuse in one market to cause effects in another market. For example, a refusal to supply can cause such a 'related market' abuse. Those subject to the abusive behaviour may be customers of the dominant firm, competing in a downstream market. The dominant firm may itself compete in the downstream market and its abusive behaviour in the upstream market may be aimed at creating an advantage for itself on the downstream market where it is not already dominant. It is not entirely clear if it is a requirement for a finding of an infringement of Article 102 in this context that the dominant firm obtains a competitive advantage. Usually, the aim of the dominant firm's behaviour will be to acquire a competitive advantage but there may be cases, for example involving a dominant standards-setting body, where no economic advantage arises.[25]

19. Article 101 is breached where an agreement or practice has an anti-competitive object or effect. Unlike Article 101, Article 102 contains no reference to the anti-competitive aim or anti-competitive effect of the practice referred to. However, 'in the light of the context of Article [102], conduct will be regarded as abusive only if it restricts competition'.[26]

20. It is not necessary to show that anti-competitive effects are likely or that anti-competitive effects have occurred in the market. It is sufficient to show that the dominant undertaking's conduct 'tends to restrict competition or, in other words, that the conduct is capable of having that effect'.[27]

21. Fifth, Article 102 applies only if there is an effect on trade between Member States. It is sufficient to show that the conduct is *capable* of having an effect on trade.[28] The effect on trade concept is the same in respect of Article 101 and is discussed in Question 6.

---

24. See, eg, Chappatte, 'FRAND Commitments – The Case for Antitrust Intervention' (2009) 5(2) *European Competition Journal* 319; Geradin and Rato, 'FRAND Commitments and EC Competition Law: A Reply to Philippe Chappatte (2010) 6(1) *European Competition Journal* 129.

25. See *Sel-Imperial Ltd v British Standards Institution* [2010] EWHC 854 (Ch), [2010] UKCLR 493, paras 56–67 (Roth J stating that the law under Article 102 was still developing and that a claim of abuse where there was no competitive advantage to a standards setting body should not be struck out). Cf Case T–155/04 *SELEX Sistemi Integrati SpA v Commission* [2006] ECR II–4797, [2007] 4 CMLR 372, para 108 (suggesting that the possibility of a competitive advantage may be required (overruled on other grounds, Case C–113/07P *SELEX Sistemi Integrati SpA v Commission* [2009] ECR I–2207, [2009] 4 CMLR 1083)).

26. Case T–203/01 *Michelin v Commission ('Michelin II')* [2003] ECR II–4071, [2004] 4 CMLR 923, para 237.

27. Case T–203/01 *Michelin v Commission ('Michelin II')* [2003] ECR II–4071, [2004] 4 CMLR 923, para 239. See also Case T–219/99 *British Airways plc v Commission* [2003] ECR II–5917, [2004] 4 CMLR 1008, para 293 (equating 'tends' with 'capable of having, or likely to have') and Case C–95/04P *British Airways v Commission* [2007] ECR I–2331, [2007] 4 CMLR 982, para 100 ('tended').

28. Case 322/81 *Michelin NV v Commission* [1983] ECR 3461, [1985] 1 CMLR 282, paras 103–104.

Has the approach to Article 102 become more 'economic'?

22. The Commission initiated a review of Article 102 in 2004 and published a Discussion Paper in 2005.[29] The review culminated in the adoption of the Commission Article 102 Guidance in December 2008.[30] The Guidance applies only to exclusionary abuses.

23. The review process can be seen as an attempt to adopt a more 'economic approach' to Article 102.[31] Such an approach can loosely be described as a move away from a formalistic analysis, where abuse is established on the basis of the form that particular conduct takes, to a more effects-based methodology, which highlights the actual competitive effects of the conduct in the particular circumstances and places greater emphasis on effects on consumers and the role of efficiencies. The Commission states that in applying or enforcing Article 102 in the case of exclusionary abuses, it 'will focus on those types of conduct that are most harmful to consumers', 'take into account the specific facts and circumstances of each case' and intervene only where 'on the basis of cogent and convincing evidence, the allegedly abusive conduct is likely to lead to anti-competitive foreclosure'.[32]

24. The Commission Article 102 Guidance should be treated with caution. It is a statement of the Commission's enforcement priorities, not a statement of the law on Article 102. Any change to a more 'economic approach' to Article 102 ultimately depends on how the EU courts interpret the law on abuse of dominance in future cases. To date, there is little sign of a move to a more economic approach to Article 102. In *Tomra*, decided in September 2010, the General Court confirmed previous case law in holding that it was not necessary to consider the actual effects of exclusivity agreements and fidelity rebates in establishing a breach of Article 102, stating that:

    > ... for the purposes of establishing an infringement of Article [102], it is not necessary to show that the abuse under consideration had an actual impact on the relevant markets. It is sufficient in that respect to show that the abusive conduct of the undertaking in a dominant position tends to restrict competition or, in other words, that the conduct is capable of having that effect.[33]

25. It can be questioned whether the Commission itself has truly embraced a more 'economic approach'. In its decision in *Intel*, delivered after the adoption of the Article 102 Guidance, even though it demonstrated that fidelity rebates were

---

29. DG Competition discussion paper on the application of Article 82 of the Treaty to exclusionary abuses (December 2005) (the 'Commission Article 102 Discussion Paper').
30. Commission Guidance on the Commission's enforcement priorities in applying Article 82 of the EC Treaty to abusive exclusionary conduct by dominant undertakings [2009] OJ C45/7 ('Commission Article 102 Guidance').
31. For commentary, see, e.g., Kellerbauer, 'The Commission's new enforcement priorities in applying article 82 EC to dominant companies' exclusionary conduct: a shift towards a more economic approach?' [2010] *European Competition Law Review* 175.
32. Commission Article 102 Guidance [2009] OJ C45/7, paras 5, 8, 20.
33. Case T–155/06 *Tomra Systems ASA v Commission,* judgment of 9 September 2010, para 289.

capable of causing or likely to cause anticompetitive foreclosure, the Commission relied on previous case law to the effect that for a fidelity rebate to constitute an abuse, it was not necessary to show any actual impact on the market.[34] In *Tomra*, the General Court approved of the Commission's use of a brief effects-based analysis as merely complementing its finding of an infringement. This has the consequence that any errors in the effect-based analysis did not affect the legality of the Commission's decision.[35]

Key Sources

Article 102 TFEU.

Cases 40/73 etc *Coöperatieve Vereniging 'Suiker Unie' UA v Commission* [1975] ECR 1663, [1976] 1 CMLR 295.

Ireland

Competition Act 2002, s 5.

UK

Competition Act 1998, s 18.

---

34. Case COMP/C–3/37.990 *Intel*, Commission Decision of 13 May 2009, paras 922–925 (appeal pending, Case T–286/09 *Intel v Commission*).
35. Case T–155/06 *Tomra Systems ASA v Commission*, judgment of 9 September 2010, paras 288, 290.

53. What are the key factors in establishing dominance?

Summary

- Market share is generally the most important factor.

- A firm will not usually be dominant if its market share is 40 per cent or less.

- A share of 50 per cent is evidence of dominance and a 60 per cent market share raises a strong presumption of dominance.

- But market share is not determinative by itself and other factors have to be considered, including:

  - The market position of competitors;

  - Barriers to entry and expansion;

  - Countervailing buyer power.

1. For a breach of Article 102 to arise, it must first be established that the undertaking in question (or *undertakings* in the case of collective dominance) holds a dominant position. In *United Brands*, the Court of Justice stated that the concept of a dominant position

    > ... relates to a position of economic strength enjoyed by an undertaking which enables it to prevent effective competition being maintained on the relevant market by giving it the power to behave to an appreciable extent independently of its competitors, customers and ultimately of its consumers.[36]

2. A dominant position can arise not only with respect to suppliers but also in respect of purchasers, so that an undertaking can be a dominant buyer vis-à-vis its suppliers.[37]

3. The ability of the firm to act independently to an appreciable extent is related to the degree of the competitive constraint exercised by competitors. The Commission notes that:

    > Dominance entails that these competitive constraints are not sufficiently effective and hence that the undertaking in question enjoys substantial market power over a period of time. This means that the undertaking's decisions are largely insensitive to the actions and reactions of competitors, customers and, ultimately, consumers.[38]

---

36. Case 27/76 *United Brands Company v Commission* [1978] ECR 207, [1978] 1 CMLR 429, para 65. See also, Case 85/76 *Hoffmann-La Roche & Co. AG v Commission* [1979] ECR 461, [1979] 3 CMLR 211, para 38; Case 322/81 *Michelin NV v Commission* [1983] ECR 3461, [1985] 1 CMLR 282, para 30.
37. See, e.g., Case T–219/99 *British Airways plc v Commission* [2003] ECR II–5917, [2004] 4 CMLR 1008, para 101 (appeal dismissed, Case C–95/04P *British Airways plc v Commission* [2007] ECR I–2331, [2007] 4 CMLR 982); *Blemings v David Patton Ltd.* [2001] 1 IR 385, 418 (in a market that was not contestable, a monopsonist was dominant within the meaning of section 5 of the Irish Competition Act 1991).
38. Commission Article 102 Guidance [2009] OJ C45/7, para 10.

4.   In general, a dominant position derives from a combination of several factors which, taken separately, are not necessarily determinative.[39] These can include structural factors (e.g. barriers to entry) as well as behavioural factors (e.g. pricing behaviour).[40]

Can a firm be dominant if its market share is less than 40 per cent?

5.   The statement by the Court of Justice in *Hoffmann-La Roche* that among the factors relevant to an assessment of dominance, 'a highly important one is the existence of very high market shares'[41] remains true and market share should be examined first in assessing dominance. To establish market share, the relevant product and geographic markets will have to be defined. This exercise is crucial as a narrow market definition will usually produce much higher shares than a broad one.[42]

6.   An undertaking will not usually be in a dominant position if its market share is less than 40 per cent. The Court of Justice has held that a market share of between 5 per cent and 10 per cent precludes the existence of a dominant position save in exceptional circumstances.[43] The Commission indicates that from its experience, dominance is unlikely if the undertaking's market share is below 40 per cent.[44] However, this is not an absolute rule and while a market share of 40 per cent or less would not in itself indicate dominance, an undertaking with a share of less than 40 per cent can occupy a dominant position if other factors in combination with its market share are sufficient to establish dominance. The closer the market share to the 40 per cent level, the more likely that dominance would be a possibility.

7.   The Commission found British Airways to be dominant with a market share of 39.7 per cent for sales of airline tickets through travel agents in the UK. It was significant that the market share held by BA was more than twice the combined

---

39.   Case 27/76 *United Brands Company v Commission* [1978] ECR 207, [1978] 1 CMLR 429, para 66. There is no exhaustive list of factors that are relevant to determining if an undertaking has a dominant position. The main factors are discussed here. For other factors that have been considered relevant, see Van Bael & Bellis, *Competition Law of the European Community* (5th edn, 2010) 113–117.

40.   For an example of a court weighing structural and behavioural factors in considering if an undertaking was dominant, see *Meridian Communication Limited v Eircell Limited* [2002] 1 IR 17, 28–36. For a review of factors relevant to establishing dominance, see also Dec No 05/002 *Greenstar*, Decision of the Irish Competition Authority of 30 August 2005, para 2.43; *Masterfoods Ltd t/a Mars Ireland v H.B. Ice Cream Ltd* [1993] ILRM 145 (Keane J).

41.   Case 85/76 *Hoffmann-La Roche & Co. AG v Commission* [1979] ECR 461, [1979] 3 CMLR 211, para 39.

42.   On market definition, see Question 10.

43.   Case 75/84 *Metro SB-Großmärkte GmbH & Co. KG v Commission ('Metro II')* [1986] ECR 3021, [1987] 1 CMLR 118, para 86 (the market consisted of highly technical products that were readily interchangeable).

44.   Commission Article 102 Guidance [2009] OJ C45/7, para 14.

share of its four nearest rivals, that the share had been even higher in previous years and that BA had a 57 per cent share if only 'top 10' airlines were considered.[45] In the earlier *Gøttrup-Klim* case, the Court of Justice indicated that an undertaking with shares of 32 per cent and 36 per cent would not be considered dominant absent other factors:

> While an undertaking which holds market shares of that size may, depending on the strength and number of its competitors, be considered to be in a dominant position, those market shares cannot on their own constitute conclusive evidence of the existence of a dominant position.[46]

Is an undertaking dominant if its market share is above 40 per cent?

8. Just because it has a share in excess of 40 per cent does not necessarily mean that an undertaking is dominant. But the larger the market share, the longer the duration over which it is held and the smaller the share held by competitors, the more likely that dominance can be established.

9. In *United Brands*, the Court of Justice found that an undertaking with a market share ranging from 45 per cent to 50 per cent was dominant when additional factors, in particular the relative strength of competitors and the existence of barriers to entry, were considered.[47] In one of the vitamins markets considered in *Hoffmann-La Roche*, dominance was established with a market share of 47 per cent in light of the 'narrow oligopolistic' features of the market which by its nature had a weakened degree of competition, with competitors having shares of 27 per cent, 18 per cent, 7 per cent and 1 per cent respectively.[48]

10. An extremely high market share may, in itself, be considered as evidence of a dominant position. The Court of Justice has held that a market share of 50 per cent is, 'save in exceptional circumstances, evidence of the existence of a dominant position'.[49] A market share of between 70 per cent and 80 per cent has been held to be in itself 'a clear indication of the existence of a dominant position'[50] and the

---

45. *Virgin/British Airways* [2000] OJ L244/56, [2000] 4 CMLR 999, paras 88, 93 (appeals dismissed, Case T–219/99 *British Airways plc v Commission* [2003] ECR II–5917, [2004] 4 CMLR 1008; Case C–95/04P *British Airways plc v Commission* [2007] ECR I–2331, [2007] 4 CMLR 982).

46. Case C–250/92 *Gøttrup-Klim v Dansk Landbrugs Grovvareselskab AmbA* [1994] ECR I–5641, [1996] 4 CMLR 191, para 48.

47. Case 27/76 *United Brands Company v Commission* [1978] ECR 207, [1978] 1 CMLR 429, paras 108–129.

48. Case 85/76 *Hoffmann-La Roche & Co. AG v Commission* [1979] ECR 461, [1979] 3 CMLR 211, paras 50–52.

49. Case C–62/86 *AKZO Chemie BV v Commission* [1991] ECR I–3359, [1993] 5 CMLR 215, para 60. See also Case T–228/97 *Irish Sugar plc v Commission* [1999] ECR II–2969, [1999] 5 CMLR 1300, para 70 and case law cited therein.

50. Case T–30/89 *Hilti AG v Commission* [1991] ECR II–1439, [1992] 4 CMLR 16, para 92 (upheld on appeal, Case C–53/92P *Hilti v Commission* [1994] ECR I–667, [1994] 4 CMLR 614).

General Court has confirmed that a 60 per cent market share gives rise to a 'strong presumption' of a dominant position.[51] The fact that a high market share has held stable over time may reinforce a finding of dominance[52] and while a declining market share may be relevant, it will not necessarily indicate that an undertaking is not dominant.[53]

11. Any presumption of dominance based on market share 'is subject to further verification in any given case by reference to contextual factors such as barriers to entry and expansion and buyer power'.[54]

12. The following table provides a summary of the effect of different market share levels based on the case law discussed at paras 5–10 above. As it is difficult to make definitive conclusions about dominance on the basis of market share only, these figures should be treated as nothing more than a rough guide and when assessing dominance in a particular case, all relevant factors will need to be considered.

Below 10 per cent	Presumed not dominant.
10 per cent–40 per cent	Dominance possible the higher the share plus other factors. Asymmetry of shares is important, *i.e.* if competitors are numerous and small.
40 per cent–50 per cent	May be dominant depending on other factors.
50 per cent	The share is evidence of a dominant position.
60 per cent	A strong presumption of dominance.
70 per cent and above	A clear indication of dominance.

Are market shares relevant to a finding of dominance in bidding markets?

13. The characteristics of some markets may be such that market share is not a particularly good indicator of market strength. For example, in bidding markets

---

51. Cases T–191/98 etc *Atlantic Container Line v Commission ('TACA')* [2003] ECR II–3275, [2005] 4 CMLR 1283, para 908.

52. See Case 85/76 *Hoffmann-La Roche & Co. AG v Commission* [1979] ECR 461, [1979] 3 CMLR 211, para 41.

53. See Case T–219/99 *British Airways plc v Commission* [2003] ECR II–5917, [2004] 4 CMLR 1008, para 223 (BA still dominant despite a fall in its market share from 47.7 per cent to 39.7 per cent) (appeal dismissed, Case C–95/04P *British Airways plc v Commission* [2007] ECR I–2331, [2007] 4 CMLR 982).

54. Case COMP/C–3/37.990 *Intel*, Commission Decision of 13 May 2009, para 852 (appeal pending, Case T–286/09 *Intel v Commission*). See also, e.g., Case T–30/89 *Hilti AG v Commission* [1991] ECR II–1439, [1992] 4 CMLR 16, paras 93–94 (in addition to a 70 to 80 per cent market share, the fact that Hilti held a patent was relevant to the conclusion that it held a dominant position).

characterised by high value infrequent tenders, the market share of an undertaking may understate or overstate its market strength although even on such a market, a stable or growing market share over a number of years may indicate market strength.[55]

Are barriers to entry and expansion relevant in assessing dominance?

14. The threat of potential entry by new competitors or expansion by existing competitors is a factor in measuring the competitive constraints placed on an undertaking. Barriers to entry and expansion can take different forms, including:

   - Legal barriers (e.g. tariffs, quotas, statutory monopoly power).[56]

   - Economic disadvantages[57] (e.g. the allegedly dominant undertaking has economies of scale, exclusive access to inputs or an established sales network; it has already made significant investments that others would have to match; it has concluded long-term contracts with customers; network effects).[58]

   - Costs (e.g. customers would face switching costs).

15. If such competitors face significant barriers, then the threat of their expansion or entry will not be real and therefore will not be sufficient to constrain the allegedly dominant undertaking from actions such as raising prices. This is emphasised by the Commission in its Article 102 Guidance:

> For the Commission to consider expansion or entry likely it must be sufficiently profitable for the competitor or entrant, taking into account factors such as the barriers to expansion or entry, the likely reactions of the allegedly dominant undertaking and other competitors, and the risks and costs of failure. For expansion or entry to be considered timely, it must be sufficiently swift to deter or defeat the exercise of substantial market power. For expansion or entry to be considered sufficient, it cannot be simply small-scale entry, for example into some market niche, but must be of such

55. See Case T–210/01 *General Electric Company v Commission* [2006] ECR II–5575, [2006] 4 CMLR 686, paras 149–151.

56. Case 311/84 *CBEM – Télémarketing v CLT* [1985] ECR 3261, [1986] 2 CMLR 558 (the Court of Justice confirmed that Article 102 applied to a dominant position held by reason of a statutory monopoly).

57. See, e.g., COMP 38.784 *Wanadoo España v Telefónica*, Commission Decision of 4 July 2007, paras 224–228 (competitors facing significant costs in entering broadband market; Telefónica benefiting from considerable economies of scale) (appeals pending, Case T–336/07 *Telefónica v Commission* and Case T–398/07 *Spain v Commission*).

58. See Case COMP/C–3/37.792 *Microsoft* [2005] 4 CMLR 965, paras 448–464 (in respect of the PC operating systems market, network effects derived from the fact that users liked platforms on which they could use a large number of applications and, second, from the fact that software designers wrote applications for the client PC operating systems that were the most popular among users) and paras 515–522 (network effects in the work group server operating systems market) (upheld on appeal, Case T–201/04 *Microsoft Corp. v Commission* [2007] ECR II–3601, [2007] 5 CMLR 846).

a magnitude as to be able to deter any attempt to increase prices by the putatively dominant undertaking in the relevant market.[59]

Are undertakings with strong brands more likely to be dominant?

16. If a supplier has a particularly strong brand, such that retailers must stock the supplier's products in order to appear credible in the marketplace, this may be another factor going to dominance. In *Michelin I*, the Court of Justice acknowledged that tyre dealers in The Netherlands could not afford not to stock Michelin tyres in view of its strong worldwide presence and the special extent of its range of products, which resulted in a large number of users having a preference for Michelin tyres.[60] In the *Virgin/BA* case, the Commission highlighted the fact that travel agents were in a situation where a very large number of the tickets they sold would be BA tickets. This would allow BA, in its purchases of air travel agency services, to act independently of other airlines who purchased those services. The agents would have to deal with BA for a large portion of their income regardless of the conditions on which BA bought their services.[61] In *Intel*, the Commission found that computer manufacturers depended on Intel for what was the most important single hardware component and as such, Intel was a 'must-stock brand'.[62]

Is abusive behaviour relevant to a finding of dominance?

17. Behaviour that constitutes an abuse may itself support a finding of dominance. In *United Brands*, the Court of Justice indicated that it may be advisable to take account of such behaviour in establishing if an undertaking is in a dominant position, without necessarily having to acknowledge that the behaviour is an abuse within the meaning of Article 102.[63]

What is the relevance of customers' buyer power in assessing dominance?

18. If customers have sufficient buyer power, this may prevent an allegedly dominant undertaking, even one with a high market share (including, possibly an

---

59. Commission Article 102 Guidance [2009] OJ C45/7, para 16. See, also, Whish, *Competition Law* (6th edn, 2009) 179–181.

60. Case 322/81 *Michelin NV v Commission* [1983] ECR 3461, [1985] 1 CMLR 282, paras 55, 56.

61. *Virgin/British Airways* [2000] OJ L244/56, [2000] 4 CMLR 999, para 92 (appeals dismissed, Case T–219/99 *British Airways plc v Commission* [2003] ECR II–5917, [2004] 4 CMLR 1008; Case C–95/04P *British Airways plc v Commission* [2007] ECR I–2331, [2007] 4 CMLR 982).

62. Case COMP/C–3/37.990 *Intel*, Commission Decision of 13 May 2009, para 896 (appeal pending, Case T–286/09 *Intel v Commission*).

63. Case 27/76 *United Brands Company v Commission* [1978] ECR 207, [1978] 1 CMLR 429, para 68. See also *Meridian Communication Limited v Eircell Limited* [2002] 1 IR 17, 34 (the facts alleged to be abuses, including the refusal to renew a volume discount agreement without its restrictive terms, were not 'particularly indicative of dominance' (O'Higgins J)).

undertaking with a 100 per cent share),[64] from acting independently of its customers.

19. A customer may have buyer power by virtue of its size or its significance for the supplier. A powerful buyer may be able to use its bargaining power to stimulate competition among suppliers, driving prices down and obtaining discounts, by threatening to switch its purchases to another supplier, to sponsor the entry of new suppliers or by vertically integrating itself. In order for the threat to switch suppliers to be credible, the buyer (or group of buyers where they engage in joint purchasing) must account for a sufficiently high level of demand. Otherwise, the allegedly dominant undertaking will be able to price discriminate, offering a competitive price to the entities with buyer power but charging a monopoly price to other purchasers. The Commission maintains that buyer power will not be considered a sufficiently effective constraint if it only applies vis-à-vis a particular or limited segment of customer.[65] To show buyer power, it is not sufficient simply to establish that a small number of customers account for a large number of the allegedly dominant firm's sales.[66]

20. Buyer power may be negated where the allegedly dominant undertaking is an unavoidable trading partner for purchasers. The Commission found this to be so in *Intel*, in light of Intel's strong brand, making Intel processors a 'must have' in computers, a position reinforced by significant entry barriers. While it was natural for purchasers to attempt to exert leverage vis-à-vis Intel using the threat of switching to Intel's competitor, AMD, the fact that Intel was an unavoidable trading partner meant that it was not plausible to argue that the purchasers had buyer power.[67]

---

64. See *Hutchison 3G UK Ltd v The Office of Communications* [2009] EWCA Civ 683, [2009] All ER (D) 174 (Jul) para 2 (in applying the concept of 'significant market power' under the Communications Act 2003, Lloyd LJ stating that in a market where there is one buyer and one seller, it does not necessarily follow that the seller has significant market power because the buyer may have sufficient countervailing buyer power). See also, *Hutchison 3G Ireland Ltd v Commission for Communications Regulation*, Decision of the Electronic Communications Appeal Panel of 26 September 2005, para 6.57 (criticising the presumption of dominance in respect of a 100 per cent market share and the failure to recognise the possibility that the presumption may not apply in the particular circumstances); Dec No 06/ 001 *Ticketmaster Ireland Limited*, Decision of the Irish Competition Authority of 26 September 2005, para 3.5 (significant countervailing buying power and other factors provided 'compelling evidence' that Ticketmaster, despite a 100 per cent market share, was not dominant; however the Authority held it was unnecessary to reach a conclusion on dominance given its view that there was no abuse).
65. Commission Article 102 Guidance [2009] OJ C45/7, para 18.
66. Case T–66/01 *Imperial Chemicals Industries Ltd v Commission*, judgment of 25 June 2010, paras 276–277 (applicant arguing that four customers accounting for 50 per cent of its sales had buyer power but it did not give details of individual shares and had not shown they actually had countervailing buyer power).
67. Case COMP/C–3/37.990 *Intel*, Commission Decision of 13 May 2009, para 894 (appeal pending, Case T–286/09 *Intel v Commission*).

If an undertaking makes a loss, can it be dominant?

21. In *United Brands*, the Court of Justice rejected the argument that the generation of losses was incompatible with a finding of dominance:

> An undertaking's economic strength is not measured by its profitability; a reduced profit margin or even losses for a time are not incompatible with a dominant position, just as large profits may be compatible with a situation where there is effective competition. The fact that UBC's profitability is for a time moderate or non-existent must be considered in the light of the whole of its operations. The finding that, whatever losses UBC may make, the customers continue to buy more goods from UBC which is the dearest vendor, is more significant and this fact is a particular feature of the dominant position and its verification is determinative in this case.[68]

If an undertaking has been conferred with a monopoly by statute, does it hold a 'dominant position' within the meaning of Article 102?

22. The Court of Justice has confirmed that an undertaking which has a statutory monopoly may be regarded as having a dominant position within the meaning of Article 102.[69] Such an undertaking may be able to benefit from the Article 106 exemption where it is entrusted with the performance of services of general economic interest.[70]

If an undertaking is regulated, can it be dominant?[71]

23. In the *Hutchison 3G* case, in assessing whether a mobile phone operator had significant market power ('SMP') in the market for mobile call termination on its own network, the English Court of Appeal considered the constraining effect of the regulatory regime imposed by a group of EU directives known as the Common Regulatory Framework, as implemented by the UK Communications Act 2003. The possession of SMP was defined in the relevant EU regulatory regime as the power to behave to an appreciable extent independently of competitors, customers and ultimately consumers and so was comparable to the concept of dominance under Article 102.

24. While *ex post* regulation, such as fixing a reasonable price by dispute resolution, might operate as a constraint on the freedom of an undertaking which had a large market share, the Court of Appeal held, adopting the so-called 'modified Greenfield' approach, that it was not relevant to a decision as to whether that undertaking had SMP:

> SMP is not to be found to be absent from a market if its absence is the result of regulation which is in place. Correspondingly, looking forward, an undertaking which

---

68. Case 27/76 *United Brands Company v Commission* [1978] ECR 207, [1978] 1 CMLR 429, paras 126–128.
69. See, e.g., Case 311/84 *CBEM – Télémarketing v CLT* [1985] ECR 3261, [1986] 2 CMLR 558, para 16; Case C–260/89 *Elliniki Radiophonia Tiléorassi AE v Dimotiki Etairia Pliroforissis* [1991] ECR I–2925, [1994] 4 CMLR 540, para 31.
70. See Question 125.
71. See also Question 55, para 20–22 on whether regulation provides a defence to a charge of abuse.

would otherwise have SMP is not to be entitled to argue that it does not have it because its freedom of operation is or would be limited (directly or indirectly) by regulatory provisions such as are designed to be put in place in order to constrain the exercise of SMP. Whether a market is 'effectively competitive' must be assessed regardless of the regulatory constraints that might be imposed if it is found that it is not. Otherwise the regulatory regime would in this respect be self-defeating.[72]

25. The fact that an undertaking itself exercises regulatory power may be a relevant factor in establishing that it is dominant. In the *Panda* case, the Irish High Court emphasised the regulatory power enjoyed by a number of local authorities in finding that they were dominant in their respective household waste collection markets:

> The undertakings involved are unlike private dominant undertakings in that not only do they have a significant share of the market, but more importantly, they have the power to regulate it: to decide entry or no entry, to decide conditions of entry, and if allowed, to decide operative conditions. It is that regulation, independently of any given market share which they might enjoy, which gives them the power to act independently and therefore makes them dominant in their respective markets.[73]

Key Sources

Case 27/76 *United Brands Company v Commission* [1978] ECR 207, [1978] 1 CMLR 429.

Case 85/76 *Hoffmann-La Roche & Co. v Commission* [1979] ECR 461, [1979] 3 CMLR 211.

Case 322/81 *Nederlandsche Banden Industrie Michelin v Commission* ('Michelin I') [1983] ECR 3461, [1985] 1 CMLR 282.

Case C–62/86 *AKZO Chemie BV v Commission* [1991] ECR I–3359, [1993] 5 CMLR 215.

Case T–30/89 *Hilti AG v Commission* [1991] ECR II–1439, [1992] 4 CMLR 16.

Virgin/British Airways [2000] OJ L244/56, [2000] 4 CMLR 999.

Hutchison 3G UK Ltd v The Office of Communications [2009] EWCA Civ 683, [2009] All ER (D) 174 (Jul).

---

72. *Hutchison 3G UK Ltd v The Office of Communications* [2009] EWCA Civ 683, [2009] All ER (D) 174 (Jul) para 53 (Lloyd LJ). See also at para 64, noting that 'one of the critical aspects of the modified Greenfield approach is that it requires that a feature of the regulatory regime be ignored, in a market assessment as to whether an undertaking has SMP or not, if otherwise it would itself provide the answer to the question whether the undertaking does or does not have SMP'. See also Case DE/2005/0144, *Call termination on individual public telephone networks provided at a fixed location*, COM(2005)1442 final, Commission Decision of 17 May 2005, on which the Court of Appeal relied.
73. *Nurendale Ltd t/a Panda Waste Services v Dublin City Council* [2009] IEHC 588, para 133.

54. WHEN ARE UNDERTAKINGS IN A POSITION OF COLLECTIVE DOMINANCE?

Summary

Collective dominance may be established in a number of ways, in particular:

- On the basis of formal links – such as agreements, cross-shareholdings, interlocking directorships; or

- On the basis of the characteristics of an oligopolistic market, in which case three conditions are necessary:

  - Transparency;

  - A deterrent mechanism;

  - Absence of significant competitive constraints that will jeopardise a common policy on the market.

- These three conditions should not be applied mechanically but rather in light of the overall economic context.

1. The concept of collective dominance is implicit in Article 102, which speaks of the abuse of a dominant position by 'one or more undertakings'. This language implies that 'a dominant position may be held by two or more economic entities legally independent of each other, provided that from an economic point of view they present themselves or act together on a particular market as a collective entity'.[74]

2. The concept of collective dominance has been established in the context of the Merger Regulation as well as under Article 102.[75] The concept appears to have the same meaning in both contexts and in applying Article 102, the General Court has adopted the analysis of collective dominance in Merger Regulation cases.[76]

3. The Commission's Article 102 Guidance is limited to addressing single firm dominance only and does not deal with collective dominance.[77] However, the earlier discussion paper, which formed part of the Commission's review of Article 102, provides guidance on collective dominance.[78]

---

74. Cases C–395 & 396/96P *Compagnie Maritime Belge Transports SA v Commission* [2000] ECR I–1365, [2000] 4 CMLR 1076, para 36. See also Case T–68/89 *Società Italiana Vetro SpA v Commission* [1992] ECR II–1403, [1992] 5 CMLR 302.

75. See also Question 75.

76. See Case T–193/02 *Piau v Commission* [2005] ECR II–209, [2005] 5 CMLR 42, para 111 (referring to the conditions for collective dominance set out in Case T–342/99 *Airtours plc v Commission* [2002] ECR II–2585, [2002] 5 CMLR 317) (appeal dismissed, Case C–171/05P *Piau v Commission* [2006] ECR I–37).

77. Commission Article 102 Guidance [2009] OJ C45/7, para 4.

78. Commission Article 102 Discussion Paper, paras 43–50.

4.   It is well established that Article 101 and 102 can apply simultaneously.[79] Where undertakings have entered into an agreement or other practice that facilitates a collective dominant position, they may also be subject to Article 101. However, it is not sufficient for the Commission to merely 'recycle the facts'[80] giving rise to a violation of Article 101 to establish that the parties to that agreement or practice are collectively dominant and that they are in breach of Article 102. Each Article must be applied on its own terms.[81]

5.   Collective dominance may be established in a number of ways. If there are concrete links between undertakings that facilitate the coordination of their activities on the market, this may lead to a finding of collective dominance. The links to establish collective dominance in this way need not be as strong as links between entities of the same corporate group that are found to constitute one undertaking. Different undertakings can be collectively dominant even if there is a degree of competition between them but a showing of significant competition between them may negate a finding of collective dominance.[82]

6.   Relevant links could include an agreement between the undertakings which leads to them acting as a collective entity or licenses held by them affording a technological advantage.[83] An agreement may 'by its very nature and in light of its objectives' set the conditions for collective dominance.[84] Other factors that may indicate collective dominance include 'ownership interest and other links in law' that lead undertakings to coordinate.[85] In *TACA*, a number of links among members of a shipping liner conference, including a common tariff, enforcement

---

79. See, e.g., Cases C–395 & 396/96P *Compagnie Maritime Belge Transports SA v Commission* [2000] ECR I–1365, [2000] 4 CMLR 1076, para 33.

80. Case T–68/89 *Società Italiana Vetro SpA v Commission* [1992] ECR II–1403, [1992] 5 CMLR 302, para 360.

81. But see *Nurendale Ltd t/a Panda Waste Services v Dublin City Council* [2009] IEHC 588, para 137 (McKechnie J, relying on the High Court decision in *Donovan v The Electricity Supply Board* [1994] 2 IR 305, holding that a dominant undertaking engaged in an agreement or concerted practice contrary to section 4 of the Competition Act 2002 would also be in breach of section 5). Cf *Vicat SA v Le Ministre de l'Economie, de l'Industrie et de l'Emploi* (n 2009/14634) judgment of the Paris Court of Appeal of 15 April 2010 (holding that a finding of collective abuse of a dominant position was inconsistent with a finding of cartel practices infringing the French equivalent of Article 101).

82. See Cases T–191/98 etc. *Atlantic Container Line AB v Commission ('TACA')* [2003] ECR II–3275, [2005] 4 CMLR 1283, para 695 (the General Court finding that it was valid for the applicants to argue that there was significant internal competition within a liner conference capable of showing that in spite of the various links between them, they were not in a position of collective dominance; however, the applicants failed to establish this argument on the facts).

83. See Case T–68/89 *Società Italiana Vetro SpA v Commission* [1992] ECR II–1403, [1992] 5 CMLR 302, para 358.

84. Cases C–395 & 396/96P *Compagnie Maritime Belge Transports SA v Commission* [2000] ECR I–1365, [2000] 4 CMLR 1076, para 48.

85. Commission Article 102 Discussion Paper, para 45.

provisions and penalties, a common secretariat and annual business plans were factors going to a finding of collective dominance.[86]

7.   In *Suiker Unie*, the Court of Justice had regard to 'the personal and financial links', which included interlocking directorships and cross-shareholdings, between certain sugar producers and the largest sugar producer on the Belgian market together with the fact that they adopted a 'sales policy fixed by' that producer. The Court concluded that the market shares of all the producers should be aggregated in establishing the extent of the dominant position enjoyed by the largest of them.[87] Although this finding was made in respect of attribution of market shares in the context of single firm dominance, similar factors could be relevant in establishing a collective dominant position. In *Irish Sugar*, cross-shareholdings and interlocking directorships, the joint allocation of tasks and an undertaking by one entity to obtain its supplies exclusively from the other were considered as factors establishing a vertically collective dominant position.[88]

8.   Legislation may also supply the necessary links to establish collective dominance. In *Panda*, the Irish High Court held that local authorities were collectively dominant in the greater Dublin area market for household waste collection services. In reaching this conclusion, McKechnie J took account of the fact that collaboration between the local authorities was provided for by statute. While acknowledging that 'the collaboration of the councils in this regard could not be condemned', the judge held that 'the fact that such collusion is provided for by statute will not prevent a finding of collective dominance'. The authorities acted in concert on many issues and viewed from outside constituted, in many respects, a collective entity and so were found to be collectively dominant.[89]

Can collective dominance arise in the absence of formal links?

9.   Formal links such as agreements or cross-shareholdings are not required for a finding of collective dominance, which may be established without such links in oligopolistic markets that contain certain characteristics. This was confirmed by the General Court in *Gencor*, rejecting the submission that structural links between the parties were required:

> [There] is no reason whatsoever in legal or economic terms to exclude from the notion of economic links the relationship of interdependence existing between the parties to a tight oligopoly within which, in a market with the appropriate characteristics, in particular in terms of market concentration, transparency and product homogeneity, those parties are in a position to anticipate one another's behaviour and are therefore

86.   Cases T–191/98 etc. *Atlantic Container Line AB v Commission ('TACA')* [2003] ECR II–3275, [2005] 4 CMLR 1283, paras 611–629.
87.   Cases 40/73 etc. *Suiker Unie UA v Commission* [1975] ECR 1663, [1976] 1 CMLR 295, paras 377–378.
88.   Case T–228/97 *Irish Sugar plc v Commission* [1999] ECR II–2969, [1999] 5 CMLR 1300, paras 50–52. On the vertical collective dominance aspect, see O'Donoghue and Padilla, *The Law and Economics of Article 82 EC* (2006) 163–164.
89.   *Nurendale Ltd t/a Panda Waste Services v Dublin City Council* [2009] IEHC 588, para 135.

strongly encouraged to align their conduct in the market, in particular in such a way as to maximise their joint profits by restricting production with a view to increasing prices. In such a context, each trader is aware that highly competitive action on its part designed to increase its market share (for example a price cut) would provoke identical action by the others, so that it would derive no benefit from its initiative. All the traders would thus be affected by the reduction in price levels.[90]

10. In the *Airtours* case, which involved an appeal against a Commission decision under the Merger Regulation, the General Court examined the factors that would allow firms to arrive at and sustain coordination in the market. These were:

(i) **Transparency** – to enable each member of the dominant oligopoly to know how the other members are behaving in order to monitor whether or not they are adopting the common policy. '[It] is not enough for each member of the dominant oligopoly to be aware that interdependent market conduct is profitable for all of them but each member must also have a means of knowing whether the other operators are adopting the same strategy and whether they are maintaining it. There must, therefore, be sufficient market transparency for all members of the dominant oligopoly to be aware, sufficiently precisely and quickly, of the way in which the other members' market conduct is evolving'.

(ii) **A sufficient deterrent mechanism** – to make tacit coordination sustainable over time, there must be a deterrent mechanism to incentivise the undertakings not to depart from the common policy on the market.

(iii) **Competitive constraints must not jeopardise the common policy** – the foreseeable reaction of current and future competitors, as well as consumers, should not be such as to jeopardise the results expected from the common policy. This will involve an assessment of the strength of competitors and countervailing buyer power.[91]

11. These criteria must be applied in light of the overall economic context. In *Bertlesmann*, the Court of Justice confirmed that in applying the test of collective dominance set out in *Airtours*, 'it is necessary to avoid a mechanical approach involving the separate verification of each of those criteria taken in isolation, while taking no account of the overall economic mechanism of a hypothetical tacit co-ordination'.[92]

12. In overturning the decision of the General Court, which had annulled the Commission decision clearing a joint venture between Bertelsmann and Sony, the Court of Justice reinstated the Commission's finding that the requisite degree of transparency was not established to enable a finding of collective dominance among the five largest labels in the market for recorded music. The Court of Justice criticised the approach of the General Court, pointing out that it was essential that an investigation into whether there was a collective dominant

---

90. Case T–102/96 *Gencor Ltd v Commission* [1999] ECR II–879, [1999] 4 CMLR 971, para 276.

91. Case T–342/99 *Airtours plc v Commission* [2002] ECR II–2585, [2002] 5 CMLR 317, para 62.

92. Case C–413/06P *Bertelsmann AG v Impala* [2008] ECR I–4951, [2008] 5 CMLR 1073, para 125.

position be carried out carefully and that 'it should adopt an approach based on the analysis of such plausible co-ordination strategies as may exist in the circumstances'.[93]

Must the collective market share be higher than in a case of single firm dominance?

13. There is no set market share level that undertakings must collectively hold before they will be found to occupy a collective dominant position. In *TACA*, the General Court rejected as 'misplaced' the argument that the market share threshold from which the existence of a collective dominant position may be inferred is higher than in the case of a simple individual dominant position. The General Court pointed out that:

> [A] collective entity is of course composed of undertakings between which a certain amount of competition may subsist and whose market shares may be somewhat asymmetrical. However, although such a circumstance is capable where appropriate of precluding a collective assessment of the position of those undertakings on the relevant market ... it is of no relevance for the purpose of determining whether that collective position is dominant. The dominant nature of a market position is to be assessed by reference to the degree of dependence vis-à-vis competitors, customers and suppliers, so that only the latter factors relating to external competition must be taken into account.[94]

Key Sources

Cases C–395&396/96P *Compagnie maritime belge transports SA v Commission* [2000] ECR I–1365, [2000] 4 CMLR 1076.

Cases T–191/98 etc. Atlantic Container Line AB v Commission ('TACA') [2003] ECR II–3275, [2005] 4 CMLR 1283.

Case T–342/99 *Airtours plc v Commission* [2002] ECR II–2585, [2002] 5 CMLR 317.

Case T–139/02 *Piau v Commission* [2005] ECR II–209, [2005] 5 CMLR 42.

Case C–413/06P *Bertelsmann AG and Another v Independent Music Publishers and Labels Association (Impala)* [2008] ECR I–4951, [2008] 5 CMLR 1073.

---

93. Case C–413/06P *Bertelsmann AG v Impala* [2008] ECR I–4951, [2008] 5 CMLR 1073, para 129.
94. Cases T–191/98 etc. *Atlantic Container Line AB v Commission ('TACA')* [2003] ECR II–3275, [2005] 4 CMLR 1283, para 933.

55. WHAT GENERAL FACTORS ARE IMPORTANT IN ESTABLISHING AN ABUSE OF DOMINANCE?

Summary

- There is often a fine line between legitimate and abusive conduct.

- The list of abusive conduct in Article 102 is not exhaustive.

- There are many possible forms of abuse, which can be categorised as exclusionary (foreclosing competition) or exploitative (e.g. excessive pricing).

- Many factors may be relevant to a finding of exclusionary abuse, including the market position of the dominant undertaking and competitors and any evidence that competitors have been foreclosed.

- A dominant undertaking can argue that its conduct was objectively justified and so should not fall foul of Article 102.

- The fact that a dominant undertaking is regulated does not mean that its conduct will not be considered abusive.

1. Given the requirement of self-assessment under the competition rules, it is important for dominant firms to be able to determine if their conduct gives rise to an abuse of dominance. Article 102 can be difficult to apply in practice. There is often a fine line between legitimate conduct and the prohibited abuse of a dominant position. Legitimate and abusive conduct may appear the same on the surface, for example, in the form of low prices. This can make it difficult for dominant firms to determine if and when their behaviour gives rise to a beach of Article 102. The case law on Article 102 does not always provide useful guidance. The law on abusive pricing practices has been described as 'complex and controversial'.[95]

2. The concept of an abuse of a dominant position is an 'objective concept' that was described by the Court of Justice in *Hoffmann-La Roche* as follows:

> The concept of abuse is an objective concept relating to the behaviour of an undertaking in a dominant position which is such as to influence the structure of a market where, as a result of the very presence of the undertaking in question, the degree of competition is weakened and which, through recourse to methods different from those which condition normal competition in products or services on the basis of the transactions of commercial operators, has the effect of hindering the maintenance of the degree of competition still existing in the market or the growth of that competition.[96]

---

95. Whish, *Competition Law* (6th edn, 2009) 706.
96. Case 85/76 *Hoffmann-La Roche & Co. AG v Commission* [1979] ECR 461, [1979] 3 CMLR 211, para 91.

3. The list of abusive practices set out in the second paragraph of Article 102 is not exhaustive and the practices mentioned there are merely examples of abuse of a dominant position.[97] These examples are expressed somewhat vaguely, with phrases such as 'unfair prices'. The wording of Article 102 does not identify precisely when particular conduct will be abusive or when it will be legitimate. A dominant firm will have to consider the structure of the market, the nature of its conduct and various other factors particular to the situation in assessing whether it is engaging in abusive conduct. An abuse cannot be established merely by reference to a specific benchmark and ultimately the 'question whether an abuse exists is highly fact-sensitive and dependent upon an evaluation of a wide range of factors'.[98] However, benchmarks, such as measurements of cost, may play a role in indentifying an abuse and the Commission endorses the use of various benchmarks in its Article 102 Guidance.[99]

What is the difference between an exclusionary abuse and an exploitative abuse?

4. A distinction can be made between exclusionary abuses and non-exclusionary, or exploitative, abuses. Particular abusive conduct may have both exclusionary and exploitative effects.

5. Exclusionary abuse impedes effective competition by foreclosing competitors. Exclusionary abuses include predatory pricing, exclusive purchasing obligations, fidelity rebates, tying and bundling, refusal to supply and margin squeeze. A common feature of exclusionary conduct, although not a necessary requirement for a finding of abuse, involves the dominant undertaking reserving to itself an activity or market that is ancillary to that in which it holds a dominant position, thereby foreclosing competition in the ancillary market. An early example can be seen in *Commercial Solvents*. The Court of Justice held that a dominant supplier of a raw material, which refused to supply a customer that made derivatives because the dominant firm had the object of reserving the raw material for the manufacture of its own derivatives, abused a dominant position when the dominant firm thereby risked the elimination of all competition on the part of that customer.[100]

---

97. See, e.g., Case C–333/94P *Tetra Pak International SA v Commission* [1996] ECR I–5951, [1997] 4 CMLR 662, para 37; Case T–201/04 *Microsoft Corp. v Commission* [2007] ECR II–3601, [2007] 5 CMLR 846, para 861 (confirming that bundling by a dominant undertaking may infringe Article 102 even where it does not correspond to the bundling example given in Article 102(d)).

98. *National Grid plc v Gas and Electricity Markets Authority* [2010] EWCA Civ 114, [2010] UKCLR 386, para 54 (Richards LJ). See also Bellamy & Child (6th edn, 2008) para 10.058, listing ten relevant factors.

99. See Commission Article 102 Guidance [2009] OJ C45/7, para 26.

100. Cases 6–7/73 *Commercial Solvents Corporation v Commission* [1974] ECR 223, [1974] 1 CMLR 309, para 25.

6. An exploitative abuse involves anti-competitive conduct directed towards a supplier or customer that relies on the dominant undertaking. An example would be the charging of an excessive price.[101]

What factors indicate that exclusionary conduct will tend to result in foreclosure?

7. The main concern with exclusionary conduct is that it results in anti-competitive foreclosure, 'where effective access of actual or potential competitors to supplies or markets is hampered or eliminated as a result of the conduct of the dominant undertaking whereby the dominant undertaking is likely to be in a position to profitably increase prices to the detriment of consumers'.[102]

8. Certain types of exclusionary conduct will be so blatantly anti-competitive that abuse of a dominant position can be inferred. Examples include where a dominant undertaking provides a financial incentive to customers not to test rival products or pays a distributor to delay, cancel or restrict the commercialisation of a rival product.[103] In other cases, it will be necessary to consider various factors.

9. The Commission has outlined a number of general factors that it considers relevant to a finding of foreclosure, which can be summarised as follows:[104]

Factor	Explanation
The position of the dominant undertaking.	The stronger the position, the more likely that foreclosure will result. Market share is important.
The position of competitors.	In addition to market share, are certain competitors particularly innovative or mavericks? Is one competitor an especially close competitor?
Conditions on the relevant market.	Barriers to entry and expansion; the existence of economies of scale (which mean that competitors are less likely to enter or stay if the dominant firm forecloses a significant part of the market) and network effects.
The position of customers or input suppliers.	Buyer power. Does the abusive conduct target a supplier with whom the dominant undertaking has an exclusive agreement?

---

101. See also Cases C–468 to 478/06 *Sot Lélos kai Sia EE v GlaxoSmithKline* [2008] ECR I–7139, [2008] 5 CMLR 1382, opinion of Advocate General Colomer, para 74 (noting that it is common to divide the circumstances in which Article 102 applies into two categories, those that harm consumers (exploitative abuses) and those that harm actual or potential competitors (exclusionary abuses).
102. Commission Article 102 Guidance [2009] OJ C45/7, para 19.
103. Commission Article 102 Guidance [2009] OJ C45/7, para 22; Case COMP/C–3/37.990 *Intel*, Commission Decision of 13 May 2009, para 1641 *et seq.* (appeal pending, Case T–286/09 *Intel v Commission*).
104. Commission Article 102 Guidance [2009] OJ C45/7, para 20.

Factor	Explanation
The extent of the allegedly abusive conduct.	Share of sales affected, duration, frequency.
Evidence of actual foreclosure.	E.g. a competitor has exited.
Direct evidence of an exclusionary strategy.	E.g. from internal documents.

10. In addition to these general factors, there may be additional specific factors relevant to the particular type of abuse in question or related to the circumstances that need to be taken into account.

11. In respect of price-based exclusionary conduct, the Commission has stated that certain cost benchmarks may be relevant to the assessment. The benchmarks that the Commission considers most likely to be useful are average avoidable cost ('AAC') and long-run average incremental cost ('LRAIC').

12. AAC is the average of the costs that could have been avoided if the firm had not produced a discrete amount of (extra) output, here the amount allegedly the subject of abusive conduct. AAC will usually be the same as average variable cost ('AVC') as it is often only variable costs that can be avoided. A failure to cover AAC indicates that a dominant firm is sacrificing profits in the short-term. This could be relevant in a predatory pricing case, for example.

13. LRAIC is the average of all costs (both variable and fixed) that a company incurs to produce a particular product. Average total cost ('ATC') is a good proxy for LRAIC and the two will be the same in the case of an undertaking making a single product, with LRAIC being lower than ATC for each individual product in a multi-product undertaking.[105] A failure by a dominant firm to cover LRAIC indicates that it is not recovering all fixed costs and so an equally efficient competitor could be foreclosed from the market.

How can an abuse be objectively justified?

14. Conduct of a dominant undertaking that would otherwise constitute an abuse of a dominant position may escape the Article 102 prohibition if it is objectively justified. In *Sot Lélos*, Advocate General Colomer identified three general grounds of justification for a dominant undertaking's conduct, 'grounds relating to the market in which they are operating, the legitimate protection of their business interests and proof of net positive economic effect'.[106] Of these, the Advocate General considered that the protection of legitimate business interests was 'the only category of objective justifications to have really taken shape' in the case law under Article 102.[107]

---

105. See Commission Article 102 Guidance [2009] OJ C45/7, para 26.
106. Cases C–468 to 478/06 *Sot Lélos kai Sia EE v GlaxoSmithKline* [2008] ECR I–7139, [2008] 5 CMLR 1382, opinion, para 79. See also the opinion of Advocate General Jacobs in Case C–53/03 *Syfait v GlaxoSmithKline AEVE* [2005] ECR I–4609, [2005] 5 CMLR 7.
107. Cases C–468 to 478/06 *Sot Lélos kai Sia EE v GlaxoSmithKline* [2008] ECR I–7139, [2008] 5 CMLR 1382, opinion, para 99.

15. An example of grounds relating to the market would be health and safety reasons related to the nature of the product. However, it is generally not for the dominant undertaking to decide what measures should be taken to protect health and safety or achieve other similar goals. Rather 'the remedy must lie in appropriate legislation or regulations, and not in rules adopted unilaterally by manufacturers'.[108]

16. A dominant undertaking can also defend its conduct under Article 102 on the basis of objective economic justification. In the *British Airways* loyalty rebates case, the Court of Justice considered the application of Article 102 to discounts linked to individual sales targets in commercial passenger aviation granted by BA, which was dominant in the UK market for air travel, to travel agencies. The Court held that 'an undertaking is at liberty to demonstrate that its bonus system producing an exclusionary effect is economically justified'.[109] The Court went on to state:

> Assessment of the economic justification for a system of discounts or bonuses established by an undertaking in a dominant position is to be made on the basis of the whole of the circumstances of the case. It has to be determined whether the exclusionary effect arising from such a system, which is disadvantageous for competition, may be counterbalanced, or outweighed, by advantages in terms of efficiency which also benefit the consumer. If the exclusionary effect of that system bears no relation to advantages for the market and consumers, or if it goes beyond what is necessary in order to attain those advantages, that system must be regarded as an abuse.[110]

17. Dominant undertakings have also sought to argue that the application of Article 102 would result in an interference with their property rights contrary to Article 345 TFEU. This is a difficult argument to make out as the application of Article 102 (and Article 101) constitutes 'one of the aspects of public interest' in the Union and consequently, pursuant to the competition rules, 'restrictions may be applied on the exercise of the right to property, provided that they are not disproportionate and do not affect the substance of that right'.[111]

---

108. Case T–83/91 *Tetra Pak International SA v Commission ('Tetra Pak II')* [1994] ECR II–755, [1997] 4 CMLR 726, para 84 (appeal dismissed, Case C–333/94P *Tetra Pak International SA v Commission* [1996] ECR I–5951, [1997] 4 CMLR 662).

109. Case C–95/04P *British Airways v Commission* [2007] ECR I–2331, [2007] 4 CMLR 982, para 69.

110. Case C–95/04P *British Airways v Commission* [2007] ECR I–2331, [2007] 4 CMLR 982, para 86 (references omitted).

111. Case T–65/98 *Van den Bergh Foods Ltd v Commission* [2003] ECR II–4653, [2004] 4 CMLR 14, para 170 (General Court rejecting the argument that the application of Articles 101 and 102 to exclusivity clauses in HB Ice Cream contracts with retailers, which required that only HB products could be stored in provided freezer cabinets, would breach HB's property rights) (appeal dismissed, Case C–552/03P *Unilever Bestfoods (Ireland) Ltd v Commission* [2006] ECR I–9091, [2006] 5 CMLR 1494). A contrary decision had been reached earlier by the Irish High Court in *Masterfoods Ltd t/a Mars Ireland v H.B. Ice Cream Ltd* [1993] ILRM 145.

18. The Commission also recognises that conduct may be justified on objective necessity and efficiencies grounds.[112] Potential justifications are discussed further in this chapter in questions dealing with particular forms of abuse.

What elements must be shown to make out an efficiencies defence in an Article 102 case?

19. The Commission's Article 102 Guidance accepts that there is an efficiencies defence under Article 102. The Commission considers that foreclosure that would otherwise be abusive may be justified on the basis of efficiencies 'that are sufficient to guarantee that no net harm to consumers is likely to arise'. The dominant undertaking should be able to show that the following cumulative conditions are met:

• The efficiencies are the result of the exclusionary conduct.

• The conduct is indispensable for achieving the efficiencies and there must be no less anti-competitive alternative capable of producing the same results.

• The efficiencies outweigh the negative effects on competition.

• The conduct does not eliminate effective competition, by removing all or most existing sources of actual or potential competition (if the conduct maintains, creates or strengthens a monopoly (or near-monopoly) position, an efficiencies defence is not normally available).[113]

If conduct is regulated, may it still give rise to an abuse of dominance?

20. The relevance of the degree of regulation to which an allegedly dominant undertaking is subject has been addressed in the context of telecommunications regulation. The fact that network access prices were regulated by the German telecoms regulator was relied on by Deutsche Telekom in arguing against a finding of an abusive margin squeeze. The Court of Justice held that this regulation did not remove Deutsche Telekom from the reach of Article 102.[114]

21. Deutsche Telekom had scope to adjust its end-user prices through applications to the regulator for authorisation (an increase in those prices could have reduced the margin squeeze between wholesale and retail prices). The General Court had found that Deutsche Telekom's special responsibility as a dominant undertaking meant that it was 'obliged to submit applications for adjustment of its charges at a time when those charges had the effect of impairing genuine undistorted competition'.[115] In upholding the General Court's judgment, the Court of Justice held that the pricing practice was attributable to Deutsche Telekom, since it had

---

112. See Commission Article 102 Guidance [2009] OJ C45/7, paras 28–31.
113. Commission Article 102 Guidance [2009] OJ C45/7, para 30.
114. Case C–280/08P *Deutsche Telekom AG v Commission*, judgment of 14 October 2010, paras 80–92.
115. Case T–271/03 *Deutsche Telekom AG v Commission* [2008] ECR II–477, [2008] 5 CMLR 631, para 122.

scope to adjust its retail prices for end-user access services (even if this required authorization from the German telecoms regulator).[116] The case did not fall into the category of cases, such as *Ladbroke Racing*,[117] where anti-competitive activity was *required* by national legislation or such legislation had precluded all scope for competitive conduct. The mere fact that the German regulator encouraged it to maintain pricing practices which led to the margin squeeze could not in any way absolve Deutsche Telekom from its responsibility under Article 102.[118]

22. The Court also held that even if it were assumed that Deutsche Telekom did not have any scope to adjust its wholesale prices, it could not rely on the premise that the wholesale prices for local loop access services set by the national regulator were excessive in order to demonstrate the inappropriateness of applying the margin squeeze test to Deutsche Telekom.[119]

Key Sources

Commission Article 102 Guidance.

Case 85/76 *Hoffmann-La Roche & Co. v Commission* [1979] ECR 461, [1979] 3 CMLR 211.

---

116. Case C–280/08P *Deutsche Telekom AG v Commission*, judgment of 14 October 2010, para 88.
117. Cases C–359, 379/95 *Commission v Ladbroke Racing Ltd.* [1997] ECR I–6265, [1998] 4 CMLR 27.
118. Case C–280/08P *Deutsche Telekom AG v Commission*, judgment of 14 October 2010, para 83.
119. Case C–280/08P *Deutsche Telekom AG v Commission*, judgment of 14 October 2010, paras 164–165.

56. MAY A DOMINANT SELLER OF PRODUCT A REQUIRE ITS CUSTOMERS TO PURCHASE PRODUCT B WHEN THEY BUY A?

Summary

- Tying and bundling may give rise to an abuse of a dominant position.

- The undertaking must hold a dominant position in the 'tying' product market, which is leveraged to distort competition in the 'tied' product market (in respect of mixed bundling, a dominant position in one of the products that is part of the bundle is required).

- Before Article 102 can apply to a tie, it must be established that the tying and tied products are distinct. If they are in fact parts of the same product, no issue of tying arises.

- Various factors may be relevant in deciding if there is a breach of Article 102, e.g. that the tie is a lasting one that is difficult to reverse or there are insufficient customers for the tied product alone to sustain competitors supplying that product.

- Arguments that tying of products was justified on health and safety grounds were raised in Hilti and Tetra Pak II but were not successful.

1. One of the specific forms of abuse outlined in Article 102 is 'making the conclusion of contracts subject to acceptance by the other parties of supplementary obligations which, by their nature or according to commercial usage, have no connection with the subject of such contracts'. The strategies of 'tying' and 'bundling' fall squarely within these parameters.

2. A tying strategy by a dominant undertaking involves placing a requirement on customers who buy one product in respect of which the undertaking has a dominant position (the tying product) to also purchase a separate, distinct product (the tied product). The firm must be dominant in the tying product if an abuse is to be established.[120]

3. Tying may be achieved through a technical tie, where the design or features of the tying product are such that it will only work with the tied product and be incompatible with alternative products supplied by competitors. An example would be a MP3 player that could only play music files sold through the MP3 supplier's music business. The dominant undertaking may also enforce tying

---

120. See Commission Article 102 Guidance [2009] OJ C45/7, paras 49–50; Case T–201/04 *Microsoft Corp. v Commission* [2007] ECR II–3601, [2007] 5 CMLR 846, paras 842, 870.

through contractual terms that require the purchaser to buy the tied product together with the tying product.

4. The concept of bundling is often used interchangeably with tying, the one possible difference being that the tied product (but not the tying product) may be sold separately in a 'tying' scheme, whereas with 'bundling', the products are only made available together.[121] 'Pure bundling' involves the tying of sales by means of a commercial obligation to purchase two or more products as a bundle or by means of technical integration. Another form of bundling is 'mixed bundling', also known as a multi-product rebate. In this case, a number of products can be purchased as a package on more favourable terms than if the products are purchased separately.[122] As with tying, to establish an abuse, the firm must hold a dominant position in the tying product (in the case of pure and technical bundling) or in one of the products that are part of a mixed bundle.

5. Tying and bundling will often provide customers with better products at lower prices. However these practices can also harm consumers. By engaging in a tying or bundling strategy, the dominant undertaking may be able to leverage its market power in the market where it holds a dominant position to distort competition on another market. The leverage derives from the tying market and is applied to the tied market. The main competition concern is that this will result in the foreclosure of rivals in the tied market and possibly, indirectly, in the tying market. In addition, tying and bundling can also lead to price discrimination and higher prices.[123]

6. Dominant firms have been found to infringe Article 102 in a number of cases involving tying and bundling. In *Tetra Pak II*, it was held that Tetra Pak took advantage of a dominant position on the aseptic market in machines and cartons for liquid foods. The company infringed Article 102 on both these aseptic markets and on the neighbouring and associated markets in non-aseptic machines and cartons. Tetra Pak tied sales of machinery with sales of cartons. By preventing its customers from obtaining supplies of aseptic cartons from competitors, other carton manufacturers were prevented from accessing the aseptic carton market, something they could otherwise have achieved through technical modifications. The tying of sales of cartons and machines contributed to preventing the development of effective competition in the aseptic sector.[124]

7. Other findings of abuse through bundling and tying include in *Hilti* (tying nails for use in nail guns with cartridge strips – illustrating that a dominant firm cannot tie

---

121. See Bellamy & Child (6th edn, 2008) para 10.120.
122. See Commission Article 102 Guidance [2009] OJ C45/7, para 48. See also Case T–210/01 *General Electric Company v Commission* [2005] ECR II–5575, [2006] 4 CMLR 686, para 406, categorising three forms of bundling – pure, technical and mixed.
123. See Commission Article 102 Staff Working Paper, paras 179–181.
124. Case T–83/91 *Tetra Pak International SA v Commission ('Tetra Pak II')* [1994] ECR II–755, [1997] 4 CMLR 726, para 242 (appeal dismissed, Case C–333/94P *Tetra Pak International SA v Commission* [1996] ECR I–5951, [1997] 4 CMLR 662).

spare parts)[125] and in the *Microsoft* case (tying sales of Windows Media Player to the Windows operating system).[126]

When are products 'distinct'?

8.　A key threshold question in tying and bundling cases is whether the products that are the subject of the tie or bundle are distinct products or merely components of the same product. Where the products are components, Article 102 will not be relevant.

9.　It is not always obvious if products that make up a tie or bundle are distinct products or components of the same product. In *Microsoft,* it was argued that media functionality was not a separate product from the Windows PC operating system, so that versions of Windows that incorporated Windows Media Player did not involve the bundling of two separate products. The Commission rejected this argument. The General Court, upholding the Commission's finding, confirmed that the distinctness of products had to be assessed by reference to customer demand and that in the absence of independent demand for the allegedly tied product, there can be no question of separate products and no abusive tying.[127] However, just because most customers wished to receive complementary products together, this did not transform separate products into a single product for purposes of Article 102.[128]

10.　The General Court pointed to *Hilti*, where it may have been assumed that there was no demand for a nail gun magazine without nails, since a magazine without nails is useless. However, that did not prevent the EU courts concluding that those two products belonged to separate markets.[129] In the case of media players and PC operating systems, it was quite possible that consumers would wish to obtain them together but from different sources. If computer manufacturers had been able to obtain Windows without Windows Media Player, they could still have responded to that consumer demand by pre-installing a media player on the operating system but this could be one of a number of media players, not necessarily Windows

---

125.　Case T–30/89 *Hilti AG v Commission* [1991] ECR II–1439, [1992] 4 CMLR 16 (upheld on appeal, Case C–53/92P *Hilti v Commission* [1994] ECR I–667, [1994] 4 CMLR 614).

126.　Case COMP/37.792 *Microsoft* [2005] 4 CMLR 965 (upheld on appeal, Case T–201/04 *Microsoft Corp. v Commission* [2007] ECR II–3601, [2007] 5 CMLR 846). See also COMP/ C–3/39.530 *Microsoft (Tying)*, Commission Decision of 16 December 2009 (tying of Internet Explorer and Windows; commitments offered by Microsoft allowing OEMs to switch Internet Explorer off and on and enabling OEMs to pre-install other web browsers).

127.　Case T–201/04 *Microsoft Corp. v Commission* [2007] ECR II–3601, [2007] 5 CMLR 846, paras 917–918.

128.　Case T–201/04 *Microsoft Corp. v Commission* [2007] ECR II–3601, [2007] 5 CMLR 846, para 922.

129.　Case T–201/04 *Microsoft Corp. v Commission* [2007] ECR II–3601, [2007] 5 CMLR 846, paras 917–922; Case T–30/89 *Hilti AG v Commission* [1991] ECR II–1439, [1992] 4 CMLR 16 (upheld on appeal, Case C–53/92P *Hilti v Commission* [1994] ECR I–667, [1994] 4 CMLR 614).

Media Player.[130] In any event, the General Court went on to consider that there was evidence of separate consumer demand for media players.[131]

11. In *Tetra Pak II*, it was argued that machines and cartons were part of the same market as there was a natural commercial link between them. In rejecting this view, the General Court pointed out that in the non-aseptic market, there were a number of independent competitors specialising in the manufacture of cartons but which did not produce machines, so consideration of commercial usage did not support a finding that machinery for packaging a product was indivisible from the cartons.[132]

12. In the *Credit Unions* case, the Irish Supreme Court examined whether the savings protection scheme ('SPS') provided by the Irish League of Credit Unions ('ILCU') and credit union representation services were distinct products. The High Court had found that they were distinct products and that the ILCU had abused its dominant position on the market for SPS by tying access to SPS to the provision of credit union representation.[133] Rejecting this analysis, the Supreme Court held that SPS was an integral part of a bundle of services provided by ILCU to its members. Giving the judgment of the court, Fennelly J relied on arguments to the effect that for two products to be distinct, they must belong to separate product markets and, also, that a distinct market for the tied item would not imply separate products absent widespread sales of the tying item in unbundled form.[134] It was clear that there was no stabilisation fund for credit unions other than SPS and that no competing product had been available for sale. SPS itself always existed as an integral part of the bundle of services that ILCU provided to its own members and it had never been provided independently.[135] As there were no unbundled sales of SPS and no similar stabilisation fund at all (not to mind 'widespread' sales), SPS and representation services were not distinct products in distinct product markets.[136]

---

130. Case T–201/04 *Microsoft Corp. v Commission* [2007] ECR II–3601, [2007] 5 CMLR 846, paras 922–923.
131. Case T–201/04 *Microsoft Corp. v Commission* [2007] ECR II–3601, [2007] 5 CMLR 846, paras 924–933.
132. Case T–83/91 *Tetra Pak International SA v Commission ('Tetra Pak II')* [1994] ECR II–755, [1997] 4 CMLR 726, para 82 (appeal dismissed, Case C–333/94P *Tetra Pak International SA v Commission* [1996] ECR I–5951, [1997] 4 CMLR 662).
133. *Competition Authority v O'Regan* [2004] IEHC 330 (Kearns J).
134. *Competition Authority v O'Regan* [2007] IESC 22, [2007] 4 IR 737, paras 119–126. Fennelly J cited with approval the discussion in O'Donoghue and Padilla, *The Law and Economics of Article 82 EC* (2006) 101.
135. *Competition Authority v O'Regan* [2007] IESC 22, [2007] 4 IR 737, paras 130, 136.
136. Cf the subsequent judgment of the General Court in Case T–201/04 *Microsoft Corp. v Commission* [2007] ECR II–3601, [2007] 5 CMLR 846, paras 919–922 (the General Court did not require that the tying product (the Windows PC operating system) be the subject of widespread sales in unbundled form before it could be considered a distinct product from a media player).

What specific factors are relevant in assessing whether tying or bundling is abusive?

13.   As well as the general factors indicating abuse, the Commission considers a number of specific factors that add to the risk of abuse in tying and bundling cases, including:

- The tying strategy is a lasting one, e.g. through technical tying that is difficult to reverse.

- In bundling, the more products in respect of which a dominant position is held.

- There are insufficient customers for the tied product alone to sustain competitors supplying that product, therefore leading to higher prices for those customers who purchase only the tied product.

- Where there is a degree of substitutability between the tying and tied products (e.g. both are inputs, the amount of which can be varied), the tie may prevent switching to the tied product where the price of the tying product is raised and lead to an overall increase in prices.

- Where the price of the tying product is regulated, the tie may allow the dominant undertaking to raise the price of the tied product to compensate.[137]

When are multi-product rebates anti-competitive?[138]

14.   The Commission suggests that mixed bundling or a multi-product rebate 'may be anti-competitive on the tied or the tying market if it is so large that equally efficient competitors offering only some of the components cannot compete against the discounted bundle'.[139]

15.   The Commission also suggests a methodology for measuring the effect of the rebate vis-à-vis competitors who are not able to offer competing bundles. Ideally, this would involve assessing whether the incremental revenue generated by the dominant undertaking would cover the incremental costs for each product in the bundle. If incremental revenue is above long-run average incremental cost ('LRAIC') from inclusion of a particular product in the bundle, the Commission will not usually intervene under Article 102. The rationale is that an equally efficient competitor with only one product should be able to compete profitably against the bundle. However, if incremental revenue is below LRAIC, this may be grounds for intervention as here, an equally efficient competitor may be prevented from expanding or entering the market. The Commission acknowledges that it may be difficult to derive the incremental revenue in practice and suggests that incremental price can instead be used as a good proxy.[140] Where competitors are

---

137. Commission Article 102 Guidance [2009] OJ C45/7, paras 52–58.
138. See also Question 59.
139. Commission Article 102 Guidance [2009] OJ C45/7, para 59.
140. Commission Article 102 Guidance [2009] OJ C45/7, para 60.

able to offer competing bundles, the dominant firm's rebate scheme will only be abusive if the price of the bundle as a whole is predatory.[141]

May a dominant undertaking require customers to purchase only its own spare parts?

16.   This issue arose in *Hilti*, where it was argued that the tying of nails with nail guns and cartridges was justified on grounds of public safety. Rejecting this argument, the General Court indicated that Hilti could have notified the relevant UK authorities of its concerns that competing products were dangerous but it had not done so. In those circumstances, it was 'not the task of an undertaking in a dominant position to take steps on its own initiative to eliminate products which, rightly or wrongly, it regards as dangerous or at least as inferior in quality to its own products'.[142]

17.   Similarly, in *Tetra Pak II*, the General Court rejected the argument that the tying of packaging and machines was justified on public health grounds. The tied-sale clauses were wholly unreasonable in the context of public health. The reliability and hygiene of packaging equipment could be ensured by disclosing to users of Tetra Pak machines all the technical specifications concerning the cartons to be used on those systems, without the applicant's intellectual property rights being prejudiced.[143]

18.   The argument that the tied sales of two products is in accordance with commercial usage or that there is a natural link between the two products in question does not amount to objective justification for the tie.[144]

Key Sources

Commission Article 102 Guidance, paras 47–62.

Case T–30/89 *Hilti AG v Commission* [1991] ECR II–1439, [1992] 4 CMLR 16, para 118.

Case T–83/91 *Tetra Pak International SA v Commission ('Tetra Pak II')* [1994] ECR II–755, [1997] 4 CMLR 726.

Competition Authority v O'Regan [2007] IESC 22, [2007] 4 IR 737.

Case T–201/04 *Microsoft Corp. v Commission* [2007] ECR II–3601, [2007] 5 CMLR 846.

---

141. Commission Article 102 Guidance [2009] OJ C45/7, para 61.
142. Case T–30/89 *Hilti AG v Commission* [1991] ECR II–1439, [1992] 4 CMLR 16, para 118 (appeal dismissed, Case C–53/92P *Hilti v Commission* [1994] ECR I–667, [1994] 4 CMLR 614).
143. Case T–83/91 *Tetra Pak International SA v Commission ('Tetra Pak II')* [1994] ECR II–755, [1997] 4 CMLR 726, paras 138–139.
144. Case C–333/94P *Tetra Pak International SA v Commission* [1996] ECR I–5951, [1997] 4 CMLR 662, para 37.

57. MAY A DOMINANT SUPPLIER CHARGE DIFFERENT PRICES FOR THE SAME PRODUCT TO DIFFERENT CUSTOMERS?

Summary

- Not every instance of price discrimination by a dominant undertaking is abusive.

- For price discrimination to infringe Article 102, it must be shown that the transactions being compared are 'equivalent' and that a customer of the dominant undertaking suffers a 'competitive disadvantage'. In practice, these criteria are usually found to be satisfied without much difficulty.

- Price discrimination can be justified for objective reasons, e.g. it was much cheaper to supply one customer because of economies of scale.

- Differential prices based purely on the home Member State of the customer are likely to be abusive.

- Selective price cutting by a dominant firm in response to competition has been found abusive in cases involving dominant firms with very strong market positions.

1. Price discrimination usually involves charging different prices for similar transactions but it could also include charging the same price for transactions that are different. Article 102(c) provides that one form of abuse is 'applying dissimilar conditions to equivalent transactions with other trading parties, thereby placing them at a competitive disadvantage' and this provision has been applied in many price discrimination cases. However, it should be remembered that the instances of abuse listed in Article 102 are not exhaustive so that even if the criteria of Article 102(c) were not strictly met, it may still be possible to find that discriminatory pricing constitutes an abuse within the meaning of Article 102 more generally.

2. It is clear that not all price discrimination by a dominant firm is abusive but 'the boundaries of abusive price discrimination remain uncertain'.[145] In applying Article 102(c), it must be determined if the transactions that are the subject of differential pricing are in fact 'equivalent' and whether customers are as a result placed at a 'competitive disadvantage'. It must also be considered whether there is a justification for the differential pricing. Fidelity rebates, as well as headline prices, may be found to have a discriminatory effect.[146]

---

145. Bellamy & Child (6th edn, 2008) para 10.080.
146. See Question 59, para 18 for cases where fidelity rebates have been found to have a discriminatory effect.

When are transactions equivalent?

3.   If different prices are applied to transactions that are not truly equivalent, then no issue of price discrimination under Article 102(c) arises. In some cases, it may be obvious whether or not transactions are equivalent but in others, a close analysis of various factors may be required. Such factors may include cost differences of providing goods or services to two customers, the timing of the transactions or the precise composition of goods or services in each transaction. It is not apparent that the Commission or the European courts have developed clear criteria for applying such factors and the conclusion that transactions are equivalent is often reached without a great deal of analysis.[147]

4.   There is some doubt about the extent to which the different circumstances of buyers can be considered in assessing whether transactions between them and a dominant supplier are equivalent. The fact that customers operate on different downstream markets has not provided justification for a finding of non-equivalence. In *Irish Sugar,* it was argued that sales of industrial sugar to different customers, only some of which received rebates, were not equivalent as one group of buyers exported the sugar while another group resold it on the Irish market. The General Court rejected this argument and found that there was a distortion of market mechanisms when Irish Sugar priced not by reference to supply and demand on the industrial sugar market but by reference to the location of the buyers from its own customers further downstream.[148] However, the fact that customers had different degrees of purchasing power has been cited as a reason why different groups of purchasers were not comparable.[149]

---

147. Geradin and Petit, 'Price discrimination under EC competition law: another antitrust doctrine in search of limiting principles?' [2006] *Journal of Competition Law and Economics* 479, 486–487. See, e.g., the judgment of the General Court in Case T–301/04 *Clearstream Banking AG v Commission* [2009] ECR II–3155, [2009] 5 CMLR 2677, paras 169–179 (that clearing and settlement services provided to two types of providers of secondary clearing services were equivalent); *Attheraces Ltd v British Horseracing Board Ltd* [2007] EWCA Civ 38, [2007] UKCLR 309, para 270 (different transactions for the sale of pre-race data accepted as being equivalent). For an example of services found not to have been equivalent, see COMP/36.568 *Scandlines v Port of Helsingborg* [2006] 4 CMLR 1224, para 252 (land-side port facilities provided to ferry operators and cargo vessels were held to differ significantly).

148. Case T–228/97 *Irish Sugar plc v Commission* [1999] ECR II–2969, [1999] 5 CMLR 1300, para 141.

149. Case C–62/86 *AKZO Chemie BV v Commission* [1991] ECR I–3359, [1993] 5 CMLR 215, para 120 (an argument that was unsuccessfully relied on by Clearstream in Case T–301/04 *Clearstream Banking AG v Commission* [2009] ECR II–3155, [2009] 5 CMLR 2677, para 179).

What amounts to a competitive disadvantage for a customer subject to differential pricing?

5.   For Article 102(c) to apply, the price discrimination must lead to a 'competitive disadvantage'. The Commission and the European courts have generally concluded without much difficulty that this criterion has been met.[150] For example, in the *Portuguese Airports* case, different landing charges were imposed on international and domestic flights but the fact that international flights would almost certainly have operated in a different product market was not an issue.[151]

6.   In *British Airways* the Court of Justice addressed the question whether concrete evidence of a competitive disadvantage was required in order to establish an infringement of Article 102(c). It held that it was sufficient if the discrimination *tended* to lead to a distortion of competition:

> ... there is nothing to prevent discrimination between business partners who are in a relationship of competition from being regarded as being abusive as soon as the behaviour of the undertaking in a dominant position tends, having regard to the whole of the circumstances of the case, to lead to a distortion of competition between those business partners. In such a situation, it cannot be required in addition that proof be adduced of an actual quantifiable deterioration in the competitive position of the business partners taken individually.[152]

7.   In the *Aeroports de Paris* case, licenses to operate groundhandling services were made available to airlines at a cheaper rate than to third party groundhandlers and this was found to be an abuse under Article 102(c). The argument that there was no competitive disadvantage to the third party groundhandlers was rejected. The lower prices charged to the airlines could incentivise them to take up self-handling rather than employ the services of a third party, placing third party groundhandlers at a competitive disadvantage.[153]

8.   The judgment of the General Court in *Clearstream* adopts a similarly low threshold to the 'competitive disadvantage' criterion. The Court held that the application by a *de facto* monopoly supplier of different prices to a customer over five years 'could not fail to cause that partner a competitive disadvantage'.[154] The finding that prolonged differential pricing was in itself sufficient to establish abuse shows a strict approach to the law on price discrimination that seems less focused on an effects-based analysis.

---

150. See Van Bael & Bellis, *Competition Law of the European Community* (5th edn, 2010) 813.
151. Case C–163/99 *Portugal v Commission* [2001] ECR I–2613, [2002] 4 CMLR 1319, para 66.
152. Case C–95/04P *British Airways plc v Commission* [2007] ECR I–2331, [2007] 4 CMLR 982, para 145.
153. Case T–128/98 *Aéroports de Paris v Commission* [2000] ECR II–3929, [2001] 4 CMLR 1376, para 215 (upheld on appeal, Case C–82/01 *Aéroports de Paris v Commission* [2002] ECR I–9297, [2003] 4 CMLR 609).
154. Case T–301/04 *Clearstream Banking AG v Commission* [2009] ECR II–3155, [2009] 5 CMLR 2677, para 194.

9.   This can be contrasted to some extent with the earlier judgment of the Court of Justice in *Kanal 5*, which suggests that a more nuanced approach to the 'competitive disadvantage' criterion may be required in some cases. The Court held, on a preliminary reference, that by charging different royalties in respect of broadcasting of copyrighted music to commercial and public service broadcasters, a copyright management organisation was likely to abuse its dominant position by applying dissimilar conditions to equivalent services, unless such a practice was objectively justified. It was for the national court to determine whether the transactions were in fact equivalent and whether the commercial broadcasters were placed at a competitive disadvantage. In making that determination, the national court would have to take account of the fact that, in contrast to the commercial broadcasters, the public service broadcaster did not generate revenue from advertising or subscription contracts and that royalties paid by it were collected without taking account of the quantity of musical works protected by copyright actually broadcast. The national court would also have to determine whether the public service broadcaster was in competition with the commercial broadcasters.[155]

10.   The difference in the position of customers was also emphasised by the English Court of Appeal in *Attheraces*. The Court held that differences in the position of customers downstream could be taken into account in coming to the conclusion that there was no abuse of a dominant position as a result of differential pricing:

> Once it is accepted that in a market such as this not all customers are similarly placed, and that the reason may be that their own onward markets are significantly different, differential pricing may legitimately reflect the distinct value of the product to each customer.[156]

Is a selective price cut in response to competition abusive?

11.   May a dominant firm issue price cuts only in respect of customers that have been approached by a competitor? Such action may seem defensible as the dominant firm is lowering its prices in response to competition. However, such selective price cutting has been condemned in cases where the dominant undertaking held a particularly strong position.

12.   This was the case in *Irish Sugar*, where 'border rebates' were granted to Irish customers of Irish Sugar located close to the Northern Ireland border and aimed at meeting competition from Northern Irish competitors. Irish Sugar, which had an 88 per cent share of the Irish retail sugar market, was found to have abused its dominant position.[157] A finding of abuse was also made in *Cewal* in respect of selective price cuts aimed at meeting competition by a liner conference that had a

---

155. Case C–52/07 *Kanal 5 Ltd v STIM* [2008] ECR I–9275, [2009] 5 CMLR 2175, paras 45–48.

156. *Attheraces Ltd v British Horseracing Board Ltd* [2007] EWCA Civ 38, [2007] UKCLR 309, para 274.

157. Case T–228/97 *Irish Sugar plc v Commission* [1999] ECR II–2969, [1999] 5 CMLR 1300, para 183.

90 per cent market share. It has been suggested that in both these cases, the dominant undertakings' 'super-dominance', as evidenced by their very high market shares, was important in finding an abuse and that conduct of this type aimed at meeting competition may not otherwise have resulted in a breach of Article 102.[158]

Is it legitimate to charge different prices to customers located in different geographic areas?

13. Price discrimination by a dominant firm based purely on the nationality of the customer is likely to constitute an abuse. In *United Brands*, a practice whereby bananas were sold to European distributors at different prices depending on the Member State in which the distributor was established created a rigid partitioning of national markets, obstructed the free movement of goods, had no justifiable basis and was found to be an abuse under Article 102(c).[159]

What other justifications are there for charging different prices?

14. A dominant firm can escape a finding of abuse if its differential pricing is objectively justified. However, the factors that may be relied on to establish an objective justification 'have not been fully identified'.[160] It is unclear when a 'meeting competition' defence will be made out and based on *Irish Sugar* and *Cewal*, it seems that such a justification will be less likely to succeed the more powerful the position of the dominant undertaking. A better justification would be to show that economies of scale justify the charging of a lower price to a particular customer or that price differences can be explained by other objective factors such as differences in transport costs.

Key Sources

Case 27/76 *United Brands Company v Commission* [1978] ECR 207, [1978] 1 CMLR 429.

Case T–228/97 *Irish Sugar plc v Commission* [1999] ECR II–2969, [1999] 5 CMLR 1300.

Case T–128/98 *Aéroports de Paris v Commission* [2000] ECR II–3929, [2001] 4 CMLR 1376.

Case C–95/04P *British Airways plc v Commission* [2007] ECR I–2331, [2007] 4 CMLR 982.

Case T–301/04 *Clearstream Banking AG v Commission* [2009] ECR II–3155, [2009] 5 CMLR 2677.

---

158. Bellamy & Child (6th edn, 2008) para 10.082.
159. Case 27/76 *United Brands Company v Commission* [1978] ECR 207, [1978] 1 CMLR 429, paras 226–234.
160. Bellamy & Child (6th edn, 2008) para 10.090.

58. HOW LOW CAN A DOMINANT SUPPLIER DROP ITS PRICES WITHOUT VIOLATING ARTICLE 102?

Summary

- If a dominant firm lowers its prices to loss making levels, this could constitute predatory pricing and an abuse of dominance.

- Prices below average variable cost are presumed to be predatory.

- Prices between average variable cost and average total cost are predatory if an intention to eliminate competitors is shown.

- In theory, predatory pricing may be justified on efficiency grounds but in practice this defence is unlikely to be successful.

- It is not a defence for the dominant firm to say that it was aligning its prices to those of competitors.

- To establish predatory pricing, it is not necessary to show that the dominant firm has the possibility of recouping its losses.

1. Predatory pricing involves a dominant undertaking lowering its prices to a level at which it incurs losses with the aim of eliminating or disciplining actual or potential competitors.[161] Predatory pricing usually takes place in the market in which the undertaking engaging in the practice holds its dominant position (it is generally an 'own market abuse') but Article 102 can also be infringed if the dominant undertaking engages in predation in a related market in which it is not dominant.[162] In practice, it may be difficult to distinguish between predatory and legitimate pricing, which may also involve low prices and be the result of competition.

---

161. The Commission adds that predatory pricing can also occur where the dominant firm deliberately foregoes profits (see Commission Article 102 Guidance [2009] OJ C45/7, para 63).
162. See, e.g., Case C–62/86 *AKZO Chemie BV v Commission* [1991] ECR I–3359, [1993] 5 CMLR 215, paras 35–45 (predation in the flour additives market, in which Akzo had only a minor interest, in order to reinforce its dominant position in the related organic peroxides sector by discouraging a competitor, for which the flour additives market was important, from extending its activities in organic peroxides); Case C–333/94P *Tetra Pak International SA v Commission* [1996] ECR I–5951, [1997] 4 CMLR 662, paras 27–31 (predation in a market that was related to the one in which the dominant position was held to an extent that Tetra Pak's position was comparable to holding a dominant position on the markets as a whole). Cf the judgment of the French Supreme Court in *Ministre des Finances, De L'Economie et de L'Emploi v Société Laboratoire Glaxosmithkline France* [2009] ECC 25 (rejecting the French Competition Authority's case of predatory pricing in a market in which Glaxo was not dominant and which was not sufficiently related to a market in which it held a dominant position).

2. To establish whether prices are so low as to be predatory, they must be compared to the costs of the dominant undertaking. A firm has both fixed costs, which remain the same no matter what level of output it generates (e.g. depreciation, management overheads) and variable costs, which are costs that vary depending on the firm's level of output (e.g. energy bills, the cost of raw materials). Another way to think of variable costs is as costs that could have been avoided had the output subject to the allegedly abusive conduct not been produced. The firm's total cost is the sum of fixed and variable costs. Two measures of cost are particularly relevant to predatory pricing analysis: (i) the average total cost ('ATC'); and (ii) the average variable cost ('AVC').[163]

3. Prices below AVC are assumed to be predatory. Prices below ATC but above AVC may be predatory if they are based on an intention to eliminate a competitor.[164] In *AKZO* the Court of Justice explained the position as follows:

    > Prices below average variable costs (that is to say, those which vary depending on the quantities produced) by means of which a dominant undertaking seeks to eliminate a competitor must be regarded as abusive. A dominant undertaking has no interest in applying such prices except that of eliminating competitors so as to enable it subsequently to raise its prices by taking advantage of its monopolistic position, since each sale generates a loss, namely the total amount of the fixed costs (that is to say, those which remain constant regardless of the quantities produced) and, at least, part of the variable costs relating to the unit produced.

    > Moreover, prices below average total costs, that is to say, fixed costs plus variable costs, but above average variable costs, must be regarded as abusive if they are determined as part of a plan for eliminating a competitor. Such prices can drive from the market undertakings which are perhaps as efficient as the dominant undertaking but which, because of their smaller financial resources, are incapable of withstanding the competition waged against them.[165]

---

163. The Commission suggests that the firm's average avoidable costs ('AAC') be used rather than AVC, although in most cases the two will be the same as it is often only variable cost that can be avoided. Where they are different, the Commission explains that AAC better reflects the sacrifice made by the dominant firm as AAC would, for example, include sunk costs generated by having to increase capacity in order to predate but these costs would not be reflected in AVC (see Commission Article 102 Guidance [2009] OJ C45/7, para 64). Variable costs are generally understood to be costs that vary according to the quantities produced. The Court of Justice pointed out in *Akzo* that 'an item of cost is not fixed or variable by nature'. Rather, costs must be categorised as either fixed or variable according to the context. In *Akzo*, the Commission had argued that labour costs were variable. However, the Court found from the relevant data that there was no correlation between the quantities produced and labour costs so that these costs could not be considered as variable. (See Case C–62/86 *AKZO Chemie BV v Commission* [1991] ECR I–3359, [1993] 5 CMLR 215, paras 92–95).

164. See also Case C–209/10 *Post Danmark A/S v Konkurrencerådet* (pending), a preliminary reference from the Danish Supreme Court, asking whether it is abusive for a dominant postal undertaking to selectively price below ATC but above average incremental cost in the absence of eliminatory intent.

165. Case C–62/86 *AKZO Chemie BV v Commission* [1991] ECR I–3359, [1993] 5 CMLR 215, paras 71–72.

4. This approach was confirmed by the Court of Justice in *France Télécom*, in which Wanadoo was found to have engaged in below cost selling of ADSL-based Internet access:

> [First] ... prices below average variable costs must be considered prima facie abusive inasmuch as, in applying such prices, an undertaking in a dominant position is presumed to pursue no other economic objective save that of eliminating its competitors. Secondly, prices below average total costs but above average variable costs are to be considered abusive only where they are fixed in the context of a plan having the purpose of eliminating a competitor.[166]

5. The presumption that prices below AVC are abusive may be capable of rebuttal by a dominant undertaking 'by showing that such pricing was not part of a plan to eliminate its competitor'.[167] The question of justification for below cost selling is considered below.

What evidence is required to show eliminatory intent where prices are between AVC and ATC?

6. In the case of prices above AVC but below ATC, an intention to eliminate competition must be established on the basis of sound and consistent evidence.[168] In *Tetra Pak II*, for example, this eliminatory intent was evidenced by factors such as the duration, the continuity and the scale of the loss-making sales over a six-year period; accounting data showing deliberate importation of products in order to resell them below their purchase price; the fact that prices in one Member State were 20 per cent to 50 per cent lower than in other Member States; and board reports that referred to the need to make major financial sacrifices in the area of prices and supply terms in order to fight competition.[169] Internal documents may expressly reveal an intention to eliminate competition.[170]

Is the possibility of recoupment of losses a necessary requirement to establish predatory pricing?

7. Under US federal antitrust law, to establish predatory pricing, it must be shown that the dominant firm has the possibility to recover the losses it made as part of its predatory strategy at a later stage.[171] In *France Télécom*, the Court of Justice confirmed that no such recoupment test applies under Article 102.[172] The previous

---

166. Case C–202/07 *France Télécom SA v Commission* [2009] ECR I–2369, [2009] 4 CMLR 1149, para 109.

167. Cases C–395 & 396/96P *Compagnie Maritime Belge Transports SA v Commission* [2000] ECR I–1365, [2000] 4 CMLR 1076, opinion of Advocate General Fennelly, para 127.

168. See Case T–340/03 *France Télécom SA v Commission* [2007] ECR II–107, [2007] 4 CMLR 919, para 197 (appeal dismissed, Case C–202/07 *France Télécom SA v Commission* [2009] ECR I–2369, [2009] 4 CMLR 1149).

169. Case T–83/91 *Tetra Pak International SA v Commission ('Tetra Pak II')* [1994] ECR II–755, [1997] 4 CMLR 726, para 151.

170. See Case T–340/03 *France Télécom SA v Commission* [2007] ECR II–107, [2007] 4 CMLR 919, para 199 *et seq.*

case law had not established such a requirement and in *Tetra Pak II*, in the context of prices below AVC, it was specifically held that it would be inappropriate to require proof that the dominant firm had a realistic chance of recouping its losses.[173]

8. Although not a requirement, the possibility of recoupment may be a relevant factor in assessing whether pricing is abusive. For example, where prices are above AVC but below ATC, a showing that the dominant firm has the possibility to recoup its losses may 'assist in establishing that a plan to eliminate a competitor exists'.[174] The Commission indicates that consumers are likely to be harmed if the dominant undertaking can reasonably expect to recoup its losses and benefit from the sacrifice it has made.[175]

9. The Court of Justice explained that the lack of any possibility of recoupment of losses was not sufficient to prevent the undertaking reinforcing its dominant position, in particular, following the withdrawal from the market of one or a number of its competitors. The degree of competition existing on the market, already weakened precisely because of the presence of the dominant undertaking, would be further reduced and customers would suffer loss as a result of the limitation of the choices available to them.[176]

10. The Commission states that consumers are more likely to be harmed if the dominant undertaking can expect to be in a position to benefit from its sacrifice.[177] So, while proof of increased profits is not required to establish predatory pricing, the Commission's statement indicates, at least at the level of enforcement practice, a focus not only on the sacrifice, but also on the likely benefit from it.[178]

---

171. *Brooke Group Ltd. v Brown & Williamson Tobacco Corp.* 509 US 209, 225, 113 S Ct 2578, 2589 (1993). See also *Weyerhaeuser Co. v Ross-Simmons Hardwood Lumber Co., Inc.* 549 US 312, 127 S Ct 1069 (2007) (in an 'overbidding' case (paying excessive prices for raw material saw logs to foreclose a sawmill competitor), the plaintiff had to show that the defendant had a dangerous probability of recouping the losses incurred).

172. Case C–202/07 *France Télécom SA v Commission* [2009] ECR I–2369, [2009] 4 CMLR 1149, para 110.

173. Case C–333/94P *Tetra Pak International SA v Commission* [1996] ECR I–5951, [1997] 4 CMLR 662, para 44.

174. Case C–202/07 *France Télécom SA v Commission* [2009] ECR I–2369, [2009] 4 CMLR 1149, para 111.

175. Commission Article 102 Guidance [2009] OJ C45/7, para 70.

176. Case C–202/07 *France Télécom SA v Commission* [2009] ECR I–2369, [2009] 4 CMLR 1149, para 112.

177. Commission Article 102 Guidance [2009] OJ C45/7, para 70.

178. Cf the views of the Irish Competition Authority in an earlier case, Dec No 05/001 *Drogheda Independent Company Limited*, Decision of the Irish Competition Authority of 7 December 2004, para 2.55 ('If the alleged predation appears to be implausible, there is a sound business justification and the feasibility of recoupment is remote, then there may be no need to deal with the issue of whether prices are below cost'). (contd \...)

Can below cost selling by a dominant firm be justified on efficiencies grounds?

11. In *France Télécom*, the Court of Justice noted that the possibility of recoupment of losses could assist in excluding legitimate economic justifications for below AVC pricing.[179] The fact that it referred to economic justification in the context of predatory pricing may be an implied acknowledgment by the Court that such a justification was possible.

12. The Commission also suggests that predatory pricing can be defended on the basis of efficiencies generated and states that it will consider claims by a dominant undertaking that low pricing enables it to achieve economies of scale or efficiencies related to expanding the market. However, the Commission acknowledges that it is unlikely that predatory conduct will generate efficiencies.[180]

13. A justification based on economies of scale was advanced in the *France Télécom* case but was rejected. In seeking to justify below cost selling for ADSL-based Internet access, Wanadoo sought to rely on an economies of scale argument. It pointed out that the variable cost of some products diminishes with quantity produced, while a high production volume may reduce future costs by building up experience. The Commission's rejection of this argument illustrates how difficult it will be for a dominant firm to successfully invoke an efficiencies defence in a predatory pricing case:

> One of the objectives of below-cost pricing may be to reserve for the company engaging in the practice the benefit of economies of scale on the market and to delay accordingly for competitors their arrival at the same volume threshold allowing the economies of scale. For an argument based on efficiency gains to be admissible, it must be possible to prove that such gains could not have been achieved by means other than a below-cost selling strategy. In the present case, there is no guarantee that such gains could not have been achieved had the market developed in a balanced manner. Moreover, a combination of being at a higher point on the learning curve than competitors and having higher output thanks to below-cost pricing may have exclusion effects capable of consolidating the dominant company's hegemony.[181]

14. The General Court's endorsement of the Commission's reasoning on appeal begs the question whether an efficiencies defence has any real possibility of success in a predatory pricing case:

> An undertaking which charges predatory prices may enjoy economies of scale and learning effects on account of increased production precisely because of such pricing.

---

178. (contd) This decision should now be read in light of the judgment in *France Télécom* and the confirmation by the Court of Justice that proof of the possibility of recoupment of losses is not a necessary precondition for a finding of abusive predatory pricing.
179. Case C–202/07 *France Télécom SA v Commission* [2009] ECR I–2369, [2009] 4 CMLR 1149, para 111.
180. Commission Article 102 Guidance [2009] OJ C45/7, para 74.
181. COMP/38.233 *Wanadoo Interactive* [2005] 5 CMLR 120, para 307.

The economies of scale and learning effects cannot therefore exempt that undertaking from liability under Article [102].[182]

Can the 'meeting competition' defence be invoked against a charge of predatory pricing?

15. It also seems that a dominant firm pricing below cost will have difficulty invoking the justification that it is merely matching the prices of its competitors. The General Court explained in *France Télécom* that whereas a dominant firm was allowed to take reasonable steps to protect its commercial interests, the position was different if the purpose of the action was to strengthen and abuse a dominant position. This stems from the nature of the obligations (*i.e.* the special responsibility) on the dominant firm:

> WIN cannot therefore rely on an absolute right to align its prices on those of its competitors in order to justify its conduct. Even if alignment of prices by a dominant undertaking on those of its competitors is not in itself abusive or objectionable, it might become so where it is aimed not only at protecting its interests but also at strengthening and abusing its dominant position.[183]

What are the Commission's enforcement priorities in respect of predatory pricing?

16. The Commission states that in deciding whether to investigate possible predatory pricing, it will focus on whether there is evidence of sacrifice by the dominant undertaking and anti-competitive foreclosure of competitors. The sacrifice analysis examines whether the dominant undertaking is incurring losses that could have been avoided. In line with the case law, pricing below AAC/AVC will generally be viewed as a clear indication of sacrifice as at this price, the firm is incurring a loss that could have been avoided. However, the Commission notes that a dominant firm may be incurring avoidable losses even at pricing levels above AAC/AVC. The Commission states that in this case, it will not consider hypothetical alternative pricing but rather focus on economically rational and realistic alternatives that could be expected to be more profitable.[184]

Key Sources

Case C–62/86 *AKZO Chemie BV v Commission* [1991] ECR I–3359, [1993] 5 CMLR 215.

COMP/38.233 *Wanadoo Interactive* [2005] 5 CMLR 120; appeal dismissed, Case T–340/03 *France Télécom SA v Commission* [2007] ECR II–107, [2007] 4 CMLR 919; further appeal dismissed, Case C–202/07 *France Télécom SA v Commission* [2009] ECR I–2369, [2009] 4 CMLR 1149.

---

182. Case T–340/03 *France Télécom SA v Commission* [2007] ECR II–107, [2007] 4 CMLR 919, para 217.
183. Case T–340/03 *France Télécom SA v Commission* [2007] ECR II–107, [2007] 4 CMLR 919, para 187.
184. Commission Article 102 Guidance [2009] OJ C45/7, paras 64–65.

59. **MAY A DOMINANT SUPPLIER OFFER A CUSTOMER A DISCOUNT IN RETURN FOR AGREEING TO PURCHASE ALL OF ITS REQUIREMENTS FROM THAT SUPPLIER?**

Summary

• Discounts granted by a dominant firm in return for increased business from customers may give rise to an abuse under Article 102.

• It is not necessary for the customer to be forced to carry out all its business or a certain percentage with the dominant undertaking. It may be sufficient if the customer is induced to do more business with the dominant firm.

• All the circumstances must be examined to determine if the discount scheme will give rise to an exclusionary effect.

• The level of the discount would not necessarily determine if an abuse occurs. An abuse could occur whatever the percentage discount granted, although a more significant discount may be more loyalty-inducing.

• The actual foreclosure of competitors does not have to be proved. It is sufficient if the discount scheme is capable of making market entry very difficult or impossible for competitors of the dominant undertaking and of making it more difficult or impossible for its co-contractors to choose between various sources of supply or commercial partners.

• A scheme that grants different levels of discounts as targets are met will be considered especially loyalty-inducing and more likely to constitute an abuse when the discounts retrospectively apply to all the business carried out rather than just the additional business that triggers the increased discount.

• If a fidelity rebate scheme operates in a discriminatory way, it may breach Article 102(c).

• It is open to a dominant undertaking to show that its fidelity rebate scheme is objectively justified. However, the case law does not provide a great deal of guidance as to what arguments might be successful to justify a rebate scheme.

1. Fidelity rebates granted by a dominant undertaking (also referred to as loyalty discounts or conditional rebates) may breach Article 102. Such rebates may take different forms. The key feature is that more favourable terms are offered to the business partner for carrying out more of its business with the dominant undertaking.

2. The main competition concern with fidelity rebates is the foreclosure of the dominant undertaking's competitors. As Advocate General Kokott put it in *British Airways*:

> ... loyalty rebates and loyalty bonuses can in practice bind business partners so closely to the dominant undertaking (the 'fidelity-building effect'), that its competitors find it

inordinately difficult to sell their products ('exclusionary', or 'foreclosure' effect), with the result that competition itself can be damaged and, ultimately, the consumer can suffer.[185]

3.   In contrast to predatory pricing, it is not necessary to show that a fidelity rebate entails a sacrifice for the dominant undertaking before concluding that it will entail exclusionary effects.[186]

4.   A fidelity rebate may be abusive whether or not it involves a formal obligation on the customer to purchase all or a certain proportion of its supplies from the dominant undertaking. Such a rebate was condemned as an abuse of a dominant position in *Hoffmann-La Roche*:

> An undertaking which is in a dominant position on a market and ties purchasers – even if it does so at their request – by an obligation or promise on their part to obtain all or most of their requirements exclusively from the said undertaking abuses its dominant position within the meaning of Article [102] of the Treaty, whether the obligation in question is stipulated without further qualification or whether it is undertaken in consideration of the grant of a rebate.
>
> The same applies if the said undertaking, without tying the purchasers by a formal obligation, applies, either under the terms of agreements concluded with these purchasers or unilaterally, a system of fidelity rebates, that is to say discounts conditional on the customer's obtaining all or most of its requirements – whether the quantity of its purchases be large or small – from the undertaking in a dominant position.
>
> Obligations of this kind to obtain supplies exclusively from a particular undertaking, whether or not they are in consideration of rebates or of the granting of fidelity rebates intended to give the purchaser an incentive to obtain his supplies exclusively from the undertaking in a dominant position, are incompatible with the objective of undistorted competition within the common market.[187]

5.   It does not affect the abusive nature of a rebate scheme whether the purchase volume commitment is expressed in absolute terms or by reference to a percentage.[188] A loyalty obligation can still be abusive despite the fact that the customer was not pressured into accepting it[189] and even if the obligation was included at the customer's request.[190]

185. Case C–95/04P *British Airways plc v Commission* [2007] ECR I–2331, [2007] 4 CMLR 982, opinion of Advocate General Kokott, para 26. On general competition concerns with fidelity rebate schemes, see also, e.g., Case T–228/97 *Irish Sugar plc v Commission* [1999] ECR II–2969, [1999] 5 CMLR 1300, paras 197, 214.

186. Commission Article 102 Guidance [2009] OJ C45/7, para 37.

187. Case 85/76 *Hoffmann-La Roche & Co. AG v Commission* [1979] ECR 461, [1979] 3 CMLR 211, paras 89–90.

188. COMP/E–1/38.113 *Prokent-Tomra*, Commission Decision of 29 March 2006, para 297 (upheld on appeal, Case T–155/06 *Tomra Systems ASA v Commission,* judgment of 9 September 2010).

189. Case 85/76 *Hoffmann-La Roche & Co. AG v Commission* [1979] ECR 461, [1979] 3 CMLR 211, para 120.

190. Case 85/76 *Hoffmann-La Roche & Co. AG v Commission* [1979] ECR 461, [1979] 3 CMLR 211, paras 89, 120. See also Case C–393/92 *Almelo v NV Energiebedrijf Ijsselmij* [1994] ECR I–1477, para 44.

6.   If the rebate scheme includes an exclusivity obligation requiring the customer to purchase a certain proportion of its sales in order to obtain the discount, a particularly important factor is the duration of such an obligation. The Commission has indicated that in its view, an exclusive purchasing obligation is unlikely to hamper effective competition unless the duration of the obligation makes it difficult for customers to switch to another supplier. Therefore, 'the longer the duration of the obligation, the greater the likely foreclosure effect'.[191] However, the Commission acknowledges the point made in the case law that where the dominant undertaking is an unavoidable trading partner, which it may be if its market share is significantly higher than competitors, even a short exclusivity obligation can lead to foreclosure. As will be seen at paragraph 8 below, the duration over which target rebate schemes operate is also a factor in assessing whether they are abusive.

To constitute an abuse, must the rebate be conditional on the customer doing all or most of its business with the dominant undertaking?

7.   No, to constitute an abuse, the rebate scheme does not have to be linked to exclusivity. It is sufficient if it is loyalty-inducing.

8.   In *Michelin I*, the Court of Justice confirmed that a rebate scheme could breach Article 102 even if it were not based on the partner carrying out all or most of its business with the dominant undertaking. Here, annual rebates took the form of 'target rebates', whereby sales targets, based on annual sales of Michelin tyres, had to be met before the rebate would be granted. Other factors leading to the finding of an abuse included that the rebate system was based on a 'relatively long reference period' of one year, which had 'the inherent effect, at the end of that period, of increasing pressure on the buyer to reach the purchase figure needed to obtain the discount or to avoid suffering the expected loss for the entire period'.[192] The rebate system was also not transparent from the business partner's perspective and Michelin's market share was significantly higher than its main competitors.

9.   Target rebate schemes were also condemned in *British Airways*. Travel agents could earn bonuses and extra commissions depending on the amount of BA ticket sales they made. Upholding the General Court's judgment dismissing an appeal against the Commission's decision finding an abuse, the Court of Justice confirmed that the categories of fidelity rebates that may give rise to an abuse are not limited and that there is no requirement that the rebate be granted in return for the customer's agreement to conduct all or a certain percentage of its business with the dominant firm.

10.   Rather, all the circumstances surrounding the rebate scheme, in particular the rules governing the grant of rebates, had to be examined to determine if there could be an exclusionary effect by foreclosure of competitors, *i.e.* whether the rebates were:

> … capable, first, of making market entry very difficult or impossible for competitors of the undertaking in a dominant position and, secondly, of making it more difficult or

---

191. Commission Article 102 Guidance [2009] OJ C45/7, para 36.
192. Case 322/81 *Michelin NV v Commission* [1983] ECR 3461, [1985] 1 CMLR 282, para 81.

      impossible for its co-contractors to choose between various sources of supply or commercial partners.[193]

11.   If so, it would have to be examined whether there was an objective justification for the scheme. The Court noted that an exclusionary effect may result from goal-related rebates, where rebates applied when certain sales targets were met. Foreclosure was more likely where the rebate applied to all sales made by the business partner, the rate of the rebates depending on the evolution of turnover over a given period. In such a case, the commitment of co-contractors towards the dominant undertaking and the pressure exerted upon them may be particularly strong, with modest variations in turnover having disproportionate effects.[194]

12.   It is not necessary to show evidence of actual foreclosure to prove that a rebate scheme is abusive. It is sufficient that the rebate scheme *tends* to restrict competition, *i.e.* that the conduct is capable of having an exclusionary effect.[195]

13.   In *British Airways*, the Court also pointed to the fact that the dominant undertaking's market share was significantly higher than competitors, as discounts granted by such an undertaking on the basis of overall turnover would largely take precedence in absolute terms, even over more generous offers of its competitors. For competitors to attract the co-contractors of the dominant undertaking, or to receive a sufficient volume of orders from them, those competitors would have to offer significantly higher rates of discount or bonus.[196] The loyalty-inducing impact of a similar type of rebate scheme had earlier been emphasised by the General Court in *Michelin II*:

> ... a quantity rebate system in which there is a significant variation in the discount rates between the lower and higher steps, which has a reference period of one year and in which the discount is fixed on the basis of total turnover achieved during the reference period, has the characteristics of a loyalty-inducing discount system.[197]

14.   In *Michelin II*, the General Court had considered that it could be inferred from previous cases that any loyalty-inducing rebate system applied by a dominant undertaking had foreclosure effects prohibited by Article 102.[198]

---

193. Case C–95/04P *British Airways plc v Commission* [2007] ECR I–2331, [2007] 4 CMLR 982, para 68.
194. Case C–95/04P *British Airways plc v Commission* [2007] ECR I–2331, [2007] 4 CMLR 982, para 73.
195. See, e.g., Case T–203/01 *Michelin v Commission ('Michelin II')* [2003] ECR II–4071, [2004] 4 CMLR 923, para 239; Case COMP/C–3/37.990 *Intel*, Commission Decision of 13 May 2009, paras 922–923, 925 (appeal pending, Case T–286/09 *Intel v Commission*).
196. Case C–95/04P *British Airways plc v Commission* [2007] ECR I–2331, [2007] 4 CMLR 982, para 75.
197. Case T–203/01 *Michelin v Commission ('Michelin II')* [2003] ECR II–4071, [2004] 4 CMLR 923, para 95.
198. Case T–203/01 *Michelin v Commission ('Michelin II')* [2003] ECR II–4071, [2004] 4 CMLR 923, para 65.

How may fidelity rebate schemes be objectively justified?

15. The Court of Justice confirmed in *British Airways* that it is open to a dominant firm to argue that its fidelity rebate scheme is objectively justified. The whole of the circumstances are relevant to the question of economic justification. The Court stated:

> It has to be determined whether the exclusionary effect arising from such a system, which is disadvantageous for competition, may be counterbalanced, or outweighed, by advantages in terms of efficiency which also benefit the consumer. If the exclusionary effect of that system bears no relation to advantages for the market and consumers, or if it goes beyond what is necessary in order to attain those advantages, that system must be regarded as an abuse.[199]

16. The General Court had examined whether the high level of fixed costs in air transport and the importance of aircraft occupancy rates could provide the basis for an economic justification of the performance reward schemes. It concluded there was no economic justification for the schemes, particularly in light of the fact that increased commissions applied retrospectively to all sales made by the travel agents. This meant that the schemes could not be regarded as consideration for efficiency gains or cost savings resulting from the sale of BA tickets after attainment of the sales objectives that triggered the additional commissions.[200]

17. Neither the General Court nor the Court of Justice indicated in what circumstances a fidelity rebate scheme might be objectively justified on the basis of efficiencies and benefits for consumers.

When will fidelity rebate schemes be found to be discriminatory?

18. In *British Airways,* it was held that the performance reward schemes breached the prohibition on discrimination in Article 102(c) as the rebates granted when targets were met applied not only to the marginal purchases or sales but on the whole of the purchases or sales handled by the agents in the period in question. This meant that equivalent transactions were remunerated differently. The Court of Justice rejected the contention that proof was required of an actual quantifiable deterioration in the competitive position of the business partners taken individually.[201] In *Michelin II*, a bonus was fixed according to the quality of service a dealer was able to provide. Michelin had a considerable margin of discretion in deciding whether certain commitments were met that would have

199. Case C–95/04P *British Airways plc v Commission* [2007] ECR I–2331, [2007] 4 CMLR 982, para 86.
200. Case T–219/99 *British Airways plc v Commission* [2003] ECR II–5917, [2004] 4 CMLR 1008, para 284.
201. Case C–95/04P *British Airways plc v Commission* [2007] ECR I–2331, [2007] 4 CMLR 982, para 145.

entitled the dealer to be awarded a bonus. Such a discretionary system was unfair and discriminatory and constituted an abuse of a dominant position.[202]

Does the size of the discount matter?

19. An abuse of Article 102 through a fidelity rebate will not depend on the size of the discount offered by the dominant undertaking. The key factor is whether the discount is such that its effect is capable of giving rise to the foreclosure of competitors. This might be achieved with a relatively modest discount that nevertheless induces a customer to carry out more of its business with the dominant supplier.

Key Sources

Case 85/76 *Hoffmann-La Roche & Co. v Commission* [1979] ECR 461, [1979] 3 CMLR 211.

Case 322/81 *Nederlandsche Banden Industrie Michelin v Commission ('Michelin I')* [1983] ECR 3461, [1985] 1 CMLR 282.

Case T–203/01 *Manufacture française des pneumatiques Michelin v Commission ('Michelin II')* [2003] ECR II–4071, [2004] 4 CMLR 923.

Case C–95/04P *British Airways plc v Commission* [2007] ECR I–2331, [2007] 4 CMLR 982.

---

202. Case T–203/01 *Michelin v Commission ('Michelin II')* [2003] ECR II–4071, [2004] 4 CMLR 923, paras 140–141. Rebate schemes were also found to be discriminatory in Case C–163/99 *Portugal v Commission* [2001] ECR I–2613, [2002] 4 CMLR 1319, paras 50–57 and Case T–228/97 *Irish Sugar plc v Commission* [1999] ECR II–2969, [1999] 5 CMLR 1300, paras 162, 167–171.

60. WHEN WILL THE PRICE CHARGED BY A DOMINANT UNDERTAKING BE 'EXCESSIVE' SO AS TO CONSTITUTE AN ABUSE?

Summary

- Excessive prices charged by a dominant undertaking may be unfair and give rise to an abuse.

- No clear definition of what is excessive has been provided in the Article 102 case law.

- The Court of Justice has stated that prices will be excessive if they bear no reasonable relation to the 'economic value' of the costs.

- Relevant factors in making this assessment may include the firm's profit margin, price comparisons and the 'economic value' of the product or service from the customer's perspective, which may be demonstrated by the amount it is prepared to pay.

1. Article 102(b) provides that 'directly or indirectly imposing unfair purchase or selling prices' is an abuse of a dominant position. An excessive price may be unfair. The extraction of an unfairly low price by a dominant buyer could also be an abuse.[203]

2. However, the role of Article 102 and equivalent laws of the Member States is not to regulate prices in themselves. This was explained by the English Court of Appeal in *Attheraces*, when overturning a finding of the High Court that prices charged for access to an essential facility (pre-race data sold to betting shops) were excessive:

> ... the law on abuse of dominant position is about distortion of competition and safeguarding the interests of consumers in the relevant market. It is not a law against suppliers making 'excessive profits' by selling their products to other producers at prices yielding more than a reasonable return on the cost of production, *i.e.* at more than what the judge described as the 'competitive price level'. Still less is it a law under which the courts can regulate prices by fixing the fair price for a product on the application of the purchaser who complains that he is being overcharged for an essential facility by the sole supplier of it.[204]

---

203. See Case 298/83 *CICCE v Commission* [1985] ECR 1105, [1986] 1 CMLR 486 (unfairly low price not found but principle confirmed).

204. *Attheraces Ltd v British Horseracing Board Ltd* [2007] EWCA Civ 38, [2007] UKCLR 309, para 119. Cf Dec No 05/002 *Greenstar*, Decision of the Irish Competition Authority of 30 August 2005, para 3.7 (after considering a complaint about excessive pricing in the household waste collection market, the Authority took the view that competition law was 'neither an appropriate nor effective tool to remedy' the competition problems in the market, suggesting regulatory reform or a system of competitive tendering instead).

3. There have not been very many Article 102 cases on excessive pricing.[205] In *United Brands*, although the Court of Justice ultimately rejected the Commission's case on excessive pricing, it made the general finding that 'charging a price which is excessive because it has no reasonable relation to the economic value of the product supplied' would be an abuse.[206] This excess could be determined by establishing the profit margin, *i.e.* the difference between the selling price of the product and its cost of production. If it were established that the price was excessive, then the question was whether the price was unfair in itself or when compared to competing products.[207]

4. The formulation in *United Brands* does not give a clear indication of what prices will be considered excessive and there is no absolute rule that a profit margin above a certain level will be excessive. The assessment will depend on the particular circumstances and the somewhat vaguely expressed and undefined concept of 'economic value'.[208] It is apparent from the Court's judgment that it considered the position that would prevail had there been 'normal and sufficiently effective competition' to be relevant[209] but it did not provide guidance on what level of prices above the competitive level would be considered so excessive as to be unfair.

5. A number of factors have been considered in the Article 102 cases assessing whether prices are excessive, including: (i) the level of profit; (ii) price comparisons; and (iii) the value of the product from the customer's perspective.

What profit margin is excessive?

6. The level of profit may be an important factor but as the Commission noted in *Scandlines*, it cannot be conclusive of an abuse. Even if it is determined that the

---

205. The Court of Justice recently invoked an excessive pricing analysis in Case C–385/07P *Der Grüne Punkt v Commission* [2009] ECR I–6155, [2009] 5 CMLR 2215, para 143 (requiring payment of a fee for all packaging bearing the DGP logo and put into circulation in Germany, even where customers of the company showed that they did not use the DGP system for some or all of that packaging, was an abuse).

206. Case 27/76 *United Brands Company v Commission* [1978] ECR 207, [1978] 1 CMLR 429, para 250. See also Case 226/84 *British Leyland Plc v Commission* [1986] ECR 3263, [1987] 1 CMLR 185, para 27 ('an undertaking abuses its dominant position where it has an administrative monopoly and charges for its services fees which are disproportionate to the economic value of the service provided'); Case 26/75 *General Motors Continental NV v Commission* [1975] ECR 1367, [1976] 1 CMLR 95, para 12.

207. Case 27/76 *United Brands Company v Commission* [1978] ECR 207, [1978] 1 CMLR 429, para 251–252.

208. See the decision of the South African Competition Appeal Court in *Mittal Steel South Africa Limited v Harmony Gold Mining Company Limited* (Case No. 70/CAC/Apr 07), 29 May 2009, para 40 (discussing a definition of 'economic value' as the notional price 'under assumed conditions of long-run competitive equilibrium'. The decision includes discussion of the approach to excessive pricing under Article 102).

209. Case 27/76 *United Brands Company v Commission* [1978] ECR 207, [1978] 1 CMLR 429, para 249.

profit is 'excessive', this would not be sufficient to establish that the price charged had no reasonable relation to the economic value of the product or service provided.[210] The difficulty of establishing any precise test based on margin can be appreciated in considering the Court of Appeal's observation in *Attheraces*, that 'where profit is obtainable, the margin of profit will be as great as the market will yield'.[211]

7. In order to establish profit, the undertaking's costs must be determined. These may be difficult to calculate in practice and should not be limited to costs actually incurred in the production or provision of the particular product or service or those costs reflected in an undertaking's audited accounts. In taking account of the costs of providing port services in *Scandlines*, the Commission included the very high sunk costs of the port and the opportunity cost for the City shareholder of the port of keeping ferry services there instead of using the land for other purposes.[212] A further question may arise in some cases about the duration over which costs should be measured. If an undertaking has made a loss for several years after making significant capital investments, to what extent should this be taken into account in determining if its prices in subsequent years are excessive? It can also be argued that 'only costs that would be recovered in the long-run competitive equilibrium'[213] should be taken into account and that increased costs caused by inefficiencies should not be considered. Such questions raise further complexities in calculation of the profit margin.

What is the relevance of price or profit comparisons?

8. A comparison with prices or profits of competing or related products may be relevant in assessing whether the dominant undertaking's prices are excessive. Such comparisons have been invoked in some cases under Article 102 but in others, they have not been found to be useful. The most useful comparison in many cases would be with prices charged by competitors in the same market. However, in many abuse cases, the market at issue will not be competitive and where the dominant undertaking has a monopoly, it may not be possible to draw any comparison with prices charged by competitors.[214] It is difficult to derive any general principles on the use of price comparisons from the cases and whether a comparison will be appropriate in a particular case will largely depend on the circumstances.

---

210. COMP/36.568 *Scandlines v Port of Helsingborg* [2006] 4 CMLR 1224, paras 214–216.
211. *Attheraces Ltd v British Horseracing Board Ltd* [2007] EWCA Civ 38, [2007] UKCLR 309, para 119.
212. COMP/36.568 *Scandlines v Port of Helsingborg* [2006] 4 CMLR 1224, para 209.
213. *Mittal Steel South Africa Limited v Harmony Gold Mining Company Limited* (Case No. 70/CAC/Apr 07), judgment of the South African Competition Appeal Court, 29 May 2009, para 43.
214. See COMP/C–1/36.915 *Deutsche Post AG – Interception of cross-border mail* [2001] OJ L 331/40, para 159.

9.   In *Scandlines*, the Commission found that comparisons with returns on capital at other ports and Swedish industry more generally had limited use. In principle, such comparisons could at most provide an indication but were not sufficient evidence in determining if port prices were unfair.[215] In rejecting price comparisons of tranquilizers sold in Germany and The Netherlands, the German Supreme Court highlighted various differences between sales in the two countries, including that the Dutch seller was infringing patents.[216]

10. In *Bodson*, the Court of Justice drew a comparison between prices charged by a monopoly and prices charged for the same types of services in a competitive market. In deciding whether the prices charged for funeral services by holders of concessions were unfair, the Court of Justice suggested that a comparison could be drawn with the prices charged in other areas of France, where the market had been left unregulated.[217]

11. In *Lucazeau*, comparisons were made between the fees charged by copyright-management societies in different Member States. The Court of Justice held that when a dominant undertaking imposes fees that are appreciably higher than those charged in other Member States and where a comparison of the fee levels has been made on a consistent basis, that difference must be regarded as indicative of an abuse of a dominant position. It was then for the undertaking to justify the difference by reference to objective dissimilarities between the situation in the different Member States.[218]

12. In its decision in *Napp*, the UK Competition Appeal Tribunal adopted a broad approach to price comparisons. The CAT held that in establishing if Napp's prices for pharmaceuticals were excessive, it was reasonable to make comparisons of '(i) Napp's prices with Napp's costs, (ii) Napp's prices with the costs of its next most profitable competitor, (iii) Napp's prices with those of its competitors and (iv) Napp's prices with prices charged by Napp in other markets'.[219]

---

215. COMP/36.568 *Scandlines v Port of Helsingborg* [2006] 4 CMLR 1224, paras 152–158, 225. See also Case T–306/05 *Scippacercola v Commission* [2008] 4 CMLR 1418, paras 100–105 (Commission had found that prices for security, terminal facility and car parking at Athens airport were not excessive when compared to prices at other European airports; General Court dismissing appeal against Commission decision rejecting excessive pricing complaints) (appeal dismissed, Case C–159/08P *Scippacercola v Commission* [2009] ECR I–46, [2010] 4 CMLR 1205).

216. Case KVR 2/76 *Valium I*, 16 December 1976, WuW/E BGH 1445 (see the discussion in Bellamy & Child (6th edn, 2008) para 10.107).

217. Case 30/87 *Bodson v SA Pompes funèbres des régions libérées* [1988] ECR 2479, [1989] 4 CMLR 984, para 31. See also Case 78/70 *Deutsche Grammophon Gesellschaft mbH v Metro-SB-Großmärkte GmbH & Co. KG.* [1971] ECR 487, [1971] CMLR 631, para 19 (the fact that the controlled selling price for sound recordings in a Member State was higher than an original reimported product, might, unless justified, be a determining factor in establishing abuse).

218. Case 395/87 *Ministère public v Tournier* [1989] ECR 2521, [1991] 4 CMLR 248, para 38. See also Cases 110/88 etc *Lucazeau v SACEM* [1989] ECR 2811, [1991] 4 CMLR 248.

219. *Napp Pharmaceutical Holdings Ltd v Director General of Fair Trading* [2002] CAT 1, [2002] CompAR 13, para 392.

What is the relevance of the position of the customer?

13.   A further factor that has been considered in determining the economic value is the position of the customer. In *Scandlines*, the Commission accepted that the amount the customer was prepared to pay could be relevant:

> The demand-side is relevant mainly because customers are notably willing to pay more for something specific attached to the product/service that they consider valuable. This specific feature does not necessarily imply higher production costs for the provider. However it is valuable for the customer and also for the provider, and thereby increases the economic value of the product/service.[220]

14.   In *Attheraces*, in deciding whether the prices of pre-race data sold to betting shops were excessive, the Court of Appeal held that the trial judge, in determining the economic value of the pre-race data, had been wrong to reject the relevance of the value of the pre-race data to the customer. The Court clearly approved of taking into account the value of the product to the customer, as evidenced, in particular, by the amount that customer could charge its own customers downstream.[221]

15.   A similar approach, emphasising the value to the customer of the product, was taken in *Kanal 5*. Collecting societies levied performing rights royalties on commercial broadcasters in Sweden based on broadcasting revenue and the amount of music broadcast. The Court of Justice approved of this method holding that 'in so far as such royalties are calculated on the basis of the revenue of the television broadcasting societies, they are, in principle, reasonable in relation to the economic value of the service provided'.[222]

Key sources

Case 27/76 *United Brands Company v Commission* [1978] ECR 207, [1978] 1 CMLR 429.

COMP/36.568 *Scandlines v Port of Helsingborg* [2006] 4 CMLR 1224.

Attheraces Ltd v British Horseracing Board Ltd [2007] EWCA Civ 38, [2007] UKCLR 309.

---

220.   COMP/36.568 *Scandlines v Port of Helsingborg* [2006] 4 CMLR 1224, para 227.
221.   *Attheraces Ltd v British Horseracing Board Ltd* [2007] EWCA Civ 38, [2007] UKCLR 309, paras 214–218. See also the Court's discussion of the appellant's argument at para 189 (that 'the economic value of a product was a different concept from its cost, as it reflects its revenue-earning potential to the person who acquires it'). See also *BHB Enterprises plc v Victor Chandler (International) Limited* [2005] EWHC 1074 (Ch), [2005] UKCLR 787, in particular at para 56 (Laddie J stating that 'in a case where unfair pricing is alleged, assessment of the *value* of the asset both to the vendor and the purchaser must be a crucial part of the assessment').
222.   Case C–52/07 *Kanal 5 Ltd v STIM* [2008] ECR I–9275, [2009] 5 CMLR 2175, para 37. The Court did acknowledge at para 40 that there might be an abuse had there been a more precise method of identifying musical works with the audience.

61. MAY A DOMINANT SUPPLIER REFUSE TO SUPPLY A PARTICULAR CUSTOMER?

Summary

- Dominant undertakings are generally allowed to choose with whom they contract. However, a refusal to supply a customer can amount to abuse in some circumstances.

- Most concern arises when the dominant undertaking competes with the customer on a downstream market.

- A refusal to supply a customer without any objective justification will likely amount to an abuse where the refusal results in the elimination of a competitor. This can occur when the dominant supplier is in competition with the customer on a downstream or neighbouring market.

- A dominant firm cannot stop supplying a long-standing customer who abides by regular commercial practice, if the orders placed are in no way out of the ordinary.

- A dominant firm may be entitled to refuse to fulfil orders that are out of the ordinary in order to prevent parallel imports.

1. Competition law does not impose any general requirement on undertakings to trade with each other.[223] The concept of freedom of contract means that companies may choose their trading partners and are not required to provide justification for refusing to supply a particular customer. From a competition perspective, even a requirement on a dominant firm, which prescribes its trading partners, may have negative effects. For example, it may undermine a supplier's incentive to invest and innovate and may tempt competitors to 'free ride' on investments made by the dominant undertaking. These consequences are not desirable from a consumer welfare perspective and the Commission has cited such factors as reason for caution in taking refusal to supply cases.[224]

2. Nevertheless, in certain circumstances a refusal by a dominant undertaking to supply a customer may constitute an abuse contrary to Article 102. As well as a flat refusal to supply, a dominant firm may offer terms of supply that are so unreasonable or that it knows are unacceptable so as to amount to a 'constructive'

---

223. A requirement to supply may be imposed in regulatory regimes in particular sectors. See, e.g., the decision of OFCOM under section 3(4) of the Broadcasting Act 1990 and section 316(2) of the Communications Act 2003, requiring BSkyB to offer its most important sports channels to retailers on other pay-TV platforms (OFCOM, Pay TV Statement, 31 March 2010 (on appeal before the CAT, Case 1158/8/3/10 *British Sky Broadcasting Limited v Office of Communications*)).

224. Commission Article 102 Guidance [2009] OJ C45/7, para 75. See also generally on refusal to supply, the Irish Competition Authority Guidance Note: Refusal to Supply (December 2005).

refusal to supply.[225] A requirement that the customer identify the ultimate geographical destination of goods that it purchases may also be treated as a constructive refusal.[226] A margin squeeze where, instead of outrightly refusing to supply, the dominant undertaking supplies an input to a downstream competitor at a price that does not enable the competitor to compete effectively on the downstream market, can be viewed as a form of refusal to supply. The Commission treats margin squeeze as a form of refusal to supply[227] and the UK CAT has also taken this approach.[228]

3.   The EU law on refusal to supply does not easily lend itself to neat categorisations. However, it may be useful to draw a distinction between refusals to license intellectual property rights, refusals to allow access to essential facilities and other refusals to supply.[229] Specific aspects of the first two categories are discussed separately in Questions 62 and 63 respectively. As with other forms of abuse under Article 102, it is open to the dominant undertaking to defend its refusal to supply on the basis of an objective justification.

What is the competition concern with a refusal to supply?

4.   The primary competition concern is that a refusal to supply will distort competition in a market downstream from that in which the refusal takes place. This may be the case in particular when a dominant supplier is itself a competitor in the downstream market and refuses to supply a competitor in that downstream market with an input that is necessary to enable the competitor to compete. However a refusal to supply can be abusive even if the dominant undertaking does not compete downstream.

5.   A refusal to supply an existing customer is more likely to give rise to abuse than a refusal to supply a new or occasional customer. As a general rule, a refusal to supply an existing customer constitutes abuse under Article 102 where, without any objective justification, that conduct is liable to eliminate a trading party as a competitor. In *Commercial Solvents*, the Court of Justice considered this question in the context of a dominant undertaking that produced raw materials for secondary products, holding that

> ... an undertaking which has a dominant position in the market in raw materials and which, with the object of reserving such raw material for manufacturing its own

225. COMP/C–1/36.915 *Deutsche Post AG – Interception of cross-border mail* [2001] OJ L 331/40, para 141; Commission Article 102 Guidance [2009] OJ C45/7, para 79.

226. *Polaroid/SSI Europe*, Commission's Thirteenth Report on Competition Policy (1983) para 156 (the file was closed when Polaroid agreed to supply SSI).

227. Commission Article 102 Guidance [2009] OJ C45/7, para 75 *et seq.*

228. *Albion Water Ltd v Water Services Regulation Authority* [2006] CAT 23, [2007] CompAR 22, para 863 (upheld on appeal, *Albion Water Ltd v Water Services Regulation Authority* [2008] EWCA Civ 536, [2008] UKCLR 457). Margin squeeze is discussed separately in Question 64.

229. See Cases C–468 to 478/06 *Sot Lélos kai Sia EE v GlaxoSmithKline* [2008] ECR I–7139, [2008] 5 CMLR 1382, opinion of Advocate General Colomer, para 76.

derivatives, refuses to supply a customer, which is itself a manufacturer of these derivatives, and therefore risks eliminating all competition on the part of this customer, is abusing its dominant position within the meaning of Article [102].[230]

6.   In *Télémarketing*, a similar approach was adopted. On a preliminary reference, the Court of Justice held that it would be an abuse for a dominant television company to require that advertisers use the telemarketing services of its subsidiary when they advertised on the television station. The television station's dominant position was in respect of a service that was 'indispensable for the activities of another undertaking on another market'[231] and its policy was a refusal to supply its services to other telemarketing firms. The Court of Justice stated that

> ... an abuse within the meaning of Article [102] is committed where, without any objective necessity, an undertaking holding a dominant position on a particular market reserves to itself or to an undertaking belonging to the same group an ancillary activity which might be carried out by another undertaking as part of its activities on a neighbouring but separate market, with the possibility of eliminating all competition from such undertaking.[232]

Can the refusal to supply be abusive if the customer is not a competitor?

7.   In *United Brands*, a refusal to supply *Chiquita* bananas to a distributor that had promoted the rival *Dole* banana brand was condemned as abusive even though the dominant undertaking was not in downstream competition with the rejected distributor. The Court of Justice held that a dominant supplier 'cannot stop supplying a long standing customer who abides by regular commercial practice, if the orders placed by that customer are in no way out of the ordinary'.[233] The Court explained that the refusal to supply would 'limit markets to the prejudice of consumers and would amount to discrimination which might in the end eliminate a trading party from the relevant market'.[234]

8.   Differing views have been expressed on whether *United Brands* is authority for the proposition that there is a positive duty on a dominant undertaking to supply save where the refusal is reasonably justifiable.[235] What the case does seem to make

---

230. Cases 6&7/73 *Commercial Solvents Corporation v Commission* [1974] ECR 223, [1974] 1 CMLR 309, para 25.

231. Case 311/84 *CBEM – Télémarketing v CLT* [1985] ECR 3261, [1986] 2 CMLR 558, para 26.

232. Case 311/84 *CBEM – Télémarketing v CLT* [1985] ECR 3261, [1986] 2 CMLR 558, para 27. See also *Hugin/Liptons* [1978] OJ L22/23 (refusal to supply spare parts of cash registers to a company that repaired cash registers) (overturned on other grounds, Case 22/78 *Hugin v Commission* [1979] ECR 1869, [1979] 3 CMLR 345)

233. Case 27/76 *United Brands Company v Commission* [1978] ECR 207, [1978] 1 CMLR 429, para 182.

234. Case 27/76 *United Brands Company v Commission* [1978] ECR 207, [1978] 1 CMLR 429, para 183.

235. See Nagy, 'Refusal to deal and the doctrine of essential facilities in US and EC competition law: a comparative perspective and a proposal for a workable analytical framework' [2007] *European Law Review* 664, 675–677.

clear is that abusive refusals to supply are not limited to cases in which the dominant supplier is in direct competition with the customer in a neighbouring or downstream market.[236] The case can also be seen as an example of a dominant firm using a refusal to supply as a mechanism to punish a customer that had endorsed a rival product. Such a punishment mechanism could also be exacted where the customer had refused to purchase a tie or bundle from the supplier.[237]

What arguments can be relied on in defence of a refusal to supply?

9. While the burden of proving the existence of the circumstances giving rise to an infringement of Article 102 lies on the Commission, it is for the dominant undertaking concerned, and not for the Commission, before the end of the administrative procedure, to raise any plea of objective justification and to support it with arguments and evidence. It then falls to the Commission, where it proposes to make a finding of an abuse of a dominant position, to show that the arguments and evidence relied on by the undertaking cannot prevail and, accordingly, that the justification put forward cannot be accepted.[238]

10. It may be a good argument to say that the customer was refused because of its poor credit worthiness or otherwise risky profile and in such a case 'common sense suggests that the wishes of any dominant undertaking to refuse orders should be respected'.[239] The Commission has stated that it will consider arguments that a refusal to supply was necessary to allow an adequate return on investments by the dominant undertaking or that imposing an obligation to supply would stifle innovation.[240]

11. The dominant firm could argue that it is terminating supplies because it wishes to vertically integrate downstream itself. In this case, the Commission has suggested that the firm would have the onus of showing that consumers would be better off were supplies to be terminated.[241] More generally, it could be argued that supplies are being terminated in order to protect the dominant undertaking's own commercial interest. However, its actions must be proportionate and reasonable and a complete refusal to supply may not meet this standard.[242] A justification for

---

236. For a discussion of when a refusal to supply a customer that is not a downstream rival may give rise to an abuse, see O'Donoghue and Padilla, *The Law and Economics of Article 82 EC* (2006) 463–476.
237. Commission Article 102 Guidance [2009] OJ C45/7, para 30.
238. Case T–201/04 *Microsoft Corp. v Commission* [2007] ECR II–3601, [2007] 5 CMLR 846, para 688.
239. Cases C–468 to 478/06 *Sot Lélos kai Sia EE v GlaxoSmithKline* [2008] ECR I–7139, [2008] 5 CMLR 1382, opinion of Advocate General Colomer, para 105. See also Commission Article 102 Staff Working Paper, para 224.
240. Commission Article 102 Guidance [2009] OJ C45/7, paras 89–90.
241. Commission Article 102 Staff Working Paper, para 224.
242. See Case 27/76 *United Brands Company v Commission* [1978] ECR 207, [1978] 1 CMLR 429, paras 189–191. A similar approach to a defence of commercial interests argument was taken by the Commission in *BBI/Boosey & Hawkes* [1998] 4 CMLR 67.

refusing to supply a new or occasional customer may be more convincing than a justification for a refusal in respect of a longstanding customer.

Is it justifiable to refuse to supply pharmaceuticals[243] to prevent parallel importing?

12. In *Sot. Lélos*, the Court of Justice, on a preliminary reference, considered whether a dominant pharmaceuticals company on the national market was justified in refusing to meet the orders of wholesalers involved in parallel exports to other Member States where the selling prices of those medicines were set at a higher level. While the dominant firm was allowed to protect its commercial interests in a reasonable and proportionate way, it was not entitled to refuse to meet ordinary orders of wholesalers engaged in parallel importing.[244] The Court referred to earlier case law in which it was held that a practice by which an undertaking in a dominant position aims to restrict parallel trade in the products that it puts on the market constitutes abuse of that dominant position. An abuse could arise in particular when such a practice had the effect of curbing parallel imports by neutralising the more favourable level of prices which may apply in other sales areas in the EU[245] or when it aimed to create barriers to re-importations which came into competition with the distribution network of that undertaking.[246]

13. However, the dominant supplier may have been entitled to refuse orders of wholesalers 'in quantities which are out of all proportion to those previously sold by the same wholesalers to meet the needs of the market in that Member State'.[247] It has been suggested that under this approach, it would be justifiable for a dominant undertaking to refuse to supply new wholesalers in order to prevent them engaging in parallel trade.[248]

---

243. A refusal to supply pharmaceuticals has been an issue in several cases. See, e.g., the Irish case of *A&N Pharmacy Ltd v United Drug Wholesale Ltd* [1996] 2 ILRM 42 and the English case of *Intecare Direct Ltd v Pfizer* [2010] EWHC 600 (Ch).
244. Cases C–468 to 478/06 *Sot Lélos kai Sia EE v GlaxoSmithKline* [2008] ECR I–7139, [2008] 5 CMLR 1382, para 71. Whether the orders were out of the ordinary would depend on previous business relations between the dominant firm and the wholesalers and the size of the orders in relation to the requirements of the market in the Member State concerned. The fact that there was a degree of state regulation of medicine prices did not justify the refusal to deal. The price was still affected by supply and demand and while patent protection attached, parallel imports provided the only source of price competition.
245. Case 26/75 *General Motors Continental NV v Commission* [1975] ECR 1367, [1976] 1 CMLR 95, para 12.
246. Case 226/84 *British Leyland Plc v Commission* [1986] ECR 3263, [1987] 1 CMLR 185, para 24.
247. Cases C–468 to 478/06 *Sot Lélos kai Sia EE v GlaxoSmithKline* [2008] ECR I–7139, [2008] 5 CMLR 1382, para 76.
248. Van Bael & Bellis, *Competition Law of the European Community* (5th edn, 2010), 842.

What are the Commission's enforcement priorities in respect of refusals to deal?

14.   The Commission indicates that it will consider a refusal to supply case an enforcement priority only if all three of the following conditions are met:

the refusal relates to a product or service that is objectively necessary to be able to compete effectively on a downstream market,

the refusal is likely to lead to the elimination of effective competition on the downstream market, and

the refusal is likely to lead to consumer harm.[249]

15.   It should be remembered that these criteria apply only to the Commission's enforcement priorities and do not aim to circumscribe the parameters of an abusive refusal to supply under Article 102.

Key Sources

Cases 6&7/73 *Commercial Solvents Corporation v Commission* [1974] ECR 223, [1974] 1 CMLR 309.

Case 27/76 *United Brands Company v Commission* [1978] ECR 207, [1978] 1 CMLR 429.

Case 311/84 *CBEM – Télémarketing v CLT* [1985] ECR 3261, [1986] 2 CMLR 558.

Case T–201/04 *Microsoft Corp. v Commission* [2007] ECR II–3601, [2007] 5 CMLR 846.

Cases C–468 to 478/06 *Sot Lélos kai Sia EE v GlaxoSmithKline AEVE Farmakeftikon Proionton* [2008] ECR I–7139, [2008] 5 CMLR 1382.

---

249. Commission Article 102 Guidance [2009] OJ C45/7, para 81.

62. MAY A DOMINANT UNDERTAKING REFUSE TO LICENSE ITS INTELLECTUAL PROPERTY RIGHTS?

Summary

- In general, yes. But in 'exceptional circumstances' a refusal to license may be an abuse.

  This may include where:

  - The IP is indispensible for an activity on a neighbouring market;

  - The refusal excludes effective competition on that market;

  - The refusal prevents the appearance of a new product for which there is demand.

1. It is more difficult to establish an abuse where the refusal to supply concerns a refusal to license intellectual property rights.

2. The Court of Justice has held that the refusal to grant a license of an intellectual property right cannot of itself constitute an abuse of dominance. The right to prevent third parties exploiting intellectual property was the very reason for the grant of those rights. In *Volvo v Veng*, the Court of Justice explained:

   > [The] right of the proprietor of a protected design to prevent third parties from manufacturing and selling or importing, without its consent, products incorporating the design constitutes the very subject-matter of his exclusive right. It follows that an obligation imposed upon the proprietor of a protected design to grant to third parties, even in return for a reasonable royalty, a licence for the supply of products incorporating the design would lead to the proprietor thereof being deprived of the substance of his exclusive right, and that a refusal to grant such a licence cannot in itself constitute an abuse of a dominant position.[250]

3. It has been recognised that in exceptional circumstances, the exercise of an exclusive intellectual property right may constitute an abuse of a dominant position. In *Magill*, the refusal of television companies to supply TV listings information to a publisher of a prospective weekly television guide was found to be abusive. The attempt to rely on copyright was unsuccessful. Three factors were crucial to the findings of the Court of Justice:

   - The refusal to supply prevented the emergence of a new product as the TV companies were the holders of information that was an indispensable raw material for compiling the guide.

   - There was no justification for the refusal to supply.

---

250. Case 238/87 *Volvo v Veng* [1988] ECR 6211, [1989] 4 CMLR 122, para 8.

- By their actions the TV companies reserved to themselves the secondary market of weekly television guides by excluding all competition on that market.[251]

4. The Court of Justice further clarified the circumstances under which a dominant undertaking would be required to license intellectual property in *IMS Health*[252] and the principles laid down in that case were considered by the General Court in *Microsoft*. The refusal to supply aspect of the *Microsoft* case involved the refusal by Microsoft to supply the information, protected by intellectual property rights, required to ensure interoperability between Microsoft's Windows work group server operating systems and other systems. The General Court held that the following three circumstances, in particular, must be considered exceptional so as to justify a requirement of the provision of information protected by intellectual property rights by a dominant firm:

- The refusal relates to a product or service indispensable to the exercise of a particular activity on a neighbouring market;

- The refusal is of such a kind as to exclude any effective competition on that neighbouring market; and

- The refusal prevents the appearance of a new product for which there is potential consumer demand.[253]

5. The Court stated that once it was established such circumstances were present, the refusal by the holder of a dominant position to grant a licence may infringe Article 102 unless the refusal is objectively justified. The Court noted that the third condition, that the refusal prevented the emergence of a new product for which there was potential demand, arose only in cases on the exercise of an intellectual property right.[254] However, the Court did not clarify whether the three conditions were necessary to show an abuse or merely sufficient.

6. On the requirement that the refusal relate to a product or service that was indispensible to participate on a neighbouring market, the General Court relied on *IMS Health* to clarify that it was sufficient if this second market was a potential or even hypothetical market. However, it would have to be shown that there was potential consumer demand for any new product.[255]

---

251. Cases C–241 & 242/91P *Radio Teilifís Éireann (RTE) v Commission ('Magill')* [1995] ECR I–743, [1995] 4 CMLR 718, paras 53–56.
252. Case C–418/01 *IMS Health GmbH & Co. OHG* [2004] ECR I–5039, [2004] 4 CMLR 1543 (see, in particular, paras 38, 44–49).
253. Case T–201/04 *Microsoft Corp. v Commission* [2007] ECR II–3601, [2007] 5 CMLR 846, para 332.
254. Case T–201/04 *Microsoft Corp. v Commission* [2007] ECR II–3601, [2007] 5 CMLR 846, para 333, 334.
255. Case T–201/04 *Microsoft Corp. v Commission* [2007] ECR II–3601, [2007] 5 CMLR 846, para 335; Case C–418/01 *IMS Health GmbH & Co. OHG* [2004] ECR I–5039, [2004] 4 CMLR 1543, para 38. See also Case T–504/93 *Tiercé Ladbroke SA v Commission* [1997] ECR II–923, [1997] 5 CMLR 304, para 131 (referring to 'specific, constant and regular potential demand on the part of consumers' for a new product).

7.   On the second condition, it is notable that the Court did not require that the refusal exclude *all* competition on the neighbouring market but only *effective* competition.

Key Sources

Case C–418/01 *IMS Health GmbH & Co. OHG* [2004] ECR I–5039, [2004] 4 CMLR 1543.

Case T–201/04 *Microsoft Corp. v Commission* [2007] ECR II–3601, [2007] 5 CMLR 846.

---

63. Is a dominant undertaking required to provide access to an 'essential facility'?

Summary

- A refusal by a dominant undertaking to provide access to an 'essential facility' may be abusive if access is indispensible to enable the refused undertaking to compete.

- The Court of Justice has held that refusal of access must entail the elimination of all competition on the part of that undertaking.

1. An 'essential facilities' doctrine has developed under Article 102, according to which it may be an abuse for a dominant undertaking to refuse access to a facility that is essential to enable another undertaking to compete. The facility could be of any kind, for example a vital raw material or a facility such as a port or airport. A product or service is considered necessary or essential if there is no real or potential substitute.[256]

2. The essential facilities doctrine is controversial both in US federal antitrust law (where its existence as a separate doctrine is doubtful)[257] and EU competition law. As one US commentator has described the essential facilities doctrine:

> You will not find any case that provides a consistent rationale for the doctrine or that explores the social costs and benefits or the administrative costs of requiring the creator of an asset to share it with a rival. It is less a doctrine than an epithet, indicating some exception to the right to keep one's creations to oneself, but not telling us what those exceptions are.[258]

3. The Court of Justice first considered the doctrine in the *Bronner* case.[259] It had previously been applied by the Commission in transport cases such as *Port of Rødby*. The Commission explained in that case:

> An undertaking that owns or manages and uses itself an essential facility, *i.e.* a facility or infrastructure without which its competitors are unable to offer their services to

---

256. Case T–301/04 *Clearstream Banking AG v Commission* [2009] ECR II–3155, [2009] 5 CMLR 2677, para 147.

257. The US Supreme Court has not embraced an essential facilities doctrine. Lower courts had suggested the doctrine as a separate basis for liability under section 2 of the Sherman Act (see, e.g., *MCI Communications Corp. v AT&T,* 708 F.2d 1081 (7th Cir.), *cert. denied,* 464 US 891 (1983)) but this approach must now be read in light of the Supreme Court decision in *Verizon Communications, Inc. v Trinko* 540 US 398 (2004).

258. Areeda, 'Essential Facilities: An Epithet in Need of Limiting Principles' (1990) 58 *Antitrust Law Journal* 841, 841.

259. Case C–7/97 *Oscar Bronner GmbH & Co. KG v Mediaprint* [1998] ECR I–7791, [1999] 4 CMLR 112. Although the Court discusses the concept of 'essential facilities' when discussing Oscar Bronner's arguments (para 24), it does not use the term in its judgment. The doctrine is discussed in more detail in the opinion of Advocate General Jacobs and as pointed out at para 45 of that opinion, it can be argued that the earlier Court of Justice judgments in *Télémarketing* and *Magill* endorsed the essential facilities doctrine, albeit not expressly.

customers, and refuses to grant them access to such facility is abusing its dominant position. Consequently, an undertaking that owns or manages an essential port facility from which it provides a maritime transport service may not, without objective justification, refuse to grant a shipowner wishing to operate on the same maritime route access to that facility without infringing Article [102].[260]

4. A key element of the doctrine is that the facility is indispensable for the company that is refused access. This was emphasised by the Court of Justice in *Bronner*, which concerned the refusal of the leading newspaper publisher in Austria to allow a rival newspaper publisher access to its distribution system. Even though the dominant publisher had the only home delivery system for newspapers, there were other available distribution methods such as post and shop sale, even if they were 'less advantageous' for the distribution of certain kinds of newspaper. In addition, there were no 'technical, legal or even economic obstacles capable of making it impossible, or even unreasonably difficult' for the competitor to establish its own delivery service.[261]

5. To show indispensability, it was not enough to show that alternative distribution methods were not economically viable by reason of the small number of newspapers to be distributed. Rather, it would be necessary to show that it was not economically viable to create a second home-delivery scheme for the distribution of daily newspapers with a circulation comparable to that of the daily newspapers distributed by the existing scheme.[262]

6. The Court in *Bronner*, drawing on *Commercial Solvents*, *Télémarketing* and *Magill*, also emphasised that refusal of access to the delivery system would be abusive only if it resulted in the elimination of *all* competition on the part of the undertaking.[263]

Can refusing access to an essential facility be abusive if the dominant undertaking does not compete downstream?

7. It is doubtful that a refusal of access to an essential facility will be abusive where the dominant undertaking is not itself active downstream. Certainly the formulation in *Bronner*, that the refusal would have to result in the elimination of all competition, does not seem to make sense if the owner of the essential facility is not in competition in the first place. However, older Commission authorities did

---

260. *Port of Rødby* [1994] OJ L55/52, para 12. See also *B&I Line/Sealink Harbours* [1992] 4 CMLR 255, para 41; Case IV/34.689 *Sea Containers v Stena Sealink — Interim Measures* [1994] OJ L 15/8; Case IV/33.544 *British Midland v Aer Lingus* [1992] OJ L 96/34.

261. Case C–7/97 *Oscar Bronner GmbH & Co. KG v Mediaprint* [1998] ECR I–7791, [1999] 4 CMLR 112, paras 43–44.

262. Case C–7/97 *Oscar Bronner GmbH & Co. KG v Mediaprint* [1998] ECR I–7791, [1999] 4 CMLR 112, paras 45–46.

263. Case C–7/97 *Oscar Bronner GmbH & Co. KG v Mediaprint* [1998] ECR I–7791, [1999] 4 CMLR 112, paras 38–41. For a more recent application of the essential facilities doctrine, see Case T–301/04 *Clearstream Banking AG v Commission* [2009] ECR II–3155, [2009] 5 CMLR 2677, paras 146–155.

seem to embrace a broader approach, which could have applied to situations in which the owner of the essential facility was not active downstream. So the answer from previous cases is not categorical.[264]

Key Sources

Case C–7/97 *Oscar Bronner GmbH & Co. KG v Mediaprint* [1998] ECR I–7791, [1999] 4 CMLR 112.

---

264. See also Bellamy & Child (6th edn, 2008) para 10.140.

64. WHEN DOES A 'MARGIN SQUEEZE' CONSTITUTE ABUSE OF A DOMINANT POSITION?

Summary

- An abusive margin squeeze arises when the dominant upstream undertaking charges a price to downstream competitors, against which the dominant undertaking competes, which is so high that the downstream undertakings cannot compete even if they are equally efficient as the dominant undertaking

What is a 'margin squeeze'?

1. A margin squeeze usually involves a vertically integrated supplier or network provider, which is dominant on an upstream market but which also competes on the downstream market against competitors to whom it sells inputs or provides network access. It is not necessary that the undertaking is dominant on the downstream market. The dominant undertaking will charge a price on the upstream market which leaves downstream competitors unable to make a sufficient margin to compete effectively in the downstream market.

2. To take a simple example, say that an undertaking is dominant in the supply of oranges, an essential input for the production of orange juice. As well as selling oranges to producers of orange juice, the dominant firm produces its own brand of orange juice. Now, say the dominant firm charges €20 for the number of oranges required to produce 100 litres of orange juice, while at the same time selling 100 litres of its own orange juice for €15. In this situation, the other producers of orange juice cannot make any margin (and in fact will make a loss) if they are to compete with the dominant undertaking in the orange juice market. This will be the case even if they are as efficient as the dominant firm.

3. In this example, the spread between the downstream price charged by the dominant firm for orange juice and the upstream price it charges for oranges, is negative (*i.e.* the downstream price is lower). A margin squeeze may arise even where this spread is positive.

4. *Deutsche Telekom* is the first margin squeeze case to have come before the Court of Justice.[265] There had been a previous judgment of the General Court[266] as well

---

265. Case C–280/08P *Deutsche Telekom AG v Commission*, judgment of 14 October 2010 (upholding Case T–271/03 *Deutsche Telekom v Commission* [2008] ECR II–477, [2008] 5 CMLR 631; upholding *Deutsche Telekom* [2003] OJ L263/9, [2004] 4 CMLR 790).

266. Case T–5/97 *Industrie des Poudres Sphériques SA v Commission* [2000] ECR II–3755, [2001] 4 CMLR 28, referring at para 178 to 'price squeezing'.

as decisions of the Commission[267] and at national level[268] concerning margin squeeze.

What is the test for an abusive margin squeeze?

5.   The Court of Justice confirmed in *Deutsche Telekom* that the correct test in margin squeeze cases is the 'equally efficient competitor' test. The determination of whether there is an abusive margin squeeze should be carried out by reference to the costs and prices of the dominant undertaking itself, rather than by reference to actual or potential competitors (the 'reasonably efficient competitor' test).[269] If the downstream part of the dominant undertaking could not [make a reasonable profit] if it had to pay the upstream prices charged by the dominant undertaking to competitors, a margin squeeze can be shown.

6.   In *Deutsche Telekom*, the Commission found that Deutsche Telekom operated an abusive margin squeeze. The prices that it charged telecom companies for wholesale access to its network were so expensive that those companies were forced to charge higher prices at the retail level than Deutsche Telekom charged its own end-users. Over a certain period, the spread between Deutsche Telekom's wholesale and retail prices was negative (*i.e.* the wholesale price was more expensive), while for another period, while the retail price was higher, it was insufficient to cover Deutsche Telekom's product-specific costs linked to the provision of retail services. The Commission found an abusive margin squeeze in both cases[270] and these findings were upheld on appeal by the General Court and the Court of Justice.

7.   The Court of Justice described a margin squeeze in general terms as follows:

> Article [102] prohibits a dominant undertaking from, inter alia, adopting pricing practices which have an exclusionary effect on its equally efficient actual or potential competitors, that is to say practices which are capable of making market entry very difficult or impossible for such competitors, and of making it more difficult or impossible for its co-contractors to choose between various sources of supply or commercial partners, thereby strengthening its dominant position by using methods other than those which come within the scope of competition on the merits.[271]

---

267. See, e.g., COMP 38.784 *Wanadoo España v Telefónica*, Commission Decision of 4 July 2007 (appeals pending, Case T–336/07 *Telefónica v Commission* and Case T–398/07 *Spain v Commission*); *Napier Brown/British Sugar* [1988] OJ L284/41.

268. See, e.g., *Genzyme Ltd v Office of Fair Trading* [2004] CAT 4, [2004] CompAR 358; *Albion Water Ltd v Water Services Regulation Authority* [2008] EWCA Civ 536, [2008] UKCLR 457; *Bulgarian Telecommunication Company (BTC) v Commission for Protection of Competition* (Bulgarian Supreme Administrative Court, 9 January 2008, Judgment No. 254).

269. The Commission proposed this test in *National Carbonising Company* [1976] OJ L36/6 (interim measures decision).

270. *Deutsche Telekom* [2003] OJ L263/9, [2004] 4 CMLR 790, paras 34–46.

271. Case C–280/08P *Deutsche Telekom AG v Commission*, judgment of 14 October 2010, para 177.

8.   The fact that Deutsche Telekom would have to increase its own retail prices for end-user access services in order to avoid the margin squeeze of its equally efficient competitor could not render irrelevant the test for establishing an abuse. The margin squeeze itself reduced competition on the market by reducing consumer choice and therefore lowering the prospect of long-term reduced retail prices.[272]

9.   The more specific test for establishing an abusive margin squeeze can be seen in the General Court's approval of the Commission's approach:

> According to the Commission, 'there is an abusive margin squeeze if the difference between the retail prices charged by a dominant undertaking and the wholesale prices it charges its competitors for comparable services is negative, or insufficient to cover the product-specific costs to the dominant operator of providing its own retail services on the downstream market'. In the present case, the margin squeeze is said to be abusive because the applicant itself, 'would have been unable to offer its own retail services without incurring a loss if ... it had had to pay the wholesale access price as an internal transfer price for its own retail operations'. In those circumstances, 'competitors [who] are just as efficient' as the applicant cannot 'offer retail access services at a competitive price unless they find additional efficiency gains'.[273]

10. The Court of Justice confirmed that the existence of an abusive margin squeeze was to be determined solely on the basis of the charges and costs of the dominant undertaking, rather than on the cost base of actual or potential competitors. Approving the approach of the General Court, the Court of Justice held that:

> ... since such a test can establish whether the appellant would itself have been able to offer its retail services to end-users otherwise than at a loss if it had first been obliged to pay its own wholesale prices for local loop access services, it was suitable for determining whether the appellant's pricing practices had an exclusionary effect on competitors by squeezing their margins.[274]

11. That the abusive nature of a dominant undertaking's pricing practices was to be determined on the basis of its own charges and costs, rather than on the cost base of actual or potential competitors, was supported by previous case law[275] as well as by the general principle of legal certainty.[276] This was a clear endorsement by the

---

272. Case C–280/08P *Deutsche Telekom AG v Commission*, judgment of 14 October 2010, paras 181–182.

273. Case T–271/03 *Deutsche Telekom v Commission* [2008] ECR II–477, [2008] 5 CMLR 631, para 187 (references to the Commission Decision, *Deutsche Telekom* [2003] OJ L263/9, [2004] 4 CMLR 790, omitted). For an economics-focused discussion of tests for margin squeeze, see Duncan 'No margin for error: the challenges of assessing margin squeeze in practice' (2010) 9 *Competition Law Journal* 124.

274. Case C–280/08P *Deutsche Telekom AG v Commission*, judgment of 14 October 2010, para 201.

275. In particular, Case T–5/97 *Industrie des Poudres Sphériques SA v Commission* [2000] ECR II–3755, [2001] 4 CMLR 28 and *Napier Brown/British Sugar* [1988] OJ L284/41.

276. Case C–280/08P *Deutsche Telekom AG v Commission*, judgment of 14 October 2010, para 202.

Union courts of the 'equally efficient competitor' test in preference to the 'reasonably efficient competitor' test.

What are the Commission's enforcement priorities in respect of margin squeezes?

12. In deciding whether to initiate enforcement action in respect of a margin squeeze, the Commission states that it will apply a benchmark to establish the costs of an equally efficient competitor. This will be the LRAIC of the downstream division of the integrated dominant undertaking.

Key Sources

Case C–280/08P *Deutsche Telekom AG v Commission*, judgment of 14 October 2010 (upholding Case T–271/03 *Deutsche Telekom v Commission* [2008] ECR II–477, [2008] 5 CMLR 631; upholding *Deutsche Telekom* [2003] OJ L263/9, [2004] 4 CMLR 790).

Napier Brown/British Sugar [1988] OJ L284/41.

COMP 38.784 *Wanadoo España v Telefónica*, Commission Decision of 4 July 2007.

Albion Water Ltd v Water Services Regulation Authority [2008] EWCA Civ 536, [2008] UKCLR 457.

Chapter 4

MERGERS AND ACQUISITIONS

Appeals of Merger Decisions

Merger Control in Ireland and the UK

Chapter 4

MERGERS AND ACQUISITIONS

65. WHAT IS THE JURISDICTIONAL TEST FOR TRANSACTIONS TO BE NOTIFIED UNDER THE MERGER REGULATION?[1]

Summary

A filing under the Merger Regulation will be required if:

- The parties have a combined worldwide turnover of €5 billion and at least two parties each have EU-wide turnover of €250 million (unless each party has more than two-thirds of its EU turnover in one and the same Member State).

OR

- The parties have a combined worldwide turnover of €2.5 billion and combined turnover in 3 Member States of €100 million, with at least two parties having €25 million in each of 3 of those Member States; plus, at least two parties have €100 million in EU-wide turnover (unless each party has more than two-thirds of its EU turnover in one and the same Member State).

1. Where parties are involved in a merger, acquisition, joint venture or other transaction that could involve merger control obligations, the task of establishing in which jurisdictions a filing may be required or desirable invariably begins by examining a country-by-country breakdown of the revenues of the relevant parties. A quick review of this information should allow a rough analysis to be made of filing requirements in the EU and elsewhere.

2. The merger control regimes of the European Commission and the Member States are mutually exclusive. If a transaction meets the jurisdictional thresholds under the Merger Regulation[2] for a filing with the Commission, then filings in the EU Member States can be ruled out. Where the Merger Regulation thresholds are not met, it may be necessary to consider if the national thresholds in one or more Member States are met. In contrast to the position under the antitrust rules, where Member State rules are typically substantially the same as Articles 101 and 102, the rules and procedures on merger control at national level are varied and do not always correspond to the Merger Regulation.[3]

---

1. See generally, the Commission Consolidated Jurisdictional Notice under Council Regulation (EC) No 139/2004 on the control of concentrations between undertakings [2008] OJ C95/1 (the 'Commission Jurisdictional Notice'); Broberg, *The European Commission's Jurisdiction to Scrutinise Mergers* (3rd edn, 2006).
2. Council Regulation (EC) No 139/2004 on the control of concentrations between undertakings [2004] OJ L24/1 (the 'Merger Regulation').
3. The jurisdictional thresholds in each of the EU Member States are set out in Question 67. An overview of the merger control regime in Ireland is set out at Question 85 and the UK regime is examined in Question 86.

3.   In certain circumstances, cases that meet the Merger Regulation thresholds may be transferred to a Member State competition authority, while transactions below the EU thresholds may be transferred to the Commission in certain cases.[4]

What kinds of transactions are subject to the Merger Regulation?

4.   The Merger Regulation applies to a 'concentration' with a 'Community dimension'. A 'concentration' is defined in Article 3 of the Merger Regulation as follows

> 1. A concentration shall be deemed to arise where a change of control on a lasting basis results from:
>
> (a) the merger of two or more previously independent undertakings or parts of undertakings, or
>
> (b) the acquisition, by one or more persons already controlling at least one undertaking, or by one or more undertakings, whether by purchase of securities or assets, by contract or by any other means, of direct or indirect control of the whole or parts of one or more other undertakings.[5]

5.   A number of separate transactions may give rise to one concentration under Article 3(1)(b). Separate transactions may constitute a single concentration if they are unitary in nature. As the General Court explained in *Cementbouw*

> … a concentration within the meaning of Article 3(1) of [the Merger Regulation] may be deemed to arise even in the case of a number of formally distinct legal transactions, provided that those transactions are interdependent in such a way that none of them would be carried out without the others and that the result consists in conferring on one or more undertakings direct or indirect economic control over the activities of one or more other undertakings.[6]

6.   Article 5(2) provides a specific rule which allows the Commission to consider successive transactions occurring in a fixed period of time as a single concentration for the purposes of calculating the turnover of the undertakings concerned. The purpose of this provision is to ensure that parties do not break a transaction down into a series of sales over a period of time, with the aim of avoiding the application of the Merger Regulation. The second subparagraph of Article 5(2) provides:

> However, two or more transactions within the meaning of the first subparagraph which take place within a two-year period between the same persons or undertakings shall be treated as one and the same concentration arising on the date of the last transaction.[7]

---

4.   Referrals are examined in Question 69.
5.   Merger Regulation [2004] OJ L24/1, Article 3(1). The concept of 'control' under the Merger Regulation is discussed in Question 66.
6.   Case T–282/02 *Cementbouw Handel & Industrie BV v Commission* [2006] ECR II–319, [2006] 4 CMLR 1561, para 109 (appeal dismissed, Case C–202/06P *Cementbouw Handel & Industrie BV v Commission* [2007] ECR I–12129, [2008] 4 CMLR 1324). See also Commission Jurisdictional Notice [2008] OJ C95/1, paras 36–48.
7.   Merger Regulation [2004] OJ L24/1, Article 5(2). See also Commission Jurisdictional Notice [2008] OJ C95/1, paras 49–50.

7.   The creation of a joint venture performing on a lasting basis all the functions of an autonomous economic entity also qualifies as a concentration.[8]

Are 'warehousing' transactions subject to the Merger Regulation?

8.   The issue of interrelated transactions arises in the context of 'warehousing' arrangements. An example of warehousing is where the target company is 'parked' with an interim buyer, often a bank, which purchases the shares of the target on the basis of an agreement for the future onward sale of the company to the ultimate buyer. The bank generally acquires shares 'on behalf' of the ultimate acquirer, which often bears the major part of the economic risks and may also be granted specific rights. Typically, warehousing occurs in transactions that might give rise to antitrust risk. The Commission has stated that it:

> ... will examine the acquisition of control by the ultimate acquirer, as provided for in the agreements entered into by the parties. The Commission will consider the transaction by which the interim buyer acquires control in such circumstances as the first step of a single concentration comprising the lasting acquisition of control by the ultimate buyer.[9]

9.   In *Éditions Odile Jacob*, a key question was whether the first step in a warehousing transaction – the sale of Vivendi Universal Publishing ('VUP') to a bank, Natexis Banques Populaires (with the ultimate sale to be made to Lagardère) – gave rise to a concentration under the Merger Regulation. It was argued that this transaction was not a concentration on the basis of Article 3(5)(a) of the Merger Regulation, which provides an exception from the meaning of a concentration for financial institutions acquiring securities for their own account or for the account of others with a view to holding the securities on a short-term basis. The General Court declined to answer this question directly, finding in the circumstances that it did not affect the Commission's ultimate decision approving the purchase of VUP by Lagardère. The Court's analysis focused on whether the governance rights that Lagardère had with respect to VUP during the time that VUP was under the bank's control were sufficient to give Lagardère sole control or joint control of VUP. The Court concluded that Lagardère's rights did not confer control. Consequently, regardless of whether this step in the warehousing structure could benefit from the Article 3(5)(a) exemption, the implementation of that step was not a concentration requiring prior approval.[10] The judgment seems to call into question the Commission's current position regarding warehousing transactions as set out in the Jurisdictional Notice, whereby the warehousing transaction and ultimate sale are treated as a single concentration.

---

8.   Merger Regulation [2004] OJ L24/1, Article 3(4).
9.   Commission Jurisdictional Notice [2008] OJ C95/1, para 35.
10.   Case T–279/04 *Éditions Odile Jacob SAS v Commission*, judgment of 13 September 2010.

What are the financial thresholds?

10.   The Merger Regulation has two alternate turnover thresholds. If either is met, the concentration has a 'Community dimension' and must be notified to the Commission. The thresholds are set out in Article 1 of the Merger Regulation:

> 2. A concentration has a Community dimension where:
>
> (a) the combined aggregate worldwide turnover of all the undertakings concerned is more than EUR 5 000 million; and
>
> (b) the aggregate Community-wide turnover of each of at least two of the undertakings concerned is more than EUR 250 million,
>
> unless each of the undertakings concerned achieves more than two-thirds of its aggregate Community-wide turnover within one and the same Member State.
>
> 3. A concentration that does not meet the thresholds laid down in paragraph 2 has a Community dimension where:
>
> (a) the combined aggregate worldwide turnover of all the undertakings concerned is more than EUR 2 500 million;
>
> (b) in each of at least three Member States, the combined aggregate turnover of all the undertakings concerned is more than EUR 100 million;
>
> (c) in each of at least three Member States included for the purpose of point (b), the aggregate turnover of each of at least two of the undertakings concerned is more than EUR 25 million; and
>
> (d) the aggregate Community-wide turnover of each of at least two of the undertakings concerned is more than EUR 100 million,
>
> unless each of the undertakings concerned achieves more than two-thirds of its aggregate Community-wide turnover within one and the same Member State.[11]

Which turnover is taken into account?

11.   To work out which turnover must be taken into account for purposes of applying the jurisdictional thresholds, the 'undertakings concerned' in the concentration must be identified. There is no definition of 'undertakings concerned' in the Merger Regulation but the Commission Jurisdictional Notice provides clarification as to which entities are undertakings concerned.[12]

12.   The identification of the undertakings concerned will be straightforward in many cases but may be more difficult in transactions with complex structures. In a merger, the undertakings concerned are each of the merging parties. In the acquisition of sole control of a whole undertaking, the undertakings concerned will be the acquiring undertaking and the target undertaking (not the seller). In the case of the acquisition of joint control of an existing undertaking, the undertakings

---

11.   Merger Regulation [2004] OJ L24/1, Article 1(2), (3).
12.   Commission Jurisdictional Notice [2008] OJ C95/1, paras 129–153.

concerned are each of the undertakings acquiring joint control and the target undertaking.[13]

13.   When parts of an undertaking are sold, whether or not the part sold constitutes a separate legal entity, 'only the turnover relating to the parts which are the subject of the transaction shall be taken into account with regard to the seller or sellers'.[14] So, in the acquisition of a company, on the seller side, only the turnover of the target (and not of the seller or its wider group) is taken into account for the purposes of the jurisdictional thresholds.

14.   Without prejudice to this treatment of the target, once each undertaking concerned is identified, the turnover of its parent company, or in the case of two or more companies exercising joint control over the undertaking concerned, the turnover of all of them, must be included in the calculation. Where the direct parent of the undertaking concerned is itself controlled by a further parent company, its turnover is also included (and so on to the ultimate parent).[15]

15.   The turnover of subsidiaries of the parent(s), the undertaking's own subsidiaries and any subsidiary jointly held by any of these undertakings, must be included in the calculation.[16] A useful graphic illustration of a complicated company structure is set out in the Commission Jurisdictional Notice.[17]

16.   For the purpose of including the turnover of subsidiaries of the undertaking concerned, they are:

> those undertakings in which the undertaking concerned directly or indirectly:

> (i)   owns more than half the capital or business assets, or

> (ii)   has the power to exercise more than half the voting rights, or

> (iii)   has the power to appoint more than half the members of the supervisory board, the administrative board or bodies legally representing the undertakings, or

> (iv)   has the right to manage the undertaking's affairs.[18]

17.   It is important to note that this definition of a subsidiary is not the same as the concept of 'control' in Article 3(2) of the Merger Regulation. In particular, the application of *de facto* control is broader in scope under Article 3(2) and 'a solely controlled subsidiary is only taken into account on a *de facto* basis under Article 5(4)(b) if it is clearly demonstrated that the undertaking concerned has the power

---

13.   Other possibilities are discussed in the Commission Jurisdictional Notice [2008] OJ C95/1, paras 129–153.

14.   Merger Regulation [2004] OJ L24/1, Article 5(2).

15.   See Commission Jurisdictional Notice [2008] OJ C95/1, para 182. The Commission Jurisdictional Notice replaced the following four notices: Commission Notice on the concept of a concentration [1998] OJ C66/5; Commission Notice on the concept of full-function joint ventures [1998] OJ C66/1; Commission Notice on the concept of undertakings concerned [1998] OJ C66/14; Commission Notice on the calculation of turnover [1998] OJ C66/25.

16.   Merger Regulation [2004] OJ L24/1, Article 5(4).

17.   Commission Jurisdictional Notice [2008] OJ C95/1, para 178.

18.   Merger Regulation [2004] OJ L24/1, Article 5(4)(b).

to exercise more than half of the voting rights or to appoint more than half of the board members'.[19]

18. In general, the whole amount of a subsidiary's turnover should be taken into account, regardless of the amount of shares actually held. However, the turnover of joint ventures is allocated on a per capita basis according to the number of undertakings exercising joint control. For example, if the undertaking concerned participates in a joint venture with two unrelated companies, a third of the turnover of the joint venture would be included in the undertaking's turnover.[20]

19. Where disposals or acquisitions have been made since an undertaking's annual turnover figures were calculated, adjustments should be made to reflect these disposals or acquisitions.[21]

How is turnover calculated?

20. In the majority of cases, it will be clear whether the transaction triggers the EU turnover thresholds and for this purpose, the turnover figures stated in the audited accounts can be relied on. However in some cases, the relevant turnover may hover close to the thresholds and careful scrutiny of the methodology for calculating turnover may be required to establish whether the Commission has jurisdiction.

21. Turnover figures should be amounts derived from the sale of products or provision of services in the preceding financial year from an undertaking's 'ordinary activities'. The turnover figures used should exclude sales rebates, value added tax and other taxes directly related to turnover.[22] Internal revenue generated from intra-group transactions should also be excluded.[23] Revenue generated from 'extraordinary activity', such as the sale of fixed assets or profit from investments, should not be taken into account.[24]

22. There are separate rules for calculating turnover of financial institutions and insurance companies.[25]

23. Where a company's accounting and reporting systems generate turnover data in a currency other than Euros, the annual turnover should be calculated in Euros using the average exchange rate of the European Central Bank for the relevant twelve-month period. The relevant exchange rates in respect of a range of currencies are published in the European Central Bank's monthly bulletin.[26]

---

19. Commission Jurisdictional Notice [2008] OJ C95/1, para 184.
20. Commission Jurisdictional Notice [2008] OJ C95/1, paras 185–187.
21. Commission Jurisdictional Notice [2008] OJ C95/1, paras 172–173.
22. Merger Regulation [2004] OJ L24/1, Article 5(1).
23. Merger Regulation [2004] OJ L24/1, Article 5(1).
24. Commission Jurisdictional Notice [2008] OJ C95/1, para 161.
25. Merger Regulation [2004] OJ L24/1, Article 5(3).
26. The ECB monthly bulletins are available at http://www.ecb.int/pub/mb/html/index.en.html.

What is the relevant date for establishing jurisdiction?

24.   The relevant date for establishing whether the EU thresholds are met is the date of the conclusion of a binding legal agreement, the announcement of a public bid or the acquisition of a controlling interest or the date of the first notification (where a notification is made on the basis of a good faith intention to enter an agreement or where the intention to make a public bid is announced), whichever date is earlier.[27]

25.   If changes to the concentration are made during the Commission's investigation, in particular through proposed commitments, which would bring the transaction outside the EU thresholds, this does not deprive the Commission of jurisdiction where the jurisdictional thresholds had been met when the relevant transactions were concluded and at the time the notification was made. This issue arose in *Cementbouw*. It was argued that the remedies offered, if accepted, would bring the transaction below the Merger Regulation thresholds. Rejecting this argument and for reasons of legal certainty and speed, the Court of Justice held that the Commission's jurisdiction had to be established at a fixed time:

> … the competence of the Commission to make findings in relation to a concentration must be established, as regards the whole of the proceedings, at a fixed time. Having regard to the importance of the obligation of notification in the system of control put in place by the Community legislature, that time must necessarily be closely related to the notification of the concentration.[28]

Does the Commission have jurisdiction if there are no physical assets within the EU?

26.   It is well established that once the jurisdictional thresholds in the Merger Regulation are met, the Commission has jurisdiction over the concentration 'irrespective of whether or not the undertakings effecting the concentration have their seat or their principal fields of activity in the Community, provided they have substantial operations there'.[29] In *Gencor*, the General Court examined the jurisdiction of the Merger Regulation over the merger of South African mining interests of a South African and English company. The General Court held that the Merger Regulation applied to all concentrations with a Community dimension and it was not necessary that 'the undertakings in question must be established in the Community or that the production activities covered by the concentration must be carried out within Community territory'.[30] The General Court found that the reference to 'substantial operations' did not ascribe greater importance to production operations than to sales operations. It compared the EU's jurisdiction over concentrations with that of Article 101, finding from the *Wood*

---

27.   Merger Regulation [2004] OJ L24/1, Article 4(1); Commission Jurisdictional Notice [2008] OJ C95/1, para 156.

28.   Case C–202/06P *Cementbouw Handel & Industrie BV v Commission* [2007] ECR I–12129, [2008] 4 CMLR 1324, para 43 (see also paras 38–39).

29.   Merger Regulation [2004] OJ L24/1, Recital 10.

30.   Case T–102/96 *Gencor Ltd v Commission* [1999] ECR II–753, [1999] 4 CMLR 971, para 79.

Pulp case[31] that the criterion as to the implementation of an agreement was satisfied by mere sale within the Community, irrespective of the location of the sources of supply or production. As the parties to the concentration made sales in the EU and the turnover thresholds were met, the Merger Regulation applied. The General Court went on to hold that this conclusion was compatible with public international law and that the application of the Merger Regulation was justified 'when it is foreseeable that a proposed concentration will have an immediate and substantial effect in the Community'.[32]

27. As a practical matter, companies involved in concentrations that involve assets outside the EU but which meet the EU thresholds, invariably submit to the Commission's jurisdiction. The ability of the Commission to enforce the Merger Regulation in respect of a 'foreign' transaction where the parties have resisted its application has not really been tested. However the importance of the Commission as a merger control authority means that it is unlikely that parties to large mergers, typically multinational companies, would challenge its jurisdiction.

Key Sources

Council Regulation (EC) No 139/2004 on the control of concentrations between undertakings [2004] OJ L24/1, Articles 1, 3 and 5.

Commission Consolidated Jurisdictional Notice under Council Regulation (EC) No 139/2004 on the control of concentrations between undertakings [2008] OJ C95/1, Part C.

---

31. Cases 89/85 etc., *Åhlström Osakeyhtiö v Commission ('Wood Pulp II')* [1993] ECR I–1307, [1993] 4 CMLR 407.
32. Case T–102/96 *Gencor Ltd v Commission* [1999] ECR II–753, [1999] 4 CMLR 971, para 90. The General Court did not provide any authority for this proposition of international law.

66. MAY A COMPANY THAT ACQUIRES LESS THAN 50 PER CENT OF ANOTHER COMPANY ACQUIRE 'CONTROL' FOR PURPOSES OF THE MERGER REGULATION?

Summary

- Yes.

- The concept of 'control' in the Merger Regulation is not based on the acquisition of a particular percentage of shares or seats on the board.

- The key issue is whether an acquirer can exercise 'decisive influence'.

- The concept of control includes 'negative control' (the ability to veto important decisions) as well as 'positive control' (the ability to take important decisions).

- Negative control may arise on a sole or joint basis and may be legal or *de facto* in nature.

- If a company acquires a minority stake in another company but gains the right to veto important business decisions, such as adoption of the annual budget or appointments to the board of directors, this may be sufficient to result in negative control.

1.   A concentration within the meaning of the Merger Regulation only arises if there is a change of control. The Merger Regulation defines control as follows:

> Control shall be constituted by rights, contracts or any other means which, either separately or in combination and having regard to the considerations of fact or law involved, confer the possibility of exercising decisive influence on an undertaking, in particular by:
>
> (a) ownership or the right to use all or part of the assets of an undertaking;
>
> (b) rights or contracts which confer decisive influence on the composition, voting or decisions of the organs of an undertaking.[33]

2.   The concept of control is not dependent on the acquisition of a particular percentage of shares or seats on the board. The key question in examining if there is control is whether there is 'the possibility of exercising decisive influence' over the undertaking in question. This concept of control is broader than a controlling interest in a legal sense (for example, on the basis of a majority of shares) and can arise through the acquisition of a minority stake. Conversely, the acquisition of a majority stake in an undertaking does not necessarily result in decisive influence. It will depend on what rights attach to the majority holding.

3.   The way in which control arises is not important. It can be direct or indirect and conferred on the basis of an agreement rather than through voting rights attaching to shares.[34]

---

33.   Merger Regulation [2004] OJ L24/1, Article 3(2).
34.   See, eg, COMP/M.1553 *France Telecom/Editel/Lince*, Commission Decision of 30 July 1999, para 6 (veto rights conferred through a shareholders' agreement).

4.   Control may be either positive or negative but the key issue is whether an acquirer has the possibility to exercise decisive influence. In the context of negative control, decisive influence has been described as the power to block 'actions which determine the strategic commercial behaviour of an undertaking'.[35] Positive control involves the ability to determine strategic decisions.[36]

5.   The concept of decisive influence in the context of the Merger Regulation does not necessarily have the same meaning as in the context of Article 101 or 102 when determining if two entities are part of the same undertaking because one exercises decisive influence over the other.[37]

Over what types of decisions may veto power lead to decisive influence?

6.   Certain decisions are sufficiently important to the strategic commercial behaviour of an undertaking that influence over them may result in control. The Merger Regulation does not provide any explanation on this point but it has been addressed in decisions of the Commission and in the Commission Jurisdictional Notice.[38] Each situation will have to be considered on its own facts. The following kinds of decisions are likely to be considered as commercially strategic:

- Appointment of the board of directors or management team.[39]

- Approval or modification of the annual budget.[40]

- Approval or modification of the annual business plan.[41]

- Decisions concerning important investments.[42]

- Decisions on the opening of production facilities.[43]

- Decisions on the use of technology, where this is important in the particular market circumstances.[44]

---

35.   Case T–282/02 *Cementbouw Handel & Industrie BV v Commission* [2006] ECR II–319, [2006] 4 CMLR 1561, para 42 (appeal dismissed, Case C–202/06P *Cementbouw Handel & Industrie BV v Commission* [2007] ECR I–12129, [2008] 4 CMLR 1324).

36.   Commission Jurisdictional Notice [2008] OJ C95/1, para 54.

37.   See Question 2, para 15–16.

38.   Commission Jurisdictional Notice [2008] OJ C95/1, paras 67–73.

39.   See, eg, COMP/M.5729 *Bank of America/Barclays Bank/DSI International*, Commission Decision of 25 February 2010, para 6; COMP/M.4234 *Carlson/One Equity Partners/Carlson Wagonlit*, Commission Decision of 3 July 2006, paras 7–8.

40.   See, eg, IV/M.865 *Cable & Wireless/Nynex/Bell Canada*, Commission Decision of 11 December 1996, para 20.

41.   See, eg, COMP/M.1637 *DB Investments/SPP/Öhman*, Commission Decision of 11 August 1999, para 4.

42.   See, eg, COMP/M.3722 *Nutreco/Stolt-Nielsen/Marine Harvest JV*, Commission Decision of 12 April 2005, para 6.

43.   See COMP/M.5518 *Fiat/Chrysler*, Commission Decision of 24 July 1999, para 8.

44.   Commission Jurisdictional Notice [2008] OJ C95/1, para 72.

- Decisions concerning product developments, which may be important in markets characterised by product differentiation and innovation.[45]

7. The ability to make or block any one of the above decisions may result in decisive influence. In other cases, it may be necessary to show that an acquirer has decisive influence based on two or more of these decisions. This will depend on the circumstances.

8. It is not necessary that decisive influence actually be exercised for control to arise. It is sufficient if an acquirer has the ability to exercise decisive influence. However as the General Court indicated in *Cementbouw*, this must be more than a mere possibility:

> In effect, while decisive influence ... need not necessarily be exercised in order to exist, the existence of control ... requires that the possibility of exercising that influence be effective.[46]

What is the difference between 'positive' and 'negative' control?

9. Control may be acquired on the basis of positive rights to exert decisive influence over another undertaking. This could arise where an acquirer gains rights to appoint more than half of the board of directors or where it can push through important decisions that require a majority vote because it has more than half of the votes at a shareholder meeting.

10. The concept of control under the Merger Regulation also includes negative control, which essentially means the ability to exercise decisive influence through the power of veto over important decisions. Negative control will often arise in situations of joint control, where a minority shareholder acquires veto rights over important strategic decisions.

11. It is also possible that negative and positive control in respect of the same undertaking arise at the same time. One shareholder may have decisive influence in the form of positive control as it can appoint a majority of the board, while a minority shareholder may have negative control through a veto power over the adoption of the annual budget and business plan.

When does sole control arise?

12. Where only one undertaking acquires the ability to exercise decisive influence, this gives rise to sole control. The acquisition of sole control will usually be on the basis of positive control, typically through the acquisition of a majority shareholding in a company.

---

45. Commission Jurisdictional Notice [2008] OJ C95/1, para 72.
46. Case T–282/02 *Cementbouw Handel & Industrie BV v Commission* [2006] ECR II–319, [2006] 4 CMLR 1561, para 58 (appeal dismissed, Case C–202/06P *Cementbouw Handel & Industrie BV v Commission* [2007] ECR I–12129, [2008] 4 CMLR 1324).

13. Sole control can also arise through negative control, where there is only one shareholder who has a veto power over important decisions. This could occur where the acquirer obtains a shareholding that is far bigger than the next largest shareholder and the acquirer is the only shareholder that has sufficient voting power to veto important decisions. This would be *de jure* sole control. In *Cinven Limited/Angel Street Holdings*, Cinven acquired 53 per cent of the share capital in the target, with three other acquirers obtaining 13 per cent to 17 per cent each. As Cinven could nominate only two of five board members, it could not impose its will. However, it was the only party that could exercise a veto over a range of strategic decisions and so it had sole control of the target.[47]

14. Minority protection rights that do not have significance for strategy, such as minority rights in the face of winding up or those granted for the protection of minority shareholders under company law, are not sufficient for negative control to arise. In *Aer Lingus*, the General Court upheld the Commission's decision that Ryanair's acquisition of 25 per cent of the shares of Aer Lingus (and later increase to 29.3 per cent) did not confer on Ryanair *de facto* or *de jure* control of Aer Lingus. The Commission had noted that Ryanair's right to block special resolutions pursuant to the Irish Companies Acts was associated exclusively with minority protection rights.[48] If there was no control, the Commission had no competence under the Merger Regulation to deal with an investment by one competitor in another. The General Court pointed out that if Aer Lingus considered that 'Ryanair's conduct as a shareholder is abusive or unlawful, it may bring the matter before the competent national courts or authorities'.[49]

15. Sole control could also operate on a *de facto* basis, for example, where the acquirer is highly likely to achieve a majority vote at the shareholders' meeting due to the large size of its shareholding (even though it is a minority shareholding), the wide dispersal of other shareholdings and the likely turnout at the shareholders' meeting.[50] In *Anglo America/Lonrho*, the Commission decided that Anglo American's shareholding of 27.5 per cent in Lonrho gave rise to *de facto* sole control where evidence from polls held at Lonrho shareholders' meetings over a three-year period showed that a holding of 27.5 per cent would have been sufficient to command consistently more than 50 per cent of votes cast.[51]

---

47. COMP/M.2777 *Cinven Limited/Angel Street Holdings*, Commission Decision of 8 May 2002, para 8. See, also, See COMP/M.5518 *Fiat/Chrysler*, Commission Decision of 24 July 1999, para 9 (*de jure* sole negative control).
48. Commission Decision C(2007) 4600 final in Case No COMP/M.4439 *Ryanair/Aer Lingus*, 11 October 2007, para 11. See also, Case IV/M.062 *Eridania/ISI*, Commission Decision of 30 July 1991; Commission Jurisdictional Notice [2008] OJ C95/1, para 66.
49. Case T–411/07 *Aer Lingus Group plc v Commission*, judgment of the General Court of 6 July 2010, para 68.
50. Commission Jurisdictional Notice [2008] OJ C95/1, para 59.
51. IV/M.754 *Anglo American/Lonrho*, Commission Decision of 23 April 1997, para 30. See also COMP/M.5121 *News Corp/Premiere*, Commission Decision of 25 June 2008, paras 5–10 (given attendance rates at the annual shareholders' meeting, a share of 24.2 per cent would have been sufficient to have resulted in *de facto* control).

16.   In *Electrabel/CNR*, the Commission fined Electrabel €20 million for failing to
        make a notification under the Merger Regulation where it had acquired *de facto*
        sole control over CNR. It was argued by Electrabel that it was only after it had
        been able to examine the actual voting position at three years of shareholders'
        meetings of CNR that it asked itself whether it had acquired *de facto* sole control.
        This argument was rejected by the Commission on the basis that it 'would
        necessarily mean that a company could exercise *de facto* control (without
        notification or approval) over another company for three years before notifying the
        Commission of the operation, on the basis that it would not be absolutely sure that
        it was exercising control until the three years were up'.[52] This case illustrates the
        importance of companies monitoring significant minority investments for the
        possibility of giving rise to *de facto* sole control.

When does joint control arise?

17.   Joint control arises where two or more undertakings acquire rights over the target
        so that each of them can exercise decisive influence over its business strategy. Joint
        control will usually involve negative control. Joint control involves the possibility
        of deadlock, as two or more shareholders each have the ability to veto decisions.
        To confer decisive influence and control, veto power must relate to strategic
        commercial decisions of the undertaking in question. However, it is not necessary
        that there be decisive influence over the day-to-day running of the target
        undertaking. The possibility of exercising such influence and, hence, the mere
        existence of the veto rights, is sufficient.[53]

Can change in the quality of control trigger a filing?

18.   It appears that the Merger Regulation catches not only acquisitions of control but
        also changes in the 'quality' of control. The Commission has explained its
        understanding of this concept as follows:

> First, such a change in the quality of control, resulting in a concentration, occurs if
> there is a change between sole and joint control. Second, a change in the quality of
> control occurs between joint control scenarios before and after the transaction if there
> is an increase in the number or a change in the identity of controlling shareholders.
> However, there is no change in the quality of control if a change from negative to
> positive sole control occurs. Such a change affects neither the incentives of the
> negatively controlling shareholder nor the nature of the control structure, as the
> controlling shareholder did not necessarily have to cooperate with specific
> shareholders at the time when it enjoyed negative control. In any case, mere changes in
> the level of shareholdings of the same controlling shareholders, without changes of the
> powers they hold in a company and of the composition of the control structure of the
> company, do not constitute a change in the quality of control and therefore are not a
> notifiable concentration.[54]

---

52.   COMP/M.4994 *Electrabel/Compagnie Nationale du Rhone*, C(2009) 4416 final,
        Commission Decision of 10 June 2009, para 56 (appeal pending, Case T–332/09 *Electrabel
        v Commission*).
53.   Commission Jurisdictional Notice [2008] OJ C95/1, para 67.
54.   Commission Jurisdictional Notice [2008] OJ C95/1, para 83.

19. Assuming that the Commission's view is correct and that changes to the quality of control as outlined above can give rise to filing obligations under the Merger Regulation, companies will need to be attentive in monitoring changes in the quality of control, particularly in situations involving joint control, if fines for failure to notify, as in the *Electrabel* case, are to be avoided.

Key Sources

Council Regulation (EC) No 139/2004 on the control of concentrations between undertakings [2004] OJ L24/1, Article 3.

Commission Consolidated Jurisdictional Notice under Council Regulation (EC) No 139/2004 on the control of concentrations between undertakings [2008] OJ C95/1, Part B.

67. HOW SHOULD MERGER CONTROL FILINGS BE MANAGED IN A GLOBAL TRANSACTION?

Summary

- Merger control is becoming an increasingly burdensome element of global transactions as the number of jurisdictions that require filings grows.

- It is important to identify filing requirements and possible substantive concerns as early as possible.

1. Mergers, acquisitions, joint ventures and other transactions that involve the transfer of assets or shares are subject to ever more burdensome regulation by competition authorities around the world. The regulators invariably have powers to block transactions that will result in anti-competitive effects and demand remedies, such as the disposal of overlapping businesses, as a condition for clearance. Although the majority of transactions subject to merger control will not raise substantive concerns, numerous filings with competition authorities may have to be made. This can be a time-consuming and costly process.

2. The number of jurisdictions with merger control regimes has risen dramatically in recent years and there are now more than 100 competition authorities that police mergers and acquisitions. An increasing number of laws impose a suspensory obligation on the transaction, prohibiting implementation until merger control clearance has been obtained. Parties typically have to make a filing with the relevant antitrust authority, supplying information about the transaction, the businesses of the parties and the markets in which they operate. Given the potentially burdensome nature of the merger control process and its impact on the transaction timetable, it is important to identify the filing requirements as soon as possible.

3. The starting point in assessing in which jurisdictions a filing is necessary should be a country-by-country breakdown of the revenues of each of the parties to the merger or acquisition. Typically, if neither party has turnover in a particular jurisdiction, the need for a merger control filing can be discounted. If the transaction involves an acquisition and if the target is not active in a particular country, a filing can usually be excluded in that country even if the acquiring firm generates revenue there.

4. Given that merger control laws in different jurisdictions can change regularly, it is important to confirm the requirements that are in effect at the time of filing. Where filings are required in different jurisdictions, it is usually necessary to retain local counsel to carry out the filing.

5. To the extent that filings are triggered, it is essential to establish at an early stage the likelihood that the transaction will give rise to substantive concerns.

6. The parties may have different views about the extent to which filing obligations should be complied with to the letter. Typically, a purchaser takes a more conservative view than a seller. A distinction should be drawn between

jurisdictions that present substantive risk and those where no substantive risk arises and where there are no mandatory waiting periods.

7.   The approach of the parties to the risks posed by the regulatory process will be reflected in the transaction documents. These will typically set out the regulatory approvals that are conditions to closing and the lengths to which the parties must go in order to obtain these approvals.[55]

8.   It has usefully been suggested that jurisdictions could be divided into a number of segments for the purpose of deciding where merger control filings should be made:

      (i)   Jurisdictions where significant substantive risk arises, whether a filing is mandatory or not.

      (ii) Jurisdictions without significant substantive risk and without mandatory waiting periods or where such periods are not enforced.

      (iii) Jurisdictions without significant substantive risk but where the parties have a significant presence and which have mandatory waiting periods.

      (iv) Of remaining jurisdictions, those that actively impose fines for non-compliance.

      (v)   All other jurisdictions.[56]

9.   In cases where the Merger Regulation thresholds are not met, it will be necessary to consider whether a filing in one or more EU Member States is required. Most EU jurisdictions with merger control have mandatory filings where the thresholds are met. The United Kingdom operates a voluntary regime. The following table sets out the jurisdictional thresholds in each of the EU Member States.

Jurisdiction	Filing Threshold
Austria	(i) Combined worldwide turnover of €300m; and
	(ii) Combined Austrian turnover of €30m; and
	(iii) Two parties with worldwide turnover of €5m
	But no filing if only one party has Austrian turnover above €5 million and combined worldwide turnover of all other parties is less than €30m
	An acquisition of shares that enables the acquiror to reach or exceed a shareholding of 25 per cent or 50 per cent may be notifiable
Belgium	(i) Combined Belgian turnover more than €100m; and
	(ii) At least two parties each with Belgian turnover of €40m
Bulgaria	(i) Combined turnover in Bulgaria of BGN 25m (c. €12.8m); and
	(ii) at least two parties each have Bulgarian turnover of BGN 3m (c. €1.5m) **OR** the target has BGN 3m (c. €1.5m) turnover in Bulgaria

---

55.   See Question 81, which discusses antitrust provisions in transaction documents.
56.   Scott et al, *Merger Control in the United Kingdom* (2006) 358.

Jurisdiction	Filing Threshold
Cyprus	(i) At least two parties each have €3.4m turnover worldwide; and
	(ii) At least one party carries on business in Cyprus; and
	(iii) Combined turnover on Cyprus of €3.4m
Czech Republic	(i) Combined turnover in the Czech market of CZK 1.5b (c. €62.5m); and
	(ii) Each of at least two parties have Czech turnover of CZK 250m (c. €10.4m)
	OR
	(i) One party (must be the target in an acquisition) has turnover of CZK 1.5B (c. €62.5m) in the Czech Republic; and
	(ii) Worldwide turnover of the other party is CZK 1.5B (c. €62.5m)
Denmark	(i) Combined Danish turnover of DKK 3.8b (c. €510m); and
	(ii) At least two parties each have DKK 300m (c. €40m) of Danish turnover
	OR
	(i) One party has Danish turnover of DKK 3.8b (c. €510m); and
	(ii) Another party has worldwide turnover of DKK 3.8b (c. €510m)
	The thresholds were due to be significantly reduced as of 1 October 2010, with the DKK 3.8b threshold to be reduced to DKK 900m (c. €121 m) and the DKK 300m threshold to be reduced to DKK 100m (c. €13.4m)
Estonia	(i) Combined Estonian turnover of EEK 100m (c. €6m); and
	(ii) At least two parties each have Estonian turnover of EEK 30m (c. €2m)
Finland	(i) Combined worldwide turnover of €350m; and
	(ii) At least two parties each have Finnish turnover of €20m
France	(i) Combined turnover worldwide of €150m; and
	(ii) At least two parties each have €50m French turnover
Germany	(i) Combined worldwide turnover of €500m; and
	(ii) One party has German turnover of €25m; and
	(iii) Another party has German turnover of €5m
	De minimis exception:
	One party has worldwide turnover of less than €10m
	OR
	Each of the relevant markets has existed for at least five years and has an annual sales volume of below €15 million
	Acquisitions of shares giving the acquiror a shareholding that exceeds 25 per or 50 per cent may be notifiable.

Jurisdiction	Filing Threshold
Greece	(i) Combined worldwide turnover of €150m; and
	(ii) At least two parties each have Greek turnover of €15m
	If these thresholds are not met, a post-merger filing is required if the combined market share is at least 10 per cent or at least two parties have Greek turnover of €15m
Hungary	(i) Combined Hungarian turnover of HUF 15b (c. €53m); and
	(ii) At least two parties each have Hungarian turnover of HUF 500m (c. €1.8m)
Ireland	(i) Each of at least two parties has €40 million worldwide turnover; and
	(ii) At least two parties carry on business in any part of the island of Ireland; and
	(iii) At least one party has turnover in Ireland of €40 million
Italy	Combined turnover in Italy of €472m
	OR
	The target has Italian turnover of €47m
	The turnover figures are updated annually; these figures are effective as of 31 May 2010
Latvia	(i) Combined Latvian turnover of LVL 25m (c. €35m); and
	(ii) Each of two merger parties have Latvian turnover above LVL 1.5m (c. €2.1m)
	OR
	(i) Combined market share of 40 per cent in a relevant market; and
	(ii) Each of two merger parties have Latvian turnover above LVL 1.5m (c. €2.1m)
Lithuania	(i) Combined Lithuanian turnover of LTL 30m (c. €8.7m); and
	(ii) At least two parties each have Lithuanian turnover of LTL 5m (c. €1.4m)
Luxembourg	*No merger control*
Malta	(i) Combined turnover in Malta of €2.3m; and
	(ii) Maltese turnover of each party equals at least 10 per cent of the combined Maltese turnover of all parties
The Netherlands	(i) Combined worldwide turnover of €113.45m; and
	(ii) At least two parties each have turnover in The Netherlands of €30m

Jurisdiction	Filing Threshold
Poland	(i) Combined worldwide turnover of €1b **OR** combined Polish turnover of €50m; and
	(ii) The target had turnover of €10m in Poland in the last two years
Portugal	(i) Combined turnover in Portugal of €150m; and
	(ii) At least two parties each have turnover in Portugal of €2m **OR** the combined market share in Portugal is 30 per cent
Romania	(i) Combined worldwide turnover of €10m; and
	(ii) At least two parties each have Romanian turnover of €4m
Slovak Republic	(i) Combined worldwide turnover of €46m; and
	(ii) At least two parties each with Slovak turnover of €14m
	OR
	(i) At least one party has worldwide turnover of €46m; and
	(ii) At least one other party has Slovak turnover of €19m
Slovenia	(i) Combined Slovenian turnover of €35m; and
	(ii) The target has Slovenian turnover of €1m **OR** in joint ventures, the Slovenian group turnover of at least two parties is €1m
	If the thresholds are not met but the combined market share of the parties exceeds 60 per cent in Slovenia, the parties must inform the CPO of the concentration (but are not required to submit a formal notification).
Spain	A share of 30 per cent of the national market or a market within Spain is acquired or increased
	OR
	Combined Spanish turnover of €240m and each of at least two parties has Spanish turnover of €60m
Sweden	(i) Combined Swedish turnover of SEK 1b (c. €102m); and
	(ii) At least two parties each have Swedish turnover of SEK 200m (c. € 20.5m)
United Kingdom	The target's UK turnover exceeds £70 million
	OR
	A share of at least 25 per cent of the supply or purchase of goods or services of any description in the UK or a substantial part of it will be created or enhanced.

10. A growing number of jurisdictions have merger control laws and there are specialist publications that set out the jurisdictional requirements.[57] The requirement to file will largely depend on the location of the turnover and assets of the parties. Non-EU jurisdictions with developed merger control regimes and which regularly feature in global transactions include Brazil, Canada, South Africa, South Korea, Turkey and the United States. Merger control was introduced in China in 2008 and the regime there is developing.[58]

Key Sources

http://www.gettingthedealthrough.com.

Gidley and Paul, *Worldwide Merger Notification Requirements* (2009).

---

57. See, eg, http://www.gettingthedealthrough.com; Dabbah and Lasok, *Merger Control Worldwide* (2005) and first and second supplements; Gidley and Paul, *Worldwide Merger Notification Requirements* (2009).
58. See Wang and Zhang, 'China: Merger Control' in *The Asia-Pacific Antitrust Review 2010* (2010).

68. WHEN IS A JOINT VENTURE 'FULL-FUNCTION'?

Summary

- The establishment of a joint venture is subject to the Merger Regulation only if it is 'full-function'.

- The joint venture must be operationally autonomous and set up on a lasting basis.

- To establish operational autonomy, important factors include that the joint venture is:

  - Operating on a market;

  - Independently managed;

  - Not dependent on its parents;

  - Not restricted to dealing with its parent entities in its sales and purchasing.

- If the joint venture is sufficiently resourced to operate autonomously, this usually indicates that it is set up on a lasting basis.

- If the joint venture is set up for a specific period, it may still be on a lasting basis if the period is long enough; its duration should probably be at least 10 years.

1. Only the creation of joint ventures that are 'full-function' are considered to give rise to a concentration.[59] The Merger Regulation provides that:

    > The creation of a joint venture performing on a lasting basis all the functions of an autonomous entity shall constitute a concentration.[60]

2. It is necessary to determine if the joint venture will have sufficient operational autonomy and also whether it is set up on a lasting basis. The applicable principles on these questions are set out in the Commission Jurisdictional Notice. It has been noted that while the Commission Jurisdictional Notice sets out the factors to be considered, the Commission's decisional practice on the concept of full-function joint ventures has not always been consistent and so each case should be considered carefully on its facts. It is also true that the Commission takes a broad approach to the concept of full-functionality.[61]

---

59. However the joint acquisition of one undertaking by a number of undertakings will give rise to a concentration, regardless of the fact that post-acquisition, the target would not be considered a full-function joint venture (because, for example, it would sell exclusively to its parent undertakings in the future). See Commission Jurisdictional Notice [2008] OJ C95/1, para 91.
60. Merger Regulation [2004] OJ L24/1, Article 3(4).
61. See Cook & Kerse, *EC Merger Control* (5th edn, 2009) para 2–036.

When is a joint venture autonomous?

3. The joint venture must have a degree of independence from its parents but to be considered operationally autonomous, it is not necessary that the joint venture have autonomy over its strategic decisions.[62] Three factors are particularly important in assessing operational autonomy: (i) the joint venture should have independent management; (ii) the joint venture should not be dependent on the parents for facilities, services etc.; and (iii) the joint venture should not be restricted to dealing with its parents in its commercial activities.

4. It is sufficient if the joint venture operates on a market and has the requisite resources and staff to perform the functions normally carried out by other undertakings operating on the same market.[63] If the joint venture has its own management team, which directs and controls the day-to-day business of the joint venture, the fact that some decisions of the joint venture require prior approval of the parents will not necessarily mean that the joint venture is not full-function.[64] The fact that employees of the parents are seconded to the joint venture will not result in a finding that it is insufficiently autonomous. However, if secondments are for any longer than a start-up period, the arrangement should be conducted on an arm's length basis and the joint venture should be free to recruit its own employees.[65]

5. If the joint venture is reliant on the parents for services or the use of facilities, infrastructure, intellectual property etc., this tends to indicate that it is not full-function. However, it will often make commercial sense or be necessary from a commercial perspective that the joint venture use certain established facilities or intellectual property of the parents. This does not necessarily mean that the joint venture is not full-function but the use of the parents' facilities should be on commercial terms.[66]

6. If the parents have control over the services and facilities of which the joint venture may avail, this might negate full functionality. In *American Express/Fortis/ Alpha Card*, the Alpha Card joint venture was not considered full-function when it required the consent of one of the parents before it outsourced certain processing

---

62. Case T–282/02 *Cementbouw Handel & Industrie BV v Commission* [2006] ECR II–319, [2006] 4 CMLR 1561, para 62 (appeal dismissed, Case C–202/06P *Cementbouw Handel & Industrie BV v Commission* [2007] ECR I–12129, [2008] 4 CMLR 1324).
63. See Commission Jurisdictional Notice [2008] OJ C95/1, para 94.
64. See COMP/M.3576 *ECT/PONL/Euromax*, Commission Decision of 22 December 2004, para 12.
65. Commission Jurisdictional Notice [2008] OJ C95/1, para 94. See also, eg, IV/M.994 *DuPont/Hitachi*, Commission Decision of 24 October 1997, para 8 (seconded employees to be controlled by the joint venture's management and the joint venture would employ all or most of its personnel in the medium term).
66. See Cook & Kerse, *EC Merger Control* (5th edn, 2009) para 2–038.

services to third parties. It was only when this obligation to obtain consent was removed that the joint venture became full-function.[67]

7. The scope of activities undertaken by the joint venture is also an important factor in considering whether the entity is autonomous. If any of the following factors are present, this would tend to indicate that the joint venture does not have sufficient autonomy:[68]

    - The joint venture is limited to R&D or production but does not itself sell products to the market.

    - The joint venture's only function is to distribute the parents' products.

    - The joint venture makes significant purchases from the parents, particularly where the joint venture adds little value to these goods or services at the level of the joint venture itself.

    - The parents are strong in the downstream market, resulting in significant sales from the joint venture to the parents.

8. In contrast, the following factors tend to indicate that the joint venture does have sufficient autonomy:[69]

    - The joint venture achieves more than 50 per cent of its sales with third parties.

    - If the joint venture sells more than 50 per cent of its output to its parents, it can be demonstrated that these sales are made on a commercial basis; however, the Commission suggests that in this case, at least 20 per cent of sales must be made to third parties.

    - The joint venture is active in a trade market and obtains a substantial proportion of its supplies not only from its parents but also from other competing sources.

9. However, reliance on the parents as sources of sales and purchases may be allowed for an initial start-up period, which the Commission suggests should not be more than three years.[70]

When is a joint venture established on a 'lasting basis'?

10. The joint venture must be intended to operate on a lasting basis to be considered full-function. This will not be the case where the joint venture is established only for a short finite period. That the parents contribute sufficient resources to allow the joint venture to operate independently on the market usually indicates that it is established on a lasting basis.

---

67. COMP/M.5241 *American Express/Fortis/Alpha Card*, Commission Decision of 3 October 2008, paras 13–15.
68. See Commission Jurisdictional Notice [2008] OJ C95/1, paras 95–102.
69. Commission Jurisdictional Notice [2008] OJ C95/1, paras 98–102.
70. Commission Jurisdictional Notice [2008] OJ C95/1, para 97.

11.   The inclusion of termination provisions does not prevent the joint venture from being considered as operating on a lasting basis. Even the stipulation of a specific period for which the joint venture is to last is not fatal, assuming the period is sufficiently lengthy. The Commission has considered a 10–15 year duration sufficient but it has also found that a period of three years was not long enough.[71]

Does the Commission also consider Article 101?

12.   Where a full-function joint venture is assessed under the Merger Regulation, the Commission will also consider whether the creation of the joint venture may result in the coordination of the competitive behaviour of its parents contrary to Article 101. In so doing, the Commission will consider whether the parents retain significant activities in the same market as the joint venture or in a closely related market.[72]

13.   Joint ventures that do not fall under the Merger Regulation, either because they are not 'full-function' or do not meet the jurisdictional thresholds, may still be subject to scrutiny under merger control laws in one or more Member States. They may also be subject to Articles 101 and 102.[73]

Key Sources

Commission Consolidated Jurisdictional Notice under Council Regulation (EC) No 139/2004 on the control of concentrations between undertakings [2008] OJ C95/1, paras 91–116.

---

71. COMP/M.3858 *Lehman Brothers/SCG/Starwood/Le Meridien*, Commission Decision of 20 July 2005, paras 8–9.

72. Merger Regulation [2004] OJ L24/1, Recital 27, Articles 2(4), 2(5)

73. On the different treatment of joint ventures under the Merger Regulation and Article 101, see Bellamy & Child (6th edn, 2008) Ch 7.

69. WHEN MAY CASES BE TRANSFERRED BETWEEN THE COMMISSION AND THE MEMBER STATES?

Summary

Referrals *to* the Commission:

- The parties can request that the Commission take jurisdiction if thresholds in at least three Member States are met.

- Member State competition authorities can make referrals to the Commission where a transaction has a cross-border effect but does not meet the EU thresholds.

Referrals *from* the Commission:

- The parties may request the referral of a case to one or more Member States if the transaction meets the EU thresholds but may significantly affect competition in a distinct market in a Member State.

- Member State competition authorities can request referral of all or part of a transaction that meets the EU thresholds but has significant effects in a distinct market in the Member State.

---

1.   A transaction with a 'Community dimension' falls within the exclusive jurisdiction of the Commission. Where the Merger Regulation thresholds are not met, the transaction may fall within the jurisdiction of one or more Member States. In some cases, the review of transactions can be transferred between the Commission and the Member States, according to the rules set out in Articles 4, 9 and 22 of the Merger Regulation. Referrals are also considered in the Commission's Case Referral Notice.[74]

When may the parties request that cases be transferred?

2.   If a transaction, which does not meet the Merger Regulation thresholds, meets the thresholds in at least three Member States, the parties can request that the Commission take jurisdiction. A submission must be made on a prescribed form, Form RS,[75] and an explanation provided as to why it is appropriate for the Commission to take jurisdiction. The Commission consults with the Member States before agreeing to accept jurisdiction. The Member States have 15 working days to consider the request and any one of them has the power to veto the referral to the Commission.

---

74.   Commission Notice on Case Referral in respect of concentrations [2005] OJ C 56/2.

75.   See Annex III to Commission Regulation (EC) No 802/2004 of 7 April 2004 implementing Council Regulation (EC) No 139/2004 on the control of concentrations between undertakings [2004] OJ L133/1 (the 'Merger Implementing Regulation'). The Merger Implementing Regulation was amended by Commission Regulation (EC) No 1033/2008 amending Regulation (EC) No 802/2004 implementing Council Regulation (EC) No 139/ 2004 on the control of concentrations between undertakings [2008] OJ L279/3.

3.   The Article 4(5) referral procedure allows companies to avail of a 'one-stop-shop' in a situation where the transaction does not meet the EU thresholds but would require filings in a number of Member States. As the Merger Regulation states:

> Concentrations may qualify for examination under a number of national merger control systems if they fall below the turnover thresholds referred to in this Regulation. Multiple notification of the same transaction increases legal uncertainty, effort and cost for undertakings and may lead to conflicting assessments. The system whereby concentrations may be referred to the Commission by the Member States concerned should therefore be further developed.[76]

4.   An example of the utility of the Article 4(5) procedure can be seen in *Nokia/ Navteq*, where the transaction did not meet either of the alternative thresholds under the Merger Regulation but did meet the thresholds in eleven different Member States. The parties requested that the Commission take jurisdiction, which it did as no Member State objected to the referral.[77] As of 31 August 2010, of 197 referral requests made under Article 4(5), only five were refused.[78]

5.   Under Article 4(4) of the Merger Regulation, the parties can request that a transaction that meets the EU thresholds be transferred, in whole or in part, to a Member State prior to its notification to the Commission. The procedure is available for transactions that 'may significantly affect competition' in a 'distinct market' in a Member State. The parties make a submission to the Commission and the Member State to which a referral is sought has 15 working days to accept or decline the referral. As of 31 August 2010, 55 requests had been made, resulting in 52 full referrals and one partial referral.[79]

When may a Member State refer a case to the Commission?

6.   Under Article 22 of the Merger Regulation, one or more Member States may request the Commission to examine any concentration that does not meet the EU thresholds but affects trade between Member States and threatens to significantly affect competition within the territory of the Member State or States making the request. The Commission consults the parties and all the Member States. The Commission can also invite Article 22 referrals from the Member States. Referrals under Article 22 are relatively rare. In the past 20 years there have been 24 referrals, 21 of which were accepted.[80]

When may the Commission refer a case to a Member State?

7.   Under Article 9 of the Merger Regulation, a Member State can request the referral of a transaction that has already been notified to the Commission. This can be done on the Member State's own initiative or at the invitation of the Commission.

---

76.   Merger Regulation [2004] OJ L24/1, Recital 12.
77.   COMP/M.4942 *Nokia/Navteq*, Commission Decision of 2 July 2008.
78.   See http://ec.europa.eu/competition/mergers/statistics.pdf.
79.   See http://ec.europa.eu/competition/mergers/statistics.pdf.
80.   See http://ec.europa.eu/competition/mergers/statistics.pdf.

If the Commission considers that there is a distinct market in the Member State and that the transaction threatens to significantly affect competition in that market, it may refer all or part of the transaction.

8.   Ultimately the Commission has discretion as to whether it will refer all or part of a transaction to a Member State. It may adopt a relatively lengthy decision setting out its reasons for a referral.[81] The Referral Notice discusses some of the relevant considerations in deciding whether a referral should be made:

> In principle, jurisdiction should only be reattributed to another competition authority in circumstances where the latter is more appropriate for dealing with a merger, having regard to the specific characteristics of the case as well as the tools and expertise available to the authority. Particular regard should be had to the likely locus of any impact on competition resulting from the merger. Regard may also be had to the implications, in terms of administrative effort, of any contemplated referral.[82]

9.   If the case is still in Phase I, the Commission will make the referral decision within 35 days of the notification of the concentration.[83] If in Phase II, the referral decision shall be taken within 65 days of the notification.[84]

10. This procedure is suitable for transactions which meet the EU thresholds but generate significant competition issues in only one Member State. The procedure enables an 'effective corrective mechanism in light of the principle of subsidiarity'.[85] Article 9 referrals are relatively rare, with 94 referral requests in the past 20 years, resulting in 37 full referrals, 40 partial referrals and five refusals to refer.[86]

Key Sources

Council Regulation (EC) No 139/2004 on the control of concentrations between undertakings [2004] OJ L24/1, Articles 4, 9 and 22.

Commission Notice on Case Referral in respect of concentrations [2005] OJ C 56/2.

---

81. See, eg, Case No COMP/M.4999 *Heineken/Scottish & Newcastle Assets*, Commission Decision of 3 April 2008, referring part of the transactions to the Irish Competition Authority.
82. Commission Notice on Case Referral in respect of concentrations [2005] OJ C 56/2, para 9.
83. Merger Regulation [2004] OJ L24/1, Article 9(4)(a), 10(1).
84. Merger Regulation [2004] OJ L24/1, Article 9(4)(b).
85. Merger Regulation [2004] OJ L24/1, Recital 11.
86. See http://ec.europa.eu/competition/mergers/statistics.pdf.

70. **WHAT INFORMATION MUST BE PROVIDED IN A MERGER FILING UNDER THE MERGER REGULATION?**

Summary

• Where there are no affected markets, a simplified filing may be made.

• Where there are affected markets, a filing must be made on Form CO, which requires extensive information to be provided to the Commission.

• The extent of the information required in Form CO will depend on the number of affected markets and the complexity and seriousness of the antitrust issues.

1. When the EU thresholds are met, the concentration must be notified to the Commission and clearance awaited before the transaction is implemented. The obligation to make a notification may rest on one or more parties depending on the nature of the transaction. In the case of mergers or transactions involving the acquisition of joint control, the notification must be made jointly by the parties to the merger or by those acquiring joint control as the case may be. In the case of an acquisition of sole control, only the acquiring party is required to notify.[87]

2. Formal notification must be made on the prescribed form prior to closing of the transaction. Notification can be made at any time following the conclusion of an agreement, the announcement of a public bid or the acquisition of a controlling interest. The undertakings concerned may choose to notify even earlier, where they can demonstrate a good faith intention to conclude an agreement or, in the case of a public bid, where they have publicly announced an intention to make such a bid.[88]

3. In cases eligible for review under the Commission's so-called simplified procedure, the much less onerous Short Form Notification can be used instead of Form CO. The simplified procedure can be used where there are no 'affected markets' (*ie*, in horizontal mergers, markets where the transaction will lead to a combined share of 15 per cent or more and in vertical mergers, where there is an individual or combined share of 25 per cent in a market upstream or downstream from one in which any of the parties is engaged). A Short Form Notification can usually be completed in a day or two if necessary.

4. Where the simplified procedure is not available, notification is made on Form CO, a standard form document that requires the compilation of a great deal of detailed information concerning the parties to the transaction, the markets potentially affected by the transaction, and the parties' activities in those markets.[89] In a complex transaction, the Form CO can extend to 100 pages or more in length and will also have several volumes of exhibits, most of which are prepared by the

---

87. Merger Regulation [2004] OJ L24/1, Article 4(2).
88. Merger Regulation [2004] OJ L24/1, Article 4(1).
89. The information required in Form CO is set out in Annex I to the Merger Implementing Regulation [2004] OJ L133/1, as amended.

company and its lawyers in support of the transaction. Due to the detailed nature of the information required, the preparation of a Form CO filing can be a time-consuming and resource-intensive task. The greater the overlaps between the parties and the more significant the potential competition issues, the more detailed the Form CO that will be required. Where the transaction raises competition issues, the Form CO may involve the input of numerous business people, lawyers and economists and often one or more drafts will be filed with the Commission and feedback received before the formal filing is made.

5.   The information that must be provided on Form CO includes:

S.1	A summary description of the concentration	The level of detail required will depend on the complexity of the transaction. Usually a transaction can be described adequately in a page or two. For transactions with complex structures, it may be advisable to include structure charts.
S.2	Information about the parties	Straightforward descriptions are called for.
S.3	Details of the concentration	As well as a description of the transaction, which can be similar to that provided in section 1, the parties' country-by-country turnover in the EU must be provided.
S.4	Ownership and control	List of subsidiaries and parent companies, which is often provided as an annex.
S.5	Supporting documentation	As well as transaction documents and annual reports, the parties must submit copies of analyses, reports, studies, surveys and comparable documents prepared by or for any member of the board of directors or the supervisory board or similar person for the purpose of assessing or analysing the concentration with respect to market shares, competitive conditions, competitors, the rationale for the transaction, potential for growth and general market conditions. The parties' lawyers will typically assist in indentifying what documents are required.
S.6	Market definitions	The parties set out their views on the appropriate product and geographic market definitions in respect of affected markets.
		A good starting point is sometimes provided by examining the Commission's approach to market definition in previous merger cases in the same sector. Although they are not made public, it can also be useful to review a previous Form CO in the same sector (which one of the parties may have from a previous transaction).
		In cases that raise substantive issues, the parties will often use section 6 to set out in detail their arguments in defence of the transaction, discussing market concentration, competitive dynamics, structural features such as entry barriers, and the relative strength of competitors and potential new entrants. It is not unusual in such cases for section 6 to be lengthy.

S.6   Market definitions (contd)

In a transaction that raises substantive issues, the following would often be covered (this list assumes a transaction concerning manufactured products):

• Customers and end uses for each of the products.

• Any products that customers consider as a viable alternative or that they would consider as such an alternative if prices were to increase on a permanent basis by 5–10 per cent, with concrete examples of situations where customers actually switched between the different products.

• A description of the manufacturing and marketing processes for each product or group of products.

• Whether the production equipment and processes employed could also be used (or are in fact used) for the manufacture of other products, with estimates of the time and expenses involved in switching production from one product to the other and concrete examples of situations where such switching has actually occurred.

• Descriptions of activities of either party that are vertically linked or neighbouring to the products.

• **Information on the following subjects (based on third party sources wherever possible):**

• Transportation costs (expressed as a percentage of the sales value).

• Differences in technical standards between (i) EEA Member States and (ii) the various world regions.

• The existence of customs duties for imports into the EEA.

• The existence of government regulations or other non-tariff barriers that restrain intra-EU trade and trade between world regions.

• The extent of imports into the EEA (expressed as percentage of total sales in the EEA) and the description of recent trends and expected future developments in this context.

• The extent of cross-border trade between EEA Member States (a starting point in this respect may be the location of production facilities and the final destination of the products manufactured there).

• Price differences between (i) EEA Member States and (ii) the various world regions (more detailed information on prices is required in section 7, see below) and the description of recent trends and expected future developments in this context.

S.7 &8   Information on affected markets

Sections 7 and 8 of the Form CO call for detailed description of the parties' activities and the competitive conditions in each 'affected market'. The following information would need to be collected in order to respond to sections 7 and 8:

• Market size data by value and volume in the preceding three years.

• Parties' sales by value and volume in the preceding three years.

• Parties' and competitors' shares of sales data in the preceding three years.

• Competitor contact details.

• Contact details of the five largest suppliers (of input materials) in each affected market.

• Contact details of the five largest customers in each affected market.

• Information on the parties' distribution systems (eg, the use of exclusive distribution arrangements) and service networks.

• Details about how the parties set prices and price comparisons in each Member State and comparisons between prices in the EU and other areas.

• Information on the parties' worldwide production facilities.

• Information on the parties' production capacity and capacity utilization in the EEA and worldwide. Also information concerning past developments and current trends concerning production capacity and capacity utilization.

• General information about the development of demand in recent years, and the expected development in the near and mid-term future.

• A description of existing barriers to entry.

• Information on actual market entrants in the previous five years. This includes:

• market newcomers, *i.e.*, those companies that have so far not been active in the affected markets or any neighbouring markets;

• companies that have been active in such neighbouring markets but have recently enlarged their product portfolio to include also products that form part of an affected market; and

S.7 &8	Information on affected markets (contd)	• companies that have already been active in affected markets but have recently broadened the geographic scope of their activities.
		• The same information for potential market entrants over the next five years.
		• Details on the parties' R&D expenditure (both as a total amount and as a percentage of turnover derived from the sale of the products concerned). Also information concerning the importance of R&D in the various affected markets and estimates of the industry-wide average of R&D expenses, expressed as a percentage of industry-wide turnover, major R&D achievements in the various affected markets in the past (in particular, in terms of technical innovation) and the areas that are currently the focus of the parties' and their main competitors' R&D activities.
		• Information on cooperative arrangements involving the parties (eg, in the R&D or marketing area).
		• Information on the memberships of the parties, its main suppliers and main customers in (national and international) trade associations.
S.8	General conditions in affected markets	Details about structures of supply and demand, market entry, research and development, cooperative agreements and trade associations, including contact details for the top five suppliers and customers in each affected market. Again, the completion of this section can take some time, especially where there are many affected markets.
S.9	Efficiencies	The parties can set out details about claimed efficiencies.
S.10	Cooperative effects of a joint venture	This section is only relevant for joint ventures. It requires data if parents remain in the same market as the joint venture or operate upstream or downstream.

Is there a sanction for failing to notify?

6.   The Commission may impose fines of up to 10 per cent of worldwide turnover on undertakings that intentionally or negligently fail to comply with the notification obligation.[90] The intentional or negligent provision of incorrect or misleading information in a submission under the Merger Regulation carries the risk of a fine

---

90. Merger Regulation [2004] OJ L24/1, Article 14(2). See COMP/M.4994 *Electrabel/ Compagnie Nationale du Rhone*, C(2009) 4416 final, Commission Decision of 10 June 2009, para 56 (€20 million fine for failure to notify) (appeal pending, Case T–332/09 *Electrabel v Commission*).

of up to 1 per cent of worldwide turnover.[91] In addition to these potential sanctions, the validity of the transaction is suspended until such time as it has been notified and approved.

Must the parties wait for the Commission's clearance before closing the transaction?

7.   Notifiable transactions other than public bids or on-market purchases (acquisition of shares through a stock exchange) cannot lawfully be closed until approved by the Commission.[92] The Commission may grant derogations from the suspensory obligation, for example, where the target company is in a state of rapidly declining solvency or would suffer irreparable harm from a delay in closing the sale. In making the decision, the Commission will consider the effects on competition and may attach conditions to any derogation granted.[93] Over 100 derogations have been granted since 1990.[94]

8.   The suspensory obligation does not apply to public bids and on-market transactions provided that the transaction is notified without delay and the acquirer refrains from exercising voting rights attaching to the securities in question or does so only to maintain their value on the basis of a derogation granted by the Commission.[95]

9.   The Commission's review may be completed in Phase I if the transaction does not raise concerns or where the parties negotiate remedies up-front to negate any competition concerns. If the transaction raises serious competition issues that are not resolved in Phase I, the Commission may open an in-depth investigation, a Phase II review.

Key Sources

Form CO in Annex I to Commission Regulation (EC) No 802/2004 of 7 April 2004 implementing Council Regulation (EC) No 139/2004 on the control of concentrations between undertakings.

---

91.   Merger Regulation [2004] OJ L24/1, Article 14(1).
92.   Merger Regulation [2004] OJ L24/1, Article 7(1).
93.   Merger Regulation [2004] OJ L24/1, Article 7(3).
94.   http://ec.europa.eu/competition/mergers/statistics.pdf.
95.   Merger Regulation [2004] OJ L24/1, Article 7(2).

71. **WHAT IS THE TIMETABLE FOR A MERGER REVIEW BEFORE THE COMMISSION?**

1.   The Commission's review procedure under the Merger Regulation may comprise three separate phases:

   •   Pre-notification.

   •   Phase I.

   •   Phase II, for transactions that raise 'serious doubts'.

2.   The Merger Regulation does not require a pre-notification phase but as a practical matter, merging parties will usually engage with DG Competition before the formal filing of the Form CO is made. This informal contact is encouraged by the Commission and can be conducted on a confidential basis as usually, the transaction will not have been made public at this time. It is not uncommon for parties to submit a memorandum setting out the competitive effects of the proposed transaction. Meetings may also be arranged depending on the extent and complexity of the competition issues. The pre-notification phase is also often used to submit a draft of the Form CO and allow the Commission staff to comment on it and ensure that when the formal filing is made, it is drafted to the Commission's satisfaction.

3.   The formal filing of the Form CO triggers a timetable for review under the Merger Regulation. In Phase I, the Commission may approve the transaction – either unconditionally or on the basis of remedies – or initiate an in-depth Phase II review.

4.   From the day following the receipt of the Form CO, the Commission has 25 working days to approve the transaction or initiate Phase II.[96] A working day is any day other than Saturday, Sunday or a day that the Commission recognises as a public holiday. The Phase I period is extended to 35 working days if the parties offer commitments to remedy competition problems or a referral is sought by a Member State.[97]

5.   Where the Commission finds that the transaction raises 'serious doubts as to its compatibility with the common market,' it will launch an in-depth Phase II investigation.[98] This triggers a new 90-day timetable that may be extended where the Commission or the parties 'stop the clock' or where the parties offer commitments (unless the commitments were offered less than 55 working days after the initiation of Phase II). The following is an indicative timetable of Phase II:

   •   **Start of Phase II**. The Commission decides to 'initiate proceedings', *i.e.* launch Phase II, by issuing the parties a confidential written decision, which sets out the Commission's 'serious doubts'.

---

96.   Merger Regulation [2004] OJ L24/1, Article 6(1)(b), Article 10(1).
97.   Merger Regulation [2004] OJ L24/1, Article 10(1).
98.   Merger Regulation [2004] OJ L24/1, Article 6(1)(c).

- **State of Play Meeting**. Pursuant to its Best Practices Guidelines, the Commission will usually hold a State of Play meeting within 10 days of initiating Phase II. The main purpose of the meeting is to enable the parties to understand the Commission's concerns at an early stage of Phase II.

- **Questionnaires**. During the first 6 weeks of the Phase II review, the Commission will continue to gather information on areas of concern to it. The Commission typically sends detailed questionnaires to the merging parties and their principal customers, suppliers and competitors (details of which will have had to be provided by the merging parties in the Form CO).

- **Stop the Clock**. It is possible that the clock will be stopped either on the initiation of the parties or the Commission. The parties have one opportunity to stop the clock. They must make the request within 15 days of the start of Phase II. Any time after the initiation of Phase II, the Commission may extend the timetable with the parties' agreement. The total duration of any extensions to the timetable cannot be more than 20 days.[99]

- **Triangular meetings**. DG Competition may decide to invite the notifying parties and third parties to voluntarily attend a 'triangular' meeting. Such meetings should take place 'as early as possible' in Phase II and 'would take place in situations where two or more opposing views have been put forward as to key market data and characteristics and the effects of the concentration on competition in the markets concerned'. The purpose of such meetings is seen as enabling DG Competition 'to reach a more informed conclusion as to the relevant market characteristics and to clarify issues of substance before deciding on the issuing of an SO'.[100]

- **State of Play Meeting before SO**. A state of play meeting may be held before the adoption of the SO.[101]

- **Statement of Objections**. The Commission usually issues the SO, setting out the Commission's concerns about the transaction, 7–9 weeks after the initiation of Phase II. Any objections upon which the Commission wishes to base its final decision must be set out in the SO. However, the SO is a provisional document and the Commission can amend its assessment based on observations submitted to it by the parties and subsequent findings of fact.[102] The Commission invites the parties to submit a written reply to the SO within a set time period, usually two weeks.

---

99. Merger Regulation [2004] OJ L24/1, Article 10(3).
100. Best Practices Guidelines, paras 38–39.
101. Best Practices Guidelines, paras 33(c).
102. See Case C–413/06P *Bertelsmann AG v Impala* [2008] ECR I–4951, [2008] 5 CMLR 1073, para 63 *et seq*. The requirement on the Commission to notify the parties in writing of its objections is based on Article 18(1) of the Merger Regulation and Article 13(2) of the Merger Implementing Regulation.

- **Access to the file**. The issuance of the SO triggers the parties' rights of access to the Commission's file.[103] This requires the Commission to give the merging parties copies of documents and other evidence on which it has relied in drafting the SO. Certain documents, such as internal Commission correspondence and business secrets of third parties, do not have to be disclosed.

- **Oral hearing**. The parties may request to have an oral hearing at which they can make arguments and present evidence. If so requested, the oral hearing would usually take place around two weeks after the issuance of the SO. The oral hearing is presided over by a Hearing Officer.[104]

- **State of play meeting after reply to SO**. A state of play meeting may be held after the reply to the SO and after any oral hearing. As well as affording the parties an opportunity to understand DG Competition's current position, this meeting may serve as an opportunity to discuss possible remedies.[105]

- **Final chance to submit undertakings**. Within 65 days of the initiation of Phase II (this will usually be after any oral hearing and around a month before the deadline for the Commission's final decision), the parties must submit any proposed remedies they wish the Commission to consider.[106]

- **Preparation of final decision**. In the weeks following the reply by the parties to the SO and the oral hearing if one was held, the Commission prepares its final decision.

- **State of Play Meeting before Advisory Committee meeting**. Another state of play meeting may take place prior to the meeting of the Advisory Committee. This meeting would usually be to discuss proposed remedies.[107]

- **Advisory Committee**. Approximately 14–17 weeks after the initiation of Phase II, the draft decision is reviewed by the Advisory Committee on concentrations, a body comprising representatives of the competition authorities of the Member States. The Advisory Committee delivers an opinion on the Commission's draft decision. This opinion has no binding effect but the Commission is to take 'utmost account' of it.[108]

- **Adoption of the decision**. The draft decision is presented to the College of Commissioners for adoption. Once adopted, the decision is sent to the notifying parties. A non-confidential version, redacting business secrets, will later be prepared for publication. Typically, precise market share and other

---

103. Merger Implementing Regulation [2004] OJ L133/1, as amended, Article 17(1).

104. See Merger Implementing Regulation [2004] OJ L133/1, as amended, Articles 14–16.

105. DG Competition Best Practices on the conduct of EC merger control proceedings (20 January 2004) ('Merger Best Practices') para 33(d).

106. Merger Implementing Regulation [2004] OJ L133/1, as amended, Article 19(2).

107. Merger Best Practices, para 33(e).

108. Merger Regulation [2004] OJ L24/1, Article 19(6).

sensitive data will be omitted in the non-confidential version or a range produced.

Key Sources

DG Competition, Best Practices on the conduct of EC merger control proceedings (20 January 2004).

Council Regulation (EC) No 139/2004 on the control of concentrations between undertakings [2004] OJ L24/1, Article 6, 10, 19.

Commission Regulation (EC) No 802/2004 of 7 April 2004 implementing Council Regulation (EC) No 139/2004 on the control of concentrations between undertakings.

---

72. **WHAT IS THE SUBSTANTIVE COMPETITION TEST UNDER THE MERGER REGULATION?**

Summary

- The test is whether the transaction results in a 'substantial lessening of competition'.

- This can be evidenced in particular by showing the creation or strengthening of a dominant position.

- However, the test is broader than dominance. It encompasses anti-competitive unilateral effects, which may arise even where the merged entity's market position falls short of dominance.

- The test can also be satisfied on the basis of coordinated effects, which generally corresponds to collective dominance.

---

1. The substantive test for merger control in the EU is set out in Article 2(3) of the Merger Regulation:

   > A concentration which would significantly impede effective competition, in the common market or in a substantial part of it, in particular as a result of the creation or strengthening of a dominant position, shall be declared incompatible with the common market.

2. This *significant impediment to effective competition* ('SIEC') test was adopted in 2004, replacing the substantive test in the previous version of the Merger Regulation, which was based exclusively on dominance.[109] The adoption of this test opened the door to consideration of unilateral effects (or 'non-coordinated effects' as the Commission terms them) falling short of dominance. Such unilateral effects can arise in oligopolistic markets, where, despite the fact that the merged firm does not have market power at the level of dominance, the reduction of competition brought about by the merger combined with the structure of the market and other factors, leads to a situation where the merged firm can increase price and/or reduce output regardless of the reaction of non-merging firms.[110]

3. The concept of dominance is maintained by the inclusion of the creation or strengthening of a dominant position as a particular way in which a SIEC can arise. This preserves the relevance of previous case law on dominance.[111]

---

109. The previous test was whether a concentration 'creates or strengthens a dominant position as a result of which effective competition would be significantly impeded in the common market or in a substantial part of it' (Regulation 4064/89 on the control of concentrations between undertakings [1989] OJ L395/1, Article 2(3)).
110. On unilateral effects, see Questions 73 and 74.
111. As noted in the Guidelines on the assessment of horizontal mergers under the Council Regulation on the control of concentrations between undertakings [2004] OJ C31/5 ('Commission Horizontal Merger Guidelines') para 4.

4.   In addition to single firm dominance and unilateral effects, the Commission can invoke the SIEC test where the merger gives rise to anti-competitive coordinated effects. Such effects generally correspond to collective dominance.[112]

5.   For full-function joint ventures the Commission is additionally required to assess whether they will lead to coordination among undertakings that remain independent and to assess their effects under Article 101.[113]

6.   The Commission may challenge transactions on the basis of horizontal overlaps, vertical overlaps or conglomerate effects. It is relatively rare that a transaction will significantly impede effective competition due to vertical or conglomerate effects[114] and most merger enforcement is focused on horizontal overlaps. The Commission has adopted separate guidelines setting out its approach to assessing horizontal mergers[115] and non-horizontal mergers.[116]

How does the Commission approach the question of whether there are substantive concerns?

7.   In each concentration that it reviews, the Commission starts out by defining the relevant product and geographic markets which merit competition analysis. The market shares of the parties are an important first consideration in analysing the concentration's effects on competition. So-called 'affected markets' for the purposes of Form CO are those where there is (i) a horizontal overlap with a combined share of 15 per cent or more and (ii) a vertical overlap, where one party has a share of 25 per cent or more in a market that is upstream or downstream from a market in which the other party is active (regardless of whether there is actually any supplier/customer relationship between the parties pre-merger). A significant amount of information is required in Form CO in respect of affected markets.[117]

8.   The Commission's approach to market definition is set out in its Relevant Market Notice.[118] As noted there, the most important factor in defining the relevant product market is usually demand-side substitution but supply-side substitutability is also of relevance. The relative importance of demand and supply-side

---

112. Coordinated effects are discussed in Question 75.

113. Merger Regulation [2004] OJ L24/1, Article 2(4).

114. On the assessment of non-horizontal mergers, see Questions 76 (vertical mergers) and 77 (conglomerate mergers).

115. Commission Horizontal Merger Guidelines [2004] OJ C31/5.

116. Guidelines on the assessment of non-horizontal mergers under the Council Regulation on the control of concentrations between undertakings [2008] OJ C265/6 ('Commission Non-Horizontal Merger Guidelines').

117. On the information required to be provided in Form CO, see Question 70.

118. Commission Notice on definition of the relevant market for the purposes of Community competition law [1997] OJ C 372. The approach to market definition in competition cases in general is considered in Question 10.

substitution will depend on the nature of the industry involved.[119] The relevant geographic market is often defined in merger cases as being EEA-wide but, depending on the characteristics of the market, it may also be narrower (national, regional or even local) or wider, up to worldwide in scope.

9.   The views of customers, competitors and others who are often asked by the Commission to comment on the proposed definitions of the relevant markets of the notifying party, may also play a role in the relevant market analysis. Previous Commission decisions, though not binding on new cases, are often a good guide as to how the Commission will define the relevant market in a particular sector.

How should an initial substantive antitrust assessment be made by the parties?

10.   It is important in any transaction that meets the Merger Regulation thresholds to identify at an early stage the likelihood of a SIEC and potential substantive antitrust concerns (it will obviously be important to also identify potential concerns in any other jurisdiction in which the transaction is reportable). The early involvement of specialist competition lawyers will usually be necessary. As well as identifying possible concerns, the view taken on antitrust risk may be important in developing the commercial structure of the transaction, negotiating appropriate terms in the transaction documents and minimising costs and overall risk.

11.   The aim of an early substantive antitrust assessment is to determine the likelihood that the Commission will seek to challenge the transaction or require remedies. The starting point will be to consider the overlaps in the businesses of the merging parties, keeping in mind vertical overlaps and potential conglomerate effects. The next step will usually involve identifying the relevant product and geographic markets. Previous decisions of the Commission can be useful in this respect. Market shares, the structure of the markets, the positions of competitors, entry barriers, efficiencies and various other factors may have to be considered to identify the potential ways in which the transaction could give rise to a SIEC.

12.   For an advisor required to provide a 'quick view' of the antitrust issues in a potential combination of Company X and Y, there are many sources of information that can be called on. The best method of gaining an insight into where overlaps lie and potential issues may arise is often to speak with a business person at the client. Business people often know immediately where the areas of possible concern lie. Obtaining internal company documents that discuss competition can also be valuable and the review of strategic plans and similar documents can help identify the issues. There may also be a great deal of information available in the public domain, whether freely available on the Internet on company websites etc. or in third party research reports on the industry. These various sources may contain market share data, which can be used to carry out a pre-merger and post-merger market concentration analysis. Previous decisions of the Commission and those of

---

119. It can be argued, for example, that in mergers in high-technology markets, less emphasis should be placed on short-term demand substitution and more emphasis on long-term supply-side substitution and potential entry.

other antitrust authorities may be useful, particularly where they deal with the same industry or companies. In some cases, the help of specialist economists will be needed to identify the issues.[120]

13. Various ways in which a transaction can give rise to a SIEC are discussed in further detail in this chapter in Questions 73–74 (unilateral effects), Question 75 (coordinated effects), Question 76 (vertical mergers) and Question 77 (conglomerate mergers).

Key Sources

Council Regulation (EC) No 139/2004 on the control of concentrations between undertakings [2004] OJ L24/1, Article 2.

Guidelines on the assessment of horizontal mergers under the Council Regulation on the control of concentrations between undertakings [2004] OJ C31/5.

Guidelines on the assessment of non-horizontal mergers under the Council Regulation on the control of concentrations between undertakings [2008] OJ C265/6.

---

120. For further discussion of making an initial substantive antitrust assessment, see Gotts (ed), *The Merger Review Process: A Step-by-Step Guide to U.S. and Foreign Merger Review* (3rd edn, 2006) 52–60.

73. WHAT ARE 'UNILATERAL EFFECTS'?

Summary

- Unilateral effects theory says that the merged firm will be able to profitably raise prices without regard to how competitors will react.

- This can occur where the merged entity assumes a dominant position but such effects can also arise where the merged entity will not be the market leader.

- An important consideration is the extent to which the products of the merging firms are close substitutes and how much of a competitive constraint each merging party is on the other.

- Unilateral effects short of dominance can occur in particular in mergers in differentiated product markets.

1. The exclusive dominance test that applied under the previous Merger Regulation was aimed at the prevention of monopolies and quasi-monopolies. The significant impediment to effective competition ('SIEC') test in the current Merger Regulation is broader. However, the concept of dominance is preserved by the stipulation that a SIEC can occur 'in particular as a result of the creation or strengthening of a dominant position'. The concept of dominance, which includes collective dominance, follows that applied in the context of Article 102 and was summed up in a merger case by the General Court as follows:

> The dominant position referred to is concerned with a situation where one or more undertakings wield economic power which would enable them to prevent effective competition from being maintained in the relevant market by giving them the opportunity to act to a considerable extent independently of their competitors, their customers and, ultimately, of consumers.[121]

2. As well as preventing anti-competitive effects brought about by the creation or strengthening of a dominant position, the SIEC test encompasses unilateral anti-competitive effects that arise in a situation where the merged firm falls short of dominance.[122] In this way, the SIEC test fills a gap[123] that had been left open by the exclusive dominance test:

> The notion of 'significant impediment to effective competition' ... should be interpreted as extending, beyond the concept of dominance, only to the anti-

---

121. Case T–102/96 *Gencor Ltd v Commission* [1999] ECR II–753, [1999] 4 CMLR 971, para 200.
122. In its Horizontal Merger Guidelines, the Commission uses the term 'non-coordinated effects' to encompass both a SIEC that arises through the creation or strengthening of a dominant position and a SIEC arising from unilateral effects where the merged firm does not occupy a dominant position.
123. For comparison of unilateral effects and the dominance test, see, eg, Völcker, 'Mind the Gap: Unilateral Effects Analysis Arrives in EC Merger Control' [2004] *European Competition Law Review* 395.

competitive effects of a concentration resulting from the non-coordinated behaviour of undertakings which would not have a dominant position on the market concerned.[124]

3. There had been a concern that under the exclusive dominance test, the Commission focused exclusively on a structural assessment premised upon market definition and market concentration that failed to give sufficient attention to other means to test for anticompetitive effects. In particular, the dominance test was considered to be insufficiently broad to tackle all problematic mergers in concentrated markets. This gap could be closed with the SIEC test.

4. Unilateral effects theory developed from industrialised economics in the 1980s and was first applied to merger control in the early 1990s in the United States. The focus is the ability of the merged firm to raise prices unilaterally even though it lacks the market power to be dominant. Instead, its ability to raise price is based on the oligopolistic features of the market and the removal, through the merger, of significant competitive constraints that the merging parties previously exerted on each other.[125] The merger may diminish competition because the merging firms may find it profitable to alter their behaviour unilaterally following the transaction by elevating price and suppressing output.[126] To put it another way, the merged entity finds it rational to raise price without expecting a similar reaction from non-merging rivals. The merged firm's reduction in output is inevitable as by raising price, it must accept a reduction in volume of sales.[127]

5. Unilateral effects can arise in markets with different characteristics. For example, if the merging parties are very close competitors in a market in which sales are made through auctions, the removal of that competitive force through the merger could itself result in anti-competitive effects. In a relatively homogeneous product market, the merged firm may find it profitable to unilaterally reduce output and raise price. Unilateral effects can also arise where the merging parties are close competitors in a differentiated product market, with, for example, any lost sales resulting from a price in one of the merging party's products going to the other merging party's product. The Commission has described differentiated product markets as follows:

> Products may be differentiated in various ways. There may, for example, be differentiation in terms of geographic location, based on branch or stores location; location matters for retail distribution, banks, travel agencies, or petrol stations. Likewise, differentiation may be based on brand image, technical specifications,

---

124. Merger Regulation [2004] OJ L24/1, Recital 25.
125. For an overview of the economics of unilateral effects theory and its application to merger control, see, eg, Ivaldi *et al*, 'The Economics of Unilateral Effects', Interim Report for DG Competition, European Commission (November 2003) available on the Commission's website.
126. See US Department of Justice and Federal Trade Commission, Horizontal Merger Guidelines (19 August 2010), s 6.1 (differentiated products), 6.3 (homogeneous products) (the 2010 Guidelines replace the 1992 Horizontal Merger Guidelines, which had been revised in 1997).
127. See Bishop and Walker, *The Economics of EC Competition Law* (3rd edn, 2010) para 7.019.

quality or level of service. The level of advertising in a market may be an indicator of the firms' effort to differentiate their products. For other products, buyers may have to incur switching costs to use a competitor's product.[128]

6. The magnitude of the anticompetitive unilateral effect will generally depend on the elasticity of substitution between the merging firms' products, *i.e.* the greater the degree to which the merging firms' products are close substitutes, the more severe is the anticompetitive impact of the merger. The extent of the anticompetitive impact is measured by the respective elasticities and not on the basis of market shares. This means that anti-competitive effects can arise even when the merged firm has a position below that of single firm dominance and it is not necessary that it becomes the market leader.

7. A useful definition of unilateral effects has been provided by the Irish Competition Authority as follows:

> Unilateral effects refers to the general case of a market characterised by a non-cooperative oligopoly, *i.e.* a market with a relatively small number of participants, each of which maximises its own profits, but is taking account of the actions of other participants in the market. Unilateral effects arise where, as a result of the merger, the merged firm finds it profitable to raise price, irrespective of the reactions of its competitors or customers. The term unilateral effects also captures the situation where, as a result of the merger, the non-cooperative equilibrium changes, and some or all of the firms modify their behaviour.[129]

8. A classic example of a case of unilateral effects without dominance is the US *Babyfoods* case.[130] The Federal Trade Commission sought to prohibit a combination of the second and third largest producers of baby food in the US, Heinz and Beech-Nut. Post-merger the parties would have a combined market share of 33 per cent, with the largest producer, Gerber, with 65 per cent. Despite the relatively low share of the merged entity, below the usual threshold for dominance in an EU context, the FTC considered that there would be a substantial lessening of competition. Heinz and Beech-Nut competed vigorously for second position and this competition led to innovation in product development and differentiation as well as placing competitive price pressure on Gerber. The parties ultimately abandoned the merger. The case illustrates how a transaction can raise unilateral effects even when the combined market share of the merging parties is relatively low and they are not dominant.

9. In the United States, merger enforcement in recent years has seen unilateral effects analysis play an increasingly prominent role, while the significance of market definition, market shares and structural factors has been downplayed. This de-emphasis on structural factors is evident in the 2010 Horizontal Merger Guidelines

---

128. Commission Horizontal Merger Guidelines [2004] OJ C31/5, fn. 32.
129. N/02/004 Competition Authority Notice in respect of Guidelines for Merger Analysis (16 December 2002) para 4.4. For application by the Irish Competition Authority of a unilateral effects theory resulting in a prohibition decision, see M/06/039 *Kingspan/Xtratherm*, Determination of the Competition Authority of 25 October 2006.
130. *Federal Trade Commission v HJ Heinz Co* 246 F 3d 708 (DC Cir 2001).

adopted by the FTC and DOJ. For example, there is a greater emphasis on econometric tools and the removal of the 35 per cent market share safe harbour for unilateral effects that was part of the 1992 Guidelines.[131] The 2010 Guidelines do acknowledge the role that can be played by market definition, while at the same time pointing out that the analysis need not start with market definition and that some of the analytical tools used by the DOJ and FTC to assess competitive effects do not rely on market definition.[132] However, the US courts continue to highlight the importance of market definition in the review of mergers.[133]

Key Sources

Guidelines on the assessment of horizontal mergers under the Council Regulation on the control of concentrations between undertakings [2004] OJ C31/5.

---

131. US Department of Justice and Federal Trade Commission, Horizontal Merger Guidelines (1992, revised 1997) s 2.22.
132. US Department of Justice and Federal Trade Commission, Horizontal Merger Guidelines (19 August 2010) s 4.
133. See, eg, *United States v Oracle Corporation* 331 F Supp 2d 1098 (ND Cal, 2004) (Walker CJ, rejecting the market definitions, and evidence for those definitions, proposed by the government, emphasised that market definition was 'critical' in an antitrust case challenging a merger); *Golden Gate Pharmacy Services, Inc. v Pfizer, Inc.* 2010 WL 1541257 (ND Cal, 2010) (Chesney J emphasising that market shares could be considered only after a 'cognisable product market' had been established); *City of New York v Group Health Inc.* 2010 WL 2132246 (SDNY, 2010) (in a challenge to a merger, Sullivan J dismissed the plaintiff's market definition as being deficient as a matter of law and rejected the plaintiff's attempt to use an 'upward pricing pressure' test as an alternative to market definition, noting 'the case law's clear requirement that a Plaintiff allege a particular product market in which competition will be impaired').

74. **WHAT FACTORS ARE IMPORTANT IN ASSESSING WHETHER A MERGER GIVES RISE TO ANTI-COMPETITIVE UNILATERAL EFFECTS?**

Summary

There is no 'checklist' that should be applied mechanically in assessing the competitive effects of a merger. However, the following are among the most important factors:

- Market shares.

- The closeness of competition between the merging parties.

- The strength of competitors and whether they provide alternative sources of supplies for customers.

- The extent to which competitors have excess capacity.

- Countervailing buyer power.

- Barriers to entry and expansion.

- Efficiencies generated by the merger.

- One of the merging parties is a 'failing firm'.

1.   A number of factors may be relevant in indicating that a merger will lead to anti-competitive unilateral effects. The Commission Horizontal Merger Guidelines set out a list of factors, summarised below.

How relevant are market shares?

2.   Although only providing first rather than conclusive indications of market power, market shares are a very important part of the Commission's analysis. The markets will first have to be defined before shares can be established.[134] Under the exclusive dominance test in the previous version of the Merger Regulation, it was generally presumed that a combined share below 40 per cent did not raise concerns. As market shares can significantly underestimate the competitive constraint exercised by firms on each other, the market share threshold above which a merger might give rise to unilateral anti-competitive effects is now seen as 25 per cent.[135]

3.   The Commission uses the Herfindahl-Hirschman Index ('HHI') as an indication of the degree of concentration in a post-merger market. The HHI is a commonly accepted measure of market concentration. It is calculated by squaring the market share of each firm competing in the market and then summing the resulting numbers. For example, for a market consisting of four firms with shares of 30 per

---

134. See Question 10.
135. Commission Horizontal Merger Guidelines [2004] OJ C31/5, para 18; Merger Regulation [2004] OJ L24/1, Recital 32.

cent, 30 per cent, 20 per cent, and 20 per cent, the HHI is 2600 ($30^2 + 30^2 + 20^2 + 20^2 = 2600$).

4. The HHI takes into account the relative size and distribution of the firms in a market and approaches zero when a market consists of a large number of firms of relatively equal size. The HHI increases both as the number of firms in the market decreases and as the disparity in size between those firms increases. By subtracting the pre-merger HHI from the post-merger HHI (this generates the delta), the increase in concentration brought about by the merger can be calculated. Assume in the above example that the firms with 30 per cent each merged. The combined firm would have a 60 per cent share. Post-merger, the HHI would be 4000 ($60^2 + 20^2 + 20^2 = 4000$). The delta, the difference between the post-merger HHI and the pre-merger HHI of 2600, would be 1400.

5. According to the Commission, a merger is unlikely to give rise to horizontal competition concerns where (i) the post-merger HHI is between 1000 and 2000 and the delta is below 250 or (ii) the post-merger HHI is above 2000 and the delta is below 150.[136]

6. It is often necessary in practice to calculate different HHIs using different market share estimates. When carrying out a substantive analysis for a proposed transaction, advisers may have to work with different market share estimates as in many markets, there will be no scientific source of precise market shares.

7. Different HHI calculations can be done quickly by setting up a template using Microsoft Excel. In the following table, the market shares are inputted as numbers in column B. Once the formulas are included in other columns, the same template can be used to quickly calculate HHIs with different market share estimates entered into column B. The following produces HHIs for a merger of Company W and Company Z:

	A	B	C
1	Company W	35	=B1^2
2	Company X	30	=B2^2
3	Company Y	25	=B3^2
4	Company Z	10	=B4^2
5	Merged Entity (W+Z)	=B1+B4	=B5^2
6	Pre-merger HHI		=SUM(C1:C4)
7	Post-merger HHI		=SUM(C2,C3,C5)
8	Delta		=C7-C6

---

136. Commission Horizontal Merger Guidelines [2004] OJ C31/5, para 20.

8.   In Excel, with the market shares entered in rows B1, B2, B3 and B4 as numbers and the formulas entered as above, this will produce the following result.

	A	B	C
1	Company W	35	1225
2	Company X	30	900
3	Company Y	25	625
4	Company Z	10	100
5	Merged Entity (W+Z)	45	2025
6	Pre-merger HHI		2850
7	Post-merger HHI		3550
8	Delta		700

9.   Market shares and market concentration levels do not necessarily provide an accurate measure of the competitive effects of a merger. They may understate the competitive constraint that exists between the merging parties pre-merger. For example, in highly differentiated product markets, some products may be closer competitors than others, a position that may not be reflected in the market share figures. The concept of closeness of competition can also be important in bidding markets and in homogeneous product markets in which firms are primarily distinguished by their capacities.[137] Market shares may also underestimate the competitive influence of a 'maverick' firm.[138]

How can the closeness of competition between the merging firms be assessed?

10.   Where the merging firms' products are particularly close substitutes, the merged firm may have an increased ability to raise prices significantly as the products of other competitors are less likely to act as a competitive constraint. Closeness of competition between the merging parties is a very important factor, in particular in differentiated product markets and especially where the products of the merging firms are considered as first and second choice by a large proportion of consumers. The extent to which rival products are substitutable for those of the merging parties is an important consideration in predicting the competitive constraint that those other competitors could exert on the merged firm.

---

137. See Bishop and Walker, *The Economics of EC Competition Law* (3rd edn, 2010) 371–383.
138. See COMP/M.3916 *T-Mobile Austria/tele.ring*, Commission Decision of 26 April 2006, paras 125–126 (unilateral effects concerns even though the combined firm would not be the largest and would have a share of about a third of the market, where the target, tele.ring, had, as a maverick, a much greater influence on competition than its market share would suggest).

11. A number of factors may be relevant in analysing whether the merging firms' products are particularly close substitutes including customer surveys, cross-price elasticities, diversion ratios and, in bidding markets, bidding data.

How relevant are customer surveys?

12. The Merger Regulation specifically provides for third parties to play a role in merger proceedings stating that 'so far as the Commission or the competent authorities of the Member States deem it necessary, they may also hear other natural or legal persons'.[139] This authorises the Commission to solicit the views of third parties, including customers. It may also consider unsolicited information from customers and customer organisations. The Commission may ask customers for their views on what products are the closest substitutes and to rank the products of different competitors according to different characteristics.

13. In *Johnson & Johnson/Guidant*, the Commission asked customers to identify the first and second next best alternative to the J&J and Guidant stent products they purchased. The data was used to determine the extent to which the Guidant product was considered the best or next best alternative to the J&J product and *vice versa*. The data showed that the merging parties were each other's closest competitors.[140]

14. The use to which customer surveys are put has also be questioned. In *Johnson & Johnson/Guidant*, the notifying parties had argued that because the response rate to the customer survey was only 25 per cent, of which only 30 per cent expressed concerns, this showed that there were no concerns related to the merger. Rejecting this argument, the Commission pointed out that customers were difficult to reach, other customers could not answer the questions because of a lack of knowledge of the field and the question on which the notifying parties had placed particular emphasis – *Please explain your possible concerns (if any) in detail* – had been left blank by the great majority of respondents.[141]

15. The use of customer surveys was criticised by the Irish High Court in *Rye* in overturning the determination of the Competition Authority that the merger of the Kerry and Breeo food groups would result in a substantial lessening of competition. The Competition Authority had asked retailers whether they could

---

139. Merger Regulation [2004] OJ L24/1, Article 18(4). See also the Merger Implementing Regulation [2004] OJ L133/1, as amended, Article 11, 16; DG Competition, Best Practices on the conduct of EC merger control proceedings (20 January 2004) paras 34–37, noting the important role of customers in providing information. See also, DG Competition, Best Practices for the Submission of Economic Evidence and Data Collection in Cases Concerning the Application of Articles 101 and 102 TFEU and in Merger Cases (6 January 2010).

140. Case No COMP/M.3687 *Johnson & Johnson/Guidant*, Commission Decision of 25 August 2005, paras 265–270.

141. Case No COMP/M.3687 *Johnson & Johnson/Guidant*, Commission Decision of 25 August 2005, para 322.

credibly threaten to de-list the merged firm's rasher products post-merger and switch to other brands. The responses to what the Court described as a 'somewhat leading' question were mixed but the Authority concluded that on balance, they showed that retailers would have difficulty resisting a price rise by the merged firm. Cooke J held that the Authority's interpretation of the survey responses was 'flawed and unsound' in light of the broad thrust of the evidence relating to the exercise of buyer power taken as a whole and objectively assessed.[142]

16. It has been argued in the context of US merger control, where antitrust statutes are silent on the role of customers, that customer surveys can be helpful on questions about industry structure, geographic and product demand substitution and acceptance of potential market entrants but that customers will have less information relevant to the likelihood of entry, the extent of any merger-specific efficiencies and the validity of a failing firm defence, while customers will almost never be qualified to offer legal conclusions, such as the proper market definition or likely competitive effects of a proposed merger.[143]

Are cross-price elasticities relevant?

17. The cross-price elasticity of demand of two different products measures how the level of demand for one product changes in response to a change in the price of the other product. Where the data are available to carry out an analysis of cross-price elasticities, the results may indicate the extent to which the parties' products are close substitutes. The application of the analysis will depend on the available data and different econometric tools may be capable of being employed to measure cross-price elasticities.[144]

How useful are diversion ratios?

18. Diversion ratios are another method of assessing the closeness of competition between two products and the likely effect of a merger on prices. A diversion ratio from product A to B represents the proportion of customers of A who would choose product B were the price of A to increase or were A unavailable. The higher the diversion ratio, the greater the extent to which B is a second preference for customers of A. The higher the diversion ratio between A and B, the greater the

---

142. *Rye Investments Ltd v Competition Authority* [2009] IEHC 140, paras 9.66–9.70 (appeal to the Supreme Court pending).
143. See Tucker et al., 'The Customer is Sometimes Right: The Role of Customer Views in Merger Investigations' [2007] *Journal of Competition Law and Economics* 551. On the use of surveys in UK merger control, see Makhkamova, 'What would you do if...? The power of surveys in mergers' (2010) 9 *Competition Law Journal* 43.
144. See, eg, COMP/M.5644 *Kraft Foods/Cadbury*, Commission Decision of 6 January 2010, paras 64–69 (consideration of a nested logit demand system, a particular functional form of demand from which own- and cross-price elasticities are derived; price data from a third party consultant report was used and a Bertrand model of competition employed to simulate the effect of the transaction in confectionary markets).

proportion of sales lost as a result of a price increase of A that will be captured by B, therefore offsetting any loss of profits for the combined A/B due to a decline in sales caused by a price increase.

19. Diversion ratios can be used to predict the likely price increase that will be generated by a merger. In the A/B merger, one way of doing this is to multiply the diversion ratio from A to B by the gross margin of A's product. The price increase can be predicted using the following formula:

$$(M)(D)/(1 - M - D),$$

where M is the gross margin of product A and D is the diversion ratio from A to B.

Assume that M was 40 per cent and that D was 15 per cent, in a merger of A and B, this would produce a price increase of 13 per cent $(0.40 \times 0.15)/(1 - 0.4 - 0.15)$.

20. This model was applied by the Irish Competition Authority in the *SRH/FM104* case in respect of the Irish market for radio advertising, although ultimately the results were not utilised as the evidence did not support the premise that there would be a diversion from one radio station to the other and the Authority concluded there was no firm evidence that the transaction would lead to price increases because of unilateral effects.[145] A similar methodology was applied by the UK Competition Commission in its review of the *Sommerfield/Morrison* merger.[146]

21. While the above model appears to be a fairly simple method of estimating the price rise that a horizontal merger will bring about, in practice, the use of a diversion ratio analysis based on simple formulae has significant limitations and care should be taken in relying on this tool.[147]

How can bidding data be used to assess unilateral effects?

22. In bidding markets, the results of previous bids may reveal the extent to which the merging parties are close competitors. For example, if the price of A's winning bid is significantly lower in bids where B also competes, compared to A's price when B does not participate in the bid, this may show that the presence of B is a significant competitive constraint on A.

23. Extensive bidding data was utilised in *GE/Instrumentarium*. The Commission carried out a series of statistical analyses of bidding data in the peri-operative patient monitoring market over a five-year period in order to assess the intensity of

145. M03/033 *Scottish Radio Holdings/Capital Radio Productions*, Determination of the Irish Competition Authority of 23 February 2004.
146. Competition Commission, Report on the acquisition by Somerfield plc of 115 stores from Wm Morrison Supermarkets plc (2005), Appendix D.
147. See Bishop and Walker, *The Economics of EC Competition Law* (3rd edn, 2010) 564–568.

competition between the merging firms. The Commission examined how often GE and Instrumentarium faced each other in bids and what other bidders participated in these bids. This showed a high proportion of bids where the merging parties only faced fringe players, suggesting that the merger might result in a reduction of the number of significant players from two to one in a third of tenders.[148] Other data illustrated the competitive constraint exerted by the merging parties on each other by showing that a major competitor, Phillips, was least successful when both GE and Instrumentarium were present in the tender. The Commission concluded from this that Instrumentarium bid lower when GE was present and that Phillips bid lower when both GE and Instrumentarium were present. The merger would remove these competitive constraints.[149]

How relevant is the ability of customers to switch to alternative suppliers?

24. If customers of the merging parties face difficulties in switching to alternative suppliers, they may be particularly vulnerable to price rises brought about by the merger. Their inability to switch may be because there are few other competitors or switching costs are high. The problem may be especially acute for customers who used dual sourcing from the merging parties as a means of obtaining competitive prices.[150]

How relevant is customers' countervailing buyer power?

25. As the Commission acknowledges in its Horizontal Merger Guidelines, even a merged firm with very high market shares may be unable to significantly impede effective competition if it faces countervailing buyer power on the part of customers. This is 'the bargaining strength that the buyer has vis-à-vis the seller in commercial negotiations due to its size, its commercial significance to the seller and its ability to switch to alternative suppliers'.[151]

26. In *Rye*, the Irish High Court undertook an extensive examination of arguments about countervailing buyer power. The court found that in prohibiting the merger of Kerry and Breeo, the Competition Authority had made a material and significant error in attributing insufficient weight to evidence that the large supermarkets could exercise significant countervailing buyer power vis-à-vis suppliers of rashers and non-poultry cooked meats. Supermarkets were able to exercise considerable buyer power in different forms, which included not only delisting entire brands from a particular supplier but also 'de-ranging' or limiting

---

148. COMP/M.3083 *GE/Instrumentarium* [2004] OJ L109/1, para 133.
149. COMP/M.3083 *GE/Instrumentarium* [2004] OJ L109/1, para 134.
150. Commission Horizontal Merger Guidelines [2004] OJ C31/5, para 31.
151. Commission Horizontal Merger Guidelines [2004] OJ C31/5, para 64.

the package sizes or formats of particular products within a range or refusing to support promotions, reducing purchases or moving products to less favourable display positions.[152]

Are barriers to expansion relevant?

27. If competitors are unlikely to increase supply in the face of a price increase by the merged firm, then the merged entity may have an incentive to reduce output and so increase prices (there is an incentive to reduce output because the merged firm has a larger base of sales on which it can enjoy higher margins from an increase in prices induced by the output reduction).

28. The problem is exacerbated if the merged firm is able to restrict the expansion or entry of rivals because, for example, it controls the supply of inputs or has control over intellectual property essential for competitors to be able to expand.

What kinds of efficiencies are relevant?

29. If the Commission is to take an efficiencies defence into account, the efficiencies have to 'benefit consumers, be merger-specific and be verifiable'.[153]

When will a 'failing firm' defence be successful?

30. The Commission may clear an otherwise problematic merger if one of the parties is a 'failing firm' and competitive conditions would deteriorate to at least the same extent even without the merger. The Commission considers three criteria to be particularly important for the operation of this defence:

  • The failing firm would be forced out of the market in the near future due to financial difficulties if not taken over.

  • There is no less anti-competitive alternative transaction available.

  • In the absence of the merger, the failing firm's assets would inevitably exit the market.[154]

---

152. *Rye Investments Ltd v Competition Authority* [2009] IEHC 140, para 9.39 *et seq*. See also Gorecki, 'The Kerry/Breeo Merger: Two Views of Countervailing Buyer Power – The Competition Authority and the High Court', (2009) 5 *European Competition Journal* 585. Countervailing buyer power may also be relevant in assessing dominance under Article 102 (see Question 53, paras 18–20).
153. Commission Horizontal Merger Guidelines [2004] OJ C31/5, para 78.
154. It is not enough to show that a company would have been liquidated.

31. These three factors were present in the first detailed application of the failing firm defence by the Commission in *Kali and Salz*.[155] The failing firm defence was also successful in *BASF/Eurodiol/Pantochim*[156] but it has been unsuccessful in several other cases.[157] The Commission has rejected the suggestion that a more lenient failing firm test should be applied in times of recession.[158]

32. In Ireland, the Competition Authority stipulates a fourth condition to be met for operation of the failing firm defence, that there is no possibility that the firm will be reorganised under the process of examinership.[159]

How has the Commission applied unilateral effects analyses in practice?

33. The application by the Commission of the above factors in practice will depend on the particular circumstances of the transaction under review. Some of the factors may be more relevant than others. In recent cases, the Commission has followed closely the approach in the Horizontal Merger Guidelines. For example, in *Arsenal/DSP*, in finding that the transaction would result in a significant impediment to competition on unilateral effects grounds in the EEA market for solid benzoic acid, the Commission adopted a methodical approach in considering the following factors:

•   A high combined market share (over 90 per cent), with other producers having a marginal presence.

•   The merging parties were the closest competitors in the market, evidenced by customer views of the higher quality of their products and internal documents which showed that one was considered a close competitor of the other.

---

155. IV/M.308 – *Kali & Salz/MdK/Treuhand*, Commission Decision of 14 December 1993 (upheld on appeal Cases C–68/94 and C–30/95 *France v Commission ('Kali & Salz')* [1998] ECR I–1375, [1998] 4 CMLR 829).

156. COMP/M.2314 *BASF/Eurodiol/Pantochim*, Commission Decision of 11 July 2001.

157. See, eg, COMP/M.4381 *JCI/Fiamm*, Commission Decision of 10 May 2007 (failure to establish the inevitable exit of production assets absent the merger). For a recent example of a rejection of the failing firm defence in the UK, see *Stagecoach Group Plc/Preston Bus Limited*, Report of the Competition Commission of 11 November 2009, Appendix H (appeal on other grounds allowed, *Stagecoach Group plc v Competition Commission* [2010] CAT 14). See also Competition Commission and Office of Fair Trading, Merger Assessment Guidelines (September 2010) paras 4.3.8–4.3.18, referring to the 'exiting firm' scenario. The OFT has accepted the failing firm defence in at least five cases. See, eg, ME/4036/09 *HMV/Zaavi*, OFT Decision of 28 April 2009.

158. See Note by DG Competition to OECD Roundtable on the Failing Firm Defence (21 October 2009), available on the Commission's website.

159. Competition Authority Notice in respect of Guidelines for Merger Analysis (16 December 2002) para 5.17. Examinership is a procedure under section 2 of the Companies (Amendment) Act 1990, the aim of which is to make it possible to rescue companies in difficulty. This is achieved by the grant of court protection over creditor action for up to 100 days. See, eg, *Re Gallium Limited* [2009] IESC 8, [2009] 2 ILRM 11.

- Customers had limited ability to switch to other suppliers given that the alternative US and Chinese suppliers had limited presence in the EEA, customers were reluctant to switch for quality reasons and switching would require several months' delay as tests would have to be carried out.

- There were significant entry barriers including tariff and transport costs for suppliers outside the EEA.

- In respect of spare capacity, it was found that competitors would have limited ability and incentive to supply more output to the EEA in the face of a price increase by the merged entity.

- The Commission's investigation found that the parties' customers had little or no countervailing bargaining power, a position the Commission found unsurprising given the parties' high market shares.

- Entry by new competitors was unlikely and there had not been any recent new entrants.

- The Commission rejected the parties' efficiencies defence, which was based on the merger generating increased capacity. The Commission found that capacity would increase in the absence of the merger so the claimed efficiencies were not merger-specific. In fact, capacity increases would be higher absent the merger, which also suggested that any efficiencies generated by the merger would not benefit consumers.[160]

34. Another recent case in which the Commission applied the methodology in the Horizontal Merger Guidelines in a unilateral effects analysis is *Ryanair/Aer Lingus*. The Commission found that:

- The concentration would lead to very high market shares on a large number of routes, with a monopoly on 22 routes and a share in excess of 60 per cent on other overlapping routes.

- Ryanair and Aer Lingus were the 'closest competitors' on all the affected routes and were actually competing with each other. The closeness of competition was evidenced by a number of factors including the parties' increasingly similar business models, they had an equally strong position in Ireland and faced few competitors, their cost bases were lower than those of competitors and customers considered them to be closest competitors.

- The merger eliminated actual competition as well as potential competition to the detriment of consumers.

- The merging parties' fragmented customers had no countervailing buyer power and no, or limited, switching possibilities.

- Entry was unlikely to defeat the anti-competitive effects of the merger.

---

160. COMP/M.5153 *Arsenal/DSP*, Commission Decision of 9 January 2009, paras 206–254.

- • Possible efficiencies were unlikely to outweigh the merger's competitive harm.[161]

Key Sources

Guidelines on the assessment of horizontal mergers under the Council Regulation on the control of concentrations between undertakings [2004] OJ C31/5.

---

161. COMP/M.4439 *Ryanair/Aer Lingus*, Commission Decision of 27 June 2007, s 7 (upheld on appeal, Case T–342/07 *Ryanair Holdings plc v Commission*, judgment of the General Court of 6 July 2010). For other Commission cases containing a unilateral effects analysis, see, eg, COMP/M.3751 *Novartis/Hexal*, Commission Decision of 27 May 2005 (serious unilateral effects concerns in the German OTC M2A market despite a relatively modest combined share of 35–40 per cent; a divestment was offered); COMP/M.3916 *T-Mobile Austria/ tele.ring*, Commission Decision of 26 April 2006 (unilateral effects concerns where one of the merging parties was a maverick, even though, post-merger, the merged firm would not have the highest market share; transaction cleared subject to conditions); COMP/M.5611 *Agilent/Varian*, Commission Decision of 20 January 2010, paras 111–117 (unilateral effects concerns leading to commitments); COMP/M.5529 *Oracle/Sun Microsystems*, Commission Decision of 21 January 2010 (unilateral effects analysed but concerns discounted).

75. WHEN WILL A TRANSACTION BE CHALLENGED ON THE BASIS OF 'COORDINATED EFFECTS'?[162]

Summary

- Three conditions are necessary for a finding that a merger will result in a significant impediment to effective competition as a result of coordinated effects/collective dominance:

  - Transparency;

  - A deterrent mechanism;

  - Absence of significant competitive constraints that will jeopardise a common policy on the market.

- In examining these conditions, the structure and characteristics of the market are analysed by the Commission. Various factors are relevant to the assessment, such as the symmetry in market shares, the degree of transparency of prices and whether the product market is homogeneous or differentiated.

- The three conditions should not be applied mechanically but rather in light of the overall economic context.

1. A merger may significantly impede effective competition in breach of the Merger Regulation if it facilitates competitors to coordinate by raising prices, reducing output, sharing markets or engaging in other forms of coordination that adversely affect competition. Such effects may occur in particular where the transaction results in the creation or strengthening of a collective dominant position, increasing the possibilities for coordination among the market participants.[163] Where the merger increases the likelihood that competitors will coordinate their behaviour, even if there is no explicit agreement between them, a SIEC may be found.

2. Coordinated effects are more likely to occur, the easier that a common understanding on terms of coordination can be reached. The case law has established three conditions for sustainable coordination:

   (i) Transparency that enables competitors to monitor each other's behaviour on the market, for example in respect of prices charged or customers served.

   (ii) A punishment mechanism, which can be employed if one competitor departs from the coordinated behaviour (for example, by lowering its price) and

---

162. This question can be read together with Question 54, 'When are undertakings in a position of collective dominance?', as the concept of collective dominance in Article 102 and the Merger Regulation overlaps.

163. Commission Horizontal Merger Guidelines [2004] OJ C31/5, para 39.

which serves as a deterrent from departing from the common policy on the market.

(iii)   The absence of destabilising external factors.

3.   In assessing whether the test for coordinated effects is met, the structure and characteristics of the relevant market are of central importance. In *Airtours*, the General Court described how coordinated effects could arise:

> A collective dominant position significantly impeding effective competition in the common market or a substantial part of it may thus arise as the result of a concentration where, in view of the actual characteristics of the relevant market and of the alteration in its structure that the transaction would entail, the latter would make each member of the dominant oligopoly, as it becomes aware of common interests, consider it possible, economically rational, and hence preferable, to adopt on a lasting basis a common policy on the market with the aim of selling at above competitive prices, without having to enter into an agreement or resort to a concerted practice within the meaning of Article [101] ... and without any actual or potential competitors, let alone customers or consumers, being able to react effectively.[164]

4.   In *Bertelsmann*, the Court of Justice held that in applying the three conditions for coordinated effects, established in *Airtours*, it was 'necessary to avoid a mechanical approach involving the separate verification of each of those criteria taken in isolation, while taking no account of the overall economic mechanism of a hypothetical tacit coordination'.[165] Various market factors should be considered in deciding whether the test for coordinated effects was met:

> Such correlative factors include, in particular, the relationship of interdependence existing between the parties to a tight oligopoly within which, on a market with the appropriate characteristics, in particular in terms of market concentration, transparency and product homogeneity, those parties are in a position to anticipate one another's behaviour and are therefore strongly encouraged to align their conduct on the market in such a way as to maximise their joint profits by increasing prices, reducing output, the choice or quality of goods and services, diminishing innovation or otherwise influencing parameters of competition. In such a context, each operator is aware that highly competitive action on its part would provoke a reaction on the part of the others, so that it would derive no benefit from its initiative.[166]

5.   The following factors may tend to support a finding of collective dominance:

- There are a small number of competitors (the smaller the number, the easier it will be to reach terms of coordination).

---

164. Case T–342/99 *Airtours plc v Commission* [2002] ECR II–2585, [2002] 5 CMLR 317, para 61.

165. Case C–413/06P *Bertelsmann AG v Impala* [2008] ECR I–4951, [2008] 5 CMLR 1073, para 125.

166. Case C–413/06P *Bertelsmann AG v Impala* [2008] ECR I–4951, [2008] 5 CMLR 1073, para 121.

- Homogeneous product markets, with little differentiation between the various offerings of competitors.

- Prices or other competitively important terms are easily available, for example in published price lists (this goes to transparency).

- Where the market is not particularly transparent, the use of mechanisms such as meeting-competition or most-favoured customer clauses, which may increase transparency.

- Demand and supply conditions are stable.

- Markets are not innovative.

- 'Simple' customers (which may facilitate market division).

- Customers do not have significant countervailing buyer power.

- Significant barriers to entry.

- Structural links between competitors, eg, cross-shareholdings, participation in joint ventures.

- Symmetries in competitors' market shares, cost structures, capacity levels, levels of vertical integration.

- The merger eliminates a 'maverick' firm.

- Past coordination in the relevant markets (according to the Commission, past coordination in similar markets may also be relevant).[167]

6. The Commission will also consider what factors tend against a finding of coordinated effects. Obviously, factors that are the opposite of those listed above as indicative of collective dominance, would tend against such a finding. Asymmetry in market shares of the remaining competitors post-merger or a market characterised by 'lumpy' demand (making it difficult to identify changes in price due to deviation from coordinated actions as opposed to changes driven by demand)[168] would be examples.

Key Sources

Guidelines on the assessment of horizontal mergers under the Council Regulation on the control of concentrations between undertakings [2004] OJ C31/5, paras 39–57.

Case T–342/99 *Airtours plc v Commission* [2002] ECR II–2585, [2002] 5 CMLR 317.

Case C–413/06P *Bertelsmann AG v Impala* [2008] ECR I–4951, [2008] 5 CMLR 1073.

---

167. See Commission Horizontal Merger Guidelines [2004] OJ C31/5, paras 42–57.

168. See, eg, Case M.5141 *KLM/MartinAir*, Commission Decision of 17 December 2008, para 348 (unstable demand of leisure travellers on long-haul passenger flights).

76. HOW DOES THE COMMISSION ANALYSE VERTICAL MERGERS?

Summary

- Vertical mergers are much less likely to raise competition concerns than horizontal mergers. Vertical mergers are often pro-competitive and generate efficiencies.

- The Commission adopted Non-Horizontal Merger Guidelines in 2008, which it now applies when assessing vertical and conglomerate mergers.

- The main concern with a vertical merger is that it might lead to foreclosure of competitors.

- The Guidelines emphasise that it is only 'anti-competitive foreclosure' which harms consumers that is problematic.

- This can take the form of 'input foreclosure' (downstream competitors are foreclosed from upstream supplies) or 'customer foreclosure' (upstream competitors are foreclosed from outlets downstream).

- Anti-competitive foreclosure may be total (eg, where the merged firm refuses to supply downstream competitors with inputs) or partial (eg, where prices are raised for inputs).

- It is not necessary that rivals be forced to exit the market for anti-competitive foreclosure to arise.

- The Commission will examine whether it would be profitable for the merged firm to engage in foreclosure. It has employed sophisticated economic analyses in making this determination.

- The Commission must also take account of the deterrent effect of Article 102 in light of the particular circumstances.

1. Vertical mergers involve companies operating at different levels of the supply chain. A simple example is where a manufacturer acquires a distributor.

2. Vertical mergers are considered together with conglomerate mergers in the Commission's 2008 Non-Horizontal Merger Guidelines.[169] The Guidelines have been applied by the Commission in a number of vertical merger cases under the

---

169. Guidelines on the assessment of non-horizontal mergers under the Council Regulation on the control of concentrations between undertakings [2008] OJ C265/6 ('Commission Non-Horizontal Merger Guidelines').

Merger Regulation.[170] The Commission's approach to vertical mergers has also been considered in case law of the EU courts, such as *General Electric*.[171]

3.   A merger may simultaneously raise horizontal and non-horizontal issues, for example, where the merger creates market power for the merged entity in a market that is upstream from a market in which one of the parties is active. This may result in horizontal concerns from the combination in the upstream market and vertical concerns because the merged entity will have an incentive to foreclose downstream competitors.[172]

4.   Non-horizontal mergers, whether vertical or conglomerate, do not result in the combination of substitutable products. They give rise to substantial scope for cost and price efficiencies and are therefore seen as predominantly pro-competitive. The Non-Horizontal Merger Guidelines acknowledge that as non-horizontal mergers do not involve the loss of direct competition and provide substantial scope for efficiencies, they are less likely to raise concerns than horizontal mergers.[173]

5.   The main competition concern with a vertical merger is that it will result in foreclosure of rivals from a source of supply or a market for its goods, resulting in price rises by the merged firm. In the Non-Horizontal Merger Guidelines, the former is referred to as 'input foreclosure' and the latter 'customer foreclosure'.[174]

6.   There is an important distinction between mere foreclosure and anti-competitive foreclosure. Under the approach in the Non-Horizontal Merger Guidelines, the Commission appears to be concerned only with anti-competitive foreclosure, *i.e.* foreclosure of competitors that results in harm to consumers. This is evident both from the Guidelines and the Commission's application of the Guidelines. In discussing foreclosure generally, the Guidelines suggest that it is anti-competitive foreclosure that is of concern:

> Non-coordinated effects may principally arise when non-horizontal mergers give rise to foreclosure. In this document, the term 'foreclosure' will be used to describe any instance where actual or potential rivals' access to supplies or markets is hampered or eliminated as a result of the merger, thereby reducing these companies' ability and/or incentive to compete. As a result of such foreclosure, the merging companies — and, possibly, some of its competitors as well — may be able to profitably increase the price charged to consumers. These instances give rise to a significant impediment to

---

170. See, eg, COMP/M.4731 *Google/DoubleClick*, Commission Decision of 11 March 2008; COMP/M.4854 *TomTom/Tele Atlas*, Commission Decision of 14 May 2008; COMP/M.4942 *Nokia/NAVTEQ*, Commission Decision of 2 July 2008; COMP/M.4874 *Itema/BarcoVision*, Commission Decision of 4 August 2008; COMP/M.5732 *Hewlett-Packard/3COM*, Commission Decision of 12 February 2010.

171. Case T–210/01 *GE v Commission* [2005] ECR II–5575, [2006] 4 CMLR 686.

172. See, eg, COMP/M.4494 *Evraz/Highveld*, Commission Decision of 20 February 2007, para 90.

173. Commission Non-Horizontal Merger Guidelines [2008] OJ C265/6, paras 11–13.

174. Commission Non-Horizontal Merger Guidelines [2008] OJ C265/6, para 30.

effective competition and are therefore referred to hereafter as 'anticompetitive foreclosure.[175]

7. This approach to the meaning of foreclosure in the context of non-horizontal mergers is an important development in the Commission's methodology. Had foreclosure meant only the creation of obstacles to competitors, the threshold for challenging non-horizontal mergers would arguably have been too low and at odds with the accepted view that non-horizontal mergers generally do not raise competition concerns.

8. Anti-competitive foreclosure in non-horizontal mergers can arise through unilateral effects, where the merged firm is itself able to raise price, or coordinated effects, if the transaction results in the merged firm and one or more of its rivals being significantly more likely to coordinate on prices or other aspects of competition following the transaction.

What are the conditions for a finding of anti-competitive foreclosure?

9. For anti-competitive foreclosure to arise in a non-horizontal merger, a number of conditions must be present:

- Ability to foreclose.

- Incentives to foreclose.

- The foreclosure strategy has a significant detrimental effect on competition, thereby causing harm to consumers.[176]

10. It is a pre-requisite for a finding of a significant impediment to effective competition that the merged entity has significant market power in at least one relevant market. The Commission will examine this issue before assessing the merger's impact on competition. The Commission has indicated that if the merged entity has a share below 30 per cent in a market in which the HHI is below 2000, it will not have sufficient market power to pose a threat to effective competition through non-horizontal effects.[177]

How may input foreclosure arise?

11. Consider a merger between a producer of raw materials (operating upstream) and a manufacturer that uses those raw materials as inputs to make a finished product (operating downstream). Foreclosure in respect of inputs could occur if the merged firm has market power upstream and limits the access of downstream competitors

---

175. Commission Non-Horizontal Merger Guidelines [2008] OJ C265/6, para 18. See also, COMP/M.4854 *TomTom/Tele Atlas*, Commission Decision of 14 May 2008, para 191.

176. Commission Non-Horizontal Merger Guidelines [2008] OJ C265/6, paras 32, 59, 94.

177. Commission Non-Horizontal Merger Guidelines [2008] OJ C265/6, paras 23–25. See, eg, COMP/M.5732 *Hewlett-Packard/3COM*, Commission Decision of 12 February 2010, paras 63–65 (in light of market shares that did not exceed 30–40 per cent and the presence of alternative suppliers, the merged firm did not have market power and so the merger was unlikely to give rise to any vertical or conglomerate effects).

to raw materials or makes access more expensive, thereby raising the costs of those downstream competitors. This is 'partial foreclosure'. The merged firm could refuse access to inputs altogether to downstream rivals, which would be 'total foreclosure'.

12. Input foreclosure may enable the merged entity to profitably increase price for the finished product, resulting in a significant impediment to competition. Describing how input foreclosure should be assessed, the Commission acknowledges that rivals need not be forced to exit the market but there must be harm to consumers:

> [For] input foreclosure to lead to consumer harm, it is not necessary that the merged firm's rivals are forced to exit the market. The relevant benchmark is whether the increased input costs would lead to higher prices for consumers. Any efficiencies resulting from the merger may, however, lead the merged entity to reduce price, so that the overall likely impact on consumers is neutral or positive.[178]

13. The ability and incentive to foreclose should be examined. In considering the effects of foreclosure, it is not sufficient merely for rivals' costs to be raised. Rather, the question is whether there is an overall anti-competitive effect after factors such as efficiencies have been considered.

14. The merged firm must have market power upstream to have the ability to engage in a foreclosure strategy that raises downstream rivals' costs (eg, refusals to deal, limiting supply, increasing prices to rivals). As well as its own market position, the position of upstream competitors and their ability to respond to a foreclosure strategy may be relevant. If downstream firms can produce inputs in-house, this may also tend against a finding that the merged firm has market power upstream.[179]

15. The incentive element asks whether it would be profitable for the merged firm to engage in a foreclosure strategy. This involves weighing upstream losses (eg, as a result of refusing to supply downstream competitors) with downstream gains (increased profits in the short or longer term gained downstream from increasing sales or implementing a price rise). Factors such as the extent of the merged firm's ability to increase capacity downstream and its downstream market share may be relevant. In assessing the merged firm's likely incentives, the Commission may consider past behaviour in the market and internal documents that reveal strategy,[180] although in some situations, 'the simple economic and commercial realities of the particular case may constitute the convincing evidence required' to show an incentive to foreclose.[181] The assessment may also involve using econometric tools to calculate potential downstream profit. For example, in

178. Commission Non-Horizontal Merger Guidelines [2008] OJ C265/6, para 31.
179. See, eg, COMP/M.4874 *Itema/BarcoVision*, Commission Decision of 4 August 2008, paras 94, 97.
180. See Commission Non-Horizontal Guidelines, paras 40–45.
181. Case T–210/01 *GE v Commission* [2005] ECR II–5575, [2006] 4 CMLR 686, para 297.

TomTom/Tele Atlas, by applying economic tools, the Commission concluded that the merged firm would not have an incentive to engage in foreclosure strategies.[182]

16. The merger's effect on competition should be assessed in light of efficiencies that are beneficial to consumers, merger-specific and verifiable. There are various types of efficiencies that might be generated. In particular, the merger may eliminate double mark-ups, where an upstream firm marks up the price of an input sold downstream and the downstream firm adds a further mark-up when it sells to its customers. In a merged entity, there is an incentive for the upstream arm to provide the downstream arm with inputs at marginal cost (as they are now part of the same undertaking) and this cost saving in the form of an elimination of the upstream mark-up can be passed on to customers in the form of lower prices.[183] Another common efficiency is the better coordination in the production and distribution process facilitated by the merger, allowing a saving on inventory costs.[184]

17. The pro-competitive and anti-competitive effects of the merger have to be weighed up to determine if the transaction's ultimate effect will be harmful to competition and consumers. As noted above, the efficiencies generated by the merger may result in lower prices being offered to consumers. This has to be compared with the effect of increasing downstream rivals' costs. If this cost-raising effect dominates so that consumer prices rise overall, there will be an adverse effect on competition.

How has the Commission applied input foreclosure theories in practice?

18. An example of the application of input foreclosure theories can be seen in the Commission's Phase II investigation of the vertical merger of TomTom and Tele Atlas.[185] The Commission ultimately cleared the transaction without imposing remedies.

19. TomTom was a provider of personal navigation devices (PNDs) and other satellite navigation devices. Tele Atlas supplied navigable digital map databases, a crucial input for producers of PNDs. The Commission investigated whether the transaction would foreclose downstream competitors to TomTom in the supply of PNDs, examining possible input foreclosure in the PND and navigation software markets.[186]

---

182. COMP/M.4854 *TomTom/TeleAtlas*, Commission Decision of 14 May 2008, paras 211–230.
183. Commission Non-Horizontal Merger Guidelines [2008] OJ C265/6, para 55.
184. Commission Non-Horizontal Merger Guidelines [2008] OJ C265/6, para 56.
185. Similar issues were considered in COMP/M.4942 *Nokia/NAVTEQ*, Commission Decision of 2 July 2008. See also, the UK Competition Commission's report on the merger of EWS and Marcroft, concluding that there would be a substantial lessening of competition from input foreclosure. Divestiture remedies were required (*EWS/Marcroft*, Report of the Competition Commission of 12 September 2006).
186. The Commission also considered possible foreclosure from the misuse by the merged entity of confidential information from non-integrated PND suppliers by the merged entity to gain market share in the PND market.

20. The Commission considered both possible total input foreclosure, where the merged firm would refuse to supply PND makers with Tele Atlas' maps, and partial foreclosure, which could involve raising price, providing inputs of lower quality or delaying the provision of updates to PND makers.

21. Having established that the merged entity enjoyed market power upstream, the Commission initially took the view in its Statement of Objections that since profits in the downstream PND market were much higher than profits from the sale of map databases upstream, the merged entity would have an incentive to foreclose downstream competitors. However, applying a critical loss-type analysis and by estimating downstream price elasticities, the Commission ultimately concluded that a total foreclosure strategy would not be profitable, unless the other supplier of map databases, Navteq, were to respond by raising its prices to PND makers by several hundred per cent, an unlikely prospect. An important factor in the analysis was that map database prices represented a minor proportion of the price of PNDs, so even a large upstream price rise would have little impact on the merged firm's ability to earn profits downstream.[187]

22. In respect of partial foreclosure, according to which the merged entity would increase prices or decrease quality in supplies to PND makers, the Commission recognised that the merged entity would have some incentive to raise upstream prices. However, as it would only capture a relatively small amount of additional downstream sales by increasing map prices upstream (switching costs to Navteq were low), its incentive to foreclose competitors would be limited. The Commission's 'simple profit test' showed that any price increase that would have a non-negligible impact on the downstream market would not be profitable for the merged firm as the downstream gains would be insufficient to compensate upstream losses.[188]

23. In reaching its conclusions on possible total and partial foreclosure, the Commission used economic models to assess whether the trade-off for the merged firm between upstream losses for downstream gains would be profitable.

24. The Commission also considered the efficiencies that the merger would generate, although it had already concluded that there would not be anti-competitive foreclosure. The Commission noted the statement in the Non-Horizontal Merger Guidelines that 'a vertical merger allows the merged entity to internalise any pre-existing double mark-ups resulting from both parties setting their prices independently pre-merger'.[189] The Commission recognised the elimination of double mark-ups as a merger-specific efficiency. The Commission examined whether in the absence of the merger the merging parties would be likely to conclude contracts with non-linear pricing with a price for marginal units of map databases close to their marginal cost (which was close to zero). A review of contracts showed that while volume discounts were common, they were not

---

187. COMP/M.4854 *TomTom/TeleAtlas*, Commission Decision of 14 May 2008, para 223.
188. COMP/M.4854 *TomTom/TeleAtlas*, Commission Decision of 14 May 2008, paras 226–228.
189. Commission Non-Horizontal Merger Guidelines [2008] OJ C265/6, para 55.

sufficient to eliminate double mark-ups. Therefore, the elimination of double mark-ups was largely merger-specific.[190]

How does customer foreclosure arise?

25. Vertical foreclosure can also occur where the merged entity has market power in the downstream market. Take, for example, a merger between a supplier and a large downstream distributor. Here, the merged entity may foreclose access to an important downstream outlet to rival suppliers and thereby reduce the ability or incentive of those suppliers to compete. A knock-on effect may be to raise the costs of downstream competitors of the merged firm. These downstream competitors may face higher costs, as it is more difficult for them to obtain supplies at pre-merger price levels, given the reduction in competition at the upstream level.[191]

26. Again, the analysis has three steps, asking whether the merged firm has the ability to foreclose access to the downstream market by reducing purchases from upstream rivals, the incentive to reduce purchases upstream and whether foreclosure would have a significant detrimental effect on consumers in the downstream market.[192]

27. In testing the ability to foreclose, the merged firm must first have significant market power in the downstream market. The importance of the downstream arm of the merged firm as a customer for upstream suppliers should be analysed, as well as whether rival upstream suppliers have other outlets for sales so that they are not dependent on the merged firm as a customer.[193]

28. As in the case of input foreclosure, testing the ability of the merged firm to successfully engage in customer foreclosure involves calculating whether costs associated with reducing purchases from upstream rivals are more than offset by gains generated from possibly raising price in upstream or downstream markets (or which may involve benefiting from higher downstream prices that result from foreclosure as rivals are forced to raise prices).[194]

29. If the merged firm has the ability and incentive to foreclose rivals, the overall impact on effective competition must be examined. It is only if a significant proportion of upstream output is affected by the revenue decreases resulting from the merger that competition may be significantly impeded on the upstream market.

---

190. COMP/M.4854 *TomTom/TeleAtlas*, Commission Decision of 14 May 2008, paras 241–242.
191. See Commission Non-Horizontal Merger Guidelines [2008] OJ C265/6, paras 58–77.
192. Commission Non-Horizontal Merger Guidelines [2008] OJ C265/6, para 59.
193. See, eg, COMP/M.4389 *WLR/BST*, Commission Decision of 5 December 2006, paras 33–36, illustrating the merged firm's lack of ability to engage in customer foreclosure given that the merged firm's downstream arm was not a key customer for upstream rivals with only 15–25 per cent of total EEA demand, accounted for only 10–30 per cent of the firm's upstream arm's supply and that customers exercised considerable influence over choice of suppliers and had a preference for maintaining a sufficient number of competitive supplier options.
194. Commission Non-Horizontal Merger Guidelines [2008] OJ C265/6, paras 68–70.

If reduction of upstream competition affects a significant amount of output downstream, the merger may result in significant price rises downstream.[195] Countervailing factors such as the presence of countervailing buyer power, competition from new entry, as well as efficiencies generated by the merger will also have to be taken into account.[196]

May vertical mergers give rise to coordinated effects concerns?

30. The Commission may also investigate possible coordinated effects of a vertical merger, where the merger makes it easier for firms to reach a common understanding on the terms of coordination. This may occur because foreclosure effects reduce the number of competitors, for example because a reduction of market participants increases price transparency. If foreclosure results in symmetry in the market shares and position of the remaining competitors, this could also facilitate coordination, for example because it creates an incentive for those competitors to engage in market or customer sharing.[197]

Must the Commission take account of Article 102 when assessing vertical mergers?

31. This issue is discussed at paras 16–20 of Question 77 in the context of conglomerate mergers and that analysis is also applicable to the Commission's assessment of vertical mergers.

Key Sources

Guidelines on the assessment of non-horizontal mergers under the Council Regulation on the control of concentrations between undertakings [2008] OJ C265/6.

Case COMP/M.4854 *TomTom/Tele Atlas*, Commission Decision of 14 May 2008.

Case COMP/M.4942 *Nokia/NAVTEQ*, Commission Decision of 2 July 2008.

Case T–210/01 *General Electric Company v Commission* [2005] ECR II–5575, [2006] 4 CMLR 686.

---

195. Commission Non-Horizontal Merger Guidelines [2008] OJ C265/6, paras 74.
196. Commission Non-Horizontal Merger Guidelines [2008] OJ C265/6, paras 76.
197. See COMP/M.3314 *Air Liquide/Messer Targets*, Commission Decision of 15 March 2003, para 92.

77. WHEN ARE CONGLOMERATE MERGERS PROBLEMATIC?

Summary

- Conglomerate mergers are much less likely to raise competition issues than horizontal mergers.

- The Commission's Non-Horizontal Guidelines set out the Commission's views on the competition issues raised by conglomerate mergers.

- The EU courts have emphasised that the Commission faces a significant burden when it seeks to block a merger on the basis of conglomerate effects.

- The Commission must produce 'convincing evidence' to support a conglomerate effects case.

- The Commission is required to take account of the deterrent effect of Article 102 on the merged firm's future behaviour but the extent of this obligation depends on the circumstances.

1.   Conglomerate mergers involve firms that are in neither a horizontal nor vertical relationship. Conglomerate mergers are considered together with vertical mergers in the Commission's Non-Horizontal Merger Guidelines.[198]

2.   Not all such mergers are considered worthy of even cursory scrutiny. In general, it is only mergers involving complementary products or products that are part of a range purchased by the same set of customers that might raise conglomerate effects concerns.

3.   That conglomerate mergers should be subject to competition scrutiny at all is not uncontroversial. This was highlighted in 2001, when the Commission blocked the merger of US companies GE and Honeywell on conglomerate effects grounds,[199] while the transaction was cleared in the United States. The US federal antitrust regulators are not generally concerned about conglomerate mergers and have not challenged a merger on a conglomerate theory since 1966.[200] While conglomerate mergers, like vertical mergers, are less likely to be problematic than horizontal mergers, they are still scrutinised by the Commission under the Merger Regulation.

---

198. General comments about non-horizontal mergers made in Question 76 on vertical mergers should be noted when considering conglomerate mergers.
199. COMP/M.2220 *General Electric/Honeywell*, Commission Decision of 3 July 2001 (substantially upheld on appeal, Case T–210/01 *GE v Commission* [2005] ECR II–5575, [2006] 4 CMLR 686).
200. Rosch, 'Terra Incognita: Vertical and Conglomerate Merger and Interlocking Directorate Law Enforcement in the United States', paper at the University of Hong Kong (11 September 2009) 7–8, available on the FTC's website.

4.   The main concern with conglomerate mergers is that the merged firm would be able to leverage a strong position from one market to another through the employment of exclusionary practices such as tying and bundling. These 'portfolio effects' or 'range effects' may be problematic if they foreclose competitors to the ultimate detriment of competition, though the ability of the merged firm to engage in tying and bundling is not itself sufficient to establish an anti-competitive effect. As in the case of vertical mergers, the Commission examines the merged firm's ability and incentive to foreclose and whether foreclosure would be detrimental to competition, harming consumers.[201]

When will the merged firm have the ability to foreclose competitors?

5.   The ability of the merged firm to cause foreclosure through exclusionary strategies such as bundling and tying will depend on a number of factors such as the characteristics of the products and markets at issue.

6.   Bundling may take the form of 'pure bundling', where complementary products are only available together in a bundle and 'mixed bundling', where the products are sold separately but the price of buying them together in a bundle is cheaper.

7.   Tying usually refers to a situation where a customer who buys one product (the 'tying' product) is required to purchase another product (the 'tied' product). This can be achieved contractually or through technical means, for example, if the tying product only functions when used with the tied product.

8.   To foreclose competitors, the merged entity must have significant market power in one of the markets concerned. There must also be a large common pool of customers for the individual products concerned, *i.e.* customers who buy both of the products that will be the subject of the foreclosure strategy.[202] The likely response of rivals is also a consideration in determining the merged firm's ability to foreclose. Such responses might include price reductions or the ability to offer similar bundles through teaming.[203]

When will the merged firm have the incentive to foreclose competitors?

9.   The merged firm's incentive to engage in foreclosure strategies will depend on whether such strategies are profitable. There is a trade-off between the costs associated with tying or bundling through lowering prices or losing sales of a product contained in the tie or bundle and the possible gains from expanding market share.

Is there consumer harm?

10.   The fact that an entity has the ability and incentive to engage in tying or bundling is not sufficient to give rise to a significant impediment to effective competition.

---

201. Commission Non-Horizontal Merger Guidelines [2008] OJ C265/6, paras 93–94.
202. Commission Non-Horizontal Merger Guidelines [2008] OJ C265/6, para 100.
203. COMP/M.3304 *GE/Amersham*, Commission Decision of 21 January 2004, para 39.

As the Commission's Article 102 Guidance states, tying and bundling can be pro-competitive:

> Tying and bundling are common practices intended to provide customers with better products or offerings in more cost-effective ways.[204]

11. However, if the merged firm's tying or bundling strategy results in lost sales by single product rivals, the ability or incentive of those competitors to compete effectively may be reduced.[205]

Can conglomerate mergers raise coordinated effects issues?

12. Conglomerate mergers may lead to coordinated effects, for example where the merger reduces the number of effective competitors to such an extent that tacit coordination becomes a real possibility.[206]

What onus of proof must the Commission meet in a conglomerate effects case?

13. Given that non-horizontal mergers in general, and conglomerate mergers in particular, are usually pro-competitive, the Commission faces a particularly difficult task when it seeks to block such mergers. In *Tetra Laval*, the General Court had emphasized that proof of anti-competitive conglomerate effects 'calls for a precise examination, supported by convincing evidence, of the circumstances which allegedly produce those effects'.[207] This statement was approved by the Court of Justice, which did note however that the General Court was not meant to be understood as adding a condition relating to the requisite standard of proof. Rather, it was merely drawing attention to 'the essential function of evidence, which is to establish convincingly the merits of an argument or, as in the present case, of a decision on a merger'.[208]

14. Summing up the burden on the Commission to make out a conglomerate effects theory of harm, the Court of Justice stated:

> The analysis of a 'conglomerate-type' concentration is a prospective analysis in which, first, the consideration of a lengthy period of time in the future and, secondly, the leveraging necessary to give rise to a significant impediment to effective competition mean that the chains of cause and effect are dimly discernible, uncertain and difficult to establish. That being so, the quality of the evidence produced by the Commission in order to establish that it is necessary to adopt a decision declaring the concentration incompatible with the common market is particularly important, since

---

204. Article 102 Guidance, para 49.
205. Commission Non-Horizontal Merger Guidelines [2008] OJ C265/6, para 111.
206. Commission Non-Horizontal Merger Guidelines [2008] OJ C265/6, paras 119–121.
207. Case T–5/02 *Tetra Laval BV v Commission* [2002] ECR II–4381, [2002] 5 CMLR 1182, para 155.
208. Case C–12/03P *Commission v Tetra Laval BV* [2005] ECR I–987, [2005] 4 CMLR 573, para 41.

that evidence must support the Commission's conclusion that, if such a decision were not adopted, the economic development envisaged by it would be plausible.[209]

15. These statements by the Court of Justice should not be read as setting out a higher standard of proof in conglomerate cases. The standard of proof on the Commission is the same in respect of conglomerate mergers as in other types of transaction – that the evidence establishes convincingly the Commission's decision. The Court is pointing out that the difficulties in making out a conglomerate effects theory of harm will mean that evidence of quality will inevitably be required.[210]

Must the Commission take account of Article 102 when assessing conglomerate mergers?

16. It can be argued that in applying the Merger Regulation in conglomerate cases, the Commission should not base its objections on potential conduct of the merged entity that would fall foul of Article 102. If the merged entity were to abuse a dominant position in the future, then Article 102 is the appropriate tool to deal with such conduct.

17. In *Tetra Laval*, the Commission rejected behavioural commitments by Tetra to the effect that it would comply with Article 102 post-merger. The General Court disagreed with this approach and held that the Commission had to consider the extent to which the merged entity's incentives to engage in anti-competitive leveraging would be reduced or even eliminated owing to the fact that such conduct would be prohibited under Article 102.[211] On appeal, the Court of Justice acknowledged that both incentives to engage in leveraging and factors liable to reduce or eliminate those incentives had to be considered and these included the possibility that the conduct was unlawful. However, it would run counter to the Merger Regulation's 'purpose of prevention' if the Commission were required to examine in each case the extent to which the incentives to adopt the anti-competitive conduct would be reduced or eliminated as a result of the unlawfulness of the conduct and the consequences that could ensue. The Court seemed to believe that this would place too high a burden on the Commission:

> ... at the stage of assessing a proposed merger, an assessment intended to establish whether an infringement of Article [102] is likely and to ascertain that it will be penalised in several legal orders would be too speculative and would not allow the

---

209. Case C–12/03P *Commission v Tetra Laval BV* [2005] ECR I–987, [2005] 4 CMLR 573, para 44. See also Case T–210/01 *GE v Commission* [2005] ECR II–5575, [2006] 4 CMLR 686, paras 68–69.

210. Cf ECAP 2004/01 *Hutchison 3G Ireland Ltd v Commission for Communications Regulation*, Decision of the Irish Electronic Communications Appeal Panel of 26 September 2005, para 4.23 (interpreting the *Tetra Laval* judgment in the context of an assessment of significant market power in the telecommunications sector, the Panel noted that 'because the likelihood of error is greater in a prospective analysis, the prospective analysis must be proportionately more rigorous to account for this possibility').

211. Case T–5/02 *Tetra Laval BV v Commission* [2002] ECR II–4381, [2002] 5 CMLR 1182, para 158.

Commission to base its assessment on all of the relevant facts with a view to establishing whether they support an economic scenario in which a development such as leveraging will occur.[212]

18. On the one hand the Court of Justice is acknowledging that the likelihood of future anti-competitive conduct on the part of the merged entity should be examined comprehensively by the Commission. This includes taking into account the disincentives for such conduct created by the fact of its illegality, particularly under Article 102. On the other hand, the Court holds that it would be too burdensome to *require* the Commission to examine in every case the *extent* to which the merged firm would be disincentivised by virtue of Article 102 and other laws.

19. These are fine distinctions and it is not altogether clear exactly what obligations are placed on the Commission. In applying this aspect of the *Tetra Laval* judgment in *General Electric*, the General Court held that the Commission must, *in principle*, take account of the unlawful nature of the conduct and that it 'must … identify the conduct foreseen and, *where appropriate*, evaluate and take into account the possible deterrent effect represented by the fact that the conduct would be clearly, or highly probably, unlawful…'[213]

20. The phrase 'where appropriate' suggests that the extent of the obligation on the Commission to consider Article 102 will depend on the circumstances. In *General Electric* itself, the particular circumstances were such that the Commission erred in failing to take account of the deterrent effect of Article 102. Given the 'extreme nature' of the pure bundling practices that the merged entity might engage in, it was 'incumbent on the Commission' to take account of Article 102.[214] In respect of vertical foreclosure, the General Court emphasised that the Commission 'had available all the evidence required in this case to assess, without the need to carry out a detailed investigation in that regard' to what extent the anticipated conduct would give rise to a breach of Article 102.[215]

When have conglomerate effects been assessed by the Commission?

21. Conglomerate effects cases under the Merger Regulation have been relatively rare. The following discusses aspects of some of the Commission's conglomerate effects decisions.

---

212. Case C–12/03P *Commission v Tetra Laval BV* [2005] ECR I–987, [2005] 4 CMLR 573, para 77.

213. Case T–210/01 *GE v Commission* [2005] ECR II–5575, [2006] 4 CMLR 686, paras 73–75 (emphasis added).

214. Case T–210/01 *GE v Commission* [2005] ECR II–5575, [2006] 4 CMLR 686, para 425. See also, in respect of mixed bundling, at para 468.

215. Case T–210/01 *GE v Commission* [2005] ECR II–5575, [2006] 4 CMLR 686, para 311.

GE/Honeywell

22. One of the theories put forward by the Commission in *GE/Honeywell* was that the merged entity would foreclose rivals by bundling GE's engines with Honeywell's avionics products. While mixed bundling of these products would result in a fall in prices in the short term, the Commission considered that rivals would be unable to respond to the merged firm's bundle and would be forced to exit the market.[216]

23. On appeal, the General Court did not challenge the theory of bundling itself, however it found that the Commission's case on bundling was flawed. There were practical problems in implementing a bundling strategy in general because the customers for the different products were not always the same. This meant that implementing a bundling strategy was more difficult and less likely to occur.[217] This was a particularly important factor in relation to pure bundling, which was 'conceivable only where the customers are the same for each product'.[218] Among the other factors vitiating the Commission's findings on pure bundling were its failure to consider the impact of Article 102 on the merged firm's incentive to engage in such a practice.[219]

24. The General Court also rejected the Commission's case on mixed bundling. The Commission's reliance on previous instances of mixed bundling by Honeywell were irrelevant in showing that the merged entity would have the ability or incentive to carry out the practice and the Commission's use of economic models did not show that the merged entity would have the incentive to engage in mixed bundling.[220]

25. Although it found against the Commission on conglomerate and vertical effects, the General Court did not annul the Commission's decision as it agreed with its case on horizontal effect.[221]

Tetra Laval/Sidel

26. The Commission prohibited the merger of Tetra Laval and Sidel finding, among others, that the transaction would enable Tetra to leverage its dominance in the carton packaging sector to the prejudice of competitors. The merged entity could achieve this by using Tetra's dominant position in the traditional carton packaging market as a 'lever' to enhance Sidel's leading (but not dominant) position in PET

---

216. See COMP/M.2220 *General Electric/Honeywell*, Commission Decision of 3 July 2001, paras 398–404.
217. Case T–210/01 *GE v Commission* [2005] ECR II–5575, [2006] 4 CMLR 686, paras 407–416.
218. Case T–210/01 *GE v Commission* [2005] ECR II–5575, [2006] 4 CMLR 686, paras 418.
219. Case T–210/01 *GE v Commission* [2005] ECR II–5575, [2006] 4 CMLR 686, para 425.
220. Case T–210/01 *GE v Commission* [2005] ECR II–5575, [2006] 4 CMLR 686, para 732.
221. Case T–210/01 *GE v Commission* [2005] ECR II–5575, [2006] 4 CMLR 686, paras 439–462.

packaging equipment, in particular the market for stretch blow-molding machines and thereby establish the merged firm as the dominant producer in that market.[222]

27. On appeal by Tetra, the General Court annulled the Commission's decision, finding that the Commission had failed to show that the merged entity would have the ability and incentive to engage in leveraging and that the Commission decision had been based on manifest errors of assessment by the Commission.[223] An appeal by the Commission to the Court of Justice was rejected.[224]

GE/Amersham

28. The Commission examined whether the combination of GE's diagnostic imaging equipment and Amersham's complementary diagnostic pharmaceuticals would give the merged entity the ability and incentive to foreclose competitors through exclusionary practices such as mixed bundling or tying.

29. Concerns about mixed bundling resulting in the foreclosure of competitors were dispelled given that neither of the parties were dominant pre-merger and given the existence of a number of viable and resourceful rivals which could respond to bundling with counter-strategies such as offering similar bundles and technological leapfrogging as a result of innovation.[225] The Commission concluded that the combined entity would lack the incentive to engage in pure tying (or 'forced bundling') as it would result in foregoing significant sales to customers that did not wish to purchase a tie.[226]

30. The Commission also examined whether the merged firm could engage in technical tying, which could occur as a result of lack of interconnectivity of the merged entity's products with competing products or through so-called time-to-market advantage that the merged company would gain by internalising the knowledge on development plans in products carried out by each one of the merging parties. The Commission found that technological links between imaging and pharmaceutical products were not prevalent and that no interoperability issues were foreseen with future products. On the time-to-market advantage, a third party had claimed that by gaining earlier access to Amersham's development plans, GE could adjust its imaging equipment and the merged firm could market an improved bundle earlier than competitors. The Commission's investigation questioned the feasibility of such a practice and suggested that even if feasible, any advantage would be short-lived. Finally, the incentive to engage in technical tying was lacking given the resulting sales that the merged entity would forego, in

---

222. COMP/M.2416 *Tetra Laval/Sidel*, Commission Decision of 30 October 2001, paras 342–389.
223. Case T–5/02 *Tetra Laval BV v Commission* [2002] ECR II–4381, [2002] 5 CMLR 1182.
224. Case C–12/03P *Commission v Tetra Laval BV* [2005] ECR I–987, [2005] 4 CMLR 573.
225. COMP/M.3304 *GE/Amersham*, Commission Decision of 21 January 2004, paras 38–39.
226. COMP/M.3304 *GE/Amersham*, Commission Decision of 21 January 2004, para 43.

particular sales of Amersham products to the installed base of competing imaging equipment.[227]

Procter & Gamble/Gillette

31. The merger of Procter & Gamble and Gillette combined two leading global producers of consumer branded goods. The Commission examined potential anti-competitive effects arising from the combined firm's large product portfolio of non-overlapping products. It pointed to its earlier decision in *Guinness/Grand Metropolitan*[228] as a basis for the theory that conglomerate effects might arise from the parties' significant portfolio of brands and the fact that the parties had large market shares in numerous product markets where their products did not overlap.

32. The Commission examined whether the merged entity could employ bundling to impose weak brands on their customers, to foreclose competitors from access to limited shelf space or hinder the entry of new products. It found that as the parties' products were not generally complementary in demand, pure bundling was unlikely to arise. The Commission concluded that bundling more generally was unlikely to give rise to anti-competitive effects given the presence of competitors with sufficiently broad product ranges and countervailing buyer power on the part of retailers, as well as the impact of efficiencies generated by the merger.[229]

IBM/Telelogic

33. The Commission considered technical tying issues in *IBM/Telelogic*. There was a concern that the merged firm would have less incentive to offer open interfaces that enabled integration with third parties' software development tools. It had been argued by Microsoft (a competitor) that the merged firm could use a technical tie to withhold interoperability information and that the merged firm would have the incentive to engage in this conduct because it would enable it to leverage market power in one software management market into adjacent markets.

34. While the merged firm would have the ability to withhold interoperability information, the Commission noted that the required degree of interoperability was generally quite basic and any technical ability to withhold information would be limited to new projects.[230] Moreover, the Commission found that the merged entity would not be incentivized to engage in such behaviour, noting the costs from lost sales and the loss of goodwill:

> The costs of engaging in such a strategy include (a) lost sales on the tying products when customers decide not to become locked in; (b) lost sales on the tying products when competitors decide to enter the markets to satisfy demand for interoperable high-end tools; (c) lost sales on the tied products (IDE, ASSP, SCCM) when

227. COMP/M.3304 *GE/Amersham*, Commission Decision of 21 January 2004, para 44–60.

228. COMP/M.938 *Guinness/Grand Metropolitan*, Commission Decision of 15 October 1997.

229. COMP/M.3732 *Procter & Gamble/Gillette*, Commission Decision of 15 July 2005, paras 117–132.

230. COMP/M.4747 *IBM/Telelogic*, Commission Decision of 5 March 2008, paras 254–256.

customers decide to switch away from any of the merged entity's product for fear of becoming even more locked-in in the future; (d) a general loss of good-will, especially in view of IBM's past behaviour in the markets concerned that has been rather open to interoperability and open standards. Every single one of these four categories of costs is potentially substantial; none of them can be prevented from the outset.[231]

35.   Meanwhile, the potential benefit from increased sales of the tied products would be rather limited.

Key Sources

Guidelines on the assessment of non-horizontal mergers under the Council Regulation on the control of concentrations between undertakings [2008] OJ C265/6.

Case C–12/03P *Commission v Tetra Laval BV* [2005] ECR I–987, [2005] 4 CMLR 573.

Case T–210/01 *General Electric Company v Commission* [2005] ECR II–5575, [2006] 4 CMLR 686.

Case COMP/M.3304 *GE/Amersham*, Commission Decision of 21 January 2004.

---

231. COMP/M.4747 *IBM/Telelogic*, Commission Decision of 5 March 2008, paras 267.

78. WHAT IS THE PROCEDURE FOR THE ACCEPTANCE AND IMPLEMENTATION OF REMEDIES?

Summary

- It is up to the notifying parties to offer remedies.

- The Commission can accept commitments to implement these remedies as a condition for clearance.

- Remedies can be offered in Phase I or Phase II.

- In Phase I, commitments must be offered within 20 days of filing.

- In Phase II, commitments must be offered within 65 days of the start of Phase II.

- In respect of divestitures, the parties are typically given a set time (often 6 months) to find a buyer, after which the business may be sold by a divestiture trustee at no minimum price.

- Pending sale, a monitoring trustee will be appointed to ensure the business to be divested is maintained in an independent and competitive manner.

- Failure to implement commitments may lead to revocation of clearance.

1. Where a merger gives rise to competition problems, the usual course of action is for the transaction to be cleared after the parties and the Commission have agreed on a remedies package. An outright prohibition is rare, with the Commission having issued a total of 20 prohibition decisions in merger cases since 1990, whereas remedies have featured in approximately 300 cases in the same period.[232]

2. The Commission may clear a concentration following commitments by the notifying parties to remedy competition problems in either Phase I or Phase II.[233] The Commission typically attaches to its clearance decision conditions and obligations aimed at ensuring compliance with the commitments.

What is the timetable for offering commitments?

3. Commitments may be accepted during Phase I where 'the competition problem is readily identifiable and can easily be remedied'.[234] The competition problem therefore needs to be straightforward and the proposed remedies clear-cut. Phase I commitments must be offered within 20 working days of the date of the receipt of the notification.[235] The Phase I timetable is then extended from 25 to 35 working days.[236] The Commission will consult the authorities of the Member States on the

---

232. See http://ec.europa.eu/competition/mergers/statistics.pdf.
233. Merger Regulation [2004] OJ L24/1, Article 6(2), 8(2), Recital 30.
234. Merger Regulation [2004] OJ L24/1, Recital 30.
235. Merger Implementing Regulation [2004] OJ L133/1, as amended, Article 19(1).
236. Merger Regulation [2004] OJ L24/1, Article 10(1).

proposed commitments and, where appropriate, market test the commitments with third parties.[237]

4. Commitments may also be offered within not more than 65 working days after the initiation of Phase II proceedings.[238] If the parties offer commitments, the timetable is extended from 90 to 105 working days (unless commitments were offered within 55 days of the start of Phase II, in which case time is not extended).[239] Further extensions of Phase II of up to 20 working days are possible and if such an extension applies, the 65-day period for the submission of commitments is extended by the same length.[240]

5. In exceptional circumstances, the Commission may accept commitments offered after the expiry of the time limit for their submission.[241] The parties must justify the granting of an extension and an extension is possible only where there is sufficient time for the Commission to make a proper assessment of the proposal and adequate time for consultation with Member States and third parties.[242] While the Merger Regulation does not impose an obligation on the Commission to consider remedies submitted out of time, it seems that parties can rely on the statements in the Remedies Notice, which allow for late commitments in specific circumstances. In *EDP*, the General Court held that:

> ... the parties to a notified concentration may have their commitments which were submitted out of time taken into account subject to two cumulative conditions, namely, first, that those commitments clearly, and without the need for further investigation, resolve the competition concerns previously identified and, second, that there is sufficient time to consult the Member States on those commitments.[243]

6. The Commission must issue a clearance decision where the proposed commitments result in the concentration no longer significantly impeding effective competition.[244]

What form may commitments take?

7. The parties will typically discuss remedies with the Commission case team in advance of submitting a formal document setting out the proposed commitments. The parties are required to submit, along with the commitments, detailed

---

237. Commission Notice on remedies acceptable under the Council Regulation (EC) No 139/2004 and under Commission Regulation (EC) No 802/2004 [2008] OJ C267/1 (the 'Commission Remedies Notice') para 80.
238. Merger Implementing Regulation [2004] OJ L133/1, as amended, Article 19(2).
239. Merger Regulation [2004] OJ L24/1, Article 10(3).
240. Merger Regulation [2004] OJ L24/1, Article 10(3); Merger Implementing Regulation [2004] OJ L133/1, as amended, Article 19(2).
241. Merger Implementing Regulation [2004] OJ L133/1, as amended, Article 19(2).
242. Commission Remedies Notice [2008] OJ C267/1, para 88.
243. See Case T–87/05 *EDP – Energias de Portugal SA v Commission* [2005] ECR II–3745, [2005] 5 CMLR 1436, para 163.
244. Merger Regulation [2004] OJ L24/1, Articles 8(2), 10(2).

information on the content and proposed implementation of the commitments, together with an explanation as to how the commitments will remove any significant impediment to effective competition. A prescribed form, Form RM, which is annexed to the Merger Implementing Regulation, must be used.[245] Guidance is also provided in the Remedies Notice, as well as in the Best Practice Guidelines for Divestiture Commitments, which includes a Model Text for Divestiture Commitments and a Model Text for Trustee Mandates.[246]

How are commitments implemented?

8.   Commitments are offered as a means of obtaining clearance for the transaction. Once commitments have been agreed, 'the Commission should have at its disposal appropriate instruments to ensure the enforcement of commitments and to deal with situations where they are not fulfilled'.[247] The implementation of the remedies proposed will usually take place after the Commission has issued its clearance decision. A number of safeguards to ensure effective and timely implementation are typically added to the commitments package. These can include conditions and obligations imposed on the parties.

9.   The distinction between conditions and obligations has an important consequence. If a condition is breached, the Commission's clearance decision becomes void, whereas if the parties fail to fulfill an obligation, the Commission has a power to withdraw the decision and impose fines and penalties.[248]

10.   To ensure the structural effect of a divestiture remedy, commitments normally include a non-reacquisition clause, providing that there shall be no reacquisition of material influence over the divested business for a set period, usually ten years. A waiver clause might also be included, which would allow the Commission to waive the prohibition on reacquisition were the structure of the market to change sufficiently.[249]

11.   In the case of divestitures, a fixed period will usually be designated in which the divestment business must be sold. The parties will be given a set time to find a buyer (the 'first divestiture period'), which will usually be a number of months. If they fail to divest the business, a second period will start in which a divestiture trustee may divest the business at no minimum price (the 'trustee divestiture period'). This structure provides a clear incentive to the parties (or at least to the purchaser in the case of a sale) to find a buyer themselves in the first divestiture period as leaving the sale to the divestiture trustee may result in a much lower price.

---

245. Merger Implementing Regulation [2004] OJ L133/1, as amended, Annex IV.
246. Commission Best Practice Guidelines: The Commission's Model Texts for Divestiture Commitments and the Trustee Mandate under the EC Merger Regulation (2003).
247. Merger Regulation [2004] OJ L24/1, recital 31.
248. Merger Regulation [2004] OJ L24/1, recital 31, Articles 8(3), 14(2).
249. Commission Remedies Notice [2008] OJ C267/1, para 43.

12. The first divestiture period will usually be a number of months. The Commission will make its prior approval of the proposed purchaser a condition. To ensure that the divestment remedies the competition problems posed by the transaction, the purchaser must satisfy 'purchaser requirements', typically:

- The purchaser is required to be independent of and unconnected to the parties.

- The purchaser must possess the financial resources, proven relevant expertise and have the incentive and ability to maintain and develop the divested business as a viable and active competitive force in competition with the parties and other competitors.

- The acquisition of the business by a proposed purchaser must neither be likely to create new competition problems nor give rise to a risk that the implementation of the commitments will be delayed. Therefore, the proposed purchaser must reasonably be expected to obtain all necessary approvals from the relevant regulatory authorities for the acquisition of the business to be divested.[250]

When are upfront buyers required?

13. The Commission sometimes requires that the parties do not close the transaction until a binding agreement with a purchaser for the divestment business has been signed. This requirement for an 'upfront buyer' may be imposed if the Commission considers that the efficacy of the remedy will be dependent on the identity of the purchaser. This may arise in situations where only a few potential purchasers can be considered suitable, in particular where the divestment business is not a viable stand-alone business and its viability will only be ensured by specific assets of the purchaser or where the purchaser needs to have certain characteristics in order to remedy the competition problem.[251]

14. From the Commission's perspective, the principal advantages with an up-front buyer requirement are that it ensures that the merger is not consummated until the competition concerns are resolved and it reduces risks of deterioration of the business during the interim phase. In practice, the Commission has rarely imposed the requirement of an up-front buyer.[252]

---

250. Commission Remedies Notice [2008] OJ C267/1, para 48.
251. Commission Remedies Notice [2008] OJ C267/1, para 57.
252. Cases in which up-front buyer commitments were required include COMP/M.5355 *BASF/CIBA*, Commission Decision of 12 March 2009; COMP/M.4844 *Fortis/ABN Amro Assets*, Commission Decision of 3 October 2007; COMP/M.3796 *Omya/Huber PCC*, Commission Decision of 19 July 2006; COMP/M.2972 *DSM/Roche Vitamins*, Commission Decision of 23 July 2003; COMP/M.2060 *Bosch/Rexroth*, Commission Decision of 13 December 2000; COMP/M.2337 *Nestlé/Ralston Purina*, Commission Decision of 27 July 2001; COMP/M.2544 *Masterfoods/Royal Canin*, Commission Decision of 15 February 2002; COMP/M.2947 *Verbund/Energie Allianz*, Commission Decision of 11 June 2003.

When will the Commission demand a 'crown jewel' remedy?

15.   In some cases, the Commission may require the parties to propose alternative remedies, where the successful implementation of their preferred divestiture option may not be certain. If the first remedy cannot be implemented in the prescribed time, the parties will be obliged to implement the alternative remedy. The alternative remedy usually has to be in respect of a 'crown jewel' in that it is at least as good as the first remedy in creating a viable competitor, it should not involve uncertainties as to its implementation and it should be capable of being implemented quickly.[253] A crown jewel remedy will often go beyond what is strictly necessary to solve the competition problem.

16.   An example of a crown jewel commitment can be seen in *Nestlé/Ralston Purina*. The parties agreed to divest Nestlé's branded dog and cat food business in Spain. If the sale was not implemented by a certain date, the parties would divest Ralston Purina's 50 per cent shareholding in a Spanish joint venture.[254]

17.   The Commission will not usually countenance alternative remedies other than where the alternative is a crown jewel. If there is no crown jewel, then alternative remedies may simply complicate the procedure as the Commission has to gather information on both alternatives and negotiate terms of two separate scenarios. Nevertheless, it has accepted non-crown jewel alternative remedies in exceptional circumstances. In *Panasonic/Sanyo*, the Commission accepted a commitment to divest either the Panasonic or Sanyo NiMH battery business, where each divestment alternative was suitable to eliminate serious doubts. The parties were required to ringfence both businesses until one of them was sold.[255]

Will the Commission cooperate with the US regulators in respect of remedies?

18.   The same package of commitments offered to one regulator may also remedy the competition problems raised by the transaction in another jurisdiction. This has led to the Commission cooperating with other regulators on remedies, most notably with the DOJ and FTC in the United States.

19.   The 1991 Competition Agreement between the US and EU incorporates the concept of 'traditional comity', according to which each Party undertakes to take into account the important interests of the other Party when it takes measures to enforce its competition rules. It also includes the concept of 'positive comity', according to which either Party can invite the other Party to take, on the basis of the latter's legislation, appropriate measures regarding anti-competitive behaviour implemented on its territory and which affects the important interests of the requesting Party. The Agreement also provides for the notification and exchange of information between the regulators.[256]

---

253. Commission Remedies Notice [2008] OJ C267/1, para 45.
254. COMP/M.2337 *Nestlé/Ralston Purina*, Commission Decision of 27 July 2001, paras 67–69.
255. COMP/M.5421 *Panasonic/Sanyo*, Commission Decision of 29 September 2009, paras 223–227.
256. Agreement between the Government of the United States of America and the Commission of the European Communities regarding the application of their competition laws [1995] OJ L 95/47.

20.   The Commission and the US regulators will typically scrutinise dozens of mergers a year in parallel and analyse issues in a similar way. This close cooperation has resulted in attempts to harmonise remedies in merger cases. The provision of confidentiality waivers by the parties usually facilitates this close cooperation.[257]

21.   Where the regulators have cooperated and the same remedies will solve the competition problem in each jurisdiction, the substance of the commitments may be the same.[258] However the Commission cannot simply rely on commitments offered to the US regulators as it must attach conditions and obligations to its own clearance decision. The US regulators also usually adopt their own measures, typically in the form of a consent order or decree.

22.   The US Department of Justice has granted clearance to a merger on the basis of commitments offered to the Commission in the *Cisco/Tandberg* case. Parallel investigations by the Commission and the DOJ had identified competition concerns. Cisco offered commitments to the Commission, which included the facilitation of interoperability between its videoconferencing products and those of third parties.[259] Following close cooperation with the Commission, the DOJ decided not to challenge the transaction, citing the commitments provided to the Commission as a positive development that would likely enhance competition in the sector.[260]

Key Sources

Commission Notice on remedies acceptable under Council Regulation (EC) No 139/2004 and under Commission Regulation (EC) No 802/2004 [2008] OJ C267/1.

Annex IV (Form RM) to Commission Regulation (EC) No 802/2004 implementing Council Regulation (EC) No 139/2004 on the control of concentrations between undertakings [2004] OJ L133/1.

Commission Best Practice Guidelines: The Commission's Model Texts for Divestiture Commitments and the Trustee Mandate under the EC Merger Regulation (2003).

---

257. See Question 101.
258. See, eg, COMP/M.3083 *GE/Instrumentarium* [2004] OJ L109/1 and *US v General Electric Company* (US District Court for the District of Columbia, final judgment of 23 February 2004) (same remedies in the EU and US); COMP/M.4000 *Inco/Falconbridge*, Commission Decision of 4 July 2006 and *US v Inco Limited* (US District Court for the District of Columbia, proposed final judgment of 23 June 2006) (same remedies in the EU and US); COMP/M.3558 *Cytec/UCB-Surface Specialties*, Commission Decision of 17 December 2004 and US Federal Trade Commission, *In the Matter of Cytec Industries Inc.*, Decision and Order of 1 March 2005 (the same divestiture, involving European and US assets, was offered in both jurisdictions, however the sale of US assets was not considered a condition or obligation in the Commission's decision (para 41)).
259. COMP/M.5669 *Cisco/Tandberg*, Commission Decision of 29 March 2010.
260. US Department of Justice Press Release, Justice Department will not challenge Cisco's acquisition of Tandberg (29 March 2010), available on the DOJ's website.

79. WHEN WILL BEHAVIOURAL REMEDIES, AS OPPOSED TO STRUCTURAL REMEDIES, BE ACCEPTED?

Summary

- Remedies should entirely eliminate the competition problem.

- The Commission's preferred remedy is divestment of a stand-alone business.

- The Commission may also accept a carve-out of a business that was not stand-alone or the divestment of a brand or license.

- Commitments that do not have a clearly structural nature, such as the provision of access to infrastructure to third parties, might be accepted but only if the effect is equivalent to a divestiture.

- Purely behavioural commitments consisting of promises as to future conduct are unlikely to be accepted as stand-alone remedies.

1. The commitments offered by the parties should 'entirely eliminate' the competition problem.[261] In deciding whether the proposed commitments will eliminate the competition concerns identified, the Commission:

    > ... will consider all relevant factors relating to the proposed remedy itself, including, *inter alia,* the type, scale and scope of the remedy proposed, judged by reference to the structure and particular characteristics of the market in which the competition concerns arise, including the position of the parties and other players on the market.[262]

2. Commitments offered by the parties 'should be proportionate to the competition problem and entirely eliminate it'.[263] It is ultimately the Commission's responsibility to declare a concentration compatible with the common market following modifications by the parties.[264] Consequently, the obligation to ensure that remedies are proportionate rests on the Commission.[265] However, the Merger Regulation operates a 'passive remedial system', *i.e.* it is up to the parties to propose remedies rather than having the regulator impose remedies on them.[266] Consequently, the parties are unlikely to be able to successfully challenge the proportionality of commitments, as they will themselves have proposed the

---

261. Merger Regulation [2004] OJ L24/1, recital 30.
262. Commission Remedies Notice [2008] OJ C267/1, para 12.
263. Merger Regulation [2004] OJ L24/1, recital 30.
264. See Merger Regulation [2004] OJ L24/1, Articles 6(2), 8(2); Case C–202/06P *Cementbouw Handel & Industrie BV v Commission* [2007] ECR I–12129, [2008] 4 CMLR 1324, para 54.
265. On the requirement that competition remedies in general be proportionate, see further Question 99.
266. An example of an 'active remedial system' would be that operated by the UK Competition Commission. See Question 86.

remedies.[267] A third party challenging the Commission's decision before the General Court might be in a better position to argue that the commitments accepted by the Commission were not proportionate.[268] However, it may be open to the parties to challenge the conditions and obligations that the Commission attaches to its decision to ensure that the undertakings comply with their commitments.[269] As the Commission's conditions and obligations are typically inextricably linked with the clearance decision, it will not usually be possible to challenge them in isolation and the decision as a whole would then have to be challenged.[270]

3. Commitments may take different forms and can be loosely categorised as either structural or behavioural in nature. The most obvious form of structural remedy is the divestment of a business, a company or assets. Behavioural remedies relate to the future behaviour of a party. An example, though not one the Commission would likely entertain, would be a commitment to refrain from imposing excessive prices.

4. The distinction between structural and behavioural remedies is sometimes blurred. For example, the Commission considers that the granting of access to infrastructure or inputs on a non-discriminatory basis is structural in nature[271] but this type of remedy could also be seen as behavioural,[272] as it relates to future conduct rather than encompassing the 'clean break' that is achieved with a divestment. Another example would be the termination of a long-term supply agreement.

5. As a rule, the Commission prefers structural remedies such as divestments rather than behavioural commitments and in the majority of cases, competition issues have been addressed by way of divestments. The attraction of structural remedies is that they 'prevent, durably, the competition concerns which would be raised by the merger as notified, and do not, moreover, require medium or long-term

---

267. Cf in the context of Regulation 1/2003, Case C–441/07P *Commission v Alrosa Company Ltd*, judgment of the Court of Justice of 29 June 2010, para 48 (describing the difference between Article 7, under which the Commission can impose remedies where it finds an infringement and Article 9, under which the undertakings offer commitments to meet the Commission's concerns, the Court of Justice held that 'undertakings which offer commitments on the basis of Article 9 of Regulation No 1/2003 consciously accept that the concessions they make may go beyond what the Commission could itself impose on them in a decision adopted under Article 7 of the regulation after a thorough examination').
268. On challenges to Commission decisions, see Questions 83 and 84.
269. See Merger Regulation [2004] OJ L24/1, Articles 6(2), 8(2).
270. See Case C–202/06P *Cementbouw Handel & Industrie BV v Commission* [2007] ECR I–12129, [2008] 4 CMLR 1324, opinion of Advocate General Kokott, para 66 (noting that the undertakings concerned may have a genuine interest in having elements of authorisation decisions that are detrimental to them judicially reviewed in order to obtain an authorisation that is free of conditions and obligations or at least an authorisation with less far-reaching conditions and obligations).
271. Commission Remedies Notice [2008] OJ C267/1, para 17.
272. See Bellamy & Child (6th edn, 2008) para 8.166, considering this type of remedy to be behavioural.

monitoring measures'.[273] In contrast, behavioural remedies by their nature are far less certain as they relate to future behaviour. They require future monitoring, which is difficult and costly to achieve.

6.   The General Court confirmed in *Gencor* that structural remedies were preferable but also indicated that regardless of the precise categorisation of a commitment, the most important thing is that it remedy the competition problem:

> The categorisation of a proposed commitment as behavioural or structural is therefore immaterial. It is true that commitments which are structural in nature, such as a commitment to reduce the market share of the entity arising from a concentration by the sale of a subsidiary, are, as a rule, preferable from the point of view of the Regulation's objective, inasmuch as they prevent once and for all, or at least for some time, the emergence or strengthening of the dominant position previously identified by the Commission and do not, moreover, require medium or long-term monitoring measures. Nevertheless, the possibility cannot automatically be ruled out that commitments which prima facie are behavioural, for instance not to use a trademark for a certain period, or to make part of the production capacity of the entity arising from the concentration available to third-party competitors, or, more generally, to grant access to essential facilities on non-discriminatory terms, may themselves also be capable of preventing the emergence or strengthening of a dominant position.[274]

7.   The Commission will accept divestiture commitments only if they consist of a viable business that is divested as a going concern, which if operated by a suitable purchaser, can compete effectively on a lasting basis.[275] The Commission considers that normally, 'a viable business is a business that can operate on a stand-alone-basis, which means independently of the merging parties as regards the supply of input materials or other forms of cooperation other than during a transitory period'.[276] In its clearance decision, the Commission will typically analyse the independence, viability and competitiveness of the divestment business.[277]

Will the Commission accept 'carve-outs' or the disposal of brands or licenses?

8.   The Commission has a clear preference for the divestment of an existing stand-alone business that is already in the form of a company or a business division. However, 'taking into account the principle of proportionality', the Commission may be prepared to consider the divestment of a business that has strong links or is partially or wholly integrated with businesses retained by the parties and therefore needs to be 'carved out' from its current context.[278] In addition to carving out the business to be sold, a 'reverse carve-out' may be employed, by which the parties

---

273. Commission Remedies Notice [2008] OJ C267/1, para 15.
274. Case T–102/96 *Gencor v Commission* [1999] ECR II–753, [1999] 4 CMLR 971, para 316.
275. Commission Remedies Notice [2008] OJ C267/1, para 23. This requirement is repeated in many Commission decisions. See, eg, COMP/M.5644 *Kraft Foods/Cadbury*, Commission Decision of 6 January 2010, para 176.
276. Commission Remedies Notice [2008] OJ C267/1, para 32.
277. See, eg, COMP/M.5721 *Otto/Primondo Assets*, Commission Decision of 16 February 2010, paras 101–102.
278. Commission Remedies Notice [2008] OJ C267/1, para 35.

extract the business activities they want to retain and divest the remainder of the original business, rather than taking out the activities to be divested.[279] Carve-outs must still be viable and any risks for the viability and competitiveness of the business caused by the carve-out must be reduced to a minimum.[280]

9. In exceptional cases, the Commission may consider a divestiture package including only brands and related assets but the resulting business must be immediately viable in the hands of a suitable purchaser.[281] In accepting such a remedy in *Masterfoods/Royal Canin*, the Commission noted the argument made by competitors that the viability of the divested brands as a business would depend on the market strategy, the established market connections and the commitment to the pet food business shown by the potential buyer. In these circumstances, an up-front buyer was required.[282]

10. The Commission has expressed reluctance to accept as a remedy licenses to intellectual property rights, in particular where a divestiture of a business seems feasible. However it may accept such a remedy where, for example, a divestiture would impede efficient, ongoing research or would be impossible given the nature of the business. To be considered sufficient to allow the licensee to compete effectively, the license must normally be exclusive and without field-of-use or geographical restrictions.[283]

May a combination of behavioural and structural remedies be appropriate?

11. As indicated above, the Commission sometimes accepts commitments that fall short of a divestiture but which have structural effects.[284] However, it has stated that it will only accept such commitments where they are at least equivalent in effect to a divestiture.[285] These may include the grant of access to inputs or infrastructure, where, for example, it is sufficiently clear that such a remedy would facilitate the entry of new competitors.[286]

---

279. As well as effects on their remaining businesses, the method of carve-out may have tax or accounting implications for the parties.
280. Commission Remedies Notice [2008] OJ C267/1, paras 32–36.
281. Commission Remedies Notice [2008] OJ C267/1, para 37.
282. COMP/M.2544 *Masterfoods/Royal Canin*, Commission Decision of 15 February 2002, paras 100–102.
283. Commission Remedies Notice [2008] OJ C267/1, paras 37–38. For an example of a license as a remedy, see COMP/M.3593 *Apollo/Bakelite*, Commission Decision of 11 April 2005, paras 157–163 (the grant of a royalty free license to produce phenolic resins was appropriate given the nature of the products).
284. See Commission Remedies Notice [2008] OJ C267/1, paras 61–70.
285. Commission Remedies Notice [2008] OJ C267/1, para 61; COMP/M.3680 – *Alcatel/Finmeccanica/Alcatel Alenia Space & Telespazio*, Commission Decision of 28 April 2005 (licensing remedy accepted where a divestiture was not feasible as the overlapping assets did not form a stand-alone business and were embedded in the remainder of the business).
286. See the discussion in Case T–177/04 *easyJet Airline Co. Ltd v Commission* [2006] ECR II–1931, [2006] 5 CMLR 663, paras 197–209.

12. If competition problems were to arise where the merged entity could withhold information necessary for the interoperability of different equipment, a commitment to grant competitors access to the necessary interoperability information could eliminate competition concerns.[287] Another example would be a remedy involving the termination of existing exclusive supply agreements.[288]

13. In some cases, a combination of structural and behavioural remedies may be appropriate. In *Friesland/Campina*, structural remedies in the form of divestments were sufficient to solve the horizontal competition problems but the Commission remained concerned about the potential for vertical foreclosure of downstream competitors, including the divestment business, in respect of access to raw milk. To ensure access for competitors to raw milk, the parties complemented the divestments with further commitments that contained both structural and behavioural elements. First, the divested businesses would be able to source raw milk from the merged entity under a transitional supply agreement. Second, a foundation would be set up to ensure access to raw milk for a maximum yearly volume to the divested businesses and other competitors until such time as structural changes in the market were achieved. Third, with the aim of creating a source of raw milk independent from the merged entity and thereby providing a long-term structural solution, the parties would reduce exit barriers for dairy farmers who might wish to leave the new cooperative.[289]

Will the Commission accept 'pure' behavioural remedies?

14. Remedies that are of a purely behavioural nature, such as a promise by the parties to refrain from certain practices like bundling or excessive pricing, are unlikely to be accepted on a stand-alone basis by the Commission. It is difficult to achieve the required degree of effectiveness from such a remedy, in particular in light of the difficulties of monitoring compliance. The Commission has stated that it will consider behavioural promises only exceptionally in specific circumstances and indicates that such remedies may be most relevant in conglomerate mergers.[290]

Key Sources

Commission Notice on remedies acceptable under Council Regulation (EC) No 139/2004 and under Commission Regulation (EC) No 802/2004.

---

287. See, eg, COMP/M.3083 *GE/Instrumentarium* [2004] OJ L109/1, paras 351–358 (commitment to produce medical equipment with 'open' interfaces and provide competitors with data necessary to develop open interfaces).
288. See, eg, COMP/M.2876 *Newscorp/Telepiù*, Commission Decision of 2 April 2003, paras 225 *et seq.* (providing termination rights and waiving exclusivity rights in respect of broadcasting agreements).
289. COMP/M.5046 *Friesland/Campina*, Commission Decision of 17 December 2008.
290. Commission Remedies Notice [2008] OJ C267/1, para 69.

80. WHAT INFORMATION MAY THE PARTIES SHARE WITH ONE ANOTHER PRE-CLOSING AND WHAT KIND OF PRE-CLOSING CONDUCT CAN RAISE COMPETITION ISSUES?

Summary

- 'Gun-jumping' is treated very seriously by the US antitrust regulators but is also an issue in the EU and other jurisdictions.

- Gun-jumping can result in significant fines.

- Between signing and closing, the merging parties continue to be independent entities and should compete, and be seen to be competing, vigorously.

- Merging parties should follow guidelines as to what information can be exchanged pre-closing. As a general rule of thumb, information that a party would normally be concerned about exchanging with a competitor should be treated carefully and be subject to set protocols.

- While the parties can plan for post-merger integration, they cannot generally integrate any of their activities until competition clearances have been received and the transaction has closed.

- It is advisable to set up a 'Clean Team', which is isolated from the operational side of the business, to handle particularly sensitive information that genuinely needs to be exchanged for integration planning purposes.

What is 'gun-jumping'?

1. EU competition law, as well as the law in various other jurisdictions, prohibits the implementation of mergers, acquisitions and joint ventures before antitrust clearances have been received – so-called 'gun-jumping'. In the past, it seemed that gun-jumping was rigorously enforced only in the United States but not in the EU. However, recent developments have shown that gun-jumping is not just a US issue and that integration planning in merger situations must be conducted carefully throughout the world.

2. Prior to receiving antitrust clearance for a merger or acquisition, the parties to the transaction are still viewed as separate, independent entities, who should not 'jump the gun' by exchanging certain competitively sensitive information or taking steps to integrate operations or engaging in other coordinated action. After all, the antitrust regulators may block the deal or it may fall through for another reason. If operations have been integrated or certain information exchanged, the competitive process between what continue to be two separate organisations may be damaged.

3. There is no provision of EU law that sets out a specific prohibition on gun-jumping or defines what is meant by gun-jumping. The EU law prohibition on gun-jumping stems from Article 7 of the Merger Regulation, which provides that, subject to certain exceptions, a transaction which falls within the jurisdiction of the Commission cannot be implemented 'either before its notification or until it

has been declared compatible with the common market'.[291] The potential sanctions for breach of this obligation are fines of up to 10 per cent of the turnover of each undertaking in question.[292] In addition, an improper exchange of information or improper pre-closing conduct could violate Article 101.

4. In practice, the Commission has rarely taken issue with gun-jumping. In one of the few cases where gun-jumping issues were raised, in December 2007, the Commission carried out dawn raids on two PVC manufacturers in the UK, which it suspected of gun-jumping by exchanging confidential material prior to obtaining clearance for their merger. This was the first time that the Commission used a dawn raid in connection with a suspected violation of the Merger Regulation. While no showing of gun-jumping was ultimately made and the transaction was cleared,[293] the episode shows that the Commission takes gun-jumping seriously.

5. Another case in which the Commission raised the issue of gun-jumping was the 1998 review of a joint venture between Bertelsmann, Kirch and Premiere involving a digital pay-TV channel. Before the transaction was notified to the Commission, one of the parties reportedly began marketing the products of another and using its decoder. The Commission warned the parties to cease this conduct, which effectively amounted to implementation of the transaction. The parties abided by the Commission's warning and no further action was taken. The Commission did not challenge the conduct under Article 101.[294]

6. A failure to notify a reportable transaction can be viewed as an extreme form of gun-jumping. In 2009, the Commission imposed a €20 million fine on Electrabel for failure to notify a transaction under the Merger Regulation.[295] In two previous cases, *Samsung/AST*[296] and *A.P. Møller*,[297] the Commission condemned a failure to notify a transaction prior to Commission approval, imposing fines amounting to €33,000 and €219,000 respectively.

7. Gun-jumping fines have also been issued by competition regulators in the EU Member States. For example, in 2008, the German Federal Cartel Office issued a fine of €4.5 million on Mars for a violation of the suspensory obligation in German merger control law in connection with Mars' acquisition of Nutro. Mars had received competition clearance in the United States and proceeded to close the

---

291. Merger Regulation [2004] OJ L24/1, Article 7(1).
292. Merger Regulation [2004] OJ L24/1, Article 14(2).
293. COMP/M.4734 *INEOS/Kerling*, Commission Decision of 30 January 2008.
294. Case No IV/M.993 *Bertelsmann/Kirch/Premiere*, Commission Decision of 27 May 1998.
295. COMP/M.4994 *Electrabel/Compagnie Nationale du Rhone*, Commission Decision of 10 June 2009, para 56 (appeal pending, Case T–332/09 *Electrabel v Commission*), discussed in Question 66, para 16.
296. 1999/594/EC *Samsung/AST*, Commission Decision of 18 February 1998 imposing fines for failing to notify and for putting into effect a concentration in breach of Article 4(1) and Article 7(1) of Council Regulation (EEC) No 4064/89 (Case IV/M.920 *Samsung/AST*).
297. 1999/459/EC *A. P. Møller*, Commission Decision of 10 February 1999 imposing fines for failing to notify and for putting into effect three concentrations in breach of Articles 4 and 7(1) of Council Regulation (EEC) No 4064/89 (Case IV/M.969 *A. P. Møller*).

transaction. Pending the German merger control clearance, Mars attempted to carve out the German business of the target by temporarily assigning the German distribution rights to the target's products to a separate entity held by the seller. Even though it ultimately agreed to divest the target's German business, Mars was still met with a fine for gun-jumping.[298]

8. Competition authorities in other jurisdictions may have the power to impose penalties for gun-jumping. The Irish and UK rules are discussed below. The US rules are also discussed briefly, as it is in that jurisdiction that gun-jumping issues have most frequently arisen.

Ireland

9. Under section 19 of the Competition Act 2002, putting a notifiable merger or acquisition into effect prior to receiving clearance from the Competition Authority results in the transaction being void.[299] In practice, it appears that the transaction remains void only until such time as the Authority subsequently approves it.[300] A failure to notify a merger that is notifiable under the Act can lead to criminal liability for the person in control of the undertaking, who can be fined up to €250,000 on indictment or €3,000 on summary conviction.[301]

10. Gun-jumping could also expose parties to liability under section 4 of the Competition Act and/or Article 101. While the Competition Authority has investigated at least one allegation of gun-jumping,[302] a finding of illegal gun-jumping in breach of section 4 or Article 101, which would have to be established before the courts, does not appear to have been made under the Competition Act 2002.

UK

11. Notification of mergers in the UK is voluntary and there is no general suspensory obligation preventing the implementation of a transaction before approval. The OFT and the Competition Commission could use their enforcement powers under the Enterprise Act 2002 to challenge gun-jumping by imposing orders or requiring undertakings of the merging parties.[303] Gun-jumping could also raise issues under the Chapter I prohibition in the Competition Act 1998 and/or Article 101.

---

298. See Bundeskartellamt Press Release, Fine imposed against Mars for violating the prohibition to put a merger into effect (15 December 2008). Other jurisdictions in which sanctions have been imposed for implementing transactions prior to clearance include Bulgaria, The Netherlands, Norway, Romania and Slovakia. Fines for gun-jumping may also be imposed under French merger control rules contained in Article L430–4 of the Commercial Code.

299. Competition Act 2002, s 19(2).

300. See M/04/03 *Radio 2000/Newstalk*, Competition Authority Determination of 5 March 2004.

301. Competition Act 2002, s 18(9).

302. Competition Authority Press Release, Competition Authority Warns Merging Parties About Gun Jumping (13 May 2003).

303. See Enterprise Act 2002, s 71, s 72 (OFT powers) and s 80, s 81 (Competition Commission powers).

United States

12. In the United States, gun-jumping may fall foul of section 7A of the Clayton Act, which prohibits the consummation of a reportable transaction before the end of the waiting period prescribed by the Hart-Scott-Rodino Act. Penalties include fines of up to $11,000 a day. Gun-jumping may also result in a breach of section 1 of the Sherman Act, with potential exposure to civil claims for treble damages.

13. There are a number of examples of enforcement action by the US antitrust regulators against gun-jumping and the following four illustrate the seriousness with which gun-jumping is treated in the United States and the significant penalties that can arise.

    •   *QUALCOMM/Flarion Technologies.* The merger agreement permitted the target, Flarion, to operate 'in the ordinary course' until closing but QULACOMM obtained operational control pre-closing by requiring Flarion to obtain its consent before undertaking routine business activities. QUALCOMM also discouraged the target from pursuing business opportunities. A fine of $1.8 million was paid to settle the case with the Department of Justice.[304]

    •   *Computer Associates/Platinum Technology International.* Pre-closing, Platinum had to seek CA's approval for customer discounts and standard trading terms. CA also installed a senior manager at Platinum to approve customer contracts. CA paid $638,000 in civil penalties and agreed to restrictions designed to prevent future recurrence of the conduct challenged in the government's lawsuit.[305]

    •   *Gemstar/TV Guide.* Gemstar and TV Guide agreed to stop competing for customers, decided together on prices and terms to be offered, and shared operational control during the mandatory pre-merger waiting period. A settlement of $5.67 million was paid, which amounted to the maximum fine that was available under the HSR Act.[306]

    •   *Smithfield/Premium Standard.* The Department of Justice alleged that Smithfield exercised operational control over the Premium Standard business prior to the expiration of the HSR waiting period – a number of contracts were submitted by Premium Standard to Smithfield for prior approval. Although a Second Request was issued, there was no substantive challenge to the transaction. A settlement of $900,000 was reached in respect of the gun-jumping violation.[307]

---

304. A copy of the DOJ complaint is at http://www.usdoj.gov/atr/cases/f215600/215608.htm.
305. A copy of the DOJ complaint is at http://www.usdoj.gov/atr/cases/f9200/9246.htm.
306. A copy of the DOJ complaint is at http://www.usdoj.gov/atr/cases/f200700/200737.htm.
307. A copy of the DOJ complaint is at http://www.justice.gov/atr/cases/f254300/254369.htm.

How are gun-jumping issues approached in practice?

14. The extent to which information may be exchanged and integration planning
     advanced can be a source of tension between the buyer and seller in some
     transactions. The natural inclination of the buyer may be to seek to control the
     target once an agreement has been signed. However gun-jumping concerns place
     restrictions on what the buyer can do. The seller may take a more conservative
     view of what can be done pre-closing – it will be less concerned about integration
     and may be more focused on ensuring that the transaction proceeds without
     violating competition law. It is not uncommon for the legal advisers of the buyer
     and seller to negotiate what pre-closing conduct and information exchange is
     permissible. Like many antitrust rules, gun-jumping issues can involve grey areas
     where it is difficult to establish a definitive right or wrong answer as to what is
     permissible. Ultimately, close calls may be involved and the parties will have to
     assess and negotiate the level of risk of proposed pre-closing actions and
     information exchanges.

What pre-closing conduct is prohibited?

15. The transacting parties are independent until closing and must act that way. In an
     acquisition, the acquirer must not require the seller to seek its approval before
     conducting the target's normal business or limit the way in which the target
     operates in the normal course. On the other hand, it is permissible for the acquirer
     to prevent the target taking actions outside the normal course of business without
     approval.

16. Any coordination that could be characterised as an agreement on prices or terms of
     trade, or allocation of customers or markets, should be avoided. The parties should
     avoid discussions about prices or specific customers or terms of trade offered to
     specific customers. The parties should not hold themselves out as a joint entity to
     customers or suppliers. For example, they should avoid joint advertising.

17. Similarly, the parties should not coordinate production or distribution. The parties
     should not attend each other's internal meetings. Unless meeting for integration
     planning or due diligence, personnel of the transacting parties should not meet
     without the approval of individuals designated with authority to sanction such
     meetings.

What pre-closing information exchanges are permissible?

18. It is permissible for the transacting parties to acquire a great deal of information
     about each other. A buyer will have to undertake due diligence, which will involve
     a detailed review of the target's business.

19. However, certain categories of information may be too competitively sensitive to
     be exchanged pre-closing. As a general rule of thumb, if a business person would
     be concerned about a competitor having access to the information, the parties
     should exercise caution in exchanging it. Another guide is to avoid the exchange of
     information that would place one of the merging parties at a disadvantage vis-à-vis
     the other if the transaction did not proceed.

20. It is generally permissible for merging parties to share the following information pre-closing:

   a. Aggregated customer information – eg, number of customers by region (but not lists identifying specific customers).

   b. Historical pricing information.

   c. Historical or aggregated cost data.

   d. Previous business and strategic plans.

   e. Lists and descriptions of products supplied and business activities in general.

   f. Projected revenues and profits of the merged entity by general product categories.

   g. R&D plans to the extent not commercially sensitive.

   h. Tax returns.

   i. Information about pending litigation.

   j. Environmental issues.

   k. Descriptions of IT systems, financial reporting systems etc.

   l. Human resources information.

What 'gun-jumping' guidelines should the merging parties adopt?

21. Neither regulators in Europe nor in the United States have stated what conduct or information exchanges will constitute gun-jumping. Decisions regarding what pre-closing conduct is acceptable and what information can safely be exchanged without raising competition issues should be addressed based on the facts of the particular situation.

22. An example of gun-jumping guidelines is provided after this paragraph. The guidelines are merely indicative of the kind of advice that is often provided in the context of mergers. In practice, guidelines will need to fit the particular circumstances. The following general principles may also be useful in devising guidelines:

   • Information exchanged between the parties should be limited to information that is necessary in order to evaluate the business that is the subject of the transaction or plan for integration. Such information should be confined to information relating to the business to be acquired or, in the case of a joint venture, the business or assets to be contributed to the joint venture.

   • The parties should agree a mechanism for the return or destruction of exchanged information in the event that the transaction does not proceed.

   • Information that is exchanged should be limited to a small group of people who genuinely require access to the information in order to carry out an appraisal of the business or plan for future integration. These individuals can be made to sign individual confidentiality agreements. It is important that individuals who could use exchanged information in their day-to-day roles, for example, sales personnel, do not gain access to sensitive information.

- In many transactions, an integration team will be set up to manage the process of planning the transition to the combined entity. This team will usually be made up of personnel from each of the transacting parties and should involve employees from the strategic, rather than the operational, side of the business. It is a good idea for each transacting party to nominate an Integration Leader to oversee integration efforts.

- In the case of very sensitive information, consideration should be given to limiting access to third party advisors, such as lawyers or accountants. Where necessary, such advisors could provide a non-confidential summary of the information to the client, for example, by deleting the names of customers, aggregating sales data, providing average prices.

- Another possibility is the use of 'Clean Teams', involving outside consultants and lawyers and individuals who are ring-fenced from day-to-day activities and who will not return to such activities until such time as any exchanged information to which they become privy is no longer commercially sensitive.

- While gun-jumping concerns are less likely to arise once clearance has been received, as the transaction could still fall apart before closing, gun-jumping guidelines should still be followed until closing occurs. It is also the case that the closer the parties get to completing regulatory clearances, the more integration planning will, of necessity, occur and the more concrete it can be.

Sample client memorandum in respect of general gun-jumping issues

All individuals involved in the merger planning process should be aware of the competition law issues raised by so-called 'gun-jumping'. The competition regulators can take action against merging parties that exchange certain commercially sensitive information or take steps to integrate operations in advance of receiving all merger control clearances.

Decisions on exactly what steps can be taken must be addressed on the particular facts of each situation but the following general guidelines are relevant to the merger planning process.

It is generally permissible for the merging parties to carry out integration planning before the transaction has closed. However there is a risk of breaching competition law before closing. Information exchanged and pre-closing conduct must not be such as to enable either party to limit competition with the other before closing, for example, through the fixing of prices or the allocation of customers. Pre-closing actions must not adversely affect future competition in the event that the transaction is not completed. Furthermore, the guise of integration planning cannot be used to attempt to coordinate the businesses of the parties prior to closing.

Information exchange

The merging parties should exercise great care in sharing any competitively sensitive information. Transfers of such information should only take place where there is a strong business justification and where strict protocols on the use to which the information is put are adhered to.

A number of factors are relevant in deciding whether an information transfer is permissible, including:

- The nature of the information.

- The timing of the information transfer.

- The personnel who will have access to the information.

- The business justification for the information transfer.

Competitively sensitive information

The degree of sensitivity attaching to commercial information may vary between different industries and markets and it is difficult to be categorical about types of information that may and may not be transferred in a merger setting. A general rule of thumb that is often useful to apply is whether the information is of a kind that one would normally be happy to provide to a competitor. Another important consideration is whether the exchange of information would place one of the parties at a competitive disadvantage were the transaction not to proceed.

Examples of information that is usually particularly sensitive include:

a.   Current or future prices or pricing strategies.

b.   Current business, strategic or marketing plans.

c.   Customer lists.

d.   Bidding strategies or information regarding pending bids.

e.   Current and proposed contracts or terms of trade with customers and suppliers (unless redacted to remove competitively sensitive information).

f.   Detailed cost data (eg, by product line).

g.   Profit margins by product line or customer.

h.   R&D details that would be competitively sensitive.

i.   Details about proprietary technologies.

The parties should also carefully consider whether any information is subject to confidentiality agreements. Appropriate consents from third parties may be required before any such information can be shared.

Timing of the information exchange

Competitively sensitive information should not be transferred unless there is a genuine business need for one side to obtain the data. Whether there is a genuine business need will depend on the stage which the transaction has reached. There may, for example, be greater justification for the transfer of particular information as the parties near closing than immediately after the signing of a merger agreement. Applying these principles will usually result in the staggered transfer of sensitive information at different stages in the process.

Personnel to whom access is granted

It is advisable to establish an Integration Team, comprised of individuals who are not involved in the day-to-day running of the business. These individuals can legitimately engage in integration planning but their isolation from operational matters should reduce antitrust risk from information exchanges and pre-closing conduct. Members of the Integration Team should ensure that competitively sensitive information received by them is not shared with others in the business. It may be necessary for certain particularly sensitive data to be isolated from employees altogether. In this case, outside consultants or lawyers could have access to the information and prepare non-confidential summaries.

Retention of sensitive information

Documents and information received by one party to the transaction from the other should be maintained in separate files and should not be intermingled with regular business files.

Team Leaders

It is recommended that each party appoint one or more individuals (the 'Team Leaders') to coordinate and oversee the exchange of information between the parties. The Team Leaders should work closely with the members of the Integration Team. All information requests should be channelled through the Team Leaders and be subject to their approval. Any meetings between personnel of the merging parties who are not involved in due diligence or post-closing integration should be approved by the Team Leaders. The Team Leaders should consult in-house or external lawyers on information exchanges and meetings where necessary or where there is any doubt about the legitimacy of the planned activity or information exchange.

Normal commercial activities must continue until closing

The merging parties must operate as independent businesses prior to closing. They must not coordinate in any way that could affect that independence or affect the prices and terms which each party offers on the market. The parties must not do anything that could affect whether one of them competes with the other.

Any cooperation that is susceptible to being viewed as an agreement on prices, terms or conditions or allocation of customers, geographic regions or businesses presents a very serious degree of risk. Any proposal for joint discussions about particular transactions or decisions on prices or terms must first be discussed with and cleared by in-house or external lawyers as appropriate.

Conclusion

It is likely that circumstances will present themselves where there appears to be a tension between these guidelines and the requirements of integration planning. It may be that in certain cases exceptions to these guidelines can be applied. However, it is important that the merging parties consult with the Team Leaders, in-house lawyers and external legal advisers as appropriate to ensure that antitrust risk with respect to pre-closing conduct and information exchange is minimized.

Key Sources

Vigdor, Premerger Coordination: The Emerging Law of Gun Jumping and Information Exchange (2007).

---

81. WHAT ANTITRUST/MERGER CONTROL PROVISIONS SHOULD BE INCLUDED IN M&A AGREEMENTS?

Summary

- The parties may have different perspectives on antitrust risk and hence what antitrust/merger control provisions should be included in the transaction documents.

- Antitrust/merger control provisions might cover the following:

  - Which merger control clearances are conditions precedent to the closing of the transaction;

  - Obligations on the parties to cooperate in respect of merger control filings and the regulatory process;

  - Allocation of the risk that the transaction will be challenged on antitrust grounds;

  - Right to terminate if regulatory approvals have not been obtained;

  - Reverse break-up fee;

  - Provisions dealing with the exchange of information pre-closing;

  - Seller warranties in respect of compliance with antitrust laws.

1. The parties to a merger or acquisition will typically include provisions in the transaction documents that deal with antitrust and merger control issues. If substantive competition issues are likely to arise in the review of the merger by the regulators, it will be critical for each party to protect its position. Among the most important antitrust provisions are those that allocate the 'risk' that a regulator will seek to prohibit the transaction on competition grounds or demand remedies. The merger or sale and purchase agreement may contain provisions setting out the regulatory approvals that are conditions to closing, the parties' obligations in respect of merger control filings, the lengths to which the parties must go in order to obtain these approvals and details about what conduct and information-sharing is permissible pre-closing. While detailed antitrust provisions may be important for a party to protect its position, such clauses may have the adverse effect of signalling to the competition regulators that the transaction raises substantive concerns.

2. The parties may have very different attitudes to antitrust risk. From the perspective of a purchaser, a significant potential risk is being obligated to complete a transaction that is ultimately prohibited by a competition authority or cleared on terms that destroy the value and rationale of the transaction. From the seller's perspective, the risk is that the transaction will not proceed, denying the seller the value of the sale proceeds and possibly leaving a weakened target that has seen its

customers abandon it following the uncertainty generated by the transaction and regulatory process.[308] These different risk perspectives may result in heavily negotiated antitrust provisions in transaction documents, as each side aims to protect its own position. The more likely that the transaction will raise substantive antitrust concerns, the more important these provisions will be.

3.   Agreements can include antitrust clauses of varying degrees of complexity. A basic clause may impose an obligation on each party to make the necessary merger control filings. More complex provisions may set out the obligations of each party to obtain antitrust clearances (including offering divestments), establish a break-up fee if the transaction is blocked, set out deadlines for receipt of merger approvals, provide for the extent of participation of each party (in particular the seller) in the merger control process and set out limits on information-sharing.

4.   A first step is to identify which merger control approvals are required. This process is usually carried out by the parties' lawyers, who will examine turnover and other data to determine in which jurisdictions a filing is triggered. It is desirable to know what filings are required before the merger agreement is signed as the requirement of obtaining antitrust clearance can pose risks for the transaction. These include that a competition authority will prohibit or challenge a transaction, there will be delays in approval or conditions will be attached to any approval.

5.   At the time an agreement is entered into, there may be uncertainties about what filings are required. While many jurisdictions apply a test based purely on turnover, others can involve less certain criteria, such as market shares. A further complication is raised in respect of voluntary jurisdictions, such as the UK or jurisdictions that do not impose a waiting period. Whereas a filing is not mandatory in voluntary regimes, if there is a risk of substantive antitrust issues arising, the transaction could be challenged. The purchaser will shoulder more risk in these cases as if the transaction has already closed and a challenge is made, it will be left with the economic consequences of a required divestment or prohibition.

What condition precedent should be included in respect of merger control filings?

6.   These potential uncertainties mean that a loosely drafted condition precedent clause in respect of antitrust approvals may be undesirable for both parties, in particular the buyer. However, in some cases the parties may choose a general clause. An example of such a clause (which specifically covers Irish merger control approval – say because the parties are certain that a filing is required in

---

308. For an insightful discussion about risk in the merger control process, see Scott et al, *Merger Control in the United Kingdom* (2005) Ch 18.

Ireland) and then provides a general description of other required approvals, could be drafted along the following lines:

> The obligations of Buyer and Seller to effect the Closing are subject to the satisfaction of the following conditions:
>
> All approvals required under the Antitrust Laws shall have been obtained and any waiting period applicable to the Transaction shall have terminated or expired (where 'Antitrust Laws' could be defined as: the Irish Competition Act 2002 and any other national, state or federal statutes, rules, regulations, orders, decrees, judgments, administrative and judicial doctrines and other laws that are designed or intended to govern merger control or to prohibit, restrict or regulate actions having the object or effect of restraining trade or adversely affecting competition).[309]

7. If the parties agree on what filings are required, then the condition precedent clause can be drafted with more precision to identify the relevant filings. In respect of filings to the Commission under the Merger Regulation, it may be prudent to provide for the possibility of a referral by the Commission to a Member State of all or part of the transaction, particularly where this is seen as a real possibility by the parties' legal advisors. The following is an example:

> The obligations of Buyer and Seller to effect the Closing are subject to the satisfaction or waiver prior to the Closing of the following conditions:
>
> The European Commission shall have adopted a decision pursuant to the Merger Regulation declaring the transactions contemplated hereby compatible with the common market (or such compatibility shall have been deemed to exist under Article 10(6) of the Merger Regulation) or, in the event that the European Commission adopts a decision pursuant to Article 9(3) of the Merger Regulation referring the review of all or part of the transactions contemplated hereby to a Competition Authority of a Member State (or is deemed pursuant to Article 9(5) of the Merger Regulation to have done so), such Competition Authority shall have granted approval of the transactions or parts thereof that were so referred.

8. If the purchaser has a strong bargaining position, it may be able to negotiate a condition precedent that would allow it to abandon the transaction were substantive issues to be raised by the Commission. Such a provision could provide for a condition precedent that the Commission not adopt a decision under Article 6(2) of the Merger Regulation and initiate a Phase II proceeding. A similar provision in the context of a merger that was notified to the OFT could provide for a condition precedent that the OFT not make a reference to the Competition Commission. Such clauses effectively provide the purchaser with an escape route at the first sign of regulatory trouble.

---

309. Other capitalised terms used in this example and in others in this question (such as Buyer, Seller, Transaction etc.) would be defined in the agreement. Definitions of such terms are not set out here. Some of the terms used, such as 'state or federal statutes' are aimed particularly at agreements that would include a US element.

9. The parties may also include an efforts clause requiring each party to make the necessary filings and provide information to the competition authority if requested:

> Buyer/Seller shall promptly make all filings, notifications and submissions required by the Merger Regulation, the laws of the EU Member States concerned in the case of application of Article 9(3) or Article 9(5) of the Merger Regulation, and the laws governing Other Antitrust Approvals and Other Antitrust Filings and promptly file any additional information requested as soon as practicable after receipt of a request therefor from an applicable Competition Authority or at such time as the parties hereto may mutually agree.

Should a clause setting out cooperation obligations in respect of filings be considered?

10. The seller may wish to negotiate further provisions that cover its involvement in antitrust filings. In some jurisdictions, only the acquiror may technically be required to make a filing. In such cases, the seller may wish to ensure that it has adequate input into the filings and is included in the merger review process. The following is an example of a clause providing significant protection to the seller:

> The Parties shall cooperate and assist one another in connection with all actions to be taken pursuant to Section [*Cross refer to section setting out obligations to make antitrust filings*], including the preparation and making of the filings referred to therein and, if requested, amending or furnishing additional information thereunder, providing copies of all related documents to the non-filing Party and their advisors prior to filing, and to the extent practicable neither of the Parties will file any such document or have any communication with any Competition Authority without prior consultation with the other Party. Each Party shall keep the other apprised of the content and status of any communications with, and communications from, any Competition Authority with respect to the Transaction. To the extent practicable and permitted by a Competition Authority, each Party shall permit representatives of the other Party to participate in meetings and calls with such Competition Authority.[310]

What is the range of antitrust risk-shifting provisions that may be negotiated between the parties?

11. The most heavily negotiated antitrust clause is often one that allocates the risk that the transaction will be blocked by an antitrust regulator or cleared only subject to conditions. At one end of the spectrum, such a clause could require the purchaser to do whatever is necessary, regardless of the cost, to ensure that the transaction receives regulatory approval, including offering divestitures. Such a 'hell or highwater' clause will offer most protection to the seller. At the other end of the spectrum would be a requirement to use best reasonable efforts or some similar standard. It has been noted that following the financial crisis in 2008, antitrust risk-shifting provisions more favourable to buyers have become more prevalent in

---

310. See Agreement on the Combination of General Electric Company and Instrumentarium Corporation dated 18 December 2002, s 4.2, available at http://www.secinfo.com/d139r2.2V7.d.htm.

US merger agreements, due in part to the disappearance of private equity buyers and the narrowing pool of potential acquirors, limited generally to strategic buyers.[311]

12. The following is an example of a 'hell or highwater' provision:

> The Purchaser will take any and all steps within its power necessary to avoid or eliminate each and every impediment under any antitrust or other merger control law that may be asserted by any Competition Authority[312] or any other party so as to enable the Parties to close the transactions contemplated hereby, including, without limitation, committing to and/or effecting, by undertakings, conditions, divestiture orders, hold separate orders or otherwise, the sale and disposition of such of its assets or businesses or of the assets or businesses to be acquired by it pursuant hereto as required or necessary to be divested in order to avoid the issuing of any prohibition, injunction or other order in any suit or proceeding, which would otherwise have the effect of preventing the consummation of any part or all of the transactions contemplated by this Agreement.

13. The following is a slightly shorter version of a 'hell or highwater' clause:

> The Purchaser agrees to take any and all steps within its power necessary to avoid or eliminate each and every impediment under any antitrust law that may be asserted by any competition authority or any other party so as to enable the parties to close the transactions contemplated hereby, including, without limitation, committing to and/or effecting by divestiture undertakings or agreements or otherwise, the sale or disposal of such of its assets or businesses or of the assets or businesses to be acquired by it pursuant hereto as are required to be divested in order to avoid a prohibition decision by the Commission under Article 8 of the Merger Regulation.

14. A 'hell or highwater' clause could be modified in a number of ways to qualify the purchaser's obligation. The following are examples of qualifications that could be added to the above 'hell or highwater' clause:

> ... provided however that the Purchaser shall not be obligated to make divestitures or take any other action that would be commercially unreasonable (*or some other standard, such as 'unreasonably burdensome'*);

> ... provided however that the Purchaser shall not be required to take any action pursuant to this section that would have a Material Adverse Effect[313] on the business to be acquired or the Purchaser's business taken as a whole;

> ... provided however that the Purchaser shall not be required to take any action that would, individually or in the aggregate, require the disposition of any product line or

---

311. See Tucker and Yingling, 'Antitrust Risk-Shifting Provisions in Merger Agreements After the Financial Collapse' *The Antitrust Source* (April 2009).

312. It may be desirable in this and some other clauses to include a more general term, such as Governmental Authority, that includes not only competition authorities but also other regulatory bodies from which consents may be required.

313. There are many ways in which a Material Adverse Effect could be defined. One possibility is to define it as an effect resulting in a diminution of the enterprise value of the Target in an amount in excess of a certain value. See, eg, Modrall and Cox, 'The Allocation of Antitrust-Approval Risk in M&A Agreements' *The M&A Lawyer* (July/August 2003) 16, 20.

product lines, which in the aggregate generated total sales of up to € ___ million in the business year 2009/10.

15.   A less stringent requirement might require the parties to do what was reasonably necessary or use their best reasonable efforts, commercially reasonable efforts or some similar standard to obtain antitrust approvals. The difficulty with such formulations is that they lack specificity and if there is a dispute about their meaning, it may be far from clear what interpretation a court would adopt.

> Each Party agrees, in relation to any matter for which it is responsible, expeditiously to make all filings with Competition Authorities that such Party is required to make and to take the steps reasonably necessary to complete and make effective, in an expeditious manner, the Transaction, including obtaining all necessary actions or non-actions, approvals, waivers or consents from all Competition Authorities and the making of all necessary filings and the taking of all reasonable steps as may be necessary to obtain an approval or waiver from any such Competition Authority.

16.   In some cases, the parties may be able to identify in advance, possibly based on preliminary discussions with the Commission, the divestments that are required to be made to ensure that the transaction will be approved. In this scenario, more specific obligations could be set out in the agreement. The following example relates to a divestment to be offered to both the European Commission and the US antitrust regulators:

> Buyer agrees to commit to 'hold separate' and to divest the Divestment Business under terms and conditions, including supporting and other ancillary arrangements, negotiated with and agreed to by the European Commission (or, as the case may be, a competent Competition Authority in a EU Member State) and the United States reviewing authority. Buyer agrees to offer, negotiate and agree to such commitment to divest the Divestment Business expeditiously and in a timely fashion with a view to obtaining approval or non-opposition from the European Commission (or, as the case may be, a competent Competition Authority in a EU Member State) pursuant to Article 6(1)(b) of the Merger Regulation (or, as the case may be, pursuant to the equivalent thereof in any EU Member State) and with a view to obtaining the expiration or termination of the waiting period applicable to the consummation of the transactions contemplated hereby under the HSR Act.

> Seller agrees to use its reasonable best efforts to separate, prior to the Closing Date, the Divestment Business from the remainder of the Target Business, in such manner as appropriate under the divestiture conditions negotiated with and agreed to by the European Commission (or, as the case may be, a competent Competition Authority in a EU Member State) and the United States reviewing authority; provided however that Seller need not, pursuant to this sentence, implement such separation (or preliminary steps in respect thereof) until immediately prior to the Closing. To the extent permissible under Law and the policies, practices, procedures and directions of each relevant Competition Authority, Seller shall inform Buyer of all actions that it proposes to take pursuant to the foregoing sentences and shall take all such actions in consultation with Buyer.[314]

---

314. See Stock and Asset Purchase Agreement between UCB SA and Cytec Industries Inc. dated 1 October 2004, s 5.5(c), available at http://www.secinfo.com/d13ACs.18qh.d.htm. See also, Sections 5.5(f)(i) and (ii) of this agreement, setting out obligations on the seller to cooperate in the implementation of the divestiture.

17. A potential drawback of including a specific clause in respect of divestments is that it may affect the ability of the parties to negotiate the scope of required divestitures with the Commission or other competition authorities.

Should a termination clause be included?

18. The parties may wish to include a provision giving either of them the option to terminate the agreement if antitrust approvals have not been obtained by a certain date or if the transaction is prohibited or challenged by an antitrust regulator. It may be in the seller's interest to have a shorter termination period as if there is doubt about antitrust approvals, the target business may deteriorate the longer the process carries on. A buyer is likely to prefer a longer termination provision so that it is given sufficient time to obtain clearances. The following is an example:

> This Agreement may be terminated with immediate effect at any time prior to the Closing Date as follows; provided however that the right to terminate under a specific subsection of this section shall not be available to any Party whose failure to fulfil any obligation under this Agreement has given rise to such termination right:
>
> (i) by mutual written consent duly authorised by the Board of Directors of each of the Seller and Purchaser;
>
> (ii) by either Party (a) if the Closing Date shall not have occurred within 12 months from the date of this Agreement, subject to extension by mutual agreement of the Parties; or (b) if any decision prohibiting the consummation of the Transaction shall have been issued by the European Commission or a Competition Authority of any EU Member State or if any other prohibition, order or action preventing the consummation of the Transaction shall have been issued or taken ...

What is a reverse break-up fee?

19. Some agreements provide for a reverse break-up fee that will be paid by the purchaser to the seller if the transaction does not close for antitrust reasons. Such a fee can be viewed as compensation for the seller for the damage its business may have suffered during the period when the transaction was pending. A downside of an antirust break-up fee is that its inclusion may signal to the antitrust regulators that the transaction raises substantive concerns.

> If either Party is entitled to terminate and does terminate this Agreement pursuant to Section [*Cross reference provision allowing termination if antitrust approvals not received by a certain date*] the Purchaser shall pay a termination fee equal to € __ million to the Seller within five working days following such termination.

What provisions should be made for the exchange of information pending closing?

20. Between signing and closing, the purchaser will require access to certain information of the target, in particular so it can plan for post-closing integration. The exchange of sensitive information can raise antitrust issues. It may result in 'gun-jumping', breaching merger control rules or Article 101 or similar laws.[315]

---

315. See Question 80.

The parties may wish to set out procedures for access to the target's information, for example:

> Except as required pursuant to any confidentiality agreement to which the Target or any of its subsidiaries is a party or pursuant to applicable law, including, without limitation, competition law, from the date of this agreement to the Closing Date, the Target shall (and shall cause its subsidiaries to) provide to the Purchaser and its officers, employees and authorised representatives reasonable and customary access, during normal business hours, upon reasonable prior notice and in a manner not disruptive to any of the businesses or operations of the Target or its subsidiaries, to such information concerning the business, properties, contracts, assets, liabilities and personnel, and to such officers, employees, accountants and other representatives, of the Target and its subsidiaries as the Purchaser may reasonably request. In making such requests under this provision the Purchaser shall act proportionately, taking into account the need for the Target to maintain its independence, to maintain business confidentiality and to maintain efficient operations pending the Closing, and taking into account the Seller's need to conduct its business if the Closing does not occur. All requests by the Purchaser under this section shall be co-ordinated by a committee comprising three representatives of each of the Parties. The Parties shall each comply with all of their respective obligations in the Confidentiality Agreement with respect to the information disclosed. All information provided hereunder to the other Party shall be covered by the Confidentiality Agreement, which shall survive the termination or expiration of this agreement.

Warranties in respect of competition compliance

21. The purchaser will typically require the seller to provide warranties that other than particular matters that may be disclosed, there is no pending or threatened litigation or regulatory investigations etc. of which the seller is aware. The agreement may also provide that any claims by the purchaser in respect of such a warranty can be made only up to a certain date.[316] Specific reference may be made to antitrust proceedings.[317]

> Save as disclosed in Schedule [ ] , the operations of the Target have been carried on and are being carried on in such manner so that there have been in the three years prior to Closing and are no material breaches of applicable laws, legal duties, regulations and by-laws in each country in which they are carried on and there have been and are no breaches by any group company of its constitutional documents. Save as disclosed in Schedule [ ], there is no investigation or inquiry by, or order, decree, decision or judgment of any court, tribunal, arbitrator, governmental agency or regulatory body outstanding or, to the best of Seller's knowledge, anticipated against Seller or any person for whose acts or defaults it may be vicariously liable, which has had or may have a material adverse effect upon Target, nor has any notice or other communication (official or otherwise) from any court, tribunal, arbitration, governmental agency or regulatory body been received with respect to an alleged material actual or potential

---

316. See, eg, the clauses in the agreement at issue in *Laminates Acquisition Co v BTR Australia Ltd* [2003] EWHC 2540 (Comm), [2004] 1 All ER (Comm) 737, paras 6–7.

317. For a case involving a claim for breach of such a warranty, see, eg, the three opinions of the Scottish Court of Session in *BSA International SA v Irvine* [2009] CSOH 77; [2010] CSOH 12; [2010] CSOH 78.

violation and/or failure to comply with any such applicable law, duty, regulation, by-law or constitutional document, or requiring it/them to take or omit any action.

Save as disclosed in Schedule [ ], none of the acts, omissions, practices, agreements or arrangements of Seller (i) is, to the best of Seller's knowledge, the subject of any pending investigation, inquiry, proceedings by any governmental or regulatory authority or court under any law, legislation or regulation (civil or criminal) relating to competition, restrictive trade practices, antitrust, monopolies, merger control, fair trading or restraint of trade in any part of the world ('Competition Law') or (ii) the subject of any enforceable undertaking or assurance given to any governmental or regulatory authority or court under Competition Law nor has such undertaking or assurance been requested.

82. WHAT IS THE PURPOSE OF A JOINT DEFENCE AGREEMENT IN THE MERGER CONTROL CONTEXT?

Summary

• Joint defence agreements are regularly entered into in the US and are sometimes used to also cover EU merger control proceedings.

• The aim of such agreements is to provide for the sharing of competitively sensitive information among the parties' advisors so as to enable assessment of antitrust risk, preparation of filings etc.

• It is unclear whether such arrangements attract privilege as a matter of EU law.

1.   The parties to a merger or acquisition will need to share certain information between the signing and closing of the transaction. Such an information exchange may aid the assessment of antitrust risk and enable the preparation of merger control filings.

2.   The parties remain independent competitors until the transaction is closed and the exchange of competitively sensitive information may risk breaching competition law.[318] In addition, the sharing of sensitive information may ultimately prove commercially damaging (particularly to the target) if the transaction falls apart for any reason.

3.   To the extent that competitively sensitive information needs to be exchanged, the parties can put in place procedures to nullify competition law risks. Certain information can be restricted to the parties' legal advisers, for instance, who can share it for the sole purpose of obtaining merger control clearances.

4.   To facilitate this process, transacting parties sometimes enter into a Joint Defence and Confidentiality Agreement. Such agreements are a common phenomenon in US-based transactions but they have also been used to cover exchanges of information in the context of the review process under the Merger Regulation.

5.   EU law recognises a form of legal professional privilege in respect of communications with independent lawyers. However, it does not cover in-house counsel.[319] It is unclear whether a form of joint privilege or common interest privilege is recognised in EU law and so it is doubtful that materials and communications transmitted pursuant to a joint defence effort in the context of merger control would attract privilege from the perspective of EU law.[320]

6.   Even though the privileged status of materials produced and communications made pursuant to a joint defence agreement is doubtful in EU law, in practice, such

---

318. See Question 80.

319. See Case C–550/07P *Akzo Nobel Chemicals Ltd v Commission*, judgment of the Court of Justice of 14 September 2010. See, also Question 92.

320 Were the context Irish or English law, it might be arguable that common interest privilege would be relevant. (contd \...)

agreements are entered into. The following is a sample draft of a Joint Defence and Confidentiality Agreement, to be signed by the Seller and Purchaser and their respective legal advisors. This sample could be used for a global merger and apply to exchanges of information in the context of merger reviews in both the US and EU.

Joint Defence and Confidentiality Agreement

This Joint Defence and Confidentiality Agreement (the 'Agreement') is entered into by and between the undersigned solicitors/attorneys/lawyers, each referred to individually as a 'party' and collectively as the 'parties', on their own behalf and on behalf of their respective clients, in contemplation of investigations by antitrust authorities and/or in contemplation of litigation in connection with the contemplated acquisition of Target by Buyer (the 'Transaction').

Whereas, the parties have undertaken and may undertake factual, legal and economic research concerning the possible competitive impact and antitrust aspects of the Transaction and the parties are of the opinion that it is in the best interest of their clients for counsel to exchange certain information, pool certain individual work product, and cooperate in a joint defence effort; and

Whereas, cooperation in such a joint defence effort will necessarily involve the exchange of confidential business, financial, technical and other information, as well as information which is otherwise privileged as lawyer-client communications and/or lawyer work product; and

Whereas the parties recognise that a joint defence effort would promote adequate and complete preparation of their respective defences; and

Whereas the parties and their clients rely on the joint defence and common interest exception to the waiver of the lawyer-client and lawyer work product privileges;

Now, therefore, and in consideration of the mutual terms and covenants contained herein and other good and valuable consideration the receipt and sufficiency of which is hereby acknowledged, the parties agree as follows:

i.   All factual information, documents, opinions, strategies, or other materials exchanged or communicated in the past or future by whatever means between or among any of the parties in connection with the joint defence efforts pursuant to this Agreement, except where already in the public domain at the time exchanged or communicated, or which subsequently come into the public domain otherwise than through breach of this Agreement, (hereinafter referred to collectively as 'Confidential Materials') shall be deemed subject to the terms of this Agreement.

---

320. (contd) However, there may be doubts that privilege would apply to a joint defence effort in the context of an administrative merger control procedure. For recent discussion of common interest privilege in Irish law, see the judgment of Clarke J in *Moorview Developments Limited v First Active plc* [2008] IEHC 274, [2009] 2 IR 788. See also *Redfern Limited v O'Mahony* [2009] IESC 18, [2009] 3 IR 583 (privilege not lost where there was limited disclosure for a particular purpose or to parties with a common interest). Cf in English law, *Svenska Handelsbanken v Sun Alliance and London Insurance plc* [1995] 1 Lloyd's Rep 84.

Joint Defence and Confidentiality Agreement

ii.   The parties hereby agree that to the extent that Confidential Materials are disclosed to them, they will be kept confidential and disclosed only to (i) partners, associates, staff or other employees of the signatory law firms who are working on the joint defence effort or any ensuing litigation; (ii) outside experts retained by such law firms in connection with the joint defence effort or any ensuing litigation who shall agree to abide by this Agreement.[321]

iii.   Other than to the persons identified in the preceding paragraph, Confidential Materials shall not be further disclosed to any other person or entity or agent, including, but not limited to officers or employees of the signatories' clients, unless previously authorised in writing by the party providing the Confidential Materials. If any party or the client of any party is served with a subpoena or other process seeking Confidential Materials, then the party shall promptly notify the party whose Confidential Materials are sought. Each party will cooperate to raise appropriate objections and seek appropriate protections to requests for Confidential Materials by persons not signatories to this Agreement. If such objections fail and no such protections are obtained, the party so required to disclose such information will furnish only that portion of the Confidential Materials which is legally required, and will use reasonable efforts to obtain reliable assurance that confidential treatment will be accorded such information. It shall not be a violation of this Agreement to produce Confidential Materials if compelled by a court order or other instrument imposing a legally binding obligation to comply.

iv.   Confidential Materials will be used only for the purposes of the joint defence effort and representation of the clients identified above in any related litigation, and shall not be used for any other purpose without the prior written consent of the party providing Confidential Materials.

v.   Each party understands that Confidential Materials may include information that has been communicated to counsel in confidence, by one or more of the parties' clients, for the purpose of securing legal advice and representation and lawyer work product and that all such Confidential Materials are therefore subject to the lawyer-client and/or lawyer work product privilege belonging to the client, which privilege may not be waived by any other party without the prior written consent of all clients on whose behalf this Agreement has been signed. No exchange of information on the basis of this Agreement will constitute a waiver of any legal privilege or protection that would otherwise exist. Any inadvertent or purposeful disclosure of information, documents or other material exchanged pursuant to this Agreement shall not constitute a waiver of any privilege or protection of the party providing such material.

---

321. In-house lawyers are also sometimes specified. However, as a matter of EU law, privilege is not available in respect of communications with in-house lawyers (see Case C–550/07P *Akzo Nobel Chemicals Ltd v Commission*, judgment of the Court of Justice of 14 September 2010).

Joint Defence and Confidentiality Agreement

vi.   No exchange of information on the basis of this Agreement or other communications between counsel is intended to create any lawyer-client relationship for the purposes of this transaction between the purchaser's law firm and the seller, on the one hand, or between the seller's law firm and the purchaser, on the other.

vii.   The existence of this Agreement or of a joint defence effort shall not be used in any fashion against the signatories to this Agreement or their clients other than to enforce the obligations set forth in this Agreement or otherwise as set forth in this Agreement. By way of example and not limitation, it shall not be used offensively or defensively in any litigation between the clients of the signatories to this Agreement nor will any of the parties or their clients claim that any counsel is disqualified in any such litigation by reason of the joint defence effort.

viii.   Nothing in this Agreement shall obligate any party to provide any information to any other party or exchange any information with any other party.

ix.   Nothing in this Agreement shall restrict any party from using or disclosing Confidential Materials solely originating with that party or client in any manner that it chooses.

x.   Nothing in this Agreement shall restrict any party or client from using or disclosing any information or materials received independently, and not in breach, of this Agreement.

xi.   Each party shall have the right to withdraw from this Agreement on five days' prior written notice to the other parties. The obligations imposed on each of the parties and their clients by this Agreement in respect of Confidential Information already communicated or exchanged shall remain in effect notwithstanding any party's withdrawal from this Agreement, the termination of the parties' joint defence effort, or the conclusion of the investigation of the Transaction or any ensuing litigation. Any party who withdraws from this Agreement shall not advise or represent any person or entity other than the client(s) identified above in connection with the Transaction.

xii.   At the conclusion of the investigation of the Transaction or any ensuing litigation, all Confidential Materials received pursuant to this Agreement (including all copies of such Confidential Materials and all other materials incorporating all or part of any Confidential Materials) shall either be destroyed or returned within 30 days. If any party ceases representation of his respective client(s) in connection with this Agreement or otherwise withdraws from this Agreement, that party shall destroy or return all Confidential Materials (including copies of such Confidential Materials and all other materials incorporating all or part of any Confidential Materials) received pursuant to this Agreement within seven days. If the client of any party withdraws from or otherwise ceases to be involved in the Transaction, all parties and, if applicable, their respective clients shall destroy or return all Confidential Materials (including all copies of such Confidential Materials and all other materials incorporating all or part of any Confidential Materials) within seven days. Each party shall certify his compliance with this paragraph in writing.

Joint Defence and Confidentiality Agreement

xiii.   Each party hereto acknowledges and agrees that money damages would not be a sufficient remedy for any actual or threatened breach of any provision of this Agreement by any party, and that in addition to all other remedies which the other non-breaching parties may have, such non-breaching parties shall be entitled to specific performance and injunctive or other equitable relief as a remedy for such actual or threatened breach.

xiv.   This Agreement applies to all communications and other exchanges of information (whether written, oral, or otherwise) in relation to the Transaction between or among the parties before execution of this Agreement and is intended as the written embodiment of the parties' prior oral understanding.

xv.   This Agreement may be signed in counterparts and all such counterparts shall together form one and the same Agreement.

xvi.   This Agreement shall be governed by the laws of [ ].

83. WHAT IS THE PROCEDURE FOR CHALLENGING MERGER DECISIONS OF THE COMMISSION IN THE UNION COURTS?

Summary

- The parties can challenge merger decisions of the Commission before the General Court, with the possibility of an appeal to the Court of Justice.

- Third parties have locus standi to challenge the Commission's merger decisions if they can show 'direct and individual concern'. This can usually be shown by a competitor (who may wish to challenge a clearance decision) who has participated in the Commission's administrative procedure. Other third parties, such as customers, may also have standing.

- The merger decision is not automatically suspended when a challenge is brought. Interim measures may be sought but will be granted only exceptionally.

- The challenge before the General Court can take 2–3 years but the Court may grant expedited review, which could result in a decision in approximately 6–8 months. A further appeal to the Court of Justice can often take between 1–2 years.

- If a Commission decision is overturned, it is remitted to the Commission and a new review is undertaken.

1. The appropriate legal basis for challenging a decision of the Commission under the Merger Regulation will usually be Article 263 TFEU, which provides for the review of the legality of acts of the Commission. A Commission decision can be reviewed 'on grounds of lack of competence, infringement of an essential procedural requirement, infringement of the Treaties or of any rule of law relating to their application, or misuse of powers'.[322]

2. Challenges to merger decisions lie to the General Court, with the possibility of a further appeal to the Court of Justice.[323] Such further appeal is limited to points of law. The limited nature of the review before the Union courts was addressed by the Court of Justice in *Bertelsmann*:

   > The [General Court] ... has exclusive jurisdiction, first, to find the facts, except where the substantive inaccuracy of its findings is apparent from the documents submitted to it and, second, to assess those facts. When the [General Court] has found or assessed the facts, the Court of Justice has jurisdiction under Article [256 TFEU] to review the legal characterisation of those facts by the [General Court] and the legal conclusions it has drawn from them. The Court of Justice thus has no jurisdiction to establish the facts or, in principle, to examine the evidence which the [General Court] accepted in support of those facts. Provided that the evidence has been properly obtained and the

---

322. Article 263, TFEU.
323. Article 256(1) TFEU. See also, Statute of the Court of Justice of the European Union, Article 58.

general principles of law and the rules of procedure in relation to the burden of proof and the taking of evidence have been observed, it is for the [General Court] alone to assess the value which should be attached to the evidence produced to it. Save where the clear sense of the evidence has been distorted, that appraisal does not therefore constitute a point of law which is subject as such to review by the Court of Justice.[324]

3.   Other potential legal bases, but less likely to be relevant in the context of merger control, include Article 16 of the Merger Regulation, under which the Court of Justice has unlimited jurisdiction to review decisions of the Commission fixing fines or periodic penalty payments and Article 265 TFEU, providing for an action on the basis of a failure by the Commission to act.[325]

4.   In certain circumstances, a party may also be able to sue the Commission for damages under Articles 268 and 340 TFEU:

> For the non-contractual liability of the Community to arise, a number of conditions must be met, including, where the unlawfulness of a legal measure is at issue, the existence of a sufficiently serious breach of a rule of law intended to confer rights on individuals. As regards that condition, the decisive criterion for establishing that a breach of Community law is sufficiently serious is whether the Community institution concerned manifestly and gravely disregarded the limits on its discretion.[326]

Who can appeal?

5.   Article 263 TFEU gives standing to the Member States and the Union institutions to challenge a Commission decision. It also provides that any natural or legal person may institute proceedings 'against an act addressed to that person or which is of direct and individual concern to them, and against a regulatory act which is of direct concern to them and does not entail implementing measures'. Clearly, this covers the addressees of the Commission decision. The last part of this sentence, in reference to a 'regulatory act', was introduced by the Lisbon Treaty. There is no definition of 'regulatory act' and it is unclear whether this provision, which requires only a showing of direct concern, could apply to a merger decision. The below discussion assumes that a third party would have to show both individual and direct concern.[327]

---

324. Case C–413/06P *Bertelsmann AG v Impala* [2008] ECR I–4951, [2008] 5 CMLR 1073, para 29.
325. See Case C–170/02P *Schlüsselverlag J.S. Moser GmbH v Commission* [2003] ECR I–9889, [2004] 4 CMLR 27, paras 25–30.
326. Case C–440/07P *Commission v Schneider Electric SA* [2009] ECR I–6413, [2009] 5 CMLR 2051, para 160 (the Commission was not liable to compensate Schneider for a reduction in divestiture price Schneider was forced to pay to compensate the purchaser for depreciation caused by delay in connection with an appeal against the Commission's unlawful prohibition decision; but the Commission was liable for Schneider's expenses in re-examination of merger; partly overturning Case T–351/03 *Schneider Electric SA v Commission* [2007] ECR II–2237, [2007] 4 CMLR 1533). See also, Case T–212/03 *MyTravel Group plc v Commission* [2008] ECR II–1967, [2008] 5 CMLR 1429 (damages claim arising out of unlawful prohibition decision failed).
327. See also Question 130, para 2.

6.   Third parties have to show that the merger decision is of both direct *and* individual concern to them. An obvious third party appellant is a competitor who wishes to appeal a clearance decision. Such competitors have been found to have *locus standi* in several cases. It seems that when they are competing in a market that will be affected by the merger, competitors can 'be certain of an immediate or imminent change in the state of the market' and therefore, the decision will be of direct concern to them.[328]

7.   The general test for individual concern to third parties, stated in *Plaumann*, is that the decision 'affects them by reason of certain attributes peculiar to them or by reason of circumstances in which they are differentiated from all other persons and … distinguishes them individually' in the same way as the addressee.[329] In *easyJet*, the General Court held that whether a third party is individually concerned by a clearance decision 'depends, on the one hand, on that third party's participation in the administrative procedure and, on the other, on the effect on its market position'.[330] The Court said that participation in the Commission's administrative procedure, for example as a complainant, was not sufficient to establish individual concern.[331] It is not entirely clear if such participation is a necessary requirement. The better view is probably that while it is not strictly necessary, it is an important factor and a third party who has not participated in the Commission procedure may have difficulty in establishing individual concern.

8.   In *Air France (TAT)*, an application was brought by Air France seeking to annul the clearance of the BA/TAT merger. The General Court took account of three factors in establishing Air France's individual concern: (i) it had participated in the Commission's procedure by making observations; (ii) in making its competitive assessment, the Commission mainly took into account the position of Air France; and (iii) pursuant to an agreement between Air France, the French government and the Commission, Air France had been required to give up its interest in TAT four months before the concentration was notified.[332]

9.   In *Babyliss*, a potential competitor, who had made observations to the Commission and had made a previous offer to acquire the target, was found to be individually concerned. A further factor in finding that the competitor was individually concerned was that the merger concerned oligopolistic markets characterised by substantial barriers to entry arising from strong brand loyalty and by the difficulty

---

328. Case T–177/04 *easyJet Airline Co. Ltd v Commission* [2006] ECR II–1931, [2006] 5 CMLR 663, para 32; Case T–3/93 *Air France v Commission* [[1994] ECR II–121, para 80; Case T–114/02 *Babyliss SA v Commission* [2003] ECR II–1279, para 89.

329. Case 25/62 *Plaumann & Co. v Commission* [1963] ECR 95, [1964] CMLR 29.

330. Case T–177/04 *easyJet Airline Co. Ltd v Commission* [2006] ECR II–1931, [2006] 5 CMLR 663, para 35.

331. Case T–177/04 *easyJet Airline Co. Ltd v Commission* [2006] ECR II–1931, [2006] 5 CMLR 663, para 35.

332. Case T–2/93 *Air France v Commission* [1994] ECR II–323, paras 44–47.

of access to retail trading.[333] The General Court has also recognised that a company involved in neighbouring markets that are upstream or downstream from the markets affected by a merger, may be directly and individually concerned.[334]

10. Minority shareholders have been held not to be directly and individually concerned.[335] Customers, suppliers, representative groups and others may have standing depending on the circumstances. For example, in a challenge to an acquisition in the meat processing sector, it was not disputed that a trade union representing pig farmers had standing.[336]

11. Where one action is brought by a number of applicants at least one of which has *locus standi*, it may not be necessary to consider whether the other applicants are entitled to bring proceedings.[337]

Are interim measures available?

12. A merger decision is not automatically suspended when an application for annulment is brought. The General Court has power to order interim remedies, which may include suspension of the decision.[338] The party seeking interim measures must show a *prima facie* case, that interim measures are required to avoid serious and irreparable harm to its interests and that the balance of interests is in favour of granting interim measures.[339]

13. The granting of interim measures in merger cases will occur only exceptionally. In *Kali & Salz*, interim measures were granted where implementation of one of the conditions to the merger clearance would have resulted in the dissolution of a company to the detriment of a third party. Suspending this part of the decision was unlikely to affect the interests of the acquiror and there was no adverse effect on the public interest or the Commission's interest in the immediate implementation of its decision.[340]

---

333. Case T–114/02 *Babyliss SA v Commission* [2003] ECR II–1279, [2004] 5 CMLR 21, paras 91–117.

334. Case T–158/00 *ARD v Commission* [2003] ECR II–3825, [2004] 5 CMLR 681, para 78.

335. Case T–96/92 *CCE de la Société Générale des Grandes Sources v Commission* [1995] ECR II–1213, [1995] IRLR 381, paras 25–46.

336. Case T–151/05 *Nederlandse Vakbond Varkenshouders (NVV) v Commission* [2009] ECR II–1219, [2009] 5 CMLR 1613, para 44.

337. See, eg, Case T–151/05 *Nederlandse Vakbond Varkenshouders (NVV) v Commission* [2009] ECR II–1219, [2009] 5 CMLR 1613, paras 44–48.

338. Articles 278, 279 TFEU.

339. Rules of Procedure of the General Court (Consolidated Version) [2010] OJ C177/37, Rule 104(2) and, eg, Case T–411/07R *Aer Lingus Group plc v Commission* [2008] ECR II–411, [2008] 5 CMLR 1244, para 33.

340. Case T–88/94R *Société Commerciale des Potasses et de l'Azote and Entreprise Minière et Chimique v Commission* [1994] ECR II–401.

What is the time limit for bringing an appeal?

14. An action for annulment under Article 263 must be brought 'within two months of the publication of the measure, or of its notification to the plaintiff, or, in the absence thereof, of the day on which it came to the knowledge of the latter, as the case may be'.[341] A recipient of a merger decision will usually receive notification of the decision before its publication in the *Official Journal* and so time will start to run from the day following the receipt of that notification.[342] For third parties, time will usually run from the date of publication in the *Official Journal*. That is so even if the applicant had knowledge of the decision before that date as a result of being sent a copy of the decision by the Commission.[343] However, the two-month time limit is not reckoned to run until the day after fourteen days from publication in the *Official Journal*.[344] In practice, all of these time limits are extended by ten days on account of distance from Luxembourg.[345]

How long will an appeal take?

15. In practice, many mergers will not await the outcome of an appeal. Market circumstances and business realities will be such that once the Commission issues a prohibition decision, the transaction will collapse. Parties have submitted appeals even where the transaction collapsed following the Commission's decision (perhaps to establish legal precedent) as, for example, in the case of *GE/ Honeywell*.[346]

16. A standard appeal to the General Court can take in the region of two to three years.[347] An applicant can request an expedited procedure, which can result in a judgment within six to eight months. The General Court has discretion to decide whether to grant expedited review 'having regard to the particular urgency and the circumstances of the case'.[348] Since its introduction in 2001, more than half of merger appeals have benefited from the expedited procedure, with judgments usually delivered within 12 months.[349] Appeals have been made against more than

---

341. Article 263 TFEU. See also Question 130, paras 7–10 on Article 263 time limits in the context of State aid decisions.
342. Rules of Procedure of the General Court (Consolidated Version) [2010] OJ C177/37, Article 101(1)(a).
343. Case T–48/04 *Qualcomm Wireless Business Solutions Europe BV v Commission* [2009] 5 CMLR 2121, para 56.
344. Rules of Procedure of the General Court (Consolidated Version) [2010] OJ C177/37, Articles 102(1), 101(1)(a).
345. Rules of Procedure of the General Court (Consolidated Version) [2010] OJ C177/37, Articles 102(12).
346. Case T–210/01 *GE v Commission* [2005] ECR II–5575, [2006] 4 CMLR 686.
347. See General Court Statistics of Judicial Activity, 2005–2009, available on the website of the Court of Justice.
348. Rules of Procedure of the General Court (Consolidated Version) [2010] OJ C177/37, Article 76a(1).
349. Cook and Kerse, *EC Merger Control* (5th edn, 2009) para 10.005.

40 merger decisions of the Commission, with the Commission's decision annulled in around a quarter of cases.[350]

17. If an appeal is taken against the judgment of the General Court to the Court of Justice, this will lengthen the timetable. In 2009, the average duration of appeals to the Court of Justice was 15.4 months.[351] For example, the appeal in *Bertelsmann* took almost two years, with the appeal lodged on 10 October 2006 and the Court of Justice's judgment delivered on 10 July 2008.[352]

What are the consequences of an annulment?

18. If the EU courts annul a Commission decision in whole or in part, it is remitted to the Commission for re-examination. A new Phase I review will be initiated and the transaction will be assessed in the light of then current market conditions.[353]

Key Sources

Article 263, TFEU.

Rules of Procedure of the General Court (Consolidated Version) [2010] OJ C177/37.

Case T–177/04 *easyJet Airline Co. Ltd v Commission* [2006] ECR II–1931, [2006] 5 CMLR 663.

---

350. Cook and Kerse, *EC Merger Control* (5th edn, 2009) para 10.001.
351. See Court of Justice Statistics of Judicial Activity, 2005–2009, available on the Court of Justice's website.
352. Case C–413/06P *Bertelsmann AG v Impala* [2008] ECR I–4951, [2008] 5 CMLR 1073.
353. Merger Regulation [2004] OJ L24/1, Article 10(5).

84. WHAT TEST DO THE EU COURTS APPLY WHEN REVIEWING A MERGER DECISION OF THE COMMISSION?

Summary

- The standard of review in respect of substantive assessment under the Merger Regulation is whether the Commission has committed a manifest error.

- The EU courts must take account of the discretion granted to the Commission under the Merger Regulation, especially in respect of economic assessment.

- The courts must nevertheless establish whether the evidence relied on is factually accurate, reliable and consistent and whether that evidence contains all the information which must be taken into account in order to assess a complex situation and whether it is capable of substantiating the conclusions drawn from it.

1. Most challenges to the Commission's decisions under the Merger Regulation will be brought under Article 263 TFEU, which provides for review 'on grounds of lack of competence, infringement of an essential procedural requirement, infringement of the Treaties or of any rule of law relating to their application, or misuse of powers'.[354]

2. The EU courts have full jurisdiction to review errors of law made by the Commission. Such an error may be a sufficient basis to annul the decision. However a finding that the Commission has committed an error will not necessarily result in the annulment of the decision. If other grounds support the decision, it will not be annulled.[355]

3. The extent of judicial review in merger cases is more limited in respect of complex economic assessments made by the Commission. The Court of Justice has recognised that the substantive rules of the Merger Regulation, in particular Article 2, confer on the Commission a certain discretion, especially with respect to assessments of an economic nature. Consequently, review by the EU courts 'must take account of the discretionary margin implicit in the provisions of an economic nature which form part of the rules on concentrations'.[356]

4. However, the courts will carry out a review to establish that the facts were accurately stated and whether in its assessment of complex economic matters, the

---

354. Article 263 TFEU.
355. See Case T–210/01 *GE v Commission* [2005] ECR II–5575, [2006] 4 CMLR 686, para 734. See also, Case C–12/03P *Commission v Tetra Laval BV* [2005] ECR I–987, [2005] 4 CMLR 573, para 38.
356. Case C–68/94 and C–30/95 *France v Commission ('Kali & Salz')* [1998] ECR I–1375, [1998] 4 CMLR 829, para 224.

Commission has committed a manifest error.[357] In the context of a conglomerate merger, the Court of Justice made the following general statement in *Tetra Laval*:

> Whilst the Court recognises that the Commission has a margin of discretion with regard to economic matters, that does not mean that the Community Courts must refrain from reviewing the Commission's interpretation of information of an economic nature. Not only must the Community Courts, inter alia, establish whether the evidence relied on is factually accurate, reliable and consistent but also whether that evidence contains all the information which must be taken into account in order to assess a complex situation and whether it is capable of substantiating the conclusions drawn from it.[358]

5. The test of 'manifest error' gives the Commission a wide margin in which to act. It has been described by Advocate General Kokott as follows:

> However, it is not sufficient, in order to assume a manifest error of assessment, for the [General Court] merely to take a different opinion to the Commission. If the factual and evidential position reasonably allows different assessments, there can be no legal objection if the Commission adopts one of them, even if it is not the one which the Court considers to be preferable. A manifest error of assessment exists only where the conclusions drawn by the Commission are no longer justifiable in the light of the factual and evidential position, that is to say if no reasonable basis can be discerned.[359]

6. The prospective analysis that is called for in assessing mergers, essentially predicting future conduct, 'makes it necessary to envisage various chains of cause and effect with a view to ascertaining which of them is the most likely'.[360]

7. A decision of the Commission can be vitiated by internal contradictions, incorrect inferences from the evidence and flaws of analysis, as shown in the *Airtours*[361] and *Schneider*[362] cases.

What if it is not clear-cut that a transaction would result in a significant impediment to effective competition?

8. There is no general presumption that a concentration is compatible (or incompatible) with the common market[363] and the standard of proof that the

---

357. See, eg, Case C–413/06P *Bertelsmann AG v Impala* [2008] ECR I–4951, [2008] 5 CMLR 1073, para 144.

358. Case C–12/03P *Commission v Tetra Laval BV* [2005] ECR I–987, [2005] 4 CMLR 573, para 39. See also, Case T–201/04 *Microsoft Corp. v Commission* [2007] ECR II–3601, [2007] 5 CMLR 846, para 87.

359. Case C–441/07P *Commission v Alrosa Company Ltd.*, opinion of Advocate General Kokott of 17 September 2009, para 84.

360. Case C–413/06P *Bertelsmann AG v Impala* [2008] ECR I–4951, [2008] 5 CMLR 1073, para 47.

361. Case T–342/99 *Airtours plc v Commission* [2002] ECR II–2585, [2002] 5 CMLR 317.

362. Case C–440/07P *Commission v Schneider Electric SA* [2009] ECR I–6413, [2009] 5 CMLR 2051.

363. Case C–413/06P *Bertelsmann AG v Impala* [2008] ECR I–4951, [2008] 5 CMLR 1073, para 48.

Commission faces is the same in prohibition and clearance decisions. Discussing collective dominance in *Bertelsmann*, the Court of Justice noted that:

> ... the inherent complexity of a theory of competitive harm put forward in relation to a notified concentration is a factor which must be taken into account when assessing the plausibility of the various consequences such a concentration may have, in order to identify those which are most likely to arise, but such complexity does not, of itself, have an impact on the standard of proof which is required.[364]

9. The Court then went on to state that 'the Commission is, in principle, required to adopt a position, either in the sense of approving or of prohibiting the concentration, in accordance with its assessment of the economic outcome attributable to the concentration which is most likely to ensue'.[365] This means that in 'borderline' cases, where it is not possible to adduce convincing evidence in favour of either prohibition or clearance, there is not necessarily a requirement that the Commission clear the transaction.[366] The reference to the 'more likely' scenario seems to suggest that a 'balance of probability' standard applies although the Court did not expressly describe the standard of proof in those terms.

10. It is not entirely clear from this what decision ought to be taken where there is genuine uncertainty as to the compatibility of a transaction with the common market. The Court of Justice judgment in *Bertelsmann* makes clear that there is no presumption of compatibility. The Court held that Article 10(6) of the Merger Regulation, which deems a concentration to be authorised if the Commission fails to take a decision within the Phase I or Phase II time limit, was concerned with 'the need for speed', and was an exception to the general scheme of the Merger Regulation according to which the Commission is to rule expressly on notified concentrations.[367]

Key Sources

Case C–12/03P *Commission v Tetra Laval BV* [2005] ECR I–987, [2005] 4 CMLR 573.

Case C–413/06P *Bertelsmann AG v Impala* [2008] ECR I–4951, [2008] 5 CMLR 1073.

---

364. Case C–413/06P *Bertelsmann AG v Impala* [2008] ECR I–4951, [2008] 5 CMLR 1073, para 51.
365. Case C–413/06P *Bertelsmann AG v Impala* [2008] ECR I–4951, [2008] 5 CMLR 1073, para 48.
366. Cf the opinion of Advocate General Tizzano in *Tetra Laval*, suggesting that in borderline cases, a concentration should be cleared (Case C–12/03P *Commission v Tetra Laval BV* [2005] ECR I–987, [2005] 4 CMLR 573, opinion at paras 74–81). The Court of Justice seems to have implicitly rejected this line of reasoning in *Bertelsmann*.
367. Case C–413/06P *Bertelsmann AG v Impala* [2008] ECR I–4951, [2008] 5 CMLR 1073, para 49.

85. WHAT ARE THE MAIN ELEMENTS OF MERGER CONTROL IN IRELAND?

Summary

- A merger notification is mandatory if the thresholds are met. Notifications are made to the Competition Authority on a prescribed form.

- A filing is triggered where two parties each have €40m worldwide turnover, two parties carry on business in the island of Ireland and at least one has €40m turnover in Ireland.

- The Phase I timetable is one month from notification.

- If Phase II is initiated, the timetable is 4 months from notification.

- The substantive test is whether the transaction would substantially lessen competition.

- The Authority's decision can be appealed to the High Court, which has a duty to issue a judgment within two months. There is a possibility of a further appeal on a point of law to the Supreme Court.

Which transactions are subject to Irish merger control?

1. The following types of transactions are subject to Irish merger control under the Competition Act 2002:[368]

    - Mergers.

    - Acquisition of control of an undertaking.

    - Acquisition of control of an undertaking's assets.

    - Full-function joint ventures.

2. The concept of 'control' in Irish merger control is based on the ability to exercise decisive influence.[369] In practice, the Competition Authority follows closely the approach of the European Commission to the meaning of concepts such as 'control', 'decisive influence' and 'full-function joint venture' and encourages parties to derive guidance from the Commission Jurisdictional Notice when interpreting the Irish merger control regime.[370]

3. Following the 2008 financial crisis, the Competition Authority's jurisdiction to review certain mergers of financial institutions has been removed. The Minister for Finance now has jurisdiction to review mergers of 'credit institutions' where he

---

368. Competition Act 2002, s 16(1), s 16(4). Certain acquisitions and disposals of shares in the financial services sector may require the approval of the Financial Regulator; see European Communities (Assessment of Acquisitions in the Financial Sector) Regulations 2009, implementing Directive 2007/44/EC into Irish law.
369. Competition Act 2002, s 16(2).
370. See, eg, M/09/003 *Communicorp/Boxer Sweden/Boxer*, Competition Authority Determination of 13 February 2009, paras 18–22.

is of opinion that the transaction is necessary to maintain the stability of the financial system in the State and there would be a serious threat to the stability of that system if the merger or acquisition did not proceed.[371] The Competition Authority is entitled to be consulted on such transactions and may provide advice to the Minister.[372] While the primary criteria for clearance by the Minister is that the transaction does not substantially lessen competition, the Minister may approve a transaction which, in his opinion, will substantially lessen competition if the transaction is necessary for the maintenance of the stability of the financial system, needed to avoid a serious threat to the stability of credit institutions or needed to remedy a serious disturbance in the economy of the State.[373]

What are the jurisdictional thresholds?

4.   The following jurisdictional thresholds apply:

- The worldwide annual turnover of each of at least two of the parties was not less than €40 million;

- At least two of the undertakings involved in the merger or acquisition carry on business in any part of the island of Ireland; and

- The turnover in the State of any one undertaking is not less than €40 million.[374]

5.   The Competition Authority has explained that to 'carry on business' in the island of Ireland means either (i) having a physical presence and making sales to customers in the island of Ireland (i.e. Ireland and Northern Ireland) or (ii) if no physical presence, making sales into the island of Ireland of at least €2 million in the most recent financial year.[375]

May the Authority review a transaction that does not meet the thresholds?

6.   There are two situations where the Authority may review mergers other than those that meet the jurisdictional thresholds under Section 18(1)(a). First, the Minister for Enterprise, Trade and Employment may, where of opinion that the exigencies of the common good require, make an order specifying a class of merger or acquisition that must be notified to the Authority. Pursuant to ministerial order, all media mergers are so notifiable.[376] A media merger is 'a merger or acquisition in which one or more of the undertakings involved carries on a media business in the State'.[377]

---

371. Credit Institutions (Financial Support) Act 2008, s 7(1), s 7(2).

372. Credit Institutions (Financial Support) Act 2008, s 7(6), s 7(7).

373. Credit Institutions (Financial Support) Act 2008, s 7(11), s 7(12).

374. Competition Act 2002, s 18(1).

375. Competition Authority Notice in respect of certain terms used in Part 3 of the Competition Act 2002 (12 December 2006) Article 3.

376. SI No 122 of 2007, Competition Act 2002 (Section 18(5) and (6)) Order 2007.

377. Competition Act 2002, s 23(10).

7.   Second, the parties may voluntarily make a filing in respect of a merger or acquisition that does not meet the jurisdictional thresholds.[378] Once notified, the transaction cannot then be put into effect until the Authority has issued a clearance or the relevant waiting period has expired.[379] It may be advisable to submit a voluntary notification if there is a possibility that the transaction will raise substantive concerns in Ireland. A benefit of this course of action is that clearance of the transaction renders it immune to challenge under section 4 or 5.[380]

8.   The Authority does not otherwise have jurisdiction to review mergers, even if they would result in a substantial lessening of competition. This is evident from the use of the words 'in respect of a notification received by it' as it is only in respect of such mergers that the Authority can make a determination that there is a substantial lessening of competition.[381]

9.   In *Stena/P&O (No. 2)*, as part of its clearance of the acquisition by Stena of certain ferry assets of P&O, the Authority accepted a commitment that were Stena to acquire P&O's Dublin-Liverpool ferry business at any time in the following ten years, it would notify the acquisition to the Authority.[382] This rather novel remedy was presumably to ensure that any such acquisition would be subject to the Authority's review even if it were below the financial thresholds, in which case the parties would be required to make a voluntary filing.

What form of merger filing is required?

10.   Each undertaking involved in a proposed transaction is to notify the Competition Authority within one month of the conclusion of an agreement or the making of a public bid.[383] In practice, the parties usually submit a joint notification. The notification to the Competition Authority must be made in writing on a prescribed form, available on the Authority's website. The form has similarities to Form CO but is not quite as onerous. Where the transaction does not give rise to overlaps, section 4 of the form, concerning overlapping products, can be omitted. The filing fee is €8,000. The Authority is available to engage in pre-notification discussion if this is necessary.

11.   Failure to notify a merger that meets the jurisdictional thresholds is a criminal offence. The person in control of an undertaking (in respect of a company, an officer who knowingly and wilfully authorises or permits the breach) that has

---

378. Competition Act 2002, s 18(3).
379. Competition Act 2002, s 19(1).
380. Competition Act 2002, s 4(8), s 5(3). See also, Competition Authority Notice in respect of the review of non-notifiable mergers and acquisitions (30 September 2003).
381. Competition Act 2002, s 20(1), s 21(2), s 22(2). Certain merger control systems, such as that in the US, enable the regulators to challenge a merger that raises substantive issues even if the jurisdictional thresholds for a filing are not met.
382. M/04/016 *Stena/P&O (No. 2)*, Determination of the Competition Authority of 5 April 2004.
383. Competition Authority 2002, s 18(1).

failed to notify faces a fine of up to €3,000 on summary conviction and €250,000 on conviction on indictment.[384] The transaction is also void.[385]

What is the procedure for the Competition Authority's review?

12.   The substantive test applied by the Competition Authority is to ask 'whether the result of the merger or acquisition would be to substantially lessen competition in markets for goods or services in the State'.[386] The Authority has issued guidance on its approach to the review of mergers.[387]

13.   As with the Merger Regulation, the Irish regime has a two-phase process. Phase I lasts for one month from the date of the notification. This may be extended to 45 days if the parties offer commitments.[388] If the Authority issues a formal request for additional information, this starts the Phase I clock running anew once the information is provided.[389]

14.   If the Authority initiates Phase II, the timetable extends in total to four months after the notification was made (or information was provided in response to a formal request).[390] The notifying parties, as well as interested third parties, are given an initial period of 21 days to make submissions and meetings with the Authority may ensue. If after eight weeks from the start of Phase II, the Authority is satisfied that the transaction will not substantially lessen competition, it will issue a clearance decision. If not satisfied, it will issue the parties with an assessment setting out its concerns and provide access to the file. The parties can respond to the assessment within three weeks. A failure to respond may be considered a waiver of issues raised in the assessment. The parties have the right to request an oral hearing. The parties may also discuss proposed commitments with the Authority. The Authority will then issue its final determination that the merger may be put into effect, be prohibited or be cleared subject to conditions.[391]

15.   If the Competition Authority decides in Phase I that a media merger will not substantially lessen competition, it informs the Minister, who has ten days to decide whether to order the Authority to carry out a Phase II investigation on the basis of a specified public interest.[392] If the Authority decides to clear the merger

384. Competition Act 2002, s 18(9), s 18(11).
385. Competition Act 2002, s 19(2).
386. Competition Act 2002, s 20(1)(c).
387. N/02/004 Competition Authority Notice in respect of Guidelines for Merger Analysis (16 December 2002).
388. Competition Act 2002, s 21(2), s 21(4).
389. Competition Act 2002, s 19(6)(b).
390. Competition Act 2002, s 19(1)(d).
391. Competition Act 2002, s 22(3). On the Phase II procedure and timetable, see Competition Authority, Revised Procedures for the Review of Mergers and Acquisitions (February 2006) paras 3.6–3.14.
392. Competition Act 2002, s 23(2).

at the end of Phase II, with or without conditions, the Minister has 30 days to prohibit the merger or impose new or stricter conditions in the public interest.[393]

16. The Authority has shown a willingness to accelerate its merger review timetable if the circumstances require. In *HMV/Zavvi*, the Authority issued a Phase I clearance eight days after receiving the merger notification, shortening the period for third party comments on the transaction from ten to five days. The target was in liquidation and a provisional liquidator had agreed to run the business pending what was anticipated to be an expedited clearance by the Authority.[394]

What is the procedure for agreeing remedies?

17. The parties may offer commitments in Phase I or Phase II. If the transaction is to be cleared with commitments in Phase I, the commitments must be the subject of agreement between the parties and the Authority as the Authority cannot impose conditions to its Phase I clearance decision.[395] In Phase II, while the Authority would usually seek to agree commitments with the parties, it does have the power to impose conditions to its Phase II clearance decision.[396] If a 'conditional determination' is issued after Phase II, it will include a condition that the parties put the merger into effect within 12 months.[397]

18. The Authority or any other person may seek to enforce commitments through an injunction.[398] A breach of a commitment or a determination issued by the Authority can result in criminal liability, leading on summary conviction to a fine of up to €3,000 and/or up to 6 months' imprisonment and on conviction on indictment, to a fine of up to €10,000 and/or up to two years imprisonment.[399]

When can determinations of the Authority be appealed?

20. The possibilities for appeals of merger control decisions of the Competition Authority are much more limited in comparison to appeals against decisions of the Commission under the Merger Regulation.

21. Provision for taking an appeal is made only in respect of those undertakings that made the notification to the Competition Authority.[400] Appeals can be brought only against prohibition decisions or clearance decisions that are subject to conditions.[401] The implication of these provisions seems to be that third parties do

---

393. Competition Act 2002, s 23(4).
394. M/09/002 *HMV Ireland/Zavvi*, Determination of the Competition Authority of 23 January 2009.
395. Competition Act 2002, s 20(3).
396. Competition Act 2002, s 22(3).
397. Competition Act 2002, s 22(6).
398. Competition Act 2002, s 26(2).
399. Competition Act 2002, s 26(4).
400. Competition Act 2002, s 24(3)(a).
401. Competition Act 2002, s 24(1), s 22(3).

not have standing to take an appeal and that appeals cannot be taken against clearance decisions. This is in contrast to the position under the Merger Regulation where an action for annulment can be taken against a clearance decision of the Commission and third parties have standing if the decision is of direct and individual concern to them.[402] However, it may be open to a third party to seek judicial review of the Authority's determination.[403]

22.   An appeal may be made to the High Court on a point of fact or law within one month after the date on which the undertaking was informed of the Authority's determination. The High Court has a duty to determine an appeal within two months and it may annul or confirm the Authority's determination or confirm it subject to such modifications as it determines. This appears to leave open the possibility that the High Court could impose an order stipulating new conditions to the clearance of a merger.[404] Further appeals from the High Court to the Supreme Court are limited to questions of law.[405]

23.   No provision is made for decisions that are annulled to be remitted to the Authority. An annulment by the High Court of a prohibition decision (or a clearance decision subject to conditions) appears then to effectively be a clearance decision. In such a case, there is no provision in the Act that the High Court must be satisfied that there is no substantial lessening of competition before the transaction can be cleared. This unusual position is in contrast to the position under the Merger Regulation, where Commission decisions annulled by the EU courts result in a re-examination of the concentration by the Commission.[406]

24.   As a practical matter, if the High Court overturns a prohibition decision, it appears that the parties can put the transaction into effect without waiting for the Supreme Court to determine any appeal brought by the Competition Authority (at least in the absence of any stay on the High Court's order). Presumably, if the Supreme Court were to allow such an appeal, a transaction that had been put into effect following the judgment of the High Court might have to be unwound. There is no provision in the Act as to how quickly the Supreme Court should decide an appeal. In practice, such appeals can take two to three years to be determined.

25.   In the case of the *Kerry/Breeo* merger, the Authority prohibited the merger[407] but that decision was overturned on appeal in the High Court in *Rye*.[408] The parties then put the transaction into effect even though the Authority filed an appeal in the Supreme Court.[409]

---

402. Article 263 TFEU. See Question 83.
403. See para 26 below.
404. See McCarthy and Power, *Irish Competition Law: The Competition Act 2002* (2003) para 9.482.
405. Competition Act 2002, s 24(9).
406. Merger Regulation [2004] OJ L24/1, Article 10(5).
407. M/08/009 *Kerry/Breeo*, Competition Authority Determination of 28 August 2008.
408. *Rye Investments Ltd v Competition Authority* [2009] IEHC 140.
409. The Supreme Court appeal is pending.

26. In addition to the specific appeals mechanism under the Competition Act 2002, it may be possible for a litigant to challenge a merger decision of the Competition Authority be way of judicial review. Such proceedings do not appear to have been brought in respect of merger determinations under the 2002 Act but in other contexts, actions of the Authority have been the subject of judicial review.[410] The judicial review route may provide a mechanism for third parties, who do not have standing to take appeals under the 2002 Act, to challenge merger determinations of the Authority. Whether the applicant has *locus standi* to apply for judicial review depends on whether it has 'sufficient interest'.[411] Any attempt by the parties to the transaction to seek judicial review may be met by the objection that they should first exhaust their remedy of appeal under the 2002 Act.[412]

What standard of review is applied in appeals?

27. The judgment of the High Court in *Rye* was the first to examine the appropriate standard of review in a merger appeal under the Competition Act 2002.

28. Cooke J noted that the procedural remedy created by section 24 was expressly one of appeal and was therefore wider than a judicial review. This meant that in addition to applying judicial review principles, the court could examine the correctness of the basis on which the Authority had made its determination. Even though the appeal at bar did not concern issues about findings of fact, and so Cooke J's comments in this respect were strictly *obiter*, the learned judge noted:

> That to the extent that the correctness of the determination is challenged, the court can re-open its material findings of fact and substitute its own findings having heard evidence in that regard, only if it is first satisfied on the basis of the content of the determination and in the light of the evidential material available to the Authority as of the date of making of the determination, that it was unreasonable for the Authority to have found or accepted one or more specific facts which are material to the validity of its assessment.[413]

29. In respect of the standard of review, Cooke J stated that it was desirable that the criteria for appeals be consistent with closely analogous statutory appeals under domestic legislation and also, in the area of competition law, with the Authority's obligation to ensure that its decisions were consistent with EU law where they had a EU dimension. On this latter point, the learned judge pointed to the Authority's obligations under Regulation 1/2003. Although the relationship between the

---

410. See *Law Society of Ireland v Competition Authority* [2005] IEHC 455, [2006] 2 IR 262 (a Competition Authority notice providing that, in general, a lawyer would not be entitled to represent more than one person in proceedings before the Authority, was quashed).
411. Rules of the Superior Courts, Order 84, Rule 20(4); *State (Lynch) v Cooney* [1982] IR 337, 369. See more recently, *Ryanair Ltd v Minister for Transport* [2009] IEHC 171, paras 47–53 (Finlay Geoghegan J holding that Ryanair had standing to challenge the award of a public contract even though it had not participated in the tender, where it could have participated in a new tender process that the Minister should have conducted).
412. See, eg, de Blacam, *Judicial Review* (2nd edn, 2009) Ch 25.
413. *Rye Investments Ltd v Competition Authority* [2009] IEHC 140, para 5.9.

Authority and the Commission was distinct in merger control, Cooke J held that it was desirable that 'no unnecessary discrepancies should be created in the criteria applied' given that the Authority might have to apply its merger control powers to a merger remitted to it from the Commission under Articles 4(4) and 9 of the Merger Regulation.[414]

30. The standard that had been adopted by the Supreme Court in the *Orange* case,[415] which had involved an appeal under telecommunications legislation, was the appropriate standard. This 'deferential standard' required the appellant to establish as a matter of probability that, taking the adjudicative process as a whole, the decision reached was vitiated by 'a serious and significant error or a series of such errors' and that in applying the test, the court would have regard to the degree of expertise and specialist knowledge of the Authority. Although not explicit on the point, Cooke J also appeared to recognise that the error had to go to the root of the decision if it was to vitiate it and justify an annulment.[416]

31. The learned judge noted that the scope of an appeal under section 24 was wider than that of the European courts under Article 263 TFEU but was nevertheless satisfied that the test in the *Orange* case was consistent with the standard of review applied to analogous decisions of the Commission by the EU courts. In this context, Cooke J equated the common law concept of 'curial deference' with that of 'margin of appreciation' or 'margin of discretion' accorded to the Commission on review by the EU Courts. Cooke J pointed to the judgments in *Tetra Laval*[417] and *Microsoft*[418] as examples of the application of this principle.

32. Cooke J held that the Authority's conclusion should not be set aside unless one of five conditions was met:

- **Serious error in making inferences**. The Authority committed a serious error in drawing inferences or conclusions from facts, such that the inferences or conclusions become untenable or unsound; or

- **Failure to consider evidence**. The Authority has failed to take into consideration or adequately to consider, relevant information or data such that an inference or conclusion material to the determination is unsupported by or is rendered inconsistent with the clear force and effect of the available evidence taken as a whole; or

- **Manifestly unreasonable and unsound appraisal**. A significant appraisal of economic or technical factors material to the functioning of competition

---

414. *Rye Investments Ltd v Competition Authority* [2009] IEHC 140, para 5.16.

415. *Orange Communications Limited v The Director of Telecommunications Regulation* [2000] 4 IR 159.

416. See *Rye Investments Ltd v Competition Authority* [2009] IEHC 140, paras 5.13, 6.1. Cf *M and J Gleeson & Co v Competition Authority* [1991] 1 ILRM 401 (such a requirement recognised in the context of appeals under section 9 of the Competition Act 1991).

417. Case T–5/02 *Tetra Laval BV v Commission* [2002] ECR II–4381, [2002] 5 CMLR 1182 and Case C–12/03P *Commission v Tetra Laval BV* [2005] ECR I–987, [2005] 4 CMLR 573.

418. Case T–201/04 *Microsoft Corp. v Commission* [2007] ECR II–3601, [2007] 5 CMLR 846.

in the relevant market is shown to be so inconsistent with the available evidence as to be manifestly unreasonable and unsound; or

- **Incoherent reasons for conclusions**. The Authority's statement of its reasons for reaching conclusions material to the basis of the determination is lacking in cogency or coherence or is contradicted by the evidence which was available to it; or

- **Material error of law**. The Authority has made a material error of law either in the construction and application of the Act or by otherwise infringing some applicable principle of constitutional or natural justice.[419]

33. In concluding on the standard that the Authority must apply in assessing mergers, Cooke J held:

> It is precisely because the Court defers to the Authority in matters of choice or judgment within the area of its specialist expertise that the Court must be assiduous to ensure that in appraising factual evidence upon which its expert conclusions and judgments are based, the Authority has considered all the relevant information at its disposal; that it has weighed it objectively and rationally and that it has not erred by wittingly or unwittingly selecting only those parts of it which appear best to fit a particular economic solution.[420]

34. The appellants had challenged the Authority's finding that the transaction would result in a substantial lessening of competition in each of the three markets for rashers, non-poultry cooked meats and processed cheese. The court found that the Authority's determination was vitiated by material error in two respects. In the processed cheese market, the basis of the Authority's conclusions on market definition was 'inadequate and unsound' and 'unsupported by the evidence as a whole'.[421] In the rashers and non-poultry cooked meats markets, the Authority had failed to properly consider the role of countervailing buyer power as it had 'misjudged the significance and weight of all of the evidence available to it as to the reality of the buyer power exercisable by the four main multiple chains' and it attributed undue weight to the responses of retailers who expressed concerns about the transaction.[422]

Key Sources

Competition Act 2002.

Competition Authority, N/02/004 Notice in respect of Guidelines for Merger Analysis (16 December 2002).

Rye Investments Ltd v Competition Authority [2009] IEHC 140.

---

419. *Rye Investments Ltd v Competition Authority* [2009] IEHC 140, para 5.20.
420. *Rye Investments Ltd v Competition Authority* [2009] IEHC 140, para 9.76.
421. *Rye Investments Ltd v Competition Authority* [2009] IEHC 140, paras 7.19–7.21.
422. *Rye Investments Ltd v Competition Authority* [2009] IEHC 140, para 9.75.

86. WHAT ARE THE MAIN ELEMENTS OF MERGER CONTROL IN THE UK?

Summary

- Merger filings in the UK are voluntary. This means there is no legal obligation to notify. However, as the OFT may challenge a merger that raises competition issues, a filing may be advisable if the transaction might raise issues in the UK.

- The jurisdictional threshold is £70 million of UK turnover by the target or 25 per cent share of supply or purchase of any goods/services in the UK.

- Filings are made with the OFT:

    - The OFT has a duty to refer the merger to the CC if it may be expected to result in a substantial lessening of competition;

    - The OFT has a discretion not to refer in limited circumstances;

    - The OFT may accept undertakings in lieu of a reference;

    - The OFT usually decides within 40 days following an 'informal' filing. If the statutory Merger Notice is used, it has up to 30 days to decide;

    - The CC examines if there is a relevant merger situation and whether it may be expected to result in a substantial lessening of competition;

    - The CC has 24 weeks to reach a decision, which can be extended by 8 weeks;

    - Appeals lie to the CAT, which applies judicial review principles. A further appeal lies to the Court of Appeal.

Which transactions are subject to UK merger control?

1.   The rules on UK merger control are contained in Part 3 of the Enterprise Act 2002. Merger filings are voluntary.[423] The decision whether to notify comes down to a risk assessment. A completed merger that was not notified and which raises competition issues may have to be unwound.

2.   The UK merger control regime applies to a 'relevant merger situation', which occurs when 'two or more enterprises have ceased to be distinct enterprises' and the jurisdictional thresholds are met.[424] Two enterprises cease to be distinct if they are brought under 'common ownership or control'.[425] An 'enterprise' means 'the activities, or part of the activities, of a business'.[426]

---

423. It is understood that proposals for reforming UK merger control, possibly to include the introduction of mandatory filings, have been mooted within the UK government but at the time of writing, no proposals have been published.
424. Enterprise Act 2002, s 22(1)(a), s 23(1), (2), (3), (4).
425. Enterprise Act 2002, s 26(1).
426. Enterprise Act 2002, s 129(1).

3. The concept of 'control' under the Enterprise Act includes (i) legal control, (ii) *de facto* control and (iii) material influence.[427] It does not equate exactly to the meaning of 'control' under the Merger Regulation.

4. Legal control exists where a controlling interest is acquired. This usually involves the acquisition of more than 50 per cent of the voting rights and therefore the ability to pass ordinary resolutions.

5. *De facto* control arises where a person does not have legal control but is able to control the policy of the business.[428] There are no set criteria in the Act to determine when *de facto* control is acquired. The OFT considers that the concept is similar in nature to 'decisive influence' under the Merger Regulation.[429] An example of *de facto* control would be where a shareholder has less than a majority, say 30 per cent, but because the remaining shares are fragmented, in practice the shareholder can obtain a majority at the shareholders' meeting. Another example might be where a minority shareholder has sufficient voting power to block shareholder resolutions that require a super-majority.

6. The OFT has the ability to decide whether or not to treat *de facto* control as a controlling interest but its practice is to do so whenever it considers that the test for a reference to the Competition Commission ('CC') would be met.[430]

7. The concept of control also includes the ability to 'materially influence' the policy of the business.[431] This appears to be a lower level of control than 'decisive influence' under the Merger Regulation. The concept of material influence is not defined in the Enterprise Act.

8. The OFT considers that the enterprise's policy 'means the management of its business, in particular in relation to its competitive conduct, and thus includes the strategic direction of a company and its ability to define and achieve its commercial objectives'.[432] The ability to exercise material influence over policy will usually be evidenced by exercising votes at shareholders' meetings. A 25 per cent shareholding that allowed the holder to block special resolutions would be presumed to confer material influence and the OFT considers that even shareholdings below 15 per cent could confer material influence.[433]

9. An assessment of material influence requires a case-by-case analysis of the entire relationship between the acquiring entity and the target. Some factors might suggest that the acquiring party exercises an influence disproportionate to its

---

427. See also *British Sky Broadcasting Group plc v Competition Commission* [2010] EWCA Civ 2, [2010] UKCLR 351, para 10, referring to three relevant types of control in s 26: ownership, ability to control policy and ability materially to influence policy.
428. Enterprise Act 2002, s 26(3).
429. OFT 527, Mergers: Jurisdictional and procedural guidance (June 2009) para 3.29.
430. OFT 527, Mergers: Jurisdictional and procedural guidance (June 2009) para 3.31.
431. Enterprise Act 2002, s 26(3).
432. OFT 527, Mergers: Jurisdictional and procedural guidance (June 2009) para 3.15.
433. OFT 527, Mergers: Jurisdictional and procedural guidance (June 2009) paras 3.17, 3.19, 3.20.

shareholding. An example would be where the acquirer has an agreement with the company to provide consultancy services. The degree to which the remaining shareholding is fragmented, as well as influence over the board, may also be important.[434]

10. In the *BSkyB* case, a finding by the CC, that the acquisition of a 17.9 per cent stake by Sky in ITV was sufficient to enable it to materially influence the policy of ITV, was upheld by the CAT and the Court of Appeal. The CC considered that Sky's ability to materially influence policy might not turn on the precise percentage of the vote held – a 25 per cent holding would have been required to block special resolutions. It was also not fatal that Sky would not have board representation. Among the relevant factors leading to a relevant merger situation were that Sky would be the largest shareholder in ITV; in practice Sky's large shareholding would be likely to influence ITV's policy and planning even without the matter being put to a vote; ITV might not pursue certain strategies if it was thought they would cause conflict with Sky; and Sky's industry knowledge and standing would likely increase its ability to influence other shareholders, enabling it to block a special resolution with others.[435]

11. As with *de facto* control, the OFT has the ability to decide whether or not to treat material influence as a controlling interest but its practice is to do so whenever it considers that the test for a reference to the CC would be met.[436]

12. A joint venture will constitute a relevant merger situation if the assets and other components of the venture constitute an 'enterprise' and the jurisdictional thresholds are met. The Enterprise Act does not apply the concept of a full-function joint venture as under the Merger Regulation. A joint venture that, for instance, does not itself provide goods or services to the market but only deals with its parents could still be subject to UK merger control even though it would not be considered a concentration under the Merger Regulation.

What are the jurisdictional thresholds?

13. The jurisdictional threshold is satisfied if either of the following tests are met:

- The value of the turnover in the United Kingdom of the enterprise being taken over exceeds £70 million;[437] or

- As a result of the transaction, a share of at least 25 per cent of the supply or purchase of goods or services of any description in the United Kingdom or a substantial part of it will be created or enhanced.[438]

---

434. OFT 527, Mergers: Jurisdictional and procedural guidance (June 2009) paras 3.17–3.28; Competition Commission and Office of Fair Trading, Merger Assessment Guidelines (September 2010) paras 3.2.8–3.2.12.
435. See *British Sky Broadcasting Group plc v Competition Commission* [2010] EWCA Civ 2, [2010] UKCLR 351, paras 44–47.
436. OFT 527, Mergers: Jurisdictional and procedural guidance (June 2009) para 3.16.
437. Enterprise Act 2002, s 23(1).
438. Enterprise Act 2002, ss 23(2), (3), (4).

14. In respect of the turnover test, it is only the turnover of the target generated in the UK that is taken into account.

15. The share of supply test is not a market share test. The group of goods or services to which the share of supply test applies need not amount to a relevant market, defined on the basis of economic criteria such as substitutability. The OFT will have regard to any reasonable description of a set of goods or services in determining whether the share of supply test is met.[439]

16. A merger falling below the thresholds may be reviewed if the Secretary of State considers that it is potentially against the public interest. Such a 'special merger situation' may only arise in certain sectors that are specified in section 58 of the Enterprise Act 2002. These currently are national security, newspapers and media and maintaining the stability of the UK financial system.[440]

What is the format and timetable for making a filing?

17. In contrast to the position under the Merger Regulation, where a filing can be made only when there is a binding commitment to proceed or evidence of a good faith intention to do so,[441] the requirement in the UK is that a transaction should be 'in contemplation'.[442]

18. The parties may seek informal advice from the OFT as to its views about potential competition issues with the transaction. In advance of making a filing, pre-notification discussions can also be entered into.

19. If the parties decide to make a filing, they may choose to notify the merger using a standard statutory 'Merger Notice' form or by way of informal submission.

20. The Merger Notice can only be used if the transaction has been made public and is not yet completed.[443] The OFT suggests that the Merger Notice only be used in respect of transactions that do not raise material competition concerns.[444] If the Merger Notice is used, a statutory timetable is established and the OFT has 20 working days (which may be extended to 30 working days) in which to decide

---

439. OFT 527, Mergers: Jurisdictional and procedural guidance (June 2009) para 3.55.
440. Enterprise Act 2002, s 58. The addition of the stability of the UK financial system as a specified interest was made by the by the Enterprise Act 2002 (Specification of Additional Section 58 Consideration) Order 2008 (SI 2008/2645). See also *Merger Action Group v Secretary of State for Business, Enterprise and Regulatory Reform* [2008] CAT 36, [2009] SLT 10 (application for review of the Secretary of State's decision under section 45 of the Enterprise Act not to refer the acquisition by Lloyds TSB of HBOS to the Competition Commission rejected).
441. Merger Regulation [2004] OJ L24/1, Article 4(1).
442. Enterprise Act 2002, s 33(1).
443. Enterprise Act 2002, s 96(1), s 96(2)(b); Office of Fair Trading, Mergers: Jurisdictional and procedural guidance (June 2009) para 4.53.
444. OFT 527, Mergers: Jurisdictional and procedural guidance (June 2009) para 4.54.

whether to refer the transaction to the CC.[445] The Merger Notice requires various information about the parties and the transaction.[446]

21. Where a transaction may raise competition issues, the parties usually notify by means of an informal submission. An informal submission must be used for completed mergers. There is no statutory timetable for review when this method of notification is used. The OFT has a target to reach a decision within 40 working days of receiving a complete submission.[447]

22. The OFT's power of review is subject to the rule that it cannot make a reference more than four months after a merger has been completed.[448] This means that where the parties decide not to make a filing, the potential risk of OFT intervention lasts for four months after the transaction has closed. The four-month period does not run if the transaction was being reviewed under the Merger Regulation.[449] So, for example, were a transaction reviewed by the Commission under the Merger Regulation and the Commission ultimately decided that it did not have jurisdiction or that the transaction did not give rise to a concentration etc., it seems that the OFT could make a reference within four months of the relevant Commission decision or the conclusion of any appeals against the Commission decision before the Union courts.

When must the OFT refer a merger to the CC?

23. The OFT has a duty to refer a merger to the CC if the OFT believes that a relevant merger situation has been created and this has resulted, or may be expected to result, in a substantial lessening of competition within any market or markets for goods or services in the United Kingdom.[450]

24. The scope of this duty to refer was considered in the *IBA Health* case. The CAT interpreted the duty in section 33 in respect of completed mergers to give rise to a two-part test, not only (i) that in the OFT's own mind there was no significant prospect of a substantial lessening of competition, but also (ii) there was no significant prospect of the CC reaching an alternative view on the basis of a fuller investigation.[451] The Court of Appeal rejected this approach, holding that:

> ... the relevant belief is that the merger may be expected to result in a substantial lessening of competition, not that the Competition Commission may in due course decide that the merger may be expected to result in a substantial lessening of competition. Further, the body which is to hold that belief is the OFT not the Commission.[452]

---

445. Enterprise Act 2002, s 97(1), (2).
446. A copy of the Merger Notice is available on the OFT website.
447. OFT 527, Mergers: Jurisdictional and procedural guidance (June 2009) para 4.65.
448. Enterprise Act 2002, s 24(1)(a).
449. Enterprise Act 2002, s 122(4).
450. Enterprise Act 2002, s 22(1) (completed mergers), s 33(1) (anticipated mergers).
451. *IBA Health Ltd v Office of Fair Trading* [2003] CAT 27, [2004] CompAR 235, para 228.
452. *Office of Fair Trading v IBA Health Ltd* [2004] EWCA Civ 142, [2004] ICR 1364, para 38 (Morritt VC).

25. In *Celesio*, the CAT rejected the contention that the OFT is always under an obligation to refer a merger to the CC where the prospect of there being a substantial lessening of competition is greater than fanciful.[453]

26. The OFT has a discretion to clear the transaction in certain circumstances where there would otherwise be a duty to refer:[454]

- If the merger has not yet been completed and the proposals are not sufficiently advanced or likely to proceed to justify a reference.

- Competition concerns are outweighed by customer benefits.

- The market at issue is not sufficiently important to justify a reference (the OFT considers that this exception will only be considered if the aggregate value of all markets affected by the merger is £10 million or less).[455]

27. The OFT has the power to accept undertakings in lieu of making a reference to the CC.[456]

What is the procedure before the CC?

28. Following a reference from the OFT, the CC investigates whether a relevant merger situation has been created and if so, whether it may be expected to result (and additionally in the case of completed mergers, whether it already has resulted) in a substantial lessening of competition within any markets in the United Kingdom.[457]

29. The CC has 24 weeks from the date of the reference to issue its report. The CC may extend the period by 8 weeks if it considers there are special reasons. The timetable may be extended if the parties or third parties have failed to comply with an information request.[458]

What is the substantive test?

30. As noted above, the substantive question in UK merger control is whether the merger has resulted or may be expected to result in a substantial lessening of competition within any market or markets for goods or services in the United

---

453. *Celesio AG v Office of Fair Trading* [2006] CAT 9, [2006] CompAR 515, para 74. Also on the OFT's duty to refer, see *UniChem Ltd v Office of Fair Trading* [2005] CAT 8, [2005] CompAR 907.
454. Enterprise Act 2002, s 22(2), s 33(2).
455. OFT 516B, Exceptions to the duty to refer: markets of insufficient importance (November 2007). For an example of the application of this exception, see OFT Press Release, OFT decides not to refer Arriva/Go-Ahead North East Transactions to Competition Commission (11 February 2010). The OFT is currently reviewing its guidance on this issue; see OFT 1122con, Mergers - Exceptions to the duty to refer and undertakings in lieu (October 2009). At the time of writing, the OFT had not adopted new guidance on the *de minimis* exception.
456. Enterprise Act 2002, s 73(2). See paras 31–33 below.
457. Enterprise Act 2002, s 35(1), s 36(1).
458. Enterprise Act 2002, s 39(1), (3), (4).

Kingdom.[459] New guidelines on the assessment of mergers were jointly published by the OFT and Competition Commission in September 2010.[460] Broadly speaking, the substantive review carried out by the OFT and CC is similar to that carried out under the Merger Regulation by the European Commission. There are three main ways in which a merger might lead to a substantial lessening of competition: (i) unilateral effects; (ii) coordinated effects; and (iii) vertical or conglomerate effects. The OFT and CC draw up theories of harm to provide the framework for assessing the effects of a merger and in doing so will examine how the merger might affect rivalry.[461] In general, the September 2010 guidelines place emphasis on the economic effects of mergers, with detailed guidance provided on unilateral and coordinated effects.

Can remedies be offered at the OFT stage?

31. If the OFT decides that the test for a reference to the CC is met, it has the power to accept undertakings in lieu of making a reference to the CC.[462] It is up to the parties to offer undertakings in lieu of a reference. The OFT does not have power to impose remedies. However, where undertakings offered in lieu of a reference are not complied with, the OFT can make an order requiring the parties to fulfil their commitments.[463]

32. The final opportunity for the parties to offer undertakings in lieu is immediately after the 'issues meeting' with the OFT, a meeting that provides the parties a final opportunity to present their case before the OFT decides whether to make a reference.[464]

33. The proposed remedies must be credible and clear-cut. The undertakings must be clear-cut both in the sense of remedying the competition problem and being straightforward to implement. Structural remedies are preferred to behavioural remedies. Pure behavioural remedies that propose to regulate parameters of competition such as price, quantity and quality will not generally be considered sufficiently clear-cut to be accepted by the OFT.[465]

What is the process for remedies at the CC stage?

34. When a merger is referred to the CC, it will consider whether interim measures are necessary to prevent pre-emptive action by the parties which might prejudice

---

459. Enterprise Act 2002, s 22(1) (completed mergers), s 33(1) (anticipated mergers).
460. CC and OFT Merger Assessment Guidelines (September 2010).
461. See further CC and OFT Merger Assessment Guidelines (September 2010) para 4.2.1 *et seq.*
462. Enterprise Act 2002, s 73(2).
463. Enterprise Act 2002, s 75.
464. See OFT 527, Mergers: Jurisdictional and procedural guidance (June 2009) para 8.10.
465. See OFT 1122con, Mergers - Exceptions to the duty to refer and undertakings in lieu (October 2009) paras 5.9–5.17, 5.24–5.28; OFT 527, Mergers: Jurisdictional and procedural guidance (June 2009) para 8.21.

possible remedial action by the CC were it to conclude that there was a substantial lessening of competition. The CC may accept such a remedy proposed by the parties but it also has the power to impose such an interim remedy by order.[466]

35. The CC will first reach a preliminary finding as to whether there is a substantial lessening of competition before consulting on possible remedies. The CC will consider any proposals from the parties as well as its own proposals. The CC will consult with relevant parties to explore remedy options prior to arriving at a provisional decision on remedies. The CC will then consult on this provisional decision with relevant parties prior to making a final decision. The CC's final report will contain its final decision on the competition issues and remedies.[467]

36. The CC will seek to implement the remedies attached to its final report by agreeing undertakings with the parties for that purpose.[468] However, if agreement cannot be reached, the CC has the power to impose undertakings by order.[469] There is no set deadline for agreeing undertakings or imposing an order. In straightforward cases of divestiture remedies, the CC will usually seek to agree undertakings within 8 weeks of the publication of its final report.[470]

37. In the case of completed transactions that are found to result in a substantial lessening of competition, as well as imposing remedies such as requiring divestments, it is possible that the CC could prohibit the merger, placing the burden on the acquirer to find a new buyer within a prescribed timetable, which may only be achievable at a 'knockdown' price.

How can merger decisions be appealed?

38. Under section 120 of the Enterprise Act, 'any person aggrieved' by a decision of the OFT, the CC or the Secretary of State in connection with a reference or possible reference in relation to a relevant merger situation, may apply to the CAT for a review of the decision.[471] This is a wide category. Although it may be stricter than the standard used in judicial review proceedings in England, that of a person with 'sufficient interest', the same factors are likely to be relevant in deciding standing.[472] An 'aggrieved' person can be a third party and the decision may be

---

466. Enterprise Act 2002, s 80, s 81.
467. See Merger Remedies: Competition Commission Guidelines (November 2008).
468. Enterprise Act 2002, s 82.
469. Enterprise Act 2002, s 83, s 84, Schedule 8.
470. Merger Remedies: Competition Commission Guidelines (November 2008) para 1.27.
471. Enterprise Act 2002, s 120(1).
472. *Merger Action Group v Secretary of State for Business, Enterprise and Regulatory Reform* [2008] CAT 36, [2009] SLT 10, paras 38 *et seq*. See also the comments of the CAT in *IBA Health Ltd v Office of Fair Trading* [2003] CAT 28, [2004] CompAR 294, paras 54–56.

one by the OFT not to make a reference to the CC.[473] The application to the CAT must be made within four weeks of the earlier of the date that the applicant was notified of the disputed decision or the date on which the decision was published.[474]

39. In determining an application, the CAT applies judicial review principles.[475] The CAT may dismiss the application or quash the whole or part of the decision. If it quashes the decision in whole or part, it may refer it back to the decision maker with a direction to reconsider and make a new decision in accordance with the CAT's ruling.[476]

40. An appeal from the CAT's decision lies to the Court of Appeal on a point of law.[477] Permission to appeal must be obtained from the CAT or the Court of Appeal.[478]

What is the standard of review in merger appeals?

41. Section 120(4) of the Enterprise Act 2002 provides that when hearing merger appeals, the CAT 'shall apply the same principles as would be applied by a court on an application for judicial review'.

42. Possible grounds for judicial review include that the decision maker has committed an error of law[479] or breached principles of procedural fairness.[480]

43. As to substantive review of the decision, in broad terms, the test is whether the decision was irrational. The origin of this test is the *Wednesbury* formulation that the decision was 'so unreasonable that no reasonable authority could ever come to

---

473. Applications against decisions of the OFT not to refer were involved in *IBA Health Ltd v Office of Fair Trading* [2003] CAT 27, [2004] CompAR 235 (partly upheld on appeal, *Office of Fair Trading v IBA Health Ltd* [2004] EWCA Civ 142, [2004] ICR 1364); *UniChem Ltd v Office of Fair Trading* [2005] CAT 8, [2005] CompAR 907; and *Celesio AG v Office of Fair Trading* [2006] CAT 9, [2006] CompAR 515. A decision by the Secretary of State not to refer a merger under section 45 of the Enterprise Act was at issue in *Merger Action Group v Secretary of State for Business, Enterprise and Regulatory Reform* [2008] CAT 36, [2009] SLT 10.
474. Competition Appeal Tribunal Rules 2003, SI 2003/1372, r 26.
475. Enterprise Act 2002, s 120(4).
476. Enterprise Act 2002, s 120(5).
477. Enterprise Act 2002, s 120(6).
478. Enterprise Act 2002, s 120(7).
479. See, eg, *Stagecoach Group plc v Competition Commission* [2010] CAT 14 (error of law unsuccessfully argued). On illegality as a ground of judicial review, see generally, eg, Woolf, Jowell, Le Seur and Donnelly, *De Smith's Judicial Review* (6th edn, 2007) Ch 5.
480. See, eg, *Unichem Ltd v Office of Fair Trading* [2005] CAT 8, in particular paras 268–279 (material failure of procedure in OFT's merger decision because of failure to check facts with the applicant). On procedural fairness as a ground of judicial review, see generally, eg, Woolf, Jowell, Le Seur and Donnelly, *De Smith's Judicial Review* (6th edn, 2007) Ch 7.

it'.[481] The application of the irrationality ground may include an inquiry whether there was 'adequate material' for the decision subject to review to be made.[482] The CAT noted in *BSkyB* that:

> A tribunal conducting a judicial review can … review the available factual material to see whether the decision-maker was entitled to make the finding in question. If the material is such that no reasonable decision-maker could reach that conclusion then the latter is unsustainable in law.[483]

44. If the CAT considers that a fact found by the OFT or CC has no evidential foundation, it must consider the materiality of any such 'fact' to the decision as 'not every failure in fact-finding and analysis by a decision making body requires or permits its finding or decision to be quashed'.[484]

45. In testing for irrationality, the CAT will afford the OFT or the CC a margin of appreciation.[485] In *IBA Health*, the Court of Appeal emphasised the flexibility of judicial review principles.[486] Relying on this judgment in *BSkyB*, the Court of Appeal rejected the argument that in merger appeals the CAT was obliged to apply judicial review principles with a greater intensity of review because it is a specialist judicial body. It held:

> [The] Tribunal is to apply the normal principles of judicial review, in dealing with a question which is not different from that which would face a court dealing with the same subject-matter. It will apply its own specialised knowledge and experience, which enables it to perform its task with a better understanding, and more efficiently. The possession of that knowledge and experience does not in any way alter the nature of the task.[487]

46. The Court of Appeal in *BSkyB* also provided useful guidance on the application of the standard of proof to decisions taken by the CC. It confirmed that the balance of probability standard applies to the CC's conclusion on whether there was a relevant merger situation and whether this would cause a substantial lessening of competition. However, the standard did 'not have to be applied separately to each

481. *Associated Provincial Picture Houses Ltd v Wednesbury Corp* [1948] 1 KB 223, 230.

482. *Office of Fair Trading v IBA Health Ltd* [2004] EWCA Civ 142, [2004] ICR 1364, para 93.

483. *British Sky Broadcasting Group plc v Competition Commission* [2008] CAT 25, [2008] CompAR 223, para 66 (appeal partly allowed on other grounds, *British Sky Broadcasting Group Plc v Competition Commission* [2010] EWCA Civ 2, [2010] UKCLR 351).

484. *Stagecoach Group plc v Competition Commission* [2010] CAT 14, para 46.

485. See, eg, *Somerfield plc v Competition Commission* [2006] CAT 4, [2006] Comp AR 390, paras 88, 128.

486. *Office of Fair Trading v IBA Health Ltd* [2004] EWCA Civ 142, [2004] ICR 1364, para 100.

487. *British Sky Broadcasting Group Plc v Competition Commission* [2010] EWCA Civ 2, [2010] UKCLR 351, para 37 (Lloyd LJ).

element in the analysis which is used to reach a conclusion on each of these points'.[488]

Key Sources

Enterprise Act 2002, Part 3.

OFT 527, Mergers: Jurisdictional and procedural guidance (June 2009).

Competition Commission and Office of Fair Trading, Merger Assessment Guidelines (September 2010).

British Sky Broadcasting Group Plc v Competition Commission [2010] EWCA Civ 2, [2010] UKCLR 351.

---

488. *British Sky Broadcasting Group Plc v Competition Commission* [2010] EWCA Civ 2, [2010] UKCLR 351, para 69 (Lloyd LJ).

Chapter 5

PUBLIC ENFORCEMENT

Chapter 5

PUBLIC ENFORCEMENT

87. HOW ARE CASES ALLOCATED BETWEEN THE COMMISSION AND THE COMPETITION AUTHORITIES OF THE MEMBER STATES?

Summary

- One of the goals of Regulation 1/2003 was to decentralise the enforcement of Articles 101 and 102, giving national competition authorities the power to fully apply Articles 101 and 102 while allowing the Commission to focus on the most serious infringements of competition law.

- The Commission focuses on large cases, such as international cartels and abuse of dominance by multinational companies.

- The Commission and the Member State competition authorities cooperate on case allocation through the European Competition Network ('ECN').

- A Joint Statement and a Commission Notice set out details of this cooperation.

- Ideally, one authority, which is best placed to deal with a case, will carry out an investigation alone.

- However, parallel proceedings by a number of Member State authorities may be taken in certain cases, with close cooperation through the ECN.

- The Commission is particularly well placed to take responsibility for investigations of infringements that have effects in three or more Member States.

1. Two changes brought about by the coming into effect on 1 May 2004 of Regulation 1/2003 significantly affect this question. First, whereas the Commission was previously the primary enforcer of Articles 101 and 102 and had exclusive jurisdiction to apply the Article 101(3) exemption, Regulation 1/2003 gave designated national competition authorities and national courts the power to apply Articles 101 and 102 in their entirety, including Article 101(3).[1]

2. Second, Regulation 1/2003 abolished the system of notification of agreements and practices to the Commission and introduced a system of self-assessment. Companies were no longer able to approach the Commission to find out if an agreement or practice was compatible with competition law. A self-assessment had to be made and the risk of making this assessment of compliance with competition

---

1. Regulation 1/2003, Articles 5 and 6. Articles 101(1) and 102 have direct effect and so were enforceable at national level before Regulation 1/2003.

451

law rested on the undertaking in question. Both of these developments have altered the way in which the Commission enforces Articles 101 and 102. The current enforcement regime is aimed at enabling the Commission to focus on the largest and most serious infringements, with the Member States taking greater responsibility in enforcing EU competition law generally.

3.   There are three main ways that an investigation into a potential breach of Article 101 or 102 might begin:

   •   The investigation is started on the Commission's or national authority's own initiative;

   •   Following a complaint; or

   •   Following a leniency application by a whistleblower.

4.   The rules for the allocation of cases among the Member State competition authorities and the Commission are somewhat cumbersome. Regulation 1/2003 provides that 'the Commission and the competition authorities of the Member States shall apply the Community competition rules in close cooperation'.[2] The Commission and the national competition authorities cooperate through the forum of the European Competition Network ('ECN'). As well as Regulation 1/2003, a Joint Statement[3] and a Commission Notice[4] set out further details of this cooperation. Neither the Joint Statement nor the Notice creates legal obligations.

5.   A Member State competition authority is required to inform the Commission 'before or without delay after commencing the first formal investigative measure' into a potential violation of Article 101 or 102.[5] This information is then made available to other members of the ECN. This allows the detection of multiple proceedings, for example, parallel complaints, and allows an efficient re-allocation of the case if appropriate. The ECN endeavours to effect any re-allocation within three months and aims to make case allocation a 'predictable process'.[6] The Commission itself aims to address at the initial assessment phase of a case the possible reallocation of a case to a competition authority in the ECN.[7]

6.   Case re-allocation is the exception rather than the rule and the competition authority that starts an investigation typically retains responsibility for the case. Where re-allocation of a case is found to be necessary, the members of the ECN 'endeavour to re-allocate cases to a single well placed competition authority as often as possible'.[8] Even if a number of authorities are 'well placed,' an

2.   Regulation 1/2003, Article 11(1).
3.   Joint Statement of the Council and the Commission on the functioning of the Network of Competition Authorities, 10 December 2002, Doc. 15435/02 ('ECN Joint Statement').
4.   Commission Notice on cooperation within the Network of Competition Authorities [2004] OJ C101/43 (the 'ECN Notice').
5.   Regulation 1/2003, Article 11(3).
6.   See ECN Joint Statement (2002) paras 12, 13.
7.   DG Competition, Best Practices on the conduct of proceedings concerning Articles 101 and 102 TFEU (January 2010) para 13.
8.   ECN Notice [2004] OJ C101/43, para 7.

investigation by one of them will usually be sufficient if its action can bring about the end of an entire infringement.[9] Conversely, parallel action may be appropriate where the action of one authority would not be sufficient and in this case, the different authorities should cooperate with each other.[10] Where the agreement or practice at issue has effects in three or more Member States, the Commission may be particularly well placed to take over the case.[11]

7.   The term 'well placed' is used throughout the Notice and the criteria for deciding whether a particular authority is 'well placed' to handle an investigation include that:

> ... the agreement or practice has substantial direct actual or foreseeable effects on competition within its territory, is implemented within or originates from its territory;

> the authority is able to effectively bring to an end the entire infringement; [and]

> it can gather, possibly with the assistance of other authorities, the evidence required to prove the infringement.[12]

8.   The Commission or a national competition authority may suspend proceedings before it or reject a complaint where the competition authority of another Member State is dealing with the case.[13] Similarly, a complaint may be rejected by the Commission or a national authority where another Member State authority has already dealt with the case.[14]

Does the Commission have the right to take over a case from a national competition authority?

9.   If the Commission decides to initiate proceedings in a case being dealt with by a national competition authority, that authority is relieved of its competence to apply Article 101 or 102 in that particular case.[15] The Commission must consult the national authority before it takes this step.[16]

---

9.   See ECN Notice [2004] OJ C101/43, para 11.

10.   See ECN Notice [2004] OJ C101/43, paras 12, 13.

11.   See ECN Notice [2004] OJ C101/43, para 14.

12.   ECN Notice [2004] OJ C101/43, para 8.

13.   Regulation 1/2003, Article 13(1).

14.   Regulation 1/2003, Article 13(2).

15.   See Case C–17/10 *Toshiba Corporation* (pending) in which the Regional Court of Brno has made a preliminary reference asking whether Commission proceedings in respect of an infringement of Article 101 instituted after the coming into force of Regulation 1/2003 and resulting in a Commission decision automatically relieve the national competition authority of its competence to deal with that conduct from the time the Commission brought proceedings and whether this also extends to relieving the national authority of applying national law that is equivalent to Article 101.

16.   Regulation 1/2003, Article 11(6).

10.   According to the Joint Statement, once the initial allocation period for a case has passed and one or more national competition authorities are dealing with the case, the Commission will not use its Article 11(6) power to take over the case unless one of the following situations applies:

- ECN members envisage conflicting decisions in the same case;

- ECN members envisage a decision which is obviously in conflict with consolidated case law;

- One or more ECN members are unduly drawing out proceedings;

- There is a need to adopt a Commission decision to develop Community competition policy; or

- The national competition authority does not object.

What obligation is on a national competition authority to keep the Commission informed?

11.   When acting under Article 101 or 102, a Member State competition authority must inform the Commission in writing 'before or without delay after commencing the first formal investigative measure'.[17] A Member State competition authority must inform the Commission in writing at least 30 days before it intends to adopt a decision requiring an infringement to be brought to an end, a decision accepting commitments or a decision withdrawing the benefit of a block exemption. A case summary and draft decision must be supplied.[18] Regulation 1/2003 provides that a Member State competition authority may consult the Commission on any case involving the application of EU law.[19] When a national competition authority rules on agreements, decisions or practices under Article 101 or 102 that have already been subject to a decision of the Commission, they cannot take decisions that would run counter to that of the Commission.[20]

12.   The Commission is not bound by a decision of a national court or competition authority on the application of Article 101 or 102. Indeed, the Commission is 'entitled to adopt at any time individual decisions under Articles [101] and [102] of the Treaty, even where an agreement or practice has already been the subject of a decision by a national court and the decision contemplated by the Commission conflicts with that national court's decision'.[21] The consultation requirements in Article 11 should help to ensure that such a situation does not arise and where

---

17.   Regulation 1/2003, Article 11(3).
18.   See Regulation 1/2003, Article 11(4).
19.   See Regulation 1/2003, Article 11(5).
20.   Regulation 1/2003, Article 16(2). A similar obligation, in Article 16(1), applies to national courts.
21.   Case C–344/98 *Masterfoods Ltd. v HB Ice Cream Ltd.* [2000] ECR I–11369, [2001] 4 CMLR 449, para 48.

those requirements are fulfilled, the Commission will 'normally not' take a decision that conflicts with a national one.[22]

Key Sources

Council Regulation (EC) No 1/2003 on the implementation of the rules on competition laid down in Articles 101 and 102 of the Treaty.

Joint Statement of the Council and the Commission on the functioning of the Network of Competition Authorities, 10 December 2002, Doc. 15435/02.

Commission Notice on cooperation within the Network of Competition Authorities [2004] OJ C101/43.

---

22.   See the ECN Notice [2004] OJ C101/43, para 57.

88. IS IT POSSIBLE TO CONFIRM WITH THE COMMISSION (OR A NATIONAL COMPETITION AUTHORITY) WHETHER A PARTICULAR AGREEMENT OR PRACTICE IS COMPATIBLE WITH ARTICLE 101 OR 102?

Summary

- Regulation 1/2003 abolished the previous notification system.

- It is no longer possible to obtain 'negative clearance'.

- Undertakings must themselves assess whether agreements and practices are compatible with the competition rules and they carry the risk of their own assessment.

- Informal guidance may be sought from the Commission in limited circumstances.

1. Before the adoption of Regulation 1/2003, it was possible to approach the Commission to establish whether a particular agreement or practice was compatible with Article 101 or 102 and, in the case of Article 101, whether the Article 101(3) exemption applied. This notification system operated under Regulation 17/1962, which applied from 1962 until 1 May 2004.[23] An application could be made for a negative clearance that there were no grounds for action on the Commission's part under Article 101(1) or 102 and/or an exemption under Article 101(3).

2. With the coming into force of Regulation 1/2003, the notification system was abolished. It was replaced by a system of 'self-assessment'.[24] Undertakings must themselves consider whether their agreements or actions are compatible with Article 101 or 102 or would benefit from the Article 101(3) exemption. The risk of compliance with the competition rules therefore rests with the undertaking.

3. Self-assessment may raise uncertainties in particular when considering whether the Article 101(3) exemption applies to an agreement that is caught by Article 101(1). The Commission's Article 101(3) Guidelines provide that the assessment of whether Article 101(3) applies may vary over the life of the agreement as circumstances change, as 'the assessment is sensitive to material changes in the facts'.[25] This requirement for a dynamic and ongoing assessment creates additional risk and uncertainty for companies.

---

23. EEC Council Regulation No 17/62 implementing Articles 85 and 86 of the Treaty [1962] OJ 13/204.

24. On the functioning of this and other aspects of Regulation 1/2003, see Communication from the Commission to the European Parliament and the Council – Report on the functioning of Regulation 1/2003, COM(2009) 206 final (29 April 2009).

25. Commission Guidelines on the application of Article 81(3) of the Treaty [2004] OJ C101/97, para 44.

4.   Useful tools for making a self-assessment include the various guidelines published by the Commission and the body of EU competition law developed by the European courts.

5.   The Commission may decide 'on its own initiative' that Article 101 or 102 does not apply to an agreement or practice.[26] However it is not envisaged that such decisions would be taken other than 'in exceptional cases where the public interest of the Community so requires ... with a view to clarifying the law and ensuring its consistent application throughout the Community.'[27] Such an exceptional case might concern a new type of agreement not covered by previous case law.

6.   The Commission may continue to issue block exemption Regulations by which it declares Article 101(1) inapplicable in respect of categories of agreements.[28]

When can informal guidance be obtained?

7.   Recital 38 of Regulation 1/2003 indicates that undertakings may seek informal guidance from the Commission in cases that give rise to genuine uncertainty because they raise novel or unresolved questions on the application of Article 101 or 102. Any informal guidance produced by the Commission would not be legally binding and the Commission can still take action under Regulation 1/2003 in respect of cases that have been the subject of informal guidance.

8.   The Commission's Informal Guidance Notice sets out more details of this procedure.[29] It states that informal guidance will only be considered where:

    (i)   the question raised is not covered by case law or other general guidance;

    (ii) clarification of the novel issue is useful in the light of the specific circumstances or because the agreement or practice is widespread; and

    (iii) informal guidance can be issued without further fact-finding.[30]

9.   The request for informal guidance should set out all the details of the agreement or practice in question as well as detailed reasons why the request raises novel questions.[31] The Commission had not released details of any applications for informal guidance as of 1 September 2010.

Ireland

10.   The position under Irish competition law is comparable to that at EU level. Previously, under the Competition Act 1991, an undertaking could notify an agreement or practice to the Competition Authority, which could issue a certificate

---

26. Regulation 1/2003, Article 10.
27. Regulation 1/2003, recital 14.
28. Regulation 1/2003, recital 10.
29. Commission Notice on informal guidance relating to novel questions concerning Articles 81 and 82 of the EC Treaty that arise in individual cases (guidance letters) [2004] OJ C 101/78 ('Commission Informal Guidance Notice').
30. Commission Informal Guidance Notice [2004] OJ C 101/78, para 8.
31. Commission Informal Guidance Notice [2004] OJ C 101/78, para 14.

stating that in its opinion there was no breach of section 4(1)[32] or a license to the effect that the conditions in section 4(5) were satisfied.[33] Under the Competition Act 2002 regime, it is not possible to make such notifications and undertakings must carry out a self-assessment.[34]

11. The Competition Authority does not have a policy of issuing informal guidance on the compatibility of particular agreements or conduct with competition law.

12. One of the functions of the Competition Authority is to publish notices containing practical guidance as to how the provisions of the Competition Act 2002 can be complied with.[35] The Authority has published notices on trade associations, collective action in the community pharmacy sector, pay-TV exclusivity arrangements in apartment complexes, medical fees, refusals to supply and vertical agreements and notices in respect of certain aspects of the merger control regime.[36] In some of these notices, the Authority has provided guidance in respect of both section 4 of the Competition Act 2002 and Article 101.[37]

13. The Authority may issue declarations (similar to block exemptions) in respect of a category of agreements that meet the criteria of section 4(5) of the Competition Act 2002, which mirror the criteria in Article 101(3).[38] At the time of writing, there were three such declarations in force, relating to motor fuels,[39] exclusive purchasing agreements for LPG[40] and vertical agreements between suppliers and resellers.[41]

14. The High Court has jurisdiction to apply sections 4 and 5 of the Competition Act 2002 and so it can declare in a case before it that a particular agreement or practice was not incompatible with section 4 or 5 or met the conditions for an exemption under section 4(5). The High Court can also apply Article 101 and 102 in full and

---

32. Competition Act 1991, s 4(4).
33. Competition Act 1991, s 4(2). See also *Cronin v Competition Authority* [1998] 1 IR 265 (unsuccessful challenge to the fairness of the procedures for granting a license and the constitutionality of the Authority's power to grant licenses).
34. See generally, McCarthy and Power, *Irish Competition Law: The Competition Act 2002* (2003) para 3.67 *et seq*.
35. Competition Act 2002, s 30(1)(d).
36. The notices are available on the Competition Authority's website.
37. See, e.g., Decision No. N/09/001 Notice in respect of Collective Action in the Community Pharmacy Sector (23 September 2009).
38. Competition Act 2002, ss 4(3), 4(5).
39. Competition Authority Decision No. D/08/001 issuing a Declaration pursuant to section 4(3) of the Competition Act 2002 to a category of exclusive purchasing agreements in respect of motor fuels (1 July 2008; amended 17 May 2010; due to expire on 30 November 2010).
40. Competition Authority Declaration No. D/05/001 in respect of Exclusive Purchasing Agreements for Cylinder Liquefied Petroleum Gas (8 March 2005; amended 31 March 2005) (due to expire on 31 March 2015).
41. Competition Authority Declaration No. D/03/001 in Respect of Vertical Agreements and Concerted Practices (5 December 2003, last amended 17 May 2010; due to expire on 30 November 2010); Competition Authority Notice N/03/002 in respect of Vertical Agreements and Concerted Practices (5 December 2003; amended 17 May 2010).

could make similar declarations in respect of the compatibility of the agreement or practice with the EU competition rules.[42] A party to an agreement or practice could not avail of the court's jurisdiction simply to obtain clearance for an agreement or practice as it would first have to be a party to proceedings before it could raise the matter before the court. However, once properly before the court, such declarations could be sought.

UK

15. The position in the UK is similar to that at EU-level. It is not possible to approach the OFT to obtain prior approval for an agreement or particular conduct and a self-assessment of compliance with the EU rules and the provisions of the Competition Act 1998 must be made.

16. It is possible to seek informal guidance on the applicability of Article 101/102 and the Chapter I/II prohibitions. Any views given by the OFT are not binding.[43] It may be possible to obtain a written opinion from the OFT if a case raises novel or unresolved questions of law. However, this would also be non-binding.[44] Such an opinion, on newspaper and magazine distribution, was given by the OFT in 2008.[45] It was couched in terms of an opinion 'to facilitate self-assessment' of the compatibility of agreements with the Competition Act 1998. Although non-binding, this opinion was detailed and the OFT published two draft opinions for consultation before adopting its final views.

17. The OFT may recommend to the Secretary of State to issue a block exemption from the Chapter I prohibition for a category of agreements that meet the criteria in section 9 of the Competition Act 1998, which mirror Article 101(3).[46]

Key Sources

Council Regulation (EC) No 1/2003 on the implementation of the rules on competition laid down in Articles 101 and 102 of the Treaty.

Commission Notice on informal guidance relating to novel questions concerning Articles 81 and 82 of the EC Treaty that arise in individual cases (guidance letters) [2004] OJ C 101/78.

---

42. The Irish courts have the power to apply Articles 101 and 102 in full by virtue of Article 6 of Regulation 1/2003. In addition, the courts have been designated as competition authorities for certain purposes under Regulation 1/2003 (see Regulation 1/2003, Article 5; SI No 195 of 2004 European Communities (Implementation of the Rules on Competition laid down in Articles 81 and 82 of the Treaty) Regulations 2004, as amended by SI No 525 of 2007).
43. An approach can be made by telephone (08457 224499) or by email (enquiries@oft.gsi.gov.uk).
44. The OFT seems to distinguish between informal advice and an opinion, although both are non-binding. It might be the case that the former would be given orally. See, e.g., the OFT 402, Abuse of a dominant position: Understanding competition law (December 2004) 20.
45. OFT 1025, Newspaper and Magazine Distribution: Opinion of the Office of Fair Trading: Guidance to facilitate self-assessment under the Competition Act 1998 (October 2008).
46. Competition Act 1998, ss 6, 8, 9.

89. **WHAT RIGHTS DOES A COMPLAINANT HAVE IN A COMPETITION INVESTIGATION?**

Summary

EU

- There are different categories of complainant.

- A 'legitimate interest' is required to obtain the status of a formal complainant and certain information must be provided to the Commission.

- That status brings with it certain procedural rights.

- Below this, complainants with a 'sufficient interest' are given the opportunity to make submissions.

- The Commission has discretion as to how it involves informal complainants or other third parties.

Ireland

- There is no provision for formal complainant status in a Competition Authority investigation and no special rights are provided.

UK

- To qualify as a formal complainant in an OFT investigation, one's interest must be likely to be materially affected and certain information must be provided to the OFT in a reasoned complaint.

- The OFT will consult formal complainants and give them an opportunity to make submissions.

1. Complainants play an important role in the enforcement of competition law. Many breaches of competition law would not be brought to light were it not for complaints. A determined complainant, especially one that is well-resourced, can play a significant role in a competition investigation and might even be in a position to make much of the case for the Commission or other regulator through economic and legal submissions. It is therefore important to consider what rights complainants have to be heard.

2. A formal complaint that the EU competition rules have been infringed may be made to the Commission by Member States or any 'natural or legal persons who can show a legitimate interest'.[47] A complainant who can show a legitimate interest is entitled to certain procedural rights.

---

47. Regulation 1/2003, Article 7(2).

Who has a 'legitimate interest'?

3. Only persons with a 'legitimate interest' in the subject matter of a complaint are entitled to make a formal complaint under Article 7(2) of Regulation 1/2003. Whether a person has a legitimate interest depends on the likelihood of them suffering economic damage as a result of the practice at issue.[48] Any person who suffers or is likely to suffer damage from the alleged infringement should satisfy the requirement of a legitimate interest, whether they are customers, distributors, suppliers or competitors of the undertakings involved.[49]

4. Persons with a sufficient interest include a final consumer 'who shows that his economic interests have been harmed or are likely to be harmed as a result of the restriction of competition in question'.[50] The right to make a complaint extends to consumer associations but does not extend to groups acting *pro bono*.[51]

5. To obtain the status of a complainant, it is not necessary that one's complaint was the catalyst for the Commission to launch its investigation. A formal complaint can still be made even after the preliminary investigation phase of the infringement proceeding has been opened upon the Commission's own initiative or by a separate complaint.[52]

What information should a formal complaint include?

6. The complaint should include the information required by Form C, attached to Regulation 773/2004, although the Commission may decide to dispense with this requirement with respect to some of the information.[53] Three paper copies and an electronic copy should be supplied to the Commission.

---

48. See Cases T–213&214/01 *Österreichische Postsparkasse AG v Commission* [2006] ECR II–1601, [2007] 4 CMLR 506, para 131.

49. For examples of persons who have been found to have the requisite 'legitimate interest,' see Bellamy & Child (6th edn, 2008) para 13.065.

50. Cases T–213&214/01 *Österreichische Postsparkasse AG v Commission* [2006] ECR II–1601, [2007] 4 CMLR 506, para 114. See also Cases T–259/02 etc *Raiffeisen Zentralbank Österreich AG v Commission* [2006] ECR II–5169, [2007] 5 CMLR 1142, paras 97–100.

51. See the Commission Notice on the handling of complaints by the Commission under Articles 81 and 82 of the EC Treaty [2004] OJ C101/65 (the 'Commission Complaints Notice') para 38.

52. See Cases T–213&214/01 *Österreichische Postsparkasse AG v Commission* [2006] ECR II–1601, [2007] 4 CMLR 506, para 91.

53. Commission Regulation (EC) No 773/2004 relating to the conduct of proceedings by the Commission pursuant to Articles 81 and 82 of the EC Treaty [2004] OJ L123/18, Article 5(1).

The information required by Form C is described in the form annexed to Regulation 773/2004 as follows:

Form C

COMPLAINT PURSUANT TO ARTICLE 7 OF REGULATION (EC) No 1/2003

I. Information regarding the complainant and the undertaking(s) or association of undertakings giving rise to the complaint

1. Give full details on the identity of the legal or natural person submitting the complaint. Where the complainant is an undertaking, identify the corporate group to which it belongs and provide a concise overview of the nature and scope of its business activities. Provide a contact person (with telephone number, postal and e-mail-address) from which supplementary explanations can be obtained.

2. Identify the undertaking(s) or association of undertakings whose conduct the complaint relates to, including, where applicable, all available information on the corporate group to which the undertaking(s) complained of belong and the nature and scope of the business activities pursued by them. Indicate the position of the complainant vis-à-vis the undertaking(s) or association of undertakings complained of (e.g. customer, competitor).

II. Details of the alleged infringement and evidence

3. Set out in detail the facts from which, in your opinion, it appears that there exists an infringement of Article [101] or [102] of the Treaty and/or Article 53 or 54 of the EEA agreement. Indicate in particular the nature of the products (goods or services) affected by the alleged infringements and explain, where necessary, the commercial relationships concerning these products. Provide all available details on the agreements or practices of the undertakings or associations of undertakings to which this complaint relates. Indicate, to the extent possible, the relative market positions of the undertakings concerned by the complaint.

4. Submit all documentation in your possession relating to or directly connected with the facts set out in the complaint (for example, texts of agreements, minutes of negotiations or meetings, terms of transactions, business documents, circulars, correspondence, notes of telephone conversations...). State the names and address of the persons able to testify to the facts set out in the complaint, and in particular of persons affected by the alleged infringement. Submit statistics or other data in your possession which relate to the facts set out, in particular where they show developments in the marketplace (for example information relating to prices and price trends, barriers to entry to the market for new suppliers etc.).

5. Set out your view about the geographical scope of the alleged infringement and explain, where that is not obvious, to what extent trade between Member States or between the Community and one or more EFTA States that are contracting parties of the EEA Agreement may be affected by the conduct complained of.

III. Finding sought from the Commission and legitimate interest

6. Explain what finding or action you are seeking as a result of proceedings brought by the Commission.

Form C

COMPLAINT PURSUANT TO ARTICLE 7 OF REGULATION (EC) No 1/2003

7. Set out the grounds on which you claim a legitimate interest as complainant pursuant to Article 7 of Regulation (EC) No 1/2003. State in particular how the conduct complained of affects you and explain how, in your view, intervention by the Commission would be liable to remedy the alleged grievance.

IV. Proceedings before national competition authorities or national courts

8. Provide full information about whether you have approached, concerning the same or closely related subject-matters, any other competition authority and/or whether a lawsuit has been brought before a national court. If so, provide full details about the administrative or judicial authority contacted and your submissions to such authority.

What is the Commission's procedure for dealing with a complaint?

7. A person qualifying as a formal complainant (*i.e.* one with a 'legitimate interest') in a Commission investigation under Article 7 of Regulation 1/2003 is entitled to certain rights. In general, the complainant is to be 'associated closely' with the Commission's proceedings into the alleged infringement.[54]

8. The Commission endeavours (but is not bound) to inform a complainant within 4 months of receipt of the complaint what action it proposes to take.[55] During this period, there may be informal exchanges between the Commission and the complainant.[56]

9. The Commission has significant discretion as to which investigations it will pursue and aims to focus its resources on cases in which it appears likely that an infringement could be found, in particular on cases with the most significant impact on the functioning of competition and risk of consumer harm, as well as on cases which are relevant with a view to defining EU competition policy and/or to ensuring coherent application of Articles 101 and/or 102 TFEU.[57]

10. In deciding the order of priority for dealing with complaints lodged before it, the Commission may legitimately refer to the Union interest. In this context, it is required to assess in each case how serious the alleged interferences with competition are and how persistent their consequences are. In particular, it must take into account the duration and extent of the infringements complained of and their effect on the competition situation in the EU. In deciding if there is sufficient Union interest in investigating a complaint, the Commission may assess whether an agreement or practice constitutes a serious impediment to the proper functioning of the common market. This concept is different from whether the

---

54. Regulation 1/2003, Article 27(1).
55. Commission Complaints Notice [2004] OJ C101/65, para 61.
56. Commission Complaints Notice [2004] OJ C101/65, para 55.
57. DG Competition, Best Practices on the conduct of proceedings concerning Articles 101 and 102 TFEU (January 2010) para 12.

agreement or practice has an effect on trade between Member States, which is a threshold issue for the application of Article 101 or 102.[58]

11. The Commission may reject a complaint if it does not appear to disclose a breach or potential breach of Article 101 or 102. The Commission may also reject a complaint on the grounds that a Member State authority is dealing or has dealt with the case.[59]

12. Even where there appears to be a breach of the competition rules, the Commission may reject the complaint on the basis of a lack of Union interest[60] as the Commission is 'entitled to give differing degrees of priority to the complaints brought before it and refer to the [Union] interest in order to determine the degree of priority to be applied to the various complaints it receives'.[61] Factors going to lack of Union interest would include that the complainant can bring an action in a national court, the significance of the infringement as against the scope of the investigation required and the fact that the relevant undertakings have given assurances to change their conduct.[62]

13. Although it has a wide discretion in dealing with complaints, there are certain constraints on the Commission. It 'must consider attentively all the matters of fact and of law which the complainant brings to its attention'.[63] The Commission is under an obligation to state reasons if it declines to continue with the examination of a complaint, setting out the facts justifying the decision and the legal considerations on the basis of which it was adopted.[64] The Commission is also subject to the duty of sound administration, enshrined in Article 41 of the Charter of Fundamental Rights and which requires the Commission to undertake a diligent and impartial examination of the complaint.[65]

---

58. See Case 425/07P *AEPI v Commission* [2009] ECR I–3205, [2009] 5 CMLR 1337, paras 49–53.
59. Regulation 1/2003, Article 13.
60. This was established in the case law, e.g., Case T–24/90 *Automec Srl v Commission* [1992] ECR II–2223, [1992] 5 CMLR 431, paras 76, 77.
61. Commission Complaints Notice [2004] OJ C101/65, para 41.
62. Commission Complaints Notice [2004] OJ C101/65, para 44.
63. Case T–306/05 *Scippacercola v Commission* [2008] ECR II–4, [2008] 4 CMLR 1418, para 95 (appeal dismissed, Case C–159/08P *Scippacercola v Commission* [2009] ECR I–46, [2010] 4 CMLR 1205).
64. Case T–306/05 *Scippacercola v Commission* [2008] ECR II–4, [2008] 4 CMLR 1418, paras 96, 174.
65. The obligation of diligent and impartial examination in respect of complaints is regularly referred to in State aid cases. See, e.g., Case C–290/07 *Commission v Scott SA*, judgment of 2 September 2010, para 90. For a statement of the obligation in the context of a complaint alleging a breach of Article 106 in conjunction with Article 102, see Case T–54/99 *max.mobil Telekommunikation Service GmbH v Commission* [2002] ECR II–313, [2002] 4 CMLR 1356, paras 48–49 (overruled on other grounds, Case C–141/02P *Commission v T-Mobile Austria GmbH* [2005] ECR I–1283, [2005] 4 CMLR 735).

14. If the Commission decides that there are insufficient grounds to act on a complaint, it shall inform the complainant in a so-called Article 7 letter of its reasons and set a time-limit within which the complainant may make known its views in writing. This letter is a preparatory measure and so cannot be the subject of an action for annulment before the European courts.[66] If the Article 7 letter was not issued within a reasonable time, the complainant could take an action under Article 265 TFEU for failure to act but the subsequent issue of the Article 7 letter would prevent such a challenge.[67] At this stage, the complainant is entitled to access to non-confidential documents upon which the Commission has based its provisional assessment. If the complainant's further submissions do not lead to a change in the Commission's assessment, the complaint is rejected (or if the complainant does not make its views known within the stipulated timeframe, the complaint is deemed to be withdrawn).[68]

What rights does a complainant have if a Statement of Objections is issued?

15. Where a case proceeds to the issuing of a Statement of Objections ('SO'), the complainant is entitled to a copy of the non-confidential version of the SO and may make its views on the SO known to the Commission in writing within a certain timeframe set down by the Commission.[69] However, where the settlement procedure under Regulation 773/2004 applies, the complainant does not have this right. Instead, the Commission shall inform the complainant in writing of the nature and subject matter of the procedure and set a time limit to submit written observations.[70]

16. Following a request in writing, the Commission may afford the complainant the opportunity to make submissions at the oral hearing, if appropriate.[71]

17. The complainant does not have a right of access to the Commission's file. A complainant might be able to utilise Regulation 1049/2001 to access documents in the file. There are a number of exceptions that the Commission can rely on to deny access, including that the documents are commercially confidential or contain legal advice[72] but the Commission must justify its refusal and cannot simply make a general assertion that the documents are confidential. Rather it must carry out a concrete examination to determine if one of the exceptions to disclosure applies.[73]

---

66. See Case C–282/95P *Guérin automobiles v Commission* [1997] ECR I–1503, [1997] 5 CMLR 447, para 24.
67. See Case T–38/96 *Guérin automobiles v Commission* [1997] ECR II–1223, [1997] 5 CMLR 352, para 31.
68. Regulation 773/2004, Articles 7 and 8.
69. See Regulation 773/2004, Article 6.
70. Regulation 773/2004, Article 6(1), as substituted by Regulation 622/2008, Article 1(2).
71. Regulation 773/2004, Article 6.
72. Regulation (EC) No 1049/2001 regarding public access to European Parliament, Council and Commission documents [2001] OJ L145/43, Article 4.
73. See Case T–2/03 *Verein für Konsumenteninformation v Commission* [2005] ECR II–1121, [2005] 4 CMLR 1627, para 69 *et seq*; Case T–237/05 *Éditions Odile Jacob SAS v Commission*, judgment of 9 June 2010 (contd \...)

What are the rights of complainants with merely a 'sufficient interest'?

18. A person who does not have a legitimate interest may still bring the alleged infringement of competition law to the attention of the Commission. In the case of such a person who can show a 'sufficient interest' in the subject matter of the complaint, the Commission 'shall inform them in writing of the nature and subject matter of the procedure and shall set a time-limit within which they may make known their views in writing'.[74] The Commission may invite such persons to the oral hearing if they so request.[75]

19. Although there is no definition of 'sufficient interest' in Regulation 773/2004, the Regulation provides that consumer associations that apply to be heard should generally be treated as having a sufficient interest where the complaint involves consumer goods or inputs into consumer goods.[76]

What role may informal complainants play?

20. In dealing with an informal complaint by a person who will not have any of the rights granted to a complainant with a 'legitimate interest' or 'sufficient interest', the Commission may use the information provided and it will deal with any correspondence from such person according to the principles of good administrative practice.[77]

21. Where it issues a SO and holds an oral hearing, the Commission may in its discretion invite other persons to submit written observations and express their views at the oral hearing.[78] This might include informal complainants.

If the Commission rejects a complaint, may the complainant appeal?[79]

22. If a formal complaint is rejected, the complainant is entitled to require the Commission to adopt a formal decision that can be appealed to the General Court under Article 263 TFEU.[80] Persons have standing to appeal against decisions

---

73. (contd) (on appeal, Case C–404/10P *Commission v Éditions Jacob*). For further discussion of using Regulation 1049/2001 to obtain Commission documents, in the context of private actions, see Question 120.
74. Commission Regulation (EC) No 773/2004 of 7 April 2004 relating to the conduct of proceedings by the Commission pursuant to Articles 81 and 82 of the EC Treaty, [2004] OJ L123/18, Article 13(1).
75. Regulation 773/2004, Article 13(3).
76. Regulation 773/2004, recital 11.
77. Commission Complaints Notice [2004] OJ C101/65, para 4. An informal complaint can be sent to the Commission at the following email address: comp-market-information@ec.europa.eu
78. Regulation 773/2004, Article 13(3) and recital 11.
79. See also Question 83 (appeals in merger cases) and Question 130 (appeals in state aid cases).
80. See, e.g., Case C–282/95P *Guérin automobiles v Commission* [1997] ECR I–1503, [1997] 5 CMLR 447, para 36; Regulation 773/2004, Article 7(2). On standing requirements for use of Article 263 see, in the context of merger control, Question 83.

which are 'of direct and individual concern to them' and formal complainants with a legitimate interest within the meaning of Article 7 of Regulation 1/2003 are entitled to bring an appeal.[81] It is more doubtful that a complainant with merely a 'sufficient interest' would have standing under Article 263.

23. The Commission is required to set out the reasons for its decision to reject the complaint in a sufficiently precise and detailed manner to enable the General Court effectively to review the Commission's use of its discretion to define priorities.[82] If the Commission fails to act within two months of having been called on to define its position, the complainant could bring an action before the General Court under Article 265 TFEU. Once the Commission does define its position however, an action for failure to act is no longer admissible.[83]

24. The Court of Justice has held, in the context of a State aid complaint by a company, that a letter from the Commission to the complainant stating that 'in the absence of additional information to justify continuing the investigation, the Commission has, for the purposes of administrative action, closed the file...' indicated that the Commission actually closed the file for the purposes of administrative action. This act, which prevented the complainant from submitting its comments in the context of a formal investigation procedure, produced legal effects which were capable of affecting that company's interests and, therefore, constituted an act open to challenge for the purposes of Article 263.[84]

Ireland

25. Section 30(1)(b) of the Competition Act 2002 provides that one of the functions of the Authority is to carry out investigations into breaches of competition law in response to complaints made to it by any person. Other than this, the 2002 Act does not contain details about the role of complainants.[85] The Competition Authority welcomes complaints[86] and often bases its investigations into potential breaches of competition law on complaints. The Authority's practice is to carry out a preliminary screening of each complaint. Many complaints are resolved at this stage because, for example, they really contain requests for information or are from companies facing legitimate competition. If a complaint succeeds in getting beyond preliminary screening, the Authority will carry out a more detailed

---

81. See, e.g., Case 210/81 *Schmidt v Commission* [1983] ECR 3045, [1984] 1 CMLR 63, para 14.
82. See Case C–450/98P *International Express Carriers Conference (IECC) v Commission* [2001] ECR I–3947, [2001] 5 CMLR 291, para 54.
83. Case 125/78 *GEMA v Commission* [1979] ECR 3173, [1980] 2 CMLR 177, paras 20–23.
84. Case C–521/06 *Athinaïki Techniki AE v Commission* [2008] ECR I–5829, [2008] 3 CMLR 979.
85. See also section 50 of the 2002 Act, which sets out protection for employees who report a breach of competition law to the Authority. See further on whistleblowers, McCarthy and Power, *Irish Competition Law: The Competition Act 2002* (2003) paras 6.14–6.28.
86. See, e.g., the Competition Authority's Guide to Competition Law and Policy for Businesses (November 2009) 10.

evaluation. If it rejects a complaint at this stage, the practice of the Authority is to issue a detailed statement of reasons to the complainant.[87] It might be possible for a complainant whose complaint is rejected at this stage to seek a judicial review of the Authority's decision not to pursue the matter (in particular in light of the Authority's extensive investigative powers which would not be available to a private party), although such an application for judicial review might be complicated by the fact the complainant may be able to bring its own private action in respect of the alleged breach of competition law.

UK

26.   Complaints about breaches of competition law in the UK should be made to the OFT. Other than the role accorded 'super-complaints' under the Enterprise Act 2002, complainants in competition investigations are not provided a formal role on a statutory footing.

27.   The OFT may give a complainant formal or informal status. To qualify as a formal complainant, a person must request formal complainant status and submit a written reasoned complaint with prescribed information. The type of information that must be submitted in a formal complaint is similar to that which must be provided in a formal complaint to the Commission.[88] Details of what information must be provided in a reasoned complaint are set out in detail by the OFT in an annex to its guide for complainants.[89]

28.   Formal complainant status may be granted to more than one person in respect of a single investigation but will only be granted to a person whose interests are, or are likely to be, materially affected by the agreement or conduct in question.[90] Examples of complainants that the OFT considers would usually qualify as formal complainants include:

- actual or potential competitors denied access to a market;

- a competitor who is unable to compete effectively because of the predatory behaviour of a dominant undertaking;

- a customer who has had its choice of supplier restricted by an upstream market sharing agreement;

- a retailer who is refused supply because it has priced below a recommended price;

- a consumer association or trade association, where consumers' or members' interests are likely to be materially affected.[91]

---

87.   Statistics in respect of complaints received by the Authority are set out in its annual reports, available on the Authority's website.
88.   The requirement for some of this information may be waived in certain circumstances, for example with respect to complaints from individual consumers or consumer associations.
89.   OFT 451, Involving third parties in Competition Act Investigations (2006) Annex B.
90.   OFT 451, Involving third parties in Competition Act Investigations (2006) para 2.6.
91.   OFT 451, Involving third parties in Competition Act Investigations (2006) para 2.12.

29.   A complainant seeking formal status can make an informal complaint in advance of submitting a reasoned complaint.[92]

What rights does a complainant have in respect of file closures?

30.   Before deciding not to take a case to the stage of a Statement of Objections ('SO'), the OFT will provide formal complainants with an opportunity to comment on the OFT's provisional view before the file is closed. This applies to all file closures, whether or not a formal investigation under section 25 of the Competition Act 1998 has been opened. The OFT's provisional view will be in the form of a provisional closure letter or, if it intends to adopt a reasoned decision closing the case, a non-confidential version of that proposed decision. The OFT sets a time limit in which the complainant must make submissions. If the OFT proceeds to close the file, it will inform the complainant as to why the additional submissions did not result in a change of mind.

31.   The OFT will inform other complainants of its decision to close the file but they do not have the right to make submissions before the file is closed.[93]

What role does a complainant have if a Statement of Objections is issued?

32.   The OFT will usually provide formal complainants with a non-confidential version of the SO and seek their views. It may also consult with third parties who are materially affected, have requested to be consulted and are likely to be able to materially assist the OFT's investigation. The OFT will usually invite approaches from third parties by publishing a notice about the SO on its website.

33.   Formal complainants and third parties who are provided with a non-confidential version of the SO will usually be invited to submit comments within a time period set by the OFT. Normally, comments will have to be made on the basis of the SO and the OFT will not make other documents (such as responses of the parties under investigation) available to formal complainants or third parties. The OFT will not usually invite formal complainants or third parties to give oral submissions.

34.   Consultations with formal complainants and third parties may be less extensive in cartel cases where consultation could prejudice a related criminal investigation.[94]

May a complainant appeal if the OFT closes the file or finds that there is no infringement?

35.   A complainant who is aggrieved at the OFT's closure of the file or its finding that there is no infringement of the Competition Act has two potential ways to challenge the OFT's action. It can appeal to the CAT and/or apply for judicial review.

---

92.   OFT 451, Involving third parties in Competition Act Investigations (2006) para A.11.
93.   See OFT 451, Involving third parties in Competition Act Investigations (2006) para 2.35.
94.   See OFT 451, Involving third parties in Competition Act Investigations (2006) Ch 3.

36. If the OFT has taken an appealable decision, the complainant can file an appeal before the CAT as a person with 'sufficient interest' under section 47(1)(a). Decisions which are appealable include decisions by the OFT as to whether the UK or EU competition rules have been infringed.[95] It is a question of fact whether an appealable decision has been taken. This is a question of substance, not form, to be determined objectively.[96] The issue is whether the OFT has in fact reached a decision on the question of infringement so a decision by the OFT to close the file merely for administrative priorities is not an appealable decision.[97] Assuming there is an appealable decision, the complainant would normally need to persuade the CAT that the decision was:

> incorrect or, at the least, insufficient, from the point of view of (i) the reasons given; (ii) the facts and analysis relied on; (iii) the law applied; (iv) the investigation undertaken; or (v) the procedure followed.[98]

37. It may also be open to a complainant to seek judicial review of the OFT's decision. The courts have acknowledged that the OFT has a wide discretion in deciding whether to close an investigation. Indeed, 'it is plain that the OFT must have the power to close the file on cases otherwise it would not be able to function satisfactorily'.[99] A complainant seeking to challenge a decision by the OFT to close the file will have to meet the judicial review threshold of irrationality in the *Wednesbury* sense.[100]

38. If it is unclear that an appealable decision has been taken, it may be advisable for the claimant to issue both an appeal to the CAT under section 47 and judicial review proceedings in the Administrative Court and apply for a stay of the judicial review proceedings while the CAT determines if it has jurisdiction.[101]

What are 'super-complaints'?

39. Section 11 of the Enterprise Act provides for designated consumer bodies to make 'super-complaints' to the OFT where a market in the UK is or appears to be significantly harming the interests of consumers. To date, seven bodies have been designated to make super-complaints: the Campaign for Real Ale Limited, the Consumer Council for Water, the Consumers' Association (Which?), the General Consumer Council for Northern Ireland, the National Association of Citizens

---

95. Competition Act 1998, s 46(3).
96. *Claymore Dairies Ltd v Office of Fair Trading* [2003] CAT 3, [2004] Comp AR 1, para 122.
97. See *Cityhook Ltd v Office of Fair Trading* [2007] CAT 18, [2007] Comp AR 813. A review of the law on the question of appealable decisions is set out at paras 223–237.
98. *Freeserve.com plc v Director General of Telecommunications* [2002] CAT 8, [2003] Comp AR 1, para 114.
99. *R (Cityhook Ltd) v Office of Fair Trading* [2009] EWHC 57 (Admin), [2009] UKCLR 255, para 163.
100. See *R (Cityhook Ltd) v Office of Fair Trading* [2009] EWHC 57 (Admin), [2009] UKCLR 255, para 165.
101. See Brealey and Green (eds), *Competition Litigation: UK Practice and Procedure* (2010) para 1.58.

Advice Bureaux, the National Consumer Council and the Scottish Association of Citizens Advice Bureaux.[102]

40.   The OFT must publish a response to the complaint within 90 days indicating if it has decided to take action. It must give reasons. If the OFT has decided to take action it must indicate what action it proposes to take.[103] A number of super-complaints have been made to the OFT since the procedure was introduced, some of which have led the OFT to carrying out market studies.[104]

Key Sources

Commission Notice on the handling of complaints by the Commission under Articles 81 and 82 of the EC Treaty (the 'Complaints Notice') [2004] OJ C101/65.

Commission Regulation (EC) No 773/2004 relating to the conduct of proceedings by the Commission pursuant to Articles 81 and 82 of the EC Treaty [2004] OJ L123/18.

Österreichische Postsparkasse AG v Commission [2006] ECR II–1601, [2007] 4 CMLR 506.

UK

OFT 451, Involving third parties in Competition Act Investigations (2006).

---

102. The Enterprise Act 2002 (Bodies Designated to make Super-complaints) (Amendment) Order 2009 (SI 2009/2079).
103. Enterprise Act 2002, s 11.
104. Details of super complaints made and responses by the OFT are available on the OFT's website.

90. **WHAT POWERS DOES THE COMMISSION ENJOY WHEN INVESTIGATING POTENTIAL BREACHES OF COMPETITION LAW? WHAT ARE THE INVESTIGATIVE POWERS OF THE IRISH COMPETITION AUTHORITY AND THE OFT?**

Summary

- The Commission has a wide discretion in deciding whether to carry out an investigation but the decision to launch an inspection is reviewable by the Court of Justice.

- The Commission has broad investigative powers to require 'all necessary information' and conduct 'all necessary inspections'. This gives the Commission the power to conduct 'dawn raids'.

- The Commission has the power to take copies of documents in any form.

- The Commission cannot compel individuals to make statements but it can take voluntary statements.

- The Commission has the power to inspect non-business premises in certain circumstances.

Ireland

- The Competition Authority has wide powers of investigation in respect of suspected infringements of the Competition Act 2002 and the EU competition rules.

- These include entry, search and seizure powers. Homes can be searched.

- The Authority can summon witnesses and examine them on oath.

UK

- The OFT has broad investigatory powers that include the power of entry, search and seizure.

- Non-business premises can be searched.

- When investigating the cartel offence, the OFT has additional investigatory powers such as the power to conduct covert surveillance and use informers.

1. The Commission's powers in antitrust investigations are set out in Regulation 1/2003 but the Regulation is silent about the grounds on which the Commission may order an investigation. A distinction should be drawn between an investigation, whether through inspections ('dawn raids') or requests to undertakings for information, and the formal opening of proceedings. The Commission will typically carry out an investigation first and open formal proceedings at a later date. The Commission may open formal proceedings at any time but no later than the earlier of (i) the date it issues a preliminary assessment under Article 9(1) of

Regulation 1/2003; (ii) the date of a statement of objections; or (iii) the date of publication of a notice under Article 27(4) of Regulation 1/2003.[105]

2. When it receives a complaint or a leniency application or otherwise considers carrying out an investigation, the Commission will assess the merits of proceeding with an investigation during an 'initial assessment phase'. The Commission's assessment is driven by the fact that it focuses its enforcement resources on cases in which it appears likely that an infringement could be found, in particular on cases with the most significant impact on the functioning of competition and risk of consumer harm, as well as on cases which are relevant with a view to defining EU competition policy and/or to ensuring coherent application of Articles 101 and/or 102 TFEU.[106]

3. The decision adopted by the Commission to order an investigation must specify the subject matter and purpose of the investigation. This decision is reviewable by the Court of Justice.[107] On review of an inspection decision, the court will seek to verify if the Commission 'had in its file information and evidence providing reasonable grounds for suspecting infringements of the competition rules by the applicant'.[108] If the decision is annulled, the Commission cannot use any documents or evidence it might have obtained in the course of the investigation.[109]

What powers does the Commission have during an investigation?

4. Three of the Commission's most significant powers when investigating breaches of competition law are outlined in Article 18 (requests for information), Article 19 (power to take statements) and Article 20 (powers of investigation) of Regulation 1/2003.

5. Under Article 18 of Regulation 1/2003, the Commission may require 'all necessary information' either through a simple request or a formal decision. If a decision is adopted, the undertaking has a set time period in which to respond. A failure to respond or the provision of false information may result in a fine (of up to 1 per cent of annual turnover)[110] or daily penalty payments (of up to 5 per cent of daily turnover).[111] The Commission can utilise Article 18 not only to seek information from undertakings under investigation but also from third parties such as customers and competitors. In addition, the governments and competition

---

105. Regulation 773/2004, Article 2(1).
106. DG Competition, Best Practices on the conduct of proceedings concerning Articles 101 and 102 TFEU (January 2010) para 12.
107. See Regulation 1/2003, Article 20(4).
108. Case T–339/04 *France Télécom SA v Commission* [2007] ECR II–521, [2008] 5 CMLR 502, para 62.
109. See Case C–94/00 *Roquette Frères SA v DGCCRF* [2002] ECR I–9011, [2003] 4 CMLR 46, para 49.
110. Regulation 1/2003, Article 23.
111. Regulation 1/2003, Article 24.

authorities of the Member States are required to provide the Commission with all necessary information at its request.

6. Article 19 of Regulation 1/2003 gave the Commission a new power to interview any natural or legal person who consents to be interviewed for the purpose of collecting information related to an investigation. Such statements are voluntary. The Commission does not have power to compel statements.

7. The interview may be conducted only if the person consents and there are no sanctions for non-compliance or the provision of false information. The interview can be carried out by any means, including by telephone and email.[112] The Commission may make a copy of the recording but the interviewee is entitled to receive a copy and submit corrections before the recording is finalised.[113]

8. The Commission has a wide power under Article 20 of Regulation 1/2003 to conduct 'all necessary inspections' of undertakings. It is under this power that the Commission carries out dawn raids. The inspection can be carried out pursuant to an authorisation or a decision. The Commission has carried out dawn raids not only in respect of suspected serious breaches of Articles 101 and 102 but also, for example, where it suspected undertakings of breaching the merger control 'gun-jumping' prohibition by putting a merger into effect before it had received clearance from the Commission.[114]

9. Commission officials and authorised accompanying persons (such as officials of a national competition authority assisting the Commission in a dawn raid) are empowered:[115]

    •   To enter premises of undertakings;

    •   To examine books and business records in whatever medium;

    •   To take copies in whatever form;

    •   To seal premises and books and records during the investigation; and

    •   To ask representatives and staff for explanations of facts or documents and to record answers. Recordings can be made but the Commission must give a copy to the undertaking and afford it the opportunity to make corrections.[116]

10. The Commission has the power to examine records irrespective of the medium in which they are stored and to take copies in any form. This obviously covers electronic files in emails, on computer hard drives, on servers etc. The Commission will typically have one or more IT specialists in its team when it conducts a dawn raid. It is not clear whether Article 20(2) empowers the Commission to make copies of hard drives or whole databases and examine them

---

112. Regulation 773/2004, Article 3(2).
113. Regulation 773/2004, Article 3(3).
114. See 'European Commission officers raid Ineos and Norsk Hydro', *The Times*, 14 December 2007.
115. Regulation 1/2003, Article 20(2).
116. Regulation 773/2004, Article 4(2) & (3).

at a later time off site. One potential difficulty with such an approach is that it might catch documents that turn out to be privileged (although a possible solution to this might be to store any potentially privileged files on a device that could operate as a 'sealed envelope'). The scope of the Commission's investigative powers is currently the subject of a number of appeals that have been taken against decisions authorising dawn raids and the conduct of the Commission during the investigations. In one of these cases, the appellant is arguing that Article 20 of Regulation 1/2003 does not empower the Commission to remove DVD-ROMs or remove and make copies of complete hard drives for later review.[117] Judgments in these cases may provide guidance on the extent of the Commission's powers to investigate electronic data.

11.   Regulation 1/2003 provides that the competition authority of a Member State may carry out any inspection or other fact-finding measure under its national law on behalf and for the account of the competition authority of another Member State in order to establish if there has been a violation of Article 101 or 102.[118]

12.   Investigations by the Commission may raise issues of compatibility with the rights of undertakings and natural persons under the Charter of Fundamental Rights, which has Treaty status, and the European Convention of Human Rights, to which the EU is expected to become a signatory.[119] The general principles of EU law, such as the principle of proportionality, may also be relevant. Investigations by national competition authorities into possible breaches of EU competition law may raise similar issues.

What are the Commission's powers of entry?

13.   The Commission does not have the power to force entry onto the premises of an undertaking. Forced entry would have to be effected under national search warrants. The national competition authority of the jurisdiction in which the investigation will occur would usually apply for a warrant as a precautionary measure before the Commission inspection. Where a national competition authority applies for a search warrant on the basis of a Commission inspection decision, the national court shall ensure that the Commission decision is authentic and that envisaged coercive measures are neither arbitrary nor excessive having regard to the subject matter of the investigation. The court may ask the Commission for the grounds on which it suspects an infringement of Article 101 or 102 but it cannot call into question the necessity for the inspection nor demand that it be provided with the information in the Commission's file. The lawfulness of the Commission decision is subject to review only by the Court of Justice.[120]

---

117. Case T–135/09 *Nexans France v Commission* (pending). See also Case T–140/09 *Prysmian v Commission* (pending).

118. Regulation 1/2003, Article 22(1).

119. Human rights issues in antitrust investigations are discussed in Question 97.

120. Regulation 1/2003, Article 20(8).

14. The Commission has the power to adopt a decision ordering the inspection of other premises, land and means of transport (for example, cars) of directors, managers and other members of staff, including domestic premises, if it has a 'reasonable suspicion' that relevant records related to the business are being kept there. This power can only be utilised with respect to a suspected 'serious violation' of Article 101 or 102.[121] The term 'serious violation' is not defined in Regulation 1/2003 but would certainly include hardcore cartel conduct and may include other violations. Before executing the decision, the Commission must obtain authorisation from the relevant national court, which is again limited to vetting whether the decision is authentic and that the envisaged measures are not arbitrary, excessive or disproportionate.[122]

15. Regulation 1/2003 does not make provision for the imposition of penalties on persons who refuse to submit to an investigation by the Commission of domestic premises. However, sanctions under the relevant national law might apply. The Commission used its power to search non-business premises for the first time in its investigation of the *Marine Hose* cartel, when it carried out a raid at the home of one of the executives of a cartel participant.[123]

Does the Commission have surveillance powers?

16. The Commission has no powers of surveillance so it cannot covertly record or videotape conversations. This is in contrast to the position in the United States, where powers to carry out covert surveillance are often used in antitrust investigations by enforcement authorities such as the FBI and Department of Justice.[124]

Ireland

What are the Competition Authority's powers of investigation?[125]

17. In investigating suspected infringements of competition law, whether breaches of section 4 or 5 or Article 101 or 102,[126] Authorised Officers[127] of the Competition Authority are empowered to carry out searches on production of a warrant, issued by a judge of the District Court.[128] There is a power to enter and search premises

---

121. Regulation 1/2003, Article 21(1).
122. Regulation 1/2003, Article 21(3).
123. See Commission Press Release IP/09/137, Commission fines marine hose producers €131 million for market sharing and price-fixing cartel (28 January 2009).
124. See, e.g., US Department of Justice Antitrust Division Update, Spring 2008 (available on the DOJ website) highlighting the use of covert investigations in uncovering cartels.
125. See also McCarthy and Power, *Irish Competition Law: The Competition Act 2002* (2003) Ch 6.
126. The Competition Authority has the power to carry out an investigation into any breach of the Competition Act. See Competition Act 2002, s 30(1)(b).
127. As appointed by the Competition Authority. See Competition Act 2002, s 45(1).
128. Competition Act 2002, s 45(4).

and vehicles in which 'any activity in connection with the business of supplying or distributing goods or providing a service, or in connection with the organisation or assistance of persons engaged in any such business, is carried on'.[129] The homes of directors, managers or any members of staff can also be searched.[130]

18.   The inclusion within this power of the ability to search the premises of undertakings involved in 'the organisation or assistance' of other businesses raises interesting possibilities. Could this power be used to search the offices of an adviser or consultant to a company that was the main subject of a competition probe? On the face of it, this appears to be possible although one might expect that this provision would not be interpreted broadly.

19.   The Competition Authority has very significant powers of seizure under the 2002 Act. Authorised Officers have the power to 'seize and retain any books, documents and records'[131] in whatever format[132] related to the business. This is in addition to the power to inspect and copy or take extracts of documents.[133] Any documents seized can be retained for up to six months or such longer period as allowed by a District Court judge or until the conclusion of proceedings.[134] The Authority is not required to provide copies of seized documents to the undertaking until 14 days after the date they were seized.[135] On the face of the legislation, the practical consequence of this seems to be that the undertaking could be left in the dark for a period of 14 days about what exact information the Authority has seized.

20.   The Authority can require any employee to supply documents and provide explanations as required and to provide information about the undertaking under investigation.[136] The Competition Authority has the power to summon witnesses to attend before it, examine witnesses on oath and require such a witness to produce to the Authority any document in his or her control.[137]

21.   Various presumptions attach to documents that are seized by the Authority during an investigation and used in proceedings under the Act, whether criminal or civil. These presumptions concern issues such as who was the author or owner of the

---

129. Competition Act 2002, s 45(3)(a).

130. Competition Act 2002, s 45(3)(b).

131. Competition Act 2002, s 45(3)(c).

132. See Competition Act 2002, s 45(11).

133. Competition Act 2002, s 45(3)(e).

134. Competition Act 2002, s 45(6). The High Court has indicated that a sworn information containing sufficient detail of the investigation to allow a District Court judge to exercise his discretion under section 45(6) to extend the six month period may be sufficient evidence for such relief; however, where the undertakings with an interest in the documents seized have been put on notice of such an application, they are entitled to carry out a cross-examination in relation to material relevant to the exercise of the judge's discretion and to give evidence of any hardship or ill effects suffered by them as a result of the deprivation of their property (see *The Competition Authority v District Judge O'Donnell* [2007] IEHC 390, [2008] 2 IR 275).

135. Competition Act 2002, s 45(7).

136. Competition Act 2002, s 45(3)(d), (f) and (g).

137. Competition Act 2002, s 31(1).

document.[138] For example, where a document purports to have been created by one person and sent to another, it is presumed that the document was sent and received and that statements made in the document came to the notice of the recipient.[139] Obstructing or impeding an Authorised Officer in exercising powers of investigation or failing to comply with a requirement under section 45 is an offence with a potential fine of €3,000 and/or six months imprisonment.[140]

22. The provisions of the Competition Act 2002 setting out the Competition Authority's powers of investigation do not draw any distinction between civil and criminal investigations. The investigatory powers granted by the 2002 Act can therefore be utilised in both civil and criminal investigations.

Will evidence be excluded if the search warrant is defective?

23. It is important that the warrant authorising the Competition Authority to inspect a premises is not defective. In *Irish Dental Council*,[141] the Competition Authority obtained documentary evidence from the defendant's premises on the basis of a warrant which mistakenly recorded that the defendant was in the business of selling and distributing motor vehicles (the Authority mistakenly produced an incorrect draft on which the warrant that was issued was based). The power of search in the warrant specifically referred to those premises or vehicles in or by means of which activity in connection with the motor vehicles business was carried on.

24. It was accepted by the Authority that the evidence was obtained illegally due to the defects in the warrant. The question then was whether the evidence could nonetheless be retained. McKechnie J held that the Authority's acts in searching for and taking away evidence gave rise to a conscious and deliberate violation of the defendant's constitutional rights, including the right to freedom of expression and possibly, the right to privacy. In those circumstances, the evidence would have to be disallowed in the absence of extraordinary excusing circumstances, of which there were none in this case. McKechnie J was satisfied that the exclusionary rule applied even though the case was civil and not criminal in nature. The learned judge was cognisant of the Authority's significant powers:

> The activities of the plaintiff had as their purpose the enforcement of the provisions of the Act of 2002. That Act conveys very substantial powers on authorised officers and other individuals within the plaintiff. Its width and breadth is quite substantial. The purpose of the exercise of those powers is not simply to further civil proceedings, but can also involve criminal proceedings though, of course, I appreciate that we are not dealing with criminal proceedings in this case. As a result of the exercise of those powers the documents taken away can be legitimately and legally used in court to

---

138. See Competition Act 2002, s 12.
139. Competition Act 2002, s 12(3).
140. Competition Act 2002, s 45(10).
141. *The Competition Authority v The Irish Dental Association* [2005] IEHC 361, [2005] 3 IR 208.

found an action against former owners and/or to incriminate them in criminal proceedings ...

[There] is a major public interest in underpinning public confidence in the business and commercial community with regard to the operation of the Competition Act. The Act of 2002 and its predecessor now constitute a relatively new but very vibrant and most penetrating statutory code in this jurisdiction. It is supported by several articles of the Treaty. Therefore, in my view, it is absolutely crucial that the most core and basic document which founds the searching of premises, namely the search warrant, is correct.[142]

25. The exclusionary rule has been the subject of recent judicial treatment, with Charleton J suggesting in the context of a criminal prosecution in *Cash* that the exclusionary rule may be incompatible with Ireland's obligations under the European Convention on Human Rights, which does not require the exclusion of unlawfully obtained evidence.[143] The Supreme Court did not address this question in the appeal in *Cash*[144] but the issue is likely to come before that court again.

UK[145]

What are the OFT's powers of investigation in civil cases?

26. The OFT's powers of investigation are set out in the Competition Act 1998. In order to carry out an investigation of a potential breach of Article 101 or 102 or the Chapter I or II prohibition, the OFT must have 'reasonable grounds' for suspecting the infringement.[146]

27. When conducting an investigation, the OFT has the power to require a person to produce a specified document or specified information that it considers relevant to the investigation. This includes a power to make copies and require an explanation of the document.[147] The OFT also has the power to enter a business premises without a warrant. In this case it must give at least two working days notice of intention to enter the premises unless it has a reasonable suspicion that the premises are or have been occupied by a party to an agreement which it is investigating, an undertaking the conduct of which it is investigating or if the

---

142. *The Competition Authority v The Irish Dental Association* [2005] IEHC 361, [2005] 3 IR 208, paras 39, 40.
143. *Director of Public Prosecutions v Cash* [2007] IEHC 108, [2008] 1 ILRM 443, paras 45–47. Charleton J endorsed the approach to the admissibility of illegally obtained evidence advanced by the House of Lords in *Attorney General's Reference (No. 3 of 1999)* [2001] 2 AC 91.
144. *Director of Public Prosecutions v Cash* [2010] IESC 1.
145. See generally, OFT 404, Powers of Investigation (December 2004); OFT 1263con, A Guide to the OFT's Competition Act 1998 investigation procedures (August 2010) Chs 6–8.
146. Competition Act 1998, s 25.
147. Competition Act 1998, s 26.

investigating officer has taken all reasonable steps to give notice but has been unable to do so.[148] The OFT's officer is empowered to require persons to produce documents, to take copies and to take away electronically stored information.[149]

28. The Competition Act also provides the OFT with the power to enter a business premises *with* a warrant. The warrant authorises the OFT's officer with the additional power to take possession of original documents and require any person to provide an explanation of any document that appears to be relevant.[150]

29. The OFT may apply for a warrant to enter a domestic premises and a judge may issue such a warrant if satisfied that there are reasonable grounds for suspecting that there are on the premises documents (i) that the OFT required to be produced under section 26 and which were not produced or (ii) that the OFT has the power to require to be produced under section 26 and if the documents were required to be produced, they would not be produced but would be concealed, removed, tampered with or destroyed.[151] If a warrant is issued, the OFT's officer may enter the premises and take original documents and require any person to provide an explanation of any document appearing to be relevant or state where such documents may be found.[152]

30. The Competition Act provides that any response by a person to a request made pursuant to the investigatory powers contained in sections 26 to 28A of the Act 'may not be used in evidence against him on a prosecution' for the cartel offence, subject to certain exceptions.[153]

31. The OFT does not have an equivalent power to that in Article 19 of Regulation 1/2003 to carry out interviews during a competition investigation. Any interviews it does carry out in practice will be of an informal nature.

32. The Competition Act 1998 sets out specific provisions dealing with the OFT's powers when carrying out inspections ordered by the Commission under Article 20(4) or 21 of Regulation 1/2003, inspections requested by the Commission under Article 22(2) and when carrying out inspections on behalf of a competition authority in another Member State under Article 22(1).[154]

What powers does the OFT have when investigating the cartel offence?[155]

33. The OFT has particular powers when investigating the cartel offence. It may conduct an investigation into the cartel offence if it has 'reasonable grounds' for

---

148. Competition Act 1998, ss 27(1), (2), (3).
149. Competition Act 1998, s 27(5).
150. Competition Act 1998, ss 28(2), (c), (e).
151. Competition Act 1998, s 28A(1).
152. Competition Act 1998, s 28A(2).
153. Competition Act 1998, s 30A.
154. Competition Act 1998, Part 2 and Part 2A.
155. See OFT 515, Powers for investigating criminal cartels (January 2004).

suspecting that the offence has been committed.[156] The OFT may require the person under investigation or any other person it has reason to believe has relevant information, to answer questions or provide information.[157] It can require any person to produce documents.[158] A notice in writing is to be provided to the relevant persons before effecting these powers.

34. In order to enter premises, the OFT must obtain a High Court warrant. Before issuing the warrant, the judge must be satisfied that there are reasonable grounds to believe that there are relevant documents on the premises and either the person has failed to produce the documents, it is not practicable to serve the person with a notice requesting production or the service of a notice might seriously prejudice the investigation.[159] The powers in the warrant include taking possession of documents and requiring a person to provide explanations or state where documents can be found.[160]

35. The Enterprise Act provides the OFT with powers of intrusive surveillance for purposes of investigating the cartel offence.[161] Intrusive surveillance is covert surveillance that is carried out in relation to anything taking place on any residential premises or in any private vehicle and involves the presence of an individual on the premises or in the vehicle or is carried out by means of a surveillance device.[162] The authorisation of the Chairman of the OFT is required before these powers are used.[163] The OFT has been added to the list of public authorities that can authorise the use of other methods of surveillance. This includes directed surveillance[164] (such as watching a person's office) and covert human intelligence sources, *i.e.* informants.[165] The OFT is also authorised to gain access to communications data when investigating the cartel offence.[166]

36. Where the OFT is conducting parallel civil and criminal investigations or where it does not know whether its investigation will ultimately be civil or criminal in nature, it will bear in mind the possibility that the cartel offence has been committed and adjust its procedures accordingly. For example, if an OFT officer suspects that a person has committed the cartel offence, that person will be given

---

156. Enterprise Act 2002, s 192.
157. Enterprise Act 2002, s 193(1).
158. Enterprise Act 2002, s 193(2).
159. Enterprise Act 2002, s 194(1).
160. Enterprise Act 2002, 194(2).
161. Enterprise Act 2002, s 199, s 200.
162. Regulation of Investigatory Powers Act 2000, s 26(3).
163. Regulation of Investigatory Powers Act 2000, s 32(3A).
164. Regulation of Investigatory Powers Act 2000, s 28.
165. Regulation of Investigatory Powers Act 2000, s 29.
166. SI 2010 No 480 The Regulation of Investigatory Powers (Communications Data) Order 2010 (which revoked and consolidated the provisions contained in SI 2003 No 3172 The Regulation of Investigatory Powers (Communications Data) Order 2003).

the standard criminal caution before being questioned if his answers or failure or refusal to answer may be given in evidence in a prosecution.[167]

Key Sources

Regulation 1/2003, Articles 18–22.

Regulation 773/2004, Article 3, 4.

Case C–94/00 *Roquette Frères SA v DGCCRF* [2002] ECR I–9011, [2003] 4 CMLR 46.

Ireland

Competition Act 2002, section 45.

UK

Competition Act 1998, sections 25–28, Part 2, Part 2A.

Enterprise Act 2002, sections 192–200.

OFT 515, Powers for investigating criminal cartels (January 2004).

---

167. See OFT 515, Powers for investigating criminal cartels (January 2004), Part 4.

91. WHAT FORMAL STEPS MUST THE COMMISSION TAKE BEFORE IT ISSUES AN INFRINGEMENT DECISION?

Summary

The formal steps that the Commission must take are:

- Issue the statement of objections and provide a right of reply.

- Provide access to the file.

- Provide the undertaking an opportunity to put its case in writing and orally.

Ireland

- There are no comparable procedures as only the courts can make findings of infringement.

UK

- The OFT's procedures are comparable to those of the Commission and provide for a statement of objections, access to the file and a right of reply.

What is the role of the statement of objections?

1. The Commission is required to set out in the statement of objections ('SO') details of its objections against the undertakings concerned. The purpose of the SO is to enable the undertaking to defend itself properly before the Commission adopts a final decision.[168] Respect for the rights of defence requires that:

> the statement of objections which the Commission sends to an undertaking on which it envisages imposing a penalty for an infringement of the competition rules contain the essential elements used against it, such as the facts, the characterisation of those facts and the evidence on which the Commission relies, so that the undertaking may submit its arguments effectively in the administrative procedure brought against it.[169]

2. The SO 'must set forth clearly all the essential facts upon which the Commission is relying at that stage of the procedure' so as to allow the undertaking to make known its views on the facts and circumstances alleged.[170] In *Archer Daniels Midland (Citric Acid)*, the Court of Justice held that this obligation was not

---

168. Cases C–89/85 etc. *Ahlström Osakeyhtiö v Commission ('Woodpulp II')* [1993] ECR I–1307, [1993] 4 CMLR 407, para 42.

169. Cases C–322/07P etc. *Papierfabrik August Koehler AG v Commission* [2009] ECR I–7191, [2009] 5 CMLR 2301, para 36. See also Case C–328/05P *SGL Carbon AG v Commission* [2007] ECR I–3921, [2007] 5 CMLR 16, para 71 ('Observance of the rights of the defence requires, in particular, that the undertaking under investigation is put in a position during the administrative procedure to put forward its point of view on the reality and the relevance of the alleged facts and also on the documents used by the Commission').

170. Case C–511/06P *Archer Daniels Midland Co v Commission (Citric Acid)* [2009] ECR I–5843, [2009] 5 CMLR 1963, para 87.

fulfilled by including the relevant facts, used to identify the company as the leader of a cartel, in documents annexed to the SO.[171]

3.   However, the SO is a provisional document by nature and is subject to subsequent amendments by the Commission on the basis of the observations submitted to it by the parties and other findings of fact. So in *SGL Carbon*, the fact that the Commission considered in the SO that SGL was a joint ringleader of a cartel with another undertaking but concluded in its final decision that SGL was the sole ringleader, did not alter SGL's position to the point of breaching its rights of defence.[172] The SO does not prevent the Commission from altering its position in favour of the undertakings concerned.[173]

4.   The Commission is not required to set out in the SO the criteria it proposes to follow in setting any fine to be imposed. As long as the Commission indicates expressly in the SO that it will consider whether it is appropriate to impose fines and that it sets out the principal elements of fact and of law that may give rise to a fine, such as the gravity and the duration of the alleged infringement and the fact that it has been committed 'intentionally or negligently', it fulfils its obligation to respect the undertakings' right to be heard. The Commission is not required to give specific indications of the level of the contemplated fines at the stage of the SO as such a requirement would in effect require it inappropriately to anticipate its final decision.[174]

5.   The addressees of the SO are given a timeframe in which to make written submissions. The parties can set out the facts relevant to their defence and attach documents as proof of facts set out, as well as proposing to the Commission that it hear persons who can corroborate those facts.[175] The Commission must give the parties to whom it addresses the SO an opportunity to be heard. In its final decision, the Commission can only include objections in respect of which the parties have been able to comment, *i.e.* any objections that go into the final decision must be in the SO.[176]

6.   Where the parties in a cartel case enter into a settlement with the Commission under Regulation 622/2008, a SO will be issued but different procedures apply. The role of the SO in this case is to reflect the parties' settlement submissions and

171. Case C–511/06P *Archer Daniels Midland Co v Commission (Citric Acid)* [2009] ECR I–5843, [2009] 5 CMLR 1963, paras 89–94.
172. Case C–328/05P *SGL Carbon AG v Commission* [2007] ECR I–3921, [2007] 5 CMLR 16, para 62.
173. Case 413/06P *Bertelsmann AG and Another v Independent Music Publishers and Labels Association (Impala)* [2008] ECR I–4951, [2008] 5 CMLR 1073, para 63.
174. Case C–511/06P *Archer Daniels Midland Co v Commission (Citric Acid)* [2009] ECR I–5843, [2009] 5 CMLR 1963, paras 68–69.
175. Regulation 773/2004, Article 10.
176. Regulation 773/2004, Article 11; Regulation 1/2003, Article 27(1).

it is envisaged that in response, the parties would merely confirm that the SO reflects the settlement.[177]

To what extent are parties entitled to access to the Commission's file?

7. The addressees of the SO are entitled to access to the Commission's file after the notification of the SO.[178] The right of access is limited to non-confidential material. Article 16 of Regulation 773/2004 makes provision for the protection of confidential information obtained by the Commission and sets out the procedures that must be followed to claim confidential treatment. The right of access to the file does not extend to correspondence between the Commission and the competition authorities of the Member States.[179] If the Commission is to deny access to certain documents on the basis that they contain business secrets or other confidential information of another party, it cannot simply make a general reference to confidentiality to justify a refusal to disclose and it may be required to draw up a non-confidential version of the particular document.[180]

8. A failure on the part of the Commission to provide access to the file will not automatically result in the annulment of the Commission's decision. However, if the undertaking has not been given access to an exculpatory document, the undertaking will have made out a breach of the rights of defence if it establishes that the non-disclosure was able to influence, to its disadvantage, the course of the proceedings and the content of the Commission's decision.[181]

9. In respect of incriminating documents, a failure to provide access to it results in a breach of the rights of defence only if the undertaking can show first, that the Commission relied on the document to support its objection concerning the existence of an infringement and second, the objection could be proved only by

---

177. Regulation 773/2004, Articles 10(1), 10(a) as substituted by Regulation 622/2008, Article 1; Commission Notice on the conduct of settlement procedures in view of the adoption of Decisions pursuant to Article 7 and Article 23 of Council Regulation (EC) No 1/2003 in cartel cases [2008] OJ C167/01, paras 23–27.

178. Regulation 1/2003, Article 27(2); Regulation 773/2004, Article 15(1). See also Commission Notice on the rules for access to the Commission file in cases pursuant to Articles 81 and 82 of the EC Treaty, Articles 53, 54 and 57 of the EEA Agreement and Council Regulation (EC) No 139/2004 [2005] OJ C325/07. The right of access to the file had already been recognised by the EU courts. See, e.g., Case T–7/89 *Hercules Chemicals NV v Commission* [1991] ECR II–1711, [1992] 4 CMLR 84, paras 53–54; Cases C–204/00P etc *Aalborg Portland A/S v Commission* [2004] ECR I–123, [2005] 4 CMLR 251, para 68.

179. See Regulation 773/2004, Article 15(2); Regulation 1/2003, Article 27(2).

180. See Case T–410/03 *Hoechst GmbH v Commission* [2008] ECR II–881, [2008] 5 CMLR 839, paras 153–154. Cf Case T–237/05 *Éditions Odile Jacob SAS v Commission*, judgment of 9 June 2010 (Commission's failure to justify refusal of access to certain documents under Regulation 1049/2001) (on appeal, Case C–404/10P *Commission v Éditions Jacob*).

181. See, e.g., Case T–161/05 *Hoechst GmbH v Commission* [2008] ECR II–881, [2009] 5 CMLR 839, para 166.

reference to that document.[182] It would be for the undertaking to show that the result at which the Commission arrived in its decision might have been different if the document were disallowed as evidence. [183]

Is there a right to an oral hearing?

10. If they so request, the addressees of the SO are entitled to an oral hearing.[184] Other persons who apply to be heard and show a sufficient interest are entitled to an opportunity to put their position in writing and where appropriate, the Commission may invite such persons to participate at the oral hearing. The Commission may itself invite other persons to make submissions and express their views at the oral hearing.[185]

11. The procedures to be followed at the oral hearing are set out in Article 14 of Regulation 773/2004. This provides for the oral hearing to be 'conducted by a Hearing Officer in full independence'. Oral hearings are not public. Parties may be represented by lawyers at the oral hearing.

Ireland

12. Given that the Competition Authority does not have the power to find that there has been a breach of either Irish or EU competition law, there are no comparable procedures in Ireland to those followed by the Commission in competition cases. Only the courts can make a finding that there has been a breach of competition law. The question of a potential breach of competition law may come before the court in a number of ways. In addition to criminal proceedings brought by the Authority (summarily) or the DPP (on indictment) and the possibility of private actions, the Authority has a right of action in respect of breaches of sections 4 and 5 of the Competition Act 2002 and Articles 101 and 102 under which it can seek relief by way of injunction or declaration before the Circuit Court or the High Court.[186]

13. The Authority has taken several civil actions in the High Court, a number of which have been settled.[187] Other notable actions include the claim of abuse of dominance by the Irish League of Credit Unions (in which the Authority was

---

182. Cases C–204/00P etc *Aalborg Portland A/S v Commission* [2004] ECR I–123, [2005] 4 CMLR 251, para 71.

183. Case T–161/05 *Hoechst GmbH v Commission* [2008] ECR II–881, [2009] 5 CMLR 839, para 165.

184. Regulation 773/2004, Article 12.

185. Regulation 773/2004, Article 13.

186. Competition Act 2002, ss 14(2), 14(5). On criminal proceedings, see Question 102. Private actions are discussed in Chapter VI.

187. See, e.g., *Competition Authority v Licensed Vintners Association* [2009] IEHC 439, [2010] 1 ILRM 374 ('price freeze' announcements by the defendants breached terms of settlement that had been reached with the Competition Authority in a case that alleged a breach of section 4 in relation to price fixing of alcoholic drinks). (contd \...)

ultimately unsuccessful in the Supreme Court)[188] and the *BIDS* case, involving agreements with an anti-competitive object in the beef industry, which was the subject of a preliminary reference to the Court of Justice and at the time of writing was pending in the High Court, with the remaining question whether the agreements in question could avail of the Article 101(3) exemption.[189] The Authority has also closed several investigations into breaches of competition law without instituting High Court proceedings. In some cases, the Authority has accepted commitments to the effect that the relevant undertaking would not breach competition law in the future, with a reciprocal agreement by the Authority that it would not take legal action while those commitments were complied with.[190]

UK

14. The OFT's procedures are comparable to those of the Commission. If the OFT comes to a provisional conclusion that there has been a breach of the Chapter I or II prohibitions or Article 101 or 102, it will issue a statement of objections. The undertaking under investigation is then entitled to inspect the OFT's file and has a right to reply to the statement of objections.[191]

Key Sources

Regulation 773/2004, Articles 10–16.

Regulation 1/2003, Article 27.

Cases C–322/07P etc. *Papierfabrik August Koehler AG v Commission* [2009] 5 CMLR 2301.

Case C–511/06P *Archer Daniels Midland Co v Commission (Citric Acid)* [2009] ECR I–5843, [2009] 5 CMLR 1963.

---

187. (contd) Details of other settlements that the Competition Authority has reached are available on its website, including settlements with the Irish Medical Organisation (alleged breach of section 4 in relation to recommendations by the IMO to GPs about prices; IMO agreed to refrain from issuing future communications in relation to prices and other matters); the Irish Dental Association (alleged breach of section 4 and Article 101; association to confirm to members that it was for individual dentists to manage their own commercial affairs with health insurer); and supermarkets and dairies in relation to price fixing of milk (one of these cases is ongoing).

188. *Competition Authority v O'Regan* [2007] IESC 22, [2007] 4 IR 737.

189. See *Competition Authority v Beef Industry Developments Society Limited* [2009] IESC 72, remitting the case to the High Court.

190. Details of these cases are available on the Authority's website.

191. For an overview of the OFT's procedures, see OFT 1263con, A Guide to the OFT's Competition Act 1998 investigation procedures (August 2010). For further detail on the OFT's procedures in competition investigations, see O'Neill and Sanders, *UK Competition Procedure: The Modernised Regime* (2007) and Gray, Lester, Darbon, Facenna, Brown and Holmes, *EU Competition Law: Procedure and Remedies* (2006) Ch 3.

92. WHEN CAN PRIVILEGE BE CLAIMED IN A COMPETITION INVESTIGATION?

Summary

- EU law recognises a form of legal privilege for communications between a lawyer and a client.

- However, the privilege only attaches to independent lawyers and does not cover in-house lawyers.

- It is up to the client to assert privilege. Where the Commission disputes the privileged status of a document, the sealed envelope procedure can be used.

- When the Commission carries out an investigation itself, the EU law on privilege applies. This is also the case when a national competition authority assists the Commission. However where a national competition authority carries out an investigation at the request of the Commission, national law on privilege applies. If that law covers in-house lawyer communications, they would be privileged in such an investigation.

Ireland

- For investigations pursuant to a decision of the Commission, the EU privilege rules apply.

- For investigations carried out by the Competition Authority on its own behalf or on behalf of the Commission or another competition authority, the Irish law on privilege would apply.

- Irish law recognises legal advice privilege and litigation privilege and communications with in-house lawyers may be privileged.

UK

- For investigations pursuant to a decision of the Commission, the EU privilege rules apply.

- For investigations carried out by the OFT on its own behalf or on behalf of the Commission or another competition authority in England & Wales, the English law on privilege would apply.

- Legal advice and litigation privilege is recognised and may include communications with in-house lawyers.

1. The Commission's broad powers of investigation are subject to the rights of the defence. EU law recognises a form of legal privilege for communications between a lawyer and client and the Commission is not entitled to access documents over which this legal professional privilege ('LPP') is asserted.

2. It was held in *AM&S* that the confidentiality of written communications between a lawyer and client were protected provided that two cumulative conditions were met: (i) the communications were made for the purposes and in the interests of the

client's rights of defence; and (ii) that the communications emanate from an 'independent lawyer', *i.e.* lawyers who are not bound to the client through a relationship of employment.[192] This position was confirmed by the Court of Justice in *Akzo*.[193]

3.   The first condition, that communications be made for the purposes of exercising the rights of defence, will apply to written communications exchanged after the initiation of the Commission's administrative procedure. It also covers 'preparatory documents, even if they were not exchanged with a lawyer or were not created for the purpose of being sent physically to a lawyer ... provided that they were drawn up exclusively for the purpose of seeking legal advice from a lawyer in exercise of the rights of the defence'.[194] However merely discussing a document with a lawyer is not sufficient to give rise to privilege.[195] Internal notes circulated within an undertaking, which report the text or the content of communications with independent lawyers containing legal advice, are protected.[196]

4.   The second condition, which means that privilege does not attach to communications of in-house lawyers, was unsuccessfully challenged in *Akzo*. The case arose out of an on-site inspection by the European Commission in 2003, during which internal written communications of a Dutch in-house lawyer of Akzo were seized. The Court of Justice rejected the argument that the obligations of professional conduct and discipline on an in-house lawyer who was enrolled in a Bar or Law Society meant that the lawyer was just as independent as an external lawyer. The Court stated that:

> ... the concept of the independence of lawyers is determined not only positively, that is by reference to professional ethical obligations, but also negatively, by the absence of an employment relationship. An in-house lawyer, despite his enrolment with a Bar or Law Society and the professional ethical obligations to which he is, as a result, subject, does not enjoy the same degree of independence from his employer as a lawyer working in an external law firm does in relation to his client. Consequently, an in-house lawyer is less able to deal effectively with any conflicts between his professional obligations and the aims of his client.[197]

---

192. Case 155/79 *AM&S Europe Limited v Commission* [1982] ECR 1575, [1982] 2 CMLR 264, para 21.

193. Case C–550/07P *Akzo Nobel Chemicals Ltd v Commission*, judgment of 14 September 2010, paras 40–41 (upholding Cases T–125 & 253/03 *Akzo Nobel Chemicals Ltd v Commission* [2007] ECR II–3523, [2008] 4 CMLR 97).

194. Cases T–125 & 253/03 *Akzo Nobel Chemicals Ltd v Commission* [2007] ECR II–3523, [2008] 4 CMLR 97, para 123.

195. Cases T–125 & 253/03 *Akzo Nobel Chemicals Ltd v Commission* [2007] ECR II–3523, [2008] 4 CMLR 97, para 123.

196. Case T–30/89 *Hilti AG v Commission* [1990] ECR II–163, [1990] 4 CMLR 602, paras 16–18.

197. Case C–550/07P *Akzo Nobel Chemicals Ltd v Commission*, judgment of 14 September 2010, para 45.

5. The fact remained that an in-house lawyer was 'not able to ensure a degree of independence comparable to that of an external lawyer' because the position of such a lawyer as an employee 'by its very nature, does not allow him to ignore the commercial strategies pursued by his employer, and thereby affects his ability to exercise professional independence'.[198] LPP only applies to independent lawyers entitled to practice in one of the EEA Member States.[199]

How is privilege asserted in practice?

6. It is up to the undertaking under investigation to assert LPP. How can this be done in practice, for example when the undertaking is subject to a dawn raid? May the undertaking refuse to allow the Commission's officials to even glance at documents on the basis that they are privileged?

7. In asserting LPP, the undertaking must first provide the Commission officials with 'relevant material of such a nature as to demonstrate that the communications fulfil the conditions' for the grant of LPP.[200] However the undertaking is not bound to disclose the contents of the documents. The undertaking is entitled to refuse to allow the Commission officials to take even a cursory look at the documents which it claims to be covered by LPP, provided that the undertaking considers that such a cursory look is impossible without revealing the content of those documents and that it gives the Commission officials appropriate reasons for its view.[201]

8. Where the Commission does not consider that the undertaking has provided sufficient reasons to make out LPP and in particular where it has refused to allow the Commission officials even a cursory glance at the documents, the Commission may put the documents in a sealed envelope and take them away. If the dispute is not resolved, the Commission must adopt a decision compelling production of the documents. The envelope must remain sealed and the Commission must not read

---

198. Case C–550/07P *Akzo Nobel Chemicals Ltd v Commission*, judgment of 14 September 2010, paras 46–47. The Court rejected other arguments put forward, finding that there was no predominant trend in the 27 EU Member States of granting privilege to in-house lawyers, that the exclusion of in-house privilege did not breach the principles of equal treatment or legal certainty and that changes brought about by Regulation 1/2003 were aimed at reinforcing the Commission's powers of inspection rather than requiring in-house and external lawyers to be treated in the same way in respect of privilege.

199. See Case 155/79 *AM&S Europe Limited v Commission* [1982] ECR 1575, [1982] 2 CMLR 264, paras 25, 26. On which lawyers are entitled to practice in one of the EEA Member States, see Directive 77/249/EEC to facilitate the effective exercise by lawyers of freedom to provide services [1977] OJ L78/17.

200. Case 155/79 *AM&S Europe Limited v Commission* [1982] ECR 1575, [1982] 2 CMLR 264, para 29.

201. Cases T–125 & 253/03 *Akzo Nobel Chemicals Ltd v Commission* [2007] ECR II–3523, [2008] 4 CMLR 97, para 82.

the content of the documents before giving the undertaking the opportunity to refer the matter to the General Court.[202]

9.   In *Akzo*, the Commission argued that undertakings might try to invoke LPP and the sealed envelope procedure as a delaying tactic where there was in fact no genuine case for LPP. However, the General Court pointed out that such conduct could be discouraged by imposing penalties under Article 23(1) of Regulation 1/2003 or treating such conduct as an aggravating factor when imposing fines for breach of the competition rules.[203]

10.   The provision for use of the sealed envelope appears to be subject to the rule that if the undertaking 'produces *no relevant material* of such a kind as to prove that it is actually protected by LPP',[204] the Commission can go ahead and read the document. In *Akzo*, the General Court indicated that relevant material would include in particular the author, the intended addressee, the duties and responsibilities of each, the objective and context in which the document was drafted, the context in which it was found, the way it was filed and any related documents.[205] The Commission has interpreted this to mean that it can read the document and does not have to use the sealed envelope if it considers (i) there is no evidence of LPP, (ii) the reasons invoked are clearly unfounded to justify LPP or (iii) the reasons are based on factual circumstances that are manifestly inaccurate.[206] It could be argued that this is an overly generous interpretation of the rights of the Commission in this situation. *Akzo* can also be read as saying that the production of *any* material justifying LPP (for example, simply the name of the author of the document) is sufficient to require the Commission to use the sealed envelope, regardless of the Commission's view of the merits of that evidence or of whether the justification would ultimately be found to be groundless by the General Court.

What practical steps can companies take to retain privilege?

11.   In light of the confirmation by the Court of Justice in *Akzo* that LPP does not attach to in-house lawyers in the context of EU competition investigations, steps

---

202. Cases T–125 & 253/03 *Akzo Nobel Chemicals Ltd v Commission* [2007] ECR II–3523, [2008] 4 CMLR 97, paras 83–88.

203. Cases T–125 & 253/03 *Akzo Nobel Chemicals Ltd v Commission* [2007] ECR II–3523, [2008] 4 CMLR 97, para 89.

204. Cases T–125 & 253/03 *Akzo Nobel Chemicals Ltd v Commission* [2007] ECR II–3523, [2008] 4 CMLR 97, para 80 (emphasis added).

205. See Cases T–125 & 253/03 *Akzo Nobel Chemicals Ltd v Commission* [2007] ECR II–3523, [2008] 4 CMLR 97, para 80.

206. See DG Competition, Best Practices on the conduct of proceedings concerning Articles 101 and 102 TFEU (January 2010) para 50.

that a company may wish to consider in order to protect legal communications may include:

- Avoid the creation of a paper trail. If a problematic antitrust issue arises, advice and communications with in-house lawyers should be carried out orally.

- Instruct outside lawyers. If written advice is to be obtained, it would be prudent to instruct an external lawyer, to whose communications privilege will attach. The lawyer must be qualified in the EEA.

- Preparatory documents created for the purpose of seeking legal advice from an external lawyer should be clearly marked as being created for this purpose.

- Limit the internal circulation of legal advice. Recipients should be advised not to amend any written legal advice communicated to them or to further distribute the advice.

- Documents and communications prepared for the purpose of obtaining legal advice should be clearly marked as privileged.

- Documents that are privileged (under both EU law and national law) should be maintained in clearly marked separate files. A detailed index should be maintained, specifying the author, recipient and subject matter of the document.

- If expert reports are to be commissioned in connection with a competition case, it is advisable to instruct such experts through an external lawyer.

Ireland

12. The Competition Act 2002 is silent about the scope of privilege that can be asserted over documents in the face of an investigation or who may assert such privilege. Depending on the nature of the investigation and the rules pursuant to which it is carried out, either EU law or Irish law on privilege could apply.

13. If the Competition Authority carries out an investigation on its own behalf, whether it is investigating only possible breaches of the Competition Act 2002 or also breaches of Article 101 or 102, the Irish law rules on privilege would apply. Irish law would also apply where the Competition Authority carries out an investigation at the request of the Commission or a competition authority in another Member State.[207] However, if the Competition Authority is merely assisting the Commission to carry out an investigation in Ireland, the EU law privilege rules would apply.[208] In *Akzo*, the Court of Justice, in rejecting the extension of EU law privilege to communications of in-house counsel, held that the principle of legal certainty did not require that the same privilege standard in both EU and national enforcement of EU competition rules apply. The Court's

---

207. Regulation 1/2003, Article 22.
208. Such assistance is provided for in Regulation 1/2003, Article 20(5).

argument here was that as restrictive practices are viewed differently by EU and national law, undertakings that are the subject of a competition investigation:

> ... are able to determine their rights and obligations vis-à-vis the competent authorities and the law applicable, as, for example, the treatment of documents likely to be seized in the course of such an investigation and whether the undertakings concerned are entitled to rely on legal professional privilege in respect of communications with in-house lawyers. The undertakings can therefore determine their position in the light of the powers of those authorities and specifically of those concerning the seizure of documents.[209]

14. On this basis, the Court held that the principle of legal certainty did not require identical criteria to be applied as regards privilege in the two types of procedure. The Court's reasoning on this point is not entirely convincing as the scope of protection for privileged documents in an investigation into breaches of Article 101 or 102 will depend on whether the Commission carries out the investigation itself or the national competition authority carries it out at the Commission's request. It is difficult to see, however, any substantive difference in the investigation in each of these cases. Both involve an investigation into a breach of EU competition law. In this situation, the Court's comments about the different views of restrictive practices at the national and EU level do not appear to be relevant.

15. The Irish courts have stressed that as well as being a rule of evidence, legal professional privilege is a fundamental condition for the administration of justice.[210] There are two recognised components of legal professional privilege, litigation privilege and legal advice privilege.[211] Litigation privilege covers third party communications and work product made for purposes of litigation.[212] Legal advice privilege applies to communications between a client and lawyer where these are confidential communications made in the course of a professional legal relationship for the purpose of giving or receiving legal advice. The Supreme Court has described legal advice privilege in the following terms:

> ... where it is established that a communication was made between a person and his lawyer acting for him as a lawyer for the purpose of obtaining from such lawyer legal advice, whether at the initiation of the client or the lawyer, that communication made on such an occasion should in general be privileged or exempt from disclosure, except with the consent of the client.[213]

16. The scope of legal privilege in Irish law would appear to include communications with in-house lawyers. However the Irish courts do not appear recently to have addressed the exact scope of privilege in the in-house context or the extent to

---

209. Case C–550/07P *Akzo Nobel Chemicals Ltd v Commission*, judgment of 14 September 2010, para 104.
210. See *Miley v Flood* [2001] 2 IR 50, 68 (Kelly J).
211. See generally McGrath, *Evidence* (2004) 524–536.
212. For recent consideration of litigation privilege, see *Ahern v Judge Mahon* [2008] IEHC 119, [2008] 4 IR 704.
213. *Smurfit Paribas Bank Ltd v AAB Export Finance Ltd* [1990] 1 IR 469, 478 (Finlay CJ).

which employees who create documents used to obtain legal advice come within the meaning of the 'client'.[214]

17. It is for the client to assert privilege.[215] In the context of a competition investigation, presumably the client would need to assert privilege at the time of the investigation. A failure to make this assertion may result in a waiver of the privilege.

18. While the Competition Act 2002 does not deal with the procedures for asserting privilege in Competition Authority investigations, in practice, the sealed envelope procedure is used. Electronic documents over which privilege is claimed can be downloaded onto a particular device, with Authority access limited to the extent that the party consents, until such time as the privilege issue is resolved.

UK

19. A definition of privileged documents is set out in the Competition Act 1998. A privileged communication is one:

   (a) between a professional legal adviser and his client, or

   (b) made in connection with, or in contemplation of, legal proceedings and for the purposes of those proceedings,

   which in proceedings in the High Court would be protected from disclosure on grounds of legal professional privilege.[216]

20. This definition, which adopts the English law of legal professional privilege, is broader than the LPP recognised in EU law. The English law concept of LPP includes legal advice privilege and litigation privilege and includes communications to and from in-house legal advisers in the UK. However, legal advice privilege applies only for communications with the 'client', a term which has been interpreted restrictively by the English courts. Within a company, the 'client' is the person charged with giving instructions to a lawyer and material prepared by employees which is ultimately for the purpose of instructing a lawyer will not be privileged.[217] The OFT does not consider as privileged communications

---

214. Cf *Three Rivers District Council v Bank of England (No. 3)* [2003] EWCA Civ 474, [2003] QB 1556. See also Spencer, 'Corporate Privilege – Shrinking the Zone of Silence' (2007) 3(2) *Journal of Civil Practice and Procedure* 12 (discussing English, Irish and US law). See also the comments of Laffoy J in *Martin v Legal Aid Board* [2007] IEHC 76, [2007] 2 IR 759, para 39, which make comparison to the position of in-house lawyers.

215. However, discovery of documents will not be made in litigation if the documents are *prima facie* privileged, even if the client does not assert the privilege (see, e.g., *Croke v Waterford Crystal Limited* [2009] IEHC 158, paras 10–13 (Birmingham J)).

216. Competition Act 1998, s 30 in respect of OFT investigations carried out on its own behalf. The same definition is provided in sections 65A and 65J in respect of investigations carried out by the OFT on behalf of the Commission and a competition authority of another Member State respectively.

217. See *Three Rivers District Council v Bank of England (No. 3)* [2003] EWCA Civ 474, [2003] QB 1556. In a related appeal, this question was not dealt with by the House of Lords (*Three Rivers District Council v Bank of England (No. 4)* [2004] UKHL 48, [2005] 1 AC 610).

of in-house lawyers based in other Member States where such communications are not privileged.[218]

21.   In respect of investigations carried out by the OFT on its own behalf[219] or by the OFT on behalf of the Commission[220] or a competition authority in another Member State,[221] a party wishing to claim privilege should provide the investigating official with material of such a nature as to demonstrate to his satisfaction that the document or information, or parts of it, for which privilege is claimed, fulfil the conditions for it being privileged. If the party does not give such reasons but wishes to claim privilege, it should gather the items over which privilege is claimed. If no agreement is reached with the investigating official that the materials can be examined or copied, copies will be made and placed in a sealed envelope and arrangements will be made for the safe keeping of the envelope pending resolution of the privilege issue.[222]

22.   For investigations carried out under Article 20 or 21 of Regulation 1/2003, *i.e.* those ordered by the Commission, the EU privilege rules as set out in *AM&S* and *Akzo* would apply.

23.   There are specific provisions dealing with privilege in the context of an investigation of the cartel offence. A person may not be required to disclose information or produce documents which he would be entitled to refuse to disclose or produce on grounds of legal professional privilege in High Court proceedings. However a lawyer may be required to provide the name and address of his client. There is a special protection concerning information or documents in respect of which a person owes an obligation of confidence by virtue of carrying on a banking business.[223]

Key Sources

Case C–550/07 *Akzo Nobel Chemicals Ltd v Commission*, judgment of 14 September 2010.

Case 155/79 *AM&S Europe Limited v Commission* [1982] ECR 1575, [1982] 2 CMLR 264.

Ireland

Miley v Flood [2001] 2 IR 50.

UK

Competition Act 1998, s 30, 65A, 65J.

---

218. See OFT 426, Under investigation? A guide to investigations by the OFT under the Competition Act 1998 (March 2005) 12.
219. Under Part I of the Competition Act 1998.
220. Under Article 22(2) of Regulation 1/2003. See Competition Act 1998, s 65A.
221. Under Article 22(1) of Regulation 1/2003. See Competition Act 1998, s 65J.
222. See Explanatory Note to Warrant under sections 28 and 29 of the Competition Act 1998, annexed to Practice Direction – Application for a Warrant under the Competition Act 1998.
223. Enterprise Act 2002, s 196.

93. HOW ARE SETTLEMENTS REACHED WITH THE COMMISSION IN CARTEL CASES?

Summary

- Cartel participants can engage in a settlement procedure with the Commission. In return for admitting liability, the Commission may grant a reduction of 10 per cent in the fine.

- There is a particular settlement procedure that was introduced by Regulation 622/2008 and which is described in detail in the Commission's Settlement Notice.

- The parties make submissions on matters including liability and fines. The agreed settlement is reflected in a statement of objections and an infringement decision is published.

- If only some of the cartel members agree to settle, the Commission may reach a settlement with those companies while proceeding in the normal way against others (so-called 'hybrid' cases).

1. The Commission introduced a procedure for reaching settlements in cartel cases in June 2008 with the adoption of Regulation 622/2008, which amends Regulation 773/2004.[224] Further details of the procedure are set out in a Commission Notice.[225] If a party is prepared to acknowledge participation in a cartel and reaches a settlement with the Commission, it's fine may be reduced by 10 per cent.[226]

2. After the initiation of proceedings, the Commission may set a time limit for the parties to indicate in writing that they are prepared to engage in settlement discussions.[227] The Commission has broad discretion in deciding whether a case is suitable for settlement and it may consider factors such as the likelihood of reaching a settlement in a reasonable timeframe, whether it can achieve procedural efficiencies and the possibility of setting a precedent. The Commission has discretion to discontinue settlement discussions and may do so where, for example, the parties destroy relevant evidence.[228] Discussions with the parties to a cartel are carried out on a bilateral basis. If only some members of the cartel wish to settle, the Commission can either end the settlement procedure or it can

---

224. Commission Regulation (EC) No 622/2008 amending Regulation (EC) No 773/2004, as regards the conduct of settlement procedures in cartel cases [2008] OJ L171/1.

225. Commission Notice on the conduct of settlement procedures in view of the adoption of Decisions pursuant to Article 7 and Article 23 of Council Regulation (EC) No 1/2003 in cartel cases [2008] OJ C167/01 ('Commission Settlement Notice').

226. Commission Settlement Notice [2008] OJ C167/01, para 32.

227. Regulation 773/2004, as amended, Article 10a.

228. Commission Settlement Notice [2008] OJ C167/01, para 5.

continue the procedure with the parties that wish to settle and apply the ordinary procedure vis-à-vis others. These are so-called 'hybrid' cases.

3.   The Commission points out that the settlement procedure is not a negotiation (in contrast to the plea agreement procedure that is a prevalent feature in US antitrust enforcement):

> Whilst the Commission, as the investigative authority and the guardian of the Treaty empowered to adopt enforcement decisions subject to judicial control by the Community Courts, does not negotiate the question of the existence of an infringement of Community law and the appropriate sanction, it can reward the cooperation described in this Notice.[229]

4.   The parties are entitled to make submissions and for this purpose will be supplied with information by the Commission including the objections that the Commission envisages raising, the evidence for the objections, non-confidential versions of documents in the Commission's file and the range of potential fines that the Commission is considering.[230] The development of discussions with a party and the timing of disclosure of information will reflect the overall progress being made in the settlement procedure.[231] It is only when the Commission has set a time limit for the party to make settlement submissions, which will be at least two weeks, that an entitlement to the above information is gained.[232]

5.   If the Commission and the party do not reach an understanding as to the scope of the infringement and the fine to be imposed, the settlement procedure is unlikely to progress.[233] If there is an understanding, the undertaking makes a final settlement submission. In practice, the settlement submission will be drafted according to a Commission template and reflect the settlement discussions. The content of the submission would be agreed with the Commission before it is filed.[234] The settlement submission should contain the following:

  (a)   An acknowledgement in clear and unequivocal terms of the parties' liability for the infringement summarily described as regards its object, its possible implementation, the main facts, their legal qualification, including the party's role and the duration of their participation in the infringement in accordance with the results of the settlement discussions;

  (b)   An indication of the maximum amount of the fine the parties foresee to be imposed by the Commission and which the parties would accept in the framework of a settlement procedure;

  (c)   The parties' confirmation that they have been sufficiently informed of the objections the Commission envisages raising against them and that they have been given sufficient opportunity to make their views known to the Commission;

229. Commission Settlement Notice [2008] OJ C167/01, para 2.
230. Regulation 773/2004, as amended, Article 10a(2).
231. Commission Settlement Notice [2008] OJ C167/01, para 15.
232. Regulation 773/2004, as amended, Article 10a(2).
233. Commission Settlement Notice [2008] OJ C167/01, para 17.
234. See Commission Memo/08/458 Commission introduces settlement procedure for cartels – frequently asked questions (30 June 2008).

    (d)   the parties' confirmation that, in view of the above, they do not envisage requesting access to the file or requesting to be heard again in an oral hearing, unless the Commission does not reflect their settlement submissions in the statement of objections and the decision;

    (e)   the parties' agreement to receive the statement of objections and the final decision pursuant to Articles 7 and 23 of Regulation (EC) No 1/2003 in an agreed official language of the European Community.[235]

6.   If so requested, the Commission may accept oral settlement submissions. These would be recorded and transcribed at the Commission's premises and the undertaking would be allowed to check the accuracy of the transcript without delay.[236] This provision is partly aimed at concerns about the potential discoverability of written statements submitted by an undertaking in, for example, a subsequent private action. The Commission has confirmed that it will not transmit settlement submissions to national courts without the consent of the relevant applicants.[237]

7.   The Commission will proceed to issue a statement of objections. The undertaking then confirms within a set time limit that the statement of objections reflects the settlement submissions and the Commission proceeds to adopt its infringement decision.[238] There is no oral hearing and the party does not gain access to the file. The Commission retains the right to adopt a final decision that does not reflect the settlement submissions. In this case, acknowledgements made by the party in the submissions would be deemed to be withdrawn and could not be used in evidence against it. The party would be allowed to present a new defence, exercise rights of defence such as accessing the Commission's file and a new statement of objections would be adopted.[239]

8.   The fact that a settlement is reached does not appear to guarantee the party a 10 per cent reduction in its fine. The Commission retains discretion as to the reduction in fine:

> Should the Commission decide to reward a party for settlement in the framework of this Notice, it will reduce by 10 per cent the amount of the fine to be imposed after the 10 per cent cap has been applied having regard to the Guidelines on the method of setting fines imposed pursuant to Article 23(2)(a) of Regulation (EC) No 1/2003. Any specific increase for deterrence used in their regard will not exceed a multiplication by two.[240]

9.   The settlement procedure is distinct from the possibility for participants in a cartel to seek leniency by providing information to the Commission to help it establish the existence of the cartel. The settlement procedure and the leniency procedure can therefore apply in parallel.

---

235. Commission Settlement Notice [2008] OJ C167/01, para 20.
236. Commission Settlement Notice [2008] OJ C167/01, para 38.
237. Commission Settlement Notice [2008] OJ C167/01, para 39.
238. Regulation 773/2004, as amended, Article 10a(3).
239. Commission Settlement Notice [2008] OJ C167/01, paras 27, 29.
240. Commission Settlement Notice [2008] OJ C167/01, para 32.

10.   The introduction of the settlement procedure has the potential to significantly decrease the length of cartel proceedings, which can last for several years. It remains to be seen whether the procedure will result in a significant number of settlements and whether it will achieve procedural efficiencies for the Commission. It will not be attractive to parties in all cases. The relatively modest 10 per cent reduction in fine for agreeing to settle may be insufficient recompense for companies making admissions as to liability and as to the likely range of fines and reducing their chances of successfully appealing the Commission's decision.[241]

11.   At the time of writing, the settlement procedure had been utilised in two cases. The first settlement was reached in May 2010 in the *DRAM* cartel, involving producers of memory chips used in computers and servers. All companies in the cartel (other than the immunity applicant, which was not fined) participated in the settlement and received a 10 per cent reduction in the fine.[242]

12.   The second case in which the settlement procedure was employed was the *Animal Feed Phosphates* cartel. This was a 'hybrid' case, with all but one member of the cartel reaching a settlement with the Commission, while the ordinary procedure was used against the other. The company that did not settle, Timab, had initially engaged in the settlement procedure but withdrew after the Commission informed it of the range of fines it was considering. Each of the undertakings that reached a settlement received a 10 per cent reduction in the fine.[243]

Key Sources

Commission Regulation (EC) No 622/2008 amending Regulation (EC) No 773/2004, as regards the conduct of settlement procedures in cartel cases [2008] OJ L171/1.

Commission Notice on the conduct of settlement procedures in view of the adoption of Decisions pursuant to Article 7 and Article 23 of Council Regulation (EC) No 1/2003 in cartel cases [2008] OJ C167/01.

---

241. Note Case C–407/08P *Knauf Gips KG v Commission*, judgment of 1 July 2010, para 90 ('Although an undertaking's express or implicit acknowledgement of matters of fact or of law during the administrative procedure before the Commission may constitute additional evidence when determining whether an action is well founded, it cannot restrict the actual exercise of a natural or legal person's right to bring proceedings before the General Court under the fourth paragraph of Article 263 TFEU').

242. IP/10/586 Commission fines DRAM producers €331 million for price cartel; reaches first settlement in a cartel case (19 May 2010). The Commission's decision had not been published at the time of writing.

243. IP/10/985 European Commission fines animal feed phosphates producers €175,647,000 for price-fixing and market-sharing in first 'hybrid' cartel settlement case (20 July 2010). The Commission's decision had not been published at the time of writing.

94. WHAT IS THE METHODOLOGY FOR CALCULATING FINES FOR BREACHES OF COMPETITION LAW?

Summary

- The Commission can impose fines of up to 1 per cent of turnover for procedural infringements relating to antitrust investigations.

- In setting fines for substantive infringements of the competition rules, the basic amount of the fine is calculated first. The Commission generally applies the following methodology in setting the basic amount of the fine:

  - It establishes the value of sales to which the infringement relates in the relevant geographic area (usually not wider than the EEA);

  - A proportion of this amount, usually no greater than 30 per cent, is then taken depending on the gravity of the infringement and factors such as market share;

  - This figure is multiplied by the number of years of the infringement;

  - A further amount may be added for deterrence purposes.

- Once the basic amount of the fine is established, this may be revised upwards or downwards depending on aggravating and mitigating factors.

- The Commission may increase the fine to create a general deterrent effect.

- The Commission may consider, but is not required to take account of, an undertaking's cooperation or the fact that it took preventative measures such as a compliance programme.

- Financial difficulties imposed on an undertaking by reason of being fined will be considered only exceptionally.

Ireland

- Only the courts have the power to impose fines. There are no fining guidelines. The court will issue a fine, which is a criminal sanction, based on the particular circumstances and after considering aggravating and mitigating circumstances.

UK

- The OFT has the power to impose fines for breach of Article 101 or 102 and the Chapter I or II prohibition. Its approach to fines is set out in published guidance, which it is required to follow.

- Fines may be appealed to the CAT and subsequently to the Court of Appeal.

---

1.   A distinction should be drawn between fines imposed for procedural and substantive infringements. The Commission can impose fines on undertakings for procedural infringements under Article 23(1) of Regulation 1/2003. The fine cannot exceed 1 per cent of the annual turnover of the undertaking. Grounds for imposing a fine include intentionally or negligently supplying incorrect information, producing incomplete records, giving incorrect answers in response

to questions and breaking Commission seals. In one case, the Commission imposed a fine of €38 million on an undertaking for breaking a seal affixed to secure documents collected during a dawn raid.[244]

2. The Commission can impose fines for substantive infringements of Articles 101 and 102 under Article 23(2) of Regulation 1/2003. Fines can be imposed on undertakings if:

   (a) they infringe Article [101] or Article [102] of the Treaty; or

   (b) they contravene a decision ordering interim measures under Article 8; or

   (c) they fail to comply with a commitment made binding by a decision pursuant to Article 9.[245]

3. In fixing the amount of the fine, the Commission is to have regard 'both to the gravity and to the duration of the infringement'.[246] The Court of Justice has held that 'the gravity of an infringement must be assessed in the light of numerous factors, such as the particular circumstances of the case, its context and the dissuasive effect of fines, although no binding or exhaustive list of the criteria to be applied has been drawn up'.[247] This gives the Commission a wide discretion in setting the fine.

4. The Commission's methodology for calculating fines is set out in its Guidelines on Fines.[248] Although not legally binding, the importance of the guidelines has been highlighted by the Court of Justice, which has indicated that they impose a 'limit on the exercise of [the Commission's] discretion' and that departure from the guidelines could, depending on the circumstances, result in a breach of general principles of EU law.[249] However, the Court has stated more recently that when assessing the fine, the Commission is 'entitled to assess overall the gravity of the infringement in relation to all the relevant circumstances, including factors not expressly mentioned in the Guidelines'.[250]

---

244. Case COMP/B–1/39.326 – *E.ON Energie*, Commission Decision C (2008) 377 Final of 30 January 2008 (on appeal, Case T–141/08 *E.ON Energie v Commission* (pending)). See also IP/10/627, Commission opens proceedings against Czech J&T Group for obstruction during inspection (28 May 2010) (concerning possible obstruction relating to email accounts and electronic records during a dawn raid).

245. Regulation 1/2003, Article 23(2).

246. Regulation 1/2003, Article 23(3).

247. Cases C–125/07 etc *Raiffeisen Zentralbank Österreich AG v Commission* [2009] ECR I–8681, para 91.

248. Commission Guidelines on the method of setting fines imposed pursuant to Article 23(2)(a) of Regulation No 1/2003 [2006] OJ C210/02 ('Commission Guidelines on Fines').

249. See, e.g., Case C–189/02P *Dansk Rørindustri A/S v Commission* [2005] ECR I–5425, [2005] 5 CMLR 796, paras 211, 212.

250. Cases C–125/07 etc *Raiffeisen Zentralbank Österreich AG v Commission* [2009] ECR I–8681, para 93.

5.   The Commission will first establish the basic amount of the fine. It may then adjust that amount upwards or downwards taking aggravating and mitigating factors into account.

6.   There is a maximum fine that can be imposed, which is 10 per cent of the undertaking's total turnover in the preceding business year.[251] The 10 per cent figure applies to worldwide turnover of the undertaking, not just turnover in the EEA or turnover in the product or geographic area that is the subject of the infringement. This can be contrasted with the US method of setting fines, which is based on the 'affected commerce' related to the infringement.[252] Where one subsidiary in a larger corporate group was involved in the infringement, it is the turnover of the group as a whole, rather than that of the individual subsidiary, that is relevant for the application of the 10 per cent threshold.

7.   In fixing the amount of the fine, the Commission is constrained by general principles of EU law. Principles of particular relevance include the principles of equal treatment and proportionality, the principle of legality and the *non bis in idem* rule. These principles are often invoked in appeals before the General Court against the level of fine imposed by the Commission.[253]

How is the basic amount of the fine calculated?

8.   Under the approach in its Guidelines on Fines, the Commission will take the value of the undertaking's sales of the goods or services to which the infringement relates in the relevant geographic area, usually confined to the EEA.[254] The basic amount of the fine is related to a proportion of the value of these sales, as a general rule up to 30 per cent,[255] depending on the degree of the gravity of the infringement, multiplied by the number of years of the infringement.[256]

9.   In deciding whether the proportion of the value of sales to be used should be at the lower or higher end of the scale, the Commission has regard to a number of factors, such as the nature of the infringement, the market share of the

---

251. Regulation 1/2003, Article 23(2).
252. United States Sentencing Commission Federal Sentencing Guidelines Manual, Ch 2, Part R. The status of the Guidelines is advisory rather than mandatory following the Supreme Court judgment in *United States v Booker* 543 US 220 (2005).
253. See Question 98, which considers potential arguments for challenging the Commission's decision imposing a fine.
254. Commission Guidelines on Fines [2006] OJ C210/02, paras 13, 18. The General Court has endorsed the use of turnover as an adequate criterion for setting fines despite its 'necessarily vague and imperfect nature' and that it does not distinguish between companies with different profitability levels (Case T–127/04 *KME Germany AG v Commission*, judgment of 6 May 2009, para 93 (appeal pending, Case C–272/09P *KME Germany AG v Commission*); similarly, Case T–25/05 *KME Germany AG v Commission*, judgment of 19 May 2010, para 100 (on appeal Case C–389/10P *KME Germany AG v Commission*)).
255. Commission Guidelines on Fines [2006] OJ C210/02, para 21.
256. Commission Guidelines on Fines [2006] OJ C210/02, para 19.

undertaking[257] and the geographic scope of the infringement.[258] For example, horizontal price fixing will tend to be at the higher end of the 30 per cent scale as it is considered to be one of the most serious types of infringement. The Commission may separate different undertakings involved in an infringement into different bands for purposes of setting the fine, for example by using each undertaking's turnover and then grouping into small, medium and large categories based on market share.[259]

10. To take duration into account, the amount determined on the basis of value of sales will be multiplied by the number of years of participation in the infringement.[260] Once this multiplier is applied, the basic amount of the fine is established. The Commission then makes adjustments depending on aggravating and mitigating circumstances.

What aggravating circumstances are relevant?

11. The Commission Guidelines on Fines list examples of aggravating circumstances, which include:

- Repeat infringements (with no limitation period on what previous infringements can be taken into account[261] and no requirement that the previous infringements be closely related to the current one[262]);

- Refusal to cooperate or obstruction of the Commission's investigation; and

- Whether the undertaking was a ringleader, instigator or coercer in the infringement.[263]

12. Other aggravating factors that have arisen in the cases include that the undertaking continued to infringe the competition rules after the beginning of the Commission

---

257. In some circumstances, the market shares of smaller members of a cartel may be taken into account in establishing the level of the fine to be imposed on undertakings that played a leading role in the cartel. See Cases C–125/07 etc *Raiffeisen Zentralbank Österreich AG v Commission* [2009] ECR I–8681, paras 172–177.
258. Commission Guidelines on Fines [2006] OJ C210/02, paras 20, 22.
259. See, e.g., Case T–68/04 *SGL Carbon AG v Commission* [2008] ECR II–2511, paras 69, 70 (such a categorisation was coherent and objectively justified and did 'not lead to a grossly inaccurate representation of the market concerned') (appeal dismissed, Case C–564/08P *SGL Carbon AG v Commission*, judgment of 12 November 2009).
260. Commission Guidelines on Fines [2006] OJ C210/02, para 24.
261. Cases T–101 & 111/05 etc *BASF AG v Commission* [2007] ECR II–4949, [2008] 4 CMLR 347, para 67.
262. See Case T–122/04 *Outokumpu Oyj v Commission* [2009] ECR II–1135, paras 55–59 (in imposing fines for a cartel in industrial tubes, the Commission could take into account a previous infringement in steel under the ECSC Treaty; the General Court held that 'the concept of repeat infringement implies only a previous finding of infringement of Community competition law').
263. See Commission Guidelines on Fines [2006] OJ C210/02, para 28. The General Court confirmed in *Nintendo* that the role of ringleader of a competition infringement could be found in restrictive vertical agreements as well as horizontal agreements. (contd)

investigation, such conduct showing that the undertaking was particularly determined to continue the infringement in spite of the risk of fines.[264] The institutionalised nature of the infringement has also been considered as an aggravating factor.[265]

What mitigating factors are relevant?

13. The following is a non-exhaustive list of mitigating factors that the Commission may take into account:

- Evidence of termination of the infringement as soon as the Commission intervened;

- Evidence that the infringement was committed because of negligence;

- Evidence that the undertaking's involvement in the infringement was substantially limited;

- Effective cooperation with the Commission outside the context of leniency and beyond legal requirements; and

- Where the anti-competitive conduct was authorised or encouraged by a public authority or legislation.[266]

14. In setting the fine, the Commission is not required to take into account 'preventative measures' such as the fact that the undertaking concerned had a competition law compliance programme in place at the time of the infringement. The Commission is similarly not required to take into account the fact that the undertaking cooperated during the Commission's investigation or that it offered compensation to third parties. These factors 'do not affect the reality of the infringement committed and do not have to be taken into account when evaluating the gravity of the infringement'.[267] Nevertheless, the Commission has reduced fines for such factors. For example, in the *Nintendo* case, the Commission made a reduction in the fine of €300,000 following the payment of compensation to affected third parties.[268]

---

263. (contd) The fact that the role of ringleader in a vertical conspiracy generally belongs to the manufacturer does not preclude that fact from being taken into account for the purposes of calculating the amount of the fine. In any event, the General Court recognised that the instigator of a vertical conspiracy could also be a distributor (Case T–13/03 *Nintendo Co., Ltd v Commission* [2009] ECR II–947, [2009] 5 CMLR 1421, para 131).

264. See, e.g., Case T–13/03 *Nintendo Co., Ltd v Commission* [2009] ECR II–947, [2009] 5 CMLR 1421, para 142.

265. See, e.g., *PVC* [1989] OJ L74/1, [1990] 4 CMLR 435, para 52.

266. See Commission Guidelines on Fines [2006] OJ C210/02, para 29. For a list of other mitigating factors that have been accepted, as well as mitigating factors that have been put forward but been rejected, see Van Bael & Bellis, *Competition Law of the European Community* (5th edn, 2010) 1112–1114.

267. Case T–13/03 *Nintendo Co., Ltd v Commission* [2009] ECR II–947, [2009] 5 CMLR 1421, para 74.

268. See *Nintendo* [2003] OJ L255/33, [2004] CMLR 421, para 441 (this aspect of the Commission's decision upheld on appeal, Case T–13/03 *Nintendo Co., Ltd v Commission* [2009] ECR II–947, [2009] 5 CMLR 1421, para 209).

15. A reduction in the fine for cooperation is based on the consideration that such cooperation facilitates the Commission's task of identifying an infringement.[269] To justify a reduction of the fine for cooperation, an undertaking's conduct must facilitate the Commission in identifying and penalising infringements of the EU competition rules.[270] The Commission enjoys a wide discretion in assessing the quality and usefulness of the cooperation provided by an undertaking.[271] Therefore, only a manifest error of assessment can be censured by the court on review.[272]

Is the undertaking's inability to pay a fine relevant?

16. Financial hardship caused by antitrust penalties is a very real issue, particularly in light of the Commission's tendency over time to increase fines. Inability to pay can be a factor in the Commission's analysis but only in exceptional cases. The Commission Guidelines on Fines provide that the Commission may take account of an undertaking's inability to pay a fine 'in a specific social and economic context' if imposition of the fine 'would irretrievably jeopardise the economic viability of the undertaking concerned and cause its assets to lose all their value'.[273] Such inability is relevant only in a 'specific social context', 'namely the consequences which payment of a fine could have, in particular, by leading to an increase in unemployment or deterioration in the economic sectors upstream and downstream of the undertaking concerned'.[274]

17. So, inability of an individual undertaking to pay is not, in itself, sufficient. The Commission is not required to consider financial hardship as this would be 'tantamount to giving unjustified competitive advantages to undertakings least well adapted to the market conditions'.[275] Indeed, 'the fact that a measure taken by a Community authority results in the insolvency or liquidation of a particular undertaking is not precluded as such by Community law'.[276] Despite this, the Commission has decided not to impose a fine on an undertaking that had exited

---

269. See, e.g., Case T–311/94 *BPB de Eendracht NV* v *Commission* [1998] ECR II–1129, para 325.
270. See, e.g., Cases T–67/00 etc. *JFE Engineering Corp.* v *Commission* [2004] ECR II–2501, [2005] 4 CMLR 27, para 499.
271. See Case C–328/05P *SGL Carbon AG* v *Commission* [2007] ECR I–3921, [2007] 5 CMLR 16, para 88.
272. See Case T–13/03 *Nintendo Co., Ltd* v *Commission* [2009] ECR II–947, [2009] 5 CMLR 1421, para 161.
273. Commission Guidelines on Fines [2006] OJ C210/02, para 35.
274. Case C–308/04P *SGL Carbon AG* v *Commission* [2006] ECR I–5977, [2006] 5 CMLR 922, para 106.
275. Case C–328/05P *SGL Carbon AG* v *Commission* [2007] ECR I–3921, [2007] 5 CMLR 16, para 100.
276. Cases T–71/03 etc. *Tokai Carbon Co Ltd* v *Commission* [2005] ECR II–10, [2005] 5 CMLR 489, para 333. See also Cases C–554/08P *Le Carbone-Lorraine SA* v *Commission*, judgment of 12 November 2009, paras 62–70 (the Commission did not breach the principle of equality in considering the financial situation of different cartel participants).

the market the subject of an infringement, a decision found not to breach the principle of equal treatment vis-à-vis other parties to the infringement.[277]

18. The Commission has also been willing to take the financial circumstances of undertakings into account in certain cases in imposing lesser fines. In June 2010, the Commission reduced the amount of the fines imposed on five of the participants in the *Bathroom Equipment* cartel to a level they could afford, reducing the fines of three companies by 50 per cent and two others by 25 per cent. It refused to reduce the fines of five other companies, which had also pleaded financial hardship. In making its decision, the Commission carried out due diligence as to the financial state of the companies, commenting as follows:

> [To] assess their claims, the Commission looked at recent financial statements, provisional current year statements and future projections, several financial ratios that measure a company's solidity, profitability, solvency and liquidity, and relations with banks and shareholders. The Commission also looked at the social and economic context of each company. Finally, the Commission assessed whether the companies' assets would be likely to lose significant value if the companies were to be forced into liquidation as a result of the fine. The analysis is company-specific and aims to be as objective and quantifiable as possible to ensure equal treatment and preserve the deterrence aspect of EU competition rules.[278]

What role does deterrence play?

19. The Commission may increase a fine to ensure a deterrent effect.[279] When considering the deterrent effect of a fine, the Commission is not limited to imposing a fine that will deter the addressee of the decision from engaging in future anti-competitive conduct. Its deterrent aim can be aimed at other companies more generally and this does not give the addressee of the fine grounds to argue a breach of the principle of proportionality. As the General Court has stated:

> [The] pursuit of deterrent effect does not concern solely the undertakings specifically targeted by the decision imposing fines. It is also necessary to prompt undertakings of similar sizes and resources to refrain from participating in similar infringements of the competition rules.[280]

---

277. See Cases T–24/93 etc. *Compagnie Maritime Belge Transports SA v Commission* [1996] ECR II–1201, [1997] 4 CMLR 273, para 237.
278. IP/10/790, Commission fines 17 bathroom equipment manufacturers €622 million in price fixing cartel (23 June 2010). The decision in the case, Case COMP/39092 – *Bathroom fittings & fixtures*, had not yet been published at the time of writing. See also IP/10/985 European Commission fines animal feed phosphates producers €175,647,000 for price-fixing and market-sharing in first 'hybrid' cartel settlement case (20 July 2010) (one undertaking's fine reduced by 70 per cent for inability to pay but a similar application by another addressee rejected).
279. See Commission Guidelines on Fines [2006] OJ C210/02, para 30.
280. Case T–13/03 *Nintendo Co., Ltd v Commission* [2009] ECR II–947, [2009] 5 CMLR 1421, para 73.

Ireland

20. Breaches of Articles 101 and 102 and sections 4 and 5 of the Competition Act 2002 are criminal offences in Ireland. The range of possible sanctions that can be imposed for particular infringements is set out in the 2002 Act. These include imprisonment for individuals and the imposition of fines on both individuals and undertakings. In the case of violations of Article 101 or 102 or section 4 or 5, individuals and undertakings convicted on indictment can be fined up to the greater of €4 million or 10 per cent of turnover.[281]

21. Only the courts have the power to impose fines. There are no formal sentencing guidelines and the appropriate sanction is a matter for the judge in each case, taking account of the particular circumstances and relevant mitigating and aggravating factors.[282] The general principles applicable to sentencing for competition law infringements were considered by the Central Criminal Court in *Duffy*.[283] The Court imposed a suspended prison term and a fine on Mr. Duffy and a fine on his company for participation in a cartel. The approach taken by McKechnie J in deciding the appropriate sentence should be seen in the context that an individual was involved and the sanction of imprisonment was available.[284] The learned judge indicated that in such cases 'a court might feel that a more general overview involving the imposition of a mixed type of sentence is to be preferred'.[285] In deciding the fine to be imposed on both the individual and his undertaking, the appropriate custodial sentence also had to be considered.

22. In cases that are taken against an undertaking only, this mixed approach is unlikely to be relevant. Similarly, where the individual was not as closely identifiable with the undertaking (in *Duffy*, the individual was the joint owner and co-director of the undertaking; it would be rather different were an accused individual an employee of a large multi-national organisation) it is doubtful that the sanction imposed on the individual would be relevant in determining any fine to be imposed on the undertaking.

23. When applying Article 101 or 102,[286] the Irish courts must observe certain EU law requirements in imposing fines. In particular, fines must be effective and aimed at

---

281. Competition Act 2002, ss 8(1)(b), 8(1)(2). The sanctions for breaches of competition law under the 2002 Act are discussed in further detail in Question 103.
282. Cf the approach of the Australian courts to imposing competition law fines in, e.g., *Australian Competition and Consumer Commission v Leahy Petroleum Pty Ltd (No 3)* [2005] FCA 265, (2005) 215 ALR 301 (see, in particular at para 39, that the penalty should aim to achieve specific as well as general deterrence). See also, for a detailed analysis of what is an appropriate fine, *Australian Competition and Consumer Commission v Baxter Healthcare Pty Ltd* [2010] FCA 929.
283. See Question 103, which discusses the *Duffy* case in more detail.
284. While the case was decided under the Competition Act 1991, as amended, the same principles would apply in application of the 2002 Act.
285. *Director of Public Prosecutions v Duffy* [2009] IEHC 208, [2009] 3 IR 613, para 40.
286. When applying sections 4 and 5 of the Competition Act 2002 to agreements or practices that may affect trade between Member States, the courts must also apply Articles 101 and 102 (Regulation 1/2003, Article 3(1)).

ensuring compliance with the prohibitions contained in Articles 101 and 102. In addressing the question whether a national court could find that competition law fines imposed by the Commission were tax deductible, the Court of Justice commented generally that:

> The effectiveness of the penalties imposed by the national or Community competition authorities on the basis of Article [103(2)(a)] is therefore a condition for the coherent application of Articles [101 and 102].
>
> In proceedings relating to the penalties in respect of anti-competitive practices provided for in Article [103(2)(a)], the decision that the court seised must give is capable of impairing the effectiveness of those penalties and therefore might compromise the coherent application of Articles [101 or 102].[287]

24. It is unclear whether the national court must follow exactly the methodology of the Commission for setting fines when it imposes fines for breaches of Article 101 and 102. Certainly, if the application of Articles 101 and 102 is to be coherent and uniform across the Union, it would seem that the Commission's methodology should be followed. The Commission could also make submissions before the national court in such a case.[288] However, where the position of the undertaking in question is closely intertwined with that of an individual who is also before the court and against whom a custodial sentence is available, the position may be more complex, as the effect of a sentence of imprisonment has not been considered by the Commission in setting fines.[289]

25. Appeals from sentences in the Central Criminal Court lie to the Court of Criminal Appeal, which is composed of one judge of the Supreme Court and two judges of the High Court. An appeal to the Supreme Court can be taken from the decision of the Court of Criminal Appeal, but only where the Court of Criminal Appeal, the Director of Public Prosecutions or the Attorney General certify that a point of law of exceptional public importance arises. In the case of summary convictions in the District Court, an appeal lies to the Circuit Court. There is also the possibility of an appeal from the District Court to the High Court by way of case stated, a consultative case stated from the District Court to the High Court and a case stated from the Circuit Court to the Supreme Court.[290]

UK

26. The OFT has the power to impose fines on undertakings for breaches of the Chapter I and II prohibitions and Articles 101 and 102.[291] A fine can be imposed

---

287. Case C-429/07 *Inspecteur van de Belastingdienst v X BV* [2009] 5 CMLR 1745, paras 37–38.

288. Regulation 1/2003, Article 15(3).

289. See *Director of Public Prosecutions v Duffy* [2009] IEHC 208, [2009] 3 IR 613, para 32 (McKechnie J, having discussed the Commission's approach to imposing fines, noted that the regime in which such fines were applied did not provide for imprisonment as a sanction but otherwise the EU approach to imposing fines contained 'compelling' reasoning).

290. See further on appeals, O'Malley, *The Criminal Process* (2009) Ch 23.

291. Competition Act 1998, ss 36(1), 36(2).

only if the OFT is satisfied that the infringement has been committed intentionally or negligently.[292] The maximum fine that can be imposed on an undertaking is 10 per cent of its worldwide turnover in the business year preceding the OFT's decision.[293]

27.   The OFT has published guidance on the setting of fines.[294] It must have regard to this guidance when imposing fines.[295] The guidance sets out a five-step approach:

(i)   Identifying the starting point in light of the seriousness of the infringement and the turnover of the undertaking in markets affected by the infringement in the last business year.

(ii)   Adjustment for the duration of the infringement.

(iii)   Adjustment for other factors, in particular deterrence.

(iv)   Adjustment for aggravating and mitigating factors (for example, if the undertaking has a competition compliance programme, this can reduce the fine by 10 per cent).[296]

(v)   Adjustment to prevent the maximum penalty being exceeded and to avoid double jeopardy.[297]

28.   A person found guilty of the cartel offence may also be fined. Individuals guilty of the offence on indictment are liable to a prison sentence of up to five years and/or an unlimited fine.[298] The OFT states that for the purposes of calculating the amount of fines payable by undertakings under section 36 of the 1998 Act, the prosecution or conviction of individuals for the cartel offence in connection with the same competition law infringement is not relevant.[299] It is arguable that in cases where the individual and undertaking are the same or closely intertwined (for example, the individual is also the largest shareholder of the undertaking) that the sentence imposed on the individual for the cartel offence should take account of any fines imposed by the OFT on the undertaking.

---

292. Competition Act 1998, s 36(3).
293. Competition Act 1998, s 36(8); SI 2000/309 Competition Act 1998 (Determination of Turnover for Penalties) Order 2000, as amended by SI 2004/1259, Article 3.
294. OFT 423, OFT's Guidance as to the appropriate amount of a penalty (December 2004).
295. Competition Act 1998, s 38(8).
296. OFT 1227, Drivers of Compliance and Non-Compliance with Competition Law (May 2010) para 1.14.
297. OFT 423, OFT's Guidance as to the appropriate amount of a penalty (December 2004) Ch 2. See Competition Act 1998, s 38(9) (the OFT and the CAT and Court of Appeal on appeal must take into account penalties or fines imposed by the Commission or by a court or other body in another Member State).
298. Enterprise Act 2002, s 190(1)(a).
299. OFT 423, OFT's Guidance as to the appropriate amount of a penalty (December 2004) para 1.14.

29.   The largest fine imposed by the OFT on one undertaking to date was the £121.5 million fine that British Airways agreed to pay for colluding with Virgin Atlantic in setting long-haul passenger fuel surcharges.[300]

30.   There is an exemption from fines for infringements of the Chapter I prohibition (but not Article 101) for 'small agreements' other than price fixing agreements. These are defined as agreements between undertakings with a combined turnover in the previous business year of not more than £20 million.[301] The exemption applies as long as the OFT is satisfied that the undertaking acted on the reasonable assumption that it had immunity.[302] Immunity from fines for breach of the Chapter II prohibition (but not Article 102) is available for 'conduct of minor significance', available for undertakings with annual turnover not exceeding £50 million.[303] Again, the undertaking must have acted on the reasonable assumption that immunity was available.[304]

31.   The penalty imposed by the OFT can be appealed to the CAT,[305] with a further appeal lying to the Court of Appeal.[306] The CAT is not bound to follow the OFT's guidance on penalties when considering the appeal but it will do so. The approach of the CAT has been described and endorsed by the Court of Appeal as follows:

> … the Tribunal commented on the application of the Guidance … by the OFT …, then went on to set out its own views on the seriousness of the infringement, and to make its own assessment of the penalty, on the basis of a 'broad brush' approach, taking the case as a whole. The Tribunal carried out a 'cross check' to see whether the amount so arrived at would be within the parameters set out in the Guidance, and concluded that it would be. It seems to us that this is an appropriate approach for the Tribunal.[307]

32.   A further appeal to the Court of Appeal is not limited to a point of law but the Court of Appeal is generally reluctant to interfere with the CAT's findings on the appropriate amount of the fine:

> In the case of the Court of Appeal, it seems to us that it is right for the court to recognise that the Tribunal is an expert and specialised body, and that, subject to any difference in the basis on which the infringements are to be considered as a result of

---

300. OFT Press Release, 'British Airways to pay record £121.5m penalty in price fixing investigation' (1 August 2007).
301. SI 2000/262 Competition Act 1998 (Small Agreements and Conduct of Minor Significance) Regulations 2000, r 3.
302. Competition Act 1998, s 36(4).
303. SI 2000/262 Competition Act 1998 (Small Agreements and Conduct of Minor Significance) Regulations 2000, r 4.
304. Competition Act 1998, s 36(5).
305. Competition Act 1998, s 46(3)(i).
306. Competition Act 1998, s 49(1)(a).
307. *Argos Limited v Office of Fair Trading* [2006] EWCA Civ 1318, [2006] UKCLR 1135, para 163.

any appeal on liability, the court should hesitate before interfering with the Tribunal's assessment of the appropriate penalty.[308]

33.   Nevertheless, the Court of Appeal has been prepared to adjust fines. In *National Grid*, the Court of Appeal was concerned about the CAT's assessment of the seriousness of the infringement in question, finding that the CAT had not given sufficient weight to a mitigating factor. The Court of Appeal reduced the fine that had been substituted by the CAT for abuse of dominance from £30 million to £15 million.[309]

Key Sources

Commission Guidelines on the method of setting fines imposed pursuant to Article 23(2)(a) of Regulation No 1/2003 [2006] OJ C210/02.

Case T–13/03 *Nintendo Co., Ltd v Commission* [2009] ECR II–947, [2009] 5 CMLR 1421.

UK

OFT 423, OFT's Guidance as to the appropriate amount of a penalty (December 2004).

---

308. *Argos Limited v Office of Fair Trading* [2006] EWCA Civ 1318, [2006] UKCLR 1135, para 165.
309. *National Grid Plc v Gas and Electricity Markets Authority* [2010] EWCA Civ 114, [2010] UKCLR 386, paras 90–115.

95. HOW CAN IMMUNITY FROM FINES BE OBTAINED IN CARTEL CASES BEFORE THE COMMISSION?

Summary

- Only one undertaking can receive immunity from fines in connection with a particular cartel.

- The undertaking which is 'first in the door' obtains immunity.

- There are two types of immunity, based on the provision of information that enables the Commission (i) to carry out a targeted inspection or (ii) to find an infringement of Article 101 (where it already has evidence or has already carried out an inspection).

- Conditional immunity is granted pending the adoption of the Commission's final decision. The undertaking must continue to provide full cooperation.

- An undertaking can obtain a 'marker', preserving its place as first in the queue, by providing basic information about the cartel, with the full application to follow at a later date.

- An undertaking not eligible for full immunity may be able to obtain 'partial immunity' *i.e.* a reduced fine, if it can supply evidence which represents significant added value.

1. The Commission's Leniency Notice sets out its approach to granting immunity from fines in cartel cases.[310] Under the Leniency Notice, undertakings that are willing to disclose their participation in a cartel can benefit from immunity from fines or from a reduction in fines.

What are the requirements to obtain immunity from fines?

2. Immunity from fines is only available for the first undertaking that comes forward and 'blows the whistle' on a cartel. Two types of immunity are provided for. Under paragraph 8(a) of the Leniency Notice, an undertaking will be granted immunity if it provides evidence which in the Commission's view will enable it to carry out a targeted inspection in connection with the alleged cartel. This type of immunity will not be available if the Commission had already carried out an inspection or had sufficient evidence to adopt a decision to carry out such an inspection.

3. Even if the Commission has carried out an investigation or had sufficient evidence to carry out such an inspection, immunity under paragraph 8(b) of the Leniency Notice may be available. This type of immunity is available for the provision of

---

310. Commission Notice on Immunity from fines and reduction of fines in cartel cases [2006] OJ C298/17 (the 'Commission Leniency Notice') para 10. Previous Leniency Notices had been issued in 1996 and 2002 (Commission Notice on the non-imposition of or reduction of fines in cartel cases [1996] OJ C207/4; Commission Notice on immunity from fines and reduction of fines in cartel cases [2002] OJ C45/03).

information which in the Commission's view enables it to find an infringement of Article 101 in connection with the alleged cartel. This immunity is only available if at the time the information was submitted, the Commission did not have sufficient evidence to find an infringement of Article 101 and no undertaking had been granted conditional immunity from fines under paragraph 8(a) of the Leniency Notice. The applicant must be the first to provide 'contemporaneous, incriminating evidence' of the alleged cartel. [311]

4. To avail of paragraph 8(a) or 8(b) immunity, the undertaking must provide a corporate statement setting out the full extent of its knowledge about the cartel. The corporate statement, which can be made in writing or orally, should include a detailed description of the alleged cartel arrangements, including its aims, activities and functioning, the names and addresses of the cartel participants and details of individuals who are involved in the cartel including, where necessary, their home addresses. The corporate statement should also include details about approaches to other competition authorities both inside and outside the EU.[312] The applicant for paragraph 8(a) immunity must also submit other evidence relating to the cartel in its possession, including any evidence contemporaneous to the infringement.[313]

5. A number of other conditions must be satisfied in order to obtain either paragraph 8(a) or 8(b) immunity. The immunity applicant must cooperate genuinely (*i.e.* provide accurate and complete information), fully, on a continuous basis and expeditiously throughout the Commission's procedure from the time it submits its application. The duty of cooperation includes, in particular:

    providing the Commission promptly with all relevant information and evidence relating to the alleged cartel that comes into its possession or is available to it;

    remaining at the Commission's disposal to answer promptly to any request that may contribute to the establishment of the facts;

    making current (and, if possible, former) employees and directors available for interviews with the Commission;

    not destroying, falsifying or concealing relevant information or evidence relating to the alleged cartel; and

    not disclosing the fact or any of the content of its application before the Commission has issued a statement of objections in the case, unless otherwise agreed.[314]

6. The applicant must also have ended its participation in the cartel immediately following its application, except to the extent that, in the Commission's view, continued participation was reasonably necessary to preserve the integrity of inspections. The undertaking must not have destroyed evidence before making its application or disclosed the fact or any content of its application except to another

---

311. Commission Leniency Notice [2006] OJ C298/17, para 11.
312. Commission Leniency Notice [2006] OJ C298/17, para 9(a).
313. Commission Leniency Notice [2006] OJ C298/17, para 9(b).
314. Commission Leniency Notice [2006] OJ C298/17, para 12(a).

competition authority.[315] An undertaking that coerced others into joining or remaining in the cartel is not eligible for immunity, although it may still qualify for a reduction in fines if it fulfills the relevant requirements.[316]

What is the procedure for applying for immunity?

7. Immunity applications are made by contacting DG Competition, with the approach usually being made by the undertaking's lawyers. The undertaking can apply initially for a marker or it may immediately proceed to make a full immunity application.

8. The grant of a marker will preserve the undertaking's place in the applicant queue while the necessary information and evidence for a full immunity application is gathered. As only the first applicant can obtain immunity, the marker system is an important device to protect the position of the undertaking that makes the first approach. To secure a marker, the undertaking must supply details of the cartel participants and other basic information about the cartel, as well as details of other leniency applications. It must also justify its request for a marker, *i.e.* explain why it cannot make a full application immediately. The Commission will set a date by which the marker must be perfected with the submission of a full immunity application.[317] Any disparity of treatment of applicants for markers could result in a breach of the principles of sound administration or equal treatment by the Commission.[318]

9. If the undertaking decides to apply for immunity immediately, it may initially present the application in hypothetical terms. In this case, it must present a detailed list of the evidence that it would later provide and clearly identify the product or service concerned by the cartel and its geographic scope and duration. Redacted documents may be submitted.[319] If it becomes apparent that immunity is not available or that the undertaking will not meet the paragraph 8(a) or 8(b) conditions, the Commission will inform it in writing. The undertaking can withdraw the evidence it has disclosed or convert its application into one for a reduction in fine. This does not prevent the Commission from using its normal powers of investigation to obtain the information that is withdrawn.[320]

---

315. Commission Leniency Notice [2006] OJ C298/17, paras 12(b), (c).
316. Commission Leniency Notice [2006] OJ C298/17, para 13.
317. Commission Leniency Notice [2006] OJ C298/17, para 15.
318. Cf, in the context of a 'queue' for leniency under the 1996 Leniency Notice, Case T–410/03 *Hoechst GmbH v Commission* [2008] ECR II–881, [2008] 5 CMLR 839, paras 134–137 (where the Commission initially did not tell either of two companies that other companies were providing information but subsequently informed one of the companies that it would be given 'fair warning' if it looked as though another company would overtake it in leniency requirements, the Commission failed to have regard to the principles of sound administration and equal treatment vis-à-vis the other undertaking).
319. Commission Leniency Notice [2006] OJ C298/17, para 16(b).
320. Commission Leniency Notice [2006] OJ C298/17, para 20.

10. Once the Commission has received the information and evidence required for a formal application and has verified that it meets the conditions for paragraph 8(a) or 8(b) immunity, it will grant conditional immunity in writing.[321] The grant of immunity can only be conditional at this stage because it depends on ongoing cooperation obligations which continue until the Commission has adopted a final decision.

What are the requirements to obtain 'partial immunity'?

11. An undertaking that does not meet the conditions for full immunity may be able to obtain a reduction in its fine. To qualify for this 'partial immunity', the undertaking must submit evidence which represents 'significant added value'.[322] Whether the evidence is of added value will depend on the extent to which, by its nature or level of detail, it strengthens the Commission's ability to prove the infringement of competition law. Written evidence originating from the time of the infringement is generally of greater value and the Commission will also consider the extent to which corroboration is required for the evidence to be relied on against other undertakings.[323]

12. The first undertaking to provide significant added value is eligible to receive a reduction in fine of between 30 per cent and 50 per cent. For the second undertaking providing significant added value, the potential reduction is between 20 per cent and 30 per cent. Subsequent undertakings can receive a reduction of up to 20 per cent. In deciding the level of reduction, the Commission takes into account the time when the evidence was submitted and the extent to which it represents added value.[324]

What is the procedure for partial immunity applications?

13. A formal application must be made, submitting the relevant evidence that the undertaking relies on in seeking a reduction in its fine. The Commission will not take a position on any application for partial immunity until it has taken a position on any existing applications for full immunity arising out of the same cartel. If the Commission considers that the conditions for partial immunity are met, it will inform the undertaking in writing, no later than the date on which the statement of objections is notified, of its intention to issue a reduced fine. The Commission's final decision on the fine reduction will be set out in the infringement decision.[325]

Key Sources

Commission Notice on Immunity from fines and reduction of fines in cartel cases [2006] OJ C298/17.

---

321. Commission Leniency Notice [2006] OJ C298/17, para 18.
322. Commission Leniency Notice [2006] OJ C298/17, para 24.
323. Commission Leniency Notice [2006] OJ C298/17, para 25.
324. Commission Leniency Notice [2006] OJ C298/17, para 26.
325. Commission Leniency Notice [2006] OJ C298/17, paras 27–30.

96. ARE COMPETITION LAW FINES TAX DEDUCTIBLE?

Summary

- The Court of Justice has indirectly suggested that a Member State law that allows antitrust fines imposed for a breach of EU competition law to be deducted from tax may be a breach of EU law; however, it has not yet decided the question directly.

- It is doubtful that antitrust fines are tax deductible in either the UK or Ireland.

1. If an undertaking fined by the Commission for a breach of EU competition law were able to deduct the fine from taxable income, this could have significant financial consequences. Say, for example, that two companies are each fined €100 million by the Commission. Antitrust fines are tax deductible in the jurisdiction in which the first company is tax resident but not in the jurisdiction of the second company. Say that the corporate tax rate is 35 per cent in each jurisdiction. The first company can deduct €100 million from its taxable profits, giving it a potential €35 million saving over the second company. Of course, differences in corporation tax rates will also affect this question in practice.

2. The issue of differences in taxable treatment of competition law fines in the Member States has not received significant treatment in the cases, in Commission policy or in academic literature.[326]

3. In the *X BV* case, the Court of Justice hinted strongly that a national tax regime that allowed the tax deductibility of competition law fines imposed by the Commission would compromise the application of Articles 101 and 102. The case arose as a preliminary reference from a Dutch court in proceedings between the Dutch Inspector of Taxes and X BV concerning the tax deductibility of fines imposed by the Commission for breach of EU competition law. The question referred did not relate directly to the question of tax deductibility. Rather the national court asked whether the Commission was competent under Article 15(3) of Regulation 1/2003 to submit, on its own initiative, written observations to the national court. In answering that question in the affirmative, the Court of Justice noted that the combination of the prohibitions in Articles 101 and 102 and the Commission's ability to impose fines in respect of those infringements was to be understood 'as forming part of a comprehensive set of provisions designed to prohibit and punish anti-competitive practices'. There was an 'intrinsic link' between fines imposed by the Commission and the application of Articles 101 and 102. The Court went on to state:

> The effectiveness of the penalties imposed by the national or Community competition authorities on the basis of Article [103(2)(a) is therefore a condition for the coherent application of Articles [101 and 102].

---

326. See Kuilwijk and Phelan, 'On the tax-deductibility of fines for EC competition law infringements' [2010] *European Competition Law Review* 131.

In proceedings relating to the penalties in respect of anti-competitive practices provided for in Article [103(2)(a)], the decision that the court seised must give is capable of impairing the effectiveness of those penalties and therefore might compromise the coherent application of Articles [101 or 102].

In the circumstances of the action in the main proceedings, it is quite clear that the outcome of the dispute relating to the tax deductibility of part of a fine imposed by the Commission is capable of impairing the effectiveness of the penalty imposed by the Community competition authority. The effectiveness of the Commission's decision by which it imposed a fine on a company might be significantly reduced if the company concerned, or at least a company linked to that company, were allowed to deduct fully or in part the amount of that fine from the amount of its taxable profits, since such a possibility would have the effect of offsetting the burden of that fine with a reduction of the tax burden.[327]

4.   The Commission subsequently intervened before the Amsterdam Court of Appeal, which ultimately decided that Dutch law prohibited the tax deductibility of competition law fines imposed by the Commission.[328] In a separate decision, the same court held that fines imposed by the Dutch Competition Authority were not tax deductible.[329] In contrast, in Belgium, the Antwerp Court of Appeal ruled in a June 2009 case that fines imposed by the European Commission for antitrust infringements were administrative rather than criminal in nature and so could be deducted from taxable profits under Article 53(6) of the Belgian Income Tax Code.[330]

5.   It is doubtful that competition law fines are tax deductible in the UK. The relevant domestic tax legislation provides that in calculating taxable profits of a trade, no deduction is allowed for 'losses not connected with or arising out of the trade'.[331] The OFT has stated that its understanding is that fines imposed pursuant to the Competition Act 1998 are not tax deductible.[332] The House of Lords indicated in *McKnight v Sheppard* that fines which carried a punitive element would not be tax deductible as the 'purpose is to punish the taxpayer and a court may easily conclude that the legislative policy would be diluted if the taxpayer were allowed to share the burden with the rest of the community by a deduction for the purposes of tax'.[333] A company seeking to claim tax deductions for competition law fines under Irish tax law may face similar difficulties. The Irish legislation provides, for example, that no deductions can be made in respect of 'any disbursement or

327. Case C-429/07 *Inspecteur van de Belastingdienst v X BV* [2009] 5 CMLR 1745, paras 37–39.
328. Case 06/00252 *Inspecteur van de Belastingdienst v X BV,* judgment of the Amsterdam Court of Appeal of 11 March 2010.
329. Case 08/01180 *X BV v Inspecteur van de Belastingdienst,* judgment of the Amsterdam Court of Appeal of 11 March 2010.
330. McDermott, Will & Emery, 'Belgian Court Rules in Favour of Tax Deductibility of European Commission Fines for Antitrust Infringements', *Brussels Brief* (26 October 2009).
331. Corporation Tax Act 2009, s 54(1)(b).
332. OFT 407, Enforcement (December 2004) para 5.15.
333. *McKnight v Sheppard* [1999] 1 WLR 1333, 1337–1338 (Lord Hoffmann).

expenses, not being money wholly and exclusively laid out or expended for the purposes of the trade or profession' or 'any loss not connected with or arising out of the trade or profession'.[334] It is arguable that these provisions would preclude the deduction of antitrust fines.

6. EU law clearly has no jurisdiction to apply its competition rules in such a way that affects the application of tax rules of jurisdictions outside the EU. If the undertaking is tax resident in a non-EU jurisdiction, and that jurisdiction allows for the tax deductibility of the fine, this obviously has an adverse impact on the rationale in *X BV* and the goal of achieving a uniform deterrent effect. It is difficult to see how EU law could respond. Could it, for example, increase the fine on an undertaking that was tax resident in a jurisdiction that allows the deductibility of competition law fines? Or could the Commission increase the fine where it appeared that the addressee of the Commission decision had purposely moved its tax residence to such a jurisdiction in anticipation of the Commission fine in order to benefit from the tax deduction?

7. To the extent that antitrust fines are tax deductible, this raises possibilities for efficient tax planning. Given that the imposition of fines may take place a number of years after an antitrust investigation has begun, a company that expects to be fined may consider moving its tax residence outside the EU or it could move profits from one group company to another group company that was likely to be fined, thereby enabling the latter company to utilise the tax deduction from profits.

Key Sources

Case C–429/07 *Inspecteur van de Belastingdienst v X BV* [2009] 5 CMLR 1745.

---

334. Tax Consolidation Act 1997, ss 81(2)(a), 81(2)(e).

97. MUST THE COMMISSION'S PROCEDURES IN COMPETITION CASES COMPLY WITH HUMAN RIGHTS?

Summary

• Fundamental rights are part of the general principles of EU law.

• There are two particularly important sources of rights: (i) the Charter of Fundamental Rights, which has the same status as the Treaties; and (ii) the European Convention on Human Rights, which the EU courts rely on and to which the EU is committed to acceding.

• It is arguable that the Commission's procedures are incompatible with provisions of the Charter and the ECHR. The case law in this area is still developing.

1. The procedures of the Commission in competition cases have long been criticised by lawyers, commentators and the business community. A frequent allegation is that the Commission acts as prosecutor, judge and jury when enforcing EU competition law. It can be argued that this is fundamentally unfair, in particular in light of the enormous power wielded by the Commission as evidenced by the steady increase in fines, which often reach hundreds of millions of Euros and have passed €1 billion in recent cases.[335]

2. Since the coming into force on 1 December 2009 of the Treaty of Lisbon, the Charter of Fundamental Rights of the European Union has the same legal status as the Treaties.[336] Recital 37 of Regulation 1/2003 provides as follows:

    This Regulation respects the fundamental rights and observes the principles recognised in particular by the Charter of Fundamental Rights of the European Union. Accordingly, this Regulation should be interpreted and applied with respect to those rights and principles.[337]

3. The Charter also provides that to the extent it contains rights corresponding to rights guaranteed by the European Convention on Human Rights ('ECHR'), the meaning and scope of those rights shall be the same as those laid down by the ECHR but that Union law shall not be prevented from providing more extensive protection.[338]

---

335. See http://ec.europa.eu/competition/cartels/statistics/statistics.pdf.
336. TEU, Article 6(1).
337. Regulation 1/2003, recital 37.
338. Charter of Fundamental Rights, Article 52(3).

4.   The EU is not yet a signatory to the ECHR but it is expected that it will accede to the ECHR in the near future.[339] The Treaty on European Union provides that fundamental rights, as guaranteed by the ECHR and the constitutional traditions of the Member States, constitute general principles of EU law[340] and, as noted above, the meaning of the rights in the Charter is linked to corresponding rights in the ECHR.[341] In applying EU law, the EU courts draw inspiration from a number of sources of law common to the Member States, particularly the ECHR. So even if the EU courts do not yet directly apply the ECHR, it is a very important factor in applying EU law.

5.   Once the EU accedes to the ECHR, the final say on ECHR issues raised in the context of the Commission's procedures would likely rest with the European Court of Human Rights. It is uncertain what procedures will apply in this regard, for example, whether an undertaking appealing a decision of the Commission will first have to complete appeals before the Union Courts before it is entitled to petition the Strasbourg court. New procedures, for example a preliminary reference procedure from the EU courts to Strasbourg, might be considered as part of the negotiations on the accession of the EU to the ECHR.

Do Article 6 ECHR and Articles 47 and 48 of the Charter apply to competition proceedings?

6.   Article 6 ECHR sets out the right to a fair trial and various rights of the defence. Similar rights are included in Articles 47 and 48 of the Charter. Article 6 ECHR provides as follows:

> 1. In the determination of his civil rights and obligations or of any criminal charge against him, everyone is entitled to a fair and public hearing within a reasonable time by an independent and impartial tribunal established by law. Judgement shall be pronounced publicly by the press and public may be excluded from all or part of the trial in the interest of morals, public order or national security in a democratic society, where the interests of juveniles or the protection of the private life of the parties so require, or the extent strictly necessary in the opinion of the court in special circumstances where publicity would prejudice the interests of justice.
>
> 2. Everyone charged with a criminal offence shall be presumed innocent until proved guilty according to law.
>
> 3. Everyone charged with a criminal offence has the following minimum rights:
>
> (a) to be informed promptly, in a language which he understands and in detail, of the nature and cause of the accusation against him;
>
> (b) to have adequate time and the facilities for the preparation of his defence;

---

339. See TEU, Article 6(2) and TFEU, Articles 218(6) and 218(8). Work on accession is currently ongoing. See Commission MEMO/10/84, European Commission proposes negotiation directives for Union's accession to the European Convention on Human Rights (ECHR) – frequently asked questions (17 March 2010). Official accession talks opened in July 2010.
340. TEU, Article 6(3).
341. Charter of Fundamental Rights, Article 52(3).

(c) to defend himself in person or through legal assistance of his own choosing or, if he has not sufficient means to pay for legal assistance, to be given it free when the interests of justice so require;

(d) to examine or have examined witnesses against him and to obtain the attendance and examination of witnesses on his behalf under the same conditions as witnesses against him;

(e) to have the free assistance of an interpreter if he cannot understand or speak the language used in court.

7. Articles 47 and 48 of the Charter provide as follows:

Article 47 – Right to an effective remedy and to a fair trial

Everyone whose rights and freedoms guaranteed by the law of the Union are violated has the right to an effective remedy before a tribunal in compliance with the conditions laid down in this Article.

Everyone is entitled to a fair and public hearing within a reasonable time by an independent and impartial tribunal previously established by law. Everyone shall have the possibility of being advised, defended and represented.

Legal aid shall be made available to those who lack sufficient resources in so far as such aid is necessary to ensure effective access to justice.

Article 48 – Presumption of innocence and right of defence

1. Everyone who has been charged shall be presumed innocent until proved guilty according to law.

2. Respect for the rights of the defence of anyone who has been charged shall be guaranteed.

8. Article 6(1) ECHR, which establishes the right to a fair trial before an independent and impartial tribunal, applies to civil as well as criminal proceedings. However, the rights in Article 6(2) (the presumption of innocence) and Article 6(3) (various rights of defence including the right to be informed of the nature of the prosecution's case, adequate time to prepare a defence and the right to examine witnesses) apply only with respect to a 'criminal offence'.

9. The approach of the Charter is similar. The second paragraph of Article 47 establishes the right to a fair hearing before an independent tribunal and is not confined to criminal proceedings. However Article 48, establishing the presumption of innocence and rights of defence in respect of anyone 'charged' appears to be limited to criminal offences. The Explanatory Memorandum to the Charter explains that the second paragraph of Articles 47 corresponds to Article 6(1) ECHR and that Article 48 'is the same as Article 6(2) and (3)' ECHR.[342]

10. There is no doubt that Article 6(1) ECHR applies to competition proceedings. The Court of Justice has acknowledged that:

the general principle of Community law that everyone is entitled to a fair hearing, which is inspired by Article 6(1) of the ECHR … is applicable in the context of

---

342. Council of the EU, Charter of Fundamental Rights of the European Union – Explanation relating to the complete text of the Charter (December 2000) 65, 67.

proceedings brought against a Commission decision imposing fines on an undertaking for infringement of competition law.[343]

11. The Commission has itself successfully invoked arguments based on Article 6 ECHR before the Court of Justice, for example, when challenging the procedures employed by the General Court as breaching the right to be heard and the rights of defence.[344]

12. Article 47 of the Charter would also apply to competition proceedings. In *Knauf Gips*, the Court of Justice overturned a finding of the General Court that an addressee of the Commission's statement of objections in a competition case had an onus to challenge matters of fact or law during the administrative procedure if it was not to be barred from doing so on appeal before the EU courts. There was no legal provision that provided for this. The Court of Justice stated:

> In the absence of a specific legal basis, such a restriction is contrary to the fundamental principles of the rule of law and of respect for the rights of the defence. Moreover, the rights to an effective remedy and of access to an impartial tribunal are guaranteed by Article 47 of the Charter of Fundamental Rights of the European Union which, under the first subparagraph of Article 6(1) TEU, has the same legal value as the Treaties. Under Article 52(1) of that charter, any limitation on the exercise of the rights and freedoms recognised by the charter must be provided for by law.[345]

13. The more difficult question is the extent to which the rights in Articles 6(2) and 6(3) ECHR and Article 48 of the Charter apply when these are limited to proceedings of a 'criminal' nature.

14. Under the case law of the European Court of Human Rights, an objective assessment should be made in establishing whether proceedings involve a criminal charge. Three factors are relevant:

(i)   the domestic classification of the charge;

(ii) the nature of the offence; and

(iii) the severity of the punishment.[346]

15. The classification of the charge in domestic law is relevant to the assessment but it does not carry significant weight; rather, 'the very nature of the offence in question is a factor of a greater importance'.[347] Were it otherwise, states could avoid the application of Article 6 by deeming certain charges as non-criminal. So

---

343. Cases C–322/07P etc *Papierfabrik August Koehler AG v Commission* [2009] ECR I–7191, [2009] 5 CMLR 2301, para 143.

344. See, e.g., Case C–89/08P *Commission v Ireland* [2010] 2 CMLR 450, paras 43–62.

345. Case C–407/08P *Knauf Gips KG v Commission*, judgment of 1 July 2010, para 91. See also Case C–385/07P *Der Grüne Punkt v Commission* [2009] ECR I–6155, [2009] 5 CMLR 2215, paras 176 – 179 (confirming the applicability of Article 6(1) and Article 47 rights in the context of proceedings brought against a Commission decision).

346. These are the 'Engel' criteria, from *Engel v The Netherlands (No 1)* (1979–80) 1 EHRR 647.

347. *Galstyan v Armenia* (2010) 50 EHRR 618, para 58.

the stipulation in Regulation 1/2003 that sanctions for breach of competition law 'shall not be of a criminal nature'[348] is of limited relevance in considering the application of Article 6 to competition proceedings.

16.   The Court of Justice has held that given the nature of competition law infringements and the severity of penalties, the presumption of innocence derived from Article 6(2) ECHR applies in competition proceedings that may result in the imposition of fines.[349] It appears therefore that competition proceedings before the Commission come within the Article 6 meaning of a 'criminal' charge.[350]

17.   It has been argued that the procedural protections required by Article 6 are different for 'hardcore' criminal matters and other criminal cases and that competition proceedings before the Commission fall into the non-hardcore category.[351] The European Court of Human Rights has accepted a less stringent application of Article 6 in certain cases, such as minor traffic offences[352] and disciplinary proceedings.[353] In such cases, it has been found that Article 6 is still respected when decisions at first instance are taken by an administrative body, as long as there is the possibility for an appeal before a court that fully guarantees Article 6 rights and has 'full jurisdiction, including the power to quash in all respects, on questions of fact and of law, the challenged decision'.[354] It can be argued that antitrust proceedings are not comparable to the relatively minor offences in respect of which the European Court of Human Rights has accepted a more relaxed Article 6 standard.[355] However the Strasbourg court has not yet considered the extent to which the Commission's antitrust proceedings are compatible with Article 6.

18.   Further support for the full application of Article 6 ECHR to the Commission's proceedings can be found in UK competition law. Although proceedings in respect of the Chapter I and II prohibition are not criminal in nature, they have been

---

348. Regulation 1/2003, Article 23(5).

349. See, e.g., Case C–199/92 *Hüls AG v Commission* [1999] ECR I–4287, [1999] 5 CMLR 1016.

350. See further Slater, Thomas & Waelbroeck, 'Competition law proceedings before the European Commission and the right to a fair trial: no need for reform?' (GCLC Working Paper 04/08); Bellamy & Child (6th edn, 2008) para 13.030.

351. Wils, 'The Increased Level of Antitrust Fines, Judicial Review and the ECHR' (2010) 33 *World Competition* 5. See also the comments of Advocate General Bot in Cases C–322/07P etc. *Papierfabrik August Koehler AG v Commission* [2009] ECR I–7191, [2009] 5 CMLR 2301, paras 128–136.

352. *Öztürk v Germany* (1984) 6 EHRR 409, para 56.

353. *Albert and Le Compte v Belgium* (1983) 5 EHRR 533.

354. *Janosevic v Sweden* (2002) 38 EHRR 473, para 81.

355. See Forrester, 'Due process in EC competition cases: a distinguished institution with flawed procedures', [2009] *European Law Review* 817; Riley, 'The modernisation of EU anti-cartel enforcement: will the Commission grasp the opportunity?' [2010] *European Competition Law Review* 191.

described as 'quasi-criminal'[356] and the CAT has held that the entirety of Article 6 ECHR applies to such proceedings, which should be seen as involving a 'criminal charge' or 'criminal offence'.[357]

19. The combination of investigative, prosecutorial and decision-making functions within one institution raises obvious questions about the compatibility of Commission enforcement of the competition rules with Article 6 ECHR and Articles 47 and 48 of the Charter. A number of pending cases before the European courts raise fundamental questions about the Commission's procedures. For example, in its appeal against the Commission decision in the car glass cartel, in which it was fined €896 million,[358] Saint-Gobain argues that its right to an independent and impartial tribunal was infringed as the fine was imposed by an administrative authority which simultaneously holds powers of investigation and sanction and that Regulation 1/2003 is unlawful insofar as it does not provide for the right to an independent and impartial tribunal.[359] If Article 6 ECHR does in fact apply in full to Commission competition proceedings, such arguments seem to have significant weight. As the OECD has commented in respect of the Commission's procedure:

> No other jurisdiction in the OECD assigns decision-making responsibility in competition enforcement to a body like the Commission ... [When] the Commission decides a matter, it has typically not heard directly the case against the proposed decision. No Commissioner, including even the Competition Commissioner, will have attended the hearing. All depend on briefings from staff, and there is no *ex parte* rule or other control on contacts between investigating staff and the Commissioners who decide the matter. There is no initial adjudicator that is fully independent of the investigative function.[360]

20. Other ECHR and Charter rights that could be relevant in competition investigations include Article 8 ECHR and Article 7 of the Charter, which provide for the right to respect for private and family life. These rights may be relevant in particular in the context of dawn raids and the Court of Justice has recognised the application of Article 8 ECHR to business premises.[361] The entitlement to interfere with these rights, provided for in Article 8(2) (for example, 'necessary in a democratic society' or to ensure the 'economic well-being of the country'), is likely to be more far-reaching in the case of business premises than an individual's domestic residence.[362]

---

356. *Crest Nicholson Plc v Office of Fair Trading* [2009] EWHC 1875 (Admin), [2009] UKCLR 895, para 69.
357. *Napp Pharmaceutical Holdings Limited v Director General of Fair Trading (No 4)* [2002] CAT 1, [2002] Comp AR 13, especially at paras 99–100.
358. See Case COMP/39.125 *Car glass*, Commission Decision of 11 February 2009.
359. Case T–56/09 *Saint-Gobain Glass France v Commission* (pending).
360. OECD, European Commission – Peer Review of Competition Law and Policy (2005) 63–64.
361. Case C–94/00 *Roquette Frères SA* [2002] ECR I–9011, [2003] 4 CMLR 46, para 29.
362. See *Colas Est v France* (2004) 39 EHRR 373, para 49.

Are references to non-parties in the Commission decision compatible with human rights?

21. The inclusion in a Commission decision of details about an undertaking that is not itself an addressee of the decision could raise human rights questions. In the *Z* case, an applicant applied to the General Court for orders arising out of the Commission decision in the *Marine Hose* cartel.[363] The applicant sought access to the Commission file, in particular information about whether the applicant was identified in the confidential version of the Commission's decision and if so, it sought removal of those references. The increase in criminal antitrust enforcement and private damages actions may cause such parties to be concerned that the Commission decision will be used against them in, say, damages actions. In this case, the applicant argued that the right to be granted access to the file and the removal of any references to the applicant were based on the infringement of the applicant's fundamental procedural rights, namely the right to a fair hearing and the right of access to the file, and on the principle of the presumption of innocence. However, the General Court dismissed the action as inadmissible.[364]

What issues may be part of future reform?

22. The dramatic increase in fines in recent years and the manner in which the Commission carries out investigations have lead to calls from lawyers and the business community for reforms in the Commission's procedures in antitrust investigations. Arguments for reform include:

- The Commission's decision-making procedures need to be fairer and made more transparent.

- The investigation team should be separated from the drafters of the Commission decision.

- The ultimate vote on the Commission decision should be removed from the College of Commissioners and entrusted to an 'independent' decision maker within the Commission, who is not part of the investigative process.

- The hearing process and rights of defence should be strengthened.

- The investigation team should be required to defend their reasoning before the 'independent' decision maker and the parties should be given the opportunity to question the evidence put forward by the Commission.

Key Sources

European Convention of Human Rights, Articles 6, 8.

Charter of Fundamental Rights of the European Union, Articles 7, 47, 48.

---

363. COMP/39406 *Marine Hoses*, Commission decision of 28 January 2009 (on appeal, Case T–146/09 *Parker ITR Srl v Commission* and Case 148/09 *Trelleborg AB v Commission*, pending).
364. Case T–173/09 *Z v Commission*, Order of 3 June 2010.

98. WHAT ARGUMENTS CAN BE MADE WHEN SEEKING TO HAVE COMMISSION FINES REDUCED ON APPEAL?

Summary

Common arguments include that the Commission breached general principles such as:

- Proportionality.

- Legal certainty and legitimate expectations.

- Equal treatment.

- Double punishment (*non bis in idem*).

- The right to be heard.

1. Undertakings that are fined by the Commission for breach of Article 101 or 102 may appeal to the General Court, with a right of further appeal to the Court of Justice. The General Court has unlimited jurisdiction to review decisions by the Commission imposing a fine.[365] The Court may uphold the fine, cancel it or increase or decrease it. An undertaking may appeal only the fine or include an appeal against the fine together with an appeal against the infringement decision. Appeals seeking a reduction in the fine imposed by the Commission are regularly taken.

2. The EU Courts have consistently held that the Commission enjoys a wide discretion in setting fines.[366] Arguments that this discretion was so wide as to breach the principle of legal certainty have been rejected because, among other constraints, the Commission is limited in the fine it can impose by the provisions of Article 23(2) of Regulation 1/2003 and its decision on fines is subject to unlimited review by the EU courts.[367]

3. The Commission is subject to the general principles of EU law. Appellants against fines often seek to argue that the Commission has breached one of these principles. These principles include proportionality, equal treatment, protection of legitimate expectations, *non bis in idem* and the right to be heard.[368]

---

365. Regulation 1/2003, Article 31.
366. See, e.g., Case C–510/06P *Archer Daniels Midland Co v Commission (Sodium Gluconate)* [2009] ECR I–1843, [2009] 4 CMLR 889, para 82.
367. Case T–69/04 *Schunk GmbH v Commission* [2008] ECR II–2567, [2009] 4 CMLR 40, paras 27–52. See also Case T–446/05 *Amann & Söhne GmbH & Co. KG v Commission*, judgment of 28 April 2010, paras 130–152; Case C–413/08P *Lafarge SA v Commission*, judgment of 17 June 2010, paras 94–95.
368. Other arguments could be based on the principle that penal provisions not have retroactive effect or the Commission's duty of good administration, for example. For a more general analysis of the limits placed on the exercise of the powers of the EU institutions by the general principles of EU law, see, e.g., Woolf, Jowell, Le Seur and Donnelly, *De Smith's Judicial Review* (6th edn, 2007) paras 14.086–14.111.

What is the extent of the requirement of proportionality?

4. The Commission must not impose a penalty which is disproportionately high in relation to the infringement of EU law. The Treaty on European Union provides that 'under the principle of proportionality, the content and form of Union action shall not exceed what is necessary to achieve the objectives of the Treaties'.[369] Article 49(3) of the Charter of Fundamental Rights states that 'the severity of the penalties must not be disproportionate to the criminal offence'.[370]

5. Undertakings which have been fined by the Commission for breach of competition law have sometimes argued on appeal that the fine imposed was disproportionate in relation to, for example, their market share or turnover, their participation in the infringement or the fine that was imposed on other addressees of the Commission's decision (in which case it may also be alleged that there is a breach of the principle of equal treatment).

6. It is apparent from the judgments of the EU courts that a finding of a breach of proportionality will not easily be made. So, for example, the Court of Justice has held that:

> the Commission is not required to calculate fines from amounts based on the turnover of the undertakings concerned nor to ensure, where fines are imposed on a number of undertakings involved in the same infringement, that the final amounts of the fines resulting from its calculations for the undertakings concerned reflect any distinction between them in terms of their overall turnover or their relevant turnover.[371]

7. In *Tomra*, the General Court rejected the argument that the fine imposed on Tomra for a 'serious' breach of Article 102, which amounted to 8 per cent of its turnover, was disproportionate when considered in light of the fine that had been imposed on Microsoft for a 'very serious' infringement of Article 102. The General Court found that earlier decisions of the Commission could not serve as a legal framework for antitrust fines in competition matters and that the Commission could not be 'compelled to set fines which display perfect coherence with those imposed in other cases'.[372]

---

369. Article 5(4), TEU. See also Article 49(3) of the Charter of Fundamental Rights, which states that 'the severity of the penalties must not be disproportionate to the criminal offence'. It is not certain that this provision applies to competition investigations. See Question 97, discussing whether Articles 6(2) and 6(3) ECHR and Article 48 of the Charter apply to competition investigations.

370. Article 49 of the Charter broadly corresponds to Article 7 ECHR, the principles contained in which have been found to be applicable to the setting of fines in competition cases (see, e.g., Case T–446/05 *Amann & Söhne GmbH & Co. KG v Commission*, judgment of 28 April 2010, para 125).

371. Case C–413/08P *Lafarge SA v Commission*, judgment of 17 June 2010, para 54. See also Case C–189/02P *Dansk Rørindustri v Commission* [2005] ECR I–5425, [2005] 5 CMLR 796, para 312; Case C–564/08P *SGL Carbon v Commission*, judgment of 12 November 2009 (proportionality argument rejected).

372. Case T–155/06 *Tomra Systems ASA v Commission,* judgment of 9 September 2010, para 314.

8. The General Court has held that when deciding whether a fine is proportionate to an undertaking's participation in a cartel, the 'final amount of the fine is not, in principle, an appropriate factor in assessing the possible lack of proportionality'.[373] This is because the final fine will have been based on various factors linked to individual conduct such as the duration of the infringement, aggravating and mitigating factors and the cooperation provided by the particular undertaking. However, the starting amount of the fine can be a relevant factor in assessing proportionality.[374]

9. The undertaking's total turnover and its turnover derived from the goods that are the subject of the infringement are each potentially relevant in establishing the fine. However the Court of Justice has held that it is:

    > ... important not to confer on one or the other of those figures an importance which is disproportionate in relation to other factors to be assessed and, consequently, the fixing of an appropriate fine cannot be the result of a simple calculation based on the turnover from sales of the product concerned. [375]

10. On the other hand, there is no general principle in EU law that the fine must be proportionate to the undertaking's turnover from sales of the product in respect of which the infringement was committed.[376] The fine need not necessarily be proportionate even to the overall volume of the market in which the infringement occurred. In *Hoechst*, the General Court rejected the argument that a fine which was five times the volume of the relevant EEA market was disproportionate in the context of a cartel that lasted more than 17 years.[377] The fact that the undertaking did not earn a profit from its breach of the competition rules does not have the consequence that the imposition of a fine by the Commission is disproportionate. If that were so, fines would cease to have deterrent effect.[378]

11. In *Lafarge*, it was argued that an uplift in the fine for repeat infringements of the competition rules was disproportionate. The Court of Justice confirmed that the Commission must comply with the principle of proportionality when it increases a fine for recidivism:

    > ... the principle of proportionality requires that the time elapsed between the infringement in question and a previous breach of the competition rules be taken into account in assessing the undertaking's tendency to infringe those rules ... [The]

---

373. Case T–304/02 *Hoek Loos NV v Commission* [2006] ECR II–1887, [2006] 5 CMLR 590, para 85.

374. Case T–304/02 *Hoek Loos NV v Commission* [2006] ECR II–1887, [2006] 5 CMLR 590, paras 85–86.

375. Case C–510/06P *Archer Daniels Midland Co v Commission (Sodium Gluconate)* [2009] ECR I–1843, [2009] 4 CMLR 889, para 74.

376. Case C–510/06P *Archer Daniels Midland Co v Commission (Sodium Gluconate)* [2009] ECR I–1843, [2009] 4 CMLR 889, paras 74–75.

377. Case T–410/03 *Hoechst GmbH v Commission* [2008] ECR II–881, [2008] 5 CMLR 839, para 342.

378. Case T–64/02 *Heubach GmbH & Co. KG v Commission* [2005] ECR II–5137, [2006] 4 CMLR 1157, para 184.

General Court and, where appropriate, the Court of Justice may therefore be called upon to scrutinise whether the Commission has complied with that principle when it increased, for repeated infringement, the fine imposed, and, in particular, whether such increase was imposed in the light of, among other things, the time elapsed between the infringement in question and the previous breach of the competition rules.[379]

12. The history of the previous infringements that were relevant to the fine imposed on Lafarge showed that it had a tendency not to draw appropriate conclusions from its infringements of competition law. The Court went on to hold that the principle of legal certainty had not been infringed because there was no fixed limitation period for taking repeated infringements into account.[380]

When is the principle of equal treatment (and non-discrimination) breached in setting fines?

13. The principle of equal treatment is breached where comparable situations are treated differently or different situations are treated in the same way, unless such treatment is objectively justified.[381] This principle applies in the determination of the fine in competition cases. Appellants often argue that a fine is both disproportionate and in breach of the principle of equal treatment when judged against fines imposed on other undertakings in respect of the same infringement.

14. The principle of equal treatment has been raised in many different contexts in appeals against Commission fines. For example, undertakings have argued that the Commission failed to appreciate that their cooperation was more valuable than that of other cartel members and that by failing to impose a lesser fine, the Commission was treating different situations in the same way. However, such arguments are difficult to establish as the Commission 'has a wide discretion in assessing the quality and usefulness of the cooperation provided by the various members of a cartel, and only a manifest abuse of that discretion can be censured'.[382]

---

379. Case C–413/08P *Lafarge SA v Commission*, judgment of 17 June 2010, para 70.

380. Case C–413/08P *Lafarge SA v Commission*, judgment of 17 June 2010, paras 71–72.

381. See, e.g., Case 106/83 *Sermide SpA v Cassa Conguaglio Zucchero* [1984] ECR 4209, para 28.

382. Cases T–71/03 etc. *Tokai Carbon Co Ltd v Commission* [2005] ECR II–10, [2005] 5 CMLR 489, para 371.

382. See Case T–13/03 *Nintendo Co., Ltd v Commission* [2009] ECR II–947, [2009] 5 CMLR 1421, paras 169–189. See also Cases T–67/00 etc *JFE Engineering Corp. v Commission* [2004] ECR II–2501, [2005] 4 CMLR 27, paras 575–579 (unequal treatment where the Commission wrongly failed to take into account that some addressees committed two infringements and others only one; the Court reduced the fines of the latter but the Commission had not pleaded that the fines of the former should be increased). Cf Case T–304/02 *Hoek Loos NV v Commission* [2006] ECR II–1887, [2006] 5 CMLR 590, para 113 (even if the Commission wrongly granted another party a reduction in its fine, the principle of equal treatment had to be reconciled with the principle of legality so that a party could not rely on an unlawful act committed in favour of a third party); (contd \...)

15. An equal treatment argument with respect to levels of cooperation was successfully invoked in the *Nintendo* case.[383] Nintendo argued that in awarding another undertaking that was party to the infringement, John Menzies, a reduction of 40 per cent in the fine, compared with Nintendo's 25 per cent reduction, the Commission breached the principle of equal treatment on the basis that Nintendo's voluntary cooperation with the investigation was more extensive and made earlier. The General Court partly upheld this ground of appeal and applied the higher 40 per cent reduction to Nintendo's fine. The Court stated that the principle of equal treatment applied to the assessment of both undertakings' cooperation with the investigation and that if the level of cooperation was comparable, they must be treated equally in relation to the setting of fines. A comparison should be made between the cooperation of each party from a chronological and qualitative perspective. The chronological perspective examines the stage when cooperation was provided. In order to be comparable, it is not necessary that cooperation be at the exact same time. It is sufficient if cooperation is proffered at the same stage in the Commission's administrative procedure so that the submission of documents made by one undertaking a week later than another might still be considered as comparable chronological cooperation. The qualitative point of view relates to the circumstances of the cooperation and the intrinsic value of the information provided. In *Nintendo*, as the cooperation of Nintendo was comparable to John Menzies under these criteria, it too should have received a 40 per cent reduction in its fine.

How are the principles of legal certainty and of the protection of legitimate expectations relevant to setting fines?

16. Appellants have also argued that the Commission's decision on fines violated the principles of legal certainty or legitimate expectations. The right to rely on the principle of the protection of legitimate expectations extends to any individual in a situation where the EU authorities have caused him to entertain legitimate expectations but a person may not plead infringement of the principle unless he has been given precise assurances by the administration.[384] The legitimate expectation must arise from an authorised and reliable source and the General Court has indicated that informal statements made in meetings by Commission officials are not sufficient to raise a legitimate expectation that binds the Commission.[385]

17. Given the Commission's wide discretion in setting fines, the fact that in the past, the Commission imposed a certain level of fine for a particular type of infringement does not preclude it from raising the fine in a similar subsequent

---

383. (contd) *Makers UK Ltd v Office of Fair Trading* [2007] CAT 11, [2007] Comp AR 699 (principle of equal treatment not infringed where the disparity in fines complained of was caused by an arithmetical error in calculation of the other party's penalty).

384. See, e.g., Case T–220/00 *Cheil Jedang Corp. v Commission* [2003] ECR II–2473, para 33.

385. Case T–13/03 *Nintendo Co., Ltd v Commission* [2009] ECR II–947, [2009] 5 CMLR 1421, para 208.

case.[386] However, the Court of Justice has also stated that if the Commission were to depart from its Guidelines on Fines when establishing fines, it could leave itself open to an accusation of breach of the principle of protection of legitimate expectations.[387]

18. The principle of legal certainty includes the principle of non-retroactivity and requires that sufficient information is made public to enable parties to know clearly what the law is and how the law can be complied with. The principle also requires that penalties have a proper legal basis. The Commission's Guidelines on Fines ensure legal certainty on the part of undertakings with respect to the setting of fines. However, the principle of legal certainty does not require that undertakings know precisely in advance the level of fine that the Commission will impose for a breach of competition law. As the General Court has explained:

> ... owing to the gravity of the infringements which the Commission is required to penalise, the objectives of punishment and deterrence justify preventing undertakings from being in a position to assess the benefits which they would derive from their participation in an infringement by taking account, in advance, of the amount of the fine which would be imposed on them for that unlawful conduct.[388]

19. In any event, an undertaking fined for breach of the competition rules would have the amount of that fine explained in the Commission's statement of reasons in the decision imposing the fine. This was required to show clearly and unequivocally the reasoning followed by the Commission so as to enable the undertaking to decide whether to bring an appeal before the Union courts.[389]

When will the *non bis in idem* principle be breached?

20. The Commission must respect the rule against double punishment, *non bis in idem*, so that the same undertaking cannot be punished more than once for the same conduct. The principle is subject to the threefold condition of identity of the facts, unity of offender and unity of the legal interest protected.[390] The principle is specifically provided for in the Charter of Fundamental Rights in respect of criminal proceedings.[391]

---

386. Case T–220/00 *Cheil Jedang Corp. v Commission* [2003] ECR II–2473, para 35.

387. Case C–189/02P *Dansk Rørindustri A/S v Commission* [2005] ECR I–5425, [2005] 5 CMLR 796, paras 211; Case C–167/04 *JCB Service v Commission* [2006] ECR I–8935, [2006] 5 CMLR 1337, para 208.

388. Case T–69/04 *Schunk GmbH v Commission* [2008] ECR II–2567, [2009] 4 CMLR 40, para 45.

389. Case T–69/04 *Schunk GmbH v Commission* [2008] ECR II–2567, [2009] 4 CMLR 40, para 46.

390. See Case C–204/00P etc, *Aalborg Portland A/S v Commission*, [2004] ECR I–123, [2005] 4 CMLR 251, para 338.

391. Article 50 of the Charter of Fundamental Rights states: 'No one shall be liable to be tried or punished again in criminal proceedings for an offence for which he or she has already been finally acquitted or convicted within the Union in accordance with the law'.

21. In setting fines, the Commission has to take into account any fines already imposed by it or by the competition authorities of the Member States in respect of the same infringement.[392] However, the double punishment principle does not extend to fines imposed by antitrust authorities outside the EU. The principle of territoriality applies, so no conflict arises where the Commission exercises its power to impose fines on undertakings which breach the EU rules and a non-EU authority applies its own rules to impose fines. It has been held that the comity agreement between the EU and the United States in respect of competition enforcement[393] does not affect this approach as the purpose of the agreement is solely to enable the EU and US authorities to take advantage of the practical effects of a procedure initiated by the other authority, rather than make provisions for the *non bis in idem* principle to be respected.[394] Even though it is not required to take into account fines imposed by regulators outside the EU, the Commission has discretion to consider those fines in reaching its own decision on the appropriate fine.[395]

22. In *Tokai Carbon*, it was held that just because the Commission used one set of proceedings and issued one decision to impose penalties in respect of two cartels in neighbouring markets, this did not breach the principle of *non bis in idem*. The proceedings in respect of each market were instituted on objective grounds, separate infringements were found and separate fines issued.[396]

23. Does the Commission's policy of increasing the fine for repeat infringements breach the double punishment principle? In *Hoechst* it was argued that by increasing the fine for a repeated infringement, using a finding which had already been made in an earlier case, the Commission breached the principle of *non bis in idem*. The General Court did not discuss this argument in depth, deciding simply that there was no unity of facts, as the previous decision relied on by Hoechst concerned a different cartel.[397]

---

392. See Case C–17/10 *Toshiba Corporation* (pending) which raises issues about the *non bis in idem* principle in the context of investigations into possible breaches of competition law by the Commission and a national competition authority. For recent consideration of the principle by the European Court of Human Rights, see *Zolotukhin v Russia* (2009) 26 BHRC 485.

393. Agreement between the European Communities and the Government of the United States of America on the application of positive comity principles in the enforcement of their competition laws [1998] OJ L173/28.

394. See Cases T–71/03 etc. *Tokai Carbon Co Ltd v Commission* [2005] ECR II–10, [2005] 5 CMLR 489, paras 112–116.

395. See Case C–328/05P *SGL Carbon AG v Commission* [2007] ECR I–3921, [2007] 5 CMLR 16, paras 31–34.

396. See Cases T–71/03 etc. *Tokai Carbon Co Ltd v Commission* [2005] ECR II–10, [2005] 5 CMLR 489, paras 124–125.

397. See Case T–161/05 *Hoechst GmbH v Commission* [2009] 5 CMLR 2728, para 149–150.

Are arguments based on the right to be heard relevant?

24. The argument that a Commission fine should be impugned because there was a breach of the right to be heard is a difficult one to make out. The Commission can fulfil its obligations with respect to the right to be heard by ensuring that the following criteria are adhered to:

> It is settled case-law that where the Commission expressly states in its statement of objections that it will consider whether it is appropriate to impose fines on the undertakings and it indicates the main factual and legal criteria capable of giving rise to a fine, such as the gravity and the duration of the alleged infringement and whether that infringement was committed intentionally or negligently, it fulfils its obligation to respect the undertakings' right to be heard. In doing so, it provides them with the necessary means to defend themselves not only against the finding of an infringement but also against the imposition of fines.

> It follows that, so far as concerns the determination of the amount of the fines, the rights of defence of the undertakings concerned are guaranteed before the Commission by virtue of the fact that they have the opportunity to make their submissions on the duration, the gravity and the anti-competitive nature of the matters of which they are accused. Moreover, the undertakings have an additional guarantee, as regards the setting of that amount, in that the [General Court] has unlimited jurisdiction and may in particular cancel or reduce the fine.[398]

25. The fact that the Commission did not state in the statement of objections the possibility of applying a multiplier to the fine for deterrence purposes will not give rise to a breach of the rights of defence. This is included in the Commission's Guidelines on Fines as one of the factors taken into account by reference to which the gravity of infringements is determined. Moreover, the Commission 'cannot be required to state in more detail in the statement of objections all the factors which it intends to take into account when determining the amount of the fines'.[399]

Key Sources

Case C–413/08P *Lafarge SA v Commission*, judgment of 17 June 2010.

Case T–13/03 *Nintendo Co., Ltd v Commission* [2009] ECR II–947, [2009] 5 CMLR 1421.

Cases T–71/03 etc. *Tokai Carbon Co Ltd v Commission* [2005] ECR II–10, [2005] 5 CMLR 489.

Case T–220/00 *Cheil Jedang Corp. v Commission* [2003] ECR II–2473.

---

398. Case T–23/99 *LR AF 1998 A/S v Commission* [2002] ECR-II 1705, [2002] 5 CMLR 571, paras 199–200.
399. Case T–13/03 *Nintendo Co., Ltd v Commission* [2009] ECR II–947, [2009] 5 CMLR 1421, para 87.

99. MUST COMPETITION LAW REMEDIES BE PROPORTIONATE TO THE COMPETITION LAW PROBLEM?

Summary

• In applying the antitrust rules, the Commission's obligations to act proportionately in respect of remedies are less extensive in the context of Article 9 of Regulation 1/2003 than under Article 7.

• The Commission must also satisfy the principle of proportionality when accepting remedies under the Merger Regulation.

• A number of principles can be drawn from recent UK cases on the scope of the requirement for regulators to adopt proportionate remedies.

1.   This question only becomes of importance where there is a dispute about remedies. In practice, such disputes are not common, largely because remedies are usually the subject of negotiation and agreement between the antitrust authority and the relevant undertaking. However there are a number of situations where the proportionality of remedies might be questioned, for example, when a third party is affected by a remedy.

2.   Proportionality is a well-established generally binding principle of EU law and can therefore be used to challenge action by the Commission. It is expressly incorporated in the Treaty on European Union, which provides that 'under the principle of proportionality, the content and form of Union action shall not exceed what is necessary to achieve the objectives of the Treaties.'[400]

3.   Proportionality also has a specific basis in the competition law context. Article 7(1) of Regulation 1/2003 provides:

> Where the Commission, acting on a complaint or on its own initiative, finds that there is an infringement of Article [101] or of Article [102] of the Treaty, it may by decision require the undertakings and associations of undertakings concerned to bring such infringement to an end. For this purpose, it may impose on them any behavioural or structural remedies which are proportionate to the infringement committed and necessary to bring the infringement effectively to an end. Structural remedies can only be imposed either where there is no equally effective behavioural remedy or where any equally effective behavioural remedy would be more burdensome for the undertaking concerned than the structural remedy.[401]

---

400. Article 5(4) TEU. See also the protocol to the TEU and TFEU, Protocol (No 2) on the Application of the Principles of Subsidiarity and Proportionality.
401. Regulation 1/2003, Article 7(1). See also recital 12 ('This Regulation should make explicit provision for the Commission's power to impose any remedy, whether behavioural or structural, which is necessary to bring the infringement effectively to an end, having regard to the principle of proportionality').

4.   Article 9 of Regulation 1/2003 deals with commitments and provides as follows:

> Where the Commission intends to adopt a decision requiring that an infringement be brought to an end and the undertakings concerned offer commitments to meet the concerns expressed to them by the Commission in its preliminary assessment, the Commission may by decision make those commitments binding on the undertakings. Such a decision may be adopted for a specified period and shall conclude that there are no longer grounds for action by the Commission.[402]

5.   It is apparent that the Commission may impose remedies under Article 7 of Regulation 1/2003, whereas Article 9 concerns the ability of the Commission to make binding commitments that have been voluntarily proposed by the parties.

6.   A recital to the Merger Regulation provides that where undertakings offer commitments, they 'should be proportionate to the competition problem and entirely eliminate it'.[403] In clearing a transaction following the proposal of commitments by the undertakings concerned (the proposal of such commitments is voluntary), the Commission may attach to its decision conditions and obligations in order to ensure that the undertakings comply with their commitments in a timely and effective manner.[404]

7.   Proportionality in the context of remedies of competition problems has not been heavily litigated in the Union courts. In *RTE*, the Court of Justice, in the context of the application of Article 3 of the predecessor of Regulation 1/2003, Regulation 17/63, commented:

> The principle of proportionality means that the burdens imposed on undertakings in order to bring an infringement of competition law to an end must not exceed what is appropriate and necessary to attain the objective sought, namely re-establishment of compliance with the rules infringed.[405]

8.   The Court of Justice here upheld a ruling by the General Court that the Commission had not acted disproportionately in imposing an obligation on RTE to grant licences for publication of its weekly TV listings and monitor compliance with the licences. RTE had tried to argue that this was an onerous burden involving disproportionate costs in terms of time and personnel.[406]

9.   In *Cementbouw*, the Court of Justice acknowledged that 'decisions taken by the Commission in proceedings for the control of concentrations must satisfy the requirements of the principle of proportionality', however, remedies also had to

---

402. Regulation 1/2003, Article 9(1).

403. Merger Regulation [2004] OJ L24/1, recital 30.

404. Merger Regulation [2004] OJ L24/1, recital 30, Articles 6(2), 8(2).

405. Cases C–241 & 242/91P *Radio Teilifís Éireann (RTE) v Commission ('Magill')* [1995] ECR I–743, [1995] 4 CMLR 718, para 93.

406. See also Case T–69/89 *Radio Teilifís Éireann (RTE) v Commission* [1991] ECR II–485, [1991] 4 CMLR 586, paras 105–108.

'entirely eliminate the competition problem that has been identified'.[407] The Court of Justice acknowledged the Commission's margin of discretion in making this assessment. On the facts, draft commitments offered were insufficient to resolve the competition problem and the Commission was not obliged to accept them.[408]

10.   In *easyJet*, involving a challenge to a merger cleared by the Commission, the General Court noted that the principle of proportionality required that commitments must be assessed in the light of the competition problems raised on the affected markets, because if competition could be maintained on those markets, it was not necessary for the Commission to extend the scope of the commitments to markets that were not affected.[409]

11.   More recently, there has been some consideration of the proportionality of remedies in *Alrosa*. Following an investigation into a breach of the competition rules by the diamond firm De Beers, the market leader in the worldwide diamond trade, the Commission adopted a decision making binding the commitments given by De Beers to bring to an end its long-standing purchases of rough diamonds from Alrosa, the second largest producer. Given the adverse effect on it, Alrosa applied to annul the decision, arguing that it was disproportionate. The General Court granted the application but its judgment was reversed on appeal.

12.   The Commission's decision had been made pursuant to Article 9 of Regulation 1/2003, which gives the Commission the power to make a commitment binding. Unlike Article 7, Article 9 does not expressly include a proportionality requirement, although it was common ground in the case that the principle of proportionality, as a general principle of EU law, was a criterion for the lawfulness of the Commission's decision. However the Court of Justice, in overruling the General Court, held that the extent and content of the proportionality requirement under Article 9 was different to that under Article 7. Application of the principle

---

407. Case C–202/06P *Cementbouw Handel & Industrie BV v Commission* [2007] ECR I–12129, [2008] 4 CMLR 1324, paras 52, 54 (decided on the basis of Article 9(8) of the former Merger Regulation, Regulation 4064/89). For examples of the Commission taking proportionality into account in respect of remedies in merger cases, see COMP/M.3570 *Piaggeo/Aprilia*, Commission Decision of 22 November 2004, paras 63–66; COMP/M.3680 *Alcatel/Finmeccanica/Alcatel Alenia Space & Telespazio*, Commission Decision of 28 April 2005) paras 117–118 and 120–129.

408. Case C–202/06P *Cementbouw Handel & Industrie BV v Commission* [2007] ECR I–12129, [2008] 4 CMLR 1324, para 55. Note the different reasoning of Advocate General Kokott, para 69 (stating that remedies offered by the parties had to be presumed to be proportionate and that extraordinary circumstances were required to show that the Commission breached the principle of proportionality in basing its decision on the remedies proposed by the parties).

409. Case T–177/04 *easyJet Airline Co. Ltd v Commission* [2006] ECR II–1931, [2006] 5 CMLR 663, paras 132–135. See also Case T–114/02 *Babyliss SA v Commission* [2003] ECR II–1279, [2004] 5 CMLR 21, para 173 (requiring the transfer of trade mark rights as a remedy would have 'amounted in substance to partially prohibiting the concentration, which would have been contrary to the principle of proportionality if commitments relating to a trade mark licence were likely to prevent the creation or strengthening of a dominant position').

by the Commission in the Article 9 context was confined to 'verifying that the commitments in question address the concerns it expressed to the undertakings concerned and that they have not offered less onerous commitments that also address those concerns adequately'.[410] This was explained by the different nature of the procedures that applied in Article 7 and Article 9, the Court explaining that

> Undertakings which offer commitments on the basis of Article 9 of Regulation No 1/ 2003 consciously accept that the concessions they make may go beyond what the Commission could itself impose on them in a decision adopted under Article 7 of the regulation after a thorough examination. On the other hand, the closure of the infringement proceedings brought against those undertakings allows them to avoid a finding of an infringement of competition law and a possible fine.[411]

13. The Court of Justice did confirm in *Alrosa* that the application of the principle of proportionality, even in the Article 9 context, required that the interests of third parties be taken into account by the Commission when making its decision.[412]

UK

14. When it carries out investigations into breaches of Article 101 or 102 or the Chapter I or II prohibition under the Competition Act 1998, the OFT may accept commitments pursuant to section 31A:

> (2) For the purposes of addressing the competition concerns it has identified, the OFT may accept from such person (or persons) concerned as it considers appropriate commitments to take such action (or refrain from taking such action) as it considers appropriate.
>
> (3) At any time when commitments are in force the OFT may accept from the person (or persons) who gave the commitments—
>
> (a) a variation of them if it is satisfied that the commitments as varied will address its current competition concerns;
>
> (b) commitments in substitution for them if it is satisfied that the new commitments will address its current competition concerns.[413]

15. The procedures for the acceptance of commitments are set out in Schedule 6A to the Competition Act 1998. These include a requirement that before accepting commitments or a variation to commitments, the OFT give a notice which states, among others, 'the purpose of the commitments or variation and the way in which the commitments or variation would meet the OFT's competition concerns'.[414] The

---

410. Case C–441/07P *Commission v Alrosa Company Ltd*, judgment of 29 June 2010, para 41.

411. Case C–441/07P *Commission v Alrosa Company Ltd*, judgment of 29 June 2010, para 48.

412. Case C–441/07P *Commission v Alrosa Company Ltd*, judgment of 29 June 2010, para 41. See also the opinion of Advocate General Kokott, paras 55–56 (noting that the Commission must review all alternatives to the proposed commitments known to it 'in order to ascertain whether they constitute less onerous means of resolving the competition problems identified, by which the interests of third parties are not affected or are affected less severely').

413. Competition Act 1998, s 31A(2), (3).

414. Competition Act 1998, Sch 6A, s 2(2)(b).

OFT must consider any representations made in accordance with the notice.[415] The language of the statute seems to imply a proportionality requirement. In any event, when enforcing the EU competition rules, the OFT would be bound by the general principle of proportionality. It would seem that a similar proportionality requirement to that applied to Article 9 of Regulation 1/2003 in *Alrosa* should apply, given that here the parties are also voluntarily offering commitments.

16. The Enterprise Act 2002 imposes a proportionality requirement on the Competition Commission and the OFT in the context of remedies in merger cases and on the Competition Commission in market investigations. For example, where the Commission has published a report indicating that a merger has an anti-competitive outcome, section 41 (using language which is prevalent throughout the 2002 Act[416]) imposes the following obligation:

> (2) The Commission shall take such action under section 82 or 84 as it considers to be reasonable and practicable—
>
> (a) to remedy, mitigate or prevent the substantial lessening of competition concerned; and
>
> (b) to remedy, mitigate or prevent any adverse effects which have resulted from, or may be expected to result from, the substantial lessening of competition
>
> …
>
> (4) In making a decision under subsection (2), the Commission shall, in particular, have regard to the need to achieve as comprehensive a solution as is reasonable and practicable to the substantial lessening of competition and any adverse effects resulting from it.

17. The question of the proportionality of commitments in the UK seems mainly to have arisen in the merger context.[417] In general, it has been accepted that the OFT and the Competition Commission have a certain amount of discretion as to what remedies they accept. So, in discussing a divestment remedy, the CAT has recently commented that

> The construction of a package of assets which will be sufficiently attractive to a potential purchaser to enable the anticompetitive outcome ultimately to be remedied is a difficult task involving an exercise of judgment by the Commission. This is particularly so where the merger has been completed and the purchased business has, to some extent, already been integrated into the business of the acquirer.[418]

---

415. Competition Act 1998, Sch 6A, s 2(1)(b).
416. See Enterprise Act 2002, s 73 (undertakings accepted by the OFT in lieu of a reference in merger cases; the undertakings are voluntarily proposed by the parties), s 138 (remedies in market investigations).
417. See also OFT 1122con Mergers – Exceptions to the duty to refer and undertakings in lieu (October 2009) para 5.17 *et seq*.
418. *Stagecoach Group plc v Competition Commission* [2010] CAT 14, para 137 (however, as the Competition Commission's decision was vitiated on other grounds, which potentially affected what remedy was appropriate, the case was remitted to the Competition Commission to look again at the scope of the remedy).

18. However, the regulators are also subject to the principle of proportionality in respect of remedies. The *Interbrew* case concerned the proportionality of a divestment ordered by the Competition Commission in the context of a merger that had been referred to the UK by the European Commission under Article 9 of Regulation 4064/89, the previous Merger Regulation. Article 9(8) had provided that on a reference to the Member State, it could 'take only the measures strictly necessary to safeguard or restore effective competition on the market concerned'. It was therefore plain that the Competition Commission had to act in a proportionate manner. Moses J observed from this that 'the measure adopted must be the least restrictive'. The second requirement of the principle of proportionality was that 'the value of the remedy which the measure sought to achieve should not be exceeded by the burden imposed upon the person against whom the remedy was directed'.[419]

19. In *Tesco*, the CAT considered measures adopted by the Competition Commission to remedy adverse effects on competition it had identified in the grocery trade. These included a decision to recommend that a 'competition test' be incorporated within the planning system in certain parts of the UK. After citing from the Court of Justice judgment in *Fedesa*[420], the CAT summarised the proportionality principle as follows:

> That passage [in Fedesa] identifies the main aspects of the principles. These are that the measure: (1) must be effective to achieve the legitimate aim in question (appropriate), (2) must be no more onerous than is required to achieve that aim (necessary), (3) must be the least onerous, if there is a choice of equally effective measures, and (4) in any event must not produce adverse effects which are disproportionate to the aim pursued.[421]

20. The CAT explained that element (1) of the proportionality principle was closely linked to element (4): it is necessary to know what the measure is expected to be able to achieve in terms of an aim, before one can sensibly assess whether that aim is proportionate to any adverse effects of the measure. The proportionality of a measure cannot be assessed by reference to an aim which the measure is not able to achieve.[422]

21. The CAT elaborated on the proportionality test:

> The first thing to note is that the application of these principles is not an exact science: many questions of judgment and appraisal are likely to arise at each stage of the Commission's consideration of these matters. This is perhaps most obviously the case when it comes to the balancing exercise between the (achievable) aims of the proposed measure on the one side, and any adverse effects it may produce on the other side. In resolving these questions the Commission clearly has a wide margin of appreciation,

---

419. *Interbrew SA v Competition Commission* [2001] EWHC 367 (Admin), [2001] ECC 40, para 23.

420. Case C–331/88 *R v Ministry of Agriculture, Fisheries and Food and Secretary of State for Health, ex parte Fedesa* [1990] ECR I–4023, [1991] 1 CMLR 507, para 13.

421. *Tesco plc v Competition Commission* [2009] CAT 6, [2009] Comp AR 168, para 137.

422. *Tesco plc v Competition Commission* [2009] CAT 6, [2009] Comp AR 168, para 143.

with the exercise of which a court will be very slow to interfere in an application for judicial review.

That margin of appreciation extends to the methodology which the Commission decides to use in order to investigate and estimate the various factors which fall to be considered in a proportionality analysis (and indeed in its determination of the statutory questions of comprehensiveness, reasonableness and practicability). There is nothing in the governing legislation, or in the general law, which requires the Commission to follow any particular formal procedure or methodology when it comes to consider the effectiveness of a possible remedy, or its relevant costs, adverse effects and benefits. ... The Commission can tailor its investigation of any specific factor to the circumstances of the case and follow such procedures as it considers appropriate. In this regard it may well be sensible for the Commission to apply a 'double proportionality approach': for example, the more important a particular factor seems likely to be in the overall proportionality assessment, or the more intrusive, uncertain in its effect, or wide-reaching a proposed remedy is likely to prove, the more detailed or deeper the investigation of the factor in question may need to be. Ultimately the Commission must do what is necessary to put itself into a position properly to decide the statutory questions. As the Commission itself accepts, this includes examining and taking account of relevant considerations, such as the effectiveness of the remedy, the time period within which it will achieve its aim, and the extent of any adverse effects that may flow from its implementation.[423]

22. The CAT agreed with a submission made by the Competition Commission that consideration of the proportionality of a remedy could not be divorced from the statutory context and framework under which that remedy was being imposed and that the governing legislation must be the starting point.[424] This meant that the Commission should consider the proportionality of a particular remedy as part and parcel of answering the statutory questions of whether to recommend (or itself take) a measure to remedy, mitigate or prevent the adverse effect on competition and its detrimental effects on customers, and if so what measure.

23. In *Barclays*, the CAT quashed a recommendation by the Competition Commission that credit providers be prohibited from offering payment protection insurance to non-business customers at the same time as the credit agreement. The CAT clarified that the 'double proportionality' approach referred to in *Tesco* did not introduce any new legal principle, but was simply a common sense proposition that,

> within a wide margin of appreciation, the depth and sophistication of analysis called for in relation to any particular relevant aspect of the inquiry needs to be tailored to the importance or gravity of the issue within the general context of the Commission's task.[425]

24. A number of factors have been given attention by the CAT and courts in their review of proportionality, although, given the fact-specific nature of the analyses,

---

423. *Tesco plc v Competition Commission* [2009] CAT 6, [2009] Comp AR 168, paras 138–139.

424. *Tesco plc v Competition Commission* [2009] CAT 6, [2009] Comp AR 168, para 135.

425. *Barclays Bank Plc v Competition Commission* [2009] CAT 27, [2009] Comp AR 381, para 21.

it is difficult to derive general guidance. A strict distinction is also not always drawn between other judicial review challenges (such as irrelevant considerations) and proportionality. The following factors have been considered:

- **Analysis of the problem to be solved**. It is necessary to engage in a proper analysis of the competition problem that is sought to be remedied. In *Vodafone*, involving a proportionality requirement in the Communications Act 2003, Ofcom had erred in simply stating that it should act to address the effects of network failure, without attempting adequately to assess the probability of network failure.[426]

- **A choice of equally effective remedies**. Where two or more remedies are equally comprehensive, the less onerous remedy should be adopted.[427]

- **One effective remedy**. It will not be necessary to engage in a cost-benefit analysis in circumstances where there is only one effective remedy. For example, in *Interbrew*, Moses J accepted that there was only one remedy capable of addressing the adverse affects of the merger under review, namely divestment by Interbrew of a larger holding (Bass), rather than a smaller holding (Whitbread). In such a situation, Moses J did not believe that it was necessary to engage in a balancing of the benefits to consumers as against the costs to Interbrew.[428]

- **A package of remedies.** In *Barclays*, it was argued that the Competition Commission should have addressed the incremental effect, both in terms of benefit and cost, attributable to the addition to the package of remedies of the prohibition on selling insurance at the same time that credit was agreed. The argument was rejected on the facts but the CAT noted that an 'incremental analysis' may be a valuable tool in the fashioning of an effective and proportionate remedy package where, for example, the question is whether the addition of a further remedy to a package which would be reasonably (but not totally) effective without it would be cost effective. Such an added remedy may, upon an incremental analysis, increase the overall benefits of the package by an amount that is less than the added cost.[429]

---

426. *Vodafone Ltd v Office of Communications* [2008] CAT 22, paras 108–111.

427. *Tesco plc v Competition Commission* [2009] CAT 6, [2009] Comp AR 168, paras 137. See also *British Sky Broadcasting Group Plc v Competition Commission* [2010] EWCA Civ 2, [2010] UKCLR 351, paras 72–73 (although proportionality was not emphasised by the Court of Appeal, in upholding the rationality of the remedy, it was relevant for the Court that the Commission had considered a number of different remedies; the Court also noted that the Competition Commission had rejected a total divestiture remedy as it was 'a more drastic remedy'); *British Sky Broadcasting Group Plc v Competition Commission* [2008] CAT 25, [2008] Comp AR 223, para 317 ('Where two solutions are equally comprehensive, proportionality will require the less restrictive or less costly one to be adopted').

428. *Interbrew SA v Competition Commission* [2001] EWHC 367 (Admin), [2001] ECC 40, para 61.

429. *Barclays Bank Plc v Competition Commission* [2009] CAT 27, [2009] Comp AR 381, para 118.

- **Effectiveness analysis**. It is important to demonstrate an analysis of the effectiveness of the proposed remedy and any alternative remedies, although that analysis need not be 'carried out in terms of percentages or statistics'.[430] Here, the CAT observed that there had been no express analysis by the Commission of the percentage of effectiveness of the remedies package, or even a sensitivity analysis, *i.e.* on the effect on the overall proportionality test of the remedies being, for example, 80 per cent, 60 per cent or 40 per cent effective. However, the Commission's report had engaged in 'detailed analysis' of whether the proposed remedies package would be effective as a comprehensive package and whether any other package of remedies would be effective. Furthermore, where a remedy has more than one aim, it will not suffice to demonstrate its likely effectiveness in respect of one of those aims.[431]

- **Timeframe**. When a remedy is proposed, the proportionality analysis requires that consideration is given to the timeframe for implementation of the remedy. So, if a divestiture remedy is imposed and a short time frame attached for achieving the sale, the potential for loss of value caused by a quick sale would have to be taken into account.[432]

- **Calculating the costs.** It will not suffice to balance in the proportionality analysis only the costs of implementation of and compliance with the remedies package as weighed against the anticipated benefits of remedying the adverse effect on competition. Rather, as the CAT held in *BAA*, the 'cost side of the weighing scales' should contain 'a certain element of the impact on the person on whom the remedy is to be imposed, namely the undisputed impact on its business'.[433] It was argued that the Competition Commission had failed to consider the impact on BAA's business in divesting airports. The argument was rejected on the facts, although the requirement to consider the business impact was accepted.

- **Monitoring costs.** In *BSkyB*, the Competition Commission rejected BSkyB's proposal of putting voting rights in ITV into a voting trust (which would have been a less intrusive remedy than that partial divestiture imposed). This choice was upheld by the Court of Appeal, which accepted the Competition Commission's concerns about this proposed remedy, namely: BSkyB would retain a 17.9 per cent economic interest in ITV and given that it was the largest owner of shares, even if it did not retain voting rights, other

---

430. *Barclays Bank Plc v Competition Commission* [2009] CAT 27, [2009] Comp AR 381, para 109.

431. See *Tesco plc v Competition Commission* [2009] CAT 6, [2009] Comp AR 168, paras 115–125.

432. See *BAA Ltd v Competition Commission* [2009] CAT 35, [2010] Comp AR 23, paras 249–257 (overturned on appeal on other grounds (issues of bias), *Competition Commission v BAA Ltd* [2010] EWCA Civ 1097).

433. *BAA Ltd v Competition Commission* [2009] CAT 35, [2010] Comp AR 23, para 250 (overturned on appeal on other grounds (issues of bias), *Competition Commission v BAA Ltd* [2010] EWCA Civ 1097).

shareholders could attach additional weight to BSkyB due to its substantial economic interest; monitoring the voting after any sale by BSkyB of its shares would be difficult and would require additional undertakings on the part of BSkyB not to sell to an associated person; and elimination of the voting would have distorted corporate governance at ITV. The Court of Appeal observed that the Commission was 'entitled to have regard' to monitoring difficulties.[434]

- **Convenience to consumers.** It may be important to consider inconvenience created for consumers by a proposed remedies package, particularly if such inconvenience may lead to a reduced demand for the service or good at issue. In *Barclays*, the CAT observed that where a remedy was 'radical' and had 'potential' to 'cause disadvantageous side-effects', this meant that 'rigorous investigation and analysis of its potentially adverse consequences' was required.[435] The Competition Commission did not appear to have taken into account evidence that there might be reduced take-up for payment protection insurance because of the customer's loss of convenience which would result if such insurance could not be offered at the point of sale. That failure vitiated the Commission's assessment of the proportionality of the prohibition on selling insurance at the same time that credit was agreed.[436] In *Tesco*, the CAT held that the Competition Commission had failed to take into account the detrimental effects the proposed planning 'competition test' would have on competition and consumers by preventing an incumbent retailer from expanding to meet demand and making developments which would in other respects enhance the welfare of consumers. The Competition Commission had not adequately 'taken account of the risk that the application of the test might have adverse effects for consumers as a result of their being denied the benefit of developments which would enhance their welfare, including by leaving demand "unmet"'.[437] The Competition Commission had acknowledged that there was a risk that such developments could be prevented by the test, and that there could be other unintended negative effects, but there was no attempt to assess the degree of risk either generally or in any particular local markets.[438]

---

434. *British Sky Broadcasting Group Plc v Competition Commission* [2010] EWCA Civ 2, [2010] UKCLR 351, para 77. See also *Co-operative Group (CWS) Ltd v Office of Fair Trading* [2007] CAT 24, [2007] Comp AR 899, paras 212–222 (OFT rejected a proposed purchaser of a divestment business in a merger case where the CEO of the proposed purchaser was also a director of the group that was selling the business; a 'firewalling' arrangement to prevent the transfer of confidential information was rejected given long-term enforceability concerns).
435. *Barclays Bank Plc v Competition Commission* [2009] CAT 27, [2009] Comp AR 381, para 128.
436. *Barclays Bank Plc v Competition Commission* [2009] CAT 27, [2009] Comp AR 381, paras 128–137.
437. *Tesco plc v Competition Commission* [2009] CAT 6, [2009] Comp AR 168, para 111.
438. *Tesco plc v Competition Commission* [2009] CAT 6, [2009] Comp AR 168, paras 112–114.

Ireland

25. Irish competition law does not set out a basis for formal commitments to remedy alleged breaches of section 4/5 or Article 101/102. This is partly because the Competition Authority does not itself make findings that there has been a breach of the antitrust rules and must initiate court action where it seeks to establish an infringement. The Competition Authority does sometimes enter into settlements with undertakings in the context of High Court litigation or accept commitments in return for its agreement not to sue. It is not entirely clear how issues surrounding the proportionality of the actions of the Competition Authority might arise in these contexts. On one view, the Authority is simply acting *qua* litigant and so its actions should not be subject to a proportionality constraint. However it might be arguable in certain cases, were for example a settlement of an action based on the EU competition rules to affect a third party, that the Authority was subject to the principle of proportionality as an emanation of the State. Such cases are unlikely to arise frequently in practice and when it has reached settlements, it seems that the terms have mainly consisted of the defendant or proposed defendant agreeing not to breach competition law in return for the Authority's agreement not to sue. Such settlements would hardly raise proportionality issues even if the principle were engaged.[439] The Irish courts are the designated competition authorities for purposes of accepting commitments in Article 101 or 102 cases and would be subject to the principle of proportionality when so acting.[440]

26. In its review of mergers, in Phase I, the Competition Authority may make binding, remedies proposed by the parties.[441] In Phase II, it may impose remedies as conditions to its clearance decision.[442] There is no express proportionality requirement in either case and the issue of proportionality of remedies in merger cases does not appear to have arisen before the Irish courts.

Key Sources

Case C–441/07P *Commission v Alrosa Company Ltd*, judgment of 29 June 2010.

Case C–202/06P *Cementbouw Handel & Industrie BV v Commission* [2007] ECR I–12129, [2008] 4 CMLR 1324.

---

439. Details of settlements reached between the Competition Authority and defendants or potential defendants are set out on the Authority's website.
440. See SI No 195 of 2004, European Communities (Implementation of the Rules on Competition laid down in Articles 81 and 82 of the Treaty) Regulations 2004, r 4(3)(b), as amended by SI No 525 of 2007, European Communities (Implementation of the Rules on Competition laid down in Articles 81 and 82 of the Treaty) (Amendment) Regulations 2007; Regulation 1/2003, Articles 5, 11(4) (power of national competition authorities to accept commitments in Article 101 or 102 cases).
441. Competition Act 2002, s 20(3).
442. Competition Act 2002, s 22(3).

100. WHAT ROLE DOES THE EU OMBUDSMAN PLAY IN COMPETITION CASES?

Summary

• An undertaking dissatisfied at how the Commission has carried out its functions can make a complaint to the EU Ombudsman.

• The Ombudsman can make a finding of maladministration but findings are not legally binding.

• The purpose of the Ombudsman is to promote checks and balance.

• Undertakings in a number of competition cases have availed of the complaints procedure before the Ombudsman.

1. An undertaking dissatisfied with how the Commission has conducted an investigation can make a complaint to the EU Ombudsman. The Ombudsman, established under Article 228 TFEU and elected by the European Parliament,[443] considers complaints of maladministration by the Union institutions (other than the General Court and Court of Justice). Any citizen of the Union or legal or natural person resident or with its registered office in a Member State can make a complaint. The Ombudsman will attempt to negotiate a settlement but failing this, can adopt a report setting out a finding of maladministration. The findings of the Ombudsman are not legally binding. Nevertheless, his role can be seen as an important tool that promotes checks and balances and encourages the EU institutions to make changes in procedures. The current Ombudsman is P. Nikiforos Diamandouros.

2. Recourse to the Ombudsman has been made in a number of competition cases.[444] For example, after the Commission's decision imposing a €1 billion fine for abuse of a dominant position,[445] Intel submitted a complaint to the Ombudsman.[446] It alleged maladministration on grounds including the Commission's failure to make notes of an interview with a Dell executive, which could have produced exculpatory evidence. Although the Commission was not legally obliged to make notes of the interview under Article 19 of Regulation 1/2003, the Ombudsman found maladministration. The Ombudsman noted that the concept of maladministration was broader than legality and 'when exercising a discretionary power, the administration must always have good and legitimate reasons for

---

443. See Decision of the European Parliament on the regulations and general conditions governing the performance of the Ombudsman's duties [1994] OJ L113/5, last amended [2008] OJ L189/25.

444. Among others, Ryanair, O2 and T-Mobile have made complaints. The Ombudsman's decisions are published at http://www.ombudsman.europa.eu.

445. COMP/C–3/37.990 *Intel* (Commission decision of 13 May 2009) (appeal pending before the General Court, Case T–286/09 *Intel v Commission*).

446. Decision of the European Ombudsman closing his inquiry into complaint 1935/2008/FOR against the European Commission (14 July 2009).

choosing one course of action rather than another'.[447] Failure to keep a record breached the principle of good administration. Record keeping here was even more important given that the evidence would have been particularly credible. Intel had also argued that there was a breach of its rights of defence but the Ombudsman did not make any finding on this point. In its appeal against the Commission decision before the General Court, Intel has raised the issue of the failure to take a proper note of the meeting with the Dell executive as an instance of the Commission's infringement of essential procedural requirements which materially infringed Intel's rights of defence.[448]

Key Sources

http://www.ombudsman.europa.eu

---

447. Decision of the European Ombudsman closing his inquiry into complaint 1935/2008/FOR against the European Commission (14 July 2009) para 95.
448. See Case T–286/09 *Intel v Commission* (pending) [2009] OJ C220/41.

101. MAY COMPETITION AUTHORITIES SHARE CONFIDENTIAL INFORMATION COLLECTED AS PART OF AN INVESTIGATION WITH EACH OTHER?

Summary

- Within the EU, the Commission and the competition authorities of the Member States have significant freedom to exchange information in the context of the application of Articles 101 and 102 and the Merger Regulation.

- The Commission cooperates extensively with regulators throughout the world both in the antitrust area and merger control.

- However, the Commission is subject to confidentiality restrictions in respect of information provided by undertakings. In order to share such information with a competition regulator outside the EU, the Commission must obtain a waiver from the particular undertaking.

Ireland

- The Competition Authority is also permitted to cooperate and share information with regulators outside the EU with ministerial approval.

UK

- The OFT can also share information with regulators outside the EU if the relevant undertaking consents. It can also share information if certain requirements are met and the OFT considers factors including whether the law of the other country provides appropriate protection against self-incrimination in criminal proceedings and provides sufficient protection for personal data.

1. Rules concerning the sharing of confidential information among EU competition authorities, including the Commission, in the context of the enforcement of Articles 101 and 102, are set out in Regulation 1/2003. The Merger Regulation contains its own confidentiality provisions.

2. Article 12 of Regulation 1/2003 provides as follows:

> 1. For the purpose of applying Articles [101] and [102] of the Treaty the Commission and the competition authorities of the Member States shall have the power to provide one another with and use in evidence any matter of fact or of law, including confidential information.

> 2. Information exchanged shall only be used in evidence for the purpose of applying Article [101] or Article [102] of the Treaty and in respect of the subject-matter for which it was collected by the transmitting authority. However, where national competition law is applied in the same case and in parallel to Community competition law and does not lead to a different outcome, information exchanged under this Article may also be used for the application of national competition law.

> 3. Information exchanged pursuant to paragraph 1 can only be used in evidence to impose sanctions on natural persons where:

> — the law of the transmitting authority foresees sanctions of a similar kind in relation to an infringement of Article [101] or Article [102] of the Treaty or, in the absence thereof,

— the information has been collected in a way which respects the same level of protection of the rights of defence of natural persons as provided for under the national rules of the receiving authority. However, in this case, the information exchanged cannot be used by the receiving authority to impose custodial sanction.

3.   These provisions are aimed at facilitating the effective enforcement of Articles 101 and 102 throughout the EU. Articles 12(2) and 12(3) of Regulation 1/2003 also enable EU competition authorities to use information obtained from other members of the European Competition Network to apply national competition law. Article 12(3) specifically enables exchanged information to be used for the application of criminal law. However, such information can be used with respect to a possible custodial sentence only where criminal sanctions also exist in the jurisdiction of the authority that transmits the information. This would mean that information transmitted by the Commission to the competition authorities in Ireland or the UK could not be used for purposes of seeking a criminal conviction that includes a custodial sentence.

4.   As the Merger Regulation is applied by the Commission in consultation with the competition authorities of the Member States through the Advisory Committee, provision is made for the sharing of information for this purpose.[449] Specific provision is made for the transmission of information from a national competition authority to the Commission and for that authority to have access to the Commission file in the case of a potential referral of a case from the Commission to the national authority under Article 9.[450]

May the Commission share information with competition authorities outside the EU?

5.   Recent years have seen an internationalisation of competition enforcement and increased cooperation between antitrust authorities. This has resulted in coordinated raids of suspected cartels. For example, in the *Marine Hose* case,[451] raids were carried out simultaneously in the US and EU, while in the suspected *Electrical Automotive Components* cartel, raids were conducted at the same time in the US, the EU and Japan.[452] Cooperation among antitrust agencies may last during the course of investigations into antitrust violations. In merger control, the Commission also cooperates with other regulators. The Commission's cooperation with other regulators is facilitated through bilateral agreements.[453]

---

449. Merger Regulation [2004] OJ L24/1, Article 19.
450. Merger Regulation [2004] OJ L24/1, Article 19(2).
451. COMP/39406 *Marine Hoses*, Commission decision of 28 January 2009 (on appeal, Case T–146/09 *Parker ITR Srl v Commission* and Case 148/09 *Trelleborg AB v Commission*, pending).
452. 'EU Raids Car Part Firms in Global Cartel Probe', *Wall Street Journal* (25 February 2010).
453. For details of bilateral agreements involving the Commission, see http://ec.europa.eu/competition/international/bilateral/index.html.

6. This cooperation requires the sharing of information among antitrust enforcers. However, the Commission is constrained from sharing confidential information it obtains from undertakings. In investigating breaches of Articles 101 and 102, the Commission is required to use information it collects 'only for the purpose for which it was acquired'.[454] Similarly, the Merger Regulation imposes an obligation of professional secrecy on the Commission, which constrains it from using information acquired during an investigation 'only for the purposes of the relevant request, information or hearing'.[455] This means that the Commission cannot share such information with other regulators outside the EU.

7. To facilitate coordination with other competition regulators during an investigation, the Commission will sometimes negotiate waivers from these confidentiality restrictions with the parties under investigation. While the parties cannot be forced to grant such a waiver, they will often be best advised to agree to a waiver in a merger investigation to enable the speedy running of proceedings in different jurisdictions. Undertakings under investigation for breaches of Article 101 or 102, especially in respect of cartel conduct, may be more reluctant to grant waivers, although an undertaking that is a leniency or immunity applicant in multiple jurisdictions may be quite willing to grant a confidentiality waiver to enable different antitrust authorities to cooperate.[456]

8. The following is a sample draft of a waiver letter allowing the Commission to share information with the US Department of Justice in the context of an investigation into a proposed merger. As indicated in the draft, a similar waiver letter would be sent to the Department of Justice.

    Waiver Letter in respect of exchange of confidential information between the Commission and the US Department of Justice in a merger investigation

    Ms. Z
    Merger Task Force
    DG Competition
    European Commission
    rue Joseph II
    B–1000 Brussels
    Belgium

    Dear Ms. Z,

    On behalf of Company X, I confirm that Company X agrees to a limited waiver of the confidentiality rules contained in Council Regulation (EC) No 139/2004, in particular

---

454. Regulation 1/2003, Article 28(1).
455. Merger Regulation, Article 17(1).
456. See, e.g., Report from the Commission to the Council and the European Parliament on the application of the agreements between the European Communities and the Government of the United States of America and the Government of Canada regarding the application of their competition laws 1 January 2001 to 31 December 2001, COM/2002/0505 final, noting at para 1.2.2 that one company involved in the *Fine Art Auction House* cartel provided a waiver that allowed the Commission and the US Department of Justice to exchange views regarding confidential evidence.

Article 17(2), and other applicable laws (collectively, 'Confidentiality Rules') that prevent the Commission from disclosing to the United States Department of Justice ('DOJ') confidential information obtained from Company X in connection with Company X's proposed acquisition of Company Y. Company X agrees that the staff of the Commission may share with DOJ, documents, data and information belonging to Company X which would otherwise be foreclosed by the Confidentiality Rules. This waiver is granted only in regard to disclosures to DOJ and only on condition that DOJ has agreed to maintain the confidentiality of information obtained from the Commission in accordance with the terms of the attached letter addressed to Ms. A of DOJ. This letter does not constitute a waiver by Company X of its rights with respect to protection against direct or indirect disclosure of information to any third party, other than DOJ.

The provision of this waiver is subject to the following conditions:

(i) that the Commission shall continue to protect the confidentiality of information provided to it by Company X in regard to other outside parties in accordance with the Commission's normal practices and the Confidentiality Rules;

(ii) that the Commission shall maintain the confidentiality of Company X information obtained from DOJ pursuant to the attached waiver, in particular that the Commission shall not in any circumstance make this information available to any third party (including the Member States of the EU) without the specific approval of Company X;

(iii) that the Commission shall consider all documentation and information obtained directly from Company X or indirectly from DOJ pursuant to the attached waiver as confidential information or business secrets unless it is clearly identified as having been obtained from a public source;

(iv) that the Commission shall only use the documentation and information obtained from DOJ pursuant to the attached waiver in connection with its investigation of the acquisition by Company X of Company Y;

(v) that, in the event the Commission is provided with privileged documents that DOJ subsequently returns to Company X, the Commission will not use those privileged documents and will return them promptly to Company X;

(vi) that the Commission shall not disclose to DOJ any documentation or information obtained from Company X over which Company X could assert a claim of privilege in the United States; and

(vii) that the Commission shall provide Company X with indices listing which documents, data, information etc. are being exchanged with DOJ.

A copy of this letter is being sent to the Antitrust Division of DOJ. When and if statutory filings are made with other competition authorities in the future, Company X is willing to discuss the extension of the terms of this waiver.

Yours truly etc.

Ireland

9.   Article 12 of Regulation 1/2003 applies to the Competition Authority, as well as the Commission for Communications Regulation, so that they may provide

confidential information to the Commission and other EU competition authorities pursuant to that provision.[457]

10. In addition, the Competition Act 2002 provides that the Competition Authority may, with ministerial approval, enter into arrangements with foreign competition authorities whereby each party may 'furnish to the other party information in its possession if the information is required by that other party for the purpose of performance by it of any of its functions'.[458] The parties may also 'provide such other assistance' as will facilitate the other party in carrying out its functions.[459] Before furnishing information, the Competition Authority must obtain from the foreign competition authority an undertaking in writing by it that it will comply with any requirements in respect of the confidential information that the Authority is required to impose.[460]

11. A number of issues are raised by these provisions. First, they must be considered to operate without prejudice to the provisions for the exchange of information among EU competition authorities contained in Regulation 1/2003. Article 12 of Regulation 1/2003 will govern the exchange of information among competition authorities enforcing Articles 101 and 102.

12. Second, the Competition Authority can furnish information to a foreign authority only where it is 'required' for performance of the latter's functions. It is not clear what this means in practice and what sort of evidence the Competition Authority might need to satisfy itself that the information is required rather than merely desirable, relevant or potentially necessary.

13. Third, it is unclear how the provisions of section 46 interplay with section 32, which sets out the conditions under which the Authority may disclose information that it obtains in investigations or is provided to it in the course of private meetings. Such information may be disclosed by a member or officer of the Authority in 'a communication the making of which was necessary for the performance by the member or officer of any of his or her functions under the Act'.[461] This begs the question whether disclosures under Section 46 must meet the Section 32 criteria and if so, whether a Section 46 disclosure by a member or officer of the Authority is a 'necessary' function under the Act.

---

457. SI No. 195 of 2004, European Communities (Implementation of the Rules on Competition laid down in Articles 81 and 82 of the Treaty) Regulations 2004, r 4, as amended by SI No. 525 of 2007, European Communities (Implementation of the Rules on Competition laid down in Articles 81 and 82 of the Treaty) (Amendment) Regulations 2007, designating the Authority and ComReg as the competition authority for purposes of chapter IV of Regulation 1/2003.
458. Competition Act 2002, s 46(2)(a).
459. Competition Act 2002, s 46(2)(b).
460. Competition Act 2002, s 46(3).
461. Competition Act 2002, s 32(2)(a).

14. It remains to be seen how extensively section 46 is used in practice and whether its proper interpretation is the subject of future litigation. It could have a far-reaching impact were it used, for example, to provide information to the US antitrust regulators, which was then used in criminal prosecutions and formed the basis of extradition proceedings.

UK

15. Article 12 of Regulation 1/2003 applies to the OFT and the sectoral regulators listed in section 54(1) of the Competition Act 1998, so they may provide confidential information to the Commission and other EU competition authorities pursuant to that provision.[462]

16. In addition, there are provisions of the Enterprise Act 2002 which facilitate the disclosure of information by the OFT to competition authorities in other countries.[463] Under Part 9 of the Enterprise Act, a public authority such as the OFT may disclose information obtained in the course of competition investigations to overseas public authorities for the purpose of facilitating the exercise of the overseas authority of specified functions, which are as follows:

    (a) carrying out investigations in connection with the enforcement of any relevant legislation by means of civil proceedings;

    (b) bringing civil proceedings for the enforcement of such legislation or the conduct of such proceedings;

    (c) the investigation of crime;

    (d) bringing criminal proceedings or the conduct of such proceedings;

    (e) deciding whether to start or bring to an end such investigations or proceedings.[464]

17. The possibility to provide information to an overseas authority does not apply in respect of certain information, which includes information obtained as part of a merger investigation under Part 3 of the Act or a market investigation under Part 4.[465] In these cases, the OFT could only disclose information provided by an undertaking with that undertaking's consent.[466]

---

462. See SI 2004/1261, Competition Act 1998 and Other Enactments (Amendment) Regulations 2004, rs 3(2), 3(3) designating the OFT and the sectoral regulators as competition authorities for purposes of chapter IV of Regulation 1/2003.

463. See OFT 507, The Overseas Disclosure of Information (April 2003). See also American Bar Association Section of Antitrust Law, *International Antitrust Cooperation Handbook* (2004) Ch 13.

464. Enterprise Act 2002, ss 243(1), 243(2).

465. Enterprise Act 2002, s 243(3).

466. Enterprise Act 2002, s 239.

18.   Disclosure of information under section 243 is not automatic on the request of an overseas regulator. The OFT must have regard to certain considerations before making the disclosure. These are:

(a)   whether the matter in respect of which the disclosure is sought is sufficiently serious to justify making the disclosure;

(b)   whether the law of the country or territory to whose authority the disclosure would be made provides appropriate protection against self-incrimination in criminal proceedings;

(c)   whether the law of that country or territory provides appropriate protection in relation to the storage and disclosure of personal data;

(d)   whether there are arrangements in place for the provision of mutual assistance as between the United Kingdom and that country or territory in relation to the disclosure of information of the kind to which section 237 applies.[467]

19.   As well as countries that are signatories to the European Convention of Human Rights, the OFT considers that the United States satisfies the criterion in section 243(6)(b) of providing appropriate protection against self-incrimination in criminal proceedings. The OFT also considers that the US federal antitrust regulators satisfy the requirement in section 243(6)(c) of appropriate protection in relation to the storage and disclosure of personal data.[468]

20.   Section 244 of the Enterprise Act sets out three other conditions that must be considered before disclosure is made:

(2) The first consideration is the need to exclude from disclosure (so far as practicable) any information whose disclosure the authority thinks is contrary to the public interest.

(3) The second consideration is the need to exclude from disclosure (so far as practicable)—

(a)   commercial information whose disclosure the authority thinks might significantly harm the legitimate business interests of the undertaking to which it relates, or

(b)   information relating to the private affairs of an individual whose disclosure the authority thinks might significantly harm the individual's interests.

(4) The third consideration is the extent to which the disclosure of the information mentioned in subsection (3)(a) or (b) is necessary for the purpose for which the authority is permitted to make the disclosure.

21.   In addition to the specific procedure in section 243 of the Enterprise Act, the OFT could provide information to another antitrust authority if the party who supplied the information consented,[469] disclosure was required by an EU obligation[470] or the

---

467. Enterprise Act 2002, s 243(6).
468. OFT 507, paras 4.17–4.19.
469. Enterprise Act 2002, s 239.
470. Enterprise Act 2002, s 240.

information was already legitimately in the public domain.[471] In these cases, the OFT would still have to have regard to the considerations in section 244 (but not those in section 243(6)).[472]

Key Sources

Regulation 1/2003, Articles 12, 19, 28.

Merger Regulation, Article 17.

Ireland

Competition Act 2002, s 32, s 46.

UK

Enterprise Act 2002, s 243.

OFT 507, The Overseas Disclosure of Information (April 2003).

---

471. Enterprise Act 2002, s 237(3).
472. OFT 507, para 3.9.

102. WHICH INFRINGEMENTS OF COMPETITION LAW CARRY CRIMINAL LIABILITY?

Summary

- EU law does not impose criminal liability for breaches of EU competition law.

- However, a number of EU Member States, as well as jurisdictions outside the EU, impose criminal liability for breaches of competition law.

- In the EU, these include Ireland, the United Kingdom, Austria, Cyprus, Czech Republic, Denmark, Estonia, France, Germany, Greece, Hungary, Malta, Poland, Romania and Slovenia.

- Outside the EU, criminal liability applies in jurisdictions including Australia, Brazil, Canada, Israel, Japan and the United States.

- Individuals may be subject to extradition to jurisdictions with criminal antitrust liability.

Ireland

- Under the Competition Act 2002, any breach of section 4/Article 101 or section 5/Article 102 is a criminal offence.

- An undertaking as well as an individual can face criminal liability.

- The 2002 Act sets out various subsidiary offences.

- The sanction of imprisonment applies not only in respect of the most serious infringements but also applies to some of the miscellaneous offences included in the 2002 Act.

UK

- Only the cartel offence, created by section 188 of the Enterprise Act 2002, carries criminal liability.

- The cartel offence applies only to individuals; companies do not face criminal liability under UK competition law.

- Dishonesty is an element of the cartel offence. The courts have applied the meaning of dishonesty as established in *R v Ghosh*.

1. EU law does not impose criminal liability in respect of competition law infringements. However a number of Member States, including Ireland and the United Kingdom, have adopted criminal sanctions in the antitrust field. It is important for international businesses to be aware of the jurisdictions within and

outside the EU that have criminal antitrust enforcement, in particular given the possibility of extradition.

2.   Other jurisdictions within the EU that carry criminal liability for breaches of competition law and provide for imprisonment as a sanction include Austria,[473] Cyprus,[474] Czech Republic,[475] Estonia,[476] France,[477] Germany,[478] Greece,[479] Hungary,[480] Romania[481] and Slovenia.[482] EU jurisdictions with criminal liability but without imprisonment include Denmark[483] and Malta.[484]

3.   Outside the EU, the jurisdiction with the most active criminal enforcement of antitrust law is the United States.[485] Other jurisdictions[486] that attach criminal

---

473. Only bid-rigging is criminalised with a sanction of up to three years imprisonment under s 68 of the Austrian Criminal Code (*Strafgesetzbuch*).

474. Failure to comply with a finding of a breach of the competition rules is a criminal offence punishable by up to two years imprisonment and/or a fine of €340,000 (Law No 13(I)/2008).

475. Criminal liability for price fixing, market sharing and entering anti-competitive agreements with a maximum jail term of eight years for individuals (s 248 of the Criminal Code, introduced in 2010).

476. Conviction for cartel behaviour can result in up to three years' imprisonment and/or a fine (Article 400 of the Estonian Penal Code).

477. Conviction for cartel behaviour can result in up to three years' imprisonment and/or a fine of up to €75,000 (French Commercial Code, Article L 420–6). The Competition Authority can impose fines of up to €3 million on individuals (French Commercial Code, Article L 420–1).

478. Individuals face up to five years' imprisonment on conviction for bid rigging (German Criminal Code, s 298).

479. Criminal sanctions include up to 6 months imprisonment for violations of Article 1 of the Greek Antimonopoly Act and Article 101 TFEU (Article 29 of Law 703/1977, as amended).

480. Cartel behaviour in the context of public procurement is punishable by up to five years' imprisonment (Act LVII of 1996 on Prohibition of Unfair and Restrictive Market Practices Act).

481. Cartel behaviour is criminalised with a sanction on conviction of imprisonment of between 6 months and four years and/or a fine (Competition Law No. 21/1996, Articles 5, 6).

482. Certain cartel behaviour is criminalised with a sanction of imprisonment of up to five years or a fine (Slovenian Penal Code, Article 231; see also, Slovenian Criminal Liability of Legal Entities Act).

483. Criminal sanctions are limited to fines (ss 6, 23a of the Danish Competition Act).

484. Criminal fines of up to 10 per cent of turnover (Article 5 of the Competition Act (Cap. 379 of the Laws of Malta)).

485. Sherman Act offences are punishable by up to ten years' imprisonment, a fine of up to $1million for individuals and a fine of up to $100 million for corporations (Antitrust Criminal Penalty Enhancement and Reform Act of 2004, §215).

486. For further discussion of the criminal sanctions in these jurisdictions, see O'Kane, *The Law of Criminal Cartels* (2009) Ch 8. In South Africa, a Competition Amendment Act that would impose a criminal sanction of up to ten years' imprisonment for cartel conduct, was signed by the President in August 2009 but as of 1 September 2010, it had not been brought into effect, with possible doubts about its constitutionality.

liability to antitrust violations include Australia,[487] Brazil,[488] Canada,[489] Israel[490], Japan[491] and Korea.[492]

4.   Extradition for antitrust offences has not yet become a significant feature of international criminal justice. This is largely because only the United States has a track record of significant prosecutions of antitrust offences and most international defendants in US cases have submitted to US jurisdiction. The first individual to be extradited to the US in connection with an antitrust offence was the former CEO of the British engineering firm Morgan Crucible, Ian Norris, who was extradited from the UK to face obstruction of justice charges in a criminal antitrust inquiry in March 2010 and subsequently convicted by a jury in federal court in Philadelphia in July 2010.[493] Ireland also has an extradition treaty in place with the US.[494] Extradition between Ireland or the UK and other EU Member States would be governed by the European Arrest Warrant scheme and extradition with other jurisdictions would be governed by the relevant law on extradition and bilateral arrangements in place.[495]

---

487. Cartel conduct is punishable by up to ten years' imprisonment and/or a fine of AUS$220,000 (Trade Practices Amendment (Cartel Conduct and Other Measures) Act 2009, Sch 1, ss 17, 33, 44ZZRF, 44ZZRG, amending provisions of the Trade Practices Act 1974).

488. Cartel conduct is punishable by a term of imprisonment of between two and five years and individuals may also be fined (Law 8.137/90, Article 4).

489. Cartel conduct is punishable by a term of imprisonment of up to fourteen years and/or a fine of up to C$25 million (Competition Act 1985, as amended, s 45(2)).

490. Cartel behaviour is punishable by up to three years' imprisonment or up to five years' imprisonment where there are aggravating circumstances (Restrictive Trade Practices Law 1988, ss 47, 47A). A number of prosecutions have been carried out and individuals have served jail time. Details are available on the website of the Israeli Antitrust Authority.

491. Cartel behaviour is punishable by up to five years' imprisonment and/or a fine up to ¥5 million for individuals (Law Covering Prohibition of Private Monopoly and Maintenance of Fair Trade 1947, as amended (these sanctions were applied in a 2010 amendment)).

492. Cartel conduct is punishable by up to three years' imprisonment and/or a fine not exceeding KRW200 million (Monopoly Regulation and Fair Trade Act).

493. Norris had avoided extradition for price fixing as the cartel offence had not been introduced into the UK at the relevant time and so the double criminality test was not met (see *Norris v Government of the United States of America* [2008] UKHL 16, [2008] 1 AC 920) but failed to avoid extradition on the lesser obstruction charges (see *Norris v Government of the United States* [2010] UKSC 9, [2010] 2 WLR 572).

494. Treaty on Extradition between the United States of America and Ireland (13 July 1983). Ireland also has a bilateral extradition treaty with Australia (Treaty on Extradition between Australia and Ireland (1985)).

495. See Irish European Arrest Warrant Act 2003; Irish Extradition Act 1965; UK Extradition Act 2003. For background on UK extradition in the antitrust context, see Osgood and Dunleavy, 'UK-US Extradition for Antitrust Offences' (2006) 19 *International Law Practicum* 35. There has been significant criticism of the ease of extradition from the UK to the US. In September 2010, the UK government announced a review of UK extradition arrangements, to include review of the UK-US Extradition Treaty (see Written Ministerial Statement of the Secretary of State for the Home Department of 8 September 2010).

Ireland

5.   Criminal liability for breaches of competition law was first introduced into Ireland by the Competition (Amendment) Act 1996, which provided for the incorporation of criminal sanctions into the Competition Act 1991. The relevant law is now contained in the Competition Act 2002.

6.   Any breach of the main competition law provisions is an offence. Sections 6 and 7 of the Competition Act 2002 respectively provide that any 'undertaking' that breaches section 4 or Article 101 or abuses a dominant position contrary to section 5 or Article 102 is guilty of an offence. The wording of sections 6(1) and 7(1) is as follows:

> 6(1) An undertaking which—
>
> (a) enters into, or implements, an agreement, or
>
> (b) makes or implements a decision, or
>
> (c) engages in a concerted practice,
>
> that is prohibited by section 4(1) or by Article [101(1)] of the Treaty shall be guilty of an offence.
>
> 7(1) An undertaking that acts in a manner prohibited by section 5(1) or by Article [102] of the Treaty shall be guilty of an offence.

7.   This broad statement of competition law offences is not usually the type of language found in a criminal statute and it may be arguable that the way in which the offences are stated is so vague and ambiguous as to be unconstitutional. However, the competition offences created by the 2002 Act and its predecessors do not yet appear to have been the subject of a constitutional challenge.[496]

What criminal liability do undertakings face?

8.   In any proceedings in respect of the offence of breach of section 4 or Article 101, section 6(2) provides that agreements, decisions or practices the purpose of which are to directly or indirectly fix prices, limit output or sales or share customers or markets are presumed to have an anti-competitive object.[497] The standard of proof for the defendant to overturn this presumption is the balance of probabilities.[498] Bid rigging was not specifically included in section 6(2) even though it is generally considered a 'hardcore' restriction of competition along with price fixing, market sharing and output restrictions. However, bid rigging agreements will usually involve agreements to fix prices or share markets so in practice, the exclusion of bid rigging from section 6(2) may not be significant.

---

496. For discussion of this issue in the context of the offences in the Competition (Amendment) Act 1996, see Charleton, McDermott and Bolger, *Criminal Law* (1999) 974–975. It was unsuccessfully argued in *Cronin v The Competition Authority* [1998] 2 ILRM 51 that the Competition Act 1991 involved an unconstitutional delegation of legislative functions from the Oireachtas to the Competition Authority.

497. Competition Act 2002, s 6(2).

498. Competition Act 2002, s 3(3)(a).

9. For purposes of determining an undertaking's liability under section 6 or 7, acts done by officers or employees are attributed to the undertakings.[499]

What liability do individuals face?

10. Sections 6 and 7 refer only to the liability of 'undertakings' for offences. An individual might constitute an undertaking and so be subject to these sections. However, it is not just undertakings that can be found guilty of an offence. Sections 8(6), (7) and (8) provide for the criminal liability of individuals in respect of the main competition offences:

> (6) Where an offence under *section 6* or *7* has been committed by an undertaking and the doing of the acts that constituted the offence has been authorised, or consented to, by a person, being a director, manager, or other similar officer of the undertaking, or a person who purports to act in any such capacity, that person as well as the undertaking shall be guilty of an offence and shall be liable to be proceeded against and punished as if he or she were guilty of the first-mentioned offence.[500]

11. There is a rebuttable presumption that any director or employee with management duties consented to the relevant anti-competitive acts so as to establish that person's liability.[501] If a body corporate is managed by its members, they can be liable in connection with their management functions in the same way as if they were directors.[502]

12. The individual liability provided for in section 8 applies to a class of individuals occupying fairly senior positions, encompassing directors, managers and similar officers. The framing of individual liability in this way may leave room for uncertainty in some cases about whether an employee is capable of being found guilty of an offence under section 8. The inclusion of an individual who though not a director, officer or manager 'purports to act in [such] capacity' may catch employees who are below these ranks. Further uncertainty arises from the fact that the Act does not contain definitions of the terms 'officer', or 'manager' and the definition of 'director' is non-exhaustive.[503] Courts faced with future arguments about the meaning and scope of these categories of individuals might draw

---

499. Competition Act 2002, ss 6(6) and 7(3). There may be a question about the compatibility of this provision with Article 38.1 of the Constitution, which provides for the right to a trial in due course of law. See *Re Article 26 and the Employment Equality Bill 1995* [1997] 2 IR 321 and the discussion in Charleton, McDermott and Bolger, *Criminal Law* (1999) 983–984. On the extent to which companies can avail of constitutional protection, see O'Neill, *The Constitutional Rights of Companies* (2007), Part II of which discusses Article 38 in particular.

500. Competition Act 2002, s 8(6).

501. Competition Act 2002, s 8(7).

502. Competition Act 2002, s 8(8).

503. A 'director' is defined in s 3(1) as including 'a person in accordance with whose directions or instructions the directors of the undertaking concerned are accustomed to act but does not include such a person if the directors are accustomed so to act by reason only that they do so on advice given by the person in a professional capacity.' (contd \...)

inspiration from other areas in which similar terms have been interpreted. In cases involving the enforcement of company law, for example, the Irish courts have recently taken the view that terms such as 'officer' should not be construed too narrowly.[504]

13.   Any person indicted for a section 6 or 7 offence or attempting to commit such an offence or the offence of conspiracy to commit such an offence shall be tried by the Central Criminal Court.[505]

14.   The scope of the main competition law offences in the 2002 Act is very broad, as *any* breach of section 4/Article 101 and *any* abuse of a dominant position constitutes an offence. This is much broader than in the UK, for example, where criminal liability is limited to the cartel offence. It remains to be seen how enforcement of sections 6 and 7 plays out over time but it would not be surprising if prosecutions focused on hardcore cartel conduct under section 6(2) rather than action against abuses of dominance under section 7 or less serious breaches of section 6 not corresponding to hardcore breaches of competition law.[506]

What subsidiary offences are contained in the Competition Act 2002?

15.   There are a number of other offences set out in the Competition Act 2002, as follows.

16.   Any person who aids, abets, counsels or procures the commission of a section 6 or 7 offence is liable to be indicted, tried and punished in the same way as a principal offender.[507]

17.   The Competition Act 2002 makes it an offence to fail to notify a merger under section 18(1) or fail to supply information requested by the Competition Authority pursuant to section 20(2) when investigating a merger. The person in control of the

---

503. (contd) This would include shadow directors but not professional advisers (see McCarthy and Power, *Irish Competition Law: The Competition Act 2002* (2003) para 8.05). The definition of 'director', with its self-referential character, is not easy to understand but in any event, it is not exhaustive.

504. See, e.g., *Director of Corporate Enforcement v Boner* [2008] IEHC 151 (Murphy J approved of the approach of the English Court of Appeal in interpreting the term 'manager' in the context of a criminal proceeding (*Re A Company* [1989] Ch 477) when interpreting the term 'officer' in the context of a disqualification proceeding).

505. Competition Act 2002, s 11.

506. Cf enforcement of the Sherman Act in the United States. While monopolization is a criminal offence under s 2 of the Sherman Act, as a matter of policy, criminal enforcement by the Antitrust Division of the Department of Justice is confined to violations of section 1, which prohibits anti-competitive agreements and conspiracies.

507. See Criminal Law Act 1997, s 7. As all offences under sections 6 and 7 of the Competition Act 2002 are indictable offences, section 7 of the 1997 Act would seem to apply whether or not the principal offender is tried summarily or on indictment. See also *Gormley v Judge Smyth* [2010] IESC 5 (Geoghegan J holding that an offence once indictable, in the sense of being capable of being tried on indictment, remains an indictable offence irrespective of whether it is tried summarily).

undertaking is liable on summary conviction to a fine not exceeding €3,000 and on conviction on indictment, a fine up to €250,000.[508] It is also an offence to contravene a provision of a commitment, determination or order made in respect of a merger or to aid or abet someone in such a contravention. On summary conviction, a person is liable to a fine of up to €3,000 and/or 6 months' imprisonment and on conviction on indictment, a fine of up to €10,000 and/or 2 years' imprisonment.[509]

18. If summoned to attend as a witness before the Authority, any person who refuses to attend, refuses to take an oath, produce documents or answer questions, or does anything that would give rise to contempt, is guilty of an offence. This is a summary offence with a potential sanction of €3,000 and/or 6 months' imprisonment.[510]

19. The disclosure of information that comes into the possession of the Authority is an offence. This is a summary offence with a potential sanction of €3,000 and/or 6 months' imprisonment.[511]

20. A person who obstructs or impedes an authorised officer of the Authority in the exercise of investigative powers or who does not comply with a requirement in an investigation shall be guilty of an offence. This is a summary offence with a potential sanction of €3,000 and/or 6 months' imprisonment.[512]

21. Falsely reporting that an undertaking has committed or is committing an offence under section 6 or 7 of the Act or is otherwise failing to comply with a provision of the Act which prohibits it from doing a particular thing, is guilty of an offence. This is a summary offence with a potential sanction of €3,000 and/or 6 months imprisonment.[513]

What defences are available?

22. It is a good defence to a charge in respect of a section 6 or 7 offence that the relevant acts were done pursuant to a determination made or direction given by a statutory body.[514] The definition of a 'statutory body' is limited to those bodies specified in *Column 1* of Schedule 1 of the 2002 Act.[515] In section 4(1)/Article 101(1) proceedings, it is a good defence to show that the section 4(5) exemption

---

508. Competition Act 2002, s 18(9).
509. Competition Act 2002, s 26(4), s 26(5).
510. Competition Act 2002, s 31(4).
511. Competition Act 2002, s 32(1), s 32(3).
512. Competition Act 2002, s 45(10).
513. Competition Act 2002, s 50(5).
514. Competition Act 2002, ss 6(5) and 7(2). The 2002 Act did not retain the ignorance defence, which was available under the 1996 Act if it could be shown that the defendant did not know, nor could reasonably be expected to have known, that an agreement had an anti-competitive effect or that conduct constituted an abuse of a dominant position (see Competition (Amendment) Act 1996, ss 2(2)(c)(i) and 2(7)(b)(i)).
515. Competition Act 2002, s 3(1).

(which mirrors Article 101(3)) is complied with.[516] It is also a good defence to show that the arrangement in question falls within a block exemption issued by the Competition Authority or a EU block exemption.[517]

23. It would of course be a good defence for an entity charged as an undertaking to show that it did not come within the definition of an undertaking. Similarly, if an individual could show that it is either not an undertaking or does not come within the categories of individuals to which the particular offence relates, this would be a good defence.

United Kingdom

24. Section 188 of the Enterprise Act 2002 introduced the 'cartel offence'. The section came into force on 20 June 2003 and so applies to conduct after that date.

188 Cartel Offence

(1) An individual is guilty of an offence if he dishonestly agrees with one or more other persons to make or implement, or to cause to be made or implemented, arrangements of the following kind relating to at least two undertakings (A and B).

(2) The arrangements must be ones which, if operating as the parties to the agreement intend, would—

(a) directly or indirectly fix a price for the supply by A in the United Kingdom (otherwise than to B) of a product or service,

(b) limit or prevent supply by A in the United Kingdom of a product or service,

(c) limit or prevent production by A in the United Kingdom of a product,

(d) divide between A and B the supply in the United Kingdom of a product or service to a customer or customers,

(e) divide between A and B customers for the supply in the United Kingdom of a product or service, or

(f) be bid-rigging arrangements.

(3) Unless subsection (2)(d), (e) or (f) applies, the arrangements must also be ones which, if operating as the parties to the agreement intend, would—

(a) directly or indirectly fix a price for the supply by B in the United Kingdom (otherwise than to A) of a product or service,

(b) limit or prevent supply by B in the United Kingdom of a product or service, or

(c) limit or prevent production by B in the United Kingdom of a product.

---

516. See Competition Act 2002, ss 6(3), 4(2) and 4(5).
517. See Competition Act 2002, s 6(3), s 4(2) and s 4(3). Section 4(3) refers only to block exemptions issued by the Competition Authority but it would be surprising if reliance on a Commission block exemption did not also provide a good defence.

(4) In subsections (2)(a) to (d) and (3), references to supply or production are to supply or production in the appropriate circumstances (for which see section 189).

(5) 'Bid-rigging arrangements' are arrangements under which, in response to a request for bids for the supply of a product or service in the United Kingdom, or for the production of a product in the United Kingdom—

(a)   A but not B may make a bid, or

(b)   A and B may each make a bid but, in one case or both, only a bid arrived at in accordance with the arrangements.

(6) But arrangements are not bid-rigging arrangements if, under them, the person requesting bids would be informed of them at or before the time when a bid is made.

(7) 'Undertaking' has the same meaning as in Part 1 of the 1998 Act.

25.   It is apparent from section 188(2) that the cartel offence captures the four classic types of hardcore restriction: price fixing, market sharing, output restrictions and bid rigging. Vertical price fixing and vertical market sharing are not subject to the cartel offence.[518] Where agreements are made outside the UK, a prosecution for the cartel offence will not be taken unless the agreements have been implemented in whole or in part in the UK.[519] The explanation of what constitutes bid rigging suggests that if the procurer knows of the arrangements in advance, there will be no offence. This should protect any undertakings that openly engage in joint bidding from the accusation of bid rigging.

26.   Section 189 explains that the cartel offence is limited to situations when the products or services of the two relevant undertakings, A and B, are at the same level in the supply chain. The cartel offence therefore applies only to horizontal agreements. Vertical conspiracies are excluded from its reach. There is some doubt about whether the undertakings must be competitors in the sense that the products or services at issue are in the same market but this is likely to be the case.[520]

27.   Only individuals can be found guilty of the cartel offence under the Enterprise Act. Undertakings that are not individuals cannot be held criminally liable.[521]

When does a person act 'dishonestly'?

28.   An important element of the cartel offence is the requirement that the accused acted dishonestly. There is no definition of dishonesty in the Enterprise Act. The established test for dishonesty, which was accepted by the trial judge in the aborted

---

518. Enterprise Act 2002, ss 189(1), 189(4).

519. Enterprise Act 2002, s 190(3).

520. See Brealey and Green (eds), *Competition Litigation: UK Practice and Procedure* (2010) paras 24.13–24.14.

521. For discussion of issues raised in civil and criminal proceedings that arise concurrently out of the same set of facts, see Brealey and Green (eds), *Competition Litigation: UK Practice and Procedure* (2010) paras 24.73–24.109.

prosecution of four British Airways employees for the cartel offence,[522] is the two-tier test put forward by the Court of Appeal in *R v Ghosh*:

> In determining whether the prosecution has proved that the defendant was acting dishonestly, a jury must first of all decide whether according to the ordinary standards of reasonable and honest people what was done was dishonest. If it was not dishonest by those standards, that is the end of the matter and the prosecution fails.

> If it was dishonest by those standards, then the jury must consider whether the defendant himself must have realised that what he was doing was by those standards dishonest. In most cases, where the actions are obviously dishonest by ordinary standards, there will be no doubt about it. It will be obvious that the defendant himself knew that he was acting dishonestly. It is dishonest for a defendant to act in a way which he knows ordinary people consider to be dishonest, even if he asserts or genuinely believes that he is morally justified in acting as he did.[523]

29. There is some doubt about whether factors additional to the *Ghosh* test must be made out by the prosecution to establish dishonesty in the context of the cartel offence. The source of this doubt is the House of Lords judgment in *Norris*, which involved an extradition request from the United States in respect of a price-fixing cartel. At the relevant time, the cartel offence had not been enacted. The question was whether Mr. Norris' conduct fell within the offence of conspiracy to defraud, which also contained dishonesty as an element. The House of Lords held that mere participation in a price fixing cartel, in the absence of 'aggravating factors' such as fraud or misrepresentation, did not amount to dishonesty.[524] The question then is whether the concept of dishonesty in the cartel offence also requires the showing of aggravating factors, such that mere entry or participation in a secret cartel would be insufficient to constitute the offence. The acknowledgment by their Lordships in *Norris* that '*until* the enactment of section 188 of the Enterprise Act 2002', there was no intrinsic unlawfulness and dishonesty in merely taking part in a cartel, might indicate their Lordships' understanding that the position did change with the arrival of the cartel offence.[525]

30. The requirement of dishonesty in the cartel offence itself has not yet received significant judicial treatment. Aspects of the dishonesty condition were considered in the *BA/Virgin* matter, involving the trial (subsequently aborted) of four BA

---

522. *R v George* [2010] EWCA Crim 1148, [2010] 2 Cr App R 17, para 6.

523. *R v Ghosh* [1982] QB 1053, 1064 (Lane LJ).

524. *Norris v Government of the United States of America* [2008] UKHL 16, [2008] 1 AC 920, paras 56–62 (Mr. Norris was ultimately extradited to the US in March 2010 on obstruction of justice charges, following a further appeal which failed; see *Norris v Government of the United States* [2010] UKSC 9, [2010] 2 WLR 572; he was convicted in July 2010 by a jury in federal court in Philadelphia of conspiring to obstruct a criminal antitrust inquiry). A similar view was expressed in *R v Goldshield Group plc* [2008] UKHL 17, [2009] 1 WLR 458, para 18.

525. *Norris v Government of the United States of America* [2008] UKHL 16, [2008] 1 AC 920, para 63 (emphasis added). See also Brealey and Green (eds), *Competition Litigation: UK Practice and Procedure* (2010) paras 24.34–24.37; O'Kane, *The Law of Criminal Cartels* (2009) paras 2.20–2.25.

employees who, it was alleged, had dishonestly agreed to fix the prices of passenger fuel surcharges with three Virgin employees. Virgin had received immunity and the three Virgin employees were prosecution witnesses. The defendants argued that the prosecution had to show 'mutual dishonesty' on the part of the defendants *and* the Virgin employees. In other words, it was argued that the prosecution would have to show that the Virgin employees, as well as the BA employees, acted dishonestly. In upholding the decision of the trial judge on this preliminary issue, the Court of Appeal emphatically rejected this interpretation of the cartel offence and held that it was not necessary to show that the person with whom the defendant had entered into the cartel arrangement had also acted dishonestly. Kay LJ agreed with Owen J's statement:

> In my judgment the language of the section is simple and straightforward. It provides that the offence is committed by an individual who, acting dishonestly, agrees with one or more others to make or implement one of the prescribed arrangements. The adverb 'dishonestly' may qualify the verb 'agrees' but the subject of the verb is 'an individual'.[526]

31. As well as finding that this interpretation of the dishonesty requirement was 'self-evident', the Court of Appeal doubted that the consequences of the defendants' interpretation were intended by Parliament. For example, under that interpretation, a defendant could escape liability if he was able to show that his counterpart with whom he agreed the cartel did not satisfy the subjective element of *Ghosh* dishonesty, which could well be the case if such person was based in a country where price fixing was not criminalised or where such person received legal advice that the conduct was lawful.[527]

Are there any specific defences to the cartel offence?

32. The Enterprise Act does not list any specific defences relevant to the cartel offence. The defences that would be open to an accused would depend on the circumstances. A showing that there was only one undertaking involved, for example because two companies were part of one corporate group, or that the undertakings at issue were in a vertical relationship, would be a good defence, as would a showing that none of the entities involved came within the definition of an 'undertaking'.[528] It would also be a good defence to show that the accused had not acted dishonestly. Where the underlying cartel agreement has an effect on trade between Member States, it would appear to be a good defence to show that the agreement would be permitted under Article 101.[529]

---

526. *R v George* [2010] EWCA Crim 1148, [2010] 2 Cr App R 17, para 8.
527. *R v George* [2010] EWCA Crim 1148, [2010] 2 Cr App R 17, para 10.
528. Section 188(7) of the Enterprise Act 2002 provides that the meaning of an 'undertaking' in the cartel offence context is the same as under Part 1 of the Competition Act 1998. On the meaning of an undertaking, see Question 1.
529. See Regulation 1/2003, Article 3(2), providing that national competition law may not lead to the prohibition of agreements with an effect between Member States that do not restrict competition within the meaning of Article 101 or benefit from the Article 101(3) exemption.

Which subsidiary offences are contained in the Enterprise Act?

33. It has been doubted whether either a conspiracy or an attempt to commit the cartel offence can itself give rise to an offence.[530] The Enterprise Act does not provide for an offence of aiding or abetting the commission of the cartel offence.

34. There are also a number of offences for failing to comply with an investigation. Any person who without reasonable excuse fails to comply with a requirement imposed on him during an investigation into the cartel offence is guilty of an offence and liable on summary conviction to imprisonment of up to six months and/or a fine.[531] In the context of an investigation into the cartel offence, it is an offence for a person to make a false or misleading statement, punishable on indictment by up to two years imprisonment and/or a fine and summarily to imprisonment of up to six months and/or a fine.[532] It is also an offence if a person knows or suspects that there is an investigation into the cartel offence and falsifies, conceals, destroys or disposes of documents he knows to be relevant. This is punishable on indictment by up to five years imprisonment and/or a fine and on summary conviction by up to six months imprisonment and/or a fine.[533] The intentional obstruction of a person carrying out investigatory powers pursuant to a warrant under section 194 is an offence punishable on indictment by up to two years imprisonment and/or a fine and on summary conviction to a fine only.[534]

Key Sources

Ireland

Competition Act 2002, sections 4, 5, 6, 7.

UK

Enterprise Act 2002, sections 188, 189, 190, 201.

---

530. O'Kane, *The Law of Criminal Cartels* (2009) paras 2.90–2.95.
531. Enterprise Act 2002, s 201(1).
532. Enterprise Act 2002, s 201(2), (3).
533. Enterprise Act 2002, s 201(4), (5).
534. Enterprise Act 2002, s 201(6).

103. WHAT SANCTIONS ARE IMPOSED FOR COMPETITION LAW OFFENCES?

Summary

Ireland

- The most serious offences carry potential sanctions for individuals convicted on indictment of a fine of up to €4 million/10 per cent of annual turnover and/or imprisonment of up to 5 years.

- Undertakings can be fined up to €4 million or 10 per cent of annual turnover.

- There are no sentencing guidelines. The sanction to be imposed will depend on the particular circumstances. The general principles are discussed in the *Duffy* case.

- All prison sentences imposed to date for substantive competition law offences have been suspended.

UK

- A person found guilty of the cartel offence may be imprisoned for up to 5 years and/or receive an unlimited fine.

- There is limited guidance to date on what sanctions will be imposed in particular cases but some general principles were discussed by the Court of Appeal in the *Whittle* case.

- The defendants in the *Whittle* case were imprisoned for the cartel offence, having previously reached an agreement with US prosecutors that they would plead guilty to the cartel offence in the UK.

Ireland[535]

1. The offences under sections 6 and 7 of the Competition Act 2002 may be tried either summarily or on indictment. A summary trial takes place in the District Court without a jury and may be brought by the Competition Authority.[536] An appeal lies to the Circuit Criminal Court. There is no further appeal. An application may be made to the High Court by way of consultative case stated on a point of law prior to a final decision in the District Court or such a case may be stated by way of appeal to determine whether a final decision is correct in law. Such an application can be made by the prosecution or the defence. There is an appeal from this decision of the High Court to the Supreme Court.[537]

---

535. Sanctions for miscellaneous offences in the Competition Act 2002 are summarised along with the description of those offences in Question 102, paras 15–21.

536. Competition Act 2002, s 8(9).

537. See further O'Malley, *The Criminal Process* (2009) Ch 23.

2. Persons indicted for section 6 or 7 offences are tried in the Central Criminal Court.[538] Such trials involve a jury and are prosecuted by the Director of Public Prosecutions. Appeals from convictions and/or sentences in the Central Criminal Court lie to the Court of Criminal Appeal, which is composed of one judge of the Supreme Court and two judges of the High Court.[539] An appeal to the Supreme Court can be taken from the decision of the Court of Criminal Appeal, but only where the Court of Criminal Appeal, the Director of Public Prosecutions or the Attorney General certify that a point of law of exceptional public importance arises.[540]

3. The Competition Act 2002 does not indicate the circumstances under which an offence should be tried summarily or on indictment. This is a common feature of Irish criminal legislation. The Competition Authority may itself bring summary prosecutions and it may make recommendations to the DPP that a prosecution on indictment be taken. The DPP retains the sole responsibility for prosecuting offences on indictment. If offences are prosecuted summarily, the District Court judge may still decide that the offence is not of a minor nature and refuse jurisdiction, in which case the trial must be transferred and proceed on indictment.[541] If the DPP elects to prosecute the charge on indictment, that election is not open to challenge.

4. The 2002 Act creates more severe penalties in respect of individuals for section 6(2) offences, *i.e.* hardcore cartel conduct, compared to other offences under sections 6 and 7. The level of penalty for undertakings that are not individuals is the same for all section 6 and 7 offences. The following are the potential sanctions for undertakings and individuals on conviction:

Summary conviction

Undertaking that is not an individual – All section 6 and 7 Offences.	Maximum fine of €3,000.[542]
Individual – section 6(2) Offence.	Maximum fine of €3,000 and/or 6 months imprisonment.[543]
Individual – Other section 6 and all section 7 Offences.	Maximum fine of €3,000.[544]

---

538. Competition Act 2002, s 11.
539. See further O'Malley, *The Criminal Process* (2009) para 23.05 *et seq.*
540. Courts of Justice Act 1924, s 6, as amended by the Criminal Justice Act 2006. A Supreme Court appeal can be taken by either the Attorney General or the DPP but this is without prejudice to the decision in favour of the accused. Again, a point of law of exceptional public importance must be certified.
541. For a discussion of a District Court judge's obligation to ensure that a case is tried with a jury if it involves a non-minor offence, see, e.g., *Reade v Judge Reilly* [2007] IEHC 44, [2007] 1 ILRM 504, especially at para 22 (appeal dismissed *Reade v Judge Reilly* [2009] IESC 66, [2009] 2 ILRM 467).

Conviction on Indictment

Undertaking that is not an individual – All section 6 and 7 Offences.	Maximum fine of the greater of €4 million or 10 per cent of annual turnover.[545]
Individual – section 6(2) Offence.	Maximum fine of the greater of €4 million or 10 per cent of the individual's annual turnover and/or 5 years imprisonment.[546]
Individual – Other section 6 and all section 7 Offences.	Maximum fine of the greater of €4 million or 10 per cent of the individual's annual turnover.[547]

What sentence would likely be imposed on an individual?

5.   The sentence to be imposed is a matter for the judge in each case. Ireland does not have formal sentencing guidelines but principles of sentencing have been established in case law. The leading case in the competition law context is *Duffy*, in which McKechnie J considered the principles of sentencing in Ireland and set out a framework for consideration of appropriate sentences in competition cases.[548] The *Duffy* case, which concerned a cartel among car dealers, involved an offence under section 4(1) of the Competition Act 1991, as amended, rather than the 2002 Act. The maximum prison term under the 1991 Act was two years and the maximum fine the greater of €3 million or 10 per cent of annual turnover.[549]

6.   McKechnie J first outlined the general approach to sentencing in Ireland, summarising the position as follows:

> In Irish Law it has been established for many years that any sentence imposed must reflect the crime and the criminal. It must be rational in its connection to both. It must be proportionate. Therefore, factors such as the seriousness of the offence (culpability, harm, behaviour etc.), the circumstances in which it is committed and the prescribed punishment must be looked at. As of course must be any aggravating circumstance as well as any mitigating one. The latter would include, if the evidence so established, matters such as a guilty plea, co-operation, remorse, absence of previous convictions, good character, unlikely to re-offend etc. This list must be added to by any other individual factor which is legally capable of attracting credit. Having done this exercise the appropriate sentence to fit the crime and the offender is then arrived at.[550]

---

542. See Competition Act 2002, s 8(1)(a)(i), 8(2)(a).
543. See Competition Act 2002, s 8(1)(a)(ii).
544. See Competition Act 2002, s 8(2)(a).
545. See Competition Act 2002, ss 8(1)(b)(i), 8(2)(b).
546. See Competition Act 2002, s 8(1)(b)(ii).
547. See Competition Act 2002, s 8(2)(b).
548. *Director of Public Prosecutions v Duffy* [2009] IEHC 208, [2009] 3 IR 613.
549. Competition (Amendment) Act 1996, s 3(1).
550. *Director of Public Prosecutions v Duffy* [2009] IEHC 208, [2009] 3 IR 613, para 35.

7. McKechnie J considered that where a company and individual are both involved in a competition offence, there is no question of them being treated as one for purposes of imposing a sentence. Similarly, if criminal sanctions are imposed on both the company and the individual, no question of double punishment arises.[551]

What is the relevance of deterrence?

8. McKechnie J went on to consider the deterrent element that a sentence in a competition case should encompass. The learned judge considered two factors to be especially important, the 'particularly pernicious' nature of antitrust crimes and the fact that defendants were unlikely to re-offend.[552] This had the consequence that deterrence should be aimed at potential offenders in general rather than the particular offender before the court. In addition to deterrence, there were a number of factors that had to be taken into account:

> I must in principle be conscious of: the gravity of the offences; the circumstances in which these offences were carried out; the nature of the offences and the continuing duration of their commission; the part played by Mr. Duffy in them, his personal circumstances and the corporate circumstances of the company; any aggravating and mitigating factor; and, finally, where appropriate, apply the principles of proportionality and totality.[553]

9. Turning to the nature of the sanction and noting that the Act provided both for financial penalties and the possibility of a custodial sentence, McKechnie J indicated a general preference in the case of crimes involving cartels for a mixed sentence to include both elements. Drawing on his earlier judgment in the *Manning* case,[554] he gave a number of reasons justifying the inclusion of a custodial sentence, such as its considerable deterrent effect, the fact that fines may not provide an adequate incentive to individuals to act responsibly and the ability of a custodial sentence to increase the incentive for individuals to cooperate in cartel investigations.[555]

---

551. See *Director of Public Prosecutions v Duffy* [2009] IEHC 208, [2009] 3 IR 613, paras 38–39.

552. See *Director of Public Prosecutions v Duffy* [2009] IEHC 208, [2009] 3 IR 613, para 37. Other than an academic paper cited, there does not appear to be any other basis on which McKechnie J concluded that there were low levels of recidivism among perpetrators of competition crimes. McKechnie J also commented, at para 48, that 'given the white collar nature of the crimes, it is almost invariable that persons convicted will have a low level of recidivism'. Even if this is the case in respect of individuals, it does not necessarily hold true for undertakings, as the Commission's findings of repeat infringements show (see, e.g., COMP/39.396 – *Calcium carbide and magnesium based reagents for the steel and gas industries*, Commission Decision of 22 July 2009, paras 309–312 (Akzo Nobel receiving a 100 per cent uplift in its fine because of participation in four previous cartels; Degussa receiving a 50 per cent uplift for participation in one previous cartel) (on appeal, Case T–391/09 *Evonik Degussa v Commission* (pending)).

553. *Director of Public Prosecutions v Duffy* [2009] IEHC 208, [2009] 3 IR 613, para 44.

554. *Director of Public Prosecutions v Manning* (unreported, 9 February 2007).

555. *Director of Public Prosecutions v Duffy* [2009] IEHC 208, [2009] 3 IR 613, para 42.

What mitigating factors may be relevant?

10. McKechnie J noted that the approach adopted by the English Court of Appeal in *R v Whittle*,[556] which also involved custodial sentences for a competition law offence, was more helpful than that used by the Commission and the EU courts when imposing fines for breach of the competition rules.

11. In considering mitigating arguments put forward on behalf of the defendant, McKechnie J made a number of general comments about mitigating factors in cartel cases. First, the learned judge rejected the argument that the actions of the defendant were out of character, pointing to the nine-year duration of the cartel:

> Operating a cartel is not a once off criminal act. It is not done on the spur of the moment. It is continuous and requires high levels of planning and organisation. A person seeking to successfully implement a price fixing agreement decides every day to go into work and therein to commit and conceal a criminal conspiracy ... For that person whose persona is representative of carteliers, it is very difficult to say that such behaviour is out of character.[557]

12. Second, McKechnie J held that in cartel cases, little weight should be given to factors such as the unlikelihood that the defendant would re-offend or the fact that it was a first offence. This was because of the type of individual and conduct likely to be involved.[558] Third, the judge was sceptical that any credit should be given for economic hardship, *i.e.* that the reason for entry into the cartel was survival.[559] Fourth, the fact that the trade association through which the cartel was conducted had some legitimate aims was irrelevant.[560] Fifth, for the defendant to receive credit for cheating on the cartel (e.g. by not actually imposing the higher cartel price), clear evidence of a direct breach of the cartel's rules would be required and instances of cheating that had no positive effect on consumer welfare or no negative impact on cartel activities would be of little significance.[561] Sixth, for cooperation with the authorities to count as a mitigating factor it would have to be of real beneficial value and be useful in preventing, detecting, halting or disrupting the cartel. An example was cooperation that actually brought the existence of the cartel to light.[562] Seventh, a guilty plea and the defendant's personal circumstances would be taken into account.[563]

What sentences have been imposed to date?

13. Convictions for competition law offences have been obtained in connection with several matters: (i) *Citroen dealers*; (ii) *Ford dealers*; (iii) *Heating Oil*; and (iv)

---

556. *R v Whittle* [2008] EWCA Crim 2560, [2009] UKCLR 247.
557. *Director of Public Prosecutions v Duffy* [2009] IEHC 208, [2009] 3 IR 613, para 47.
558. See *Director of Public Prosecutions v Duffy* [2009] IEHC 208, [2009] 3 IR 613, para 48.
559. See *Director of Public Prosecutions v Duffy* [2009] IEHC 208, [2009] 3 IR 613, para 49.
560. See *Director of Public Prosecutions v Duffy* [2009] IEHC 208, [2009] 3 IR 613, para 50.
561. See *Director of Public Prosecutions v Duffy* [2009] IEHC 208, [2009] 3 IR 613, para 53.
562. See *Director of Public Prosecutions v Duffy* [2009] IEHC 208, [2009] 3 IR 613, para 57.
563. See *Director of Public Prosecutions v Duffy* [2009] IEHC 208, [2009] 3 IR 613, para 58.

Grain Imports. A prosecution was unsuccessful in the *Mayo Waste* case and a further case, *Iarnród Éireann*, was ongoing at the time of writing.[564]

14. In *Duffy*, which involved one of the participants in the *Citroen dealers* cartel, McKechnie J imposed a sentence of six months imprisonment for the count of entering into a cartel agreement and nine months for implementing the agreement. However, the judge felt constrained by the principle of equality before the law, as reflected in Article 40.1 of the Constitution, to suspend these custodial sentences as in two previous cases arising out of the same cartel, the defendants had received suspended sentences in the Circuit Court. But for this constraint, it seems likely that a custodial sentence would have been imposed in this case. McKechnie J indicated that custodial sentences should be imposed in future cartel cases, commenting that 'if the first generation of carteliers have escaped prison, the second and present generation almost certainly will not'.[565] In addition, fines of €50,000 were imposed on each of Mr. Duffy and his company.

15. One of the other participants in the *Citroen dealers* cartel, who received a suspended sentence of nine months and a personal fine of €80,000 after pleading guilty to participation in the cartel, was subsequently imprisoned for 28 days by the Central Criminal Court for failure to pay the fine, thus becoming the first individual to be imprisoned in connection with a competition law offence in Ireland.[566]

16. Overall, the prosecutions by the DPP arising out of the *Citroen dealers* cartel, which were taken under the Competition Act 1991, as amended, resulted in six companies receiving fines of €12,000, €20,000, €30,000, €35,000, €50,000 and €80,000 respectively.

17. The fines and prison sentences (all of which were suspended) imposed on individuals arising out of the *Citroen dealers* cartel were as follows:

- 3 months imprisonment.

- 3 months imprisonment.

- 6 months (for entering the cartel) plus 9 months imprisonment (for implementing it), to be served concurrently plus a €50,000 fine.

- 9 months imprisonment plus a €2,000 fine.

- 6 months imprisonment plus a €30,000 fine.

- 6 months imprisonment plus a €30,000 fine.

- 9 months imprisonment plus a €80,000 fine.

18. In April 2006, Mr. Denis Manning was charged in Cork District Court on two charges of aiding and abetting the Irish Ford Dealers Association and its members

---

564. Details of criminal competition law cases are published on the website of the Competition Authority.

565. *Director of Public Prosecutions v Duffy* [2009] IEHC 208, [2009] 3 IR 613, para 67.

566. See 'Former car firm director jailed for not paying fine', *The Irish Times*, 30 November 2009.

in implementing an agreement which had the object of preventing, restricting or distorting competition in the motor trade so as to directly or indirectly fix the selling price of cars. The first charge, relating to a period before the introduction of the Competition Act 2002, was in respect of a breach of section 4 of the Competition Act 1991, as amended and section 7(1) of the Criminal Law Act 1997. The second charge was for breach of sections 4(1) and 6 of the 2002 Act and section 7(1) of the Criminal Law Act 1997. The defendant pleaded guilty to the second charge at the Central Criminal Court in January 2007 and a *nolle prosequi* was entered in relation to the first charge. Mr. Manning was sentenced to 12 months' imprisonment, suspended for five years, and a €30,000 fine.

19.   The DPP secured the first conviction on indictment of an individual under Irish competition law in 2005. Following its investigation into allegations of price fixing of home heating oil products in the west of Ireland, the Competition Authority recommended that the DPP prosecute on indictment the undertakings and individuals involved. In April 2004, proceedings on indictment were initiated against 24 defendants. Mr JP Lambe was given a suspended sentence and fined €15,000 for aiding and abetting members of a price-fixing cartel in the market for domestic heating oil operating in the west of Ireland. This was the first criminal conviction secured in Europe for membership of an anti-competitive cartel, and also made Ireland the first country to hold a jury trial for a criminal competition offence in Europe. In total there have been seventeen convictions arising out of this cartel, involving ten undertakings and seven individuals.[567] The six individuals other than Mr. Lambe received fines only, ranging in amount from €1,000 to €15,000. The fines imposed on undertakings ranged in amount from €3,500 to €15,000. One further case against an individual arising from this cartel is pending as a case stated on a point of law has been made to the Supreme Court. The defendant argued in Galway Circuit Criminal Court that his guilt was contingent on a finding that his company, of which he was a manager, had committed an offence, which in turn required the existence of a conviction against the company. However no prosecution had been taken against the company in respect of the cartel. The DPP disputed this argument and Mr. Justice Groarke agreed to the application by the prosecution that a case be stated on the question to the Supreme Court, which was expected to be heard in November 2010.[568]

20.   The *Heating Oil* cartel was not the first criminal case under the 2002 Act. In 2003, the Competition Authority brought summary proceedings in the District Court in Drogheda for breach of section 4 of the 2002 Act against individual farmers and Irish Farm Association leaders for blockading a shipload of British grain in the port of Drogheda. Convictions were secured in the District Court against six accused and fines were imposed.[569] Three of the six convictions were set aside on appeal to the Circuit Court in Dundalk.[570]

---

567. Details are set out on the website of the Competition Authority.
568. *Director of Public Prosecutions v Hegarty* (Case 350/08).
569. Sub nom *Competition Authority v Deasy* (Drogheda District Court, March 2003, unreported).
570. Sub nom *Competition Authority v Deasy* (Dundalk Circuit Court, October 2004, unreported).

21. A number of criminal competition cases in Ireland have arisen out of alleged bid rigging for contracts in the public procurement context. Five individuals and three companies were tried in 2009 for alleged bid-rigging offences in respect of a tender for the supply of domestic waste collection services in County Mayo. The charges included entering into agreements to share waste collection markets and waste collection customers contrary to the Competition Act 2002. The defendant companies had come together to submit a joint bid in response to a tender. The case was tried at the Central Criminal Court sitting in Galway and, on 2 July 2009, all of the defendants (the companies as well as the directors) were acquitted by a jury. The defendants in the case were later successful in obtaining their costs of the trial.[571]

22. A further case is pending against three parties, which involves allegations of bid-rigging of a contract for hedge cutting and vegetation clearance services put out to tender by Iarnród Éireann. The Competition Authority brought summary proceedings in this case in Athenry District Court, alleging breaches of section 4 of the Competition Act 2002. The District Judge declined jurisdiction and the case was sent to the Central Criminal Court. The jurisdiction of that court to try the case was affected by a Supreme Court judgment in respect of the Central Criminal Court's jurisdiction to hear certain cases and in consequence, the DPP entered a *nolle prosequi* on the indictments in January 2010. The DPP subsequently reinstituted proceedings in the District Court and at the time of writing, the case was pending.

Are plea bargains part of Irish law?

23. The practice of plea bargaining is not a feature of the Irish criminal justice system. In *Heeney*, Keane CJ expressed the view that plea bargaining had no place in Irish criminal law.[572] It seems that plea bargaining may be invalid in light of Article 34.1 of the Constitution, which provides that justice shall be administered in public, save in such special and limited cases as may be prescribed by law.[573]

UK[574]

24. The cartel offence, which only applies to individuals, may be prosecuted summarily or on indictment.[575] Summary trials take place in the Magistrates Court

---

571. See *Director of Public Prosecutions v Bourke Waste Removal Limited* [2010] IEHC 122, in which McKechnie J sets out the details of the case (the case has been appealed to the Supreme Court by the DPP).

572. *The People (DPP) v Heeney* [2001] 1 IR 736, 742.

573. But see *Attorney General v Murphy* [2007] IEHC 342 (Peart J, rejecting the argument that the extradition to the United States of an individual who had voluntarily entered into the plea bargaining process in a US proceeding would violate his constitutional rights, interpreted the comments of Keane CJ in *Heeney* as merely having 'discouraged' a system of plea bargaining).

574. Sanctions for miscellaneous offences in the Enterprise Act 2002 are summarised along with the description of those offences in Question 102, paras 33–34.

575. See Enterprise Act 2002, s 190(1).

whereas charges on indictment are tried in the Crown Court before a jury. Both the Office of Fair Trading and the Serious Fraud Office are empowered to prosecute and they have discretion to proceed summarily or on indictment. Even if a case is brought before the Magistrates Court, the magistrate may decline jurisdiction and send the case to the Crown Court or the defendant may opt for a jury trial in the Crown Court.

25.   Appeals from the Magistrates Court lie to the Crown Court.[576] The appeal is by way of rehearing.[577] Appeals against conviction and/or sentence on indictment lie to the Court of Appeal. An appeal against conviction shall be allowed by the Court of Appeal if they think that the conviction is 'unsafe'.[578] If they allow the appeal, the Court of Appeal shall quash the conviction,[579] unless it appears to the Court that the interests of justice require a retrial to be ordered.[580] An appeal against conviction lies only with leave of the Court of Appeal or if, within 28 days of the date of conviction, the trial judge certifies that the case is fit for appeal.[581] In dealing with an appeal against sentence, if they consider that the appellant should be sentenced differently, the Court of Appeal may quash the sentence and pass such sentence or order as appropriate. The Court of Appeal cannot increase the sentence.[582] Again, leave of the Court of Appeal or a certificate from the trial judge is required to appeal the sentence.[583]

What is the range of penalties?

26.   An individual found guilty of the cartel offence on indictment is liable to imprisonment of up to five years and/or an unlimited fine.[584]

27.   An individual found guilty of the cartel offence on summary conviction is liable to imprisonment for a term not exceeding six months and/or a fine not to exceed the statutory maximum, which is currently £5,000.[585]

---

576. Magistrates Court Act 1980, s 108.
577. Supreme Court Act 1981, s 79(3).
578. Criminal Appeal Act 1968, s 2(1).
579. Criminal Appeal Act 1968, s 2(2).
580. Criminal Appeal Act 1968, s 7(1).
581. Criminal Appeal Act 1968, s 1(2).
582. Criminal Appeal Act 1968, s 11(3).
583. Criminal Appeal Act 1968, ss 11(1), 11(1A). For further discussion of the criminal procedure in relation to the cartel offence, see O'Kane, *The Law of Criminal Cartels* (2009) Ch 6. In May 2010, the Conservative/Liberal Democrat government proposed that a new agency would be created to tackle white collar crime, taking over the functions of the OFT, SFO and others in that area. Should this proposal be implemented, it may alter how the cartel offence is prosecuted.
584. See Enterprise Act 2002, s 190(1)(a).
585. See Enterprise Act 2002, s 190(1)(b).

What sentence would likely be imposed on an individual?

28.   There are no sentencing guidelines applicable to the cartel offence. The sentence
       to be imposed is a matter for the judge in each case. To date, only one case, *R v
       Whittle*,[586] has examined the approach to sentencing for the cartel offence. This
       resulted in a decision of the Court of Appeal, which considered some of the
       relevant factors in deciding sentences in cartel cases. However, in delivering
       judgment, Hallett LJ signalled at the outset the difficulty for the court in offering
       general guidance for sentencing levels in cartel cases due to the particular
       circumstances of the case. The court had little, if any, knowledge of where to place
       the case before it in the scale of seriousness given the lack of a sufficient body of
       similar cases. Any general guidance from the case should therefore be drawn
       cautiously.

29.   The *Whittle* case involved three individuals who participated in the *Marine Hose*
       cartel, the activities of which targeted government contracts as well as private
       purchasers of marine hoses in various parts of the world. The individuals were
       arrested in the United States and admitted their involvement in the cartel and
       cooperated with the investigation of the US Department of Justice. They each
       entered into a formal plea agreement with the US authorities, which included an
       agreement to plead guilty to antitrust offences in the United States and to the cartel
       offence in the UK in the event that they were prosecuted in the UK. The plea
       agreements provided that the US authorities would not seek to bring further
       criminal charges against the individuals as long as they pleaded guilty to the cartel
       offence in the UK and did not seek from the English courts sentences lower than
       those stipulated in the plea agreements.[587]

30.   Following guilty pleas in the United States, each of the three individuals agreed
       jointly with the US authorities to recommend to the relevant US court a disposition
       of the case against him which included a term of imprisonment, to be reduced 'by
       one day for each day of the total term of the sentence of imprisonment imposed
       upon [him] following his conviction for the UK cartel offence'. The sentences
       provided for in the respective agreements were 30 months for Whittle, 24 months
       for Allison and 20 months for Brammar.

31.   On return to the UK, the three were duly charged with the cartel offence and
       pleaded guilty before Southwark Crown Court. However, the sentences imposed (3
       years each for Whittle and Allison and 30 months for Brammar) were greater than
       those in the US plea agreements and the three appealed to the Court of Appeal.

32.   The applicants did not argue for sentences below those that had been agreed to in
       the plea agreements. As such, Hallett LJ felt 'obliged to dispose of the
       applications'[588] in such a way that they corresponded to the sentences in the plea
       agreements. Given this, there was little purpose in examining mitigating factors in
       detail although Hallett LJ noted that had there been a full trial, the applicants

---

586. *R v Whittle* [2008] EWCA Crim 2560, [2009] UKCLR 247.
587. See *R v Whittle* [2008] EWCA Crim 2560, [2009] UKCLR 247.
588. *R v Whittle* [2008] EWCA Crim 2560, [2009] UKCLR 247, para 29.

would have received 'significant discounts' from their sentences to reflect that each was of good character, admitted his involvement readily, offered to assist the authorities further, pleaded guilty at the first opportunity, had lost a livelihood and would face significant financial consequences.[589] The sentences were reduced to those in the plea agreements, *i.e.* 30 months for Whittle, 24 months for Allison and 20 months for Brammar. Clearly referring to the constraining effect of the US plea agreements, Hallett LJ indicated that the Court had 'considerable misgivings' about the approach taken, with a US prosecutor effectively having constrained the sentencing options available to a UK court, but felt that it had 'no alternative'.[590]

33. Having already made the decision, Hallett LJ provided some 'guidance for the future' on sentencing, setting out a non-exhaustive list of factors that would be relevant:

- The gravity and nature of the offences;

- The duration of the offences;

- The degree of culpability of the defendant in implementing the cartel agreement;

- The degree of culpability of the defendant in enforcing the cartel agreement;

- Whether the defendant's conduct was contrary to guidelines laid down in a Company Compliance Manual; and

- Mitigating factors, for example, any co-operation the defendant may have provided in respect of an inquiry; whether or not the defendant was compelled to participate in the cartel under duress; whether the offence was a first offence; and any personal circumstances of the defendant which the courts may regard as a factor suggesting leniency.[591]

Are plea bargains part of UK law?

34. Despite the Court of Appeal's (reluctant) deference to the plea agreement reached with US prosecutors in *Whittle*, plea bargaining is not generally accepted in the UK. The courts will not give effect to an agreement between the prosecution and defence as to the appropriate sentence.[592] In the context of corruption offences, the English courts have made clear that they will not give effect to plea agreements reached between the SFO and defendants. In *R v Dougall*, the defendant entered into a cooperation agreement with the SFO pursuant to section 73 of the Serious Organised Crime and Police Act 2005. The plea agreement made representations on the defendant's behalf for a suspended sentence to be imposed. The Crown Court imposed a 12-month sentence but this was reduced by the Court of Appeal to a suspended sentence. However, the Court of Appeal emphasised that it was for

---

589. See *R v Whittle* [2008] EWCA Crim 2560, [2009] UKCLR 247, para 29.

590. See *R v Whittle* [2008] EWCA Crim 2560, [2009] UKCLR 247, para 32.

591. *R v Whittle* [2008] EWCA Crim 2560, [2009] UKCLR 247, para 34.

592. Although a limited form of plea bargaining is provided for in the Serious Organised Crime and Police Act 2005, s 71.

the court and not the SFO to make sentencing decisions and that 'a plea agreement or bargain between the prosecution and the defence in which they agree what the sentence should be, or present what is in effect an agreed package for the court's acquiescence is contrary to principle'.[593] Even so, in reaching its own conclusion on the sentence to be imposed, the court will take into account the defendant's cooperation and the fact that it entered into a plea agreement.[594]

35.   The statutory basis for the plea agreement in *R v Dougall* was section 73 of the Serious Organised Crime and Police Act 2005, which does not apply to the OFT.[595] It is unclear whether the OFT has the statutory power to enter into such a plea agreement in respect of the cartel offence. It is also unclear whether the SFO, in prosecuting the cartel offence, can reach such an agreement. Although the SFO is designated as one of the prosecuting authorities that can reach such agreements with defendants, the cartel offence is excluded from section 71 of the Serious Organised Crime and Police Act 2005, which applies to immunity agreements,[596] although section 73, in respect of plea agreements, does not specifically exclude the cartel offence. In any event, the principle that the court takes the ultimate decision on sentencing and is not bound or will not give effect to plea agreements, would still apply.[597]

What other criminal cartel cases have been brought in the UK?

36.   The OFT prosecuted four British Airways executives for the cartel offence arising out of alleged fixing of passenger fuel surcharges by BA and Virgin. The case went to trial but collapsed in May 2010 following the discovery of new evidence that had not been disclosed to the defence.[598] At the time of writing, three investigations of the cartel offence, in the automotive sector, agricultural products sector and among commercial vehicle manufacturers, respectively, were ongoing.[599]

37.   The SFO, which has yet to take a prosecution for the cartel offence, did take prosecutions in respect of alleged price fixing of generic drugs sold to the NHS. As the timing of the alleged offences pre-dated the Enterprise Act, the prosecutions were for conspiracy to defraud. However, the case fell apart due to defects in the SFO's indictments, which had proceeded on the incorrect assumption that price fixing, when carried out in circumstances of secretive and

593. *R v Dougall* [2010] EWCA Crim 1048, para 19 (Judge LCJ). See also, *R v Innospec Limited* (Southwark Crown Court, 26 March 2010).
594. See *R v P; R v Blackburn* [2007] EWCA Crim 2290, paras 34, 41.
595. Serious Organised Crime and Police Act 2005, s 71(4).
596. Serious Organised Crime and Police Act 2005, s 71(7).
597. For a general discussion about plea bargaining in cartel cases, see Lawrence, O'Kane, Rab and Nakwal, 'Hardcore Bargains: What Could Plea Bargaining Offer in UK Criminal Cartel Cases' [2008] *Competition Law Journal* 17.
598. See, e.g., 'British Airways price-fixing trial collapses' *The Financial Times* (10 May 2010).
599. See http://www.oft.gov.uk/OFTwork/competition-act-and-cartels/.

deceptive behaviour, was dishonest in itself and a sufficient basis for conspiracy to defraud.[600]

Key Sources

Ireland

Competition Act 2002, sections 8, 11.

Director of Public Prosecutions v Duffy [2009] IEHC 208, [2009] 3 IR 613.

UK

Enterprise Act 2002, section 190.

R v Whittle [2008] EWCA Crim 2560, [2009] UKCLR 247.

---

600. See *R v Goldshield Group plc* [2008] UKHL 17, [2009] 1 WLR 458. An application by the SFO to amend the indictments was subsequently refused by Pitchford J at Southwark Crown Court and an appeal was refused by the Court of Appeal (see *R v GG plc* [2008] EWCA Crim 3061).

104. CAN DECISIONS TO PROSECUTE BE CHALLENGED?

Summary

Ireland

- The DPP, who has the sole power to prosecute competition law offences on indictment, enjoys a wide discretion in deciding whether to prosecute or not to prosecute.

- However decisions to prosecute by either the DPP or the Competition Authority (summary prosecutions) can be challenged by way of judicial review.

- To succeed, an applicant must show that the decision was taken in bad faith or was influenced by an improper motive or an improper policy or on the basis that fair procedures guaranteed by Article 34.1 of the Constitution were not observed.

UK

- The OFT and the SFO, each of which has power to prosecute the cartel offence, have a wide discretion in respect of prosecutorial decisions.

- Those decisions are amenable to judicial review.

- However an applicant will succeed only where there are exceptional circumstances, such as dishonesty or bad faith.

1.   Prosecutors in both Ireland and the UK have a wide discretion in deciding whether to initiate a prosecution. It is only in exceptional circumstances that this decision can be challenged. An accused hoping to avoid liability has an obvious interest in considering if there are grounds to challenge the decision to take a prosecution. The circumstances may prompt such a challenge, for example, where the accused is aggrieved at being prosecuted when he had earlier been led to believe that no prosecution would be taken. Conversely, an accused who was involved in an international cartel and has not been charged in Ireland/UK but is faced with an extradition request from, say, the United States, may wish to challenge the decision of the prosecutor *not* to initiate a prosecution. The reason would be that if a prosecution were taken in Ireland/UK, extradition for the same conduct could be avoided on the basis of the double jeopardy rule.[601] Attempts, in the face of extradition, to challenge decisions not to prosecute have been unsuccessful in the UK.[602]

---

601. See Irish Extradition Act 1965, ss 16, 17; UK Extradition Act 2003, ss 12, 80.

602. See, e.g., *R (Bermingham) v Director of the Serious Fraud Office* [2006] EWHC 200 (Admin), [2007] QB 727, discussed at paras 10–13 below.

Ireland

2.   The Competition Authority may take summary proceedings for offences under sections 6 and 7 of the Competition Act 2002[603] but only the DPP can prosecute charges on indictment. The Competition Authority may recommend that a prosecution on indictment be brought but it is for the DPP alone to decide whether to bring such a prosecution. The remainder of this section focuses on challenges to prosecution decisions of the DPP, although the same principles would be applicable to challenges to summary prosecutions.

3.   Prosecutorial decisions of the DPP are not subject to any appeal mechanism. The only way in which they can be challenged is in judicial review proceedings. The courts have acknowledged that a 'special protection'[604] attaches to the reasons for the DPP's decision to prosecute or not to prosecute. The scope of judicial review of decisions of the DPP is 'much more circumscribed'[605] than other bodies subject to judicial review and so it can be said that the DPP enjoys a partial immunity from judicial review.[606] An application seeking to impugn the decision to prosecute will succeed in only limited circumstances.

4.   The DPP's decision to prosecute has been successfully challenged where the accused had already been informed that the DPP would not pursue a prosecution but the DPP then changed that decision. In *Eviston*,[607] the Supreme Court reviewed a decision of the DPP to carry out a prosecution for dangerous driving where the DPP had previously informed the accused that no prosecution would ensue. A majority of the Supreme Court held that a decision of the High Court prohibiting the prosecution should be upheld on the ground that fair procedures guaranteed by Article 34.1 of the Constitution had not been observed. The DPP 'had unequivocally and without any *caveat* informed the applicant that no prosecution would issue against her'[608] and there was no new evidence that might have justified the DPP's change of mind (the change came about after a review of the initial decision not to prosecute following a request from the victim's family). Although stress was not itself a ground to prohibit the prosecution, the degree of stress and anxiety to which the applicant was subjected was exacerbated by the reversal of the decision not to prosecute and this was a relevant factor.[609]

---

603. Competition Act 2002, s 8(9).
604. See, e.g., *Dunphy v Director of Public Prosecutions* [2005] IESC 75, [2005] 3 IR 585, para 40.
605. *Q.(M.) v Judge of Northern Circuit & Director of Public Prosecutions* [2003] IEHC 88, para 31 (McKechnie J).
606. See Mícheál O'Higgins, 'Reviewing Prosecution Decisions', paper delivered to the 9th Annual Prosecutors' Conference, Dublin (24 May 2008); O'Malley, *The Criminal Process* (2009) paras 12.21–12.22.
607. *Eviston v DPP* [2002] 3 IR 260.
608. *Eviston v DPP* [2002] 3 IR 260, 320 (McGuinness J).
609. *Eviston v DPP* [2002] 3 IR 260, 299 (Keane CJ).

5.   The *Eviston* case established that a failure to observe fair procedures may be a sufficient ground to impugn a decision of the DPP to prosecute. However, later cases have shown the limits of this doctrine.[610] In *Carlin*, the DPP had no new evidence before he changed his decision not to prosecute and he had not warned the accused that his decision was subject to review. Nevertheless, the Supreme Court held that fair procedures would not be violated. Fennelly J interpreted the judgment of Keane CJ in *Eviston* to mean that the key question was the degree of stress caused to the accused by the actions of the DPP,[611] which he found not to be sufficiently severe in the case before him to warrant a prohibition on the prosecution on the grounds of fair procedures. Everything turned on the particular facts of the case and here, the accused had not shown that 'the level of anxiety or stress suffered was raised beyond [the] normal level by reason of the failure of the Director to observe fair procedures'.[612]

6.   The grounds of review established in *Eviston* were clearly narrow and seem to have been further limited by *Carlin*. If these grounds are not available then the DPP's decision to prosecute is reviewable only where the decision was made in bad faith or was influenced by an improper motive or an improper policy.[613]

Can a decision *not* to prosecute be challenged?

7.   There seems to be no reason in principle why the *Eviston* grounds could not also apply to a challenge to a decision *not* to prosecute. However, it would likely be more difficult to show a breach of fair procedures in such a case, as from the perspective of Irish criminal law, the potential defendant would benefit from the decision not to prosecute. In particular, it would take a considerable extension of *Eviston* to find that a decision not to prosecute was a breach of fair procedures because it would facilitate the potential defendant's extradition to a requesting state. Realistically, a person faced with extradition and seeking to have the DPP's decision not to prosecute him in Ireland reviewed, would need to be able to invoke the grounds established in earlier cases[614] and summarised by Keane CJ in *Eviston,*

---

610. See, also, *G.E.*, in which the DPP reconsidered a charge of unlawful carnal knowledge and changed it to a charge of rape. The Supreme Court held that fair procedures required that 'any alternative charge brought should not be one which, notwithstanding the absence of new or additional evidence, is grossly different and disproportionate from the original charge (*G.E. v DPP* [2008] IESC 61, [2009] 1 IR 801, para 35 (Kearns J)). See also *Higgins v DPP* [2010] IESC 46 (it was not an abuse of process for the DPP to prosecute a charge of assault causing serious harm after the accused had entered written guilty pleas in respect of a lesser assault charge with which he had originally been charged (O'Donnell J)).

611. Fennelly J acknowledged that the judgment of McGuinness J in *Eviston* could not be interpreted in exactly the same way (see *Carlin v DPP* [2010] IESC 14, para 25–26).

612. *Carlin v DPP* [2010] IESC 14, para 29 (Fennelly J). The learned judge considered that had the accused been informed of the possibility that the DPP's decision might be reviewed, he would probably have suffered more from stress (para 24).

613. See *The State (McCormack) v Curran* [1987] ILRM 225, 237.

614. See *The State (McCormack) v Curran* [1987] ILRM 225; *H v Director of Public Prosecutions* [1994] 2 IR 589.

noting that the courts would not interfere with a decision of the DPP not to prosecute where:

(a) no *prima facie* case of *mala fides* has been made out against the [DPP];

(b) there is no evidence from which it could be inferred that he has abdicated his functions or been improperly motivated; and

(c) the facts of the case do not exclude the reasonable possibility of a proper and valid decision of the [DPP] not to prosecute the person concerned.[615]

UK

8.   In England and Wales and Northern Ireland, the cartel offence can be prosecuted by the Director of the Serious Fraud Office or the OFT.[616] Pursuant to a memorandum of understanding between the SFO and the OFT, it was envisaged that the SFO would prosecute more serious instances of the cartel offence involving serious or complex fraud.[617] However the two most significant prosecutions of the cartel offence to date, those arising out of the *Marine Hose* cartel[618] and the *BA/Virgin* matter,[619] were taken by the OFT. The SFO did take prosecutions in respect of alleged price fixing of generic drugs sold to the NHS but as the conduct pre-dated the Enterprise Act, the charge was conspiracy to defraud. Those prosecutions did not reach trial.[620]

9.   The decisions of the OFT or SFO to prosecute or not to prosecute are not immune from judicial review but 'only in highly exceptional cases will the court disturb the decisions of an independent prosecutor'.[621] The decision to take a prosecution is not amenable to judicial review 'absent dishonesty or *mala fides* or an exceptional circumstance'.[622] The same goes for refusals by a prosecutor to give an undertaking not to prosecute.[623]

Can a decision *not* to prosecute be challenged?

10.   A challenge to a decision of the SFO not to carry out an investigation, taken in the context of attempting to avoid extradition to the United States, was taken in the

---

615. *Eviston v DPP* [2002] 3 IR 260, 294.

616. Enterprise Act 2002, s 190(2). The Lord Advocate can prosecute in Scotland.

617. Memorandum of Understanding between the Office of Fair Trading and the Director of the Serious Fraud Office (October 2003).

618. See *R v Whittle* [2008] EWCA Crim 2560, para 24.

619. See *R v B* [2009] EWCA Crim 2575, [2010] 1 Cr App R 181. The trial subsequently collapsed in May 2010.

620. See *R v Goldshield Group plc* [2008] UKHL 17; *R v GG plc* [2008] EWCA Crim 3061.

621. *R (Corner House Research) v Director of the Serious Fraud Office* [2008] UKHL 60, [2008] 3 WLR 568, para 30 (Lord Bingham).

622. *R v Director of Public Prosecutions, ex parte Kebilene* [2000] 2 AC 326, 371 (Lord Steyn).

623. See *R (Pretty) v Director of Public Prosecutions* [2001] UKHL 61, [2002] 1 AC 800.

NatWest 3 case.[624] Once a person sought on extradition is charged with an offence in the UK, the extradition is halted.[625] If the offence charged in the UK is similar to the extradition offence, then extradition can ultimately be avoided based on the double jeopardy rule.[626] It is not difficult to imagine a situation arising in the context of an international cartel, where the OFT and SFO decline to prosecute but the US authorities or those in another jurisdiction seek the extradition of an accused based in the UK.

11. In the *NatWest 3* case, the US authorities sought the extradition of three former British bankers to face fraud charges connected with the collapse of the energy company, Enron. The bankers argued that any charges against them should properly be brought in England. However no English prosecution was brought even though it was argued by the bankers that to the extent anyone suffered due to the alleged fraud, it was NatWest, a British bank. The bankers sought a judicial review of the refusal of the Director of the SFO to institute a criminal investigation under section 1(3) of the Criminal Justice Act 1987.

12. The application for judicial review was rejected by the Divisional Court. Arguments made by the applicants that the Director made errors that rendered his decision irrational on *Wednesbury* grounds were rejected as 'wholly unsustainable' (they included arguments that the Director had wrongly identified the party that suffered loss as a result of the alleged fraud). Laws LJ entertained 'considerable reservation as to the propriety of the courts embarking at all on a challenge to the Director's decision' framed on *Wednesbury* grounds, finding that in making the decision whether or not to prosecute, 'there will have been expert assessments of weight and balance which are so conspicuously within the professional judgment of the statutory decision-maker that there will very rarely be legal space for a reviewing court to interfere'.[627] In the case of launching an investigation, the Director's discretion was even more open-ended than with a decision not to prosecute and ultimately it would take a 'wholly exceptional case on its legal merits to justify a judicial review' of the Director's discretionary decision.[628]

13. A further argument was made that where a crime could be prosecuted in two different jurisdictions, there was essentially a duty on the Director to decide which was the more appropriate venue for the case to be tried. The difficulty with this

---

624. *R (Bermingham) v Director of the Serious Fraud Office* [2006] EWHC 200 (Admin), [2007] QB 727.

625. Extradition Act 2003, s 22 (Category 1 territories) and s 88 and s 97 (Category 2 territories).

626. Extradition Act 2003, s 12 (Category 1 territories) and s 80 (Category 2 territories).

627. *R (Bermingham) v Director of the Serious Fraud Office* [2006] EWHC 200 (Admin), [2007] QB 727, para 63.

628. *R (Bermingham) v Director of the Serious Fraud Office* [2006] EWHC 200 (Admin), [2007] QB 727, para 64. The argument by extraditees that they should be tried in the UK rather than in the requesting state has been rejected in a number of recent extradition cases. For a list of such cases, see *R (Bary) v Secretary of State for the Home Department* [2009] EWHC 2068 (Admin) para 72.

argument was that it required to be read into section 1(3) of the Criminal Justice Act 1987 something which Parliament had not provided for. An argument based on the applicants' rights under Article 6 of the European Convention of Human Rights was also rejected. While the Director had a duty to consider the ECHR in making any decision, Laws LJ could not envisage any circumstances in which a decision *not* to investigate might breach a person's Convention rights.[629]

14.   Ultimately an applicant seeking to overturn a prosecutorial decision, whether one to prosecute or not to prosecute, faces a difficult task and will need to show that exceptional circumstances such as dishonesty or bad faith are present.

If Article 101 is engaged, must the cartel offence be tried by a designated 'national competition authority'?

15.   In a challenge to the prosecutions arising out of the *BA/Virgin passenger fuel surcharge* case, it was argued that that the Crown Court had no jurisdiction to try any offence charged under section 188 of the Enterprise Act 2002 where the agreement or conduct that was the subject of the offence had an effect on trade between Member States so as to engage Article 101. The reason relied on was that the Crown Court was not a national competition authority designated under Article 35 of Regulation 1/2003 and so, under Regulation 1/2003, it did not have jurisdiction to impose a fine or other penalty for a breach of Article 101. The question before the Court of Appeal turned on whether section 188 was a 'national competition law' as that term is used in Regulation 1/2003, in which case it would have been enforceable only by a designated national competition authority. The rationale for this situation arose from the goal of consistent application of Articles 101 and 102, as evidenced, for example, by the power conferred on the Commission to have a national case on the application of Article 101/102 transferred to it pursuant to Article 11(6) of Regulation 1/2003.

16.   The Court of Appeal, rejecting these arguments, concluded that the risk of any inconsistency arising between a prosecution under section 188 and a decision on the validity of an agreement under Article 101 or 102 was likely to be small, in particular because such a prosecution would not usually take place without parallel proceedings against an undertaking and because Articles 101 and 102 were directly effective, independent of Regulation 1/2003. So section 188 was not a 'national competition law' within the particular sense used in Regulation 1/2003.[630]

17.   In any event, the Court of Appeal considered that nothing in Regulation 1/2003 made the punishment of an offence which amounts to part of a national

---

629. *R (Bermingham) v Director of the Serious Fraud Office* [2006] EWHC 200 (Admin), [2007] QB 727, para 70.

630. *R v B* [2009] EWCA Crim 2575, [2010] 1 Cr App R 181, paras 36–37.

competition law the exclusive province of the national competition authorities designated pursuant to Regulation 1/2003.[631]

Key Sources

Ireland

Eviston v DPP [2002] 3 IR 260.

Carlin v DPP [2010] IESC 14.

UK

R v Director of Public Prosecutions, ex parte Kebilene [2000] 2 AC 326.

R (Bermingham) v Director of the Serious Fraud Office [2006] EWHC 200 (Admin), [2007] QB 727.

R v B [2009] EWCA Crim 2575, [2010] 1 Cr App R 181.

---

631. *R v B* [2009] EWCA Crim 2575, [2010] 1 Cr App R 181, para 38.

105. WHAT ARE THE RULES ON DIRECTOR DISQUALIFICATION FOR THOSE FOUND TO HAVE BREACHED COMPETITION LAW?

Summary

Ireland

- Persons found guilty on indictment of section 6 or 7 offences are automatically disqualified for 5 years.

- It is doubtful that a defendant can rely on this automatic disqualification as a mitigating factor in respect of the sentence to be imposed.

UK

- If a person is convicted of the cartel offence, that will trigger the court's discretion to impose a disqualification order.

- The OFT and certain of the sectoral regulators can apply for a disqualification order in respect of a civil breach of competition law.

- A disqualification undertaking may also be offered by the person in question.

Ireland

1. As offences under sections 6 and 7 of the Competition Act 2002 (and previously, offences under section 4(1) of the Competition Act 1991, as amended) are indictable offences relating to a company, any person convicted under those provisions in the Circuit Court or a higher court is automatically disqualified for five years from acting as a company officer, such as a director, secretary, auditor or liquidator.[632]

2. When it imposes a sentence for breach of competition law, should a court take account of the fact that the defendant will be subject to an automatic disqualification order? Such an approach would be justified if the nature of the disqualification order were considered to be penal.

3. In the *Dalton* case, the defendant pleaded guilty to price fixing arising out of the *Heating Oil* cartel in the West of Ireland. Judge Delahunt in the Circuit Criminal Court imposed a fine of €10,000 on the defendant and noted that he would be disqualified from acting as a director and acknowledged that this would be a significant penalty for him. Although there does not appear to be a written judgment that might indicate that the fact of the disqualification order was taken into account by the judge in deciding on the sentence,[633] in the view of the Competition Authority, the judge took the automatic disqualification into

---

632. See Companies Act 1990, s 160(1). For further discussion, see McFadden, 'How directors can be disqualified following competition cases', *Competition*, Vol. 14, at 158.

633. See the report in *The Irish Times*, 24 January 2007.

consideration in imposing 'a comparatively small fine with no custodial sentence'.[634]

4.   It was subsequently argued by the defendant in the *Duffy* case in the Central Criminal Court that the automatic disqualification order was penal in nature and so should be taken into account in deciding what punishment was to be imposed. McKechnie J held that on the particular facts, the disqualification would not have 'any real or substantial disabling effect'[635] on the defendant, who could likely continue to work in his family business as before, the only difference being that he could not act as a director during a limited period. However the judge left open the possibility that in an appropriate case, the fact that a defendant was disqualified might be considered as a factor in determining the sentence to be imposed.

5.   Prosecutors will likely argue that a disqualification order under section 160(1) of the Companies Act 1990 is not of a penal nature and should not be relevant to the court's decision on sentencing. It has been accepted by the Irish courts that disqualification orders made in civil cases under section 160(2) of the 1990 Act (where the court has discretion to impose an order) are not fundamentally penal in nature. Rather, the main purpose of the disqualification order is to protect the public.[636] It can be argued that the primary purpose of a section 160(1) order is not any different. The automatic application of the section 160(1) order means that the sentencing court has 'no involvement whatsoever with it [as] it follows directly as a matter of law' and to take account of it in sentencing would seem to be 'almost self-defeating to the section'.[637]

6.   Against this, a defendant may argue that the automatic five-year disqualification order is itself a primary punishment and should be a factor in sentencing. This is especially so where the effect of the disqualification order would result in the defendant losing his livelihood or main source of income. The effect of disqualification would then be closer to an 'intentional penal deprivation of property' which has been found to be a feature of a primary punishment.[638]

UK

7.   The conviction of a director for the cartel offence should trigger the jurisdiction of the court to impose a disqualification order under section 2 of the Company Directors Disqualification Act 1986. That provision states that the court may make a disqualification order against a person where he is convicted of an indictable

---

634. See letter from the Competition Authority to the Office of the Director of Corporate Enforcement dated 17 October 2008 available on the Authority's website.

635. *Director of Public Prosecutions v Duffy* [2009] IEHC 208, [2009] 3 IR 613, para 62.

636. See, e.g., *Director of Corporate Enforcement v McGowan* [2008] IESC 28, [2008] 2 ILRM 406, paras 45–46.

637. *Director of Public Prosecutions v Duffy* [2009] IEHC 208, [2009] 3 IR 613, para 60.

638. See *Conroy v Attorney General* [1965] IR 411, 441 (Walsh J). The other feature of primary punishment is loss of liberty.

offence (whether on indictment or summarily) in connection with, among others, the 'management' of the company. It should normally be possible to relate the cartel offence to the management of the company.[639] The court's power under section 2 of the 1986 Act is discretionary. A disqualification order provides that a person shall not be a director, receiver or be concerned or take part in the promotion, formation or management of a company or act as an insolvency practitioner.[640] The maximum term of disqualification is 15 years if made by the Crown Court[641] and 5 years if made by a Magistrates' Court.[642]

8. Disqualification orders were imposed on the three defendants in the *Whittle* case under section 2 of the 1986 Act, with periods of disqualification of seven years imposed on two and five years imposed on the other. On the appeal against their sentences to the Court of Appeal, none of the defendants sought to challenge the disqualification order.[643]

9. Under section 9A of the Company Directors Disqualification Act 1986, the OFT and certain sectoral regulators can apply to the court for a disqualification order. The court *must* make a disqualification order on such an application where the company has committed a breach of the Chapter I or II prohibition or Article 101 or 102 and the court considers that the director's conduct in relation to the breach makes him unfit to be concerned in the management of a company.[644] The director can be disqualified for up to 15 years.[645] In its guidance on disqualification orders, the OFT indicates that it does not expect to have to use its section 9A powers where a director is convicted of the cartel offence before a court as the court can itself consider a disqualification order in this case.[646]

10. Provision is also made for persons to offer a disqualification undertaking to the OFT or sectoral regulator in situations where the OFT or regulator thinks that an undertaking has committed or is committing a breach of competition law.[647] The OFT or specified regulator is also empowered to carry out an investigation for the purpose of deciding whether to make an application under section 9A for a disqualification order where it has reasonable grounds for suspecting that a breach of competition law has occurred.[648]

11. The OFT has stated in its 2010 guidance that it will not seek competition disqualification orders against individuals who benefit from no-action letters or

---

639. It is sufficient if the offence has 'some relevant factual connection with the management of the company' (*R v Goodman* [1994] 1 BCLC 349, 353 (Staughton LJ)).

640. Company Directors Disqualification Act 1986, s 1(1).

641. Company Directors Disqualification Act 1986, s 2(3)(b).

642. Company Directors Disqualification Act 1986, s 5(5).

643. See *R v Whittle* [2008] EWCA Crim 2560, para 14.

644. Company Directors Disqualification Act 1986, s 9A(1), (2), (3).

645. Company Directors Disqualification Act 1986, s 9A(9).

646. OFT 510, Director disqualification orders in competition cases (June 2010) para 4.28.

647. Company Directors Disqualification Act 1986, s 9B.

648. Company Directors Disqualification Act 1986, s 9C.

who are directors of companies that benefit from leniency (this is limited to breaches of competition law to which the leniency relates). However, the OFT or sectoral regulators may consider applying for a disqualification order against a director who was removed or otherwise ceases to act as a director owing to his role in a breach of competition law or a director who fails to cooperate with the leniency process.[649]

12. The OFT's guidance also indicates that the OFT will consider making applications for disqualification orders against directors who did not know of the breach of competition law but ought to have known. In considering whether a director 'ought' to have known of the infringement, the OFT will consider the director's role in the company, his relationship to those responsible for the breach, the general knowledge, skill and experience actually possessed by the director and that which should have been possessed by a person in that position and/or the information relating to the breach that was available to the director.[650] The OFT also states that in exceptional cases, it may consider it appropriate to apply for a disqualification order even though there is no prior decision or judgment finding a breach of competition law. The OFT or regulator would still have to satisfy a court that there had been an infringement of competition law.[651] Examples of exceptional circumstances might include where a company has become insolvent.

13. It is doubtful that the possibility of a disqualification order under section 2 or 9A can be taken into account in sentencing. The English courts have stated that the purpose of a disqualification order is to protect the public, whether it is issued in the context of civil or criminal proceedings.[652]

Key Sources
Ireland
Companies Act 1990, section 160(1).
Director of Public Prosecutions v Duffy [2009] IEHC 208, [2009] 3 IR 613.
UK
Company Directors Disqualification Act 1986, sections 1, 9A, 9B and 9C.
OFT 510, Director disqualification orders in competition cases (June 2010).

---

649. OFT 510, Director disqualification orders in competition cases (June 2010) paras 4.13–4.14.
650. OFT 510, Director disqualification orders in competition cases (June 2010) para 4.22.
651. OFT 510, Director disqualification orders in competition cases (June 2010) para 4.7.
652. See, e.g., *Secretary of State for Trade and Industry v Tjolle* [1998] 1 BCLC 333, 336 (Jacob J stating that it was 'self-evident that civil and criminal courts should be applying the same standards: the purpose of disqualification (to protect the public from the activities of persons unfit to be concerned in the management of a company) is the same in both kinds of court').

106. How can immunity from prosecution be obtained?

Summary

Ireland

- The decision whether to grant immunity from prosecution is for the DPP.

- The Competition Authority operates an immunity programme, pursuant to which it may recommend to the DPP that immunity be granted.

- The applicant must be the 'first in the door' and fully cooperate before the Authority will recommend it for immunity.

- An undertaking can apply for immunity on behalf of itself and its employees, directors and officers.

- A review of the Authority's immunity programme was launched in July 2010.

UK

- Individuals can obtain immunity pursuant to a corporate leniency application to the OFT or by making an application themselves.

- If Type A immunity is granted to an undertaking, its current and former employees and directors will automatically be granted criminal immunity.

- In Type B cases resulting in a 100 per cent immunity from fines, individuals will also be granted immunity. In other cases, the OFT may grant criminal immunity on an individual basis.

- In Type C cases, the decision on criminal immunity will depend on factors including the role played by the individual in the cartel and the information provided in the leniency application.

Ireland

1. The DPP has the sole power to prosecute competition law offences on indictment and the final decision whether to take a prosecution is for the DPP alone. The Competition Authority makes recommendations to the DPP in respect of prosecutions on indictment.

2. A cartel immunity programme was introduced by the Competition Authority and the DPP in 2001.[653] The programme is currently under review and the Competition Authority published a consultation paper and draft revised immunity programme document in July 2010,[654] followed by a public consultation. At the time of writing

---

653. See *Cartel Immunity Programme*, Notice of 20 December 2001 ('2001 Irish Immunity Notice').

654. Competition Authority, Cartel Immunity Programme Review – Consultation Paper (15 July 2010) ('2010 Irish Immunity Consultation Paper') and Revised Cartel Immunity Programme (15 July 2010) ('2010 Irish Immunity Proposal').

a new programme had not yet been adopted. The 2001 programme is first discussed before considering the suggested changes in the July 2010 proposal.

3.   Under the 2001 programme, applications for immunity from prosecution should be made to the Competition Authority, which will make a recommendation to the DPP whether to grant immunity.[655] Both undertakings that are not individuals and individuals can apply for immunity.

4.   The Authority will recommend immunity if the applicant is the first to come forward before the Authority has gathered sufficient evidence to warrant a referral of a completed investigation file to the DPP.[656] The applicant must meet a number of requirements before the Authority will recommend immunity and if the first applicant does not meet these requirements, a subsequent applicant can be considered for immunity. In particular, the applicant must:

- Terminate its participation in the illegal activity.

- Not do anything to alert its former associates that it has applied for immunity.

- Not have been a coercer, instigator or ringleader in the cartel.

- Provide complete and timely cooperation to the Authority in its investigation and in particular (i) reveal all Competition Act offences in which it may have been involved; (ii) fully disclose all material relevant to the offences; and (iii) cooperate fully on a continuing basis.[657]

5.   A corporate undertaking seeking immunity must make its application a corporate act.[658] Such an undertaking can make an application on behalf of employees, including directors and officers.[659] If a corporate undertaking qualifies for immunity, all past and present directors, officers and employees who admit their involvement in the cartel and who cooperate with the Authority's investigation will also qualify for immunity.[660] An employee can apply for immunity for himself, whether or not the corporate undertaking applies or cooperates.[661]

6.   There are four steps in the immunity process:

(i)   Initial contact with the Authority's designated officer, which can be made in person or by phone. The application can be made through lawyers in hypothetical terms so as to protect anonymity. Once contact is made, the applicant receives a 'marker', allowing the applicant to retain its place in the queue until its application is complete. This preserves a 'first in the door' immunity policy.

---

655. 2001 Irish Immunity Notice, para 10.
656. 2001 Irish Immunity Notice, para 12.
657. 2001 Irish Immunity Notice, paras 13–16.
658. 2001 Irish Immunity Notice, para 17.
659. 2001 Irish Immunity Notice, para 8.
660. 2001 Irish Immunity Notice, para 19.
661. 2001 Irish Immunity Notice, para 20.

   (ii)   The applicant must supply the Authority with a sufficient description of the illegal activity. If the Authority takes the view that the case falls within the immunity programme, it will refer the matter to the DPP seeking a written qualified agreement to grant immunity from the DPP.

   (iii) Once the applicant receives a written qualified agreement to grant immunity, it must make full disclosure to the Authority and the DPP. The applicant will be reminded of its legal privilege against self-incrimination.

   (iv)   Once the terms of the qualified guarantee have been satisfied, the DPP will execute an immunity agreement.[662]

7.   If the applicant fails to comply with any of the requirements set out in the programme (for example, if it fails to provide ongoing cooperation or if a corporate undertaking fails to fully promote the complete and timely cooperation of its employees), the DPP may revoke the immunity agreement.[663]

8.   Under the 2001 Immunity Programme, information provided by the applicant will not be disclosed other than in accordance with normal practices and procedures pertaining to criminal investigations and prosecutions. So, information may be disclosed if it was made public by the applicant, disclosure is required by law, disclosure is for the purpose of the administration and enforcement of the Competition Act 2002, disclosure is necessary to prevent the commission of a criminal offence or disclosure is made in the course of an investigation or subsequent proceedings.[664]

9.   The aim of the 2010 review of the immunity programme is to make the programme 'more self-contained, transparent and attractive for potential applicants and thus a more effective tool in the fight against cartels'.[665] The proposed amendments also take account of the ECN Model Leniency Programme, which Ireland signed in 2006.

10. One of the proposals is the lifting of the bar on a ringleader from the immunity programme. As the Authority explains, the roles that undertakings play in a cartel can change over time and maintaining an exclusion on ringleaders from the programme could potentially preclude a number of participants in the cartel from ever applying for immunity.[666] However, the Authority proposes maintaining the exclusion of coercers and instigators, with the provision that applicants 'must not have coerced another party to participate in the illegal cartel activity and must not have acted as the instigator of the cartel activity'.[667] The practical effect of the change may not be significant as ringleaders will often also have acted as coercers and/or instigators. There is no definition given of what constitutes coercion, instigation or ringleading.

---

662. 2001 Irish Immunity Notice, paras 21–28.
663. 2001 Irish Immunity Notice, pars 29–30.
664. 2001 Irish Immunity Notice, para 31.
665. 2010 Irish Immunity Consultation Paper, para 1.7.
666. 2010 Irish Immunity Consultation Paper, para 2.5.
667. 2010 Immunity Proposal, para 15.

11.   Other than this change, the basic structure of the revised programme is similar to the 2001 programme. The 2010 Proposal does make clear that the immunity programme is in addition to the general discretion enjoyed by the DPP in prosecutorial matters and that nothing in the programme shall affect the exercise by the DPP of his general discretion to grant immunity.[668]

12.   Unlike the Commission and UK leniency systems, leniency short of immunity is not part of the Irish system. Ireland does not have a leniency programme, pursuant to which undertakings and individuals could receive reductions in fines for breach of competition law in return for cooperating with an investigation. Ireland, like the United States, operates a prosecutorial competition law enforcement regime in which court actions must be instituted in order to impose sanctions. Neither the DPP nor the Competition Authority has the power to impose sanctions or agree a particular fine or reduction in fine. The relevant power that the DPP can exercise is his decision not to initiate a prosecution. Cooperation by a defendant in the investigation of competition law infringements would likely be considered by a court as a mitigating factor that may result in a reduction of a fine or sentence.[669]

Does immunity granted by the Commission protect individuals or undertakings from criminal prosecution in Ireland?

13.   There is no express prohibition to the prosecution of individuals in Ireland who are employees or directors of undertakings that have applied for and/or obtained immunity or leniency from the Commission. Neither the 2001 Immunity Programme nor the 2010 Immunity Proposal addresses the policy of the Competition Authority or the DPP on this issue. There would be a prohibition on the Authority or the DPP using information obtained from the Commission as evidence in a criminal prosecution for breach of the Competition Act 2002.[670]

UK

How is criminal immunity obtained as part of corporate leniency?

14.   The cartel offence only applies to individuals and undertakings that are not individuals face only civil penalties. There are two ways in which individuals may obtain immunity from criminal prosecution for the cartel offence: (i) as part of the grant of corporate leniency; (ii) following an application by an individual for a 'no-action' letter.

15.   The OFT operates a leniency programme in respect of cartels. That programme may benefit applicants by granting immunity or reduction in fines and/or immunity from criminal prosecution for individuals. Criminal immunity is in this way intertwined with the application for civil leniency by an undertaking.

---

668. 2010 Immunity Proposal, para 7.
669. See further Question 103.
670. Regulation 1/2003, Article 12.

16. The availability of immunity from prosecution for individuals will depend on the type of leniency that is granted. Under the OFT programme, there are three types of leniency that an applicant firm may be granted:

- Type A (the applicant is the first to apply where the OFT had not already begun an investigation; automatic full immunity).

- Type B (the applicant was first to apply but the OFT had already started an investigation; discretionary full immunity or partial leniency).

- Type C (the applicant is not first to apply; discretionary partial leniency only).

17. In Type A immunity, an undertaking is granted automatic civil immunity and all of its current and former employees and directors who co-operate with the OFT are granted automatic criminal immunity for cartel activity. Type A immunity is only available where the undertaking was the first to apply and there was no preexisting civil and/or criminal investigation into such activity. If these conditions are met and the firm was not a coercer, full immunity from fines will be granted, together with blanket criminal immunity for individuals.

18. Type B is sometimes divided into two parts, 'Type B immunity' and 'Type B leniency'. Under Type B immunity, an undertaking is granted discretionary civil immunity and all of its current and former employees and directors who co-operate with the OFT are granted discretionary criminal immunity for cartel activity. Type B immunity applies where the undertaking was the first to apply but there was already a pre-existing civil and/or criminal investigation into such activity but the OFT had not yet issued a statement of objections. If the applicant firm is granted 100 per cent immunity from fines, this carries with it full criminal immunity for individuals.

19. Type B leniency refers to where an undertaking is granted a reduction of, but not immunity from fines where the undertaking was the first to apply but there was already a pre-existing civil and/or criminal investigation into the relevant cartel activity. In this case, criminal immunity may be granted by the OFT on an individual basis. This will depend on the role of the employee and the nature of the information supplied in the leniency application.

20. Type C Leniency involves the grant to an undertaking of a reduction of up to 50 per cent in the fine where the undertaking was not the first to apply whether or not there was already a pre-existing civil and/or criminal investigation into the relevant cartel activity. While Type C leniency does not bring any automatic guarantee of criminal immunity for individuals, the OFT has discretion to grant criminal immunity to directors or employees where it considers it appropriate. The OFT will consider the role of the individual and the nature of the information provided in the leniency application.

21. Types A and B immunity are only available where the applicant firm did not coerce others into participating in the cartel. While it does not provide a definition of a 'coercer', the OFT has indicated that to qualify as a coercer, there must be evidence of 'clear, positive and ultimately successful steps from a participant (that

is, the coercer) to pressurize an unwilling participant to take part in the cartel'.[671] The OFT gives as examples of coercion, physical or proven threats of violence that have a realistic prospect of being carried out or blackmail or such strong economic pressure as to make market exit a real risk. The OFT does not consider as coercion harmful market pressure falling short of a risk of market exit but which may reduce profits or agreed cartel enforcement mechanisms.[672] Given this approach, an applicant will rarely be considered to be a coercer. Even if an applicant firm were later to lose full immunity having been found to be a coercer, its current and former employees or directors (other than employees who played a coercing role) remain eligible for criminal immunity.[673]

22.   Even if criminal immunity is not given, this does not mean that the OFT will carry out criminal prosecutions. There are no clear guidelines for when criminal prosecutions will be taken by the OFT (or the SFO). The OFT has stated that relevant factors would include whether there was evidence that individuals acted dishonestly (which is of course a requirement to make out the cartel offence) and the extent of consumer detriment brought about by the cartel.[674]

What is the procedure for obtaining immunity?

23.   The first step is for the firm to contact the OFT by telephone, usually through its lawyer, to inquire as to whether Type A immunity is available. If so, the next step is to obtain a 'marker'. If Type A immunity is not available, the undertaking can consider its options. It may wish to apply for Type B immunity if the OFT confirms that Type B is available.

24.   The OFT operates a 'marker' system so that a leniency applicant can maintain its position as first in the queue by providing certain basic information initially (usually specifying the nature and emerging details of the suspected infringement and the evidence uncovered so far). However, the undertaking must have a 'genuine intention to confess' in order to obtain Type A immunity, so that if it seeks to deny that it is involved in cartel conduct and makes the application merely in case the OFT is minded to take the view that there is a cartel, it will not obtain a marker.[675]

25.   The OFT will discuss with the undertaking the timing for perfecting the marker, through the provision of all information, documents and evidence available to the applicant regarding the existence and activities of the cartel. If information is not provided within the set timeframe, the undertaking may lose the marker. Once the marker is perfected, the OFT will enter into a formal leniency agreement with the applicant.

---

671. OFT 803, Leniency and no-action: OFT's guidance note on the handling of applications (December 2008) para 6.4.

672. OFT 803, paras 6.5–6.6.

673. OFT 803, paras 6.9, 7.11.

674. OFT 803, para 7.1.

675. OFT 803, para 3.1.

How does an individual obtain criminal immunity himself?

26.   Criminal immunity can be obtained by an individual other than in the context of a corporate leniency application. The individual can himself apply to the OFT. This could arise, for example, where the individual has reported cartel activity to his company but the company decides not to make a leniency application.

27.   In this case, the individual will be given immunity provided he tells the OFT about the cartel before any other individual or undertaking and provided there is no pre-existing civil or criminal investigation. If there is already an investigation but the individual is first to report, immunity may still be granted provided that the conditions for the issuing of a no-action letter are met and that the individual adds significant value to the OFT's investigation.[676]

What is the procedure for granting criminal immunity?

28.   The OFT has the statutory power to grant immunity from prosecution by virtue of section 190(4) of the Enterprise Act 2002, which provides:

> Where, for the purpose of the investigation or prosecution of offences under section 188, the OFT gives a person a written notice under this subsection, no proceedings for an offence under section 188 that falls within a description specified in the notice may be brought against that person in England and Wales or Northern Ireland except in circumstances specified in the notice.

29.   Immunity from prosecution is granted in the form of a 'no-action letter'. The letter will provide that a prosecution will not be taken except in the circumstances outlined in the letter. The OFT can only grant immunity from prosecution in respect of England and Wales and Northern Ireland. Prosecutions in Scotland are a matter for the Lord Advocate but the OFT will report on the individual's cooperation to the Lord Advocate, who may decide that the individual is immune from prosecution in Scotland.

30.   An individual must meet a number of conditions to benefit from a no-action letter. The individual must (i) admit participation in the criminal offence, including dishonesty; (ii) provide the OFT with all information available to him about the cartel; (iii) fully cooperate throughout the investigation, including until the conclusion of any criminal proceedings; (iv) not have been a coercer; and (v) cease participation in the cartel from the time of notification to the OFT.[677] Satisfaction of these conditions appears to be a minimum requirement but is not a sufficient condition for the grant of a no-action letter. Where the OFT believes that it already has, or is in the course of gathering, sufficient information to bring a successful prosecution of an individual, it will not issue a no-action letter.[678]

---

676. OFT 803, paras 7.24–7.25.
677. OFT 513, The Cartel Offence: Guidance on the issue of no-action letters for individuals (April 2003) para 3.3.
678. OFT 513, para 3.4; OFT 803, para 7.4.

31.   The limited experience with criminal immunity to date means that there may be uncertainty about certain aspects of the immunity process. For example, to what extent will an individual granted immunity be required to cooperate in a criminal prosecution taken against another individual who was involved in the cartel? In the (aborted) trial of four British Airways employees arising out of the *BA/Virgin passenger fuel surcharge* cartel, several Virgin employees, who had been granted criminal immunity, were due to testify as prosecution witnesses. Although plea bargaining is not generally accepted in the criminal justice system, this form of plea bargaining – effectively, the grant of immunity in return for testifying for the prosecution – appears to be legitimate given the express statutory basis in s 190(4) of the Enterprise Act 2002.

When will a comfort letter be issued?

32.   If admission of participation in the cartel offence is not deemed appropriate, the OFT will offer the individual a 'comfort letter'. This will state that there is insufficient evidence to implicate the individual in the cartel offence and that the OFT does not consider that there is any risk of prosecution by the OFT or any other agency. If the OFT decides to limit itself to a civil investigation, it will, where requested, issue a comfort letter to an undertaking qualifying for Type A or Type B immunity, covering all current and future employees of the undertaking.[679]

Does immunity granted by the Commission protect individuals from criminal prosecution in the UK?

33.   When an undertaking benefits from immunity pursuant to the European Commission's leniency programme, there is no express prohibition to the prosecution of individuals who are employees or directors of that undertaking for the cartel offence in the UK. Of course, if the undertaking obtains Type A immunity, the individuals will receive immunity in any event. If Type A immunity is not available but the undertaking obtains immunity from the Commission, as a matter of policy, the OFT will not 'normally' prosecute such individuals. However, it may be unwilling to grant no-action letters where (i) a criminal investigation was already underway in the UK or (ii) where it considers that the undertaking later sought immunity from the Commission having failed to gain Type A immunity in the UK as a device to obtain criminal immunity for individuals or (iii) there was an unreasonable delay between the approach to the Commission and the subsequent approach to the OFT.[680]

34.   Even if an undertaking is not eligible for immunity under the Commission's programme and cannot secure immunity from the OFT, the OFT suggests that individuals will not be placed at increased risk of prosecution for the cartel offence due to the undertaking's application to and cooperation with the Commission. This is because information disclosed by the Commission to the OFT can only be used

679. OFT 803, paras 7.4–7.5.
680. OFT 803, paras 7.34–7.39.

for applying Article 101 and 102 and any material received by the OFT from the Commission cannot be used for purposes of a criminal prosecution.[681] The OFT also appears to be prohibited from using such information as intelligence to start an investigation in the UK that could result in criminal prosecutions. The Commission's Leniency Notice provides that where corporate statements are transmitted by the Commission to the OFT under Regulation 1/2003, the conditions of the Network Notice must be met.[682] Those conditions include that the leniency applicant has provided its consent for the transmission of the information to the OFT, or, it has either made a leniency application to the OFT or the OFT has provided written confirmation that it will not use the information to impose sanctions on the undertaking or individuals.[683] Nevertheless, where an undertaking consents to the transmission to the OFT of material provided to the Commission in a leniency application, it seems open to the OFT to use this information to start an investigation that could ultimately result in criminal prosecutions for the cartel offence. This creates a vulnerability for an employee or director, particularly one whom the undertaking is prepared to 'hang out to dry'.

35.   The OFT insists however that it will not use information obtained from the Commission for purposes of a criminal investigation and as a further safeguard, the OFT will erect a Chinese wall between staff receiving information from the Commission and staff involved in prosecuting the cartel offence.[684]

Key Sources

Ireland

Cartel Immunity Programme, Notice of 20 December 2001.

Competition Authority, Cartel Immunity Programme Review – Consultation Paper and Revised Cartel Immunity Programme (15 July 2010).

UK

OFT 513, The Cartel Offence: Guidance on the issue of no-action letters for individuals (April 2003).

OFT 803, Leniency and no-action: OFT's guidance note on the handling of applications (December 2008).

---

681. Regulation 1/2003, Article 12.
682. Commission Notice on Immunity from fines and reduction of fines in cartel cases [2006] OJ C298/11, recital 35.
683. Commission Notice on cooperation within the Network of Competition Authorities [2004] OJ C101/43, paras 40–41.
684. OFT 803, para 7.45.

Chapter 6

PRIVATE ENFORCEMENT

Suits Against Employees to Recover Fines

Chapter 6

PRIVATE ENFORCEMENT

107. IN WHICH JURISDICTION CAN A PRIVATE ANTITRUST ACTION BE TAKEN?

Summary

- Jurisdiction is determined by the Judgments Regulation.

- The general rule is that a defendant is to be sued in his country of domicile.

- In contractual claims, the defendant can also be sued in the place of performance of the obligation.

- Most antitrust actions will involve claims in tort, in respect of which the defendant can also be sued in the place where the harmful event occurred. This includes both the place where damage occurred and the place of the event giving rise to the damage. If jurisdiction is based on the former, only damages arising in that country can be claimed in that court.

- In cases of multiple defendants, if there is a sufficient connection between the claims, all can be sued in the country where one is domiciled.

- The English courts have considered whether a subsidiary of a party that infringed competition law can be sued in order to ground jurisdiction in England, even if the subsidiary did not participate in or was not aware of the infringement. A definitive answer has not been provided and this question will likely be the subject of a reference to the Court of Justice in a future case.

- If the same cause of action is pending in different courts of EU Member States, any court other than the court first seised must stay its proceedings.

- If the actions are merely 'related', the second court has a discretion whether to stay its proceedings and should balance various factors in making that decision.

- If the court of a contracting state of the Judgments Regulation has jurisdiction because the defendant is domiciled there, it cannot stay its proceedings in favour of the court of a non-contracting state.

1. The rules determining which courts have jurisdiction to hear a private antitrust action are those set out in Regulation 44/2001 (the 'Judgments Regulation').[1] The general jurisdictional rule in Article 2 is that a defendant is to be sued in the courts of the Member State in which he is domiciled.

2.   In matters relating to a contract, Article 5(1) provides that a defendant may also be sued 'in the courts for the place of performance of the obligation in question'. In matters of tort, Article 5(3) provides that the claimant has the option to sue 'in the courts for the place where the harmful event occurred or may occur'.[2] This means 'both the place where the damage occurred and the place of the event giving rise to it, so that the defendant may be sued, at the option of the plaintiff, in the courts for either of those places'.[3] Because Article 5 is in derogation from the basic principle of domicile in Article 2, the provisions of Article 5 are to be construed restrictively.[4]

3.   Private antitrust actions could potentially fall within either Article 5(1) or 5(3) depending on the nature of the claim and whether there is a contractual relationship between the parties. For example, in an action seeking a declaration that a contract is void because it infringes Article 101, Article 5(1) would apply. In an action for damages arising out of a cartel or an abuse of dominance, the cause of action would usually be in tort and so Article 5(3) is more likely to apply even if there was a direct contractual relationship between the claimant and defendant.

Where is the place where the harmful event originated or the damage occurred?

4.   In the context of the tort of defamation, it was established that if the Article 5(3) jurisdiction were based on the place where the harmful event originated, all damages for the loss, wherever incurred, could be claimed in that court. However, if jurisdiction were based on the place where the damage occurred, only damages arising in that country could be claimed in that court.[5]

5.   If Article 5(3) were invoked to establish jurisdiction in an antitrust case, it would therefore be desirable from the claimant's perspective to invoke it by reference to the place where the harmful event originated. Identifying this country, in which 'the event setting the tort in motion'[6] occurred, may not always be straightforward.

---

1.   Council Regulation (EC) No 44/2001 on jurisdiction and the recognition and enforcement of judgments in civil and commercial matters [2001] OJ L 12/1. The Judgments Regulation replaced the Brussels Convention on jurisdiction and the enforcement of judgments in civil and commercial matters (1968). A new Lugano Convention on jurisdiction and the enforcement of judgments in civil and commercial matters, to which the EU Member States, Iceland, Norway and Switzerland are signatories and which is aligned with the rules in the Judgments Regulation, was signed in 2007 and replaces the 1988 Lugano Convention. The new Lugano Convention entered into force between the EU Member States and Norway on 1 April 2010, with ratifications in Iceland and Switzerland outstanding as of 1 September 2010.
2.   Judgments Regulation, Article 5(3).
3.   See, e.g., Case C–189/08 *Zuid-Chemie BV v Philippo's Mineralenfabriek NV/SA* [2009] ECR I–6917, para 23.
4.   See Case 189/87 *Kalfelis v Bankhaus Schröder, Münchmeyer, Hengst and Co* [1988] ECR 5565, para 19.
5.   Case C–68/93 *Shevill v Press Alliance SA* [1995] ECR I–415, para 33.
6.   *Sandisk Corporation v Koninklijke Philips Electronics* [2007] EWHC 332 (Ch), [2007] Bus LR 705, para 25.

In the case of a damages claim arising out of a cartel, for example, it could be argued that this is the place where the first cartel meeting took place. However, this approach may not be realistic in the context of a European-wide cartel orchestrated at meetings in several countries.[7] A further complicating factor might arise in a follow-on claim that relies on a Commission decision, where that decision acknowledges that a cartel was already in existence before the period that the Commission takes into account for purposes of establishing the infringement of competition law.[8]

Where can multiple defendants be sued?

6.   In cases involving multiple defendants domiciled in different Member States, Article 6(1) of the Judgments Regulation enables a claimant to bring a single action against all of the defendants in 'the courts for the place where any one of them is domiciled'.[9] One defendant can be used as an 'anchor' to bring in the others. To avail of this provision, there must be a sufficient connection between that claim and the claims against other defendants. The claims must be 'so closely connected that it is expedient to hear and determine them together to avoid the risk of irreconcilable judgments resulting from separate proceedings'.[10] Article 6(1) provides a claimant in a multi-defendant private damages action with the opportunity to forum shop where defendants are domiciled in different jurisdictions.

Can subsidiaries of cartel participants be sued in order to ground jurisdiction?

7.   In a multi-defendant private action arising out of a cartel, the range of forums in which a claimant can establish jurisdiction is not necessarily limited to the places where the parties to the cartel are domiciled. It may also be possible to sue in the place where a subsidiary of one of the cartel participants is domiciled, even if the subsidiary was not itself a member of the cartel or an addressee of any infringement decision by the Commission.

8.   This question has arisen before the English courts. Claimants have sought to use English subsidiaries of cartel participants as anchor defendants to ground jurisdiction in England under Article 6(1) of the Judgments Regulation, even though the subsidiaries had not themselves participated in the cartel. In *Provimi*, a

---

7.   See the comments of Teare J in *Cooper Tire & Rubber Company v Shell Chemicals UK Limited* [2009] EWHC 2609 (Comm), [2009] UKCLR 1097, para 65.

8.   See, e.g., COMP/E–2/38.359 *Electrical and mechanical carbon and graphite products*, Commission Decision of 3 December 2003, para 72, in which the Commission acknowledged that it found indications that the cartel was in operation in the 1970s and 1980s but decided to limit its proceeding to an 11-year period starting in October 1988.

9.   Judgments Regulation, Article 6(1).

10. Judgments Regulation, Article 6(1). Article 6(1) of the Lugano Convention is in similar terms.

follow-on action arising from the *Vitamins* cartel, the defendants argued in strike-out proceedings that as the subsidiaries were not parties to the cartel, they did not breach Article 101 and that mere implementation of the cartel agreement, without knowledge of it, was insufficient to ground liability. The defendants also argued that the claims were hopeless on causation grounds as no products had been bought from the English subsidiaries. Refusing to strike out the claims, Aiken J invoked the EU law concept of an undertaking to find that it was arguable that where one entity within an undertaking implemented a cartel agreement (by selling products at the cartelised price) to which another entity had been party, the former entity was also in breach of Article 101.[11] On the causation point, the learned judge found that as it was arguable that the subsidiaries had infringed Article 101, it was also arguable that the subsidiaries, by implementing the cartel, had caused the claimants' loss.[12]

9.   The approach in *Provimi* was followed by the High Court in *Cooper Tire* but the Court of Appeal was more sceptical. The claims involved a follow-on damages action arising out of the Commission's decision in the *Butadiene Rubber* cartel.[13] Twenty-six claimants brought damages actions in the English High Court against twenty-four defendants. Three of the defendants, the anchor defendants for purposes of Article 6(1) of the Judgments Regulation, were English subsidiaries of companies that were addressees of the Commission decision but the subsidiaries themselves were not addressees. Two defendants, Dow and Bayer, whose English subsidiaries were two of the anchor defendants, challenged the jurisdiction of the English court and alternatively sought a stay.[14]

10. Ultimately, the Court of Appeal in *Cooper Tire* did not have to decide the *Provimi* point as based on the pleadings, it was open to the claimants to prove that the anchor defendants were in fact parties to or aware of the cartel and this was not a claim that could be struck out at the preliminary stage. However, the Court of Appeal held in *dicta* that had it to decide the question whether subsidiaries unaware of the cartel could be used as anchor defendants, it would have been inclined to make a preliminary reference to the Court of Justice. While agreeing that the claimants' position in *Provimi* was arguable, it was also arguable the other way. It can be expected that this question will come before the Court of Justice in a future case and the concerns of the Court of Appeal are worth noting:

> Although one can see that a parent company should be liable for what its subsidiary has done on the basis that a parent company is presumed to be able to exercise (and actually exercise) decisive influence over a subsidiary, it is by no means obvious even in an Article [101] context that a subsidiary should be liable for what its parent does,

---

11. *Provimi Limited v Roche Products Limited* [2003] EWHC 961 (Comm), [2003] UKCLR 493, para 31.

12. See *Provimi Limited v Roche Products Limited* [2003] EWHC 961 (Comm), [2003] UKCLR 493, para 40.

13. Case COMP/F/38.638 – *Butadiene Rubber and Emulsion Styrene Butadiene Rubber* (29 November 2006).

14. On the stay application, see paras 14–16 below.

let alone for what another subsidiary does. Nor does the *Provimi* point sit comfortably with the apparent practice of the Commission, when it exercises its power to fine, to single out those who are primarily responsible or their parent companies rather than to impose a fine on all the entities of the relevant undertaking. If, moreover, liability can extend to any subsidiary company which is part of an undertaking, would such liability accrue to a subsidiary which did not deal in rubber at all, but another product entirely?[15]

Can jurisdiction be established if related proceedings are pending in another jurisdiction?

11. A common issue in international commercial litigation generally and one that is likely to arise in antitrust actions, in particular those based on international conspiracies or markets, is when a court must stay its proceedings because the courts of another jurisdiction have been seised.

12. A distinction should be drawn between jurisdictional disputes involving the courts of another EU Member State and those of a country outside the EU. The former situation is governed by the Judgments Regulation. Where proceedings involving 'the same cause of action and between the same parties' are brought in the courts of different Member States, any court other than the court first seised must stay its proceedings until such time as the jurisdiction of the court first seised is established. Once jurisdiction is established, other courts must decline jurisdiction in favour of that court.[16]

13. In the case of 'related actions' (*i.e.* actions 'so closely connected that it is expedient to hear and determine them together to avoid the risk of irreconcilable judgments resulting from separate proceedings')[17] pending in courts of different Member States, any court other than the court first seised *may* stay its proceedings. Where the actions are pending at first instance, a party can make an application to the court other than the court first seised, seeking to have it decline jurisdiction.[18] In this case, the court which is not first seised has a discretion

---

15. *Cooper Tire & Rubber Company Europe Limited v Dow Deutschland Inc* [2010] EWCA Civ 864, para 45. See also the approach of Teare J on this point in the High Court. The judge found that a subsidiary that did not trade in the cartelised goods (say, a shoe polish company) would not be liable and could not be used as an anchor defendant. Emphasising the relative nature of the concept of an undertaking in EU law (*i.e.* the question is whether two entities form a single undertaking in a specific context, not generally), Teare J reasoned that that the shoe polish subsidiary would not be considered to form a single undertaking with the parent for the purpose of producing and selling rubber products (see *Cooper Tire & Rubber Company v Shell Chemicals UK Limited* [2009] EWHC 2609 (Comm), [2009] UKCLR 1097, paras 56–61).

16. Judgments Regulation, Article 27.

17. Judgments Regulation, Article 28(3).

18. Judgments Regulation, Article 28.

whether to stay its proceedings. The court should consider all the circumstances of the case before it and keep in mind the object of Article 28 of the Judgments Regulation, which is to avoid the risk of conflicting judgments.[19]

14. This issue arose in *Cooper Tire*, where the defendants sought a stay pending related proceedings in Italy. One of the addressees of the *Butadiene Rubber* cartel, Enichem, brought proceedings in Italy seeking, *inter alia*, declarations that the cartel that was the subject of the Commission's decision did not exist and that manufacturers of tyres which were named as defendants in the action had not suffered loss as a result of the alleged cartel (whether they purchased from Enichem or another company).[20] The claimants in *Cooper Tire* were from the same groups as the defendants named in the Italian proceedings. The claimants sued all of the addressees of the Commission decision in England, except Enichem. The Dow and Bayer defendants in the English proceedings subsequently intervened in the Italian proceedings and adopted the claims made by Enichem. The Italian proceedings were subsequently dismissed, in part because they were contrary to Article 16(1) of Regulation 1/2003 but appeals were lodged by the defendants. The question then was whether in these circumstances, the Italian proceedings were 'related' to the proceedings brought in England and whether the English court should exercise its discretion to stay its proceedings.

15. In deciding to refuse a stay, Teare J in the High Court conducted a careful balancing exercise, considering the following three matters in particular: (i) the extent of the relatedness and the risk of mutually irreconcilable decisions; (ii) the stage reached in each set of proceedings; and (iii) the proximity of the courts to the subject matter of the case.[21]

16. The learned judge acknowledged that the Italian and English proceedings were related, that the Italian court was first seised and that the connections with England were slight. However, in favour of allowing the English proceedings to continue, Teare J noted that some of the defendants had sought to intervene in the Italian proceedings only after claims were brought against them in England, a decision on the merits in Italy was contingent on a successful appeal, the English proceedings would in any event continue against some of the defendants who had submitted to jurisdiction, the English court would probably have to quantify damage whereas this was not an issue in Italy and Italy could not be said to be the centre of gravity

---

19. See *Cooper Tire & Rubber Company v Shell Chemicals UK Limited* [2009] EWHC 2609 (Comm), [2009] UKCLR 1097, para 104.

20. This has been referred to as an 'Italian torpedo' action. The rationale for a defendant is to establish jurisdiction in a country perceived as more 'defendant friendly' (such as Italy) in order to prevent actions proceeding in what are perceived to be more 'plaintiff friendly' jurisdictions such as England.

21. See Case C–129/92 *Owens Bank Ltd. v Bracco* [1994] ECR I–117, opinion of Advocate General Lenz at para 76.

of the case.[22] In upholding this approach, the Court of Appeal held that the judge was not wrong to take into account the likely time it would take for a decision to be reached in Italy.[23] More generally, the Court approved of the judge's approach to weighing various factors. It was apparent that the Court of Appeal was cognisant of the motivations of Enichem in filing proceedings in Italy in order to 'torpedo' actions in jurisdictions such as England, and the motivations of the claimants in seeking to use subsidiaries of cartel participants as a tool to ground jurisdiction in England. The Court favoured a balanced approach to the various arguments, noting that it was

> not persuaded that the fact that the Italian court was first seised of Enichem's claim can operate as a sort of trump card or even as a primary factor where there was as much care and deliberation on the part of Enichem in starting proceedings for negative declaratory relief as there was in the Claimants' decision to make their substantive claim in England.[24]

17. Where a dispute involving the same cause of action or a related dispute is pending in the courts of a country that is not a contracting party of the Judgments Regulation, may the courts of a contracting state stay their own proceedings in favour of the jurisdiction of the court in the non-contracting state? Such a stay could be applied pursuant to a *forum non conveniens* rule of national law. In *Owusu*, the Court of Justice held that the Brussels Convention (the predecessor of the Judgments Regulation) precluded a court of a contracting state from declining the jurisdiction conferred on it by Article 2 (jurisdiction based on the defendant's domicile) on the ground that a court of a non-contracting state would be a more appropriate forum even if the jurisdiction of no other contracting state was in issue or the proceedings had no connecting factors to any other contracting state.[25] In *Goshawk*, the Irish High Court held that the doctrine of *lis alibi pendens* could not be invoked to stay proceedings which were mandated to be brought in Ireland under Article 2 of the Judgments Regulation pending the resolution of prior proceedings commenced in a non-Member State, in this case, before a court in the United States. Clarke J held that the Irish court was bound to exercise the jurisdiction conferred on it by Article 2, notwithstanding that the proceedings in the non-contracting state were first in time and involved the same subject matter and where the judgment from the US court would be recognised in Ireland.[26] This

---

22. *Cooper Tire & Rubber Company v Shell Chemicals UK Limited* [2009] EWHC 2609 (Comm), [2009] UKCLR 1097, paras 104–118.

23. *Cooper Tire & Rubber Company Europe Limited v Dow Deutschland Inc* [2010] EWCA Civ 864, paras 54–56.

24. *Cooper Tire & Rubber Company Europe Limited v Dow Deutschland Inc* [2010] EWCA Civ 864, para 53.

25. Case C–281/02 *Owusu v Jackson* [2005] ECR I–1383, [2005] QB 801, para 46.

26. *Goshawk Dedicated Ltd. v Life Receivables Ireland Ltd.* [2008] IEHC 90, [2008] 2 ILRM 460, para 6.18. The case was appealed to the Supreme Court, which decided to make a reference for a preliminary ruling to the Court of Justice (*Goshawk Dedicated Ltd. v Life Receivables Ireland Ltd.* [2009] IESC 7). However, the case was settled in the meantime.

interpretation of the Judgments Regulation has since been followed by the English High Court.[27]

Key Sources

Council Regulation (EC) No 44/2001 on jurisdiction and the recognition and enforcement of judgments in civil and commercial matters [2001] OJ L 12/1.

Case C–281/02 *Owusu v Jackson* [2005] ECR I–1383, [2005] QB 801.

UK

Cooper Tire & Rubber Company Europe Limited v Dow Deutschland Inc [2010] EWCA Civ 864.

---

27. *Catalyst Investment Group Ltd. v Lewinsohn* [2009] EWHC 1964 (Ch), [2010] Ch 218. But cf *JKN v JCN* [2010] EWHC 843 (Fam), [2010] Fam Law 796 (High Court not extending the *Owusu* principle to Council Regulation (EC) No 2201/2003 concerning jurisdiction and the recognition and enforcement of judgments in matrimonial matters and in matters of parental responsibility (Brussels II)).

108. WHAT LAW WILL APPLY TO A PRIVATE ANTITRUST ACTION?

Summary

- The Rome II Regulation determines the applicable law in actions based in tort and other non-contractual liability. Rome II contains special rules for antitrust actions.

- There is some uncertainty at present whether Rome II applies to events that occurred after 20 August 2007 or 11 January 2009. This question may be decided by the Court of Justice.

- The primary rule in Rome II is that the law of the country where the market is affected is the applicable law.

- Where markets in more than one country are affected and the action is filed in the country of the defendant's domicile, the claimant can opt to have that law apply, as long as the market in that country is 'directly and substantially' affected.

- Where there are multiple defendants, the claimant can make the same election for the lex fori, but only if there is a direct and substantial effect in that country vis-à-vis each of the defendants.

- The operation of the Rome II rules is not entirely clear and there may be future litigation as to its interpretation in the antitrust context.

- In actions based in contract, the Rome I Regulation applies from 17 December 2009. Accordingly, the law chosen by the parties applies. In the absence of choice, the applicable law depends on the nature of the contract. In cases relating to the provision of goods or services, the law of the country of habitual residence of the seller/provider of goods/services applies. In distributor/ franchise contracts, the law is determined by the habitual residence of the distributor/franchisee.

1. Private antitrust actions will usually lie in either contract or tort. Most claims, such as claims for damages arising out of agreements or practices that breach Article 101 or 102, will lie in tort.[28]

2. The Rome II Regulation ('Rome II')[29] sets out a new scheme for determining the applicable law in the context of non-contractual liability. Rome II includes specific

---

28. Even if there is a contract in place between the parties, an antitrust claim may well be tortious. For example, a customer may have a contract with a supplier which it sues for damages for breaching competition law by charging a cartel price. In *Provimi* such a claim was characterised as tortious so that a jurisdiction clause in the contract did not apply (*Provimi Limited v Roche Products Limited* [2003] EWHC 961 (Comm), [2003] UKCLR 493, para 127 (Aikens J)).

29. Regulation (EC) No 864/2007 on the law applicable to non-contractual obligations (Rome II) [2007] OJ L 199/40.

rules for competition law actions. Rome II applies to all EU Member States except Denmark.

From what point does Rome II apply?

3. Rome II applies to 'events giving rise to damage which occur after its entry into force'[30] and is stated to 'apply from 11 January 2009'.[31] There is no express provision in Rome II which defines when it enters into force. According to Article 297 TFEU, legislative acts come into force twenty days after their publication in the Official Journal. Rome II was published on 31 July 2007 and so came into force on 20 August 2007. Despite the provision that Rome II shall 'apply from 11 January 2009', there is a good argument that it in fact applies to events giving rise to damage that occurred after 20 August 2007. This was the interpretation preferred by Tomlinson J in the English High Court in *Bacon*, noting that this result, though arbitrary, was clear.[32] However in an unrelated case delivered three days earlier, Slade J also addressed the question of the temporal scope of Rome II and decided that a preliminary reference to the Court of Justice should be made on the interpretation of Articles 31 and 32 of Rome II.[33] There may therefore be a judgment of the Court of Justice on this question.

4. Whatever the exact temporal scope of Rome II, the Regulation might not apply to some private actions that are taken in the coming years. Many private actions arising out of cartel behaviour are taken years after the actual *events* giving rise to damage occurred. Where such events occurred before the coming into force of Rome II (whether that relevant date is ultimately decided to be 20 August 2007 or 11 January 2009), the private international law rules of the court seised of the claim would continue to apply in determining the applicable law.[34]

5. The choice of law could be complicated where it was found that the events giving rise to damage straddled the period both before and after the entry into force of

---

30. Rome II, Article 31.
31. Rome II, Article 32 (with the exception of Article 29, which is stated to apply from 11 July 2008).
32. *Bacon v Nacional Suiza Cia Seguros Y Reseguros SA* [2010] EWHC 2017 (QB). Tomlinson J explained (paras 43–54) that the concepts of 'entry into force' and 'application' were separate, a distinction well established in the creation of EU legislation and one supported by the legislative history.
33. *Homawoo v GMF Assurance SA* [2010] EWHC 1941 (QB).
34. However, there is also some doubt about this due to the fact that other language versions of Rome II indicate that the Regulation applies to 'damage' that occurs after the entry into force of Rome II rather than 'events giving rise to' that damage. See Segan, 'Applicable Law 'Shopping'? Rome II and Private Antitrust Enforcement in the EU' (2008) 7 *Competition Law Journal* 251, 258.

Rome II. It is not clear whether Rome II or national conflict of law rules apply in this situation.

What is the applicable law if pre-Rome II rules apply to the action?

6. If the action falls outside Rome II, national conflicts of law rules would determine the applicable law. In Ireland, the choice of law rule in tort is based on the *Grehan* case, in which Walsh J rejected the previous English 'double actionability' choice of law rule from *Phillips v Eyre* (that the tort must be actionable as a tort according to the *lex fori* and that the act must not have been 'justifiable' by the law of the place where it was done)[35] and suggested that Irish law should take a more flexible approach:

    > [So] far as choice of law in torts cases is concerned, the Irish courts should be sufficiently flexible to be capable of responding to the individual issues presented in each case and to the social and economic dimensions of applying any particular choice of law rule in the proceedings in question.[36]

7. This somewhat vague formulation has not been added to by the Irish courts with a more precise choice of law rule. In fact, the rule in *Phillips v Eyre* seems to have made a comeback in subsequent cases.[37] Where the common law choice of law rule does apply in Ireland, it cannot be said with certainty how it would operate in an antitrust action lying in tort and much will depend on the particular facts of the case. Were the action to be based in restitution, no particular choice of law rule applies and the *flexible* test laid down in *Grehan* would likely be applicable.

8. The choice of law rules applicable in England and Wales in respect of events giving rise to damage before Rome II are contained in the Private International Law (Miscellaneous Provisions) Act 1995 in respect of tort. The principal rule is that the applicable law is the law of the country in which the events constituting the tort occur.[38] Where those events occur in more than one country, the law of the country in which the most significant element or elements of the events constituting the tort occurred applies.[39] Again, it has not been established in English law that an antitrust action can lie in restitution[40] but if it did, such a claim

---

35. *Phillips v Eyre* (1870) 6 LR QB 1.

36. *Grehan v Medical Incorporated* [1986] IR 528, 541.

37. See *An Bord Trachtala v Waterford Foods Plc* [1994] FSR 516; *Intermetal Group Ltd v Worslade Trading Ltd* [1997] IEHC 231. See also Dicey, Morris & Collins, *The Conflict of Laws* (14th edn, 2006) para 35–011.

38. Private International Law (Miscellaneous Provisions) Act 1995, s 11(1).

39. Private International Law (Miscellaneous Provisions) Act 1995, s 11(2)(c).

40. See *Devenish Nutrition Ltd. v Sanofi-Aventis SA* [2008] EWCA Civ 1086, [2009] Ch 390. The reference in section 47A to a claim for 'damages or any other claim for a sum of money' with respect to claims before the CAT seemed to have left open the possibility of claims in restitution. While not accepted by the Court of Appeal in *Devenish*, this may not have been the last word on the point. See also Question 111, paras 34–38.

is governed by the proper law of the obligation in question. In obligations arising in connection with a contract, this is the law applicable to the contract and for non-contractual obligations, the proper law is the law of the country where the enrichment occurs.[41]

What is the scope of the applicable law derived from Rome II?

9.   The scope of the applicable law according to Rome II is set out in Article 15 and includes the basis and extent of liability, the grounds for exemption from liability, the nature and assessment of damage, injunctions,[42] measures to ensure compensation, persons entitled to compensation and rules on limitation and extinguishment of rights (which would include settlements).[43]

10.   Rome II provides a generic exception that it 'shall not apply to evidence and procedure',[44] which continue to be governed by the *lex fori*. However, this is subject to Article 15, which includes some rules that could be described as procedural, and Article 22, which includes 'rules which raise presumptions of law or determine the burden of proof'.

11.   The law that applies to an antitrust claim as chosen by Rome II will cover many important aspects of the claim. Given the disparities in national laws in the EU, the choice of law may be significant. For example, whereas Irish law specifically provides for exemplary damages as a remedy for breaches of competition law,[45] the concept of exemplary damages is anathema to many continental jurisdictions. The length of limitation periods is another important difference. Such differences provide an incentive for claimants to forum shop and such efforts may be aided by the uncertainties inherent in Rome II's choice of law rules for antitrust cases.

What is the applicable law under Rome II?

12.   The general rule, set out in Article 4(1), is that the applicable law is the law of the country in which damage occurs. However, there are specific rules for private antitrust actions, covering actions arising out of both EU law and national competition law.[46] These are not an exception to the Article 4(1) rule 'but rather a

---

41. See Dicey, Morris & Collins, *The Conflict of Laws* (14th edn, 2006) Rule 230, para 34R–001.

42. Injunctions are not specifically mentioned but should be covered by 'the measures which a court may take to prevent or terminate injury or damage or to ensure the provision of compensation'.

43. Rome II, Article 15.

44. Rome II, Article 1(3).

45. Competition Act 2002, s 14.

46. See Rome II, Recital 22.

clarification of it'.[47] The parties cannot agree to derogate from the choice of law as determined by these rules,[48] which are contained in Article 6(3):

(a) The law applicable to a non-contractual obligation arising out of a restriction of competition shall be the law of the country where the market is, or is likely to be, affected.

(b) When the market is, or is likely to be, affected in more than one country, the person seeking compensation for damage who sues in the court of the domicile of the defendant, may instead choose to base his or her claim on the law of the court seised, provided that the market in that Member State is amongst those directly and substantially affected by the restriction of competition out of which the non-contractual obligation on which the claim is based arises; where the claimant sues, in accordance with the applicable rules on jurisdiction, more than one defendant in that court, he or she can only choose to base his or her claim on the law of that court if the restriction of competition on which the claim against each of these defendants relies directly and substantially affects also the market in the Member State of that court.

13. Article 6(3) is to be distinguished from and should be considered mutually exclusive of Article 6(1),[49] which provides that the applicable law in an action arising out of an act of unfair competition is the law of the country 'where competitive relations or the collective interests of consumers are, or are likely to be, affected'. It is not clear, certainly as a matter of Irish law or English law, to what class of wrongs 'acts of unfair competition' are meant to apply (it appears that areas such as misleading advertising, disruption of deliveries by competitors, enticing a competitor's employees and passing off are covered[50]). However actions based on a breach of EU competition law or the competition law of a Member State are covered by Article 6(3) and not Article 6(1).[51]

14. Under Article 6(3)(a), when the market in only one Member State is affected, then the law of that State applies, whether or not that State is the forum for the dispute or the place of domicile of the defendant (or defendants). The claimant does not have the possibility to opt for another applicable law.

What if there are effects in more than one country?

15. When markets are affected in more than one country, the somewhat convoluted formula in Article 6(3)(b) may be applicable. This gives the option to a claimant who has sued in the courts of the defendant's domicile to elect the law of that State to apply to the claim. However, this is subject to the requirement that the market in

---

47. Rome II, Recital 21.
48. Rome II, Article 6(4). In other situations, the parties are free to choose the applicable law pursuant to Article 14.
49. See Dickinson, *The Rome II Regulation: The Law Applicable to Non-Contractual Obligations* (2008) paras 6.31–6.32.
50. See Commission, Proposal for a Regulation on the law applicable to non-contractual obligations (Rome II) COM (2003) 427 final (22 July 2003) 15.
51. See Rome II, Recital 23 and Article 6(3).

this State be 'directly and substantially affected' by the restriction of competition that forms the basis of the claim. There is no explanation in Rome II as to when the effect of an anti-competitive agreement or practice will be 'direct and substantial' and it is unclear exactly what this means. It appears that this extra requirement is aimed at limiting forum shopping.[52]

16. It is unclear from the scheme of Article 6(3) whether the concept of a 'market' is the economic concept used for market definition when applying Article 101 or 102. Under that concept of market definition, the relevant geographic market might be wider than national. Assume, for example, that the Commission has found a cartel in widgets and in the course of its decision establishing an infringement of Article 101, it has defined the relevant geographic market as EEA-wide in scope. Does this mean that the market in every EEA country is or is likely to be affected, even if widgets were sold in only two countries? Even if that position were accepted, it seems that for purposes of Article 6(3)(b), the market would not be 'directly and substantially' affected in a particular country if no widgets were sold there, notwithstanding that the relevant geographic market from an economic perspective, in which the cartel had effects, included that country. The better approach here may be to say that Article 6(3)(b) will only apply to countries where the cartel had a real and substantial impact through sales of the cartelised product, regardless of the definition of the relevant geographic market.

What if there are effects in several countries but not in the country of the defendant's domicile?

17. Assume the following scenario. C, an international company with operations in several locations, sues D1 in the courts of D1's domicile, Ireland. The anti-competitive practices upon which C bases its claim have had effects on C in the markets of Belgium, France and Spain. Which law applies to the claim?

18. The primary rule for this scenario is still the one in Article 6(3)(a). The law that applies is the law of the country where the market is affected. There is no requirement that there be a 'direct and substantial' effect. As markets in each of Belgium, France and Spain are affected, the law of any of these countries could apply to the claim. Article 6 does not say which law should be chosen. Article 6(3)(b) is not relevant because the market in D's country of domicile, Ireland, is not affected and so cannot be selected by the claimant.

19. A possible solution in this situation would be to choose the law of the country with which the claim is most closely connected. Article 4(3) provides, as an 'escape clause' from the general choice of law rule in Article 4(1), that where a tort is 'manifestly more closely connected' with a country other than that where the damage occurs, the law of that other country applies. While Article 6 does not refer to this escape clause, the Regulation's explanation that Article 6 is not an exception to Article 4(1) 'but rather a clarification of it'[53] might suggests that,

---

52. See Commission's Staff Working Paper accompanying the White Paper on Damages actions for breach of the EC antitrust rules, COM (2008) 165 final, para 8.
53. Rome II, Recital 22.

when applying Article 6(3), inspiration for solving the choice of law problem could be drawn from the Article 4(3) 'escape clause' notwithstanding the words of Article 4(3) referring to a country other than that where the damage occurs. Another solution would allow the claimant to elect which law should apply, even though Article 6(3)(a) is written in prescriptive terms (the applicable law 'shall be') and does not on its face provide for an election by the claimant (in contrast to Article 6(3)(b)). A further possibility might be to address liability and damage on a market-by-market basis applying, in the above example, three different systems of law.

What if there are multiple countries affected and multiple defendants?

20. The situation is further complicated if there are multiple defendants. Say that C sues D1, D2 and D3 in the courts of Ireland, the country in which D1 is domiciled.[54] Once more, the primary rule on the applicable law is that in Article 6(3)(a), *i.e.* the law of the country where the market is affected. As discussed above, there is uncertainty as to how this rule applies where markets in more than one country are affected, with one possible solution being the law of the country most closely connected with the claim.

21. Assume now that the market in Ireland, the country of D1's domicile and the chosen forum for the dispute, is one in which there is a direct and substantial effect because D1 sold products to C for delivery in Ireland. If C were suing D1 alone, it could elect Irish law under Article 6(3)(b) (although this election would be unnecessary if Irish law were selected applying Article 6(3)(a)). However, if C is also suing D2 and D3, it must show that the market in Ireland is directly and substantially affected vis-à-vis all three of the defendants before Irish law could be chosen.

22. It may be straightforward for C to establish this if each of D1, D2 and D3 have operations in Ireland or have sold products to C in Ireland. But one can imagine many cases involving multiple antitrust defendants where the anti-competitive effects caused by each of the defendants on an individual basis will arise in different countries. Assume that the defendants were party to an international cartel. D2 and D3 are German and Italian companies respectively, which supplied C with the cartelised products in France and Spain respectively. In this case, it could be argued that the restriction of competition on which C's claim against D2 and D3 relies did not have any effect in Ireland, let alone a direct or substantial effect. If that were correct, then C could not avail of Article 6(3)(b) and the court would have to decide the applicable law solely by reference to Article 6(3)(a). A possible answer to this difficulty might be that if D1, D2 and D3 are jointly liable, then it could be argued that the 'restriction of competition on which the claim against each of these defendants relies' is one and the same and so has direct and

---

54. The question whether C can sue each of D1, D2 and D3 in the Irish courts will be determined by application of the Judgments Regulation. See Question 107.

substantial effects vis-à-vis each defendant in Ireland, despite the fact that D2 and D3 have not made sales in Ireland.[55]

23.   The choice of law problems under Rome II could be even more complicated where multiple claimants brought an action (assuming this were allowed under the procedural rules of the forum). This situation is not provided for in the Regulation.

What is the applicable law for claims based in contract?

24.   The choice of law rules applicable to contractual claims are now contained in the Rome I Regulation,[56] which came into force on 17 December 2009 and replaces the Rome Convention 1980.[57] Rome I applies to all EU Member States except Denmark.

25.   The principal rule set out in Article 3 of Rome I is to give effect to the choice of law chosen by the parties in the contract.[58] If no choice of law has been made in the contract, the governing law is determined by Article 4. This provision sets out specific rules for eight particular types of contract, some of which might arise in the competition context. For example, a contract for the sale of goods/provision of services is governed by the law of the country where the seller/service provider has his habitual residence;[59] a franchise agreement is governed by the law of the country where the franchisee has his habitual residence;[60] and in a distribution contract, the applicable law is that of the country where the distributor is habitually resident.[61] If the contract does not come within one of the specific rules, it is governed by the law of the country 'where the party required to effect the characteristic performance of the contract has his habitual residence'.[62] This is subject to the rules that where it is clear that the contract is manifestly more closely connected with another country, the law of that country applies[63] and where the governing law cannot be determined with reference to characteristic performance or does not come within one of the eight listed types of contract, the governing law is that of the country with which the contract is most closely connected.[64]

---

55.   Under Article 6(1) of the Judgments Regulation, C would already have had to show that the claims against D2 and D3 were 'so closely connected' to the claim against D1 that it was expedient to hear them together.

56.   Regulation (EC) 593/2008 on the law applicable to contractual obligations (Rome I) [2008] OJ L177/6.

57.   Rome Convention on the Law Applicable to Contractual Obligations (1980).

58.   Rome I, Article 3(1).

59.   Rome I, Article 4.1(a), 4.1(b).

60.   Rome I, Article 4.1(e).

61.   Rome I, Article 4.1(f).

62.   Rome I, Article 4.2.

63.   Rome I, Article 4.3.

64.   Rome I, Article 4.4. There are specific rules in Rome I with respect to contracts of carriage, consumer contracts, insurance contracts and individual employment contracts set out in Articles 5, 6, 7 and 8 respectively.

26. The scope of the applicable law determined by Rome I includes the various ways of extinguishing obligations and the consequences of nullity.[65] This would cover an action for a declaration of nullity of the contract on the basis that it breached EU competition law.

27. In cases concerning contractual obligations, the rules in Ireland and England and Wales that applied before 17 December 2009 were those contained in the Rome Convention 1980.[66] Under the Rome Convention, contracts are governed by the law chosen by the parties.[67] In the absence of choice, the rule is that the contract shall be governed by the law of the country with which it is most closely connected.[68]

Key Sources

Regulation (EC) No 864/2007 on the law applicable to non-contractual obligations (Rome II) [2007] OJ L 199/40.

Regulation (EC) 593/2008 on the law applicable to contractual obligations (Rome I) [2008] OJ L177/6.

---

65. Rome I, Article 12.1(d), 12.1(e).
66. In Ireland, the legislative provision incorporating the Rome Convention is the Contractual Obligations (Applicable Law) Act 1991. The UK Act is the Contracts (Applicable Law) Act 1990.
67. Rome Convention 1980, Article 3.1.
68. Rome Convention 1980, Article 4.1.

109. WHO HAS STANDING TO BRING A PRIVATE ANTITRUST ACTION FOR BREACH OF EU COMPETITION LAW?

Summary

- As a matter of EU law, any person who suffers harm from a breach of EU competition law is entitled to sue for damages in the national courts.

- The national law that applies to the damages action determines precise rules surrounding standing, subject to the EU law principles of equivalence and effectiveness.

- EU law does not preclude national rules on remoteness of damage applying, again as long as the effectiveness and equivalence principles are satisfied.

- The cause of action for damages arising out of a breach of competition law in both Irish and English law is generally characterised as one for breach of statutory duty. As well as proving an infringement, for which a Commission decision can be relied on, causation and loss must be shown.

- It is not clear, either as a matter of Irish law or English law, if a third party can purchase a competition law claim and pursue it in the courts. Such an arrangement might breach the rules against maintenance and champerty in some circumstances.

- Third-party funding of competition litigation may also raise concerns about champerty but against this it can be argued that such arrangements facilitate access to justice.

- In England, it has been established that if the plaintiff loses, a third party funder of the claimant may be liable in costs up to the amount of funding provided.

1. The standing rules for private claims based on a breach of Article 101 or 102 depend on a combination of EU law and rules of the national law applicable to the action.

2. Articles 101 and 102 are both directly effective and confer rights on individuals.[69] The EU law principle of effectiveness requires that 'any individual can claim compensation for the harm suffered where there is a causal relationship between that harm and an agreement or practice' that infringes Article 101 or 102.[70] In the absence of detailed EU rules, it is for national law to determine the rules governing

---

69. See, e.g., Case 453/99 *Courage v Crehan* [2001] ECR I–6297, [2001] 5 CMLR 1058, para 23.
70. Cases C–295–298/04 *Manfredi v Lloyd Adriatico Assicurazioni SpA* [2006] ECR I–6619, [2006] 5 CMLR 980, para 61.

such damages actions, subject to the principles of equivalence (the rules must not be less favourable than those governing similar domestic actions) and effectiveness (the national rules must not render practically impossible or excessively difficult the exercise of rights conferred by EU law).[71]

3. The class of individuals who can claim compensation as a matter of EU law for harm suffered from anti-competitive agreements and practices will depend on the circumstances. In an abuse of dominance case, for example, a competitor as well as a customer may have a good argument that it suffered harm. In damages actions arising from cartels, those with standing would potentially include direct purchasers,[72] indirect purchasers[73] and possibly others (such as potential customers of the cartel who suffered loss as a result of purchasing less desirable goods).[74] However national rules on remoteness of damage may prevent some of these claimants from bringing a case (again, such national rules can apply as long as they are compatible with equivalence and effectiveness).

4. A party to an unlawful anti-competitive agreement may in principle sue for damages for loss arising from the agreement, although this right is circumscribed. In *Crehan*, the Court of Justice indicated that such a party could sue only where there was an inequality of bargaining power between the parties or the defendant bore 'significant responsibility' for the infringement. However, EU law did 'not preclude national law from denying a party who is found to bear significant responsibility for the distortion of competition the right to obtain damages from the other contracting party'.[75]

Which national law applies?

5. Subject then to the EU law principle that an individual who has suffered harm as a result of a breach of EU competition law has a right to claim compensation and subject to the twin EU law principles of equivalence and effectiveness, national law applies.

6. Under the Rome II Regulation, the standing rules that apply to a private antitrust action with an international dimension that is based on tort or other non-contractual liability (as actions for damages will be) are those of the applicable law as determined under Rome II, rather than the *lex fori*. The applicable law under

---

71. See Cases C–295–298/04 *Manfredi v Lloyd Adriatico Assicurazioni SpA* [2006] ECR I–6619, [2006] 5 CMLR 980, para 62.
72. However, direct purchasers may be faced with the passing-on defence. See Question 112.
73. The claimants in Case No: 1147/5/7/09 *Moy Park Limited v Evonik Degussa GmbH* (pending before the CAT) are indirect purchasers.
74. See also Beard, 'Damages in Competition Law Litigation' in Ward and Smith (eds) *Competition Litigation in the UK* (2005) paras 7.021–7.037.
75. Case 453/99 *Courage v Crehan* [2001] ECR I–6297, [2001] 5 CMLR 1058, para 31.

Rome II covers, among others, 'persons entitled to compensation for damage sustained personally'.[76]

Irish Law

7.   The standing rules for private competition law actions in Ireland are contained in section 14(1) of the Competition Act 2002:

> Any person who is aggrieved in consequence of any agreement, decision, concerted practice or abuse which is prohibited under *section 4* or *5* shall have a right of action under this subsection for relief...[77]

8.   Section 14(5) provides that relief by way of injunction or declaration and damages, including exemplary damages, are available. Section 14 relates to breaches of Irish competition law. Under the principle of equivalence, the procedures relating to actions in respect of breaches of Article 101 and 102 cannot be less favourable from the plaintiff's perspective.

9.   On the face of section 14, the class of claimants which is provided for, those 'aggrieved', goes at least as far as what is required by *Crehan* and *Manfredi* as a matter of EU law to give effect to a person's right to damages when harmed by a breach of Article 101 or 102. The term 'aggrieved' may indicate a wider class of claimant than just those who have suffered harm. However, it is only those who have been harmed who will be able to make out a cause of action for damages. Similarly, where an interlocutory injunction is sought, the applicant would have to show that he was suffering or would suffer harm that could not adequately be compensated by damages were an injunction not granted.[78] While the Irish courts tend to take a generous approach to *locus standi* in declaratory actions (especially where constitutional issues are raised) and even though the applicant does not have to show that other relief could be claimed,[79] a plaintiff would still likely have to show that it was suffering harm or that its interests would be adversely affected were the relief sought not granted.[80]

---

76. Regulation (EC) No 864/2007 on the law applicable to non-contractual obligations (Rome II) [2007] OJ L 199/40, Article 15(f). The application of Rome II is considered in Question 108, which also discusses the applicable law in contract cases, now determined by Regulation (EC) 593/2008 on the law applicable to contractual obligations (Rome I) [2008] OJ L177/6.
77. Competition Act 2002, s 14(1). The Competition Authority is granted a right of action under section 14(2) of the Competition Act 2002 in respect of agreements and practices breaching section 4 or 5 and Article 101 or 102 but it is limited to seeking injunctive or declaratory relief and cannot sue for damages.
78. *Campus Oil Limited v Minister for Industry and Energy (No 2)* [1983] IR 88, 105–106 (O'Higgins CJ).
79. Rules of the Superior Courts, Order 19, Rule 29.
80. See the judgment of Laffoy J in *Pierce (t/a Swords Memorials) v Dublin Cemetries Committee* [2006] IEHC 182, which contains a detailed discussion of *locus standi* in Irish law in the context of declaratory and injunctive relief for civil wrongs (this aspect of the High Court judgment was upheld on appeal in *Pierce (t/a Swords Memorials) v Dublin Cemeteries Committee* [2009] IESC 47, enabling the appellant to proceed with a substantive appeal against the High Court judgment).

10.   The right of action provided for in section 14 gives effect to the cause of action for a breach of competition law, the nature of which is generally understood to be breach of statutory duty. As the Irish government stated in its response to the Commission's 2008 White Paper on antitrust damages:

> From a very early stage it has been recognised and accepted by Irish practitioners, judges and litigants that a breach of Articles [101] and [102] gave rise to a remedy in, amongst other remedies, damages. A breach of [Article 101 or 102] is a breach of statutory duty which gives rise to a right of damages.[81]

11.   The 'any aggrieved person' formula may sound broader than 'any harmed person' but in order to make out the action for breach of statutory duty and establish a right to damages, the claimant will have to show that he suffered loss and that this was caused by the defendant's breach of competition law. In a stand-alone action, the breach of competition law will have to be proved, whereas if the action follows on from an infringement decision of the Commission, that decision can be relied on to establish the breach.[82]

12.   In the *Crehan* litigation, the English Court of Appeal considered the position in English law that a claim for breach of statutory duty can only be made out where the damage suffered is of a type that the statute was meant to protect. Even if this is also the position in Ireland with respect to a breach of statutory duty generally or could be read into section 14, the EU law requirement of effectiveness would require that this rule be disapplied in the case of antitrust claims alleging a breach of EU competition law, were it otherwise to prevent a plaintiff recovering damages.[83]

Can an action be brought for an effect on the value of a shareholding?

13.   A shareholder who claims that the value of his shareholding in a company has been reduced because of a breach of competition law cannot take a damages action for recovery of such loss. The rule against 'reflective loss' prevents a shareholder from recovering a loss which is merely reflective of the loss of the company rather than being a loss to the shareholder in his own right. In *O'Neill v Ryan,* the Supreme Court applied this rule in striking out a claim by a former shareholder for damages in respect of the reduction in the value of his shareholding as a result of alleged breaches of EU competition law by several defendants, which caused damage to the company. The Supreme Court held that the plaintiff had no right of personal action in respect of the resulting reduction in the value of his shareholding. EU law did not require that such an action be available to the former shareholder. If there had been a breach of Article 101 or 102, the party that

---

81.   Submission of the Department of Enterprise, Trade & Employment on behalf of Ireland, Response to the European Commission White Paper on Damages actions for breach of EC antitrust rules (31 July 2008) para 20.

82.   On the basis of Regulation 1/2003, Article 16.1, that the national court not take decisions 'running counter' to that of the Commission applying Articles 101 or 102 to the same agreement or practice.

83.   See below at paras 22–23.

suffered damage was the company and the company could itself institute proceedings claiming damages.[84]

May competition law claims be assigned?

14. There are already companies in the EU that are engaged in the business of 'purchasing' claims from potential claimants and then pursuing those claims in the courts or to settlement. One such firm is the Brussels-based Cartel Damages Claims.[85] Would such a company be allowed to pursue a claim in Ireland?

15. The Irish courts have not yet addressed the question whether a competition law claim can be assigned or sold by the person who has the *bona fide* claim. Order 15 of the Rules of the Superior Courts simply provides that all persons who have a 'right to relief' may join as plaintiffs.[86] The question for a court would be whether a person, whose right to relief derived from the assignment of a claim from another person who originally had the right to relief, would be entitled to act as a plaintiff under Order 15. In other jurisdictions, for example Germany, the courts have allowed 'professional' competition law claimants, who have bought a claim from an original plaintiff, to run a private action for their own benefit. In the *CDC* case, the German Supreme Court rejected a motion to dismiss claims brought by the Belgian company, Cartel Damages Claims, which had purchased the claims from victims of a cement cartel in Germany. The court confirmed that actions based on bundled claims assigned to one plaintiff were permissible in German law.[87]

16. Such arrangements might be questionable as a matter of Irish law because of the rules against maintenance and champerty. Maintenance arises where a third person financially assists a party to litigation although they do not themselves have an interest in the litigation or other motive recognised by law to justify their involvement. Champerty is an aggravated form of maintenance where assistance is given in return for the promise of a share in the proceeds of the litigation. In 1997, the Supreme Court confirmed that the rules against maintenance and champerty were still part of Irish law:

> It is clear from [the] authorities that the law relating to maintenance and champerty still exists in this State. A person who assists another to maintain or defend proceedings without having a *bona fide* interest independent of that other person in the prosecution or defence of those proceedings acts unlawfully and contrary to public policy and cannot enforce an agreement with that other person for any form of benefit,

---

84. *O'Neill v Ryan* [1993] ILRM 557, 574 (Blayney J). The rule against recovery of reflective loss was confirmed by the Supreme Court in *Madden v Anglo Irish Bank Corporation plc.* [2004] IESC 108, [2005] 1 ILRM 294.
85. See http://www.carteldamageclaims.com. The company describes claims based on antitrust infringements as 'a self-contained and marketable asset'.
86. Rules of the Superior Courts, Order 15, Rule 1.
87. *Cartel Damage Claims (CDC) v Dyckerhoff AG*, KZR 42/08, judgment of the German Supreme Court of 7 April 2009.

whether it be a share of the proceeds of the litigation or a promise of remuneration, such as money or a transfer of property if the claim is successfully defended.[88]

17.   The question of the legitimacy of assignments of competition law claims may be the subject of legislation at some point but in the meantime, it would be up to the courts to decide whether such arrangements are in line with public policy.

May a claimant obtain funding from a third party?

18.   Third party funding of competition litigation may also be viewed as problematic when set against the doctrines of maintenance and champerty. An important question will be the extent to which the funder is given influence over the running of the plaintiff's litigation.

19.   In support of third party funding, it can be argued that such arrangements should be permissible in order to give effect to the constitutional right to litigate[89] and that a ban on access to third party funding would 'deprive people of their constitutional right of access to the courts to litigate reasonably stateable claims'.[90] It can also be pointed out that the policy considerations underlying the medieval rules against maintenance and champerty – preventing officious intermeddling in litigation – should be seen in a modern light and reflect the development of society and the value to society of facilitating access to justice.[91] It remains to be seen if the Irish courts adopt a more flexible approach. In general though, Ireland has conservative positions on these issues, evidenced, for example, by the prohibition on solicitors and barristers entering into conditional fee agreements.[92]

20.   As discussed below in relation to English law, should third party funding be permissible, there is a question of the liability of a third party funder for costs of the action where the plaintiff loses.

English Law

21.   It has been accepted in a number of English cases that the nature of a competition law claim brought in the High Court, whether for breach of Articles 101 or 102, lies in the tort of breach of statutory duty. In *Garden Cottage* Lord Diplock indicated that a claimant affected by a breach of Article 102 could bring an action in domestic law for the tort of breach of statutory duty, giving rise to a remedy in

---

88.   *O'Keeffe v Scales* [1998] 1 IR 290, 295 (Lynch J).

89.   On this right, see Hogan and Whyte, *JM Kelly: The Irish Constitution* (4th edn, 2003) para 7.3.132 *et seq.*

90.   *O'Keeffe v Scales* [1998] 1 IR 290, 295 (Lynch J).

91.   For a recent discussion of the roles of maintenance and champerty in a modern legal system, see the judgment of the Hong Kong Court of Final Appeal in *Unruh v Seeberger* [2007] 2 HKLRD 414. See also the judgment of the Australian High Court in *Campbell Cash and Carry Pty Ltd* v *Fostif Pty Ltd* [2006] HCA 41.

92.   Solicitors (Amendment) Act 1994, s 68(2); Code of Conduct of the Bar of Ireland, Rule 12.1(e).

damages.[93] It is established that actions based on Article 101 are also categorised in English law as claims for breach of statutory duty.[94] Breach of statutory duty is not necessarily the only cause of action for a competition law wrong and it may be possible to base a claim in, for example, the tort of unlawful interference with trade or in restitution.[95] There are also the specific procedures for follow-on claims in the CAT under sections 47A and 47B of the Competition Act 1998.

What are the standing rules for breach of statutory duty?

22. Assuming that the claim is one for breach of statutory duty, the English law requirements to make out the claim based on a breach of Article 101 or 102 are subject to the principles of equivalence and effectiveness. In one of the *Crehan* judgments, it was found that adherence to the strict English law requirements of making out a breach of statutory duty would have rendered ineffective the EU law right to claim for damages on foot of a breach of Article 101. Under English law, the claimant is required to establish not only that a duty is owed to him, but also that it is a duty in respect of the kind of loss he has suffered.[96] The well-known circumstances of this case involved a publican, Mr. Crehan, whose lease contained a beer-tie requiring him to purchase beer from a particular brewery. In defence to a claim against him for unpaid purchases, he claimed that the beer-tie was in breach of Article 101 and that he suffered loss as a result.

23. It was argued that since the only unlawful distortion of competition occurred at the distribution level, loss at a retail level, which was the only loss that Mr. Crehan had claimed, was not loss against which he was protected by Article 101. The cause of action for breach of statutory duty therefore could not be made out because the loss suffered did not fall within the scope of the duty. While this contention was correct as a matter of English law, had it operated in this case, it would have rendered Mr. Crehan's EU law right to rely on a breach of Article 101 ineffective. The English law rule was therefore not applied so that Mr. Crehan could proceed with his claim.[97]

24. In making out the claim of breach of statutory duty, it must also be shown that the statutory duty was breached and that this breach caused the claimant's loss. The further initial requirement in English law, to show that the breach of statutory duty

---

93. *Garden Cottage Foods Ltd v Milk Marketing Board* [1984] 1 AC 130, especially at 141 and 144.
94. See, e.g., *Crehan v Inntrepreneur Pub Co CPC* [2004] EWCA Civ 637, [2004] UKCLR 1500, para 156 (reversed by the House of Lords on other grounds, *Crehan v Inntrepreneur Pub Co (CPC)* [2006] UKHL 38, [2007] 1 AC 333).
95. See Brealey and Green (eds), *Competition Litigation: UK Practice and Procedure* (2010) para 1.22.
96. See *South Australia Asset Management Corporation v York Montague Ltd.* [1997] AC 191, 211.
97. See *Crehan v Inntrepreneur Pub Co CPC* [2004] EWCA Civ 637, [2004] UKCLR 1500, para 167.

gives rise to an action in private law, is already well established in cases relying on Article 101 or 102, from *Garden Cottage* and subsequent cases.

25.   Section 58A implicitly recognises the right of a claimant to bring follow-on actions before the courts based on decisions by the OFT or CAT that the Chapter I or II prohibition or Article 101 or 102 have been infringed, stating that the court is bound by such a decision.[98] The Act does not provide that infringement decisions of the Commission are binding on the court but this is clear from Regulation 1/2003, which requires that a national court ruling on an agreement, decision or practice under Article 101 or 102 which has already been the subject of a Commission decision, cannot take a decision 'running counter' to the Commission's decision.[99]

26.   The Competition Act 1998 does not contain any provision confirming the right of a claimant to take a private action for damages for a breach of UK competition law that has not already been the subject of an infringement decision. However, it is generally accepted that such a standalone action can be taken.[100] That such actions can be taken also follows from section 60 of the Act, which seeks to ensure that questions of UK competition law arising in the UK are treated in a manner consistent with the treatment of corresponding questions arising in EU law in relation to competition within the EU.

What are the standing rules under sections 47A and 47B of the Competition Act 1998?

27.   The CAT has a special jurisdiction to hear follow-on claims for breach of competition law under Section 47A and 47B of the Competition Act 1998. The right of an individual claimant to take a case before the CAT under section 47A does not affect his right to bring a claim before the High Court.[101] The claimant has a choice of suing in the CAT or the High Court. Section 47B establishes a special right of action before the CAT for consumer groups.

28.   The right of action in a follow-on claim before the CAT under section 47A of the Competition Act 1998 is linked to the right of action before the High Court:

>   This section applies to—

>   (a) any claim for damages, or

>   (b) any other claim for a sum of money,

---

98.   Competition Act 1998, s 58A(1), (2).
99.   Regulation 1/2003, Article 16(1). This position had already been established by the Court of Justice in Case C–344/98 *Masterfoods Ltd. v HB Ice Cream Ltd.* [2000] ECR I–11369, [2001] 4 CMLR 449.
100. See, e.g., *Emerald Supplies Ltd v British Airways plc* [2009] EWHC 741 (Ch), [2009] UKCLR 801, para 1. This action involves a damages claim based on a breach of section 2 of the Competition Act 1998 as well as Article 101. It was filed before the Commission adopted any decision on the underlying alleged anti-competitive agreements and practices.
101. Competition Act 1998, s 47A(10).

which a person who has suffered loss or damage as a result of the infringement of a relevant prohibition may make in civil proceedings brought in any part of the United Kingdom.[102]

29.   The linking of the section 47A right of action to normal civil proceedings indicates that a claimant would have to establish the elements of a breach of statutory duty, in particular causation and loss. The fact of a breach of Article 101 or 102 or the Chapter I or II prohibition does not have to be made out as there will already be an infringement decision of the Commission, the OFT or the CAT (on an appeal from the OFT) establishing the infringement and the claimant can rely on this finding in the follow-on claim before the CAT.[103]

30.   The right of action under section 47A does not affect the right to bring any other proceedings in respect of the claim.[104] If a claim under section 47A were taken in the CAT but the CAT found that it did not have jurisdiction for example, the claimant would not be prevented from bringing the claim in the High Court.[105]

31.   Section 47B provides for a limited kind of class action to be taken on behalf of consumers. It enables 'specified bodies' to bring an action before the CAT on behalf of individuals who received or sought to receive goods or services as a consumer and who have a claim to which section 47A applies. Section 47B is discussed in further detail in Question 110.

Can an action be brought for an effect on the value of a shareholding?

32.   The English law rule, which prevents a claimant from recovering for 'reflective loss', would prevent a claim by a shareholder seeking damages for the loss caused to his shareholding caused by a breach of competition law that adversely affected the company.[106] The issue was briefly considered by Ferris J in *Intergraph*, in which there was a counterclaim for loss caused to a company from a breach of competition law by a competitor. Ferris J cited the approach of the Irish Supreme Court in *O'Neill v Ryan* with approval (although, for other reasons, refused to strike out the counterclaim).[107]

Can a plaintiff assign a competition law claim or obtain third party funding?

33.   While the Criminal Law Act 1967 abolished the crimes and torts of champerty and maintenance, assignments of competition law claims or third party funding arrangements could be found contrary to champerty under the common law.[108]

---

102. Competition Act 1998, s 47A(1).
103. Competition Act 1998, s 47A(6).
104. Competition Act 1998, s 47A(10).
105. Section 47A claims are discussed further in Question 116.
106. For a recent statement of the rule against recovery of reflective loss, see *Johnson v Gore Wood & Co.* [2002] 2 AC 1.
107. *Intergraph Corporation v Solid Systems CAD Services Limited* [1995] ECC 53. One of the factors for refusing to strike out the counterclaim was that it might have led to an appeal or a reference to the Court of Justice.
108. Criminal Law Act 1967, s 14(2).

However, there are indications that the English courts are prepared to take a modern and flexible approach to these doctrines. The principles involved were recently discussed by Coulson J as follows:

    (a)   the mere fact that litigation services have been provided in return for a promise in the share of the proceeds is not by itself sufficient to justify that promise being held to be unenforceable;

    (b)   in considering whether an agreement is unlawful on grounds of maintenance or champerty, the question is whether the agreement has a tendency to corrupt public justice and that such a question requires the closest attention to the nature and surrounding circumstance of a particular agreement;

    (c)   the modern authorities demonstrated a flexible approach where courts have generally declined to hold that an agreement under which a party provided assistance with litigation in return for a share of the proceeds was unenforceable;

    (d)   the rules against champerty, so far as they have survived, are primarily concerned with the protection of the integrity of the litigation process in this jurisdiction.[109]

34.   This modern and flexible approach suggests that the chances of assignments or third party funding arrangements being found to be champertous are low.

35.   The assignment of actions is relatively common in the context of liquidation, enabling a liquidator to sell causes of action to assignees in return for a share of the recovered spoils without the risk of the assignment being treated as one in maintenance or champerty. The practice has also been extending into other areas.

36.   The English courts have recognised the legitimacy of third party funding of litigation and the important role it can play in facilitating access to justice.[110] Section 58B of the Courts and Legal Services Act 1990 would put third party funding arrangements on a statutory footing, however the relevant provisions have not yet been enacted.[111] In the meantime, whether a funding agreement is deemed champertous will likely come down to its provisions and in particular, the extent to which it provides the funder with influence over the running of the litigation.

37.   A third-party funder may be liable to a costs order being made against it if the party which it funds loses the case. It was held in *Arkin* that where the third-party funding agreement is non-champertous, the third party's potential liability in costs is limited to the amount of the funding it provided.[112] However, where the arrangement is champertous, the Court of Appeal indicated that the funder was

---

109. *London and Regional (St George's Court) Limited v Ministry of Defence* [2008] EWHC 526 (TCC), 121 ConLR 26, para 103 (references omitted) (upheld on appeal, *London and Regional (St George's Court) Ltd v Ministry of Defence* [2008] EWCA Civ 1212, 121 ConLR 26).

110. See, e.g., *Hamilton v Al Fayed (No 2)* [2002] EWCA Civ 665, [2003] QB 1175.

111. Courts and Legal Services Act 1990, inserted by the Access to Justice Act 1999, s 28.

112. *Arkin v Borchard Lines Ltd* [2005] EWCA Civ 655, [2005] 1 WLR 3055, para 41.

likely to render himself liable for the opposing party's costs without limit should the claim fail.[113]

Key Sources

Case 453/99 *Courage v Crehan* [2001] ECR I–6297, [2001] 5 CMLR 1058.

Cases C–295–298/04 *Manfredi v Lloyd Adriatico Assicurazioni SpA* [2006] ECR I–6619, [2006] 5 CMLR 980.

Ireland

Competition Act 2002, Section 14.

O'Neill v Ryan [1993] ILRM 557.

UK

Competition Act 1998, ss 47A, 47B, 58A.

Arkin v Borchard Lines Ltd [2005] EWCA Civ 655, [2005] 1 WLR 3055.

---

113. *Arkin v Borchard Lines Ltd* [2005] EWCA Civ 655, [2005] 1 WLR 3055, para 40.

110. CAN MULTIPLE CLAIMANTS JOIN TOGETHER IN ONE ACTION FOR BREACH OF EU COMPETITION LAW?[114]

Summary

- There are no specific EU rules on antitrust class actions or multiple claimant actions.

- The national law applicable to the action will determine the permissibility of multiple claimants suing together.

UK

- There is a special jurisdiction under Section 47B of the Competition Act 1998 for representative actions to be brought before the CAT on behalf of consumers.

- Representative claims can be brought before the courts if claimants have the same interest. To date, the courts have not allowed this facility to be used for class actions.

- The Group Litigation Order case management tool may also be a way for multiple claimants to join together, however this procedure falls well short of a class action.

Ireland

- A limited form of representative action is provided for in Order 15 Rule 9 RSC but it is unclear if competition law actions or any actions for damages can avail of this procedure.

1. This question is not addressed by EU law and so national law applies, subject to the minimum requirements laid down by the Court of Justice in cases such as *Crehan* and *Manfredi* and subject to the principles of equivalence and effectiveness. In its White Paper on private antitrust actions, the Commission had proposed that rules be adopted to facilitate both representative actions to be taken by particular entities and opt-in collective actions[115] and related proposals were included in draft directives produced by the Commission in 2009. However none of the Commission's proposals have resulted in legislation.

UK

2. There are a number of ways in which multiple claimants can take a competition law action and the English courts have also considered whether it is permissible for a class of persons to sue for a breach of competition law.

---

114. See also the discussion in Question 109, paras 14–17, 33–35 about whether multiple claims can be assigned to one plaintiff.

115. Commission's White Paper on Damages actions for breach of the EC antitrust rules, COM (2008) 165 final (2 April 2008) para 2.1.

What claims can be brought under section 47B?

3.   Section 47B of the Competition Act 1998 provides for a limited form of follow-on class action to be taken on behalf of consumers before the CAT. The consumer claims included in the proceedings must all relate to the same infringement of competition law.

4.   The action provided for is a limited form of 'opt-in' class action, capable of being brought only on behalf of consumers who explicitly opt in to the claim. This is in contrast to the 'opt-out' system in place in the United States where a representative brings a claim on behalf of a specified class of plaintiff, with all members of the class included unless they opt out of the action. To date, the only entity approved as a specified body entitled to bring a case under section 47B is the Consumers' Association, also known as *Which?*[116]

5.   So far, one case has been taken under section 47B, which was a damages claim on behalf of 130 consumers who had purchased replica Manchester United and England football shirts.[117] The claim followed on from a decision of the OFT that the makers of sports replica kits had breached the Chapter I prohibition through price-fixing arrangements. The case was settled before trial. It was reported that consumers who joined the claim would receive £20 each, with consumers who did not join able to claim £5 or £10 provided they could show proof of purchase.[118] Although a successful outcome for the claimants, the fact that only 130 consumers, out of an estimated one million who bought football shirts, opted in to the action, illustrates the difficulties associated with using section 47B. *Which?* has reportedly indicated that it does not intend to bring any similar actions because of the up-front costs of encouraging consumers to join the action.[119] The consumer class claim might be strengthened if a rule were adopted leaving it to the court to decide whether in the particular circumstances of a case an opt-in or opt-out model would be appropriate.[120]

Can representative claims be brought under CPR 19.6?

6.   Provision for representative claims before the High Court is made in CPR 19.6. Under this rule, where more than one person has the same interest in a claim, one or more claimants may sue as representatives of any other persons who have that interest.[121] Unless the court otherwise directs, any judgment or order given in a representative claim is binding on all persons represented in the claim but it may

---

116. SI 2005 No. 2365 The Specified Body (Consumer Claims) Order 2005.
117. Case No: 1078/7/9/07 *The Consumers Association v JJB Sports PLC*.
118. See 'Thousands of football fans win 'rip-off' replica shirt refunds', *The Times* (10 January 2008).
119. See Department for Business Innovation and Skills Consultation, *The Role and Powers of the Consumer Advocate* (December 2009) para 68.
120. See Department for Business Innovation and Skills Consultation, *The Role and Powers of the Consumer Advocate* (December 2009) para 69–70.
121. CPR 19.6(1).

only be enforced by or against a person who is not a party to the claim with the permission of the court.[122]

7.   The use of CPR 19.6 in the context of an antitrust action was considered by the High Court in *Emerald v BA*[123] in which the claimants brought a representative action for damages for breach of Article 101 and the Chapter I prohibition. The claim arose out of alleged price fixing and market sharing by British Airways and other airlines in air freight services, a matter which was the subject of a Commission investigation when the action was launched. The action was brought against BA by direct and indirect air cargo customers both on their own behalf and on behalf of all other direct or indirect purchasers of air freight services the prices for which were inflated by the anti-competitive agreements or practices.

8.   The High Court granted BA's application to strike out the representative element of the claim. Based on the wording of CPR 19.6, it was a necessary requirement that all members of the class sought to be represented by the claimants had the same interest at the time the claim was launched. It was insufficient that this identity of interest would exist when judgment was issued. The requirement of the same interest, as stated by Lord MacNaghten in the *Duke of Bedford* meant that all must have 'a common interest and a common grievance' and 'the relief sought [must] in its nature [be] beneficial to all' of them.[124]

9.   The key problem with the class at issue was that the criteria for inclusion in it depended on the outcome of the action itself. The claim referred to 'direct or indirect purchasers of air freight services the prices for which were inflated by the agreements or concerted practices'. This formula referred to allegations the claimants would have to prove in the action. It was therefore impossible to say of any given person that he was a member of the class at the time the claim form was issued.

10.   In relation to the second of the *Duke of Bedford* criteria, Morritt C accepted the argument that even if the criteria for inclusion in the class were sufficient, the relief sought was not equally beneficial to each. This was partly because some members of the class would have passed on the overcharge and there would have been an inevitable conflict between different members of the class. For example, a particular indirect purchaser's claim might have depended on showing that a particular direct purchaser had passed on any overcharge and so had not suffered loss. The Chancellor noted that it was not for the English courts to make policy decisions about the treatment of the passing-on defence[125] 'by stretching the use of r 19.6 to accommodate cases such as this' and that this was a matter for

---

122. CPR 19.6(4).
123. *Emerald Supplies Ltd v British Airways plc* [2009] EWHC 741 (Ch), [2009] UKCLR 801 (on appeal to the Court of Appeal).
124. *Duke of Bedford v Ellis* [1901] AC 1 (HL) at 8.
125. As the US Supreme Court did in deciding in *Hanover Shoe Inc. v United Shoe Machinery Corp.* 392 US 481 (1968) that the passing-on defence was not available in federal antitrust actions. See Question 112.

Parliament.[126] A suggested amendment to exclude claimants for damage which had been passed on would not solve these difficulties and might increase them as such an exclusion would make it impossible to ascertain the members of the class even when judgment in the action had been given. This would necessitate further proceedings before it could be established which claimants were entitled to recover damages from BA.

11. The decision in *Emerald v BA*, which is understood to be on appeal to the Court of Appeal, makes the utility of CPR 19.6 somewhat doubtful as a means of bringing antitrust class actions.[127]

Can Group Litigation Orders under CPR 19.11 be used for a private antitrust action?

12. CPR 19.11 provides for a Group Litigation Order ('GLO') which is essentially a managerial tool that enables the court to gather similar cases together before a single judge who can make appropriate case management decisions best suited to the particular litigation. The court may make a GLO 'where there are or are likely to be a number of claims giving rise to the GLO issues'.[128] This requirement of showing common issues is easier to satisfy than that of the 'same interest' under CPR 19.6. The GLO will contain directions about the establishment of a group register on which the claims to be managed under the GLO will be entered. Proceedings must already have been issued before a particular claim will be entered on the register. Where a judgment or order is given in relation to a claim on the group register, the judgment is binding on parties to all other claims that are on the group register. Like the representative action, the GLO works on an opt-in basis.

13. GLOs were introduced in 2000[129] but have not yet been used in an antitrust case. However, in *Emerald v BA*, the High Court suggested that a GLO rather than CPR 19.6 could have been used, indicating that 'the avoidance of multiple actions based on the same or similar facts can equally well be achieved by a Group Litigation Order' and that the various potential claimants 'are more conveniently accommodated under that procedure.'[130]

---

126. *Emerald Supplies Ltd v British Airways plc* [2009] EWHC 741 (Ch), [2009] UKCLR 801, para 37.
127. On the plus side for potential claimants, Chancellor Morritt noted, at para 30, that there was no limit on the number of persons in the class to be represented and the mere fact that the relevant class was both numerous and geographically widespread was not itself an objection to a representative action. See also for discussion of this case and representative actions in the UK, O'Donoghue, 'Recent Developments in Antitrust Class Actions in the United Kingdom' *The CPI Antitrust Journal* (August 2010) 1.
128. CPR 19.11(1).
129. Since 2000, some 72 GLOs have been issued. See http://www.hmcourts-service.gov.uk/cms/150.htm.
130. *Emerald Supplies Ltd v British Airways plc* [2009] EWHC 741 (Ch), [2009] UKCLR 801, para 38 (Morritt C).

Ireland

14. Irish law contains limited rules facilitating multiple claimant cases. Order 15 Rule 9 of the Rules of the Superior Courts provides as follows:

> Where there are numerous persons having the same interest in one cause of action or matter, one or more of such persons may sue or be sued, or may be authorised by the court to defend, in such cause or matter, on behalf, or for the benefit, of all persons so interested.

15. Order 15 Rule 9 works on an opt-in basis and the court will not grant a representative order if there is no evidence that the members of the group have authorised the named plaintiff to take the action on their behalf.[131] A relatively positive attitude to representative actions is discernible from the judgment of Murphy J in *Greene*. Here, five plaintiffs challenged compensation schemes introduced by the Minister for Agriculture and pleaded that they brought the proceedings on behalf of themselves and 1,390 listed farmers, who had contributed to a fighting fund. Although in *obiter dictum*, Murphy J concluded that it might be inferred that the farmers had authorised the proceedings to be brought on their behalf, notwithstanding their belief that they would not render themselves liable for additional costs as a result of being *listed* in the action, when they were not named plaintiffs.[132]

16. There are a number of potential difficulties in using the Order 15 Rule 9 procedure to bring a representative claim in the antitrust context. First, it would have to be shown that all the members of the group had the 'same interest'. As discussed above,[133] the claimants in *Emerald v BA* failed on this point in the English High Court and the analysis in that case (which is on appeal) would be persuasive authority in a similar action before the Irish courts. Second, there is uncertainty whether the representative action can be used in tort claims and in particular whether the court's jurisdiction in such actions is limited to awarding injunctive or declaratory relief rather than damages. This position is based on a traditional view of representative actions, which, it could be argued, is outdated. However it may require a rule change or a new interpretation by the Irish courts before representative actions based in tort can be taken.[134]

17. In addition to representative claims, Order 15 Rule 1 may be used to join several plaintiffs in one action. It provides as follows:

> All persons may be joined in one action as plaintiffs in whom any right to relief in respect of or arising out of the same transaction or series of transactions is alleged to exist, whether jointly, severally, or in the alternative, where, if such persons brought separate actions, any common question of law or fact would arise.

---

131. See *Madigan v Attorney General* [1986] ILRM 136, 148 (O'Hanlon J discussing what was then Order 19, Rule 29 of the Rules of the Superior Courts).
132. *Greene v Minister for Agriculture* [1990] 2 IR 17, 28–29.
133. See paras 8–10 above.
134. See Law Reform Commission, *Consultation Paper on Multi-Party Litigation (Class Actions)* (LRC CP 25–2003) (July 2003) paras 1.09–1.17.

18.   This provision could be useful in an antitrust action where, for example, several claimants sought to argue that the same defendants had breached Article 101 by engaging in a cartel. This would raise common issues, in particular whether there had been an infringement in the first place. The application of Order 15 Rule 1 is limited to cases where the plaintiffs have already instituted their own actions and it does not provide any basis for taking a representative or class action.

Key Sources

UK

Competition Act 1998, s 47B.

CPR 19.6, 19.11.

Emerald Supplies Ltd v British Airways plc [2009] EWHC 741 (Ch), [2009] UKCLR 801.

Ireland

Rules of the Superior Courts, Order 15, Rules 1, 9.

---

111. WHAT TYPE OF MONETARY COMPENSATION IS AVAILABLE IN ACTIONS ALLEGING A BREACH OF EU COMPETITION LAW?

Summary

- EU law requires that persons harmed by a breach of Article 101 or 102 be entitled to sue for damages in the national courts for actual loss and loss of profit, plus interest.

- Beyond this minimum requirement, the scope of remedies available is a matter for national law. The principles of equivalence and effectiveness must be respected.

Ireland

- As well as compensatory damages, a claimant may seek exemplary damages for a breach of competition law.

- Restitutionary remedies may be available but there is little guidance on this question.

UK

- A claimant may seek compensatory damages. It is unclear to what extent exemplary damages are available. It has been held that in a follow-on action where the defendant has already been fined by the Commission, the availability of exemplary damages would breach the principle against double punishment.

- There is doubt as to whether restitutionary awards are available. They have been denied in one case where compensatory damages were the more appropriate remedy.

---

1. The remedies available in a private antitrust action alleging a breach of Article 101 or 102 are determined by the applicable national law subject to minimum requirements of EU law. The minimum EU law requirements are that Member States must provide at least compensatory damages for actual loss and loss of profit, plus interest, as a remedy for a claimant who has suffered loss as a result of a breach of Article 101 or 102. National law may provide for additional remedies, including exemplary damages. The Court of Justice stated in *Manfredi*:

> [It] follows from the principle of effectiveness and the right of any individual to seek compensation for loss caused by a contract or by conduct liable to restrict or distort competition that injured persons must be able to seek compensation not only for actual loss (*damnum emergens*) but also for loss of profit (*lucrum cessans*) plus interest.[135]

---

135. Cases C–295–298/04 *Manfredi v Lloyd Adriatico Assicurazioni SpA* [2006] ECR I–6619, [2006] 5 CMLR 980, para 100.

2.   The parameters of actual loss may be an issue of contention in private actions. In a damages action arising from a straightforward price fixing cartel, for example, it could be argued that actual loss is not limited to the overcharge on purchased goods that was caused by the cartel. Actual loss could also extend to items such as loss of sales caused by the fact that the inflated price was passed on by the direct purchaser to its own customers or loss of sales volumes of other products as a result of brand damage.[136]

3.   EU law 'does not prevent national courts from taking steps to ensure that the protection of the rights guaranteed by Community law does not entail the unjust enrichment of those who enjoy them'.[137] This leaves open the possibility for national law to provide for the passing-on defence, *i.e.* a defence that the claimant has passed on any loss arising from the anti-competitive agreement or conduct to others such as its own customers.[138]

4.   EU law does not preclude national law from denying one party to an agreement who is found to bear significant responsibility for the distortion of competition the right to obtain damages from the other contracting party. This is based on the principle that a litigant should not profit from his own unlawful conduct.[139] This rule could operate, for example, to prevent a member of a cartel obtaining damages from other members of the cartel for lost sales as a result of the inflated cartel price.

5.   The EU law principle of equivalence plays an important role in determining what remedies are available at the national level. The principle requires that national rules applicable to private actions based on a breach of EU competition law are not less favourable than those governing similar actions based on breaches of national competition law.[140] Where a specific remedy is provided for in actions based on a breach of national competition law, which is equivalent to Article 101 or 102, the same remedy should be available in actions invoking Article 101 or 102.

6.   EU law does not prevent the award of damages above the compensatory level, whether punitive damages, exemplary damages, double damages etc. as there is no absolute principle of EU law 'that prevents victims of a competition law infringement from being economically better off after a successful damages claim than the situation they would be in 'but for' the infringement'.[141] The only EU

---

136. These two items of loss were claimed in *Emerald Supplies Ltd v British Airways plc* [2009] EWHC 741 (Ch), [2009] UKCLR 801, para 2.

137. Case C–453/99 *Courage Ltd v Crehan* [2001] ECR I–6297, [2001] 5 CMLR 1058, para 30.

138. See Question 112.

139. See Case C–453/99 *Courage Ltd v Crehan* [2001] ECR I–6297, [2001] 5 CMLR 1058, para 31.

140. See Case C–453/99 *Courage Ltd v Crehan* [2001] ECR I–6297, [2001] 5 CMLR 1058, para 29.

141. Commission's Staff Working Paper accompanying the White Paper on Damages actions for breach of the EC antitrust rules, COM (2008) 165 final, 58; see also Cases C–295–298/04 *Manfredi v Lloyd Adriatico Assicurazioni SpA* [2006] ECR I–6619, [2006] 5 CMLR 980, para 92.

jurisdictions in which the remedy of exemplary damages is known are Ireland, England and Wales, Northern Ireland and Cyprus. In some Member States, such as Germany, an award of exemplary or punitive damages is considered to be contrary to public policy.[142]

Ireland

7.   Section 14 of the Competition Act 2002 sets out the private law remedies that are available in respect of a breach of sections 4 and 5, the Irish law equivalents of Articles 101 and 102:

> (1) Any person who is aggrieved in consequence of any agreement, decision, concerted practice or abuse which is prohibited under *section 4* or *5* shall have a right of action under this subsection for relief against either or both of the following, namely—
>
> (a) any undertaking which is or has at any material time been a party to such an agreement, decision or concerted practice or has done any act that constituted such an abuse,
>
> (b) any director, manager or other officer of such an undertaking, or a person who purported to act in any such capacity, who authorised or consented to, as the case may be, the entry by the undertaking into, or the implementation by it of, the agreement or decision, the engaging by it in the concerted practice or the doing by it of the act that constituted the abuse.[143]
>
> (5) Without prejudice to *subsection (7)*,[144] the following reliefs, or any of them, may be granted to the plaintiff in an action under *subsection (1)*:
>
> (a) relief by way of injunction or declaration,
>
> (b) damages, including exemplary damages.[145]

8.   Additionally in the case of an abuse of dominance contrary to section 5, a potentially significant remedy, empowering the court to break up a dominant position, is provided for:

> ... the Court may, either at its own instance or on the application of the Authority, by order either—
>
> (a) require the dominant position to be discontinued unless conditions specified in the order are complied with, or

---

142. See *Devenish Nutrition Ltd. v Sanofi-Aventis SA* [2007] EWHC 2394 (Ch), [2009] Ch 390, para 33. Exemplary damages are not known in Scotland. On the availability of exemplary damages in Northern Ireland, see, e.g., *Clinton v Chief Constable of the Royal Ulster Constabulary* [1999] NI 215.

143. Competition Act 2002, s 14(1).

144. This enables the court, in an abuse of dominance case, to require the dominant position to be discontinued unless conditions in the court's order are complied with or require an adjustment of the dominant position, by a sale of assets or as otherwise may be ordered. See Competition Act 2002, s 14(7).

145. Competition Act 2002, s 14(5).

      (b) require the adjustment of the dominant position, in a manner and within a period specified in the order, by a sale of assets or otherwise as the Court may specify.[146]

9.   Section 14 does not cover actions based on breaches of the EU antitrust rules but pursuant to the principle of equivalence, the remedies provided for in section 14 would also be available in actions based on a breach of Article 101 or 102. Section 14 provides claimants in such cases with potential remedies above the minimum provided for in *Manfredi*. Actions for damages can be taken not only against infringing undertakings but also against individual directors, managers and officers. This right could be significant where, for example, the undertaking that infringed Article 101 or 102 is insolvent but the individual directors, managers or officers who were involved in the infringement have assets. There is also a specific right to sue for exemplary damages although, as discussed below, this does not mean that exemplary damages will be granted as a matter of course.

10.   Compensatory damages are included as a remedy in section 14, which provides for 'damages'. In any event, compensatory damages are available as a matter of EU law for breaches of Article 101 or 102. Based on *Manfredi*, the award must be capable of including damages for loss of profits and interest.[147]

11.   To date, there has been no reported case in which damages have been awarded for breach of the EU competition rules in Ireland.[148] Two recent private actions involving claims for damages arising from the Commission's decision finding that Irish Sugar had abused its dominant position in the Irish sugar market[149] were both settled.[150]

12.   The only case in which antitrust damages have been awarded involved a breach of Irish competition law. In *Donovan v ESB*,[151] the plaintiffs were awarded damages for loss suffered as a result of the defendant's abuse of a dominant position contrary to section 5 of the Competition Act 1991. It was reported that the amount of damages paid amounted to approximately IR£360,000 (€457,000) with an additional sum of a similar amount paid to the plaintiffs in respect of costs.[152]

---

146. Competition Act 2002, s 14(7). An order under s 14(7) was initially sought by the Competition Authority in the High Court in the *Credit Unions* case but this submission was not advanced as the litigation progressed (see *Competition Authority v O'Regan* [2004] IEHC 330).

147. The award of compensatory damages in Ireland typically includes interest.

148. Claims for damages based on a breach of Article 101 and/or 102 were unsuccessful in *Chanelle Veterinary Limited v Pfizer (Ireland) Limited* [1999] 1 IR 365.

149. Case IV/34.621 *Irish Sugar plc* [1997] OJ L258/1.

150. These cases were *Gem Pack Foods v Irish Sugar plc* and *ASI v Greencore plc*. (1996/8200P)

151. *Donovan v Electricity Supply Board* [1994] 2 IR 305 (appeal dismissed, *Donovan v Electricity Supply Board* [1997] 3 IR 573).

152. See *Competition*, Vol. 12(5), 105.

13. There is little in the way of judicial guidance on the quantification of damages in antitrust cases in Ireland.[153] It is up to the plaintiff to prove causation and loss on the balance of probabilities.[154] The 'but for' test is generally used by the Irish courts in determining causation.[155] This asks whether the plaintiff would have suffered loss had it not been for the breach. It is open to a defendant to argue that the causal connection between the breach of competition law and the loss caused is too remote to give rise to liability.[156]

Are exemplary damages available?

14. It would seem that the *possibility* of exemplary damages must be available in actions for breach of the EU antitrust rules in Ireland. In *Manfredi*, the Court of Justice stated that

> in accordance with the principle of equivalence, it must be possible to award particular damages, such as exemplary or punitive damages, pursuant to actions founded on the Community competition rules, if such damages may be awarded pursuant to similar actions founded on domestic law.[157]

15. As exemplary damages are provided for in respect of actions based on a breach of Irish competition law,[158] pursuant to the principle of equivalence, they ought also be available in actions for breach of EU competition law.

16. As a general matter of Irish law, exemplary damages are a discretionary remedy:

> The Court has a wide discretion in determining the circumstances in which a separate award for exemplary damages ought or ought not to be made.[159]

17. The significance of the fact that exemplary damages are specifically provided for in section 14 of the Competition Act 2002 is unclear but it would be surprising if the award of exemplary damages in a particular case were not still at the discretion

---

153. See the Oxera-led Study produced for the European Commission, 'Quantifying antitrust damages – Towards non-binding guidance for courts' (December 2009). For a discussion of quantification of antitrust damages in the UK, which would also be relevant to Ireland, see Brealey and Green (eds), *Competition Litigation: UK Practice and Procedure* (2010) Ch 17.

154. See, e.g., *Masterfoods Ltd t/a Mars Ireland v H.B. Ice Cream Ltd* [1993] ILRM 145, 183 (Keane J) (the standard of proof was found to be the standard normally applicable in civil proceedings, proof on the balance of probabilities; while this finding was made in respect of making out a breach of Article 101 or 102, the same standard should apply to showing causation and loss).

155. See the Irish report annexed to the Ashurt Study on the conditions of claims for damages in case of infringement of EC competition rules (2004) 14 and case law cited (available on the Commission's website).

156. On the requirement that loss be foreseeable, see e.g., *William Egan & Sons Ltd v John Sisk & Sons Ltd* [1986] ILRM 283.

157. Cases C–295–298/04 *Manfredi v Lloyd Adriatico Assicurazioni SpA* [2006] ECR I–6619, [2006] 5 CMLR 980, para 93.

158. Competition Act 2002, s 14(5)(b).

159. *Shortt v Commissioner of An Garda Síochána* [2007] IESC 9, [2007] 4 IR 587, para 114 (Murray CJ).

of the court. The Irish courts have acknowledged that exemplary damages can serve several different purposes including a punitive purpose, deterrence and to mark the court's disapproval of a defendant's outrageous conduct.[160]

18.   If an award of exemplary damages were to be countenanced by a court in an antitrust case, it is difficult to speculate at what level they might be assessed and this would depend on the circumstances. The facts of some antitrust cases, particularly those involving cartels, may well persuade a court to award exemplary damages to punish a defendant, deter potential violations of competition law and mark the court's disapproval of cartel conduct. However, other factors may have to be weighed, such as the punitive and deterrent effect of any related criminal prosecutions.

19.   Most awards of exemplary damages by the Irish courts have been modest, reflecting a small fraction of the compensatory damages awarded. However there have been cases where the amount of exemplary damages was larger than the related compensatory award. In one defamation case, involving misbehaviour by a company director that was considered to be quite beyond the bounds of normal civilised behaviour and far outside any accepted commercial relationships, exemplary damages amounting to five times the compensatory damages were awarded.[161] While the amount of exemplary damages was reduced on appeal, the final figure still amounted to twice the compensatory award.[162]

20.   The English High Court has held that exemplary damages are not available in follow-on actions where the defendants have already been fined for the antitrust infringements that form the basis of the claim. This decision, which would have persuasive effect in Ireland,[163] is discussed below at paras 32–33.

21.   Even if exemplary damages were not available in a follow-on action against the undertaking that had been fined, it may be open to a claimant in an appropriate case to argue that exemplary damages should be awarded against a director, manager or officer who was involved in the infringement and may have acted in a particularly egregious manner. Section 14(1)(b) of the Competition Act 2002 provides a right of action against such defendants. It can be argued that in this case the EU law principle of *non bis in idem* does not apply. As the undertaking, rather than the individual director or officer, would have been fined in any Commission proceedings, it could be argued that one of the conditions required for the

---

160. *Shortt v Commissioner of An Garda Síochána* [2007] IESC 9, [2007] 4 IR 587, paras 108, 109.

161. *Crofter Properties Ltd. v Genport Ltd.* [2002] 4 IR 73 (McCracken J).

162. *Crofter Properties Ltd. v Genport Ltd. (No 2)* [2005] IESC 20, [2005] 4 IR 28. The award of exemplary damages was reduced from IR£250,000 to IR£100,000; compensatory damages were left at IR£50,000.

163. In *Shortt v Commissioner of An Garda Síochána* [2007] IESC 9, [2007] 4 IR 587, the Supreme Court held that 'exemplary damages cannot be characterised as involving double compensation' (Murray CJ, para 116). However, the only other award in issue was compensatory damages. The context would be different in a case that involved a Commission fine and where the EU law principle against double punishment was relevant.

operation of the *non bis in idem* principle – unity of offender – would not be met.[164]

Are restitutionary remedies available?

22. The Irish courts have not yet addressed the availability of a restitutionary remedy in an antitrust case. However, the Competition Act 2002 envisages that restitution might be available in respect of an agreement, decision or concerted practice which contravenes section 4 and which creates or, but for the Act, would have created legal relations between the parties thereto. In such a case, the court 'may make such order as to recovery, restitution or otherwise between the parties'.[165] The principle of equivalence suggests that the possibility of a restitutionary remedy also applies in the case of an agreement or practice in breach of Article 101.

23. However, this provision would only apply in limited circumstances, *i.e.* where one party to an agreement that breaches section 4 seeks to recover from the other party to the agreement. There is no suggestion in the Act that restitution is available in say, a claim arising out of a cartel or abuse of dominance, where the claimant was not a party to the impugned agreement or practice. On the contrary, section 14(5), which sets out the right of action for breaches of competition law, provides only for relief by way of injunction, declaration, damages and exemplary damages.

UK

24. The English law rules on remedies are subject to the minimum EU law requirement that compensatory damages be available in an action for breach of EU competition law. It has been recognised that the cause of action in English law in such actions is one for breach of statutory duty and that compensatory damages are available as a remedy. This was held to be so in *Garden Cottage* in respect of a breach of Article 102[166] and confirmed in respect of a breach of Article 101 in *Crehan*.[167] The basis of the statutory duty is section 2(1) of the European Communities Act 1972, which provides a statutory basis for the recognition of directly effective EU law rights and duties in the English legal system. Breach of statutory duty is not necessarily the only cause of action for a competition law

---

164. Three cumulative conditions are necessary for the *non bis in idem* principle to operate: identity of the facts, the unity of offender and the unity of legal interest protected (see Cases C–204/00P etc *Aalborg Portland A/S v Commission* [2004] ECR I–123, [2005] 4 CMLR 2514 (*Cement*) para 338).

165. Competition Act 2002, s 4(7).

166. See *Garden Cottage Foods Ltd v Milk Marketing Board* [1984] 1 AC 130, especially at 141 and 144.

167. *Crehan v Inntrepreneur Pub Co CPC* [2004] EWCA Civ 637, [2004] UKCLR 1500, para 156 (reversed by the House of Lords on other grounds, *Crehan v Inntrepreneur Pub Co (CPC)* [2006] UKHL 38, [2007] 1 AC 333).

wrong and it may be possible to base a claim in, for example, the tort of unlawful interference with trade or in restitution.[168]

25.   The Competition Act 1998 specifically recognises the right to sue for damages for breach of competition law. Section 58A refers to proceedings before a court in which 'damages or any other sum of money is claimed' and Section 47A provides for 'any claim for damages ... or any other claim for a sum of money' in follow-on actions before the CAT.

26.   To date, there has only been one reported English case in which a claimant recovered damages for breach of EU competition law and that decision was overturned on appeal. This was the long-running beer-tie case involving Mr. Crehan. The basic action was for damages for loss caused to Mr. Crehan as a result of the beer-tie to which he was subject, which, it was claimed, was in breach of Article 101. The High Court found that there was no breach of Article 101 but that had there been a breach, damages would have been assessed at £1,311,500. On appeal, the Court of Appeal held that there was a breach of Article 101 but it entered a lower assessment of damages at £131,336. That decision was reversed by the House of Lords, which held that the High Court was entitled to find that there was no breach of Article 101 and was not bound by the duty of sincere cooperation to give effect to a Commission decision on the beer-ties.[169]

27.   In *Genzyme*, the CAT made an interim award of damages to a claimant in a follow-on action arising out of the breach of the Chapter II prohibition in the Competition Act 1998. In making the interim award, the CAT estimated what it thought would be the likely award after trial.[170] The case ultimately settled.

28.   A number of other antitrust actions seeking damages (and, in some cases, other remedies) have been taken both before the courts and the CAT. None of these have yet resulted in an award of damages but settlements were reached in some of the actions, which would have involved a payment to the claimants.[171]

29.   Given the limited number of cases to date, there is little in the way of detailed guidance as to how the courts would quantify damages in an antitrust case. The claimant must show causation (generally on the 'but for' standard) and loss. It is open to the defendant to argue that the causal connection between the infringement and the loss is too remote to give rise to liability. Other defences that could be expected to be raised in antitrust cases include arguments that the claimant's loss was caused by other factors or by the way in which it ran its own business. The

---

168. See Brealey and Green (eds), *Competition Litigation: UK Practice and Procedure* (2010) para 1.22.

169. This aspect of the case is discussed in Question 121.

170. *Healthcare at Home Limited v Genzyme Limited* [2006] CAT 29, [2007] Comp AR 474, para 70.

171. For example, the *Provimi* case settled following judgment in the High Court in *Provimi Limited v Roche Products Limited* [2003] EWHC 961 (Comm), [2003] UKCLR 493. Details of actions taken before the CAT under section 47A and 47B of the Competition Act 1998 are set out in Question 116.

method of quantification will depend on the type of antitrust injury at issue. In a claim brought by a customer of a cartel, the court will likely look to establish the amount of the overcharge relative to the competitive price that would have been charged had the cartel not been in existence. In claims arising out of exclusionary infringements brought by a competitor of a dominant firm, it may be more appropriate to assess damages taking into account the loss of profit suffered by the claimant because of its loss of opportunity caused by the infringement.[172]

Are exemplary damages available?

30. Exemplary damages are available in English law in limited circumstances. There are three categories of cases in which exemplary damages can be awarded, as set out in *Rookes v Barnard*: (i) of oppressive, arbitrary or unconstitutional acts by government servants; (ii) where the defendant's conduct had been calculated by him to make a profit for himself which might well exceed the compensation payable to the plaintiff; and (iii) where expressly authorised by statute.[173] These categories are not necessarily exhaustive of the situations in which exemplary damages are available.[174]

31. The second *Rookes v Barnard* category is of most potential relevance in an antitrust case and in *Devenish*, it was common ground that the pleaded facts, which involved a cartel, came within this second category.[175] There are no statutory provisions in the UK with respect to exemplary damages in antitrust cases.[176] To date, exemplary damages have not been awarded in an antitrust case before the English courts or the CAT.

32. It was held by the High Court in *Devenish* that exemplary damages are not available in follow-on cases where the defendant had already received a fine from the Commission. First, as a matter of EU law, it was found that the award of exemplary damages for a breach of Article 101 or 102 in this situation would

---

172. For a more detailed discussion of quantification of damages in the UK, see Brealey and Green (eds), *Competition Litigation: UK Practice and Procedure* (2010) Ch 17. See also, the Oxera-led Study produced for the European Commission, 'Quantifying antitrust damages – Towards non-binding guidance for courts' (December 2009).

173. *Rookes v Barnard* [1964] AC 1129, 1226–1227.

174. *Kuddus v Chief Constable of Leceistershire* [2001] UKHL 29, [2002] 2 AC 122, para 66 (Lord Nicholls suggesting that the first category could be extended to include oppressive acts by private parties).

175. *Devenish Nutrition Ltd. v Sanofi-Aventis SA* [2007] EWHC 2394 (Ch), [2009] Ch 390, para 43.

176. For discussion, see Jones, *Private Enforcement of Antitrust Law in the EU, UK and USA* (1999) Ch 19. See also the discussion of treble damages in US law, noting that the failure to provide for pre-judgment interest may leave plaintiffs less than fully compensated in US actions. See also Randall, 'Does De-Trebling Sacrifice Recoverability of Antitrust Awards?' (2006) 23 *Yale Journal of Regulation* 311.

breach the principle of double punishment, *non bis in idem*.[177] Lewison J found that the aim of exemplary damages would be the same as the fines that had been imposed on the defendants by the Commission – punishment and deterrence – and so their award would breach the *non bis in idem* principle.[178]

33. Second, if a fine has already been imposed by the Commission, it can be argued that the Commission has decided on the adequacy of punitive measures and that for a national court to impose exemplary damages in this case would 'run counter' to the Commission decision and be in breach of Article 16 of Regulation 1/2003. This argument seems to be based on a rather expansive interpretation of Article 16 but it was accepted by the High Court in *Devenish*.[179] The exemplary damages point was not raised in the appeal in *Devenish*, which was dismissed.[180]

Are restitutionary awards available?

34. May a claimant seek a restitutionary award in an antitrust action? In particular, in a claim by a purchaser against a supplier which had been party to a cartel, may the purchaser claim an account of the supplier's profits as a remedy? This could be a useful remedy for a claimant who was unable to prove the loss which was caused to him as a result of anti-competitive agreements or conduct. Other forms of restitutionary claim that may be relevant in an antitrust context include claims for money paid by mistake (for example, where a cartel resulted in higher prices being charged) or actions for the return of money paid under a contract that was found to be in breach of competition law.

35. The reference to a claim 'for a sum of money' in section 47A of the Competition Act 1998 led the former President of the CAT to ask whether, other than damages,

---

177. The EU law principle of *non bis in idem* would not seem relevant in standalone actions based on a breach of Article 101 or 102 in a national court. However, the argument has been made that awards above the compensatory level would be incompatible with EU law in standalone actions because the consequence of such an award would be that the Commission could not issue fines for an infringement that had already been the subject of the decision of a national court without breaching the *non bis in idem* principle (see Wils, 'The Relationship between Public Antitrust Enforcement and Private Actions for Damages' (2009) 32(1) *World Competition* 3). Were such an argument accepted, it would seem to nullify the Court of Justice finding in *Manfredi* that EU law does not preclude the award of exemplary damages.

178. See *Devenish Nutrition Ltd. v Sanofi-Aventis SA* [2007] EWHC 2394 (Ch), [2009] Ch 390, paras 40–52.

179. See *Devenish Nutrition Ltd. v Sanofi-Aventis SA* [2007] EWHC 2394 (Ch), [2009] Ch 390, paras 53–55. The first sentence of Article 16(1) of Regulation 1/2003 states: 'When national courts rule on agreements, decisions or practices under Article [101] or Article [102] of the Treaty which are already the subject of a Commission decision, they cannot take decisions running counter to the decision adopted by the Commission'.

180. Cf the finding in the Court of Appeal that the award of restitutionary damages was not precluded by EU law on the basis of Article 16 of Regulation 1/2003 and that such a finding would be contrary to the Court of Justice decision in *Manfredi* (*Devenish Nutrition Ltd. v Sanofi-Aventis SA* [2008] EWCA Civ 1086, [2009] Ch 390, para 155). The same could be said of this second argument that was accepted in the High Court in respect of exemplary damages.

claims based on a breach of competition law 'can be looked at in some other way, for example, as some kind of claim that could perhaps go under the general heading of 'Unjust Enrichment' – unjust enrichment in the sense of a defendant who has made an undue or 'secret' profit, as a result of breaking the law'.[181] The availability of a restitutionary remedy for a breach of competition law was considered more fully in *Devenish*.[182]

36. It was held by the High Court and confirmed by the Court of Appeal in *Devenish* that a restitutionary award was not available. The case involved an action by direct and indirect purchasers of vitamins that followed on from the Commission's decision in the *Vitamins* cartel. The High Court addressed itself to the preliminary issue as to whether the claimants were entitled to any of exemplary damages, restitutionary damages and/or an account of profits, holding that only compensatory damages were available.[183] The claimants appealed the decision on the availability of a restitutionary award, arguing that the defendants should be required to disgorge the profits they had made from the cartel.

37. Dismissing that appeal, the Court of Appeal held that the exceptional circumstances that would have to be present before a restitutionary award could be made were not evident, a restitutionary award was only available where necessary to do justice and it was not an appropriate remedy in principle where damages were an adequate remedy. A key factor in the case was that the loss to the purchasers could be worked out – Devenish's economic expert was able to calculate the overcharge caused by the cartel.[184] Compensatory damages were therefore an adequate remedy.[185] The fact that damages might be difficult to prove did not justify an account of profits from the defendants. The Court also seemed uneasy at the prospect of a restitutionary award (or a damages award) being granted where the claimant had passed on the overcharge to its own customers, suggesting that the passing-on defence would likely be available in English law.[186]

38. *Devenish* was not an appropriate case for a restitutionary award, as compensatory damages were adequate to address the losses caused to the claimants by the cartel.

---

181. Case nos. 1028/5/7/04 & 1029/5/7/04 *BCL Old Co Ltd v Aventis* and *Deans Foods v Roche Products Limited*, hearing of 26 July 2004 (transcript at 2) (Sir Christopher Bellamy).
182. The classification of different types of restitutionary remedies has not always been clear-cut in the cases and the distinction between compensatory damages and a restitutionary award is sometimes difficult, such as when a defendant is required to pay the claimant a fair price in respect of his wrongful conduct. For a comprehensive discussion, see Brealey and Green (eds), *Competition Litigation: UK Practice and Procedure* (2010) para 16.33 *et seq.*
183. *Devenish Nutrition Ltd. v Sanofi-Aventis SA* [2007] EWHC 2394 (Ch), [2009] Ch 390.
184. *Devenish Nutrition Ltd. v Sanofi-Aventis SA* [2008] EWCA Civ 1086, [2009] Ch 390, paras 157–158.
185. See also *Attorney General v Blake* [2001] 1 AC 268, 285 (Lord Nicholls stating that it was only in exceptional cases, where damages and other remedies were inadequate, that an account of profits could be ordered for a breach of contract).
186. See *Devenish Nutrition Ltd. v Sanofi-Aventis SA* [2008] EWCA Civ 1086, [2009] Ch 390, para 147 (Longmore LJ) and para 114 (Arden LJ). See on the passing-on defence, Question 112.

The case leaves open the possibility that a restitutionary remedy could be available in an appropriate future case, for example, where it is established that an anti-competitive agreement or conduct caused loss but the economic evidence is not available or too complex to work out the quantum of that loss.

Key Sources

Cases C–295–298/04 *Manfredi v Lloyd Adriatico Assicurazioni SpA* [2006] ECR I–6619, [2006] 5 CMLR 980.

Case C–453/99 *Courage Ltd v Crehan* [2001] ECR I–6297, [2001] 5 CMLR 1058.

Ireland

Competition Act 2002, s 14.

UK

Competition Act 1998, s 47A, 58A.

Devenish Nutrition Ltd. v Sanofi-Aventis SA [2007] EWHC 2394 (Ch), [2008] EWCA Civ 1086, [2009] Ch 390.

---

112. IS THE 'PASSING ON' DEFENCE AVAILABLE?

Summary

- EU law does not preclude the passing on defence applying but this is a question for national law.

- It is likely that both Irish and English law would recognise the defence.

1.   The 'passing on' defence enables the defendant to an antitrust action to plead that the claimant has passed on any loss arising from the anti-competitive agreement or conduct to others such as its own customers. An example would be where a retailer sues a wholesaler for damages on the basis that the products sold by the wholesaler to the retailer were the subject of a cartel. The retailer was therefore overcharged for the goods and claims the difference between what it paid and what it would have paid had the cartel not been in existence. However, the retailer was able to pass on this overcharge to its own customers. Were the passing on defence available, the wholesaler could rely on the fact that the overcharge was passed on. In this case, only the indirect purchasers, the retailer's customers, would be able to claim for the loss caused by the cartel.

2.   Whether or not the passing on defence is available is significant for private antitrust actions. In many cases, it may be unrealistic to expect that indirect purchasers will act as claimants. They may be widely dispersed, they may have no interest in taking a case, they may have difficulty in proving a loss etc.[187] A direct purchaser would usually be in a better position to sue. If the direct purchaser has passed on the loss and the passing on defence is unavailable, there is a good chance that no action will be taken at all.

3.   The availability of the passing on defence therefore raises policy issues. If private actions are to be effective, there is a good argument to say that the passing on defence should not be available and that direct purchasers should be able to claim even where they have passed on an overcharge. As a concomitant, a rule could be adopted that indirect purchasers were not entitled to sue. This rule would prevent the possibility of a defendant having to pay twice.

4.   In the United States, the Supreme Court held in *Hanover Shoe* that the passing on defence was not available in private actions based on a breach of the federal antitrust laws. This conclusion was partly driven by the concern that were such a defence available, defendants would frequently seek to establish its applicability and antitrust proceedings would be greatly complicated.[188] The Supreme Court later established in *Illinois Brick* the concomitant, that indirect purchasers were not entitled to sue. Keeping in mind 'the longstanding policy of encouraging vigorous

---

187. However, claims have been filed by indirect purchasers. See, e.g., Case No: 1147/5/7/09 *Moy Park Limited v Evonik Degussa GmbH* (pending before the CAT) which involves claims by indirect purchasers from the *Methionine* cartel.

188. *Hanover Shoe Inc. v United Shoe Machinery Corp.* 392 US 481 (1968), in particular at 493.

private enforcement of the antitrust laws' the Court was again concerned that were a different rule to apply and indirect purchasers allowed to sue, this would greatly complicate private actions and 'could seriously impair this important weapon of antitrust enforcement'.[189] While this is the position in US federal antitrust law, the laws of many US states allow both direct and indirect purchasers to sue for antitrust damages. The Californian Supreme Court has held that the passing on defence is not generally available in this situation, despite the risks of potential windfalls for direct purchasers who had passed on the overcharge and the possibility of double recovery against plaintiffs.[190]

5.   The availability of the passing on defence in private antitrust actions is, at present, not governed by EU law and like many aspects of private actions, is a matter for national law. A national law that allowed the passing on defence would not be contrary to EU law as EU law 'does not prevent national courts from taking steps to ensure that the protection of the rights guaranteed by Community law does not entail the unjust enrichment of those who enjoy them'.[191] Were the defence not available, then a claimant who had passed on the overcharge caused by an anti-competitive agreement or practice to its own customers, could benefit from a windfall were it allowed to obtain damages. In its White Paper on private actions, the Commission expressed approval of the passing on defence, arguing that a denial of the defence could result in the unjust enrichment of direct purchaser plaintiffs while leaving defendants exposed to multiple payments for their infringement.[192] Recognising the difficulties that indirect purchasers would face in bringing a claim, the Commission also proposed that such claimants be entitled to rely on a rebuttable presumption that the overcharge was passed on to them in its entirety.[193]

6.   While EU law does not preclude national law from applying the passing on defence, a rule that denied the right of indirect purchasers to sue would likely fall foul of EU law, which guarantees the right of any person harmed by a breach of Article 101 or 102 to bring an action for damages.[194]

---

189. *Illinois Brick Co v Illinois* 431 US 720, 745 (1977).

190. See *Clayworth v Pfizer, Inc.* No S166435, 2010 WL 2721021 (California Supreme Court, 12 July 2010). The Supreme Court found that exceptions to the rule prohibiting the passing on defence could be developed to deal with double recovery situations.

191. See Case C–453/99 *Courage Ltd v Crehan* [2001] ECR I–6297, [2001] 5 CMLR 1058, para 30. The legitimacy of the passing on defence has been recognised in tax cases; see Case 199/82 *Amministrazione delle Finanze dello Stato v SpA San Giorgio* [1983] ECR 3595, [1985] 2 CMLR 658.

192. Commission's White Paper on Damages actions for breach of the EC antitrust rules, COM (2008) 165 final (2 April 2008) para 2.6.

193. Commission's White Paper on Damages actions for breach of the EC antitrust rules, COM (2008) 165 final (2 April 2008) para 2.6.

194. See Cases C–295–298/04 *Manfredi v Lloyd Adriatico Assicurazioni SpA* [2006] ECR I–6619, [2006] 5 CMLR 980, para 95 (referring to 'the right of any individual to seek compensation for loss caused by a contract or by conduct liable to restrict or distort competition').

Ireland

7. The Competition Act 2002 does not address the passing on defence and the Irish courts have not yet decided whether it is available in an antitrust case. Given that the Irish courts would assess damages in an antitrust case on the basis of harm suffered, there is a good chance that the defence would be recognised as a means of showing that the claimant had not in fact suffered the loss claimed.

UK

8. There are no legislative provisions on the passing on defence and the courts have not expressly decided whether the defence is available. However, the tentative indications from recent cases are that the passing on defence would likely be recognised. In *Emerald*, the High Court indicated that it was not open to the English courts to adopt the position as the US Supreme Court had in *Hanover Shoe* that the passing on defence was not available in antitrust actions. This was a matter better addressed by Parliament.[195]

9. In *Devenish*, although the availability of the passing-on defence was not a matter that had to be decided, the Court of Appeal was prepared to countenance its availability in an antitrust damages action. Longmore LJ, discussing whether an account of profits was available as a remedy for breach of competition law, implied that a passing on defence would be available:

    > No one suggests that, to the extent the claimant has in fact suffered a loss because it has paid too high a price which it has been unable (for any reason) to pass on to its own purchasers, that loss cannot be recovered. If, however, the claimant has in fact passed the excessive price on to its purchasers and not absorbed the excess price itself, there is no very obvious reason why the profit made by the defendants (albeit undeserved and wrongful) should be transferred to the claimant without the claimant being obliged to transfer it down the line to those who have actually suffered the loss. Neither the law of restitution nor the law of damages is in the business of transferring monetary gains from one undeserving recipient to another undeserving recipient even if the former has acted illegally while the latter has not.[196]

10. Similarly, Arden LJ reached her conclusions about the unavailability of a restitutionary award 'on the basis that the passing on defence would apply to a claim for an account of profits as it does to a claim for damages.'[197]

Key Sources

Hanover Shoe Inc. v United Shoe Machinery Corp. 392 US 481 (1968).

Illinois Brick Co v Illinois 431 US 720 (1977).

---

195. *Emerald Supplies Ltd v British Airways plc* [2009] EWHC 741 (Ch), [2009] UKCLR 801, para 37 (the case is on appeal to the Court of Appeal).
196. *Devenish Nutrition Ltd. v Sanofi-Aventis SA* [2008] EWCA Civ 1086, [2009] Ch 390, para 147. For a critical note of this reasoning and other aspects of the case, see Sheehan, 'Competition Law Meets Restitution for Wrongs', (2009) 125 *Law Quarterly Review* 222.
197. *Devenish Nutrition Ltd. v Sanofi-Aventis SA* [2008] EWCA Civ 1086, [2009] Ch 390, para 114.

113. Is injunctive and declaratory relief available as a remedy in actions alleging a breach of EU competition law?

Summary

- The availability of injunctive and declaratory relief is a question of national law, subject to the EU law principles of equivalence and effectiveness.

Ireland and UK

- Injunctions are available as a remedy. Prohibitory or mandatory injunctions may be awarded.

- Competition law arguments have also been raised in defence to applications for an injunction.

- A plaintiff may apply for a declaration, for example, that a particular agreement or practice is in breach of competition law.

1. The availability of injunctive and declaratory relief as remedies for a breach of EU competition law is a matter for the national law that applies to the action. As in the case of other remedies, the national rules must comply within the EU law principles of equivalence and effectiveness.

Ireland

What kinds of injunction can be sought in an antitrust case?

2. It is open to a plaintiff in an antitrust case to seek an injunction as a remedy, whether a permanent injunction or an interlocutory injunction and whether mandatory or prohibitory.[198] Section 14(5) of the Competition Act 2002 specifically provides for relief by way of injunction. An example of a mandatory injunction in a competition law context might be an order requiring one company to supply goods to another that it had refused to supply. A prohibitory injunction might require companies to cease engaging in anti-competitive practices.

3. The availability of an interlocutory injunction may be especially useful in certain circumstances, for example where there is urgency in ensuring that anti-competitive conduct is brought to an end so as to prevent irreparable damage that might otherwise be caused were the conduct allowed to continue pending a lengthy damages action. The court considers a number of principles when deciding whether to grant an interlocutory injunction. It will consider whether (i) there is a fair question to be tried, (ii) damages would not be an appropriate remedy and (iii) the balance of convenience is in the applicant's favour.[199] If the balance of

---

198. For a detailed exposition of the law and practice on injunctions in Irish law, see Kirwan, *Injunctions: Law and Practice* (2008).

199. See *Campus Oil Limited v Minister for Industry and Energy (No 2)* [1983] IR 88, 107, following the House of Lords decision in *American Cyanamid Co (No 1) v Ethicon Ltd.* [1975] AC 396.

convenience is even, it seems that the court may come down on the side of preserving the status quo.[200]

4. In a competition law case, the complexity of the issues will often be such that a court will quickly conclude that there is a fair issue to be tried. Even if the prospects of the injunction being granted are good, the applicant for an interlocutory injunction faces a financial risk as he is usually required to give an undertaking in damages to the effect that if his claim is unsuccessful, he will compensate the defendant for loss incurred arising from the grant of the interlocutory injunction.[201] This undertaking may be in respect of a considerable sum in a competition case. If an applicant is unlikely to be able to honour such an undertaking, the injunction might not be granted. This may make the interlocutory injunction an unattractive option for claimants without significant financial resources.

5. Injunctions may be granted *ex parte* on an interim basis where there is urgency and will remain in place usually only until an *inter partes* motion can be heard. An applicant for an *ex parte* injunction has a duty to disclose all material facts to the court. Given that complex issues will often arise in competition cases, it may be difficult for an applicant to feel confident that it has complied with this duty. A later finding that full disclosure had not been made can result in the order being discharged.[202] Many competition cases will not in any event require that an *ex parte* application be made.

6. The award of an injunction in the competition law context has been considered by the Irish courts in several cases. A prohibitory interlocutory injunction was granted to the plaintiffs in *Donovan v ESB*. The defendant, the ESB, the sole supplier of electricity in Ireland, established an approved register of electrical contractors, the Register of Electrical Contractors of Ireland Ltd. (RECI). The ESB adopted the position that it would only supply electricity to installations carried out by a RECI contractor or approved by a RECI inspector. The plaintiffs, who were not members of RECI, argued that the RECI regime amounted to abuse of a dominant position contrary to section 5 of the Competition Act 1991 as it imposed unfair trading conditions on them. The plaintiffs sought damages but in the meantime, sought and obtained an interlocutory injunction from the High Court preventing the ESB from implementing the RECI scheme.[203]

---

200. See *B & S Ltd v Irish Auto Trader Ltd* [1995] 2 IR 142, 146, (McCracken J stating that 'it is normally a counsel of prudence, although not a fixed rule, that if all other matters are equally balanced, the court should preserve the status quo'.)

201. See, e.g., *Pasture Properties Ltd v Evans* (unreported, High Court, Laffoy J, 5 February 1999).

202. See *Bambrick v Cobley* [2005] IEHC 43, [2006] 1 ILRM 81, 89 (Clarke J).

203. *Donovan v Electricity Supply Board* [1994] 2 IR 305 (appeal dismissed, *Donovan v Electricity Supply Board* [1997] 3 IR 573).

7. In *Leanort*, the High Court granted a prohibitory interlocutory injunction in a predatory pricing case.[204] A new entrant to the insulating panels market, Hytherm, alleged that a number of competitors in the market dropped their prices to uneconomic levels in an attempt to defeat Hytherm's entry and put it out of business. In arguing that there was a breach of Articles 101 and 102, it was alleged that the pricing behaviour of the defendants could only have resulted from an agreement between those who controlled the market or alternatively because dominant firms in the market had forced the predatory pricing and other firms had no alternative but to go along with the scheme. Blayney J held that there was a serious issue to be tried, that Hytherm would be driven into receivership or liquidation were the status quo to prevail pending trial, so damages were not an adequate remedy and that the balance of convenience favoured the granting of an injunction (the only risk to the defendants was being faced with continued competition from the plaintiff). Blayney J issued an order restraining the defendants from selling insulating panels 'at unreasonably low prices'. The learned judge declined to add the words 'designed to damage the plaintiff's business viability' to the order, as that would have constituted a finding on an issue (the competitors' intentions) that could only be dealt with at trial.[205]

8. The Irish courts have also granted mandatory injunctions in competition cases. In *A&N Pharmacy*, the plaintiff pharmacy claimed that a refusal by a wholesaler to supply it with essential non-generic drugs amounted to an abuse of a dominant position contrary to Article 102 and/or section 5 of the Competition Act 1991 and also a breach of Article 101/section 4. The plaintiff sought interlocutory relief pursuant to section 6 of the Competition Act 1991 compelling the defendant to supply it with non-generic pharmaceutical products. In granting the mandatory injunction requiring the defendant to supply the plaintiff with pharmaceutical products on terms of cash on delivery, Carroll J held that there was a serious issue to be tried and that damages would not be an adequate remedy as the plaintiff claimed it would be forced out if business if it did not obtain supplies. In considering the balance of convenience, the learned judge noted:

> [Since] the advent of competition law commercial enterprises are being forced to do business with other persons against their will. Since the defendant is a commercial enterprise supplying drugs there would be no inconvenience to it if cash is

---

204. *Leanort Ltd v Southern Chemicals Ltd ('Hytherm')* (High Court, 15 August 1988, Blayney J). A report of this case is available in Cregan, *Competition Law in Ireland: Digest and Commentary* (1997) F1. See also *Dunlea v Nissan (Ireland) Ltd* (High Court, 24 May 1990, Barr J) reported in Cregan at F20 (interlocutory injunction granted to restrain the defendant from terminating a franchise agreement, where it might be shown at the trial that such termination was an abuse of dominance contrary to Article 102).

205. It was reported (*Competition,* Vol. 2(2)) that prices in the market rose by around 50 per cent in the six months following the grant of the injunction and that the case settled before trial.

forthcoming for orders from the plaintiff. Its averred lack of confidence and worries about creditworthiness simply do not arise if cash is paid.[206]

How can competition law arguments be used to oppose the granting of an injunction?

9.   Competition law arguments have been raised as a defence against applications for an injunction.[207] In *Masterfoods*,[208] HB Ice Cream provided freezer cabinets to retailers on condition that only HB products be stored in the cabinets. HB sought injunctions to restrain Mars from inducing retailers to breach the terms of their exclusivity with HB and from allowing Mars ice cream to be sold in the HB cabinets. Mars argued that the exclusivity was in breach of Articles 101 and 102 and on this basis, it sought orders restraining HB from enforcing its cabinet agreements with retailers so as to prevent retailers from storing or stocking the Mars' products. In granting interlocutory injunctions in favour of HB, Lynch J held that HB had a serious case to be tried on the issue of wrongful interference with its contractual rights vis-á-vis the retailers to whom it had supplied cabinets and that the balance of convenience favoured the granting of the interlocutory relief sought. The interference with HB's contractual rights was *prima facie* unlawful and therefore the onus of establishing that it was not unlawful rested on Mars. The learned judge was not satisfied that a serious case had been made out on the basis of either Article 101 or 102.[209]

---

206. *A&N Pharmacy Ltd v United Drug Wholesale Ltd* [1996] 2 ILRM 42. Although not a private action, as the plaintiff was the Competition Authority, in the Credit Unions case, the High Court was prepared to issue an injunction requiring the Irish League of Credit Unions ('ILCU') to share access to its savings protection scheme with credit unions not affiliated to ILCU and to prevent it from disaffiliating credit unions which sought savings protection from other providers. The court had held that ILCU had abused its dominant position on the market for savings protection by 'tying' access to the scheme to the provision of credit union representation. The tie also breached section 4/Article 101 (*Competition Authority v O'Regan* [2004] IEHC 330 (it is not entirely clear from the judgment of Kearns J what the exact terms of the injunction were but it seems that it would have included both a mandatory and prohibitory element)). The substantive case was overturned on appeal by the Supreme Court (*Competition Authority v O'Regan* [2007] IESC 22, [2007] 4 IR 737).

207. See also *Radio Telefís Éireann v Magill TV Guide Ltd. (No. 2)* [1989] IR 554, in which the defendants, who relied on arguments based on Articles 101 and 102, failed to prevent the grant of an interlocutory injunction for breach of copyright (as the issue of whether the plaintiff had breached Article 102 was the subject of a Commission decision that was under appeal at the time, the court's consideration of that issue was limited to finding relevant facts and no determination on the infringement would be made).

208. *Masterfoods Ltd v HB Ice-cream Ltd* [1990] 2 IR 463.

209. A permanent injunction was subsequently granted to HB in *Masterfoods Ltd t/a Mars Ireland v H.B. Ice Cream Ltd* [1993] ILRM 145. However, on appeal, the Supreme Court made a preliminary reference to the Court of Justice, resulting in the judgment in Case C–344/98 *Masterfoods Ltd. v HB Ice Cream Ltd.* [2000] ECR I–11369, [2001] 4 CMLR 449. Ultimately, the HB arrangements were found by the Commission to be in breach of Article 101 and 102, findings upheld on appeal (see Case T–65/98 *Van den Bergh Foods Ltd v Commission* [2003] ECR II–4653, [2004] 4 CMLR 14 (appeal dismissed, Case C–552/03P *Unilever Bestfoods (Ireland) Ltd v Commission* [2006] ECR I–9091, [2006] 5 CMLR 1494)).

10. In *Premier Dairies v Doyle*, the plaintiff dairy argued that the defendant, which had been its exclusive distributor of milk products until the plaintiff terminated the agreement for default in payment, was in breach of a 12-month non-compete clause in the agreement. An interlocutory injunction was granted to the plaintiff preventing the defendant from selling competing products. The defendant argued that the non-compete was in breach of section 4 or 5 of the Competition Act 1991. The Supreme Court accepted that the defendant had the potential to make an argument based on the 1991 Act, in particular because it was a complex piece of legislation that had not been judicially considered to any extent at that time. It would not hold the defendant to the non-compete without considering the balance of convenience, which it decided in favour of the plaintiff, thus affirming the grant of the interlocutory injunction.[210]

11. In *Mantruck*, a parallel importer defendant partly relied on Article 101 in successfully overturning an interlocutory injunction restraining it from selling a particular brand of refrigerator, of which the plaintiff was the sole authorised distributor in Ireland. On the competition law argument, the Supreme Court, citing *Consten & Grundig*,[211] held that as the distributorship agreement was potentially in violation of Article 101 (and not, on the face of it, valid, as the High Court had held), the plaintiffs had not made out a fair case to be tried on this point.[212]

12. In *Tejo Ventures*, the plaintiff, following termination of a franchise agreement with the defendant, obtained an interlocutory injunction enforcing a 9-month non-compete clause contained in that agreement. In contesting the application for the interlocutory injunction, the defendant argued that the non-compete clause was in breach of section 4 of the Competition Act 2002. Laffoy J held that it would be open to the plaintiff in due course to argue that the non-compete clause did not breach section 4(1), came within a Competition Authority exemption pursuant to section 4(3) or that it met the conditions for exemption under section 4(5). In determining whether there was a fair issue to be tried, the learned judge found compelling the plaintiff's argument that it would be a worthless exercise for a company to grant a franchise, if the franchisee was entitled to terminate the franchise and immediately enter into competition with the franchisor, although there would be a question whether the restraint was reasonable. Ultimately, there was a fair question to be tried, damages would not provide the plaintiff with an adequate remedy given its complaint of damage to the goodwill and reputation of

---

210. *Premier Dairies Ltd v Doyle* [1996] 1 IR 37, 53–54 (O'Flaherty J). The High Court had been reluctant to consider the competition argument as it was raised at a late stage. See the judgment of Kinlen J at [1996] 1 IR 37, 48.

211. Cases 56&58/64 *Établissements Consten S.à.R.L. and Grundig-Verkaufs-GmbH v Commission* [1966] ECR 299.

212. *Mantruck Services Ltd v Ballinlough Electrical Refrigeration Company Ltd* [1992] 1 IR 351, 359–360.

its business and the balance of convenience favoured the granting of the injunction.[213]

What kinds of declaration can be sought?

13.   Section 14(5) of the Competition Act 2002 also specifically provides for relief by way of declaration in competition actions. A plaintiff may apply for a declaration, for example that a particular agreement or particular conduct is contrary to Article 101/section 4 or Article 102/section 5. A declaration that such agreements and practices are therefore invalid and accordingly ought to be set aside as null and void might also be sought. A litigant might also seek a declaration that it is not an undertaking and that the competition rules do not apply to it.[214] A plaintiff is entitled to seek *only* declaratory relief in an action and the court may make binding declarations of right whether any consequential relief is or could be claimed or not.[215] However an applicant 'must show that it is just and convenient that the declaratory order be made'.[216]

UK

What kinds of injunction can be sought in an antitrust case?

14.   The approach to injunctive relief in the English High Court is similar to the Irish approach described above. In deciding to grant an interlocutory injunction, the court considers the principles established in *American Cyanamid*, namely whether (i) there is a fair question to be tried, (ii) damages would not be an adequate remedy and (iii) the balance of convenience is in the applicant's favour.[217] These principles apply in the case of both mandatory and prohibitory injunctions. The court may require greater assurance that the claim is well founded before granting a mandatory injunction, given the greater risk of injustice in having required a positive step if the injunction turns out to have been wrongly ordered.[218]

---

213. *Tejo Ventures International Ltd v O'Callaghan* [2009] IEHC 410. See also *Sibra Building Company Limited v Ladgrove Stores Limited* [1998] 2 IR 589 (unsuccessful competition law defence to an application for an injunction to enforce a restrictive covenant that prohibited the use of a premises as a public house, Barron J holding, at 594, that the Competition Act 1991 was not intended to deal with restrictive covenants).

214. See *Deane v The Voluntary Health Insurance Board* [1992] 2 IR 319 (prior to the hearing of an action alleging a breach of section 5 of the Competition Act 1991, the defendant obtained a declaration in the High Court that it did not come within the definition of an undertaking contained in section 3 of the 1991 Act. On appeal, this finding was reversed by the Supreme Court, which held that the defendant was an undertaking).

215. Rules of the Superior Courts, Order 19, Rule 29.

216. *Shannon v McGuinness* [1999] 3 IR 274, 284 (Kelly J).

217. *American Cyanamid Co (No 1) v Ethicon Ltd.* [1975] AC 396 (HL).

218. See *Nottingham Building Society v Eurodynamics Systems plc* [1993] FSR 468, 474, approved by the Court of Appeal in *Zockoll Group Ltd v Mercury Communications Ltd* [1998] FSR 354, 366.

15. Interim relief may also be granted in the CAT pursuant to Rule 61 of the CAT Rules. This jurisdiction is most likely to be invoked where an applicant seeks a stay of an OFT direction in an infringement decision. The CAT does not have jurisdiction to issue interim relief in damages actions brought under section 47A or 48A of the Competition Act 1998.[219]

16. The English courts have considered applications for prohibitory and mandatory injunctions in competition cases. A prohibitory injunction was granted in *Attheraces*. The defendant, which was the owner of pre-race data required by the claimant bookmakers, threatened to cut off the supply of that data to the claimant via its licensee. Arguing that this was an abuse of a dominant position contrary to section 18 of the Competition Act 1998, Attheraces sought an injunction preventing the defendant from causing its licensee to cut off its supply of pre-race data. In granting the injunction, Morritt VC, as he then was, emphasised the complex nature of the claim of an abuse of dominance. Not only did the question of abuse (and the existence of a dominant position itself) involve 'substantial and complex issues of fact as well as of law', the defendant's argument that its conduct was objectively justified raised 'points of novelty and considerable public importance' which were fact sensitive and may have required a reference to the Court of Justice. These complexities meant that there was a seriously arguable case. If the injunction were not granted, the claimant would be denied data that was essential for its business and the loss of that business could not properly be compensated by damages. Therefore the balance of convenience as well as maintenance of the status quo both favoured the grant of an injunction.[220]

17. The English courts have also considered applications for mandatory injunctions in the antitrust context. In *Intecare*, the High Court refused a mandatory injunction that would have required Pfizer to provide Intecare with the SUTENT drug, for the treatment of kidney and gastrointestinal cancers. It was assumed for purposes of the application that Pfizer had a dominant position and Intecare argued that the refusal to supply it was abusive. Pfizer's supply policy was not an outright refusal, rather it supplied SUTENT only where a customer had a hospital subscription or there was an emergency. This policy was to combat stock shortages. Roth J held that Pfizer did not seek to secure an advantage for itself by the application of its supply policy nor was it attempting to distort competition between Intecare and its competitors. The learned judge also did not discount as fanciful Pfizer's argument that if it accepted Intecare's orders without proof of Intecare's hospital

---

219. Competition Appeal Tribunal Rules 2003, SI 2003/1372, r 61(13). On interim remedies in the CAT, see Brealey and Green (eds), *Competition Litigation: UK Practice and Procedure* (2010) paras 8.52 *et seq.*

220. *Attheraces Ltd v British Horseracing Board Ltd* [2005] EWHC 1553 (Ch), [2005] UKCLR 757, paras 53–66 (reversed on the substance on appeal, *Attheraces Ltd v British Horseracing Board Ltd* [2007] EWCA Civ 38, [2007] Bus LR D77). A prohibitory interim injunction was also granted to a claimant alleging abuse of dominance in *Network Multimedia v Jobserve* [2001] EWCA Civ 2018, [2002] UKCLR 184. A prohibitory injunction was refused in *Claritas (UK) Ltd v The Post Office* [2001] UKCLR 2 (no possible basis in the evidence to suggest an abuse of a dominant position).

prescriptions, it would be obliged to treat other purchasers in the same way, opening the flood-gates and jeopardising its supply to UK patients.[221]

18. A mandatory injunction was granted to a provider of VoiP services, Truphone, requiring T-Mobile to activate its numbers on the T-Mobile network so that Truphone could launch a new telephone service. Truphone alleged that T-Mobile's refusal to activate its numbers amounted to an abuse of dominance. In considering the application, the judge, Knowles QC, took particular account of the mandatory nature of the orders sought, the fact that the interim orders were intrusive, and the consequences it if turned out that orders of this nature should not have been made. Even though the learned judge did not have a 'high degree of assurance' that the claimant would succeed on the substantive claim, the risk of injustice caused to T-Mobile were it ultimately successful was outweighed by the greater risk of injustice to Truphone in the form of potential destruction of its business were the injunction not granted.[222]

Key Sources

Ireland

A&N Pharmacy Ltd v United Drug Wholesale Ltd [1996] 2 ILRM 42.

UK

Software Cellular Network Limited v T-Mobile (UK) Limited [2007] EWHC 1790 (Ch), [2007] All ER (d) 314 (Jul).

---

221. *Intecare Direct Ltd v Pfizer* [2010] EWHC 600 (Ch), [2010] UKCLR 477. See also *AAH Pharmaceuticals Ltd v Pfizer Ltd* [2007] EWHC 565 (Ch), [2007] UKCLR 1561 (mandatory injunction for supply of drugs in an abuse of dominance claim refused); *Getmapping plc v Ordnance Survey* [2002] EWHC 1089 (Pat), [2003] ICR 1 (mandatory injunction to enable the claimant to advertise on the defendant's website denied where the claimant's case that there was an abuse of dominance was 'very weak' (para 57)).
222. *Software Cellular Network Limited v T-Mobile (UK) Limited* [2007] EWHC 1790 (Ch), [2007] UCLR 1663, in particular at paras 46–49.

114. IF ALL PARTIES TO AN ANTI-COMPETITIVE ARRANGEMENT ARE SUED FOR DAMAGES TOGETHER, HOW MUCH WILL EACH DEFENDANT BE LIABLE FOR?

Summary

UK

- The court attempts to allocate contributions on a 'just and equitable' basis having regard to each defendant's degree of responsibility for the damage.

- Contributions among antitrust defendants are likely to be based on the gain each has made from the anti-competitive conduct, where that information is available.

- Next, the court looks to degrees of causative potency and blameworthiness.

- Solvent defendants will have to pay an insolvent defendant's contribution.

- Other factors, such as the behaviour of a defendant during an antitrust investigation and even the market shares of co-conspirators, could be relevant.

- If it is otherwise unable to decide contributions, the court may divide them equally.

Ireland

- The Irish statute apportions liability on a 'just and equitable basis' having regard to fault.

- There is a good argument that, like in England, retention of gains should apply first as a principle of apportionment.

- Irish law considers blameworthiness or fault but, unlike English law, does not take account of causative responsibility.

- Solvent defendants will have the burden of paying an insolvent defendant's contribution.

- It is uncertain whether the Irish courts would consider other non-causative factors to be relevant in deciding contributions.

1. How liability is apportioned among multiple defendants in a private action based on a breach of EU competition law is a matter for the national law that applies to the action. In Ireland and England & Wales (and probably most other EU jurisdictions), it is likely that multiple defendants in antitrust cases, such as members of a cartel sued for damages by customers, will often be jointly and severally liable for the damage caused to a claimant.[223] Depending on the

---

223. See Ashurst Study on the conditions of claims for damages in case of infringement of EC competition rules (31 August 2004) and accompanying national reports, available on the Commission's website.

circumstances, a claimant may be able to elect to sue only one defendant for all of its loss, leaving it to that defendant to obtain contribution from the other responsible parties. If all defendants are sued, contributions may have to be worked out after the plaintiff's total damages are decided.[224]

2.   Joint and several liability is an important safeguard for claimants. As long as there is one defendant capable of paying all of the claimant's damages, the claimant should obtain full compensation, even if other defendants are insolvent or otherwise beyond the reach of the court. The ability to obtain contribution is an important safeguard for a defendant and the manner in which contributions are apportioned can have significant financial consequences. The issue of contribution is important not only for defendants in private antitrust actions but also for plaintiffs. The extent to which a defendant will ultimately be liable in damages may influence its strategy to defending the action and also affect how settlements are reached in a multi-defendant case.[225]

3.   The availability of contribution in antitrust cases under the relevant general legislation in both Ireland and England & Wales is assumed here[226] (there does not appear to be any reason why the relevant law would not apply), although as yet, the courts in neither jurisdiction have decided a contribution case in the antitrust context.[227] In *Arkin*, multiple defendants in a private antitrust action issued claims against each other for contribution and indemnity in the event that the claimant would be successful. However, the claimant was unsuccessful and so the contribution issues were never tried. In case managing the action, the judge ordered that to the extent issues of contribution became relevant, they should be resolved in a separate phase of the trial, which would take place following the

---

224. Given the different factual scenarios that may arise and the dearth of case law on joint liability in antitrust actions, issues of joint liability and whether one defendant can be sued for damage caused by all etc. should be considered in light of the particular facts.

225. See generally, on contribution and settlement in antitrust cases, Dunleavy, 'Contribution among Antitrust Defendants in English Law' [2009] *European Competition Law Review* 22.

226. Described as an attempt to 'measure the immeasurable' (Williams, *Joint Torts and Contributory Negligence* (1951) 158), the rules on contribution in both jurisdictions are complex and readers should refer to the detailed provisions of the relevant statutes, discussed below.

227. In the United States, there was an extensive debate about antitrust contribution in the late 70s and early 80s. Contribution among antitrust defendants is not available as a matter of federal law (*Texas Industries Inc v Radcliff Materials Inc* 415 US 630 (1981)). Once a defendant settles with a claimant, it is out of the case and cannot be sued for contribution by another defendant. This 'no-contribution' rule is considered to be an important factor in encouraging settlements as no defendant wishes to be the last to settle, potentially facing much higher liability than expected. However many commentators have criticised the injustice of the no-contribution rule. The Antitrust Modernization Commission in its Report and Recommendations (2007) at 252 recommended that Congress enact a contribution and claim reduction rule in antitrust cases. For a recent argument in favour of contribution see England, 'The Case for Contribution and Claim Reduction under US Antitrust Law' [2010] *Global Competition Litigation Review* 106.

judgment on matters of liability and quantum in the main action.[228] This is a sensible approach and means that a successful claimant would not have to await what might be a complicated trial of contribution issues before obtaining the main verdict.

4.   The English and Irish rules on contribution are similar. As there have been significant developments in English law in a number of recent cases, it is considered first.

UK

5.   There are a number of sources of the right to contribution in English law but claims arising from a common liability for the same damage are governed by the Civil Liability (Contribution) Act 1978. Section 1(1) provides that 'any person liable in respect of any damage suffered by another person may recover contribution from any other person liable in respect of the same damage (whether jointly with him or otherwise)'. In many antitrust cases involving multiple defendants, such as claims against a cartel, it is likely that the defendants would be classed as joint tortfeasors and found to be liable for the same damage. In particular cases it may be arguable that the defendants are not liable for the same damage but the discussion here assumes that this could be established.[229]

6.   In measuring contribution against a person under section 2(1) of the Contribution Act, the court is to make a just and equitable apportionment 'having regard to the extent of that person's responsibility for the damage in question.'

7.   This apportionment formula has not yet been interpreted in the antitrust context. However the courts have developed a number of general principles used to apply the statute.[230] Based on how the courts have applied those principles, the following is a suggestion about how contribution would work in an antitrust case.

8.   To the extent it can be established how much each defendant benefited from the anti-competitive conduct, it can be argued that contribution should be based on direct gains made.[231] The way this 'retention of gains' principle has been applied by the House of Lords in *Dubai Aluminium*[232] and by the English courts in a

---

228. See *Arkin v Borchard Lines Ltd* [2005] EWCA Civ 655, [2005] 1 WLR 3055, para 61.
229. On the meaning of the 'same damage', see *Royal Brompton Hospital NHS Trust v Hammond (No. 3)* [2002] UKHL 14, [2002] 1 WLR 1397 (see at para 30, Lord Steyn rejecting a flexible and broad view of the meaning of the 'same damage' and emphasising that a legal analysis of the claims was required to determine whether they were claims for the same damage). On when wrongdoers are joint tortfeasors, see *Clerk & Lindsell on Torts* (19th edn, 2006) 235–236.
230. See Dunleavy, 'Principles of apportionment in contribution cases' (2009) 125 *Law Quarterly Review* 239.
231. This would be limited to gains made directly from the anti-competitive agreement or conduct. It would not involve assessing whether further gains were made by investing the original gain etc.
232. *Dubai Aluminium Co. Ltd. v Salaam* [2002] UKHL 48, [2003] 2 AC 366.

number of subsequent cases,[233] suggests that it acts as an overriding principle to apportion liability. Essentially, if apportionment can be made using gains, the court will do so and need not consider other factors. This approach is 'obviously just and equitable'[234] as otherwise, a defendant who retained an illegal gain but was not made to contribute according to that gain, would be unjustly enriched at the expense of his co-defendant who had not made the gain.

9. Basing apportionment on gains made would be particularly suitable in horizontal price fixing cases, where defendants could be made to contribute based on their relative sales to the claimant. To take a very simple example, assume that the claimant, C, suffered a loss of £100,000 through overcharges on its purchases of widgets from members of a widget cartel. C made 60 per cent of its purchases from D1, 30 per cent from D2 and 10 per cent from D3. C may sue any or all of the defendants to recover the total amount of its loss as each is jointly and severally liable. In a related contribution action, the defendants would have to contribute according to their respective gains, which would correspond to the percentage of sales each made to C. So, D1's contribution would be £60,000, D2's would be £30,000 and D3's would be £10,000.

10. The difficulty is that real-life cases are hardly ever this simple and basing apportionment on gains may not work in other types of antitrust cases, such as vertical conspiracies, bid rigging or market allocation, where it will likely be more difficult to work out the gain that has accrued to each defendant.

11. Where 'retention of gains' does not solve apportionment, the court would next consider the causative potency and blameworthiness of each defendant's actions in causing loss to the claimant. The use of these principles is less scientific and ultimately, the trial judge enjoys wide discretion in how they are applied. In a private action arising out of a cartel, one might expect that a judge would consider factors such as the role played by each participant in the cartel (were they a ringleader, an enforcer or an 'innocent' party who was coerced?) and the duration of involvement in the conspiracy.[235] In a follow-on case, the court will have the benefit of the Commission's decision (or that of the OFT), which may provide evidence of causative potency and degrees of blameworthiness.

---

233. See, e.g., *Cressman v Coys of Kensington* [2004] EWCA Civ 47, [2004] 1 WLR 2775, paras 37, 48; *Niru Battery v Milestone Trading Ltd (No 2)* [2004] EWCA Civ 487, [2004] 2 All ER (Comm) 289, paras 51, 78.

234. *Dubai Aluminium Co. Ltd. v Salaam* [2002] UKHL 48, [2003] 2 AC 366, para 164 (Lord Millett).

235. There is an argument that a defendant should not be liable at all for loss caused while it was outside the conspiracy, on which, see *O'Keeffe v Walsh* [1903] 2 IR 681 (one defendant who joined a boycott conspiracy later than the others was held not liable for damage accruing before he joined; note, however, at this time, the rule in *Merryweather v Nixan* (1799) 8 Term Rep 186 precluding the recovery of contribution by joint and several tortfeasors *inter se* applied) and Williams, *Joint Torts and Contributory Negligence* (1951) 66 ('a party is not liable for the damage flowing from the conspiracy before the date of his joining it'). (contd \...)

12. If one of the defendants is insolvent, his contribution will be apportioned among the remaining solvent defendants in proportions corresponding with their own contributions.[236] This can extend to factoring in a potential future insolvency.[237]

13. There is recent authority that the court may also take into account factors that have not caused loss to the claimant. Of course, retention of gains and insolvency are non-causative factors but are best viewed as being exceptional factors. Examples of other non-causative factors that have been considered include reprehensible conduct that took place after loss was caused in an attempt to deflect blame for the loss[238] and a non-causative breach of duty.[239] It has been suggested that the relative size of a defendant company can be considered in apportioning contributions.[240] However, in another case, Steel J ruled that the extent of insurance cover held by a party from whom one defendant sought contribution was irrelevant[241].

14. In a follow-on case, relevant non-causative factors might include the behaviour of the defendant during the Commission's investigation and whether the defendant was cooperative or obstructive towards the claimant's attempts to recover damages. Market share could also be relevant. If non-causative factors are included, it seems they should only have moderate weight attached to them and not play a significant role in deciding contributions.[242]

15. If the court is otherwise unable to apportion contributions, it can divide the amount equally among all defendants.[243] This appears to be a 'last resort'.

16. A two-year limitation applies to claims for contribution.[244] If the defendant claiming contribution was held liable in respect of the damage that is the subject of the contribution claim, the period runs from the date of a judgment or

---

235. (contd) This could have significant consequences for private actions arising out of a cartel where the participants may have been involved at different times, a common occurrence. In follow-on actions, this raises questions about the binding effect of findings by the Commission that a particular defendant was jointly and severally liable for the whole of an infringement, on the basis that there was a 'single continuous infringement', even where such a defendant may have joined the conspiracy later than others. See Question 121 on the binding effect of Commission decisions in follow-on actions.

236. See *Dubai Aluminium Co. Ltd. v Salaam* [2002] UKHL 48, [2003] 2 AC 366, paras 52, 167.

237. See *Dubai Aluminium Co Ltd v Salaam* [2002] UKHL 48, [2003] 2 AC 366, para 167.

238. *Re-Source America International Ltd v Platt Site Services Ltd* [2004] EWCA Civ 665, 95 Con LR 1.

239. *Brian Warwicker Partnership plc v HOK International Ltd* [2005] EWCA Civ 962, 103 Con LR 112.

240. *Gray v Fire Alarm Fabrication Services Ltd* [2006] EWCA Civ 1496, [2007] ICR 247, para 71.

241. *West London Pipeline and Storage Ltd v Total UK Ltd* [2008] EWHC 1296, [2008] 1 CLC 935.

242. See *Brian Warwicker Partnership plc v HOK International Ltd* [2005] EWCA Civ 962, 103 Con LR 112, paras 44, 45, 51.

243. See Mitchell, *The Law of Contribution and Reimbursement* (2003) 183.

244. Limitation Act 1980, s 10(1).

award.[245] This has been interpreted to mean a judgment or award that ascertained quantum and not merely the existence of liability.[246] Where contribution is sought after a settlement, the two-year period runs from the earliest date on which the amount paid under the settlement was agreed.[247]

Ireland

17. For purposes of Part III of the Civil Liability Act 1961, 'two or more persons are concurrent wrongdoers when both or all are wrongdoers and are responsible to [the plaintiff] ... for the same damage.'[248] The Act further provides that persons may become concurrent wrongdoers as a result of 'conspiracy, concerted action to a common end or independent acts causing the same damage' and that 'it is immaterial whether the acts constituting concurrent wrongs are contemporaneous or successive'.[249] It is likely that in many antitrust cases involving multiple defendants, the defendants would be concurrent wrongdoers and it is assumed for purposes of the discussion here that this could be established.

18. The basis of apportionment of liability against a concurrent wrongdoer is 'such as may be found to be just and equitable having regard to the degree of that contributor's fault.'[250] It is well established that apportionment is based on the extent of blameworthiness and not the respective causative effect of each party's actions:

> [Degrees] of fault between the parties are not to be apportioned on the basis of the relative causative potency of their respective causative contributions to the damage, but rather on the basis of the moral blameworthiness of their respective causative contributions.[251]

19. While causative potency is not used in the apportionment formula in Ireland, that actions are causative of loss seems to be a threshold issue for them to be taken into account in assessing levels of blameworthiness, *i.e.* the blameworthiness at issue is the 'blameworthiness of the *causative* contributions'[252] of each concurrent wrongdoer.

---

245. Limitation Act 1980, s 10(3).
246. *Aer Lingus plc v Gildacroft Ltd* [2006] EWCA Civ 4, [2006] 1 WLR 1173
247. Limitation Act 1980, s 10(4).
248. Civil Liability Act 1961, s 11(1). For recent analysis of the meaning of the 'same damage', see *Larkin v Joosub* [2006] IEHC 51, [2007] 1 IR 521, 532–534 (Finlay Geoghegan J).
249. Civil Liability Act 1961, s 11(2). On the impact of the plaintiff being found guilty of contributory negligence, see section 38.
250. Civil Liability Act 1961, s 21(2). If the plaintiff is found guilty of contributory negligence, under s 38(1), the court will only award the plaintiff a several judgment against each defendant for such apportioned part of his total damages as the court thinks just and equitable.
251. *O'Sullivan v Dwyer* [1971] 1 IR 275, 286 (Walsh J).
252. *Ward v McMaster* [1985] 1 IR 29, 54 (Costello J) (emphasis added) (appeal dismissed, *Ward v McMaster* [1988] IR 337.

20.   It was confirmed by the Supreme Court in *Iarnród Éireann v Ireland* that the insolvency of one of the concurrent wrongdoers can be considered in contribution proceedings, with the risk of such an insolvency falling on other solvent defendants, 'a solution that is in harmony with the core principles underlying civil liability.'[253]

21.   The Irish courts do not appear to have recently considered whether retention of gains should be applied as the first principle in apportioning contributions, as it was by the House of Lords in *Dubai Aluminium*. However, the persuasive reasoning in that case, that it is *obviously* just and equitable to base contributions according to the various gains retained by the wrongdoers is one that goes to the heart of the purpose of contribution (restitution of unjust enrichment rather than punishment of defendants) and seems equally applicable in the context of the Irish Act. Moreover, Ireland has accepted at least one non-causative factor (insolvency) so there would not appear to be any principled objection to the inclusion of another non-causative factor in terms of retention of gains (unlike, for example, certain Canadian jurisdictions, which although basing contribution like in England in terms of responsibility, do not take account of non-causative factors, even insolvency[254]).

22.   The Irish courts also do not seem to have recently decided whether other factors that are non-causative of loss, such as a defendant's reprehensible behaviour or breach of duty after loss had been caused to a plaintiff, are relevant in apportioning contributions. It can be argued that the 'having regard to … fault' language in section 21(2) of the 1961 Act does not limit the inquiry and that consideration of factors beyond fault is permitted by the legislation. This comes down to whether the words 'having regard to' are interpreted as limiting the inquiry to fault or merely pointing the court to consider fault as one factor among many. If the latter interpretation were taken (and in interpreting similar language in the English Court of Appeal, the latter interpretation was preferred)[255] and non-causative factors considered relevant, it is likely that the Irish courts would not give significant weight to such factors in deciding contributions.

23.   It is likely that the Irish courts would adopt a position of equal apportionment were they unable to divide contributions based on fault, retention of gains, taking the insolvency of defendants into account or on the basis of other non-causative factors (were they accepted as being applicable). It is noteworthy that the Civil

---

253.   *Iarnród Éireann v Ireland* [1996] 3 IR 321, 377 (O'Flaherty J). See also section 28 of the 1961 Act, which provides that a wrongdoer who obtains a contribution judgment against two or more concurrent wrongdoers but cannot enforce his judgment against one, 'shall have liberty to apply for secondary judgments having the effect of distributing the deficiency among the other defendants in such proportions as may be just and equitable'.

254.   These Canadian jurisdictions include Alberta, Manitoba, Nova Scotia and New Brunswick. See Cheifetz, 'Joint and Several Liability: Show me the Principle but Hold the Metaphysics' (paper dated 29 April 2006) 40.

255.   See *Brian Warwicker Partnership plc v HOK International Ltd* [2005] EWCA Civ 962, 103 Con. LR 112, para 38.

Liability Act provides that in contributory negligence[256] and maritime cases,[257] liability may be apportioned equally where different degrees of fault cannot be established.

24. A contribution action can be brought within the same period as the underlying plaintiff could have sued the contributor, or within two years after the liability of the defendant seeking contribution is ascertained or damages are paid to the underlying plaintiff, whichever is greater.[258]

Key Sources

UK

Civil Liability (Contribution) Act 1978.

Dubai Aluminium v Salaam [2002] UKHL 48, [2003] 2 AC 366.

Ireland

Civil Liability Act 1961.

---

256. Civil Liability Act 1961, s 34(1).
257. Civil Liability Act 1961, s 46(1). See also section 12(2), providing that in cases involving persons who are not concurrent wrongdoers but have caused independent items of damage of the same kind, if apportionment based on the probabilities of the case cannot be established, damages may be apportioned or divided equally.
258. Civil Liability Act 1961, s 31. On the limitations of this section, owing to its general nature, see *Keane v Western Health Board* [2006] IEHC 370, [2007] 2 IR 555.

115. IF ONE DEFENDANT REACHES A SETTLEMENT, CAN IT LATER BE BROUGHT BACK INTO THE CASE BY OTHER DEFENDANTS WHO DID NOT SETTLE?

Summary

UK

- A defendant who settles can still be sued for contribution by other defendants.

Ireland

- It can be argued that it is implied in section 17 of the Civil Liability Act 1961 that a settling defendant is protected from a future contribution claim.

1. The question of settlement is an important element of antitrust actions, as it is with civil litigation more generally. Difficult issues may arise in multi-defendant actions in which defendants are jointly liable, in particular where defendants do not wish to cooperate with each other in settling the action. Defendants may have different views about how contributions should be apportioned or some may be more willing to contest a case than others. If one or only some of the defendants wish to settle, can they do this and safely extricate themselves from the litigation? Or could they be brought back into the case by the non-settling defendants and sued for contribution?

UK

2. The position in English law appears to be that a defendant who reaches a settlement with the claimant can still be sued for contribution by others liable for the same damage. Section 1(3) of the Civil Liability (Contribution) Act 1978 provides that a person liable to contribution remains liable 'notwithstanding that he has ceased to be liable in respect of the damage in question since the time when the damage occurred.'[259] The Court of Appeal has held that this provision is unambiguous and means that a defendant who has settled with the claimant is still exposed to contribution.[260]

3. The rationale behind the rule is that an unreleased tortfeasor, who can still be sued by the claimant, should not be prejudiced by the settlement between the claimant and the released tortfeasor, which, from the unreleased defendant's point of view,

---

259. Civil Liability (Contribution) Act 1978, s 1(3).
260. See *Logan v Uttlesford District Council* (1984) 136 NLJ 541 (CA).

is *res inter alios acta*.[261] If the unreleased tortfeasor could not claim contribution from the settling tortfeasor, he would be potentially exposed to greater than his fair share of liability if the settlement amount were less than the true liability of the settling tortfeasor (as the claimant's claim against the unreleased tortfeasor is reduced only by the amount of the settlement). No comprehensive defence of the rule is discernible from the law reports – it has been said that, '[if] this solution is not perfect, it at least has the merit of promoting more sensible results than any other solution.'[262]

4.   The rule that a settling defendant is exposed to contribution clearly creates a major disincentive for a defendant in a multi-defendant case to settle alone. If he can later be sued for contribution, the settlement does not 'buy peace' and may hold little value. The only way a defendant can protect himself is to obtain an indemnity from the claimant to cover a contribution action or obtain an enforceable undertaking that the claimant will not pursue claims against the other defendants. Persuading a claimant to agree to either of these propositions may be difficult and would probably require a generous settlement to be paid. While it would be open to the settling defendant to sue the other defendants for contribution, such an approach may be risky and puts the burden of recovery on the settling defendant.

5.   The upshot of the settlement rule is that, in England, where defendants to a private action are not prepared to collectively settle the case, and where there is disagreement among defendants as to what their respective contributions to the damages should be, no defendant can safely reach a settlement with the claimant.

6.   This is a problematic rule and is not in line with the policy goal 'to encourage settlement of cases without going to court or trial wherever possible.'[263] However, for the time being, defendants in antitrust cases should be wary of this rule.

Ireland

7.   The disincentive for settlements created by the English position that a settling defendant is exposed to contribution has a solution – an 'identification' or 'claim reduction' rule. There are various formulas that can be used in a claim reduction

---

261. A thing done between others.

262. *Watts v Aldington, Tolstoy v Aldington*, The Times 16 December 1993 (CA) (Steyn LJ). His Lordship cited Williams, *Joint Obligations* (1949) 138–129 in support but in his later work, Williams acknowledged the problem with the rule and suggested it be changed in favour of, essentially, a claim reduction rule, discussed here in para 7 (see Williams, *Joint Torts and Contributory Negligence* (1951) 151–152). However, the position in *Watts v Aldington* has been defended elsewhere; see, New South Wales Law Reform Commission, Report 89 (1999) – Contribution Between Persons Liable for the Same Damage, paras 4.30–4.36, as well as *Jameson v Central Electricity Generating Board* [1998] QB 323 (CA) 336, 347.

263. OFT 916resp, Private actions in competition law: effective redress for consumers and business (November 2007) 12.

rule but a typical feature is that the claim against unreleased defendants is reduced by the greater of the amount of the settlement or an amount representing the settling defendant's true share of liability. In this sense, the plaintiff is *identified* with the settling defendant (and the extent of the settling defendant's liability) when he sues the non-settling defendants. The settling defendant is then immune from contribution.

8.   The Civil Liability Act 1961 includes a claim reduction rule that appears to protect a settling defendant from contribution claims. Section 17 of the Act provides as follows:

> (1) The release of, or accord with, one concurrent wrongdoer shall discharge the others if such release or accord indicates an intention that the others are to be discharged.

> (2) If no such intention is indicated by such release or accord, the other wrongdoers shall not be discharged but the injured person shall be identified with the person with whom the release or accord is made in any action against the other wrongdoers in accordance with paragraph (h) of subsection (1) of section 35; and in any such action the claim against the other wrongdoers shall be reduced in the amount of the consideration paid for the release or accord, or in any amount by which the release or accord provides that the total claim shall be reduced, or to the extent that the wrongdoer with whom the release or accord was made would have been liable to contribute if the plaintiff's total claim had been paid by the other wrongdoers, whichever of those three amounts is the greatest.

9.   While it is not made explicit, it seems to be a necessary implication of this provision that the settling defendant would be immune from claims for contribution by non-settling defendants, who may subsequently be sued by the plaintiff. Were the settling defendant open to be sued for contribution in this case, it would largely defeat the purpose and rationale behind the identification theory in section 17(2).

10.   The settling defendant may himself claim contribution from the non-settling defendants. Where the settlement bars the underlying plaintiff from suing these other defendants, the contribution action by the settling defendant can proceed if it is shown that the settlement is reasonable or, if the court finds that the settlement was excessive, it may fix the amount at which the claim should have been settled for purposes of the contribution action.[264]

11.   The settling defendant can also seek contribution from the other defendants where the settlement did not bar claims by the plaintiff against those defendants (or where that defendant has been forced to pay damages). However, if one of those defendants is subsequently compelled to pay a settlement to the plaintiff in respect

---

264. Civil Liability Act 1961, s 22(1).

of his own liability, he will have the right to claim repayment of the whole or part of the sum paid in contribution, if just and equitable.[265]

Key Sources

UK

Civil Liability (Contribution) Act 1978, s 1(3).

Watts v Aldington, Tolstoy v Aldington, The Times 16 December 1993 (CA).

Logan v Uttlesford District Council (1984) 136 NLJ 541 (CA).

Ireland

Civil Liability Act 1961, s17, s 22.

---

265. Civil Liability Act 1961, s 22(2). See also Carey and Leonowicz, 'Litigating Settlement Contributions' (2001) 8 *Commercial Law Practitioner* 85.

116. ARE THERE SPECIAL PROCEDURES GOVERNING FOLLOW-ON ACTIONS?

Summary

•   As a matter of EU law, any person who suffers harm from a breach of the EU competition rules can obtain reparation from the infringing party.

•   Where the Commission has found a violation, that decision can be relied on in a follow-on action for damages in the national courts.

•   The procedures governing follow-on actions are largely a matter of national law.

Ireland

•   Ireland has no special procedures governing follow-on actions.

UK

•   A claimant can take a follow-on action in either the High Court or the CAT.

•   Special procedures, under sections 47A and 47B of the Competition Act 1998, apply to claims before the CAT. There must be an infringement decision of the Commission, the OFT or one of the UK sectoral regulators before a claim can be brought in the CAT.

1.   Many of the private antitrust damages actions instituted in Europe have been so-called 'follow-on' actions. These are actions taken after the Commission or another antitrust regulator has issued a decision finding an infringement of the competition rules. The private action 'piggy backs' on this decision, using it as evidence of a violation of competition law and more generally as an aid in other aspects of the claim.

2.   Actions that follow-on from a Commission decision ʳe taken in the national courts.[266] When national courts rule on agreements, deci.   ns or practices under Article 101 or 102 which have been the subject of a Comɴ ʌsion decision, 'they cannot take decisions running counter to the decisi adopted by the Commission'.[267] The consequence of this rule is that in follov on actions, it is not open to a national court to question the finding made in the C ʋmmission decision that the competition rules have been infringed.[268] Beyond this, the rules that apply to the follow-on action are largely a matter of national law but the principles of equivalence and effectiveness must be complied with.[269]

---

266. Issues of jurisdiction and choice of law are discussed in Questions 107 and 108 respectively.
267. Regulation 1/2003, Article 16(1). A similar requirement is placed on national competition authorities by Article 16(2) of Regulation 1/2003.
268. See Question 121. The rule is subject to any appeal to the General Court or the Court of Justice that may overturn the Commission decision.
269. See Cases C–295–298/04 *Manfredi v Lloyd Adriatico Assicurazioni SpA* [2006] ECR I–6619, [2006] 5 CMLR 980, para 54.

Ireland

3. No special provision for follow-on actions is made in the Irish legislation or procedural rules. The Competition Act 2002 provides that any aggrieved person has a right of action for relief, to include injunctions, declarations, damages and exemplary damages, in respect of a breach of section 4 or 5 of the Act.[270] Although not specifically provided for in the Act, the principle of equivalence would require that the same right of action apply in respect of breaches of Article 101 or 102. This would apply whether the action is standalone or a follow-on action.

UK

4. A claimant in a follow-on action in the UK has a choice of venue in which to institute proceedings. It can bring its action before the High Court or, if the claim falls within the parameters of the CAT's special jurisdiction to hear follow-on claims, it can bring the action under section 47A of the Competition Act 1998. A limited form of representative action can be taken under section 47B on behalf of consumers who individually would have a claim under section 47A.[271] The CAT's ability to hear follow-on claims is limited to the jurisdiction set out in sections 47A and 47B, whereas the High Court has general jurisdiction.

5. Section 47A of the Competition Act 1998, which was inserted by the Enterprise Act 2002 and came into effect on 20 June 2003, contains the following provisions:

    (1) This section applies to–

    (a) any claim for damages, or

    (b) any other claim for a sum of money,

    which a person who has suffered loss or damage as a result of the infringement of a relevant prohibition may make in civil proceedings brought in any part of the United Kingdom.

    (2) In this section "relevant prohibition" means any of the following–

    (a) the Chapter I prohibition;

    (b) the Chapter II prohibition;

    (c) the prohibition in Article [101(1)] of the Treaty;

    (d) the prohibition in Article [102] of the Treaty ...

    (3) For the purpose of identifying claims which may be made in civil proceedings, any limitation rules that would apply in such proceedings are to be disregarded.

    (4) A claim to which this section applies may (subject to the provisions of this Act and Tribunal rules) be made in proceedings brought before the Tribunal.

---

270. See Competition Act 2002, s 14.
271. On section 47B actions, see Question 110.

(5) But no claim may be made in such proceedings–

(a) until a decision mentioned in subsection (6) has established that the relevant prohibition in question has been infringed; and

(b) otherwise than with the permission of the Tribunal, during any period specified in subsection (7) or (8) which relates to that decision.

(6) The decisions which may be relied on for the purposes of proceedings under this section are–

(a) a decision of the OFT that the Chapter I prohibition or the Chapter II prohibition has been infringed;

(b) a decision of the OFT that the prohibition in Article [101(1)] or Article [102] of the Treaty has been infringed;

(c) a decision of the Tribunal (on an appeal from a decision of the OFT) that the Chapter I prohibition, the Chapter II prohibition or the prohibition in Article [101(1)] or Article [102] of the Treaty has been infringed; [or]

(d) a decision of the European Commission that the prohibition in Article [101(1)] or Article [102] of the Treaty has been infringed ...

(7) The periods during which proceedings in respect of a claim made in reliance on a decision mentioned in subsection (6)(a), (b) or (c) may not be brought without permission are–

(a) in the case of a decision of the OFT, the period during which an appeal may be made to the Tribunal under section 46, section 47 or the EC Competition Law (Articles 84 and 85) Enforcement Regulations 2001 (SI 2001/2916);

(b) in the case of a decision of the OFT which is the subject of an appeal mentioned in paragraph (a), the period following the decision of the Tribunal on the appeal during which a further appeal may be made under section 49 or under those Regulations;

(c) in the case of a decision of the Tribunal mentioned in subsection (6)(c), the period during which a further appeal may be made under section 49 or under those Regulations;

(d) in the case of any decision which is the subject of a further appeal, the period during which an appeal may be made to the *House of Lords [Supreme Court]* from a decision on the further appeal;

and, where any appeal mentioned in paragraph (a), (b), (c) or (d) is made, the period specified in that paragraph includes the period before the appeal is determined.

(8) The periods during which proceedings in respect of a claim made in reliance on a decision or finding of the European Commission may not be brought without permission are–

(a) the period during which proceedings against the decision or finding may be instituted in the European Court; and

(b) if any such proceedings are instituted, the period before those proceedings are determined.

(9) In determining a claim to which this section applies the Tribunal is bound by any decision mentioned in subsection (6) which establishes that the prohibition in question has been infringed.

(10) The right to make a claim to which this section applies in proceedings before the Tribunal does not affect the right to bring any other proceedings in respect of the claim.

6. Section 47A should be read together with the Competition Appeal Tribunal Rules, which set out further rules on time limits and procedure.[272]

7. The reference to decisions of the OFT in section 47A(6) should be read as including decisions made by the sectoral regulators.[273]

8. The nature of the right of action under section 47A was considered by the Court of Appeal in the *Enron Coal* case. The claimant sued under section 47A alleging loss and damage in that it had been overcharged for coal haulage by the defendant, which had been found by the Office of Rail Regulation ('ORR') to have abused a dominant position contrary to the Chapter II prohibition. The question arose, in strike out proceedings, as to what findings of infringement of the Chapter II prohibition had been made by the ORR. Overruling a decision of the CAT not to strike out the proceedings, the Court of Appeal found that the ORR had made no finding of competitive disadvantage as had been pleaded by the claimant. In the course of the leading judgment, Patten LJ commented on the CAT's section 47A jurisdiction in respect of a Chapter II/Article 102 infringement:[274]

> The jurisdiction of the tribunal is therefore limited to determining what are commonly referred to as follow-on claims for damages based on a finding of infringement of the Ch II prohibition or art [102] which has been made by the OFT or one of the sectoral regulators ... The existence of such a finding is not only a pre-condition to the making of a claim under s 47A(1). It also operates to determine and define the limits of that claim and the tribunal's jurisdiction in respect of it.
>
> For there to be such a claim (and, with it, the jurisdiction of the tribunal to adjudicate upon it) the regulator must have made a decision of the kind described in s 47A(6). The use of the word "decision" makes it clear that s 47A is differentiating between findings of fact as to the conduct of the Defendant made as part of the overall decision and a determination by the regulator that particular conduct amounts to an infringement of the Ch II prohibition. It is not open to a Claimant such as ECSL to seek to recover damages through the medium of s 47A simply by identifying findings of fact which could arguably amount to such an infringement. No right of action exists unless the regulator has actually decided that such conduct constitutes an infringement of the relevant prohibition as defined. The corollary to this is that the tribunal (whose jurisdiction depends upon the existence of such a decision) must satisfy itself that the regulator has made a relevant and definitive finding of infringement. The purpose of s 47A is to obviate the necessity for a trial of the question of infringement only where the regulator has in fact ruled on that very issue. We were not referred to any

---

272. Competition Appeal Tribunal Rules 2003, SI 2003/1372. Time limits are considered separately in Question 117.

273. See Competition Act 1998, s 54.

274. The judgment would also be applicable to actions based on a breach of Chapter I/Article 101.

procedure for seeking clarification of any points of uncertainty from the decision-maker. The tribunal ought therefore, in my judgment, to be astute to recognise and reject cases where there is no clearly identifiable finding of infringement and where they are in effect being asked to make their own judgment on that issue.[275]

9.   This judgment holds that there must be a finding on the part of the regulator that the relevant competition law provision has been infringed.[276] A mere finding of fact, which it might be arguable leads to the conclusion that competition law has been infringed, is not sufficient. In other words, the Court of Appeal is holding that in invoking section 47A, the claimant can only rely on findings of fact which the regulator has found give rise to an infringement of competition law.

When may follow-on actions be transferred between the High Court and Competition Appeal Tribunal?

10.   The CAT may at any stage, on application of one of the parties or on its own initiative, transfer a section 47A claim to the High Court, County Court (or Court of Session or a sheriff court in Scotland).[277] A claim that could have been brought before the CAT under section 47A but which was instituted in the High Court, may be transferred to the CAT by the High Court.[278] A practice direction sets out factors the court should consider in deciding whether to make a transfer to the CAT. These are whether:

(1) there is a similar claim under section 47A of the 1998 Act based on the same infringement currently before the CAT;

(2) the CAT has previously made a decision on a similar claim under section 47A of the 1998 Act based on the same infringement; or

---

275. *English Welsh & Scottish Railway Ltd v Enron Coal Services Ltd (in liquidation)* [2009] EWCA Civ 647, [2009] UKCLR 816, paras 30–31. The claimant was refused leave to appeal by the Supreme Court. See also the subsequent decision of the CAT in *Enron Coal Services Ltd (in liquidation) v English Welsh & Scottish Railway Ltd* CAT [2010] CAT 4, [2010] Comp AR 229 (in refusing permission to the claimant to appeal against the judgment of the CAT in *Enron Coal Services Limited (in liquidation) v English Welsh & Scottish Railway Limited* [2009] CAT 36, [2010] Comp AR 108, in which the CAT found against the claimant in its damages claim, the CAT held that it was not inconsistent with the judgment of the Court of Appeal for the CAT to hear evidence from the parties on the question of causation and that this was one of the CAT's functions in a section 47A case).

276. See also the comments of Carnwath LJ that 'it is not enough to be able to point to findings in the decision from which an infringement might arguably be inferred' and that 'it is important that in drafting such a decision the regulator should leave no doubt as to the nature of the infringement (if any) which has been found' (*English Welsh & Scottish Railway Ltd v Enron Coal Services Ltd (in liquidation)* [2009] EWCA Civ 647, [2009] UKCLR 816, para 64).

277. See Competition Appeal Tribunal Rules 2003, SI 2003/1372, r 48.

278. See Competition Appeal Tribunal Rules 2003, SI 2003/1372, r 49.

(3) the CAT has developed considerable expertise by previously dealing with a significant number of cases arising from the same or similar infringements.[279]

What section 47A and 47B actions have been brought to date?

11. To date, at least thirteen section 47A claims have been filed with the CAT. Six of these claims were settled before coming to trial.[280] At the time of writing, six cases were pending. The *Albion Water* case involves claims arising out of the findings of the Tribunal in an earlier case in respect of abusive pricing practices. The claimant seeks compensatory damages and/or restitution, aggravated damages, exemplary damages, interest and an order for costs.[281] The *Moy Park* case involves claims for damages and interest by indirect purchasers of products allegedly cartelised by the *Methionine* cartel.[282] The *Marshall Food Group* case arises out of the same cartel and as well as damages and interest, an account of profits is also claimed.[283] In *Emerson* the claimant seeks damages, exemplary damages, restitution, and interest for direct purchasers of electrical and mechanical carbon and graphite products, also the subject of a Commission decision finding an infringement of Article 101.[284] The *BCL* case involves a claim by indirect purchasers from the *Vitamins* cartel for damages and interest.[285] The *Grampian* case also involves claims arising from the *Vitamins* cartel by direct and indirect purchasers who seek damages, alternatively restitution and interest.[286]

12. The thirteenth case, *Enron Coal*, was partly struck out and the claimant was unsuccessful in the remainder of the claim for damages for loss of opportunity to win a four-year contract to supply coal to a power plant owned by the defendant. The CAT held that the claimant had failed to establish that the defendant's unlawful conduct had caused the loss claimed.[287]

---

279. Practice Direction – Transfer, supplementing CPR Part 30, para 8.4.
280. Case No: 1028/5/7/04 *BCL Old Co Limited v Aventis SA*; Case No: 1029/5/7/04 *Deans Foods Limited v Roche Products Limited*; Case No: 1060/5/7/06 *Healthcare at Home Ltd v Genzyme Ltd*; Case No: 1088/5/7/07 *ME Burgess v W Austin & Sons (Stevenage) Limited*; Case No: 1105/5/7/08 *Freightliner Limited v English Welsh & Scottish Railway Limited*; Case No: 1108/5/7/08 *NJ and DM Wilson v Lancing College Limited*.
281. Case No 1166/5/7/10 *Albion Water Ltd v Dwr Cymru Cyfyngedig*.
282. Case No: 1147/5/7/09 *Moy Park Limited v Evonik Degussa GmbH*.
283. Case No: 1153/5/7/10 *Marshall Food Group Limited v Evonik Degussa GmbH*.
284. Case No: 1077/5/7/07 *Emerson Electric Co. v Morgan Crucible Company plc*.
285. Case No: 1098/5/7/08 *BCL Old Co Ltd v BASF SE*. The CAT dismissed applications by the claimants to extend time for lodging their claims, *BCL Old Co Ltd v BASF SE* [2009] CAT 29, [2010] Comp AR 1 (on appeal to the Court of Appeal).
286. Case No: 1101/5/7/08 *Grampian Country Foods Group Limited*.
287. *Enron Coal Services Limited (in liquidation) v English Welsh & Scottish Railway Limited* [2009] CAT 36, [2010] Comp AR 108.

13. The only case to date under section 47B was a damages claim on behalf of 130 consumers who had purchased replica Manchester United and England football shirts, which ultimately settled.[288]

> *Key Sources*
>
> **UK**
>
> Competition Act 1998, s 47A, s 47B.
>
> Practice Direction – Transfer, supplementing CPR Part 30.
>
> *English Welsh & Scottish Railway Ltd v Enron Coal Services Ltd (in liquidation)* [2009] EWCA Civ 647, [2009] UKCLR 816.

---

288. Case No: 1078/7/9/07 *The Consumers Association v JJB Sports PLC*. See Question 110.

117. WHAT IS THE TIME LIMIT FOR BRINGING A COMPETITION LAW CLAIM BASED ON A BREACH OF EU COMPETITION LAW?

Summary

Ireland

- Six years from accrual of the cause of action.

UK

High Court

- Six years from accrual of the cause of action.

Competition Appeal Tribunal – Follow-on Actions

- For actions that follow-on from a Commission decision, two years, two months and ten days from the Commission's decision.

- Appeals against the Commission's infringement decision stop time but appeals against only the penalty do not.

- The CAT has held that if one defendant appeals against the infringement decision, time is stopped against all defendants.

- The CAT may give permission for a claim to proceed even if time has not yet started running or if the claimant is out of time.

1. Limitation periods in private actions based on a breach of EU competition law are a matter for the national law that applies to the action,[289] subject to EU law principles, in particular the principles of equivalence and effectiveness. A very short limitation period might render practically impossible or excessively difficult the exercise of the right to seek compensation for the harm suffered and so breach the principle of effectiveness.[290] There is a considerable diversity of limitation periods in the Member States with the length of relevant limitation periods ranging from between one and thirty years.[291]

Ireland

2. The Competition Act 2002 is silent on the limitation period for bringing actions based on a breach of section 4 or 5 of the Act or Article 101 or 102. The limitation period is therefore governed by the Statute of Limitations 1957.[292]

---

289. See Regulation (EC) No 864/2007 on the law applicable to non-contractual obligations (Rome II) [2007] OJ L 199/40, Article 15(b), which includes rules on the 'grounds for exemption from liability' and rules on 'limitation of liability' as coming within the applicable law determined by Rome II.

290. See Cases C–295–298/04 *Manfredi v Lloyd Adriatico Assicurazioni SpA* [2006] ECR I–6619, [2006] 5 CMLR 980, para 78.

291. See Commission Staff Working Paper – Annex to the Green Paper – Damages actions for the Breach of EC Antitrust Rules, Com(2005) 672 final, 19 December 2005, para 265.

292. See Statute of Limitations 1957, s 7(a).

3.   Assuming that the cause of action in a particular competition law claim is to be characterised as a breach of statutory duty,[293] then this is an action in tort,[294] to which a six-year limitation period applies.[295] Alternatively, the action might be categorised as one to 'recover any sum recoverable by virtue of any enactment', to which a six-year limitation period also applies.[296] However, it is more likely that the action would be characterised as one simply in tort.[297] A six-year limitation period also applies to contract actions.[298] Each of these limitation periods runs from the date on which the cause of action accrued. Expiry of the limitation period does not extinguish the cause of action and it will bar an action only where it is raised successfully by the defendant.[299]

4.   In contract claims, the limitation period begins on the date of the breach of the contract.[300] In tort actions, a leading authority is the judgment of the Supreme Court in *Hegarty v O'Loughran*, which considered when the cause of action in a personal injury action accrued.[301] McCarthy J held that the cause of action accrues not on the date of discovery of its existence but 'on the date on which, if it had been discovered, proceedings could lawfully have been instituted'.[302] This rejection of a 'discoverability' rule in tort cases has been repeated in recent cases.[303] However, it is apparent from other judgments in *Hegarty* that where damage was not manifest until a later date, the limitation period should not run from the earlier date of the wrongful act. Griffin J stated:

> In such cases as these, if time were to run from the date of the occurrence of the wrongful act, the period of limitation ... might very well expire before there is any manifestation of the damage suffered in consequence of the wrongful act. However, in s. 11, sub-s. 2 (b) of the Act of 1957, time is not expressed to run from the date of the occurrence of the wrongful act and should not in my view be interpreted as if it was. The relevant date under the subsection is the date on which the cause of action accrues. Until and unless the plaintiff is in a position to establish by evidence that damage has been caused to him, his cause of action is not complete and the period of limitation fixed by that sub-section does not commence to run.[304]

---

293. On the characterisation of causes of action in competition cases, see Question 109.
294. See, e.g., *Tate v Minister for Social Welfare* [1995] 1 IR 418 (HC) 439.
295. See the Statute of Limitations 1957, s 11(2)(a).
296. Statute of Limitations 1957, s 11(1)(a).
297. See para 10 below and *R v Secretary of State for Transport, ex p Factortame Ltd (No. 6)* [2001] 1 WLR 942, para 163.
298. Statute of Limitations, s 11(1).
299. See Rules of the Superior Courts, Order 19, Rule 15.
300. See, e.g., *Irish Equine Foundation Ltd v Robinson* [1999] 2 IR 442 (HC).
301. The limitation period in personal injury actions is now governed the Civil Liability and Courts Act 2004.
302. *Hegarty v O'Loughran* [1990] 1 IR 148 (SC) 164 (McCarthy J).
303. See *Murphy v McInerney Construction Limited* [2008] IEHC 323 (Dunne J).
304. *Hegarty v O'Loughran* [1990] 1 IR 148 (SC) 158 (Griffin J).

5. It may be arguable from this authority[305] that in a competition case, the limitation period does not run until it is evident that there has been a breach of competition law, where the plaintiff is not aware of the damage until the breach has been established. This may not arise until well after the wrongful acts involved have occurred. For example, a customer may not realise that it was the victim of a price fixing cartel and so suffered damage until after the Commission has published a decision finding an infringement of Article 101. This could be years after the cartel had ceased operating.

6. Even if the courts did not take that view and rejected the 'discoverability' rule in a competition action, there are a number of possible arguments open to a plaintiff who is faced with a defence that his claim is statute barred in such circumstances. It may be arguable in EU competition law actions that the way in which the limitation period operates breaches the EU law principles of effectiveness and/or legal certainty.[306] In *Manfredi*, the Court of Justice explained that:

    > A national rule under which the limitation period begins to run from the day on which the agreement or concerted practice was adopted could make it practically impossible to exercise the right to seek compensation for the harm caused by that prohibited agreement or practice, particularly if that national rule also imposes a short limitation period which is not capable of being suspended.[307]

7. A plaintiff may also be able to rely on section 71 of the Statute of Limitations 1957, which provides that where the action is based on the fraud of the defendant or the right of action is concealed by the fraud of the defendant, time will only begin to run from the date the plaintiff discovers the fraud or could with reasonable diligence have discovered it.[308] Given that many competition law violations, such as those based on cartels or predatory strategies to eliminate a competitor, will have been deliberately concealed, section 71 could operate to extend the limitation period. In a follow-on action, a plaintiff may even be able to show that he was only

---

305. See also the comments of Finlay CJ in the same case, *Hegarty v O'Loughran* [1990] 1 IR 148 (SC) 155–157, and the discussion of the case by Geoghegan J in *Irish Equine Foundation Ltd v Robinson* [1999] 2 IR 442 (HC) 446–447 (noting the possibility that the views of Griffin J and Finaly CJ in *Hegarty* could be adapted to actions for property damage). See also Canny, *Limitation of Actions* (2010) para 7.10, noting that the Irish courts have consistently applied the 'manifestation' approach set out in *Hegarty*.

306. Although not a direct comparison, see the approach of the Court of Justice to national time limits in procurement cases in Case C–406/08 *Uniplex (UK) Ltd v NHS Business Services Authority* [2010] PTSR 1377 and Case C–456/08 *Commission v Ireland* [2010] 2 CMLR 1138.

307. Cases C–295–298/04 *Manfredi v Lloyd Adriatico Assicurazioni SpA* [2006] ECR I–6619, [2006] 5 CMLR 980, para 78. See also Case C–445/06 *Danske Slagterier v Germany* [2009] ECR I–2119, [2009] 3 CMLR 311, paras 49–52 (the fact that the limitation period laid down by national law for a *Francovich* claim begins to run when the first injurious effects have been produced was unlikely to breach the principle of effectiveness; however, in the case at bar, it was clear that the limitation period could not begin to run until the injured party had become aware of the loss or damage and of the identity of the person required to pay compensation).

308. Statute of Limitations 1957, s 71.

able to establish that the competition law violation affected him after the Commission had published the details in its infringement decision.

8. The limitation period question may be complicated when the infringement is one that is continuing over time, which will often be the case with breaches of competition law. The Court of Justice pointed to the difficulty in *Manfredi*, noting that 'where there are continuous or repeated infringements, it is possible that the limitation period expires even before the infringement is brought to an end, in which case it would be impossible for any individual who has suffered harm after the expiry of the limitation period to bring an action'.[309] The national rule will again be subject to the principle of effectiveness. An Irish court would probably take an approach similar to that of the English High Court in *Arkin*, finding that where the infringement continued after the expiry of the limitation period vis-à-vis the beginning of the infringement and caused damage after that date, a claim in respect of that damage would not be time-barred.[310]

9. There are no specific rules of limitation for follow-on actions in Ireland so it can be assumed that the same limitation period applies in such cases.

UK

10. Follow-on actions as well as stand-alone actions can be brought before the High Court. Competition law claims will generally be characterised as claims for breach of statutory duty.[311] This is a tort and the limitation period under the Limitation Act 1980 is six-years from the date on which the cause of action accrued.[312] Alternatively, the claim could be characterised as an action to recover a sum recoverable by virtue of an enactment and again, there is a six-year limitation period.[313] It is more likely however that the claim will be viewed as simply one in tort.[314] The limitation period for contract actions is also six years, which runs from the date of the breach of contract.[315]

11. The cause of action for a tort actionable on proof of damage accrues once the claimant has suffered 'real damage', which is more than 'minimal damage'.[316] While the Limitation Act 1980 provides for special time limits in certain cases

---

309. Cases C–295–298/04 *Manfredi v Lloyd Adriatico Assicurazioni SpA* [2006] ECR I–6619, [2006] 5 CMLR 980, para 79.
310. See paras 13–14 below.
311. See Question 109.
312. Limitation Act 1980, s 2.
313. Limitation Act 1980, s 9.
314. Cf *R v Secretary of State for Transport, ex p Factortame Ltd (No. 6)* [2001] 1 WLR 942, para 163 (Toulmin HHJ holding that in the context of section 9 of the Limitation Act 1980, 'sums recoverable by virtue of any enactment' referred to cases 'where those sums which are recoverable by the claimant are specified in or directly ascertainable from the enactment').
315. Limitation Act 1980, s 5.
316. See, e.g., discussing negligence claims, *Haward v Fawcetts* [2006] UKHL 9, [2006] 1 WLR 682, para 3.

where the facts relevant to the cause of action were not known, none of these would usually apply in a competition case.[317] As discussed above in the context of the Irish rules, a claimant may have an argument that the EU law principle of effectiveness (and possibly the principle of legal certainty) requires the limitation period to be disapplied where it operates to bar a claim, where the claimant's knowledge of the relevant facts arose after the limitation period had expired.

12.   An antitrust claimant faced with a limitation defence may also be able to rely on section 32 of the Limitation Act 1980. It provides that in the case of fraud or deliberate concealment, the limitation period does not begin to run until the claimant discovered the fraud or concealment or could with reasonable diligence have discovered it.[318]

13.   The High Court addressed the issue of limitation in the context of continuing infringements when ruling on a preliminary issue in *Arkin*. Colman J held that the alleged breaches of Articles 101 and 102 were continuing infringements. If the limitation period, starting when the infringement first caused the claimant real damage, had expired, a claim in respect of damage occurring after the end of that limitation period would not be barred. The learned judge distinguished this situation of a continuous infringement from that of a single infringement causing a chain of damage:

> [An] isolated event amounting to such a breach may cause a chain of damage development commencing when the effects of the breach first affect the claimant and those efforts may continue for a long period of time. If that period commences prior to the cut-off date for the purposes of a period of limitation, the claim will *prima facie* be time-barred notwithstanding that the effects of the breach may continue beyond that date. The position is similar to a claim in tort for negligence.

> By contrast, there may be a continuing or repeated breach of statutory duty, over an extended period, such as an unlawful emission of toxic fumes which continues to affect and injure those exposed to it over the whole period of that breach. In such a case, if the limitation cut-off date occurs during the period, the claimant's cause of action for the damage suffered after the date in question will not be time-barred. He is then in the position where he can identify a continuing or repeated breach of duty within the limitation period.

14.   So, if implementation of the agreements and practices contrary to Articles 101 and 102

> continued after the commencement of the limitation period, and subsequently caused loss or damage to the claimant a claim in respect of that damage would not be time-barred. Similarly ... if implementation prior to the cut-off date could be shown first to have caused damage after that date, a claim in respect of that damage would not be

---

317. See, in particular, Limitation Act 1980, s 14A (negligence actions).
318. Limitation Act 1980, s 32(1).

time-barred, the cause of action in respect of that implementation only having arisen when that damage was sustained.[319]

15. It is doubtful that the limitation period will be affected by any appeals brought against the Commission's decision in the General Court or subsequent appeals to the Court of Justice. However, in one such follow-on case where the defendants had appealed against the Commission's infringement decision, *National Grid v ABB*, it was argued that the High Court should stay the proceedings until after the conclusion of the appeals before the EU courts. While accepting that the national court should take all steps required to ensure that the trial did not come on before appeals against the Commission decision were concluded, Morritt C rejected the argument that the national court was *required* to abstain from taking further steps in the action on the basis of the principle that a national court must avoid giving decisions which would conflict with a decision of the Commission or EU courts.[320]

16. The Chancellor acknowledged that if an immediate stay was not ordered, the defendants would sustain some prejudice and expense because they would be required to prepare for a trial which might not occur (if the appeals before the EU courts were successful). On the other hand, if a stay were granted immediately, the claimant would sustain prejudice from the further delay that would ensue before its claim could be heard. The extent of that prejudice on, for example, the availability of evidence, could not be foreseen. The Chancellor found that the balance of justice required that the action proceed at least to the close of pleadings. Unless the preparation of the action continued, the parties would not be on an equal footing because the claimant would not know what the relevant issues were or what documents relevant to those issues, particularly causation, were available. As well as requiring the defendants to file a defence, the Chancellor did not rule out that some disclosure should take place before the conclusion of the appeals against the Commission decision. It was ordered that the action should not be listed for hearing against any of the defendants until after three months from the conclusion of the appeals against the Commission decision before the EU courts.

17. The situation in *National Grid v ABB*, where the national court hearing a follow-on damages claim is faced with deciding what steps in that action should proceed before the conclusion of appeals against the Commission infringement decision, is likely to arise frequently in such cases. The resulting orders of the court will have to take account of the principle of sincere cooperation[321] and avoid conflicting

---

319. *Arkin v Borchard Lines Ltd (Preliminary Issue)* [2000] UKCLR 495 (references omitted). For further examples of the application of limitation periods to continuing breaches, see Brealey and Green (eds), *Competition Litigation: UK Practice and Procedure* (2010) para 4.22.

320. See *National Grid Electricity Transmission plc v ABB Ltd* [2009] EWHC 1326 (Ch), [2009] UKCLR 838.

321. See Article 4(3) TEU.

decisions while having regard 'to the overriding objective to deal with the follow on action justly'.[322]

What is the time limit for follow-on actions under section 47A of the Competition Act 1998?[323]

18. Section 47A of the Competition Act 1998 provides a specific jurisdiction for follow-on claims in the CAT.[324] The time limit for bringing a follow-on claim in the CAT from a Commission decision is set out in Rule 31 of the CAT's Rules[325] read together with section 47A(8) of the Competition Act 1998. The claim must be brought within two years from one of the following dates:

    (a) the period during which proceedings against the decision or finding may be instituted in the European Court; and

    (b) if any such proceedings are instituted, the period before those proceedings are determined.[326]

19. If the cause of action accrues after the later of these two dates, then the claim would not have to be brought until two years from the date that the cause of action accrued.[327] It is unlikely that the date of accrual of the cause of action would prove to be the later date.[328]

20. If no appeal is brought against the decision of the Commission, then the time limit will be two years from the last date for filing an appeal against the Commission decision, which is two months and ten days from publication of the decision.[329] If an appeal is brought, the two-year time limit does not run until conclusion of that appeal. If a claimant wishes to bring a section 47A action before the two-year period has started to run, it must obtain permission from the CAT. The CAT also has the power to extend the time limit where an action is brought out of time.[330]

21. In section 47A claims that follow on from a decision of the OFT or the CAT, the time limit is calculated in a similar way, with the two-year time limit running only from the end of the period in which an appeal against the infringement decision could have been brought or, if appeals are brought, two years from the conclusion of the appeals.[331]

---

322. *National Grid Electricity Transmission plc v ABB Ltd* [2009] EWHC 1326 (Ch), [2009] UKCLR 838, para 32.

323. See also Brealey and Green (eds), *Competition Litigation: UK Practice and Procedure* (2010) paras 4.67–4.82.

324. On the section 47A procedure, see Question 116.

325. Competition Appeal Tribunal Rules 2003, SI 2003/1372, r 31.

326. Competition Act 1998, s 47A(8).

327. Competition Appeal Tribunal Rules 2003, SI 2003/1372, r 31(2)(b).

328. See para 11 on when the cause of action accrues.

329. Article 263 TFEU read together with Article 102(2) of the Rules of Procedure of the General Court [2010] OJ C177/02.

330. Competition Appeal Tribunal Rules 2003, SI 2003/1372, r 19(2)(i).

331. Competition Act 1998, s 47A(7).

What is the time limit if only the Commission's fine is appealed?

22.   What if the appeals against the Commission's decision are only against the penalty imposed and do not challenge the finding of an infringement of Article 101 or 102? In *BCL v BASF*, the Court of Appeal held that where appeals were brought only against the fine, this was insufficient to stop the running of the two-year time period for bringing a section 47A action.

23.   The claimants had brought a follow-on action just inside two years after the conclusion of appeals by the defendants against the Commission decision in the *Vitamins* cartel. Those appeals were limited to appealing the fines imposed by the Commission and did not challenge the finding of infringement of Article 101. On this basis the Court of Appeal held that the relevant decision, by reference to which the time limit under section 47A was calculated, was the decision finding an infringement of the competition rules. This was different to the decision imposing a penalty.[332] The CAT had found that it was the Commission's decision as a whole that was the relevant decision.[333]

24.   Richards LJ found support for his interpretation that the infringement decision was decisive from section 47A(5)(a), which provides that no claim can be made until 'a decision mentioned in subsection (6) has established that the relevant prohibition in question has been infringed'. The relevant decision listed in section 47A(6) was that Article 101 had 'been infringed', not that a fine had been applied in respect of an infringement. They were two separate decisions, even if the Commission's practice was to cover both in a single decision document. As BASF had only appealed against the Commission's decision on the amount of the fine and not on the infringement decision, the two-year time period for section 47A purposes began to run from the date on which BASF could have appealed the infringement decision, *i.e.* two months and ten days after the Commission's decision. The claim was brought outside this time limit and was therefore time barred and could only be brought if the CAT granted an extension of time. The CAT subsequently refused to grant an extension of time.[334]

If only some defendants have appealed the Commission's decision, does this affect the time limit vis-à-vis all defendants?

25.   If only some of the defendants in a follow-on action have appealed against the Commission's infringement decision, does the time limit start to run against other defendants who did not appeal? This situation may occur frequently in follow-on actions as one of the defendants may be a leniency applicant, which probably received no fine from the Commission and therefore had little incentive to file an appeal against the Commission's infringement decision.

---

332. *BCL Old Co Ltd v BASF SE* [2009] EWCA Civ 434, [2009] UKCLR 789.
333. *BCL Old Co Ltd v BASF SE* [2008] CAT 24, [2008] Comp AR 210, para 35.
334. *BCL Old Co Ltd v BASF SE* [2009] CAT 29, [2010] Comp AR 1 (on appeal to the Court of Appeal; the effect of the CAT's decision on the EU and ECHR rights of the claimants may be an issue in the appeal).

26. In *Emerson*, the CAT decided that where *any* appeal had been brought against the Commission's decision (even one by a party who was not a defendant in the follow-on action), time for purposes of applying the two-year time limit in Rule 31 of the CAT's Rules had not begun to run against any of the addressees of the Commission decision. The time limit would only begin to run at the conclusion of all of the appeals before the European Courts.[335] This decision was not appealed to the Court of Appeal. Given the subsequent approach of the Court of Appeal in *BCL v BASF*, distinguishing between appeals of different types of decision, the safest course for a claimant wishing to utilise the section 47A jurisdiction will be to file its claim sooner rather than later, where there is any doubt about when the two-year window for bringing a claim starts.

27. Where the time limit has not yet begun, the CAT has the power to grant permission for a claim to be brought under Rule 31(3) of the CAT's Rules. In *Emerson*, the CAT decided to grant permission for the claim to proceed against Morgan Crucible,[336] which had not appealed the Commission decision, while denying permission to proceed against the other defendants, which had appeals seeking annulment of the Commission decision pending before the European Courts. The very basis of the follow-on claim – the Commission's infringement decision – could be annulled in those appeals. The CAT thought that the likelihood of the defendants succeeding in the appeals was irrelevant to its decision as this was a matter entirely for the General Court and possibly the Court of Justice, if there was a further appeal.[337]

When will the CAT extend the Section 47A time limit?

28. Even if the two-year time limit for bringing a section 47A action has expired, there is a possibility of having the time limit extended. However, the *BCL v BASF* case suggests that the CAT considers the extension of this time limit to be a 'serious matter' and that extensions will not be granted lightly.

29. Rule 19(2)(i) of the CAT's Rules provides that the CAT may give directions as to 'the abridgement or extension of any time limits, whether or not expired'. In *BCL v BASF*, following the Court of Appeal's decision that the section 47A time limit had expired when they filed their claims in the CAT,[338] in further proceedings before the CAT, BCL and Grampian sought to have the time limit extended.

30. Drawing a comparison with cases on the extension of a time limit under maritime legislation, the CAT adopted a two-part test to the question of whether time should

335. *Emerson Electric Co. v Morgan Crucible Company plc* [2007] CAT 28, [2008] Comp AR 9.
336. *Emerson Electric Co. v Morgan Crucible Company plc* [2007] CAT 30.
337. *Emerson Electric Co. v Morgan Crucible Company plc* [2008] CAT 8, [2008] Comp AR 118, para 87. SGL Carbon and Le Carbone lost their appeals to the General Court (Case T–68/04 *SGL Carbon AG v Commission* [2008] ECR II–2511, [2009] 4 CMLR 7; Case T–73/04 *Le Carbone-Lorraine SA v Commission* [2008] OJ C301/31) and subsequent appeals to the Court of Justice (Case C–564/08 *SGL Carbon AG v Commission*, 12 November 2009; Case C–554/08 *Le Carbone-Lorraine SA v Commission*, 12 November 2009).
338. *BCL Old Co Ltd v BASF SE* [2009] EWCA Civ 434, [2009] UKCLR 789.

be extended: (i) whether the claimants had shown that there was a good reason for not having issued their proceedings in time; and (ii) if so, whether other factors relevant to the exercise of the CAT's discretion, including the prejudice that would be caused to either side, were present.[339]

31.   BCL (but not the other claimant, Grampian) satisfied the first part of the test, having made the mistake of thinking that the time in which it could bring its claim had not yet started to run while appeals against the Commission's decision were pending. This view was based on legal advice, which at the time (before the Court of Appeal later clarified the position) was not an untenable position.

32.   However, BCL did not satisfy the second leg of the test. During the period when appeals by the defendants against the Commission decision were pending before the General Court, it should at least have alerted BASF that it intended to lodge a claim when the two-year period opened. Even after the General Court's judgment on the appeals, it took six months for BCL to notify BASF of its intention to sue and this was a substantial delay. In considering potential prejudice, the CAT held that the possibility that the six-year limitation period for BCL to bring an action in the High Court had expired, was not a relevant consideration. Any prejudice from this was simply 'part and parcel of the application of the relevant rules and not an additional factor to weigh in the balance'.[340]

Key Sources

Ireland

Statute of Limitations 1957, s 11(2)(a).

UK

Competition Act 1998, s 47A.

Competition Appeal Tribunal Rules, r 19, r 31.

BCL Old Co Ltd v BASF SE [2009] EWCA Civ 434, [2009] UKCLR 789.

National Grid Electricity Transmission plc v ABB Ltd [2009] EWHC 1326 (Ch), [2009] UKCLR 838.

BCL Old Co Ltd v BASF SE [2009] CAT 29, [2010] Comp AR 1.

---

339. *BCL Old Co Ltd v BASF SE* [2009] CAT 29, [2010] Comp AR 1, para 19.

340. *BCL Old Co Ltd v BASF SE* [2009] CAT 29, [2010] Comp AR 1, para 32 (on appeal to the Court of Appeal).

118. Do SPECIAL DISCOVERY RULES APPLY IN COMPETITION LAW CASES?

Summary

Ireland

• The standard discovery rules apply to competition law actions.

• Discovery will not be ordered unless it is relevant and necessary.

• The Irish courts have acknowledged that competition cases may have special features, e.g. deliberate concealment of documents, which should be taken into account.

UK

• The standard disclosure rules apply in competition law actions in the High Court.

• The standard rules cover disclosure of documents on which a party relies, documents that adversely affect his own or another party's case and documents that support another party's case.

• The High Court has considered an application for pre-action disclosure in a competition law case but refused it in the particular circumstances.

• The CAT also has the power to order disclosure.

Ireland

1. Discovery in competition law cases as in other civil cases in the High Court is governed by Order 31, Rule 12 of the Rules of the Superior Courts. The court shall not order discovery 'if and so far as the Court shall be of the opinion that it is not necessary either for disposing fairly of the cause or matter or for saving costs'.[341]

2. The application for discovery is by notice of motion, specifying precise categories of documents in respect of which discovery is sought. A grounding affidavit must verify that the discovery is necessary for the fair disposal of the case and reasons must be furnished as to why each category of documents is required.[342]

3. The Irish Supreme Court has considered the application of the discovery rules in a competition law context in a number of decisions, the most important of which are *Framus*[343] and *Ryanair*.[344] The general approach of the Irish courts to discovery will first be considered before examining whether special rules apply in competition cases.

---

341. Rules of the Superior Courts, Order 31 Rule 12(3).
342. Before bringing an application in the court, the applicant must seek voluntary discovery from the other party by letter. See Rules of the Superior Courts, Order 31, Rule 12(4).
343. *Framus Limited v CRH plc* [2004] 2 IR 20.
344. *Ryanair plc v Aer Rianta cpt* [2003] 4 IR 264.

4.   The Irish courts have often repeated the requirement that discovery must be both relevant to the issues pleaded and necessary for the fair disposal of the case or to save costs. An applicant is not entitled to discovery based on mere speculation or on the basis of what has been traditionally characterised as 'fishing':

> [A] party may not seek discovery of a document in order to find out whether the document may be relevant. A general trawl through the other party's documentation is not permitted under the Rules.[345]

5.   The Irish courts have endorsed the statement of Brett LJ in *Compagnie Financière du Pacifique*[346] to the effect that 'every document [relating] to the matters in question in the action, which not only would be evidence upon any issue, but also which, it is reasonable to suppose contains information which may – not which must – either directly or indirectly enable the party requiring the affidavit either to advance his own case or to damage the case of his adversary' should be discovered. This is the accepted test of the primary requirement for discovery.

6.   Murray J, as he then was, pointed out in *Aquatechnologie*[347] that there is nothing in the statement of Brett LJ in *Compagnie Financière du Pacifique* to qualify the principle that documents discovered must be relevant to the issues between the parties. In addition, it must be shown that it is reasonable for the court to suppose that the documents contain information which may reasonably advance the applicant's case or damage the case of his opponent.

7.   In *Ryanair*, Fennelly J made the point that most disputes about discovery centre on whether documents are relevant, rather than whether they are necessary. There was good reason for this as 'if there are relevant documents in the possession of one party, it will normally be unfair if they are not available to the opposing party'.[348] In other words, if a document is relevant, it will usually be necessary as well.

8.   To show necessity, the applicant does not have to prove that the documents are 'in any sense absolutely necessary'.[349] Although Fennelly J did not favour adopting as a test whether the discovery of the documents would give the applicant a 'litigious advantage' (or that he would suffer a litigious disadvantage by not seeing the document), the learned judge did acknowledge that the framework of litigious advantage was a useful context in which to examine the necessity for discovery.[350] As well as considering the relevance of documents based on the pleadings, the court 'should also consider the necessity for discovery having regard to all the relevant circumstances, including the burden, scale and cost of the discovery

---

345. *Hannon v Commissioners for Public Works* [2001] IEHC 59 (McCracken J).
346. *Compagnie Financière du Pacifique v Peruvian Guano Company* (1882) 11 QBD 55. For Irish cases endorsing the statement see, for example, *Sterling-Winthrop Group Ltd v Farbenfabriken Bayer AG* [1967] IR 97.
347. *Aquatechnologie Limited v National Standards Authority of Ireland* [2000] IESC 64.
348. *Ryanair plc v Aer Rianta cpt* [2003] 4 IR 264, 276.
349. *Ryanair plc v Aer Rianta cpt* [2003] 4 IR 264, 276.
350. The adoption of a test of 'litigious advantage' had been proposed by Kelly J in the High Court in *Cooper Flynn v Radio Telefís Éireann* [2000] 3 IR 344.

sought'.[351] This is all subject to the position that the 'overriding interest in the proper conduct of the administration of justice will be the guiding consideration, when evaluating the necessity for discovery'.[352]

9. The proportionality of the discovery sought is an important consideration. In *Framus*, Murray J stated:

> [There] must be some proportionality between the extent or volume of the documents to be discovered and the degree to which the documents are likely to advance the case of the applicant or damage the case of his or her opponent in addition to ensuring that no party is taken by surprise by the production of documents at a trial. That is not to gainsay in any sense that the primary test is whether the documents are relevant to the issues between the parties. Once that is established it will follow in most cases that their discovery is necessary for the fair disposal of those issues.[353]

10. In *Ryanair*, Fennelly J explained that the change made to Order 31, rule 12 in 1999, which shifted to the applicant the burden of proving that discovery is necessary, exemplified

> growing concern about the dangers of unnecessarily costly and protracted litigation and, in particular, the burdens on parties and the courts arising from excessive resort to automatic blanket discovery. The public interest in the proper administration of justice is not confined to the relentless search for perfect truth. The just and proper conduct of litigation also encompasses the objectives of expedition and economy.[354]

Is the special nature of competition law infringements considered?

11. The same discovery rules set out in Order 31, Rule 12 apply to competition law cases as they do to other types of civil cases in the High Court. Nevertheless, there is an argument that special consideration should be given to discovery applications because competition law claims will often be based on alleged illicit anti-competitive agreements or practices, which of their nature are likely to be concealed.

12. This was acknowledged by Fennelly J in *Ryanair*, stating that antitrust cases have

> ... the special feature that any documents relating to anti-competitive behaviour, whether by being party to agreements or concerted practices or protecting a dominant position, are likely to be in the possession of the party engaged in that behaviour. Anti-competitive agreements or practices will be kept secret.[355]

13. Similar comments were made by Kearns J, as he then was, in the Supreme Court in *Dome Telecom* to the effect that:

> Competition cases generally may have the special feature that anti-competitive practices may be kept secret and that any documents relating to anti-competitive

---

351. *Ryanair plc v Aer Rianta cpt* [2003] 4 IR 264, 277.
352. *Ryanair plc v Aer Rianta cpt* [2003] 4 IR 264, 276.
353. *Framus Limited v CRH plc* [2004] 2 IR 20, 38.
354. *Ryanair plc v Aer Rianta cpt* [2003] 4 IR 264, 277.
355. *Ryanair plc v Aer Rianta cpt* [2003] 4 IR 264, 277–278.

behaviour are more likely to be in the possession of the party engaging in that behaviour.[356]

14. These various statements by the Supreme Court on the special features of competition law cases are an important acknowledgment of the particular difficulties faced by antitrust claimants. The secret nature of anti-competitive agreements and practices seems to be a factor to be taken into account when the court decides what discovery should be ordered. With perhaps a more sceptical tone, Murray J in *Framus* acknowledged the special characteristics of competition cases in agreeing that there was:

> some substance in the plaintiffs' arguments that in a case of this nature, that is to say, where the wrongful activities alleged against a party are ones which by their nature are likely to be concealed, thus making it difficult for an opposing party to identify particular documents or specify categories in a limited way, it may indeed be appropriate for a court to order discovery of documents relating to anti-competitive agreements or practices which are not directly related to particular acts or conduct which a party, perhaps fortuitously, is in a position to set out in their pleadings.[357]

15. Murray J agreed that where discovery is sought in a case where the wrongful acts are likely to be peculiarly within the defendant's knowledge and unlikely to be within the plaintiff's knowledge 'because of a propensity to conceal them', this was a factor to be taken into account.[358]

16. However, the secret nature of alleged anti-competitive agreements and conduct is only one factor in deciding what discovery should be ordered. It has to be balanced against other factors, such as the burden and expense on the other party of making discovery, whether discovery would result in nothing more than marginal advantage to the applicant and whether there was a speculative element in the application. These factors are all subject to the requirement that discovery be confined to what is necessary for the fair disposal of the case in the context of the applicable facts and issues.[359]

17. It is also apparent from *Framus* that the Irish courts will not consider relevant the much more generous approach to discovery in antitrust cases in the United States. The plaintiffs in *Framus* had argued for a broader approach to discovery in competition law cases on the basis of US case law. However Murray J was not persuaded of the relevance of US authorities 'given the indigenous traditions and practices of United States courts in the whole area of discovery which are very much different from ours'.[360]

18. One specific area where the courts may give more leeway in a discovery application in a competition law case is in the identification of the categories of documents sought. In *Ryanair*, McCracken J considered whether the applicant had

---

356. *Dome Telecom Limited v Eircom Limited* [2007] IESC 59, [2008] 2 IR 726, para 103.
357. *Framus Limited v CRH plc* [2004] 2 IR 20, 39–40.
358. *Framus Limited v CRH plc* [2004] 2 IR 20, 47.
359. See *Framus Limited v CRH plc* [2004] 2 IR 20, in particular at 40.
360. *Framus Limited v CRH plc* [2004] 2 IR 20, 47.

identified with sufficient precision the categories of documents sought in discovery. Finding that Ryanair specified sufficiently precise categories, McCracken J stated:

> In many cases and this is particularly so in relation to competition cases, a plaintiff cannot know whether documents exist, and if so what those documents are. For example, meetings may have been held between a defendant and third parties, or indeed between members of the staff of a defendant, relating to a number of the matters in issue. A plaintiff has no means of knowing whether those meetings were ever held, or whether any record or minutes of such meetings exist. All he can do is seek documents in relation to any such discussions which may have taken place, and cannot be any more specific than that.[361]

19. While acknowledging that the 1999 amendments to the discovery rules had sought to do away with blanket discovery, McCracken J nevertheless found that:

> ... the reference to categories of documents recognises that a person seeking discovery may not know what documents exist and may not be able to specify the individual documents with precision ... The situation in a competition case is very different from that in a personal injuries action and any reference to precision in categories of documents must be considered in the light of the particular cause of action and the likely knowledge of the party claiming discovery as to what documents exist.[362]

20. These statements indicate a more lenient approach to the identification of precise categories of documents sought through discovery in competition cases. That view is supported by Murray J's finding in *Framus* that in a competition law case he would 'not exclude the possibility of granting discovery for a specified class of documents which did not relate directly to a specific event pleaded but which was nonetheless relevant to the issues'.[363] Whatever the extent of this more generous approach to categories of discovery in competition cases, it will not save categories of documents that are vague or irrelevant or unnecessary to issues in the case.

Are the EU law principles of equivalence and effectiveness relevant?

21. In *Framus*, Murray J rejected the argument that to the extent the plaintiffs were seeking to enforce EU law rights under Articles 101 and 102, the principles of equivalence and effectiveness were not complied with. Equivalence was guaranteed as the same discovery rules under Order 31, Rule 12 applied whether the claim was based on national law or EU law. The principle of effectiveness was not infringed as there was no basis for finding that remedies open to the plaintiff were rendered 'virtually impossible or excessively difficult'.[364]

---

361. *Ryanair plc v Aer Rianta cpt* [2003] 4 IR 264, 279–280.
362. *Ryanair plc v Aer Rianta cpt* [2003] 4 IR 264, 280.
363. *Framus Limited v CRH plc* [2004] 2 IR 20, 40.
364. *Framus Limited v CRH plc* [2004] 2 IR 20, 48, quoting Cases C–430 & 431/1993 *Van Schijndel v Stichting Pensioenfonds* [1995] ECR I–4705, para 19.

Is pre-action discovery available?

22. The general rule is that a party should not seek discovery at the pre-pleading stage. However an order for pre-action discovery (or, in the case of the defendant, an order for discovery before the delivery of the defence) may be granted in exceptional circumstances, where the demands of justice so require.[365] The Irish courts do not appear to have considered the question of pre-action discovery in the competition law context specifically.

23. A party may apply pre-discovery or even at the pre-action stage for an injunction to search for and preserve documents (an *Anton Piller* order).[366]

UK[367]

24. The standard disclosure rule in England and Wales is set out in CPR 31.6:

> Standard disclosure requires a party to disclose only –
>
> (a) the documents on which he relies; and
>
> (b) the documents which –
>
> > (i) adversely affect his own case;
> >
> > (ii) adversely affect another party's case; or
> >
> > (iii) support another party's case; and
>
> (c) the documents which he is required to disclose by a relevant practice direction.

25. This provision replaced the previous disclosure rules which had been based on *Compagnie Financière du Pacifique*,[368] which still forms the basis of discovery in Ireland and other jurisdictions. While standard disclosure under CPR 31.6 is narrower in scope, how much difference this has made in practice is open to debate.[369] It does not seem that the English courts have recently had an opportunity to comment on whether the special features of competition cases should be taken into account in ordering disclosure.

Is pre-action disclosure available?

26. An application for pre-action disclosure can be made under CPR31.16, which provides in part:

> (3) The court may make an order under this rule only where-
>
> (a) the respondent is likely to be a party to subsequent proceedings;
>
> (b) the applicant is also likely to be a party to those proceedings;

---

365. See, e.g., *Law Society of Ireland v Rawlinson* [1997] 3 IR 592.
366. See Kirwan, *Injunctions: Law and Practice* (2008) paras 8.129–8.183.
367. For more detailed treatment of disclosure in UK competition actions, see Brealey and Green (eds), *Competition Litigation: UK Practice and Procedure* (2010) paras 9.02–9.52.
368. *Compagnie Financière du Pacifique v Peruvian Guano Company* (1882) 11 QBD 55.
369. See *Nichia Corpn v Argos Ltd* [2007] EWCA Civ 741, [2007] FSR 38 (the judgments of the Court of Appeal emphasise the requirement that disclosure be proportionate).

     (c) if proceedings had started, the respondent's duty by way of standard disclosure, set out in rule 31.6 , would extend to the documents or classes of documents of which the applicant seeks disclosure; and

     (d) disclosure before proceedings have started is desirable in order to-

         (i) dispose fairly of the anticipated proceedings;

         (ii) assist the dispute to be resolved without proceedings; or

         (iii) save costs.[370]

27.   The availability of pre-action disclosure in a competition case was considered by the High Court in *Hutchison 3G*. The applicant sought wide-ranging pre-action disclosure against four of its mobile phone competitors, which it claimed were engaged in activities that were contrary to Article 101/Chapter I prohibition and Article 102/Chapter II prohibition. Hutchison claimed that the Mobile Number Portability ('MNP') system in operation in the UK constituted a significant barrier to entry and growth for a new mobile operator such as itself and that the defendants prevented the development of an efficient MNP system.

28.   In refusing disclosure, Steel J found that the applicants would have to show that it was more probable than not that the documents they sought were within the scope of standard disclosure in regard to the issues that were likely to arise.[371] The scope of the disclosure sought, which had identified very few specific documents and the vast bulk of which sought groups or classes of documents, was well beyond any probable scope of standard disclosure. In any event, the request was so lacking in specificity, that Steel J could not accept that the entirety of the classes of documents were 'likely' or 'may well' have fallen within standard disclosure.[372]

29.   On the desirability of disclosure (another cumulative condition), the applicant had made two arguments, that its action might be abandoned depending on what materials were disclosed and, if not, pre-action disclosure would achieve a focused pleading. The learned judge rejected both arguments, noting that it was improbable that the applicant would unearth material that convincingly demonstrated that its suspicions about a breach of competition law were ill-founded rather than well-founded. A cost-benefit analysis, taking account of the fact that pre-action disclosure would have to be made without inference to any pleaded materials among other factors, clearly favoured the respondent.[373]

30.   In some circumstances, it may be desirable for a party seeking pre-action disclosure (or simply disclosure in the normal course) to apply for a search order (formerly *Anton Piller* orders) requiring the other party to admit it to premises for the purpose of preserving evidence.[374]

---

370. CPR 31.16(3).

371. *Hutchison 3G UK Ltd v O2 (UK) Ltd* [2008] EWHC 55 (Comm), [2008] UKCLR 83, para 44.

372. *Hutchison 3G UK Ltd v O2 (UK) Ltd* [2008] EWHC 55 (Comm), [2008] UKCLR 83, paras 46–47.

373. *Hutchison 3G UK Ltd v O2 (UK) Ltd* [2008] EWHC 55 (Comm), [2008] UKCLR 83, paras 53–61.

374. CPR 25.1(h).

What disclosure rules apply in the CAT?

31. The CAT Rules provide that the CAT may give directions 'for the disclosure between, or the production by, the parties of documents or classes of documents'.[375] To date, disclosure issues in the CAT have generally arisen in the context of regulatory appeals or judicial review proceedings, rather than in private actions.[376]

Key Sources

Ireland

Rules of the Superior Courts, Order 31, Rule 12.

Framus Limited v CRH plc [2004] 2 IR 20.

Ryanair plc v Aer Rianta cpt [2003] 4 IR 264.

UK

CPR 31.6, 31.16.

Hutchison 3G UK Ltd v O2 (UK) Ltd [2008] EWHC 55 (Comm), [2008] UKCLR 83.

---

375. Competition Appeal Tribunal Rules 2003, SI 2003/1372, r 19(2)(k).
376. See, e.g., *Durkan Holdings v Office of Fair Trading* [2010] CAT 12.

119. MAY THE EUROPEAN COMMISSION INTERVENE IN A PRIVATE ANTITRUST ACTION BASED ON A BREACH OF EU COMPETITION LAW?

Summary

- Article 15 of Regulation 1/2003 facilitates the Commission's involvement in national cases involving the application of Article 101 or 102.

- The national court may ask the Commission to transmit information or issue an opinion.

- The Commission may submit observations and, with the approval of the national court, make oral submissions.

- The Commission will not use its ability to intervene to favour one side over the other in an *inter partes* dispute.

1. Article 4(3) TEU (which corresponds to what was previously Article 10 TEC) provides that pursuant to the principle of sincere cooperation, the Union and the Member States shall assist each other in carrying out tasks which flow from the Treaties. The Court of Justice has found that this allows the national court to contact the Commission 'where the concrete application of Article [101(1)] or of Article [102] raises particular difficulties, in order to obtain the economic and legal information which that institution can supply to it'.[377]

2. Specific provisions on cooperation between the Commission and national courts in competition matters are included in Regulation 1/2003.[378] Article 15 of Regulation 1/2003 deals with cooperation between the Commission and the national courts. It provides for the intervention of the Commission in any national court proceedings involving the application of Article 101 or 102, whether a private action or another type of proceeding. Article 15 provides in part as follows:

    > 1. In proceedings for the application of Article [101] or Article [102] of the Treaty, courts of the Member States may ask the Commission to transmit to them information in its possession or its opinion on questions concerning the application of the Community competition rules.

---

377. Case C–234/89 *Delimits v Henninger Bräu AG* [1991] ECR I–935, [1992] 5 CMLR 210, para 53. See also Case C–2/88 *Zwartveld* [1990] ECR I–3365, [1990] 3 CMLR 457, paras 17–18.

378. Article 11 of Regulation 1/2003 provides for cooperation between the Commission and the national competition authorities. Although courts in certain Member States are designated as competition authorities for purposes of Regulation 1/2003 (for example, in Ireland; see SI No 195 of 2004 European Communities (Implementation of the Rules on Competition laid down in Articles 81 and 82 of the Treaty) Regulations 2004), in the context of private actions, Article 15 is the appropriate basis for cooperation between the national court and the Commission.

2. Member States shall forward to the Commission a copy of any written judgment of national courts deciding on the application of Article [101] or Article [102] of the Treaty. Such copy shall be forwarded without delay after the full written judgment is notified to the parties.

3. Competition authorities of the Member States, acting on their own initiative, may submit written observations to the national courts of their Member State on issues relating to the application of Article [101] or Article [102] of the Treaty. With the permission of the court in question, they may also submit oral observations to the national courts of their Member State. Where the coherent application of Article [101] or Article [102] of the Treaty so requires, the Commission, acting on its own initiative, may submit written observations to courts of the Member States. With the permission of the court in question, it may also make oral observations.

3.   An intervention by the Commission could carry weight before a national judge. There is a danger that such an intervention could favour one side over the other in what is an *inter partes* dispute. This may have implications for the protection of the 'equality of arms' between litigants and the fairness of the litigation.

4.   However, the goal of cooperation between the Commission and national courts is to ensure consistency in the application of the EU competition rules rather than encourage the Commission to support the case of one of the parties to the action. The Commission makes clear in its 2004 Notice on cooperation with the national courts that it will not seek to intervene in the merits of a case before the national court:

> [The] Commission is committed to remaining neutral and objective in its assistance. Indeed, the Commission's assistance to national courts is part of its duty to defend the public interest. It has therefore no intention to serve the private interests of the parties involved in the case pending before the national court. As a consequence, the Commission will not hear any of the parties about its assistance to the national court. In case the Commission has been contacted by any of the parties in the case pending before the court on issues which are raised before the national court, it will inform the national court thereof, independent of whether these contacts took place before or after the national court's request for co-operation.[379]

5.   The Commission's involvement in a case before a national court may take one of three forms: transmission of information, providing an opinion on questions concerning the application of the EU competition rules and submitting observations to the national court.[380]

When can the national court request an opinion from the Commission?

6.   Article 15(1) also provides for the national court to request an opinion from the Commission on questions concerning the application of Articles 101 and 102. Any opinion issued by the Commission is not legally binding and when giving an

---

379. Commission Notice on the co-operation between the Commission and the courts of the EU Member States in the application of Articles 81 and 82 EC [2004] OJ C101/54 ('Commission Cooperation Notice') para 19.
380. Transmission of information is dealt with in Question 120.

opinion, the Commission states that it 'will limit itself to providing the national court with the factual information or the economic or legal clarification asked of it, without considering the merits of the case pending before the national court'.[381]

7.   Nevertheless, the provision by the Commission of an opinion could raise difficulties. The Commission has stated that the parties would not be able to make representations to the Commission before it issues its opinion.[382] This could cause concerns about the protection of the parties' rights of defence. The parties in the national proceedings may also change their position in response to the opinion and in this sense, the opinion could become 'a sort of informal judgment outside the scope of the normal procedural safeguards', raising questions about the status of evidence supplied by the Commission.[383]

8.   Article 15(1) has been used on a number of occasions to request opinions from the Commission. In 2005, the Commission issued six opinions; in 2006, it issued two opinions; in 2007, it issued three opinions; and in 2009, it issued five opinions under Article 15(1).[384] No opinions appear to have been issued to Irish or UK courts.

What observations may the Commission submit to the national court?

9.   Where the Commission makes submissions under Article 15(3) of Regulation 1/2003, it shall 'limit its observations to an economic and legal analysis of the facts underlying the case pending before the national court'.[385]

10.   Article 15(3) was considered by the Court of Justice on a preliminary reference from a Belgian court, which asked whether the Commission was competent under Article 15(3) to submit written observations of its own initiative to a national court in proceedings relating to the deductibility from taxable profits of the amount of a fine imposed by the Commission for infringement of Articles 101 or 102. The national proceedings involved a dispute between the undertaking involved and the Inspector of Taxes about whether it was permissible to deduct the fine for the calculation of corporation tax.

11.   The Court of Justice held that the Commission was entitled to submit observations of its own initiative. The first sub-paragraph of Article 15(3) meant that the option for the Commission to submit observations on its own initiative was 'subject to the sole condition that the coherent application of arts. [101] or [102] so requires' and that condition could be fulfilled 'even if the proceedings concerned do not pertain to issues relating to the application of art.[101] or art.[102] of the Treaty'.[386] The

---

381. Commission Cooperation Notice [2004] OJ C101/54, para 29.
382. Commission Cooperation Notice [2004] OJ C101/54, para 30.
383. Van Bael & Bellis, *Competition Law of the European Community* (5th edn, 2010) 1249.
384. Sources: Commission's Annual Reports on Competition Policy, 2005–2009. The Commission has published some of these opinions; see, e.g., http://ec.europa.eu/competition/court/uab_en.pdf.
385. Commission Cooperation Notice [2004] OJ C101/54, para 32.
386. Case C–429/07 *Inspecteur van de Belastingdienst v X BV* [2009] 5 CMLR 1745, para 30.

power to impose fines was designed to ensure compliance with the EU competition rules and the effectiveness of the penalties imposed was a condition for the coherent application of Articles 101 and 102. The outcome of the dispute before the national court on the deductibility of fines was capable of impairing the effectiveness of the penalty imposed by the Commission and so this was sufficient to allow the Commission to take advantage of its right to make submissions under Article 15(3). The Court of Justice held that its analysis was not contradicted by paragraphs 31–35 of the Cooperation Notice but that in any event the contents of the Notice could not prevail over the provisions of Regulation 1/2003.[387]

12.   To date, the Commission has used its *amicus curiae* role in one case in Ireland, *BIDS* (pending at the time of writing),[388] in which the High Court was to consider the application of Article 101(3) to agreements in the beef industry which required capacity reductions to be implemented. The Supreme Court had made a preliminary reference to the Court of Justice, before which the Commission made observations. The Court of Justice ruled to the effect that the agreements had an anti-competitive object contrary to Article 101(1).[389] Following that judgment, the Supreme Court remitted the case back to the High Court to consider the application of Article 101(3) to the agreements and the Commission decided to submit written observations to the High Court in 2010 but subsequently took no further part in the proceedings. The *BIDS* action is not strictly a private action as it was taken by the Competition Authority using its right of action under section 14(2) of the Competition Act 2002.

13.   The Commission has also invoked Article 15(3) to submit observations before the Paris Court of Appeal on questions concerning the interpretation of quantitative selective distribution under the Motor Vehicles Block Exemption[390] and in a separate case before the Paris Court of Appeal relating to a restriction of online sales in selective distribution agreements,[391] which is now the subject of a preliminary reference before the Court of Justice.[392]

14.   Article 15(3) also provides for the competition authority of a Member State to make written observations to the courts of its own State and, with the court's permission, oral observations.[393] There is no provision for national competition authorities to make observations before the courts of another Member State.

---

387. See Case C–429/07 *Inspecteur van de Belastingdienst v X BV* [2009] 5 CMLR 1745, paras 34–40.
388. Case 2003/7764P *Competition Authority v Beef Industry Development Society Ltd.* (pending).
389. See Case C–209/07 *Competition Authority v BIDS* [2008] ECR I–8637, [2009] 4 CMLR 310; *Competition Authority v Beef Industry Developments Society Limited* [2009] IESC 72.
390. *Garage Grémeau v Daimler Chrysler France* (Paris Court of Appeal, 7 June 2007, No. 05/17909).
391. *Pierre Fabre Dermo-Cosmétique* (Paris Court of Appeal, No. RG 2008/23812).
392. Case C–439/09 *Pierre Fabre Dermo-Cosmétique SAS v Président de l'Autorité de la Concurrence* (pending).
393. See Case C–439/08 *VEBIC* (pending), concerning a Belgian law which provided that in appeals against decisions of the Belgian Competition Council, (contd \...)

What is the procedure for Commission interventions under Article 15?

15.   A request by the national court to the Commission for information or an opinion should be made in writing to the Commission by email or post. The Commission aims to provide information within a month and an opinion within four months.[394]

16.   It is largely up to the national courts to provide the procedural framework to facilitate the Commission's involvement in national proceedings through the submission of observations under Article 15(3). Those rules should be compatible with the general principles of EU law, in particular the fundamental rights of the parties involved in the case, and should respect the principles of equivalence and effectiveness.[395] It would be seem prudent and may even be a requirement of procedural fairness for the national court to ensure that the parties have an opportunity to properly address any submissions made by the Commission.

Ireland

17.   In Ireland, Order 63B of the Rules of the Superior Courts includes provisions dealing with cooperation between the High Court and the Commission. These rules provide that where the judge requests the Commission to transmit information or an opinion to the court under Article 15(1) of Regulation 1/2003, copies of communications between the court and the Commission shall be provided to the parties as soon as possible after being sent or received.[396] Order 63B, Rule 22 makes provision for the Commission (and the Competition Authority)[397] to make written or oral observations, in response to which the parties may reply. The relevant provisions are as follows:

> (2) Where the Authority or the Commission submits written observations to the Court in competition proceedings in accordance with Article 15(3) of the Regulation, the Registrar shall furnish a copy of such observations to each of the parties to the proceedings?
>
> (3) Where the Authority or the Commission wishes to submit oral observations to a Judge in competition proceedings in accordance with Article 15(3) of the Regulation,

---

393. (contd) the Minister of the Economy was the appropriate respondent, while the Council itself was not allowed to intervene in the appeal. Advocate General Mengozzi (opinion of 25 March 2010) found that Article 15(3) of Regulation 1/2003 was applicable and that national competition authorities should enjoy the status of parties to court proceedings involving the application of Article 101 and 102 so as to be able to exercise a power of intervention. At the time of writing, the Court of Justice had not yet issued its judgment. In one Irish private action, the Competition Authority applied to submit observations but following a stay of the proceedings, it was unnecessary for the High Court to rule on the Authority's application (Case 2003/5034P *Calor Teoranta v Tervas Ltd.*).

394. Commission Cooperation Notice [2004] OJ C101/54, paras 18, 22, 28.

395. See Commission Cooperation Notice [2004] OJ C101/54, para 17.

396. Rules of the Superior Courts, Order 63B, Rule 21(2).

397. Order 63B, Rule 22(1) provides for the Competition Authority to make submissions in cases in which it is not a party, either on the application of a party or on application of the Authority.

an application for leave to make such observations shall be made by the Authority or the Commission, as the case may be, by motion on notice to the parties?

(4) Where the Authority or the Commission submits observations to the Court, each of the parties may file an affidavit in reply to such observations, or a reply in such other form as the Judge may direct, within such period as the Judge may allow, and shall within that period serve a copy of any such affidavit or other form of reply on the other party or parties and on the Authority or the Commission (as the case may be).[398]

18.   As discussed at para 12 above, the Commission has intervened in one Irish case to date, the pending *BIDS* action.

UK

19.   A practice direction has been adopted in England and Wales setting out the procedure for Commission interventions. When it wishes to submit written observations to the English court, the Commission (or the OFT or the UK sectoral regulators) must give notice of its intention to do so to the court at the earliest reasonable opportunity. If it wishes to make oral representations at the hearing of a claim, it must submit an application in advance. The court may give directions or make orders in respect of applications by the Commission to make written or oral observations and such directions or orders will be served on every party to the claim. A pre-trial review will be ordered to take place shortly before the trial.[399] The Commission does not yet appear to have applied to make observations in any UK proceedings.

Key Sources

Commission Notice on the co-operation between the Commission and the courts of the EU Member States in the application of Articles 81 and 82 EC [2004] OJ C101/54.

Case C–429/07 *Inspecteur van de Belastingdienst v X BV* [2009] 5 CMLR 1745.

Case T–353/94 *Postbank NV v Commission* [1996] ECR II–921, [1997] 4 CMLR 33.

Ireland

Rules of the Superior Courts, Order 63B, Rules 21–22.

UK

Practice Direction – Competition Law – Claims Relating to the Application of Articles 81 and 82 of the EC Treaty and Chapters I and II of Part I of the Competition Act 1998, paras 4.1–4.8.

---

398. Rules of the Superior Courts, Order 63B, Rule 22(2), (3), (4).
399. Practice Direction – Competition Law – Claims Relating to the Application of Articles 81 and 82 of the EC Treaty and Chapters I and II of Part I of the Competition Act 1998, paras 4.1–4.8.

120. MAY A CLAIMANT IN A PRIVATE ACTION OBTAIN DOCUMENTS FROM THE COMMISSION TO ASSIST ITS CASE?

Summary

- The claimant will obviously be able to use whatever information the Commission makes public.

- If the claimant is a complainant in the Commission case, it is entitled to receive a non-confidential version of the Statement of Objections; however, that document cannot be used in evidence in a private action.

- An application may be made to the Commission for disclosure of documents under Regulation (EC) No 1049/2001. This could be a way to obtain documents before deciding whether to launch an action but the Commission has shown reluctance to make documents available under this provision.

- Under Article 15 of Regulation 1/2003, the national court can ask the Commission for documents but it is doubtful that this tool could be utilised by a claimant to obtain documents to assist its case.

1. The Commission may be in possession of many documents that would assist a claimant in a private antitrust action. This is particularly so where the Commission has already carried out an investigation and made an infringement decision, on which the private action follows. Whether documents held by the Commission should be available to a claimant raises conflicting policy issues. Providing the documentation would aid the policy goal of encouraging private actions. On the other hand, it might adversely impact the Commission's leniency programme because companies may be less willing to disclose documents that can later be discovered in private actions. That dichotomy is the subject of a case which, at the time of writing, was pending before the Court of Justice.[400]

2. In addition to the specific provisions relating to the disclosure of information discussed below, pursuant to the duty of sincere cooperation in Article 4(3) TEU (which corresponds to what was previously Article 10 TEC), it is incumbent on the Commission to assist national courts applying EU law 'by producing documents to the national court and authorizing its officials to give evidence in the national proceedings'.[401] The Commission must supply the requested documents unless it

---

400. Case C–360/09 *Pfleiderer AG v Bundeskartellamt* (pending). This is a preliminary reference from the Bonn District Court which asks whether EU law is to be interpreted to mean that parties adversely affected by a cartel may not, for the purpose of bringing civil claims, be given access to leniency applications or to information and documents voluntarily provided by leniency applicants which the national competition authority of a Member State has received, pursuant to a national leniency programme, within the framework of proceedings for the imposition of fines which are (also) intended to enforce Article 101.

401. Case C–2/88 *Zwartveld* [1990] ECR I–3365, [1990] 3 CMLR 457, para 22. See also Case C–234/89 *Delimits v Henninger Bräu AG* [1991] ECR I–935, [1992] 5 CMLR 210, para 53.

can give 'imperative reasons relating to the need to avoid any interference with the functioning and independence' of the EU.[402]

3.   The published version of any infringement decision may provide useful information to potential claimants who wish to pursue damages actions against the undertakings identified in the decision. However the Commission only makes public a non-confidential version of the decision, redacting confidential information pursuant to its obligation to 'have regard to the legitimate interest of undertakings in the protection of their business secrets'.[403] This can result in the removal from the published version of the decision of information that would be useful to a claimant in a damages action.

What documents may be used by claimants who were complainants?

4.   Under Regulation 773/2004, a party who was a complainant in the Commission case is entitled to a non-confidential version of the Statement of Objections.[404] If the Commission rejects a complaint, the complainant is entitled to request documents on which the Commission has based its provisional assessment. The complainant will not be given access to business secrets or confidential information of third parties but what information is provided can be used by the complainant in a damages action for breach of Article 101 or 102.[405] The Commission states that it will provide access to such documents only on a single occasion.[406]

Can Regulation 1049/2001 be availed of?

5.   Regulation 1049/2001 sets out rules and principles governing rights of access to documents held by the EU institutions. While the Regulation's aim is to advance the general right of public access to documents, it sets out a number of specific exceptions that may be invoked to refuse access.

6.   The exceptions include refusals to disclose where the 'commercial interests of a natural or legal person', 'court proceedings and legal advice' or 'the purpose of inspections, investigations and audits' would be undermined.[407] The 'commercial interest' exception is of particular relevance in competition cases. The concept of 'commercial interest' is not defined but it is a wider concept than 'business secrets',[408] which the Commission must not disclose.

---

402. Case C–2/88 *Zwartveld* [1990] ECR I–3365, [1990] 3 CMLR 457, para 25.
403. Regulation 1/2003, Article 30(2).
404. Regulation 773/2004, Article 6(1).
405. Regulation 773/2004, Article 8.
406. Commission Notice on the rules for access to the Commission file in cases pursuant to Articles 81 and 82 of the EC Treaty, Articles 53, 54 and 57 of the EEA Agreement and Council Regulation (EC) No 139/2004 [2005] OJ C325/7, para 31.
407. See Regulation 1049/2001, Article 4(2).
408. See Case T–353/94 *Postbank v Commission* [1996] ECR II–921, [1997] 4 CMLR 33.

7. The exceptions in Article 4(2) are to be applied restrictively and 'the Commission is required to carry out a specific review of each document, and to assess whether there is a specific and foreseeable risk that disclosure will undermine the protection of one of the interests specified in Art 4(2).'[409] The Commission must carry out 'a concrete, individual examination of the documents referred to in the request in order to determine whether any exceptions applied or whether partial access was possible'.[410] This obligation can only exceptionally be derogated from, 'where the administrative burden entailed by a concrete, individual examination of the documents proves to be particularly heavy.'[411]

8. These statements of principle were made by the General Court in a competition case, in which a consumer organisation, pursuing claims in the national court against members of the *Austrian Banks Cartel* made a request under Regulation 1049/2001 for access to the Commission's file. The Commission had refused access on the basis that the documents fell within exceptions in the Regulation and that it would be disproportionate for the Commission to be required to examine each individual document, the file running to 47,000 pages. The Commission erred in law by its outright refusal to grant the applicant access and the General Court annulled the Commission's decision. In a more recent case, the General Court found that the Commission's refusal to provide documents to a party which had challenged a merger decision of the Commission was vitiated by error of law. The Commission's reliance on the exceptions in Regulation 1049/2001 was found to have been vague, general and abstract and the Court found that the Commission should have conducted a concrete and individual examination of each document before refusing its release.[412] These cases illustrate the potential utility of document requests under Regulation 1049/2001.[413]

9. Were the Commission, in refusing access to the documents sought, to invoke one of the exceptions under Regulation 1049/2001, an appeal could be taken before the EU courts under Article 263 TFEU.

---

409. Willis and Chisholm, 'Access to Commission Evidence for Follow-on Damages Claims' [2008] *Competition Law Journal* 145 at 155. See also Cases T–391/03 and T–70/04 *Franchet and Byk v Commission* [2006] ECR II–2023; Case T–36/04 *Association de la presse internationale ASBL (API) v Commission*, [2007] ECR II–3201, [2007] 3 CMLR 51.

410. Case T–2/03 *Verein für Konsumenteninformation v Commission* [2005] ECR II–1121, [2005] 4 CMLR 1627, para 92.

411. Case T–2/03 *Verein für Konsumenteninformation v Commission* [2005] ECR II–1121, [2005] 4 CMLR 1627, para 112.

412. Case T–237/05 *Éditions Odile Jacob SAS v Commission*, judgment of 9 June 2010 (on appeal, Case C–404/10P *Commission v Éditions Jacob*).

413. See also, on the wide scope of Article 1049/2001, Cases C–39&52/05 *Sweden v Council* [2008] ECR I–4723, [2008] 3 CMLR 493 (Regulation 1049/2001 imposes, in principle, an obligation to disclose the opinions of the Council's legal service relating to a legislative process). But cf Case C–139/07P *Commission v Technische Glaswerke Ilmenau GmbH*, judgment of 29 June 2010 (possibly indicating a more restrictive approach to disclosure in state aid cases).

What documents can be obtained under Article 15 of Regulation 1/2003?

10.   Article 15(1) of Regulation 1/2003 states that a national court may request the Commission to transmit to it information in its possession on the application of the EU competition rules. This provision could have a significant impact in a private action if it were capable of being used to obtain information in the Commission's file relating to the relevant competition law infringement. It could, for example, enable the retrieval of data that could be used to quantify damages.

11.   The extent to which Article 15(1) can be used to gain access to information that may aid one of the parties to the litigation before the national court is yet to be worked out and may be the subject of future rulings by the Court of Justice. The Court of Justice has previously referred to the possibility for national courts to obtain from the Commission details of the status of a pending case, as well as 'economic and legal information'.[414]

12.   The national court appears to have a discretion to request information. A key issue is whether the national court should exercise its discretion to request the transmission of information from the Commission. A defendant could be expected to oppose the exercise of this discretion. It is arguable that the principle of effectiveness requires the national court to at least closely consider using Article 15(1) to request information from the Commission that may aid the claimant in exercising rights under Article 101 or 102. In a different context, the General Court has stated that a prohibition, based on protecting professional secrecy, on an undertaking submitting to a national court information it had obtained through the Commission's administrative procedure, in this case a statement of objections, might 'deprive certain undertakings of the protection, afforded by national courts, of the rights conferred on them by virtue of the direct effect of Articles [101] and [102] of the Treaty'.[415]

13.   Assuming the national court made the request to the Commission, the next question is to what extent the Commission would disclose documents. The Commission has a duty of sincere cooperation under Article 4 TEU to transmit documents relating to an administrative investigation for use in civil proceedings before a national court.[416] On the other hand, the Commission must ensure that obligations with respect to confidentiality are respected. In its Cooperation Notice, the Commission stresses that the provisions of Article 339 TFEU relating to the non-disclosure of information covered by professional secrecy requires the Commission to ensure that before it transmits information, the national court will

---

414. Cases C–319/93, 40/94 & 224/94 *Dijkstra v Friesland (Frico Domo) Coöperatie BA* [1995] ECR I–4471, [1996] 5 CMLR 178, para 34.

415. Case T–353/94 *Postbank NV v Commission* [1996] ECR II–921, [1997] 4 CMLR 33, para 89.

416. Case C–2/88 *Zwartveld* [1990] ECR I–3365, [1990] 3 CMLR 457, paras 22–25; Case T–353/94 *Postbank NV v Commission* [1996] ECR II–921, [1997] 4 CMLR 33, para 75.

guarantee the protection of confidential information and business secrets.[417] This may lead to disputes between the parties to a private action, with the party whose information is requested arguing that disclosure would reveal business secrets.

14. There is also the issue of the Commission's reluctance to take sides in a dispute before a national court. Would this give the Commission pause when faced with an information request under Article 15(1) arising out of a private action before the national court? In a follow-on damages claim, it can be argued that the fact an infringement decision has already been taken by the Commission means that by providing documents that formed the basis of the decision, the Commission is hardly taking sides in a case before a national court, which is, in any event, bound by the finding of infringement. By providing information in its file, the Commission would also be acting in pursuit of its clear policy goal of encouraging private actions.

15. On the other hand, the Commission is concerned to protect its leniency programme, which could be undermined if it were to disclose information received from leniency applicants for use in a damages action. In the Cooperation Notice, the Commission states that it will not transmit to the national court information supplied to it by a leniency applicant without that applicant's consent.[418] However, by stating this, the Commission seems to imply first, that such information may properly be the subject of an Article 15(1) request and second, that it may not insist on the consent of other parties, who are not leniency applicants (for example, parties to a cartel other than the leniency applicant) before it discloses information provided by them to the Commission.

16. To date, there have only been a few cases in which national courts have requested the Commission to provide information under Article 15(1). In 2005, the Commission provided information to national courts in three cases but no information requests seem to have been made in 2006, 2007, 2008 or 2009.[419] The EU Ombudsman has advocated the use of Article 15 as a means of making Commission documents available for use in private actions.[420]

Are national discovery rules relevant?

17. It is doubtful that national discovery rules could be used to obtain documents from the Commission (or a competition authority located in another Member State).[421]

---

417. Commission Cooperation Notice [2004] OJ C101/54, para 25. See also Case T–353/94 *Postbank NV v Commission* [1996] ECR II–921, [1997] 4 CMLR 33, paras 90–93.
418. Commission Cooperation Notice [2004] OJ C101/54, para 26.
419. Sources: Commission's Annual Reports on Competition Policy, 2005–2009, available on the Commission's website.
420. See Decision of the European Ombudsman closing his inquiry into complaint 3699/2006/ELB against the European Commission (6 April 2010).
421. Note the possibility for national competition authorities to exchange information between themselves and the Commission. See Commission Notice on cooperation within the network of Competition Authorities [2004] OJ C101/43, paras 26–28.

The Commission would not usually be a party to the national proceedings and unless it submitted to the jurisdiction of the national court, it seems unlikely that a third party discovery order would be made against it.[422] It could also be argued that the provisions of Regulation 1049/2001 and Regulation 1/2003 discussed above have, in any event, 'occupied the field' with respect to the disclosure of Commission documents.

18. To the extent that a litigant sought correspondence between the Commission and a Member State or national competition authority, an additional hurdle in invoking discovery rules would be the argument that such documents attract a public immunity privilege as a matter of EU law. This privilege has applied in respect of correspondence between the Commission and a Member State in the context of Article 258 TFEU infringement proceedings against the Member State.[423] It is arguable that this principle should extend to, for example, correspondence between a national competition authority and the Commission related to infringements of competition law by undertakings that were subsequently defendants in a private action. However, if the Member State were a party to the proceedings, it could be argued that such a privilege should not apply and that relevant correspondence between the Member State and the Commission should be obtainable on discovery. This could arise, for example, in an action where the State was a defendant and it was alleged that there was a breach of Article 106(1) in conjunction with Article 101 or 102.

19. National discovery rules may be relevant in obtaining documents from the competition authority of the Member State in which the action is taking place. In both Ireland[424] and England and Wales[425] it is possible to obtain discovery from third parties but the courts are generally reluctant to do so. The Irish High Court has said that third party discovery 'should only be ordered when there is no realistic alternative available,'[426] and the English Court of Appeal has emphasised that non-party disclosure is the 'exception rather than the rule.'[427] National freedom of information legislation could also be relevant but the exceptions that generally apply (e.g. for confidential information) may limit its utility.[428]

---

422. See, e.g., *Fusco v O'Dea* [1994] 2 IR 93 (discovery from the UK government would not be ordered unless it had submitted to the jurisdiction of the Irish courts).
423. See Case T–105/95 *WWF UK (World Wide Fund for Nature) v Commission* [1997] ECR II–313, [1997] 2 CMLR 55, para 63; C–191/99 *Petrie v Commission* [2001] ECR II–3677, [2002] 1 CMLR 519, para 67; *Sweetman v An Bord Pleanála* [2009] IEHC 174.
424. See Rules of the Superior Courts, Order 31, Rule 29.
425. See CPR 31.17; Supreme Court Act 1981, s 34.
426. *Chambers v Times Newspapers Ltd* [1999] 2 IR 424, 430 (Morris P).
427. *Frankson v Home Office* [2003] EWCA Civ 655, [2003] 1 WLR 1952, para 10 (Scott Baker LJ).
428. For Ireland, Freedom of Information Act 1997, as amended (see, e.g., sections 26 and 27, providing exceptions for information provided in confidence and commercially sensitive information, respectively); for the UK, Freedom of Information Act 2000 (see, e.g., sections 41 and 43).

20. It should also be possible to use discovery rules to obtain documents from a defendant such as confidential unredacted versions of a Commission infringement decision.[429]

Key Sources

Regulation 1049/2001.

Regulation 773/2004, Article 6(1).

Regulation 1/2003, Articles 15, 28.

Case T–2/03 *Verein für Konsumenteninformation v Commission* [2005] ECR II–1121, [2005] 4 CMLR 1627.

---

429. Note also the possibility of obtaining discovery in US courts. The US Supreme Court held in *Intel Corp. v Advanced Micro Devices, Inc.* 542 US 241 (2004) that US discovery procedures may be used to obtain access to relevant information for non-US legal proceedings even if such broad discovery is not available in the forum where those legal proceedings are pending. The proceedings in respect of which discovery is sought need not be pending; it is sufficient if they are in 'reasonable contemplation'. The Supreme Court held that the relevant US statute covered complainants before the European Commission.

121. IN A FOLLOW-ON ACTION, WHAT ELEMENTS OF THE COMMISSION'S INFRINGEMENT DECISION ARE BINDING ON THE NATIONAL COURT?

Summary

- In applying Article 101 or 102, national courts are obliged not to take decisions 'running counter' to those of the Commission.

- Decisions of the Commission are therefore binding on a national court if the anti-competitive agreement or practice at issue is the same.

- Addressees of the Commission decision, as well as complainants and third parties with locus standi to challenge the Commission decision, are bound.

- The finding of infringement cannot be departed from in the national proceeding. As to other findings by the Commission, it has been suggested that findings that 'carry weight' in the final decision are binding.

- Decisions by the Commission on agreements or practices, the legal and factual context of which are not the same as that before the national court, may have evidential value but are not binding.

1. Article 16(1) of Regulation 1/2003 provides in part:

    > When national courts rule on agreements, decisions or practices under Article [101] or Article [102] of the Treaty which are already the subject of a Commission decision, they cannot take decisions running counter to the decision adopted by the Commission. They must also avoid giving decisions which would conflict with a decision contemplated by the Commission in proceedings it has initiated. To that effect, the national court may assess whether it is necessary to stay its proceedings. This obligation is without prejudice to the rights and obligations under Article [267] of the Treaty.[430]

2. National competition authorities are also required not to take decisions running counter to those already adopted by the Commission on Article 101 or 102.[431]

3. If an action for annulment of the Commission decision is pending before the European courts when the follow-on action comes before the national court, it is for the national court to decide whether to stay proceedings until a definitive decision has been given in the action for annulment or in order to refer a question to the Court of Justice for a preliminary ruling. When the outcome of the dispute before the national court depends on the validity of the Commission decision, it follows from the obligation of sincere cooperation that the national court should stay its proceedings pending final judgment in the action for annulment (unless it

---

430. Regulation 1/2003, Article 16(1). This codifies findings that had previously been made by the Court of Justice. See Case C–344/98 *Masterfoods Ltd. v HB Ice Cream Ltd.* [2000] ECR I–11369, [2001] 4 CMLR 449, para 52; Case C–234/89 *Delimitis v Henninger Bräu AG* [1991] ECR I–935, [1992] 5 CMLR 210, paras 47–52.
431. Regulation 1/2003, Article 16(2).

considers that a preliminary reference to the Court of Justice is warranted).[432] This would usually be the case in a follow-on action.

4.   The form of any 'stay' is up to the national court. In *National Grid*, the English High Court dealt with an application to stay follow-on actions where appeals against the Commission decisions on which the actions were based were pending before the General Court. Rather than order a stay, the High Court made orders with respect to various pre-trial procedures (including requiring the defendants to file a defence and requiring the parties to seek to agree the scope of disclosure) and ordered that the action not be fixed for hearing until after three months from the conclusion of appeals before the EU courts.[433] This approach allowed the court to progress the action before it without running any risk of adopting a decision that conflicted with that of the Commission.[434]

Who is bound?

5.   Who is bound by the Commission decision? Clearly, an addressee of the decision is bound. This is evident from Article 288 TFEU[435] as well as Article 16 of Regulation 1/2003 and the *Masterfoods* case. This should cover defendants in a follow-on case, where they are addressees of the Commission decision.

6.   In this case, the defendant cannot challenge in the national court the finding of the Commission that it has infringed the competition rules. In *Iberian v BPB*, the English High Court accepted that it was not open to a defendant in a damages

---

432. See Case C–344/98 *Masterfoods Ltd. v HB Ice Cream Ltd.* [2000] ECR I–11369, [2001] 4 CMLR 449, paras 55, 57.

433. *National Grid Electricity Transmission plc v ABB Ltd* [2009] EWHC 1326 (Ch), [2009] UKCLR 838.

434. Cf *Ringaskiddy and District Residents' Association Limited v Environmental Protection Agency* [2008] IESC 55 (the Irish Supreme Court dismissed an appeal against a High Court decision that refused to stay or adjourn Irish proceedings pending the outcome of *potential* proceedings between the Commission and Ireland in respect of an alleged failure by Ireland to transpose the environmental Council Directive 85/337/EEC. The appellants had not established a substantial risk of a conflict between decisions of the Court of Justice and Irish courts). See also, *Belgium v Ryanair Limited* [2006] IEHC 213, [2009] 3 IR 417 (High Court refused to stay an action by Belgium for recovery of illegal State aid while Ryanair's appeal against the Commission's decision was pending in the General Court; the Commission decision was subsequently annulled in Case T–196/04 *Ryanair Ltd v Commission* [2008] ECR II–3643, [2009] 2 CMLR 137); *Conex Banninger Ltd v Commission* [2010] EWHC 1978 (Ch) (Floyd J declined to make a reference to the Court of Justice where the applicant sought declarations that would have confirmed that it was not liable for breaches of Article 101 in respect of an ongoing proceeding by the Commission, the applicant being the economic successor of the party that participated in a breach of Article 101; the learned judge left open the question whether the English court had jurisdiction to grant such declarations).

435. Article 288 provides: 'A decision shall be binding in its entirety. A decision which specifies those to whom it is addressed shall be binding only on them'.

action to challenge findings of infringement made by the Commission, Laddie J stating that:

> [Where], as here, the parties have disputed the same issues before the Commission and have had real and reasonable opportunities to appeal from an adverse decision, there is no injustice in obliging them to accept the result obtained in Europe. The position is a *fortiori* when, as here, the opportunities of appeal have been used to the full.[436]

7. Third parties who participated in the Commission investigation, such as complainants, are also bound as well as persons to whom the decision is of 'direct and individual concern' and who would have *locus standi* under Article 263 TFEU to appeal the Commission decision to the European courts.[437]

8. While other parties may be free to challenge findings of the Commission in national proceedings, the obligation on the national court under Article 16 of Regulation 1/2003 appears to limit the scope for any meaningful departure from the Commission's findings. It should be recalled though that the obligation is not to reach an identical decision but rather avoid decisions that 'run counter' to the Commission decision.

What effect do related decisions have?

9. The situation is different if the Article 101 or 102 decision which the national court faces is merely *related* to one that the Commission has taken. In *Crehan*, the legal and factual context of a decision taken by the Commission was not identical to that before the national court. The national court was examining the legality of an exclusivity agreement between a particular supplier and certain retailers and the Commission was assessing a similar agreement in respect of the same products in the same market between another supplier and other retailers. The House of Lords held that in this case, there was no risk of the national court adopting a conflicting decision. In *Masterfoods*, Advocate General Cosmas had considered when a conflicting decision arose:

> In order to establish such a form of conflict, a connection between the legal problem which arises before the national courts and that being examined by the Commission is not in itself sufficient. Nor is the similarity of the legal problem where the legal and factual context of the case being examined by the Commission is not completely identical to that before the national courts. The Commission's decision may provide important indications as to the appropriate way to interpret Articles [101(1)] and [102], but in this case there is no risk, from a purely legal point of view, of the adoption of conflicting decisions. Such a risk only arises when the binding authority which the decision of the national court has or will have conflicts with the grounds and operative part of the Commission's decision. Consequently the limits of the

---

436. *Iberian U.K. Limited v BPB Industries Plc* [1996] 2 CMLR 601, [1997] ICR 164, para 72.
437. See the speech of Lord Hoffmann in *Crehan v Inntrepreneur Pub Co (CPC)* [2006] UKHL 38, [2007] 1 AC 333, para 61, discussing the opinion of Advocate General Van Gerven in Case 128/92 *H. J. Banks & Co. Ltd v British Coal Corporation* [1994] ECR I–1209, [1994] 5 CMLR 30.

binding authority of the decision of the national court and the content of the Commission's decision must be examined every time.[438]

10.   Having referred to this opinion, Lord Hoffmann went on to state:

> [When] there is no question of a conflict of decisions in the sense which I have discussed, the decision of the Commission is simply evidence properly admissible before the English court which, given the expertise of the Commission, may well be regarded by that court as highly persuasive. As a matter of law, however, it is only part of the evidence which the court will take into account.[439]

11.   Following this logic, a claimant in a follow-on action will be able to rely on a Commission decision as binding only where the parties and the subject matter of the decision overlap with the follow-on action.[440] Where the follow-on action is based on a claim that is related to the subject matter of the Commission decision, for example, where it is taken against a defendant who operates in the same market as those found by the Commission to have breached the competition rules, at most, the Commission decision can form part of the evidence before the national court. It may be open to the national court in this case to make its own decision as to whether such a defendant had breached the competition rules.

Are all parts of the Commission decision binding?

12.   Commission decisions finding an infringement of the competition rules are often lengthy documents containing numerous findings of fact and economic assessment. Are all of these findings binding on the national court in a follow-on action? The finding of infringement of the competition rules is certainly binding. The binding nature of other findings (for example, the definition of the relevant market) was addressed by Advocate General Van Gerven in *Banks*. It was suggested that if the national court has a doubt about findings made by the Commission, 'in the case of findings which carried no weight in the final decision and do not therefore underlie the reasoning of the Commission, the national court is at liberty to adopt a different interpretation'.[441] Where the court disagrees with findings that have an influence on the decision of the Commission, the Advocate General suggested that it could seek information from the Commission or make a preliminary reference to the Court of Justice.[442] However it is doubtful that the Court of Justice could revisit findings of fact in a preliminary reference.[443]

---

438. Case C–344/98 *Masterfoods Ltd. v HB Ice Cream Ltd.* [2000] ECR I–11369, [2001] 4 CMLR 449, opinion of Advocate General Cosmas, para 16.

439. *Crehan v Inntrepreneur Pub Co (CPC)* [2006] UKHL 38, [2007] 1 AC 333, para 69.

440. On the requirement that a regulator has made a clear finding of infringement before a follow-on action can be brought under section 47A of the Competition Act 1998, see the discussion of *English Welsh & Scottish Railway Ltd v Enron Coal Services Ltd (in liquidation)* [2009] EWCA Civ 647, [2009] UKCLR 816 in Question 116.

441. Case 128/92 *H. J. Banks & Co. Ltd v British Coal Corporation* [1994] ECR I–1209, [1994] 5 CMLR 30, opinion of Advocate General Van Gerven, para 61.

442. Case 128/92 *H. J. Banks & Co. Ltd v British Coal Corporation* [1994] ECR I–1209, [1994] 5 CMLR 30, opinion of Advocate General Van Gerven, para 61.

443. See Bellamy & Child (6th edn, 2008) para 14.079.

13.   As more follow-on actions for damages come before the national courts, disputes about the binding effect of findings made in the Commission decision might arise more frequently between claimants and defendants. It would not be surprising if questions in this area made their way to the Court of Justice on preliminary references in due course.

Key Sources

Regulation 1/2003, Article 16.

Case C–344/98 *Masterfoods Ltd. v HB Ice Cream Ltd.* [2000] ECR I–11369, [2001] 4 CMLR 449.

Crehan v Inntrepreneur Pub Co (CPC) [2006] UKHL 38, [2007] 1 AC 333.

---

122. ARE DECISIONS OF NATIONAL COMPETITION AUTHORITIES BINDING ON NATIONAL COURTS?

Summary

- This is a question of national law.

- In Ireland, decisions of national competition authorities of EU Member States may have evidential value but are not binding in proceedings before the courts.

- Similarly, in English law, decisions of competition authorities of other EU Member States are not binding. However, pursuant to the Competition Act 1998, certain decisions of the OFT and other UK regulators are binding.

1. As a matter of EU law, there are no provisions dealing with this question. In its White Paper on private antitrust damages the Commission proposed a rule that would make final decisions of national competition authorities or final judgments of national courts finding an infringement of Article 101 or 102 binding on Member State courts in subsequent damages actions.[444] The adoption of such a proposal would promote private actions, enhance legal certainty, save costs and bring greater uniformity to the application of Articles 101 and 102.

2. On the other hand, there are potential difficulties in according decisions of all national competition authorities the status of binding effect. For example, the scope of the decision of a national authority may be unclear and disputes among parties as to the meaning of a particular decision could lead to more litigation. According the decisions of another country's competition authority binding effect might also raise constitutional or separation of powers issues in some Member States.[445]

3. None of the provisions of the White Paper have been adopted into EU legislation. A European Parliament resolution on the White Paper in March 2009 took the view that 'a national court should not be bound by a decision of the national competition authority of another Member State'.[446]

---

444. Commission, White Paper on Damages actions for breach of the EC antitrust rules COM (2008) 165 final, 2 April 2008, para 2.3.

445. Although at least one Member States has already adopted such a provision. Section 33(4) of the German Competition Act (*Gesetz gegen Wettbewerbsbeschränkungen*), provides for the binding effect of Article 101 or 102 infringement decisions of the EU Member State national competition authorities and, on appeal, the national courts, in actions before the German civil courts.

446. European Parliament resolution of 26 March 2009 on the White Paper on damages actions for breach of the EC antitrust rules, T6–0187/2009, Article 14.

UK

4. The Competition Act 1998 contains a number of specific provisions on the binding effect of decisions of the OFT, sectoral regulators and the CAT. Under section 58A, the court is bound in follow-on actions by decisions of the OFT, or by the CAT on appeal, finding an infringement of the Chapter I or II prohibition or Article 101 or 102.[447] Section 58 provides that unless the court otherwise directs, findings of fact of the OFT relevant to an issue arising in such proceedings are binding on the parties (assuming the finding was not overturned on appeal in the CAT).[448]

5. In follow-on actions before the CAT under section 47A, claimants can rely on similar infringement decisions of the OFT, by the CAT on appeal or the Commission.

6. There is no UK rule providing that decisions of national competition authorities in other Member States have binding effect in a subsequent action in the UK. A court may consider such a decision as evidence but it would not have binding effect.

Ireland

7. In Ireland, the Competition Authority is not empowered to take decisions finding an infringement of section 4 or 5 of the Competition Act 2002 or Article 101 or 102.[449] Only the courts can make such findings. The question of the binding power of Competition Authority decisions in respect of breaches of the antitrust rules does not therefore arise.

8. There are no provisions in Ireland dealing with the binding effect of a decision of a competition authority of another Member State in a subsequent action in Ireland. Other than a few limited exceptions, the Constitution of Ireland requires that justice be administered by the courts.[450] The adoption of a rule giving binding effect to decisions of national competition authorities could therefore raise constitutional difficulties in Ireland. In its submission commenting on the Commission's White Paper on private antitrust actions, the Irish government argued strongly against the adoption of such a rule at EU level. As that submission argues, the basis of the *Masterfoods* decision on the binding effect of Commission decisions and Article 16 of Regulation 1/2003 stems from the fact that the Commission is a EU institution subject to the appellate jurisdiction of the EU courts. The national competition authorities are in a different position and to give the same status to their decisions would go far beyond the recognition of judgments already provided for in Regulation 44/2001 (which involves recognition

---

447. Competition Act 1998, s 58A(2).
448. Competition Act 1998, s 58(1).
449. The Commission for Communications Regulation (ComReg) is also designated a competition authority under Article 35 of Regulation 1/2003 by SI 195 of 2004 as amended by SI 525 of 2007.
450. Irish Constitution, Article 34.

of a final decision of a competent court of another Member State as to the rights and obligations *inter se* of the parties to proceedings before the Court).[451]

Key Sources

Commission, White Paper on Damages actions for breach of the EC antitrust rules COM (2008) 165 final (2 April 2008).

UK

Competition Act 1998, s 47A, 58, 58A.

---

451. Department of Trade, Enterprise and Employment on behalf of Ireland, 'Response to the European Commission White Paper on Damages actions for breach of the EC antitrust rules', 31 July 2008, available on the Commission's website.

123. DOES ALTERNATIVE DISPUTE RESOLUTION HAVE A ROLE TO PLAY IN COMPETITION CASES?

Summary

- Forms of alternative dispute resolution such as mediation and arbitration are regularly used to resolve commercial disputes and may play an increasing role in antitrust matters.

- Both the English and Irish courts make efforts to facilitate the resolution of disputes in this way.

- It is important that the outcome of alternative dispute resolution does not itself raise antitrust issues.

- Arbitration has been used in the enforcement of competition law by the European Commission, for example, as an aid to monitor compliance with commitments in merger and antitrust cases.

1. The use of alternative dispute resolution ('ADR') is increasingly important in civil litigation. Competition disputes may be suitable for ADR, in particular mediation or arbitration. Mediation involves the parties entering into voluntary negotiations with the assistance of a third party mediator. Arbitration is a more formal method of ADR, involving both sides putting a case to an arbitral tribunal, which will then take a decision. In addition to the potential use of ADR in private antitrust actions, competition authorities may make use of ADR techniques, for example, to provide for the resolution of disputes about whether a party is complying with commitments made in a merger or antitrust case.

2. Mediation has a number of potential advantages as a means of resolving disputes. These include cost savings and privacy. The parties may also be able to consider a broader set of resolutions than would be possible before a court and come to agreements on their commercial relationship going forward. They may be able to agree the terms of new contracts or vary existing contracts, for instance. It is of course vitally important that any agreements or understandings reached in the course of mediation do not themselves raise competition concerns. For example, if the parties were to enter into a long-term or exclusive contract, this might raise issues under Article 101. Competition issues may also arise in the mediation and settlement of other types of cases. In the pharmaceutical industry, patent infringement actions between originator and generic companies can raise concerns under Article 101 or 102 where the settlement is used to delay the market entry of a generic drug. The originator company might make payments to the generic manufacturer in return for delayed market entry or place other limitations on the extent of entry, which can raise antitrust concerns.[452]

---

452. See Commission Pharmaceutical Sector Inquiry Final Report (8 July 2009); Commission First Report on the Monitoring of Patent Settlements (5 July 2010).

3.   It is difficult to estimate the extent to which mediation has been used to settle disputes raising competition law issues given the confidential nature of this form of ADR. Details have been provided about two high-profile competition disputes in the UK that resulted in mediation.[453]

4.   Arbitration is a more formal method of ADR. It will usually involve an arbitrator or arbitration panel deciding on the merits of the dispute referred for arbitration and making an arbitral award. There are a number of potential advantages to using arbitration. An expert arbitral panel could be appointed to arbitrate, containing an expert competition lawyer and economist. A broader range of remedies may be available in arbitration than before a court. Arbitration may also be quicker and cheaper than litigation, though this is not necessarily the case. Examples of where arbitration might be used in the antitrust context could include in a damages claim, where liability had been established and only issues of quantum remained to be decided or in the context of a dispute between a supplier and distributor, where one party seeks to enforce the agreement while the other seeks to argue that it breaches competition law. In contrast to mediation, arbitration is a more concrete form of ADR as it involves the issuance of final awards, subject to court review where applicable.

Are competition issues arbitrable?

5.   There is a question as to whether competition law issues are capable of being arbitrated at all. There is a public interest in the enforcement of competition law and one school of thought suggests that antitrust issues should not be resolved in the private forum of arbitration in preference to the courts or before regulators. Accordingly, a court should refuse to enforce contracts requiring the parties to arbitrate antitrust claims. In the US, this approach was initially adopted at the federal appeals court level, the Second Circuit holding that Sherman Act claims were 'inappropriate for arbitration'.[454] However, the Supreme Court decided in *Mitsubishi Motors* that an obligation in an international contract to submit an antitrust dispute to arbitration should be enforced.[455] This decision was limited to holding that antitrust claims arising out of international transactions were arbitrable. While the Supreme Court has yet to directly consider the arbitrability of antitrust claims arising out of domestic US transactions, lower courts have typically enforced clauses in domestic contracts requiring the arbitration of antitrust claims.[456]

---

453. See Brealey and Green (eds), *Competition Litigation: UK Practice and Procedure* (2010) para 22.13(c).

454. *American Safety Equipment Corp. v JP Maguire & Co, Inc.* 391 F 2d 821, 828 (2d Cir. 1968)

455. *Mitsubishi Motors Corp. v Soler Chrysler-Plymouth* 473 US 614, 105 S Ct 3346 (1985).

456. See, e.g., *In re Cotton Yarn Antitrust Litigation* 505 F 3d 274, 282 (4th Cir. 2007). In *Gilmer*, an employment case, the Supreme Court commented that claims under a number of statutes, including the Sherman Act, 'were appropriate for arbitration' (*Gilmer v Interstate/Johnson Lane Corp* 500 US 20, 27, 111 S Ct 1647, 1653 (1991) (White J)).

6. The arbitrability of antitrust disputes as a matter of EU law has not been directly addressed by the Union courts.[457] However the Court of Justice judgment in *Eco Swiss* implies that EU law has no objection to antitrust disputes being arbitrated, as respect for the EU competition rules can be ensured at the stage of enforcement of an arbitral award before the national court. The case involved a preliminary reference from The Netherlands. An unsuccessful party to an arbitration argued that the arbitration award should be set aside as the underlying agreement was in breach of Article 101. The Court of Justice noted that Article 101 could be applied by the national court on review of the arbitration award:

> ... a national court to which application is made for annulment of an arbitration award must grant that application if it considers that the award in question is in fact contrary to Article [101] of the Treaty, where its domestic rules of procedure require it to grant an application for annulment founded on failure to observe national rules of public policy[458].

7. In England, the prevailing view seems to be that competition issues can be arbitrated. In *ET Plus*, Gross J in the High Court held that claims based on Article 101 or 102 could be arbitrated if they came within the scope of the relevant arbitration clause[459] and the Court of Appeal suggested in *Attheraces* that complex antitrust issues might better be resolved satisfactorily 'by arbitration or by a specialist body equipped with appropriate expertise and flexible powers'.[460]

8. If an arbitration clause provides for a dispute to be arbitrated in a place and by a law that would not give effect to mandatory provisions of EU law, the English High Court has found that an action based on those mandatory EU law provisions should not be stayed in favour of the foreign arbitration. This finding was made in respect of a claim for compensation under Regulation 17 of the Commercial Agents (Council Directive) Regulations 1993.[461] The same principle should apply to actions seeking to enforce the EU competition rules, which are also mandatory provisions of EU law.

---

457. The use of arbitration in public enforcement of the merger control and antitrust rules by the Commission supports the view that arbitration is a suitable method of resolving private antitrust disputes based on the EU antitrust rules. See paras 18–20 below.

458. Case C–126/97 *Eco Swiss China Time Ltd v Benetton International NV* [1999] ECR I–3055, [2000] 5 CMLR 816, para 41.

459. *ET Plus SA v Welter* [2005] EWHC 2115 (Comm) [2006] 1 Lloyd's Rep 251, para 51 (Gross J stating that 'There is no realistic doubt that such "competition" or "anti-trust" claims are arbitrable; the issue is whether they come within the scope of the arbitration clause, as a matter of its true construction').

460. *Attheraces Ltd v British Horseracing Board Ltd* [2007] EWCA Civ 38, [2007] Bus LR D77, para 7 (Mummery LJ). But see Brealey and Green (eds), *Competition Litigation: UK Practice and Procedure* (2010) para 23.18, noting that the position may not be so clear-cut in CAT proceedings.

461. *Accentuate Ltd v Asigra Inc* [2009] EWHC 2655 (QB), [2009] 2 Lloyd's Rep 599 (Tugendhat J finding that a Canadian arbitration clause was 'null and void' within the meaning of section 9(4) of the Arbitration Act 1996 in so far as it purported to require the submission to arbitration of 'questions pertaining to' mandatory provisions of EU law).

9.   The Irish courts have also endorsed the view that competition law issues can be arbitrated. In *McCormack*, a plaintiff distributor alleging breach of a petrol distribution and supply agreement alleged that the defendant supplier had incited him to engage in price fixing. On an application by the defendant that the proceedings should be stayed and subject to arbitration according to the arbitration clause in the agreement, the plaintiff relied on section 39(2) of the Arbitration Act 1954, which provided that the court could revoke the authority of an arbitrator where there was a question that a party was guilty of fraud. In rejecting the plaintiff's arguments and granting the defendant's application to a stay pending arbitration, Dunne J stated:

> I am not satisfied that the issues in this case are of such magnitude or complexity that they cannot properly be dealt with by arbitration. The allegation of incitement to engage in price fixing made in this case by Mr. McCormack does not seem to me to be such as to create a special public interest arising from the allegation such that it is inappropriate from the public point of view that the matter should be dealt with by way of arbitration rather than in open court. Indeed, I have to say that the issue of incitement to engage in price fixing as raised by Mr. McCormack seems to me to be peripheral to the real dispute at issue between the parties.[462]

10.   This judgment should probably not be taken as definitive support for the arbitrability of competition issues in general given that the price fixing allegations were a 'peripheral' aspect of the dispute.

11.   Assuming that there is no policy objection to the arbitration of antitrust disputes, it will have to be determined whether the antitrust issues fall within the scope of the particular arbitration clause. In *ETI*, Gross J in the English High Court held that an arbitration clause whereby the parties had agreed 'to submit any potential disputes regarding the performance or the interpretation' of the contract to arbitration did cover claims based on Articles 101 and 102. The learned judge had initially doubted that the antitrust claims were covered but was persuaded that they were given their close connection to other tortious claims that were covered by the arbitration clause.[463]

How can a court facilitate ADR?

12.   In High Court actions in England and Wales, the judge may encourage the use of ADR at the case management conference and may stay the proceedings to allow for ADR to take place. However, the judge will not order ADR without the consent of the parties.[464] The CAT may also encourage the use of ADR, its Rules specifically providing that it may 'encourage and facilitate the use of an alternative dispute resolution procedure if the Tribunal considers that appropriate'.[465]

---

462. *McCormack Fuels Ltd v Maxol Ltd* [2008] IEHC 197.

463. *ET Plus SA v Welter* [2005] EWHC 2115 (Comm) [2006] 1 Lloyd's Rep 251, para 51. See further Brealey and Green (eds), *Competition Litigation: UK Practice and Procedure* (2010) paras 23.21–23.22.

464. See Brealey and Green (eds), *Competition Litigation: UK Practice and Procedure* (2010) para 22.09.

465. Competition Appeal Tribunal Rules 2003, SI 2003/1372, r 44(3).

13. In a multi-defendant case in which the defendants are liable to the claimant for the same damage, defendants should exercise caution in carrying out ADR or entering into settlements that do not involve all defendants. Under English law, a defendant who agrees a settlement with the claimant (for example, following mediation) may still be subject to a contribution claim from a non-settling defendant.[466]

14. The procedural rules applicable to competition law actions in the Irish High Court make specific provision for the judge to direct that the parties engage in ADR. Order 63B, Rule 5 of the Rules of the Superior Courts states that the judge hearing a competition case may give such directions and make such orders for the conduct of the proceedings 'as appears convenient for the determination of the proceedings in a manner which is just, expeditious and likely to minimise the costs of those proceedings'.

15. Order 63B, Rule 6 provides that the judge may, of his own motion and after hearing the parties or by application of a party on notice to the other party, give directions at the initial directions hearing, including

> (xiii) that the proceedings or any issue therein be adjourned for such time, not exceeding twenty-eight days, as he considers appropriate to allow the parties time to consider whether such proceedings or issue ought to be referred to a process of mediation, conciliation or arbitration, and where the parties decide so to refer the proceedings or issue, to extend the time for compliance by any party with any provision of these Rules or any order of the Court.[467]

16. In order to assist the judge in making any such order or direction, he may direct the parties to provide him with information in respect of the proceedings including 'particulars of any mediation, conciliation or arbitration arrangements which may be available to the parties'.[468]

17. More generally, there seems to be increasing use of ADR in Ireland. Order 56A of the Rules of the Superior Courts, which was to come into effect on 16 November 2010, provides that the High Court may in any proceedings invite the parties to engage in mediation or conciliation (but not arbitration) or refer proceedings to such a process where the parties consent. A new Arbitration Act was introduced in

---

466. See Question 115.
467. Rules of the Superior Courts, Order 63B, Rule 6(1)(xiii). Similar rules enabling the judge to adjourn proceedings for ADR apply to the Commercial List of the High Court (Rules of the Superior Courts, Order 63A, Rule 6(1)(xiii)). Cases in the Commercial List are frequently adjourned to allow for alternative dispute resolution, particularly mediation. There might be cost consequences for a party who does not cooperate with a court-facilitated ADR procedure (see, e.g., the comments of Kelly J in *Kay-El (Hong Kong) Ltd v Musgrave Ltd* [2005] IEHC 418 that 'the parties came to the mediation in good faith and made genuine efforts to reach a compromise. Such being so the lack of success at mediation carries no costs implication for the litigation').
468. Rules of the Superior Courts, Order 63B, Rule 6(2).

2010, which grants a new power to the High Court and Circuit Court to adjourn a case for arbitration on the consent of the parties.[469]

What role does arbitration play in public enforcement by the Commission?

18. Arbitration has played a role in the public enforcement of the merger control and antitrust rules by the Commission. In merger cases, as part of a package of commitments, parties have agreed that disputes about compliance with their commitments can be arbitrated. For example, in *GE/Instrumentarium*, an aspect of the remedies package was a commitment by GE to ensure the interoperability of patient monitors, anaesthesia machines and clinical information systems of the merged firm with those of third parties and the provision of interfacing information to third parties. Compliance with these commitments would be overseen by a monitoring trustee. In addition, third parties would have recourse to a 'fast track' arbitration procedure before a panel of three arbitrators, one chosen by the third party, one by GE/Instrumentarium and the third chosen by the other two arbitrators. The arbitration would be conducted in accordance with the rules of the London Court of Arbitration. An important aspect of this procedure from the Commission's perspective was that it would retain control of the procedure as arbitrators would have to seek and be bound by the Commission's interpretation of the commitments where necessary.[470]

19. Arbitration can also play a role in the enforcement of the antitrust rules. An interesting example is the public undertaking that Microsoft adopted to address concerns raised in a Commission investigation into potential abuse of dominance in relation to interoperability of different software products.[471] Based partly in response to the General Court's judgment in *Microsoft v Commission*,[472] Microsoft adopted a unilateral commitment to ensure that third-party software products could interoperate with Microsoft software using the same interoperability information on an equal footing as other Microsoft products. This commitment was provided while the Commission investigation was still pending and although informal vis-à-vis the Commission, it has said that it will carefully monitor the impact of the undertaking on the market and take its findings into account in the pending antitrust investigation regarding interoperability.[473]

---

469. Arbitration Act 2010, s 32. See also Rules of the Superior Courts, Order 56. The purpose of the Arbitration Act 2010 is to apply the UNCITRAL Model Law on International Commercial Arbitration to all arbitrations that take place in Ireland. Note also powers of the Circuit Court to adjourn proceedings to allow for ADR (SI 539 of 2009 Circuit Court Rules (Case Progression (General)) 2009).

470. COMP/M.3083 *GE/Instrumentarium* [2004] OJ L109/1, para 355.

471. COMP/C–3/39.294 *Microsoft* (interoperability) (pending).

472. Case T–201/04 *Microsoft Corp. v Commission* [2007] ECR II–3601, [2007] 5 CMLR 846.

473. Commission Press Release IP/09/1941, Commission accepts Microsoft commitments to give users browser choice (16 December 2009) (the commitments accepted by the Commission related to COMP/C–3/39.530 *Microsoft* (tying)).

20. The Microsoft commitment includes a standard warranty agreement to be entered into between Microsoft and third parties, with Microsoft warranting to provide complete and accurate interoperability information. The agreement, governed by English law, includes an arbitration clause, providing for a 'fast track' arbitration process in the event that the third party claims that Microsoft is failing to comply with its obligations under the warranty agreement. The arbitration is to be conducted according to the Rules of Arbitration of the International Chamber of Commerce before a three-person or one-person panel. The Commission is given a significant role in any arbitration, being provided with all submissions and other relevant documents, being afforded the opportunity to file *amicus curiae* briefs and, upon the request of the arbitral tribunal, being present at the arbitration hearing.[474]

Key Sources

Case C–126/97 *Eco Swiss China Time Ltd v Benetton International NV* [1999] ECR I–3055, [2000] 5 CMLR 816.

---

474. Copies of the Public Undertaking by Microsoft (24 July 2009) and the Warranty Agreement are available on Microsoft's website. For in-depth coverage of antitrust arbitration, see Blanke & Landolt, *EU and US Antitrust Arbitration: A Handbook for Practitioners* (forthcoming, 2010).

124. MAY AN UNDERTAKING THAT IS FINED FOR BREACHING COMPETITION LAW RECOVER THE FINE FROM RESPONSIBLE EMPLOYEES?

Summary

- This is a question of national law.

- In England, it was found as a preliminary matter in the *Safeway* case that a company seeking to retrieve competition law fines from employees was not bound to fail.

- Irish law does not appear to have addressed this question. There are differences with the UK competition regime in respect of individual liability and attribution of responsibility to companies that may be relevant.

1. Whether a fine is imposed on a company for breach of EU competition law or a national statute, any claim to recover the fine from directors or employees would have to be taken under national law.

2. If such a claim were capable of succeeding, it would have consequences not only for the employees who are involved in conduct that results in an antitrust infringement but also for insurers providing directors' and officer's insurance cover, who might ultimately have to compensate the company.

3. A key issue that arises in considering this question is whether there is a public policy objection in allowing a company that has breached competition law to recover sums it has had to pay by way of fines.

UK

4. The most significant judicial guidance on this question to date is the decision of the High Court in the *Safeway* case.[475] In anticipation of receiving a penalty following a settlement with the OFT regarding alleged collusion between supermarkets and dairy producers concerning dairy products, a number of companies in the Safeway group sued the employees who had participated in the anti-competitive activity, seeking an indemnity against liability for the penalty. The claim was based on breach of employment contracts, breach of fiduciary duties and negligence.

5. The defendants brought a strike out application and sought to obtain summary judgment on the basis that, as a matter of public policy, the claim must fail. The defendants' main argument was that the claim infringed the principle of public policy expressed in the maxim *ex turpi causa non oritur actio*, and in particular the rule that a person who commits an illegal or unlawful act cannot maintain an

---

475. *Safeway Stores Limited v Twigger* [2010] EWHC 11 (Comm), [2010] Bus LR 974 (it is understood that an appeal before the Court of Appeal is pending).

action for an indemnity against the liability which results from the act. It was also argued that the claim was fundamentally inconsistent with the UK's competition law regime.

6. Two conditions would have to be met before the *ex turpi causa* principle could apply: (i) the claimants committed an illegal or unlawful act; and (ii) that illegal or unlawful act was of sufficient seriousness to engage the *ex turpi causa* rule. Flaux J accepted that infringement of the Chapter I prohibition, though not a criminal offence, was sufficiently serious to engage the *ex turpi causa* principle as it had the necessary element of moral reprehensibility or turpitude.[476]

7. On the first condition, if it were shown that the unlawful conduct was that of the claimants, they could not succeed in the claim because they would be benefiting from their own illegal acts. The learned judge analysed a number of authorities to decipher the circumstances in which the acts of employees would be attributed to a company for purposes of application of the *ex turpi causa* rule. Those authorities indicated that a company can be bound by the actions of its employees on the basis of vicarious liability and the principles of agency but for purposes of application of the *ex turpi causa* rule, a narrower concept of attribution applies. The company will only be bound on the basis of *primary* rules of attribution, for example, where a decision was taken by a majority of the company's shareholders or by resolution of its board or where the act was committed by an individual who wholly owned and controlled the company or who was the directing mind and will of the company:

> [The *ex turpi causa*] rule does not apply where the company is only liable for the acts of its employees or agents either by virtue of the application of the doctrine of vicarious liability or where the act or conduct of an employee or agent is attributed to the company under the general principles of the law of agency. In neither of those cases is the liability of the company 'personal' or primary or direct, nor can it be said that the company is guilty of turpitude.[477]

8. The defendants argued that the claimants were primarily liable because under section 2 of the Competition Act 1998, it was only undertakings that could be found liable for the breach of the competition rules, so it was the company's own wrongdoing that would be penalised by the OFT. However, Flaux J was more concerned with the question of the 'true basis' for the company's liability, which was the acts of its employees or agents. Whereas it may have been the case that in the scheme of the Competition Act 1998, the issue of attribution did not arise because the wrongdoing was inevitably that of the claimants as the 'undertakings', the context here – whether the *ex turpi causa* rule applied to the claim against the defendants – was different. The Competition Act simply did not address this situation. The answer depended instead upon the correct analysis of the liability which the claimants were under. That liability was not primary or direct so as to attract the necessary degree of turpitude. Therefore the claimants had a real

---

476. *Safeway Stores Limited v Twigger* [2010] EWHC 11 (Comm), [2010] Bus LR 974, paras 28–43.
477. *Safeway Stores Limited v Twigger* [2010] EWHC 11 (Comm), [2010] Bus LR 974, para 54.

possibility of success of defeating an *ex turpi causa* defence at trial and the strike out motion was dismissed.[478]

9.   Two other points considered by the court, although not necessary for the decision, are worth noting. First, Flaux J dismissed the defendants' arguments that there was a public policy against the recovery of fines by those on whom the fines were imposed. This was evident from a number of authorities, discussed in detail in the judgment. The fact that the damages which the claimant sought to recover consisted of a fine did not preclude recovery, provided that the claimant was not negligent or otherwise personally at fault in relation to the incurring of the fine.[479] Among the authorities supporting this view was the judgment of Denning LJ in *Strongman v Sincock*:

> It is, of course, a settled principle that a man cannot recover for the consequences of his own unlawful act, but this has always been confined to cases where the doer of the act knows it to be unlawful or is himself in some way morally culpable. It does not apply when he is an entirely innocent party.[480]

10.   The other point argued by the defendants was that to allow the retrieval of a penalty imposed on an undertaking to be recovered from directors or employees, would be contrary to the scheme of competition law in the UK. It was argued that personal consequences for individuals for breaching competition law were provided only in respect of the cartel offence and the possibility of making disqualification orders and that to allow recovery of penalties imposed on undertakings (which under the Competition Act could only be imposed on undertakings) would undermine the scheme of UK competition law and result in the courts deciding issues of policy that should be left to Parliament. The deterrent effect of the fines would also be undermined if the claimants could pass on the fines to the defendants.

11.   In the view of Flaux J, the fact that the Competition Act applied to undertakings and not individuals, which was true of any legislation regulating companies, did not mean that individuals could not owe the company duties on normal common law principles to ensure that the company complied with its statutory obligations. The Competition Act 1998 and the Enterprise Act 2002 were 'not intending to affect any common law remedies which an undertaking might have against its directors or employees which ... arise wholly independent of the statute'.[481] The learned judge dismissed the suggestion that undertakings would only be deterred from breaching competition law if they were prevented from suing the individuals who caused the breach as 'completely illogical'.[482]

---

478. See *Safeway Stores Limited v Twigger* [2010] EWHC 11 (Comm), [2010] Bus LR 974, para 77.
479. See *Safeway Stores Limited v Twigger* [2010] EWHC 11 (Comm), [2010] Bus LR 974, para 87.
480. *Strongman v Sincock* [1955] 2 QB 525, 535.
481. *Safeway Stores Limited v Twigger* [2010] EWHC 11 (Comm), [2010] Bus LR 974, para 127.
482. *Safeway Stores Limited v Twigger* [2010] EWHC 11 (Comm), [2010] Bus LR 974, para 130.

12.   It should be stressed that *Safeway* involved a preliminary issue. The judgment decided only that the claimants had a real prospect of successfully defeating at trial any defence of *ex turpi causa* or that their claims were contrary to the UK's competition regime.

13.   Nevertheless, the *Safeway* case may well encourage companies that are fined for breach of competition law to seek to recover those fines from the executives who were responsible. Companies may be particularly inclined to pursue such actions where there has been a takeover subsequent to the anti-competitive activity and the relevant executives are no longer employed with the company (as was the case in *Safeway*).

14.   Potentially, the rationale in this case could be extended to apply to private damages actions, so that companies that are forced to pay damages for breaches of competition law could recover those damages from the relevant executives.

15.   Given the enormous sums that can be involved in antitrust fines and damages actions, in most cases, the claimant company will only pursue such claims where there is a Directors' and Officers' insurance policy or some other type of insurance that can be targeted. The judgment clearly has implications then for D&O insurance. Exposing employees to liability for fines could also have implications for competition investigations more generally. Conflicts of interest between employees and their companies may be more likely to arise and employees may be less willing to cooperate, which in turn could affect a company's ability to apply for leniency.

Ireland

16.   The Irish courts do not yet appear to have addressed this question.[483] While the decision in *Safeway* may have persuasive effect in a comparable Irish case, there are important differences in the Irish and UK competition regimes that should be kept in mind. In the UK, an individual faces liability for breaches of competition law only under the cartel offence.[484] The potential exposure of individuals in Irish competition law is much broader. Essentially, all violations of sections 4 and 5 and Articles 101 and 102 are criminal offences and prosecutions can be taken and fines imposed on both undertakings and individuals, including certain employees. Where the undertaking has committed an offence and the relevant acts were 'authorised or consented to, by a person, being a director, manager or other similar officer of the undertaking, or a person who purports to act in such capacity,' that person may also be guilty of a criminal offence and can be prosecuted and fined

---

483. In something of a reverse situation, in one Irish case, an employee sued an employer for mistreatment at work, alleging that the employer required him to engage in an illegal cartel and exposed the employee to risk of sanction under the Competition Acts 1991 and 1996, putting the plaintiff to expense, inconvenience and distress. The proceedings were settled but details of the claim are set out in a judgment of Ó Caoimh J concerning taxation of costs. See *Doyle v Deasy* (High Court, unreported, 21 March 2003).

484. Enterprise Act 2002, s 188.

(as well as imprisoned for certain offences).[485] An employee faced with an indemnity claim from an undertaking that was fined may wish to argue that had he or she been primarily responsible, there was ample scope for an action to be taken on an individual basis.

17.   The Competition Act 2002 also makes specific provision for the attribution of acts of employees to the undertaking in question.[486] An employee might argue that this specific attribution mechanism makes the undertaking's responsibility more 'direct' than under vicarious liability or agency principles and consequently, that there is a stronger argument for an *ex turpi causa* defence.[487]

Key Sources

Safeway Stores Limited v Twigger [2010] EWHC 11 (Comm), [2010] Bus LR 974.

---

485. Competition Act 2002, s 8(6).
486. Competition Act 2002, s 6(6).
487. Cf *Safeway Stores Limited v Twigger* [2010] EWHC 11 (Comm), [2010] Bus LR 974, para 54.

Chapter 7

COMPETITION AND THE STATE

Chapter 7

COMPETITION AND THE STATE

125. WHAT ARE THE CONDITIONS FOR APPLICATION OF THE ARTICLE 106(2) DEROGATION?

Summary

- The undertaking must have been entrusted with the performance of a service of general economic interest.

- Application of the Treaty's rules would obstruct or jeopardise the performance, in law or in fact, of those services. It is not necessary to show that the undertaking could not survive were the derogation unavailable. It is sufficient to show that the special or exclusive rights granted to the undertaking are necessary to enable it to perform the tasks of general economic interest assigned to it under economically acceptable conditions.

- The development of trade must not be affected to such an extent as is incompatible with the interests of the Union.

1. Article 106 TFEU provides as follows:

    1. In the case of public undertakings and undertakings to which Member States grant special or exclusive rights, Member States shall neither enact nor maintain in force any measure contrary to the rules contained in the Treaties, in particular to those rules provided for in Article 18 and Articles 101 to 109.

    2. Undertakings entrusted with the operation of services of general economic interest or having the character of a revenue-producing monopoly shall be subject to the rules contained in this Treaty, in particular to the rules on competition, in so far as the application of such rules does not obstruct the performance, in law or in fact, of the particular tasks assigned to them. The development of trade must not be affected to such an extent as would be contrary to the interests of the Community.

    3. The Commission shall ensure the application of the provisions of this Article and shall, where necessary, address appropriate directives or decisions to Member States.

2. Article 106(1) makes clear that the Treaty rules, in particular the rules on competition and State aid, apply to public undertakings and undertakings granted special or exclusive rights. Article 106(2) provides a potential exemption from the competition and State aid rules of the Treaty in particular, but also other Treaty rules, for undertakings performing services of general economic interest.

3. An undertaking could seek to rely on Article 106(2) as a defence to a claim that the undertaking is in breach of Article 101 or 102 or other rules of the Treaty. This

may arise in national proceedings so that a national court will have to consider the application of Article 106(2).[1]

4.   Even though it is addressed to undertakings, Article 106(2), in conjunction with Article 106(1), may be relied on, under certain conditions, to justify the grant by a Member State to an undertaking entrusted with the operation of services of general economic interest of special or exclusive rights which are contrary to the provisions of the Treaty.[2] So either the undertaking in question or the Member State could rely on Article 106(2) depending on the circumstances of the case. Member States have sought to rely on Article 106(2) as a derogation not only from the competition rules but also, for example, from the EU public procurement rules.[3]

5.   Article 106(2), as a derogation from the Treaty, must be interpreted strictly[4] and it must be shown that the task of general economic interest 'cannot be achieved equally well by other means'.[5] It is incumbent on the Member State or undertaking which invokes Article 106(2) to show that all the conditions for its application are fulfilled.[6] So, when a Member State invokes the derogation, it:

> ... must set out in detail the reasons for which, in the event of elimination of the contested measures, the performance, under economically acceptable conditions, of the tasks of general economic interest which it has entrusted to an undertaking would, in its view, be jeopardised.[7]

What is meant by 'entrusted'?

6.   To invoke Article 106(2), it must first be shown that the undertaking has been entrusted with the performance of a service of general economic interest.[8]

---

1.   See, e.g., *O'Neill v Minister for Agriculture* (unreported, Irish High Court, 5 July 1995) (Budd J) (Article 106(2) considered but as the court found that Article 102 was not breached, it was not ultimately required to apply Article 106(2)).
2.   See, e.g., Case C–340/99 *TNT Traco SpA v Poste Italiane SpA* [2001] ECR I–4109, [2002] 4 CMLR 454, para 52.
3.   See, e.g., Case C–160/08 *Commission v Germany*, judgment of 29 April 2010, paras 125– 130 (Germany failed to show how compliance with the procurement rules was liable to prevent the accomplishment of the task of general economic interest of universal provision of ambulance services).
4.   Cases C–157/94 etc *Commission v The Netherlands* [1997] ECR I–5699, [1998] 2 CMLR 373, para 37.
5.   Case C–203/96 *Dusseldorp BV* [1998] ECR I–4075, [1998] 3 CMLR 873, para 67.
6.   Case C-159/94 *Commission* v *France* [1997] ECR I-5815, [1998] 2 CMLR 373, para 101. But the burden on the Member State is qualified. It does not have to prove positively that no other conceivable measure could be used to achieve the tasks of general economic interest. See para 9 below.
7.   Case C–463/00 *Commission v Spain ('Golden Shares')* [2003] ECR I–4581, [2003] 2 CMLR 557, para 82.
8.   Or has the character of a revenue producing monopoly. Such undertakings may also benefit from a commercial monopoly, in which case they are also subject to Article 37 TFEU, requiring Member States to adjust commercial monopolies so as to ensure there is no discrimination regarding the conditions under which goods are procured and marketed between nationals of Member States.

Entrustment requires that there be a positive act of a public authority,[9] whether legislation or another public act (for example, entrustment could take place through the grant of a public contract or concession to the undertaking).[10] There is no requirement to show that the entrustment of the service of general economic interest was made pursuant to a competitive tendering procedure.[11]

Which services are 'services of general economic interest'?

7.   There is no definition in the Treaty of what constitutes a service of general economic interest and this term has been left to be interpreted by the courts. The Union courts have stated that there must be a strict definition of the undertakings which can take advantage of Article 106(2).[12] It has also been acknowledged by the General Court that the Member States enjoy a wide discretion in defining what they regard to be services of general economic interest and the definition of such services by a Member State can be questioned by the Commission only in the event of manifest error.[13] The division of powers between the Member States and the Union in the context of services of general economic interest is also reflected in Article 14 TFEU. That Article recognises the place occupied by services of general economic interest in the shared values of the Union and calls on the Union and the Member States to take care that these services operate on the basis of principles and conditions which enable them to fulfil their missions.[14] The Lisbon Treaty annexed a Protocol on services of general interest to the TEU and TFEU, which recognises the shared values of the Union in respect of services of general economic interest as including 'the essential role and the wide discretion of national, regional and local authorities in providing, commissioning and organising services of general economic interest as closely as possible to the needs of the users'.[15]

8.   Services that have been found to come within the meaning of services of general economic interest include, among many others, television broadcasting, including advertising and commercial activities,[16] the establishment and operation of the

---

9.   See, e.g., Case 66/86 *Ahmed Saeed Flugreisen v Zentrale zur Bekämpfung unlauteren Wettbewerbs e.V.* [1989] ECR 803, [1990] 4 CMLR 102, para 55; Case 172/80 *Züchner v Bayerische Vereinsbank AG* [1981] ECR 2021, [1982] 1 CMLR 313, para 7; Case C–203/96 *Dusseldorp BV* [1998] ECR I–4075, [1998] 3 CMLR 873 (responsibility for waste management attributed to an undertaking under a plan for disposal of dangerous waste).

10. Case C–393/92 *Almelo v NV Energiebedrijf Ijsselmij* [1994] ECR I–1477, [1994] 2 CEC 281, para 47.

11. Case T–442/03 *SIC v Commission* [2008] ECR II–1161, para 145.

12. Case 127/73 *BRT v SABAM* [1974] ECR 313, para 19; Case C–242/95 *GT-Link A/S v De Danske Statsbaner (DSB)* [1997] ECR I–4449, [1997] 5 CMLR 601, para 50.

13. Case T–289/03 *BUPA v Commission* [2008] ECR II–81, [2009] 2 CMLR 1043, para 166. See also Commission Communication – Services of general interest, including social services of general interest: a new European commitment COM(2007) 725 final (20 November 2007), noting at 2 that services of general interest cover a broad range of activities.

14. Article 14 TFEU.

15. Protocol (No 26) on services of general interest, annexed to the TEU and TFEU, Article 1.

16. Case 155/74 *Sacchi* [1974] ECR 409, [1974] 2 CMLR 177, para 15.

public telecommunications network,[17] a supplementary pension scheme,[18] mooring services at a port[19] and the provision of emergency ambulance services.[20]

Is it necessary to show that the undertaking could not survive could it not avail of Article 106(2)?

9.   Article 106(2) provides that the undertaking is subject to the Treaty's rules only to the extent that the application of those rules 'does not obstruct the performance, in law or in fact, of the particular tasks assigned' to the undertaking. The Court of Justice has interpreted this to mean that it is not necessary to show that the undertaking could not survive were it not able to avail of the derogation.[21] In the *Commission v The Netherlands* case, involving an undertaking with an exclusive right to import electricity, the Court held that to successfully invoke the Article 106(2) derogation, it is sufficient to establish that the maintenance of the special or exclusive rights

> … is necessary to enable the holder of them to perform the tasks of general economic interest assigned to it under economically acceptable conditions.
>
> Whilst it is true that it is incumbent upon a Member State which invokes Article [106(2)] to demonstrate that the conditions laid down by that provision are met, that burden of proof cannot be so extensive as to require the Member State, when setting out in detail the reasons for which, in the event of elimination of the contested measures, the performance, under economically acceptable conditions, of the tasks of general economic interest which it has entrusted to an undertaking would, in its view, be jeopardized, to go even further and prove, positively, that no other conceivable

---

17.   Case C–18/88 *RTT v GB-INNO-BM* [1991] ECR I–5941, [1992] 4 CMLR 78, para 16.
18.   Case C–67/96 *Albany* [1999] ECR I–5751, [2000] 4 CMLR 446, paras 104–110.
19.   Case C–266/96 *Corsica Ferries France SA v Gruppo Antichi Ormeggiatori del porto di Genova Coop arl* [1998] ECR I–3949, [1998] 5 CMLR 402, para 45 ('Mooring groups are obliged to provide at any time and to any user a universal mooring service, for reasons of safety in port waters').
20.   Case C–475/99 *Ambulanz Glöckner v Landkreis Südwestpfalz* [2001] ECR I–8089, [2002] 4 CMLR 726, para 55.
21.   Cases C–157–160/94 *Commission v The Netherlands, Italy, France and Spain* [1997] ECR I–5699, [1998] 2 CMLR 373, para 43. See also Case C–320/91 *Corbeau* [1993] ECR I–2533, [1995] 4 CMLR 621 (that it would be contrary to Article 106 for a prohibition to lie against an economic operator performing services that did 'not compromise the economic stability of the service of general economic interest performed by the holder of the exclusive right'.) Cf earlier approaches before the Court had applied a principle of proportionality, in, e.g., Case 155/73 *Sacchi* [1974] ECR 409, [1974] 2 CMLR 177, para 15 (the prohibitions in the competition rules apply 'so long as it is not shown that the said prohibitions are incompatible with the performance' of their general interest tasks); Case C–41/90 *Höfner & Elser v Macrotron GmbH* [1991] ECR I–1979, [1993] 4 CMLR 306, para 25 (Article 102 could not obstruct the performance of the particular task assigned to a public employment agency in so far as it was 'manifestly not in a position to satisfy demand' in an area of the market and allowed its exclusive rights to be encroached on by those companies).

measure, which by definition would be hypothetical, could enable those tasks to be performed under the same conditions.[22]

10. It follows from the requirement that the restrictions be necessary for performing the entrusted tasks that the restrictions also be proportionate. This proportionality test requires that there be a causal link between the measure and the service of general economic interest, that the restrictions are balanced by the benefits to the general interest and that the objective of general interest cannot be achieved by less restrictive means.[23] In cases involving the payment of compensation to the undertaking performing the services of general economic interest (for example, in State aid cases or where the undertaking is subsidised by other undertakings in the market) it would seem to be a requirement of the proportionality test that the compensation does not exceed the amount necessary to offset the losses incurred in providing the general interest service.[24]

11. This in turn raises the issue of the efficiency of the undertaking performing the service of general economic interest. The amount of compensation required for it to perform its tasks without making a loss will obviously be higher the lower its efficiency levels. An efficiency test is included in the fourth *Altmark* condition, referring to a 'typical efficient undertaking'[25] but the efficiency requirement has not yet been specifically answered in the context of the Article 106(2) derogation.[26]

12. The judgment of the General Court in *BUPA* indicates that in relying on Article 106(2) as a derogation from the State aid rules, a Member State enjoys a wide discretion in determining what measures are necessary to ensure the performance of a service of general economic interest. The *BUPA* case concerned the Irish government's risk equalisation scheme ('RES'), which required private health insurers ('PMI' insurers) with lower risk profiles to make payments to PMI insurers with higher risk profiles. The insurer with the higher risk profile was the State-owned health insurer, VHI. The obligations placed on private health insurers,

22. Cases C–157–160/94 *Commission v The Netherlands, Italy, France and Spain* [1997] ECR I–5699, [1998] 2 CMLR 373, paras 53, 58.

23. Buendia Sierra, 'Article 86(2): Services of General Economic Interest' in *Faull & Nikpay: The EC Law of Competition* (2nd edn, 2007) para 6.162.

24. Case C–340/99 *TNT Traco SpA v Poste Italiane* [2001] ECR I–4109, [2002] 4 CMLR 454, para 57.

25. Where the *Altmark* criteria are met (from Case C–280/00 *Altmark Trans GmbH v Nahverkehrsgesellschaft Altmark GmbH* [2003] ECR I–7747, [2003] 3 CMLR 339), compensation for the performance of a public service obligation will not constitute State aid and so it will be unnecessary to apply Article 106(2). See Question 128.

26. This question was raised directly in *BUPA* but the General Court found it unnecessary to provide an answer (Case T–289/03 *BUPA v Commission* [2008] ECR II–81, [2009] 2 CMLR 1043, paras 139, 297). Buendia Sierra suggests that in principle, the only relevant cost in the application of Article 106(2) is the actual cost incurred by the undertaking irrespective of its level of efficiency (Buendia Sierra, 'Article 86(2): Services of General Economic Interest' in *Faull & Nikpay: The EC Law of Competition* (2nd edn, 2007) para 6.199).

which included community rating (an obligation to apply the same premium to all policy-holders for the same type of product irrespective of their health status, age or sex), open enrolment, lifetime cover and minimum benefits constituted services of general economic interest.[27] Even though it found that RES did not give rise to State aid and so the application of Article 106(2) was unnecessary to exempt it,[28] the General Court nonetheless examined the applicant's case on Article 106(2), which disputed the necessity and proportionality of the introduction of RES. The Court upheld the Commission's review of the necessity and the proportionality of RES for purposes of the application of Article 106(2).[29] The Court emphasised that its own review was limited to the application of judicial review principles and in particular, in respect of the necessity of the RES system for achieving the performance of the services of general economic interest at issue, examining whether RES was manifestly inappropriate for achieving the objectives pursued. The Court held, regarding the extent of the Commission's review, that:

> ... the review of necessity does not require that the Commission be convinced that the Member State, in the light of present or future market conditions, cannot abandon the notified measures, but is limited to ascertaining whether there has been a manifest error in the exercise of the wide discretion of the Member State as regards the way of ensuring that the SGEI mission may be achieved under economically acceptable conditions.[30]

13.   The General Court went on to hold that the Commission could reasonably consider that RES was necessary for the services of general economic interest to be discharged in economically acceptable conditions.[31] The Court added that the proportionality of the scheme was supported by the fact that decisions taken by the Irish authorities in connection with the activation of RES were amenable to judicial review.[32]

---

27. Case T–289/03 *BUPA v Commission* [2008] ECR II–81, [2009] 2 CMLR 1043, paras 182–184.

28. Case T–289/03 *BUPA v Commission* [2008] ECR II–81, [2009] 2 CMLR 1043, para 258.

29. Case T–289/03 *BUPA v Commission* [2008] ECR II–81, [2009] 2 CMLR 1043, paras 259–310.

30. Case T–289/03 *BUPA v Commission* [2008] ECR II–81, [2009] 2 CMLR 1043, para 268. See also *BUPA Ireland Ltd v Health Insurance Authority* [2006] IEHC 431, paras 233–234, in which the Irish High Court (McKechnie J) held that the same RES scheme met the conditions for the application of Article 106(2) (overturned by the Supreme Court on other grounds, *BUPA Ireland Ltd v Health Insurance Authority* [2008] IESC 42, [2009] 1 ILRM 81). Cf Case C–67/96 *Albany* [1999] ECR I–5751, [2000] 4 CMLR 446, para 108 (the exclusive right of a pension fund to manage employers' supplementary pensions could benefit from Article 106(2) as otherwise undertakings with young employees who were good risks would move to private providers, leaving the pension fund with bad risks and thereby increasing the cost of pensions to workers and undermining the important social function performed by the fund).

31. Case T–289/03 *BUPA v Commission* [2008] ECR II–81, [2009] 2 CMLR 1043, para 295.

32. Case T–289/03 *BUPA v Commission* [2008] ECR II–81, [2009] 2 CMLR 1043, para 304 (such a challenge was ultimately successful, *BUPA Ireland Ltd v Health Insurance Authority* [2008] IESC 42, [2009] 1 ILRM 81).

14. The *BUPA* case may indicate a more flexible application of Article 106(2) vis-à-vis the State aid rules. However, there have also been cases in which the conditions for the application of the Article 106(2) derogation were not met. In *Corbeau*, the Court of Justice considered on a preliminary reference the extent to which exclusive rights were necessary to enable the Belgian postal monopoly to carry out its universal service obligations, in light of a Belgian law, which prohibited, with criminal sanctions, any form of competition in the distribution of mail of any kind. The Court recognised the legitimacy of placing some restrictions on competition so as to prevent competitors from 'cherry-picking' the most lucrative sectors, which could leave the undertaking with the universal service obligation with unprofitable sectors. However, a complete ban on competition was not justified:

> … the exclusion of competition is not justified as regards specific services dissociable from the service of general interest which meet special needs of economic operators and which call for certain additional services not offered by the traditional postal service, such as collection from the senders' address, greater speed or reliability of distribution or the possibility of changing the destination in the course of transit, in so far as such specific services, by their nature and the conditions in which they are offered, such as the geographical area in which they are provided, do not compromise the economic equilibrium of the service of general economic interest performed by the holder of the exclusive right.[33]

To what extent must the development of trade not be affected?

15. Article 106(2) also provides that for the derogation to apply, 'the development of trade must not be affected to such an extent as would be contrary to the interests of the Union'. This additional requirement is clearly narrower than the concept of an effect on trade between Member States but its parameters have not been fully explored by the Union courts.[34] Advocate General Colomer opined in *Federutility* that in order to find that there is a detrimental effect on intra-community trade within the meaning of Article 106(2), unlike the classic concept of measures having an effect equivalent to a quantitative restriction, 'proof would be required that the measure in issue has substantially disrupted the operation of the internal market'.[35]

Is there an equivalent of Article 106(2) in national law?

16. In the UK, the Competition Act 1998 has a corresponding provision to Article 106(2), which provides:

> Neither the Chapter I prohibition nor the Chapter II prohibition applies to an undertaking entrusted with the operation of services of general economic interest or

---

33. Case C–320/91 *Corbeau* [1993] ECR I–2533, [1995] 4 CMLR 621, para 19.
34. See Cases C–157–160/94 *Commission v The Netherlands, Italy, France and Spain* [1997] ECR I–5699, [1998] 2 CMLR 373, paras 66–71 (the Commission failed to define the Union interest and provided no explanation as to how the Union interest was affected).
35. Case C–265/08 *Federutility and Others v Autorità per l'energia elettrica e il gas*, opinion of Advocate General Colomer of 20 October 2009, para 78.

having the character of a revenue-producing monopoly in so far as the prohibition would obstruct the performance, in law or in fact, of the particular tasks assigned to that undertaking.[36]

17. The Irish Competition Act 2002 does not have a provision that corresponds to Article 106(2). This leaves open the possibility that an undertaking could have an Article 106(2) defence to what would otherwise be infringements of Article 101 or 102 but not in respect of an infringement of sections 4 and 5 of the Competition Act 2002. In the *Panda* case, the respondent local authorities against which breaches of both Irish and EU competition law were alleged, argued that they could benefit from Article 106(2). It is not entirely clear from the judgment whether this argument was invoked only vis-à-vis EU competition law or whether the respondents attempted to make a similar argument in respect of the Irish competition rules. McKechnie J ultimately held that there was no affect on inter-State trade but that even if there had been, the Article 106(2) derogation would not have applied.[37]

Key Sources

Case C–320/91 *Corbeau* [1993] ECR I–2533, [1995] 4 CMLR 621.

Case C–157/94 *Commission v The Netherlands* [1997] ECR I–5699, [1998] 2 CMLR 373.

Case T–289/03 *BUPA v Commission* [2008] ECR II–81, [2009] ECR II–1043.

---

36. Competition Act 1998, Sch 3, para 4.
37. *Nurendale Ltd t/a Panda Waste Services v Dublin City Council* [2009] IEHC 588, paras 3, 144.

126. WHAT MEASURES AMOUNT TO STATE AID?

Summary

Four cumulative conditions must be fulfilled for a measure to constitute State aid. The measure must:

(i)   Be financed directly or indirectly through State resources and be imputable to the State.

(ii)   Confer an economic advantage to certain undertakings or the production of certain goods.

(iii) Distort or threaten to distort competition.

And

(iv)   Have an effect on trade between Member States.

There is a *de minimis exception* for certain types of aid of €200,000 over three years

1.   The rationale for the control of State aids is to prevent distortions of competition in the market. The Treaty contains rules aimed at preventing the granting of aid by a Member State that distorts or threatens to distort competition and affects inter-state trade. Although State aid can be used for protectionist and anti-competitive purposes, it can also have a positive effect in terms of saving jobs and industries and State aid may be a necessary part of preventing economic collapse, as demonstrated by the recent financial crisis. The State aid rules in the Treaty balance these positive and negative effects in establishing which State aids are illegal and which are permissible.[38]

2.   The key State aid rules are set out in Article 107 TFEU, which provides as follows:

    Article 107(1)

    Save as otherwise provided in the Treaties, any aid granted by a Member State or through State resources in any form whatsoever which distorts or threatens to distort competition by favouring certain undertakings or the production of certain goods shall, in so far as it affects trade between Member States, be incompatible with the internal market.[39]

3.   It is apparent from Article 107 that for a transaction to give rise to State aid, the following cumulative conditions must be met:

    •   The transaction is financed directly or indirectly through State resources;

---

38.   For specialist works on State aid, see, e.g., Bacon, *European Community Law of State Aid* (2009); Quigley, *European State Aid Law and Policy* (2nd edn, 2009); Hancher, Ottervanger and Slot, *EC State Aids* (3rd edn, 2006).

39.   Article 93 TFEU may also be relevant in the transport sector ('Aids shall be compatible with the Treaties if they meet the needs of coordination of transport or if they represent reimbursement for the discharge of certain obligations inherent in the concept of a public service').

- The transaction confers an economic advantage to certain undertakings or the production of certain goods;

- The transaction distorts or threatens to distort competition; and

- The transaction has an effect on trade between Member States.

When is aid financed through 'State resources'?

4. The State aid rules only apply to measures involving advantages granted 'by a Member State or through State resources'. No distinction should be drawn between cases where aid is granted directly by the State and by public or private bodies established or designated by the State with a view to administering the aid. As the Court of Justice clarified in *PreussenElektra*:

> ... the case-law of the Court of Justice shows that only advantages granted directly or indirectly through State resources are to be considered aid within the meaning of Article [107(1)]. The distinction made in that provision between aid granted by a Member State and aid granted through State resources does not signify that all advantages granted by a State, whether financed through State resources or not, constitute aid but is intended merely to bring within that definition both advantages which are granted directly by the State and those granted by a public or private body designated or established by the State.[40]

5. For an advantage to give rise to aid it must, first, be funded directly or indirectly through State resources and, second, be imputable to the State.[41] So, for example, in *Pearle*, there was no aid because an advertising campaign run by a trade association governed by public law was funded entirely by compulsory levies on undertakings that were members of the association and the funds were not made available to public authorities. Therefore there was no funding from state resources.[42] This can be contrasted with the situation in cases such as *GEMO*, where particular benefits were granted out of monies generated by a tax levied and administered by State authorities so that there was no question that the benefits were funded from State resources.[43]

6. It is not necessary for resources to come directly from taxation or a State's budget or the funds or assets of central government in order to be 'State resources'. The resource could be from a public undertaking if the funds are under State control:

> Article [107(1)] of the Treaty covers all the financial means by which the public sector may actually support undertakings, irrespective of whether or not those means are permanent assets of the public sector. Consequently, even though the sums involved in

---

40. Case C–379/98 *PreussenElektra AG v Schhleswag AG* [2001] ECR I–2099, [2001] 2 CMLR 833, para 58.

41. See, e.g., Case C–482/99 *France v Commission ('Stardust Marine')* [2002] ECR I–4397, [2002] 2 CMLR 1069, para 24.

42. Case C–345/02 *Pearle BV v Hoofdbedrijfschap Ambachten* [2004] ECR I–7139, [2004] 3 CMLR 182, para 36.

43. Case C–126/01 *Ministre de l'Économie, des Finances et de l'Industrie v GEMO SA* [2003] ECR I–13769, [2004] 1 CMLR 259, paras 7, 27.

the measure … are not permanently held by the Treasury, the fact that they constantly remain under public control, and therefore available to the competent national authorities, is sufficient for them to be categorised as State aid and for the measure to fall within Article [107(1)] of the Treaty.[44]

7. Article 107(1) can encompass the acts of bodies such as local and regional authorities and public undertakings, which can be imputed to the State. However, just because an undertaking is funded by the State or governed by public law does not necessarily mean that its acts are capable of giving rise to 'aid'. The role and oversight of the State in the measure may need to be examined, as the Court of Justice indicated in *Stardust Marine*:

> Even if the State is in a position to control a public undertaking and to exercise a dominant influence over its operations, actual exercise of that control in a particular case cannot be automatically presumed. A public undertaking may act with more or less independence, according to the degree of autonomy left to it by the State. That might be the situation in the case of public undertakings such as Altus and SBT. Therefore, the mere fact that a public undertaking is under State control is not sufficient for measures taken by that undertaking, such as the financial support measures in question here, to be imputed to the State. It is also necessary to examine whether the public authorities must be regarded as having been involved, in one way or another, in the adoption of those measures.[45]

What measures constitute 'aid'?

8. State aid can take many forms. It is not limited to transfers of money or the grant of subsidies. It extends to measures 'constituting an additional charge for the State or for bodies designated or established by the State for that purpose'.[46] Therefore, an actual *transfer* of State resources is not required. A measure may be State aid if the State foregoes revenue that it is otherwise entitled to receive, for example by waiving taxes or other charges.[47] The provision of a guarantee for a loan could

---

44. Case C–83/98P *France v Ladbroke Racing Limited* [2000] ECR I–3271, [2000] 3 CMLR 555, para 50 (funds derived from unclaimed winnings held by a body controlled by the French State were State resources where allocation of the funds to the treasury depended on whether certain statutory conditions were met). See also Case C–482/99 *France v Commission ('Stardust Marine')* [2002] ECR I–4397, [2002] 2 CMLR 1069, paras 32, 37–38 (loans and guarantees granted by public undertakings were from State resources).

45. Case C–482/99 *France v Commission ('Stardust Marine')* [2002] ECR I–4397, [2002] 2 CMLR 1069, para 52.

46. Case C–200/97 *Ecotrade Srl v AFS* [1998] ECR I–7907, [1999] 2 CMLR 804, para 35. Advocate General Kokott has suggested that 'an additional financial burden of any kind for the State or regional body to which the measure is attributable is sufficient for a *presumption* that it is financed by the State or through State resources' (Case C–169/08 *Presidente del Consiglio dei Ministri v Regione Sardegna* [2009] ECR I–10821, [2010] 2 CMLR 159, opinion of Advocate General Kokott, para 144).

47. Case C–387/92 *Banco Exterior de España SA v Ayuntamiento de Valencia* [1994] ECR I–877, [1994] 3 CMLR 473 (grant by public authorities of tax exemptions was State aid).

constitute State aid.[48] The provision of goods or services at an undercharge[49] or the purchase by the State or public body of goods that were not required could also amount to State aid.[50]

What constitutes an economic advantage?

9.   The key criterion in the assessment of whether there is State aid will often be that of economic advantage. It is necessary to establish whether the recipient undertaking receives an economic advantage which it would not have obtained under 'normal market conditions'.[51] To answer this question, it may be appropriate in certain contexts to ask whether the terms of the State measure are ones that would be acceptable to a commercial investor. This is the 'private investor' test or 'market economy investor' test. Essentially, if the recipient undertaking could not have obtained comparable terms from a commercial investor seeking a normal return, the State measure will be seen as conferring an economic advantage. Different considerations apply if the measure is the provision of credit, in which case a 'private creditor' test is used.[52] Where aid arises from the sale of an asset to the recipient at an undervalue, it would be necessary to ask whether the price is lower than the price that would have been paid under normal market conditions.[53]

10.   In applying the private investor test, 'it is necessary to consider whether in similar circumstances a private investor of a size comparable to that of the bodies administering the public sector might have provided capital of such an amount'.[54] However, it is not necessary that the comparator be with a private investor that seeks maximum short-term profitability:

>   ... although the conduct of a private investor, with which the intervention of a public investor pursuing economic policy aims must be compared, need not be the conduct of an ordinary investor laying out capital with a view to realizing a profit in the relatively short term, it must at least be the conduct of a private holding company or a private

---

48.   Case C–288/96 *Germany v Commission* [2000] ECR I–8237, paras 30–32, 41–42 (guarantee for a bank loan was State aid; undertaking would not otherwise have been able to obtain financing).

49.   Case C–39/94 *SFEI v La Poste* [1996] ECR I–3547, para 57 (provision by a public undertaking to private subsidiaries of logistical and commercial assistance without normal consideration was State aid).

50.   Case T–14/96 *BAI v Commission* [1999] ECR II–139, [1999] 3 CMLR 245 (it could not be excluded that an agreement by a public authority to purchase travel services it did not need constituted State aid).

51.   See, e.g., Case C–256/97 *Déménagements-Manutention Transport SA (DMT)* [1999] ECR I–3913, [1999] 3 CMLR 1, para 22.

52.   See, e.g., Case C–342/96 *Spain v Commission ('Tubacex')* [1999] ECR I–2459, [2000] 2 CMLR 415, paras 46–49.

53.   See, e.g., Cases C–341 & 342/06P *Chronopost SA v Union française de l'express (UFEX)* [2008] ECR I–4777, [2008] 3 CMLR 568 (the Court of Justice held that there was no State aid in this case).

54.   Case C–305/89 *Italy v Commission ('Alfa Romeo')* [1991] ECR I–1603, para 19.

group of undertakings pursuing a structural policy – whether general or sectoral – and guided by prospects of profitability in the longer term.[55]

11. Various factors may be relevant to the assessment of whether a comparable private investor would have carried out the transaction on similar terms. The underlying market conditions and the nature of the funds being contributed may be relevant. The announcement of an aid measure, such as the offer of a loan, may constitute a financial advantage, even if the measure is never implemented, as the announcement itself could have a positive and stabilising effect on the undertaking's credit rating.[56]

12. The private investor test also applies in the case of benefits granted to public undertakings. The benefits granted to public undertakings may fall outside Article 107(1) on the basis of the *Altmark* test or the Article 106(2) exemption may apply. Otherwise, the State aid rules apply equally to public undertakings. Again, however, the particular circumstances of the public undertaking may be relevant:

> Since the Commission must always examine all the relevant features of the transaction at issue and its context, it must take into account the question whether an informed private investor, in the place of the public investor in question, would have accepted a lower return than the average return in the sector concerned as an appropriate return because of economic considerations other than the optimisation of his return.[57]

Must aid favour certain undertakings over others?

13. Article 107(1) involves aid that distorts or threatens to distort competition 'by favouring certain undertakings or the production of certain goods'. In considering this requirement of selectivity, 'it is necessary to determine whether or not the measure in question entails advantages accruing exclusively to certain undertakings or certain sectors of activity'.[58]

14. In practice, it is not always easy to determine whether there is selectivity. A measure may appear to be of general application but in fact favour some undertakings over others. For example, a measure reducing employers' sickness insurance contributions to a greater extent in respect of women than men was an aid as it favoured undertakings in sectors with higher numbers of women workers such as textiles.[59]

15. Conversely, where undertakings are treated differently, this will not always result in some being favoured over others. Such a difference of treatment may be

---

55. Case C–42/93 *Spain v Commission ('Merco')* [1994] ECR I–4175, [1995] 2 CMLR 702, para 14.
56. Cases T–425/04 etc *France v Commission,* judgment of 21 May 2010, paras 212–261 (however, the open, imprecise and conditional nature of the announcement meant that it was not a guarantee and so there was no transfer of State resources and no State aid).
57. Cases T–228/99 & T–233/99 *Westdeutsche Landesbank Girozentrale v Commission* [2003] ECR II–435, [2004] 1 CMLR 529, para 270.
58. Case T–55/99 *Confederación Española de Transporte de Mercancías (CETM) v Commission* [2000] ECR II–3207, para 39.
59. Case 203/82 *Commission v Italy* [1983] ECR 2525, [1985] 1 CMLR 653, para 4.

objectively justified. The condition of selectivity is not satisfied by a measure which, although conferring an advantage on its recipient, is justified by the nature or general scheme of the system of which it is part. So in *GIL* a system of taxation of insurance premiums characterised by the existence of two different rates was not aid where the application of the higher rate to a specific part of the insurance contracts previously subject to the standard rate was justified by the nature and the general scheme of the national system of taxation of insurance, even if the introduction of the higher rate involved an advantage for operators offering contracts subject to the standard rate.[60]

16.   Even if an aid is granted to some undertakings before others, this may not give rise to selectivity if the earlier recipients have not taken advantage of the aid. In *Bouygues*, 3G licenses granted by French regulators to Orange and SFR did not have a higher economic value than a 3G license granted at a later date to Bouygues, where Orange and SFR had not yet been able to launch services under the license by the time of the award to Bouygues.[61]

When will the 'distortion of competition' criterion be met?

17.   The criterion of distortion of competition is often considered together with the effect on trade criterion, although the two are separate conditions. It is enough that the measure is liable to distort competition. It is not necessary to show an actual anti-competitive effect. In many cases, the Commission does not have much difficulty in finding that the distortion of competition criterion is satisfied. However, the Commission must at least set out in its statement of reasons for the decision, circumstances showing that the aid is capable of distorting or threatening to distort competition (and capable of affecting trade between Member States). In *Leeuwarder*, the Commission failed this requirement since its decision did 'not contain the slightest information concerning the situation of the relevant market, the place of [the recipient] in that market, the pattern of trade between Member States in the products in question or the undertaking's exports'.[62]

18.   Setting out the circumstances which show that the measure is liable to distort competition does not require the Commission to define the market in question or analyse its structure and the ensuing competitive relationships.[63] In *Brandt*, the

---

60.   Case C–308/01 *GIL Insurance Ltd v Commissioners of Customs & Excise* [2004] ECR I–4777, [2004] 2 CMLR 22, para 78.

61.   Case C–431/07P *Bouygues SA v Commission* [2009] ECR I–2665, [2009] 3 CMLR 407, para 120.

62.   Cases 296 & 318/82 *The Netherlands and Leeuwarder Papierwarenfabriek BV v Commission* [1985] ECR 809, [1985] 3 CMLR 380, para 24. The requirement to state reasons derives from Article 296 TFEU which provides that 'legal acts shall state the reasons on which they are based'.

63.   Cases T–298/97 etc *Alzetta v Commission* [2000] ECR II–2319, para 95.

following finding by the Commission in its State aid decision was sufficient to satisfy the distortion of competition (and effect on trade) criteria:

> The third and fourth conditions for the application of Article [107(1)] are that the measure must distort or threaten to distort competition and must affect trade between Member States. The scheme under examination threatens to distort competition because it reinforces the financial position of some undertakings compared to those of their competitors. In particular, it threatens to distort competition and affect trade in cases where the recipients compete with products coming from other Member States, even if they do not export their own products. If they do not export their own products there is nevertheless an advantage to domestic production, because undertakings established in other Member States have less chance of exporting their products to the market in question.[64]

19. In principle, 'aid which is intended to release an undertaking from costs which it would normally have had to bear in its day-to-day management or normal activities, distorts the conditions of competition'.[65] It is not necessary to carry out an economic analysis of the actual situation on the relevant market or to show the real effect of the aid at issue on prices.[66]

When will the 'effect on trade' criterion be met?

20. In contrast to Articles 101 and 102, which refer to practices which *may* affect inter-state trade, Article 107(1) simply refers to aid that affects trade between Member States. There does not appear to be any material difference however and like the distortion of competition criterion, it can often quickly be concluded that an aid affects trade between Member States.

21. It is not necessary to establish that there is a real effect on trade between Member States, but only to examine whether the aid is liable to affect inter-state trade.[67] The fact that the amount of the aid is relatively small or that the recipient undertaking is not large, does not necessarily exclude the possibility that trade between Member States might be affected.[68] For example, in respect of tax legislation, it can be presumed that trade between Member States is affected where those favoured by the legislation perform an economic activity in the field of cross-border trade or where it is conceivable that they are in competition with firms established in other Member States.[69]

---

64. See Cases T–239 & 323/04 *Italy v Commission (Brandt)* [2007] ECR II–3265, para 128 (quoting the Commission decision) and going on to find (para 130) that the reasons of the Commission were appropriate and sufficient.
65. Case C–172/03 *Heiser v Finanzamt Innsbruck* [2005] ECR I–1627, [2005] 2 CMLR 402, para 55.
66. Case C–494/06P *Re Loans for Foreign Investment: Commission v Italy* [2009] ECR I–3639, [2009] 3 CMLR 943, para 58.
67. See, e.g., Case C–66/02 *Italy v Commission* [2005] ECR I–10901, para 111.
68. See, e.g., Cases C–393/04 & 41/05 *Air Liquide Industries Belgium SA v Ville de Seraing* [2006] ECR I–5293, [2006] 3 CMLR 23, para 36.
69. Case C–494/06P *Re Loans for Foreign Investment: Commission v Italy* [2009] ECR I–3639, [2009] 3 CMLR 943, para 51.

Is there a *de minimis* rule?

22.   It has been noted that the EU courts and the Commission have been less than clear in their approach to the question of whether aid below a certain value can be treated as *de minimis* so that it does not fulfil the criteria of distortion of competition and effect on inter-state trade.[70] However, there is no requirement in the State aid case law that the distortion of competition, or the threat of such distortion, or the effect on intra-EU trade, must be significant or substantial.[71] This can be contrasted with the position under Article 101, where the effect on competition and on inter-state trade must be appreciable.[72]

23.   The Commission's practice has been to apply a *de minimis* exception and the position is now encompassed in Regulation 1998/2006. A grant of up to €200,000 in aid to an undertaking over a three-year period will be considered *de minimis*.[73] The figure is €100,000 for undertakings in road transport. Guarantees of up to €1.5 million (€750,000 in road transport) are considered *de minimis*.[74] Regulation 1998/2006 does not apply in every industry sector and it does not cover aid in the fishery and aquaculture sectors, aid in respect of certain agricultural products, export-related activities, aid favouring domestic over imported goods, aid in the coal sector, road freight transport and aid granted to undertakings in difficulty.[75] There are specific rules applicable to aid in agriculture, fisheries, transport and coal.

24.   In response to the financial crisis, the Commission decided to temporarily allow the granting of a limited amount of aid that would not fall within the *de minimis* thresholds. The amount of aid permitted per undertaking is €500,000 and it must be granted no later than 31 December 2010. Various other conditions apply, including that the firm was not in difficulty on 1 July 2008.[76]

---

70.   Quigley, *European State Aid Law and Policy* (2nd edn, 2009) 60.
71.   See Cases T–227/01 etc *Territorio Histórico de Álava v Commission*, judgment of 9 September 2009, para 148.
72.   See Questions 6 and 19.
73.   Commission Regulation (EC) No 1998/2006 on the application of Article 87 and 88 of the Treaty to *de minimis* aid, Article 2(2).
74.   Regulation 1998/2006, Article 2(4)(d).
75.   Regulation 1998/2006, Article 1(1).
76.   Commission Communication – Temporary Community framework for State aid measures to support access to finance in the current financial and economic crisis [2009] OJ C83/01, para 4.2.2. There are also new measures in respect of aid in the form of guarantees, subsidised interest rates, aid for the production of green products and measures to promote risk capital investments. The provisions on guarantees were amended by the Commission Communication amending the Temporary Community Framework for State aid measures to support access to finance in the current financial and economic crisis [2009] OJ C303/04. For crisis aid in respect of undertakings active in the primary production of agricultural products (up to €15,000), see Commission Communication amending the Temporary Community Framework for State aid measures to support access to finance in the current financial and economic crisis [2009] OJ C261/02.

Must the recipient be an 'undertaking'?

25. Article 107(1) refers to aid which favours 'certain undertakings or the production of certain goods'. The term 'undertaking' has the same meaning in this context as it does in Articles 101 and 102.[77]

Key Sources

Article 107, TFEU.

Case C–379/98 *PreussenElektra AG v Schhleswag AG* [2001] ECR I–2099, [2001] 2 CMLR 833.

Case C–482/99 *France v Commission ('Stardust Marine')* [2002] ECR I–4397, [2002] 2 CMLR 1069.

---

77. See Question 1.

127. WHICH TYPES OF AID ARE COMPATIBLE WITH THE COMMON MARKET?

Summary

• Article 107(2) specifies three types of aid that are compatible with the common market.

• Article 107(3) lists four types of aid that may be compatible with the common market.

• The Commission determines whether Article 107(3) can be relied on. The Council is empowered to specify additional categories.

• Both Article 107(2) and Article 107(3), as derogations from the State aid rules, are to be construed narrowly.

1. Article 107(2) sets out three types of State aid that are compatible with the common market:

    Article 107(2)

    The following shall be compatible with the internal market:

    (a) aid having a social character, granted to individual consumers, provided that such aid is granted without discrimination related to the origin of the products concerned;

    (b) aid to make good the damage caused by natural disasters or exceptional occurrences;

    (c) aid granted to the economy of certain areas of the Federal Republic of Germany affected by the division of Germany, in so far as such aid is required in order to compensate for the economic disadvantages caused by that division. Five years after the entry into force of the Treaty of Lisbon, the Council, acting on a proposal from the Commission, may adopt a decision repealing this point.

2. The types of aid listed in Article 107(2) are automatically compatible with the common market. Such aids must be notified to the Commission but the Commission has no discretion in making its assessment and must declare the aid compatible with the common market if it comes within Article 107(2). As Article 107(2) provides a derogation from the State aid rules, it must be construed narrowly.[78]

3. Examples of aid that have benefited from the Article 107(2) exemption include aid granted to airlines following 11 September 2001. This included compensation for costs from the closure of US airspace and the assumption of the extra cost of insurance.[79] The Commission also considered that the disruption caused by the

---

78. Case C–156/98 *Germany v Commission* [2000] ECR I–6857, para 49.
79. See Case T–268/06 *Olympiaki Aeroporia Ypiresies AE v Commission* [2008] ECR II–1091.

volcanic ash cloud in the Spring of 2010 might justify the provision of aid compatible with Article 107(2).[80]

4. Article 107(3) sets out categories of aid that *may* be considered compatible with the internal market:

> **Article 107(3)**
>
> The following may be considered to be compatible with the internal market:
>
> (a) aid to promote the economic development of areas where the standard of living is abnormally low or where there is serious underemployment, and of the regions referred to in Article 349, in view of their structural, economic and social situation;
>
> (b) aid to promote the execution of an important project of common European interest or to remedy a serious disturbance in the economy of a Member State;
>
> (c) aid to facilitate the development of certain economic activities or of certain economic areas, where such aid does not adversely affect trading conditions to an extent contrary to the common interest;
>
> (d) aid to promote culture and heritage conservation where such aid does not affect trading conditions and competition in the Union to an extent that is contrary to the common interest;
>
> (e) such other categories of aid as may be specified by decision of the Council on a proposal from the Commission.

5. Before considering whether the Commission might grant an exemption under Article 107(3), it should be checked whether the aid at issue could benefit from Regulation 800/2008, which contains a general block exemption for certain aids.[81] Regulation 800/2008 grants exemption to 26 specific types of aid. Aid that comes within Regulation 800/2008 does not need to be notified to the Commission. The Regulation, which came into force on 29 August 2008 is due to expire on 31 December 2013.

6. The Commission enjoys a wide discretion in applying Article 107(3). The exercise of that discretion involves complex economic and social assessments and in reviewing the Commission's actions, the EU courts will confine themselves to applying judicial review principles, *i.e.* examining whether there was a manifest error of assessment etc.[82]

7. As with the competition rules of the Treaty, the Commission has adopted numerous notices and guidelines that discuss the criteria and principles applied by the Commission in assessing aid under Article 107(3).[83] These include sector-

---

80. Commission Note – The impact of the volcanic ash cloud crisis on the air transport industry SEC(2010) 533 (27 April 2010).

81. Commission Regulation (EC) No 800/2008 declaring certain categories of aid compatible with the common market in application of Articles 87 and 88 of the Treaty [2008] OJ L 214.

82. See, e.g., Cases C–75/05P & 80/05P *Germany v Kronofrance SA* [2008] ECR I–6619, [2009] 1 CMLR 89, para 59.

83. These documents are available on the Commission's website.

specific guidelines and guidelines more generally applicable to different types of aid.

8. As Article 107(3) is a derogation from the State aid rules of the Treaty, it should be construed narrowly. The aid must be necessary for the objective that is covered by Article 107(3):

    > ... aid which improves the financial situation of the recipient undertaking without being necessary for the attainment of the objectives specified in Article [107(3)] cannot be considered compatible with the common market.[84]

9. Regional aid may be compatible with the common market under Article 107(3)(a) or (b).[85] The 'abnormally low' standard of living or 'serious underemployment' criteria in Article 107(3)(a) must be judged on a EU-wide rather than a national standard.[86] Article 107(3)(c) provides for a wider exemption in that it permits regional aid to areas of a Member State that are disadvantaged vis-à-vis the national standard rather than the EU standard.[87] However, a greater distortion of competition can be accepted in the case of the most disadvantaged regions covered by Article 107(3)(a) than those covered by Article 107(3)(c).[88]

10. Article 107(3)(b) refers to two types of aid. The first is important projects of common European interest. Such projects will usually involve research and development and must involve a specific project that is of common European interest. An example is the channel tunnel rail link project.[89]

11. The second type of aid referred to in Article 107(3)(b) is aid 'to remedy a serious disturbance in the economy of a Member State'. The serious disturbance must be in the entire economy of the Member State, not just a particular region or area within the Member State.[90] This provision has been used extensively to approve aid provided by Member States in response to the financial crisis, such as guarantee schemes and recapitalisations of banks.[91] Banks in receipt of aid have

---

84. Case C–390/06 *Nuova Agricast Srl v Ministero delle Attività Produttive* [2008] ECR I–2577, para 68.
85. See Commission Guidelines on National Regional Aid for 2007–2013 [2006] OJ C54/08.
86. Case 73/79 *Philip Morris Holland BV v Commission* [1980] ECR 2671, [1981] 2 CMLR 321, paras 24–25.
87. Case 248/84 *Germany v Commission* [1987] ECR 4013, [1989] 1 CMLR 591, para 19.
88. See Case T–380/94 *AIUFFASS v Commission* [1996] ECR II–2169, [1997] 3 CMLR 542, para 54.
89. Case N706/2001 *Channel Tunnel Rail Link*, Commission Decision of 24 April 2002.
90. Case C–301/96 *Germany v Commission* [2003] ECR I–9919, para 106.
91. See, e.g., NN48/2008 *Guarantee scheme for banks in Ireland*, Commission Decision of 13 October 2008; N149/2009 *Recapitalisation of Bank of Ireland by the Irish State*, Commission Decision of 26 March 2009; Commission Communication – The application of State aid rules to measures taken in relation to financial institutions in the context of the current global financial crisis [2008] OJ C270/8; Commission Communication – The recapitalisation of financial institutions in the current financial crisis: limitation of aid to the minimum necessary and safeguards against undue distortions of competition [2009] OJ C10/2.

been required to provide restructuring plans demonstrating that the institution will return to viability free of aid, that the institution bears a fair share of the costs of restructuring and that distortions of competition will be kept to a minimum. To offset negative effects on competition, Member States and banks have been required to provide commitments covering the disposal of shareholdings and other assets, reductions in balance sheets, limits on future growth (including in core businesses) and restrictions regarding the bank's behaviour in terms of competition and market entry.[92]

12. Article 107(3)(b) has also provided the underlying rationale for the approval of the transfer of impaired banking assets to State run institutions such as Ireland's National Asset Management Agency (NAMA), where the amount of the State aid corresponds to the difference between the transfer value of the assets and the market price.[93]

13. Article 107(3)(d) refers to aid to promote heritage and culture conservation. This provision has been used to authorise aid such as that for the film industry[94] and aid for theatre activities.[95]

Key Sources

Articles 107(2), 107(3) TFEU.

Commission Regulation (EC) No 800/2008 declaring certain categories of aid compatible with the common market in application of Articles 87 and 88 of the Treaty [2008] OJ L 214.

Commission Communication on the treatment of impaired assets in the Community banking sector [2009] OJ C72/1.

Commission Communication – The application of State aid rules to measures taken in relation to financial institutions in the context of the current global financial crisis [2008] OJ C270/8.

Commission Communication – The recapitalisation of financial institutions in the current financial crisis: limitation of aid to the minimum necessary and safeguards against undue distortions of competition [2009] OJ C10/2.

---

92. See, e.g., N244/2009 *Commerzbank*, Commission Decision of 7 May 2009, paras 66–78.
93. See Commission Communication on the treatment of impaired assets in the Community banking sector [2009] OJ C72/1; N725/2009 *NAMA*, Commission Decision of 26 February 2010 (the Commission has required ongoing notification of individual asset transfers to NAMA in order to assess market value); C17/09 (ex N265/09) *Landesbank Baden-Württemberg* [2010] OJ L188/1 (Commission initially had competition law doubts about the scheme but these were subsequently dispelled following modification of the measure).
94. See, e.g., N151/2006 *Ireland – Tax relief for investment in film*, Commission Decision of 16 May 2006.
95. See, e.g., N577/2008 *Aid for production of theatre, music and dance*, Commission Decision of 23 January 2009.

128. CAN COMPENSATION FOR PUBLIC SERVICE OBLIGATIONS GIVE RISE TO STATE AID?

Summary

- If the compensation does not exceed the costs incurred, in accordance with the four conditions in Altmark, there will be no State aid.

- Even if the compensation qualifies as State aid, it may be possible to avail of the Article 106(2) derogation.

- The Commission has adopted a Decision setting out conditions which, if met, result in an exemption under Article 106(2).

- Article 106(2) cannot be availed of where the compensation exceeds the necessary costs of the provision of the public service (allowing for a reasonable profit).

1.   Payments by the State to an undertaking for performing public service obligations could give rise to State aid if the amount paid is too high and gives the undertaking more than a reasonable profit. However, if there is a sufficient degree of equivalence between the compensation paid and the additional costs incurred in performing the public service obligation, the undertaking 'will not be enjoying any real advantage' for the purposes of Article 107(1) and therefore the payment will not give rise to State aid.[96]

2.   How is the line to be drawn between acceptable compensation and an over-payment that confers an economic advantage? In *Altmark*, the Court of Justice laid down four conditions which, if satisfied, would show that the compensation paid for public service obligations was not State aid:

   (i)   The recipient undertaking must actually have public service obligations to discharge, and the obligations must be clearly defined.

   (ii) The parameters on the basis of which the compensation is calculated must be established in advance in an objective and transparent manner.

   (iii) The compensation cannot exceed what is necessary to cover all or part of the costs incurred in the discharge of public service obligations, taking into account the relevant receipts and a reasonable profit for discharging those obligations.

   (iv) Where the undertaking is not chosen pursuant to a public procurement procedure which would allow for the selection of the tenderer capable of providing the services at the least cost, the level of compensation needed must be determined on the basis of an analysis of the costs, which a typical efficient undertaking with

---

96.   Case C–53/00 *Ferring SA v ACOSS* [2001] ECR I–9067, [2003] 1 CMLR 1001, para 27. See generally the opinion of Advocate General Jacobs in Case C–126/01 *Ministre de l'économie, des finances et de l'Industrie v GEMO SA* [2003] ECR I–13769, [2004] 1 CMLR 259.

the means to meet the public service requirements, would have incurred in discharging those obligations, taking into account relevant receipts and a reasonable profit. [97]

3.   The Commission must find that one or more of these conditions are not met before deciding that the compensation provided to an undertaking performing a public service obligation is State aid. So, where the Commission failed to check whether the total amount of payments made to an undertaking performing services of general economic interest exceeded the total amount of the net additional costs in respect of providing those services, its decision finding State aid was annulled.[98]

4.   The *Altmark* conditions were initially applied quite strictly[99] but the judgment of the General Court in *BUPA* suggests a more lenient approach, particularly towards the third *Altmark* condition. The case concerned the Irish government's risk equalisation scheme ('RES'), which required private health insurers (PMI insurers) with a lower risk profile to make payments to PMI insurers which had a higher risk profile. The PMI insurer with the higher risk profile and the beneficiary of RES turned out to be the dominant State-owned health insurer, VHI. While it found that the third *Altmark* condition was not strictly fulfilled (there was no direct relationship between the risk equalisation payments and the additional costs of the VHI and no comparison had been made between VHI's costs and those of an efficient operator), the General Court nevertheless held that the *Altmark* test was satisfied, stating that

> … the quantification of the additional costs by means of a comparison between the actual risk profile of a PMI insurer and an average market risk profile in light of the amounts paid by all PMI insurers subject to the RES is consistent with the purpose and the spirit of the third *Altmark* condition in so far as the compensation is calculated on the basis of elements which are specific, clearly identifiable and capable of being controlled.[100]

5.   The Court held that the fourth *Altmark* condition could not be strictly applied in the circumstances of the case and that the Commission had not been required to draw a comparison between potential recipients of RES and an efficient operator. RES payments were not determined solely by reference to the payments made by the PMI insurer in receipt of the compensation, but also by reference to the payments made by the contributing PMI insurer, which reflected the risk profile differentials of those two insurers by comparison with the average market risk profile. In addition, at the time the scheme was adopted, the Commission could not

---

97.   Case C–280/00 *Altmark Trans GmbH v Nahverkehrsgesellschaft Altmark GmbH* [2003] ECR I–7747, [2003] 3 CMLR 339, paras 89–93.

98.   Case C–399/08 *Commission v Deutsche Post AG*, judgment of 2 September 2010, paras 44–47.

99.   See Bacon, *European Community Law of State Aid* (2009) para 2.67 *et seq*.

100. Case T–289/03 *BUPA v Commission* [2008] ECR II–81, [2009] 2 CMLR 1043, para 237.

identify precisely the beneficiaries of RES and so could not compare their situation with that of an efficient operator anyway.[101]

If the *Altmark* conditions are not met, can the aid be justified under Article 106(2)?

6.   If an undertaking has been entrusted with the performance of services of general economic interest, Article 106(2) provides that it is subject to the competition and State aid rules only in so far as the application of those rules does not obstruct the performance, in law or in fact, of the particular tasks assigned to it.[102]

7.   Compensation for the performance of public service obligations that constitutes State aid could be exempted under Article 106(2) if the conditions for that Article's application were met. The compensation will have failed to meet the *Altmark* criteria (otherwise, it would fall outside the scope of State aid), which, to a large extent, overlap with the criteria required to invoke Article 106(2).[103] However, as the General Court has emphasised, in laying down the *Altmark* conditions, the Court of Justice was not indicating that it wished to cease applying Article 106(2) when assessing the compatibility with the common market of State measures for the financing of services of general economic interest.[104] In principle then, if a measure fails to meet the *Altmark* criteria and so gives rise to aid, it may still benefit from the Article 106(2) derogation if the conditions for the application of that provision are met.

8.   Where the measure has failed the third *Altmark* condition (compensation exceeds what is necessary to perform the public service), it is difficult to see how the criteria of Article 106(2) could be satisfied. The advantage conferred by the payment of compensation exceeding the additional costs of performing the public service would not be regarded as necessary to enable the undertaking to perform that service under economically acceptable conditions, a requirement for Article 106(2) to apply.[105] The General Court has acknowledged that the third *Altmark* condition broadly coincides with the criterion of proportionality as established by the case law in the context of the application of Article 106(2).[106] In other words, the failure to satisfy the third *Altmark* condition will, almost by definition, result in a failure to satisfy Article 106(2).

---

101. Case T–289/03 *BUPA v Commission* [2008] ECR II–81, [2009] 2 CMLR 1043, para 249.

102. See Question 125 on the Article 106(2) derogation.

103. See Case T–289/03 *BUPA v Commission* [2008] ECR II–81, [2009] 2 CMLR 1043, paras 160–162 (noting that the first *Altmark* condition, that there be a public service obligation, corresponds to the requirement in Article 106(2) that an undertaking be entrusted with the performance of services of general economic interest).

104. Case T–354/05 *Télévision française 1 SA (TF1) v Commission*, judgment of 11 March 2009, para 135.

105. Case C–53/00 *Ferring SA v ACOSS* [2001] ECR I–9067, [2003] 1 CMLR 1001, paras 31–33.

106. Case T–289/03 *BUPA v Commission* [2008] ECR II–81, [2009] 2 CMLR 1043, para 224.

9.   Nevertheless, Article 106(2) may be relevant where other of the *Altmark* conditions are not satisfied, for example, where the parameters of the compensation were not established in advance or where a public procurement procedure was not used or where the application of the 'typical efficient undertaking' comparator was not possible.

10.   Following *Altmark*, the Commission adopted a Decision[107] and Framework[108] on the application of Article 106(2) to State aids in 2005. The Decision sets out the conditions under which State aid in the form of public service compensation to undertakings entrusted with the performance of services of general economic interest is to be regarded as compatible with the common market. The Decision effectively works as a block exemption. Where the conditions are met, the aid does not have to be notified to the Commission. There is a general threshold of €30 million in annual compensation for the service, with specific exemptions for certain sectors including hospitals, social housing, maritime transport, ports and airports.[109] Overall, the conditions for exemption seem to be more generous than the *Altmark* criteria, in particular in light of the absence of a requirement that the compensation be set pursuant to a public procurement procedure or 'typical efficient undertaking' comparator.[110]

11.   State aid that does not come within the terms of the Article 106 Decision must be notified to the Commission. The Commission will exempt the aid if the conditions of Article 106(2) are met. The aid would have to be necessary for the operation of the services of general economic interest entrusted to the undertaking and not affect the development of trade to an extent that would be contrary to the interests of the Union.[111]

12.   Article 106(2) has been found to have direct effect in the context of the competition provisions of the Treaty so that a national court can decide if the derogation applies in such cases.[112] However, given that the Commission has exclusive jurisdiction to decide whether State aid is compatible with the common market, a national court would not have jurisdiction to apply Article 106(2) in the

107. Commission Decision on the application of Article 86(2) of the EC Treaty to State aid in the form of public service compensation granted to certain undertakings entrusted with the operation of services of general economic interest [2005] OJ L312/67 ('Article 106 Decision').

108. Community framework for State aid in the form of public service compensation [2005] OJ C297/4 ('Article 106 Framework'). The Framework will apply until November 2011 (para 25).

109. Article 106 Decision, Article 2.

110. The Commission carried out a consultation on the workings of the Article 106 Decision and the Article 106 Framework in the summer of 2010. It is possible that this will lead to changes in the Commission's approach to State aid rules on services of general economic interest.

111. The Article 106 Framework discusses in more detail the conditions that should be met to satisfy these requirements.

112. See, e.g., Case C–393/92 *Almelo v NV Energiebedrijf Ijsselmij* [1994] ECR I–1477, [1994] 2 CEC 281, para 50; Bellamy & Child (6th edn, 2008) para 11.055.

context of a State aid scheme. Only the Commission can decide on the availability of Article 106(2) as a means of avoiding the State aid rules.

Key Sources

Case C–53/00 *Ferring SA v ACOSS* [2001] ECR I–9067, [2003] 1 CMLR 1001.

Case C–280/00 *Altmark Trans GmbH v Nahverkehrsgesellschaft Altmark GmbH* [2003] ECR I–7747, [2003] 3 CMLR 339.

Commission Decision on the application of Article 86(2) of the EC Treaty to State aid in the form of public service compensation granted to certain undertakings entrusted with the operation of services of general economic interest [2005] OJ L312/67.

Community framework for State aid in the form of public service compensation [2005] OJ C297/4.

---

129. WHAT IS THE PROCEDURE FOR THE APPROVAL OF STATE AID?

Summary

- State aid must be notified to the Commission, which has the exclusive jurisdiction to determine whether aid is compatible with the common market.

- The relevant procedures are set out in Regulation 659/1999.

- The Commission first carries out a preliminary examination. It may decide that a measure does not constitute aid or that there are no doubts about its compatibility with the common market.

- If the Commission has doubts about an aid's compatibility with the common market, it will carry out an in-depth investigation. The decision to open a full investigation should be taken within two months of the aid being notified.

- The Commission endeavours to make a final decision within 18 months of opening a full investigation. It may decide that there is no aid, it may approve the aid unconditionally or attach conditions or it may decide that the aid is incompatible with the common market.

- The Commission may in certain circumstances issue an injunction to recover aid that had been granted pending its final decision.

- On application of a Member State, the Council, acting unanimously, may also approve an aid scheme.

1. The Commission has the power under Article 108 TFEU to oversee State aid. The detailed procedures for the notification, approval and recovery of aid are set out in Regulation 659/1999[113] and the case law of the EU courts. Article 108 provides as follows:

   Article 108

   1. The Commission shall, in cooperation with Member States, keep under constant review all systems of aid existing in those States. It shall propose to the latter any appropriate measures required by the progressive development or by the functioning of the internal market.

   2. If, after giving notice to the parties concerned to submit their comments, the Commission finds that aid granted by a State or through State resources is not compatible with the internal market having regard to Article 107, or that such aid is being misused, it shall decide that the State concerned shall abolish or alter such aid within a period of time to be determined by the Commission.

   If the State concerned does not comply with this decision within the prescribed time, the Commission or any other interested State may, in derogation from the provisions of Articles 258 and 259, refer the matter to the Court of Justice of the European Union direct.

---

113. Council Regulation (EC) No 659/1999 laying down detailed rules for the application of Article 93 of the EC Treaty [1999] OJ L 83/1.

On application by a Member State, the Council may, acting unanimously, decide that aid which that State is granting or intends to grant shall be considered to be compatible with the internal market, in derogation from the provisions of Article 107 or from the regulations provided for in Article 109, if such a decision is justified by exceptional circumstances. If, as regards the aid in question, the Commission has already initiated the procedure provided for in the first subparagraph of this paragraph, the fact that the State concerned has made its application to the Council shall have the effect of suspending that procedure until the Council has made its attitude known.

If, however, the Council has not made its attitude known within three months of the said application being made, the Commission shall give its decision on the case.

3. The Commission shall be informed, in sufficient time to enable it to submit its comments, of any plans to grant or alter aid. If it considers that any such plan is not compatible with the internal market having regard to Article 107, it shall without delay initiate the procedure provided for in paragraph 2. The Member State concerned shall not put its proposed measures into effect until this procedure has resulted in a final decision.

4. The Commission may adopt regulations relating to the categories of State aid that the Council has, pursuant to Article 109, determined may be exempted from the procedure provided for by paragraph 3 of this Article.

2.   If aid comes within any of the categories of Article 107(2), it will be declared compatible with the common market. For other aids, the Commission will examine whether they are compatible with the common market pursuant to Article 107(3). The Commission weighs the positive and negative effects of the measure:

> The assessment of aid compatibility is essentially a balancing of the positive effects of aid (in terms of contributing to the achievement of a well-defined objective of common interest) and its negative effects (namely the resulting distortion of competition and trade) (the 'balancing test'). In order to be declared compatible, aid must be necessary and proportionate to achieve a particular objective of common interest.[114]

3.   The system of State aid supervision by the Commission involves *ex ante* authorisation. Before a Member State grants or alters aid, it must notify the Commission and observe a standstill period, *i.e.* it must not put the aid into effect until it has been authorised by the Commission.[115] If a Member State is uncertain that a measure constitutes State aid, it may be advisable to make a notification for purposes of legal certainty.

4.   There is a prescribed standard form for notifying new aid.[116] On notification, the Commission carries out a preliminary examination. If it finds that the measure does not constitute State aid, it will issue a decision to that effect.[117] If it concludes

---

114. Commission Vademecum – Community law on State aid (30 September 2008) 11.
115. Article 108(3).
116. Commission Regulation (EC) No 794/2004 implementing Council Regulation (EC)No 659/ 1999 laying down detailed rules for the application of Article 93 of the EC Treaty [2004] OJ L 140/1, Annex I.
117. Regulation 659/1999, Article 4(1).

that the measure is aid but that there are no doubts about its compatibility with the common market, the Commission takes a decision that the aid is compatible with the common market.[118] If it has doubts about the aid's compatibility with the common market, it will adopt a decision to initiate a formal investigation procedure.[119] The Commission must initiate the formal procedure where it 'experiences serious difficulties in establishing whether or not aid is compatible with the common market'.[120] The Commission has two months from notification to take a decision following a preliminary assessment and that period can be extended with the consent of the Member State.[121]

5.   Where the Commission adopts a decision to initiate a formal investigation, it will set out its preliminary assessment and call on the Member State and concerned parties to express their views within a prescribed time, usually a month. The parties that are concerned potentially form an indeterminate class but a notice in the Official Journal is sufficient notice.[122] The Member State is given the opportunity to reply to comments from other parties. The Commission is to endeavour to take its final decision within 18 months of opening the procedure, a time limit which may be extended with the agreement of the Member State.[123]

6.   The Commission's final decision could be that there is no aid,[124] that the aid is compatible with the common market[125] (in either case, where appropriate, following modification by the Member State) or that the aid is not compatible with the common market.[126] The Commission may attach to a positive decision conditions subject to which an aid may be considered compatible with the common market and it may lay down obligations to enable compliance with the decision to be monitored.[127] The Commission may require that the aid not be paid until the Member State has recovered previous unlawful aid to the same company.[128]

7.   Member States are required to submit annual reports on all existing aid schemes that do not have specific reporting obligations.[129] If the Commission has serious doubts that conditions in a conditional decision are not being complied with, it

---

118. Regulation 659/1999, Article 4(2).
119. Regulation 659/1999, Article 4(4).
120. Case T–375/04 *Scheucher-Fleisch GmbH v Commission* [2010] 2 CMLR 121, para 70.
121. Regulation 659/1999, Article 4(5).
122. Case 323/82 *Intermills v Commission* [1984] ECR 3809, [1986] 1 CMLR 614, para 16; Regulation 659/1999, Article 26(2).
123. Regulation 659/1999, Article 7(6)
124. Regulation 659/1999, Article 7(2).
125. Regulation 659/1999, Article 7(3).
126. Regulation 659/1999, Article 7(5).
127. Regulation 659/1999, Article 7(4).
128. See Cases T–244 & 486/93 *TWD Textilwerke Deggendorf GmbH v Commission* [1995] ECR II–2265, [1998] 1 CMLR 332, paras 54–60 (upheld on appeal, Case C–355/95P *Textilwerke Deggendorf GmbH (TWD) v Commission* [1997] ECR I–2549, [1998] 1 CMLR 234).
129. Regulation 659/1999, Article 21(1).

can, after allowing the Member State to submit comments, undertake on-site monitoring visits.[130]

8.   The Commission has the power under Article 108 to take a decision that, where State aid is not compatible with the common market or is being misused, the State shall abolish or alter the aid. If the Member State fails to comply with that decision in the prescribed time, the Commission or any other interested party may refer the matter to the Court of Justice under Article 108(2). The Commission can use this power of referral in the case of a negative or conditional decision with which the Member State is not complying.[131]

9.   When confronted with a situation where it considers that the grant of aid by a Member State is illegal because it was granted in breach of a previous decision authorising aid to the same undertaking subject to certain conditions, the Commission cannot simply adopt a decision in such a situation that the grant of aid was illegal.[132] The Commission must either refer the matter to the Court of Justice directly under the second subparagraph of Article 108(2) (if it considers that the Member State has not complied with certain conditions in the previous decision), or institute the special examination procedure provided for by the first subparagraph of Article 108(2) (if it considers that the Member State has granted new aid which had not been examined under the procedure leading to the adoption of its previous decision).

When may the Commission issue 'recovery injunctions'?

10.   The Commission's ability to issue preliminary injunctions requiring the recovery of aid is subject to strict requirements and can be invoked only in narrow circumstances. Under Article 11(1) of Regulation 659/1999, the Commission may adopt a decision requiring the Member State to suspend any unlawful aid until the Commission has made its decision as to whether the aid is compatible with the common market.[133] Article 11(2) provides for the issuance of a preliminary recovery injunction.

> The Commission may, after giving the Member State concerned the opportunity to submit its comments, adopt a decision requiring the Member State provisionally to recover any unlawful aid until the Commission has taken a decision on the compatibility of the aid with the common market (hereinafter referred to as a 'recovery injunction'), if the following criteria are fulfilled:
>
> –   according to an established practice there are no doubts about the aid character of the measure concerned
>
> and
>
> –   there is an urgency to act

---

130. Regulation 659/1999, Article 22.
131. Regulation 659/1999, Article 23(1).
132. See Case C–294/90 *British Aerospace Public Ltd Company v Commission* [1992] ECR I–493, [1992] 1 CMLR 853.
133. See also Case 301/87 *France v Commission ('Boussac')* [1990] ECR I–307, para 19.

and

– there is a serious risk of substantial and irreparable damage to a competitor.

11. The strict requirements imposed in respect of recovery injunctions highlights the importance of redress before the national courts as a means of protection for competitors and other third parties affected by the grant of aid in breach of the Article 108(3) standstill obligation.[134]

What is the effect of the opening by the Commission of a formal investigation into an aid that has already been or is being implemented?

12. Unlike a suspension injunction issued under Article 11 of Regulation 659/1999, which is immediately binding on a Member State, it is up to the Member State and the undertakings at issue to draw the appropriate consequences from a decision by the Commission to open the formal investigative procedure in respect of an aid that has been or is being implemented. There will be an element of doubt about the compatibility of the measure with the State aid rules after the adoption of the decision to open the formal procedure. The General Court has held that this:

> must lead the Member State to suspend its application, since the initiation of the formal investigation procedure excludes the possibility of an immediate decision that the measure is compatible with the common market, which would enable it to continue to be lawfully implemented. Such a decision might also be invoked before a national court called upon to draw all the consequences arising from infringement of the last sentence of Article [108(3)].[135]

If the Member State breaches the conditions of a State aid decision before all the aid is paid out, what must occur before further tranches can be paid out?

13. In the *Ryanair* case, Ireland failed to comply with conditions in a State aid decision before it paid a second tranche of aid. The Commission granted a derogation, allowing for the aid to be paid, without taking a formal decision. This action was challenged by Ryanair. The General Court held that Ireland's failure to comply with the conditions attached to the original decision raised a presumption that the payment of further tranches of the aid was incompatible with the common market. It followed that subsequent tranches of aid could not be released without a new Commission decision granting a formal derogation from the condition in question. The Court went on to explain the ramifications:

> In those circumstances, the Commission must initially consider whether such a derogation can be granted, whilst ensuring that the subsequent tranches of the aid are still compatible with the common market under the conditions laid down by Article [107(3)(c)] of the Treaty ... If such an examination leads the Commission to conclude that the subsequent tranches of the aid are no longer compatible with the common market, or if it does not enable it to overcome all the difficulties involved in

---

134. See also Commission Notice on the enforcement of State aid law by national courts [2009] OJ C85/1 ('National Court State Aid Notice') para 25.

135. Cases T–269/99 etc *Territorio Histórico de Guipúzcoa v Commission* [2002] ECR II–4217, [2003] 1 CMLR 298, para 38.

determining whether the subsequent tranches of the aid are compatible with the common market, the Commission is under a duty to carry out all the requisite consultations and, for that purpose, to initiate or, where appropriate, to re-open, the procedure under Article [107(2)] of the Treaty ... It also follows, by analogy with Article [107(3)] of the Treaty, that in such a case payment of the aid at issue must be suspended until the Commission adopts its final decision.

Furthermore, the Court considers that, once the Commission has adopted a decision approving aid subject to conditions at the end of a procedure under Article [107(2)], it is not entitled to depart from the scope of its initial decision without re-opening that procedure. It follows that, if one of the conditions to which approval of an aid was subject is not satisfied, the Commission may normally adopt a decision derogating from that condition without re-opening the procedure under Article [107(2)] of the Treaty only in the event of relatively minor deviations from the initial condition, which leave it with no doubt as to whether the aid at issue is still compatible with the common market.[136]

Does the Council have a role in approving State aid?

14.   Article 108(2) provides a potential role for the Council, allowing a Member State to apply to the Council for approval of aid. The Council may decide that the aid is compatible with the common market if justified by exceptional circumstances. The Council has a wide discretion in deciding what constitutes exceptional circumstances and its decision is reviewable by the EU courts only to the extent that it has committed a manifest error.[137] The Council must act only on the application of a Member State and its decision must be unanimous. The application by the Member State to the Council has the effect of suspending the procedure before the Commission but if the Council rejects the application, the Commission procedure is reactivated.[138] The Council has issued State aid decisions under Article 108(2) in a range of cases.[139]

What role can complainants play in Commission State aid investigations?

15.   Many State aid investigations are triggered by complaints, often from competitors of a firm that has allegedly received illegal State aid. In practice, the Commission may afford a complainant significant input in a State aid case.[140]

---

136. Case T–140/95 *Ryanair Limited v Commission* [1998] ECR II–3322, [1998] 3 CMLR 1022, paras 87–88.
137. Case C–122/94 *Commission v Council* [1996] ECR I–881, para 18.
138. See Article 108(2) TFEU.
139. See, e.g., *Hungarian aid for the purchase of agricultural land,* 2009/1017/EU [2009] OJ L348/55 (aid granted where Hungarian farmers could not obtain commercial loans for the purchase of land following the financial crisis).
140. See, e.g., N725/2009 *NAMA*, Commission Decision of 26 February 2010, which devotes several pages (paras 75–78, 134–140) to dealing with arguments made by a complainant, Senator Eugene Regan SC.

16.   To comply with the principle of sound administration, the Commission must deal
      with State aid complaints in a diligent manner. The General Court has summed up
      this duty as follows:

> Since the assessment of the compatibility of State aid with the common market falls
> within its exclusive competence, the Commission is bound, in the interests of sound
> administration of the fundamental rules of the Treaty relating to State aid, to conduct a
> diligent and impartial examination of a complaint alleging the existence of aid that is
> incompatible with the common market. It follows that the Commission cannot prolong
> indefinitely its preliminary investigation into State measures that have been the
> subject of a complaint. Whether or not the duration of the investigation of a complaint
> is reasonable must be determined in relation to the particular circumstances of each
> case and, especially, its context, the various procedural stages to be followed by the
> Commission and the complexity of the case.[141]

17.   The role that will be afforded to a complainant will depend on the stage of the
      procedure before the Commission that has been reached. When making its
      preliminary assessment in a State aid case, the Commission is not required to
      consult with anybody and it is not obliged to give complainants an opportunity to
      state their views at the stage of the initial review provided for by Article 108(3).[142]

18.   The Commission's decision to initiate the formal investigation procedure must
      summarise the relevant issues of fact and law, include a preliminary assessment of
      the Commission as to the aid character of the proposed measure and set out the
      doubts as to its compatibility with the common market. It must also call upon the
      Member State concerned and upon 'other interested parties' to submit
      comments.[143] An 'interested party' is defined as 'any Member State and any
      person, undertaking or association of undertakings whose interests might be
      affected by the granting of aid, in particular the beneficiary of the aid, competing
      undertakings and trade associations'.[144] An interested party is entitled to submit
      comments following the initiation of the formal investigation procedure.[145]

19.   Comments must be submitted in a period set by the Commission, which will
      usually not be more than a month after the decision to open the formal
      investigation procedure.[146] In some circumstances, the Commission may be
      required to extend the period for providing comments. This has applied in respect
      of a beneficiary of potentially illegal aid, as the Commission was in that case
      subject to the general principle 'that any person against whom an adverse decision
      may be taken must be given the opportunity to make his views known effectively
      regarding the facts held against him by the Commission as a basis for the disputed

---

141. Case T–167/04 *Asklepios Kliniken GmbH v Commission* [2007] ECR II–2379, [2007] 3
     CMLR 902, para 81 (references omitted).
142. Case C–367/95 *Commission v Sytraval* [1995] ECR II–2651, para 59.
143. Regulation 659/1999, Article 6(1).
144. Regulation 659/1999, Article 1(h).
145. Regulation 659/1999, Article 20(1).
146. Regulation 659/1999, Article 6(1).

decision'.[147] While beneficiaries may generally be entitled to rely on this principle, it may not be applicable to many complainants.

20. In comparison, in *Scott*, the Court of Justice overturned a judgment of the General Court which had found that the Commission could not refuse the recipient the opportunity to make further submissions after the one month deadline. The documents provided details of valuations carried out years after the sale of the land at issue and the valuations had been made in the context of a tax audit, which did not necessarily show market value. In those circumstances, the Commission was entitled not to consider the submissions.[148]

21. In general, interested parties are only entitled to be involved in the administrative procedure to the extent appropriate in the light of the circumstances of the case.[149]

Key Sources

Article 108 TFEU.

Council Regulation (EC) No 659/1999 laying down detailed rules for the application of Article 93 of the EC Treaty [1999] OJ L 83/1.

Commission Regulation (EC) No 794/2004 implementing Council Regulation (EC) No 659/1999 laying down detailed rules for the application of Article 93 of the EC Treaty [2004] OJ L 140/1.

---

147. Case T–34/02 *Le Levant 001 v Commission* [2005] ECR II–267, paras 95–97.
148. Case C–290/07P *Commission v Scott SA*, judgment of 2 September 2010, paras 90–98.
149. See, e.g., Case T–62/08 *ThyssenKrupp Acciai Speciali Terni SpA v Commission*, judgment of 1 July 2010, para 149. For a detailed account of the role of complainants in State aid cases, see Quigley, *European State Aid Law and Policy* (2nd edn, 2009) 402–410.

130. HOW CAN STATE AID DECISIONS OF THE COMMISSION BE CHALLENGED?

Summary

- An action for annulment can be brought before the General Court under Article 263 TFEU. There is a right of appeal on a point of law to the Court of Justice.

- As well as Member States, third parties who are directly and individually concerned can bring actions for annulment.

- The Commission decision must be a reviewable act within the meaning of Article 263 before an action for annulment can be taken.

- In certain circumstances, the challenge can be initiated in the national court.

1. An action for annulment of a Commission State aid decision (or a Council decision[150]) can be brought before the General Court under Article 263 TFEU, with a further right of appeal on points of law to the Court of Justice.[151] Another way of challenging the decision would be to invite the Commission to use its powers under Article 9 of Regulation 659/1999 to revoke a positive decision. This can only be done where the decision was based on incorrect information provided during the procedure which was a determining factor for the decision.[152] In certain cases, the Commission decision can be challenged before a national court by a person whose standing to challenge the Commission decision before the General Court under Article 263 TFEU was not obvious.[153]

Who has standing under Article 263?[154]

2. The Member States and EU institutions have a right of action in respect of any legally binding acts of the Union institutions under the second paragraph of Article 263 TFEU. Under the fourth paragraph of Article 263, any natural or legal person can institute proceedings against an act addressed to that person or 'which is of direct and individual concern to them, and against a regulatory act which is of direct concern to them and does not entail implementing measures'. The last part of this sentence, which omits the need to show individual concern in respect of

---

150. Although less frequent, the Council can make decisions approving State aid under the third paragraph of Article 108(2) TFEU.
151. Article 256 TFEU; Protocol on the Statute of the Court of Justice of the European Union [2008] OJ C115/210, Articles 56–58.
152. Regulation 659/1999, Article 9.
153. See Question 131.
154. See also Question 83 (standing to challenge merger decisions of the Commission).

'regulatory acts' that do not entail implementing measures, was introduced by the Lisbon Treaty. There is no definition of a 'regulatory act' and it is unclear whether it could refer to a State aid decision.[155] Were it applicable, it would lower the standing requirement as the applicant would only have to show direct concern.

3. Assuming that a third party must show both direct and individual concern, it is the latter requirement that is more difficult to satisfy. Third parties must show that the decision 'affects them by reason of certain attributes peculiar to them or by reason of circumstances in which they are differentiated from all other persons and ... distinguishes them individually' just as in the case of the addressee.[156] Article 108(2) specifically refers to 'parties concerned', who are entitled to be given notice to submit comments when the Commission carries out a full investigation into an aid.[157] That notice requirement is fulfilled by the Commission placing a notice in the *Official Journal*.[158] The Court of Justice has recognised that the category of persons who are 'concerned' is potentially wide:

> According to Article [108(2)], the Commission is to take a decision in relation to aid granted after giving notice to the parties concerned to submit their comments. It must be noted that the parties concerned referred to in that provision are not only the undertaking or undertakings receiving aid but equally the persons, undertakings or associations whose interests might be affected by the grant of the aid, in particular competing undertakings and trade associations. In other words, there is an indeterminate group of persons to whom notice must be given.[159]

4. If a person is 'concerned' within the meaning of Article 108(2), it seems that the person must be directly and individually concerned within the meaning of Article 263 by a decision of the Commission in respect of the aid in question.[160] Persons who may have standing under Article 263 TFEU include those that were complainants in the procedure before the Commission. In achieving the status of direct and individual concern, 'it is useful to complain as early as possible and be identifiable to the Commission'.[161]

---

155. See Case T–16/04 *Arcelor SA v Parliament*, judgment of 2 March 2010, para 123 (a directive on greenhouse gas emission allowance trading (Directive 2003/87/EC) was held not to be a regulatory act not entailing implementing measures within the meaning of the fourth paragraph of Article 263 TFEU as Member States had a broad discretion as to how the directive was implemented). See also Balthasar, 'Locus standi rules for challenges to regulatory acts by private applicants: the new art.263(4) TFEU' [2010] *European Law Review* 542 (but discussing only challenges to Regulations).

156. Case 25/62 *Plaumann & Co. v Commission* [1963] ECR 95, [1964] CMLR 29.

157. Article 108(2) TFEU.

158. Case 323/82 *Intermills v Commission* [1984] ECR 3809, [1986] 1 CMLR 614, para 16; Regulation 659/1999, Article 26(2).

159. Case 323/82 *Intermills v Commission* [1984] ECR 3809, [1986] 1 CMLR 614, para 16.

160. See Case C–198/91 *William Cook v Commission* [1993] ECR I–2487, [1993] 3 CMLR 206, para 26.

161. Power, *Competition Law and Practice* (2001) para 57.94.

Which kinds of decision are open to challenge?

5.   The Commission decision must be a reviewable act within the meaning of Article 263 if it is to be the subject of annulment proceedings before the General Court:

> According to settled case-law, any measure the legal effects of which are binding on, and capable of affecting the interests of, the applicant by bringing about a distinct change in his legal position is an act or decision which may be the subject of an action for annulment under Article [263]. The form in which such acts or decisions are cast is, in principle, immaterial as regards the question whether they are open to challenge by an action for annulment. In order to ascertain whether or not an act which has been challenged produces such effects it is necessary to look to its substance.[162]

6.   State aid decisions that have been challenged under Article 263 include the following:

- A decision adopted by the Commission pursuant to Article 108(3) not to initiate the second phase of the procedure and to approve the grant of new aid notified by a Member State was open to challenge by a competitor of the proposed aid recipient.[163]

- A decision that an aid was not subject to the obligation of prior notice under Article 108(3) was open to challenge by an association whose membership consisted of the main international manufacturers in the relevant sector and which had taken action connected with the policy of restructuring the sector and had actively pursued negotiations with the Commission in respect of the measures it claimed were notifiable.[164]

- A decision to initiate the formal investigation procedure in relation to a measure in the course of implementation and which the Member State did not regard as falling within the scope of Article 107(1), taken by the Commission on the ground that the measure in question was new aid, was open to challenge by an intra-State body, which was the author of the tax measures in question.[165]

- A decision prohibiting the grant of an aid was open to challenge by a potential recipient of the aid.[166] General State aid measures, pursuant to which there may be many potential beneficiaries, will not usually be open to

---

162. Case T–109/06 *Vodafone España, SA v Commission* [2007] ECR II–5151, [2008] 4 CMLR 1378, para 69 (references omitted).

163. Case C–198/91 *William Cook v Commission* [1993] ECR I–2487, [1993] 3 CMLR 206, paras 23–26. See also, e.g., Case T–375/04 *Scheucher-Fleisch GmbH v Commission* [2010] 2 CMLR 121, paras 34–64 (note the distinction between standing for the purpose of enforcing procedural rights and the more difficult showing of standing to challenge the substance of the decision).

164. Case C–313/90 *CIRFS v Commission* [1993] ECR I–1125, paras 29–30.

165. Case T–272/99 *Territorio Histórico de Guipúzcoa v Commission* [2002] ECR II–4217, [2003] 1 CMLR 298, paras 37–40.

166. Case 73/79 *Philip Morris v Commission* [1980] ECR 2671, [1981] 2 CMLR 321, para 5.

challenge by one of those potential beneficiaries.[167] On the other hand, 'where a contested measure affects a group of persons who were identified or identifiable when that measure was adopted by reason of criteria specific to the members of the group, those persons might be individually concerned by that measure inasmuch as they form part of a limited class of traders'.[168] A trade association, which has participated as a negotiator in respect of the aid, may have standing.[169] A trade association that merely participated in the procedure before the Commission and whose involvement went no further than exercising the procedural rights guaranteed by Article 108(2), did not have standing.[170] The General Court has summed up the standing of trade associations in State aid cases by stating that trade associations may challenge State aid decisions in three situations:

> where they represent the interests of undertakings which themselves have standing to bring proceedings; where they are distinguished individually because of the impact on their own interests as associations, in particular because their position as a negotiator has been affected by the measure sought to be annulled; and where a legal provision expressly confers on them a number of rights of a procedural nature.[171]

- A decision requiring that aid paid in breach of an earlier decision be repaid was open to challenge by the recipient.[172]

- A decision requiring the repayment of aid has been challenged by Member States in several cases.[173]

What is the time limit for bringing an action for annulment?

7.   An action for annulment under Article 263 must be brought 'within two months of the publication of the measure, or of its notification to the plaintiff, or, in the

---

167. Cases 67/85 etc *Kwekerij Gebroeders van der Kooy BV v Commission* [1988] ECR 219, [1989] 2 CMLR 804, para 15 (measure favoured all Dutch growers who used natural gas to heat their glasshouses and therefore had legal effects for 'categories of persons envisaged in a general and abstract manner' and could not be regarded as being of individual concern to the applicants).

168. Case C–519/07P *Commission v Koninklijke FrieslandCampina NV* [2009] ECR I–8495, [2010] 1 CMLR 385, paras 54–57 (applicant was individually concerned where its application under the relevant scheme was one of 14 that were pending at the time of the Commission decision).

169. Cases 67/85 etc *Kwekerij Gebroeders van der Kooy BV v Commission* [1988] ECR 219, [1989] 2 CMLR 804, paras 18–24 (trade association which negotiated tariffs and took an active part in the procedure before the Commission had standing).

170. Case C–78/03P *Commission v Aktionsgemeinschaft Recht und Eigentum eV ('ARE')* [2005] ECR I–10737, [2006] 2 CMLR 1197, para 58.

171. Case T–189/08 *Forum 187 ASBL v Commission*, judgment of 10 March 2010, para 58.

172. Case C–294/90 *British Aerospace Public Ltd Company v Commission* [1992] ECR I–493, [1992] 1 CMLR 853.

173. See, e.g., Case C-142/87 *Belgium v Commission ('Tubemeuse')* [1990] ECR I-959, [1991] 3 CMLR 213.

absence thereof, of the day on which it came to the knowledge of the latter, as the case may be'.[174] In practice, all time limits are extended by a period of ten days on account of distance from Luxembourg.[175]

8.   A Member State will typically receive notification of a State aid decision before its publication in the *Official Journal* and so will have to bring an action under Article 263 within two months and ten days from the day after receipt of notification.[176]

9.   For third parties, time will usually run from the date of publication in the *Official Journal*. In this case, the two-month (and ten day) time limit is not reckoned to run until the day after fourteen days from publication of the decision in the *Official Journal*.[177] Full publication of the decision on the Internet coupled with a summary notice in the *Official Journal* is a sufficient form of publication.[178]

10.   The third possibility provided for in Article 263, that time runs from the date of knowledge of the applicant, is relevant only if the measure is subject to neither notification nor publication.[179] As all State aid decisions (or at least a summary) are required to be published in the *Official Journal*,[180] the issue of time limits for unpublished decisions should not arise in practice. It has been confirmed that where a third party applicant had knowledge of the decision before it was published in the *Official Journal*, for example because the Commission forwarded that person a copy of the decision, the time limit still ran from the date of publication rather than from the earlier date of knowledge. The knowledge criterion is only relevant via-à-vis the addressee of the decision.[181]

On what grounds may an action for annulment be brought?

11.   The General Court can review the legality of Commission decisions under Article 263. A Commission decision can be reviewed 'on grounds of lack of competence, infringement of an essential procedural requirement, infringement of the Treaties or of any rule of law relating to their application, or misuse of powers'.[182] Grounds on which State aid decisions could be challenged include procedural irregularities,

---

174. Article 263 TFEU. See also Question 83 on Article 263 time limits in the context of merger decisions.
175. Rules of Procedure of the General Court (Consolidated Version) [2010] OJ C177/37, Articles 102(12).
176. Rules of Procedure of the General Court (Consolidated Version) [2010] OJ C177/37, Article 101(1)(a).
177. Rules of Procedure of the General Court (Consolidated Version) [2010] OJ C177/37, Articles 102(1), 101(1)(a).
178. Case T–354/05 *Télévision française 1 SA (TF1) v Commission*, judgment of 11 March 2009, para 35.
179. Cases T–273 & 297/06 *ISD Polska v Commission*, judgment of 1 July 2009, para 55.
180. Regulation 659/1999, Article 26.
181. Cases T–273 & 297/06 *ISD Polska v Commission*, judgment of 1 July 2009, paras 55.
182. Article 263 TFEU.

lack of reasoning, a failure to provide reasons for rejecting a complaint, a manifest error of assessment, misuse of powers, breach of another provision of the Treaty, an error of law such as a failure to respect the principles of legitimate expectation or equality or failure to categorise an aid as an existing aid.[183]

How else may State aid decisions come before the Union courts?

12. State aid issues may also come before the EU courts where the Commission takes enforcement action against a Member State for its failure to comply with the State aid rules of the Treaty. Such actions can be taken under Article 108(2) or under the normal infringement procedure pursuant to Article 258 TFEU. State aid issues may also come before the Court of Justice where a national court makes a preliminary reference on State aid questions under Article 234.

Key Sources

Article 263 TFEU.

Case 323/82 *Intermills v Commission* [1984] ECR 3809, [1986] 1 CMLR 614.

Cases 67/85 etc *Kwekerij Gebroeders van der Kooy BV v Commission* [1988] ECR 219, [1989] 2 CMLR 804.

Case C–198/91 *William Cook v Commission* [1993] ECR I–2487, [1993] 3 CMLR 206.

Case C–78/03P *Commission v Aktionsgemeinschaft Recht und Eigentum eV ('ARE')* [2005] ECR I–10737, [2006] 2 CMLR 1197.

Case C–519/07P *Commission v Koninklijke FrieslandCampina NV* [2009] ECR I–8495, [2010] 1 CMLR 385.

---

183. For a detailed review of grounds on which State aid decisions have been challenged, see, e.g., Bellamy & Child (6th edn, 2008) paras 15.118–15.123; Bacon, *European Community Law of State Aid* (2009) paras 17.53–17.73.

131. WHAT ROLE DO NATIONAL COURTS PLAY WITH RESPECT TO THE STATE AID RULES?

Summary

- Article 108(3), which requires that aid be notified to the Commission, is directly effective and can be enforced in the national courts.

- This enables an affected third party, such as a competitor of a recipient of aid, to seek a remedy before the national court when aid has been granted in breach of the Article 108(3) notification requirement.

- The national court can decide whether a measure is State aid, whether it is new aid or falls within an existing scheme and whether the notification requirement in Article 108(3) has been breached. However, the national court cannot decide whether aid is compatible with the common market. This is the exclusive jurisdiction of the Commission.

- Possible remedies before a national court include injunctive relief preventing the grant of aid in violation of Article 108(3), the recovery of illegally granted aid and interest and damages.

- Even if the Commission subsequently approves the aid, this does not affect the availability of remedies for breach of the Article 108(3) standstill obligation.

- Challenges to a Commission State aid decision can be brought in a national court by a person whose standing to challenge the Commission decision before the General Court under Article 263 TFEU was not obvious.

1.   The Commission views private litigation before the national courts as an important tool in contributing to the Union's commitment to a strict approach towards illegal State aid.[184] An obvious way in which State aid issues may come before the national court is when aid has been granted in breach of the obligation to notify the Commission under Article 108(3). A private party can sue in the national court where it is affected by the grant of unnotified State aid. A Commission decision finding that State aid is incompatible with the common market and ordering its recovery can also be enforced in the national court. The Member State which granted the aid may itself sue for recovery.[185]

2.   Article 107(1) does not have direct effect so a national court cannot declare that an existing aid is contrary to the Treaty. However a national court will have to apply and interpret Article 107(1) in determining whether a particular measure is State

---

184.   National Court State Aid Notice [2009] OJ C85/1, paras 1, 5. See also the Commission's handbook, Enforcement of State Aid Law by the National Courts (October 2010) (Commissioner Almunia stating that national judges are 'increasingly one of the key actors' in the State aid field).

185.   See, e.g., *Belgium v Ryanair Limited* [2006] IEHC 213, [2009] 3 IR 417.

aid.[186] As well as the possibility of making a reference to the Court of Justice under Article 267 TFEU, a national court can ask the Commission for an opinion as to whether a measure constitutes State aid.[187]

3.   Article 108(3), which prohibits the implementation of new aids without Commission approval, does have direct effect. A national court has a duty to provide a remedy to an individual who is affected by a violation of Article 108(3).[188] The Court of Justice has stated:

> National courts must offer to individuals the certain prospect that all the appropriate conclusions will be drawn from an infringement of the last sentence of Article [108(3)] of the Treaty, in accordance with their national law, as regards the validity of measures giving effect to the aid, the recovery of financial support granted in disregard of that provision and possible interim measures.[189]

4.   As well as preserving the interests of individuals, the national court must also take fully into consideration the interests of the Union.[190]

5.   The circumstances and extent to which remedies are available in the national court depends on national law and national procedural rules, subject to the principles of equivalence and effectiveness. Certain other basic EU law requirements may also be relevant. So, the Court of Justice has stated that a finding that aid has been granted in breach of the Article 108(3) notification requirement 'must in principle lead to its repayment in accordance with the procedural rules of domestic law'.[191] The national court therefore has a EU law obligation to provide a remedy that involves the repayment of unnotified aid. An action before a national court may be a much faster way of recovering unnotified aid than making a complaint to the Commission.[192]

6.   The Commission has summarised the available remedies before national courts as follows:

         (a)   preventing the payment of unlawful aid;

         (b)   recovery of unlawful aid (regardless of compatibility);

         (c)   recovery of illegality interest;

---

186. The power of national courts to interpret and apply the notion of State aid was confirmed in Case 78/76 *Steinike & Weinlig v Germany* [1977] ECR 595, para 14.
187. National Court State Aid Notice [2009] OJ C85/1, paras 89–96.
188. See, e.g., Cases C–261 & 262/01 *Belgium v Van Calster* [2003] ECR I–12249, [2004] 1 CMLR 607, para 75.
189. Case C–39/94 *SFEI v La Poste* [1996] ECR I–3547, [1996] 3 CMLR 369, para 40. See also Case C–354/90 *Fédération Nationale du Commerce Extérieur des Produits Alimentaires ('FNCEPA') v France* [1991] ECR I–5505, para 12.
190. Case C–368/04 *Transalpine Ölleitung in Österreich GmbH v Finanzlandesdirektion für Tirol* [2006] ECR I–9957, [2007] 1 CMLR 588, para 48.
191. Case C–39/94 *SFEI v La Poste* [1996] ECR I–3547, [1996] 3 CMLR 369, para 68.
192. National Court State Aid Notice [2009] OJ C85/1, para 31.

(d) damages for competitors and other third parties; and

(e) interim measures against unlawful aid.[193]

7. The type of action that is brought in the national court will depend on national procedures. In Ireland and England and Wales, State aid actions, particularly in respect of breaches of Article 108(3), may be brought as actions for judicial review of the State authority's actions. Remedies normally available in judicial review actions, such as an injunction or an order quashing the decision of the State, could be applied for. Actions for damages might simply be framed as such, although it may be possible to include a damages claim in a judicial review action.[194]

What interim remedies are available?

8. The Commission considers that where unlawful aid is about to be disbursed, the national court is obliged to prevent the payment from taking place. Where, for example, the claimant in national proceedings seeks to challenge the validity of the national act granting the unlawful State aid, the Commission considers that 'preventing the unlawful payment will usually be the logical consequence of finding that the granting act is invalid as a result of the Member State's breach of Article [108(3)] of the Treaty'.[195] The Commission's 2009 update on its State aid study states that national courts have ordered interim measures in several State aid cases.[196]

9. Where illegal aid has already been paid, the national court will usually be required to order full recovery without undue delay.[197] However if the court's final judgment is delayed, it may be necessary to apply interim measures available under national law:

> Where it is likely that some time will elapse before it gives its final judgment, it is for the national court to decide whether it is necessary to order interim relief such as the suspension of the measures at issue in order to safeguard the interests of the parties.[198]

10. The Commission suggests that the unlawful aid and illegality interest could be placed in a blocked account pending the final outcome of the case.[199]

---

193. National Court State Aid Notice [2009] OJ C85/1, para 26.
194. See generally, de Blacam, *Judicial Review* (2nd edn, 2009) Ch 25; Woolf, Jowell, Le Seur and Donnelly, *De Smith's Judicial Review* (6th edn, 2007) Chs 18, 19; Commission Study on enforcement of State aid law at national level (March 2006) 277–282 (Ireland), 461–496 (UK). For a recent Irish case, see *National Broadband Ltd v Minister for Communications, Energy and Natural Resources* [2008] IEHC 240 (judicial review application, which included claims that the Minister breached the EU State aid rules, unsuccessful).
195. National Court State Aid Notice [2009] OJ C85/1, para 29.
196. 2009 Update of the 2006 Study on enforcement of State aid rules at national level (October 2009) 4.
197. National Court State Aid Notice [2009] OJ C85/1, para 59.
198. Case C–39/94 *SFEI v La Poste* [1996] ECR I–3547, [1996] 3 CMLR 369, para 52.
199. National Court State Aid Notice [2009] OJ C85/1, para 61.

When can the national court order recovery of aid?

11. When the national court finds that an aid has been granted in breach of the standstill obligation in Article 108(3), this must, in principle, lead to its repayment in accordance with national procedural rules.[200] National courts also have the power to enforce decisions of the Commission taken under Article 108(2) that aid is not compatible with the common market[201] and decisions adopted under Article 14 of Regulation 659/1999 that illegal aid shall be recovered by the Member State. Article 14 of Regulation 659/1999 provides that:

> recovery shall be effected without delay and in accordance with the procedures under the national law of the Member State concerned, provided that they allow the immediate and effective execution of the Commission's decision. To this effect and in the event of a procedure before national courts, the Member States concerned shall take all necessary steps which are available in their respective legal systems, including provisional measures, without prejudice to Community law.[202]

12. The enforcement of a Commission decision may arise before a national court if the beneficiary of the illegal aid resists its recovery by, for instance, challenging the legality of the recovery request by the national authorities. Depending on national law, it may also be possible for the national authority to bring an action against the beneficiary aimed at full implementation of the Commission's recovery decision. While national procedural rules govern such an action, the principle of effectiveness requires that those rules must be applied in such a way that the recovery required by EU law is not rendered practically impossible or excessively difficult.[203]

13. When ordering the recovery of aid granted in breach of Article 108(3), the national court must also order the repayment of interest for the period during which the aid was unlawful.[204]

14. If a Member State has imposed a tax or charge that formed a part of an illegal State aid measure, any person who paid the tax or charge can bring an action for its

---

200. Case C–39/94 *SFEI v La Poste* [1996] ECR I–3547, [1996] 3 CMLR 369, para 68. See also *Belgium v Ryanair Limited* [2006] IEHC 213, [2009] 3 IR 417 (High Court refused to stay an action by Belgium for recovery of illegal State aid while Ryanair's action for annulment of the Commission's decision was pending in the General Court; the Commission decision was annulled in Case T–196/04 *Ryanair Ltd v Commission* [2008] ECR II–3643, [2009] 2 CMLR 137).

201. See Case 77/72 *Capolongo v Azienda Agricole Maya* [1973] ECR 611, para 6.

202. Regulation 659/1999, Article 14(3).

203. See, e.g., Case C–368/04 *Transalpine Ölleitung in Österreich GmbH v Finanzlandesdirektion für Tirol* [2006] ECR I–9957, para 45.

204. Case C–199/06 *CELF v SIDE* [2008] ECR I–469, [2008] 2 CMLR 561, paras 52, 54; Regulation 659/1999, Article 14(2).

recovery, whether or not such person is a competitor of the undertaking that benefited from the aid:

> An individual may have an interest in relying before the national court on the direct effect of the prohibition on implementation referred to in the last sentence of Article [108(3)] of the Treaty not only in order to erase the negative effects of the distortion of competition created by the grant of unlawful aid, but also in order to obtain a refund of a tax levied in breach of that provision. In the latter case, the question whether an individual has been affected by the distortion of competition arising from the aid measure is irrelevant to the assessment of his interest in bringing proceedings. The only fact to be taken into consideration is that the individual is subject to a tax which is an integral part of a measure implemented in breach of the prohibition referred to in that provision.[205]

When can a damages action be taken?

15. Actions for damages by third parties, such as competitors of the aid recipient, may involve claims against the State or, if national law enables such an action, against the beneficiary of the aid. Whatever actions are available in national law against the State, as a matter of EU law, a *Francovich* claim could be brought against the State for breach of the Article 108(3) standstill obligation.[206] To succeed, the claimant would have to show a direct causal link between the breach of Article 108(3) by the Member State and the damage it had suffered. This could be done, for example, by showing that the breach was directly responsible for a loss of profit.[207] As of October 2009 and the update of the Commission study on national enforcement of State aid rules, there did not appear to be any cases in the EU where a competitor obtained damages for a breach of the State aid rules.[208]

16. A recipient of illegal State aid may also be able to sue the Member State for damages. The recipient may have suffered damage from being required to repay illegal aid. This could include financial and administrative costs linked to the recovery of the aid, costs resulting from commitments made pursuant to the aid scheme and loss of profits. National rules on quantification of damages, remoteness etc. would have a bearing on what damages could be recovered.

---

205. Case C–174/02 *Streekgewest Westelijk Noord-Brabant v Staatssecretaris van Financiën* [2005] ECR I–85, para 19.

206. Cases C–6 & 90/90 *Francovich v Italy* [1991] ECR I–5357.

207. See the National Court State Aid Notice [2009] OJ C85/1, paras 45–52. There are two other conditions to be made out to succeed in a *Francovich* claim, (i) that the EU law that was infringed was intended to confer rights on individuals and (ii) that the breach is sufficiently serious. The first is met in the case of Article 108(3) and the Commission, at least, considers that the second would also generally be met.

208. Study on enforcement of State aid law at national level (March 2006) and 2009 Update of the 2006 Study on enforcement of State aid rules at national level (October 2009), available on the Commission's website.

Another potential claimant would be a creditor of a recipient of illegal State aid who is adversely affected by the recovery of the aid.

17. In addition to damages actions in the national court, it may be possible for a party that is damaged by a State aid decision of the Commission (or the Council) to bring an action for damages before the General Court. Article 340 TFEU provides:

> In the case of non-contractual liability, the Union shall, in accordance with the general principles common to the laws of the Member States, make good any damage caused by its institutions or by its servants in the performance of their duties.[209]

18. The Court of Justice held in *SFEI* that as a matter of EU law, there is no right to claim damages from the recipient of the aid as Article 108(3) does not place any specific obligations on the recipient.[210] However, the Court also held that this does not prevent national law providing a remedy against the recipient:

> If, according to national law, the acceptance by an economic operator of unlawful assistance of a nature such as to occasion damage to other economic operators may in certain circumstances cause him to incur liability, the principle of non-discrimination may lead the national court to find the recipient of aid paid in breach of Article [108(3)] of the Treaty liable.[211]

19. The English High Court has held that a Commission decision finding that a company had misused State aid did not provide a EU law cause of action against that company on the ground that it had used the aid to the detriment of competitors. At best, the claimant would have had a claim against the Member State to whom the Commission's decision was addressed.[212] Actions by competitors against recipients of illegal aid may be available as a matter of national law in some Member States, for example on the basis of unfair competition law.[213]

If the Commission approves unnotified aid, does this affect national proceedings?

20. The fact that the Commission subsequently approves aid that had been implemented before that approval does not validate measures taken in breach of Article 108(3). The prohibition on the implementation of aid without approval by the Commission is absolute. Depending on which national law remedies are available, a national court may be called upon to order recovery of unlawful aid from its recipient, even if that aid has subsequently been declared compatible with

---

209. Article 340 TFEU. The claimant must show that the rule of law infringed was intended to confer rights on individuals, the breach was sufficiently serious and there is a direct causal link between the breach and the damage suffered (see, e.g., Case C–312/00P *Commission v Camar Srl* [2002] ECR I–11355, para 53).

210. Case C–39/94 *SFEI v La Poste* [1996] ECR I–3547, [1996] 3 CMLR 369, paras 73–74.

211. Case C–39/94 *SFEI v La Poste* [1996] ECR I–3547, [1996] 3 CMLR 369, para 75.

212. *Betws Anthracite Ltd v DSK Anthrazit Ibbenburen GmbH* [2003] EWHC 2403 (Comm), [2004] 1 CMLR 381, para 37 (Morison J).

213. See Bacon, *European Community Law of State Aid* (2009) para 18.24.

the common market by the Commission. In the same way, the national court may be required to provide for compensation for the damage caused by reason of the unlawful nature of that aid.[214] Any other approach would have the effect of encouraging the Member States to disregard the prohibition on implementation of planned aid.[215]

How should a national court treat challenges to State aid in the form of tax breaks?

21. Many State aid cases have come before the national courts where an undertaking seeks relief from a tax or other charge from which its competitor was exempted. The aid that was granted in breach of Article 108(3) may have taken the form of an exemption from the tax or charge granted to the competitor. The Court of Justice has held that in such a situation it would not be compatible with the interest of the Union to order that such a rebate be applied also in favour of other undertakings if such a decision would have the effect of extending the circle of recipients, thus leading to an increase in the effects of that aid instead of their elimination. The national court must ensure that whatever remedies it grants negate the effects of the aid granted in breach of Article 108(3) and do not merely extend them to a further class of beneficiaries.[216]

Do national courts have a role in respect of State aid block exemptions?

22. The national courts have the power to apply the State aid block exemption regulations, *i.e.* the national court can assess whether the conditions for application of the exemption are met but it cannot find that a measure is incompatible with the common market where those conditions are not met.[217]

When may a Commission decision fall to be interpreted by a national court?

23. A national court has the jurisdiction to consider and decide whether a particular State measure involves State aid. In answering that question, the national court may have to consider whether the measure falls within an approved aid scheme. That task in turn will require the Commission decision that approved the scheme to be examined to determine whether the State measure comes within its scope. It can be argued that this function of the national court is recognised by the General Court's statement in *Salt Union* that it is open to undertakings challenging the grant of State aid to competitor companies before the national court to contest the decision of the national authorities to grant State aid.[218]

---

214. See Case C–368/04 *Transalpine Ölleitung in Österreich GmbH v Finanzlandesdirektion für Tirol* [2006] ECR I–9957, [2007] 1 CMLR 588, para 56.
215. Case C–39/94 *SFEI v La Poste* [1996] ECR I–3547, [1996] 3 CMLR 369, para 45.
216. Case C–368/04 *Transalpine Ölleitung in Österreich GmbH v Finanzlandesdirektion für Tirol* [2006] ECR I–9957, [2007] 1 CMLR 588, paras 49–50.
217. National Court State Aid Notice [2009] OJ C85/1, para 16.
218. Case T–330/94 *Salt Union Ltd v Commission* [1996] ECR II–1475, para 39.

24. In the National Court State Aid Notice, the Commission states that 'if the national court needs to determine whether the measure falls under an approved aid scheme, it can only verify whether all conditions of the approval decision are met'.[219] It is not entirely clear what the Commission envisages here. Is it suggesting that the national court has a role to play only in respect of the interpretation of conditional State aid decisions adopted by the Commission, *i.e.* decisions adopted under Article 7(4) of Regulation 659/1999, to which formal conditions are attached? A better view would be that the national court can consider more broadly whether the State measure in question falls within the scope of a positive Commission decision as a whole, whether it is a conditional decision under Article 7(4) or not. Otherwise, the national court may be unable to decide whether a particular State measure fell within a particular approved scheme. There are therefore at least two potential questions for the national court in respect of a State measure that is challenged: (i) does the measure come within an approved State aid scheme?; and (ii) if the relevant Commission decision is one to which formal conditions are attached, does the measure also comply with those formal conditions? To assist it in answering these questions, the national court can request information or an opinion from the Commission.[220]

Is it possible to challenge a Commission State aid decision in the national court?

25. A national court may have occasion to consider whether a Commission decision is invalid as a matter of EU law. It may decide that the Commission decision is valid but the court does not have jurisdiction to declare the decision invalid.[221] That is the exclusive jurisdiction of the Court of Justice.[222] The most then that a national court can do when the validity of a Commission State aid decision is raised in proceedings before it is to make a reference to the Court of Justice. If the national court considers that an argument for the invalidity of the Commission decision put forward by a party or raised by the court of its own motion is well founded, then it must make a reference.[223]

26. An applicant will not be entitled to indirectly challenge the validity of a Commission decision in the national court if it could have challenged the

---

219. National Court State Aid Notice [2009] OJ C85/1, para 17.

220. National Court State Aid Notice [2009] OJ C85/1, paras 82–96.

221. Case 314/85 *Firma Fotofrost v Hauptzollamt Lübeck-Ost* [1987] ECR 4199, [1988] 3 CMLR 57, paras 14–15.

222. Case C–119/05 *Ministero dell'Industria, del Commercio e dell'Artigianato v Lucchini SpA* [2007] ECR I–6199, para 53.

223. Case C–344/04 *R(International Air Transport Association (IATA)) v Department of Transport* [2006] ECR I–403, [2006] 2 CMLR 557, para 32. See, in a different context, *Digital Rights Ireland Ltd v Minister for Communications* [2010] IEHC 221 (where the compatibility of Directive 2006/24/EC on data retention was challenged as breaching EU law before the Irish High Court, McKechnie J granted an application for an Article 267 reference to the Court of Justice). A failure by a court of last instance to make a preliminary reference, in breach of the obligation in the third sub-paragraph of Article 267 TFEU, may give rise to an action for damages against a Member State; (contd \...)

Commission's decision under Article 263 but allowed the time limit to expire. In *TWD*, the Court held:

> To accept that in such circumstances the person concerned could challenge the implementation of the decision in proceedings before the national court on the ground that the decision was unlawful would in effect enable the person concerned to overcome the definitive nature which the decision assumes as against that person once the time-limit for bringing an action has expired.[224]

27. However in *Atzeni*, the Court of Justice allowed a preliminary reference from national proceedings which questioned the validity of a Commission decision declaring aid illegal and ordering recovery. The applicants before the national court were recipients of the aid. The Court of Justice distinguished *TWD* as the Commission decision at issue in that case had made explicit reference to the recipient of individual aid and the State had communicated the decision to the recipient, stating that it could bring an action for annulment of the Commission decision. In *Atzeni*, the Commission decision concerned aid schemes intended for categories of persons defined in a general manner and Italy had not notified the decision to the applicants or any other recipients of the aid. In those circumstances, 'it was not self-evident that an action for annulment brought against the contested decision brought by the recipients of the four aid measures would have been admissible' under Article 263 TFEU.[225] The preliminary reference was therefore admissible, an implicit acknowledgement by the Court that the Commission decision could be challenged indirectly via national proceedings, at least by applicants who did not clearly have standing under Article 263 TFEU.

28. There is a distinction to be made between an applicant who *allows* the Article 263 TFEU time limit to expire and a person whose ability to institute Article 263 proceedings was not obvious or self-evident. As Advocate General Kokott has stated in respect of the second category:

> An indirect challenge before the national courts and the submission of a reference for a preliminary ruling to the Court should only be considered inadmissible, however, if the individual could *undoubtedly* have instituted an action for annulment in the Community Courts.[226]

---

223. see Case C–224/01 *Köbler v Austria* [2003] ECR I–10239, [2003] 3 CMLR 1003, para 55; see also Case C–173/03 *Traghetti del Mediterraneo SpA (in liquidation) v Italy* [2006] ECR I–5177, [2006] 3 CMLR 586 (the Italian Supreme Court had refused to make a preliminary reference in a State aid/competition case); *Cooper v Attorney General* [2010] EWCA Civ 464, [2010] 3 CMLR 775 (failure to make a reference had not been so manifest as to give rise to *Köbler* liability).

224. Case C–188/92 *TWD Textilwerke Deggendorf GmbH v Germany* [1994] ECR I–833, [1995] 2 CMLR 145, para 18.

225. Cases C–346 & 529/03 *Atzeni v Regione autonoma della Sardegna* [2006] ECR I–1875, para 34.

226. Case C–333/07 *Societe Regie Networks v Direction de Controle Fiscal Rhone-Alpes Bourgogne* [2008] ECR I–10807, [2009] 2 CMLR 467, opinion, para 36 (emphasis in the original).

May the Commission participate in national proceedings involving the application of the State aid rules?

29. A national court may ask the Commission to transmit information or to provide an opinion on questions concerning the application of the State aid rules. Information requests can relate to the status of pending procedures before the Commission. For example, the national court can ask when the Commission expects to decide on the compatibility of a particular aid measure with the common market. The national court may also ask the Commission to transmit documents in its possession. The Commission aims to provide requested information to the national court within a month.[227]

30. The national court can also request an opinion from the Commission which can relate to any factual, legal or economic matters that arise in national State aid proceedings. This could include, for example, an opinion on whether a particular measure constitutes State aid or whether an aid measure falls under a specific aid scheme which has been approved by the Commission.[228] Commission opinions are not legally binding but it would seem, based on the principle of sincere cooperation, that the national court would have to take any Commission opinion into account.[229] The Commission aims to provide opinions within four months. The Commission has no intention of serving the interests of any party before the national court and it will not hear the parties before providing an opinion.[230] A number of requests for information/opinions have been made by national courts since the National Court State Aid Notice was issued in 2009.[231]

Key Sources

Commission Notice on the enforcement of State aid law by national courts [2009] OJ C85/1.

Case C–188/92 *TWD Textilwerke Deggendorf GmbH v Germany* [1994] ECR I–833, [1995] 2 CMLR 145.

Case C–39/94 *SFEI v La Poste* [1996] ECR I–3547, [1996] 3 CMLR 369.

Case C–368/04 *Transalpine Ölleitung in Österreich GmbH v Finanzlandesdirektion für Tirol* [2006] ECR I–9957, [2007] 1 CMLR 588.

Cases C–346 & 529/03 *Atzeni v Regione autonoma della Sardegna* [2006] ECR I–1875.

---

227. National Court State Aid Notice [2009] OJ C85/1, para 84.
228. See Case C–39/94 *SFEI v La Poste* [1996] ECR I–3547, [1996] 3 CMLR 369, para 50.
229. See Article 4(3) TEU.
230. National Court State Aid Notice [2009] OJ C85/1, paras 89–96. The ability of the national courts to seek the opinion of the Commission in State aid cases had earlier been recognised in Case C–39/94 *SFEI v La Poste* [1996] ECR I–3547, [1996] 3 CMLR 369, para 50. See also the Notice on cooperation between national courts and the Commission in the State aid field [1995] OJ C312/8.
231. Commission Staff Working Document accompanying the Report from the Commission on Competition Policy 2009 COM(2010) 282 final, para 36. See also Question 119, discussing cooperation between the national courts and the Commission in application of the antitrust rules.

132. IF A CONTRACT IS AWARDED UNDER THE PUBLIC PROCUREMENT RULES, DOES THIS NEGATE STATE AID CONCERNS?

Summary

- The award of a public contract could involve State aid where, for example, the price paid by the contracting authority is too high or there was no genuine requirement for the contract in the first place.

- A proper procurement procedure tends to show that the award of the public contract does not involve State aid.

- Nevertheless, it may not always be possible to rule out the presence of State aid, in particular where the restricted or negotiated procedure or competitive dialogue are used.

- Where the award of a public contract includes financial support from the State to carry out a public service, State aid may be present regardless of whether the public procurement rules have been complied with.

- There are a number of features that a contracting authority can include in the procurement to lower the likelihood of a finding of State aid.

- If State aid is present, a proper procurement can support a finding that the aid is compatible with the common market.

1.   The EU public procurement directives[232] require public bodies to award contracts on an open, competitive and non-discriminatory basis. The directives, as implemented in the Member States,[233] set out detailed procedures for advertising and awarding public contracts. These rules apply when certain financial thresholds are met.[234] Even if a public contract is not caught by the public procurement directives, if the contract is of cross-border interest, the contracting authority will

---

232. The two main directives are Directive 2004/18/EC on the coordination of procedures for the award of public works contracts, public supply contracts and public service contracts [2004] OJ L134/114 and Directive 2004/17/EC coordinating the procurement procedures of entities operating in the water, energy, transport and postal services sectors [2004] OJ L134/1. See generally Arrowsmith, *The Law of Public and Utilities Procurement* (2nd edn, 2005).

233. In Ireland, Directive 2004/18 is implemented in SI No 329 of 2006, European Communities (Award of Public Authorities' Contracts) Regulations 2006 and Directive 2004/17 is implemented in SI No 50 of 2007, European Communities (Award of Contracts by Utilities Undertakings) Regulations 2007. In the UK, Directive 2004/18 is implemented in SI No 5 of 2006, The Public Contracts Regulations 2006 and Directive 2004/17 is implemented in SI No 6 of 2006, The Utilities Contracts Regulations 2006.

234. As of 1 January 2010, the main thresholds are €125,000 for public supply and service contracts awarded by central government, €193,000 for other public supply and service contracts and €4,845,000 for public works contracts (Commission Regulation (EC) No 1177/2009 amending Directives 2004/17/EC, 2004/18/EC and 2009/81/EC in respect of their application thresholds for the procedures for the award of contracts [2009] OJ L314/64).

have to comply with general principles of EU law. The courts have subjected such contracts to ever increasing requirements that in some cases are comparable to or come close to the requirements in the formal public procurement rules.[235]

2.   The award of a public contract might give rise to State aid if the amount paid for the contract is excessive or if there is no real need for the procurement in the first place. To the extent that the contracting authority has followed the EU public procurement rules, this *tends* to show that no State aid is involved in the award. The underlying rationale of this argument is that a properly conducted procurement should produce a commercial transaction with the best market price and therefore not result in any advantage for the winning bidder.[236] A showing of proper procurement practice can also be used to support the argument that when there is an element of State aid in the award, it should be exempted. The same principle should apply in respect of a public contract that falls below the thresholds of the public procurement directives, where the contracting authority has carried out an open and competitive tendering process and, to the extent the contract is of cross-border interest, has complied with the general principles of EU law.

3.   The *BAI* case confirmed the parallel application of the public procurement and State aid rules.[237] BAI had complained to the Commission about subsidies received by its competitor on UK-Spanish ferry routes by two Spanish authorities. The subsidies, which had social and cultural aims, included an agreement by the authorities to purchase a set number of travel vouchers. After changes to the arrangements, the Commission declared the scheme compatible with the common market and BAI challenged that decision. The General Court held that the agreement could not be excluded in principle from the concept of State aid merely because the parties undertook reciprocal commitments.[238] The Court also found that the social and cultural motivation of the Spanish authorities had no bearing on the finding that the arrangements constituted State aid but these aims could be taken into account by the Commission in considering if State aid was exempted.[239] The Court ultimately concluded that the Commission's decision that the arrangements did not give rise to State aid misinterpreted Article 107 and it

---

235. See Commission Communication on the Community law applicable to contract awards not or not fully subject to the provisions of the Public Procurement Directives [2006] OJ C179/2 (a challenge to this communication was rejected in Case T–258/06 *Germany v Commission*, judgment of 20 May 2010). See also, on the requirements for below threshold contracts, *Sidey Limited v Clackmannanshire Council* [2010] CSIH 37, [2010] SLT 607; *R(Chandler) v Secretary of State for Children, Schools and Family* [2009] EWCA Civ 1011, [2010] 1 CMLR 612; Cases C–147 & 148/06 *SECAP SpA v Comune di Torino* [2008] ECR I–3565, [2008] 2 CMLR 1558.

236. For discussion of this point, including its application to the sale of State assets, see Nicolaides, 'State aid, Advantage and Competitive Selection: What is a Normal Market Transaction?' [2010] *European State aid Law Quarterly* 65.

237. Case T–14/96 *BAI v Commission* [1999] ECR II–139, [1999] 3 CMLR 245.

238. Case T–14/96 *BAI v Commission* [1999] ECR II–139, [1999] 3 CMLR 245, para 71.

239. Case T–14/96 *BAI v Commission* [1999] ECR II–139, [1999] 3 CMLR 245, para 81.

annulled the Commission's decision to terminate its State aid review.[240] The *BAI* case is an example of State aid arising where a public authority contracts for something it does not really need. In theory, this should not occur with contracts that follow from procurement as public procurement functions to satisfy a public sector need, however in practice there may be cases where the need is not in fact real.

4.   The Commission seemed to have a practice of presuming that transactions that properly followed the public procurement rules would not give rise to State aid. This is apparent from the *London Underground* case, which involved a Public-Private-Partnership ('PPP') for operation of the London underground. The Commission, in analyzing whether the scheme gave the operators an economic advantage, applied the presumption that a properly run procurement process should not result in the grant of State aid:

> [When] these types of infrastructure arrangements are concluded after the observance of an open, transparent and non-discriminatory procedure, it is, in principle, presumed that the level of any public sector support can be regarded as representing the market price for the execution of a project. This conclusion should lead to the assumption that, in principle, no State aid is involved.[241]

5.   The key question then was whether the procurement process had been open, transparent and non-discriminatory. The Commission examined the advertisement of the PPP (which was sufficient for an open tendering process), the methodology for selecting preferred bidders (bidders were chosen on the basis of best value for money) and whether modifications to the contracts after selection of preferred bidders caused discrimination or unequal treatment (the nature of the contract required a flexible approach and the modifications did not change the nature and scope of the PPP beyond what was contemplated in the notices published in the *Official Journal*; any improvements the preferred bidders could achieve in the terms of the contracts were reasonable in this type of novel and complex contract that had been awarded under the negotiated procedure; and ultimately, it was possible for contract modifications to be made without automatically vitiating the presumption that the final price was a market price). The Commission concluded that the tendering process was open, transparent and non-discriminatory. On this basis, the PPP arrangements were considered to reflect a market price and so did not constitute State aid.

6.   Even though the negotiated procedure was used in *London Underground*, the Commission applied the presumption that an open, transparent and non-discriminatory procedure should not result in State aid. However, later cases illustrate that the presumption may not fully apply to the negotiated procedure or the competitive dialogue (understandably, it also may not fully apply to the restricted procedure). In the *Clonee/Kells Motorway* decision,[242] Ireland notified

---

240. The Commission subsequently re-opened the State aid procedure and found that there was State aid, a decision upheld by the EU courts (see Case C–442 & 471/03P *P&O European Ferries (Vizcaya) SA v Commission* [2006] ECR I–4845).
241. N264/02 *London Underground,* Commission Decision of 2 December 2002, para 79.
242. N149/2006 *Clonee/Kells,* Commission Decision of 16 May 2006.

two PPP road-building transactions (the M3 motorway and the Limerick tunnel) that involved certain grants and guarantees for the private partners. For each project, an open, transparent and non-discriminatory procurement process that complied with the EU directives was to be used, with selection under the negotiated procedure. Ireland took the position that as the private companies would be selected through a competitive tender process, they would not receive any economic advantage and therefore, no State aid was involved. The Commission, however, could not rule out the possibility that the schemes would result in the grant of State aid. Its view of the salutary effect of a procurement process in compliance with EU rules was less emphatic than it had been in *London Underground*:

> The Commission in general considers that a call for tender can be an appropriate means for establishing the market value of a given good or service. The Commission notes that an open, transparent and non-discriminatory tender procedure *tends to minimize* potential advantages to the service providers and thus possible elements of State aid. However, an element of State aid may remain.

In the present case, the Irish authorities have opted for a negotiated procedure. As the outcome of this procedure, which is very complex, is not yet known, the Commission considers that it cannot exclude that the financing measures proposed by the Irish authorities may confer an economic advantage to the successful bidder.[243]

7.   The particular concern expressed by the Commission stemmed from the fact that at the time it considered the project, its details had not been worked out sufficiently so that the possibility of State aid could not be ruled out. Nevertheless, the Commission decided that any State aid at issue would be compatible with the common market, persuaded in part by the fact that the Irish government had received numerous requests for bidding documents and that bidding was very competitive.

8.   Contracting authorities may be able to include particular features in the tender that will tend to show that no economic advantage is being conferred and therefore that State aid is not present. In *Welsh Networks*,[244] the Welsh Assembly carried out a procurement process pursuant to the competitive dialogue procedure in Directive 2004/18 to select a provider of consolidated network services for the public sector in Wales. Concerned that the complex transaction might give rise to State aid, the UK notified the Commission in advance of making the award. The Commission found that there would be no economic advantage for the winning bidder. It considered that the award was a 'pure procurement transaction' aimed at satisfying a clearly defined public need. The Commission then examined the procurement process. It found that there was a competitive procurement process – which employed the criterion of most economically advantageous tender – in line with Directive 2004/18, which was suitable for achieving best value for money. The

---

243. N149/2006 *Clonee/Kells*, Commission Decision of 16 May 2006, paras 38–39 (emphasis added).
244. N46/2007 *Welsh Public Sector Network Scheme*, Commission Decision of 30 May 2007.

Commission noted a number of particular mechanisms of the procedure which would ensure cost effectiveness over the entire duration of the contract:

- A 'benchmarking' requirement, involving regular independent reviews of tariffs and service performance;

- A 'gain sharing' mechanism to cover situations where market prices for networking services would fall during the term of the contract; the difference between the reduced costs to the service provider and the fees paid by the Welsh authorities would be shared between the parties – this would prevent increased return for the provider while providing an incentive for it to reduce costs; and

- Price control for connectivity services through a system of mini-competitions – enabling individual authorities to continually test the market.

9.   The Commission concluded that there was no economic advantage conferred and therefore no State aid.

10. Other ways of showing that the service provider does not gain an economic advantage might include a comparison with a similar transaction in the private sector (although identifying a sufficiently similar transaction and obtaining data may be problematic) or independent valuation.

11. In some cases involving contracts with public service obligations, the Commission has considered the effect of the use of a public procurement procedure on the potential application of the *Altmark* test. If that test is satisfied, there is no State aid.[245]

12. The *Cumbria Broadband* decision[246] involved a contract for the provision of broadband services in Cumbria and North Lancashire. There was little incentive for companies to invest in broadband services in this remote area given the high costs involved so the contract was to provide public funding to the winning bidder, in effect, compensation for carrying out a public service obligation. The Commission considered that the conditions for State aid were met, one of the advantages to the winning bidder being its ability to commercially exploit the infrastructure that would be built after the contract had expired. The Commission examined whether the *Altmark* criteria were satisfied. The Commission noted that the conclusion that the contract gave rise to State aid was not altered by the fact that the service provider would be chosen through a tendering procedure. As the negotiated procedure was to be used, the terms of the eventual agreement were not yet clear, so the second *Altmark* condition was not fulfilled (the second condition is that the parameters on the basis of which compensation is calculated must have been established *in advance* in an objective and transparent manner so as to avoid the conferral of an economic advantage). In addition, as the infrastructure would be in the ownership of the service provider after termination of the agreement, it could not be excluded that the compensation awarded to the winning bidder would

---

245. See Question 128.
246. N282/2003 *Cumbria Broadband*, Commission Decision of 10 December 2003.

eventually exceed what was necessary to cover all or part of the costs incurred in discharging its obligations.[247]

If State aid is present, will the use of a public procurement procedure support a finding that the State aid is compatible with the common market?

13. It is apparent from the above discussion that in some cases, State aid may be present even if the procurement rules are followed. This scenario has arisen, for instance, in several of the Commission's *Broadband* decisions. The question then is whether the use of a public procurement procedure supports a finding that the aid is compatible with the common market.

14. In *Northern Irish Broadband*, the Commission found that the State aid, which was provided to achieve 100 per cent broadband coverage in Northern Ireland, was designed in such a way as to minimise the amount of State aid and potential distortions of competition. Among the factors supporting this conclusion was the fact that the recipient of State aid was selected through an open tender procedure which, by applying the criterion of economically most advantageous tender, minimised the potential advantage to the provider. Under the terms of the tender, the bidder with the lowest amount of aid requested received more priority points within the overall assessment of the bid.[248]

15. In its decision in *Irish National Broadband Scheme ('NBS')*, the Commission also concluded that the State aid was compatible with the common market. The scheme involved the selection of a service provider to roll out and operate broadband networks in rural areas of Ireland that would not otherwise be served by broadband. An open tender process following the competitive dialogue procedure would be used to select the service provider. The Irish government would provide aid, the amount of which would be determined during negotiations as part of the competitive dialogue, with the remaining costs being funded by the winning bidder. In concluding that the scheme constituted State aid but was, nonetheless, compatible with the common market (by reference to Article 107(3)(c) in particular), the Commission highlighted the fact that an open tender process in compliance with the procurement rules was being used to select the winning bidder. By requiring bidders to indicate the amount of aid they considered necessary, Ireland's objective was to ensure that the State aid awarded would 'provide a direct and appropriate investment incentive limited to the amount

---

247. The Commission did go on to find that the aid was compatible with Article 107(3)(c) of the Treaty, taking into account that an open, transparent and competitive tender procedure was used.

248. N418/2009 *United Kingdom (Northern Ireland) – Next Generation Broadband*, Commission Decision of 5 November 2009, para 44. See also, e.g., N62/2010 *High-speed broadband construction aid in sparsely populated areas of Finland*, Commission Decision of 6 May 2010, para 42.

required for the Preferred Bidder to provide the requested services'.[249] The use of a competitive bidding process would minimise the public funding required and so helped ensure that any aid measure would be proportionate in light of the objectives sought. On balance, the overall effect of the State aid was positive.[250]

16.   The inclusion of particular features in the tender procedure or the public contract may also support an argument that any State aid which is present is compatible with the common market. One of the *Scottish Broadband* cases involved the scrutiny of the tender by an independent audit body, a factor supporting the conclusion that the State aid provided to the relevant service provider was compatible with the common market.[251]

Key Sources

Case T–14/96 *Bretagne Angleterre Irlande (BAI) v Commission* [1999] ECR II–139, [1999] 3 CMLR 245.

N264/02 *London Underground*, Commission Decision of 2 December 2002.

N46/2007 *Welsh Public Sector Network Scheme*, Commission Decision of 30 May 2007.

N418/2009 *United Kingdom (Northern Ireland) – Next Generation Broadband*, Commission Decision of 5 November 2009.

---

249. N475/2007 *Ireland – National Broadband Scheme*, Commission Decision of 25 September 2007, para 44. The contract was awarded to '3' and entered into on 23 December 2008. The Irish government are contributing €80 million of the €223 million cost.

250. The NBS appeared to involve a public service obligation on the winning bidder – there was a requirement to offer connections with specified requirements in specified areas and a wholesale product at an appropriate tariff – but the Commission did not carry out an *Altmark* analysis. Had it done so, it seems that the second condition – parameters of compensation to be established in advance – would not have been met as the overall budget was to be determined during negotiations.

251. N117/2005 *Aggregated public sector procurement of broadband in Scotland*, Commission Decision of 21 November 2005, para 21.

133. IS A RECIPIENT OF STATE AID PROHIBITED FROM PARTICIPATING IN A PUBLIC PROCUREMENT TENDER?

Summary

- There is no absolute rule requiring the exclusion of a recipient of State aid from participating in a public tender.

- A bid may be rejected if it is abnormally low because the bidder received State aid and the bidder cannot show that the State aid was obtained legally.

1. Should an undertaking that has received State aid be allowed to participate in a public bid? A possible concern is that such an undertaking would be enabled, through the financial advantage gained from the aid, to undercut other bidders and gain an unfair advantage. In turn, this might breach the principle of equal treatment.

2. The Court of Justice addressed this issue in *ARGE*. It held that recipients of State aid were not automatically excluded from participating in a public procurement tender and that their inclusion did not necessarily give rise to a breach of the principle of equal treatment. Were such bidders meant to be excluded, this would have been made explicit in the public procurement directives.[252] This view was confirmed by the Court of Justice in *CoNISMa*, when it stated that

    > ... the fact that an economic operator may enjoy an unfair advantage because it receives public finance or State aid cannot justify the exclusion of entities, such as the applicant in the main proceedings, from a public tendering procedure *a priori* and without further consideration.[253]

3. In *ARGE*, the Court went on to consider whether the recipient of illegal State aid could be barred from participation in a particular tender. While there was no automatic exclusion of recipients of illegal State aid, the Court stated:

    > [It] is not excluded that, in certain specific circumstances, Directive 92/50 requires, or at the very least allows, the contracting authorities to take into account the existence of subsidies, and in particular of aid incompatible with the Treaty, in order, where appropriate, to exclude tenderers in receipt of such aid. The Commission correctly states in this connection that a tenderer may be excluded from a selection procedure where the contracting authority considers that it has received aid incompatible with the Treaty and that the obligation to repay illegal aid would threaten its financial well-being, so that that tenderer may be regarded as unable to offer the necessary financial or economic security.[254]

4. The reference in this passage to Directive 92/50 is to a provision now found in Article 55 of Directive 2004/18. Article 55 provides that where a tender is

---

252. Case C–94/99 *ARGE Gewässerschutz* [2000] ECR I–11037, [2002] 3 CMLR 1107, paras 25–26.
253. Case C–305/08 *CoNISMa v Regione Marche*, judgment of 23 December 2009, para 34.
254. Case C–94/99 *ARGE Gewässerschutz* [2000] ECR I–11037, [2002] 3 CMLR 1107, paras 29–30.

abnormally low due to what the contracting authority considers to be the receipt of illegal State aid, the bidder may be excluded but only after a consultation has been carried out:

> Where a contracting authority establishes that a tender is abnormally low because the tenderer has obtained State aid, the tender can be rejected on that ground alone only after consultation with the tenderer where the latter is unable to prove, within a sufficient time limit fixed by the contracting authority, that the aid in question was granted legally. Where the contracting authority rejects a tender in these circumstances, it shall inform the Commission of that fact.[255]

5.   The Commission's 2006 State aid study highlights the difficulty for aggrieved bidders in showing that the effect of State aid is to make a competitor's bid abnormally low. The study suggests that 'in practice, it is almost impossible to make such a showing unless the aid is specifically related to the tender'.[256] Nevertheless, the study contains at least one Belgian example where a participant in a public tender successfully argued that another bidder should be excluded because it had been awarded State aid in breach of the Article 108(3) notification requirement. The participation by the aid recipient in the tender gave rise to a breach of a national unfair competition law.[257]

6.   It should also be noted that according to Recital 4 of Directive 2004/18, Member States are obliged to ensure that the participation of a body governed by public law in a public tendering procedure does not cause a distortion of competition. That obligation also applies in respect of entities in receipt of State funding and State aid.[258]

Can an undertaking that has breached competition law be excluded from tendering for a public tender?

7.   A related question is whether an undertaking that has breached competition law, for example through participation in a cartel, can be excluded from participating in a public tender under the public procurement rules.

8.   The EU public procurement directives exclude from participation in public tenders carried out under those rules any tenderer who has been convicted of certain offences, including those involving 'corruption' or 'fraud'.[259] Those terms are in turn defined by reference to other EU instruments.[260] The implementing Regulations in both the UK and Ireland provide for exclusion of tenderers who

---

255. Directive 2004/18, Article 55(3).
256. Commission Study on enforcement of State aid law at national level (March 2006) 51.
257. *Breda Fucine Meridionali v Manoir Industries*, JTDE (1995/p72), summarised in the Commission Study on enforcement of State aid law at national level (March 2006) 87–89. See also at 61 (Austrian rule providing for the exclusion of a bidder whose bid is not 'plausible' is potentially applicable to a beneficiary of State aid).
258. See Case C–305/08 *CoNISMa v Regione Marche*, judgment of 23 December 2009, para 32.
259. Directive 2004/18, Article 45(1). The same exclusion applies in respect of utilities tenders carried out by public contracting authorities (see Directive 2004/17, recital 54).
260. See, in particular, Convention relating to the protection of the financial interests of the European Communities [1995] OJ C316/48; (contd \...)

have been involved in such offences. The Irish Regulations repeat the language of the directive, excluding persons convicted of 'corruption' or 'fraud'.[261] The UK Regulations include reference to the offences of 'fraud' and 'corruption' but also set out a more detailed list of offences which will trigger exclusion.[262] The Regulations in neither jurisdiction provide for exclusion on the basis of competition law offences. However competition law offences may overlap with fraud or corruption offences in certain cases. For example, the relevant definition of 'corruption' could encompass conduct that would also give rise to a breach of the cartel offence in the UK or section 4 of the Irish Competition Act 2002. It refers in part to 'conduct which involves, or could involve, the distortion of competition, as a minimum within the common market, and which results, or might result, in economic damage to others by the improper award or improper execution of a contract'.[263]

9.   Some jurisdictions have adopted specific rules excluding violators of competition law from participating in public procurement contracts. For example, in Portugal, if an undertaking is found to breach the national law equivalent of Article 101, in addition to imposing fines of up to 10 per cent of turnover, the Portuguese Competition Authority may withdraw the right of the undertaking to participate in public procurement tenders where the breach of the competition rules itself occurred within the context of a procurement procedure. This ancillary sanction can be used to exclude the undertaking from participating in public tenders for up to two years from the date of the Competition Authority's decision.[264]

Key Sources

Directive 2004/18/EC on the coordination of procedures for the award of public works contracts, public supply contracts and public service contracts [2004] OJ L134/114.

Case C–94/99 *ARGE Gewässerschutz* [2000] ECR I–11037, [2002] 3 CMLR 1107.

Case C–305/08 *Consorzio Nazionale Interuniversitario per le Scienze del Mare (CoNISMa) v Regione Marche*, judgment of 23 December 2009.

---

260. (contd) Joint Action adopted by the Council on the basis of Article K.3 of the Treaty on European Union, on corruption in the private sector [1998] OJ L358/2.
261. SI No 329 of 2006, European Communities (Award of Public Authorities' Contracts) Regulations 2006, r 53(1). While SI No 50 of 2007, European Communities (Award of Contracts by Utilities Undertakings) Regulations 2007 provides definitions of 'fraud' and 'corruption' in r 3, the terms are not used again in the Regulations. This may be an oversight.
262. SI No 5 of 2006, The Public Contracts Regulations 2006, r 23; SI No 6 of 2006, The Utilities Contracts Regulations 2006, r 26.
263. Joint Action adopted by the Council on the basis of Article K.3 of the Treaty on European Union, on corruption in the private sector [1998] OJ L358/2, Articles 2(2), 3(2).
264. Section 45(3) of the Portuguese Competition Act 2003, as amended in July 2008.

134. MUST A CONTRACTING AUTHORITY, SUBJECT TO THE PUBLIC PROCUREMENT RULES, COMPLY WITH COMPETITION LAW?

Summary

- A contracting authority will be subject to the competition rules if it comes within the meaning of an 'undertaking'.

- If the contracting authority is engaged in 'economic activity', it will be subject to competition law. The key characteristic of an economic activity is offering goods or services on a market.

- A contracting authority could be an undertaking in respect of its procurement activities if the goods or services procured were subsequently used in an economic activity.

- Potential arguments alleging a breach of competition law by a contracting authority could include that the authority is abusing a dominant position by failing to pay suppliers on time (imposing unfair trading conditions) or that a public procurement contract breaches Article 101 where it is of an excessively long duration.

- In addition to the competition rules in the Treaty, the public procurement directives make specific reference to the need to ensure that contracting authorities do not distort competition.

1. A contracting authority will be subject to Articles 101 and 102 (and national law equivalents) if it comes within the meaning of an 'undertaking'. The key question is whether the contracting authority is engaged in 'economic activity'. The central characteristic of an economic activity consists in offering goods or services on a market.[265]

2. The Union's procurement rules apply to 'contracting authorities' which includes the State, local and regional authorities and 'bodies governed by public law'.

3. Any type of public body, including emanations of the State, can constitute an undertaking if it is engaged in economic activity. There is therefore no immunity from the competition rules for contracting authorities.

4. Local and regional authorities, which are contracting authorities under the procurement rules, may well be engaged in economic activity. In England, for example, local authorities are specifically empowered to engage in trade.[266]

---

265. See Question 1, which discusses the concept of an undertaking in detail.
266. See SI 2009/2393 Local Government (Best Value Authorities) (Power to Trade) (England) Order 2009.

5. Bodies governed by public law are ones that meet 'needs in the general interest, not having an industrial or commercial character'.[267] This is not a straightforward concept. The underlying rationale is summed up by Arrowsmith:

    > [It] excludes entities which, whilst connected with government, are not likely to apply national preferences because they are subject to commercial pressures to purchase efficiently. Most notably this applies to public entities providing goods or services to the market in competition with other firms: applying national preferences increases their costs and makes it more difficult to compete, and this pressure can serve as an alternative to bureaucratic regulation for ensuring non-discriminatory behaviour.[268]

6. It might at first be thought doubtful that a body falling within the definition of a body governed by public law engages in 'economic activity' and that therefore, such bodies falls outside the definition of an undertaking. However the EU courts have not drawn such a connection between the concepts of an undertaking and a body governed by public law. On the contrary, it is apparent from some of the public procurement cases that a body governed by public law may still face competition, in which case, it is likely to be engaged in economic activity.[269] So, like local and regional authorities and emanations of the State, a body governed by public law may qualify as an undertaking.

7. The concept of an undertaking is tied to the context in which the entity operates so that it must be asked whether an entity is an undertaking when it performs a particular activity. An entity may be an undertaking when it engages in one activity and not be an undertaking when it carries out a different function. If a contracting authority is engaged in economic activity through offering goods or services and qualifies as an undertaking for that purpose, it may also be an undertaking when it carries out procurement of goods or services that are employed in its downstream activity. Take the example of a health authority that purchases medical equipment. If that equipment were used in delivering services of, say, a semi-private nature in competition with private hospitals and for which patients were charged, the authority may well be considered an undertaking when offering medical services and consequently may be an undertaking when it procured the equipment.[270]

---

267. Directive 2004/18, Article 1(9). Directive 2004/18 sets out non-exhaustive lists of bodies that are governed by public law, listed both as specific bodies and categories. The Irish Regulations implementing Directive 2004/18 refer to a 'public authority', the definition of which is similar to a body governed by public law (SI No 329 of 2006, European Communities (Award of Public Authorities' Contracts) Regulations 2006, r 3(1)). The UK Regulations incorporate the definition of a body governed by public law (SI No 5 of 2006, The Public Contracts Regulations 2006, r 3(1)(w)).

268. Arrowsmith, *The Law of Public and Utilities Procurement* (2nd edn, 2005) para 5.10. For a more general discussion of the concept of a body governed by public law in EU law, see Chiti, 'The EC Notion of Public Administration: The Case of the Bodies Governed by Public Law' [2002] *European Public Law* 473.

269. See, e.g., Case C–393/06 *Ing. Aigner, Wasser-Wärme-Umwelt, GmbH v Fernwärme Wien GmbH* [2008] ECR I–2339, [2008] 2 CMLR 1183, paras 46–47.

270. Cf Case C–205/03P *FENIN v Commission* [2006] ECR I–6295, [2006] 5 CMLR 559.

When might the actions of a contracting authority give rise to competition law concerns?

8. Assuming that the contracting authority was an undertaking when engaged in procurement, there are a number of ways in which potential competition issues could arise. It is possible that the public contract with the winning bidder could itself breach Article 101 (or national equivalents) where it had an anti-competitive object or effect. An example might be where the duration of the contract is unnecessarily long and results in the foreclosure of competitors. Whether an anti-competitive effect was created would depend on the circumstances and economic context of the agreement. In certain cases an agreement of, say, five years might be considered to be anti-competitive but in other circumstances, an agreement of much longer duration may be justified. In the *London Underground* case, contracts for the management and maintenance of the London tube system were of 30 years duration.[271] This was acceptable and considered to be proportionate in light of the particular complexities involved. Another feature of a public contract that could potentially raise concerns is an exclusivity clause. Again, it should be considered if there is foreclosure of competitors.[272] If the agreement was caught by Article 101(1), it might benefit from the exemption under Article 101(3). An agreement that does not benefit from the exemption is void under Article 101(2).

9. It is also possible that a tenderer or a contracting authority could abuse a dominant position in breach of Article 102 (or national law equivalents) through its conduct in a public procurement context. Again, the contracting authority could only ever breach competition law in this way if it qualifies as an undertaking. In areas such as health, defence and education, such a contracting authority may well be the largest or only purchaser and therefore hold a dominant position on the particular purchasing market. A narrow geographic market will increase the likelihood of dominance. Abuses of a dominant position could take various forms. The *FENIN* case involved an allegation of abuse of a dominant position by a contracting authority, through its alleged continuous failures to make payments on time.[273] Other possible breaches might involve the imposition of unreasonable contract terms, for example, if a dominant contracting authority reduces prices further after negotiations with bidders or later bargains down the winning bidder or imposes non-negotiable pricing.

What general competition requirements are placed on contracting authorities?

10. Competition is a 'fundamental principle' of public procurement[274] and if a contracting authority were to run a procurement that distorted competition in the

---

271. N264/02 *London Underground*, Commission Decision of 2 December 2002.
272. See Question 44 for an analysis of vertical agreements under Article 101.
273. Case C–205/03P *FENIN v Commission* [2006] ECR I–6295, [2006] 5 CMLR 559.
274. See Case C–247/02 *Sintesi SpA v Autorita per la Vigilanza sui Lavori Pubblici* [2004] ECR I–9215, [2005] 1 CMLR 269, opinion of Advocate General Stix-Hackl, para 33 and the Court, paras 35–42 (public procurement rules precluded a national law that required contracting authorities to only use the award criterion of lowest price, contrary to the objective of developing effective competition).

general sense (whether or not the formal competition rules were applicable), this could result in a breach of the public procurement Regulations.[275]

11. There are some specific competition requirements built into the public procurement directives. For example, Directive 2004/18 provides that public contracts should be awarded on the basis of objective criteria which ensure that 'tenders are assessed in conditions of effective competition'.[276] The Directive also provides that while a pre-tender 'technical dialogue' may be used by the contracting authority to seek advice, it should not have the effect of 'precluding competition'.[277] This might occur were a bidder allowed, through the technical dialogue, to have some influence over technical specifications or gain a time advantage in making preparations for the bid.

12. Directive 2004/18 specifically provides that framework agreements, dynamic purchasing systems and electronic auctions shall not be used to prevent, restrict or distort competition.[278] Taking a framework agreement, it could potentially have an adverse effect on competition, for example:

- Where the duration of the agreement is excessive (a framework agreement may exceed 4 years only exceptionally, justified by factors such as the subject matter of the contract;[279] justifications might be based on the nature of the product or market, security of supply or the need for long term investment, for instance);

- The product range covered by the framework is excessively wide resulting in the foreclosure of suppliers;

- The range of users is too wide (again, resulting in foreclosure of suppliers; for example, a framework covering all local councils in a Member State would probably be too wide);

- Breach of the framework agreement itself may distort competition, for example, if mini-competitions are not run competitively.

13. If the procedure carried out to award a public procurement contract is anti-competitive in this more general sense, then the procedure or contract award may

---

275. See, e.g., *Henry Brothers (Magherafelt) Ltd v Department of Education for Northern Ireland* [2007] NIQB 116, [2008] CILL 2630, para 21 (on an application for interim relief, Coghlin J was satisfied that there was a serious question to be tried as to whether the contracting authority's procedure complied with the Regulations and the '*general principles* of domestic and European competition law') (emphasis added); in respect of amendments requiring a new tendering procedure, Case C–454/06 *pressetext Nachrichtenagentur GmbH v Austria* [2008] ECR I–4401, opinion of Advocate General Kokott, para 48 ('Only material contractual amendments which are such as to distort competition on the relevant market and to favour the contracting authority's contractual partner as against other possible service providers justify conducting a new procurement procedure'.)

276. Directive 2004/18, Recital 46.

277. Directive 2004/18, Recital 8.

278. Directive 2004/18, Articles 32, 33, 54.

279. Directive 2004/18, Article 32(2).

not be compliant with the public procurement rules. Where a contracting authority breaches the public procurement rules, the remedies available to a plaintiff follow from the Remedies Directive.[280]

Key Sources

Directive 2004/18/EC on the coordination of procedures for the award of public works contracts, public supply contracts and public service contracts [2004] OJ L134/114.

Case C–205/03P *FENIN v Commission* [2006] ECR I–6295, [2006] 5 CMLR 559.

Henry Brothers (Magherafelt) Ltd v Department of Education for Northern Ireland [2007] NIQB 116, [2008] CILL 2630.

---

280. Directive 2007/66/EC amending Council Directives 89/665/EEC and 92/13/EEC with regard to improving the effectiveness of review procedures concerning the award of public contracts [2007] OJ L335/31. The implementing Regulations in Ireland are SI No 130 of 2010 European Communities (Public Authorities' Contracts) (Review Procedures) Regulations 2010. The UK implementing Regulations are the Public Contracts (Amendment) Regulations 2009, SI 2009 No 2992.

135. CAN MEASURES OF MEMBER STATES, SUCH AS LEGISLATION, BE CHALLENGED AS BREACHING EU COMPETITION LAW?

Summary

- Yes.

- The basis for the Member States' obligations lies in particular in Article 4(3) TEU and Article 106(1) TFEU.

- Even though Articles 101 and 102 are addressed to undertakings, Member States have a duty not to introduce measures that would deprive the competition rules of their effectiveness and in the case of public undertakings and undertakings to which the Member State grants special or exclusive rights, Member States are specifically required not to enact or maintain measures contrary to the competition rules.

1. Even though the rules on competition are addressed to undertakings, the Member States have a duty not to adopt or maintain measures that would deprive Union competition law of its effectiveness or enact measures that would breach the rules in the Treaty, in particular the competition rules. There are two important Treaty provisions which give effect to this principle, Article 106(1) TFEU and the more general Article 4(3) TEU.

When does Article 106(1) apply?

2. Article 106(1) TFEU, which is addressed to Member States (it has been suggested that it may also apply to the Commission[281]), provides as follows:

> In the case of public undertakings and undertakings to which Member States grant special or exclusive rights, Member States shall neither enact nor maintain in force any measure contrary to the rules contained in the Treaties, in particular to those rules provided for in Article 18 and Articles 101 to 109.

3. The prohibition in Article 106(1) is aimed at 'measures' of Member States, which would include legislative, executive and administrative measures. Article 106(1) must be applied in conjunction with another Treaty provision. Article 106(1) has direct effect so that it can be relied on directly in the national court[282] but it appears that the other Treaty article on which reliance is placed must also be directly effective.[283] Article 106(1) can be applied not only with the competition rules but

---

281. See Case C–313/04 *Franz Egenberger GmbH Molkerei v Bundesanstalt für Landwirtschaft und Ernährung* [2006] ECR I–6331, opinion of Advocate General Geelhoed, paras 51–54 (the issue was not addressed by the Court).

282. See Case 155/73 *Sacchi* [1974] ECR 409, [1974] 2 CMLR 177, para 18; Case C–179/90 *Merci convenzionali porto di Genova SpA* [1991] ECR I–5889, [1994] 4 CMLR 422, para 23.

283. See Bellamy & Child (6th edn, 2008) para 11.009.

also with other Treaty provisions such as those on free movement of goods (Article 34 TFEU) or freedom to provide services (Article 56 TFEU).

4.   Article 106(1) applies only in respect of undertakings. The meaning of an 'undertaking' in this context is the same as that under the competition rules. The key criterion is that the entity is engaged in 'economic activity'.[284] Article 106(1) applies either to 'public undertaking' or undertakings that have been granted 'special or exclusive rights'.

5.   There is no definition in the Treaty of a 'public undertaking'. In the Transparency Directive, a public undertaking was defined as any undertaking over which the public authorities may exercise directly or indirectly a dominant influence by virtue of their ownership of it, their financial participation in it, or the rules which govern it. A dominant influence is presumed when the public authorities hold the major part of the undertaking's subscribed capital, or control the majority of the votes attaching to shares issued by the undertaking; or can appoint more than half of the members of the undertaking's administrative, managerial or supervisory body.[285] The Court of Justice has upheld this definition, although it noted that the definition in the Transparency Directive was not meant to define the concept as it appears in Article 106.[286] Nevertheless, it appears that this can be taken as a working definition.

6.   There is again no definition of 'special or exclusive rights'. If the undertaking is a public undertaking, there is no need to establish whether it has been granted special or exclusive rights as it will automatically be caught by Article 106(1) in any event. The Court has referred to special or exclusive rights as arising where 'protection is conferred by a legislative measure on a limited number of undertakings which may substantially affect the ability of other undertakings to exercise the economic activity in question in the same geographical area under substantially equivalent conditions'.[287]

7.   It is evident from Article 106(1) that public undertakings and undertakings to which the State grants special or exclusive rights themselves continue to be subject to the rules in the Treaty and in particular the competition rules.

Must the Member State measure inevitably lead to a breach of the competition rules?

8.   In applying Article 106(1) in conjunction with Article 102, it does not seem to be necessary that the grant of exclusive rights or other State measure inevitably results in an abuse of a dominant position. There will be a breach where 'the

---

284. See Question 1 on the meaning of an 'undertaking'.

285. Directive 80/723/EEC of 25 June 1980 on the transparency of financial relations between Member States and public undertakings as well as on financial transparency within certain undertakings [1980] OJ L195/35, as amended, Articles 1, 2.

286. Cases 188–190/80 *France v Commission* [1982] ECR 2545, para 24.

287. Case C–475/99 *Ambulanz Glöckner v Landkreis Südwestpfalz* [2001] ECR I–8089, [2002] 4 CMLR 726, para 24 (see also the opinion of Advocate General Jacobs, paras 83–89).

undertaking in question, merely by exercising the special or exclusive rights conferred upon it, is led to abuse its dominant position or where such rights are liable to create a situation in which that undertaking is led to commit such abuses'.[288]

9. A Member State can be found in breach of Article 106(1) in conjunction with Article 102 even if no particular case of abuse of dominance is made out. In *Raso*, the Court of Justice held that Italian legislation, which granted a dock-work company the exclusive right to supply temporary labour to terminal concessionaires and to other undertakings authorised to operate in the port, while also enabling it to compete with them on the market in dock services, was contrary to Article 106 in conjunction with Article 102. The Court held that it was immaterial that the national court did not identify any particular case of abuse.[289] This approach would hold equally to breaches based on Article 101 (or where Article 4(3), rather than Article 106(1) was employed).

10. In *Dusseldorp*, the Court of Justice confirmed that

> ... a Member State breaches the prohibitions laid down by Article [106] in conjunction with Article [102] if it adopts any law, regulation or administrative provision which enables an undertaking on which it has conferred exclusive rights to abuse its dominant position.[290]

11. The Court went on to hold that a Dutch rule that required undertakings to deliver their waste for recovery to a Dutch undertaking which had exclusive rights to incinerate dangerous waste (unless the processing of their waste in another Member State was of a higher quality than that performed by that undertaking) was in breach of Article 106 in conjunction with Article 102 if, without any objective justification and without being necessary for the performance of a task in the general interest, the rule had the effect of favouring the Dutch undertaking and increasing its dominant position.[291]

12. In *MOTOE*, the Court of Justice found that a Greek rule which provided the Automobile and Touring Club of Greece (ELPA) with powers of authorisation over motorcycling was a breach of Article 102 in conjunction with Article 106 when ELPA was at the same time engaged in organising and commercialising such

---

288. Case C–451/03 *Servizi Ausiliari Dottori Commercialisti Srl v Calafiori* [2006] ECR I–2941, [2006] 2 CMLR 1135, para 23. Cf a slightly less broad statement of this principle in earlier cases such as Case C–323/93 *Centre d'Insémination de la Crespelle v Coopérative de la Mayenne* [1994] ECR I–5077, para 18 (there was a breach of Article 106(1) in conjunction with Article 102 'only if, in merely exercising the exclusive right granted to it, the undertaking in question cannot avoid abusing its dominant position').
289. Case C–163/96 *Raso* [1998] ECR I–533, [1998] 5 CMLR 737, para 31. The extension of a dominant position into a neighbouring market that was a result of a State measure has also resulted in a breach of Article 106(1) in conjunction with Article 102 without any requirement that the dominant position have been abused (Case C–18/88 *RTT v GB-INNO-BM* [1991] ECR I–5941, paras 20–28).
290. Case C–203/96 *Dusseldorp BV* [1998] ECR I–4075, [1998] 3 CMLR 873, para 61.
291. Case C–203/96 *Dusseldorp BV* [1998] ECR I–4075, [1998] 3 CMLR 873, para 68.

events itself. The rule was tantamount *de facto* to conferring upon ELPA the power to designate the persons authorised to organise motorcycling events and to set the conditions in which those events were organised, thereby placing ELPA at an obvious advantage over its competitors. ELPA was in a position to deny competitors access to the relevant market while at the same time ELPA was not itself required to obtain authorisation for motorcycling events. It could also use its power of authorisation to distort competition by favouring events which it organised or those in whose organisation it participated.[292]

13. If the undertaking is compelled by the State measure to abuse a dominant position, it can rely on the State compulsion defence against any charge that it is in breach of Article 102.[293]

14. If a Member State measure is in breach of the competition rules, in conjunction with Article 106(1), it may nevertheless be justified if the conditions for the application of the Article 106(2) derogation are fulfilled.[294]

When is Article 4(3) TEU applicable?

15. Article 4(3) TEU is very similar to what was previously Article 10 TEC, although the wording of the two provisions is slightly different.[295] There are two main additions in Article 4(3). It has added the idea of 'mutual respect' and it applies the duty of cooperation to tasks that 'flow from the Treaties'.[296] Article 4(3) TEU provides as follows:

> Pursuant to the principle of sincere cooperation, the Union and the Member States shall, in full mutual respect, assist each other in carrying out tasks which flow from the Treaties.
>
> The Member States shall take any appropriate measure, general or particular, to ensure fulfilment of the obligations arising out of the Treaties or resulting from the acts of the institutions of the Union.
>
> The Member States shall facilitate the achievement of the Union's tasks and refrain from any measure which could jeopardise the attainment of the Union's objectives.

16. Member State measures may also be challenged under Article 4(3) TEU read in conjunction with one of the other provisions of the Treaty, including Article 101 or

---

292. Case C–49/07 *MOTOE v Elliniko Dimosio* [2008] ECR I–4863, [2008] 5 CMLR 790, paras 51–53.
293. See Question 4 and Cases C–359 & 379/95P *Commission v Ladbroke Racing Ltd.* [1997] ECR I–6265, [1998] 4 CMLR 27, para 33.
294. See Question 125 on the conditions for the application of the Article 106(2) derogation.
295. Article 10 TEC had provided: 'Member States shall take all appropriate measures, whether general or particular, to ensure fulfilment of the obligations arising out of this Treaty or resulting from action taken by the institutions of the Community. They shall facilitate the achievement of the Community's tasks. They shall abstain from any measure which could jeopardise the attainment of the objectives of this Treaty'.
296. It remains to be seen how significant these changes are. See for discussion, Chalmers, Davies and Monti, *European Union Law* (2nd edn, 2010) 223.

102. While Article 106(1) refers only to measures in respect of public undertakings and undertakings that have been granted special or exclusive rights, the effect of Article 4(3) is to apply the same prohibition on Member State measures that apply vis-à-vis undertakings in general, whether they are public undertakings or have been conferred with special or exclusive rights or not.[297] The Court of Justice has explained that Article 106(1) is a specific application of the general duties of the Member States under Article 4(3).[298]

17. The general principle prohibiting Member State measures that result in a breach of the competition rules has been stated many times by the Court of Justice in the following or similar terms:

> As regards ... [Articles 101 and 102], although it is true that they are concerned solely with the conduct of undertakings and not with laws or regulations emanating from Member States, those articles, read in conjunction with [Article 4(3) TFEU], which lays down a duty to cooperate, none the less require Member States not to introduce or maintain in force measures, even of a legislative or regulatory nature, which may render ineffective the competition rules applicable to undertakings.[299]

18. Article 4(3) can be applied together with Article 102 as well as with Article 101 but in practice, the Court of Justice has applied Article 106(1) mainly in conjunction with Article 102, while Article 10 EC (and now Article 4(3)) TEU) has been used frequently in conjunction with Article 101 in finding that a national law is unenforceable as it gives rise to agreements that would breach the EU competition rules.[300]

19. Not all national legislation that adversely affects competition gives rise to a breach of Article 4(3) in conjunction with the competition rules. In the Article 101 context, the Court of Justice has identified in *Van Eycke* different kinds of cases in which the national measure would result in an infringement. Those cases were described more recently in *Cipolla*:

> Articles [4(3) TEU] and [101] are infringed where a Member State requires or encourages the adoption of agreements, decisions or concerted practices contrary to Article [101] or reinforces their effects, or where it divests its own rules of the character of legislation by delegating to private economic operators responsibility for taking decisions affecting the economic sphere.[301]

---

297. See Temple Lang, 'European Union Law Rules on State Measures Restricting Competition' [2003] *Finnish Yearbook of European Law* 9.
298. Case 13/77 *INNO v ATAB* [1977] ECR 2115, [1978] 1 CMLR 283, para 42.
299. Case C–393/08 *Sbarigia v Azienda USL RM/A,* judgment of 1 July 2010, para 31. This principle was first stated in Case 13/77 *INNO v ATAB* [1977] ECR 2115, [1978] 1 CMLR 283, paras 30–31.
300. See Vaughan, Lee, Kennelly & Riches, *EU Competition Law: General Principles* (2006) paras 319, 380–387.
301. Cases C–94 & 202/04 *Cipolla v Fazari* [2006] ECR I–11421, [2007] 4 CMLR 286, para 47; Case 267/86 *Van Eycke v ASPA NV* [1988] ECR 476, [1990] 4 CMLR 330, para 16 (using the term 'favour' rather than 'encourage').

20. It is apparent that there must be a link between the national measure and the agreements or conduct of undertakings that come within Article 101.[302] The effects of an anti-competitive agreement, decision or concerted practice are 'reinforced' where a Member State merely reproduces all or some of the elements of that agreement or practice between undertakings.[303] The necessary link can also be shown if the measure 'encourages' the adoption of agreements or practices that breach Article 101. This does not seem to be a particularly high threshold to give rise to an infringement of Article 4(3) in combination with Article 101 and 'encouragement, in any form whatsoever' will be caught.[304]

21. In respect of the other class of cases mentioned in *Van Eycke*, where the Member State delegates decision-making in the economic sphere to private parties, the State will not generally be liable if the private parties are 'independent' or the State retains ultimate control of the relevant decision. So, for example, in *Arduino*, Italian legislation that fixed legal fees on the basis of a proposal prepared by a committee of lawyers did not result in an infringement by Italy because the State retained ultimate control over setting fees. The draft produced by the lawyers' committee was not compulsory and the relevant Minister had the power to amend the draft before it came into effect. Also, in setting fees, the courts could depart from the maximum and minimum amounts set out in the measure in certain exceptional circumstances.[305] In contrast, in the *Italian customs agents* case, there was an improper delegation in allowing an association of undertakings composed of representatives of customs agents to set compulsory tariffs for all customs agents. The Italian legislation 'wholly relinquished to private economic operators the powers of the public authorities as regards the setting of tariffs'.[306]

22. In the past, the Court has sometimes cited what was formerly Article 3(1)(g) of the EC Treaty together with Article 101 when examining a Member State's duty of good faith under Article 10 TEC. Article 3(1)(g) TEC had provided that the activities of the Community would include 'a system ensuring that competition in the internal market is not distorted'. It was repealed by the Lisbon Treaty but the substance of the provision was retained in a new Protocol to the TEU and TFEU.[307]

---

302. One Advocate General has considered that there must be a 'demonstrable direct link' (Case C–72/03 *Carbonati Apuani Srl v Comune di Carrara* [2004] ECR I–8027, [2004] 3 CMLR 1282, opinion of Advocate General Maduro, para 20).

303. Case C–2/91 *Meng* [1993] ECR I–5751, para 19.

304. Case 66/86 *Ahmed Saeed Flugreisen v Zentrale zur Bekämpfung unlauteren Wettbewerbs e.V.* [1989] ECR 803, [1990] 4 CMLR 102, para 52. For a recent discussion, see Case C–531/07 *Fachverband der Buch- und Medienwirtschaft v LIBRO Handelsgesellschaft mbH* [2009] ECR I–3717, [2009] 3 CMLR 26, opinion of Advocate General Trstenjak, paras 125–138.

305. Case C–35/99 *Arduino* [2002] ECR I–1529, [2002] 4 CMLR 866, paras 40–43. See also Case C–185/91 *Reiff* [1993] ECR I–5801, [1995] 5 CMLR 145, para 22 (if tariffs decided on by a board were inimical to the public interest, the Minster could fix tariffs instead).

306. Case C–35/96 *Commission v Italy ('CNSD')* [1998] ECR I–3851, [1998] 5 CMLR 889, para57. On legal issues surrounding delegation of governmental power more generally, see Donnelly, *Delegation of Governmental Power to Private Parties: A Comparative Perspective* (2007).

307. Protocol (No 27) on the internal market and competition, annexed to the TEU and TFEU.

It is doubtful that this change would affect challenges to Member State measures based on a breach of what is now Article 4(3) TEU in conjunction with the competition rules.[308]

23.   If a Member State measure is in breach of the competition rules, in conjunction with Article 4(3), as in the case of a breach of Article 106(1), the measure may be justified if the conditions for the application of the Article 106(2) derogation are fulfilled.

How can action be taken against a Member State for breach of Article 106(1) or Article 4(3) in conjunction with the competition rules?

24.   The Commission can take action against a Member State for breach of Article 106(1), either under Article 106(3), through directives or decisions, or under Article 258 TFEU, which can result in proceedings before the Court of Justice. The Commission can also avail of Article 258 TFEU when challenging a Member State measure as a breach of Article 4(3) TEU.

25.   National courts are under a duty under Article 4(3) TEU to ensure that individuals' rights derived from EU law are protected.[309] The precise procedural rules that apply for safeguarding those rights is a matter of national law but the principles of equivalence and effectiveness must be complied with. Both Articles 106(1) and 4(3) have direct effect so that a private party can rely on the fact that a national law measure is in breach of Article 106(1)/4(3) in conjunction with the competition rules to render that measure ineffective. In such a case, the national judge must disapply the national measure.[310] In *CIF*, the Court of Justice confirmed that a national competition authority had a duty to disapply a national measure, including legislation, that was contrary to Article 101 in conjunction with Article 10 EC (now, essentially, Article 4(3) TEU).[311] This duty applies to any national competition authorities which are designated pursuant to Regulation 1/2003 for the purposes of applying Articles 101 and 102.[312]

26.   Several such cases have involved a situation where a measure of national law, involving a sanction, is being enforced against the private party and in its defence

---

308. See also Question 11.
309. See, e.g., Case C–312/93 *Peterbroeck v Belgium* [1995] ECR I–4599, [1996] 1 CMLR 793, para 12.
310. See, generally, Temple Lang, 'The Principle of Loyal Cooperation and the Role of the National Judge in Community, Union and EEA Law' (2006) 7(4) *ERA Forum* 476.
311. Case C–198/01 *CIF* [2003] ECR I–8055, [2003] 5 CMLR 829, para 50.
312. However it may extend further. The Irish Competition Authority, for example, does not have the power to take decisions finding an infringement of Article 101 or 102 but it does have power to carry out investigations into breaches of the Competition Act 2002, which, it is arguable, extends to carrying out investigations into breaches of Article 101 or 102 (see Competition Act 2002, s 30(1)(b), giving the Authority the power to carry out an investigation into any breach of the Act; while a breach of Article 101 or 102 may not strictly constitute a breach of the Competition Act 2002, a breach of either Article is a criminal offence under the Competition Act 2002, ss 6(1), 7(1)).

the party raises the incompatibility of the measure with EU law. The *Meng* case illustrates how such a scenario may arise. The Court of Justice, on a preliminary reference, concluded that the relevant national measure – a German insurance law pursuant to which an insurance broker was fined for passing commission to clients – did not breach Article 10 EC in conjunction with Article 101 as the law, which was self-contained, was not linked to any unlawful agreement contrary to Article 101. However, it has been noted that had the legislation authorised an association of insurance brokers to adopt rules prohibiting the passing of commission to clients and adopted related criminal sanctions, the broker could successfully have invoked a breach of Article 10 EC (and now Article 4(3) TEU) in conjunction with Article 101.[313]

Key Sources

Article 106(1) TFEU.

Article 4(3), TEU.

Case C–203/96 *Dusseldorp BV* [1998] ECR I–4075, [1998] 3 CMLR 873.

Case 267/86 *Van Eycke v ASPA NV* [1988] ECR 476, [1990] 4 CMLR 330.

---

312. (contd) In *CIF*, the Court stated that a competition authority had a duty to disapply national measures contrary to the combined provisions of Article 10 EC (now, essentially, Article 4(3) TEU) and Article 101 'in the course of an investigation' into a breach of Article 101 (Case C–198/01 *CIF* [2003] ECR I–8055, [2003] 5 CMLR 829, para 50). This raises the possibility that a body such as the Competition Authority could disapply an Irish measure were it found to be in breach of Article 4(3) in conjunction with Article 101 or 102 and hindered the Authority's investigation.
313. Bellamy & Child (6th edn, 2008) para 11.034.

136. DO SPECIFIC COMPETITION RULES APPLY IN PARTICULAR SECTORS?

Summary

There are specific rules for certain sectors, including:

- Transport.

- Electronic Communications.

- Electricity and Gas.

- Post.

1. This question aims to briefly identify some of the main sector-specific competition rules that apply. In general, undertakings in a particular sector are subject to the Articles 101 and 102 even if they are also subject to a sector-specific regulatory regime. Sectors that are wholly or partly outside the reach of the Treaty's competition rules are nuclear energy, military equipment and agriculture.[314] Other sectors have been the subject of liberalisation in recent years, moving from a prevalence of state monopolies to a competitive environment. Specific rules have been required to effect such liberalisation and competition policy plays an important role in bringing about the change to competitive markets. Specific rules can also be required to ensure universal service provision. The sectors considered below are transport, electronic communications, electricity, gas, post and water.

What rules apply to the transport sector?

2. Special provisions on transport are set out in Title VI TFEU, in Articles 90–100. Article 100(1) provides that these provisions apply to transport by rail, road and inland waterway. Article 100(2) provides that the Parliament and the Council have the power to lay down appropriate provisions for sea and air transport.

3. The transport sector has been the subject of extensive liberalisation in recent years and there are now only a limited number of EU transport-specific regulations. In general, Articles 101 and 102 apply to the transport sector.

4. Articles 101 and 102 apply to transport by rail, road and inland waterway other than to the extent provided for in Regulation 169/2009. This Regulation sets out certain exceptions to the application of the competition rules. There is an exemption from Article 101(1) for certain types of technical agreements and for small and medium-sized undertakings in road and inland waterway.[315]

---

314. See Whish, *Competition Law* (6th edn, 2009) 956–961.
315. Council Regulation (EC) No 169/2009 of 26 February 2009 applying rules of competition to transport by rail, road and inland waterway [2009] OJ L61/1.

5.   In the maritime transport sector, Regulation 1419/2006[316] repealed Regulation 4056/86, which had set out a specific regime for applying the competition rules in the maritime sector. Regulation 1/2003 therefore applies to all maritime transport services. The Commission has adopted guidelines on the application of Article 101 to maritime transport services.[317]

6.   There is a general block exemption Regulation in respect of liner shipping companies (consortia).[318] The Commission has adopted a specific block exemption under Article 101(3) for consortia.[319] This exempts from Article 101(1) certain activities of a consortium including the joint operation of liner shipping services, capacity adjustments in response to fluctuations in supply and demand, the joint operation and use of port terminals and ancillary activities. The block exemption does not cover price fixing, limitations of capacity other than in response to fluctuations in supply and demand or market allocation. The block exemption entered into force on 26 April 2010 and applies until 25 April 2015.

7.   The rail sector has gradually been liberalised in recent years with the adoption of a number of directives. EU action to liberalise freight rail was completed in 2007 and passenger rail was liberalised as of 1 January 2010, with all railway undertakings having a right of cross-border access to railway infrastructure in the EU for the purposes of operating international passenger services.[320]

8.   Whereas there had previously been special competition rules applicable to air transport, the Commission now applies Regulation 1/2003 to all air routes, including those between the EU and other jurisdictions.[321] The 'Open Skies' judgments of the Court of Justice established that the Commission had exclusive competence to negotiate bilateral air transport agreements with third countries in

---

316. Council Regulation (EC) No 1419/2006 repealing Regulation (EEC) No 4056/86 laying down detailed rules for the application of Articles 85 and 86 of the Treaty to maritime transport, and amending Regulation (EC) No 1/2003 as regards the extension of its scope to include cabotage and international tramp services [2006] OJ L269/1.

317. Guidelines on the application of Article 81 of the EC Treaty to maritime transport services [2008] OJ C245/2.

318. Council Regulation (EC) No 246/2009 of 26 February 2009 on the application of Article 81(3) of the Treaty to certain categories of agreements, decisions and concerted practices between liner shipping companies [2009] OJ L79/1.

319. Commission Regulation (EC) 906/2009 on the application of Article 81(3) of the Treaty to certain categories of agreements, decisions and concerted practices between liner shipping companies (consortia) [2009] OJ L256/31.

320. See Directive 2007/58/EC amending Council Directive 91/440/EEC on the development of the Community's railways and Directive 2001/14/EC on the allocation of railway infrastructure capacity and the levying of charges for the use of railway infrastructure [2007] OJ L315/44.

321. See Council Regulation (EC) No 411/2004 repealing Regulation (EEC) No 3975/87 and amending Regulations (EEC) No 3976/87 and (EC) No 1/2003, in connection with air transport between the Community and third countries [2004] OJ L68/1.

certain areas.[322] Among the most significant agreements is the 'open skies' agreement with the United States. This lifted capacity, frequency and designation requirements on flights between the US and EU and enables US and EU carriers to fly between any EU and US airport regardless of their nationality.[323] A general block exemption Regulation sets out the types of block exemptions that the Commission may adopt in the air transport sector.[324]

9.   In the UK, the Office of Rail Regulation has concurrent powers with the OFT to apply Article 101 and 102 (and the Chapter I and II prohibitions under the Competition Act 1998) to agreements and conduct relating to the supply of services relating to railways.[325] The Civil Aviation Authority has similar concurrent powers in respect of agreements and conduct relating to the supply of air traffic services.[326] In Ireland, certain aspects of the air transport sector are regulated by the Commission for Aviation Regulation. There is no comparable rail regulator in Ireland to the UK's Office of Rail Regulation.

What rules apply to electronic communications?

10.   The competition rules apply to telecommunications together with sector-specific rules that have been adopted under Article 114 TFEU for the purpose of opening up to competition an industry that had previously been controlled by state monopolies.[327] A system of *ex ante* regulation applies, which requires mandatory access to networks and the regulation of access fees, so that new entrants can compete. In 2002, a EU regulatory framework for electronic communications networks and services was adopted so that all transmission networks and associated services would be subject to the same regulatory framework. This consists of Directive 2002/21[328] and other specific directives. In December 2009, new legislation for regulating the telecoms sector was adopted by the Parliament and the Council. This consists of Regulation 1211/2009,[329] Directive

---

322. Cases C–466/98 etc *Commission v United Kingdom* [2002] ECR I–9427, [2003] 1 CMLR 143.

323. Air Transport Agreement between the United States and the European Community [2007] OJ L134/4.

324. Council Regulation (EC) No 487/2009 on the application of Article 81(3) of the Treaty to certain categories of agreements and concerted practices in the air transport sector [2009] OJ L148/1.

325. Railways Act 1993, s 67(3).

326. Transport Act 2000, s 86(3).

327. There are several specialist works on EU telecommunications law. See, e.g., Koenig, Bartosch, Braun and Romes (eds) *EC Competition and Telecommunications Law* (2nd edn, 2009).

328. Directive 2002/21/EC on a common regulatory framework for electronic communications networks and services [2002] OJ L108/33.

329. Regulation (EC) No 1211/2009 establishing the Body of European Regulators for Electronic Communications (BEREC) and the Office [2009] OJ L337/1.

2009/136[330] and Directive 2009/140.[331] The deadline for the transposition of the two directives in the Member States is 25 May 2011.

11. The 2002 framework established a mechanism allowing national regulatory authorities, where there is no effective competition on a relevant market, to impose *ex ante* regulatory obligations on undertakings in the electronic communications sector designated as having significant market power following an analysis of the market concerned. There is a need for *ex ante* regulation in certain circumstances to ensure the development of a competitive market. This arises where one or more undertaking has 'significant market power', a concept that is equivalent to the competition law concept of dominance. As the Directive 2002/21 states:

> It is essential that *ex ante* regulatory obligations should only be imposed where there is not effective competition, *i.e.* in markets where there are one or more undertakings with significant market power, and where national and Community competition law remedies are not sufficient to address the problem.[332]

12. An example of the specific type of regulation under the framework can be seen in the operation of Regulation 717/2007, which caps the wholesale and retail charges terrestrial mobile operators may charge for the provision of roaming services on public mobile networks for voice calls between Member States.[333]

13. The December 2009 legislative package provides for further reform in electronic communications regulation. Regulation 1211/2009 provides for a new EU telecoms body, the Body of European Regulators of Electronic Communications ('BEREC') which will establish more formal cooperation between the EU's national telecoms regulators. Directives 136/2009 and 140/2009 provide for various reforms to the regulatory framework, strengthening mechanisms for

---

330. Directive 2009/136/EC amending Directive 2002/22/EC on universal service and users, rights relating to electronic communications networks and services, Directive 2002/58/EC concerning the processing of personal data and the protection of privacy in the electronic communications sector and Regulation (EC) No 2006/2004 on cooperation between national authorities responsible for the enforcement of consumer protection laws [2009] OJ L337/11.

331. Directive 2009/140/EC amending Directives 2002/21/EC on a common regulatory framework for electronic communications networks and services, 2002/19/EC on access to, and interconnection of, electronic communications networks and associated facilities, and 2002/20/EC on the authorisation of electronic communications networks and services [2009] OJ L337/37.

332. Directive 2002/21/EC, Recital 27.

333. Regulation (EC) No 717/2007 on roaming on public mobile telephone networks within the Community and amending Directive 2002/21/EC [2007] OJ L171/32. The validity of this Regulation was upheld by the Court of Justice in Case C–58/08 *R (Vodafone Ltd) v Secretary of State for Business, Enterprise and Regulatory Reform* [2010] All ER (EC) 741. A previous set of directives adopted under Article 106(3) had been aimed at removing exclusive rights in the area of terminal equipment and opening up telecommunications markets to competition, including the fields of satellite, cable and mobile telecommunications. See Commission Directive 2002/77/EC on competition in the markets for electronic communications networks and services [2002] OJ L249/21.

regulating operators with significant market power and adopting measures to accelerate broadband access across the EU, among others.

14. A new European Telecoms Body that will help ensure fair competition and more consistency of regulation on the telecoms markets has been set up. It will be called BEREC (Body of European Regulators of Electronic Communications) and will replace the loose cooperation between national regulators that exists today in the European Regulators Group with a better structured, more efficient approach. BEREC decisions will be taken, as a rule, by majority of heads of the 27 national telecoms regulators. A decision on the seat of BEREC still needs to be taken by the Governments of the 27 Member States.

15. National regulatory authorities, which oversee telecommunications regulation, play an important role with respect to competition in the sector. In the UK, the Office of Communications (Ofcom) has concurrent powers with the OFT to apply Articles 101 and 102 to the telecommunications sector.[334] Ofcom also has concurrent powers with the OFT in relation to market investigations concerning commercial activities connected with communications matters.[335] Numerous cases in the telecommunications sector have come before the CAT in recent years. Under Part 2 of the Communications Act 2003, Ofcom has the power to regulate the provision of electronic communications networks. Its regulatory decisions are appealable to the CAT on the merits by any person who is affected by the decision.[336] Appeals on points of law lie to the Court of Appeal.[337] Competition issues are often integral in such cases.[338] Ofcom has various enforcement powers in relation to the EU regulatory framework.

16. In Ireland, the Commission for Communications Regulation (ComReg) has a number of functions in relation to the enforcement of competition law in the electronic communications sector. These powers are found in amendments to the Competition Act 2002 brought about by the Communications Regulation (Amendment) Act 2007. ComReg is designated as a national competition authority in the electronic communications sector for purposes of investigatory and procedural functions surrounding the enforcement of Articles 101 and 102 pursuant to Regulation 1/2003.[339] However, like the Competition Authority,

---

334. Communications Act 2003, s 371.
335. Enterprise Act 2002, Part 4; Communications Act 2003, s 370.
336. Communications Act 2003, ss 192(2), 195(2).
337. Communications Act 2003, s 196(6).
338. See as an example of an appeal to the CAT against a decision of OFCOM, which was subsequently appealed to the Court of Appeal, resulting in a preliminary reference to the Court of Justice, *The Number (UK) Ltd v Office of Communications* [2009] EWCA Civ 1360.
339. SI No. 195 of 2004, European Communities (Implementation of the Rules on Competition laid down in Articles 81 and 82 of the Treaty) Regulations 2004, r 4, as amended by SI No. 525 of 2007, European Communities (Implementation of the Rules on Competition laid down in Articles 81 and 82 of the Treaty) (Amendment) Regulations 2007, designating the Authority and (contd \...)

ComReg does not have power to take decisions that Article 101 or 102 or section 4 or 5 of the Competition Act 2002 have been infringed. ComReg is empowered to take a civil action in the High Court in respect of breaches of section 4 or 5 or Article 101 or 102, in which it can seek an injunction or declaration.[340] ComReg has the function of investigating possible breaches of sections 4 and 5 in the electronic communications sector.[341] ComReg is required to notify the Competition Authority in advance in writing of its intention to exercise any of its functions under the Competition Act 2002.[342] Like other national regulators, ComReg has various powers relating to the EU regulatory framework.[343]

What rules apply in the electricity and gas sectors?

17. A number of liberalising measures have been adopted in the electricity and gas industries, with liberalisation directives adopted in the 1990s and more recently.[344] Among the goals of these measures have been the provision of non-discriminatory and fairly priced access to networks and other infrastructure for energy companies, the unbundling of transmission and distribution systems and effective regulation by national regulatory authorities. Article 194 TFEU, which was added by the Lisbon Treaty, provides that the Parliament and Council may adopt measures to achieve the objectives of a Union energy policy which aims, in a spirit of solidarity between the Member States, to:

 (a) ensure the functioning of the energy market;

 (b) ensure security of energy supply in the Union;

 (c) promote energy efficiency and energy saving and the development of new and renewable forms of energy; and

 (d) promote the interconnection of energy networks.[345]

18. The antitrust and State aid rules apply to the energy sector and the Commission has carried out several competition and State aid investigations in the sector. For example, the Commission conducted an investigation into an abuse of a dominant position by the French energy company, EDF, arising from its long-term electricity supply contracts. Following a statement of objections which set out grounds for a

---

339. (contd) ComReg as the competition authority for purposes of certain parts of Regulation 1/ 2003. The assigned functions include the ability to withdraw the benefit of block exemptions in electronic communications, which can only be done in concurrence with the Competition Authority.

340. Competition Act 2002, ss 14(2), 14(6).

341. Competition Act 2002, s 47A.

342. Competition Act 2002, s 47C.

343. For a detailed review of the role and powers of ComReg, see Connery and Hodnett, *Regulatory Law in Ireland* (2009) Ch 6.

344. See Council Directive 2003/54 concerning common rules for the internal market in electricity and repealing Directive 96/92EC [2003] OJ L176/37; Council Directive 2003/55 concerning common rules for the internal market in natural gas and repealing Directive 98/ 30/EC [2003] OJ L176/57.

345. Article 194 TFEU.

finding that EDF has breached Article 102, the company submitted commitments to the Commission under Article 9 of Regulation 1/2003, resulting in the adoption of a settlement decision. The settlement included a commitment to make available every year on average 65 per cent of volumes contracted on the relevant market for recontracting by alternative suppliers and a commitment not to conclude new contracts with a duration exceeding five years and to offer customers non-exclusive contracts.[346]

19. In the UK, the Office of the Gas and Electricity Markets (Ofgem) has concurrent powers with the OFT to apply Article 101 and 102 (and the Chapter I and II prohibitions under the Competition Act 1998) to agreements and conduct relating to the supply of gas and commercial activities connected with the generation, transmission or supply of electricity or the use of electricity interconnectors.[347]

20. In Ireland, the Commission for Energy Regulation is the regulator for the energy sector. While its functions include the monitoring of competition in the electricity and gas sectors, it does not have a formal role in applying competition law.[348]

What rules apply in the postal sector?

21. Postal services in the EU have been liberalised pursuant to Directive 97/67/EC of 1997, as amended by Directive 2002/39 and as further amended by Directive 2008/06/EC.[349] The first two directives have aimed to promote competition in the postal sector while maintaining universal postal provision. Under the second directive, Member States were entitled to reserve from competition postal services in respect of domestic correspondence weighing less than 50g. The main elements of the EU regulatory framework include the provision of universal service, the setting of quality standards for universal service provision, tariff principles and transparency of accounts, the harmonisation of technical standards and the creation of independent national regulators. The third postal directive is aimed at full liberalisation, requiring Member States to abolish any remaining reserved areas by 2010 and in some cases, 2012. The Commission has adopted a decision designating postal regulators in each of the Member States.[350]

22. Article 101 and 102 are applied to the postal sector and the Commission has adopted a Notice discussing the application of the competition rules to

---

346. Case COMP/39.386 *Long-term Contracts France*, Commission Decision of 17 March 2010.

347. Gas Act 1986, s 36A(3); Electricity Act 1989, s 43(3).

348. See, e.g., SI No 60 of 2005 European Communities (Internal Market in Electricity) Regulations 2005, r 3(c)(h) providing that the Commission's functions include monitoring the levels of transparency and competition in the electricity sector.

349. Directive 2008/6/EC amending Directive 97/67/EC with regard to the full accomplishment of the internal market of Community postal services [2008] OJ L52/3.

350. Commission Decision establishing the European Regulators Group for Postal Services [2010] OJ C217/7.

postal services.[351] The Commission also applies the State aid rules to postal services.[352]

23. In the UK, the Postal Services Commission (Postcomm) regulates the postal sector. Unlike some of the other sectoral regulators, Postcomm does not have the power to apply the Chapter I or II prohibition or Article 101 or 102.

24. ComReg is the designated postal regulator in Ireland.[353] ComReg does not have the power to apply competition law in the postal sector, however it works closely with the Competition Authority on relevant competition issues in post.[354]

What rules apply in the water sector?

25. There is no specific EU law regulatory regime for the water industry. In the UK, the Office of Water Services (Ofwat) has concurrent powers with the OFT to apply Article 101 and 102 (and the Chapter I and II prohibitions under the Competition Act 1998) to agreements and conduct relating to commercial activities connected with the supply of water or securing a supply of water or with the provision or securing of sewerage services.[355] In Ireland, the water supply industry has not been liberalised. The supply of water is the responsibility of local authorities and the funding for maintaining the water supply system is provided by central government.

---

351. Notice from the Commission on the application of the competition rules to the postal sector and on the assessment of certain State measures relating to postal services [1998] OJ C39/2.

352. See, e.g., Case C–399/08P *Commission v Deutsche Post AG*, judgment of 2 September 2010 (General Court's annulment of a Commission decision finding State aid was upheld by the Court of Justice; Commission had not shown a financial advantage to Deutsche Post from transfers by Deutsche Telekom).

353. See SI No 616/2002 European Communities (Postal Services) Regulations 2002.

354. See further Connery and Hodnett, *Regulatory Law in Ireland* (2009) para 6.135.

355. Water Industry Act 1991, s 31(3).

INDEX

Vertical agreements (contd)

most favoured nation clauses

generally, 47.3–7

introduction, 47.1

negative effects, 44.1–2

non-compete clauses

franchise agreements, 51.3

justification for restraints, and, 44.2

selective distribution agreements, 50.8

passive sales

generally, 49.1–6

selective distribution agreements, 50.2

potential negative effects, 44.2

resale restrictions, 49.1–6

selective distribution agreements, 50.1–8

supply agreements, 43.1

types of vertical restraints, 44.2

Vertical mergers

abuse of dominant position, and, 76.31

conditions for finding of anti-competitive foreclosure, 76.9–10

coordinated effects concerns, and, 76.30

customer foreclosure, 76.25–29

foreclosure

customer foreclosure, 76.25–29

input foreclosure, 76.11–24

introduction, 76.5–8

generally, 76.1–8

input foreclosure

application by Commission in practice, 76.18–24

generally, 76.11–17

Non-Horizontal Merger Guidelines, 76.2

Void agreements

severance, and, 20.1–6

Warehousing transactions

mergers and acquisitions, and, 65.8–9

Warranties as to competition compliance

merger control agreements, and, 81.2

Water sector

application of competition rules, and, 136.25